WEBSTER'S
SCHOLASTIC
DICTIONARY

A New Edition Set in Modern Type
Based on the Lexicography of
Noah Webster

AIRMONT

AIRMONT PUBLISHING COMPANY, INC.
22 EAST 60TH STREET · NEW YORK 10022

ISBN: 0-8049-2001-X

FOREWORD

Webster's Scholastic Dictionary is designed for the use of the pupil in schools, but it can be of equal value for everyone for general use.

In a dictionary of this size, the problems of abridgment and condensed definitions are of major concern. In selecting the more than 30,000 entries, the editors have, by diligent research, retained what they consider the necessary words of the English language.

The rigid rule for simplicity implicit in this format has been carried through to word definitions, without detracting from or changing the value of the meanings. This simplicity also applies to the key to pronunciation. Examples for the use of words have been retained where possible.

The British spellings are given following the American spellings, which is rarely done in a dictionary of this size.

The entries in *Webster's Scholastic Dictionary* are set in modern, easy-to-read boldface type, with clear and concise definitions.

—THE EDITORS

Key to Pronunciation

ā	*as in*	fate, paid, gray, great
a	*as in*	fat, had, pad, shall
a̤	*as in*	fall, author, fought, false, waltz
ä	*as in*	father, far, calm, far
ē	*as in*	meat, machine, feet, even
e	*as in*	met, set, terrible, equity
ė	*as in*	her, firm, transfer, over
ī	*as in*	mine, light, height, kite
i	*as in*	lip, abyss, little, mit
ō	*as in*	note, load, snow, go
o	*as in*	odd, not, folly, lot
ö	*as in*	tool, move, rule, food
ū	*as in*	cube, union, futile, use
u	*as in*	rustic, hurry, dull, up
ụ	*as in*	woman, wolf, book
oi	*as in*	join, oyster, boy
ou	*as in*	house, town, bound
ch	*as in*	church, chain, bunch, match
th	*as in*	thin, worth, breath
ᴛʜ	*as in*	breathe, then, father
g	*as in*	go, get, give, dog
w	*as in*	will, wig, win, wager
wh	*as in*	whip, white, whiff
zh	*as in*	azure, closure, measure

Abbreviations Used in this Dictionary

a	adjective	*obs*	obsolete
abbr	abbreviated	*p*	past
adv	adverb	*p.a*	participle adjective
art	article	*p.p*	past participle
colloq	colloquial	*pers*	person
comp	comparative	*pl*	plural
conj	conjunction	*pref*	prefix
contr	contraction	*prep*	preposition
exclam	exclamation	*pres*	present
fem	feminine	*pret*	preterite
fut	future	*pron*	pronoun
gram	grammar	*pr.p*	present participle
imp	imperfect	*sing*	singular
ind	indicative	*superl*	superlative
indef	indefinite	*syn*	synonym
interj	interjection	*v*	verb
irreg	irregular	*vi*	verb intransitive
n	noun	*vt*	verb transitive
neut	neuter		

ABBREVIATIONS

AA, A.A., achievement age (*Psychol.*); Alcoholics Anonymous; antiaircraft.
AAA, A.A.A., Amateur Athletic Association; American Automobile Association.
AAAA, A.A.A.A., Amateur Athletic Association of America.
A.A.A.L., American Academy of Arts and Letters.
A.A.A.S., AAAS, American Association for the Advancement of Science.
AAF, Army Air Forces.
A.A.U., Amateur Athletic Union.
A.B., Artium Baccalaureus (L., Bachelor of Arts).
abbr., abbrev., abbreviated; abbreviation.
ab init., ab initio (L., from the beginning).
Abp., Archbishop.
abr., abridged; abridgment.
AC, A.C., a.c., alternating current. *Elec.*
ACC, Air Co-ordinating Committee.
acct., account; accountant.
ack., acknowledge; acknowledgment.
A.C.P., American College of Physicians.
A.D., A.D., anno Domini.
ad., advertisement.
A.D.C., ADC, a.d.c., aide-de-camp.
ad inf., ad infinitum (L., to infinity).
ad init., ad initium (L., to, or at, the beginning).
ad int., ad interim (L., in the meantime).
Adj., Adjt., Adjutant.
ad lib., ad libit., ad libitum (L., at one's pleasure, to the amount desired).
Adm., Admiral; Admiralty.
ad val., ad valorem (L., according to value).
advt., advertisement.
A.E. and P., Ambassador Extraordinary and Plenipotentiary.
AEC, Atomic Energy Commission.
A.E.F., AEF, American Expeditionary Force, *or* Forces.

AF, Air Force.
A.F.A.M., A.F. & A.M., Ancient Free and Accepted Masons.
AFL, A.F. of L., American Federation of Labor.
A.G., Adjutant General; Attorney General.
agcy., agency.
Agt., agt., agent; agreement.
AKC, American Kennel Club.
Ala., Alabama.
A.L.A., ALA, American Library Association; Automobile Legal Association.
Alas., Alaska.
Alb., Albanian; Alberta.
ALP, American Labor Party.
alt., alternate; alternating; alternations; altitude; alto.
AM, A.M., a-m, a.m., amplitude modulation.
A.M., Artium Magister (L., Master of Arts).
A.M., A.M., a.m., ante meridiem.
A.M.A., AMA, American Medical Association.
AMG, Allied (*also*, American) Military Government.
amp., ampere; amperage.
amp.-hr., ampere-hour.
AMVETS, American Veterans (of World War II).
anon., anonymous.
ANZAC, Australian and New Zealand Army Corps.
AP, A.P., AP, Associated Press.
APO, Army Post Office.
Apoc., Apocalypse; Apocrypha; Apocryphal.
approx., approximately.
Apr., April.
ARA, Agricultural Research Administration.
A.R.A., Associate of the Royal Academy.
ARC, A.R.C., American (National) Red Cross.
Ariz., Arizona.
Ark., Arkansas.
Ar.M., Architecture Magister (L., Master of Architecture).
Arty., Artillery.
ASA, American Standards Association.

ASC, A.S.C., Air Service Command; Army Service Corps.
ASCAP, A.S.C.A.P., American Society of Composers, Authors and Publishers.
ASCE, A.S.C.E., American Society of Civil Engineers.
ASF, Army Service Forces.
asst., assistant.
ASTP, Army Specialized Training Program.
AT, A.T., antitank.
ATC, Air Transport Command.
Atl., Atlantic.
ATS, A.T.S., Army Transport Service.
att., attn., attention.
Atty., Attorney.
Atty. Gen., Attorney General.
at. wt., atomic weight.
Aug., August.
Austral., Austl., Australia.
Aust., Austria; Austrian.
aux., auxil., auxiliary.
a.v., A/V., ad valorem.
av., avdp., avoir., avoirdupois.
AVC, A.V.C., American Veterans Committee.
Ave., Avenue.
AWOL, A.W.O.L., absent without leave.
AWVS, American Women's Volunteer Services.

B.A., Baccalaureus Artium (L., Bachelor of Arts).
B.Ag., B.Agr., Baccalaureus Agriculturae (L., Bachelor of Agriculture).
bal., balance; balancing.
Bapt., Baptist.
B.Ar., B.Arch., Bachelor of Architecture.
bat., batt., battalion; battery.
Bav., Bavarian.
B.B.A., Bachelor of Business Administration.
B.B.C., BBC, British Broadcasting Corporation.
B.C., Bachelor of Chemistry; British Columbia.
B.C., B.C., before Christ.

B.C.E., Bachelor of Chemical Engineering; Bachelor of Civil Engineering.

B.C.L., Bachelor of Civil Law.

B.D., Bachelor of Divinity.

B.D.S., Bachelor of Dental Surgery.

B.E., Bachelor of Education; Bachelor of Engineering.

B.E.E., Bachelor of Electrical Engineering.

Belg., Belgian; Belgium.

bf, b.f., bold-faced (type).

Bib., Bible; Biblical.

Bibl., bibliographical.

B.J., Bachelor of Journalism.

B.L., Bachelor of Laws.

B/L, bill of lading.

bldg., building.

B.L.E., Brotherhood of Locomotive Engineers.

B.Lit(t)., Baccalaureus Lit(t)erarum (L., Bachelor of Literature, *or* of Letters).

BLS, Bureau of Labor Statistics.

B.L.S., Bachelor of Library Science.

blvd., boulevard.

B.M., Baccalaureus Medicinae (L., Bachelor of Medicine).

BMR, basal metabolic rate.

B.Mus., Bachelor of Music.

bor., borough.

B.P.E., Bachelor of Physical Education.

BPI, Bureau of Public Inquiries.

B.P.O.E., BPOE, Benevolent and Protective Order of Elks.

Brig., Brigade; Brigadier.

Brig. Gen., Brigadier General.

Brit., Britain; Britannia; Britannica; British.

B.S., Bachelor of Science.

b.s., B/S, bill of sale.

B.S.A., Boy Scouts of America.

B.Sc., Baccalaureus Scientiae (L., Bachelor of Science).

B.S.Ed., Bachelor of Science in Education.

B.T., B.Th., Baccalaureus Theologiae (L., Bachelor of Theology).

B.T.U., B.Th.U., b.t.u., btu, British thermal unit.

bu., bureau; bushel.

Bulg., Bulgaria; Bulgarian.

B.W.I., British West Indies.

c., C, c-., c, centimeter.

C.A., Central America; Coast Artillery.

ca., cathode; circa.

CAA, Civil Aeronautics Administration.

CAB, Civil Aeronautics Board; Consumers' Advisory Board.

cal., calendar; caliber; calorie(s).

Calif., California.

Camb., Cambridge.

Can., Canada; Canadian.

canc., canceled.

Cantab., Cantabrigiensis (L., of Cambridge).

CAP, Civil Air Patrol.

Capt., Captain.

CAR, C.A.R., Civil Air Regulations.

car., carat.

Card., Cardinal.

CARE, Co-operative for American Remittances to Everywhere.

Cath., Catholic.

cav., cavalry.

C.B., Chirurgiae Baccalaureus (L., Bachelor of Surgery).

CBC, Canadian Broadcasting Corporation.

CBS, Columbia Broadcasting System.

cc., cc, c.c., cubic centimeters.

CCC, Civilian Conservation Corps; Commodity Credit Corporation.

C.C.F., CCF, Cooperative Commonwealth Federation (of Canada).

CCS, Combined Chiefs of Staff.

CDB, Cdr., Commander.

C.E., Christian Endeavor; Church of England; Civil Engineer.

CEA, Council of Economic Advisers.

CED, Committee for Economic Development.

C.G., Coast Guard.

Chanc., Chancellor; chancery.

chap., chaplain; chapter.

Ch.B., Chirurgiae Baccalaureus (L., Bachelor of Surgery).

Ch. Clk., Chief Clerk.

Ch.D., Doctor of Chemistry.

Ch.E., Chemical Engineer.

Chin., China; Chinese.

chm., chairman.

Chron., Chronicles.

CIA, Central Intelligence Agency.

CIAA, Coordinator of Inter-American Affairs.

C. in C., C in C, Commander in Chief.

CIO, C.I.O., Congress of Industrial Organizations.

civ., civil; civilian.

ck., check.

c.m., court-martial.

Cmdr., Commander.

CO, C.O., Commanding Officer; conscientious objector.

Co., co., company; county.

c.o., c/o, care of; carried over.

C.O.D., cash on delivery.

C. of S., Chief of Staff.

Col., Colonel; Columbia.

Colo., Colorado.

Com., Commander; Commodore.

comdg., commanding.

Comdr., Commander.

Comdt., Commandant.

Com. in Ch., Commander in Chief.

Comr., Commissioner.

conf., conference; confessor.

Confed., Confederate.

Cong., Congregational; Congress; Congressional.

Conn., Connecticut.

Cont., Continental.

co-op., co-operative.

Cor., Corinthians.

Corp., Corporal; Corporation.

corresp., correspondence.

CP, command post; Communist Party.

C.P.A., CPA, Certified Public Accountant.

Cpl., Corporal.

CPO, C.P.O., Chief Petty Officer.

C.R., Costa Rica.

C.S., Christian Science; Christian Scientist.

C.S.C., Conspicuous Service Cross.

CSC, Civil Service Commission.

CST, C.S.T., Central Standard Time.

CWA, Civil Works Administration.

CWAC, C.W.A.C., Canadian Women's Army Corps.

cwt., hundredweight.

CYO, Catholic Youth Organization.

C.Z., Canal Zone (Panama).

Czech., Czechoslovakia.

D.A., District Attorney.

D.A.R., DAR, Daughters of the American Revolution.

DAV, D.A.V., Disabled American Veterans.

D.C., District of Columbia.

DC, D.C., d.c., direct current.

D.C.L., Doctor of Canon Law; Doctor of Civil Law.

D.C.M., Distinguished Conduct Medal. *British Army.*

D.D., Divinitatis Doctor (L., Doctor of Divinity).

D.D.S., Doctor of Dental Surgery.

Dec., December.

D.E.I., Dutch East Indies.

Del., Delaware.

Dem., Democrat, Democratic.

Den., Denmark.

dept., department; deputy.

desc., descendant.

Deut., Deuteronomy.

D.F.C., DFC, Distinguished Flying Cross.

di., dia., diam., diameter.

dir., director.

disc., discount.

disch., discharged.

dist., distance; district.

div., divided; dividend; division; divisor.

D.Lit., D.Litt., Doctor Lit(t)erarum (L., Doctor of Literature, *or* of Letters).

do., ditto (It., the same).

dom., dominion.

doz., dozen; dozens.

DP, displaced person.

Dr., Dr, debit; debtor; Doctor.

dr., dram; drams.

D.S., D.Sc., Doctor of Science.

D.S.C., DSC, Distinguished Service Cross.

D.S.M., DSM, Distinguished Service Medal.

D.S.O., (Companion of the) Distinguished Service Order; District Staff Officer.

D.S.T., Daylight Saving Time.

d.t., delirium tremens.

D.Th., D.Theol., Doctor of Theology.

dup., duplicate.

D.V.M., Doctor of Veterinary Medicine.

E, E., e., east; eastern.

ea., each.

Eccles., Ecclesiastes.

Ecua., Ecuador.

ed., edited; edition; editor.

Ed.B., Bach. of Education.

Ed.D., Doctor of Education.

Ed.M., Master of Education.

E.E., Electrical Engineer.

e.g., exempli gratia (L., for example).

E.I., East Indian; East Indies.

EKG, electrocardiogram.

elev., elevation.

E. long., east longitude.

enc., encl., enclosure.

encycl., encyclopedia.

Ency. Brit., Encyc. Brit., Encyclopaedia Britannica.

ENE, east-northeast.

Eng., England; English.

Eng. D., Doctor of Engineering.

Ens., Ensign.

env., envelope.

Epis., Episc., Episcopal.

ERA, Emergency Relief Administration.

E.R.V., English Revised Version (of the Bible).

ESE, east-southeast.

ESP, extrasensory perception.

Esq., Esqr., Esquire.

E.S.T., Eastern Standard Time.

est., established.

et al., et alibi (L., and elsewhere); et alii (L., and others).

etc., et cetera.

Eth., Ethiopia.

ETO, European Theater of Operations.

et seq., et sequens (L., and the following); et sequentes *or* sequentia (L., and those that follow).

Eur., Europe; European.

exam., examination.

excl., exclusive.

exec., executive; executor.

ex lib., ex libris (L., from the books [of]).

F, Fahrenheit; fathom; fluorine (*Chem.*).

F., Fahrenheit; Fellow.

FA, F.A., field artillery.

fac., facsim., facsimile.

F.A.C.P., Fellow of the American College of Physicians.

F.A.C.S., Fellow of the American College of Surgeons.

F.A.I.A., Fellow of the American Institute of Architects.

F.A.M., F. and A.M., Free and Accepted Masons.

F.A.S., Fellow of the Actuarial Society (*Canada*); Fellow of the Antiquarian Society (*Brit.*); Fellow of the Anthropological Society (*Brit.*).

F.B.A., Fellow of the British Academy.

FBI, Federal Bureau of Investigation.

FCA, Farm Credit Administration.

FCC, Federal Communications Commission.

F.C.C., First Class Certificate.

F.C.I.C., Fellow of the Canadian Institute of Chemistry.

F.C.S., Fellow of the Chemical Society.

FDA, Food and Drug Administration.

FDIC, Federal Deposit Insurance Corporation.

FEB, Fair Employment Board.

Feb., February.

fed., federal; federation.

fem., feminine.

FEPC, Fair Employment Practice Committee.

FERA, Federal Emergency Relief Administration.

F.F.V., First Families of Virginia.

FHA, Farmers Home Administration; Federal Housing Administration.

F.H.S., Fellow of the Horticul'ural Society.

F.I.A., Fellow of the Institute of Actuaries. *Brit.*

F.I.J., Fellow of the Institute of Journalists. *Brit.*

Fin., Finland; Finnish.

Fl, Flanders; Flemish.

FLA, Federal Loan Agency.

Fla., Florida.

fl. oz., fluid ounce, *or* ounces.

FM, F.M., f-m, f.m., frequency modulation.

FMCS, Federal Mediation and Conciliation Service.

F.M.S.A., Fellow of the Mineralogical Society of America.

fn., footnote.

FNMA, Federal National Mortgage Association.

F.O., Foreign Office.

F.O.B., .f.o.b, free on board.

fol., folio; following.

FPC, Federal Power Commission.

f.p.m., fpm, feet per minute.

F.R.A.M., Fellow of the Royal Academy of Music.

F.R.A.S., Fellow of the Royal Astronomical Society.

FRC, Federal Radio Commission.

F.R.C.M., Fellow of the Royal College of Music.

F.R.C.P., Fellow of the Royal College of Physicians.

F.R.C.S., Fellow of the Royal College of Surgeons.

F.R.G.S., Fellow of the Royal Geographical Society.

Fri., Friday.

F.R.S., Fellow of the Royal Society (scientific).

F.R.S.C., Fellow of the Royal Society of Canada.

F.R.S.L., Fellow of the Royal Society of Literature; Fellow of the Royal Society, London.

F.R.S.N.Z., Fellow of the Royal Society of New Zealand.

frt., freight.

FSA, Federal Security Agency.

ft., feet; fort.

FTC, Federal Trade Commission.

FWA, Federal Works Agency.

fwd., forward.

F.Z.S., Fellow of the Zoological Society.

g., g, gram.

Ga., Georgia.

G.A., GA, General Agent; General Assembly.

gal., gallon; gallons.

GAO, General Accounting Office.

G.A.R., GAR, Grand Army of the Republic.

gaz., gazette; gazetteer.

G.B., Great Britain.

G.C.B., (Knight) Grand Cross of the Bath.

G.C.L.H., Grand Cross of the Legion of Honor.

GCT, G.C.T., Greenwich civil time.

gds., goods.

Gen., General (*Army*); Genesis; Geneva.

gent., gentleman.

geol., geologic; geological; geologist; geology.

geom., geometer; geometric; geometrical; geometry.

Ger., German; Germany.

Gestapo, Geheime Staatspolizei (G., Secret State Police).

GHQ, G.H.Q., General Headquarters. *Mil.*

GI, G.I., member of the U.S. armed forces (government issue).

Gib., Gibraltar.

Gk., Greek.

G.M., General Manager; Grand Master.

GMT, G.M.T., Greenwich mean time.

G.O.P., GOP, Grand Old Party (a rhetorical name for the Republican party).

Gov., gov., governor.

Govt., govt., government.

G.P., general practitioner.

G.P.O., GPO, General Post Office; Government Printing Office.

GQ, G.Q., g.q., general quarters. *Nav.*

Gr., Greece.

grad., graduate; graduated.

gram., grammar; grammarian; grammatical.

Gr. Br., Gr. Brit., Great Britain.

gr. wt., gross weight.

GS, G.S., General Staff.

G.S.A., GSA, Girl Scouts of America.

GSC, G.S.C., General Staff Corps.

GSO, General Staff Officer.

h.a., hoc anno (L., in this year).

Hb, hemoglobin.

H.C., House of Commons.

hdqrs., headquarters.

H.E., His Eminence; His Excellency.

Heb., Hebr., Hebrews(s).

her., heraldry.

H.F., HF, h.f., hf, high-frequency.

H.H., His, or Her, Highness; His Holiness (the Pope).

H.I., Hawaiian Islands.

Hind., Hindu; Hindustan.

H.M., His (Her) Majesty.

H.M.S., His (Her) Majesty's Service, Ship, or Steamer.

HOLC, Home Owners' Loan Corporation.

Hon., Honorable.

hon., honorary.

hosp., hospital.

H.P., HP, h.p., hp, high pressure; horsepower.

HQ, H.Q., hq, h.q., headquarters.

H.R., House of Representatives.

hr., hour; hours.

H.R.H., His (Her) Royal Highness.

ht., height; heat.

Hts., Heights.

Hung., Hungarian; Hungary.

I., Island(s), Isle(s).

ib., ibid., ibidem (L., in the same place).

ICAO, International Civil Aviation Organization.

ICC, Interstate Commerce Commission.

ICJ, International Court of Justice.

I.D., Intelligence Department.

IE, I.E., Indo-European.

i.e., id est (L., that is).

I.F.S., Irish Free State.

Ill., Illinois.

ill., illus., illust., illustrated; illustration.

ILO, I.L.O., International Labor Organization.

in., inch; inches.

incl., inclosure; inclusive.

Ind., India; Indian; Indiana; Indies.

ind., index.

inf., information.

inf., Inf., infantry.

init., initial.

in loc. cit., in loco citato (L., in the place cited).

INS, I.N.S., International News Service.

insp., inspector.

Inst., Institute; Institution.

Int. Rev., Internal Revenue.

introd., introduction.

inv., invoice.

invt., inventory.

I.O.O.F., Independent Order of Odd Fellows.

I.O.R.M., Improved Order of Red Men.

IOU, I.O.U., I owe you.

IQ, I.Q., intelligence quotient.

i.q., idem quod (L., the same as).

Ire., Ireland.

IRO, International Refugee Organization.

Is., is., island; isle.

Isr., Israel.

It., Ital., Italian; Italy.

ital., italic (type).

ITO, International Trade Organization.

IWW, I.W.W., Industrial Workers of the World.

J., Judge, Justice.

JA, J.A., Judge Advocate.

J.A.G., Judge Advocate General.

Jam., Jamaica.

Jan., January.

Jap., Japan; Japanese.

Jav., Javanese.

J.D., Jurum Doctor (L., Doctor of Laws).

jg, j-g., junior grade.

J.P., justice of the peace.

Jr., jr., junior.

Jur. D., Juris Doctor (L., Doctor of Law.

Kans., Kansas.

K.B., King's Bench; Knight Bachelor.

K.C., King's Counsel; Knights of Columbus.

K.C.B., Knight Commander (of the Order) of the Bath.

K.G., Knight (of the Order) of the Garter.

kg., kg, kilogram(s).

kilo., kilogram; kilometer.

K.K.K., Ku Klux Klan.

km., km, kilometer; kingdom.

KO, K.O., k.o., knockout. *Pugilism.*

K. of C., Knight, *or* Knights, of Columbus.

K. of P., Knight, *or* Knights, of Pythias.

K.P., Knight (of the Order) of St. Patrick; Knights of Pythias.

K.P., KP, kitchen police.

K.T., Knight Templar.

kt., carat.

kw., kilowatt.

K.W.H., kw-h, kw-hr, kilowatt-hour.

Ky., Kentucky.

£, L, l, libra (L., pound).

La., Louisiana.

Lab., Labrador.

lab., laboratory.
Lam., Lamentations.
Lat., Latin.
lat., latitude.
L.B., Lit(t)erarum Baccalaureus (L., Bachelor of Letters); Local Board.
lb., **lb.**, libra (L., pound).
L.C., Library of Congress.
L.C.M., **l.c.m.**, lowest, or least, common multiple.
L.F., **LF.**, **l.f.**, **lf**, low-frequency.
lge., large.
L.H.D., Litterarum Humaniorum Doctor (L., Doctor of Humanities).
L.I., Long Island.
Lib., Liberal.
lib., librarian; library.
Lieut., Lieutenant.
lit., literature.
Lit.B., **Litt.B.**, Lit(t)erarum Baccalaureus (L., Bachelor of Letters, Bachelor of Literature).
Lit.D., Literarum Doctor (L., Doctor of Literature).
Litt.D., Literarum Doctor (L., Doctor of Letters).
LL.B., Legum Baccalaureus (L., Bachelor of Laws).
LL.D., Legum Doctor (L., Doctor of Laws).
lon., **long.**, longitude.
L.O.O.M., Loyal Order of Moose.
L.P.S., Lord Privy Seal.
L.S.S., (U.S.) Lifesaving Service.
Lt., Lieutenant.
Ltd., **ltd.**, limited.
lv., leave.

M, thousand.
MA, **M.A.**, mental age.
M.A., Magister Artium (L., Master of Arts); Military Academy.
M.Agr., Master of Agriculture.
Maj., Major.
Man., Manitoba.
mar., maritime.
marg., margin; marginal.
masc., masculine.
Mass., Massachusetts.
MATS, Military Air Transport Service.
max., maximum.
M.B., Medicinae Baccalaureus (L., Bachelor of Medicine); Militia Bureau.
M.B.A., Master in, or of, Business Administration.
M.C., Master of Ceremonies; Medical Corps; Member of Congress.
M.C.L., Master of Civil Law.
M.D., Medical Department; Doctor of Medicine.
Md., Maryland.
mdse., merchandise.

M.E., Methodist Episcopal; Mining, or Mechanical, Engineer.
M.Ed., Master of Education.
med., medical; medicine.
Medit., Mediterranean.
meg., megacycle.
memo., memorandum.
mer., meridian.
Messrs., **Messrs**, Messieurs.
Meth., Methodist.
Mex., Mexico.
mfg., manufacturing.
MG, Military Government.
mg., milligram(s).
Mgr., Manager.
MH, Medal of Honor.
mi., mile.
Mich., Michigan.
mil., military; militia.
Minn., Minnesota.
misc., miscellaneous.
Miss., Mississippi.
mm., millimeter; millia (L., thousands).
Mo., Missouri.
MO, **M.O.**, Medical Officer.
M.O., **m.o.**, money order.
mo., **mos.**, month(s).
M.O.I., Ministry of Information (Brit.).
Mon., Monday; Monsignor.
Mont., Montana.
MP, **M.P.**, military police.
M.P., Member of Parliament.
M.P.E., Master of Physical Education.
mph, **m.p.h.**, miles per hour.
Ms., **MS.**, **ms.**, **ms**, manuscript.
M.S., Master of Science.
Msgr., Monsignor.
M/Sgt, **M.Sgt.**, Master Sergeant.
MSS., **mss.**, manuscripts.
M.S.T., Mountain Standard Time.
Mt., **mt.**, mount; mountain
mtge., mortgage.
MTO, Mediterranean Theater of Operations.
Mus.B., **Mus.Bac.**, Musicae Baccalaureus (L., Bachelor of Music).
Mus.D., **Mus.Doc.**, **Mus.Dr.**, Musicae Doctor (L., Doctor of Music).
MVA, Missouri Valley Authority.
mythol., mythology.

N, **n.**, **n.**, north; northern.
N.A., National Academician; North America.
NAA, **N.A.A.**, National Aeronautic Association.
NAACP, National Association for the Advancement of Colored People.

NACA, National Advisory Committee for Aeronautics.
NAB, National Association of Broadcasters.
N.A.D., National Academy of Design.
NAM, National Association of Manufacturers.
NATO, North Atlantic Treaty Alliance.
naut., nautical.
nav., naval; navigation.
N.B., New Brunswick.
N.B., **n.b.**, nota bene (L., note well).
NBA, **N.B.A.**, National Boxing Association.
NBC, National Broadcasting Company.
N.B.S., National Bureau of Standards.
NC, Nurse Corps.
N.C., North Carolina.
NCAA, **N.C.A.A.**, National Collegiate Athletic Association.
NCO, **N.C.O.**, **n.c.o.**, noncommissioned officer.
N.Dak., North Dakota.
NE, **N.E.**, **n.e.**, northeast.
N.E., New England.
NEA, **N.E.A.**, National Education Association.
Nebr., Nebraska.
Neth., Netherlands.
neut., neuter.
Nev., Nevada.
New Test., New Testament.
N.F., Newfoundland.
N.F., **n/f.**, no funds.
NG, **N.G.**, National Guard.
N.G., **n.g.**, no good.
N.H., New Hampshire.
NHA, National Housing Agency.
Nicar., Nicaragua.
N.J., New Jersey.
N. lat., north latitude.
NLRB, National Labor Relations Board.
N. Mex., New Mexico.
NNE, north-northeast.
NNW, north-northwest.
No., north; northern.
No., **no.**, number.
noncom., noncommissioned officer.
non pros., non prosequitur (L., he does not prosecute).
non seq., non sequitur (L., it does not follow).
Nor., Norway; Norwegian.
Nov., November.
NP, neuropsychiatric.
N.P., no protest; Notary Public.
NRAB, National Railroad Adjustment Board.
N.S., Nova Scotia.
NSC, National Security Council.

N.S.P.C.A., National Society for the Prevention of Cruelty to Animals.

N.S.P.C.C., National Society for the Prevention of Cruelty to Children.

NSRB, National Security Resources Board.

N.S.W., New South Wales.

N.T., New Testament.

nt. wt., net weight.

num., numeral; numerals.

NW, N.W., n.w., northwest.

N.W.T., Northwest Territories. *Can.*

N.Y., New York.

NYA, National Youth Administration.

N.Y.C., New York City.

N.Z., N.Zeal, New Zealand.

ob., obiit (L., he (she) died); obiter (L., in passing, i. e. incidentally).

O.B.E., Officer (of the Order) of the British Empire.

obs., obsolete.

obstet., obstetrical.

OCD, Office of Civilian Defense.

OCIAA, Office of Co-ordinator of Inter-American Affairs.

OCS, Officer Candidate School.

Oct., October.

O.D., Officer of the Day; ordinary seaman; overdraft, *or* overdrawn.

ODT, Office of Defense Transportation.

OEM, Office for Emergency Management.

O.E.S., Order of the Eastern Star.

off., officer; official.

O.G., Officer of the Guard.

O.H.M.S., On His (Her) Majesty's Service.

O.K., all correct.

Okla., Oklahoma.

Old Test., Old Testament.

O.M., Order of Merit (*Brit.*).

ONI, Office of Naval Intelligence.

Ont., Ontario.

O.P., OP, o.p., op, out of print; overprint (*Philately*); overproof.

OPA, Office of Price Administration.

ORC, Officers' Reserve Corps.

Ore., Oreg., Oregon.

OSS, Office of Strategic Services.

OSSR, Office of Selective Service Records.

OTC, O.T.C., Officers' Training Camp, *or* Corps.

OTS, O.T.S., Officers' Training School.

OWI, Office of War Information.

Oxf., Ox., Oxford.

Pa., Pennsylvania.

P.A., Passenger Agent; Post Adjutant; public address (system); Purchasing Agent.

P.A., P/A, power of attorney; private account.

p.a., participial adjective; per annum.

PAC, Political Action Committee.

Pac., Pacif., Pacific.

Pan., Panama.

par., paragraph.

Para., Paraguay.

pat., patent; patented.

patd., patented.

Pat. Off., Patent Office.

P.A.U., PAU, Pan American Union.

PBA, Public Buildings Administration.

P.C., Past Commander; Post Commander; Privy Council, *or* Councilor.

pc., piece; price(s).

p.c., per cent; post card.

P.D., Police Department.

P.D., p.d., per diem (L., by the day).

pd., paid.

P.E., Protestant Episcopal.

P.E.N., (International Association of) Poets, Playwrights, Editors, Essayists and Novelists.

Pen., pen., peninsula.

per an., per ann., per annum.

Pers., Persia; Persian.

Peruv., Peruvian.

Pfc, Pfc., Private, First Class.

pfd., preferred.

P.G., Past Grand; postgraduate.

PGA, Professional Golfers Association.

P.H., Purple Heart.

PHA, Public Housing Authority.

Phar., Pharm., pharmaceutical; pharmacopoeia; pharmacy.

Phar.D., Pharm.D., Doctor of Pharmacy.

Ph.B., Philosophiae Baccalaureus (L., Bachelor of Philosophy).

Ph.D., Philosophiae Doctor (L., Doctor of Philosophy).

Phila., Philadelphia.

photo., photograph.

PHS, Public Health Service.

phys., physician; physics.

pk., pack; park; peck.

pkg., package, *or* packages.

pl., plural.

plat., platoon.

P.M., Past Master; Paymaster; Police Magistrate; Postmaster; Provost Marshal.

P.M., P.M., p.m., post meridiem.

p.m., post-mortem.

PMA, Production and Marketing Administration.

pmkd, postmarked.

P.O., p.o., petty officer; postal order; post office.

po., p.o., put-out. *Baseball.*

P.O.D., Post Office Department.

pop., population.

Port., Portugal; Portuguese.

POW, P.O.W., prisoner of war.

P.P., p.p., parcel post; postpaid.

pp., pages.

ppd., postpaid; prepaid.

P.P.S., p.p.s., post postscriptum (L., an additional postscript).

P.Q., Province of Quebec.

P.R., Puerto Rico.

pr., pair; pairs.

PRA, Public Roads Administration.

prelim., preliminary.

Pres., President.

pres., present; presidency.

Presb., Presbyterian.

Prof., prof., professor.

pron., pronoun.

propr., proprietor.

Prot., Protestant.

pro tem., pro tempore.

prov., province; provincial; provost.

P.S., Privy Seal; Public School.

P.S., p.s., passenger steamer; post scriptum (L., postscript).

pseud., pseudonym.

P.S.T., Pacific Standard Time.

pt., part; payment; pint; point; port.

P.T.A., PTA, Parent-Teacher Association.

PT boat, patrol torpedo boat.

ptg., printing.

pub., public; published.

PWA, Public Works Administration.

P.W.D., PWD, Public Works Department.

PX, post exchange.

Q., q., quarts; question.

Q.E.D., quod erat demonstrandum (L., which was to be demonstrated).

Q.E.F., quod erat faciendum (L., which was to be done).

QMC, Q.M.C., Quartermaster Corps.

QMG, Q.M.G., Q.M. Gen., Quartermaster-General.

qr., quarter; quire.

qt., quantity; quart.

q.t., quiet. *Slang.*

qu., query; question.

Que., Quebec.

quot., quotation.

q.v., quod vide (L., which see).

R.A., Rear Admiral; Royal Academy, *or* Academician; Royal Artillery.

RA, R.A., Regular Army.

R.A.A.F., RAAF, Royal Australian Air Force.

R.A.F., RAF, Royal Air Force.

R.A.M., Royal Academy of Music.

R.C., RC, Red Cross; Reserve Corps; Roman Catholic.

R.C.A.F., RCAF, Royal Canadian Air Force.

R.C.Ch., Roman Catholic Church.

Rd., rd., road.

RDB, Research Development Board.

R.E., Royal Engineers.

rec., receipt; recipe; recorded.

recd., received.

rec. sec., recording secretary.

ref., referee; reference; referred; reformed.

Ref.Ch., Reformed Church.

rel., relating; relative.

rel. pron., relative pronoun.

Rep., Republican.

resp., respectively.

Resurr., Resurrection.

ret., retired; returned.

Rev., Reverend.

rev., review.

R.F., r.f., radio frequency; rapid-fire.

RFC, Reconstruction Finance Corporation.

R.F.C., Royal Flying Corps.

R.F.D., Rural Free Delivery.

R.I., Rhode Island.

R.I.P., requiescat, *or* requiescant, in pace (L., may he (she), *or* they, rest in peace).

rm., ream. *Paper.*

R.M.A., Royal Military Academy (Woolwich).

R.M.C., Royal Military College (Sandhurst).

R.N., Registered Nurse; Royal Navy.

R.N.R., Royal Naval Reserve.

Rom., Roman; Romance; Romania; Romanian.

Rom. Cath., Roman Catholic.

ROTC, R.O.T.C., Reserve Officers' Training Corps, *or* Camp.

rpm, r.p.m., revolutions per minute.

R.R., railroad; Right Reverend.

RRB, Railroad Retirement Board.

R.S.V.P., r.s.v.p., Répondez, s'il vous plaît (F., please reply).

Rt. Hon., Right Honorable.

Rt. Rev., Right Reverend.

Rus., Russ., Russia.

Ry., Railway.

S.A., sex appeal. *Slang.*

s.a., sine anno (L., without year); semiannual.

S.A.E., SAE, Society of Automotive Engineers.

Salv., Salvador.

S.Am., S.Amer., South America, *or* American.

S.A.R., SAR, Sons of the American Revolution.

Sask., Saskatchewan.

Sat., Saturday; Saturn.

Sax., Saxon; Saxony.

S.B., Scientiae Baccalaureus (L., Bachelor of Science).

Sc., science.

SC, Security Council (of United Nations).

S.C., Sanitary Corps; Signal Corps; South Carolina; Supreme Court.

Sc.B., Scientiae Baccalaureus (L., Bachelor of Science).

Sc.D., Scientiae Doctor (L., Doctor of Science).

Sch., School.

Sc.M., Scientiae Magister (L., Master of Science).

Scot., Scotch; Scotland; Scottish.

Script., Scripture.

SCS, Soil Conservation Service.

s.d., sine die.

S.Dak., South Dakota.

SE, S.E., s.e., southeast.

SEC, Securities and Exchange Commission.

secy., secretary.

Sem., Seminary; Semitic.

Sen., sen., senate; senator; senior.

Sept., September.

seq., sequel.

ser., series.

sg, s.g., senior grade.

s.g., specific gravity.

sgd., signed.

Sgt., Sergeant.

SHAEF, Supreme Headquarters, Allied Expeditionary Forces.

shpt., shipment.

S.I., Sandwich Islands; Staten Island (N.Y.).

S. lat., south latitude.

sld., sailed; sealed.

S.M., Scientiae Magister (L., Master of Science); Sergeant Major; Soldier's Medal; State Militia.

So., South; Southern.

soc., soc., society.

sol., solution.

Sp., Spain; Spaniard; Spanish.

SPARS [from Coast Guard motto "Semper Paratus—Always Ready"], Women's Coast Guard Reserves.

S.P.C.A., Society for Prevention of Cruelty to Animals.

S.P.C.C., Society for Prevention of Cruelty to Children.

S.P.R., Society for Psychical Research.

spt., seaport.

Sq., Squadron.

sq., square; sequence sequentia (L., the following).

Sr., Senior; Sir; Sister.

S.R., Sons of the Revolution.

S.R.O., standing room only.

SS., Sancti (L., Saints); Saints.

S.S., Silver Star; Sunday School.

SS, S.S., S/S, steamship.

SSE, south-southeast.

S/Sgt., S.Sgt., Staff Sergeant.

SSS, Selective Service System.

SSW, south-southwest.

St., Saint; Strait; Street.

Sta., Station.

S.T.D., Sacrae Theologiae Doctor (L., Doctor of Sacred Theology).

Ste., Sainte (F., *fem.* of saint).

St. Ex., Stock Exchange.

Sun., Sunday.

Supt., supt., superintendent.

surg., surgeon; surgery.

SW, S.W., s.w., southwest; southwestern.

syn., synonym.

Syr., Syria; Syrian.

tab., tables.

Tass, TASS, Telegraphnoye Agentstvo Sovyetskovo Soyuza (Russ., The Soviet News Agency).

T.B., Tb., t.b., tubercle bacillus; tuberculosis.

tbsp., tablespoon.

TC, Trusteeship Council (of the United Nations).

tech., technical; technology.

Tech. Sgt., Technical Sergeant.

temp., temperature.

Tenn., Tennessee.

Tex., Texan; Texas.

Th.D., Theologiae Doctor (L., Doctor of Theology).

Thur., Thurs., Thursday.

tit., title.

TKO, T.K.O., t.k.o., technical knockout. *Pugilism.*

tn., ton; train.

tng., training.

TNT, T.N.T., trinitrotoluene; trinitrotoluol.

tp., township.

trans., transactions; transitive.

treas., treasurer; treasury.

trop., tropic; tropical.

tsp., teaspoon.

Tues., Tuesday.

Turk., Turkey; Turkish.

TV, television.

TVA, Tennessee Valley Authority.

UAW, U.A.W., United Auto, Aircraft and Agricultural Implements Workers.

U.D.C., United Daughters of the Confederacy. *U.S.*

UHF, UHF, u.h.f., uhf, ultra-high-frequency.

ult., ultimate; ultimately.

ult., ulto., ultimo.

UMW, U.M.W., United Mine Workers.

UN, U.N., United Nations.

UNCIO, United Nations Conference on International Organization.

UNESCO, United Nations Educational, Scientific and Cultural Organization.

univ., universal; university.

UNRRA, United Nations Relief and Rehabilitation Administration.

UP, U.P., United Press.

Uru., Uruguay.

U.S., US, United States.

U.S.A., USA, Union of South Africa; United States Army; United States of America.

USAF, United States Air Force.

USCG, U.S.C.G., United States Coast Guard.

USDA, United States Department of Agriculture.

USES, United States Employment Service.

U.S.M., United States Mail.

U.S.M.A., USMA, United States Military Academy.

USMC, U.S.M.C., United States Marine Corps.

USN, U.S.N., United States Navy.

U.S.N.A., USNA, United States National Army; United States Naval Academy.

USNG, U.S.N.G., United States National Guard.

USNR, U.S.N.R., United States Naval Reserve.

USO, United Service Organizations.

USS, U.S.S., United States Ship, *or* Steamer.

USSR, Union of Soviet Socialist Republics.

U.S.V., United States Volunteers.

V, v, volt.

VA, Veterans' Administration.

Va., Virginia.

V.A., Vice-Admiral.

Vat., Vatican.

vb., verb.

V.C., Veterinary Corps; Vice-Chancellor; Vice-Consul; Victoria Cross.

VD, V.D., v.d., venereal disease.

Ven., Venerable; Venice.

Venez., Venezuela.

ver., verse, *or* verses.

Vet., vet., veteran; veterinarian; veterinary.

VFW, V.F.W., Veterans of Foreign Wars (of the U.S.).

V.I., Virgin Islands.

VIP, V.I.P., very important person. *Informal.*

viz., videlicet (L., namely).

V.M.D., Veterinariae Medicinae Doctor (L., Doctor of Veterinary Medicine).

vocab., vocabulary.

vol., volcano; volume.

vox pop., vox populi (L., voice of the people).

V.P., Vice-President.

V.S., Veterinary Surgeon.

vs., versus.

Vt., Vermont.

v.v., vice versa.

W, w, watt; western.

W.A., West Africa; Western Australia.

WAAC, Women's Army Auxiliary Corps. *U.S. Army.*

WAAF, Women's Auxiliary Air Force. *Brit.*

WAAS, Women's Auxiliary Army Service. *Brit.*

WAC, Women's Army Corps. *U.S.*

WAF, Women in the Air Force. *U.S.*

WAFS, Women's Auxiliary Ferrying Squadron. *U.S. Army.*

Wash., Washington.

WASP, Women's Air Force Service Pilots.

watt-hr., watt-hour.

WAVES, Women Accepted for Volunteer Emergency Service. *U.S. Navy.*

W.C.T.U., Woman's Christian Temperance Union.

Wed., Wednesday.

WFTU, World Federation of Trade Unions.

WHO, World Health Organization.

W.I., West India; West Indian; West Indies.

Wis., Wisc., Wisconsin.

wk., week; work.

WL, w.l., water line; wave length.

WLB, War Labor Board.

WMC, War Manpower Commission.

wmk., watermark.

WNW, west-northwest.

WO, W.O., wait order; Warrant Officer.

WPA, Works Progress Administration.

WPB, War Production Board.

WRAC, Women's Royal Army Corps.

WRAF, Women's Royal Air Force.

WRENS, W.R.N.S., Women's Royal Naval Service. *Brit.*

WSW, west-southwest.

wt., weight.

W. Va., West Virginia.

WVS, Women's Voluntary Service. *Brit*

Wyo., Wyoming.

x, an unknown quantity.

Xmas, Christmas.

Y.M.C.A., Young Men's Christian Association.

Y.M.H.A., Young Men's Hebrew Association.

Y.P.S.C.E., Young People's Society of Christian Endeavor.

Y.W.C.A., Young Women's Christian Association.

Y.W.H.A., Young Women's Hebrew Association.

Z., z., zone.

A

a, the indefinite article, used before a consonant. *See* **an.**

aback, a-bak′, *adv.* Backwards; by surprise.

abacus, ab′a-kus, *n.*; pl. **-ci**, or **-cuses**. 1. A square slab forming the crowning of a column. 2. An Oriental calculating device.

Abacus.

abalone, ab′a-lō′nĕ, *n.* An edible shellfish; the shell is lined with mother-of-pearl.

abandon, a-ban′dun, *vt.* To forsake entirely; to desert. **abandoned**, a-ban′-dund, *p.a.* Depraved. **abandonment**, a-ban′dun-ment, *n.* A total desertion.

abase, a-bās′, *vt.* (abasing, abased). To bring low; degrade; disgrace. **abasement**, a-bās′ment, *n.* State of being abased; degradation.

abash, a-bash′, *vt.* To put to confusion; to make ashamed.

abate, a-bāt′, *vt.* (abating, abated). To lessen. *vi.* To become less. **abatement**, a-bāt′ment, *n.* Act of abating; a mitigation; deduction.

abattoir, a-ba-twär′, *n.* A public slaughterhouse.

abbot, ab′ut, *n.* The male superior of an abbey.

abbacy, ab′a-si, *n.*; pl. **-cies.** The dignity, rights, and privileges of an abbot.

abbé, ab-ā, *n.* An inferior R. Catholic ecclesiastic with no benefice.

abbess, ab′es, *n.* A female superior of a nunnery.

abbey, ab′i, *n.*; pl. **-eys.** A monastery, or convent.

abbreviate, ab-brē′vi-āt, *vt.* To shorten. **abbreviation**, ab-brē′vi-ā″shun, *n.* A shortening; contraction. **abbreviator**, ab-brē′vi-ā-tėr, *n.* One who abbreviates or abridges.

abdicate, ab′di-kāt, *vt.* (abdicating, abdicated). To resign voluntarily; to relinquish. *vi.* To resign power. **abdication**, ab-di-kā′shon, *n.* Act of abdicating an office.

abdomen, ab-dō′men, *n.* The lower belly. **abdominal**, ab-dom′in-al, *a.* Pertaining to the lower belly.

abduct, ab-dukt′, *vt.* To entice or lead away wrongly. **abduction**, ab-duk′shon, *n.* The felonious carrying off a man's daughter, wife, &c.

abeam, a-bēm′, *adv.* or *pred. a.* At right angles to the length of a ship.

aberrant, ab-e′rant, *a.* Wandering from; deviating from an established rule. **aberration**, abe-rā′shun, *n.* A wandering from; alienation of the mind.

abet, a-bet′, *vt.* (abetting, abetted). To urge on; to encourage. (Chiefly in a bad sense.) **abetment**, a-bet′ment, *n.* Act of abetting. **abetter**, **abettor**, a-bet′-ėr, *n.* One who abets.

abeyance, a-bā′ans, *n.* Temporary extinction. (With *in* before it.)

abhor, ab-hor′, *vt.* (abhorring, abhorred). To shrink from with horror; to loathe, detest.

abide, a-bīd′, *vi.* (abiding, abode or abided). To stay in a place; to dwell— *vt.* To wait for; to endure. **abiding**, a-bīd′ing, *p.a.* Permanent.

ability, a-bil′li-ti, *n.* Power to do anything; talent; skill; in *pl.* the powers of the mind.

abject, ab′jekt, *a.* Mean; despicable.

abjure, ab-jūr′, *vt.* (abjuring, abjured). To renounce upon oath; to reject. **abjuration**, ab-jū-rā′shun, *n.* Act of abjuring; oath taken for that end.

ablative, ab′lat-iv, *a.* or *n.* Applied to a case of nouns in Latin and other languages.

ablaze, a-blāz′, *adv.* On fire; in a blaze.

able, ā′bl, *a.* Having power sufficient; capable; skillful.

ablution, ab-lu′shun, *n.* A washing away from; a purification by water.

abnegate, ab′nē-gāt, *vt.* To deny; to renounce. **abnegation**, ab-nē-gā′shon, *n.* A denial.

abnormal, ab-norm′al, *a.* Deviating from a fixed rule: irregular.

aboard, a-bōrd′, *adv.* or *prep.* On board; in a ship or vessel.

abode, a-bōd′, *n.* Residence; habitation.

abolish, a-bol′ish, *vt.* To destroy; to abrogate. **abolition**, ab-ō-li′shun, *n.* Act of abolishing; state of being abolished. **abolitionist**, ab-ō-li′shon-ist, *n.* One who seeks to abolish anything, especially slavery.

abominable, a-bom′in-a-bl, *a.* Loathsome. **abominably**, a-bom′in-a-bli, *adv.* Odiously. **abominate**, a-bom′in-āt, *vt.* (abominating, abominated). To hate extremely; to abhor. **abomination**, a-bom′in-ā″shun, *n.* Hatred; object of hatred; loathsomeness.

aboriginal, ab-ō-rig′in-al, *a.* Primitive. **aborigines**, ab-ō-rij′in-ēz, *n. pl.* The original inhabitants of a country.

abort, a-bort′, *vi.* To miscarry in giving birth. **abortion**, a-bor′shun, *n.* A miscarriage. **abortive**, a-bort′iv, *a.* Immature; causing abortion; coming to nought. **abortively**, *adv.* Immaturely.

abound, a-bound′, *vi.* To be, or have, in great plenty. **abounding**, a-bound′ing, *p.a.* In great plenty; prevalent.

about, a-bout′, *prep.* Around; near to; relating to; engaged in. *adv.* Around; round; nearly; here and there.

above, a-buv′, *prep.* To or in a higher place than; superior to; more than; beyond; before. *adv.* To or in a higher place; chiefly.

aboveboard, a-buv'bōrd, *adv.* Without concealment or deception.

abrade, a-brād, *vt.* (abrading, abraded). To scrape off; to waste by friction.

abrasion, ab-rā'zhon, *n.* A rubbing off; substance worn off by rubbing.

abreast, a-brest', *adv.* In a line; side by side.

abridge, a-brij', *vt.* To shorten; to condense. **abridgment**, a-brij'ment, *n.* An epitome; a summary.

abroad, a-brad', *adv.* At large; away from home; in a foreign country.

abrogate, ab'rō-gāt, *vt.* (abrogating, abrogated). To repeal; to make void. **abrogation**, ab-rō-gā'shun, *n.* Act of abrogating; a repeal; annulment.

abrupt, ab-rupt', *a.* Broken off; steep; sudden; unceremonious. **abruptly**, ab-rupt'li, *adv.* Suddenly; unceremoniously. **abruptness**, ab-rupt'nes, *n.* Suddenness; unceremonious haste.

abscess, ab'ses, *n.* A gathering of purulent matter in some part of the body.

abscond, ab-skond', *vi.* To hide one's self; to fly from justice.

absent, ab-sent', *vt.* To keep away from. (With refl. pron.)

absent, ab'sent, *a.* Being away from; not present; wanting in attention.

absence, ab'sens, *n.* State of being absent; inattention to things present.

absentee, ab-sen-tē', *n.* One who absents himself.

absinthe, ab'sinth, *n.* A liquor consisting of spirit flavored with wormwood.

absolute, ab'sō-lūt, *a.* Unlimited; unconditional; certain; despotic. **absolutely**, ab'sō-lūt-li, *adv.* Unconditionally; peremptorily. **absoluteness**, ab'sō-lūt-nes, *n.* State or quality of being absolute. **absolution**, ab-sō-lū'shun, *n.* A loosing from guilt, or its punishment.

absolve, ab-solv', *vt.* To free from, as from guilt or punishment; acquit; pardon.

absorb, ab-sorb', *vt.* To drink in; to engross. **absorbable**, ab-sorb'a-bl, *a.* That may be absorbed or swallowed up. **absorbent**, ab-sorb'ent, *a.* Imbibing; swallowing—*n.* That which absorbs. **absorption**, ab-sorp'shun, *n.* Act or process of imbibing or swallowing up. **absorptive**, ab-sorp'tiv, *a.* Having power to absorb or imbibe.

abstain, ab-stān', *vi.* To keep back from; to refrain; to forbear.

abstemious, ab-stē'mi-us, *a.* Sparing in food or drink; temperate; sober.

abstinence, ab'sti-nens, *n.* A keeping from the indulgence of the appetites, especially from intoxicating liquors. **abstinent**, ab'sti-nent, *a.* Abstaining from; refraining from indulgence. **abstinently**, ab'sti-nent-li, *adv.* With abstinence.

abstract, ab-strakt', *vt.* To draw from; to separate and consider by itself; to epitomize. **abstract**, ab'strakt, *a.* Existing in the mind only; not concrete; general in language or in reasoning.—*n.* A summary; an abridgment. **abstracted**, ab-strakt'ed, *a.* Absent in mind. **abstractedly**, ab-strakt'ed-li, *adv.* In an

absent manner. **abstraction**, ab-strak'-shon, *n.* Act of abstracting; deep thought; absence of mind. **abstractive**, ab-strakt'iv, *a.* Having the power or quality of abstracting. **abstractly**, ab-strakt'li, *adv.* Separately; absolutely.

abstruse, ab-strūs', *a.* Difficult of comprehension; profound in meaning; obscure.

absurd, ab-sèrd', *a.* Contrary to reason or common sense; ridiculous. **absurdity**, ab-sèrd'i-ti, *n.* Quality of being absurd; that which is absurd. **absurdly**, ab-sèrd'li, *adv.* In an absurd manner; against common sense; ridiculously.

abundant, a-bun'dant, *a.* Abounding; plentiful; ample. **abundantly**, a-bun'-dant-li, *adv.* Fully; amply; plentifully. **abundance**, a-bun'dans, *n.* Plenteousness; copiousness; wealth.

abuse, a-būz', *vt.* (abusing, abused). To turn from the proper use; to ill-use; to deceive; to vilify; to violate. **abuse**, a-būs', *n.* Misuse; bad language addressed to a person; insulting words; violation. **abusive**, a-būs'iv, *a.* Practicing abuse; containing abuse; insulting.

abut, a-but', *vi.* (abutting, abutted). To border; to meet. (With *upon.*) **abutment**, a-but'ment, *n.* That which abuts; solid support for the extremity of a bridge, arch, &c.

abyss, a-bis', *n.* A bottomless gulf; a deep pit or mass of waters; hell.

academy, a-kad'ē-mi, *n.* A seminary of arts or sciences; a society of persons for the cultivation of arts and sciences. **academic, academical**, ak-a-dem'ik, ak-a-dem'ik-al, *a.* Belonging to an academy or university. **academic**, ak-a-dem'ik, *n.* A student in a university or academy. **academician**, ak'a-dē-mi''-shi-an, *n.* A member of an academy.

acanthus, a-kan'thus, *n.* A prickly plant, the model of the foliage of the Corinthian order.

accede, ak-sēd', *vi.* (acceding, acceded). To assent to; to comply with.

accelerate, ak-sel'lè-rāt, *vt.* (accelerating, accelerated). To hasten; to quicken the speed of. **acceleration**, ak-sel'lè-rā''shun, *n.* Act of accelerating; increase of velocity. **accelerative**, ak-sel'lè-rāt-iv, *a.* Adding to velocity; accelerating.

accent, ak'sent, *n.* A tone or modulation of the voice; stress of the voice on a syllable or word; the mark which indicates this stress; manner of speaking. **accent**, ak-sent', *vt.* To express or note the accent of. **accented**, ak-sent'ed, *p.a.* Uttered or marked with accent. **accentuate**, ak-sent'ū-āt, *vt.* (accentuating, accentuated). To mark or pronounce with an accent or accents; to emphasize. **accentuation**, ak-sent'ū-ā''shun, *n.* Act of marking with the proper accents.

accept, ak-sept', *vt.* To receive; to admit; to promise to pay, by attaching one's signature. **acceptability**, ak-sept'a-bil''li-ti, *n.* Quality of being acceptable. **acceptable**, ak-sept'a-bl, *a.* That may be accepted; pleasing; gratifying. **acceptably**, ak-sept'a-bli, *adv.*

In an acceptable manner. **acceptance**, ak-sept'ans, *n.* Reception; reception with approbation; a bill of exchange accepted. **acceptation**, ak-sep-tā'shun, *n.* Kind reception; meaning in which a word is understood.

access, ak'ses, *n.* Approach; admission; means of approach; increase. **accessary**, ak'ses-a-ri. *See* **accessory**. **accessibility**, ak-ses'i-bil''li-ti, *n.* Quality of being accessible. **accessible**, ak-ses'i-bl, *a.* Easy of approach; affable. **accessibly**, ak-ses'i-bli, *adv.* So as to be accessible. **accession**, ak-se'shun, *n.* The act of acceding; augmentation; succession to a throne. **accessory**, ak'ses-sō-ri, *a.* Additional, contributing to.—*n.* An accomplice; an adjunct.

accident, ak'si-dent, *n.* Quality of a being not essential to it; an unfortunate event occurring casually. **accidental**, ak-si-dent'al, *a.* Happening by chance; not necessarily belonging to.—*n.* A property or thing not essential. **accidentally**, ak-si-dent'al-li, *adv.* By accident or chance; casually.

acclaim, ak-klām', *n.* Acclamation.—*vt.* To applaud; to declare by acclamation. **acclamation**, ak-kla-mā'shun, *n.* A shout of applause, assent, or approbation.

acclimatize, ak-klī'mat-īz, *vt.* To habituate to a climate different from the native one.

accolade, ak-kō-lād', *n.* A ceremony used in conferring knighthood, usually a blow on the shoulder with the flat of a sword.

accommodate, ak-kom'mō-dāt, *vt.* (accommodating, accommodated). To make suitable; to adjust; to furnish with. **accommodating**, ak-kom'mō-dāt-ing, *p.a.* Obliging; complying. **accommodation**, ak-kom'mō-dā''shun, *n.* Act of accommodating; a convenience; lodgings; loan.

accompany, ak-kum'pa-ni, *vt.* (accompanying, accompanied). To go with; to associate with; to perform music along with. **accompaniment**, ak-kum'pa-ni-ment, *n.* That which accompanies; the subordinate part or parts, in music.

accomplice, ak-kom'plis, *n.* An associate, especially in a crime.

accomplish, ak-kom'plish, *vt.* To fulfill; to execute fully; to perfect. **accomplished**, ak-kom'plisht, *p.a.* Elegant; having a finished education. **accomplishment**, ak-kom'plish-ment, *n.* Fulfillment; acquirement; embellishment.

accord, ak-kord', *n.* Harmony; agreement; will.—*vt.* To make to agree; to grant, or concede.—*vi.* To agree; to be in correspondence. **accordance**, ak-kord'ans, *n.* Agreement; conformity; harmony. **accordant**, ak-kord'ant, *a.* Corresponding; consonant; agreeable. **according**, ak-kord'ing, *p.a.* Agreeing; harmonizing; agreeable. **accordingly**, ak-kord'ing-li, *adv.* Agreeably; consequently.

accordion, ak-kord'i-on, *n.* A small melodious, keyed wind-instrument.

accost, ak-kost', *vt.* To speak to first; to address.

account, ak-kount', *n.* A reckoning; a register of facts relating to money; narration; advantage; end; importance.—*vt.* To reckon; to consider; to deem; to value.—*vi.* To give or render reasons; to explain (with *for*). **accountability**, ak-kount'a-bil''li-ti, *n.* State of being accountable; liability. **accountable**, ak-kount'a-bl, *a.* Liable to be called to account; amenable. **accountably**, ak-kount'a-bli, *adv.* In an accountable manner. **accountant**, ak-kount'ant, *n.* One skilled or employed in accounts; one whose profession is to examine accounts. **accountantship**, ak-kount'ant-ship, *n.* The office or duties of an accountant.

accouter, ak-kö'ter, *vt.* (accoutering, accoutered). To furnish with a military dress and arms. **accouterments**, ak-kö'tēr-ments, *n. pl.* Military dress and arms; dress.

accredit, ak-kred'it, *vt.* To give credit or authority to; to receive, as an envoy; to bring into vogue, as a word. **accredited**, ak-kred'it-ed, *p.a.* Authorized; sanctioned.

accretion, ak-krē'shun, *n.* A growing to, or increase by natural growth.

accrue, ak-krö', *vi.* (accruing, accrued). To arise or come; to be added.

accumulate, ak-kū'mū-lāt, *vt.* (accumulating, accumulated). To heap up; to amass.—*vi.* To increase. **accumulation**, ak-kū'mū-lā''shun, *n.* Act of accumulating; a heap; a collection. **accumulative**, ak-kū'mū-lāt-iv, *a.* That accumulates, or is accumulated.

accurate, ak'kū-rāt, *a.* Done with care; exact; without error. **accurately**, ak'kū-rāt-li, *adv.* Exactly. **accuracy**, ak'kū-ra-si, *n.* State of being accurate; precision; exactness.

accursed, ak-kėrs'ed, *a.* Lying under a curse; doomed; wicked.

accuse, ak-kūz', *vt.* (accusing, accused). To charge with a crime; to impeach; to censure. **accused**, ak-kūzd', *n.* A person charged with a crime or offense. **accuser**, ak-kūz'ėr, *n.* One who accuses. **accusation**, ak-kū-zā'shun, *n.* Act of accusing; impeachment; that of which one is accused.

accustom, ak-kus'tum, *vt.* To inure to a custom; to make familiar with by use. **accustomed**, ak-kus'tumd, *p.a.* Familiar by custom; usual; often practiced.

ace, ās, *n.* A unit; a single point on cards or dice.

acerbity, a-sėrb'i-ti, *n.* Sourness; bitterness or severity of language.

acetic, a-set'ik, *a.* Relating to vinegar; sour. **acetify**, a-set'i-fī, *vt.* or *i.* (acetifying, acetified). To turn into acid or vinegar. **acetous**, as-ēt'us, *a.* Having the quality of vinegar; sour; acid.

acetylene, a-set'i-lēn, *n.* A gas used for lighting houses, &c.

ache, āk, *vi.* (aching, ached). To be in pain; to be distressed.—*n.* Continued pain.

achieve, a-chēv', *vt.* (achieving, achieved). To bring to an end; to accomplish). To obtain by effort. **achieve-**

ment, a-chēv'ment, *n.* Act of achieving; exploit; an escutcheon.

achromatic, ak-rō-mat'ik, *a.* Free from color.

acid, as'id *a.* Sharp, or sour to the taste.—*n.* A sour substance; a substance that with certain other substances forms salts. **acidity,** as-id'i-ti, *n.* Sourness. **acidosis,** ac-i-dō'sis, *n.* A condition of acidity.

acknowledge, ak-nol'lej, *vt.* (acknowledging, acknowledged). To own the knowledge of; to avow; to own or confess. **acknowledgment,** ak-nol'lej-ment, *n.* Act of acknowledging; recognition.

acme, ak'mē, *n.* The top or highest point.

acolyte, ak'ol-īt, *n.* One of the lowest order in the Roman church; an attendant.

acorn, ā'korn, *n.* The fruit of the oak. **acorned,** a'kornd, *p.a.* Loaded or fed with acorns.

acoustic, a-kous'tik, *a.* Pertaining to the sense of hearing, or to the doctrine of sounds. **acoustics,** a-kous'-tiks, *n.* The science of sound.

Acorn.

acquaint, ak-kwānt', *vt.* To make to know; to make familiar; to inform. **acquaintance,** ak-kwānt'ans, *n.* Familiar knowledge; intimacy; a person well known. **acquaintanceship,** ak-kwānt'ans-ship, *n.* State of being acquainted.

acquiesce, ak-kwi-es', *vi.* (acquiescing, acquiesced). To rest satisfied; to admit without opposition; to comply. **acquiescence,** ak-kwi-es'ens, *n.* Assent. **acquiescent,** ak-kwi-es'ent, *a.* Resting satisfied; submitting.

acquire, ak-kwir', *vt.* (acquiring, acquired). To obtain; to procure. **acquirable,** ak-kwīr'a-bl, *a.* That may be acquired. **acquirement,** ak-kwir'ment, *n.* Act of acquiring; the thing acquired; attainment.

acquisition, ak-kwi-zi'shun, *n.* Act of acquiring; the thing acquired; gain. **acquisitive,** ak-kwiz'it-iv, *a.* Prone or eager to acquire.

acquit, ak-kwit', *vt.* (acquitting, acquitted). To set free from a charge or blame; to absolve; to bear or conduct (with refl. pron.). **acquittal,** ak-kwit'al, *n.* A setting free from a charge; a judicial discharge. **acquittance,** ak-kwit'ans, *n.* Discharge or release from a debt.

acre, ā'kėr, *n.* A quantity of land, containing 4840 square yards. **acreage,** ā'kėr-āj, *n.* The number of acres in a piece of land. **acred,** ā'kėrd, *a.* Possessing acres or landed property.

acrid, ak'rid, *a.* Sharp; hot or biting to the taste; corroding; harsh. **acridity,** ak-rid'i-ti, *n.* Acrid quality. **acrimonious,** ak-ri-mō'ni-us, *a.* Full of acrimony; severe; sarcastic. **acrimoniously,** ak-ri-mō'ni-us-li, *adv.* With sharpness or acrimony. **acrimony,** ak'ri-mo-ni, *n.* Sharpness; harshness; severity.

acropolis, a-krop'o-lis, *n.* The citadel of a Greek city, as of Athens.

across, a-kros', *prep.* or *adv.* From side to side; transversely; crosswise.

acrostic, a-kros'tik, *n.* A composition in verse, in which the first (or other) letters of the lines form the name of a person, &c.

act, akt, *vi.* To be in action; to exert power; to conduct one's self.—*vt.* To do; to perform, as an assumed part; to counterfeit.—*n.* A deed; power, or the effect of power, put forth; a state of reality; a part of a play; law, as an act of parliament. **acting,** akt'ing, *n.* Action; mode of performing a part of a play.

action, ak'shon, *n.* A deed; operation; a series of events; gesture; a suit or process; an engagement, battle. **actionable,** ak'shon-a-bl, *a.* Furnishing ground for an action at law.

active, ak'tiv, *a.* That acts or is in action; busy; quick; denoting action. **actively,** ak'tiv-li, *adv.* In an active manner. **activity,** ak-tiv'i-ti, *n.* Quality of being active; agility; nimbleness.

actual, ak'tū-al, *a.* Existing in act; real; certain; positive. **actuality,** ak-tū-al'li-ti, *n.* State of being actual; reality. **actually,** ak'tū-al-li, *adv.* In fact; really.

actuary, ak'tū-a-ri, *n.* A registrar or clerk; a specially able accountant. **actuate,** ak'tū-āt, *vt.* (actuating, actuated). To put into action; to incite.

acumen, a-kū'men, *n.* Sharpness of perception; sagacity.

acute, a-kūt', *a.* Sharpened; sharp; ending in a sharp point; penetrating; having nice sensibility; sharp in sound. **acutely,** a-kūt'li, *adv.* Sharply. **acuteness,** a-kūt'nes, *n.* Sharpness; shrewdness; faculty of nice perception.

adage, ad'āj, *n.* A proverb; a maxim.

adagio, a-dä'jō, *a.* and *adv.* In *music,* slow; with grace.—*n.* A slow movement.

adamant, ad'a-mant, *n.* Any substance of impenetrable hardness; the diamond. **adamantine,** ad-a-mant'in, *a.* Made of adamant; very hard.

adapt, a-dapt', *vt.* To fit; to adjust; to suit. **adaptability,** a-dapt'a-bil''li-ti, *n.* Capability of being adapted. **adaptable,** a-dapt'a-bl, *a.* That may be adapted. **adaptation,** a-dap-tā'shun, *n.* Act of adapting; the result of adapting.

add, ad, *vt.* To join to; to annex; to say further.

addendum, ad-den'dum, *n.;* pl. **-da.** A thing to be added; an appendix.

adder, ad'ėr, *n.* A venomous serpent.

addict, ad-dikt', *vt.* To apply habitually; generally in a bad sense (with refl. pron.) **addicted,** ad-dikt'ed, *p.a.* Habitually given to a practice; inclined; prone. **addiction,** ad-dik'shun, *n.* The state of being addicted; devotion.

addition, ad-di'shon, *n.* Act of adding; the thing added; increase. **additional,** ad-di'shon-al, *a.* Added on.

additive, ad'it-iv, *a.* That is to be or may be added.

addle, ad'l, *a.* Rotten; barren.—*vt.*

(addling, addled). To make corrupt or barren.—*vt.* and i. to muddle.

address, ad-dres', *vt.* To direct; to apply to by words or writing; to speak to; to apply (one's self); to write a name and destination on.—*n.* Verbal or written application; speech or discourse to a person; tact; courtship (generally in *plural*); direction of a letter. **addressee,** ad-dres'ē, *n.* One addressed.

adduce, ad-dūs', *vt.* (adducing, adduced). To bring forward; to cite. **adducible,** ad-dūs'i-bl, *a.* That may be adduced.

adenoid, ad'en-oid, *a.* Glandular.

adept, a-dept', *n.* One fully skilled in any art.—*a.* Well skilled; completely versed or acquainted.

adequate, ad'ē-kwāt, *a.* Equal to; proportionate; fully sufficient. **adequately,** ad'ē-kwāt-li, *adv.* In an adequate manner.

adequacy, ad'ē-kwa-si, *n.* State or quality of being adequate.

adhere, ad-hēr', *vi.* (adhering, adhered). To stick; to cling; to remain firm. **adherence,** ad-hēr'ens, *n.* State of adhering; attachment; fidelity. **adherent,** ad-hēr'ent, *a.* Sticking to; united with. —*n.* A follower; a partisan. **adhesion,** ad-hē'zhun, *n.* Act or state of sticking to; adherence. **adhesive,** ad-hē'siv, *a.* Apt or tending to adhere; sticky; tenacious.

adipose, ad'i-pōs, *a.* Consisting of or resembling fat; fatty.

adjacent, ad-jā'sent, *a.* Lying near; adjoining; contiguous; neighboring. **adjacence, adjacency,** ad-jā'sens, ad-jā'sen-si, *n.* State of lying close or contiguous.

adjective, ad'jek-tiv, *n.* A word used with a noun, to express some quality or circumstance. **adjectival,** ad'jek-tiv-al, *a.* Belonging to or like an adjective.

adjoin, ad-join', *vt.* To join to.—*vi.* To lie or be next; to be contiguous. **adjoining,** ad-join'ing, *p.a.* Adjacent.

adjourn, ad-jėrn', *vt.* To put off to a future day; to postpone.—*vi.* To leave off for a future meeting. **adjournment,** ad-jėrn'ment, *n.* Act of adjourning; interval during which a public body defers business.

adjudge, ad-juj', *vt.* To decree judicially; to decide. **adjudicate,** ad-jū'di-kāt, *vt.* To adjudge; to determine judicially. **adjudication,** ad-jū'di-kā″shon, *n.* Judicial sentence; judgment or decision. **adjudicator,** ad-jū'di-kāt-or, *n.* One who adjudicates.

adjunct, ad'jungkt, *n.* A thing (or person) joined to another.—*a.* United with.

adjure, ad-jūr', *vt.* (adjuring, adjured). To charge on oath; to charge earnestly and solemnly. **adjuration,** ad-jū-rā″shun, *n.* Act of adjuring; an oath or solemn charge.

adjust, ad-just', *vt.* To rectify; to make exact; to regulate; to adapt; to settle. **adjustable,** ad-just'a-bl, *a.* That may or can be adjusted. **adjustment,** adjust'ment, *n.* Act of adjusting; arrangement; settlement.

adjutant, ad'jū-tant, *n.* An officer who assists a commanding officer; a large species of bird allied to the stork. **adjutancy,** ad'jū-tan-si, *n.* Office of an adjutant.

administer, ad-min'is-ter, *vt.* To manage; to dispense; to distribute. **administration,** ad-min'is-trā″shun, *n.* Management; executive part of a government. **administrative,** ad-min'is-trāt-iv, *a.* That administers. **administrator,** ad-min-is-trāt'or, *n.* One who manages an intestate estate.

admirable, ad'mi-ra-bl, *a.* Worthy of admiration; excellent. **admirably,** ad'mi-ra-bli, *adv.* In an admirable manner.

admiral, ad'mi-ral, *n.* The chief commander of a fleet or navy. **admiralty,** ad'mi-ral-ti, *n.* A board of officials for administering naval affairs; the official buildings of this board.

admire, ad-mīr', *vt.* (admiring, admired). To regard with delight or affection. **admiration,** ad-mi-rā′shun, *n.* Wonder mingled with delight; esteem.

admit, ad-mit', *vt.* (admitting, admitted). To allow to enter; to grant; to concede. **admissible,** ad-mis'ibl, *a.* That may be admitted. **admission,** ad-mi'shon, *n.* Admittance; access; introduction; concession. **admittance,** ad-mit'ans, *n.* Permission to enter; entrance; allowance.

admixture, ad-miks'tūr, *n.* That which is mixed with something else; a mixing.

admonish, ad-mon'ish, *vt.* To warn; to reprove solemnly or quietly; to exhort. **admonition,** ad-mō-ni'shun, *n.* Gentle or solemn reproof; instruction; caution. **admonitory,** ad-mon'i-tō-ri, *a.* Containing admonition.

ado, a-dö', *n.* Stir; bustle; difficulty.

adolescent, ad-ō-les'ent, *a.* Advancing to manhood. **adolescence,** ad-ō-les'ens, *n.* A growing up to manhood; the age of youth.

adopt, a-dopt', *vt.* To take and treat as a child, giving a title to the rights of a child; to embrace. **adoption,** a-dop'shun, *n.* Act of adopting; state of being adopted. **adoptive,** a-dopt'iv, *a.* Adopting or adopted.

adore, a-dōr, *vt.* (adoring, adored). To address in prayer; to worship with reverence and awe; to love intensely. **adorable,** a-dōr'a-bl, *a.* Worthy to be adored. **adorably,** a-dōr'a-bli, *adv.* In a manner worthy of adoration. **adorer,** a-dōr'ėr, *n.* One who adores. **adoringly,** a-dōr'ing-li, *adv.* With adoration. **adoration,** a-dōr-ā'shun, *n.* Worship paid to God; profound reverence.

adorn, a-dorn', *vt.* To deck with ornaments; to embellish; to beautify.

adrenal, ad-rē'nal, *n.* Anat. A small glandlike body situated above each kidney, a suprarenal capsule; also used attributively.

Adrenalin, ad-rē'nal-in, *n.* A powerful hemostatic astringent principle of the suprarenal gland.

adrift, a-drift', *adv.* Floating at random; at the mercy of any impulse.

adroit, a-droit', *a.* Dexterous; skillful; ready. **adroitly,** a-droit'li, *adv.* With dexterity.

adulation, ad-ū-lā'shun, *n.* Servile flattery; excessive praise. **adulatory,** ad'-ū-lā-tō-ri, *a.* Flattering; praising excessively or servilely.

adult, a-dult', *a.* Grown to maturity.— *n.* A person grown to manhood.

adulterate, a-dul'tēr-āt, *vt.* (adulterating, adulterated). To change to a worse state by mixing; to contaminate with base matter. **adulterate,** a-dul'tēr'āt, *a.* Adulterated. **adulterated,** a-dul'-tēr-āt-ed, *p.a.* Debased by admixture. **adulteration,** a-dul'tēr-ā"shun, *n.* Act of adulterating, or state of being adulterated.

adulterer, a-dul'tēr-ēr, *n.* A man guilty of adultery. **adulteress,** a-dul'tēr-es, *n.* A woman guilty of adultery.

adultery, a-dul'tēr-i, *n.* Sexual intercourse between a married person and another (not the spouse).

advance, ad-vans', *vt.* (advancing, advanced). To put forward; to promote; (in *commerce*) to pay beforehand; to supply.—*vi.* To go forward; to be promoted.—*n.* A going forward; preferment; first hint or step; rise in value; a giving beforehand. **advanced,** ad-vanst', *p.a.* In the van of intellectual or religious progress. **advancement,** ad-vans'ment, *n.* Act of moving forward; improvement.

advantage, ad-van'tāj, *n.* Favorable state; superiority; gain.—*vt.* (advantaging, advantage). To benefit; to promote. **advantageous,** ad-van-tāj'us, *a.* Profitable; beneficial; useful. **advantageously,** ad-van-tāj'us-li, *adv.* In an advantageous manner.

Advent, ad'vent, *n.* Arrival; the coming of Christ; the four weeks before Christmas. **adventitious,** ad-ven-ti'shi-us, *a.* Accidental; casual; accessory; foreign.

adventure, ad-ven'tūr, *n.* Hazardous enterprise; a bold undertaking.—*vt.* To risk or hazard.—*vi.* To dare; to venture. **adventurer,** ad-ven'tūr-ēr, *n.* One who risks hazards, or braves. **adventuress,** ad-ven'tūr-es, *n.* A female adventurer. **adventurous,** ad-ven'tūr-us, *a.* Prone to incur hazard; daring; full of hazard. **adventurously,** ad-ven'tūr-us-li, *adv.* In a manner to incur hazard.

adverb, ad'vėrb, *n.* A word which modifies a verb, adjective, or another adverb. **adverbial,** ad-vėrb'i-al, *a.* Pertaining to an adverb.

adversary, ad'vėr-sa-ri, *n.* An enemy; an antagonist.

adverse, ad'vėrs, *a.* Hostile; unprosperous. **adversely,** ad-vėrs'li, *adv.* In an adverse manner. **adversity,** ad-vėrs'-i-ti, *n.* Misfortune; affliction; calamity; distress.

advert, ad-vėrt', *vi.* To refer or allude to; to regard. (With *to.*) **advertence,** ad-vėrt'ens, *n.* Regard; attention; heedfulness. **advertent,** ad-vėrt'ent, *a.* Attentive.

advertise, ad-vėr-tīz', *vt.* (advertising, advertised). To inform; to announce; to publish a notice of. **advertisement,** ad-vėr'tiz-ment, *n.* Information; public

notice. **advertiser,** ad-vėr-tīz'ėr, *n.* One who advertises. **advertising,** ad-vėr-tīz'ing, *p.a.* Containing or furnishing advertisements.

advice, ad-vīs', *n.* Opinion offered; counsel; information.

advise, ad-vīz', *vt.* (advising, advised). To counsel; to warn; to inform.—*vi.* To deliberate or consider. **advisable,** ad-vīs'a-bl, *a.* Fitting or proper to be done; expedient; fit. **advised,** ad-vīzd', *p.a.* Cautious; done with advice. **advisedly,** ad-vīz'ed-li, *adv.* With deliberation or advice.

advocate, ad'vō-kāt, *n.* One who pleads for another; an intercessor.—*vt.* (advocating, advocated). To plead in favor of; to vindicate. **advocacy,** ad'vō-kā-si, *n.* Act of pleading for; defense; vindication.

adz, adz, *n.* A kind of ax, with the edge at right angles to the handle.

aegis, ē'jis, *n.* A shield; protection.

aeration, ā-ėr-ā'shon, *n.* Impregnation of a liquid with carbonic acid gas.

aerial, ā-ē'ri-al, *a.* Belonging to the air; high; lofty, *n.* An antenna or the horizontal portion of an antenna.

aerie, ē'rē, *n.* The nest of a bird of prey; a brood of such birds.

aeriform, ā'ėr-i-form, *a.* Having the form or nature of air.

aerify, ā'ėr-i-fī, *vt.* (aerifying, aerified). To infuse air into.

aero-, ā'ėr-ō, Air-, of aeroplane or airship. **aerobatics,** ā-er-o-bat'ics, *n.*; *pl.* Feats of expert aviation.

aeronaut, ā-ėr-ō-nat, *n.* One who sails or floats in the air.

aeronautic, ā'ėr-ō-nat"ik, *a.* Pertaining to aerial sailing.

aeronautics, ā'ėr-ō-nat"iks, *n.* The science or art of sailing in the air.

aeroplane, ā'ėr-ō-plān, *n,* A motordriven flying machine made of planes on the kite principle.

aesthetic, aesthetical, ēs-thet'ik, ēs-thet'-ik-al, or es-, *a.* Pertaining to æsthetics. **aesthetics,** ēs-thet'iks, or es-, *n.* The science of the beautiful; the philosophy of taste.

afar, a-fär', *adv.* At, to, or from a distance.

affable, af'fa-bl, *a.* Easy to be spoken to; courteous; accessible. **affably,** af'-fa-bli, *adv.* In an affable manner. **affability,** af-fa-bil'i-ti, *n.* Courteousness; civility; urbanity.

affair, af-fār', *n.* That which is to do, or in which is done; business.

affect, af-fekt', *vt.* To act upon; to move the feelings of; to aim at; to pretend. **affectation,** af-fek-tā'shun, *n.* False pretense; an artificial air put on by a person. **affected,** af-fekt'ed, *p.a.* Inclined to; full of affectation; assumed artificially. **affectedly,** af-fekt'ed-li, *adv.* In an affected manner; feignedly. **affecting,** af-fekt'ing, *p.a.* Pathetic; tender; exciting. **affectingly,** af-fekt'-ing-li, *adv.* In an affecting manner. **affection,** af-fek'shon, *n.* The state of being affected; fondness; love. **affectionate**, af-fek'shon-āt, *a*. Tender; loving; fond. **affectionately**, af-fek'shon-āt-li, *adv*. Fondly. **affectioned**, af-fek'shond, *a*. Inclined.

affidavit, af-fi-dā'vit, *n*. A written declaration upon oath.

affiliate, af-fil'li-āt, *vt*. (affiliating, affiliated). To adopt; to assign to a father; to unite to a chief society or body. **affiliation**, af-fil'li-ā"shon, *n*. Act of affiliating; association.

affinity, af-fin'i-ti, *n*. Relation by marriage; resemblance; chemical attraction.

affirm, af-ferm', *vt*. To assert; to declare; to ratify.—*vi*. To declare solemnly. **affirmable**, af-ferm'a-bl, *a*. That may be affirmed. **affirmation**, af-fèrm-ā'shon, *n*. Act of affirming; declaration; ratification. **affirmative**, af-firm'at-iv, *a*. That affirms, positive.—*n*. That which expresses assent. **affirmatively**, af-ferm'at-iv-li, *adv*. In an affirmative manner.

affix, af-fiks', *vt*. To fasten to; to subjoin.—*n*. af'fiks. A syllable or letter added to a word.

afflatus, af-flā'tus, *n*. Inspiration.

afflict, af-flikt', *vt*. To distress; to grieve; to harass. **afflicting**, af-flikt'-ing, *p.a*. Distressing. **affliction**, af-flik'shon, *n*. State of being afflicted; distress; grief. **afflictive**, af-flikt'iv, *a*. Containing affliction; painful.

affluent, af'flū-ent, *a*. Flowing to; wealthy; abundant.—*n*. A river that flows into another river. **affluence**, af'flū-ens, *n*. A flowing to; abundance; opulence; wealth.

afford, af-fōrd', *vt*. To yield; to supply; to be able to give, grant, buy, or expend.

affront, af-frunt', *vt*. To insult; to offend.—*n*. Open defiance; insult. **affronting**, af-frunt'ing, *p.a*. Contumelious; abusive; insulting.

affusion, af-fū'shon, *n*. The act of pouring upon, or sprinkling with a liquid.

afraid, a-frād', *a*. Struck with fear; fearful.

aft, äft, *a*. or *adv*. Abaft; astern.

after, äft'èr, *a*. Later in time; subsequent.—*prep*. Later in time than; behind; according to; in imitation of.—*adv*. Later in time.

after-birth, äft'èr-bèrth, *n*. That which is expelled from the uterus after the birth of a child.

aftermath, äft'èr-math, *n*. A second crop of grass in the same season.

afterward, **afterwards**, äft'èr-wèrd, äft'èr-wèrdz, *adv*. In subsequent time.

again, a-gen', *adv*. Once more; further.

against, a-genst', *prep*. In opposition to; in expectation of.

agape, a-gāp', *a*. With the mouth wide open.

agate, ag'āt, *n*. A semi-pellucid mineral.

age, āj, *n*. A period of time; an epoch; number of years during which a person has lived; decline of life; oldness; legal maturity.—*vi*. and *t*. (aging, aged). To grow or make old; to show signs of advancing age.

aged, āj'ed, *a*. Old; having a certain age.

agency, ā'jen-si, *n*. Instrumentality; office or business of an agent.

agenda, a-jen'da, *n. pl*. Memoranda; business to be transacted at a meeting.

agent, ā'jent, *n*. One who acts; a deputy; an active cause or power.

agglomerate, ag-glom'mè-rāt, *vt*. To gather into a mass.—*vi*. To grow into a mass. **agglomeration**, ag-glom'mè-rā"shun, *n*. Act of agglomerating; heap.

agglutinate, ag-glö'tin-āt, *vt*. To glue to; to cause to adhere. **agglutination**, ag-glö'tin-ā"shun, *n*. Act of agglutinating; in *philolog_*, the loose combination of roots to form words. **agglutinant**, ag-glö'tin-ant, *n*. Any viscous or gluey substance.

aggrandize, ag'gran-dīz, *vt*. To make great; to magnify. **aggrandizement**, ag'gran-dīz-ment, *n*. Act of aggrandizing; augmentation.

aggravate, ag'gra-vāt, *vt*. (aggravating, aggravated). To intensify; to exasperate. **aggravating**, ag'gra-vāt-ing, *p.a*. Making worse; provoking. **aggravation**, ag-gra-vā'shun, *n*. Act of aggravating; provocation.

aggregate, ag'grē-gāt, *vt*. To bring together; to heap up.—*a*. Formed of parts collected.—*n*. A sum, mass, or assemblage of particulars. **aggregately**, ag'grē-gāt-li, *adv*. Collectively. **aggregation**, ag-grē-gā'shon, *n*. Act of aggregating; an aggregate or collection.

aggression, ag-gre'shun, *n*. The first act of hostility; attack. **aggressive**, ag-gres'iv, *a*. Taking the first step against; prone to encroachment. **aggressor**, ag-gres'or, *n*. The person who commences hostilities.

aggrieve, ag-grēv', *vt*. To pain, oppress, or injure.

aghast, a-gast', *a*. or *adv*. Amazed; stupefied. Also *agast*.

agile, aj'il, *a*. Ready to act; nimble. **agility**, a-jil'i-ti, *n*. Nimbleness; activity.

agitate, aj'it-āt, *vt*. (agitating, agitated). To put in violent motion; to shake briskly; to excite; to consider; to discuss. **agitated**, aj'it-āt-ed, *p.a*. Disturbed. **agitation**, aj-it-ā'shun, *n*. Excitement; emotion; discussion. **agitator**, aj'it-āt-or, *n*. One who excites discontent, sedition, or revolt.

agnostic, ag-nos'tik, *n*. One who disclaims any knowledge of God or of anything but material phenomena.—*a*. Pertaining to agnostics or their doctrines. **agnosticism**, ag-nos'ti-sizm, *n*. The doctrines or belief of agnostics.

ago, a-gō', *adv*. or *a*. Past; gone.

agog, a-gog', *adv*. In eager excitement.

agony, ag'ō-ni, *n*. Extreme pain of body or mind; anguish; the pangs of death. **agonize**, ag'ō-nīz, *vi*. (agonizing, agonized). To writhe with extreme pain.—*vt*. To distress with extreme pain; to torture. **agonizing**, ag'ō-nīz-ing, *p.a*. Giving extreme pain.

agrarian, a-grā'ri-an, *a*. Relating to lands. **agrarianism**, a-grā'ri-an-izm, *n*. The principles of those who favor an equal division of lands.

agree, a-grē', *vi*. (agreeing, agreed). To

be in concord; to correspond; to suit. **agreeable,** a-grē'a-bl, *a.* Suitable to; pleasing; grateful. **agreeableness,** a-grē'a-bl-ness, *n.* Quality of being agreeable; suitableness. **agreeably,** a-grē'a-bli, *adv.* In an agreeable manner; conformably. **agreement,** a-grē'ment, *n.* Harmony; conformity; stipulation.

agriculture, ag'ri-kul-tūr, *n.* The art or science of cultivating the ground. **agricultural,** ag-ri-kul'tūr-al, *a.* Pertaining to agriculture. **agriculturist,** ag-ri-kul'tūr-ist, *n.* One skilled in agriculture.

aground, a-ground', *adv.* Stranded.

ague, ā'gū, *n.* An intermittent fever, with cold fits and shivering.

ah, ä, *interj.* Expressing surprise, pity, &c.

aha, ä-hä', *interj.* Expressing triumph or contempt.

ahead, a-hed', *adv.* Before; onward.

ahoy, a-hoi', *exclam.* A sea-term used in hailing.

aid, ād, *vt.* To help; to relieve.—*n.* Help; assistance; a helper.

aide-de-camp, ād-de-kong, *n.*; pl. **aides-de-camp.** An officer attendant on a general.

aigret, aigrette, ā'gret, ā-gret', *n.* A plume or ornament for the head composed of feathers or precious stones.

ail, āl, *vt.* To pain; to affect with uneasiness.—*vi.* To be in pain or trouble.

ailment, āl'ment, *n.* Pain; disease.

aim, ām, *vi.* To point with a missive weapon; to intend; to endeavor.—*vt.* To level or direct as a firearm.—*n.* That which is aimed at; direction; purpose; drift. **aimless,** ām'les, *a.* Without aim.

air, ār, *n.* The fluid which we breathe; a light breeze; a tune; mien; *pl.* affected manner.—*vt.* To expose to the air; to ventilate; to dry. **air base,** ār'bās. *n.* A base of operations for aircraft and for the housing of the craft. **air bladder,** ār'blad-dèr, *n.* The bladder of a fish containing air. **aircraft,** ār'kraft, *n.* Any form of craft designed for navigation of the air. **air cushion,** ār'kụsh-on, *n.* An inflated bag of air-tight cloth. **airdrome,** ār'drōm, *n.* A field providing facilities for aircraft to land and take off. **airgun,** ār'gun, *n.* A gun to discharge bullets by means of condensed air. **airily,** ār'i-li, *adv.* In an airy manner. **airiness,** ār'i-nes, *n.* Openness; gayety. **airing,** ār'ing, *n.* An exposure to the air or to a fire; an excursion in the open air. **airless,** ār'les, *a.* Destitute of fresh air. **airplane,** ār'plān, *n.* A form of aircraft, heavier than air, which obtains support by the dynamic reaction of the air against the wings and which is driven through the air by a screw propeller. (The form **airplane** has been officially adopted by the United States Army and Navy, Bureau of Standards, &c.; **aeroplane** is still generally used by British writers) **air-port,** ār'pōrt", *n.* A landing place or loading and delivering center for aircraft. **air-pump,** ār'pump, *n.* A machine for pumping the air out of a vessel. **air-shaft,** ār'shaft, *n.* A passage for air into a mine. **airtight,** ār'tīt, *a.* So tight or compact as

not to let air pass. **airy,** ār'i, *a.* Open to the free air; high in air; light, thin; vain; gay.

aisle, īl, *n.* A wing or side of a church; a passage in a church.

ajar, a-jär', *adv.* Partly open, as a door.

akimbo, a-kim'bō, *pred. a.* or *adv.* With the elbow outwards and the hand on the hip.

akin, a-kin', *a.* Of kin; related to; partaking of the same properties.

ababaster, al'a-bas-tèr, *n.* A soft marblelike mineral.—*a.* Made of alabaster.

alack, a-lak', *interj.* Expressing sorrow.

alacrity, a-lak'ri-ti, *n.* Liveliness, cheerful readiness; promptitude.

alamode, ä-lä-mōd', *adv.* According to fashion.—*n.* A thin black silk.

alarm, a-lärm', *n.* A call to arms; sudden surprise; fright; a notice of danger. —*vt.* To give notice of danger; to disturb. **alarming,** a-lärm'ing, *p.a.* Terrifying. **alarmingly,** a-lärm'ing-li, *adv.* So as to excite apprehension. **alarmist,** a-lärm'ist, *n.* One prone to excite alarm.—*a.* Exciting unnecessary alarm.

alas, a-las', *interj.* Expressing grief, pity, &c.

alb, alb, *n.* A long robe of white linen.

albatross, al'ba-tros, *n.* An aquatic bird of southern seas, the largest sea-bird known.

albeit, al-bē'it. *adv.* Be it so; although.

albino, al-bi'nō, *n.* A person with abnormally white skin and hair, and pink eyes.

album, al'bum, *n.* A book for autographs; sketches, &c.

Albatross.

albumen, al-bū'men, *n.* The white of an egg; a substance of the same kind found in animals and vegetables.

alcohol, al'kō-hol, *n.* Pure spirit of a highly intoxicating nature. **alcoholic,** al-kō-hol'ik, *a.* Pertaining to alcohol. **alcoholism,** al'kō-hol-izm, *n.* The condition of habitual drunkards.

alcove, al'kōv, *n.* A recess.

aldehyde, al'dē-hīd, *n.* A colorless liquid produced by oxidation of alcohol.

alder, al'dèr, *n.* A tree generally growing in moist land.

alderman, al'dèr-man, *n.*; pl. **-men.** A magistrate of a town.

ale, āl, *n.* A fermented malt liquor; beer.

alert, a-lèrt', *a.* Vigilant; quick; prompt. **alertness,** a-lèrt'nes, *n.* Briskness; activity.

alfalfa, al-fal'fa, *n.* A clover-like plant; lucerne; a valuable fodder.

alga, al'ga, *n.*; pl. **-gae.** A sea-weed.

algebra, al'je-bra, *n.* The science of computing by symbols. **algebraically,** al-jē-brā'ik-al-li, *adv.* By algebraic process.

alias, ā'li-as, *adv.* Otherwise.—*n.*; pl. **-ses.** An assumed name.

alibi, al'i-bī, *n.* The plea of a person who, charged with a crime, alleges that he was elsewhere when the crime was committed.

alien, āl'yen, *a.* Foreign; estranged from. —*n.* A foreigner. **alienable,** āl'yen-a-bl, *a.* That may be alienated or transferred to another. **alienate,** āl'yen-āt, *vt.* (alienating, alienated). To transfer to another; to estrange. **alienation,** āl-yen-ā'shun, *n.* Act of alienating.

alight, a-līt', *vi.* To get down; to settle on.

alight, a-līt', *pred. a.* or *adv.* Lighted; kindled.

alike, a-līk', *a.* Like; similar.—*adv.* In the same manner, form, or degree.

aliment, al'i-ment, *n.* Nourishment; food.

alimony, al'i-mo-ni, *n.* Allowance to a woman legally separated from her husband.

alive, a-līv', *a.* Living; lively; susceptible.

alkali, al'ka-li, *n.*; pl. **-ies** or **-is.** A substance, as potash and soda, which neutralizes acids and unites with oil or fat to form soap. **alkaline,** al'ka-līn, *a.* Having the properties of an alkali.

alkaloid, al'ka-loid, *n.* A substance resembling an alkali, or having alkaline properties.

all, al. *a.* Every part; every one.—*n.* The whole; everything.—*adv.* Wholly; entirely.

Allah, al'la. *n.* The Arabic name of God.

allay, al-lā', *vt.* To repress; to assuage.

allege, al-lej', *vt.* (alleging, alleged). To adduce; to assert; to plead in excuse. **allegation,** al-lē-gā'shun, *n.* Affirmation; declaration.

allegiance, al-lē'ji-ans, *n.* Loyalty.

allegory, al'li-gō-ri, *n.* A speech or discourse which conveys a meaning different from the literal one. **allegorize,** al'li-gō-riz, *vt.* To turn into allegory. —*vi.* To use allegory. **allegoric, allegorical,** al-li-gor'ik, al-li-gor'ik-al, *a.* Pertaining to allegory; figurative.

allegro, al-lā'grō, *a.* and *adv.* A word denoting a brisk, sprightly movement.

alleluiah, al-lē-lū'ya, *n.* Praise to Jehovah; a word used to express pious joy.

allergy, al'er-ji, *n.* A hypersensitivity to a special substance, food, plants, chemicals, allergen, &c.

allergic, a-lur'jik, *a.* Possessing allergy.

alleviate, al-lē'vi-āt, *vt.* (alleviating, alleviated). To make light; to assuage. **alleviation,** al-lē-vi-ā'shun, *n.* Act of alleviating; mitigation.

alley, al'i, *n.* A narrow walk or passage.

alliance, al-lī'ans, *n.* State of being allied; confederacy; league.

allied, al-līd', *p.a.* United by treaty.

alligation, al-li-gā'shon, *n.* Act of tying together; a rule of arithmetic.

alligator, al'li-gā-tor, *n.* The American crocodile.

alliteration, al-lit-ēr-ā'shun, *n.* The repetition of a letter at the beginning of two or more words in close succession. **alliterative,** al-lit'ēr-at-iv, *a.* Pertaining to alliteration.

allocate, al'lō-kāt, *vt.* (allocating, allocated). To distribute; to assign to each his share. **allocation,** al-lō-kā'shun, *n.* Distribution; assignment.

allot, al-lot', *vt.* (allotting, allotted).

To give by lot; to apportion. **allotment,** al-lot'ment, *n.* Act of allotting; a share allotted.

allow, al-lou', *vt.* To grant; to admit; to abate; to bestow, as compensation. **allowable,** al-lou-a-bl, *a.* That may be allowed. **allowably,** al-lou'a-bli, *adv.* In an allowable manner. **allowance,** al-lou'ans, *n.* Act of allowing; that which is allowed; abatement.

alloy, al-loi', *vt.* To mix with baser metals; to abate by mixture.—*n.* A baser metal mixed with a finer; a metallic compound.

All Saints' Day, al sānts dā, *n.* 1st November.

All Souls' Day, al sölz dā, *n.* 2nd November.

allude, al-lūd', *vi.* (alluding, alluded). To refer to; to hint at.

allure, al-lūr', *vt.* (alluring, allured). To draw by some lure; to entice; to decoy. **allurement,** al-lūr'ment, *n.* That which allures; temptation; enticement. **alluring,** al-lūr'ing, *p.a.* Attractive. **alluringly,** al-lūr'ing-li, *adv.* In an alluring manner.

allusion, al-lū'zhun, *n.* The act of alluding; a hint; a reference. **allusive,** **allusory,** al-lū'siv, al-lū'so-ri, *a.* Containing allusion.

alluvial, al-lū'vi-al, *a.* Deposited by water.

alluvium, al-lū'vi-um, *n.*; pl. **-via.** Soil deposited by the action of water.

ally, al-lī', *vt.* (allying, allied). To unite by friendship, marriage, or treaty; to associate.—*n.* One related by marriage or other tie; an associate.

almanac, al'ma-nak. *n.* A calendar of days, weeks, and months, &c.

Almighty, al-mī'ti, *a.* Omnipotent.—*n.* God.

almond, ä'mund, *n.* The nut of the almond tree; *pl.* the tonsils of the throat.

almost, al'most, *adv.* Nearly; well-nigh; for the greatest part.

alms, ämz, *n. pl.* A charitable gift.

aloe, al'ō, *n.* A succulent plant; *pl.* a bitter purgative medicine. **aloetic,** al-ō-et'ik, *a.* Pertaining to aloes.

aloft, a-loft', *adv.* In the sky; on high.

alone, a-lōn', *a.* Solitary.—*adv.* Separately.

along, a-long', *adv.* Lengthwise; forward.—*prep.* By the side of, lengthwise.

aloof, a-lōf', *adv.* At a distance; apart.

alp, alp, *n.* A high mountain.

alpaca, al-pak'a, *n.* A Peruvian animal, with long, soft, and woolly hair; cloth made of its hair, or a similar cloth.

alpenstock, al'pen-stok, *n.* A long stick shod with iron, used in climbing mountains.

alpha, al'fa, *n.* The first letter in the Greek alphabet; the first or beginning.

alphabet, al'fa-bet, *n.* The letters of a language arranged in the customary order.

alphabetical, al-fa-bet'ik-al, *a.* In the order of an alphabet.

alpine, al'pīn, *a.* Pertaining to high mountains.

already, al-red'i, *adv.* Before or by this time; even now.

also, ạl'sŏ, *adv.* Likewise; in the same manner; further.

altar, ạl'tẽr, *n.* An elevated place on which sacrifices were offered; the communion table.

alter, ạl'tẽr, *vt.* To make some change in; to vary.—*vi.* To vary. **alterable,** ạl'tẽr-a-bl, *a.* That may alter, or be altered. **alteration,** ạl-tẽr-ā'shun, *n.* Partial change or variation.—*n.* A medicine which induces a change in the habit or constitution.

altercate, ạl'tẽr-kāt, *vi.* (altercating, altercated). To dispute; to wrangle. **altercation,** ạl-tẽr-kā'shun, *n.* Heated dispute; wrangle.

alternate, al-tẽrn'āt, *a.* Being by turns. *vt.* (alternating, alternated). To cause to follow by turns; to interchange.—*vi.* To happen or act by turns. **alternately,** al-tẽrn'āt-li, *adv.* By turns. **alternation,** al-tẽrn-ā'shun, *n.* Reciprocal succession; interchange. **alternative,** al-tẽrn'at-iv, *n.* A choice of two things. **alternatively,** al-tẽrn'at-iv-li, *adv.* In the manner of alternatives.

although, ạl-тнō', *conj.* Be it so; admit all that.

altitude, al'ti-tūd, *n.* Height; eminence; elevation.

alto, al'tŏ, *a.* High.—*n.* In *music,* contralto.

altogether, ạl-tŏ-geтн'ẽr, *adv.* Wholly; entirely; without exception.

altruism, al'trŏ-izm, *n.* Devotion to others or to humanity; the opposite of selfishness. **altruistic,** al-trŏ-ist'ik, *a.* Pertaining or relating to altruism.

alum, al'um, *n.* An astringent salt of great use in medicine and the arts. **alumina,** al-ū'min-a, *n.* The oxide of aluminium; the chief ingredient of clay. **aluminium,** al-ū-min'i-um, *n.* A very light metal of a silvery white color.

aluminum, aluminium, a-lū'mi-num, al-ū-min'i-um, *n.* A malleable silver-white metal.

alumnus, a-lum'nus, *n.*; pl. **-ni.** A pupil; a graduate of a university.

always, ạl'wāz, *adv.* At all times; continually.

am, am. The first person singular, present tense, indicative mood, of the verb *to be.*

amalgam, a-mal'gam, *n.* A compound of quicksilver with another metal; a compound. **amalgamate,** a-mal'gam-āt, *vt.* To mix, as quicksilver with another metal.—*vi.* To unite in an amalgam; to blend. **amalgamation,** a-mal'gam-ā''shon, *n.* The act or operation of amalgamating.

amaranth, a'ma-ranth, *n.* The unfading flower; a color inclining to purple. **amaranthine,** am-a-ran'thin, *a.* Unfading.

amaryllis, am-a-ril'lis, *n.* Lily-asphodel.

amass, a-mas', *vt.* To form into a mass; to accumulate; to heap up.

amateur, am-a-tūr', *n.* A lover of any art of science, not a professor.

amatory, am'a-tŏ-ri, *a.* Relating to love; causing love; amorous.

amaze, a-māz', *vt.* (amazing, amazed). To astonish; to bewilder. **amazedly,** a-māz'ed-li, *adv.* With amazement.

amazement, a-māz'ment, *n.* Wonder; perplexity. **amazing,** a-māz'ing, *p.a.* Very wonderful. **amazingly,** a-māz'-ing-li, *adv.* In an astonishing degree.

amazon, am'a-zon, *n.* A warlike or masculine woman; a virago. **amazonian,** am-a-zŏ'ni-an, *a.* Relating to the Amazons.

ambassador, am-bas'sa-dor, *n.* A representative of a sovereign or state at a foreign court.

amber, am'bẽr, *n.* A mineralized pale-yellow resin of extinct pine-trees.

ambergris, am'bẽr-grēs, *n.* A fragrant, solid, opaque, ash-colored substance.

ambidexter, am-bi-deks'tẽr, *n.* One who uses both hands with equal facility. **ambidextrous,** am-bi-deks'trus, *a.* Using both hands alike.

ambient, am'bi-ent, *a.* Encompassing.

ambiguity, am-bi-gū'i-ti, *n.* Doubtfulness of signification. **ambiguous,** am-big'ū-us, *a.* Of uncertain signification; doubtful. **ambiguously,** am-big'ū-us-li, *adv.* In an ambiguous manner.

ambition, am-bi'shon, *n.* Desire of preferment or power. **ambitious,** am-bi'-shus, *a.* Aspiring. **ambitiously,** am-bi'shus-li, *adv.* In an ambitious manner.

amble, am'bl, *vi.* (ambling, ambled). To move as a horse, by lifting the two legs on each side alternately; to go between a walk and a trot.—*n.* A peculiar motion of a horse; a pace between a walk and a trot.

ambrosia, am-brŏ'zhi-a, *n.* The imaginary food of the gods, which conferred immortality. **ambrosial,** am-brŏ'zhi-al, *a.* Of the nature of ambrosia; fragrant; delicious.

ambulance, am'bū-lans, *n.* An itinerant hospital; a wagon for the sick or wounded.

ambulatory, am'bū-lā-tŏ-ri, *a.* Movable.—*n.* A part of a building to walk in.

ambuscade, am-bus-kād', *n.* The act or place of lying in wait in order to surprise; the troops lying in wait; ambush.

ambush, am'bush, *n.* Ambuscade.

ameliorate, a-mel'yor-āt, *vt.* To make better. **amelioration,** a-mēl'yor-ā''-shun, *n.* A making better; improvement.

amen, ā-men', *adv.* So be it.

amenable, a-mēn'a-bl, *a.* Accountable; responsible.

amend, a-mend', *vt.* To correct; to improve. **amende,** ä-mängd, *n.* A fine; reparation. **amendment,** a-mend'ment, *n.* A change for the better; correction; reformation. **amends,** a-mendz', *n. pl.* Compensation; satisfaction; recompense.

amenity, a-men'i-ti, *n.* Pleasantness; agreeableness of situation.

American, a-me'ri-kan, *n.* A native of America.—*a.* Pertaining to America. **Americanism,** a-me'ri-kan-izm, *n.* An American idiom or custom.

amethyst, am'ē-thist, *n.* A variety of quartz, a precious stone of a bluish violet or purple color. **amethystine,** a-mē-thist'in, *a.* Pertaining to or resembling amethyst.

amiable, ā'mi-a-bl, *a.* Lovable; sweet-tempered. **amiably,** ā'mi-a-bli, *adv.* In an amiable manner. **amiability,** ă'mi-a-bil''i-ti, *n.* Sweetness of temper.

amicable, am'ik-a-bl, *a.* Friendly; kind. **amicably,** am'ik-a-bli, *adv.* In a friendly manner.

amid, amidst, a-mid', a-midst', *prep.* In the midst of; enveloped with. **amidships,** a-mid'ships, *adv.* or *pred. a.* In or towards the middle of a ship.

amiss, a-mis', *a.* In error; improper.— *adv.* In a faulty manner; improperly.

amity, am'i-ti, *n.* Friendship; harmony.

ammonia, am-mō'ni-a, *n.* Volatile alkali.

amnesia, am-nē'zhi-a, *n.* Loss of memory.

amnesty, am'nes-ti, *n.* A general pardon of offenses against a government.

amoeba, a-mē'ba, *n.;* pl. -bæ. A microscopic animal commonly found in fresh water. **amoebean,** am-ē-bē'an, *a.* Exhibiting persons speaking alternately (an amoebean poem).

among, amongst, a-mung', a-mungst', *prep.* Amidst; throughout; of the number.

amorous, am'or-us, *a.* Inclined to love; enamored; fond; relating to love. **amorously,** am'or-us-li, *adv.* In an amorous manner.

amorphous, a-mor'fus, *a.* Without shape; of irregular shape.

amortize, a-mor'tiz, *vt.* (amortizing, amortized). To extinguish a debt or obligation by a series of payments, usually at the same time as the interest payments are made.

amount, a-mount', *vi.* To mount up to; to result in.—*n.* The sum total; effect or result.

amour, a-mör', *n.* A love intrigue.

ampere, am-pār', *n.* The unit in measuring the strength of an electric current.

amphibian, am-fib'i-an, *n.:* pl. **amphibia,** am-fib'i-a. An animal capable of living both in water and on land; an animal that has both lungs and gills; an airplane designed to arise from and alight on either land or water. **amphibious,** am-fib'i-us, *a.* Able to live under water and on land.

amphitheater, am-fi-thē'a-tēr, *n.* An edifice of an oval form, with rows of seats all round, rising higher as they recede from the area.

ample, am'pl, *a.* Spacious; copious; rich. **ampleness,** am'pl-nes, *n.* Spaciousness; abundance. **amplification,** am'pli-fi-kā''shun, *n.* Act of amplifying; enlargement; discussion. **amplifier,** am'pli-fī-ēr, *n.* One who or that which amplifies or enlarges. **amplify,** am'plif-ī, *vt.* (amplifying, amplified). To enlarge; to treat copiously.—*vi.* To speak copiously; to be diffuse. **amplitude,** am'pli-tūd, *n.* Ampleness; extent; abundance. **amply,** am'pli, *adv.* Largely; liberally; fully; copiously.

amputate, am'pū-tāt, *vt.* (amputating, amputated). To cut off, as a limb. **amputation,** am-pū-tā'shun, *n.* Act of amputating.

amuck, a-muk', *n.* or *adv.* Only in phrase *to run amuck,* to rush about frantically, to attack all and sundry.

amulet, am'ū-let, *n.* A charm against evils or witchcraft.

amuse, a-mūz', *vt.* (amusing, amused). To entertain; to beguile. **amusement,** á-mūz'ment, *n.* Diversion; entertainment. **amusing,** a-mūz'ing, *a.* Giving amusement; diverting. **amusingly,** a-mūz'ing-li, *adv.* In an amusing manner.

an, an, *a.* The indefinite article, used before words beginning with a vowel-sound.

anachronism, an-ak'ron-izm, *n.* An error in chronology.

anaconda, an-a-kon'da, *n.* A large species of the serpent tribe.

anaemia, a-nē'mi-a, *n.* Bloodlessness. A condition in which the red corpuscles of the blood are deficient in number or lacking in hemoglobin.

anaesthetic, an-es-thet'ik, *a.* Producing insensibility.—*n.* A substance, as chloroform, which produces insensibility.

anagram, an'a-gram, *n.* A transposition of the letters of a name or sentence, by which a new word or sentence is formed.

analogy, an-al'o-ji, *n.* Likeness; similarity.

analogical, an-a-loj'ik-al, *a.* According to analogy.

analogous, an-al'og-us, *a.* Having analogy; corresponding.

analogously, an-al'og-us-li, *adv.* In an analogous manner.

analysis, an-al'i-sis, *n.;* pl. -ses. A resolution of a thing into its elements; synopsis.

analyze, an'a-liz, *vt.* (analyzing, analyzed). To subject to analysis; to resolve into its elements. **analyst,** an'a-list, *n.* One who analyzes. **analytic, analytical,** an-a-lit'ik, an-a-lit'ik-al, *a.* Pertaining to analysis. **analytically,** an-a-lit'ik-al-li, *adv.* In the manner of analysis. **analytics,** an-a-lit'iks, *n.* The science of analysis.

anarchy, an'ar-ki, *n.* State of being without rule; political confusion. **anarchic, anarchical,** an-ärk'ik, an-ärk'ik-al, *a.* Without rule or government. **anarchist,** an'ärk-ist, *n.* An author or promoter of anarchy; one who opposes all systems of government.

anathema, a-nath'e-ma, *n.* An ecclesiastical denunciation; curse. **anathematize,** a-nath'e-mat-iz, *vt.* (anathematizing, anathematized). To pronounce an anathema against; to excommunicate.

anatomy, a-nat'o-mi, *n.* The art of dissection; doctrine of the structure of the body learned by dissection. **anatomical,** an-a-tom'ik-al, *a.* Relating to anatomy. **anatomist,** a-nat'ō-mist, *n.* One skilled in anatomy. **anatomize,** a-nat'ō-miz, *vt.* (anatomizing, anatomized). To cut up or dissect.

ancestor, an'ses-tēr, *n.* A progenitor; forefather. **ancestral,** an-ses'tral, *a.* Relating or belonging to ancestors. **ancestry,** an'ses-tri, *n.* Lineage; descent.

anchor, ang'kēr, *n.* An iron for holding a ship at rest in water.—*vt.* To hold fast by an anchor.—*vi.* To cast anchor. **anchorage,** ang'kēr-āj, *n.* A place where a

Anchor.

ship can anchor; duty on ships for anchoring.

anchorite, ang'kō-rīt, *n.* A hermit.

anchovy, an-chō'vi, *n.* A small fish of the herring kind, furnishing a fine sauce.

ancient, ān'shent, *a.* That happened in former times; old, antique. **anciently,** ān'shent-li, *adv.* In old times. **ancientness,** ān'shent-nes, *n.* Antiquity.

and, and, *conj.* A particle which connects words and sentences together.

andante, an-dan'te, *a.* In *music,* with slow, graceful movement.

andiron, and'ī-ėrn, *n.* A metallic support for logs of wood burned on an open hearth.

anecdote, an'ek-dōt, *n.* A short story. **anecdotical,** an-ek-dot'ik-al, *a.* Pertaining to an anecdote.

anemometer, an-e-mom'et-ėr, *n.* An instrument for measuring the force of the wind.

anemone, a-nem'o-nē, *n.* Wind-flower, a genus of plants.

anent, a-nent', *prep.* About; regarding.

angel, ān'jel, *n.* A divine messenger; a spirit; an old English gold coin worth ten shillings. **angelic, angelical,** an-jel'ik, an-jel'ik-al, *a.* Belonging to or resembling an angel. **angelically,** an-jel'ik-al-li, *adv.* Like an angel.

anger, ang'gėr, *n.* A violent passion, excited by real or supposed injury; resentment.—*vt.* To excite anger; to irritate.

angle, ang'gl, *n.* The inclination of two lines which meet in a point but have different directions; a corner.

angle, ang'gl, *n.* A fishing-hook, or hook with line and rod.—*vi.* (angling, angled). To fish with an angle. **angler,** ang'glėr, *n.* One that fishes with an angle.

Anglican, ang'glik-an, *a.* Pertaining to England, or to the English Church. **Anglicism,** ang'gli-sizm, *n.* An English idiom. **Anglicize,** ang'gli-sīz, *vt.* To make English.

Anglo-Saxon, ang-glō-sak'son, *n.* One of the English race; the English language in its first stage.—*a.* Pertaining to the Anglo-Saxons, or their language.

angry, ang'gri, *a.* Affected with anger; provoked; wrathful; resentful. **angrily,** ang'gri-li, *adv.* In an angry manner.

anguish, ang'gwish, *n.* Extreme pain, either of body or mind; agony; grief.

angular, ang'gū-lėr, *a.* Having an angle; stiff. **angularity,** ang-gū-la'ri-ti, *n.* Quality of being angular.

animal, an'i-mal, *n.* A living being having sensation and voluntary motion; a quadruped.—*a.* Belonging to animals; gross.

animalcule, an-i-mal'kūl, *n.* A minute animal seen by means of a microscope. **animalcular,** an-i-mal'kūl-ėr, *a.* Pertaining to animalcules.

animate, an'i-māt, *vt.* (animating, animated). To give natural life to; to enliven. **animated,** an'i-māt-ed, *p.a.* Lively; living. **animating,** an'i-māt-ing. *p.a.* Enlivening. **animation,** an-i-mā'shun, *n.* Life; vigor.

animosity, an-i-mos'i-ti, *n.* Violent hatred; active enmity; malignity.

animus, an'i-mus, *n.* Intention; hostile spirit.

anise, an'is, *n.* An aromatic plant, the seeds of which are used in making cordials.

ankle, ang'kl, *n.* The joint which connects the foot with the leg. **ankled,** ang'kld, *a.* Having ankles.

annals, an'nalz, *n. pl.* A record of events under the years in which they happened. **annalist,** an'nal-ist, *n.* A writer of annals.

anneal, an-nēl', *vt.* To temper glass or metals by heat; to fix colors laid on glass.

annex, an-neks', *vt.* To unite at the end; to subjoin; to take possession of. **annexation,** an-neks-ā'shon, *n.* Act of annexing.

annihilate, an-nī'hil-āt, *vt.* (annihilating, annihilated). To reduce to nothing; to destroy the existence of. **annihilation,** an-nī'hil-ā'shon, *n.* Act of annihilating; state of being annihilated. **annihilable,** an-nī'hil-a-bl, *a.* That may be annihilated.

anniversary, an-ni-vėrs'a-ri, *a.* That returns every year.—*n.* A day on which some event is annually celebrated.

annotate, an'nō-tāt, *vt.* (annotating, annotated). To write notes upon. **annotation,** an-nō-tā'shon, *n.* A remark on some passage of a book, &c. **annotator,** an'nō-tāt-ėr, *n.* A writer of notes.

announce, an-nouns', *vt.* (announcing, announced). To declare; to proclaim. **announcement,** an-nouns'ment, *n.* Declaration.

annoy, an-noi', *vt.* To hurt; to molest; to vex. **annoyance,** an-noi'ans, *n.* Act of annoying; state of being annoyed.

annual, an'nū-al, *a.* Yearly; lasting a year.—*n.* A plant whose root dies yearly; a book published yearly. **annually,** an'nū-al-li, *adv.* Yearly.

annuity, an-nū'i-ti, *n.* A sum of money payable yearly, &c. **annuitant,** an-nū'-it-ant, *n.* One who receives an annuity.

annul, an-nul', *vt.* (annulling, annulled). To make void or of no effect; to repeal. **annulment,** an-nul'ment, *n.* Act of annulling.

annular, an'nū-lėr, *a.* Having the form of a ring; pertaining to a ring.

annunciation, an-nun'si-ā'shun, *n.* The angel's salutation to the Virgin Mary, and its anniversary, the 25th of March.

anode, an'ōd, *n.* The positive pole of a voltaic current.

anodyne, an'ō-dīn, *n.* Any medicine which allays or mitigates pain.—*a.* Assuaging pain.

anoint, a-noint', *vt.* To rub over with oil; to consecrate by unction.

anomalous, a-nom'a-lus, *a.* Deviating from common rule.

anomaly, a-nom'a-li, *n.* Irregularity; deviation from common rule.

anon, a-non', *adv.* Immediately.

anonymous, a-non'im-us, *a.* Nameless; without the real name of the author. **anonymously,** a-non'im-us-li, *adv.* Without a name.

another, an-uTH'ėr, *a.* Not the same; different; any other.

answer, an'sèr, *vt.* To reply to; to satisfy; to suit.—*vi.* To reply; to be accountable; to succeed.—*n.* A reply; a solution. **answerable,** an'sèr-a-bl, *a.* That may be answered; accountable; suitable. **answerably,** an'sèr-a-bli, *adv.* In due proportion; suitably.

ant, ant. *n.* An emmet; a pismire.

antagonism, an-tag'ō-nizm, *n.* Opposition; contest. **antagonist,** an-tag'ō-nist, *n.* One who struggles with another in combat; an opponent; that which acts in opposition. **antagonistic,** an-tag'ō-nist'ik, *a.* Opposing in combat; contending against.

Antarctic, ant-ärk'tik, *a.* Relating to the south pole, or the region near it.

antecedent, an-tē-sē'dent, *a.* Going before; prior.—*n.* That which goes before; the noun to which a relative refers; *pl.* a man's previous history, &c. **antecedently,** an-tē-sē'dent-li, *adv.* Previously; at a time preceding.

ante-chamber, an'tē-chām-bèr, *n.* An apartment leading into a chief apartment. **antedate,** an'tē-dāt, *n.* Prior date.—*vt.* To date before the true time.

antediluvian, an-tē-di-lū''vi-an, *a.* Before the flood.—*n.* One who lived before the flood.

antelope, an'tē-lōp, *n.* An animal resembling the deer, but with hollow, unbranched horns.

antemeridian, an'tē-mē-rid''i-an, *a.* Before mid-day; pertaining to the forenoon.

antennae, an-ten'nē, *n. pl.* The feelers of an insect.

anterior, an-tē'ri-èr, *a.* Before; prior; in front.

anteroom, an'tē-röm, *n.* A room in front of a principal apartment.

anthem, an'them, *n.* A sacred song sung in alternate parts; a piece of Scripture set to music.

anther, an'thèr, *n.* The summit of the stamen in a flower, containing the pollen.

anthology, an-thol'o-ji, *n.* A collection of poems. **anthological,** an-tho-loj'ik-al, *a.* Pertaining to anthology.

anthracite, an'thra-sīt, *n.* A hard, compact coal which burns almost without flame.

anthropoid, an'thrō-poid, *a.* Resembling man; applied to the higher apes.

anthropology, an-thrō-pol'o-ji, *n.* The science of man and mankind; the study of the physical and mental constitution of man.

anthropomorphism, an-thrō'pō-mor''fizm, *n.* The representation of a deity in human form, or with human attributes.

anthropophagi, an-thrō-pof'a-jī, *n. pl.* Maneaters; cannibals. **anthropophagy,** an-thrō-pof'a-ji, *n.* Cannibalism.

antiaircraft, an-ti-är'kraft, *a.* A gun &c. (for shooting down hostile aircraft).

antic, an'tik, *a.* Grotesque; fantastic.—*n.* A buffoon; buffoonery.

Antichrist, an'ti-krīst, *n.* The great adversary of Christ. **Antichristian,** an-ti-kris'ti-an, *a.* Pertaining to Antichrist.

anticipate, an-tis'i-pāt, *vt.* (anticipating, anticipated). To forestall; to foretaste; to foresee; to expect, **anticipa-**

tion, an-tis'i-pā''shun, *n.* Act of anticipating; foretaste; expectation.

anti-climax, an-ti-klī'maks, *n.* A sentence in which the ideas become less striking at the close.

antidote, an'ti-dōt, *n.* A remedy for poison or any evil. **antidotal,** an'ti-dōt-al, *a.* Acting as an antidote.

anti-macassar, an'ti-ma-kas''ar, *n.* A movable covering for chairs, sofas, &c.

antimony, an'ti-mo-ni, *n.* A brittle, white-colored metal used in the arts and in medicine.

antipathy, an-tip'a-thi, *n.* Instinctive aversion; dislike; opposition.

antiphon, an'ti-fōn, *n.* The chant or alternate singing in choirs of cathedrals.

Antipodes, an-tip'ō-dēz, *n.pl.* Those who live on opposite sides of the globe; the opposite side of the globe.

antique, an-tēk', *a.* Old; of genuine antiquity.—*n.* Anything very old; an ancient relic. **antiquity,** an-tik'wi-ti, *n.* Ancient times; great age; *pl.* remains of ancient times. **antiquarianism,** an-ti-kwā'ri-an-izm, *n.* Love or knowledge of antiquities. **antiquary,** an'ti-kwa-ri, *n.* One versed in antiquities. **antiquated,** an'ti-kwāt-ed, *a.* Grown old; obsolete. **antiquarian,** an-ti-kwā'ri-an, *a.* Pertaining to antiquaries.—*n.* One versed in antiquities.

antiseptic, an-ti-sep'tik, *a.* Counteracting putrefaction.—*n.* A substance which resists or corrects putrefaction.

antithesis, an-tith'e-sis, *n.*; *pl.* -theses. Opposition of thoughts or words; contrast. **antithetical,** an-ti-thet'ik-al, *a.* Pertaining to antithesis.

antitoxin, an-ti-tox'in, *n.* A preparation to neutralize the poison of a micro-organism.

antler, ant'lèr, *n.* A branch of a stag's horn. **antlered,** ant'lèrd, *p.a.* With antlers.

anus, ā'nus, *n.* The opening of the body by which excrement is expelled.

anvil, an'vil, *n.* An iron block on which smiths hammer and shape their work.

anxious, angk'shus, *a.* Suffering mental distress; solicitous; concerned. **anxiously,** angk'shus-li, *adv.* In an anxious manner. **anxiety,** ang-zī'e-ti, *n.* State of being anxious; concern.

any, en'i, *a.* One indefinitely; whatever; some.—*adv.* At all; in any degree.

Apache, a-pach'è, *n.* One of a tribe of Athapascan stock of the American race; in Paris, a vagrant given to violence.

apart, a-pärt', *adv.* Separately; aside. **apartment,** a-pärt'ment, *n.* A room.

apathy, ap'a-thi, *n.* Want of feeling; insensibility; indifference. **apathetic,** ap-a-thet'ik, *a.* Void of feeling; free from passion; indifferent.

ape, āp, *n.* A monkey; an imitator.—*vt.* (aping, aped). To imitate servilely; to mimic.

aperture, ap'èr-tūr, *n.* An opening; a hole.

apex, ā'peks, *n.*; *pl.* -exes and -ices. The summit of anything.

aphorism, af'or-izm, *n.* A precept expressed in few words; a maxim.

apiary, ā'pi-a-ri, *n.* A place where bees are kept.

apish, āp'ish, *a.* Resembling an ape.

aplomb, a-plom', *n.* Self-possession.

apocalypse, a-pok'a-lips, *n.* Revelation; the last book of the New Testament.

apocrypha, a-pok'ri-fa, *n. pl.* Certain books whose authenticity as inspired writings is not generally admitted. **apocryphal,** a-pok'ri-fal, *a.* Pertaining to the Apocrypha; not canonical; fictitious.

apogee, ap'ō-jē, *n.* The point in the moon's orbit farthest from the earth.

apology, a-pol'ō-ji, *n.* That which is said in defense; vindication; excuse. **apologetic,** a-pol'ō-jet"ik, *a.* Containing apology; defending; excusing. **apologetics,** a-pol'ō-jet"iks, *n. pl.* The branch of theology which defends Christianity. **apologist,** a-pol'ō-jist, *n.* One who apologizes; an excuser, or defender. **apologize,** a-pol'ō-jiz, *vi.* (apologizing, apologized). To make an apology.

apoplexy, ap'ō-plek-si, *n.* A sudden privation of sense and voluntary motion. **apoplectic,** ap-o-plek'tik, *a.* Pertaining to apoplexy.

apostasy, a-pos'ta-si, *n.* Departure from one's faith; desertion of a party. **apostate,** a-pos'tāt, *n.* One who renounces his religion or his party.—*a.* False; traitorous. **apostatize,** a-pos'ta-tiz, *vi.* To abandon one's religion or party.

apostle, a-pos'l, *n.* One sent to preach the gospel; one of the twelve disciples. **apostleship,** a-pos'l-ship, *n.* Office of an apostle. **apostolic, apostolical,** ap-os-tol'ik, ap-os-tol'ik-al, *a.* Pertaining to an apostle.

apostrophe, a-pos'tro-fē, *n.* An addressing of the absent or the dead as if present; a mark (') indicating contraction of a word, or the possessive case. **apostrophize,** a-pos'trof-iz, *vi.* To address by apostrophe.

apothecary, a-poth'e-ka-ri, *n.* One who prepares and sells drugs or medicines.

appall, ap-pal', *vt.* (appalling, appalled). To depress with fear; to dismay. **appalling,** ap-pal'ing, *a.* Causing dread or terror.

apparatus, ap-pa-rā'tus, *n.; pl.* **-tus,** or **-tuses.** Set of instruments or utensils for performing any operation.

apparel, ap-pa'rel, *n.* Equipment; clothing.—*vt.* (appareling, appareled). To dress; to array.

apparent, ap-pa'rent, *a.* That may be seen; evident; seeming; not real. **apparently,** ap-pa'rent-li, *adv.* Openly; seemingly.

apparition, ap-pa-ri'shon, *n.* An appearance; a specter; a ghost or phantom.

appeal, ap-pēl', *vi.* To call; to refer to a superior court; to have recourse.—*vt.* To remove to a superior court.—*n.* The removal of a cause to a higher tribunal; a reference to another.

appear, ap-pēr', *vi.* To be or become visible; to seem. **appearance,** ap-pēr'ans, *n.* Act of coming into sight; semblance; likelihood.

appease, ap-pēz', *vt.* (appeasing, appeased). To pacify; to tranquilize.

appellant, ap-pel'ant, *n.* One who appeals. **appellate,** ap-pel'āt, *a.* Pertaining to appeals. **appellation,** ap-pel-ā'shun, *n.* Name, title. **appellative,** ap-pel'at-iv, *a.* Naming; designating.—*n.* A name; an appellation.

append, ap-pend', *vt.* To add; to annex. **appendage,** ap-pend'āj, *n.* Something added; a subordinate part. **appendant,** ap-pend'ant, *a.* Annexed.—*n.* Something subordinate or incidental. **appendix,** ap-pen'diks, *n.; pl.* **-ixes,** or **-ices.** An adjunct or appendage; a supplement.

appertain, ap-pèr-tān', *vi.* To belong; to relate.

appetite, ap'pē-tīt, *n.* A desire or relish for food or other sensual gratifications. **appetize,** ap'pē-tiz, *vt.* (appetizing, appetized). To give an appetite to; to whet the appetite. **appetizer,** ap'pē-tiz-èr, *n.* That which appetizes.

applaud, ap-plad', *vt.* To praise by clapping the hands, &c.; to extol. **applause,** ap-plaz', *n.* Praise loudly expressed; acclamation.

apple, ap'l, *n.* The fruit of the appletree; the pupil of the eye.

apply, ap-plī', *vt.* (applying, applied). To fasten or attach; to use; to employ with assiduity.—*vi.* To suit; to solicit; to have recourse to. **appliance,** ap-plī'ans, *n.* Act of applying; thing applied; article of equipment. **applicability,** ap'pli-ka-bil"li-ti, *n.* Quality of being applicable. **applicable,** ap'pli-ka-bl, *a.* That may be applied;- suitable. **applicably,** ap'pli-ka-bli, *adv.* In an applicable manner. **applicant,** ap'pli-kant, *n.* One who applies. **application,** ap-pli-kā'shun, *n.* Act of applying; request; close study; assiduity; the thing applied.

appoint, ap-point', *vt.* To fix; to allot; to nominate; to equip.—*vi.* To determine. **appointment,** ap-point'ment, *n.* Act of appointing; office held; arrangement; decree; *pl.* equipments.

apportion, ap-pōr'shon, *vt.* To portion out; to assign in just proportion. **apportioner,** ap-pōr'shon-èr, *n.* One who apportions. **apportionment,** ap-pōr'shon-ment, *n.* Act of apportioning.

apposite, ap'pō-zit, *a.* Suitable; applicable; pat. **appositely,** ap'pō-zit-li, *adv.* Suitably. **appositeness,** ap'pō-zit-nes, *n.* Fitness.

apposition, ap-pō-zi'shun, *n.* In *grammar,* the relation of one noun to another, when it explains its meaning, while agreeing in case.

appraise, ap-prāz', *vt.* (appraising, appraised). To fix or set a price on: to estimate. **appraisement,** ap-prāz'ment, *n.* Valuation. **appraiser,** ap-prāz'èr, *n.* One who values; a valuator.

appreciate, ap-prē'shi-āt, *vi.* (appreciating, appreciated). To value; to estimate justly. **appreciation,** ap-prē'shi-ā"shun, *n.* Act of appreciating; a just valuation. **appreciable,** ap-prē'shi-a-bl, *a.* That may be appreciated.

apprehend, ap-pre-hend', *vt.* To take hold of; to arrest; to conceive; to fear. —*vi.* To think; to imagine. **apprehensible,** ap-prē-hen'si-bl, *a.* That may be apprehended or conceived. **appre-**

hension, ap-prē-hen'shon, *n.* Seizure; faculty of conceiving ideas; dread. **apprehensive,** ap-prē-hen'siv, *a.* Fearful; suspicious.

apprentice, ap-pren'tis, *n.* One who is indentured to a master to learn a trade, an art, &c.—*vt.* To bind as an apprentice. **apprenticeship,** ap-pren'tis-ship, *n.* The term an apprentice serves; state or condition of an apprentice.

apprise, ap-prīz', *vt.* (apprising, apprised). To inform; to make known to.

approach, ap-prōch', *vi.* To come near; to approximate.—*vt.* To come near to; to resemble.—*n.* Act of drawing near; an avenue; access. **approachable,** ap-prōch'a-bl, *a.* That may be approached.

approbation, ap-prō-bā'shun, *n.* Approval; attestation; a liking.

appropriable, ap-prō'pri-a-bl, *a.* That may be appropriated.

appropriate, ap-prō'pri-āt, *vt.* (appropriating, appropriated). To take to one's self as one's own; to set apart for.—*a.* Set apart for a particular use or person; suitable; adapted. **appropriately,** ap-prō'pri-āt-li, *adv.* In an appropriate manner. **appropriateness,** ap-prō'pri-āt-nes, *n.* Peculiar fitness. **appropriation,** ap-prō'pri-ā"shon, *n.* Act of appropriating; application to special use.

approve, ap-prōv', *vt.* (approving, approved). To deem good; to like; to sanction.—*vi.* To feel or express approbation (with *of*). **approvable,** ap-prōv'a-bl, *a.* That may be approved. **approval,** ap-prō'val, *n.* Approbation.

approximate, ap-prok'si-māt, *a.* Near; approaching.—*vt.* (approximating, approximated). To bring near.—*vi.* To come near; to approach. **approximately,** ap-prok'si-māt-li, *adv.* Nearly. **approximation,** ap-prok'si-mā"shun, *n.* Act of approximating; approach.

appurtenance, ap-pèr'ten-ans, *n.* That which pertains to; an appendage.

apricot, ā'pri-kot, *n.* Stone-fruit, resembling the peach.

April, ā'pril, *n.* The fourth month of the year.

apron, ā'prun, *n.* A cloth, or piece of leather, worn in front to protect the clothes.

apropos, ap'rō-pō, *adv.* To the purpose; opportunely.

apt, apt, *a.* Suitable; liable; ready.

aptitude, ap'ti-tūd, *n.* Fitness; readiness.

aqua, ak'wa, *n.* Water.

aqualung, ak'wa-lung', *n.* A breathing device of one or more cylinders of compressed air and a watertight face mask for underwater diving.

aquaplane, ak'wa-plān, *n.* A plank attached by ropes behind a power boat, on which a person may stand and control to some degree the plank as it is dragged over the water.

aquarium, a-kwā'ri-um, *n.*; pl. **-iums** or **-ia.** A vessel or tank for aquatic plants and animals; a collection of such vessels.

Aquarius, a-kwā'ri-us, *n.* The water-bearer, a sign in the zodiac.

aquatic, a-kwat'ik, *a.* Living or growing in water.—*n.* A plant which grows in water; *pl.* sports or exercises in water.

aqueduct, ak'wē-dukt, *n.* A conduit made for conveying water.

aquiline, ak'wil-in, *a.* Belonging to the eagle; hooked like the beak of an eagle.

Arab, a'rab, *n.* A native of Arabia; a street urchin; an Arabian horse.

arabesque, ar'ab-esk, *n.* A species of ornamentation consisting of fanciful figures and floral forms.

arable, a'ra-bl, *a.* Fit for plowing

Aramaic, Aramean, a-ra-mā'ik, a-ra-mē'an, *a.* Pertaining to the language, &c., of the Syrians and Chaldeans.

arbiter, är'bit-ėr, *n.* A person appointed by parties in controversy to decide their differences; an umpire.

arbitrament, är-bit'ra-ment, *n.* Decision.

arbitrarily, är'bi-tra-ri-li, *adv.* By will only; despotically.

arbitrary, är'bi-tra-ri, *a.* Depending on one's will; despotic.

arbitrate, är'bi-trāt, *vi.* (arbitrating, arbitrated). To act as an arbiter; to decide. **arbitration,** är-bi-trā'shun, *n.* The act of arbitrating. **arbitrator,** är'bi-trāt-ėr, *n.* A person chosen to decide a dispute; umpire.

arbor, är'bėr, *n.* A bower; a shelter in a garden, formed of trees, &c.

arboreous, är-bōr'rē-us, *a.* Belonging to trees. **aborescence,** är-bor-es'sens, *n.* The state of being arborescent. **arborescent,** är-bor-es'sent, *a.* Growing like a tree; becoming woody. **arboretum,** är-bo-rē'tum, *n.* A place where trees are cultivated for scientific purposes. **arboriculture,** är-bo'ri-kul"tūr, *n.* The art of cultivating trees and shrubs.

arbutus, är-bū'tus, *n.* An evergreen shrub, with berries like the strawberry.

arc, ärk, *n.* A part of a circle or curve.

arcade, är-kād', *n.* A walk arched above; an arched gallery; a covered passage containing shops.

arch, ärch, *a.* Chief; cunning; sly; roguish.

arch, ärch, *n.* A concave structure supported by its own curve; a vault.—*vt.* To cover with an arch; to form with a curve.

archæological, är-kē-ō-loj'ik-al, *a.* Relating to archæology.

archæology, är-kē-ol'o-ji, *n.* The science of antiquities; knowledge of ancient art.

archaic, är-kā'ik, *a.* Antiquated; obsolete.

archangel, ärk-ān'jel, *n.* An angel of the highest order. **archangelic,** ärk-an-jel'ik, *a.* Belonging to archangels.

archbishop, ärch-bish'up, *n.* A chief bishop; a bishop who superintends other bishops, his suffragans, in his province. **archbishopric,** ärch-bish'up-rik, *n.* The province of an archbishop.

archdeacon, ärch-dē'kn, *n.* A church dignitary next in rank below a bishop. **archdeaconry,** ärch-dē'kn-ri, *n.* The office or residence of an archdeacon. **archdeaconship,** ärch-dē'kn-ship, *n.* The office of an archdeacon.

archduke, ärch-dūk′, *n.* A title of princes of the House of Austria.

archer, ärch′ẽr, *n.* A bowman; one who shoots with a bow and arrow. **archery,** ärch′ē-ri, *n.* The practice, art, or skill of archers.

archetype, är′kē-tīp, *n.* The original model from which a thing is made.

archidiaconal, är′ki-dī-ak″on-al, *a.* Pertaining to an archdeacon.

archiepiscopal, är′ki-ē-pis″kō-pal, *a.* Belonging to an archbishop.

archipelago, är-ki-pel′a-gō, *n.* The Ægean Sea; a sea abounding in small islands.

architect, är′ki-tekt, *n.* One who plans buildings, &c.; a contriver. **architectural,** är-ki-tek′tūr-al, *a.* Pertaining to architecture.

architecture, är′ki-tek-tūr, *n.* The art or science of building; structure.

archive, är′kīv, *n.* A record: generally *pl.*; records of a kingdom, city, family, &c.

archness, ärch′nes, *n.* Roguishness.

archon, är′kon, *n.* One of the chief magistrates of ancient Athens.

archway, ärch′wā, *n.* A way or passage under an arch.

Arctic, ärk′tik, *a.* Pertaining to the regions about the north pole; frigid; cold.

ardent, är′dent, *a.* Burning; fervent; eager.

ardor, är′dẽr, *n.* Warmth; fervency; eagerness.

arduous, är′dū-us, *a.* Difficult; laborious. **arduously,** är′dū-us-li, *adv.* In an arduous manner; with effort.

are, är. The plural pres. indic. of verb *to be.*

area, ā′rē-a, *n.* Any open surface; superficial contents; any inclosed space.

arena, a-rē′na, *n.* An open space of ground, strewed with sand or saw-dust, for combatants; any place of public contest.

argent, är′jent, *a.* Silvery; like silver.

Argonaut, är′gō-naṭ, *n.* One who sailed in the ship *Argo* in quest of the golden fleece.

argue, är′gū, *vi.* (arguing, argued). To offer reasons; to dispute.—*vt.* To show reasons for; to discuss. **argument,** är′gū-ment, *n.* A reason offered; a plea; subject of a discourse; heads of contents; controversy. **argumentation,** är-gū-ment-ā″shun, *n.* Act, art, or process of arguing. **argumentative,** är-gū-ment′at-iv, *a.* Consisting of or prone to argument.

arid, a′rid, *a.* Dry; dried; parched. **aridity,** a-rid′i-ti, *n.* Dryness.

Aries, ā′ri-ēz, *n.* The Ram, the first of the twelve signs in the zodiac.

aright, a-rīt′, *adv.* Rightly; justly.

arise, a-riz′, *vi.* (arising, pret. arose, pp. arisen). To rise up; to proceed from.

aristocracy, a-ris-tok′ra-si, *n.* Government by the nobility; the nobility. **aristocrat,** a-ris′tō-krat, *n.* A noble; one who favors aristocracy. **aristocratic,** a-ris-tō-krat′ik, *a.* Pertaining to aristocracy. **aristocratically,** a-ris-tō-krat′-ik-al-li, *adv.* In an aristocratic manner.

arithmetic, a-rith′met-ik, *n.* The science of numbering; the art of computation. **arithmetical,** a-rith-met′ik-al, *a.* Pertaining to arithmetic. **arithmetically,** a-rith-met′ik-al-li, *adv.* By means of arithmetic. **arithmetician,** a-rith′-me-ti″shan, *n.* One skilled in arithmetic.

ark, ärk, *n.* A chest; a large floating vessel.

arm, ärm, *n.* The limb from the shoulder to the hand; anything extending from a main body; a weapon; *pl.* war; armor; armorial bearings; *vt.* To furnish with arms; to fortify.— *vi.* To take up arms.

armada, är-mä′da, *n.* A fleet of armed ships; a squadron.

armadillo, är-ma-dil′lō, *n.* A quadruped of S. America with a hard bony shell.

armament, ärm′a-ment, *n.* A force armed for war; war-munitions of a ship.

Armenian, är-mē′ni-an, *a.* Pertaining to Armenia.—*n.* A native of Armenia; the language of the country.

armistice, är′mis-tis, *n.* A cessation of hostilities for a short time; a truce.

armor, ärm′ẽr, *n.* Defensive arms. **armorer,** ärm′ẽr-er, *n.* One who makes or has the care of arms. **armorial,** är-mō′ri-al, *a.* Belonging to armor, or to the arms of a family. **armory,** ärm′ē-ri, *n.* A repository of arms.

armpit, ärm′pit, *n.* The hollow place under the shoulder.

army, är′mi, *n.* A body of men armed for war; a great number.

arnica, är′ni-ka, *n.* Kinds of plant including mountain tobacco; medicine made from arnica.

aroma, a-rō′ma, *n.* Perfume; the fragrant principle in plants, &c. **aromatic,** a-rō-mat′ik, *a.* Fragrant; spicy. —*n.* A fragrant plant or drug.

around, a-round′, *prep.* About; on all sides of; encircling.—*adv.* On every side.

arouse, a-rouz′, *vt.* (arousing, aroused). To rouse; to stir up.

arraign, a-rān′, *vt.* To indict; to censure. **arraigner,** a-rān′ẽr, *n.* One who arraigns. **arraignment,** a-rān′ment, *n.* Act of arraigning; accusation.

arrange, a-rānj′, *vt.* (arranging, arranged). To put in order; to classify. **arrangement,** a-rānj′ment, *n.* Orderly disposition; adjustment; classification.

arrant, a′rant, *a.* Downright; thorough.

array, a-rā′, *n.* Order; order of battle; apparel.—*vt.* To draw up in order; to adorn.

arrear, a-rēr′, *n.* That which remains unpaid. Generally in plural.

arrest, a-rest′, *vt.* To stop; to apprehend.—*n.* A seizure by warrant; stoppage.

arrive, a-rīv′, *vi.* (arriving, arrived). To come; to reach; to attain. **arrival,** a-rīv′al, *n.* Act of coming to a place; persons or things arriving.

arrogant, a′rō-gant, *a.* Assuming; haughty. **arrogantly,** a′rō-gant-li, *adv.* In an arrogant manner. **arrogance,** a′rō-gans, *n.* Assumption; haughtiness; insolent bearing.

arrogate, a′rō-gät, *vt.* (arrogating, arrogated). To claim unduly; to assume.

arrow, a′rō, *n.* A straight-pointed weapon, to be discharged from a bow. **arrow-headed**, a'rō-hed-ed, a. Shaped like the head of an arrow.

arrowroot, a'rō-röt, n, A W. Indian plant; the starch of the plant, a medicinal food.

arsenal, är'sė-nal, n. A public establishment where naval and military engines are manufactured or stored.

arsenic, är'sen-ik, n. A virulent mineral poison; an oxide of a brittle metal, called also arsenic. **arsenical**, är-sen'-ik-al, a. Consisting of or containing arsenic.

arson, är'son, n. The malicious setting on fire of a house, &c.

art, ärt. The second person, present indicative of the verb to be.

art, ärt, n. Practical skill; a system of rules for certain actions; cunning; profession of a painter, &c.

arterial, är-tē'ri-al, a. Pertaining to an artery or the arteries.

artery, är'tė-ri, n. A tube which conveys blood from the heart.

artesian, är-tē'zi-an, a. Designating a well made by boring till water is reached.

artful, ärt'ful, a. Full of art; skillful; crafty. **artfully**, ärt'ful-li, adv. With art. **artfulness**, ärt'ful-nes, n. Craft; address.

arthritis, är-thri'tis, n. The gout.

artichoke, är'ti-chōk, n. An esculent plant somewhat resembling a thistle.

article, är'ti-kl, n. A separate item; stipulation; a particular commodity; a part of speech used before nouns, as the.—vt. To bind by articles.—vi. To stipulate.

articulate, är-tik'ū-lāt, a. Distinct; clear.—vi. To utter distinct sounds, syllables, or words.—vt. To speak distinctly. **articulately**, är-tik'ū-lāt-li, adv. Distinctly. **articulation**, är-tik'ū-la'shun, n. Juncture of bones; joint; distinct utterance.

artifice, ärt'i-fis, n. An artful device; fraud; stratagem. **artificer**, är-tif'is-ėr, n. A contriver; a mechanic.

artificial, ärt-i-fi'shal, a. Made by art; not natural. **artificially**, ärt-i-fi'shal-li, adv. In an artificial manner.

artillery, är-til'lė-ri, n. Cannon; the troops who manage them; gunnery.

artisan, ärt'i-zan, n. One trained to manual dexterity; a mechanic.

artist, ärt'ist, n. One skilled in some art, especially the fine arts, as painting, &c. **artiste**, är-tēst, n. One skilled in some art not one of the fine arts, as singing, dancing.

artless, ärt'les, a. Wanting art; unaffected. **artlessly**, ärt'les-li, adv. In an artless manner. **artlessness**, ärt'les-nes, n. Quality of being artless; simplicity.

Aryan, ä'ri-an or ä'ri-an, a. Indo-European; belonging to the Hindus, Persians, and most Europeans (except Turks, Hungarians, Finns, &c.), and to their languages.

as, az, adv. and conj. Like; even; equally; while; since; for example. **asbestos**, as-bes'tos, n. A mineral fibrous substance which is incombustible.

ascend, as-send', vi. To rise; to go backward in order of time.—vt. To move upward upon; to climb. **ascendancy**, **ascendency**, as-send'an-si, as-send'en-si, n. Controlling power; sway. **ascendant**, as-send'ant, a. Rising; superior; predominant.—n. Ascendancy; superiority. **ascension**, as-sen'shun, n. Act of ascending.

Ascension Day, as-sen'shon dā, n. The Thursday but one before Whitsuntide, to commemorate Christ's ascension into heaven.

ascent, as-sent', n. Rise; a mounting upward; the means of ascending.

ascertain, as-sėr-tān', vt. To make certain; to find out. **ascertainable**, as-sėr-tān'a-bl, a. That may be ascertained.

ascetic, as-set'ik, a. Unduly rigid in devotion.—n. One rigidly austere. **asceticism**, as-set'i-sizm, n. State or practice of ascetics.

ascribe, as-krīb', vt. (ascribing, ascribed). To attribute; to assign. **ascribable**, as-krīb'a-bl, a. That may be ascribed. **ascription**, as-krip'shun, n. Act of ascribing; the thing ascribed.

aseptic, a-sep'tik, a. Not liable to putrefy.

ash, ash, n. A well-known timber tree.

ashamed, a-shāmd', a. Affected by shame.

ashen, ash'en, a. Pertaining to ash; made of ash.

ashes, ash'ez, n.pl. The dust produced by combustion; the remains of a dead body.

Ash-Wednesday, ash-wenz'dā, n. The first day of Lent, so called from a custom of sprinkling ashes on the head.

aside, a-sīd', adv. On one side; apart; at a small distance.

asinine, as'i-nīn, a. Belonging to or resembling the ass.

ask, ask, vt. To request; to question; to invite.—vi. To request or petition; to make inquiry.

askance, **askant**, a-skans', a-skant', adv. Awry; obliquely.

askew, a-skū, adv. or pred.a. Awry.

aslant, a-slant', pred.a. or adv. On slant; obliquely; not perpendicularly.

asp, asp, n. A small venomous serpent of Egypt.

asparagus, as-pa'ra-gus, n. A well-known esculent plant.

aspect, as'pekt, n. Appearance; situation.

aspen, asp'en, n. A species of the poplar.

asperity, as-pe'ri-ti, n. Roughness; harshness.

asperse, as-pėrs', vt. (aspersing, aspersed). To calumniate; to slander. **aspersion**, as-pėr'shon, n. Calumny.

asphalt, as-falt', n. A bituminous, hard substance, used for pavement, &c.

asphyxia, as-fik'si-a, n. Suspended animation from suffocation, &c.

asphyxiate, as-fik'si-āt, vt. To bring to a state of asphyxia.

aspire, as-pīr', vi. (aspiring, aspired). To aim at high things; to soar. **aspiringly**, as-pīr'ing-li, adv. In an aspiring manner. **aspirant**, as-pīr'ant, n.

A candidate. **aspiration,** as-pi-rā′shon, *n.* Ardent desire; an aspirated sound.

aspirin, as′pi-rin, *n.* A white crystalline compound, used as a drug for the salicylic acid liberated from it in the intestines.

asquint, a-skwint′, *adv.* Out of the corner or angle of the eye; obliquely.

assail, as-sāl′, *vt.* To attack; to assault. **assailable,** as-sāl′a-bl, *a.* That may be assailed. **assailant,** as-sāl′ant, *n.* One who assails.

assassin, as-sas′sin, *n.* One who kills, or attempts to kill, by surprise or secretly. **assassinate,** as-sas′sin-āt, *vt.* (assassinating, assassinated). To murder by surprise or secretly. **assassination,** as-sas′sin-ā″shon, *n.* Act of murdering by surprise.

assault, as-salt′, *n.* An attack; a storming.—*vt.* To assail; to storm. **assaulter,** as-salt′ér, *n.* One who assaults.

assay, as-sā′, *n.* Proof; trial; determination of the quantity of metal in an ore or alloy.—*vt.* To try; to ascertain the purity or alloy of.—*vi.* To try or endeavor. **assayer,** as-sā′ér, *n.* One who assays. **assaying,** as-sā′ing, *n.* Act of ascertaining the purity of the precious metals.

assemble, as-sem′bl, *vt.* (assembling, assembled). To bring together.—*vi.* To come together. **assembly,** as-sem′bli, *n.* An assemblage; a convccation.

assemblage, as-sem′blāj, *n.* A collection of individuals or things.

assent, as-sent′, *n.* Act of agreeing to anything; consent.—*vi.* To agree; to yield.

assert, as-sèrt′, *vt.* To affirm; to maintain; to vindicate. **assertion,** as-sèr′-shon, *n.* Act of asserting. **assertive,** as-sèrt′iv, *a.* Affirming confidently; peremptory.

assess, as-ses′, *vt.* To fix a charge to be paid upon; to rate. **assessable,** as-ses′a-bl, *a.* That may be assessed. **assessment,** as-ses′ment, *n.* Act of assessing; the sum levied; a tax. **assessor,** as-ses′ér, *n.* A legal adviser who assists a magistrate or judge.

assets, as′sets, *n.pl.* Goods available to pay debts.

asseverate, as-sev′ē-rāt, *vt.* (asseverating, asseverated). To declare seriously or solemnly; to protest. **asseveration,** as-sev′ē-rā″shon, *n.* Positive and solemn declaration.

assiduous, as-sid′ū-us, *a.* Constantly diligent. **assiduity,** as-si-dū′i-ti, *n.* Close application; diligence.

assign, as-sīn′, *vt.* To designate; to allot; to make over to another.—*n.* A person to whom property or any right may be or is transferred.

assignable, as-sīn′a-bl, *a.* That may be- assigned. **assignation,** as-sig-nā′-shon, *n.* An appointment to meet, as of lovers; a making over by transfer of title. **assignee,** as-sī-nē′, *n.* One to whom an assignment is made. **assigner,** as-sīn′ér, *n.* One who assigns. **assignment,** as-sīn′ment, *n.* Act of assigning; thing assigned; a writ of transfer.

assimilate, as-sim′il-āt, *vt.* (assimilating, assimilated). To make like to; to digest.—*vi.* To become similar or of the same substance. **assimilation,** as-sim′-il-ā″shun, *n.* Act of assimilating.

assist, as-sist′, *vt.* To help.—*vi.* To lend help; to contribute. **assistance,** as-sist′ans, *n.* Help; aid. **assistant,** as-sist′ant, *n.* One who assists.

assize, as-sīz′, *n.* A statute regulating weights, measures, or prices; in *pl.* the periodical courts held in the counties of England and Wales.

associate, as-sō′shi-āt, *vt.* (associating, associated). To join in company with; to combine.—*vi.* To keep company with. —*n.* A companion; friend. **association,** as-sō′si-ā″shon, *n.* Act of associating; union; confederacy. **associable,** as-sō′shi-a-bl, *a.* Companionable.

assonance, as′sō-nans, *n.* Resemblance of sounds.

assort, as-sort′, *vt.* To sort; to arrange. —*vi.* To suit; to agree. **assortment,** as-sort′ment, *n.* Act of assorting; quantity of things assorted; variety.

assuage, as-swāj′, *vt.* (assuaging, assuaged). To allay; to calm.—*vi.* To abate or subside. **assuagement,** as-swāj′ment, *n.* Mitigation.

assume, as-sūm′, *vt.* (assuming, assumed). To take for granted; to usurp. —*vi.* To claim more than is due; to be arrogant. **assuming,** as-sum′ing, *a.* Arrogant. **assumption,** as-sump′shun, *n.* Act of assuming; the thing assumed; the taking up of any person into heaven.

assure, a-shōr′, *vt.* (assuring, assured). To make sure; to confirm; to insure. **assuredly,** a-shōr′ed-li, *adv.* Certainly. **assuredness,** a-shōr′ed-nes, *n.* State of being assured. **assurer,** a-shōr′ér, *n.* One who assures or insures. **assurance,** a-shōr′ans, *n.* Act of assuring; secure confidence; impudence; positive declaration; insurance.

Assyrian, as-sir′i-an, *a.* Pertaining to Assyria or its inhabitants.—*n.* A native of Assyria; the language of the Assyrians.

aster, as-tèr, *n.* A genus of composite plants, with flowers somewhat like stars.

asterisk, as′tē-risk, *n.* The figure of a star thus *, used in printing.

astern, a-stèrn′, *adv.* In or at the hinder part of a ship.

asteroid, as′tèr-oid, *n.* A small planet.

asthma, as′ma or as′thma, *n.* A disorder of respiration, characterized by difficulty of breathing, cough, and expectoration. **asthmatic,** as-mat′ik, *a.* Pertaining to asthma; affected by asthma.

astigmatism, a-stig′mat-izm, *n.* A malformation of the eye, in which rays of light do not properly converge to one point.

astir, a-stèr′, *adv.* or *pred.a.* On stir; active.

astonish, as-ton′ish, *vt.* To surprise; to astound. **astonishing,** as-ton′ish-ing, *a.* Marvelous. **astonishment,** as-ton′ish-ment, *n.* Amazement.

astound, as-tound′, *vt.* To astonish; to stun; to strike dumb with amazement.

astounding, as-tound'ing, *a.* Adapted to astonish; most astonishing.

astrakhan, as'tra-kan, *n.* A rough kind of cloth with a curled pile.

astral, as'tral, *a.* Belonging to the stars.

astride, a-strid', *adv.* or *pred.a.* With the legs apart or across a thing.

astringent, as-trinj'ent, *a.* Contracting tissues of the body; strengthening.—*n.* A medicine which contracts and strengthens. **astringency,** as-trinj'en-si, *n.* Power of contracting, or of giving firmness.

astrolabe, as'trō-lāb, *n.* An old instrument for taking the altitude at sea.

astrology, as-trol'o-ji, *n.* The pretended art of foretelling future events from the stars. **astrologer,** as-trol'o-jer, *n.* One versed in astrology. **astrological,** as-trō-loj'ik-al, *a.* Pertaining to astrology.

astronaut, astra-naut', *n.* A trained space traveler.

astronomy, as-tron'o-mi, *n.* The science of the heavenly bodies. **astronomer,** as-tron'o-mèr, *n.* One versed in astronomy. **astronomical,** as-trō-nom'ik-al, *a.* Pertaining to astronomy.

astute, as-tūt', *a.* Shrewd; crafty. **astutely,** as-tūt'li, *adv.* Shrewdly. **astuteness,** as-tūt'nes, *n.* Shrewdness.

asunder, a-sun'dèr, *adv.* or *pred.a.* Apart; into parts; in a divided state.

asylum, a-sī'lum, *n.* A place of refuge; an institution for the care or relief of the unfortunate.

at, at, *prep.* Denoting presence or nearness; in a state of; employed in, on, or with; with direction towards.

atavism, at'a-vizm, *n.* The resemblance of offspring to a remote ancestor.

atheism, ā'thē-izm, *n.* The disbelief in the existence of a God. **atheist,** ā'thē-ist, *n.* One who disbelieves the existence of a God. **atheistic, atheistical,** ā-thē-ist'ik, ā-thē-ist'ik-al, *a.* Pertaining to atheism.

atheneum, ath-e-nē'um, *n.* An establishment connected with literature, science, or art.

Athenian, a-thēn'i-an, *a.* Pertaining to Athens.—*n.* A native of Athens.

athlete, ath-lēt', *n.* One skilled in exercises of agility or strength. **athletic,** ath-let'ik, *a.* Pertaining to an athlete; strong; robust; vigorous. **athleticism,** ath-let'i-sizm, *n.* The practice of athletics. **athletics,** ath-let'iks, *n.pl.* Athletic exercises.

athwart, a-thwart', *prep.* Across; from side to side.—*adv.* Crossly; wrong.

Atlantic, at-lan'tik, *a.* Pertaining to the ocean between Europe, Africa, and America.—*n.* This ocean.

atlas, at'las, *n.* A collection of maps.

atmosphere, at'mos-fēr, *n.* The whole mass of air surrounding the earth; air; pervading influence. **atmospheric,** at-mos-fe'rik, *a.* Pertaining to the atmosphere.

atoll, a-tol', *n.* A ring-shaped coral island.

atom, at'om, *n.* A minute particle of matter; anything extremely small. **atomic,** a-tom'ik, *a.* Pertaining to or consisting of atoms.

atone, a-tōn', *vi.* (atoning, atoned). To make satisfaction.—*vt.* To expiate. **atonement,** a-tōn'ment, *n.* Reconciliation; satisfaction.

atrocious, a-trō'shus, *a.* Extremely cruel or wicked; flagitious. **atrociously,** a-trō-shus-li, *adv.* In an atrocious manner. **atrocity,** a-tros'i-ti, *n.* Horrible wickedness.

atrophy, at'rō-fi, *n.* A wasting away; emaciation.

attach, at-tach', *vt.* To affix; to connect; to arrest; to win.—*vi.* To adhere. **attache,** at-ta-shā, *n.* One attached to the suit of an ambassador. **attachment,** at-tach'ment, *n.* State of being attached; fidelity; tender regard.

attack, at-tak', *vt.* To assault; to assail.—*n.* An assault; seizure by a disease.

attain, at-tān', *vi.* To come or arrive.—*vt.* To reach; to gain; to obtain.

attainable, at-tān'a-bl, *a.* That may be attained.

attainment, at-tān'ment, *n.* Act of attaining; acquirement; accomplishment.

attainder, at-tān'dèr, *n.* Extinction of civil rights, in consequence of a capital crime.

attaint, at-tānt', *vt.* To affect with attainder.

attar, at'tär, *n.* An essential oil made from roses forming a valuable perfume.

attempt, at-temt', *vt.* To try to do; to make an effort upon.—*n.* An essay; enterprise.

attend, at-tend', *vt.* To wait on; to accompany or be present at.—*vi.* To pay regard; to hearken; to wait.

attendance, at-tend'ans, *n.* Act of attending; service; retinue.

attendant, at-tend'ant, *a.* Accompanying, as subordinate.—*n.* One who waits on, is present, or accompanies.

attention, at-ten'shon, *n.* Act of attending; heed; courtesy. **attentive,** at-tent'iv, *a.* Heedful. **attentively,** at-tent'iv-li, *adv.* With attention. **attentiveness,** at-tent'iv-nes, *n.* State of being attentive; heedfulness.

attenuate, at-ten'ū-āt, *vt.* (attenuating, attenuated). To make slender or thin (as liquids).—*vi.* To diminish. **attenuation,** at-ten'ū-ā'shun, *n.* Act of attenuating; thinness; slenderness.

attest, at-test', *vt.* To bear witness to; to certify; to call to witness. **attestation,** at-test-ā'shon, *n.* Testimony.

Attic, at'tik, *a.* Pertaining to Attica or to Athens; pure; elegant in style or language.—*n.* The dialect of Attica or Athens; the uppermost story of a building; garret.

attire, at-tīr, *vt.* (attiring, attired). To dress; to array.—*n.* Dress.

attitude, at'ti-tūd, *n.* Posture. **attitudinise,** at-ti-tūd'in-iz, *vi.* To assume affected attitudes or airs.

attorney, at-tér'ni, *n.* One who acts in place of another; one who practices in law-courts.

attract, at-trakt', *vi.* To draw to; to entice. **attractable,** at-trakt'a-bl, *a.* That may be attracted. **attraction,** at-trak'shon, *n.* Act of attracting; allurement; charm. **attractive**, at-trakt'iv, a. Having the power of attracting; enticing. **attractively**, at-trakt'iv-li, adv. In an attractive manner.

attribute, at-trib'ūt, vt. (attributing, attributed). To ascribe; to impute.—n. at'tri-būt; inherent property; characteristic; an adjectival word or clause. **attribution**, at-tri-bū'shun, n. Act of attributing, or the quality ascribed. **attributable**, at-trib'ūt-a-bl, a. That may be attributed. **attributive**, at-trib'ūt-iv, a. That attributes.—n. That which is attributed.

attrition, at-tri'shun, n. Act of wearing, or state of being worn, by rubbing.

attune, at-tūn', vt. (attuning, attuned). To put in tune; to adjust to another sound.

auburn, a-bērn, a. Reddish-brown.

auction, ak'shun, n. A public sale in which the article falls to the highest bidder. **auctioneer**, ak-shun-ēr', n. The person who sells at auction.

audacious, a-dā'shus, a. Daring; impudent. **audacity**, a-das'i-ti, n. Daring; reprehensible boldness; impudence.

audible, a'di-bl, a. That may be heard. **audibly**, a'di-bli, adv. In an audible manner.

audience, a'di-ens, n. Act of hearing; an assembly of hearers; admittance to a hearing; ceremonial interview.

audit, a'dit, n. An official examination of accounts.—vt. To examine and adjust, as accounts. **auditor**, a'dit-ēr, n. One who examines and adjusts accounts. **auditorship**, a'dit-ēr-ship, n. The office of auditor.

auditory, a'di-tō-ri, a. Pertaining to the sense or organs of hearing.—n. An audience; an auditorium.

auger, a'gēr, n. An instrument for boring holes.

augment, ag'ment, n. Increase; a prefix to a word. **augmentable**, ag-ment'a-bl, a. Capable of augmentation. **augmentation**, ag-ment-ā'shon, n. Act of augmenting; increase; addition. **augmentative**, ag-ment'at-iv, a. Having the quality of augmenting.—n. A word formed to express greatness.

augur, a'gēr, n. One who foretold the future by observing the flight of birds; a soothsayer.—vi. To predict; to bode.—vt. To predict or foretell. **augural**, a'gū-ral, a. Pertaining to an augur or augury. **augurer**, a'gēr-ēr, n. One who augurs. **augury**, a'gū-ri, n. Omen; prediction.

august, a-gust', a. Grand; majestic; awful.

August, a'gust, n. The eighth month of the year.

auk, ak, n. A swimming bird found in the British seas, with very short wings.

aunt, ant, n. The sister of one's father or mother.

aureola, **aureole**, a-rē'o-la, a'rē-ōl, n. An illumination represented as surrounding a holy person, as Christ; a halo.

auricle, a'ri-kl, n. The external ear; either of the two ear-like cavities over the two ventricles of the heart.

auricular, a-rik'ū-lēr, a. Pertaining to the ear; confidential.

aurora, a-rō'ra, n. The dawn. Roman mythology—the goddess of the dawn.

aurora borealis, a-rō'ra bō-rē-ā'lis, n. The northern lights or streamers. **aurora australis**, a-stra'lis, n. A similar phenomenon in the S. hemisphere.

auspice, a'spis, n. Augury from birds; protection; influence. **auspicious**, a-spi'shus, a. Fortunate; propitious. **auspiciously**, a-spi'shus-li, adv. Prosperously; favorably.

austere, a-stēr', a. Rigid: sour; stern; severe. **austerely**, a-stēr'li, adv. In an austere manner. **austerity**, a-ste'ri-ti, n. Severity of manners or life; rigor.

authentic, a-then'tik, a. Genuine; authoritative. **authentically**, a-then'tik-al-li, adv. In an authentic manner. **authenticate**, a-then'ti-kāt, vt. To render or prove authentic. **authentication**, a-then'ti-kā"shon, n. Act of authenticating; confirmation. **authenticity**, a-then-tis'i-ti, n. Quality of being authentic; genuineness.

author, a'thēr, n. One who creates; an originator; the writer of a book, &c.

authoress, a'thēr-es, n. A female author.

authority, a-tho'ri-ti, n. Legal power or right; influence conferred by character or station; person in power; testimony; credibility; precedent.

authorize, a'thor-īz, vt. (authorizing, authorized). To give authority to; to make legal; to sanction.

authoritative, a-tho'ri-tā-tiv, a. Having due authority; peremptory.

authoritatively, a-tho'ri-tā-tiv-li, adv. In an authoritative manner.

autobiographer, a'tō-bī-og"ra-fēr. n. One who writes his own life. **autobiography**, a'tō-bī-og"ra-fi, n. Memoirs of a person written by himself. **autobiographical**, a-tō-bī'ō-graf"ik-al, a. Pertaining to or containing autobiography.

autocracy, a-tok'ra-si, n. Absolute government by one man. **autocrat**, a'tō-krat, n. An absolute prince or sovereign.

autograph, a'tō-graf, n. A person's own handwriting; signature.

automatic, **automatical**, a-tō-mat'-ik, a-tō-mat'ik-al, a. Self-acting; moving spontaneously.

automaton, a-tom'a-ton, n.; pl. **-ta**. A self-moving machine, or one which moves by invisible machinery.

automobile, a'to-mo'bil, n. A vehicle propelled usually by a gasoline motor.

autonomy, a-ton'o-mi, n. The power or right of self-government.

autopsy, a'top-si, n. Personal observation; post-mortem examination.

autumn, a'tum, n. The third season of the year, between summer and winter.

auxiliary, ag-zil'i-a-ri, a. Aiding.—n. One who aids; a verb which helps to form the moods and tenses of other verbs; pl. Foreign troops employed in war.

avail, a-vāl', vt. To profit; to promote.

—*vi.* To be of use; to answer the purpose.—*n.* Advantage; use.

avalanche, av'a-lansh, *n.* A large body of snow or ice sliding down a mountain.

avarice, av'a-ris, *n.* Covetousness. **avaricious**, av-a-ri'shus, *a.* Covetous; greedy of gain; niggardly. **avariciously**, av-a-ri'shus-li, *adv.* In an avaricious manner.

Ave, ā've, *n.* Hail; an abbreviation of the Ave-Maria, or Hail-Mary.

avenge, a-venj', *vt.* (avenging, avenged). To vindicate; to take satisfaction for. **avenger**, a-venj'èr, *n.* One who avenges.

avenue, av'e-nū, *n.* An approach to; an alley of trees leading to a house, &c.

aver, a-vèr', *vt.* (averring, averred). To declare positively; to assert. **averment**, a-vèr'ment, *n.* Affirmation; declaration.

average, av'èr-āj, *n.* Medium; mean proportion.—*a.* Medial; containing a mean proportion.—*vt.* To find the mean of.—*vi.* To form a mean.

averse, a-vèrs', *a.* Disinclined; not favorable. **averseness**, a-vèrs'nes, *n.* Aversion. **aversion**, a-vèr'shon, *n.* Dislike; antipathy.

avert, a-vert', *vt.* To turn aside or away from; to keep off or prevent.

aviary, ā'vi-a-ri, *n.* A place for keeping birds.

aviator, ā'vi-ā-tèr, *n.* The operator or pilot of a heavier-than-air craft.

aviatress, **aviatrix**, ā-vi-ā'triks, *n.* A woman aviator.

avidity, a-vid'i-ti, *n.* Eager desire; greediness; strong appetite.

avocation, av-o-kā'shun, *n.* Business; occupation.

avoid, a-void', *vt.* To shun; to evade; to make void. **avoidable**, a-void'a-bl, *a.* That may be avoided. **avoidance**, a-void'ans, *n.* Act of avoiding.

avoirdupois, av'èr-dū-poiz', *n.* or *a.* A system of weight, in which a pound contains sixteen ounces.

avow, a-vou', *vt.* To declare with confidence; to confess frankly. **avowable**, a-vou'a-bl, *a.* That may be avowed. **avowal**, a-vou'al, *n.* An open declaration; frank acknowledgment. **avowedly**, a-vou'ed-li, *adv.* In an open manner; with frank acknowledgment.

await, a-wāt', *vt.* To wait for; to expect; to be in store for.

awake, a-wāk', *vt.* (awaking, awoke, awaked, pp. awaked). To rouse from sleep or from a state of inaction.—*vi.* To cease from sleep; to rouse one's self.—*a.* Not sleeping; vigilant.

awaken, a-wāk'n, *vt.* and *i.* To awake.

awakening, a-wāk'n-ing, *n.* Act of awaking.

award, a-wąrd', *vt.* To adjudge.—*vi.* To make an award.—*n.* A judgment; decision of arbitrators.

aware, a-wār', *a.* Informed; conscious.

away, a-wā', *adv.* Absent; at a distance; in motion from; by degrees; in continuance.—*exclam.* Begone!

awe, ą, *n.* Fear; fear mingled with reverence.—*vt.* (awing, awed). To strike with fear and reverence.

awful, ą'ful, *a.* Filling with awe; terrible. **awfully**, ą'ful-li, *adv.* In an awful manner. **awfulness**, ą'ful-nes, *n.* Quality or state of being awful.

awhile, a-whil', *adv.* For some time.

awkward, ąk'wèrd, *a.* Inexpert; inelegant. **awkwardly**, ąk'wèrd-li, *adv.* In a bungling manner; inelegantly.

awl, ąl, *n.* A pointed iron instrument for piercing small holes in leather.

awning, ąn'ing, *n.* A cover of canvas, &c., to shelter from the sun or wind.

awry, a-ri', *pred.a.* or *adv.* Twisted toward one side; distorted; asquint.

ax, **axe**, aks, *n.* An instrument for hewing and chopping.

axial, aks'i-al, *a.* Pertaining to an axis.

axiom, aks'i-om, *n.* A self-evident truth; an established principle. **axiomatic**, aks'i-ō-mat"ik, *a.* Pertaining to an axiom. **axiomatically**, aks'i-ō-mat"ik-al-li, *adv.* By the use of axioms.

axis, aks'is, *n.*; pl. **axes**, aks'ēz. The straight line, real or imaginary, passing through a body, on which it revolves.

axle, **axle-tree**, aks'l, aks'l-trē, *n.* The pole on which a wheel turns.

ay, **aye**, ī, *adv.* Yea; yes.—*n.* An affirmative vote.

aye, ā, *adv.* Always; ever; continually.

azalea, a-zā'lē-a, *n.* The generic name of certain showy plants of the heath family.

azimuth, az'i-muth, *n.* An arc of the horizon between the meridian of a place and a vertical circle.

Azores, ā-zōrz, *n.* A group of islands in the N. Atlantic Ocean belonging to Portugal.

Aztec, az'tek, *n.* 1. An Indian of the Nahuatlan tribe which founded the Mexican Empire conquered by Cortez in 1519. 2. Any Indian of Aztecan or Nahuatlan stock.

azure, a-shūr, *a.* Sky-colored.—*n.* The fine blue color of the sky; the sky.

B

baa, bä, *n.* The cry of a sheep.—*vt.* To cry or bleat as sheep.

babble, bab'bl, *vi.* (babbling, babbled). To talk idly; to prate.—*vt.* To utter idly.—*n.* Idle talk; murmur as of a stream. **babblement**, bab'bl-ment, *n.* Babble. **babbler**, bab'bl-èr, *n.* One who babbles.

babe, bāb, *n.* An infant; a young child.

babel, bā'bel, *n.* Confusion; disorder.

baboon, ba-bōn′, n. A large kind of monkey.

baby, bā′bi, n. A babe; a young child.— a. Pertaining to a baby.

Babylonian, Babylonish, ba-bi-lōn′i-an, ba-bi-lōn′ish, a. Pertaining to Babylon.

baccalaureate, bak′a-lo′re-at, n. A bachelor's degree conferred by a college or university.

baccarat, baccara, bak-ka-rä′, n. A game of cards played by any number and a banker.

bacchanal, bak′ka-nal, n. A votary of Bacchus; a revel.—a. Characterized by intemperate drinking.

Bacchanalia, bak-a-nä′li-a, n. pl. Feasts in honor of Bacchus.

Bacchanalian, bak-ka-nä′li-an, a. Bacchanal.—n. A reveler; a votary of Bacchus.

bachelor, bach′el-ėr, n. An unmarried man; one who has taken the university degree below that of Master or Doctor. **bachelorhood, bachelorship,** bach′-el-ėr-hyd″, bach′el-ėr-ship″, n. The state of being a bachelor.

bacillus, ba-sil′lus, n.; pl. -illi. A microscopic organism which causes disease.

back, bak, n. The hinder part of the body in man and the upper part in beasts; the hinder part.—vt. To support; to cause to recede; to endorse.—vi. To move back. —adv. To the rear; to a former state; in return.

backbite, bak′bīt, vt. To speak evil of secretly.

backbone, bak′bōn, n. The spine; strength.

backer, bak′ėr, n. One who backs or supports another in a contest.

backgammon, bak-gam′mon, n. A game played by two persons on a board, with men and dice.

background, bak′ground, n. The part of a picture represented as farthest away; a situation little noticed.

backhand, backhanded, bak′hand, bak′hand-ed, a. With the hand turned backward; indirect.

backslide, bak-slīd′, vi. To apostatize; to relapse. **backslider,** bak-slīd′ėr, n. An apostate.

backward, backwards, bak′wėrd, bak′wėrdz, adv. With the back towards; towards past times, back; from better to worse.

backward, bak′wėrd, a. Lagging behind; reluctant; late; dull.

backwardly, bak′wėrd-li, adv. In a backward manner; unwillingly. **backwardness,** bak′wėrd-nes, n. Unwillingness; reluctant; dilatoriness.

backwoods, bak′wydz, n.pl. Outlying forest districts.

bacon, bā′kn, n. Swine's flesh cured and dried.

bacteriology, bak-tē′ri-ol″o-ji, n. The doctrine or study of bacteria.

bacterium, bak-tē′ri-um, n.; pl. -ia. A disease germ.

bad, bad, a. Not good; wicked; immoral; injurious; incompetent.

badge, baj, n. A mark or cognizance worn.

badger, baj′ėr, n. A burrowing quadruped, nocturnal in habits. —vt. To worry; to pester.

badly, bad′li, adv. In a bad manner.

badminton, bad′min-ton, n. A game like lawn-tennis played with shuttlecocks.

baffle, baf′l, vt. (baffling, baffled). To elude; to frustrate, to defeat.

bag, bag, n. A sack; what is contained in a bag; a certain quantity of a commodity.—vt. (bagging, bagged). To put into a bag; to distend.—vi. To swell like a full bag.

baggage, bag′ij, n. The necessaries of an army; luggage; lumber.

bagpipe, bag′pīp, n. A musical wind-instrument.

bail, bāl, vt. To liberate from custody on security for reappearance; to free (a boat) from water; to bale.—n. Security given for release; the person who gives such security. **bailable,** bāl′a-bl, a. That may be bailed.

bailiff, bā′lif, n. A subordinate civil officer; a steward.

bailiwick, bā′li-wik, n. The extent or limit of a bailiff's jurisdiction.

bait, bāt, n. A substance used to allure fish, &c.; an enticement.—vt. To furnish with a lure; to give food and drink to a beast when traveling; to harass; to annoy.—vi. To take refreshment on a journey.

bake, bāk, vt. (baking, baked). To heat, dry, and harden by fire or the sun's rays; to cook in an oven.—vi. To do the work of making bread; to be baked. **baker,** bāk′ėr, n. One whose occupation is to bake bread, &c. **bakery,** bāk′ė-ri, n. A place for baking. **baking,** bāk′ing, p.n. The action of the verb to bake; the quantity baked at once.

balance, bal′ans, n. A pair of scales; equilibrium; surplus; difference of two sums; the sum due on an account.—vt. (balancing, balanced). To bring to an equilibrium; to weigh, as reasons; to settle, as an account.—vi. To be in equilibrium; to be equal when added up; to hesitate.

balcony, bal′ko-ni, n. A platform projecting from a window.

bald, bald, a. Wanting hair; unadorned; bare; paltry. **baldly,** bald′li, adv. Nakedly; meanly. **baldness,** bald′nes, n. State of being bald; inelegance of style; want of ornament.

bale, bāl, n. A bundle or package of goods.—vt. (baling, baled). To make up in a bale; to free from water; to bail.

baleen, ba-lēn′, n. The whalebone of commerce.

baleful, bāl′fyl, a. Calamitous; deadly.

balk, bak, n. A ridge of land left unplowed; a great beam; a barrier; a disappointment.—vt. To baffle; to disappoint.

ball, bal, n. A round body; a globe; a

bullet; an entertainment of dancing.—*vi.* To form, as snow, into balls, as on horses' hoofs.

ballad, bal'lad, *n.* A short narrative poem; a popular song.

ballast, bal'last, *n.* Heavy matter carried in a ship to keep it steady; that which confers steadiness.—*vt.* To load with ballast; to make or keep steady.

ballet, bal'lā, *n.* A theatrical dance.

ballistic, bal-lis'tik, *a.* Pertaining to projectiles.

balloon, bal-lön', *n.* A spherical hollow body; a large bag filled with a gas which makes it rise and float in the air.

ballot, bal'lot, *n.* A ball, paper, &c., used for voting in private; the system of voting by such means.—*vi.* To vote by ballot.

balm, bäm, *n.* Balsam; that which heals or soothes; the name of several aromatic plants.—*vt.* To anoint with balm; to soothe. **balmy**, bäm'i, *a.* Aromatic; soothing.

balsam, bal'sam, *n.* An oily, aromatic substance got from trees; a soothing ointment. **balsamic**, bal- or bal-sam'ik, *a.* Balmy; mitigating.

bamboo, bam-bö', *n.* A tropical plant of the reed kind.

ban, ban, *n.* A public proclamation; curse; excommunication; *pl.* proclamation of marriage.—*vt.* (banning, banned). To curse.

banal, ban'al, or ba-nal', *a.* Hackneyed; vulgar. **banality**, ba-nal'i-ti, *n.* State of being banal.

banana, ba-nä'na, *n.* A plant allied to the plantain, with soft luscious fruit.

band, band, *n.* That which binds; a bond; a fillet; a company; a body of musicians.—*vt.* To bind together; to unite in a troop or confederacy.—*vi.* To unite in a band.

bandage, band'ij, *n.* A band; a cloth for a wound, &c.—*vt.* (bandaging, bandaged). To bind with a bandage.

bandbox, band'boks, *n.* A slight box for caps, bonnets, &c.

banded, band'ed. *p.a.* United in a band.

bandit, ban'dit, *n.*; pl. **-itti-**, **-its.** An outlaw; a robber; a highwayman.

bandoleer, **bandolier**, ban-do-lēr', *n.* A shoulder-belt for carrying cartridges.

bandy, ban'di, *n.* A bent club for striking a ball; a play at ball with such a club.—*vt.* (bandying, bandied). To strike to and fro; to exchange (compliments, &c.).

bane, bān, *n.* That which causes hurt or death; ruin; poison; mischief. **baneful**, bān'fụl, *a.* Pernicious; poisonous.

bang, bang, *vt.* To thump; to treat with violence.—*n.* A heavy blow.

banish, ban'ish, *vt.* To drive away; to exile. **banishment**, ban'ish-ment, *n.* Act of banishing; exile.

banister, ban'is-tėr, *n.* A baluster.

banjo, ban'jō, *n.* A six-stringed musical instrument.

bank, bangk, *n.* Ground rising from the side of a river, lake, &c.; any heap piled up; a bench of rowers; place where money is deposited; a banking company.—*vt.* To fortify with a bank; to deposit in a bank. **banker**, bangk'ėr, *n.* One

who deals in money. **banking**, bangk'-ing, *p.n.* The business of a banker.

bank-note, bangk'nōt, *n.* A promissory note issued by a banking company.

bankrupt, bangk'rupt, *n.* One who cannot pay his debts.—*a.* Unable to pay debts. **bankruptcy**, bangk'rupt-si, *n.* State of being a bankrupt; failure in trade.

banner, ban'nėr, *n.* A flag bearing a device or national emblem; a standard.

banns, banz, *n.pl.* The proclamation in church necessary for a regular marriage.

banquet, bang'kwe:, *n.* A feast; a sumptuous entertainment.—*vt.* To treat with a feast.—*vi.* To feast.

banshee, ban'shē, *n.* An Irish fairy believed to attach herself to a house or family.

Bantam, ban'tam, *n.* A small breed of domestic fowl with feathered shanks.

banter, ban'tėr, *vt.* To attack with jocularity; to rally.—*n.* Raillery; pleasantry.

banyan, ban'yan, *n.* An Indian tree of the fig genus.

banzai, bän-zä-ē', *n.* A Japanese exclamation of honor, meaning 10,000 years.

baptism, bap'tizm, *n.* An immersing in or sprinkling with water, as a religious ceremony. **Baptist**, bap'tist, *n.* One of those Protestants who believe in baptism by immersion. **baptistery**, bap'-tis-te-ri, *n.* A place where baptisms take place. **baptize**, bap-tīz', *vt.* (baptizing, baptized). To administer baptism to; to christen.

bar, bär, *n.* A bolt; obstacle; a long piece of wood or metal; inclosure in an inn or court; a tribunal; body of barristers; obstruction at the mouth of a river; a counter where liquors are served.—*vt.* (barring, barred). To secure; to hinder; to prohibit; to except.

barb, bärb, *n.* The points which stand backward in an arrow, hook, &c.; a Barbary horse.—*vt.* To furnish with barbs or points.

barbarian, bär-ba'ri-an, *a.* Belonging to savages; uncivilized.—*n.* A savage. **barbarism**, bär'bär-izm, *n.* Barbarity; an impropriety of speech. **barbarity**, bär-ba'ri-ti, *n.* The state or qualities of a barbarian; ferociousness. **barbarize**, bär'bär-īz, *vt.* (barbarizing, barbarized). To make barbarous. **barbarous**, bär'bär-us, *a.* In a state of barbarism; cruel; inhuman. **barbarously**, bär'bär-us-li, *adv.* In a savage, cruel, or inhuman manner.

barbecue, bär'be-kū, *n.* A hog, &c., roasted whole; a feast in the open air.—*vt.* To dress and roast whole.

barbed, bärbd, *a.* Jagged with hooks or points.

barber, bär'bėr, *n.* One who shaves beards and dresses hair.

barberry, bär'be-ri, *n.* A thorny shrub bearing red berries.

barbiturate, bär'bi-tū'rāt, *n.* A class of drugs used as sedatives, hypnotics, &c.

bard, bärd, *n.* A Celtic minstrel; a poet. **bardic**, bärd'ik, *a.* Pertaining to bards.

bare, bär, *a.* Uncovered; empty; scanty;

worn.—*vt.* (baring, bared). To make naked.

barebacked, bār'bakt, *a.* Unsaddled.

barefaced, bār'fāst, *a.* Shameless; glaring.

barely, bār'li, *adv.* Nakedly, scarcely.

bargain, bär'gin, *n.* A contract; a gainful transaction; a thing bought or sold. —*vi.* To make a bargain.—*vt.* To sell.

bargainer, bär'gin-ėr, *n.* One who makes a bargain.

barge, bärj, *n.* A boat of pleasure or state; a flat-bottomed boat of burden.

bargee, bärj-ē', *n.* One of a barge's crew. **bargeman**, bärj'man, *n.* The man who manages a barge.

baritone, ba'ri-tōn, *a.* Having a voice ranging between tenor and bass.—*n.* A male voice between tenor and bass.

bark, bärk, *n.* The outer rind of a tree; a barque; the noise made by a dog, wolf, &c.—*vt.* To strip bark off; to treat with bark; to make the cry of dogs, &c.

bark, barque, bärk, *n.* A sailing vessel; a three-masted ship, the mizzen-mast without yards.

barley, bär'li, *n.* A species of grain used especially for making malt.

barn, bärn, *n.* A building for grain, hay, &c.

barnacle, bär'na-kl, *n.* A shell-fish, often found on ships' bottoms; a species of goose. **barnacles**, bär'na-klz, *n.pl.* An instrument put on a horse's nose; a pair of spectacles.

barograph, ba'rō-graf, *n.* A barometer that records changes in the atmosphere.

barometer, ba-rom'et-ėr, *n.* An instrument for measuring the weight of the atmosphere. **barometric**, ba-rō-met'rik, *a.* Pertaining or relating to the barometer. **barometrically**, ba-rō-met'rik-al-li, *adv.* By means of a barometer.

baron, ba'ron, *n.* A peer of the lowest rank; a title of certain judges, &c. **baronage**, ba'ron-ij, *n.* The whole body of barons; the dignity or estate of a baron. **baroness**, ba'ron-es, *n.* A baron's wife. **baronet**, ba'ron-et, *n.* One of the hereditary rank next below a baron, with title of "Sir." **baronetage**, ba'ron-et-ij, *n.* The collective body of baronets. **baronetcy**, ba'ron-et-si, *n.* The condition or rank of a baronet. **baronial**, ba-rō'ni-al, *a.* Pertaining to a baron. **barony**, bar'on-i, *n.* The lordship, honor, or fee of a baron.

barrack, ba'rak, *n.* A building for soldiers, especially in garrison (generally in *pl.*).

barracuda, bar-a-kūd'a, *n.* A large and voracious deep-sea fish.

barratry, ba'ra-tri, *n.* The practice of a barrator; fraud by a shipmaster.

barrel, ba'rel, *n.* A round wooden cask; the quantity which a barrel holds; a hollow cylinder.—*vt.* (barreling, barreled). To pack in a barrel. **barreled**, ba'reld, *a.* Having a barrel or barrels.

barren, ba'ren, *a.* Sterile; unfruitful; unsuggestive. **barrenness**, ba'ren-nes, *n.* The state or quality of being barren.

barricade, ba-ri-kād', *n.* A temporary fortification to obstruct an enemy; a barrier.—*vt.* To obstruct; to bar.

barrier, ba'ri-ėr, *n.* Fence; obstruction.

barrister, ba'ris-tėr, *n.* A counselor at law; a lawyer whose profession is to speak in court on behalf of clients.

barrow, ba'rō, *n.* A small hand or wheel carriage; a sepulchral mound.

barter, bär'tėr, *vi.* To traffic by exchange.—*vt.* To exchange in commerce. —*n.* Traffic by exchange.

basalt, ba-zalt', *n.* A dark volcanic rock, often found in columnar form. **basaltic**, ba-zalt'ik, *a.* Pertaining to basalt.

base, bās, *a.* Low in value or station, worthless; despicable.—*n.* Foundation; lower side; support; chief ingredient of a compound; the gravest part in music. —*vt.* (basing, based). To place on a basis; to found.

baseball, bās'bal, *n.* An American game played with bat and ball by two sides.

base-born, bās'born, *a.* Illegitimate.

baseless, bās'les, *a.* Without base; groundless.

base-line, bās'līn, *n.* A line taken as a base of operations.

basement, bās'ment, *n.* The ground floor of a building.

baseness, bās'nes, *n.* Lowness; meanness; vileness.

bash, bash, *vt.* To beat violently. (Eng.)

bashful, bash'ful, *a.* Modest; wanting confidence. **bashfully**, bash'ful-li, *adv.* In a shy manner. **bashfulness**, bash'ful-nes, *n.* Quality of being bashful; extreme modesty.

basic, bās'ik, *a.* Relating to a base.

basil, baz'il, *n.* An aromatic pot-herb.

basilica, ba-sil'i-ka, *n.* An ancient Roman public hall; a church in imitation thereof.

basin, bā'sn, *n.* A broad circular dish; a reservoir; a dock; tract of country drained by a river.

basis, bās'is, *n.*; pl. **-ses**. A base; foundation; groundwork.

bask, bask, *vi.* To lie in warmth, or in the sun; to enjoy ease and prosperity.— *vt.* To warm by exposure to heat.

basket, bas'ket, *n.* A domestic vessel made of twigs, &c.; the contents of a basket.—*vt.* To put in a basket.

bas-relief, bas'rē-lēf, or bä', *n.* Low relief; sculpture in which the figures do not stand out prominently.

bass, bas, *n.* The American linden; a mat made of bast; a fish allied to the perch.

bass, bās, *n.* The lowest part in musical harmony; the lowest male voice.

bassinet, bas'si-net, *n.* A wicker cradle.

bassoon, bas-sön', *n.* A musical wind-instrument which serves for a bass.

bass-relief, bās'rē-lēf, *n.* Bas-relief.

bastard, bas'tėrd, *n.* An illegitimate child.—*a.* Illegitimate; not genuine. **bastardize**, bas'tėrd-īz, *vt.* (bastardizing, bastardized). To prove to be a bastard. **bastardy**, bas'tėrd-i, *n.* The state of being a bastard.

baste, bāst, *vt.* (basting, basted). To beat with a stick; to drip fat or butter on meat while roasting; to sew with temporary stitches.

bastion, bas'ti-on, *n.* A large mass of earth or masonry standing out from a rampart.

bat, bat, *n.* A flying mammal, like a mouse; a heavy stick; a club used to strike the ball in baseball or cricket, &c.—*vi.* (batting, batted). To play with a bat.

batch, bach, *n.* Quantity of bread baked at one time; a quantity.

bate, bāt, *vt.* (bating, bated). To abate.

bath, bäth, *n.* Place to bathe in; immersion in water, &c.; a Jewish measure.

bathe, bāTH, *vt.* (bathing, bathed). To immerse in water, &c.—*vi.* To take a bath.

bathos, bā'thos, *n.* A ludicrous sinking in writing or speech; anti-climax.

baton, ba'ton, *n.* A staff; a truncheon; a badge of office.

battalion, bat-ta'li-on, *n.* A body of infantry, consisting of from 300 to 1000 men.

batten, bat'n, *n.* A piece of wood from 4 to 7 inches broad, and from ½ to 2½ thick; a plank.—*vi.* To fasten with battens; to fatten.

batter, bat'tėr, *vt.* To beat with violence; to wear by hard usage.—*n.* A mixture beaten together with some liquid.

battering-ram, bat'tėr-ing-ram, *n.* An ancient engine for battering down walls.

battery, bat'tė-ri, *n.* A number of cannon prepared for field operations; a parapet covering guns; an apparatus for originating an electric current; a violent assault.

battle, bat'l, *n.* Encounter of two armies; a combat.—*vi.* (battling, battled). To contend in fight.

battlement, bat'l-ment, *n.* A parapet with openings to discharge missiles through.

bauble, ba'bl, *n.* A trifling piece of finery; a gewgaw.

bawd, bad, *n.* A procurer or procuress; a pimp.

bawdy, ba'di, *a.* Obscene; unchaste.

bawl, bal, *vi.* To shout; to clamor.

bay, bā, *a.* Reddish-brown.—*n.* An arm of the sea; the laurel tree; a laurel-crown, fame (generally in *pl.*); a deep-toned bark of a dog.—*vi.* To bark.—*vt.* To bark at; to follow with barking. at bay, so pressed by enemies as to be compelled to face them.

bayonet, bā'on-et, *n.* A dagger-like weapon fixed to a rifle.—*vt.* (bayoneting, bayoneted). To stab with a bayonet.

bay-window, bā'win-dō, *n.* A projecting window which forms a recess within.

bazaar, ba-zär', *n.* A place of sale; a sale of articles for a charitable purpose.

be, bē, *vi. substantive* (being, been; pres. am, art, is, are; pret. was, wast, or wert, were). To exist; to become; to remain.

beach, bēch, *n.* The shore of the sea.—*vt.* To run (a vessel) on a beach.

beached, bēcht, *p.a.* Having a beach; stranded.

beacon, bē'kn, *n.* A light to direct seamen; a signal of danger.—*vt.* To afford light, as a beacon; to light up.

bead, bēd, *n.* A little ball strung on a thread; any small globular body; a small molding.

beagle, bē'gl, *n.* A small hunting dog.

beak, bēk, *n.* The bill of a bird; anything like a bird's beak.

beaked, bēkt, *a.* Having a beak.

beaker, bēk'ėr, *n.* A large drinking-cup.

beam, bēm, *n.* A main timber in a building; part of a balance which sustains the scales; pole of a carriage; a ray of light.—*vt.* To send forth, as beams; to emit.—*vi.* To shine. **beaming**, bēm'ing, *a.* Emitting beams or rays; radiant; expressing joy in the face. **beamy**, bēm'i, *a.* Emitting beams or rays; radiant; shining.

bean, bēn, *n.* The edible seed of many leguminous plants.

bear, bār, *vt.* (bearing; pret. bore; pp. borne). To carry; to suffer; to produce; to have; to permit; to behave (one's self).—*vi.* To suffer; to be patient; to produce; to take effect; to be situated as to the point of the compass; to refer (with *upon*).

bear, bār, *n.* A large carnivorous plantigrade quadruped; one of two constellations, the Greater and Lesser; an uncouth person; one who tries to bring down the price of stock.

bearable, bār'a-bl, *a.* That can be borne.

beard, bērd, *n.* The hair on the chin, &c.; the awn of corn.—*vt.* To defy to the face. **bearded**, bērd'ed, *a.* Having a beard. **beardless**, bērd'les, *a.* Without a beard.

bearer, bār'ėr, *n.* One who bears; one who carries a letter, &c.; a support.

bearing, bār'ing, *n.* A carrying; deportment; mien; relation; tendency.

bearish, bār'ish, *a.* Partaking of the qualities of a bear.

beast, bēst, *n.* Any four-footed animal, a brutal man. **beastly**, bēst'li, *a.* Brutal; filthy; bestial.

beat, bēt, *vt.* (beating, pret. beat, pp. beat, beaten). To strike repeatedly; to overcome; to crush; to harass.—*vi.* To throb, as a pulse; to sail against the wind.—*n.* A stroke; a pulsation; a course frequently trodden.

beatific, bē-a-tif'ik, *a.* Blessing or making happy. **beatification**, bē-at'i-fi-kā"shon, *n.* Act of beatifying; a kind of canonization. **beatify**, bē-at'i-fī, *vt.* (beatifying, beatified). To make happy; to declare a person blessed.

beating, bēt'ing, *n.* Act of striking; chastisement by blows; a conquering; defeat.

beatitude, bē-at'i-tūd, *n.* Blessedness; bliss; one of the declarations of blessedness to particular virtues made by Christ.

beau, bō, *n.*; pl. **-aux** or **-aus**, bōz. A man fond of fine dress; a gallant; a lover.

beauteous, bū'tē-us, *a.* Beautiful; fair.

beautiful, bū'ti-ful, *a.* Full of beauty;

lovely.—*n.* That which possesses beauty. **beautifully,** bū'ti-ful-li, *adv.* In a beautiful manner.

beautify, bū'ti-fī, *vt.* (beautifying, beautified). To make beautiful; to adorn. —*vi.* To become beautiful.

beauty, bū'ti, *n.* Loveliness; elegance; grace; a beautiful woman.

beaver, bē'vėr, *n.* A rodent quadruped; beaver-fur, or a hat made of it; the face-guard of a helmet; a visor.—*a.* Made of beaver, or of its fur.

becalm, bē-kam', *vt.* To make calm.

because, bē-kaz'. By cause; on this account that.

beck, bek, *n.* A sign with the hand or head.—*vi.* To make a sign or nod.—*vt.* To notify by a sign or nod.

beckon, bek'n, *vi.* To make a sign by nodding, &c.—*vt.* To make a sign to.

becloud, bē-kloud', *vt.* To cloud; to obscure.

become, bē-kum', *vi.* (becoming; pp. become; pret. became). To come to be; to change to.—*vt.* To suit, to add grace to; to be worthy of. **becoming,** bē-kum'ing, *a.* Fit; graceful. **becomingly,** bē-kum'ing-li, *adv.* In a becoming or proper manner.

bed, bed, *n.* Something to sleep or rest on; the channel of a river; place where anything is deposited; a layer; a stratum.—*vt.* (bedding, bedded). To lay in a bed; to sow; to stratify.—*vi.* To go to bed.

bedchamber, bed'chām-bėr, *n.* An apartment for a bed.

bedding, bed'ing, *n.* The materials of a bed.

bedeck, bēdek', *vt.* To deck; to adorn.

bedlam, bed'lam, *n.* A madhouse; a place of uproar.—*a.* Belonging to a madhouse.

Bedouin, bed'ö-in, *n.* A nomadic Arab living in tents in Arabia, Syria, Egypt, &c.

bedraggle, bē-drag'l, *vt.* To soil by drawing along on mud.

bedrid, bedridden, bed'rid, bed'rid-n, *a.* Confined to bed by age or infirmity.

bedroom, bed'röm, *n.* A sleeping apartment.

bedstead, bed'sted, *n.* A frame for supporting a bed.

bee, bē, *n.* The insect that makes honey.

beech, bēch, *n.* A large smooth-barked tree yielding a hard timber and nuts.

beef, bēf, *n.* The flesh of an ox, bull, or cow.—*a.* Consisting of such flesh.

beer, bēr, *n.* A fermented alcoholic liquor made from barley and hops.

beet, bēt, *n.* A vegetable with thick, fleshy roots, yielding sugar.

beetle, bē'tl, *n.* A coleopterous insect; a heavy wooden mallet.—*vi.* (beetling, beetled). To jut; to hang over.

beeves, bēvz, *n.pl.* of beef. Cattle; black cattle.

befall, bē-fal', *vt.* To happen to.—*vi.* To happen.

befit, bē-fit', *vt.* To suit; to become. **befitting,** bē-fit'ing, *a.* Suitable.

before, bē-fōr', *prep.* In front of; in presence of; earlier than; in preference

to.—*adv.* In time preceding; further; onward; in front.

beforehand, bē-fōr'hand, *a.* In good pecuniary circumstances.—*adv.* In advance.

befoul, bē-foul', *vt.* To make foul.

befriend, bē-frend', *vt.* To act as a friend to.

beg, beg, *vt.* (begging, begged). To ask in charity; to ask earnestly; to take for granted.—*vi.* To ask or live upon alms.

beget, bē-get', *vt.* (begetting, pp. begotten, pret. begot). To procreate; to produce.

beggar, beg'gėr, *n.* One who begs.—*vt.* To impoverish. **beggarliness,** beg'gėr-li-nes, *n.* Meanness; extreme poverty. **beggarly,** beg'gėr-li, *a.* Like a beggar; poor.—*adv.* Meanly; despicably. **beggary,** beg'gė-ri, *n.* Extreme indigence.

begin, bē-gin', *vi.* (pp. begun, pret. began). To take rise; to do the first act; to commence.—*vt.* To enter on; to originate.—**beginner,** bē-gin'ėr, *n.* One who begins; a novice. **beginning,** bē-gin'ing, *n.* The first cause, act, or state; origin; commencement.

begird, bē-gėrd', *vt.* To gird round about; to bind.

begone, bē-gon', *interj.* Get you gone; go away!

begonia, bē-gō'ni-a, *n.* A showy tropical plant much cultivated in hothouses.

begrudge, bē-gruj', *vt.* To envy the possession of.

beguile, bē-gīl', *vt.* (beguiling, beguiled). To practice guile on; to dupe; to while away. **beguilement,** bē-gīl'ment, *n.* Act of beguiling. **beguiler,** bē-gīl'ėr, *n.* One who or that which beguiles.

behalf, bē-haf', *n.* Interest; support.

behave, bē-hāv', *vt.* (behaving, behaved). To conduct (one's self).—*vi.* To act; to conduct one's self. **behaviour, behavior,** bē-hāv'i-ėr, *n.* Conduct; deportment.

behead, bē-hed', *vt.* To cut off the head of.

behemoth, bē-hē'moth, *n.* Supposed to be an elephant or hippopotamus.

behest, bē-hest', *n.* Command; precept.

behind, bē-hīnd', *prep.* In the rear of; remaining after; inferior to.—*adv.* In the rear; backwards; remaining.

behold, bē-hōld', *vt.* (beholding, beheld). To look upon; to regard with attention.—*vi.* To look; to fix the mind.

beholden, bē-hōld'n, *a.* Obliged; indebted.

behoove, bē-höv', *vt.* (behooving, behooved). To be meet or necessary for (used impersonally).

being, bē'ing, *n.* Existence; a creature.

belabor, belabour, bē-lā'bėr, *vt.* To beat soundly; to thump; to attack verbally.

belated, bē-lāt'ed, *p.a.* Made late; benighted.

belay, bē-lā', *vt. Nautical,* to fasten by winding round something.

belch, belch, *vt.* To eject, as wind from the stomach; to cast forth violently.—*vi.* To eject wind from the stomach; to issue out, as by eructation.—*n.* Eructation.

beleaguer, bē-lē'gėr, *vt.* To surround with an army; to blockade; to besiege.

belfry, bel'fri, *n.* A bell-tower; place where a bell is hung.

belie, bē-lī', *vt.* (belying, belied). To represent falsely; to be in contradiction to; to fail to equal.

belief, bē-lēf', *n.* Assent of the mind; persuasion; creed; opinion. **believe**, bē-lēv', *vt.* (believing, believed). To give belief to; to credit; to expect with confidence.—*vi.* To have a firm persuasion. **believer**, bē-lēv'ėr, *n.* One who believes.

belittle, bē-lit'l, *vt.* To make smaller; to speak disparagingly of.

bell, bel, *n.* A metallic vessel used for giving sounds by being struck; anything in form of a bell.—*vi.* To flower.—*vt.* Te put a bell on.

belladonna, bel-la-don'na, *n.* A European plant yielding a powerful medicine.

belle, bel, *n.* A lady of great beauty.

belles-lettres, bel-let'tr, *n.pl.* Polite literature, including poetry, rhetoric, history, &c.

bellicose, bel'li-kōs, *a.* Warlike, pugnacious.

bellied, bel'lid, *a.* Swelled in the middle.

belligerent, bel-lij'ėr-ent, *a.* Waging war.—*n.* A nation or state waging war.

bellow, bel'ō, *vi.* To make a hollow loud noise, as a bull; to roar.—*n.* A roar.

bellows, bel'ōz, *n. sing.* and *pl.* An instrument for blowing fires, supplying wind to organ-pipes, &c.

bell-wether, bel'weᴛн-ėr, *n.* A sheep which leads the flock with a bell on his neck.

belly, bel'li, *n.* That part of the body which contains the bowels.—*vt.* and *i.* (bellying, bellied). To swell, bulge.

belong, bē-long', *vi.* To be the property; to appertain; to be connected; to have original residence.

belonging, bē-long'ing, *n.* That which pertains to one; generally in *pl.*

beloved, bē-luvd', bē-luv'ed, *a.* Greatly loved.

below, bē-lō', *prep.* Under in place; beneath; unworthy of.—*adv.* In a lower place; beneath: on earth; in hell.

belt, belt, *n.* A girdle; a band.—*vt.* To encircle.

bemoan, bē-mōn', *vt.* To lament; bewail.

bemused, bē-mūzd', *a.* Muddled; stupefied.

bench, bensh, *n.* A long seat; seat of justice; body of judges.—*vt.* To furnish with benches.

bend, bend, *vt.* (pp. and pret. bent and bended). To curve; to direct to a certain point; to subdue.—*vi.* To become crooked; to lean or turn; to yield.—*n.* A curve.

beneath, bē-nēth', *prep.* Under; lower in place, rank, dignity, &c.; unworthy of.—*adv.* In a lower place; below.

benediction, ben-ē-dik'shon, *n.* Act of blessing: invocation of happiness.

benefit, ben'ē-fit, *n.* An act of kindness; a favor; advantage.—*vt.* To do a service

to.—*vi.* To gain advantage. **benefaction**, ben-ē-fak'shon, *n.* The doing of a benefit; a benefit conferred. **benefactor**, ben-ē-fak'tėr, *n.* He who confers a benefit. **benefactress**, ben-ē-fak'tres, *n.* A female who confers a benefit. **benefice**, ben'ē-fis, *n.* An ecclesiastical living. **beneficed**, ben'ē-fist, *p.a.* Possessed of a benefice or church preferment. **beneficence**, bē-nef'i-sens, *n.* Active goodness. **beneficent**, bē-nef'i-sent, *a.* Kind; bountiful. **beneficently**, bē-nef'i-sent-li, *adv.* In a beneficent manner. **beneficial**, ben-ē-fi'shal, *a.* Conferring benefit. **beneficially**, ben-ē-fi'shal-li, *adv.* Helpfully. **beneficiary**, ben-ē-fi'shi-a-ri, *n.* A person who is benefited or assisted.

benevolent, bē-nev'ō-lent, *a.* Kind; charitable. **benevolently**, bē-nev'ō-lent-li, *adv.* In a kind manner; with good-will. **benevolence**, bē-nev'ō-lens, *n.* Kindness; active love of mankind.

benign, bē-nīn, *a.* Gracious; kind; mild. **benignant**, bē-nig'nant, *a.* Gracious; favorable. **benignantly**, bē-nig'nant-li, *adv.* In a benignant manner. **benignity**, bē-nig'ni-ti, *n.* Kindness; graciousness; beneficence. **benignly**, bē-nīn'li, *adv.* Graciously.

benison, ben'i-zn, *n.* A blessing, benediction.

bent, bent, pret. and pp. of *bend.*—*n.* Bias of mind; inclination; a wiry grass; a wild piece of land.

benzene, ben'zēn, *n.* A petroleum product; a liquid used to remove grease spots, &c.

benzoin, benzoine, ben-zō'in or ben'-zoin, *n.* A fragrant resinous juice.

bequeath, bē-kwēᴛн', *vt.* To leave by will; to hand down. **bequest**, bē-kwest', *n.* A legacy.

berate, bē-rāt', *vt.* To scold vehemently.

bereave, bē-rēv', *vt.* (bereaving, pp. and pret. bereaved and bereft). To deprive of. **bereavement**, bē-rēv'ment, *n.* Act of bereaving; state of being bereft.

berry, be'ri, *n.* A pulpy fruit containing many seeds.

berserker, bėr'sėr-kėr, *n.* A furious Scandinavian warrior of heathen times.

berth, bėrth, *n.* A station in which a ship lies; a place for sleeping in a ship, &c.—*vt.* To allot a berth to.

beryl, be'ril, *n.* A hard greenish mineral.

beseech, bē-sēch', *vt.* (beseeching, besought). To entreat; to solicit.

beseeming, bē-sēm'ing, *a.* Becoming.

beset, bē-set', *vt.* (besetting, beset). To surround; to press on all sides. **besetting**, bē-set'ing, *a.* Habitually assailing.

beshrew, bē-shrō', *vt.* To wish a curse to.

beside, besides, bē-sīd', bē-sīdz', *prep.* By the side of; near; over and above; distinct from.—*adv.* Moreover; in addition.

besiege, bē-sēj', *vt.* (besieging, besieged). To lay siege to; to beset.

besmear, bē-smēr', *vt.* To smear; to soil.

besot, bē-sot', *vt.* (besotting, besotted). To make sottish. **besotted**, bē-sot'ed, *p.a.* Made sottish; stupid.

bespeak, bē-spēk', *vt.* (pp. bespoke, bespoken; pret. bespoke). To speak for beforehand; to indicate.

best, best, *a.superl.* Most good; having good qualities in the highest degree; exceeding all.—*n.* The utmost; highest endeavor.—*adv.* In the highest degree; beyond all others.

bestial, bes'ti-al, *a.* Belonging to a beast; brutish; vile. **bestiality**, bes-ti-al'i-ti, *n.* The quality of being bestial; brutal conduct. **bestially**, bes'ti-al-li, *adv.* Brutally.

bestir, bē-stėr', *vt.* To stir up; to put into brisk action. (Usually with *refl.* pron.)

bestow, bē-stō', *vt.* To lay up; to give; to confer; to dispose of; to apply. **bestowal**, bē-stō'al, *n.* Act of bestowing; disposal. **bestower**, bē-stō'ėr, *n.* One who bestows; a giver; a disposer.

bestrew, bē-strō', *vt.* To scatter over.

bestride, bē-strīd', *vt.* (pp. bestrid, bestridden, pret. bestrid, bestrode). To stride over; to place a leg on each side of.

bet, bet, *n.* A wager; that which is pledged in a contest.—*vt.* (betting, betted). To wager.

bethink, bē-thingk', *vt.* To call to mind; to recollect.

betide, bē-tīd', *vt.* (pp. betid, pret. betid, betided). To happen to; to befall. —*vi.* To happen.

betimes, bē-tīmz', *adv.* Seasonably; early.

betoken, bē-tō'kn, *vt.* To portend; to signify.

betray, bē-trā', *vt.* To disclose treacherously; to entrap. **betrayal**, bē-trā'al, *n.* Act of betraying. **betrayer**, bē-trā'ėr, *n.* One who betrays.

betroth, bē-trōTH', *vt.* To affiance; to pledge to marriage. **betrothal, betrothment**, bē-trōTH'al, bē-trōTH'ment, *n.* Mutual contract of marriage.

better, bet'tėr, *a.comp.* More good; improved.—*adv.* More excellently; in a higher degree.—*vt.* To make better; to advance.—*n.* A superior (generally in *pl.*).

bettor, bet'ėr, *n.* One who bets.

between, bē-twēn', *prep.* In the middle; from one to another of; belonging to two.

betwixt, bē-twikst', *prep.* Between.

bevel, be'vel, *n.* An instrument for taking angles; an angle not a right angle. —*a.* Slant; oblique.—*vt.* (beveling, beveled). To cut to a bevel angle.

beverage, bev'ėr-ij, *n.* Drink; liquor.

bevy, be'vi, *n.* A flock of birds; a company of females.

bewail, bē-wāl', *vt.* To lament.—*vi.* To utter deep grief.

beware, bē-wār', *vi.* To take care (with *of*).

bewilder, bē-wil'dėr, *vt.* To confuse; to perplex. **bewilderment**, bē-wil'dėr-ment, *n.* State of being bewildered.

bewitch, bē-wich', *vt.* To enchant; to fascinate; to overpower by charms. **bewitchery**, bē-wich'ėr-i, *n.* Fascination. **bewitching**, bē-wich'ing, *p.a.* Fascinating; captivating. **bewitchingly**, bē-wich'ing-li, *adv.* In a fascinating manner. **bewitchment**, bē-wich'ment, *n.* Fascination.

beyond, bē-yond', *prep.* On the further side of; farther onward than; out of the reach of; above.—*adv.* At a distance.

bias, bī'as, *n.;* pl. **-ses.** Weight on one side; a leaning of the mind; bent.—*vt.* To incline to one side; to prejudice.

biased, biassed, bī'ast, *p.a.* Prejudiced.

bib, bib, *n.* A cloth worn by children over the breast.

Bible, bī'bl, *n.* The Holy Scriptures. **biblical**, bib'lik-al, *a.* Pertaining to the Bible. **biblically**, bib'lik-al-li, *adv.* In accordance with the Bible. **biblicist**, bib'li-sist, *n.* One skilled in biblical knowledge. **bibliographical**, bib'li-ō-graf''ik-al, *a.* Pertaining to bibliography. **bibliography**, bib-li-og'ra-fi, *n.* An account of books. **bibliology**, bib-li-ol'o-ji, *n.* Biblical literature; bibliography.

bibulous, bib'ū-lus, *a.* Spongy; addicted to intoxicants.

bicarbonate, bi-kär'bon-āt, *n.* A carbonate containing two equivalents of carbonic acid to one of a base.

bicentenary, bī-sen'te-na-ri, *n.* Two hundred years.

biceps, bī'seps, *n.* A muscle of the arm and of the thigh.

bicker, bik'ėr, *vi.* To skirmish; to quarrel.

bicycle, bī'si-kl, *n.* A two-wheeled vehicle propelled by the rider. **bicyclist**, bī'sik-list, *n.* One who rides a bicycle.

bid, bid, *vt.* (bidding; pp. bid, bidden; pret. bid, bade). To ask; to order; to offer.—*n.* An offer, as at an auction. **biddable**, bid'a-bl, *a.* Obedient; docile. **bidding**, bid'ing, *n.* Invitation; order; offer.

bide, bīd, *vi.* (biding, bode). To dwell; to remain.—*vt.* To endure; to abide.

biennial, bī-en'ni-al, *a.* Continuing for two years; taking place once in two years.—*n.* A plant which lives two years. **biennially**, bī-en'ni-al-li, *adv.* Once in two years; at the return of two years.

bier, bēr, *n.* A carriage or frame for conveying a corpse to the grave.

big, big, *a.* Great; large; pregnant; arrogant.

bigamy, big'a-mi, *n.* The crime of having two wives or husbands at once. **bigamist**, big'am-ist, *n.* One who has two wives or husbands at once.

bight, bit, *n.* A small bay; a loop.

bigot, big'ot, *n.* A person obstinately wedded to a particular creed. **bigoted**, big'ot-ed, *a.* Obstinately attached to some creed. **bigotry**, big'ot-ri, *n.* Blind zeal in favor of a creed, party, sect, or opinion.

bilateral, bī-lat'ėr-al, *a.* Two-sided.

bile, bīl, *n.* A yellow bitter liquid secreted in the liver; spleen; anger.

bilge, bilj, *n.* The protuberant part of a cask; the breadth of a ship's bottom.—*vi.* (bilging, bilged). To leak in the bilge.

bilingual, bī-lin'gwal, *a.* In two languages.

bilious, bil'i-us, *a.* Affected by bile.

bilk, bilk, *vt.* To defraud; to elude.

bill, bil, *n.* The beak of a bird; anything

resembling a bird's beak; an instrument for pruning, &c.; a military weapon; an account of money due; draught of a proposed new law; a placard.—*vi.* To join bills, as doves; to fondle.—*vt.* To announce by bill; to stick bills on.

billet, bil′et, *n.* A small note in writing; a ticket directing soldiers where to lodge; a situation; a stick of wood.—*vt.* To quarter, as soldiers.—*vi.* To be quartered.

billet-doux, bil-e-dö′, *n.* A love-letter.

billiards, bil′yĕrdz, *n.pl.* A game played on a table with balls and cues.

billingsgate, bil′lingz-gāt, *n.* Foul language.

billion, bil′yon, *n.* A thousand millions.

billow, bil′lō, *n.* A great wave of the sea.—*vi.* To roll in large waves.

billowy, bil′lō-i, *a.* Swelling into large waves.

bimonthly, bī-munth′li, *a.* Occurring every two months.

bin, bin, *n.* A receptacle for grain, &c.; a partition in a wine-cellar.

binary, bī′na-ri, *a.* Twofold.

bind, bind, *vt.* (binding, bound). To tie; to confine; to oblige; to cover (a book); to render costive; to make firm; to form a border round.—*vi.* To grow hard; to be obligatory. **binder,** bīnd′ĕr, *n.* One who binds books or sheaves; a bandage.

binding, bīnd′ing, *p.n.* Act of binding; the cover and sewing, &c., of a book.

binnacle, bin′a-kl, *n.* A case in which a ship's compass is kept.

binocular, bī-nok′ū-lĕr, *a.* Adapted for both eyes.—*n.* A small telescope for using with both eyes at once.

binomial, bī-nō′mi-al, *a.* or *n.* An algebraic expression consisting of two terms.

biography, bi-og′ra-fi, *n.* An account of one's life and character. **biographer,** bī-og′ra-fĕr, *n.* A writer of biography. **biographical,** bī-ō-graf′ik-al, *a.* Pertaining to biography.

biology, bī-ol′o-ji, *n.* The science of life. **biologist,** bī-ol′o-jist, *n.* One skilled in biology.

biped, bī′ped, *a.* Two-footed.—*n.* Such animal. **bipedal,** bī′ped-al, *a.* Having two feet; biped.

birch, bĕrch, *n.* A tree having small leaves, white bark, and a fragrant odor.

bird, bĕrd, *n.* One of the feathered race.

bird-lime, bĕrd′līm, *n.* A viscous substance used to catch birds.

birds-eye, bĕrdz′ī, *a.* Seen as by a flying bird; wide and rapid.—*n.* A tobacco.

biretta, beretta, bi-ret′ta, be-ret′ta, *n.* A square cap worn by ecclesiastics.

birth, bĕrth, *n.* Act of bearing or coming into life; extraction. **birthday,** bĕrth′dā, *n.* The day on which a person is born, or its anniversary. **birthplace,** bĕrth′plās, *n.* Place where one is born. **birthright,** bĕrth′rit, *n.* Any right to which a person is entitled by birth.

biscuit, bis′ket, *n.* Hard bread made into cakes; unglazed porcelain.

bisect, bī-sekt′, *vt.* To cut into two equal parts. **bisection,** bī-sek′shon, *n.* Act of bisecting; division into two equal parts.

bishop, bish′up, *n.* Head of a diocese.

bishopric, bish′up-rik, *n.* Office of a bishop; a diocese.

bismuth, bis′muth, *n.* A brittle yellowish or reddish-white metal.

bison, bī′zon, *n.* A quadruped of the ox family; the American buffalo.

bisque, bisk, *n.* Unglazed white porcelain; odds given at tennis, &c.

bit, bit, *n.* A morsel; fragment; the metal part of a bridle inserted in a horse's mouth; a boring tool.—*vt.* (bitting, bitted). To put the bit in the mouth.

bitch, bich, *n.* A female dog; a name of reproach for a woman.

bite, bit, *vt.* (biting; pp. bit, bitten; pret. bit). To crush or sever with the teeth; to cause to smart; to wound by reproach, &c.; to corrode.—*a.* Act of biting; wound made by biting; a mouthful. **biting,** bit′ing, *p.a.* Sharp; severe; sarcastic. **bitingly,** bit′ing-li, *adv.* In a biting or sarcastic manner.

bitter, bit′ĕr, *a.* Sharp to the taste; severe; painful; calamitous; distressing. **bitterish,** bit′ĕr-ish, *a.* Somewhat bitter. **bitterly,** bit′ĕr-li, *adv.* In a bitter manner. **bitterness,** bit′ĕr-nes, *n.* Quality of being bitter; hatred; deep distress.

bittern, bit′ern, *n.* A bird of the heron kind.

bitters, bit′ĕrz, *n.pl.* A liquor in which bitter herbs or roots are steeped.

bitumen, bi-tū′men, *n.* A mineral, pitchy, inflammable substance. **bituminous,** bi-tū′min-us, *a.* Having the qualities of or containing bitumen.

bivalve, bī′valv, *n.* A molluscous, bivalvular animal. **bivalve, bivalvular,** bī′valv, bi-valv′ū-lĕr, *a.* Having two shells which open and shut, as the oyster.

bivouac, bi′vö-ak, *n.* Encampment of soldiers for the night in the open air.—*vi.* (bivouacking, bivouacked). To encamp during the night without covering.

bizarre, bi-zär′, *a.* Odd; fantastical.

black, blak, *a.* Destitute of light; dark; gloomy; sullen; atrocious; wicked.—*n.* The darkest color; a negro.—*vt.* To make black.

black-ball, blak′bal, *n.* A composition for blacking shoes; a ball used as a negative in voting.—*vt.* To reject by private voting.

blackberry, blak′be-ri, *n.* A plant of the bramble kind, and its fruit.

blackbird, blak′bĕrd, *n.* A species of thrush.

blackboard, blak′bōrd, *n.* A board for writing on with chalk for instruction.

blacken, blak′n, *vt.* To make black; to defame.—*vi.* To grow black or dark.

blackguard, blak′gärd, *n.* A scoundrel.—*vt.* To revile in scurrilous language. **blackguardism,** blak′gärd-izm, *n.* The conduct or language of a blackguard.

blacking, blak′ing, *n.* A substance used for blacking shoes.

black-list, blak′list, *n.* A list of bankrupts.

black-mail, blak′māl, *n.* Money paid for protection; extortion by intimidation.

black-sheep, blak′shĕp, *n.* One whose conduct is discreditable.

blacksmith, blak'smith, *n*. A smith who works in iron.

bladder, blad'ér, *n*. A thin sac in animals containing the urine, bile, &c.; a blister; anything like the animal bladder.

blade, blād, *n*. The spire of grass; a leaf; cutting part of a sword, knife, &c.; flat part of an oar.

blame, blām, *vt*. (blaming, blamed). To censure; to reprimand.—*n*. Censure; fault. **blameless**, blām'les, *a*. Free from blame. **blamable**, blām'a-bl, *a*. Deserving of blame.

blanch, blansh, *vt*. To make white.—*vi*. To grow white; to bleach.

bland, bland, *a*. Mild; soothing; gentle. **blandish**, bland'ish, *vt*. To soothe; to caress; to flatter. **blandishment**, bland'ish-ment, *n*. Soft words; artful caresses; flattery.

blank, blangk, *a*. White; pale; void; void of writing; without rhyme.—*n*. A white unwritten paper; a void space; the white mark which a shot is to hit. **blankly**, blangk'li, *adv*. In a blank manner; with paleness or confusion. **blank-verse**, blangk'vérs, *n*. Any kind of verse without rhyme.

blanket, blang'ket, *n*. A woolen covering for a bed, horses, &c. **blanketing**, blang'ket-ing, *n*. Cloth for blankets.

blare, blār, *vi*. (blaring, blared). To give forth a loud sound.—*vt*. To sound loudly; to proclaim noisily.—*n*. Sound like that of a trumpet; roar.

blarney, blär'ni, *n*. Excessively complimentary language; gammon.—*vt*. To flatter.

blasé, blä-zä', *a*. Satiated; used up.

blaspheme, blas-fēm', *vt*. (blaspheming, blasphemed). To speak irreverently of, as of God; to speak evil of.—*vi*. To utter blasphemy. **blasphemer**, blas-fēm'ér, *n*. One who blasphemes. **blasphemous**, blas'fēm-us, *a*. Impiously irreverent. **blasphemy**, blas'fēm-i, *n*. Profane speaking; an indignity offered to God.

blast, blast, *n*. A gust of wind; sound of a wind-instrument; violent explosion of gunpowder; pernicious influence, as of wind; blight.—*vt*. To blight; to strike with some sudden plague, &c.; to destroy; to blow up by gunpowder.—*vi*. To wither; to be blighted.

blatant, blā'tant, *a*. Bellowing; noisy.

blaze, blāz, *n*. A flame; brilliance; a bursting out; a white spot.—*vi*. (blazing, blazed). To flame; to send forth a bright light.—*vt*. To noise abroad; to proclaim.

blazon, blāz'on, *vt*. To display; to adorn; to explain in heraldic terms.—*n*. A coat of arms; description of coats of arms.

bleach, blēch, *vt*. To make white or whiter.—*vi*. To grow white. **bleacher**, blēch'ér, *n*. One whose occupation is to whiten cloth. **bleachery**, blēch'ér-i, *n*. A place for bleaching.

bleak, blēk, *a*. Exposed; chill; dreary.

blear, blēr, *a*. Sore; dimmed, as the eyes.—*vt*. To dim or impair.

bleat, blēt, *vi*. To cry as a sheep.—*n*. The cry of a sheep.

bleed, blēd, *vi*. (bleeding, bled). To emit blood; to die by slaughter; to feel agony, as from bleeding; to drop, as blood.—*vt*. To take blood from; to extort money from. **bleeding**, blēd'ing, *n*. A discharge of blood; the operation of letting blood; the drawing of sap from a tree.

blemish, blem'ish, *vt*. To mar; to tarnish.—*n*. A mark of imperfection; dishonor.

blench, blensh, *vi*. To shrink; to flinch.

blend, blend, *vt*. To mix together.—*vi*. To be mixed.—*n*. A mixture.

bless, bles, *vt*. (blessing, blessed or blest). To make happy; to wish happiness to; to consecrate. **blessed**, bles'ed, *a*. Happy; prosperous; holy and happy; happy in heaven. **blessedness**, bles'-ed-nes, *n*. Sanctity; joy. **blessing**, bles'ing, *n*. A prayer imploring happiness upon; piece of good fortune. **blest**, blest, *a*. Blessed; cheering.

blight, blīt, *n*. That which withers up; mildew.—*vt*. and *i*. To wither up; to corrupt with mildew; to frustrate.

blimp, blimp, *n*. A small nonrigid airship driven by an engine installed in an airplane fuselage slung beneath the gas bag.

blind, blind, *a*. Destitute of sight; wanting discernment; having no outlet.—*n*. A screen; something to mislead; a pretext.—*vt*. To make blind; to obstruct the view. **blindfold**, blind'fōld, *a*. Having the eyes covered.—*vt*. To cover the eyes of. **blindly**, blind'li, *adv*. Heedlessly. **blindness**, blind'nes, *n*. Want of sight or discernment; ignorance.

blink, blingk, *vi*. To wink; to twinkle.—*vt*. To shut the eyes upon; to avoid.—*n*. A twinkle; a glimpse or glance.

blinker, bling'kér, *n*. A flap to prevent a horse from seeing sideways.

bliss, blis, *n*. Blessedness; perfect happiness. **blissful**, blis'ful, *a*. Full of bliss.

blister, blis'tér, *n*. A thin bladder on the skin; a pustule; something to raise a blister.—*vi*. To rise in blisters.—*vt*. To raise a blister or blisters on; to apply a blister to. **blister-fly**, blis'tér-flī, *n*. The Spanish fly, used in raising a blister. **blistery**, blis'tér-i, *a*. Full of blisters.

blithe, blīTH, *a*. Joyful; gay; mirthful. **blithely**, blīTH'li, *adv*. In a blithe manner. **blithesome**, blīTH'som, *a*. Gay; merry.

blizzard, bliz'érd, *n*. A violent snowstorm, with high wind and intense cold.

bloat, blōt, *vt*. To make turgid; to cure by salting and smoking.—*vi*. To grow turgid. **bloated**, blōt'ed, *p.a*. Inflated; overgrown.

blob, blob, *n*. A small globe of liquid.

block, blok, *n*. A heavy piece of wood or stone; a lump of solid matter; piece of wood in which a pulley is placed; a mass of buildings; an obstacle; a stupid person.—*vt*. To shut up; to obstruct; to form into blocks.

blockade, blok-ād', *n*. A close siege by troops or ships.—*vt*. (blockading, blockaded). To besiege closely.

blockhead, blok′hed, *n.* A stupid fellow.

blockhouse, blok′hous, *n.* A building used for defense, chiefly of timber.

blockish, blok′ish, *a.* Stupid; dull.

block-tin, blok′tin, *n.* Tin cast into blocks.

blond, blonde, blond, *a.* Of a fair complexion.—*n.* A person of fair complexion.

blood, blud, *n.* The fluid which circulates in animals; kindred; high birth; the juice of fruits.—*a.* Pertaining to blood; of a superior breed.—*vt.* To bleed; to stain with blood; to inure to blood.

blood-horse, blud′hors, *n.* A horse of the purest breed.

bloodhound, blud′hound, *n.* A hound of remarkably acute smell.

bloodily, blud′i-li, *adv.* Cruelly.

bloodshed, blud′shed, *n.* The shedding of blood; slaughter.

blood shot, blud′shot, *a.* Inflamed.

blood sucker, blud′suk-èr, *n.* Any animal that sucks blood; an extortioner.

bloodthirsty, blud′thèrs-ti, *a.* Eager to shed blood.

bloody, blud′i, *a.* Stained with blood; cruel; given to the shedding of blood.

bloom, blöm, *n.* A blossom; a flower; state of youth; native flush on the cheek; the powdery coating on plums, &c.; a lump of puddled iron.—*vi.* To blossom; to flourish; to show the freshness of youth. **bloomy,** blöm′i, *a.* Full of bloom.

blossom, blos′om, *n.* The flower of a plant.—*vi.* To bloom; to flower; to flourish.

blot, blot, *vt.* (blotted, blotting). To spot; to stain; to cancel (with *out*); to dry.—*n.* A spot or stain; an obliteration.

blotch, bloch, *n.* Pustule upon the skin; an eruption; a confused patch of color. **blotchy,** bloch′i, *a.* Having blotches.

blotter, blot′èr, *n.* One who blots; a piece of blotting paper; a waste-book.

blouse, blouz, *n.* A light loose upper garment.

blow, blö, *vi.* (blowing, pp. blown, pret. blew). To make a current of air; to emit air or breath; tó pant; to sound by being blown; to bloom, to flourish.— *vt.* To impel by wind; to inflate; to sound by the breath; to infect with the eggs of flies.—*n.* A blast; a blossoming; bloom; a stroke; a calamitous event. **blower,** blö′èr, *n.* One who blows; a contrivance to increase the draught of a chimney.

blow-out, blö′out, *n.* The bursting of a pneumatic tire from pressure of contained air on a weakened spot.

blowpipe, blö′pip, *n.* A tube by which a current of air is driven through a flame.

blubber, blub′bèr, *n.* The fat of whales and other large sea-animals; the sea-nettle.—*vi.* To weep in a noisy manner.

bludgeon, blud′jon, *n.* A short club with one end loaded.

blue, blü, *n.* The color which the sky exhibits; one of the seven primary colors.—*a.* Of a blue color; sky-colored.— *vt.* (bluing, blued). To dye of a blue color.

bluebell, blü′bel, *n.* The wild hyacinth (in England), the harebell (in Scotland).

bluejacket, blü′jak-et, *n.* A sailor.

bluestocking, blü′stok-ing, *n.* A learned and pedantic lady.

bluff, bluf, *a.* Steep; blustering; burly; hearty.—*n.* A steep projecting bank.— *vt.* and *i.* To impose on by a show of boldness or strength.

blunder, blun′dèr, *vi.* To err stupidly; to stumble.—*vt.* To confound.—*n.* A gross mistake; error.

blunt, blunt, *a.* Dull on the edge or point; not sharp; dull in understanding; unceremonious.—*vt.* To make blunt or dull. **bluntly,** blunt′li, *adv.* In a blunt manner. **bluntness,** blunt′nes, *n.* Dullness of edge or point; rude sincerity or plainness.

blur, blèr, *n.* A stain; a blot.—*vt.* (blurring, blurred). To stain; to obscure; to render indistinct.

blurt, blèrt, *vt.* To utter suddenly or unadvisedly.

blush, blush, *vi.* To redden in the face; to bear a blooming red color.—*n.* A red color caused by shame, confusion, &c.; sudden appearance or glance. **blushing,** blush′ing, *a.* Reddening in the cheeks or face; roseate.

bluster, blus′tèr, *vi.* To roar like wind; to swagger.—*n.* A violent gust of wind; swagger. **blusterer,** blus′tèr-èr, *n.* A swaggerer. **blustering,** blus′tèr-ing, *a.* Noisy; windy.

boa, bō′a, *n.* A genus of large serpent without fangs and venom; a long piece of fur. &c., worn round the neck.

boar, bōr, *n.* The male of swine.

board, bōrd, *n.* A piece of timber broad and thin; a table; food; persons seated round a table; a council; the deck of a ship; a thick stiff paper.—*vt.* To cover with boards; to supply with food; to place as a boarder; to enter a ship by force.—*vi.* To live in a house at a certain rate. **boarder,** bōrd′èr, *n.* One who receives food and lodging at a stated charge; one who boards a ship in action. **boarding,** bōrd′ing, *n.* Act of one who boards; boards collectively.

boast, bōst, *vi.* To brag; to talk ostentatiously.—*vt.* To brag of; to magnify. —*n.* A vaunting; the cause of boasting. **boaster,** bōst′èr, *n.* One who boasts. **boastful,** bōst′ful, *a.* Given to boasting. **boastingly,** bōst′ing-li, *adv.* In an ostentatious manner; with boasting.

boat, bōt, *n.* A small open vessel, usually impelled by oars; a small ship.—*vt.* To transport in a boat.—*vi.* To go in a boat.

boatswain, bōt′swān, *n.* A ship's officer who has charge of boats, sails, &c.

bob, bob, *n.* A pendant; something that plays loosely; a short jerking motion; a docked tail.—*vt.* (bobbing, bobbed). To move with a short jerking motion.—*vi.* To play backward and forward, or loosely.

bobbin, bob′in, *n.* A small pin of wood to wind the thread on in weaving lace, &c.

bode, bōd, *vt.* (boding, boded). To por-

tend; to be the omen of.—*vi.* To presage.

bodice, bod'is, *n.* Something worn round
the waist; a corset.

body, bo'di, *n.* The trunk of an animal;
main part; matter; a person; a system;
strength; reality; any solid figure.—*vt.*
(bodying, bodied). To give a body to;
to embody (with *forth*). **bodied,** bo'did,
a. Having a body. **bodiless,** bo'di-les,
a. Having no body. **bodily,** bo'di-li, *a.*
Relating to the body; actual.—*adv.* Corporeally; entirely.

bodyguard, bo'di-gärd, *n.* The guard
that protects or defends the person.

Boer, bör, *n.* A Dutch colonist of S.
Africa.

bog, bog, *n.* A quagmire; a morass.—*vt.*
(bogging, bogged). To whelm, as in mud.

bogey, bogy, bo'gi, *n.* A goblin.

bogus, bo'gus, *a.* Counterfeit; sham.

Bohemian, bō-hē'mi-an, *n.* A native of
Bohemia; a gipsy; an artist who leads
an unconventional life.

boil, boil, *vi.* To bubble from the action
of heat; to seethe; to be cooked by boiling; to be in a state of agitation.—*vt.*
To heat to a boiling state; to prepare by
boiling.—*n.* A sore swelling or tumor.

boiler, boil'ėr, *n.* One who boils; a vessel in which a thing is boiled, or steam
generated.

boisterous, bois'tėr-us, *a.* Stormy;
noisy. **boisterously,** bois'tėr-us-li,
adv. In a boisterous manner.

bold, bōld, *a.* Daring; courageous; impudent; steep and abrupt. **boldly,**
bōld'li, *adv.* In a bold manner. **boldness,** bōld'nes. *n.* Quality of being bold;
intrepidity; assurance.

bole, bōl, *n.* The body or stem of a
tree; a kind of fine clay.

bolero, bo-lār'ō, *n.* A Spanish dance.

boll, bōl, *n.* A pod; an old Scotch dry
measure of 6 bushels.—*vi.* To form into
a pericarp.

Bolshevik, bol-she-vik', *n.* In Russian
politics a member of the radical wing of
the Social Democratic party.

bolster, bōl'stėr, *n.* A long pillow; a
pad.—*vt.* To support with a bolster; to
hold up; to maintain.

bolt, bōlt, *n.* An arrow; a thunderbolt;
a bar of a door; anything which fastens
or secures; a roll of cloth, &c.—*vi.* To
leave suddenly.—*vt.* To fasten; to swallow hurriedly; to sift.

bomb, bom, *n.* An iron shell filled with
explosive material. **bombard,** bom-
bärd', *vt.* To attack with shot and shell.
—*n.* An old short cannon. **bom-
bardier,** bom-bärd-ėr', *n.* A non-commissioned officer who serves artillery.
bombardment, bom-bärd'ment, *n.*
The act of bombarding.

bombast, bom'bast, *n.* High-sounding
words. **bombastic,** bom-bast'ik, *a.* Inflated; turgid. **bombastically,** bom-
bas'tik-al-li, *adv.* In a bombastic or inflated manner.

bona fide, bō'na fī'dē, *adv.* and *a.* With
good faith.

bonbon, bong'bong, *n.* A sweetmeat.

bond, bond, *n.* That which binds; obligation; state of being bonded; a writing

by which a person binds himself; in *pl.*
chains; imprisonment.—*a.* In a servile
state.—*vt.* To grant a bond in security
for money; to store till duty is paid.

bondage, bond'ij, *n.* Slavery; thraldom. **bonded,** bond'ed, *a.* Secured by
bond; under a bond to pay duty; containing goods liable to duties. **bonder,**
bon'dėr, *n.* One who bonds; one who de-
posits goods in a bonded warehouse.
bond-holder, bond'hōld-ėr, *n.* A person who holds a bond for money lent.
bondman, bondsman, bond'man,
bondz'man, *n.* A m.an slave.

bone, bōn, *n.* A hard substance forming
the framework of an animal; something
made of bone.—*vt.* (boning, boned). To
take out bones from. **boned,** bōnd, *a.*
Having bones; deprived of bones.

bonfire, bon'fir, *n.* A large fire in the
open air.

bonnet, bon'net, *n.* A covering.for the
head.

bonus, bō'nus, *n.* A premium; extra
dividend to shareholders.

bony, bon'i, *a.* Pertaining to or consisting of bones; full of bones; stout;
strong.

book, buk, *n.* A printed or written literary work; a volume; division of a
literary work.—*vt.* To enter in a book.

booking-office, buk'ing-of-is, *n.* An
office where passengers receive tickets,
&c. (Eng.).

bookish, buk'ish, *a.* Given to books or
reading; fond of study.

bookkeeper, buk'kēp-ėr, *n.* One who
keeps the accounts of a business house.
bookmaker, buk'māk-ėr, *n.* One who
compiles books; one who bets systematically.

bookworm, buk'wėrm, *n.* A worm that
eats holes in books; a close student of
books.

boom, bōm, *n.* A long pole to extend
the bottom of a sail; a chain or bar
across a river or mouth of a harbor; a
hollow roar; briskness in commerce.—*vi.*
To make a humming sound; to roar, as
waves or cannon.

boomerang, bōm'e-rang, *n.* An Australian missile of hard wood, which can return to hit an object behind the thrower.

boon, bōn, *n.* Answer to a prayer; a
favor, gift, or grant.—*a.* Merry; pleasant.

boor, bör, *n.* A rustic; an ill-mannered
or illiterate fellow. **boorish,** bör'ish, *a.*
Clownish; rustic.

boot, böt, *vt.* To benefit; to. put on
boots.—*n.* Profit; a covering for the foot
and leg; *pl.* A male servant in a hotel.
booted, böt'ed, *a.* Having boots on.

booth, bōтн, *n.* A temporary shed.

boot-jack, böt'jak, *n.* An instrument
for drawing off boots.

bootless, böt'les, *a.* Unavailing; without
profit.

boot-tree, boot-last, böt'trē, böt'last,
n. An instrument for stretching a boot.

booty, bö'ti, *n.* Spoil; plunder.

borax, bō'raks, *n.* A salt found crude,
or prepared from boracic acid and soda.

border, bor'dėr, *n.* The outer edge of
anything; boundary; margin.—*vi.* To

approach near; to touch at the confines; to be contiguous.—*vt.* To surround with a border. **borderer**, bor'dèr-èr, *n.* One who dwells on a border.

bore, bōr, *vt.* (boring, bored). To make a hole in; to pester.—*vi.* To pierce.—*n.* The hole made by boring; the diameter of a round hole; a person or thing that wearies; a sudden rise of the tide in certain estuaries.

born, born, *pp.* of *bear*. To bring forth.

borne, born, *pp.* of *bear*. To carry.

borough, bu'ro, *n.* A town with a municipal government.

borrow, bo'rō, *vt.* To ask or receive as a loan; to appropriate. **borrower**, bo'-rō-èr, *n.* One who borrows.

bosh, bosh, *n.* Nonsense.

bosky, bosk'i, *a.* Woody or bushy.

bosom, bö'zum, *n.* The breast; the seat of the affections.—*vt.* To conceal.—*a.* Much beloved; confidential.

boss, bos, *n.* A knob; an ornamental projection; a master. **bossy**, bos'i, *a.* Ornamented with bosses.

botany, bot'a-ni, *n.* The science which treats of plants. **botanic, botanical**, bō-tan'ik, bō-tan'ik-al, *a.* Pertaining to botany. **botanist**, bot'an-ist, *n.* One skilled in botany.

botch, boch, *n.* A swelling on the skin; a clumsy patch; bungled work.—*vt.* To mend or perform clumsily. **botcher**, boch'èr, *n.* One who botches. **botchy**, boch'i, *a.* Marked with botches.

both, bōth, *a.* and *pron.* The two, taken by themselves; the pair.—*conj.* As well; on the one side.

bother, boTH'èr, *vt.* To annoy.—*vi.* To trouble one's self.—*n.* A trouble, vexation. **botheration**, boTH-èr-ā'shon, *n.* The act of bothering; state of being bothered. **bothersome**, boTH'èr-sum, *a.* Causing trouble.

bottle, bot'l, *n.* A narrow-mouthed vessel of glass, leather, &c., for liquor; the contents of a bottle.—*vt.* (bottling, bottled). To put into a bottle or bottles.

bottle-nose, bot'l-nōz, *n.* A kind of whale.

bottom, bot'tom, *n.* The lowest part; the ground under water; foundation; a valley; native strength; a ship; dregs.—*vt.* To found or build upon. **bottomless**, bot'tom-les, *a.* Without a bottom; fathomless.

boudoir, bö-dwar', *n.* A lady's private room.

bough, bou, *n.* A branch of a tree.

boulevard, böö'le-värd, *n.* A wide street planted with trees.

bounce, bouns, *vi.* (bouncing, bounced). To spring or rush out suddenly; to thump; to boast or bully.—*n.* A strong sudden thump; a rebound, a boast (col. Eng.). **bouncer**, bouns'èr, *n.* A boaster; a liar. **bouncing**, bouns'ing, *p.a.* Big; strong; boasting.

bound, bound, *n.* A boundary; a leap.—*vt.* To limit; to restrain.—*vi.* To leap; to rebound.—*p.a.* Obliged; sure.—*a.* Ready; destined. **boundary**, bound'a-ri, *n.* A mark designating a limit; border.

bounden, bound'en, *a.* Obligatory.

boundless, bound'les, *a.* Unlimited.

bounty, boun'ti, *n.* Liberality; generosity; a gratuity; premium to encourage trade. **bounteous**, boun'te-us, *a.* Liberal; bountiful. **bounteously**, boun'tē-us-li, *adv.* Liberally; generously; largely. **bountiful**, boun'ti-ful, *a.* Munificent; generous.

bouquet, bö-kā', *n.* A bunch of flowers; a nosegay; an agreeable aromatic odor.

bourgeois, börzh-wä', *n.* A citizen; a man of middle rank.

bourgeoisie, börzh-wa-zē', *n.* The middle classes, especially those dependent on trade.

bout, bout, *n.* As much of an action as is performed at one time; turn; debauch.

bovine, bō'vin, *a.* Pertaining to oxen.

bow, bou, *vt.* To bend; to bend the head or body in token of respect; to depress. —*vi.* To bend; to make a reverence; to yield.—*n.* A bending of the head or body, in token of respect; the rounding part of a ship's side forward.

bow, bō, *n.* An instrument to shoot arrows; the rainbow; a curve; a fiddlestick; an ornamental knot.

bowed, bōd, *p.a.* Bent like a bow.

bowel, bou'el, *n.* One of the intestines; *pl.* the intestines; the seat of pity; compassion.

bower, bou'èr, *n.* An anchor carried at the bow; a shady recess; an arbor.

bowl, bōl, *n.* A large roundish cup; a ball, of wood, &c., used for rolling on a level plat of ground; *pl.* the game played with such bowls.—*vi.* To play with bowls, to deliver a ball at cricket; to move rapidly.—*vt.* To roll as a bowl; to deliver (a ball), &c., at cricket.

bowlder, bōl'dèr, *n.* A large roundish stone.

bowlegged, bō'legd, *a.* With crooked legs.

bowler, bōl'èr, *n.* One who bowls.

bowline, bō'lin, *n.* A rope to make a sail stand towards the bow to catch the wind.

bowling, bōl'ing, *n.* Act or art of playing with bowls; art or style of a bowler.

bowling-green, bōl'ing-grēn, *n.* A level piece of ground for bowling.

bowman, bō'man, *n.* An archer.

bowshot, bō'shot, *n.* The distance which an arrow flies when shot from a bow.

bowsprit, bō'sprit, *n.* A large spar which projects over the bow of a ship.

box, boks, *n.* A case of wood, metal, &c.; quantity that a case contains; a seat in a playhouse, &c.: driver's seat on a coach; a sportsman's house; a blow on the ear; a tree or shrub, yielding a dense wood.—*vt.* To put in a box; to strike with the hand.—*vi.* To fight with the fists.

boxer, boks'èr, *n.* One who boxes; a pugilist.

boxing, boks'ing, *n.* The act or art of fighting with the fist; pugilism.

boxwood, boks'wud, *n.* The hard-grained wood of the box-tree; the plant itself.

boy, boi, *n.* A male child; a lad. **boyhood**, boi'hud, *n.* The state of a boy. **boyish**, boi'ish, *a.* Like a boy; puerile.

boycott, boi'kot, *vt.* To combine in refusing to have dealings with.

brace, brās, *n.* That which holds; a bandage; a couple.—*vt.* (bracing, braced). To tighten; to strain up; to strengthen.

bracelet, brās'let, *n.* An ornament for the wrist.

bracing, brās'ing, *a.* Invigorating.

bracket, brak'et, *n.* A support for something fixed to a wall; a mark in printing to inclose words, &c.—*vt.* To place within or connect by brackets. **bracketing**, brak'et-ing, *n.* A series of brackets for the support of something.

brackish, brak'ish, *a.* Salt; saltish.

brag, brag, *vi.* (bragging, bragged). To bluster; to talk big.—*n.* A boast.

braggadocio, brag-a-dō'shi-ō, *n.* A boasting fellow; boastful words.

braggart, brag'ärt, *a.* Boastful.—*n.* A boaster.

braid, brād, *vt.* To weave, knit, or wreathe; to intertwine.—*n.* A narrow woven band of silk, cotton, &c.; something braided. **braided**, brād'ed, *a.* Edged with braid.

brail, brāl, *n.* A small rope attached to sails.—*vt.* To haul in by means of brails (with *up*).

brain, brān, *n.* The nervous matter within the skull; seat of sensation and of the intellect; the understanding.—*vt.* To dash out the brains of. **brainless**, brān'les, *a.* Silly; thoughtless. **brain-sick**, brān'sik, *a.* Disordered in the understanding; crazed.

braise, **braize**, brāz, *vt.* (braising, braised). To cook with herbs, &c., in a close pan.

brake, brāk, *n.* A place overgrown with brushwood, &c.; a thicket; the bracken; an instrument to break flax; a harrow for breaking clods; a contrivance for retarding the motion of wheels; a large wagonette. **braky**, brāk'i, *a.* Full of brakes; thorny.

bramble, bram'bl, *n.* A prickly shrub of the rose family; its berry.

brambling, bram'bling, *n.* A British finch, like the chaffinch, but larger.

bran, bran, *n.* The husks of ground corn.

branch, branch, *n.* The shoot of a tree or plant; the offshoot of anything, as of a river, family, &c.; a limb.—*vi.* To spread in branches.—*vt.* To divide or form into branches. **branchy**, bransh'i, *a.* Full of branches.

brand, brand, *n.* A burning piece of wood; a sword; a mark made with a hot iron; a note of infamy; a trademark; a kind of quality.—*vt.* To mark with a hot iron; to stigmatize as infamous.

brandish, brand'ish, *vt.* To shake, wave, or flourish.—*n.* A waving; a flourish.

brandy, bran'di, *n.* An ardent spirit distilled from wine.

brash, brash, *n.* A confused heap of fragments; small fragments of crushed ice.

brasier, brā'zhėr, *n.* One who works in brass; a pan for holding coals.

brass, bras, *n.* A yellow alloy of copper and zinc; a utensil, &c., made of brass; impudence.

brassy, bras'i, *a.* Made of brass; like brass.

brat, brat, *n.* A child, so called in contempt.

bravado, bra-vā'dō, *n.* A boast or brag; would-be boldness.

brave, brāv, *a.* Daring; bold; valiant; noble.—*n.* A daring person; a savage warrior.—*vt.* (braving, braved). To challenge; to defy; to encounter with courage. **bravely**, brāv'li. *adv.* Courageously. **bravery**, brāv'ė-ri, *n.* Courage; heroism.

bravo, brā'vo, *n.* A bandit; an assassin. —*interj.* Well done!

brawl, brạl, *vi.* To quarrel noisily.—*n.* A noisy quarrel; uproar. **brawler**, brạl'ėr, *n.* A noisy fellow. **brawling**, brạl'ing, *p.a.* Quarrelsome.

brawn, brạn, *n.* The flesh of a boar; the muscular part of the body; muscle. **brawny**, brạn'i, *a.* Muscular; fleshy.

bray, brā, *vt.* To beat or grind small.— *vi.* To make a loud harsh sound, as an ass.—*n.* The cry of an ass.

braze, brāz, *vt.* (brazing, brazed). To cover with brass; to solder with brass.

brazen, brāz'n, *a.* Made of brass; impudent.—*vt.* To behave with insolence (with *it*). **brazen-faced**, brāz'n-fāst, *a.* Impudent; bold to excess; shameless.

breach, brēch, *n.* The act of breaking, or state of being broken; infringement; quarrel.—*vt.* To make a breach or opening in.

bread, bred, *n.* Food made of flour or meal baked; food; sustenance.

breadfruit-tree, bred'fröt-trē, *n.* A tree of the Pacific Islands producing a fruit which forms a substitute for bread.

breadth, bredth, *n.* The measure across any plane surface; width; liberality.

break, brāk, *vt.* (breaking, pret. broke; pp. broke, broken). To sever by fracture; to rend; to open; to tame; to make bankrupt; to discard; to interrupt; to dissolve any union; to tell with discretion.—*vi.* To come to pieces; to burst; to burst forth; to dawn; to become bankrupt; to decline in vigor; to change in tone.—*n.* An opening; breach; pause; the dawn; a brake for vehicles; a large wagonette. **breakage**, brāk'ij, *n.* A breaking; damage by breaking; allowance for things broken.

breakdown, brāk'doun, *n.* An accident; a downfall; a lively dance.

breaker, brāk'ėr, *n.* One who or that which breaks; a rock; a wave broken by rocks.

breakfast, brek'fast, *n.* The first meal in the day.—*vi.* To eat the first meal in the day.—*vt.* To furnish with breakfast.

break-up, brāk'up, *n.* Disruption; dissolution.

breast, brest, *n.* The fore part of the body, between the neck and the belly; the heart; the conscience; the affections.—*vt.* To bear the breast against; to meet in front.

breastbone, brest'bōn, *n.* The bone of the breast.

breastplate, brest'plāt, *n.* Armor for the breast.

breath, breth, *n.* The air drawn into and expelled from the lungs; life; a single respiration; pause; a gentle breeze.

breathe, brēŧH, *vi.* (breathing, breathed). To draw into and eject air from the lungs; to live; to take breath; to rest.—*vt.* To inspire, and exhale; to infuse; to utter softly or in private; to suffer to take breath. **breathing**, brēŧH'ing, *n.* Respiration; inspiration; breathing-place; an aspirate. **breathless**, breth'les, *a.* Being out of breath; spent with labor; dead.

bred, bred, *pp.* of *breed*.

breech, brēch, *n.* The lower part of the body behind; the hinder part of a gun, &c.—*vt.* To put into breeches.

breeches, brēch'ez, *n.pl.* A garment worn on the legs by men.

breed, brēd, *vt.* (breeding, bred). To bring up; to educate; to engender; to bring forth; to occasion; to rear, as live stock.—*vi.* To produce offspring; to be with young; to be produced.—*n.* Offspring; kind; a brood. **breeder**, brēd'ėr, *n.* One that breeds. **breeding**, brēd'ing, *n.* The raising of a breed or breeds; education; deportment.

breeze, brēz, *n.* A light wind. **breezy**, brēz'i, *a.* Subject to breezes; airy.

breviary, brē'vi-e-ri, *n.* A book containing the daily service of the R. Catholic Church.

brevity, brē'vi-ti, *n.* Shortness; conciseness.

brew, brō, *vt.* To prepare, as ale or beer, from malt, &c.; to concoct; to plot.—*vi.* To make beer; to be forming.—*n.* The mixture formed by brewing. **brewage**, brō'ij, *n.* Drink brewed. **brewer**, brō'ėr, *n.* One who brews. **brewery**, brō'e-ri, *n.* A house where brewing is carried on. **brewing**, brō'ing, *n.* The act of making beer; the quantity brewed at once.

briar, *See* **brier.**

bribe, brib, *n.* A gift to corrupt the conduct or judgment.—*vt.* (bribing, bribed). To gain over by bribes. **briber**, brib'ėr, *n.* One who gives bribes. **bribery**, brib'ė-ri, *n.* The act or practice of giving or taking bribes.

bric-a-brac, brik-a-brak, *n.* Articles of interest or value from rarity, antiquity, &c.

brick, brik, *n.* A rectangular mass of burned clay, used in building, &c.; a loaf shaped like a brick.—*a.* Made of brick.—*vt.* To lay with bricks.

bricklayer, brik'lā-ėr, *n.* One who builds with bricks.

bridal, brid'al, *n.* A wedding-feast; a wedding.—*a.* Belonging to a bride or to a wedding.

bride, brid, *n.* A woman about to be or newly married.

bridegroom, brid'gröm, *n.* A man about to be or newly married.

bridesmaid, **bride'smaid**, brid'mād, brīdz'mād, *n.* A woman who attends on a bride at her wedding.

bridge, brij, *n.* A structure across a river, &c. to furnish a passage; the up-

per part of the nose.—*vt.* (bridging, bridged). To build a bridge over.

bridle, bri'dl, *n.* The part of harness with which a horse is governed; a curb; a check.—*vt.* (bridling, bridled). To put a bridle on; to restrain.—*vi.* To hold up the head and draw in the chin; to bristle.

brief, brēf, *a.* Short; concise.—*n.* A short writing; a writ or precept; an abridgment of a client's case. **briefless**, brēf'les, *a.* Having no brief. **briefly**, brēf'li, *adv.* Concisely.

brier, bri'ėr, *n.* A prickly shrub, species of the rose. **briery**, bri'ėr-i, *a.* Full of briers; rough.

brig, brig, *n.* A vessel with two masts, square-rigged.

brigade, bri-gād', *n.* A body of troops consisting of several battalions.

brigadier, bri-ga-dēr', *n.* The officer who commands a brigade.

brigand, bri'gand, *n.* A freebooter.

brigantine, brig'an-tin, *n.* A light swift vessel, two-masted and square-rigged.

bright, brit, *a.* Clear; shining; glittering; acute; witty; lively; cheerful.

brighten, brit'n, *vt.* To make bright or brighter.—*vi.* To become bright; to clear up.

brightly, brit'li, *adv.* With lustre; cheerfully.

brilliant, bril'yant, *a.* Shining; sparkling; splendid; of great talents.—*n.* A diamond of the finest cut; a small printing type.

brilliantly, bril'yant-li, *adv.* Splendidly. **brilliance**, **brilliancy**, bril'yans, bril'yan-si, *n.* State of being brilliant; splendor.

brim, brim, *n.* The rim of anything; the upper edge of the mouth of a vessel.—*vi.* (brimming, brimmed). To be full to the brim. **brimful**, brim'ful', *a.* Full to the brim. **brimmer**, brim'ėr, *n.* A bowl full to the top.

brimstone, brim'stōn, *n.* Sulphur.

brindled, brin'dld, *a.* Marked with brown streaks.

brine, brin, *n.* Salt water; the sea.

bring, bring, *vt.* (bringing, brought). To lead or cause to come; to fetch; to produce; to attract; to prevail upon.

brink, bringk, *n.* The edge of a steep place.

briny, brin'i, *a.* Pertaining to brine.

brisk, brisk, *a.* Lively; bright; effervescing.

brisket, brisk'et, *n.* The breast of an animal, or that part next to the ribs.

briskly, brisk'li, *adv.* Actively; vigorously.

bristle, bris'l, *n.* A stiff hair of swine; stiff hair of any kind.—*vt.* (bristling, bristled). To erect in bristles.—*vi.* To stand erect, as bristles; to show anger, &c. **bristly**, bris'li, *a.* Thick set with bristles.

Britannic, bri-tan'ik, *a.* Pertaining to Britain.

British, brit'ish, *a.* Pertaining to Britain or its inhabitants.

Briton, brit'on, *n.* A native of Britain.

brittle, brit'l, *a.* Apt to break; not tough or tenacious.—*vt.* To cut up a deer.

broach, brōch, *n.* A spit; a brooch.—*vt.* To pierce, as with a spit; to tap; to open up; to publish first.

broad, brąd, *a.* Having extent from side to side; wide; unrestricted; indelicate.

broaden, brąd'n, *vi.* To grow broad.—*vt.* To make broad. **broadside,** brąd'sid, *n.* A discharge of all the guns on one side of a ship; a sheet of paper printed on one side.

broadsword, brąd'sōrd, *n.* A sword with a broad blade and a cutting edge.

brocade, brō-kād', *n.* A silk or satin stuff variegated with gold and silver. **brocaded,** brō-kād'ed, *a.* Worked like brocade; dressed in brocade.

broccoli, brok'o-li, *n.* A kind of cauliflower.

brochure, brō-shōr', *n.* A pamphlet.

brogue, brōg, *n.* A shoe of raw hide; the pronunciation of English peculiar to the Irish.

broil, broil, *n.* A brawl; a noisy quarrel. —*vt.* To cook over a fire; to subject to strong heat.—*vi.* To be subjected to heat; to be greatly heated.

broken, brōk'n, *a.* Subdued; bankrupt.

broker, brō'kėr, *n.* An agent who buys and sells for others; a pawnbroker.

brokerage, brō'kėr-ij, *n.* The business of a broker; the pay or commission of a broker.

bromide, brō'mīd, *n.* A compound of bromine with another element.

bronchial, brong'ki-al, *a.* Belonging to the tubes branching from the windpipe through the lungs.

bronchitis, brong-kī'tis, *n.* Inflammation of the bronchial tubes.

bronze, bronz, *n.* An alloy of copper and tin; a color to imitate bronze; a figure made of bronze.—*vt.* (bronzing, bronzed). To make appear on the surface like bronze. **bronzed,** bronzd, *p.a.* Made to resemble bronze.

brooch, brōch, *n.* An ornamental pin or buckle used to fasten dress.

brood, brōd, *vi.* To sit on eggs; to ponder anxiously (with *over* or *on*).—*n.* That which is bred; birds of one hatching; offspring.

brook, bryk, *n.* A natural stream smaller than a river.—*vt.* To bear; to endure.

broom, brōm, *n.* A shrub with yellow flowers and angular branches; a brush. **broomy,** brōm'i, *a.* Full of broom.

broth, broth, *n.* Liquor in which flesh, or some other substance, has been boiled.

brothel, broth'el, *n.* A house of ill-fame.

brother, bruᴛн'ėr, *n.*; pl. **brothers, brethren,** bruᴛн'ėrz, breᴛн'ren, *n.* A male born of the same parents; an associate; a fellow-creature. **brotherhood,** bruᴛн'ėr-hyd, *n.* The state or quality of being a brother; an association. **brotherly,** bruᴛн'ėr-li, *a.* Like a brother.

brow, brou, *n.* The ridge over the eye; the forehead; the edge of a steep place.

browbeat, brou'bēt, *vt.* To bear down with stern looks or arrogant speech.

brown, broun, *a.* Of a dusky color, inclining to red.—*n.* A color resulting from the mixture of red, black, and yellow.—*vt.* To make brown. **brownish,** broun'ish, *a.* Somewhat brown.

brownie, brou'ni, *n.* A domestic spirit of benevolent character.

browse, brouz, *vt.* (browsing, browsed). To pasture or feed upon.—*vi.* To crop and eat food.

bruin, brō'in, *n.* A familiar name of a bear.

bruise, brōz, *vt.* (bruising, bruised). To crush; to make a contusion on.—*n.* A contusion; a hurt from a blow.

bruiser, brōz'ėr, *r.* A boxer; a prize-fighter.

bruit, brōt, *n.* Report; rumor.—*vt.* To noise abroad.

brunette, brō-net', *n.* A woman with a brownish or dark complexion.

brunt, brunt, *n.* The heat of battle; onset; shock.

brush, brush, *n.* An instrument to clean by rubbing or sweeping; a painter's large pencil; a skirmish; a thicket; the tail of a fox.—*vt.* To sweep, rub, or paint with a brush; to touch lightly in passing.—*vi.* To move nimbly or in haste; to skim.

brusque, brusk, *a.* Abrupt in manner; rude.

Brussels sprouts, brus'elz-sprouts, *n. pl.* A variety of cabbage.

brute, brōt, *a.* Senseless; bestial; uncivilized.—*n.* A beast; a brutal person. **brutish,** brōt'ish, *a.* Brutal; grossly sensual. **brutal,** brōt'al, *a.* Cruel; ferocious. **brutality,** brōt-al'i-ti, *n.* Quality of being brutal; savageness; cruelty. **brutalize,** brōt'al-iz, *vt.* (brutalizing, brutalized). To make brutal.—*vi.* To become brutal. **brutally,** brōt'al-li, *adv.* In a brutal manner.

bubble, bub'l, *n.* A small vesicle of fluid inflated with air; a vain project; a swindle.—*vi.* (bubbling, bubbled). To rise in bubbles.—*vt.* To cheat; to swindle.

bubo, bū'bō, *n.*; pl. **-oes.** A swelling or abscess in a glandular part of the body. **bubonic,** bū-bon'ik, *a.* Pertaining to bubo.

buccaneer, bucanier, buk-a-nēr', *n.* A pirate. **buccaneering,** buk-a-nēr'ing, *n.* The employment of buccaneers.

buck, buk, *n.* The male of deer, goats, &c.; a gay young fellow; a lye for steeping clothes in.—*vt.* To steep in lye.—*vi.* To leap, as a horse, so as to dismount the rider.

bucket, buk'et, *n.* A vessel in which water is drawn or carried.

buckle, buk'l, *n.* An instrument to fasten straps, &c.—*vt.* (buckling, buckled). To fasten with a buckle; to bend or warp. —*vi.* To apply with vigor (with *to*).

buckram, buk'ram, *n.* A coarse linen cloth stiffened with glue.—*a.* Stiff; formal.

buckshot, buk'shot. *n.* A large kind of shot used for killing large game.

buckwheat, buk'whēt, *n.* A plant bearing small seeds which are ground into meal.

bucolic, bū-kol'ik, *a.* Pastoral.—*n.* A pastoral poem.

bud, bud, *n.* The first shoot of a leaf, &c.; a germ.—*vi.* (budding, budded). To put forth buds or germs; to begin to grow.—*vt.* To graft by inserting a bud.

Buddhism, bud'izm, *n.* The religion founded in India by Buddha.

Buddhist, bud'ist, *n.* One who adheres to Buddhism.

budding, bud'ing, *n.* A mode of grafting buds.

budge, buj, *vt.* (budging, budged). To move; to stir.

budget, buj'et, *n.* A little sack with its contents; a stock; the annual statement respecting the government's finances.

buff, buf, *n.* Leather prepared from the skin of the buffalo, elk, &c.; a dull light yellow.—*a.* Light yellow; made of buff.

buffalo, buf'fa-lō, *n.* A species of ox, larger than the common ox; the American bison.

buffer, buf'èr, *n.* An apparatus for deadening concussion.

buffet, buf'et, *n.* A cupboard for wine, glasses, &c.; a place for refreshments (pron. bu-fe').

buffet, buf'et, *n.* A blow; a slap.—*vt.* To beat; to box; to contend against.

buffoon, bu-fön', *n.* One who makes sport by low jests and antic gestures; a droll. **buffoonery,** bu-fön'é-ri, *n.* The arts and practices of a buffoon.

bug, bug, *n.* A name for various insects, particularly one infesting houses and inflicting severe bites.

buggy, bug'i, *n.* A light one-horse carriage.

bugle, bū'gl, *n.* A hunting-horn; a military instrument of music; a long glass bead, commonly black.

bugler, bū'glèr, *n.* A soldier who conveys officers' commands by sounding a bugle.

build, bild, *vt.* (building, built). To construct; to raise on a foundation; to establish.—*vi.* To form a structure.—*n.* Construction; make; form. **builder,** bil'dèr, *n.* One who builds. **building,** bil'ding, *n.* The art of constructing edifices; an edifice.

bulb, bulb, *n.* A round root; a round protuberance. **bulbous,** bulb'us, *a.* Pertaining to a bulb; swelling out.

bulge, bulj, *n.* A swelling; bilge.—*vi.* (bulging, bulged). To swell out; to be protuberant.

bulk, bulk, *n.* Magnitude; the majority; extent. **bulky,** bul'ki, *a.* Of great bulk.

bull, bul, *n.* The male of cattle; a sign of the zodiac; one who raises the price of stock; a letter or edict of the pope; a ludicrous contradiction in language.

bulldog, bul'dog, *n.* A species of dog.

bullet, bul'et, *n.* A small ball; a ball of lead, &c., used to load firearms.

bulletin, bul'e-tin, *n.* An official report.

bullfight, bul'fīt, *n.* A combat between armed men and bulls in a closed arena.

bullfinch, bul'finch, *n.* A British songbird.

bullfrog, bul'frog, *n.* A large species of frog, with a loud bass voice.

bullion, bul'yon, *n.* Uncoined gold or silver.

bullock, bul'ok, *n.* An ox or castrated bull.

bull's-eye, bulz'ī, *n.* A circular opening for light or air; the center of a target.

bully, bul'i, *n.* An overbearing, quarrelsome fellow.—*vt.* (bullying, bullied). To insult and overbear.—*vi.* To bluster or domineer.

bulrush, bul'rush, *n.* A large, strong kind of rush.

bulwark, bul'wèrk, *n.* A bastion; a fortification; a means of defense or safety.

bumblebee, bum'bl-bē, *n.* A large bee.

bump, bump, *n.* A heavy blow, or the noise of it; a lump produced by a blow. —*vi.* To make a loud, heavy, or hollow noise.—*vt.* To strike heavily against.

bumper, bump'èr, *n.* A cup or glass filled to the brim; something completely filled.

bumpkin, bump'kin, *n.* An awkward rustic; a lout.

bumptious, bump'shus, *a.* Self-assertive.

bun, bun, *n.* A kind of cake or sweet bread.

bunch, bunch, *n.* A knob or lump; a cluster.—*vi.* To swell out in a protuberance; to cluster. **bunchy,** bunch'i, *a.* Like a bunch.

bundle, bun'dl, *n.* A number of things bound together; a package.—*vt.* (bundling, bundled). To tie in a bundle; to dispose of hurriedly.—*vi.* To depart hurriedly (with *off*).

bung, bung, *n.* The stopper of a cask. —*vt.* To stop with a bung; to close up.

bungalow, bung'ga-lō, *n.* In India, a house or residence, generally of a single floor.

bungle, bung'gl, *vi.* (bungling, bungled). To perform in a clumsy manner.—*vt.* To make or mend clumsily; to manage awkwardly.—*n.* A clumsy performance. **bungler,** bung'glèr, *n.* A clumsy workman. **bungling,** bung'gling, *p.a.* Clumsy; awkwardly done.

bunion, bun'yon, *n.* An excrescence on some of the joints of the feet.

bunk, bungk, *n.* A wooden box serving as a seat and bed; a sleeping berth.

bunker, bungk'èr, *n.* A large bin or receptacle; a sandy hollow on a golf course.

bunkum, buncombe, bung'kum, *n.* Talking for talking's sake; mere words.

bunting, bun'ting, *n.* A bird allied to finches and sparrows; stuff of which flags are made; flags.

buoy, bö'i, boi, *n.* A floating mark to point out shoals, &c.; something to keep a person or thing up in the water.—*vt.* To keep afloat; to bear up.—*vi.* To float. **buoyancy,** bö'yan-si, *n.* The quality of being buoyant; vivacity; cheerfulness. **buoyant,** bö'yant, *a.* Floating; light; elastic.

bur, burr, bèr, *n.* A guttural sounding of the letter *r*; a rough or projecting ridge; bur.

burden, burthen, bèr'dn, bèr'тнn, *n.* That which is borne; load; freight; that which is oppressive; chorus of a song; that which is often repeated.—*vt.* To load; to oppress. **burdensome,** bėr'-dn-sum, *a.* Heavy; oppressive.

burdock, bėr'dok, *n.* A plant with a rough prickly head.

bureau, bū'rō', *n.;* pl. **-eaux,** rōz, or **-eaus.** A writing table with drawers; an office or court; a government office. **bureaucracy,** bū-ro'kra-si, *n.* Centralized administration of a country, through regularly graded officials; such officials collectively.

burglar, bėrg'lėr, *n.* One who robs a house by night. **burglary,** bėrg'la-ri, *n.* Act of nocturnal house-breaking.

burgomaster, bėr'gō-mas"tėr, *n.* The chief magistrate of a Dutch and German town.

burgundy, bėr'gun-di, *n.* A kind of wine so called from Burgundy in France.

burial, be'ri-al, *n.* Act of burying; interment.

burlesque, bėr-lesk', *a.* Tending to excite laughter.—*n.* A composition tending to excite laughter; caricature.—*vt.* (burlesquing, burlesqued). To turn into ridicule; to make ludicrous.

burly, bėr'li, *a.* Great in size; boisterous.

Burmese, bur'mēz, *a.* Pertaining to Burma.—*n.* An inhabitant or inhabitants of Burma; their language.

burn, bėrn, *vt.* (burning, burnt or burned). To consume with fire; to scorch; to inflame; to harden by fire.—*vi.* To be on fire; to be inflamed with desire; to rage fiercely.—*n.* A hurt caused by fire; a rivulet. **burner,** bėrn'ėr, *n.* One who burns; that which gives out light or flame. **burning,** bėrn'ing, *p.a.* Fiery; vehement. **burning-glass,** bėrn'ing-glas, *n.* A glass which collects the rays of the sun into a focus, producing an intense heat.

burnish, bėr'nish, *vt.* To polish.—*vi.* To grow bright or glossy.—*n.* Gloss; luster.

burnt offering, bėrnt'of-fėr-ing, *n.* A sacrifice burnt on an altar.

burrow, bu'rō, *n.* A hole in the earth made by rabbits, &c.—*vi.* To excavate a hole underground; to hide.

burst, bėrst, *vi.* (bursting, burst). To fly or break open; to rush forth; to come with violence.—*vt.* To break by force; to open suddenly.—*n.* A violent disruption; a rupture.

bury, be'ri, *vt.* (burying, buried). To put into a grave; to overwhelm; to hide.

bus, bus, *n.;* pl. **buses.** An omnibus.

bush, bush, *n.* A shrub with branches; a thicket; the backwoods of Australia; a lining of hard metal in the nave of a wheel, &c.—*vi.* To grow bushy.

bushel, bush'el, *n.* A dry measure containing eight gallons or four pecks.

bushman, būsh'man, *n.* A settler in the bush or forest districts of a new country.

bushy, būsh'i, *a.* Full of bushes; like a bush.

business, biz'nes, *n.* Occupation; concern; trade.—*a.* Pertaining to traffic, trade, &c.

buss, bus, *n.* A kiss.—*vt.* To kiss.

bust, bust, *n.* The chest and thorax; a sculptured figure of the head and shoulders.

bustard, bus'tėrd, *n.* A large heavy bird of the order of runners.

bustle, bus'l, *vi.* (bustling, bustled). To hurry and be busy.—*n.* Hurry; tumult; a pad worn by ladies at the back below the waist.

busy, bi'zi, *a.* Occupied; actively engaged; officious.—*vt.* (busying, busied). To make or keep busy. **busily,** bi'zi-li, *adv.* In a busy manner.

busybody, bi'zi-bo-di, *n.* An officious meddling person.

but, but, *conj., prep., adv.* Except; unless; only; however; nevertheless.

butcher, buch'ėr, *n.* One who kills animals for market; one who sells meat; one who delights in bloody deeds.—*vt.* To kill animals for food; to slaughter cruelly. **butchery,** buch'ėr-i, *n.* A slaughter-house; massacre.

butler, but'lėr, *n.* A male servant who has the care of wines, &c.

butt, but, *n.* The end of a thing; a mark to be shot at; the person at whom ridicule, &c. is directed; a cask holding 126 gallons of wine.—*vt.* To thrust the head forward.—*vt.* To strike with the head or horns.

butter, but'ėr, *n.* An oily substance obtained from cream by churning; any substance resembling butter.—*vt.* To spread with butter; to flatter grossly.

butter-cup, but'ėr-kup, *n.* A wild yellow cup-shaped flower.

butterfly, but'ėr-fil, *n.* The name of a group of winged insects.

buttermilk, but'ėr-milk, *n.* The milk that remains after the butter is separated.

buttock, but'ok, *n.* The protuberant part of the body behind; the rump.

button, but'n, *n.* A knob to fasten the parts of dress; a knob or stud; *pl.* A page-boy.—*vt.* To fasten with buttons.

button-hole, but'n-hōl, *n.* A hole for a button; a flower for putting in this.—*vt.* To detain in conversation against one's will.

buttress, but'res, *n.* A projecting support for a wall; a prop.—*vt.* To support by a buttress; to prop.

buy, bī, *vt.* (buying, bought). To acquire by payment; to purchase; to bribe. *vi.* To negotiate or treat about a purchase.

buyer, bī'ėr, *n.* One who buys.

buzz, buz, *vi.* To hum, as bees; to whisper.—*vt.* To whisper.—*n.* The noise of bees; a confused bumming noise.

buzzard, buz'ėrd, *n.* A species of hawk; a blockhead.

by, bī, *prep.* Used to denote the instrument, agent, or manner; at; near; beside; through or with; in; for; according to; at the rate of; not later than.— *adv.* Near; passing. In *composition,* secondary, side.

by-and-by, bī-and bī. In the near future.

ygone, bī′gon, *a.* Past; gone by.

ygones, bī′gonz, *n.pl.* Past troubles, offenses, &c.

ylaw, bī′lą, *n.* A local law of a city, society, &c.; an accessory law.

yplay, bī′plā, *n.* Action carried on aside, and commonly in dumb-show.

ystander, bī′stand-èr, *n.* One who stands near; a spectator; a mere looker-on.

by-the-by (or **bye**). bī-THĒ-bī. By the way; in passing.

byway, bī′wā, *n.* A private or obscure way.

byword, bī′wèrd, *n.* A common saying; a proverb.

Byzantine, biz-an′tin or biz′, *a.* Pertaining to Byzantium or Constantinople and the Greek Empire of which it was the capital.

C

ab, kab, *n.* A covered one-horse carriage; an automobile for hire.

abal, ka-bal′, *n.* An intrigue; persons united in some intrigue.—*vi.* (caballing, caballed). To combine in plotting.

abala, cabbala, kab′a-la, *n.* A mysterious tradition among Jewish rabbins.

aballer, ka-bal′èr, *n.* An intriguer.

abaret, kab′a-ret, ka-ba-rā, *n.* A tavern.

abbage, kab′ij, *n.* A culinary vegetable.—*vt.* (cabbaging, cabbaged). To purloin, especially pieces of cloth.

abbage-rose, kab′ij-rōz, *n.* A species of rose; called also *Provence rose.*

abby, kab′i, *n.* A cabman.

abin, kab′in, *n.* A hut; an apartment in a ship.—*vt.* To confine, as in a cabin.

abinet, kab′in-et, *n.* A closet; a small room; a set of drawers for curiosities; the ministers of state.

abinet-council, kab′in-et-koun-sil, *n.* A council of state.

abinet-maker, kab′in-et-māk″èr, *n.* One who makes articles of furniture.

able, kā′bl, *n.* The strong rope or chain to hold a ship at anchor; a large rope or chain; a submarine telegraph wire.—*vt.* (cabling, cabled). To furnish with a cable; to send by ocean telegraph. **cablegram,** kā′bl-gram, *n.* A message sent by an oceanic telegraph cable.

abman, kab′man, *n.* The driver of a cab.

abriolet, kab′ri-ō-lā″, *n.* A one-horse chaise.

acao, ka-kā′ō, *n.* The chocolate-tree.

ackle, kak′l, *vi.* (cackling, cackled). To make the noise of a goose or hen; to chatter.—*n.* The noise of a hen, &c.; idle talk.

acophony, ka-kof′ō-ni, *n.* Unpleasant vocal sound; a discord.

actus, kak′tus, *n.*; pl. **-tuses** or **-ti.** A spiny shrub of numerous species.

ad, kad, *n.* A mean, vulgar fellow.

adaverous, ka-dav′èr-us, *a.* Resembling a dead human body; pale; ghastly.

addie, kad′i, *n.* A golfer's attendant.

adence, kā′dens, *n.* A fall of the voice at the end of a sentence; rhythm; the close of a musical passage or phrase.—*vt.* To regulate by musical measures.

adet, ka-det′, *n.* A younger brother; a young man in a military school.

adge, kaj, *vt.* and *i.* (cadging, cadged). To carry about for sale; to go about

begging. **cadger,** kaj′èr, *n.* An itinerant hawker.

cadmium, kad′mi-um, *n.* A whitish metal resembling tin.

caduceus, ka-dū′sē-us, *n.* Mercury's rod.

café, kaf-ā′, *n.* A coffee-house; a restaurant.

caffeine, kaf′ēn, *n.* A slightly bitter alkaloid found in coffee, tea, &c.

cage, kāj, *n.* An enclosure of wire, &c., for birds and beasts.—*vt.* (caging, caged). To confine in a cage.

cairn, karn, *n.* A rounded heap of stones.

caisson, kās′un, *n.* An ammunition chest; a structure to raise sunken vessels; a structure used in laying foundations in deep water.

cajole, ka-jōl′, *vt.* (cajoling, cajoled). To coax; to court; to deceive by flattery. **cajolery,** ka-jōl′è-ri, *n.* Flattery.

cake, kāk, *n.* A composition of flour, butter, sugar, &c., baked; a mass of matter concreted.—*vt.* (caking, caked). To form into a cake of mass.—*vi.* To form into a hard mass.

calabash, kal′a-bash, *n.* A gourd shell dried.

calamity, ka-lam′i-ti, *n.* Misfortune; disaster.

calamitous, ka-lam′it-us, *a.* Miserable; afflictive.

calcareous, kal-ka′rē-us, *a.* Of the nature of lime or chalk; containing lime.

calcination, kal-sin-ā′shon, *n.* Act or operation of calcining.

calcine, kal-sīn′. *vt.* (calcining, calcined). To reduce to a powder by fire. —*vi.* To be converted by heat into a powder.

calculate, kal′kū-lāt, *vt.* (calculating, calculated). To compute; to adjust; to make suitable.—*vi.* To make a computation. **calculable,** kal′kū-la-bl, *a.* That may be calculated. **calculating,** kal′kū-lāt-ing, *p.a.* Scheming. **calculation,** kal-kū-lā′shon, *n.* Estimate. **calculator,** kal′kū-lāt-èr, *n.* One who calculates.

calculus, kal′kū-lus, *n.*; pl. **-li.** The stone in the bladder, kidneys, &c.; a method of calculation in mathematics.

caldron, kąl′dron, *n.* A large kettle or boiler.

Caledonian, kal-e-dō′ni-an, *a.* Pertaining to Scotland.—*n.* A Scotchman.

calendar, ka′len-dèr, *n.* A register of the

months and days of the year; an almanac.

calender, ka'len-dèr, n. A machine for smoothing and glazing cloth.—vt. To press between rollers to make smooth, glossy, wavy, &c.

calf, käf, n.; pl. **calves,** kävz. The young of the cow; a kind of leather; the fleshy part of the leg below the knee.

caliber, ka'li-bèr, n. Diameter of the bore of a gun; extent of mental qualities; a sort or kind.

calico, ka'li-kō, n. Cotton cloth.

calisthenics, kal-is-then'iks, n. Exercise for health, strength, or grace of movement.

calk, kak, vt. To drive oakum into the seams of (a ship).

call, kal, vt. To name; to style; to summon; to ask, or command to come; to appoint; to appeal to; to utter aloud; to awaken.—vi. To utter a loud sound; to make a short visit.—n. A vocal utterance; summons; demand; divine vocation; a short visit.

calligraphy, kal-lig'ra-fi, n. The art of beautiful writing; penmanship.

calling, kal'ing, n. Vocation; profession,

callipers, kal'i-pèrz, n.pl. Compasses for measuring caliber.

callous, kal'us, a. Hardened; unfeeling; obdurate.

callow, kal'ō, a. Destitute of feathers; unfledged.

calm, käm, a. Still; free from wind; peaceable; composed.—n. Absence of wind; tranquillity.—vt. To make calm; to still; to assuage.—vi. To become calm.

calmly, käm'li, adv. In a calm manner.

calmness, käm'nes, n. Quietness; composure.

calomel, ka'lō-mel, n. A preparation of mercury, much used in medicine.

caloric, ka-lo'rik, n. The principle or simple element of heat; heat.

calorie, kal'o-ri, n The large or great calorie used as a unit in expressing the heat-producing or energy-producing value of food.

calumny, ka'lum-ni, n. False and malicious defamation; backbiting. **calumniate,** ka-lum'ni-āt, vt. (calumniating, calumniated). To defame maliciously; to slander.—vi. To utter calumnies. **calumniation,** ka-lum'ni-ā'shon, n. False and malicious accusation. **calumniator,** ka-lum'ni-āt-èr, n. One who calumniates. **calumnious,** ka-lum'ni-us, a. Partaking of calumny. **calumniously,** ka-lum'ni-us-li, adv. Slanderously.

Calvary, kal'va-ri, n. A place of skulls, particularly the place where Christ was crucified.

calve, käv, vi. (calving, calved). To give birth to a calf.

Calvinism, kal'vin-izm, n. The theological tenets of Calvin.

Calvinist, kal'vin-ist, n. One who embraces the doctrines of Calvin.

Calvinistic, kal-vin-is'tik, a. Pertaining to Calvin, or to his tenets.

calyx, kā'liks, n.; pl. **-yces,** or **-yxes.** The outer covering of a flower; the flower-cup.

cam, kam, n. A projection on a wheel to give alternating motion to another wheel &c.

cambric, käm'brik, n. A fine white linen.

camel, kam'el, n. A large ruminant hoofed quadruped used in Asia and Africa for carrying burdens.

camellia, ka-mel'i-a or ka-mēl'ya, n. A genus of beautiful shrubs of the tea family.

cameo, kam'ē-ō, n. A stone or shell of different colored layers cut in relief.

camera, kam'ē-ra, n. An arched roof; a council chamber; an apparatus for taking photographs.

camouflage, cam-o-fläzh', n. Disguise of guns, ships, &c., effected by obscuring outline with splashes of various colors: use of smoke-screens, boughs, &c., for same purpose;—vt. Hide by camouflage

camp, kamp, n. The ground on which an army pitch their tents; an encampment —vi. To pitch a camp; to encamp.

campaign, kam-pān', n. Series of military operations in a definite theatre or with one objective or from taking the field to a temporary or final cessation of hostilities.

camphor, kam'fèr, n. A whitish, bitter, strong-smelling substance used in medicine. **camphorate,** kam'fèr-āt, vt (camphorating, camphorated). To impregnate with camphor.

can, kan, n. A cup or vessel for liquors.

can, kan, vi. (pret. could). To be able; to have sufficient moral or physical power.

Canada, kan'a-da, n. A British dominion of North America.

canal, ka-nal', n. A channel; an artificial watercourse for boats; a duct of the body.

canard, ka-när' or ka-närd', n. An absurd story; a false rumor.

canary, ka-nā'ri, n. Wine made in the Canary Isles; a finch from the Canary Isles.

cancel, kan'sel, vt. (canceling, canceled). To obliterate; to revoke; to set aside.—n. Act of canceling.

cancer, kan'sèr, n. One of the signs of the zodiac; a malignant growth in the body. **cancerous,** kan'sèr-us, a. Having the qualities of a cancer.

candelabrum, kan-de-lā'brum, n.; pl. **-ra.** A branched ornamental candle-stick.

candid, kan'did, a. Sincere; ingenuous. **candidly,** kan'did-li, adv. In a candid manner.

candidate, kan'di-dāt, n. One who proposes himself, or is proposed for some office; one who aspires after preferment

candied, kan'did, a. Preserved with sugar, or incrusted with it.

candle, kan'dl, n. A cylindrical body of tallow, wax, &c., surrounding a wick and used for giving light.

Candlemas, kan'dl-mas, n. A church festival on 2nd February, in honor of the purification of the Virgin Mary.

candlestick, kan'dl-stik, n. An instrument to hold a candle.

candor, kan'dèr, n. Frankness; sincerity

candy, kan'di, vi. (candying, candied)

o conserve with sugar; to form into crystals.—*vi.* To take on the form of candied sugar.—*n.* Crystallized sugar; a sweetmeat.

ane, kān, *n.* A reed; a walking-stick.—*t.* (caning, caned). To beat with a cane.

anine, ka'nīn, *a.* Pertaining to dogs.

aning, kān'ing, *n.* A beating with a cane.

anister, kan'is-tèr, *n.* A small box for tea, coffee, &c.; a case containing shot which bursts on being discharged.

anker, kang'kèr, *n.* A malignant ulcer; disease of trees; a disease in horses' feet; something that gnaws or corrodes.—*vt.* and *i.* To corrode or corrupt. **cankerous,** kang'kèr-us, *a.* Corroding.

ankerworm, kang'kèr-wèrm, *n.* A worm destructive to trees or plants.

annibal, kan'i-bal, *n.* A savage who eats human flesh.—*a.* Relating to cannibalism. **cannibalism,** kan'ni-bal-izm, *n.* The eating of human flesh by mankind.

annon, kan'un, *n.* A great gun; the striking of the players' ball on two other balls successively at billiards (Eng.).—*vi.* To strike with rebounding collision. **cannonade,** kan-un-ād', *n.* An attack with cannon.—*vt.* (cannonading, cannonaded). To attack with cannon; to batter with cannon-shot. **cannoneer,** kan-un-nēr', *n.* A man who manages cannon.

annot, kan'not. The negative of *can.*

anny, cannie, kan'i, *a.* Cautious; wary.

anoe, ka-nö', *n.* A boat made of the trunk of a tree, or of bark or skins; a light boat propelled by paddles.

anon, kan'on, *n.* A rule of doctrine or discipline; a law in general; the genuine books of the Holy Scriptures; a member of the cathedral chapter; a catalogue of saints canonized; a formula; a large kind of printing type. **canoness,** kan'on-es, *n.* A female canon. **canonical,** kan-on'ik-al, *a.* According to the canon; ecclesiastical. **canonicals,** kan-on'ik-alz, *n.pl.* The full dress of the clergy worn when they officiate. **canonist,** kan'on-st, *n.* One versed in canon or ecclesiastical law. **canonization,** kan'on-īz-ā"shon, *n.* Act of canonizing; state of being canonized. **canonize,** kan'on-īz, *vt.* (canonizing, canonized). To enroll in the canon as a saint.

anopy, kan'ö-pi, *n.* A covering over a throne, bed, or person's head. &c.—*vt.* (canopying, canopied). To cover with a canopy.

ant, kant, *vi.* To speak in a whining tone; to sham piety.—*vt.* To tilt up; to bevel.—*n.* A whining, hypocritical manner of speech; jargon; slang; inclination from a perpendicular or horizontal line; a toss or jerk.—*a.* Of the nature of cant or slang.

antankerous, kan-tang'kèr-us, *a.* Ill natured; cross; contentious.

antata, kan-tä'ta, *n.* A short musical composition in the form of an oratorio.

anteen, kan-tēn', *n.* A vessel used by soldiers for carrying liquor; a place in barracks where provisions, &c., are sold.

canter, kan'tèr, *n.* A moderate gallop.—*vi.* To move in a moderate gallop.

canticle, kan'ti-kl, *n.* A song; a passage of Scripture for chanting; in *pl.* the Song of Solomon.

cantilever, kan'ti-le"vèr, *n.* A bracket to carry moldings, eaves, balconies, &c.; one of two long arms projecting toward each other from opposite banks or piers, used in bridge-making.

cantle, kan'tl, *n.* A corner; a piece; the hind part of a saddle.

canto, kan'tō, *n.* A division of a poem; the treble part of a musical composition.

canton, kan'ton, *n.* A division of territory or its inhabitants.—*vt.* To divide into cantons; to allot separate quarters to different parts of an army. (In *milit. lan.* pron. kan-tön'.)

canvas, kan'vas, *n.* A coarse cloth; sailcloth; sails of ships; cloth for painting on; a painting.

canvass, kan'vas, *vt.* To scrutinize; to solicit the votes of.—*vi.* To solicit votes or interest; to use efforts to obtain.—*n.* Scrutiny; solicitation of votes. **canvasser,** kan'vas-èr, *n.* One who solicits votes, &c.

canyon, cañon, kan'yun, *n.* A long and narrow mountain gorge.

cap, kap, *n.* A covering for the head; something used as a cover; a top piece.—*vt.* (capping, capped). To put a cap on; to complete; to crown; to excel.

capable, kā'pa-bl, *a.* Having sufficient skill or power; competent; susceptible. **capability,** kā-pa-bil'i-ti, *n.* Quality of being capable.

capacity, ka-pas'i-ti, *n.* Power of holding; extent of space; ability; state.

capacious, ka-pā'shus, *a.* Wide; large; comprehensive.

caparison, ka-pa'ri-son, *n.* A covering laid over the saddle of a horse; clothing.—*vt.* To cover with a cloth; to dress richly.

cape, kāp, *n.* The point of a neck of land extending into the sea; a loose cloak hung from the shoulders.

caper, kā'pèr, *vi.* To prance; to spring.—*n.* A skip, spring, jump; the flower-bud of the caper-bush, much used for pickling. **caperer,** kā'pèr-èr, *n.* One who capers.

capillary, kap'i-la-ri or ka-pil'a-ri, *a.* Resembling a hair; having a bore of very small diameter.—*n.* A tube with a very small bore; a fine vessel or canal in an animal body.

capital, kap'i-tal, *a.* First in importance; metropolitan; affecting the head; punishable with death.—*n.* The uppermost part of a column; the chief city; the stock of a bank, tradesman, &c.; a large letter or type. **capitalist,** kap'i-tal-ist. *n.* A man who has a capital or wealth. **capitalize,** kap'i-tal-īz, *vt.* (capitalizing, capitalized). To convert into capital. **capitally,** kap'i-tal-i, *adv.* In a capital manner; so as to involve life.

Capitol, kap'it-ol, *n.* The temple of Jupiter in Rome; a citadel; a statehouse.

capitulate, ka-pit'ū-lāt, *vi.* (capitulating, capitulated). To surrender on conditions. **capitulation**, ka-pit'ū-lā"shun, *n.* Surrender on certain conditions.

capon, kā'pon, *n.* A young castrated cock.

caprice, ka-prēs', *n.* A freak; a sudden or unreasonable change of opinion or humor. **capricious**, ka-pri'shus, *a.* Full of caprice. **capriciously**, ka-pri'shus-li, *adv.* In a capricious manner; whimsically.

Capricorn, ka'pri-korn, *n.* The he-goat; one of the signs of the zodiac; the southern tropic.

capsize, kap-sīz', *vt.* (capsizing, capsized). To upset or overturn.

capstan, kap'stan, *n.* An apparatus in ships to raise great weights, weigh anchors, &c.

capsule, kap'sūl, *n.* A dry, many-seeded seed-vessel; an envelope for drugs. **capsular**, kap'sūl-ėr, *a.* Pertaining to a capsule; hollow like a capsule.

captain, kap'tin, *n.* A head officer; the commander of a ship, troop of horse, or company of infantry; a leader. **captaincy**, kap'tin-si, *n.* The rank, post, or commission of a captain.

caption, kap'shun, *n.* Text with picture, explaining it; or heading of article, chapter, page, &c.

captious, kap'shus, *a.* Ready to find fault; carping. **captiously**, kap'shus-li, *adv.* In a captious manner.

captivate, kap'ti-vāt, *vt.* (captivating, captivated). To take captive; to fascinate.

captive, kap'tiv, *n.* One taken in war; one ensnared by love, beauty, &c.—*a.* Made prisoner; kept in bondage. **captivity**, kap-tiv'i-ti, *n.* State or condition of being a captive; slavery. **captor**, kap'tėr, *n.* One who captures. **capture**, kap'tūr, *n.* Act of taking; the thing taken.—*vt.* (capturing, captured). To take by force or stratagem.

Capuchin, ka-pū-shēn', *n.* A Franciscan monk; a cloak with a hood.

car, kär, *n.* A chariot; a vehicle in pageants; a railway coach; an automobile.

caramel, ka'ra-mel, *n.* Burnt sugar, used to color spirits; a species of candy.

carat, ka'rat, *n.* A weight of four grains, for weighing diamonds, &c.; a word employed to denote the fineness of gold, pure gold being of twenty-four carats.

caravan, ka'ra-van, *n.* A company of travelers associated together for safety; a large close carriage.

caravansary, ka-ra-van'sa-ri, *n.* A house in the East, where caravans rest at night.

caraway, ka'ra-wä, *n.* A biennial, aromatic plant whose seeds are used in baking, &c.

carbide, kär'bīd, *n.* A compound of carbon with a metal.

carbine, carabine, kär'bīn, ka'ra-bīn, *n.* A short gun or rifle used chiefly by cavalry. **carbineer, carabineer**, kär-bin-ēr', ka'ra-bi-nēr", *n.* One who carries a carbine; a sort of light horseman.

carbolic, kär-bol'ik, *a.* An antiseptic and disinfecting acid obtained from coal tar.

carbon, kär'bon, *n.* Pure charcoal; elementary substance bright and britt **carbonaceous**, kär'bon-ā'shus, *a.* Pertaining to or containing carbon. **carbonate**, kär'bon-āt, *n.* A salt formed by the union of carbonic acid with a bas **carbonic**, kär-bon'ik, *a.* Pertaining carbon, or obtained from it. **carboniferous**, kär-bon-if'ėr-us, *a.* Producing containing carbon. **carbonize**, kär'boniz, *vt.* (carbonizing, carbonized). To convert into carbon.

carbuncle, kär'bung-kl, *n.* A fiery red precious stone; an inflammatory tumor.

carburetor, kar'bu-rā-tėr, *n.* An apparatus for sending air past a liquid fuel so as to provide an explosive mixture.

carcass, kär'kas, *a.* A dead body; anything decayed; a framework; a kind bomb.

card, kärd, *n.* A piece of pasteboard with figures, used in games; a piece of pasteboard containing a person's name, &c.; printed invitation; a note; the dial of compass; a large comb for wool or fla —*vt.* To comb wool, flax, hemp, &c.

cardamom, kär'da-mum, *n.* The aromatic capsule of various plants of th ginger family.

cardboard, kärd'bõrd, *n.* A stiff kind paper or pasteboard for making card &c.

cardiac, kär'di-ak, *a.* Pertaining to th heart; stimulating.—*n.* A cordial.

cardigan, kär'di-gan, *n.* A knitted waistcoat.

cardinal, kär'din-al, *a.* Chief; fundamental.—*n.* A dignitary in the Roma Catholic Church next to the pope; lady's short cloak.

care, kār, *n.* Solicitude; attention; objec of watchful regard.—*vi.* (caring, cared) To be solicitous; to be inclined; to hav regard. **careful**, kār'ful, *a.* Solicitous cautious. **carefully**, kär'ful-li, *adv.* I a careful manner. **carefulness**, kär'ful-nes, *n.* Quality of being careful **careless**, kär'les, *a.* Heedless; incau tious. **carelessly**, kär'les-li, *adv.* In careless way. **carelessness**, kär'les nes, *n.* Quality of being careless.

careen, ka-rēn', *vt.* To lay (a ship) o one side, for the purpose of repairing.— *vi.* To incline to one side.

career, ka-rēr', *n.* A race; course action.—*vi.* To move or run rapidly.

caress, ka-res', *vt.* To fondle; to em brace affectionately.—*n.* An act of en dearment. **caressingly**, ka-res'ing-l *adv.* In a caressing manner.

caret, kā'ret, *n.* In writing, this mark A, noting insertion.

caretaker, kär'tā-kėr, *n.* A person pu in charge of a house, farm, or the like.

cargo, kär'gō, *n.* The freight of a ship.

caribou, ka'ri-bö, *n.* An American va riety of the reindeer.

caricature, ka'ri-ka-tūr, *n.* A portrai or description so exaggerated as to excit ridicule.—*vt.* (caricaturing, caricatured) To represent by caricature.

caries, kā'ri-ēz, *n.* Ulceration of a bone

rillon, kar'i-lon, *n.* A chime of bells; simple air adapted to a set of bells.

rmine, kär'min, *n.* A bright crimson lor.

rnage, kär'nij, *n.* Great slaughter in ar; massacre; butchery.

rnal, kär'nal, *a.* Fleshly; sensual.

rnality, kär-nal'i-ti, *n.* Sensuality.

rnally, kär'nal-i, *adv.* In a carnal anner; according to the flesh.

rnation, kär-nä'shon, *n.* Flesh-color; sweet-scented plant with pink flowers.

rnival, kär'ni-val, *n.* A festival during he week before Lent; a revel.

rnivora, kär-niv'o-ra, *n.pl.* Animals at feed on flesh.

rnivorous, kär-niv'o-rus, *a.* Feeding flesh.

rol, kar'ul, *n.* A song of joy or devo-on; a warble.—*vi.* (caroling, caroled). sing; to warble.—*vt.* To celebrate in ng.

rotid, ka-rot'id, *a.* Pertaining to the vo great arteries in the neck conveying he blood to the head.

rouse, ka-rouz', *vi.* (carousing, ca-oused). To drink freely with noisy ollity.—*n.* A drinking bout. **carousal,** a-rouz'al, *n.* A noisy revel.

rp, kärp, *vi.* To cavil; to find fault.— A voracious fish, found in rivers and onds.

rpenter, kär'pen-tèr, *n.* One who orks in timber. **carpentry,** kär-pen-i, *n.* The trade, art, or work of a car-enter.

rpet, kär'pet, *n.* A woven fabric for overing floors, &c.—*vt.* To cover with a arpet.

rpetbag, kär'pet-bag, *n.* A traveling ag made of the same material as carpets. **rpetbagger,** kär'pet-bag-èr, *n.* An utsider who holds or seeks political of-ce.

rping, kär'ping, *a.* Caviling.

rriage, kar'ij, *n.* Act of carrying; hat which carries; a vehicle; convey-nce; price of carrying; behavior; de-neanor.

rrier, kar'i-èr, *n.* One who carries for ire.

rrion, kar'i-on, *n.* Dead and putrefy-ng flesh.—*a.* Relating to putrefying arcasses; feeding on carrion.

rrot, kar'ot, *n.* A yellowish or reddish sculent root of a tapering form. **car-oty,** kar'ot-i, *a.* Like a carrot in color.

rry, kar'i, *vt.* (carrying, carried). To ear, convey, or transport; to gain; to apture; to import; to behave.—*vi.* To onvey; to propel.—*n.* Onward motion.

rt, kärt, *n.* A carriage of burden with wo wheels.—*vt.* To carry or place on . cart. **cartage,** kärt'ij, *n.* Act of car-ying in a cart; the price paid for cart-ng.

rte blanche, kärt blänsh, *n.* A blank aper; unconditional terms.

rtel, kär-tel', *n.* A challenge; an agree-nent for the exchange of prisoners.

rtilage, kär'ti-lij, *n.* Gristle; an elas-ic substance from which bone is formed.

rtilaginous, kär-ti-laj'in-us, *a.* Per-aining to or resembling a cartilage.

cartography, kär-tog'ra-fi, *See* **char-tography.**

cartoon, kär-tön', *n.* A drawing for a fresco or tapestry; a pictorial sketch re-lating to a prevalent topic.

cartridge, kär'trij, *n.* A case containing the charge of a gun or any firearm.

carve, kärv, *vt.* (carving, carved). To cut; to engrave; to shape by cutting.—*vi.* To cut up meat; to sculpture.

carver, kärv'èr, *n.* One who carves; a large table-knife for carving.

carving, kärv'ing, *n.* The act or art of cutting meat or sculpturing figures; sculpture.

cascade, kas'kād, *n.* A waterfall.

case, kās, *n.* That which contains; a box; a receptacle; covering; an event; condition; a suit in court; a form in the inflection of nouns, &c.—*vt.* (casing, cased). To cover with a case; to put in a case.

caseharden, käs'här'dn, *vt.* To harden on the outside, as iron.

casein, caseine, kä'sē-in, *n.* That in-gredient in milk which forms curd and cheese.

casement, käs'ment, *n.* A case for a window.

cash, kash, *n.* Money; ready money; coin.—*vt.* To turn into money.

cashier, kash-ēr', *n.* One who has charge of money.—*vt.* To deprive of office; to dismiss; to break.

cashmere, kash'mēr, *n.* A rich kind of shawl; a fine woolen stuff.

casing, käs'ing, *n.* Act of putting in a case; a covering.

casino, ka-sē'nō, *n.* A public dancing, singing, or gaming saloon.

cask, kask, *n.* A vessel for containing liquors.

casket, kask'et, *n.* A small chest for jewels.

casserole, kas'e-röl, *n.* A saucepan; a kind of stew.

cassimere, kas'si-mēr, *n.* A twilled woolen cloth.

cassock, kas'uk, *n.* A close garment worn by clergymen under the gown.

cast, kast, *vt.* (casting, cast). To throw; to impel; to throw off; to let fall; to condemn; to compute; to model; to found; to scatter (seed); to bring forth immaturely.—*vi.* To revolve in the mind; to contrive (with *about*); to warp.—*n.* A throw; the thing thrown; manner of throwing; distance passed by a thing thrown; a squint; form; a tinge; manner; that which is formed from a mold; a company of actors.

castanet, kas-ta-net', *n.* Small pieces of wood or ivory struck together in dancing.

castaway, kast'a-wä, *n.* A person aban-doned; a reprobate.

caste, kast, *n.* A distinct hereditary or-der among the Hindus; a class of society.

castigate, kas'ti-gāt, *vt.* (castigating, castigated). To chastise; to punish by stripes. **castigation,** kas-ti-gā'shun, *n.* Chastisement. **castigator,** kas'ti-gā-tèr, *n.* One who corrects.

casting, kast'ing, *n.* Act of casting; that which is cast in a mold.

cast iron, kast' i'ẽrn, *n.* Iron which has been cast into pigs or molds.

castle, kas'l, *n.* A fortified building; a large and imposing mansion; a piece in chess.

castoff, kast'of, *a.* Laid aside; rejected.

caster, kas'tẽr, *n.* A small cruet; a small wheel on the leg of a table; &c.

castor oil, kas'tẽr oil, *n.* A medicinal oil obtained from a tropical plant.

castrate, kas'trāt, *vt.* (castrating, castrated). To geld; to emasculate; to expurgate. **castration,** kas-trā'shun, *n.* Act of castrating.

casual, kazh'ū-al, *a.* Happening by chance; occasional; contingent. **casually,** kazh'ū-al-li, *adv.* In a casual manner; by chance. **casualty,** kazh'ū-al-ti, *n.* Accident, especially one resulting in death or injury.

casuist, kazh'ū-ist, *n.* One who studies and resolves cases of conscience. **casuistic,** kazh-ū-is'tic, *a.* Relating to cases of conscience or conduct.

cat, kat, *n.* A domestic animal of the feline tribe; a strong tackle; a double tripod; an instrument for flogging.

cataclysm, kat'a-klizm, *n.* A deluge; a sudden overwhelming catastrophe.

catacomb, ka'ta-kōm, *n.* A subterranean place for the burial of the dead.

Cat

catalepsy, ka'ta-lep-si, *n.* A nervous affection suspending motion and sensation. **cataleptic,** ka-ta-lep'tik, *a.* Pertaining to catalepsy.

catalogue, ka'ta-log, *n.* A list; a register.—*vt.* (cataloguing, catalogued). To make a list of.

catapult, kat'a-pult, *n.* An apparatus for throwing stones, &c.

cataract, kat'a-rakt, *n.* A great waterfall; a disease of the eye.

catarrh, ka-tär', *n.* A flow of mucus from the nose, &c.; a cold. **catarrhal,** ka-tär'al, *a.* Pertaining to or produced by catarrh.

catastrophe, ka-tas'trō-fē, *n.* Calamity or disaster; final event.

catch, kach, *vt.* (catching, caught). To lay hold on; to stop the falling of; to grasp; to entangle; to receive by contagion; to be seized with; to get.—*vi.* To lay hold; to be contagious.—*n.* Act of seizing; anything that takes hold; a sudden advantage taken; something desirable; a capture; a song. **catching,** kach'ing, *a.* Infectious; charming.

catchup, catsup, kach'up, kat'sup. *n.* A sauce made from mushrooms, &c.; ketchup.

catchword, kach'wẽrd, *n.* A word under the last line of a page, repeated at the top of the next; the last word of a preceding speaker.

catechetic, ka-tē-ket'ik, *a.* Relating to a catechism or catechisms. **catechetically,** ka-tē-ket'ik-al-li, *adv.* In a catechetic manner.

catechise, ka-tē-kīz, (catechising, catechised). To instruct by question and answer; to question. **catechism,** ka-tē-kizm, *n.* A manual of instruction by questions and answers, especially in religion. **catechist,** ka-tē-kist, *n.* One who catechises.

category, kat'ē-gō-ri, *n.* One of the highest classes to which objects of thought can be referred; class; a general head. **categorical,** ka-tē-go'ri-kal, *a.* Pertaining to a category; absolute; positive. **categorically,** ka-tē-go'ri-kal-li, *adv.* Absolutely; directly; positively.

cater, kā-tẽr, *vi.* To buy or procure provisions, food, entertainment, &c. **caterer,** kā'tẽr-ẽr, *n.* One who caters. **cateress,** kā'tẽr-es, *n.* A woman who caters.

caterpillar, kat'ẽr-pil-ẽr, *n.* The hairy wormlike grub of butterflies and moths.

caterpillar tractor, *n.* A tractor which travels upon two endless belts, one on each side of the machine kept in motion by cogged driving wheels so that the tractor moves forward with the revolution of the belts which carries it over very rough ground.

caterwaul, kat'ẽr-wal, *vi.* To cry as cats.

catgut, kat'gut, *n.* The intestines of sheep prepared for the strings of musical instruments, &c.; a kind of linen or canvas.

cathartic, ka-thär'tik, *a.* Purging.—*n.* A medicine that purges.

cathedral, ka-thē'dral, *n.* The principal church in a diocese.

cathode, kath'ōd, *n.* The negative pole of an electric current.

catholic, ka'thol-ik, *a.* Universal; liberal; pertaining to the universal Church; pertaining to the Roman Catholic Church.—*n.* A member of the universal Christian Church; an adherent of the Roman Catholic Church. **catholicism,** ka-thol'i-sizm, *n.* Adherence to the Catholic Church; adherence to the Roman Catholic Church; the Roman Catholic religion. **catholicity,** kath'o-lis'i-ti, *n.* Universality; liberality.

catmint, catnip, kat'mint, kat'nip, *n.* A strong-scented labiate plant.

cat's-eye, kats'ī, *n.* A variety of chalcedony.

cat's-paw, kats'pa, *n.* A light breeze; a dupe; a tool.

cattle, kat'l, *n.pl.* Domestic quadrupeds serving for tillage or food; bovine animals.

caucus, ka̦'kus, *n.* A private committee to manage election matters.

caudal, ka̦'dal, *a.* Pertaining to a tail.

cauliflower, ka̦'li-flou-ẽr, *n.* A variety of cabbage.

caulk, kak, *vt.* To drive oakum into the seams of (a ship) to prevent leaking; to calk.

cause, ka̦z, *n.* That which produces an effect; reason; origin; sake; purpose; a suit in court; that which a person or party espouses.—*vt.* (causing, caused). To effect; to bring about. **causal,** ka̦z'al, *a.* Implying cause. **causality,** ka̦z-al'i-ti, *n.* The agency of a cause. **causation,**

tion, kąz-ā′shun, n. The act or agency by which an effect is produced. causative, kąz′a-tiv, a. That expresses a cause or reason; that effects.

causeless, kąz′les, a. Having no cause.

causeway, causey, kąz′wā, kąz′i, n. A raised road; a paved way.

caustic, kąs′tik, a. Burning; corroding; cutting.—n. A substance which burns the flesh. caustically, kąs′tik-al-li, adv. In a caustic manner; severely. causticity, kąs-tis′i-ti, n. Quality of being caustic; severity; cutting remarks.

cauterize, ką′tėr-iz, vt. To burn with caustics, or hot iron as morbid flesh. cautery, ką′tė-ri, n. A burning or searing by a hot iron, or caustic substances. cauterization, ką′ter-i-zā′shun, n. Act of cauterizing.

caution, ką′shun, n. Care; wariness; warning; pledge.—vt. To warn. cautionary, ką′shun-a-ri, a. Containing caution; given as a pledge. cautious, ką′shus, a. Using caution; wary; circumspect; prudent. cautiously, ką′shus-li, adv. With caution.

cavalcade, kav′al-kād, n. A procession of persons on horseback.

cavalier, kav-a-lėr′, n. A horseman; a gay military man; a beau.—a. Gay; brave; haughty; supercilious. cavalierly, kav-a-lėr′li, adv. Haughtily.

cavalry, kav′al-ri, n. A body of troops mounted.

cave, kāv, n. A hollow place in the earth; a den.

caveat, kā′vē-at, n. A warning; a process to stop proceedings in a court.

cavern, ka′vėrn, n. A large cave. caverned, ka′vėrnd, a. Full of caverns; forming or inhabiting a cavern. cavernous, ka′vėr-nus, a. Hollow; full of caverns.

caviare, caviar, kav-i-är′, n. The roe of the sturgeon salted and prepared for food.

cavil, kav′il, vi. (caviling, caviled). To carp; to find fault with insufficient reason.—n. A captious objection. caviler, ka′vil-ėr, n. One who cavils.

cavity, kav′i-ti, n. A hollow place.

caw, ką, vi. To cry like a crow, rook, or raven.—n. The cry of the rook or crow.

cayenne, ką-en′, n. A pepper made from capsicum seeds.

cease, sēs, vi. (ceasing, ceased). To leave off; to fail; to stop; to become extinct.—vt. To put a stop to. ceaseless, sēs′les, a. Incessant; perpetual. ceaselessly, sēs′les-li, adv. Incessantly.

cedar, sē′dėr, n. A large coniferous tree. —a. Made of cedar; belonging to cedar.

cede, sēd, vt. (ceding, ceded). To give up; to surrender.—vi. To yield; to lapse.

ceiling, sēl′ing, n. The upper inside surface of a room.

ceiling, sēl′ing, n. The highest altitude to which an aircraft can attain under given conditions.

celebrant, sel′ē-brant, n. One who performs a public religious rite.

celebrate, sel′ē-brāt, vt. (celebrating, celebrated). To honor by solemn rites; to praise; to commemorate. celebrated, se′lē-brāt-ed, a. Famous. celebration, se-lē-brā′shun, n. The act of celebrating; ceremonious performance.

celebrity, se-leb′ri-ti, n. Fame; eminence.

celerity, sē-ler′i-ti, n. Speed; quickness.

celery, sel′e-ri, n. An umbelliferous plant cultivated for the table.

celestial, sē-les′chal, a. Heavenly; pertaining to heaven.—n. An inhabitant of heaven.

celibacy, sel′i-ba-ṣi, n. The unmarried state; a single life. celibate, se′li-bāt, n. One who intentionally remains unmarried.—a. Unmarried.

cell, sel, n. A small room; a cave; a small mass of protoplasm forming the structural unit in animal tissues.

cellar, sel′lėr, n. An apartment underground used for storage.

cello, chel′ō, n. A stringed instrument of the violin family.

cellophane, sel′ō-fān, n. A transparent film made from cellulose.

cellular, sel′ū-lėr, a. Consisting of cells.

celluloid, sel′ū-loid, n. An artificial substitute for ivory, bone, coral, &c.

Celt, selt, n. One of a race of Western Europe; a prehistoric cutting instrument. Celtic, sel′tik, a. Pertaining to the Celts.—n. Their language.

cement, sē-ment′, n. An adhesive substance which unites bodies; mortar; bond of union.—vt. To unite closely.—vi. To unite and cohere. cementation, sē-men-tā′shun, n. Act of cementing.

cemetery, se′mē-te-ri, n. A burial-place.

censor, sen′sėr, n. One who examines manuscripts, &c., before they are published; one who censures. censorial, sen-sō′ri-al, a. Belonging to a censor. censorious, sen-sō′ri-us, a. Addicted to censure. censoriously, sen-sō′ri-us-li, adv. In a censorious manner. censorship, sen′sėr-ship, n. The office or dignity of a censor.

censure, sen′shūr, n. Severe judgment; reproof.—vt. (censuring, censured). To judge unfavorably of; to blame. censurable, sen′shūr-a-bl, a. Blamable. censurably, sen′shūr-a-bli, adv. In a manner worthy of blame.

census, sen′sus, n. An enumeration of the inhabitants of a country.

cent, sent, n. A hundred; a copper coin, the hundredth part of a dollar.—Per cent, a certain rate by the hundred.

centaur, sen′tąr, n. A fabulous being, half man and half horse.

centenarian, sen-te-nā′ri-an, n. A person a hundred years old.

centenary, sen′te-na-ri, a. Pertaining to a hundred.—n. Period of a hundred years; commemoration of an event a hundred years earlier.

centennial, sen-ten′i-al, a. Consisting of a hundred years; happening every hundred years.

center, sen′tėr, n. The middle point; a nucleus.—vt. (centering, centered). To fix on a center; to collect to a point.—

vi. To be collected to a point; to have as a center.

centerboard, sen'tēr-bōrd, *n.* A movable keel in yachts.

centesimal, sen-tes'i-mal, *a.* The hundredth.—*n.* The hundredth part.

centigrade, sen'ti-grād, *a.* Divided into a hundred degrees.

centimeter, sen'ti-mē-tr, *n.* The hundredth part of a meter, about two-fifths of an inch.

centipede, sen'ti-pēd, *n.* An insect having a great number of feet.

central, sen'tral, *a.* Placed in the center; relating to the center. **centralization,** sen'tral-I-zā'shun, *n.* Act of centralizing. **centralize,** sen'tral-īz, *vt.* (centralizing, centralized). To render central; to concentrate. **centrally,** sen'tral-li, *adv.* In a central manner.

centurion, sen-tū'ri-on, *n.* Among the Romans, the captain of a hundred men.

century, sen'tū-ri, *n.* A hundred; the period of a hundred years.

cephalic, se-fal'ik, *a.* Pertaining to the head.

ceramic, se-ram'ik, *a.* Pertaining to the manufacture of porcelain and earthenware.

cere, sēr, *n.* The waxlike skin that covers the base of the bill in some birds. —*vt.* (cering, cered). To wax or cover with wax.

cereal, sē'rē-al, *a.* Pertaining to grain.— *n.* A grain plant.

cerebral, ser'ē-bral, *a.* Pertaining to the brain. **cerebration,** ser-ē-brā'shun, *n.* Action of the brain, conscious or unconscious.

ceremony, ser'ē-mō-ni, *n.* Outward rite; form; observance; formality. **ceremonial,** ser-ē-mō'ni-al, *a.* Relating to ceremony.—*n.* Sacred rite; outward form. **ceremonially,** ser-ē-mō'ni-al-li, *adv.* In a ceremonial or formal manner. **ceremonious.** ser-ē-mō'ni-us, *a.* Formal. **ceremoniously,** se-rē-mō'ni-us-li, *adv.* In a ceremonious manner.

cerise, se-rēz', *n.* Cherry-color.

certain, sēr'tin, *a.* Sure; undeniable; decided; particular; some; one. **certainly,** sēr'tin-li, *adv.* Without doubt. **certainty,** sēr'tin-ti, *n.* A fixed or real state; truth; fact; regularity.

certificate, sēr-tif'i-kit, *n.* A written testimony; a credential. **certifier,** sēr'ti-fī-ēr, *n.* One who certifies. **certify,** sēr'ti-fī, *vt.* (certifying, certified). To give certain information; to testify to in writing.

cessation, se-sā'shun, *n.* Stoppage.

cession, sesh'un, *n.* Surrender; a yielding up.

cesspool, ses'pōl, *n.* A receptacle for sewage.

chafe, chāf, *vt.* (chafing, chafed). To make warm by rubbing; to fret by rubbing; to enrage.—*vi.* To be fretted by friction; to rage.—*n.* A heat; a fretting.

chaff, chaf, *n.* The husk of corn and grasses; batter.—*vt.* To banter.

chagrin, sha-grin', *n.* Ill-humor; vexation.—*vt.* To vex; to mortify.

chain, chān, *n.* A series of links; a line

of things connected; that which binds; a line formed of links, 66 feet long; (*pl.*) bondage; slavery.—*vt.* To bind with a chain; to confine.

chair, chār, *n.* A movable seat; an official seat; professorship.—*vt.* To place or carry in a chair.

chairman, chār'man, *n.* The presiding officer of an assembly; a president.

chairmanship, chār'man-ship, *n.* The office of a chairman.

chaise, shāz, *n.* A light horse carriage.

chalcedony, kal-sed'ō-ni, *n.* A variety of quartz, having a whitish color.

Chaldaic, Chaldean, Chaldee, kal-dā'ik, kal-dē'an, kal'dē, *a.* Pertaining to Chaldea.—*n.* The language of the Chaldeans.

chalice, chal'is, *n.* A drinking-cup.

chalk, chak, *n.* A white calcareous earth or carbonate of lime.—*vt.* To mark with chalk. **chalky,** chak'i, *a.* Resembling chalk; consisting of or containing chalk.

challenge, chal'enj, *n.* A summons to fight; a calling in question; an exception taken.—*vt.* (challenging, challenged). To summon to a fight; to defy; to call in question; to object to. **challengeable,** chal'enj-a-bl, *a.* That may be challenged. **challenger,** chal'en-jer, *n.* One who challenges.

chamber, chām'bēr, *n.* An apartment; an office; a hall of justice or legislation; a legislative body. **chambered,** chām'bērd, *a.* Having chambers; shut up in a chamber.

chamberlain, chām'bēr-lin, *n.* One who has charge of the chambers of a monarch or noble; an officer of state; a city treasurer; a steward.

chambermaid, chām'bēr-mād, *n.* A female servant who has the care of chambers.

chameleon, ka-mē'lē-un, *n.* A species of lizard whose color changes.

chamois, sham'i, or sha'mwą, *n.* A species of antelope; a soft leather.

champ, champ, *vt.* To devour with violent action of the teeth; to bite the bit, as a horse. —*vi.* To keep biting.

Chamois.

champagne, sham-pān', *n.* A kind of brisk sparkling wine.

champaign, sham'pān, *a.* Open; level. *n.* A flat open country.

champion, cham'pi-un, *n.* A combatant for another, or for a cause; a hero; one victorious in contest.—*vt.* To fight for. **championship,** cham'pi-un-ship, *n.* State of being a champion; support of a cause.

chance, chans, *n.* That which happens; accident; possibility of an occurrence; opportunity.—*vi.* (chancing, chanced). To happen.—*a.* Happening by chance; casual.

chancel, chan'sel, *n.* That part of a church where the altar is placed.

chancellor, chan'se-lēr, *n.* A high judicial officer who presides over a court of chancery, &c.; a presiding official. **chancellorship,** chan'se-lėr-ship, *n.* The office of a chancellor.

chancery, chan'se-ri, *n.* A court of public affairs; in England, a division of the High Court of Justice.

chancre, shang'kėr, *n.* An ulcer which arises from the venereal virus.

chandelier, shan-dē-lēr', *n.* A frame with branches for candles or lamps.

chandler, chan'dlėr, *n.* A maker and seller of candles; a retail dealer.

change, chānj, *vt.* (changing, changed). To cause to turn from one state to another; to substitute; to give one kind of money for another.—*vi.* To be altered. —*n.* Variation; small money. **changeable,** chān'ja-bl, *a.* Subject to alteration; fickle; wavering. **changeably,** chān'ja-bli, *adv.* Inconstantly. **changeful,** chānj'ful, *a.* Full of change; inconstant; mutable; fickle; uncertain. **changeling,** chānj'ling, *n.* A child substituted for another; a fool; one apt to change.

channel, chan'el, *n.* A watercourse; a narrow sea; means of passing or transmitting.—*vt.* (channeling, channeled). To form into a channel; to groove.

channeled, chan'eld, *a.* Grooved longitudinally.

chant, chant, *vt.* and *i.* To sing; to sing after the manner of a chant.—*n.* Song; a kind of sacred music; a part of church service.

chanter, chan'tėr, *n.* A singer; a bagpipe tube with finger-holes.

chanticleer, chan'ti-klėr, *n.* A cock.

chantry, chan'tri, *n.* A chapel where priests sing or say mass for the souls of others.

chaos, kā'os, *n.* Confused mass; disorder. **chaotic,** kā-ot'ik, *a.* Pertaining to chaos.

chap, chap, *vt.* (chapping, chapped). To cause to crack.—*vi.* To open in slits.— *n.* A crack in the skin; the jaw; a young fellow.

chapel, chap'el, *n.* A place of worship; a church; a sanctuary.

chaperon, shap'e-rōn, *n.* A married lady who attends a young lady to public places.—*vt.* To act as chaperon to.

chaplain, chap'lin, *n.* A clergyman of the army, navy, court, &c. **chaplaincy,** chap'lān-si, *n.* The office of a chaplain.

chapter, chap'tėr, *n.* Division of a book; a society of clergymen belonging to a cathedral or collegiate church; an organized branch of some fraternity.

char, chär, *vt.* (charring, charred). To reduce to carbon by burning; to burn slightly.—*n.* A charred body; a lake fish of the salmon kind.

character, kar'ak-tėr, *n.* A mark engraved; a letter or figure; manner of writing; distinctive qualities of a person or thing; certificate of qualifications; a person in fiction or drama; a peculiar person. **characteristic,** kar'ak-tėr-is"-tik, *a.* Constituting character; marking distinctive qualities.—*n.* That which constitutes character. **characteristically,** kar'ak-tėr-is"tik-al-li, *adv.* In a

characteristic manner. **characterize,** kar'ak-tėr-īz, *vt.* To give a character to; to designate.

charade, sba-räd', *n.* A species of riddle upon the syllables of a word.

charcoal, chär'kōl, *n.* Coal made by charring wood; the residue of animal, vegetable, and many mineral substances, when heated to redness in close vessels.

charge, chärj, *vt.* (charging, charged). To load; to put a price on; to entrust; to impute, as a debt or crime; to command; to confide; to attach.—*vi.* To make a charge or onset.—*n.* That which is laid on; that which loads a rifle, &c.; an assault or onset; order; instruction; person or thing committed to another's care; accusation; cost. **chargeable,** chär'ja-bl, *a.* That may be charged.

chargé d'affaires, shär-zhä'dä-far', *n.* One who transacts diplomatic business in place of an ambassador.

charger, chär'jer, *n.* A large dish; a warhorse.

chariot, char'i-ot, *n.* A stately carriage with four wheels.

charioteer, char'i-ot-ēr", *n.* The person who drives or conducts a chariot.

charity, cha'ri-ti, *n.* A disposition to relieve the wants of others; benevolence; alms; a charitable institution. **charitable,** char'it-a-bl, *a.* Liberal to the poor; pertaining to charity; indulgent. **charitably,** char'it-a-bli, *adv.* In a charitable manner; kindly; liberally.

charlatan, shär'la-tan, *n.* A quack.

charm, chärm, *n.* A spell; fascination; a locket, &c.—*vt.* To enthrall; to delight. **charmer,** chär'mėr, *n.* One who charms. **charming,** chär'ming, *a.* Enchanting. **charmingly,** chär'ming-li, *adv.* In a charming manner.

charnel-house, chär'nel-hous, *n.* A place for bones of the dead.

chart, chärt, *n.* A map; delineation of coasts, &c.; tabulated facts.

charter, chär'tėr, *n.* A writing given as evidence of a grant, contract, &c.—*vt.* To establish by charter; to hire or to let (a ship). **chartered,** chär'tėrd, *a.* Granted by charter; privileged.

chartography, kär-tog'ra-fi, *n.* The art or practice of drawing up charts.

charwoman, chär'wųm-un, *n.* A woman hired for odd work, or for single days.

chary, chā'ri, *a.* Careful; wary; frugal.

chase, chäs, *vt.* (chasing, chased). To pursue; to hunt; to enchase; to cut into the form of a screw.—*n.* Pursuit; hunt; that which is pursued; a printer's frame.

chassis, shas'i, *n.* Frame of an automobile.

chaste, chäst, *a.* Free from impure desires; undefiled; pure in taste and style. **chastely,** chäst'li, *adv.* In a chaste manner; purely. **chasten,** chās'n, *vt.* To afflict in order to reclaim; to chastise; to correct. **chastise,** chas-tīz', *vt.* (chastising, chastised).—To correct by punishment. **chastisement,** chas'tiz-ment, *n.* Correction. **chastity,** chas'ti-ti, *n.* Purity of the body, mind, language, or style.

chat, chat, *vi.* (chatting, chatted). To

talk familiarly.—*n.* Familiar talk; a small songbird.

chateau, sha'tō, *n.* A castle; a country seat.

chattel, chat'l, *n.* Any article of movable goods; in law, all goods except such as have the nature of freehold.

chatter, chat'ẻr, *vi.* To make a noise by repeated clashing of the teeth; to jabber. —*n.* Sounds like those of a magpie or monkey; idle talk.

chatterbox, chat'ẻr-boks, *n.* One that talks incessantly; applied chiefly to children.

chatty, chat'i, *a.* Talkative.

chauffeur, shō-fẻr', *n.* The motorist of an automobile; a stoker. **chauffeuse,** shō-fōs', *n.* A female motorist.

cheap, chēp, *a.* Of a low price; common; not respected. **cheapness,** chēp'-nes, *n.* State or quality of being cheap; lowness in price.

cheat, chēt, *vt.* To defraud; to deceive. —*n.* A deceitful act; a swindler.

check, chek, *vt.* To stop; to curb; to chide; to compare with corresponding evidence.—*vi.* To stop; to clash or interfere.—*n.* An attack made on the king in chess; a stop; control; a counterfoil; a token; cloth with a square pattern; an order for money. **checker,** chek'ẻr, *n.* One who checks; a square pattern; an exchequer or treasury; *pl.* the game of draughts.—*vt.* To mark with little squares; to variegate. **checkered,** chek'ẻrd, *p.a.* Marked with squares; crossed with good and bad fortune.

checkmate, chek'māt, *n.* A movement in chess which ends the game; defeat.—*vt.* To give checkmate to; to frustrate; to defeat.

Cheddar, ched'ẻr, *n.* A rich English cheese.

cheek, chēk, *n.* The side of the face below the eyes on each side; impudence.

cheep, chēp, *vi.* and *t.* To pule; to chirp. —*n.* A chirp.

cheer, chēr, *n.* Expression of countenance; gayety; viands; a shout of joy. —*vt.* To brighten the countenance of; to gladden; to applaud. *vi.* To grow cheerful. **cheerful,** chēr'ful, *a.* Gay; sprightly; willing. **cheerfully,** chēr'-ful-li, *adv.* In a cheerful manner. **cheerily,** chēr'i-li, *adv.* With cheerfulness. **cheering,** chēr'ing, *a.* Encouraging. **cheerless,** chēr'les, *a.* Gloomy; dejected. **cheery,** chēr'i, *a.* Blithe; sprightly; promoting cheerfulness.

cheese, chēz, *n.* Coagulated milk pressed into a firm mass, and used as food; anything in the form of cheese. **cheesemonger,** chēz'mung-gẻr, *n.* One who deals in or sells cheese (Eng.). **cheeseparing,** chēz'pār-ing, *n.* The rind of cheese.—*a.* Meanly economical. **cheesepress,** chēz'pres, *n.* A press or engine for making cheese. **cheesy,** chēz'i, *a.* Resembling cheese.

chef, shef, *n.* A head cook.

chemical, kem'ik-al, *a.* Pertaining to chemistry. **chemically,** kem'ik-al-li, *adv.* By chemical process or operation.

chemist, kem'ist, *n.* One versed in chemistry. **chemistry,** kem'is-tri, *n.*

The science which treats of the properties and nature of elementary substances.

chemise, she-mēz', *n.* An under garment worn by females.

cheque, chequer. *See* **check, checker.**

cherish, cher'ish, *vt.* To treat with tenderness; to encourage.

cherry, cher'i, *n.* A tree and its fruit, of the plum family.—*a.* Like a cherry in color.

cherub, cher'ub, *n.*; *pl.* **-ubs** and **-ubim.** An angel of the second order; a beautiful child. **cherubic,** che-rū'bik, *a.* Angelic.

chess, ches, *n.* A game played by two parties, with 16 pieces each on a board of 64 squares.

chessboard, ches'bōrd, *n.* The checkered board used in the game of chess.

chessman, ches'man, *n.* A piece used in the game of chess.

chest, chest, *n.* A large close box; the part of the body containing the heart, lungs, &c.—*vt.* To reposit in a chest.

chestnut, ches'nut, *n.* A kind of tree; its fruit or nut.—*a.* Of the color of a chestnut; reddish-brown.

chevalier, she'va-lẻr, *n.* A horseman; a knight.

chevron, shev'run, *n.* A heraldic figure representing two rafters of a house meeting at the top; similar mark on uniform.

chew, chö, *vt.* To grind with the teeth; to masticate.

chic, shek, *n.* Easy elegance; smartness.

chicane, chicanery, shi-kān', shi-kān'ẻr-i, *n.* Trickery; artifice. **chicane,** *vi.* (chicaning, chicaned). To use chicane or artifices. **chicaner,** shi-kān'ẻr, *n.* One who uses chicane.

chick, chicken, chik, chik'en, *n.* The young of various birds; a child.

chickenhearted, chik'en-här-ted, *a.* Timid; fearful; cowardly.

chicken pox, chik'en poks, *n.* An eruptive disease, generally appearing in children.

chickweed, chik'wēd, *n.* A weed of which chickens and birds are fond.

chicory, chik'o-ri, *n.* A common English plant, often used to mix with coffee.

chide, chīd, *vt.* and *i.* (chiding, pret. chid, pp. chid, chidden). To reprove; to scold.

chief, chēf, *a.* Being at the head; first; leading.—*n.* A principal person; a leader. **chiefly,** chēf'li, *adv.* Mainly; especially. **chieftain,** chēf'tin, *n.* A chief; the head of a troop, army, or clan. **chieftaincy, chieftainship,** chēf'-tin-si, chēf'tin-ship, *n.* Rank or office of a chieftain.

chiffonier, shif'fon-ẻr, *n.* A small sideboard.

chilblain, chil'blān, *n.* A blain or sore produced on the hands or feet by cold.

child, child, *n.*; *pl.* **children,** An infant; one very young; a son or daughter; offspring.

childbearing, chīld'bār-ing, *n.* The act of bringing forth children.

childbed, child'bed, *n.* The state of a woman in labor.

childbirth, child'bẽrth, *n.* The act of bringing forth a child; travail; labor.

childe, child, *n.* A noble youth; a squire.

childhood, child'hud, *n.* State of a child.

childish, child'ish, *a.* Like a child; trifling.

childless, child'les, *a.* Destitute of children.

childlike, child'lik, *a.* Like a child; innocent.

chill, chil, *n.* A shivering with cold; a cold fit; that which checks or disheartens.—*a.* Cold; tending to cause shivering; dispiriting.—*vt.* To make cold; to discourage. **chilling,** chil'ing, *a.* Causing to shiver; tending to repress enthusiasm. **chilly,** chil'i, *a.* Moderately chill.

chime, chim, *n.* A set of bells tuned to each other; their sound; harmony; the brim of a cask.—*vi.* (chiming, chimed). To sound in consonance; to agree.—*vt.* To cause to sound in harmony; to cause to sound.

chimera, ki-mẽr'a, *n.* A fire-breathing monster of fable; a vain or idle fancy. **chimerical,** ki-mer'ik-al, *a.* Wildly or vainly conceived.

chimney, chim'ni, *n.* The funnel through which the smoke is conveyed; a flue; a glass funnel for a lamp, &c.

chimpanzee, chim-pan'zē or chim'pan-zē, *n.* A large W. African ape.

chin, chin, *n.* The lower part of the face; the point of the under jaw.

china, chī'na, *n.* A species of fine porcelain.

chinchilla, chin-chil'a, *n.* A genus of S. American rodent animals; their fur.

Chinese. chī-nēz', *n.sing.* and *pl.* A native of China; the language of China.

chink, chingk, *n.* A narrow opening; a cleft; a sharp metallic sound; money.—*vi.* To crack; to make a sound as by the collision of coins.—*vt.* To jingle, as coins. **chinky,** chingk'i, *a.* Full of fissures.

chintz, chints, *n.* Cotton cloth printed with colored designs.

chip, chip, *n.* A fragment; a small piece. —*vt.* (chipping, chipped). To cut into chips; to cut off chips.—*vi.* To fly off in small pieces.

chiropodist, kī-rop'o-dist, *n.* One who extracts corns, removes bunions, &c.

chirp, chẽrp, *vi.* To make the lively noise of small birds.—*n.* A short, shrill note of birds.

chisel, chiz'l, *n.* A cutting tool, used in woodwork, masonry, sculpture, &c.—*vt.* (chiseling, chiseled). To cut, gouge, or engrave with a chisel. **chiseled,** chiz'ld, *p.a.* Cut with a chisel; clearcut.

chit, chit, *n.* A child; a shoot or sprout.

chitchat, chit'chat, *n.* Prattle.

chivalry, shiv'al-ri, *n.* Knighthood; customs pertaining to the orders of knighthood; heroic defense of life and honor. **chivalric, chivalrous,** shiv'al-rik,

shiv'al-rus, *a.* Pertaaining to chivalry; gallant.

chive, chiv, *n.* A perennial plant of the onion family.

chloral, klō'ral, *n.* An oily liquid produced from chlorine and alcohol; a narcotic.

chloride, klō'rid, *n.* A compound of chlorine and some other substance.

chlorine, klō'rēn, *n.* A gaseous substance obtained from common salt, used in bleaching and disinfecting.

chlorodyne, klō'rō-dēn, *n.* An anodyne, containing morphia, chloroform, and prussic acid.

chloroform, klō'rō-form, *n.* A volatile thin liquid, an anæsthetic.

chlorophyll, klō'rō-fil, *n.* The green coloring matter of plants.

chocolate, chok'ō-lit, *n.* A preparation from the kernels of the cacao-nut.—*a.* Dark, glossy brown.

choice, chois, *n.* Act of choosing; option; the thing chosen; best part of anything; the object of choice.—*a.* Select; precious.

choir, kwir, *n.* A body of singers in a church; part of a church set apart for the singers.

choke, chōk, *vt.* (choking, choked). To strangle by compressing the throat of; to block up; to stifle.—*vi.* To be suffocated; to be blocked up.

choler, kol'ẽr, *n.* Anger; wrath.

cholera, kol'ẽr-a, *n.* A disease accompanied by purging and vomiting.

choleric, kol'ẽr-ik, *a.* Irascible; peevish.

choose, chöz, *vt.* (choosing; pret. chose; pp. chosen). To take by preference.—*vi.* To make choice; to prefer. **chooser,** chöz'ẽr, *n.* One who chooses.

chop, chop, *vt.* (chopping, chopped). To cut into small pieces; to barter or exchange.—*vi.* To change; to turn suddenly.—*n.* A piece chopped off; a small piece of meat; a crack or cleft; a turn or change; the jaw; the mouth. **chopfallen,** chop'fal-en, *a.* Dejected. **choppy,** chop'i, *a.* Full of clefts; having short, abrupt waves.

chopsticks, chop'stiks, *n.* Two sticks of wood, ivory, &c., used by the Chinese in eating.

choral, kō'ral, *a.* Belonging to a choir.

chord, kord, *n.* String of a musical instrument; the simultaneous combination of different sounds; a straight line joining the ends of the arc of a circle or curve.

chorus, ko'rus, *n.* A company of singers; a piece performed by a company in concert; verses of a song in which the company join the singer; any union of voices in general.

chosen, chō'zn, *a.* Select; eminent.

Christ, krist, *n.* **The Anointed;** the Messiah; the Savior.

christen, kris'n, *vt.* To baptize; to name.

Christendom, kris'n-dum, *n.* The countries inhabited by Christians; the whole body of Christians.

christening, kris'n-ing, *n.* Baptism.

Christian, kris'ti-an, *n.* A follower of Christ. **Christian-Science,** kris'ti-an si-ens, *n.* The religion, based on the Bible, founded by Mary Baker Eddy.

Christianity, kris-ti-an'i-ti, *n.* The religion of Christians.

Christmas, kris'mas, *n.* The festival of Christ's nativity, observed annually on 25th December.—*a.* Belonging to Christmas time.

chromatic, krō-mat'ik, *a.* Relating to color; proceeding by semitones.

chrome, chromium, krōm, krō'mi-um, *n.* A steel-gray, hard metal, from which colored preparations are made. **chromic,** krōm'ik, *a.* Pertaining to chrome.

chronic, kron'ik, *a.* Continuing a long time; lingering; continuous.

chronicle, kron'i-kl, *n.* An historical account of events in order of time.—*vt.* (chronicling, chronicled). To record.

chronicler, kron'i-klėr, *n.* An historian.

chronological, kron-ō-loj'i-kal, *a.* Relating to chronology; in order of time.

chronologist, kro-nol'o-jist, *n.* One who studies or is versed in chronology.

chronology, kro-nol'o-ji, *n.* Arrangement of events according to their dates.

chronometer, kro-nom'et-ėr, *n.* An instrument that measures time.

chrysalis, kris'a-lis, *n.* *pl.* **-ides** or **ises.** The form of certain insects before they arrive at their winged state.

chrysanthemum, kris-an'thē-mum, *n.* The name of numerous composite plants.

chrysolite, kris'ō-līt, *n.* A gem of a yellowish or greenish color.

chub, chub, *n.* A small river fish of the carp family.

chubby, chub'i, *a.* Round or full-cheeked; plump; having a large fat face.

chuck, chuk, *vi.* To make the noise of a hen.—*vt.* To call, as a hen her chickens; to tap under the chin; to throw with quick motion; to pitch.—*n.* The call of a hen; a slight blow under the chin; a short throw.

chuckle, chuk'l, *vi.* (chuckling, chuckled). To laugh in the throat; to feel inward triumph or exultation.—*n.* A short and suppressed laugh in the throat.

chum, chum, *n.* A sharer of one's rooms; an intimate friend.

chump, chump, *n.* A short, thick piece of wood; a fool.

chunk, chungk, *n.* A short thick piece.

church, chėrch, *n.* A house consecrated to the worship of God among Christians; the collective body of Christians; a particular body of Christians; the body of clergy; ecclesiastical authority.—*vt.* To give or receive a service in church, as after childbirth.

churchman, chėrch'man, *n.* An ecclesiastic; an adherent of the Church.

churchyard, chėrch'yärd, *n.* The ground adjoining a church in which the dead are buried.

churl, chėrl, *n.* A rude, ill-bred man; a rustic laborer; a miser. **churlish,** chėr'lish, *a.* Surly; sullen.

churn, chėrn, *n.* A vessel in which butter is made.—*vt.* To agitate cream for making butter; to shake with violence.

cider, sī'dėr, *n.* A fermented drink prepared from the juice of apples.

n'ar-r, si-gär', *n.* A roll of tobacco for smoking.

cigarette, sig'a-ret", *n.* A little cut tobacco rolled up in tissue paper, used for smoking.

cilia, sil'i-a, *n. pl.* Minute hairs on plants or animals. **ciliary,** sil'i-a-ri, *a.* Belonging to or of the nature of eyelashes.

cinchona, sin-kō'na, *n.* A genus of S. American trees whose bark yields quinine; Peruvian bark.

cincture, singk'tūr, *n.* A girdle.

cinema, sin'e-ma, *n.* A motion picture or motion picture theater.

cinnabar, sin'a-bär, *n.* Red sulphide of mercury; vermilion.

cinnamon, sin'a-mon, *n.* The inner bark of a tree, native to Ceylon; a spice.

cipher, sī'fėr, *n.* The figure O or nothing; any numeral; a person or thing of no importance; a device; a secret writing.—*vi.* To use figures.—*vt.* To write in secret characters.

circle, sėr'kl, *n.* A plane figure contained by a curved line, every point of which is equally distant from a point within the figure, called the center; the curved line itself; a ring; enclosure; a class; a coterie.—*vt.* (circling, circled). To move round; to inclose.—*vi.* To move circularly.

circlet, sėr'klet, *n.* A little circle; a chaplet.

circuit, sėr'kit, *n.* Act of going round; space measured by traveling round; the journey of judges to hold courts; the district visited by judges; path of an electric current. **circuitous,** ser-kū'i-tus, *a.* Going in a circuit; round about; not direct. **circuitously,** ser-kū'i-tus-li, *adv.* In a circuit.

circular, sėr'kū-lėr, *a.* Round; addressed to a number of persons.—*n.* A paper addressed to a number of persons. **circulate,** sėr'kū-lāt, *vi.* (circulating, circulated). To move in a circle; to have currency.—*vt.* To spread; to give currency to. **circulating,** sėr'kū-lāt-ing, *a.* That circulates; repeating, as figures in decimals. **circulation,** sėr-kū-lā'-shun, *n.* Act of circulating; diffusion; currency. **circulatory,** sėr"kū-la-tō'ri, *n.* Circulating.

circumcise, sėr'kum-sīz, *vt.* (circumcising, circumcised). To cut off the foreskin, according to Jewish and Mohammedan law. **circumcision,** sėr-kum-si'zhun, *n.* The act of circumcising.

circumference, sėr-kum'fėr-ens, *n.* The bounding line of a circle.

circumflex, sėr'kum-fleks, *n.* An accent on long vowels, generally marked thus (^).

circumlocution, sėr-kum'lō-kū"shon, *n.* A roundabout mode of speaking. **circumlocutory,** sėr-kum-lok"ū-to'ri, *a.* Pertaining to circumlocution; periphrastic.

circumnavigate, sėr-kum-na'vi-gāt, *vt.* To sail round. **circumnavigation,** sėr-kum-nav-i-gā'shun, *n.* Act of circumnavigating. **circumnavigator,** sėr-kum-nav'i-gāt-ėr, *n.* One who sails round.

circumpolar, sėr-kum-pō'lėr, *a.* Surrounding either pole of the earth or heavens.

circumscribe, sėr-kum-skrīb, *vt.* To draw a line round; to limit; to restrict.

circumspect, sėr"kum-speckt, *a.* Watchful on all sides; wary; thoughtful. **circumspection,** sėr-kum-spek'shon, *n.* Watchfulness; deliberation; wariness. **circumspectly,** sėr"kum-spekt'li, *adv.* With circumspection.

circumstance, sėr"kum-stans, *n.* Something attending, or relative to a main fact or case; event; (*pl.*) state of affairs; condition. **circumstantial,** sėr-kum-stan'shal, *a.* Consisting in or pertaining to circumstances; attending; detailed. **circumstantiality,** sėr-kum-stan'shi-al"-i-ti, *n.* Minuteness; fullness of detail. **circumstantially,** sėr-kum-stan'shal-li, *adv.* With full detail; minutely. **circumstantiate,** sėr-kum-stan'shi-āt, *vt.* To confirm by circumstances.

circumvent, sėr-kum-vent", *vi.* To encompass; to outwit. **circumvention,** sėr"kum-ven'shun, *n.* Outwitting; overreaching.

circus, sėr-kus, *n.*; *pl.* -ses. Among the Romans, a place for horse-races; a place for feats of horsemanship and acrobatic displays.

cirrus, sir'us, *n.*; *pl.* cirri. A tendril; a light fleecy cloud at a high elevation.

cistern, sis'tėrn, *n.* An artificial receptacle for water, &c.; a natural reservoir.

citadel, sit'a-del, *n.* A fortress in or near a city.

cite, sīt, *vt.* (citing, cited). To summon to appear in a court; to quote; to adduce.

citation, sī-tā'shun, *n.* Quotation; a summons.

citizen, sit'i-zen, *n.* An inhabitant of a city; one who has full municipal and political privileges.—*a.* Having the qualities of a citizen. **citizenship,** sit"i-zen-ship', *n.* State of being vested with the rights of a citizen.

citron, sit'run, *n.* The fruit of the citron tree, a large species of lemon; the tree itself. **citric,** sit'rik, *a.* Belonging to citrons, or to lemons or limes.

city, sit'i, *n.* A large town; a borough or town corporate; the inhabitants of a city.

civet, siv'et, *n.* A substance taken from the anal glands of the civet-cat, used as a perfume.

civet cat, siv'et kat, *n.* A carnivorous animal, native of N. Africa and Asia.

civic, siv'ik, *a.* Pertaining to a city or citizen; relating to civil affairs. **civil,** siv'il, *a.* Relating to the government of a city or state; polite; political; lay; legislative, not military; intestine, not foreign. **civilian,** si-vil'yan, *n.* One skilled in the civil law; one engaged in civil, not military or clerical pursuits. **civility,** si-vil'i-ti, *n.* Quality of being civil; good breeding; (*pl.*) acts of politeness. **civilly,** siv'il-li, *adv.* In a civil manner.

civilize, siv'il-īz, *vt.* (civilizing, civilized). To reclaim from a savage state.

civilized, si'vil-īzd, *a.* Having civilization; refined. **civilization,** siv'i-li-za'-shun, *n.* Act of civilizing, or the state of being civilized.

clad, klad, *pp.* of *clothe.*

claim, klām, *vt.* To ask; to demand as due.—*n.* A demand as of right; a title to something in the possession of another; a pretension. **claimable,** klām'a-bl, *a.* That may be claimed. **claimant,** klām'ant, *n.* One who claims.

clairvoyance, klār-voi'ans, *n.* A power attributed to a mesmerized person, by which he discerns objects concealed from sight, &c.

clam, klam, *vt.* (clamming, clammed). To smear with viscous matter.—*n.* A clamp; a bivalve shell-fish.

clamber, klam'bėr, *vi.* To climb with difficulty, or with hands and feet.

clammy, klam'i, *a.* Sticky; adhesive.

clamor, clamour, klam'ėr, *n.* Loud and continued noise; uproar.—*vi.* To call aloud; to make importunate demands. **clamorer,** klam'ėr-ėr, *n.* One who clamors. **clamorous,** klam'ėr-us, *a.* Noisy. **clamorously,** klam'ėr-us-li, *adv.* With loud noise.

clamp, klamp, *n.* A piece of timber or iron, used to strengthen or fasten; a heavy footstep.—*vt.* To fasten or strengthen with clamps; to tread heavily.

clan, klan, *n.* A family; a tribe; a sect.

clandestine, klan-des'tin, *a.* Secret; underhand. **clandestinely,** klan-des'tin-li, *adv.* Secretly.

clang, klang, *vt.* or *i.* To make a sharp sound, as by striking metallic substances. —*n.* A loud sound made by striking together metallic bodies.

clangor, klang'ėr, *n.* A clang; a ringing sound.

clank, klangk, *n.* The loud sound made by the collision of metallic bodies.—*vt.* or *i.* To sound or cause to sound with a clank.

clannish, klan'ish, *a.* Devoted to the members of one's own clan and illiberal to others.

clansman, klanz'man, *n.* One belonging to the same clan.

clap, klap, *vt.* (clapping, clapped or clapt). To strike together so as to make a noise; to strike with something broad; to shut hastily; to pat.—*vi.* To move together suddenly with noise; to strike the hands together in applause.—*n.* A noise made by sudden collision; a sudden explosive sound; a striking of hands in applause.

clapper, klap'ėr, *n.* He or that which claps; the tongue of a bell.

claptrap, klap"trap', *n.* Words used merely to gain applause.—*a.* Showy in sentiment.

claret, klar'et, *n.* A French red wine.— *a.* Of the color of claret wine.

clarify, klar'i-fī, *vt.* (clarifying, clarified). To purify; to make clear.—*vi.* To become clear, pure, or fine. **clarification,** klar'i-fi-kā"shun, *n.* The clearing of liquids by chemical means. **clarifier,** klar'i-fī-ėr, *n.* That which clarifies.

clarinet, clarionet, kla'rin-et, kla'ri-on-et, *n.* A musical wind instrument of wood.

clarion, klar′i-un, *n.* A kind of trumpet with a shrill tone.

clash, klash, *vi.* To make a noise by collision; to meet in opposition; to interfere.—*vt.* To strike noisily together.—*n.* Noisy collision; opposition.

clasp, klasp, *n.* An embrace; a hook, for fastening; a catch.—*vt.* To fasten together with a clasp; to enclose in the hand; to embrace closely.

class, klas, *n.* A rank of persons or things; an order; group.—*vt.* To arrange in classes.

classic, klas′ik, *a.* Of the first rank; standard in literary quality; pertaining to Greek and Roman antiquity; pure in style.—*n.* An author of the first rank; a Greek or Roman author of this character; a work of the first rank. **classical,** klas′i-kal, *a.* Pertaining to writers of the first rank; pertaining to ancient Greece or Rome; correct; refined (taste, style, &c.). **classicism,** klas′i-sizm, *n.* A class idiom or style. **classicist,** klas′i-sist, *n.* One versed in the classics; one imbued with classicism.

classify, klas′i-fī, *vt.* (classifying, classified). To distribute into classes. **classification,** klas′i-fi-kā″shun, *n.* Act of forming into a class or classes.

clatter, klat′ėr, *vi.* To make repeated rattling noises; to talk fast and idly.—*vt.* To cause to rattle.—*n.* A rattling, confused noise.

clause, klaz, *n.* A member of a sentence; a distinct part of a contract, will, &c.

clavicle, klav′i-kl, *n.* The collarbone.

clavier, klav′i-ėr, *n.* The keyboard of the pianoforte, &c.

claw, kla, *n.* The sharp hooked nail of an animal; that which resembles a claw.—*vt.* To scrape, scratch, or tear.

clay, klā, *n.* A tenacious kind of earth; earth in general; the body.—*vt.* To cover with clay; to purify and whiten with clay, as sugar. **clayey,** klā′ē, *a.* Partaking of clay; like clay.

clean, klēn, *a.* Free from dirt; pure.—*adv.* Quite; fully.—*vt.* To purify; to cleanse. **cleanliness,** klen′li-nes, *n.* State of being cleanly; purity. **cleanly,** klen′li, *a.* Clean in habits; neat.—*adv.* In a clean manner; neatly. **cleanness,** klēn′nes, *n.* Freedom from dirt; purity; innocence. **cleanse,** klenz, *vt.* (cleansing, cleansed). To make clean or pure; to free from guilt. **cleanser,** klenz′ėr, *n.* One who or that which cleanses.

clear, klēr, *a.* Bright; shining; open; fair; plain; shrill; cheerful; acute; free from debt; free from guilt; exempt.—*adv.* Manifestly; quite; indicating entire separation.—*vt.* To make clear; to free from obstructions or obscurity; to cleanse; to justify; to make gain as profit; prepare, as waste land for tillage or pasture; to leap over; to pay customs on a cargo.—*vi.* To become clear; to become fair; to exchange checks. **clearance,** klēr′ans, *n.* Act of clearing; a certificate that a ship has been cleared at the custom-house. **clearer,** klēr′ėr, *n.* One who or that which clears. **clearheaded,** klēr′hed′ed, *a.* Having a clear understanding. **clearing,** klēr′ing, *n.* Act of making clear; act of distributing the proceeds of traffic passing over several railways; among bankers, the act of exchanging drafts on each other's houses; a tract of land cleared of wood. **clearly,** klēr′li, *adv.* In a clear manner.

cleat, klēt, *n.* A piece of wood or iron in a ship to fasten ropes upon; a wedge.

cleavage, klēv′ij, *n.* The act or manner of cleaving.

cleave, klēv, *vi.* (pret. clave, cleaved pp. cleaved). To stick; to adhere.

cleave, klēv, *vt.* (pret. clove, cleaved, cleft; pp. cloven, cleaved, cleft). To split; to sever.—*vi.* To part asunder.

cleaver, klēv′ėr, *n.* One who cleaves; that which cleaves; a butcher's ax.

cleck, klek, *n.* A large hook; an ironheaded club used in golf.

clef, klef, *n.* A character prefixed to a staff in music to determine the pitch.

cleft, kleft, *n.* A crevice; a fissure.

clematis, klem′a-tis, *n.* The generic name of woody climbing plants.

clement, klem′ent, *a.* Mild; humane. **clemently,** klem′ent-li, *adv.* With clemency. **clemency,** klem′en-si, *n.* Mercifulness; mildness; tenderness.

clench, klench, *vt.* To secure; to confirm; to grasp.

clergy, klėr′ji, *n.pl.* The body or order of men set apart to the service of God, in the Christian church. **clergyman,** klėr′ji-man, *n.* A man in holy orders; a minister of the gospel.

cleric, kler′ik, *a.* Clerical.—*n.* A clergyman. **clerical,** kler′ik-al, *n.* Pertaining to the clergy, or to a clerk. **clericalism,** kler′i-kal-izm, *n.* Clerical power or influence; sacerdotalism.

clerk, klėrk, *n.* A clergyman; one who reads the responses in church; one who is employed under another as a writer. **clerkship,** klėrk′ship, *n.* The office or business of a clerk.

clever, klev′ėr, *a.* Adroit; talented; executed with ability. **cleverly,** klev′ėr-li, *adv.* In a clever manner. **cleverness,** klev′ėr-nes, *n.* Quality of being clever; smartness; skill.

clew, klū, *n.* A clue; the corner of a sail.—*vt.* To truss up (sails) to the yard.

click, klik, *vi.* To make a small, sharp noise, or a succession of such sounds.—*n.* A small sharp sound.

client, klī′ent, *n.* A person under patronage; one who employs a lawyer.

clientele, klī′en-tēl″, *n.* One's clients collectively.

cliff, klif, *n.* A precipice; a steep rock.

climate, klī′mit, *n.* The condition of a country in respect of temperature, dryness, wind, &c. **climatic,** klī-mat′ik, *a.* Pertaining to a climate; limited by a climate.

climax, klī′maks, *n.* A figure of rhetoric, in which the language gradually rises in strength and dignity; culmination; acme.

climb, klim, *vi.* To creep up step by step; to ascend.—*vt.* To ascend.

climber, klīm′ėr, *n.* One who climbs; a plant that rises on a support.

clime, klīm, *n.* A region of the earth.

clinch, klinch, *vt.* To rivet; to clench; to make conclusive.—*n.* A catch; a pun.

clincher, klinch′ėr, *n.* A kind of nail; a conclusive argument.

cling, kling, *vi.* (clinging, clung). To hang by twining round; to adhere closely.

clinic, clinical, klin′ik, klin′i-kal, *a.* Pertaining to a sick bed.—*n.* One confined to bed.

clink, klingk, *vt.* To cause to ring or jingle.—*vi.* To ring.—*n.* A sound made by the collision of small sonorous bodies.

clinker, klingk′ėr, *n.* A partially vitrified brick; a mass of incombustible slag.

clip, klip, *vt.* (clipping, clipped). To shear; to trim with scissors; to cut short. —*n.* Act or product of sheep-shearing.

clipper, klip′ėr, *n.* One who clips; a sharp, fast-sailing vessel. **clipping**, klip′ing, *n.* The act of cutting off; a piece separated by clipping.

clique, klēk, *n.* A party; a coterie; a set.

cloak, klōk, *n.* A loose outer garment; a disguise; a pretext.—*vt.* To cover with a cloak; to hide; to veil.

clock, klok, *n.* A machine which measures time. **clockwork**, klok″wėrk′, *n.* The machinery of a clock; well-adjusted mechanism.

clod, klod, *n.* A lump of earth; a stupid fellow.—*vt.* (clodding, clodded). To pelt with clods. **cloddy**, klod′i, *a.* Consisting of clods; earthy; gross. **clodhopper**, klod′hop″-ėr, *n.* A clown, dolt.

clog, klog, *vt.* (clogging, clogged). To hinder; to impede; to trammel.—*vi.* To be loaded.—*n.* Hindrance; a shoe with a wooden sole. **cloggy**, klog′i, *a.* That clogs; viscous.

cloister, klois′tėr, *n.* A monastery or nunnery; an arcade round an open court. —*vi.* To shut up in a cloister, to immure.

close, klōz, *vt.* (closing, closed). To shut; to finish.—*vi.* To come close together; to end; to grapple; to come to an agreement.—*n.* End.

close, klōs, *a.* Shut fast; tight; dense, near; stingy; trusty; intense; without ventilation; disposed to keep secrets.— *adv.* Tightly; in contact, or very near. —*n.* An enclosed place; precinct of a cathedral. **closefisted**, klōs′fist′ed, *a.* Niggardly. **closely**, klōs′li, *adv.* In a close manner. **closing**, klōz′ing, *p.a.* That concludes. **closure**, klō′zher, *n.* The act of closing; the act of ending a parliamentary debate.

closet, kloz′et, *n.* A small private apartment.—*vt.* To take into a private apartment.

clot, klot, *n.* A mass of soft or fluid matter concreted.—*vi.* (clotting, clotted). To become thick; to coagulate. **clotty**, klot′i, *a.* Full of clots.

cloth, kloth, *n.* A woven material or fabric; the covering of a table; the clerical profession.

clothe, klōтн, *vt.* (clothing, clothed or clad). To put clothes on; to cover or spread over. **clothes**, klōтнz, *n.pl.* of *cloth.* Garments for the body; blankets, &c., on a bed. **clotheshorse**, klōтнz″-

hors′, *n.* A frame to hang clothes on. **clothier**, klōтн′i-ėr, *n.* A maker or seller of cloths or clothes. **clothing**, klōтн′ing, *n.* Garments in general.

cloud, kloud, *n.* A collection of visible vapor, suspended in the air; something similar to this; what obscures, threatens, &c.; a great multitude; a mass.—*vt.* To obscure; to darken; to sully; to make to appear sullen.—*vi.* To grow cloudy. **cloudiness**, kloud′i-nes, *n.* State of being cloudy; gloom. **cloudless**, kloud′-les, *a.* Without a cloud; clear. **cloudlet**, kloud′let, *n.* A little cloud. **cloudy**, kloud′i, *a.* Overcast with clouds; dark; not easily understood; indicating gloom.

clout, klout, *n.* A patch of cloth, leather, &c.; a rag; a blow.—*vt.* To patch; to join clumsily.

clove, klōv, *n.* The dried spicy bud of an East Indian tree; the tree itself; a small bulb in a compound bulb, as in garlic.

cloven-footed, cloven-hoofed, klō′ven-fut′ed, klō′ven-höft, *a.* Having the foot or hoof divided into two parts, as the ox.

clover, klō′vėr, *n.* A leguminous plant with three-lobed leaves.

clown, kloun, *n.* An awkward country fellow; a lout; a professional jester. **clownish**, kloun′ish, *a.* Coarse; rude.

cloy, kloi, *vt.* To glut; to fill to loathing.

club, klub, *n.* A cudgel; a card of the suit marked with trefoils; a staff with a heavy head for driving the ball in golf, &c.; an association for some common object; the meeting-place of such an association.—*vt.* To beat with a club.—*vi.* To join for some common object.

clubfooted, klub′fut′ed, *a.* Having short, crooked, or deformed feet.

cluck, kluk, *vi.* To make the noise of the hen when calling chickens.—*n.* Such a sound.

clue, klö, *n.* A ball of thread; a thread serving to guide; something helping to unravel a mystery.

clump, klump, *n.* A lump; a cluster of trees or shrubs.

clumsy, klum′zi, *a.* Unwieldy; ungainly; rude in make. **clumsily**, klum′-zi-li, *adv.* In a clumsy manner. **clumsiness**, klum′zi-nes, *n.* Quality of being clumsy.

cluster, klus′tėr, *n.* A bunch, as of grapes; a knot; a small crowd.—*vi.* To be or to keep close together; to grow in bunches; to collect in masses.—*vt.* To collect into a body.

clutch, kluch, *vt.* To seize hold of; to grasp.—*n.* A grasp; talon; a merciless hand; something that holds fast.

clutter, klut′ėr, *n.* A confused noise; a bustle.—*vt.* To crowd together in disorder.—*vi.* To make a bustle.

coach, kōch, *n.* A large four-wheeled close vehicle; a tutor.—*vi.* To ride in a coach; to tutor. **coachbox**, kōch′-boks, *n.* Seat on which the driver of a coach sits. **coachman**, kōch′man, *n.* The person who drives a coach.

coadjutor, kō′ad-jū″ter, *n.* An assistant; a colleague. **coadjutrix**, kō′ad-jū″triks, *n.* A female assistant.

coagulate, kŏ-ag'ū-lāt, *vt.* (coagulating, coagulated). To change from a fluid into a fixed state.—*vi.* To curdle; to congeal. **coagulable**, kŏ-ag'ū-la-bl, *a.* Capable of being coagulated. **coagulation**, kŏ-ag'ū-la″shon, *n.* Act of coagulating; mass coagulated.

coal, kōl, *n.* Any combustible substance in a state of ignition; charcoal; a solid, black, fossil substance used as fuel.—*vt.* or *i.* To supply with coals; to take in coal.

coalesce, kŏ'al-es″, *vi.* (coalescing, coalesced). To grow together; to unite. **coalescence**, kŏ-a-les'ens, *n.* Act of coalescing; state of being united; union. **coalescent**, kŏ-a-les'ent, *a.* Coalescing. **coalition**, kŏ-a-lish'un, *n.* Act of coalescing; union of persons, parties, &c., into one body; alliance; confederation.

coarse, kŏrs, *a.* Rude; not refined; crude; inelegant; gross. **coarsely**, kŏrs'li, *adv.* In a coarse manner.

coast, kōst, *n.* The seashore; the country near the sea.—*vi.* To sail along a shore; to sail from port to port. **coaster**, kōs'tēr, *n.* A trading vessel which trades from port to port. **coast guard**, kōst'gärd, *n.* A force employed to guard the coast. **coasting**, kōst'ing, *a.* Sailing along a coast; employed in trade along a coast. **coastwise**, kōst'wīz, *adv.* By way of or along the coast.

coat, kōt, *n.* An upper garment; vesture, as indicating office; hair or fur covering of animals; a layer; a covering; that on which ensigns armorial are portrayed.—*vt.* To cover; to spread over. **coating**, kōt'ing, *n.* A covering; a thin external layer; cloth for coats.

coax, kōks, *vt.* To wheedle; to persuade by fondling and flattering. **coaxer**, kōks'ēr, *n.* A wheedler. **coaxingly**, kōks'ing-li, *adv.* By coaxing.

cob, kob, *n.* A round knob; the head of clover or wheat; a strong pony.

cobalt, kō'balt, *n.* A mineral of grayish color, and a metal obtained from it yielding a permanent blue; the blue itself.

cobble, kob'l, *vt.* (cobbling, cobbled). To mend coarsely, as shoes; to botch. *—n.* A roundish stone. **cobbler**, kob'l-ēr, *n.* A mender of shoes; a clumsy workman; a cooling beverage.

cobra, **cobra-de-capello**, kō'bra, kō'bra-de-ka-pel-ō, *n.* A hooded venomous snake.

cobweb, kob'web, *n.* A spider's net; something flimsy; old musty rubbish.

coca, kō'ka, *n.* The dried leaf of a S. American plant which gives power of enduring fatigue.

cocaine, kō'kān, *n.* The active principle of coca, used as a local anæsthetic.

cochineal, koch'i-nēl″, *n.* An insect which forms a scarlet dye; a dye-stuff consisting of the bodies of these insects.

cock, kok, *n.* The male of the domestic fowl; the male of other birds; a vane; a person or thing having resemblance to a cock; a chief man; a tap for drawing off liquids; the hammer of a gun; a small pile of hay.—*vt.* To set erect; to set on the head with an air of pertness; to draw back the cock of a gun.

cockade, kok-ād', *n.* A knot of ribbon worn on the hat.

cock-and-bull, kok'and-bul', *a.* Idle; without foundation (applied to stories).

cockatoo, kok-a-tö', *n.* A crested bird of the parrot kind.

cock-crow, **cock-crowing**, kok'krō, kok'krō-ing, *n.* Early morning.

cockle, kok'l, *n.* A weed that chokes grain; a small shellfish; a kind of stove (Eng.).—*vi.* or *t.* To wrinkle; to shrink.

cockney, kok'nē, *n.* An effeminate citizen; a native of London.—*a.* Pertaining to a cockney. **cockneyism**, kok'nē-izm, *n.* The peculiar dialect, pronunciation, &c., of a cockney.

cockpit, kok'pit, *n.* A pit where game-cocks fight; an apartment in a ship of war, where wounds are dressed.

cockroach, kok'rōch, *n.* The black beetle.

cock's-comb, koks'kōm, *n.* The comb of a cock; a plant. *See* **coxcomb**.

cockswain, **coxswain**, kok'swän or kok'sn, *n.* The person who steers a boat, or who has the care of a boat and its crew.

cocktail, kok'tāl, *n.* A species of beetle; a half-bred horse; a kind of beverage.

cocoa, kō'kō, *n.* A tropical palm-tree.

cocoa, kō'kō or kō'kō'a, *n.* The seed of the cocoa prepared for a beverage; the beverage itself.

coconut, kō'kō-nut, *n.* The fruit of the cocoa palm.

cocoon, kō-kön', *n.* The silky case in which the silkworm involves itself when still a larva; the envelope of other larvae.

cod, kod, *n.* A species of sea fish allied to the haddock; a husk; a pod.

coddle, kod'l, *vt.* (coddling, coddled). To fondle.

code, kōd, *n.* A digest of laws; a collection of rules; a system of signals, &c. **codification**, kōd'i-fi-kā″shun, *n.* Act or process of reducing laws to a code. **codify**, kōd'i-fī, *vt.* (codifying, codified). To reduce to a code.

codling, **codlin**, kod'ling, kod'lin, *n.* A variety of cooking apple.

codling, kod'ling, *n.* A young codfish.

cod-liver oil, kod'liv-ēr-oil, *n.* A medicinal oil obtained from the livers of the cod.

coefficient, kō-e-fish'ent, *a.* Jointly efficient; co-operating.—*n.* That which co-operates; a number or quantity that multiplies or measures another.

coerce, kō-ērs', *vt.* (coercing, coerced). To restrain by force; to compel. **coercion**, kō-ēr'shun, *n.* Act of coercing; restraint; compulsion. **coercive**, kō-ēr'siv, *a.* That has power to coerce; constraining; compulsory. **coercively**, kō-ēr'siv-li, *adv.* By constraint.

coeval, kō-ē'val, *a.* Of the same age; contemporary.—*n.* One of the same age.

coexist, kō-eg-zist′, To live at the same time with another. **coexistence**, kō-eg-zist′ens, *n*. Existence at the same time with another. **coexistent**, kō-eg-zist′ent, *a*. Existing at the same time with another.

coffee, kof′i, *n*. A tree and its fruit or berries; a beverage made from the seeds.

coffer, kof′ėr, *n*. A chest for holding gold, jewels, &c.

cofferdam, kof′ėr-dam, *n*. A case of piling, water-tight, serving to exclude water in laying the foundations.

coffin, kof′in, *n*. The chest in which a dead human body is buried.—*vt*. To enclose in a coffin.

cog, kog, *n*. The tooth of a wheel.—*vt*. (cogging, cogged). To furnish with cogs; to trick, deceive; to load (dice).—*vi*. To cheat; to lie.

cogent, kō′jent, *a*. Forcible; convincing. **cogently**, kō′jent-li, *adv*. In a cogent manner. **cogency**, kō′jen-si, *n*. Force; persuading power.

cogitate, koj-i-tāt, *vi*. (cogitating, cogitated). To ponder; to meditate. **cogitation**, koj-i-tā′shun, *n*. Act of thinking much or deeply; reflection. **cogitative**, kōj′i-tā-tiv, *a*. Having the power of thinking; given to thought.

cognac, kō′nyak, *n*. A kind of brandy.

cognate, kog′nāt, *a*. Born of the same stock; akin; of the same nature.

cognition, kog-nish′un, *n*. Knowledge from personal view or experience. **cognizable**, kog′ni-za-bl, *a*. That may be known; that may be tried and determined. **cognizance**, kog′ni-zans, *n*. Knowledge; judicial notice; trial, or right to try; a badge. **cognizant**, kog′-ni-zant, *a*. Having knowledge of.

cognomen, kog-nō′men, *n*. A name added to a family name; a surname. **cognominal**, kog-nom′in-al, *a*. Pertaining to a cognomen or surname.

cohabit, kō-hab′it, *vi*. To dwell together; to live as husband and wife, though not married. **cohabitation**, kō-hab′i-tā″·un, *n*. Act or state of cohabiting.

cohere, kō-hēr′, *vi*. (cohering, cohered). To stick together; to be consistent. **coherence**, **coherency**, kō-hēr′ens, kō-hēr′en-si, *n*. The state of being coherent; cohesion; congruity. **coherent**, kō-hēr′ent, *a*. Sticking together; consistent. **coherently**, kō-hēr′ent-li, *adv*. In a coherent manner. **cohesion**, kō-hē′zhun, *n*. Act of sticking together; the attraction by which bodies are kept together; coherence. **cohesive**, kō-hē′siv, *a*. That has the power of cohering; tending to unite in a mass.

cohort, kō′hort, *n*. A company of soldiers, among the Romans the tenth part of a legion.

coif, koif, *n*. A kind of caul or cap.—*vt*. To cover or dress with a coif. **coiffure**, kwä-fūr′, *n*. A head-dress.

coil, koil, *vt*. To wind into a ring.—*n*. A ring or rings into which a rope, &c., is wound.

coin, koin, *n*. A piece of metal stamped as money; that which serves for payment.—*vt*. To stamp and convert it into money; to mint; to invent; to fabricate. **coinage**, koin′ij, *n*. The act or art of coining; coined money; fabrication.

coincide, kō′in-sīd″, *vi*. (coinciding, coincided). To agree in position; to happen at the same time; to concur. **coincidence**, kō-in′si-dens, *n*. Concurrence; agreement. **coincident**, kō-in′si-dent, *a*. Having coincidence; concurrent; corresponding.

coition, kō-ish′on, *n*. Sexual intercourse.

coke, kōk, *n*. Coal charred and deprived of gas.—*vt*. (coking, coked). To turn into coke.

cola, kō′la, *n*. An African tree with nuts containing much caffeine and yielding an invigorating beverage.

colander, ku′lan-dėr, *n*. A strainer; sieve.

cold, kōld, *a*. Not hot; chill; indifferent; reserved; stoical; unaffecting.—*n*. Absence of heat; sensation produced by the escape of heat; an ailment occasioned by cold. **cold-blooded**, kōld′blud′ed, *a*. Having cold blood; without sensibility or feeling. **coldish**, kōld′ish, *a*. Somewhat cold. **coldly**, kōld′li, *adv*. In a cold manner. **coldness**, kōld′nes, *n*. Want of heat; unconcern; frigidity of temper; reserve.

cole, kōl, *n*. A kind of cabbage.

colic, kol′ik, *n*. A painful affection of the intestines.

collaborator, ko-lab″o-ra′tėr, *n*. An associate in literary or scientific labor.

collapse, ko-laps′, *n*. A wasting of the body; a sudden and complete failure.—*vi*. (collapsing, collapsed). To fall together, as the sides of a vessel; to break down.

collar, kol′ėr, *n*. A part of dress that surrounds the neck; something worn round the neck.—*vt*. To seize by the collar; to put a collar on; to roll up and bind with a cord.

collarbone, kol″ėr-bōn′, *n*. Each of the two bones of the neck.

collate, ko′lāt′, *vt*. (collating, collated). To lay together and compare, as books, &c.; to place in a benefice; to gather and place in order.—*vi*. To place in a benefice.

collateral, ko-lat′ėr-al, *a*. Placed side by side; running parallel; descending from the same stock, but not one from the other; connected.—*n*. A kinsman.

colleague, kol′ēg, *n*. An associate in office.

collect, ko′lekt, *n*. A short comprehensive prayer; a short prayer adapted to a particular occasion.

collect, ko-lekt′, *vt*. To bring together; to gain by information; to infer or deduce.—*vi*. To run together; to accumulate. **collected**, ko-lek′ted, *p.a*. Cool; self-possessed. **collectedly**, ko-lek′ted-li, *adv*. In a collected state or manner. **collection**, ko-lek′shun, *n*. Act of collecting; that which is collected. **collective**, ko-lek′tiv, *a*. Gathered into a mass; congregated; united. **collectively**, ko-lek′tiv-li, *adv*. In a collected state; in a mass or body. **collectivism**, ko-lek′tiv-izm, *n*. The doctrine that the state should own or control the land and all means of production. **collector**, ko-lekt'ẽr, *n.* One who collects customs or taxes.

college, kol'ej, *n.* A society of men invested with certain powers, engaged in some common pursuit; a seminary of the higher learning; the building occupied for such purposes. **collegian**, ko-lē'ji-an, *n.* A member of a college; a student. **collegiate**, ko-lē'ji-it, *a.* Pertaining to a college.

collide, ko-līd', *vi.* (colliding, collided). To strike against each other; to meet in opposition.

collie, colly, kol'i, *n.* A dog common in Scotland, much used for sheep.

collier, kol'yẽr, *n.* One who works in a coalmine; a ship that carries coal. **colliery**, kol'yẽr-i, *n.* A coal mine.

collingual, kol-ling'gwal, *a.* Speaking the same language.

collision, ko-lizh'un, *n.* Act of striking together; state of contrariety; conflict.

collodion, kol-lō'di-on, *n.* A solution of gun-cotton in ether, forming a thin film.

colloquy, kol'ō-kwi, *n.* A speaking together; mutual discourse; dialogue. **colloquial**, ko-lō'kwi-al, *a.* Pertaining to common conversation or discourse. **colloquialism**, ko-lō'kwi-al-izm, *n.* A colloquial form of expression.

collude, kol-lūd', *vi.* (colluding, colluded). To conspire in a fraud; to connive. **collusion**, kol-lū'zhon, *n.* Fraud by concert. **collusive**, kol-lū'siv, *a.* Fraudulently concerted.

colon, kō'lon, *n.* A mark of punctuation, thus (:); the largest of the intestines.

colonel, kẽr'nel, *n.* The chief commander of a regiment of troops. **colonelcy**, kẽr'nel-si, *n.* The office, rank, or commission of a colonel.

colonnade, kol-on-ād', *n.* A range of columns placed at regular intervals.

colony, kol'ō-ni, *n.* A body of people transplanted from their mother country to inhabit some distant place; the country colonized. **colonial**, ko-lō'ni-al, *a.* Pertaining to a colony.—*n.* A person belonging to a colony. **colonialism**, ko-lō'ni-al-izm, *n.* A phrase, idom, or practice peculiar to a colony. **colonist**, kol'on-ist, *n.* An inhabitant of a colony. **colonization**, kol'on-I-zā''shun, *n.* Act of colonizing, or state of being colonized. **colonize**, kol'on-īz. *vt.* (colonizing, colonized). To establish a colony in; to migrate to and settle in as inhabitants.

colophon, kol'ō-fon, *n.* An inscription or device on the last page of a book.

color, colour, kul'ẽr, *n.* That which gives bodies different appearances independently of form; a pigment; complexion; appearance to the mind; pretense; *pl.* a flag.—*vt.* To give some kind of color to; to give a specious appearance to; to exaggerate in representation.—*vi.* To show color; to blush. **colorable**, kul'ẽr-a-bl, *a.* Designed to cover or conceal; specious; plausible. **color blindness**, kul'ẽr-blind'nes, *n.* Inability to distinguish colors. **colored**, kul'ẽrd, *a.* Tinged; having a specious appearance;

of a dark skin. **coloring**, kul'ẽr-ing, *n.* Act of giving a color; color applied; a specious appearance; fair artificial representation. **colorist**, kul'ẽr-ist, *n.* One who colors; a painter who excels in coloring. **colorless**, kul'ẽr-les, *a.* Destitute of color.

colossal, kō-los'al, *a.* Huge; gigantic. **colossus**, kō-los'us, *n.*; pl. **-lossi**. A statue of gigantic size.

colporteur, kol''põr'tẽr, *n.* One who travels for the sale or distribution of moral books, &c.

colt, kōlt, *n.* A young male of the horse kind; a young foolish fellow. **coltish**, kōlt'ish, *a.* Like a colt; wanton; gay.

columbine, ko'lum-bīn, *n.* A plant of the buttercup family; the female companion of Harlequin in pantomines.

column, ko'lum, *n.* A pillar; a body of troops; a perpendicular section of a page; a perpendicular line of figures. **columnar**, ko-lum'nẽr, *a.* Formed in columns; having the form of columns.

coma, kō'ma, *n.* Deep sleep; stupor; the hair-like envelope round the nucleus of a comet. **comatose, comatous**, kō'ma-tōs, kō'ma-tus, *a.* Pertaining to coma; lethargic.

comb, kōm, *n.* An instrument for separating hair, wool, &c.; the crest of a cock; honeycomb.—*vt.* To separate and adjust with a comb.

combat, kom'bat, *vi.* To fight; to act in opposition.—*vt.* To oppose; to resist.—*n.* A fighting; an engagement; a duel. **combatable**, kom-bat'a-bl, *a.* That may be combated, disputed, or opposed. **combatant**, kom'bat-ant, *a.* Contending.—*n.* One who combats. **combative**, kom'bat-iv, *a.* Disposed to combat.

combine, kom-bīn', *vt.* (combining, combined). To cause to unite; to join.—*vi.* To come into union; to coalesce; to league together.—*n.* A union. **combined**, kom-bīnd', *a.* United closely; produced by combination. **combinable**, kom-bīn'a-bl, *a.* Capable of combining. **combination**, kom-bi-nā'shun, *n.* Act of combining; state of being combined; union; confederacy; a close-fitting under-garment.

combustible, kom-bus'ti-bl, *a.* Capable of catching fire; inflammable.—*n.* A substance easily set on fire. **combustibility**, kom-bus'ti-bil''i-ti, *n.* The quality of being combustible. **combustion**, kom-bus'chun, *n.* A burning; chemical combination, attended with heat and light.

come, kum, *vi.* (coming, pret. came, pp. come). To move hitherward; to draw nigh; to arrive; to happen; to appear; to rise; to result.

comedy, kom'ē-di, *n.* A drama of the lighter kind. **comedian**, ko-mē'di-an, *n.* An actor or writer of comedies.

comely, kum'li, *a.* Good-looking; handsome; becoming. **comeliness**, kum'li-nes, *n.* The quality of being comely; good looks.

comet, kom'et, *n.* A heavenly body having a luminous tail or train. **cometary**, kom'e-ter-i, *a.* Pertaining to or like a comet.

mfort, kum'fèrt, vt. To console; to ladden.—n. Consolation; relief; moderate enjoyment. **comfortable**, kum'ért-a-bl, a. Enjoying or giving comfort. **comfortably**, kum'fèrt-a-bli, adv. In comfortable manner. **comforter**, um'fèrt-èr, n. One who comforts; the Holy Spirit; a woolen scarf. **comfortless**, kum'fèrt-les, a. Destitute of comfort; forlorn; wretched.

mic, kom'ik, a. Relating to comedy. **omical**, kom'ik-al, a. Raising mirth; unny. **comically**, kom'i-kal-li, adv. In a comical manner.

ming, kum'ing, p.a. Future.—n. Approach.

mique, kom-ēk', n. A comic actor or inger.

mity, ko'mi-ti, n. Courtesy; civility. **mma**, kom'a, n. A mark of punctuation, thus (,); an interval in music. **mmand**, ko-mand', vt. To order; to overn; to have at one's disposal.—vi. To have chief power.—n. Order; control; power of overlooking; power of defending. **commandant**, ko"mandant', n. A commanding officer of a place r forces. **commander**, kom-mand'ér, n. One who commands; an officer in the avy, between a lieutenant and captain. **commanding**, ko-mand'ing, a. Exercising command; overlooking a wide iew. **commandment**, ko-mand'ment, n. A command; a precept of the moral law.

mmemorate, ko-mem'ō-rāt, vt. To all to remembrance by a solemn act; to elebrate with honor and solemnity. **commemorable**, ko-mem'ō-ra-bl, a. Worthy to be commemorated. **commemoration**, ko-mem'ō-rā"shun, n. Solemn celebration. **commemorative**, o-mem'ō-rā-tiv, a. Tending to preserve in remembrance.

mmence, ko-mens', vi. (commencing, commenced). To take the first step; o begin to be.—vt. To begin; to originate. **commencement**, ko-mens'ment, n. Beginning; rise; origin; first existence.

mmend, ko-mend', vt. To commit o the care of; to recommend; to praise. **commendable**, ko-mend'a-bl, a. Worthy of praise. **commendation**, com-en-dā'shun, n. Praise; recommendation; compliments. **commendatory**, ko-men'da-to-ri, a. That serves o commend; containing praise.

mmensurable, ko-men'sūr-a-bl, a. Having a common measure. **commensurability**, ko-men'sūr-a-bil"i-ti, n. The capacity of having a common measure. **commensurate**, ko-men'sūr-āt, a. Proportional; having equal measure. **commensurately**, ko-men'sūr-āt-li, adv. Correspondingly; adequately.

mment, kom'ent, vi. To make remarks or criticisms.—vt. To annotate.—n. An explanatory note; a remark or criticism. **commentary**, kom-en-ter'i, n. Book of comments; an historical narrative. **commentator**, kom-en-tā'ter, n. One who writes annotations; one who

broadcasts current events on radio or television.

commerce, kom' èrs, n. Exchange of goods by barter or purchase; trade; intercourse. **commercial**, kom-mèr'shal, a. Pertaining to commerce; trading; mercantile. **commercially**, ko-mèr'shal-li, adv. In a commercial manner or view. **commingle**, ko-ming'gl, vt. To blend. —vi. To unite together.

commiserate, ko-miz'èr-āt, vt. (commiserating, commiserated). To pity; to condole with. **commiseration**, ko-miz'èr-ā"shun, n. Act of commiserating. **commissary**, kom''i-ser'i, n. A delegate; an officer of a bishop; an officer who has the charge of furnishing provisions, clothing, &c., for an army. **commissariat**, kom''i-ser'i-at, n. The department of an army which supplies provisions, &c.; the officers in this department.

commission, ko-mish'un, n. Trust; warrant; a written document, investing one with an office; allowance made to an agent, &c., for transacting business; a body of men joined in an office or trust, or their appointment; perpetration.—vt. To appoint; to depute. **commissioned**, ko-mish'und, a. Furnished with a commission. **commissioner**, ko-mish'un-er, n. One commissioned to perform some office.

commit, ko-mit', vt. (committing, committed). To entrust; to consign; to send to prison; to perpetrate; to endanger or compromise (one's self). **commitment**, ko-mit'ment, n. The act of committing; a sending to prison. **committal**, ko-mit'al, n. The act of committing in the various senses of the verb. **committee**, ko-mit'tē, n. A body of persons appointed to manage any matter. **commode**, ko-mōd', n. A kind of small sideboard; a lady's headdress; a nightstool.

commodious, ko-mō'di-us, a. Convenient; spacious and suitable. **commodiously**, ko-mō'di-us-li, adv. In a commodious manner; suitably.

commodity, ko-mod'i-ti, n. Something useful; any article of commerce; (pl.) goods; merchandise.

commodore, kom'o-dōr, n. A naval officer lower than an admiral.

common, kom'un, a. Having no separate owner; general; usual; of no rank; of little value.—n. An open public ground; pl. untitled people; the lower House of Parliament; food at a common table; food in general. **commonable**, kom'un-a-bl, a. Held in common; that may be pastured on. **commonage**, kom'un-ij, n. The right of pasturing on a common. **commonalty**, **commonality**, kom'un-al-ti, kom-un-al'i-ti, n. The common people. **commoner**, kom'un-èr, n. One of the common people; a member of the House of Commons; a student of Oxford, not dependent for support on the foundation. **commonly**, kom'un-li, adv. Usually. **commonplace**, kom'un-plās, n. A usual topic; a trite saying.—*a.* Ordinary; trite.

common sense, kom'mon sens, *n.* Sound practical judgment.

commonweal, kom'un-wēl, *n.* A commonwealth; the state.

Commonwealth, kom'un-welth, *n.* The public good; the state; body politic; a form of government; a republic.

commotion, ko-mō'shun, *n.* Violent agitation; tumultuous disorder.

commune, ko'mūn, *n.* A small administrative district in France; a socialist body who ruled over Paris in 1871.

commune, ko-mūn', *vi.* (communing, communed). To confer; to meditate.

communicable, kom-mū'ni-ka-bl, *a.* Capable of being imparted to another.

communicably, ko-mū'ni-ka-bli, *adv.* With communication. **communicant,** ko-mū'ni-kant, *n.* One who communicates; a partaker of the Lord's supper.

communicate, ko-mū'ni-kāt, *vt.* (communicating, communicated). To cause to be common to others; to impart, as news, disease, &c.; to bestow; to reveal.—*vi.* To share with others; to partake of the Lord's supper; to have intercourse; to correspond. **communication,** ko-mū'ni-kā"shun, *n.* Act of communicating; that which is communicated; a letter or despatch received; a passage from one place to another. **communicative,** ko-mū'ni-kā-tiv, *a.* Ready to communicate; not reserved.

communion, ko-mūn'yun, *n.* A mutual participation in anything; mutual intercourse; concord; celebration of the Lord's supper.

communism, kom'ū-nizm, *n.* The doctrine of a community of property. **communist,** kom'mūn-ist, *n.* One who holds the doctrines of communism.

community, kom-ū'ni-ti, *n.* Mutual participation; the public; a society of persons under the same laws.

commute, ko-mūt', *vt.* (commuting, commuted). To exchange; to put one thing for another; to travel daily at reduced rates. **commutability,** ko-mūt'a-bil"i-ti, *n.* Quality of being commutable. **commutable,** ko-mūt'a-bl, *a.* That may be exchanged; convertible into money. **commutation,** kom-ū-tā'shun, *n.* Exchange; change; substitution of a less for a greater penalty; reduced railroad fares. **commutative,** ko-mū'ta-tiv, *a.* Relative to exchange; interchangeable.

compact, kom-pakt', *a.* Closely united; solid; dense; brief.—*vt.* To consolidate; to unite firmly.—*n.* kom'pakt. An agreement; a contract. **compactly,** kom-pakt'li, *adv.* Closely; densely; tersely.

companion, kom-pan'yun, *n.* A comrade; an associate; one of the lowest rank in an order of knighthood; a raised cover to the cabin stair of a merchant vessel. **companionable,** kom-pan'yun-a-bl, *a.* Fitted to be an agreeable companion; sociable. **companionship,** kom-pan'yun-ship, *n.* Fellowship; association.

company, kum'pa-ni, *n.* Companion-

ship; an assembly of persons; partners a firm; a division of a regiment un a captain; the crew of a ship.—*vi.* associate with.

comparable, kom'pa-ra-bl, *a.* That m be compared; being of equal rega **comparably,** kom'pa-ra-bli, *adv.* comparison; so as to be compared.

comparative, kom-par'a-tiv, *a.* Es mated by comparison; not positive absolute. **comparatively,** kom-par tiv-li, *adv.* By comparison.

compare, kom-pār', *vt.* (comparin compared). To bring together and e amine the relations between; to estima one by another; to inflect in the degre of signification.—*vi.* To hold compariso **comparison,** kom-pa'ri-sun, *n.* Act comparing; state of being compare relation; the formation of an adjective its degrees of signification; a simile.

compartment, kom-pärt'ment, *n.* A d vision or part of a general design.

compass, kum'pas, *n.* A round; a ci cuit; limit; extent; range; an instrumen for directing the course of ships; an i strument for describing circles (often *pl.*)—*vt.* To pass round; to enclose; obtain; to contrive.

compassion, kom-pash'un, *n.* Fello suffering; pity; sympathy. **compas sionate,** kom-pash'un-it, *a.* Ready pity; sympathizing.—*vt.* To pity. **com passionately,** kom-pash'un-it-li, *ad* With compassion; mercifully.

compatible, kom-pat'i-bl, *a.* Consis ent; suitable; not incongruous. **com patibility,** kom-pat'i-bil"i-ti, *n.* Qua ity of being compatible. **compatibly** kom-pat'i-bli, *adv.* Fitly.

compatriot, kom-pā'tri-ut, *n.* One o the same country.

compel, kom-pel', *vt.* (compelling, com pelled). To drive; to urge; to necessitat **compellable,** kom-pel'a-bl, *a.* Tha may be compelled. **compellatio** kom-pe-lā'shun, *n.* An addressing; ceremonious appellation.

compend, compendium, kom'pen kom-pen'di-um, *n.* An abridgment; summary; an epitome.

compensate, kom-pen'sāt, *vt.* (compen sating, compensated). To give equa value to; to make amends for; to re quite.—*vi.* To make amends; to suppl an equivalent. **compensation,** kom pen-sā'shun, *n.* Act of compensating; rec ompense. **compensatory,** kom-pen' sa-to-ri, *a.* Serving for compensation making amends.

compete, kom-pēt', *vi.* (competing competed). To strive for the same thin as another; to contend.

competent, kom'pē-tent, *a.* Suitable sufficient; qualified; having adequa right. **competently,** kom'pē-tent-l *adv.* Sufficiently; adequately. **compe tence, competency,** kom'pē-tens kom'pē-ten-si, *n.* Suitableness; sufficien cy; legal capacity or right.

competition, kom'pē-tish"un, *n.* Con test for the same object; rivalry.

competitive, kom-pet'i-tiv, *a.* Relatin

to competition; carried out by competition.

competitor, kom-pet'i-tèr, *n.* One who competes; a rival; an opponent.

compile, kom-pil', *vt.* (compiling, compiled). To gather from various sources; to draw up by collecting parts from different authors. **compiler,** kom-pil'èr, *n.* One who compiles. **compilation,** kom-pi-lā'shun, *n.* Act of compiling; that which is compiled; a work made up of parts from various authors.

complacent, kom-plā'sent, *a.* Showing complacency; complaisant. **complacently,** kom-plā'sent-li, *adv.* In a complacent manner; softly. **complacence, complacency,** kom-plā'sens, kom-plā'sen-si, *n.* A feeling of quiet satisfaction; complaisance.

complain, kom-plān', *vi.* To express grief or distress; to lament; to express dissatisfaction; to make a formal accusation. **complainant,** kom-plān'ant, *n.* One who complains; a plaintiff. **complaint,** kom-plānt', *n.* Expression of grief, censure, &c.; accusation; malady. **complaisant,** kom-plā-zant, *a.* Pleasing in manners; desirous to please; courteous. **complaisantly,** kom-plā-zant-li, *adv.* With complaisance. **complaisance,** kom-plā-zans, *n.* A pleasing deportment; courtesy; urbanity.

complement, kom'plē-ment, *n.* That which fills up; full quantity or number. **complementary,** kom-plē-ment'a-ri, *a.* Completing; supplying a deficiency.

complete, kom-plēt', *a.* Having no deficiency; finished; total; absolute.—*vt.* (completing, completed). To make complete; to finish; to fulfill. **completely,** kom-plēt'li, *adv.* Fully. **completeness,** kom-plēt'nes, *n.* State of being complete; perfection. **completion,** kom-plē'shun, *n.* Act of completing; state of being complete; fulfillment; accomplishment.

complex, kom'pleks, *a.* Of various parts; involved; composite. **complexity,** kom-plek'si-ti, *n.* State of being complex; intricacy. **complexly,** kom'pleks-li, *adv.* In a complex manner; not simply.

complexion, kom-plek'shun, *n.* The color of the face; general appearance. **complexional,** kom-plek'shun-al, *a.* Pertaining to complexion.

compliance, kom-pli'ans, *n.* Submission; consent. **compliant,** kom-pli'ant, *a.* Yielding; bending; submissive; obliging. **compliantly,** kom-pli'ant-li, *adv.* In a yielding manner.

complicate, kom'pli-kāt, *vt.* (complicating, complicated). To make complex or intricate; to entangle. **complicated,** kom'pli-kāt-ed, *p.a.* Involved; intricate. **complication,** kom-pli-kā'shun, *n.* That which consists of many things involved; entanglement; intricacy.

complicity, kom-plis'i-ti, *n.* State or condition of being an accomplice.

compliment, kom'pli-ment, *n.* Act or expression of civility or regard; delicate flattery; a favor bestowed.—*vt.* To pay a compliment to; to congratulate; to praise. **complimentary,** kom-pli-men'ta-ri, *a.* Containing compliment; flattering.

comply, kom-pli', *vi.* (complying, complied). To yield; to assent; to acquiesce.

comport, kom-pōrt', *vi.* To agree; to suit.—*vt.* To bear or carry (one's self); to behave.

compose, kom-pōz', *vt.* (composing, composed). To form by uniting; to constitute; to write; to calm; to set types in printing. **composed,** kom-pōzd', *p.a.* Calm; sedate. **composedly,** kom-pōz'ed-li, *adv.* Calmly. **composer,** kom-pōz'èr, *n.* An author, especially a musical author.

composite, kom-poz'it, *a.* Compound; noting a rich order of architecture; noting plants whose flowers are arranged in dense heads.

composition, kom-pō-zish'un, *n.* Act of composing; a mixture; a literary or musical work; arrangement; agreement to receive or pay part of a debt in place of the whole; the part paid; act of setting types. **compositor,** kom-poz'i-èr, *n.* One who sets types.

compost, kom'pōst, *n.* A mixture for manure.

composure, kom-pō'zhèr, *n.* A settled frame of mind; calmness; tranquillity.

compound, kom-pound', *vt.* and *i.* To put together; to mix; to adjust; to discharge a debt by paying a part.—*a.* kom'pound. Composed of two or more ingredients, words, or parts.—*n.* A mass composed of two or more elements; inclosure in which houses stand.

comprehend, kom-prē-hend', *vt.* To embrace within limits; to understand. **comprehensible,** kom-prē-hen'si-bl, *a.* That may be comprehended; intelligible. **comprehension,** kom-prē-hen'shon, *n.* Act of comprehending; power of comprehending; understanding.

comprehensive, kom-prē-hen'siv, *a.* Comprising much; capacious; able to understand. **comprehensively,** kom-prē-hen'siv-li, *adv.* In a comprehensive manner.

compress, kom-pres', *vt.* To press together; to squeeze; to condense.—*n.* kom'pres. A soft mass or bandage used in surgery. **compressed,** kom-prest', *p.a.* Pressed together; flattened; condensed. **compressibility,** kom-pres'i-bil''i-ti, *n.* The quality of being compressible. **compressible,** kom-pres'i-bl, *a.* Capable of being compressed. **compression,** kom-presh'un, *n.* Act of compressing; state of being compressed.

comprise, comprize, kom-prīz', *vt.* (comprising, comprised). To embrace; to contain; to inclose.

compromise, kom'prō'mīz, *n.* An amicable agreement to settle differences; mutual concession.—*vt.* To settle by mutual concessions; to involve; to endanger the interests of.

comptroller, kon-trōl'èr, *n.* A controller; an officer who examines the accounts of collectors of public money.

compulsion, kom-pul'shun, *n.* Act of compelling; state of being compelled;

force. **compulsive**, kom-pul'siv, *a.* Having power to compel. **compulsively**, kom-pul'siv-li, *adv.* By force. **compulsory**, kom-pul'so-ri, *a.* Constraining; coercive; obligatory.

compunction, kom-pungk'shun, *n.* Remorse; contrition. **compunctious**, kom-pungk'shus, *a.* Implying or feeling compunction.

compute, kom-pūt', *vt.* (computing, computed). To count; to estimate. **computable**, kom-pūt'a-bl, *a.* Capable of being computed. **computation**, kom-pū-tā'shun, *n.* Act or process of computing; reckoning.

comrade, kom'rad, *n.* A mate; a companion; an associate. **comradeship**, kom'rad-ship, *n.* State of being a comrade or comrades.

con, kon, *vt.* (conning, conned). To learn; to fix in the mind; to peruse carefully; to direct the steering of (a ship).

concave, kon'kāv, *a.* Hollow, as the inner surface of a sphere; opposed to convex.—*n.* A hollow; an arch or vault. **concavity**, kon-kav'i-ti, *n.* Hollowness; a concave surface.

conceal, kon-sēl', *vt.* To hide; to secrete; to disguise. **concealable**, kon-sēl'a-bl, *a.* That may be concealed. **concealment**, kon-sēl'ment, *n.* Act of concealing; state of being concealed; a hiding-place.

concede, kon-sēd', *vt.* (conceding, conceded). To yield; to grant.—*vi.* To make concession.

conceit, kon-sēt', *n.* Conception; fancy; self-flattering opinion; vanity. **conceited**, kon-sēt'ed, *a.* Vain; egotistical.

conceive, kon-sēv', *vt.* (conceiving, conceived). To form in the womb; to take into the mind; to comprehend.—*vi.* To become pregnant; to have or form an idea. **conceivable**, kon-sēv'a-bl, *a.* That may be imagined or understood. **conceivably**, kon-sēv'a-bli, *adv.* In a conceivable or intelligible manner.

concentrate, kon-sen'trāt or kon', *vt.* (concentrating, concentrated). To bring together; to direct to one object; to condense. **concentration**, kon-sen-trā'-shun, *n.* Act of concentrating; state of being concentrated. **concentrative**, kon-sen'trā-tiv, *a.* Tending to concentrate.

concentric, kon-sen'trik, *a.* Having a common center.

concept, kon'sept, *n.* An object conceived by the mind; a general notion of a class of objects. **conception**, kon-sep'shun, *n.* Act of conceiving; state of being conceived; thing conceived; image in the mind; mental faculty which originates ideas. **conceptualist**, kon-sep'tū-al-ist, *n.* One who holds that the mind can give independent existence to general conceptions.

concern, kon-sèrn', *vt.* To belong to; to affect the interest of; to make anxious. —*n.* That which relates to one; affair; care; anxiety; a commercial establishment. **concerned**, kon-sèrnd', *a.* Interested; anxious. **concerning**, kon-sèrn'ing, *prep.* Having relation to; re-

specting. **concernment**, kon-sèrn'-ment, *n.* Affair; concern; solicitude.

concert, kon-sèrt', *vt.* To plan together; to contrive.—*n.* kon'sèrt. Agreement in a design; harmony; performance of a company of players, singers, &c. **concerted**, kon-sèrt'ed, *p.a.* Mutually contrived; done in concert.

concertina, kon-sèr-tē'na, *n.* A musical instrument of the accordion species.

concerto, kon-cher'tō, *n.* A musical composition for one principal instrument, with accompaniments for a full orchestra.

concession, kon-sçsh'un, *n.* Act of conceding; the thing yielded; a grant.

conch, kongk, *n.* A marine shell.

conciliate, kon-sil'i-āt, *vt.* (conciliating, conciliated). To bring to friendliness; to win the favor or consent; to reconcile; to propitiate. **conciliation**, kon-sil'i-ā"shun, *n.* Act of gaining favor of affection. **conciliator**, kon-sil'i-ā-tèr, *n.* One who conciliates or reconciles. **conciliatory**, kon-sil'i-a-to-ri, *a.* Tending to conciliate; pacific.

concise, kon-sīs', *a.* Brief; abridged; comprehensive. **concisely**, kon-sīs'li, *adv.* Briefly. **conciseness**, kon-sīs'nes, *n.* Brevity. **concision**, kon-sizh'un, *n.* Cutting off; conciseness.

conclave, kon'klāv, *n.* A private apartment; the assembly of cardinals for the election of a pope; a close assembly.

conclude, kon-klūd', *vt.* (concluding, concluded). To end; to decide; to deduce.—*vi.* To end; to form a final judgment. **conclusion**, kon-klū'zhun, *n.* Act of concluding; that which is concluded; inference; consequence; final decision; end. **conclusive**, kon-klū'siv, *a.* That concludes or determines; final; convincing. **conclusively**, kon-klū'siv-li, *adv.* Decisively; with final determination.

concoct, kon-kokt', *vt.* To devise; to plot. **concoction**, kon-kok'shun, *n.* Act of concocting; a mixture or preparation.

concomitant, kon-kom'it-ant, *a.* Accompanying; concurrent.—*n.* An accompaniment; a connected circumstance.

concord, kong'kord, *n.* Union in feelings, opinions, &c.; harmony; agreement of words in construction. **concordance**, kon-kor'dans, *n.* Agreement; index of the principal words of a book. **concordant**, kon-kor'dant, *a.* Agreeing together; correspondent; harmonious. **concordat**, kon-kor'dat, *n.* An agreement made by a sovereign with the pope relative to ecclesiastical matters.

concourse, kong'kōrs, *n.* Confluence; an assembly; crowd.

concrete, kon'krēt, *a.* Composed of particles united in one mass; congealed; existing in a subject; not abstract.—*n.* A mass formed by concretion; a hard mass formed of lime, sand, &c.—*vi.* kon-krēt' (concreting, concreted). To unite in a mass; to become solid. **concretely**, kon-krēt'li, *adv.* In a concrete manner. **concretion**, kon-krē'shun, *n.* Act of concreting; state of being concreted; a mass concreted.

concubine, kong'kū-bīn, *n.* A woman

who cohabits with a man; a mistress. **concubinage,** kon-kū'bin-ij, *n.* The living together as husband and wife without being married.

concupiscent, kon-ku'pi-sent, *a.* Lustful. **concupiscence,** kon-ku'pi-sens, *n.* Lust.

concur, kon-kur', *vi.* (concurring, concurred). To unite; to agree; to assent. **concurrence,** kon-kur'ens, *n.* Act of concurring; union; joint action. **concurrent,** kon-kur'ent, *a.* Acting together.—*n.* That which concurs; joint cause. **concurrently,** kon-kur'ent-li, *adv.* With concurrence; unitedly.

concuss, kon-kus', *vt.* (concussing, concussed). To force by threats; to intimidate.

concussion, kon-kush'un, *n.* A violent shock. **concussive,** kon-kus'iv, *a.* Having the power or quality of shaking; agitating.

condemn, kon-dem', *vt.* To pronounce to be wrong; to censure; to sentence. **condemnation,** kon-dem-nā'shun, *n.* Act of condemning; state of being condemned; sentence; cause of blame. **condemnatory,** kon-dem'na-tō-ri, *a.* Condemning; bearing condemnation.

condense, kon-dens', *vt.* (condensing, condensed). To reduce in compass; to reduce from a gaseous to a liquid or solid state.—*vi.* To become dense; to grow thick. **condensable,** kon-dens'a-bl, *a.* Capable of being condensed. **condensation,** kon-dens-ā'shun, *n.* Act of condensing; state of being condensed. **condenser,** kon-den'sèr, *n.* One who or that which condenses; a vessel in which vapors are reduced to liquid by coldness; a chamber in which steam is condensed.

condescend, kon-dē-send', *vi.* To descend from the privileges of superior rank; to deign. **condescending,** kon-dē-sen'ding, *a.* Yielding to inferiors; patronizing. **condescendingly,** kon-dē-sen'ding-li, *adv.* In a condescending manner. **condescension,** kon-dē-sen'shun, *n.* Act of condescending; courtesy; complaisance.

condign, kon-dīn', *a.* Deserved; suitable. **condiment,** kon'di-ment, *n.* Seasoning; relish.

condition, kon-dish'un, *n.* State; case; external circumstances; temper; stipulation. **conditional,** kon-dish'un-al, *a.* Depending on conditions; not absolute. **conditionally,** kon-dish'un-al-li, *adv.* With certain limitations. **conditioned,** kon-dish'und, *a.* Having a certain condition, state, or qualities.

condole, kon-dōl', *vi.* (condoling, condoled). To grieve with another; to sympathize. **condolement,** kon-dōl'ment, *n.* Sympathetic grief; sorrow with others. **condolence,** kon-dō'lens, *n.* Act of condoling; expression of sympathy.

condone, kon-dōn', *vt.* (condoning, condoned).

condor, kon'dor, *n.* A S. American vulture.

conduce, kon-dūs', *vi.* (conducing, conduced). To lead; to tend; to contribute.

conducive, kon-dū'siv, *a.* Having a tendency to promote.

conduct, kon'dukt, *n.* Personal behavior; management; escort.—*vt.* kon-dukt'. To lead or guide; to escort; to manage; to behave (one's self); to transmit, as heat, &c. **conductible,** kon-duk'ti-bl, *a.* That may be conducted. **conduction,** kon-duk'shun, *n.* Property by which bodies transmit heat or electricity. **conductive,** kon-duk'tiv, *a.* Having the physical property of conducting. **conductor,** kon-duk'tèr, *n.* A leader; a director; a body that transmits heat, electricity, &c.

conduit, kon'dwit or kon'dit, *n.* A channel or pipe to convey water, &c., or to drain off filth; a channel or passage.

cone, kōn, *n.* A solid body having a circle for its base, and tapering to a point; the fruit of firs, pine-trees, &c.

confection, kon-fek'shun, *n.* A mixture; a sweet-meat. **confectionary,** kon-fek'shun-eri, *a.* Pertaining to confections.—*n.* A place where sweetmeats are made. **confectioner,** kon-fek'shun-èr, *n.* One who makes or sells sweetmeats.

confederate, kon-fed-er-āt, *a.* Allied by treaty, *n.* One united with others in a league.—*vt.* and *i.* (confederating, confederated). To unite in a league. **confederation,** kon-fed'er-a-"shun, *n.* A league; alliance, particularly of states, &c. **confederacy,** kon-fed'er-a-si, *n.* A confederation; the parties united by a league.

confer, kon-fèr', *vi.* (conferring, conferred). To consult together.—*vt.* To give or bestow. **conference,** kon'fèr-ens, *n.* A meeting for consultation, or for the adjustment of differences; bestowal.

confess, kon-fes', *vt.* To own, as a crime, debt, &c.; to admit; to declare adherence to; to hear a confession, as a priest.—*vi.* To make confession. **confessedly,** kon-fes'ed-li, *adv.* Avowedly. **confession,** kon-fesh'un, *n.* Act of confessing; that which is confessed; a formulary of articles of faith; a creed. **confessional,** kon-fesh'un-al, *n.* The place where a priest sits to hear confessions. **confessor,** kon-fes'èr, *n.* One who confesses; a priest who hears confession.

confide, kon-fīd', *vi.* (confiding, confided). To trust wholly; to have firm faith (with *in*).—*vt.* To entrust; to commit to the charge of. **confidant,** kon'fi-dant, *n.m.*; **confidante,** kon-fi-dant', *n.f.* A confidential friend.

confidence, kon'fi-dens, *n* Firm belief or trust; self-reliance; boldness; assurance; a secret. **confident,** kon'fi-dent, *a.* Having confidence; trusting; assured; dogmatical. **confidential,** kon-fi-den'shal, *a.* Enjoying confidence; trusty; private; secret.

confidentially, kon-fi-den'shal-li, *adv.* In confidence. **confidently,** kon'fi-dent-li, *adv.* In a confident manner; positively. **confiding,** kon-fīd'ing, *a.* Trusting; reposing confidence.

configuration, kon-fig'ū-rā'shun, *n.* External form; contour.

confine, kon'fīn, *n.* Boundary; territory near the end; border (generally in *pl.*).—*vt.* kon-fīn', (confining, confined). To restrain; to limit; to shut up; to imprison. **To be confined,** to be in childbed.

confined, kon-fīnd', *a.* Limited; secluded.

confinemnt, kon-fīn'ment, *n.* Imprisonment; seclusion; childbirth.

confirm, kon-fèrm', *vt.* To make firm or more firm; to establish; to make certain; to administer rite of confirmation to. **confirmation,** kon-fèr-mā'shun, *n.* Act of confirming; additional evidence; ratification; the laying on of a bishop's hands in the rite of admission to the privileges of a Christian. **confirmed,** kon-fèrmd', *a.* Fixed; settled in certain habits, state of health, &c.

confiscate, kon'fis-kāt or kon-fis'kāt, *vt.* (confiscating, confiscated). To seize as forfeited to the public treasury. **confiscation,** kon-fis-kā'shun, *n.* Act of confiscating.

conflagration, kon-fla-grā'shun, *n.* A great fire.

conflict, kon'flikt, *n.* A struggle; clashing of views or statements.—*vi.* kon-flikt'. To meet in opposition; to be antagonistic. **conflicting,** kon-flikt'ing, *a.* Contradictory.

confluence, kon'flū-ens, *n.* A flowing together; meeting, or place of meeting, of rivers; a concourse; a crowd. **confluent,** kon'flū-ent, *a.* Flowing together, running into each other; united.

conform, kon-form', *vt.* To cause to be of the same form; to adapt.—*vi.* To comply. **conformable,** kon-for'ma-bl, *a.* In harmony or conformity; suitable; compliant; *geol.* lying in parallel planes. **conformably,** kon-for'ma-bli, *adv.* Suitably. **conformation,** kon-for-mā'shun, *n.* The act of conforming; structure; configuration. **conformist,** kon-for'mist, *n.* One who conforms; one who complies with the worship of the established church. **conformity,** kon-for'mi-ti, *n.* Agreement; resemblance; compliance with.

confound, kon-found', *vt.* To confuse; to astound; to overthrow; to mistake. **confounded,** kon-foun'ded, *a.* Excessive; odious; detestable; reprehensible. **confoundedly,** kon-foun'ded-li, *adv.* Shamefully; odiously; detestably.

confrère, kong-frär, *n.* A colleague.

confront, kon-frunt', *vt.* To face; to oppose; to bring into the presence of; to set together for comparison.

Confucian, kon-fū'shi-an, *a.* and *n.* Pertaining to, or a follower of, Confucius, the famous Chinese philosopher.

confuse, kon-fūz', *vt.* (confusing, confused). To mix without order; to derange; to confound; to disconcert. **confused,** kon-fūzd', *p.a.* Perplexed; disconcerted. **confusedly,** kon-fūz'ed-li, *adv.* In a confused manner. **confusion,** kon-fū'zhun, *n.* Disorder, embarrassment.

confute, kon-fūt', *vt.* (confuting, confuted). To prove to be false; to refute. **confutable,** kon-fūt'a-bl, *a.* That may be confuted. **confutation,** kon-fū-tā'shun, *n.* Act of confuting; refutation; overthrow.

congeal, kon-jēl', *vt.* To freeze; to coagulate.—*vi.* To pass from a fluid to a solid state.

congenial, kon-jē'ni-al, *a.* Of like taste or disposition; kindly; adapted. **congeniality,** kon-jē'ni-al″i-ti, *n.* Natural affinity; suitableness.

congenital, kon-jen'i-tal, *a.* Pertaining to an individual from his birth.

conger, kong'gèr, *n.* The sea eel.

congest, kon-jest', *vt.* and *i.* To accumulate to excess, as blood, population, &c. **congestion,** kon-jes'chun, *n.* Excessive accumulation; undue fullness of blood-vessels in an organ.

conglomerate, kon-glom'ėr-it, *a.* Gathered into a ball; composed of fragments of rock cemented together.—*n.* A rock composed of pebbles cemented together. —*vt.* To gather into a ball or round mass. **conglomeration,** kon-glom'ėr-ā″shun, *n.* Act of conglomerating; state of being conglomerated; a mixed mass.

congratulate, kon-grat'ū-lāt, *vt.* (congratulating, congratulated). To express sympathy to in good fortune; to felicitate. **congratulation,** kon-grat'ū-lā″shun, *n.* Act of congratulating; expression of sympathetic joy at another's good fortune. **congratulator,** kon-grat'ū-lāt-ėr, *n.* One who offers congratulations. **congratulatory,** kon-grat'ū-lā-tō-ri, *a.* Expressing congratulation.

congregate, kong'grē-gāt, *vt.* (congregating, congregated). To collect together. —*vi.* To come together; to assemble. **congregation,** kong'grē-gā″shun, *n.* Act of congregating; an assembly; an assembly met for divine worship. **congregational,** kong'grē-gā″shun-a′ *a.* Pertaining to a congregation, or to the Congregationalists. **congregationalist,** kong'grē-gā″shun-al-ist, *n.* One who adheres to the system in which each separate congregation or church forms an independent body.

congress, kong'gres, *n.* An assembly; a meeting of ambassadors, &c., for the settlement of affairs between different nations; the legislature of the United States. **congressional,** kon-gresh'un-al, *a.* Pertaining to a congress.

congruity, kon-grū'i-ti, *n.* Suitableness; accordance; consistency. **congruence,** **congruency,** kong'grū-ens, kong'grū-en-si, *n.* Accordance; consistency. **congruent,** kong'grū-ent, *a.* Suitable; agreeing; correspondent.

congruous, kong'grū-us, *a.* Accordant; suitable; consistent. **congruously,** kong'grū-us-li, *adv.* Suitably; consistently.

conic, conical, kon'ik, kon'i-kal, *a.* Having the form of a cone; pertaining to a cone. **conically,** kon'i-kal-li, *adv.* In the form of a cone.

conics, kon'iks, *n.* That part of geometry which treats of the cone.

coniferous, kŏ-nif'ẽr-us, *a.* Bearing cones as the pine, fir, &c.

conjecture, kon-jek'tūr, *n.* Supposition; opinion without proof; surmise.—*vt.* (conjecturing, conjectured). To judge by guess; to surmise.—*vi.* To form conjectures. **conjecturable**, kon-jek'tur-a-bl, *a.* That may be conjectured or guessed. **conjectural**, kon-jek'tūr-al, *a.* Depending on conjecture.

conjoin, kon-join', *vt.* To join together; to unite; to associate. **conjoint**, kon-joint', *a.* United; connected; associated. **conjointly**, kon-joint'li, *adv.* Jointly.

conjugal, kon'jū-gal, *a.* Pertaining to marriage; connubial. **conjugally**, kon'jū-gal-li, *adv.* Matrimonially; connubially.

conjugate, kon'jū-gāt, *vt.* (conjugating, conjugated). To join together; to inflect (a verb) through its several forms. —*a.* Joined in pairs; kindred in origin and meaning. **conjugation**, kon-jū-gā'shun, *n.* The act of conjugating; the inflection of verbs; a class of verbs similarly conjugated.

conjunction, kon-jungk'shun, *n.* Act of joining; state of being joined; connection; a connecting word. **conjunctive**, kon-jungk'tiv, *a.* Serving to unite; subjunctive. **conjunctively**, kon-jungk'tiv-ly, *adv.* In conjunction. **conjunctly**, kon-jungkt'li, *adv.* Jointly. **conjuncture**, kon-jungk'tūr, *n.* A combination of important events; a crisis.

conjuration, kon-jū-rā'shun, *n.* The act of conjuring; an incantation; a spell. **conjure**, kon-jūr', *vt.* (conjuring, conjured). To call upon solemnly; to beseech. **conjure**, kun'jẽr, *vt.* (conjuring, conjured). To summon up by enchantments.—*vi.* To practice the arts of a conjurer. **conjurer, conjuror**, kun'-jẽr-ẽr, *n.* An enchanter; one who practices legerdemain. **conjury**, kun'jẽr-i, *n.* Magic; legerdemain.

connect, ko-nekt', *vt.* To conjoin; to combine; to associate.—*vi.* To unite or cohere together; to have a close relation. **connectedly**, ko-nekt'ed-li, *adv.* In a connected manner. **connection, connexion**, ko-nek'shun, *n.* Act of connecting; state of being connected; a relation by blood or marriage; relationship. **connective**, ko-nek'tiv, *a.* Having the power of connecting; tending to connect. —*n.* A word that connects other words and sentences; a conjunction. **connector**, ko-nek'tẽr, *n.* One who or that which connects.

connive, ko-nīv', *vi.* (conniving, connived). To wink; to pretend ignorance or blindness; to forbear to see (with *at*). **connivance, connivence**, ko-nīv'ans, ko-nīv'ens, *n.* Voluntary blindness to an act; pretended ignorance. **conniver**, ko-nīv'ẽr, *n.* One who connives.

connoisseur, kon'i-sẽr, *n.* A judge of any art; particularly painting and sculpture.

connote, ko-nōt', *vt.* (connoting, connoted). To include in the meaning; to imply. **connotation**, kon-ō-tā'shun, *n.* That which constitutes the meaning of a word.

connubial, ko-nū'bi-al, *a.* Pertaining to marriage; conjugal; matrimonial.

conquer, kong'kẽr, *vt.* To gain by force; to vanquish; to subjugate; to surmount. —*vi.* To overcome; to gain the victory. **conquerable**, kong'kẽr-a-bl, *a.* That may be conquered or subdued. **conqueror**, kong'kẽr-ẽr, *n.* A victor. **conquest**, kong'kwest, *n.* Act of conquering; that which is conquered; a gaining by struggle.

consanguinity, kon'sang-gwin"i-ti, *n.* Relationship by blood. **consanguineous**, kon'sang-gwin"ē-us, *a.* Of the same blood; related by birth.

conscience, kon'shens, *n.* Internal knowledge or judgment of right and wrong; the moral sense; morality. **conscientious**, kon-shi-en'shus, *a.* Regulated by conscience; scrupulous. **conscientiously**, kon-shi-en'shus-li, *adv.* In a conscientious manner.

conscious, kon'shus, *a.* Knowing in one's own mind; knowing by sensation or perception; aware; sensible; self-conscious. **consciously**, kon'shus-li, *adv.* In a conscious manner. **consciousness**, kon'shus-nes, *n.* State of being conscious; perception of what passes in one's own mind; sense of guilt or innocence.

conscript, kon'skript, *a.* Registered; enrolled.—*n.* One compulsorily enrolled to serve in the army or navy. **conscription**, kon-skrip'shun, *n.* A compulsory enrollment for military or naval service.

consecrate, kon'sē-krāt, *vt.* (consecrating, consecrated). To appropriate to sacred uses; to dedicate to God.—*a.* Sacred; consecrated. **consecration**, kon-sē-krā'shun, *n.* Act of consecrating; ordination of a bishop.

consecutive, kon-sek'ū-tiv, *a.* Following in regular order; following logically. **consecutively**, kon-sek'ū-tiv-li, *adv.* In a consecutive manner.

consent, kon-sent', *n.* Agreement to what is proposed; concurrence; compliance.—*vi.* To be of the same mind; to assent; to comply. **consentient**, kon-sen'shent, *a.* Consenting; agreeing; accordant.

consequence, kon'sē-kwens, *n.* That which follows as a result; inference; importance. **consequent**, kon'sē-kwent, *a.* Following, as the natural effect, or by inference.—*n.* Effect; result; inference. **consequential**, kon-sē-kwen'shal, *a.* Following as the effect; pompous. **consequentially**, kon-sē-kwen'shal-li, *adv.* By consequence; pompously. **consequently**, kon'sē-kwent-li, *adv.* By consequence; therefore.

conserve, kon-sẽrv', *vt.* (conserving, conserved). To keep in a sound state; to candy or pickle.—*n.* kon'sẽrv. That which is conserved, particularly fruits. **conservancy**, con-sẽr'van-si, *n.* Conservation; preservation; official supervision. **conservation**, kon-sẽr-vā'shun, *n.* Preservation; the keeping of a thing entire. **conservatism**, kon-sẽrv'at-izm, *n.* The political principles of Conservatives. **conservative**, kon-sẽr'va-tiv, *a.* Preservative; adhering to existing institutions.—*n.* One opposed to political changes of a radical nature; a Tory.

conservatoire, kong-sėr-vȧ-twär', *n.* A public establishment for the study of music.

conservatory, kon-sėr'va-to-ri, *n.* A greenhouse for exotics.

consider, kon-sid'ėr, *vt.* To fix the mind on; to ponder; to have respect to; to regard to be.—*vi.* To think seriously; to ponder. **considerable**, kon-sid'ėr-a-bl, *a.* Worthy of consideration; moderately large. **considerably**, kon-si'dėr-a-bli, *adv.* In a considerable degree. **considerate**, kon-sid'ėr-it, *a.* Given to consideration; mindful of others; deliberate. **considerately**, kon-sid'ėr-āt-li, *adv.* In a considerate manner. **consideration**, kon-sid'ėr-ā"shun, *n.* Mental view; serious deliberation; importance; motive of action; an equivalent. **considering**, kon-sid'ėr-ing, *prep.* Taking into account; making allowance for.

consign, kon-sīn', *vt.* To deliver over to another by agreement; to entrust; to commit; to deposit. **consignee**, kon-sī-nē', *n.* The person to whom goods are consigned. **consigner**, **consignor**, kon-sīn'er, kon-sīn'or, *n.* The person who consigns. **consignment**, kon-sīn'ment, *n.* Act of consigning; the thing consigned.

consist, kon-sist', *vi.* To be in a fixed state; to be comprised; to be made up; to be compatible; to agree. **consistence, consistency**, kon-sis'tens, kon-sis'ten-si, *n.* A degree of density; firmness or coherence; harmony; agreement. **consistent**, kon-sis'tent, *a.* Fixed; firm; not contradictory; compatible. **consistently**, kon-sis'tent-li, *adv.* In a consistent manner.

consistory, kon'sis-to-ri, *n.* A spiritual court; the court of a diocesan bishop; college of cardinals.

console, kon-sōl', *vt.* (consoling, consoled). To comfort; to soothe; to cheer. **consolation**, kon-sō-lā'shun, *n.* A solace; alleviation of misery; what helps to cheer; what gives comfort. **consolatory**, kon-sol'a-to-ri, *a.* Tending to give solace; assuaging grief.

consolidate, kon-sol'id-āt, *vt.* (consolidating, consolidated). To make solid or firm; to unite into one; to compact.—*vi.* To grow firm and solid. **consolidation**, kon-sol'i-dā"shun, *n.* Act of consolidating; state of being consolidated.

consonance, kon'sō-nans, *n.* Concord; agreement; consistency.

consonant, kon'sō-nant, *a.* Having agreement; accordant; consistent.—*n.* A letter always sounded with a vowel.

consort, kon'sort, *n.* A partner; a wife or husband; a companion.—*vi.* kon-sort'. To associate; to accord.

conspicuous, kon-spik'ū-us, *a.* Standing clearly in view; manifest; distinguished. **conspicuously**, kon-spik'ū-us-li, *adv.* In a conspicuous manner.

conspiracy, kon-spir'a-si, *n.* A plot; a treasonable combination. **conspirator**, kon-spir'āt-ėr, *n.* One who engages in a plot or conspiracy. **conspire**, kon-spir', *vi.* (conspiring, conspired). To plot; to

combine for some evil purpose; to tend to one end.

constable, kun'sta-bl, *n.* An officer of the peace; a policeman. **constabulary**, kon-stab'ū-le-ri, *a.* Pertaining to constables.—*n.* The body of constables in a city, county, &c.

constancy, kon'stan-si, *n.* Uniformity; steadfastness; lasting affection.

constant, kon'stant, *a.* Steadfast; perpetual; assiduous; resolute.—*n.* That which remains unchanged; a fixed quantity. **constantly**, kon'stant-li, *adv.* In a constant manner.

constellation, kon-ste-lā'shun, *n.* A group of fixed stars; an assemblage of splendors or excellences.

consternation, kon-stėr-nā'shun, *n.* Prostration of the mind by terror, dismay, &c.

constipate, kon'sti-pāt, *vt.* (constipating, constipated). To make costive. **constipation**, kon-sti-pā'shun, *n.* Costiveness.

constituent, kon-stit'ū-ent, *a.* Forming; existing as an essential part.—*n.* An elector; an essential part. **constituency**, kon-stit'ū-en-si, *n.* The body of constituents.

constitute, kon'sti-tūt, *vt.* (constituting, constituted). To set up or establish; to compose; to appoint; to make and empower.

constitution, kon-sti-tū'shun, *n.* The particular frame or character of the body or mind; established form of government; a system of fundamental laws; a particular law. **constitutional**, kon-sti-tū'shun-al, *a.* Adherent in the human constitution; consistent with the civil constitution; legal.—*n.* A walk for the sake of health. **constitutionalism**, kon-sti-tū'shun-al-izm, *n.* The theory of constitutional rule; adherence to a constitution. **constitutionalist, constitutionist**, kon-sti-tū'shun-al-ist, kon-sti-tū'shon-ist, *n.* An adherent to the constitution. **constitutionally**, kon-sti-tū'shun-al-li, *adv.* In consistency with the constitution.

constrain, kon-strān', *vt.* To urge by force; to necessitate; to restrain. **constrainable**, kon-strān'a-bl, *a.* That may be constrained. **constrained**, kon-strānd', *a.* With a certain constraint or want of freedom; forced. **constraint**, kon-strānt', *n.* Necessity; reserve; restraint.

constrict, kon-strikt', *vt.* To draw together; to contract. **constriction**, kon-strik'shun, *n.* Contraction. **constrictive**, kon-strik'tiv, *a.* Tending to contract or compress. **constrictor**, kon-strikt'ėr, *n.* That which constricts; a muscle that closes an orifice; a serpent which crushes its prey.

construct, kon-strukt', *vt.* To build; to frame with contrivance; to devise. **construction**, kon-struk'shun, *n.* Structure; arrangement of words in a sentence; sense; interpretation. **constructional**, kon-struk'shun-al, *a.* Pertaining to construction. **constructive**, kon-struk'tiv, *a.* Having ability to construct; created or deduced by construction; inferred. **constructively,** kon-struk'tiv-li, *adv.* In a constructive manner; by fair inference.

construe, kon'strū, *vt.* (construing, construed). To arrange words so as to discover the sense of a sentence; to interpret.

consul, kon'sul, *n.* One of the two chief magistrates of ancient Rome; a person appointed by government to reside in a foreign country, and protect the commercial interests of his own country. **consular,** kon'sū-lėr, *a.* Pertaining to a consul. **consulate,** kon'sūl-āt, *n.* The office, jurisdiction, or residence of a consul. **consulship,** kon'sul-ship, *n.* The office of a consul, or the term of his office.

consult, kon-sult', *vi.* To seek the opinion of another; to deliberate in common; to consider.—*vt.* To ask advice of; to refer to for information; to have regard to. **consultation,** kon-sul-tā'shun, *n.* Act of consulting; a meeting for deliberation. **consulter,** kon-sul'tėr, *n.* One who consults. **consulting,** kon-sul'ing, *a.* Giving advice; used for consultations.

consume, kon-sūm', *vt.* (consuming, consumed). To reduce to nothing; to burn up; to squander.—*vi.* To waste away slowly; to be exhausted. **consumer,** kon-sūm'ėr, *n.* One who consumes.

consummate, kon'sum-it, *vt.* To finish; to perfect.—*a.* Complete; perfect. **consummately,** kon-sum'it-li, *adv.* Completely; perfectly. **consummation,** kon-sum-ā'shun, *n.* Act of consummating; end; perfection.

consumption, kon-sum'shun, *n.* Act of consuming; quantity consumed; a gradual wasting away of the body; phthisis. **consumptive,** kon-sump'tiv, *a.* Affected with or inclined to consumption or phthisis.

contact, kon'takt, *n.* A touching together; close union or juncture of bodies.

contagion, kon-tā'jun, *n.* Communication of a disease by contact; poisonous emanation; infection. **contagious,** kon-tā'jus, *a.* Caught or communicated by contact; infectious.

contain, kon-tān', *vt.* To hold; to be able to hold; to comprise; to restrain. **containable,** kon-tān'a-bl, *a.* That may be contained or comprised. **container,** kon-tān'ant, kon-tān'ėr, *n.* One who or that which contains.

contaminate, kon-tam'i-nāt, *vt.* To corrupt; to taint; to vitiate. **contamination,** kon-tam'i-nā"shun, *n.* Pollution; defilement; taint.

contemplate, kon-tem'plāt or kon'tem-plāt, *vt.* To view with continued attention; to meditate on; to design; to purpose.—*vi.* To study; to meditate. **contemplation,** kon-tem-plā'shun, *n.* Act of contemplating; meditation. **contemplative,** kon-tem'plā-tiv, *a.* Given to contemplation; thoughtful.

contemporary, kon-tem'pō-re-ri, *a.* Living or occurring at the same time.—*n.* One who lives at the same time with another. **contemporaneous,** kon-tem'pō-rā"nē-us, *a.* Living or being at the same time. **contemporaneously,** kon-tem'pō-rā"nē-us-li, *adv.* At the same time.

contempt, kon-tempt', *n.* Act of contemning; scorn; disregard; disobedience to the rules, &c., of a court. **contemptible,** kon-temp'ti-bl, *a.* Worthy of contempt; despicable; vile; mean. **contemptibly,** kon-temp'ti-bli, *adv.* In a contemptible manner; meanly. **contemptuous,** kon-temp'tū-us, *a.* Manifesting contempt; scornful; insolent. **contemptuously,** kon-temp'tū-us-li, *adv.* In a contemptuous manner.

contend, kon-tend', *vi.* To strive; to vie; to dispute; to wrangle. **contender,** kon-tend'ėr, *n.* One who contends.

content, kon-tent', *a.* Easy in mind; satisfied.—*vt.* To satisfy the mind of; to please or gratify.—*n.* State of being contented; contentment. Kon-tent' or kon'tent, things contained in a vessel, book, &c.; in these senses, *pl.*; capacity; space occupied; in these senses, *sing.* **contented,** kon-ten'ted, *a.* Satisfied; easy in mind. **contentedly,** kon-ten'ted-li, *adv.* In a contented manner. **contentment,** kon-tent'ment, *n.* State of being contented; satisfaction; content. **contention,** kon-ten'shun, *n.* Struggle; quarrel; debate; emulation. **contentious,** kon-ten'shus, *a.* Quarrelsome.

contest, kon-test', *vt.* To call in question; to strive for.—*vi.* To strive; to contend; to emulate.—*n.* kon'test. Struggle for victory; encounter; debate; competition. **contestable,** kon-test'a-bl, *a.* That may be contested; disputable; controvertible.

context, kon'tekst, *n.* The parts which precede or follow a passage quoted. **contexture,** kon-teks'tūr, *n.* The interweaving of several parts into one body; disposition of parts; texture.

contiguous, kon-tig'ū-us, *a.* Touching one another; in contact; adjacent. **contiguously,** kon-tig'ū-us-li, *adv.* In a contiguous manner or position. **contiguity,** kon-ti-gū'i-ti, *n.* State of being contiguous; proximity.

continence, continency, kon'ti-nens, kon'ti-nen-si, *n.* Restraint of the desires and passions; chastity; temperance. **continent,** kon'ti-nent, *a.* Chaste; moderate.—*n.* A connected tract of land of great extent; the mainland of Europe. **continental,** kon-ti-nen'tal, *a.* Pertaining to a continent, particularly Europe. **continently,** kon'ti-nent-li, *adv.* In a continent manner; chastely.

contingent, kon-tin'jent, *a.* Happening by chance; incidental; dependent upon an uncertainty.—*n.* A contingency; a quota; a quota of troops for a joint enterprise. **contingently,** kon-tin'jent-li, *adv.* Accidentally; dependently. **contingence, contingency,** kon-tin'jens, kon-tin'jen-si, *n.* Quality of being contingent; an event which may occur; chance; juncture.

continual, kon-tin'ū-al, *a.* Not intermitting; uninterrupted; often repeated. **continuation,** kon-tin'ū-ā"shun, *n.* Succession; extension; prolongation.

continue, kon-tin'ū, *vi.* (continuing, continued). To remain in a state or place; to be durable; to persevere; to be steadfast.—*vt.* To prolong; to extend; to persevere in.

continuity, kon-ti-nū'i-ti, *n.* Close union of parts; unbroken texture; cohesion.

continuous, kon-tin'ū-us, *a.* Joined together closely; conjoined; continued.

contort, kon-tort', *vt.* To twist; to writhe; to draw or pull away.

contortion, kon-tor'shun, *n.* A writhing; wry motion; distortion.

contortionist, kon-tor'shun-ist, *n.* An acrobat who practices contortions of the body.

contour, kon-tör', *n.* The line that bounds a body; outline.

contraband, kon'tra-band, *n.* Illegal traffic; smuggling.—*a.* Prohibited.

contract, kon-trakt', *vt.* To draw together; to cause to shrink; to reduce; to betroth; to bring on; to incur.—*vi.* To shrink up; to make a mutual agreement. —*n.* kon'trakt. Agreement; bond; the writing which contains stipulations; betrothment.

contracted, kon-trakt'ed, *a.* Limited; narrow; mean.

contractible, kon-trak'ti-bl, *a.* Capable of contraction.

contraction, kon-trak'shun, *n.* Shrinking; shortening; abbreviation.

contractor, kon-trak'tèr, *n.* One who contracts.

contradict, kon-tra-dikt', *vt.* To assert to be the contrary; to deny; to oppose.

contradiction, kon-tra-dik'shun, *n.* A contrary assertion; inconsistency with itself.

contradictorily, kon-tra-dik'to-ri-li, *adv.* In a contradictory manner.

contradictory, kon-tra-dik'to-ri, *a.* Implying contradiction; inconsistent.

contralto, kon-tral'tō, *n.* The lowest voice of a woman or boy.

contraposition, kon'tra-po-zish'un, *n.* A placing over against; opposite position.

contrapuntal, kon-tra-pun'tal, *a.* Pertaining to counterpoint.

contrarily, kon'trer-i-li, *adv.* In a contrary manner; on the other hand.

contrariwise, kon'tra-ri-wīz, *adv.* On the contrary; on the other hand.

contrary, kon'trer-i, *a.* Opposite; repugnant; inconsistent.—*adv.* In an opposite manner; in opposition.—*n.* A thing that is contrary.

contrast, kon-trast', *vt.* To set in opposition; to show the difference or heighten the effect.—*vi.* To stand in contrast to.—*n.* kon'trast. Opposition or comparison of things; a person or thing strikingly different.

contravene, kon-tra-vēn', *vt.* (contravening, contravened). To oppose; to transgress. **contravention,** kon-tra-ven'shun, *n.* Transgression; violation.

contribute, kon-trib'ūt, *vt.* (contributing, contributed). To give in common with others.—*vi.* To give a part; to conduce. **contribution,** kon-tri-bū'shun, *n.* Act of contributing; that which is contributed; an article sent to a periodical, &c. **contributive,** kon-trib'ū-tiv, *a.* Tending to contribute; lending aid to promote. **contributor,** kon-trib'ū-tèr, *n.* One who contributes; a writer to a periodical. **contributory,** kon-trib'ū-tō-ri, *a.* Contributing to the same end.

contrite, kon'trīt, *a.* Broken-hearted for sin; penitent. **contritely,** kon'trīt-li, *adv.* In a contrite manner; with penitence. **contrition,** kon-tri'shun, *n.* Grief of heart for sin.

contrive, kon-trīv', *vt.* (contriving, contrived). To invent; to devise.—*vi.* To form or design. **contrivable,** kon-trīv'a-bl, *a.* That may be contrived, invented, or devised. **contrivance,** kon-trīv'ans, *n.* Scheme; invention; artifice.

contriver, kon-trīv'èr, *n.* Inventor; schemer.

control, kon-trōl', *n.* Restraint; superintendence; authority.—*vt.* (controlling, controlled). To restrain; to regulate. **controllable,** kon-trōl'a-bl, *a.* That may be controlled; subject to command. **controller,** kon-trōl'ér, *n.* An officer who checks the accounts of collectors of public moneys.

controversy, kon'trō-vèr-si, *n.* A disputation, particularly in writing; litigation. **controversial,** kon-trō-vèr'shal, *a.* Relating to controversy. **controversialist,** kon-trō-vèr'shal-ist, *n.* One who carries on a controversy.

controvert, kon'trō-vèrt, *vt.* To dispute by reasoning; to attempt to disprove or confute. **controvertible,** kon-trō-vèrt'-i-bl, *a.* That may be controverted. **controvertibly,** kon-trō-vèrt'i-bli, *adv.* In a controvertible manner.

contumacy, kon'tū-ma-si, *n.* Resistance to authority; perverseness. **contumacious,** kon-tū-mā'shus, *a.* Opposing rightful authority; obstinate.

contumely, kon'tū-me-li, *n.* Haughty insolence; contemptuous language. **contumelious,** kon-tū-mē'li-us, *a.* Contemptuous; insolent; proudly rude.

contusion, kon-tū'zhun, *n.* A severe bruise; injury without breaking of the skin.

conundrum, kō-nun'drum, *n.* A sort of riddle turning on some odd resemblance between things quite unlike.

convalesce, kon-va-les', *vi.* (convalescing, convalesced). To recover health. **convalescence, convalescency,** kon-va-les'ens, kon-va-les'en-si, *n.* The state of one convalescent; gradual recovery after disease. **convalescent,** kon-va-les'ent, *a.* Recovering health after sickness.—*n.* One recovering from sickness.

convene, kon-vēn', *vi.* (convening, convened). To assemble.—*vt.* To cause to assemble; to convoke. **convener,** kon-vēn'èr, *n.* One who calls an assembly together. **convenable,** kon-vēn'a-bl, *a.* That may be convened or assembled.

convenient, kon-vēn'i-ent, *a.* Suitable; adapted; opportune. **conveniently,** kon-vēn'i-ent-li, *adv.* Suitably; with ease. **convenience, conveniency,** kon-vēn'i-ens, kon-vēn'i-en-si, *n.* Ease; comfort; suitable opportunity; an appliance or utensil.

convent, kon'vent, *n.* A body of monks or nuns; a monastery; a nunnery.

convention, kon-ven'shun, *n.* An assembly; an agreement; recognized social custom. **conventional**, kon-ven'shun-al, *a.* Formed by agreement; tacitly understood; resting on mere usage. **conventionalism**, kon-ven'shun-al-izm, *n.* Arbitrary custom; a conventional phrase, ceremony, &c. **conventionally**, kon-ven'shun-al-li, *adv.* In a conventional manner.

converge, kon-vėrj', *vi.* (converging, converged). To tend to the same point; to approach in position or character. **convergence**, **convergency**, kon-vėr'jens, kon-vėr'jen-si, *n.* Tendency to one point. **convergent**, kon-vėr'jent, *a.* Tending to one point or object; approaching.

conversation, kon-vėr-sā'shun, *n.* Familiar intercourse; easy talk. **conversational**, kon-vėr-sā'shun-al, *a.* Pertaining to conversation. **conversationalist**, **conversationist**, kon-vėr-sā'shun-al-ist, kon-vėr-sā'shun-ist, *n.* One who excels in conversation. **conversably**, kon-vėrs'a-bli, *adv.* In a conversable manner. **conversant**, kon'vėr-sant, *a.* Having intercourse or familiarity; versed in; proficient; occupied or concerned.

converse, kon-vėrs', *vi.* (conversing, conversed). To hold intercourse; to talk familiarly; to commune.—*n.* kon'vėrs. Conversation; familiarity; something forming a counterpart.—*a.* Put the opposite or reverse way. **conversely**, kon'vėrs-li, *adv.* In a converse manner; with inversion of order. **conversion**, kon-vėr'shun, *n.* Change from one state, religion, or party to another; interchange of terms in logic.

convert, kon-vėrt', *vt.* and *i.* To change from one state, use, religion, or party to another; to turn from a bad life to a good; to interchange conversely.—*n.* kon'vėrt. One who has changed his opinion, practice, or religion. **convertibility**, kon-vėr'ti-bil'i-ti, *n.* Condition or quality of being convertible. **convertible**, kon-vėr'ti-bl, *a.* Transformable; interchangeable.

convex, kon'veks, *a.* Rising on the exterior surface into a round form; opposed to *concave.* **convexity**, kon-vek'si-ti, *n.* State of being convex; roundness. **convexly**, kon'veks-li, *adv.* In a convex form.

convey, kon-vā', *vt.* To transport; to deliver; to impart. **conveyable**, kon-vā'a-bl, *a.* That may be conveyed. **conveyance**, kon-vā'ans, *n.* Act or means of conveying; a carriage; transference; a deed which transfers property. **conveyer**, kon-vā'ėr, *n.* One who or that which conveys.

convict, kon-vikt', *vt.* To prove or decide to be guilty.—*n.* kon'vikt. A person found guilty; one undergoing penal servitude. **conviction**, kon-vik'shun, *n.* Act of finding a person guilty; strong belief; state of being sensible of wrong-doing.

convince, kon-vins', *vt.* (convincing, convinced). To persuade by argument; to satisfy by evidence or proof. **convincing**, kon-vin'sing, *a.* Compelling assent; leaving no doubt. **convincingly**, kon-vin'sing-li, *adv.* In a convincing manner.

convivial, kon-vi'vi-al, *a.* Festive; festal; jovial; social. **conviviality**, kon-vi'vi-al'i-ti, *n.* Convivial disposition; mirth at an entertainment.

convocate, kon'vō-kāt, *vt.* To convoke. **convocation**, kon-vō-kā'shun, *n.* Act of convoking; an assembly, particularly of clergy or heads of a university.

convolute, **convoluted**, kon'vō-lūt, kon-vō-lūt'ed, *a.* Rolled on itself; presenting convolutions. **convolution**, kon-vō-lū'shun, *n.* Act of rolling together or on itself; a winding; a spiral.

convoy, kon-voi', *vt.* To accompany for defense; to escort.—*n.* kon'voi. A protecting force; escort.

convulse, kon-vuls', *vt.* (convulsing, convulsed). To contract violently, as the muscles; to affect by irregular spasms; to disturb. **convulsion**, kon-vul'shun, *n.* A violent involuntary contraction of the muscles; a violent irregular motion; disturbance.

coo, kö, *vi.* (cooing, cooed). To make a low sound, as doves; to act in a loving manner.

cook, kuk, *vt.* To prepare food by fire or heat; to concoct; to tamper with.—*n.* One who prepares victuals for the table. **cookery**, kuk'ė-ri, *n.* Art of preparing victuals for the table.

cool, köl, *a.* Moderately cold; dispassionate; self-possessed; impudent.—*n.* A moderate degree or state of cold.—*vt.* To make cool; to moderate; to calm; to render indifferent.—*vi.* To lose heat, ardor, affection, &c. **cooler**, köl'ėr, *n.* That which cools; anything which debates heat or excitement. **cool-headed**, köl'hed-ed, *a.* Having a temper not easily excited. **coolly**, köl'li, *adv.* In a cool or indifferent manner; with calm assurance. **coolness**, köl'nes, *n.* Moderate degree of cold; indifference; calm assurance.

coolie, kö'li, *n.* An East Indian porter.

coop, köp, *n.* A barrel or cask; a box for poultry, &c.—*vt.* To confine in a coop; to shut up in a narrow compass.

cooper, köp'ėr, *n.* One who makes barrels.—*vt.* and *i.* To do the work of a cooper. **cooperage**, köp'ėr-ij, *n.* The work of a cooper; workshop of a cooper.

co-operate, kō-op'ėr-āt, *vi.* To act with another; to concur in producing the same effect. **co-operation**, kō-op'ėr-ā'shun, *n.* Act of co-operating; concurrent effort or labor. **co-operative**, kō-op'ėr-ā-tiv, *a.* Operating jointly to the same end. **co-operator**, kō-op'ėr-ā-tėr, *n.* One who co-operates.

co-ordinate, kō-or'di-nāt, *a.* Holding the same rank or degree.—*vt.* To arrange in due order. **co-ordinately**, kō-or'di-nat-li, *adv.* In the same order or rank. **co-ordination**, kō-or'di-nā'shun, *n.* State of being co-ordinate; act of co-ordinating.

coot, köt, *n.* A black wading bird.

copartner, kō-pärt'nėr, *n.* An associate.

cope, kōp, *n.* A sacerdotal cloak; the

arch of the sky; the roof of a house; the arch over a door, &c.—*vt.* (coping, coped). To cover, as with a cope; to strive or contend; to oppose with success (with *with*).

Copernican, kŏ-pèr'ni-kan, *a.* Pertaining to Copernicus, or to his astronomical system.

coping, kōp'ing, *n.* The covering course of a wall, parapet, &c.

copious, kō'pi-us, *a.* Abundant; exuberant; diffuse. **copiously**, kō'pi-us-li, *adv.* Abundantly.

copper, kop'ėr, *n.* A reddish colored ductile and malleable metal; a large boiler; a copper coin.—*a.* Consisting of or resembling copper—*vt.* To cover with sheets of copper. **copperas**, kop'ėr-as, *n.* Green vitriol or sulphate of iron.

coppice, copse, kop'is, kops, *n.* A wood of small growth; a thicket.

copulate, kop'ū-lāt, *vi.* (copulating, copulated). To come together, as different sexes. **copulation**, kop-ū-lā'shun, *n.* Coition.

copy, kop'i, *n.* An imitation; a transcript; a pattern; a single example of a book, &c.; matter to be set up in type. —*vt.* (copying, copied). To imitate; to transcribe. **copyhold**, kop'i-hōld, *n.* A tenure for which the tenant has nothing to show except the rolls made by the steward of the lord's court; land held in copyhold. **copyist**, kop'i-ist, *n.* A transcriber; imitator. **copyright**, kop'i-rīt, *n.* The exclusive right to print or produce, given for a limited number of years to an author, artist, &c., or his assignee.—*a.* Relating to, or protected by copyright.—*vt.* To secure by copyright.

coquette, kŏ-ket', *n.* A vain, trifling woman; a flirt. **coquettish**, kŏ-ket'ish, *a.* Practicing coquetry. **coquet**, kŏ-ket', *vi.* (coquetting, coquetted). To trifle in love; to endeavor to excite admiration from vanity. **coquetry**, kŏ'ket-ri, *n.* Arts of a coquette; trifling in love.

coral, kor'al, *n.* A hard calcareous substance found in the ocean; a piece of coral.—*a.* Made of coral; resembling coral. **coralliferous**, ko-ral-if'ėr-us, *a.* Producing or containing coral. **coralline**, kor'al-in, *a.* Consisting of, like, or containing coral.—*n.* A sea-weed; an orange-red color; a coral zoophyte. **coralloid**, kor'al-oid, *a.* Having the form of coral; branching like coral.

cord, kord, *n.* A small rope; a band; a sinew; a pile of wood, 8 feet long, 4 high, and 4 broad.—*vt.* To bind with a cord. **cordage**, kord'ij, *n.* Cords collectively; the ropes used in the rigging of a ship.

cordial, kor'jal, *a.* Hearty; heartfelt; invigorating.—*n.* A medicine or beverage which increases strength; anything that gladdens or exhilarates. **cordiality**, kor-jal'i-ti, *n.* Heartiness; sincerity. **cordially**, kor'jal-li, *adv.* Heartily.

cordite, kor'dīt, *n.* A smokeless explosive.

cordon, kor'don, *n.* A line of military posts; a ribbon worn across the breast by knights.

cordovan, kor'dō-van, *n.* Spanish leather.

corduroy, kor-dė-roi', *n.* A thick cotton stuff corded or ribbed.

core, kōr, *n.* The heart or inner part; the central part of fruit.

corespondent, kō-rē-spon'dent, *n.* A joint respondent; a man charged with adultery in a divorce case.

cork, kork, *n.* The bark of a species of oak; the tree itself; a stopple made of cork.—*vt.* To stop with a cork. **corked**, korkt, *a.* Stopped with a cork; tasting of cork; blackened with burnt cork. **corky**, kor'ki, *a.* Consisting of or like cork.

cormorant, kor'mō-rant, *n.* A large voracious sea bird; a glutton.

corn, korn, *n.* Grain; the seeds of plants which grow in ears, and are made into bread; a horny excrescence on a toe or foot.—*vt.* To preserve with salt in grains; to granulate.

cornea, kor'nē-a, *n.* The horny transparent membrane in the fore part of the eye.

corned, kornd, *a.* Cured by salting.

corner, kor'nėr, *n.* A projecting extremity; angle; a secret or retired place; a nook.

cornerstone, kor'nėr-stōn, *n.* The stone which lies at the corner of two walls, and unites them; the principal stone.

cornet, kor'net, *n.* A sort of trumpet; a cavalry officer who bore the standard.

cornice, kor'nis, *n.* A molded projection crowning a part; uppermost molding of a pediment, room, &c.

cornucopia, kor-nū-kō'pi-a, *n.* The representation of a horn filled with fruit, flowers, and grain, a symbol of plenty and peace.

corny, kor'ni, *a.* Producing corn; containing corn; tasting of corn or malt; trite.

corollary, kor'o-ler-i, ko-rol'a-ri, *n.* Something added to a proposition demonstrated; an inference, deduction.

coronation, ko-rō-nā'shun, *n.* Act or solemnity of crowning a sovereign.

coroner, kor'ō-nėr, *n.* An officer who holds a court of inquiry in a case of sudden death.

coronet, kor'ō-net, *n.* An inferior crown worn by noblemen; an ornamental headdress; something that surmounts.

corporal, kor'po-ral, *n.* The lowest officer of a company of infantry.—*a.* Belonging or relating to the body; material. **corporally**, kor-po-ral-li, *adv.* Bodily.

corporate, kor'po-rit, *a.* Formed into a legal body, and empowered to act in legal processes as an individual. **corporately**, kor'po-rit-li, *adv.* In a corporate capacity. **corporation**, kor-po-rā'shun, *n.* A body corporate, empowered to act as an individual; the human body or frame.

corporeal, kor-pō'rē-al, *a.* Having a body; material; opposed to spiritual. **corporeally**, kor-pō'rē-al-li, *adv.* In a bodily form or manner.

corps, kōr, *n.*; pl. **corps**, kōrz. A body of troops; any division of an army.

corpse, korps, *n.* The dead body of a human being; a carcass; remains.

corpulent, kor'pū-lent, *a.* Having gross or fleshy body; very fat; stout; lusty. **corpulence, corpulency,** kor'-pū-lens, kor'pū-len-si, *n.* The state of being corpulent; excessive fatness.

corpuscle, kor'pus-l, *n.* A minute particle or physical atom; a minute animal cell. **corpuscular,** kor-pus'kū-lèr, *a.* Pertaining to corpuscles.

corral, ko-ral', *n.* A pen for cattle; an enclosure formed by wagons; a stockade for capturing elephants.

correct, ko-rekt', *a.* Right; accurate; exact.—*vt.* To make right; to chastise; to counteract. **correction,** ko-rek'shun, *n.* Act of correcting; state of being corrected; discipline; chastisement; counteraction. **correctional,** ko-rek'shun-al, *a.* Tending or pertaining to correction. **corrective,** ko-rek'tiv, *a.* Having the power to correct; tending to rectify.—*n.* That which corrects; restriction. **correctly,** ko-rekt'li, *adv.* Exactly; accurately. **correctness,** ko-rekt'nes, *n.* Freedom from faults or errors; accuracy; exactness.

correlate, kor'ē-lāt, *n.* A correlative.—*vi.* (correlating, correlated). To be reciprocally related.—*vt.* To place in reciprocal relation; to determine the relations between. **correlation,** ko-rē-lā'-shun, *n.* Reciprocal relation.

correspond, kor-ē-spond', *vi.* To answer one to another; to be congruous; to fit; to hold intercourse by letters. **correspondence,** kor-ē-spond'ens, *n.* Act or state of corresponding; fitness; congruity; intercourse by letters; the letters interchanged. **correspondent,** kor-ē-spond'ent, *a.* Corresponding; suitable; congruous.—*n.* One who has intercourse by letters. **correspondently,** kor-ē-spond'ent-li, *adv.* In a corresponding manner. **corresponding,** kor-ē-spond'-ing, *a.* Answering; agreeing; suiting.

corridor, kor'i-dōr, *n.* A passage in a building, or round a court.

corroborate, ko-rob'ō-rāt, *vt.* (corroborating, corroborated). To strengthen; to confirm. **corroboration,** ko-rob'ō-rā''-shun, *n.* Act of corroborating; confirmation. **corroborative,** ko-rob'ō-rā-tiv, *a.* Tending to strengthen or confirm. **corroborant,** ko-rob'ō-rant, *a.* Strengthening.

corrode, ko-rōd', *vt.* (corroding, corroded). To eat or wear away by degrees; to prey upon; to poison, blight, canker. **corrodent,** ko-rō'dent, *a.* Having the power of corroding.—*n.* A substance that corrodes. **corrodible,** ko-rōd'i-bl, *a.* That may be corroded. **corrosion,** ko-rō'zhun, *n.* Action of corroding; state of being corroded. **corrosive,** ko-rō'siv, *a.* Having the power of corroding; vexing; blighting.—*n.* That which has the quality of corroding.

corrugate, kor'ū-gāt, *vt.* To wrinkle; to contract into folds or furrows. **corrugated,** kor'ū-gāt-ed, *a.* Wrinkled; having prominent ridges and grooves. **corrugation,** kor-ū-gā'shun, *n.* A wrinkling; contraction into wrinkles.

corrupt, ko-rupt', *vt.* To make putrid; to deprave; to taint; to bribe; to infect with errors.—*vi.* To become putrid or vitiated.—*a.* Tainted; depraved; infected with errors. **corruption,** ko-rup'shun, *n.* Act or process of corrupting; depravity; pollution; taint of blood; bribe-taking; bribery.

corsair, kor'sar, *n.* A pirate; a piratical vessel.

corset, kor'set, *n.* An article of dress laced closely round the body; stays.

cortège, kor'tāzh, *n.* A train of attendants.

cortisone, kor'ti-sōn, *n.* A hormone extract used in the treatment of certain diseases.

coruscant, ko-rus'kant, *a.* Flashing. **coruscate,** kor-us'kāt, *vi.* (coruscating, coruscated). To flash intermittently; to glitter. **coruscation,** kor-us- kā'shun, *n.* A glittering or flashing; a quick vibration of light; intellectual brilliancy.

corvette, kor-vet', *n.* A sloop of war with only one tier of guns.

cosmetic, koz-met'ik, *a.* Improving beauty.—*n.* An external application to improve the complexion.

cosmic, cosmical, koz'mik, koz'mi-kal, *a.* Relating to the whole frame of the universe; rising or setting with the sun.

cosmopolitanism, cosmopolitism, koz-mō-pol'i-tan-izm, koz-mop'ō-lit-izm, *n.* The state of being a cosmopolitan; disregard of local prejudices, &c. **cosmopolitan, cosmopolite,** koz-mō-pol'i-tan, koz-mop'ō-lit, *n.* One who is at home in every place.—*a.* Free from local prejudices; common to all the world.

cosmos, koz'mos, *n.* The universe; the system of order and harmony in creation.

cost, kost, *vi.* (costing, cost). To be bought for; to require to be laid out or borne.—*n.* That which is paid for anything; expenditure; loss; (*pl.*) expenses of a lawsuit.

costly, kost'li, *a.* Of a high price; valuable; precious; dear; sumptuous. **costliness,** kost'li-nes, *n.* State of being costly; expensiveness; sumptuousness.

costume, kos'tūm, *n.* An established mode of dress; garb; attire.

cosy, kō'zi, *a.* Snug; comfortable. Also **cosie, cozie, cozy.**—*n.* A cover put over a teapot to keep in the heat. **cosily,** kō'zi-li, *adv.* In a cosey manner.

cot, kot, *n.* A small house; a hut; a small bed.

cote, kōt, *n.* A shelter for animals (as a dove-*cote*); a sheepfold; a cottage or hut.

cotemporaneous, cotemporary, kō-tem'po-rā''nē-us, kō-tem'po-ra-ri. *See* CONT-.

coterie, kō'te-rē, *n.* A circle of familiar friends who meet for social or literary intercourse; an exclusive society; a clique.

cotillion, ko-til'yun, *n.* A brisk dance; a kind of quadrille.

cottage, kot'ij, *n.* A cot; a small country or suburban house. **cottager,** kot'-ij-ér, *n.* One who lives in a cottage.

cotton, kot'n, *n.* A soft, downy substance in the pods of several plants;

cloth made of cotton.—*a.* Pertaining to, or consisting of cotton.—*vi.* To agree; to become friendly. **cotton wool,** kot'n wul, *n.* Cotton in the raw state. **cottony,** kot'n-i, *a.* Soft like cotton; downy.

cottonwood, kot'n-wud, *n.* A large tree of the poplar kind.

couch, kouch, *vi.* To lie down; to bend down; to lie close and concealed.—*vt.* To lay down; to place upon a bed; to comprise; to express; to fix a spear in rest; to depress a cataract in the eye.—*n.* A bed; a place for rest and ease.

cougar, kö'ger, *n.* A large carnivorous quadruped of the cat kind; the puma.

cough, kof, *n.* A violent convulsive effort of the lungs to throw off offending matter.—*vi.* To make a violent effort, with noise, to expel the air from the lungs, and throw off any offensive matter. —*vt.* To expel from the lungs by a violent effort with noise; to expectorate.

could, kud, *pret.* of *can.* Was able.

council, koun'sil, *n.* An assembly for consultation; a body of men designated to advise a sovereign or chief magistrate; a convocation.

council board, koun'sil börd, *n.* The table round which a council holds consultation; the council itself.

councilor, koun'si-lér, *n.* A member of a council.

counsel, koun'sel, *n.* Deliberation; consultation; advice; design; a barrister.— *vt.* (counseling; counseled). To advise; to warn. **counselor,** koun'se-lér, *n.* A person who gives counsel; an adviser; a barrister.

count, kount, *vt.* To enumerate; to compute; to consider; to judge.—*vi.* To reckon; to rely; to be reckoned.—*n.* Reckoning; a particular change in an indictment; a continental title of nobility, equivalent to the English earl.

countenance, koun'te-nans, *n.* The human face; air; aspect; favor; encouragement.—*vt.* To favor; to encourage; to vindicate.

counter, koun'tér, *n.* One who or that which counts; anything used to reckon, as in games; a store table.—*adv.* Contrary; in an opposite direction.—*a.* Adverse; opposing.

counteract, koun-tér-akt', *vt.* To act in opposition to; to render ineffectual. **counteraction,** koun'tér-ak″shun, *n.* Action in opposition; hindrance. **counteractive,** koun'tér-ak″tiv, *a.* Tending to counteract.—*n.* That which counteracts.

counterbalance, koun-tér-bal'ans, *vt.* To weigh against with an equal weight; to act against with equal power.—*n.* Equal weight, power or agency, acting in opposition.

counterfeit, koun'tér-fit, *vt.* and *i.* To forge; to copy; to feign.—*a.* Made in imitation; fraudulent.—*n.* An impostor; a forgery. **counterfeiter,** koun'tér-fit-ér, *n.* A forger.

counterirritant, koun'tér-ir'i-tant, *n.* An irritant employed to relieve another irritation or inflammation.

countermand, koun'tér-mand', *vt.* To annul or revoke a former command.—*n.* A contrary order; revocation of a former order.

countermarch, koun'tér-märch, *vi.* To march back.—*n.* A marching back; a returning; a change of measures.

counterpart, koun'tér-pärt, *n.* A corresponding part; a duplicate; a supplement.

counterplot, koun-tér-plot', *vi.* To oppose one plot by another.—*vt.* To plot against in order to defeat another plot; to baffle by an opposite plot.—*n.* A plot to frustrate another.

counterpoint, koun'tér-point, *n.* The art, in music, of adding to a given melody one or more melodies.

counterpoise, koun'tér-poiz, *vt.* To counterbalance.—*n.* A weight which balances another; equivalence of power or force; equilibrium.

countersign, koun-tér-sin', *vt.* To sign with an additional signature.—*n.* A military watchword.

countess, kount'es, *n.* The consort of an earl or count.

countless, kount'les, *a.* Innumerable.

country, kun'tri, *n.* A large tract of land; a region; a kingdom or state; the inhabitants of a region; the public; rural parts.—*a.* Pertaining to the country; rural.

countryman, kun'tri-man, *n.* One born in the same country with another; one who dwells in the country; a rustic.

countryside, kun'tri-sid, *n.* A tract of country, or the people inhabiting such.

county, koun'ti, *n.* A particular portion of a state or kingdom; a shire.—*a.* Pertaining to a county.

coupé, kö-pä', *n.* A low four-wheeled close carriage.

couple, kup'l, *n.* A band or leash; a pair; a brace; a man and his wife.—*vt.* and *i.* (coupling, coupled). To join together; to unite.

couplet, kup'let, *n.* Two lines that rhyme.

coupling, kup'ling, *n.* The act of one who couples; that which couples; a hook, chain, or other contrivance forming a connection.

coupon, kö'pon, *n.* An interest certificate attached to a bond; one of a series of tickets which guarantee the holder to obtain a certain value or service for each at different periods.

courage, ku'rij, *n.* Intrepidity; dauntlessness; hardihood. **courageous,** ku-rä'jus, *a.* Bold; brave; heroic; fearless. **courageously,** ku-rä'jus-li, *adv.* With courage; bravely; boldly; stoutly.

courier, kör'i-ér, *n.* A messenger sent express with despatches; a traveling attendant.

course, körs, *n.* A running; passage; route; career; ground run over; line of conduct; order of succession; series of lectures, &c.; range of subjects taught; a layer of stones in masonry; part of a meal served at one time.—*vt.* (coursing, coursed). To hunt; to run through or over.—*vi.* To move with speed. **courser,** kör'sér, *n.* A swift horse. **coursing,**

kōr'sing, *n.* The act or sport of chasing and hunting hares with greyhounds.

court, kōrt, *n.* An enclosed area; residence of a sovereign; the family and retinue of a sovereign; judges assembled for deciding causes; the place where judges assemble; a judicial body; attention directed to gain favor; flattery.—*vt.* To endeavor to please by civilities; to woo; to seek.

courteous, kėr'tē-us, *a.* Polite; complaisant; affable; respectful. **courteously**, kėr'tē-us-li, *adv.* In a courteous manner.

courtesan, courtezan, kōr'tē-zan, *n.* A loose woman; a prostitute.

courtesy, kėrt'e-si, *n.* Urbanity; complaisance; act of kindness or civility.

courthouse, kōrt'hous, *n.* A house in which established courts are held.

courtier, kōr'ti-er, *n.* A man who attends courts; a person of courtly manners; one who solicits favors.

courtly, kōrt'li, *a.* Relating to a court; elegant; polite with dignity; flattering. **courtliness**, kōrt-li-nes, *n.* Quality of being courtly; complaisance with dignity.

court-martial, kōrt'mär'shal, *n.*; pl. **courts-martial.** A court consisting of military or naval officers for the trial of offenses of a military or naval character.

courtship, kōrt'ship, *n.* Act of courting a woman in view of marriage; wooing.

courtyard, kōrt'yärd, *n.* A court or inclosure round or near a house.

cousin, kuz'n, *n.* The son or daughter of an uncle or aunt; a kinsman.

cove, kōv, *n.* A small inlet or bay; a sheltered recess in the sea-shore; a concave molding; a man, fellow.—*vt.* To arch over.

covenant, kuv'e-nant, *n.* A contract; compact; a writing containing the terms of an agreement.—*vi.* To enter into a formal agreement; to stipulate.—*vt.* To grant by covenant.

cover, kuv'ėr, *vt.* To overspread; to cloak; to secrete; to defend; to wrap up; to brood on; to be sufficient for; to include.—*n.* Anything spread over another thing; disguise; shelter; articles laid at table for one person. **covering**, kuv'ėr-ing, *n.* Envelope; cover. **coverlet**, kuv'ėr-let, *n.* The cover of a bed.

covert, kuv'ėrt, *a.* Kept secret; private; insidious.—*n.* A shelter; a thicket. **covertly**, kuv'ėrt-li, *adv.* Secretly; insidiously.

covet, kuv'et, *vt.* To long for (in a good sense); to desire unlawfully; to hanker after.—*vi.* To have inordinate desire. **covetable**, kuv'et-a-bl, *a.* That may be coveted. **covetous**, kuv'et-us, *a.* Eager to obtain; inordinately desirous; avaricious. **covetously**, kuv'et-us-li, *adv.* In a covetous manner. **covetousness**, kuv'et-us-nes, *n.* Cupidity.

covey, kuv'i, *n.* A hatch of birds; a small flock of birds together; a company.

cow, kou, *n.* The female of the bull, or of bovine animals generally.—*vt.* To sink the spirits or courage of; to dishearten.

coward, kou'ėrd, *n.* A person who wants courage to meet danger; a craven; a dastard.—*a.* Destitute of courage; dastardly.

cowardice, kou'ėr-dis, *n.* Want of courage to face danger. **cowardliness**, kou'ėrd-li-nes, *n.* Cowardice. **cowardly**, kou'ėrd-li, *a.* Wanting courage to face danger; faint-hearted; mean; base. —*adv.* In the manner of a coward.

cowcatcher, kou'kach-ėr, *n.* A frame in front of locomotives to remove obstructions.

cower, kou'ėr, *vi.* To crouch; to sink by bending the knees; to shrink through fear.

cowhide, kou'hīd, *n.* The hide of a cow; a leather whip.—*vt.* To flog with a leather whip.

cowl, koul, *n.* A monk's hood; a chimney cover which turns with the wind; a vessel carried on a pole by two persons.

cowpox, kou'poks, *n.* The vaccine disease, which appears on the teats of the cow.

cowslip, kou'slip, *n.* A species of primrose.

coxcomb, koks'kōm, *n.* The comb worn by fools in their caps; the cap itself; a fop; a vain, showy fellow. **coxcombry**, koks'kōm-ri, *n.* Foppishness.

coxswain. See cockswain.

coy, koi, *a.* Shy; reserved; bashful. **coyly**, koi'li, *adv.* With reserve; shyly. **coyness**, koi'nes, *n.* Shyness; bashfulness.

cozen, kuz'n, *vt.* To cheat; to defraud; to beguile.—*vi.* To act deceitfully. **cozenage**, knz'n-ij, *n.* Trickery; fraud. **cozener**, kuz'n-ėr, *n.* One who cheats.

cozy, kō'zi, *a.* Snug; comfortable.

crab, krab, *n.* A crustaceous fish with strong claws; a portable windlass, &c.; Cancer, a sign of the zodiac; a wild sour apple; a morose person. **crabbed**, krab'ed, *a.* Perverse; peevish; perplexing. **crabbedly**, krab'ed-li, *adv.* Peevishly.

crack, krak, *n.* A chink or fissure; a sudden or sharp sound; a sounding blow; a chat.—*vt.* and *i.* To break with a sharp, abrupt sound; to break partially; to snap; to boast of; to utter with smartness; to chat.

crackbrained, krak'brānd, *a.* Crazy.

cracked, krakt, *a.* Having fissures but not in pieces; impaired; crazy.

cracker, krak'ėr, *n.* One who or that which cracks; a small firework; a hard biscuit.

crackle, krak'l, *vi.* (crackling, crackled). To make small abrupt noises rapidly repeated. **crackling**, krak'ling, *n.* The act or noise of the verb to crackle; the brown skin of roasted pork.

cradle, krā'dl, *n.* A small bed in which infants are rocked; a frame to support or hold together.—*vt.* (cradling, cradled). To lay or rock in a cradle.

craft, kraft, *n.* Ability; skill; artifice; guile; manual art; trade; a vessel or ship. **craftily**, kraf'ti-li, *adv.* Artfully; cunningly. **craftiness**, kraf'ti-nes, *n.* Artfulness. **craftsman**, krafts'man, *n.* An artificer. **crafty**, kraf'ti, *a.* Skillful; artful.

crag, krag, *n.* A steep rugged rock; a cliff; gravel or sand mixed with shells. **cragged**, krag'ed, *a.* Full of crags; rugged. **craggy**, krag'i, *a.* Cragged.

cram, kram, *vt.* (cramming, crammed). To thrust in by force; to stuff; to coach for an examination.—*vi.* To stuff; to eat beyond satiety; to prepare for an examination.

cramp, kramp, *n.* A spasmodic contraction of a limb or muscle; restraint; piece of iron bent at the ends, to hold together pieces of timber, stones, &c.—*vt.* To affect with spasms; to restrain, hinder. cramped, krampt, *a.* Affected with spasm; restrained.

cranberry, kran'ber-i, *n.* A wild sour berry.

crane, krān, *n.* A migratory bird with long legs and neck; a machine for raising great weights; a crooked pipe for drawing liquor out of a cask.—*vi.* To stretch out one's neck.

crank, krangk, *n.* A contrivance for producing a horizontal or perpendicular motion by means of a rotary motion, or the contrary; a bend or turn.—*a.* Liable to be overset; loose.

cranky, krangk'i, *a.* Liable to overset; full of whims; crazy.

cranny, kran'i, *n.* A narrow opening; chink. crannied, kran'id, *a.* Having crannies.

crape, krāp, *n.* A thin, transparent stuff of a crisp texture, much used in mourning.

crash, krash, *vi.* To make the loud, clattering sound of many things falling and breaking at once.—*n.* The sound of things falling and breaking; a commercial collapse.

crass, kras, *a.* Gross; coarse; dense.

crate, krāt, *n.* A basket of wickerwork, for crockery, &c.

crater, krā'tėr, *n.* A bowl; the circular cavity or mouth of a volcano.

cravat, kra-vat', *n.* A neck-cloth.

crave, krāv, *vt.* (craving, craved). To ask earnestly or submissively; to desire strongly.—*n.* Strong desire.

craven, krā'vn, *n.* A coward; a weak-hearted, spiritless fellow.—*a.* Cowardly.

craving, krā'ving, *n.* Vehement desire; morbid demand of appetite.

craw, kra, *n.* The crop or first stomach of fowls.

crawfish, kra'fish, *n.* A crustacean found in streams; also the spiny lobster, a sea crustacean.

crawl, kral, *vi.* To creep; to advance slowly, slyly, or weakly.

crawler, kral'ėr, *n.* One who or that which crawls; a creeper; a reptile.

crayfish, krā'fish. See crawfish.

crayon, krā'on, *n.* A pencil of colored clay, or charcoal, used in drawing; a drawing made with crayons.—*vi.* To sketch.

crazy, krā'zi, *a.* Decrepit; deranged; weakened or disordered in intellect. craze, krāz, *vt.* (crazing, crazed). To shatter; to impair the intellect of.—*vi.* To become crazy.—*n.* An inordinate desire. crazed, krāzd, *a.* Decrepit; crazy.

creak, krēk, *vi.* To make a grating sound.—*n.* A sharp, harsh, grating sound.

cream, krēm, *n.* That part of a liquor which collects on the surface; the richer part of milk; best part of a thing.—*vt.*

To take off cream from.—*vi.* To gather cream; to mantle. creamery, krēm'ėr-i, *n.* A place where milk is made into butter and cheese. creamy, krēm'i, *a.* Full of cream; like cream; luscious.

crease, krēs, *n.* A mark made by folding; a hollow streak like a groove.—*vt.* (creasing, creased). To make a mark in by compressing or folding; lines near the wickets in cricket.

creasote, creosote, krē'a-sōt, krē'ō-sōt, *n.* An antiseptic liquid obtained from wood-tar.

create, krē-āt', *vt.* (creating, created). To bring into being from nothing; to cause to be; to shape; to beget; to bring about; to invest with a new character; to constitute or appoint. creation, krē-ā'shun, *n.* Act of creating; the aggregate of created things; the universe; conferring of a title or dignity. creative, krē-ā'tiv, *a.* Having the power to create, or exerting the act of creation. creator, krē-ā'tėr, *n.* The being that creates; a producer; the Supreme Being. creature, krē'tūr, *n.* Something created; a human being; something imagined; a person who owes his rise to another; a mere tool.

credence, krē'dens, *n.* The act of believing; credit; trust. credendum, krē-den'dum, *n.*; pl. -da. A thing to be believed; an article of faith. credential, krē-den'shal, *n.* That which gives a title to credit; (*pl.*) documents showing that one is entitled to credit, or is invested with authority.

credible, kred'i-bl, *a.* Worthy of credit. credibly, kred'i-bli, *adv.* In a credible manner. credibility, kred-i-bil'i-ti, *n.* State or quality of being credible.

credit, kred'it, *n.* Reliance on testimony; faith; reputed integrity; transfer of goods, &c., in confidence of future payment; reputation for pecuniary worth; time given for payment of goods sold on trust; side of an account in which payment is entered; money possessed or due. —*vt.* To trust; to believe; to sell or lend to, in confidence of future payment; to procure credit or honor to; to enter on the credit side of an account; to attribute. creditable, kred'it-a-bl, *a.* Estimable. creditably, kred'it-a-bli, *adv.* In a creditable manner; with credit. creditor, kred'i-tėr, *n.* One to whom a debt is due.

credulity, kre-dū'li-ti, *n.* A disposition to believe on slight evidence. credulous, kred'ū-lus, *a.* Apt to believe without sufficient evidence; unsuspecting.

creed, krēd, *n.* A system of principles believed or professed; a brief summary of the articles of Christian faith.

creek, krēk, *n.* A small bay; a small harbor; a brook. creeky, krēk'i, *a.* Containing creeks.

creel, krēl, *n.* An osier basket or pannier.

creep, krēp, *vi.* (creeping, crept). To move as a reptile; to crawl; to grow along the ground, or on another body; to move secretly, feebly, or timorously; to be servile; to shiver.

creeper, krēp'ėr, *n.* A creeping plant; a

small bird; a kind of grapnel for dragging.

remate, krē'māt, vt. To burn; to dispose of (a human body) by burning.

cremation, krē-mā'shun, n. Act or custom of cremating.

creole, krē'ōl, n. A native of the W. Indies or Spanish America, but not of indigenous blood.

creosote, krē'ō-sōt, n. See creasote.

crescent, kres'ent, n. The moon in her state of increase; anything resembling the shape of the new moon; the Turkish standard; buildings in the form of a crescent.

cress, kres, n. The name of various plants, mostly cruciferous, used as a salad.

crest, krest, n. A tuft on the head of certain birds; the plume of feathers or tuft on a helmet; the helmet itself; the top; a lofty mien; a sort of heraldic badge.—vt. To furnish with a crest. **crested**, kres'ted, p.a. Having a crest. **crestfallen**, krest'fal-en, a. Dejected.

cetaceous, krē-tā'shus, a. Chalky.

cretin, krē'tin, n. One afflicted with cretinism.

cretinism, krē'tin-izm, n. A disease resembling rickets, but accompanied with idiocy.

cretonne, kre-ton', n. A cotton cloth printed with colored patterns.

crevice, krev'is, n. A crack; cleft; cranny.

crew, krö, n. A company; a gang; the company of sailors belonging to a vessel. **crib**, krib, n. A child's bed; a small habitation; a rack; a stall for oxen; a framework; a literal translation.—vt. (cribbing, cribbed). To shut up in a narrow habitation; to pilfer.

cribbage, krib'ij, n. A game at cards.

crick, krik, n. A local spasm or cramp; a stiffness of the neck.

cricket, krik'et, n. An insect which makes a creaking or chirping sound; an open-air game played with bats, ball, and wickets.

crier, cryer, krī'ēr, n. One who cries; one who makes proclamation.

crime, krīm, n. A breach of law, divine or human; any great wickedness. **criminal**, krim'in-al, a. Guilty; wicked; relating to crime.—n. A malefactor; a convict. **criminality**, krim-in-al'i-ti, n. The quality of being criminal; guiltiness. **criminally**, krim'in-al-li, adv. In a criminal manner; wickedly.

crimp, krimp, a. Easily crumbled; friable; brittle.—vt. To curl or crisp; to seize; to pinch; to decoy for the army or navy.

crimple, krimp'l, vt. (crimpling, crimpled). To contract; to cause to shrink; to curl.

crimson, krim'zn, n. A deep-red color; a red tinged with blue.—a. Of a beautiful deep-red.—vt. To dye of a deep-red color.—vi. To become of a deep-red color; to blush.

cringe, krinj, vi. (cringing, cringed). To bend; to bend with servility; to fawn.—n. A bow; servile civility.

crinkle, kring'kl, vi. (crinkling, crinkled). To bend in little turns; to wrinkle.—vt. To form with short turns or wrinkles.—n. A winding or turn; a wrinkle.

crinoline, krin'o-lin, n. A fabric of horse-hair and linen thread; a hooped petticoat.

cripple, krip'l, n. A lame person.—vt. (crippling, crippled). To lame; to disable.

crisis, krī'sis, n.; pl. -ses. Turning-point of a disease; a decisive stage time when anything is at its height; conjuncture.

crisp, krisp, a. Brittle; easily broken or crumbled; fresh; brisk.—vt. To curl; to make wavy.—vi. To form little curls. **crisper**, kris'pēr, n. One who or that which crisps; an instrument for crisping cloth. **crisply**, krisp'li, adv. With crispness. **crispy**, kris'pi, a. Crisp; curled; brittle.

criterion, krī-tēr'i-un, n.; -ia. Standard of judging; a measure; test.

critic, krit'ik, n. One skilled in judging literary or artistic work; a reviewer; a severe judge.—a. Relating to criticism. **critical**, krit'i-kal, a. Relating to or containing criticism; nicely judicious; inclined to find fault; relating to a crisis; momentous. **critically**, krit'i-kal-li, adv. In a critical manner; at the crisis. **criticize, criticise**, krit'i-sīz, vi. or t. (criticizing, criticized). To examine or judge critically; to pick out faults; to animadvert upon. **criticism**, krit'i-sizm, n. Act or art of criticising; exhibition of the merits of a literary or artistic work; a critical essay; censure. **critique**, kri-tēk', n. A written estimate of the merits of a literary or artistic work.

croak, krōk, vi. To make a low hoarse noise in the throat, as a frog or crow; to forebode evil without much cause; to murmur.—n. The low harsh sound of a frog, raven, &c. **croaker**, krōk'ēr, n. A grumbler. **croaking, croaky**, krōk'-ing, krōk'i, a. Uttering a croak; foreboding evil; grumbling.

crochet, krō-shā', n. A species of knitting performed by means of a small hook.

crock, krok, n. An earthen vessel; a pot; soot or smut from pots, kettles, &c.

crockery, krok'ēr-i, n. Earthenware; vessels formed of clay, glazed and baked.

crocodile, krok'ō-dīl, n. A large aquatic reptile of the lizard kind.—a. Pertaining to or like a crocodile; affected (tears).

crocus, krō'kus, n. A bulbous plant of the iris family; saffron.

crone, krōn, n. An old woman.

crony, krō'ni, n. A familiar friend.

crook, krök, n. A bend; a curving instrument; a shepherd's staff; a pastoral staff.—vt. and i. To bend; to make a hook on. **crooked**, krök'ed, a. Bent; wry; deceitful.

crop, krop, n. The first stomach of birds; the craw; harvest; grain, &c., while growing; act of cutting, as hair; a short whip without a lash.—vt. (cropping, cropped or cropt). To cut off the ends of; to cut close; to browse; to gather before it falls; to cultivate.

cropper, krop'ēr, n. A breed of pigeons

with a large crop; a fall as from horse-back.

croquet, krō'kā, *n.* An open-air game played with mallets, balls, hoops, and pegs.

crosier, crozier, krō'zhėr, *n.* A bishop's crook or pastoral staff.

cross, kros, *n.* An instrument of death, consisting of two pieces of timber placed transversely; the symbol of the Christian religion; the religion itself; a monument or sign in the form of a cross; anything that thwarts; a hybrid.—*a.* Athwart; adverse; fretful.—*vt.* To draw a line or lay a body across; to mark with a cross; to cancel; to pass from side to side of; to thwart; to perplex; to interbreed.—*vi.* To be athwart; to move across.

crossbones, kros'bōnz, *n.pl.* A symbol of death; two human bones placed crosswise, generally in conjunction with a skull.

crossbow, kros'bō, *n.* A weapon for shooting, formed by fixing a bow crosswise on a stock.

crossbreed, kros'brēd, *n.* A breed from a male and female of different breeds.

cross-examine, kros'eg-zam-in, *vt.* To examine a witness of the opposite party.

cross-examination, kros'eg-zam-in-ā-shun, *n.* The examination of a witness called by one party by the opposite party.

cross-grained, kros'grānd, *a.* Having the fibers across or irregular; perverse.

crossing, kros'ing, *n.* Act of one who or that which crosses; a place where passengers cross.

crossly, kros'li, *adv.* Peevishly; adversely.

cross-purpose, kros'pėr-pus, *n.* A contrary purpose; a misunderstanding.

cross-question, kros'kwes-chun, *vt.* To cross-examine.

crossroad, kros'rōd, *n.* A road which crosses the country or other roads.

crosstrees, kros'trēz, *n. pl.* Horizontal pieces of timber on masts, to sustain the tops and extend the shrouds.

crosswise, kros'wiz, *adv.* Transversely.

crotch, kroch, *n.* A fork or forking.

crotchet, kroch'et, *n.* A note in music, half the length of a minim; a whim; a perverse conceit; a bracket in printing.

crotchety, kroch'e-ti, *a.* Whimsical.

crouch, krouch, *vi.* To bend low; to lie close to the ground; to cringe.

croup, krōp, *n.* A disease of the windpipe in children; the rump of certain animals; the place behind the saddle.

croupier, krō'pē-ėr, *n.* One who at a public dinner sits at the lower end of the table.

crow, krō, *n.* A black bird of the genus Corvus, including the raven, rook, jackdaw, &c.; a crowbar; the sound which a cock utters.—*vi.* (crowing; pret. crew, crowed; pp. crowed). To cry as a cock; to exult; to boast.

crowbar, krō'bär, *n.* A bar of iron with a bent or forked end, used as a lever.

crowd, kroud, *n.* A number of persons or things; a throng; the populace.—*vt.* To fill by pressing together; to fill to excess. —*vi.* To press in numbers; to throng.

crowded, kroud'ed, *a.* Filled by promiscuous multitude.

crowfoot, krō'fut, *n.* Cords used ships to suspend the awnings, &c; a bu tercup.

crown, kroun, *n.* An ornament for th head in the form of a wreath; a diadem; a badge of royalty; perfection; completion; the top of anything, especially the head; a coin of five shillings; value $1.21.—*vt.* To invest with a crown; to cover; to adorn; finish; to perfect. **crowned**, kroun *p.a.* Invested with a crown; surmounte

crowning, kroun'ing, *p.a.* Highest; pe fecting; final.

crown-prince, kroun'prins, *n.* Th prince who is apparently successor the crown.

crow's-feet, krōz'fēt, *n.pl.* The wrinkle under the eyes, the effects of age.

crucial, krō'shal, *a.* Relating to cross; severe; searching; decisive.

crucible, krō'si-bl, *n.* A melting pe used by chemists and others.

crucifix, krō'si-fiks, *n.* A cross with th figure of Christ crucified on it.

crucifixion, krō-si-fik'shun, *n.* The ac of crucifying; the death of Christ.

crucify, krō'si-fī, *vt.* (crucifying, cruc fied). To put to death by nailing th hands and feet of to a cross; to mortify to torment.

crude, krōd, *a.* Raw; unripe; in its na ural state; not brought to perfectior

crudely, krōd'li, *adv.* In a crude man ner. **crudity**, krō'di-ti, *n.* State of be ing crude; something in a crude state.

cruel, krō'el, *a.* Unmerciful; hare hearted; ferocious; brutal; sever **cruelly**, krō'el-li, *adv.* In a cruel man ner. **cruelty**, krō'el-ti, *n.* Quality o being cruel; inhumanity; barbarity; cruel act.

cruet, krō'et, *n.* A vial or small glas bottle for holding vinegar, oil, &c.

cruise, krōz, *vi.* (cruising, cruised). T sail hither and thither.—*n.* A sailing t and fro in search of an enemy's ships, o for pleasure. **cruiser**, krōz'ėr, *n.* A pe son or a ship that cruises; a swift arme vessel to protect or destroy shipping.

crumb, **crum**, krum, *n.* A fragment; small piece of bread broken off; the sof part of bread.—*vt.* To break into sma pieces with the fingers; to cover wit bread-crumbs.

crumble, krum'bl, *vt.* (crumbling crumbled). To break into small frag ments; to pulverize.—*vi.* To part int small fragments; to decay.

crumpet, krum'pet, *n.* A sort of muffin

crumple, krum'pl, *vt.* (crumpling crumpled). To press into wrinkles; t rumple.—*vi.* To shrink; to shrive **crumpled**, krum'pld, *p.a.* Wrinkled curled.

crunch, **krunch**, krunch, *vt.* To crush betwee the teeth.

crupper, krup'ėr, *n.* A strap of leathe to prevent a saddle from shifting for ward; the buttocks.

crusade, krō-sād', *n.* A military exped tion against the infidels of the Hol

Land; a romantic or enthusiastic enterprise. **crusader**, krö-sȧd′ẽr, *n.* A person engaged in a crusade.

ruse, krös or kröz, *n.* A small cup; cruet.

rush, krush, *vt.* To squeeze; to bruise; to pound; to overpower; to oppress.—*vi.* To be pressed; to force one's way amid a crowd.—*n.* A violent pressing or squeezing; a crowding. **crushing**, krush′ing, *p.a.* Overwhelming.

rust, krust, *n.* The hard outer coat of anything; the outside of a loaf; a piece of hard bread; a deposit from wine.—*vt.* and *i.* To cover with a crust or hard coat. **crustily**, krust′i-li, *adv.* Peevishly. **crusty**, krust′i, *a.* Pertaining to, having, or like a crust; snappish; surly. **crustacea**, krus-tā′shē-a, *n. pl.* A division of animals, comprising crabs, shrimps, &c., having an external skeleton or shell. **crustacean**, krus-tā′shan, *n.* and *a.* One of, or pertaining to, the crustaceans. **crustaceous**, krus-tā′shus, *a.* Having a shell; belonging to the Crustacea.

rutch, kruch, *n.* A staff with a crosspiece used by cripples; a support.—*vt.* To support on crutches; to prop with miserable helps.

ry, krī, *vi.* (crying, cried). To utter the loud shrill sounds of weeping, joy, fear, surprise, &c.; to clamor; to weep.—*vt.* To shout; to proclaim.—*n.* The loud voice of man or beast; a shriek or scream; acclamation; weeping; importunate call; a political catchword. **crying**, krī′ing, *p.a.* Calling for vengeance or punishment; notorious; clamant.

crypt, kript, *n.* A subterranean cell for burying purposes; a subterranean chapel. **cryptic**, **cryptical**, krip′tik, krip′tik-al, *a.* Hidden; secret; occult. **cryptogam**, krip′tō-gam, *n.* One of those plants which do not bear true flowers, such as lichens, mosses, ferns, &c. **cryptogamy**, krip-tog′a-mi, *n.* Concealed fructification, as in cryptogams.

cryptogram, **cryptograph**, krip′tō-gram, krip′tō-graf, *n.* Something written in secret characters. **cryptography**, krip-tog′ra-fi, *n.* Art of writing in secret characters; cipher.

rystal, kris′tal, *n.* Pure transparent quartz; a superior kind of glass; articles, collectively, made of this material; a regular solid mineral body with smooth surfaces.—*a.* Consisting of or like crystal; clear; pellucid. **crystalline**, kris′tal-īn, *a.* Pure; pellucid. **crystallization**, kris′tal-ī-zā″shun, *n.* Act or process of crystallizing. **crystallize**, kris′tal-īz, *vt.* and *i.* To form into crystals; to unite, and form a regular solid.

ub, kub, *n.* The young of certain quadrupeds, as the bear and fox.—*vi.* (cubbing, cubbed). To bring forth cubs.

ube, kūb, *n.* A regular solid body, with six equal square sides; the third power, or the product from multiplying a number twice by itself.—*vt.* To raise to the third power. **cubic**, **cubical**, kūb′ik, kūb′i-kal, *a.* Having the form or properties of a cube.

ubicle, kū′bi-kl, *n.* A sleeping-place; a

compartment for one bed in a dormitory. **cubit**, kū′bit, *n.* The forearm; the length from the elbow to the extremity of the middle finger, usually taken at 18 inches.

cuckold, kuk′uld, *n.* A man whose wife is false to his bed.—*vt.* To make a cuckold of.

cuckoo, ky′kö, *n.* A migratory bird, so named from the sound of its note.

cucumber, kū′kum-bẽr, *n.* An annual plant of the gourd family.

cud, kud, *n.* The food which ruminating animals bring up from the first stomach to chew; a quid.

cuddle, kud′l, *vi.* (cuddling, cuddled). To lie close and snug.—*vi.* To hug; to embrace; to fondle.

cudgel, kuj′el, *n.* A short thick stick; a club.—*vt.* (cudgeling, cudgeled). To beat with a cudgel; to beat in general.

cue, kū, *n.* The last words of an actor's speech; catchword; hint; the part which any man is to play in his turn; humor; the straight rod used in billiards.

cuff, kuf, *n.* A blow; slap; part of a sleeve near the hand.—*vt.* To beat; to strike with talons or wings, or with fists.

cuisine, kwē-zēn′, *n.* Style of cooking.

cul-de-sac, kul′dė-sȧk, *n.* A blind alley.

culinary, kū′li-ner-i, *a.* Relating to the kitchen, or cookery; used in kitchens.

cull, kul, *vt.* To pick out; to gather.

culminate, kul′mi-nāt, *vi.* To come or be in the meridian; to reach the highest point, as of rank, power, size, &c. **culmination**, kul-mi-nā′shun, *n.* The transit of a heavenly body over the meridian; highest point; consummation.

culpable, kulp′a-bl, *a.* Blameworthy; guilty; criminal; immoral; sinful. **culpably**, kul′pa-bli, *adv.* In a culpable manner; blamably. **culpability**, kul-pa-bil′i-tī, *n.* Blamableness; guiltiness.

culprit, kul′prit, *n.* A person arraigned in court for a crime, or convicted of a crime; a criminal; an offender.

cult, kult, *n.* A system of belief and worship; a subject of devoted study.

cultivate, kul′ti-vȧt, *vt.* To till; to refine; to foster; to improve.

cultivation, kul-ti-vā′shun, *n.* Tillage; practice, care, or study directed to improvement; refinement; advancement.

cultivator, kul′ti-vȧt-ẽr, *n.* One who cultivates; a kind of harrow.

culture, kul′tur, *n.* Cultivation; the rearing of certain animals, as oysters; the application of labor; or other means of improvement; the result of such efforts; refinement.—*vt.* To cultivate. **cultured**, kul′tūrd, *a.* Having education and taste; refined.

culvert, kul′vẽrt, *n.* An arched drain under a road, railway, &c., for the passage of water.

cumber, kum′bẽr, *vt.* To embarrass; to entangle; to obstruct; to distract. **cumbersome**, kum′bẽr-sum, *a.* Troublesome; unwieldly; unmanageable. **cumbrous**, kum′brus, *a.* Burdensome; troublesome; oppressive.

cummerbund, kum′ẽr-bund. *n.* A girdle or waistband.

cumulate, kū′mū-lȧt, *vt.* (cumulating,

cumulated). To form a heap; to heap together. **cumulation**, kū-mū-lā'shun, *n.* A heaping up; a heap; accumulation. **cumulative**, kū'mū-lā-tiv, *a.* Forming a mass; that augments by addition.

cumulus, kū'mū-lus, *n.*; pl. **-li.** A cloud in the form of dense convex or conical heaps.

cuneiform, kū-nē'i-form, *a.* Wedge-shaped; applied to the arrow-headed characters on old Babylonian and Persian inscriptions.

cunning, kun'ing, *a.* Astute; artful.—*n.* Faculty or act of using stratagem; craftiness; artifice. **cunningly**, kun'ing-li, *adv.* In a cunning manner; craftily.

cup, kup, *n.* A small vessel to drink out of; anything hollow, like a cup; a glass vessel for drawing blood; liquor in a cup. —*vt.* (cupping, cupped). To apply a cupping-glass.

cupboard, kub'erd, *n.* A case or inclosure for cups, plates, dishes, &c.

cupellation, kū-pe-lā'shun, *n.* The process of refining gold or silver in a cupel.

Cupid, kū'pid, *n.* The god of love.

cupidity, kū-pid'i-ti, *n.* A longing to possess; inordinate or unlawful desire; covetousness.

cupola, kū'pō-la, *n.* A spherical vault on the top of a building; a dome.

cur, kėr, *n.* A mongrel dog; a contemptible man.

curaçao, **curaçoa**, kö-ra-sō', *n.* A liqueur flavored with orange-peel, &c.

curacy, **curateship**, kū'ra-si, kū'rāt-ship, *n.* The office of a curate.

curate, kū'rāt, *n.* One to whom the cure of souls is committed; a clergyman employed to perform the duties of a rector or vicar.

curative, kūr'ā-tiv, *a.* Relating to the cure of diseases; tending to cure.

curator, kū-rā'tėr, *n.* A superintendent; custodian; guardian.

curb, kėrb, *vt.* To control; to check; to restrain with a curb, as a horse; to strengthen by a curbstone.—*n.* Check; restraint; part of a bridle; a curb-stone.

curbstone, kėrb'stōn, *n.* The outer edge of a foot-pavement.

curd, kėrd, *n.* Coagulated milk.—*vt.* and *i.* To curdle; to congeal.

curdle, kėr'dl, *vt.* and *i.* (curdling, curdled). To change into curds; to coagulate.

cure, kūr, *n.* Act of healing; a remedy; the care of souls; spiritual charge.—*vt.* (curing, cured). To heal; to remedy; to pickle.—*vi.* To effect a cure.

curfew, kėr'fū, *n.* An evening bell; an old utensil for covering a fire.

curia, kū'ri-a, *n.* The Roman see in its temporal aspect.

curio, kū'ri-ō, *n.*; pl. **-os.** A curiosity; an interesting and curious article.

curious, kū'ri-us, *a.* Inquisitive; addicted to research or inquiry; strange; singular. **curiously**, kū'ri-us-li, *adv.* In a curious manner; inquisitively; unusually. **curiosity**, kū-ri-os'i-ti, *n.* Inquisitiveness; a thing unusual; a rarity.

curl, kėrl, *vt.* To form into ringlets.—*vi.* To take a twisted or coiled form; to

play at the game of curling.—*n.* A rin[g] let of hair, or anything of a like form; waving; flexure.

curler, kėr'lėr, *n.* One who or th[e] which curls; one who plays the game [of] curling.

curlew, kėr'lū, *n.* A bird allied to t[he] snipe and woodcock.

curling, kėr'ling, *n.* A winter game which large smooth stones are propell[ed] on the ice.

curly, kėr'li, *a.* Having curls; tending [to] curl.

curmudgeon, kėr-muj'on, *n.* An av[a]ricious churlish fellow; a miser; a chu[rl].

currant, kur'ant, *n.* A small dri[ed] grape; the name of several shrubs and their fruit.

currency, kur'en-si, *n.* Circulation; ci[r] culating medium; the aggregate of coi[n] notes, &c., in circulation.

current, kur'ent, *a.* Running; circ[u] lating; general; present in its course.— *n.* A running; a stream; progressive m[o] tion of water; successive course. **cur rently**, kur'ent-li, *adv.* In a curren[t] manner; generally.

curriculum, ku-rik'ū-lum, *n.* A cour[se] of study in a university, school, &c.

curry, kur'i, *n.* A highly spiced sauce [or] mixture; a dish cooked with curry.—*v[t]* (currying, curried). To flavor with cu[r] ry; to dress leather; to rub and clean [a] horse) with a comb; to seek (favor).

currycomb, kur'i-kōm, *n.* A comb f[or] rubbing and cleaning horses.

curse, kėrs, *vt.* (cursing, cursed curst). To utter a wish of evil agains[t] to blight; to torment with calamities.— *vi.* To utter imprecations; to blasphem[e] —*n.* Imprecation of evil; execratio[n] torment. **cursed**, kėr'sed, *a.* Deservi[ng] a curse; under a curse; execrable; d[e] testable. **cursedly**, kėr'sed-li, *adv.* In [a] cursed manner; confoundedly. **cursin[g]** kėr'sing, *n.* The uttering of a curs[e] execration. **cursive**, kėr'siv, *a.* Ru[n] ning; flowing.

cursory, kėr'sō-ri, *a.* Hasty; superficia[l] **cursorily**, kėr'sō-ri-li, *adv.* In a has[ty] manner; slightly; hastily.

curt, kėrt, *a.* Short; concise; somewh[at] rude.

curtail, kėr-tāl', *vt.* To cut short; abridge.

curtain, kėr'tin, *n.* A hanging cloth f[or] a window, bed, &c.; a screen in [a] theater.—*vt.* To inclose or furnish wi[th] curtains.

curtly, kėrt'li, *adv.* Shortly; briefly.

curtsy, curtsey, kėrt'si, *n.* A gestu[re] of respect by a female.—*vi.* (curtsyi[ng] or curtseying; curtsied or curtseyed). [To] drop or make a curtsy.

curvature, kėr'va-tūr, *n.* A curving.

curve, kėrv, *a.* Bending; inflected.— A bending without angles; a bent lin[e] —*vt.* (curving, curved). To bend.

cushion, kush'on, *n.* A pillow for a sea[t] something resembling a pillow.—*vt.* [To] seat on a cushion; to furnish wi[th] cushions.

cusp, kusp, *n.* The point of the moon, [or] other luminary; a point formed by t[he] meeting of two curves.

custard, kus'tẽrd, n. A composition of milk and eggs, sweetened, and baked or boiled.

custard apple, kus'tẽrd ap'l, n. A W. Indian tree or fruit.

custody, kus'tō-di, n. A keeping; guardianship; imprisonment; security. custodial, kus-tō'di-al, a. Relating to custody or guardianship. custodian, kus-tō'di-an, n. One who has care of a library, public building, &c. custodier, kus-tō'di-ẽr, n. One who has something in custody; a keeper; a guardian.

custom, kus'tum, n. Habit; established practice; fashion; a buying of goods; business support; a tax on goods; pl. duties on merchandise imported or exported. customable, kus'tum-a-bl, a. Subject to the payment of customs. customarily, kus'tum-er'i-li, adv. Habitually. customary, kus'tum-er'i, a. According to custom; habitual; usual. customer, kus'tum-ẽr, n. An accustomed buyer at a shop, &c.; one who buys goods. custom house, kus'tum hous', n. The house where customs are paid.

cut, kut, vt. (cutting, cut). To divide into pieces; to fell or mow; to clip; to carve; to affect deeply; to intersect; to castrate; to divide, as cards; to refuse to recognize.—vi. To make an incision; to be severed by a cutting instrument; to pass straight and rapidly.—a. Gashed; carved; intersected; deeply affected.—n. The action of an edged instrument; a wound; a stroke with a whip; a severe remark; a channel; any small piece; a lot; a near passage; a carving or engraving; act of dividing a pack of cards; form; fashion; refusal to recognize a person.

cutaneous, kū-tā'nē-us, a. Pertaining to the skin.

cuticle, kū'ti-kl, n. The thin exterior coat of the skin; a vesicular membrane in plants.

cutlass, kut'las, n. A broad, curving sword.

Cutlass

cutlery, kut'lẽr-i, n. Knives and edged instruments collectively.

cutlet, kut'let, n. A small piece of meat for cooking, generally off the ribs.

cutter, kut'ẽr, n. One who or that which cuts; a vessel with one mast and a straight running bowsprit.

cutthroat, kut"thrōt', n. A murderer.

cutting, kut'ing, p.a. Serving to cut; wounding the feelings; severe.—n. A piece cut off; an incision; an excavation; a twig or scion.

cuttle, cuttle-fish, kut'l, kut'l-fish, n. A mollusk which ejects a black fluid to conceal itself.

cyanide, si'a-nid, n. A combination of cyanogen with a metallic base.

cybernetics, si-bẽr-net'iks, n. The science that relates the principles of controls of the human organism and that of machines.

cycle, si'kl, n. An orbit in the heavens; a circle of years; a bicycle or tricycle.—vi. To recur in a cycle; to ride a bicycle. cyclic, cyclical, si'klick, si'kli-kal, a. Pertaining to a cycle; connected with a series of legends. cyclist, si'klist, n. One who uses a cycle.

cycloid, si'kloid, n. A geometrical curve.

cyclometer, si-klom'e-tẽr, n. An instrument for measuring circles, or for giving the distance traveled by a cycle.

cyclone, si'klōn, n. A circular storm; a rotatory system of winds revolving round a calm center and advancing.

cyclopædia, cyclopedia, si'klō-pē'di-a, n. A kind of dictionary, giving accounts on a branch or all branches of science, art, or learning. cyclopædic, cyclopedic, si-klō-pē'dik, a. Belonging to a cyclopædia.

cygnet, sig'net, n. A young swan.

cylinder, sil'in-dẽr, n. An elongated round body of uniform diameter. cylindric, cylindrical, si-lin'drik, si-lin'dri-kal, a. Having the form of a cylinder, or partaking of its properties.

cymbal, sim'bal, n. A basin-shaped musical instrument of brass, used in pairs.

cynic, sin'ik, n. One of a sect of Greek philosophers who professed contempt of riches, arts, &c.; a morose man. cynic, cynical, sin'ik, sin'i-kal, a. Belonging to the Cynics; surly; sneering; captious.

cynicism, sin'i-sizm, n. A morose contempt of the pleasures and arts of life.

cynosure, si'nō-zhōr, n. The constellation of the Little Bear; a center of attraction.

cypress, si'pres, n. An evergreen tree; the emblem of mourning.

cyst, sist, n. A bag in animal bodies containing matter.

czar, zär, n. A title of the Emperor of Russia.

czarevitch, zär'e-vich, n. The eldest son of the czar; also cesarevitch (tsä-zä-rä'vich).

czarina, zä-rē'na, n. A title of the Empress of Russia.

Czech, chek, n. One of the Slavonic inhabitants of Bohemia; the language of the Czechs.

Czechoslovakia, chek-ō-slō-va'ki-a, n. A country in central Europe.

D

dab, dab, vt. (dabbing, dabbed). To hit lightly with something soft or moist.—n. A gentle blow; a small mass of anything soft or moist; a small flat fish; an adept or expert.

dabble, dab'l, vt. (dabbling, dabbled).

To wet; to sprinkle.—*vi.* To play in water; to do anything in a superficial manner; to meddle. **dabbler**, dab'lėr, *n.* One who dabbles; a superficial meddler.

dachshund, däks'hunt, *n.* A long-bodied short-legged dog, with short hair.

Dacron, dā'kron, *n.* A synthetic fabric of great strength and resistance to wrinkling. A trade-mark.

dad, daddy, dad, dad'i, *n.* A childish or pet name for father.

dado, dā'dō, *n.* That part of a pedestal between the base and the cornice; the finishing of the lower part of the walls in rooms.

daffodil, daf'ō-dil, *n.* A plant of the amaryllis family with yellow flowers.

dagger, dag'ėr, *n.* A short sharp-pointed sword.

daggle, dag'l, *vt.* (daggling, daggled). To trail in mud or wet grass; to dirty.

daguerreotype, da-ger'ō-tip, *n.* A photograph fixed on a metallic plate.

dahlia, dāl'ya, *n.* A genus of composite plants, consisting of tuberous-rooted herbs.

daily, dā'li, *a.* Happening or being every day; diurnal.—*adv.* Day by day.

dainty, dān'ti, *a.* Toothsome; nice; delicate; elegant.—*n.* Something nice; a delicacy.

daintily, dān'ti-li, *adv.* Nicely; delicately.

dairy, dār'i, *n.* The place where milk is converted into butter or cheese; a store where milk, butter, &c., are sold.—*a.* Pertaining to the keeping of cows, managing of milk, &c.

dais, dā'is, *n.* The high table at the upper end of the dining-hall; the raised floor on which the table stood; a canopy.

daisy, dā'zi, *n.* The day's eye; a well-known plant, bearing a white flower with a tinge of red, and a yellow center.

dale, dāl, *n.* A valley; a place between hills.

dally, dal'i, *vi.* (dallying, dallied). To trifle; to wanton; to linger. **dalliance**, dal'yans, *n.* Acts of fondness; interchange of caresses; toying.

dam, dam, *n.* A female parent; a bank to confine or raise water.—*vt.* (damming, dammed). To obstruct or confine by a dam.

damage, dam'ij, *n.* Hurt; injury; money; compensation (generally in *pl.*).—*vt.* (damaging, damaged). To injure; to impair. **damageable**, dam'ij-a-bl, *a.* That may be damaged.

damask, dam'ask, *n.* A fabric of various materials, with figures of flowers, &c.; a pink color.—*a.* Pink or rosy.—*vt.* To form or imprint flowers or figures on. **damaskeen**, dam'as-kēn, *vt.* To inlay iron, steel, &c., with another metal, as gold or silver.

dame, dām, *n.* A lady; the wife of a knight or baronet.

damn, dam, *vt.* To send to hell; to condemn. **damnable**, dam'na-bl, *a.* Deserving damnation; odious; pernicious. **damnably**, dam'na-bli, *adv.* In a damnable manner. **damnation**, dam-nā'shun, *n.* Condemnation; sentence to punishment in the future state. **damnatory**, dam'na-tō-ri, *a.* Containing condemnation; condemnatory. **damned**, damd, *a.* Hateful; detestable. **damning**, dam'ing or dam'ning, *a.* That condemns or exposes to damnation.

damp, damp, *a.* Moist; humid.—*n.* Moist air; fog; noxious exhalation from the earth; depression of spirits; discouragement.—*vt.* To moisten; to dispirit; to restrain. **dampen**, damp'en, *vt.* and *i.* To make or become damp or moist. **damper**, damp'ėr, *n.* One who or that which damps; a plate across a flue of a furnace, &c., to regulate the draught of air. **dampish**, damp'ish, *a.* Moderately damp. **dampness**, damp'nes, *n.* Moisture; fogginess; moistness; moderate humidity.

damsel, dam'zel, *n.* A young unmarried woman; a girl.

damson, dam'zun, *n.* A small dark plum.

dance, dans, *vi.* (dancing, danced). To move with measured steps regulated by a tune; to leap and frisk.—*vt.* To make to dance; to dandle.—*n.* A leaping or stepping to the measure of a tune; the tune itself. **dancer**, dan'sėr, *n.* One who dances. **dancing-girl**, *n.* A girl who dances professionally, as in Egypt or India.

dandelion, dan'dē-li-un, *n.* A composite plant bearing a bright yellow flower.

dandle, dan'dl, *vt.* (dandling, dandled). To shake on the knee, as an infant; to fondle; to trifle with.

dandruff, dan'druf, *n.* A scurf on the head.

dandy, dan'di, *n.* A fop; a coxcomb. **dandyish**, dan'di-ish, *a.* Like a dandy. **dandyism**, dan'di-ism, *n.* Manners and dress of a dandy.

danger, dān'jėr, *n.* Exposure to injury; jeopardy; risk. **dangerous**, dān'jėr-us, *a.* Perilous; causing risk of harm; unsafe; insecure. **dangerously**, dān'jėr-us-li, *adv.* With danger; perilously.

dangle, dang'gl, *vi.* (dangling, dangled). To hang loose; to follow officiously.—*vt.* To carry suspended loosely; to swing. **dangler**, dang'glėr, *n.* One who dangles; a man who hangs about women.

dank, dangk, *a.* Damp; moist; humid.

danseuse, däng-sėz, *n.* A female stage-dancer.

dapper, dap'ėr, *a.* Little and active; neat.

dapple, dap'l, *n.* A spot.—*a.* Marked with spots.—*vt.* (dappling, dappled). To variegate with spots. **dappled**, dap'ld, *a.* Spotted.

dare, dār, *vi.* (daring, *pret.* dared or durst, *pp.* dared). To have courage; to be bold enough; to venture.—*vt.* To challenge; to defy; to venture on. **daredevil**, dār''dev'l, *n.* A desperado; one who will fearlessly attempt anything. **daring**, dār'ing, *a.* Bold; intrepid; fearless.—*n.* Courage; audacity. **daringly**, dār'ing-li, *adv.* Boldly; fearlessly.

dark, därk, *a.* Destitute of light; clouded: black or blackish; disheartening; involved in mystery; keeping designs in concealment.—*n.* Darkness; obscurity;

secrecy; state of ignorance. **darken,** därk'n, vt. To make dark.—vi. To grow dark or darker. **darkly,** därk'li, adv. Obscurely; dimly. **darkness,** därk'nes, n. Absence of light; blackness; gloom; ignorance; privacy.

darkroom, dark'röm, n. A room protected from rays of light, used for the development of film and printing of photographs.

darling, där'ling, a. Dearly beloved.—n. One much beloved; a favorite.

darn, därn, vt. To mend by imitating the texture of the stuff with thread and needle; to sew together.—n. A place so mended.

dart, därt, n. A pointed missile thrown by the hand; a sudden rush or bound.—vt. To throw with a sudden thrust; to shoot.—vi. To fly or shoot, as a dart; to start and run.

Darwinism, där'win-izm, n. The doctrine as to the origin and modifications of species taught by Darwin; evolution.

dash, dash, vt. To cause to strike suddenly or violently; to throw or cast; to sprinkle; to mix slightly; to sketch out hastily; to obliterate; to frustrate; to abash.—vi. To rush with violence; to strike or be hurled.—n. A violent striking of two bodies; admixture; a rushing or onset; vigor in attack; bluster; a mark in writing or printing (—). **dashing,** dash'ing, a. Spirited; showy.

dastard, das'tĕrd, n. A coward.—a. Cowardly; base.

data, dā'ta, n.pl. See **datum.**

date, dāt, n. The time when any event happened; era; age; a soft fleshy drupe, the fruit of the date-palm.—vt. (dating, dated). To note time of.—vi. To reckon time; to have origin.

date palm, date tree, dāt'päm, dāt'trē, n. The kind of palms which bear dates.

dative, dā'tiv, a. or n. A grammatical case, following verbs that express giving, &c.

datum, dā'tum, n.; pl. **-ta.** A fact, proposition, &c., granted or known, from which other facts, &c., are to be deduced.

daub, dab, vt. To smear; to cover with mud or other soft substance; to paint coarsely; to flatter grossly.—n. Coarse painting; a smear. **dauber,** dab'ĕr, n. One who daubs; a coarse painter; a gross flatterer.

daughter, da'tĕr, n. A female child or descendant. **daughter-in-law,** da'tĕr-in-la, n. A son's wife.

daunt, dant, vt. To subdue the courage of; to intimidate; to discourage. **dauntless,** dant'les, a. Fearless; intrepid.

dauphin, da'fin, n. The eldest son of the king of France.

davenport, dav'en-port, n. Kind of sofa.

davit, da'vit, n. One of a pair of projecting pieces over a ship's side, with tackle to hoist or lower a boat by.

dawdle, da'dl, vi. (dawdling, dawdled). To waste time; to trifle; to saunter.

dawn, dan, vi. To begin to grow light in the morning; to glimmer obscurely; to begin to open or appear.—n. The break of day; beginning; first appearance.

dawning, dan'ing, n. The first appearance of light in the morning; beginning.

day, dā, n. The time between the rising and setting of the sun; the time of one revolution of the earth, or 24 hours; light; time specified; age; time; anniversary.

daybreak, dā'brāk, n. The dawn; first appearance of light in the morning.

daydream, dā'drēm, n. A vision to the waking senses; a reverie.

daylight, dā'lit, n. The light of the day.

daytime, dā'tim, n. The time of daylight.

daze, dāz, vt. (dazing, dazed). To stupefy; to stun.

dazzle, daz'l, vt. (dazzling, dazzled). To overpower with light or splendor.—vi. To be intensely bright; to be overpowered by light.—n. A dazzling light; glitter.

deacon, dē'kun, n. A person in the lowest degree of holy orders; a church officer; the president of an incorporated trade. **deaconess,** dē'kon-es, n. A female deacon.

dead, ded, a. Without life; deceased; perfectly still; dull; cold; tasteless; spiritless; utter; unerring.—n. Stillness; gloom; depth; (pl.) the deceased. **deaden,** ded'n, vt. To abate in vigor, force, or sensation; to darken, dull, or dim.

dead heat, ded hēt, n. A race in which the competitors finish at the same time.

dead letter, ded let'ĕr, n. A letter which cannot be delivered, and is returned to the sender.

deadlock, ded'lok, n. Complete standstill.

deadly, ded'li, a. That may cause death; mortal; implacable.—adv. In a deadly manner.

dead-set, ded'set, n. The fixed position of a dog in pointing game; a pointed attack.

dead weight, ded wāt, n. A heavy or oppressive burden.

deaf, def, a. Wanting the sense of hearing; not listening or regarding. **deafen,** def'en, vt. To make deaf; to render impervious to sound. **deafening,** def'en-ing, n. Matter to prevent the passage of sound through floors, &c. **deaf-mute,** def'mūt', n. A deaf and dumb person.

deal, dēl, n. A part; an indefinite quantity, degree, or extent; the distribution of playing cards; a board or plank; fir or pine timber.—vt. (dealing, dealt). To distribute.—vi. To traffic; to behave; to distribute cards. **dealer,** dēl'ĕr, n. A trader; one who distributes cards. **dealing,** dēl'ing, n. Conduct; behavior; intercourse; traffic.

dean, dēn, n. A dignitary in cathedral and collegiate churches who presides over the chapter; an officer in a university or college.

dear, dēr, a. Bearing a high price; valuable; expensive; in high estimation; beloved.—n. A darling.—adv. Dearly. **dearly,** dēr'li, adv. At a high price; with great fondness.

dearth, dĕrth, n. Scarcity; want; famine.

death, deth, *n.* Extinction of life; decease; cause of decease; damnation. **deathbed**, deth'bed, *n.* The bed on which a person dies. **deathless**, deth'-les, *a.* Not subject to death. **deathlike**, deth'līk, *a.* Resembling death; gloomy; quiet; motionless. **deathly**, deth'li, *a.* Deadly; fatal.

death-rate, deth'rāt, *n.* The proportion of deaths in a town, country, &c.

debacle, de-bäk'l, *n.* A sudden breaking up of ice; a confused rout; a crash in the social or political world.

debar, dē-bär', *vt.* (debarring, debarred). To hinder from approach, entry, or enjoyment.

debase, dē-bās', *vt.* (debasing, debased). To lower; to degrade; to vitiate. **debased**, dē-bāsd', *p.a.* Adulterated; degraded; vile. **debasement**, dē'bās'-ment, *n.* Act of debasing; state of being debased. **debatable**, dē-bāt'a-bl, *a.* Disputable.

debate, dē-bāt', *n.* Contention in words or arguments; discussion; controversy.—*vt.* (debating, debated). To dispute; to argue; to discuss.—*vi.* To examine different arguments in the mind; to deliberate. **debater**, dē-bāt'ėr, *n.* One who debates.

debauch, dē'bäch', *vt.* To corrupt; to pervert.—*vi.* To riot; to revel.—*n.* Excess in eating or drinking; lewdness. **debauched**, dē'bächt', *p.a.* Vitiated in morals; profligate. **debauchery**, dē-bäch'ė-ri, *n.* Gluttony; intemperance; habitual lewdness.

debenture, dē-ben'tūr, *n.* A deed charging property with the repayment of money lent, and with interest; a certificate of drawback.

debility, dē-bil'i-ti, *n.* Weakness; feebleness. **debilitate**, dē-bil'i-tāt, *vt.* (debilitating, debilitated). To enfeeble; to enervate.

debit, deb'it, *n.* A recorded item of debt; the left-hand page or debtor side of a ledger or account.—*vt.* To charge with debt.

debonair, deb-ō-nār', *a.* Gracious; courteous.

debris, de-brē, *n.sing.* or *pl.* Fragments; rubbish.

debt, det, *n.* That which is due from one person to another; obligation; guilt. **debtor**, det'ėr, *n.* One who owes money, goods, or services; one indebted.

début, dā-bū', *n.* First appearance in public. **débutant**, dā-bū-tänt'; *fem.* **débutante**, dā-bu-tängt', *n.* One who makes a debut.

decade, dek'ād, *n.* The number of ten; a period of ten years. **decadence**, **decadency**, dē-kā'dens, dē-kā'den-si, or dek'a-, *n.* A falling off; decay. **decadent**, dē-kā'dent or dek'a-, *a.* Decaying; deteriorating.

decagon, dek'a-gon, *n.* A figure having ten sides.

decahedron, de-ka-hē'dron, *n.* A solid figure or body having ten sides.

Decalogue, dek'a-log, *n.* The ten commandments given by God to Moses.

decamp, dē-kamp', *vi.* To depart from

a camp; to march off; to take one's self off. **decampment**, dē-kamp'ment, *n.* Departure from a camp; a marching off.

decant, dē'kant', *vt.* To pour from one vessel into another. **decanter**, dē-kan'tėr, *n.* A glass bottle used for holding wine or other liquors.

decapitate, dē-kap'i-tāt, *vt.* (decapitating, decapitated). To behead. **decapitation**, dē-kap'i-tā'shun, *n.* Act of beheading.

decay, dē-kā', *vi.* To pass from a sound or prosperous state; to waste; to wither; to fail.—*n.* Gradual loss of strength, excellence, &c.; corruption; putrefaction.

decease, dē-sēs', *n.* Departure from this life; death.—*vi.* (deceasing, deceased). To die. **deceased**, dē-sēst', *a.* Dead; often as a noun *with (the)*.

deceit, dē-sēt', *n.* Fraud; guile; cunning. **deceitful**, dē-sēt'ful, *a.* Fraudulent; delusive; false; hollow. **deceitfully**, dē-sēt'ful-li, *adv.* In a deceitful manner.

deceive, dē-sēv', *vt.* (deceiving, deceived). To mislead the mind of; to impose on; to delude; to frustrate (hopes, &c.). **deceivable**, de-sēv'a-bl, *a.* Capable of being deceived; exposed to imposture. **deceiver**, dē-sēv'ėr, *n.* One who deceives.

decelerate, dē-sel'er-āt, *vt.* and *vi.* To slow down. **deceleration**, dē-sel-er-ā'shun, *n.* Act of slowing down.

December, dē-sem'bėr, *n.* The twelfth and last month of the year.

decency, dē'sen-si, *n.* The state or quality of being decent; decorum; modesty.

decennial, dē-sen'i-al, *a.* Consisting of ten years; happening every ten years.

decent, dē'sent, *a.* Becoming; seemly; respectable; modest; moderate. **decently**, dē'sent-li, *adv.* In a decent manner.

decentralize, dē-sen'tral-īz, *vt.* To remove from direct dependence on a central authority.

deception, dē-sep'shun, *n.* Act of deceiving; state of being deceived; artifice practiced; fraud; double-dealing. **deceptive**, dē-sep'tiv, *a.* Tending to deceive; misleading; false; delusive.

decide, dē-sīd', *vt.* (deciding, decided). To determine; to settle; to resolve.—*vi.* To determine; to pronounce a judgment. **decided**, dē-sīd'ed, *a.* Clear; resolute. **decidedly**, dē-sīd'ed-li, *adv.* Clearly; indisputably.

deciduous, dē-sid'ū-us, *a.* Not permanent; having leaves that fall in autumn.

decimal, des'i-mal, *a.* Tenth; reckoned by ten.—*n.* A tenth. **decimate**, des'i-māt, *vt.* (decimating, decimated). To kill every tenth man of; to tithe; to destroy a large number of. **decimation**, des'i-mā'shun, *n.* Act of decimating; a tithing.

decipher, dē-sī'fėr, *vt.* To explain what is written in ciphers; to read what is not clear; to interpret. **decipherable**, dē-sī'fėr-a-bl, *a.* That may be deciphered. **decipherer**, dē-sī'fėr-ėr, *n.* One who deciphers.

decision, dē-sizh'un, *n.* Determination of a difference, doubt, or event; final judgment; firmness of purpose or character. **decisive**, dē-sī'siv, *a.* Conclusive;

absolute; marked by prompt determination. **decisively**, dĕ-sī'siv-li, *adv*. Conclusively.

deck, dek, *vt*. To clothe; to adorn; to furnish with a deck, as a vessel.—*n*. The platform or floor of a ship. **decker**, dek'ĕr, *n*. One who decks; a ship having decks, as, a three-decker.

declaim, dĕ-klām', *vi*. To make a formal speech; to harangue; to inveigh. **declaimer**, dĕ-klām'ĕr, *n*. One who declaims. **declamation**, dek-la-mā'shun, *n*. The art or act of declaiming; a harangue. **declamatory**, dĕ-klam'a-tō-ri, *a*. Relating to the practice of declaiming; rhetorical, without solid sense or argument.

declare, dĕ-klār', *vt*. (declaring, declared). To show clearly; to tell explicitly; to testify; to reveal.—*vi*. To make a declaration. **declared**, dĕ-klārd', *p.a*. Made known; avowed; openly professed. **declarable**, dĕ-klār'a-bl, *a*. That may be declared or proved. **declaration**, dek-la-rā'shun, *n*. Act of declaring; that which is declared; an explicit statement; a solemn affirmation. **declarative**, dĕ-klār'a-tiv, *a*. Explanatory; making proclamation.

decline, dĕ-klīn', *vi*. (declining, declined). To bend downward; to swerve; to fail; not to comply.—*vt*. To bend downward; to refuse; to change the termination of a noun, &c.—*n*. A falling off; decay; deterioration; consumption. **declension**, dĕ-klen'shun, *n*. The act or state of declining; refusal; the change of the terminations of nouns, adjectives, and pronouns to form the oblique cases. **declinable**, dĕ-klīn'a-bl, *a*. That may be declined. **declination**, de-klin-ā'shun, *n*. A bending downwards; decay; deviation from rectitude; angular distance of a heavenly body north or south from the equator; variation of the magnetic needle from the true meridian of a place.

declivity, dĕ-kliv'i-ti *n*. Inclination downward; a downward slope.

decoct, dĕ'kokt', *vt*. To prepare by boiling; to digest by heat. **decoction**, dĕ-kok'shun, *n*. The act of boiling a substance in water to extract its virtues; the preparation thus obtained.

decode, dĕ-kōd', *vt*. To translate into ordinary language.

decompose, dĕ-kom-pōz', *vt*. To resolve into original elements.—*vi*. Te become resolved into elementary particles; to decay.

decomposition, dĕ-kom'pō-zish"un, *n*. Act or process of decomposing; analysis; decay.

decorate, dek'ō-rāt, *vt*. (decorating, decorated). To adorn; to embellish. **decoration**, dek-ō-rā'shun, *n*. Act of decorating; that which adorns; a badge or medal. **decorative**, dek'ō-rā-tiv, *a*. Suited to adorn. **decorator**, dek'ō-rā-tĕr, *n*. One who decorates buildings by painting, &c.

decorous, dĕk-ō'rus, *a*. Seemly; becoming; behaving with strict propriety. **decorously**, dĕk-ō'rus-li, *adv*. In a decorous manner. **decorum**, dē-kō'rum, *n*. Propriety of speech or behavior; seemliness.

decoy, dĕ-koi', *n*. An inclosure for catching ducks or wild fowls; a lure.—*vt*. To lure into a snare; to entice.

decrease, dĕ-krēs', *vi*. (decreasing, decreased). To grow less.—*vt*. To cause to become less.—*n*. Gradual diminution; decay; the wane of the moon.

decree, dĕ-krē', *n*. An edict; an order or law; predetermined purpose; judicial decision.—*vt*. (decreeing, decreed). To enact; to award; to determine judicially.—*vi*. To make an edict; to appoint by edict.

decrepit, dĕ-krep'it, *a*. Broken down with age; being in the last stage of decay.

decrepitate, dĕ-krep'i-tāt, *vt*. To calcine in a strong heat, with a continual crackling of the substance.—*vi*. To crackle when roasting. **decrepitation**, dĕ-krep'i-tā"shun, *n*. The separation of parts with a crackling noise.

decrepitude, dĕ-krep'i-tūd, *n*. The crazy state of the body produced by decay or age.

decry, dĕ-krī', *vt*. To cry down; to rail against; to censure; to depreciate. **decrial**, de-krī'al, *n*. The act of decrying.

dedicate, ded'i-kāt, *vt*. (dedicating, dedicated). To consecrate to a sacred purpose; to devote (often refl.); to inscribe to a friend. **dedication**, ded-i-kā'shun, *n*. Act of devoting to some person, use, or thing; inscription or address.

deduce, dĕ-dūs', *vt*. (deducing, deduced). To draw or bring; to gather from premises; to infer; to derive. **deducible**, dĕ-dūs'i-bl, *a*. That may be deduced or inferred.

deduct, dĕ-dukt', *vt*. To subtract. **deduction**, dĕ-duk'shun, *n*. Inference; abatement; discount. **deductive**, dĕ-duk'tiv, *a*. That is or may be deduced from premises. **deductively**, dĕ-duk'-tiv-li, *adv*. In a deductive manner; by deduction.

deed, dēd, *n*. That which is done; an act; feat; reality; a written agreement; an instrument conveying real estate.

deem, dēm, *vt*. To judge; to think.—*vi*. To judge; to be of opinion; to estimate.

deep, dēp, *a*. Being far below the surface; descending far downward; low in situation; not obvious; sagacious; designing; grave in sound; very still or solemn; thick; strongly colored; mysterious; heartfelt; absorbed.—*n*. The sea; the abyss of waters; any abyss. **deepen**, dēp'n, *vt*. To make deep or deeper.—*vi*. To become more deep. **deep-laid**, dēp'-lād, *a*. Formed with great skill or artifice. **deeply**, dēp'li, *adv*. At or to a great depth; profoundly.

deer, dēr, *n.sing*. and *pl*. A quadruped of several species, as the stag, the fallow-deer, the roebuck, the reindeer, &c. **deerstalking**, dēr'stak-ing, *n*. The hunting of deer on foot, by stealing within shot of them unawares.

deface, dĕ'fās', *vt*. To destroy or mar the surface of a thing; to disfigure; to erase. **defacement**, dē-fās'ment, n. Injury to the surface or beauty; obliteration; that which mars or disfigures.

defalcate, dē-fal'kāt, vt. To take away or deduct. **defalcation**, dē-fal-kā'shun, n. A deficit; a fraudulent abstraction of money. **defalcator**, de'fal-kāt-ėr, n. One guilty of defalcation or embezzlement.

defame, dē-fām', vt. (defaming, defamed). To accuse falsely and maliciously; to slander. **defamer**, dē-fām'ėr, n. A slanderer. **defamation**, dē-fa-mā'shun, n. Act of defaming; slander; calumny. **defamatory**, dē-fam'a-tō-ri, a. Calumnious; slanderous.

default, de-falt', n. An omission; neglect to do what duty or law requires; failure to appear in court.—vi. To fail in fulfilling an engagement, contract, &c. **defaulter**, dē-falt'ėr, n. One who makes default; one who fails to account for money intrusted to his care; a delinquent.

defeat, dē-fēt', n. Frustration; overthrow; loss of battle.—vt. To frustrate; to foil, to overthrow; to conquer.

defecate, de'fē-kāt, vt. To clear from lees; to purify.—vi. To void excrement. **defecation**, de-fē-kā'shun, n. Act of separating from lees; purification.

defect, dē-fekt', n. Want; a blemish; fault; flaw. **defection**, dē-fek'shun, n. Act of abandoning a person or cause; apostasy. **defective**, dē-fek'tiv, a. Having a defect; deficient; faulty. **defectively**, dē-fek'tiv-li, adv. In a defective manner.

defend, dē-fend', vt. To guard; to support; to resist; to vindicate; to act as defendant.—vi. To make defense or opposition. **defendant**, dē-fen'dant, n. A defender; in law, the person that opposes a charge, &c. **defender**, dē-fen'dėr, n. One who defends; a protector, supporter, or vindicator. **defense, defence**, dē-fens', n. A guarding against danger; protection; fortification; vindication; apology; plea; method adopted by one against whom legal proceedings are taken; skill in fencing. **defenseless**, dē-fens'les, a. Without defense; unprotected; weak. **defensible**, dē-fen'si-bl, a. That may be vindicated, maintained, or justified. **defensive**, dē-fen'siv, a. Proper for defense; carried on in resisting attack; in a state or posture to defend.—n. That which defends; state or posture of defense. **defensively**, dē-fen'siv-li, adv. In a defensive manner.

defer, dē-fėr', vt. (deferring, deferred). To put off to a future time; to postpone.—vi. To yield to another's opinion; to submit courteously or from respect. **deference**, def'er-ens, n. A yielding in opinion; regard; respect; submission. **deferential**, de-fėr-en'shal, a. Expressing or implying deference; respectful. **deferentially**, de-fėr-en'shal-li, adv. With deference. **deferment**, dē-fėr'ment, n. Postponement.

defiance, dē-fi'ans, n. Act of defying; a challenge to fight; contempt of opposition or danger. **defiant**, dē-fi'ant, a. Characterized by defiance, boldness, or insolence.

deficient, de-fish'ent, a. Defective; imperfect; not adequate. **deficiency, deficience**, de-fish'en-si, de-fish'ens, n. Want; defect.

deficit, def'i-sit, n. Deficiency of revenue.

defile, dē-fīl', vt. (defiling, defiled). To make foul; to pollute; to violate the chastity of; to march off in a line, or file by file.—n. A narrow way in which troops may march only in a line, or with a narrow front; a long narrow pass. **defilement**, dē-fīl'ment, n. Act of defiling, or state of being defiled.

define, dē-fīn', vt. (defining, defined). To limit; to explain exactly. **definable**, dē-fīn'a-bl. a. That may be defined. **definite**, def'i-nit, a. Having fixed limits; precise; exact; clear. **definitely**, def'-i-nit-ly, adv. Precisely **definition**, def'-i-nish''un, n. The act of defining; a brief description of a thing by its properties; an explanation in words. **definitive**, dē-fin'i-tiv, a. Limiting; positive; determining; final.—n. A word used to limit the signification of a noun. **definitively**, dē-fin'i-tiv-li, adv. In a definitive manner.

deflect, dē-flekt', vi. To deviate; to swerve.—vt. To cause to turn aside. **deflection, deflexion, deflexure**, dē-flek'shun, dē-flek'sūr, n. Deviation; a turning from a true line or regular course.

deflower, deflour, dē-flou'ėr, dē-flour', vt. To strip of flowers, or of bloom and beauty; to deprive of virginity.

defoliation, dē-fō'li-ā''shun, n. The fall of the leaf, or shedding of leaves.

deform, dē-form', vt To mar in form; to disfigure. **deformation**, dē-for-mā''shun, n. A disfiguring or defacing. **deformed**, dēformd', a. Disfigured; distorted; misshapen. **deformity**, dē-for'mi-ti, n. Want of proper form; distortion; gross deviation from propriety.

defraud, dē-frad', vt. To deprive of or withhold from wrongfully.

defray, dē-frā', vt. To discharge or pay, as the expenses of anything. **defrayal, defrayment**, dē-frā'al, dē-frā'ment, n. The act of defraying.

deft, deft, a. Apt; clever. **deftly**, deft'li, adv. Aptly; fitly; neatly.

defunct, dē-fungkt', a. Dead; deceased. —n. A dead person; one deceased.

defy, dē-fī', vt. (defying, defied). To provoke to combat; to dare; to challenge; to set at nought.

degenerate, dē-jen'ė-rāt, vi. To become worse than one's kind; to decay in good qualities.—a. dē-jen'ė-rit, Fallen from primitive or natural excellence; mean; corrupt. **degeneracy**, dē-jen'ėr-a-si, n. A growing worse or inferior; decline in good qualities; departure from the virtue of ancestors. **degeneration**, dē-jen'ėr-ā''shun, n. A degenerate state; degeneracy; deterioration.

degrade, dē-grād', vt. (degrading, degraded). To reduce to a lower rank; to strip of honors; to debase; to depose; to dishonor. **degradation**, de-gra-dā′shun, n. Act of degrading; state of being degraded; debasement; disgrace; a gradual wasting away. **degraded**, dē-grād′ed, p.a. Sunk to an abject state; exhibiting degradation; debased. **degrading**, dē-grād′ing, p.a. Dishonoring.

degree, dē-grē′, n. A step; step in relationship, rank, quality, &c.; measure; extent; the 360th part of the circumference of a circle; a mark of distinction conferred by universities; divisions marked on scientific instruments.

dehydration, de-hī-drā′shun, n. Process of freeing a compound from water.

deify, dē′i-fī, vt. (deifying, deified). To exalt to the rank of a deity; to extol as an object of supreme regard.

deign, dān, vi. To vouchsafe; to condescend.—vt. To condescend to give.

deity, dē′i-ti, n. Godhead; the Supreme Being; a fabulous god or goddess; a divinity.

deject, dē-jekt′, vt. To dispirit; to depress. **dejected**, dē-jek′ted, p.a. Cast down; depressed; grieved; discouraged. **dejection**, dē-jek′shun, n. Depression; melancholy; lowness of spirits.

delay, dē-lā′, vt. To defer; to retard; to stop; to protract.—vi. To linger; to stop for a time.—n. A lingering; stay; hindrance.

delectable, dē-lek′ta-bl, a. Delightful.

delegate, del′ē-gāt, vt. (delegating, delegated). To send as a representative; to depute; to commit to another's care.—n. A representative; a deputy. **delegation**, del-ē-gā′shun, n. Act of delegating; persons delegated; a commission.

delete, dē-lēt′, vt. (deleting, deleted). To blot out; to erase; to efface. **deletion**, dē-lē′shun, n. Act of deleting; an erasure; passage deleted.

deleterious, del-ē-tēr′i-us, a. Hurtful; poisonous; pernicious.

deliberate, dē-lib′ē-rāt, vi. To weigh well in one's mind; to consider; to consult; to debate.—vt. To balance well in the mind; to consider.—a. dē-lib′ē-rit. Cautious; discreet; well advised. **deliberately**, dē-lib′ē-rit-li, adv. In a deliberate manner; slowly; cautiously. **deliberation**, dē-lib′ēr-ā′shun, n. Thoughtful consideration; prudence; discussion of reasons for and against a measure. **deliberative**, dē-lib′ēr-ā-tiv, a. Proceeding or acting by deliberation; having a right to deliberate.

delicate, de′li-kit, a. Pleasing to the taste or senses; choice; fine; soft; smooth; nice in forms; minute; easily hurt or affected; tender; not robust. **delicacy**, del′i-ka-si, n. The quality of being delicate; fineness of texture; tenderness; minute accuracy; refined taste; a dainty. **delicately**, de′li-kit-li, adv. In a delicate manner; finely.

delicious, dē-lish′us, a. Highly pleasing to the taste; delightful. **deliciously**, dē-lish′us-li, adv. In a delicious manner.

delight, dē-līt′, n. That which yields great pleasure; a high degree of pleasure; joy.—vt. To affect with great pleasure;

to give high satisfaction to.—vi. To take great pleasure; to be rejoiced. **delighted**, dē-līt′ed, a. Experiencing delight; charmed. **delightful**, dē-līt′ful, a. Affording great pleasure and satisfaction; charming. **delightfully**, dē-līt′-ful-li, adv. In a delightful manner.

delineate, dē-lin′ē-āt, vt. To draw the lines showing the form of; to sketch; to describe. **delineation**, dē-lin′ē-ā′shun, n. Act of delineating; outline; sketch; description.

delinquent, dē-ling′kwent, a. Neglecting duty.—n. One who fails to perform his duty; one who commits a fault or crime. **delinquency**, dē-ling′kwen-si, n. An omission of duty; fault; offense; crime.

deliquesce, del-i-kwes′, vi. To melt by absorbing moisture from the air. **deliquescence**, dēl-i-kwes′ens, n. Act or process of deliquescing. **deliquescent**, dē-li-kwes′ent, a. That deliquesces; liquefying in the air.

delirium, dē-lir′i-um, n. Temporary disorder of the mind; violent excitement. **delirious**, de-lir′i-us, a. Disordered in intellect; raving; frenzied; insane.

deliver, dē-liv′ēr, vt. To free, as from danger or bondage; to disburden a woman of a child; to surrender; to commit; to give forth in words or in action. **deliverance**, dē-liv′ēr-ans, n. Release; rescue; an authoritative judgment. **deliverer**, dē-liv′ēr-ēr, n. One who delivers. **delivery**, dē-liv′ē-ri, n. Act of delivering; childbirth; rescue; surrender; distribution (of letters); manner of speaking.

dell, del, n. A small valley; a glen.

delta, del′ta, n. The space between diverging mouths of a river, as the Nile. **deltoid**, del′toid, a. Triangular.

delude, dē-lūd′, vt. (deluding, deluded). To impose on; to deceive; to circumvent.

deluge, del′ūj, n. A flood; an inundation; the flood in the days of Noah; a sweeping or overwhelming calamity.—vt. (deluging, deluged). To inundate; to drown; to overwhelm.

delusion, dē-lū′zhun, n. Act of deluding; a false belief; illusion; fallacy. **delusive**, dē-lū′siv, a. Apt to deceive. **delusively**, dē-lū′siv-li, adv. In a delusive manner. **delusory**, dē-lū′so-ri, a. Delusive.

delve, delv, vt. and i. (delving, delved). To dig. **delver**, delv′ēr, n. One who delves.

demagogue, dem′a-gog, n. A leader of the people; a factious orator.

demand, dē-mand′, vt. To seek as due by right; to require; to interrogate.—n. A claim by virtue of a right; an asking with authority; debt; the calling for in order to purchase; desire to purchase or possess.

demarcation, dē-mär-kā′shun, n. Act of setting a limit; a limit fixed.

demean, dē-mēn′, vt. To conduct; to behave; to debase (one's self).

demeanor, dē-mēn′ēr, n. Manner of conducting one's self; behavior.

demented, dē-men′ted, a. Insane; infatuated.

demerit, dē-mer′it, n. Fault; vice.

demigod, dem'i-god, *n.* Half a god; one partaking of the divine nature.

demise, dē-miz', *n.* Death; conveyance of an estate by lease or will.—*vt.* (demising, demised). To transfer; to lease; to bequeath.

demitasse, dem'i-tas, *n.* A small cup of coffee.

demobilize, dē-mō'bi-līz, *vt.* To disband.

democracy, dē-mok'ra-si, *n.* A form of government in which the supreme power is vested in the people. **democrat,** dem'ō-krat, *n.* One who adheres to democracy. **democratic, democratical,** dem-ō-krat'ik, dem-ō-krat'ik-al, *a.* Pertaining to democracy. **democratically,** dem-ō-krat'i-kal-li, *adv.* In a democratical manner.

demolish, dē-mol'ish, *vt.* To pull down; to destroy. **demolition,** dem-ō-lish'un, *n.* Act of demolishing; ruin; destruction.

demon, dē'mun, *n.* A spirit, holding a place below the celestial deities of the pagans; an evil spirit; a devil; a fiendlike man.

demoniac, dē-mō'ni-ak, *n.* A human being possessed by a demon. **demoniac, demoniacal, demonian,** dē-mō'ni-ak, dē-mō-ni'a-kal, dē-mō'ni-an, *a.* Pertaining to demons; influenced or produced by demons. **demoniacally,** dē-mō-ni'a-kal-li, *adv.* In a demoniacal manner.

demonstrate, dem-on-strāt', *vt.* (demonstrating, demonstrated). To prove beyond doubt; to make evident; to exhibit. **demonstrable,** dē-mon'stra-bl, *a.* That may be demonstrated or proved. **demonstrably,** dē-mon'stra-bli, *adv.* In a manner to preclude doubt. **demonstration,** dem-on-strā'shun, *n.* Act or process of demonstrating; proof; massing of troops to deceive the enemy; a gathering to exhibit sympathy with a person or cause. **demonstrative,** dē-mon'stra-tiv, *a.* Serving to demonstrate; outwardly expressive of feelings; indicating clearly. **demonstrator,** dem"on-strā'tėr, *n.* One who demonstrates.

demoralize, dē-mor'al-īz, *vt.* To corrupt the morals of; to deprave. **demoralization,** dē-mor'al-īz-a"shun, *n.* Act of demoralizing.

demoralizing, dē-mor'al-īz-ing, *p.a.* Tending to destroy morals or moral principles.

demur, dē-mėr', *vi.* (demurring, demurred). To hesitate; to object.—*n.* Pause; suspense of proceeding or decision; objection stated.

demure, dē-mūr', *a.* Consciously grave; affectedly modest. **demurely,** dē-mūr'li, *adv.* In a demure manner.

demurrage, dē-mur'ij, *n.* Delay of a vessel, railway car, &c., in loading or unloading; compensation for such delay; charge for the exchange of notes or coin into bullion.

den, den, *n.* A cave; a dell; a haunt.

denature, dē-nā'tur, *vt.* Change the essential qualities of (*denatured alcohol,* so treated as to be unfit for drinking).

denial, dē-nī'al, *n.* Act of denying; con-

---

tradiction; refusal to grant or acknowledge.

denim, den'im, *n.* Twined cotton fabric used for overalls, &c.

denizen, den'i-zen, *n.* A stranger admitted to residence in a foreign country. —*vt.* To naturalize.

denominate, dē-nom'i-nāt, *vt.* (denominating, denominated). To name; to designate.

denomination, dē-nom'i-nā"shun, *n.* Act of naming; title; class; religious sect. **denominational,** dē-nom'i-nā"shun-al, *a.* Pertaining to denomination. **denominationalism,** dē-nom'i-nā"shun-al-izm, *n.* A class spirit; system of religious sects having each their own schools.

denominative, dē-nom'i-nā-tiv, *a.* That confers a distinct appellation.

denominator, dē-nom'in-ā-tėr, *n.* One who or that which denominates; that number placed below the line in vulgar fractions.

denotable, dē-nōt'a-bl, *a.* That may be denoted or marked.

denote, dē-nōt', *vt.* To indicate; to imply.

dénouement, dā-nö'mäng, *n.* The winding up of a plot in a novel or drama; solution of a mystery; issue; the event.

denounce, dē-nouns', *vt.* (denouncing, denounced). To threaten; to accuse publicly; to stigmatize.

denouncement, dē-nouns'ment, *n.* Act of denouncing; denunciation.

dense, dens, *a.* Thick; close; compact. **densely,** dens'li, *adv.* In a dense manner. **density,** den'si-ti, *n.* Closeness of constituent parts; compactness.

dent, dent, *n.* A mark made by a blow on a solid body.—*vt.* To make a dent on.

dental, den'tal, *a.* Pertaining to the teeth; pronounced by the teeth and the tip of the tongue.—*n.* A dental letter or sound, as *d, t, th.*

dentifrice, den'ti-fris, *n.* A powder or other substance for cleansing the teeth.

dentist, den'tist, *n.* One whose occupation is to extract, repair, or replace teeth.

denude, dē-nūd', *vt.* (denuding, denuded). To make bare; to divest; to uncover.

denunciation, dē-nun'si-ā"shun, *n.* Act of denouncing; public menace; arraignment.

denunciator, dē-nun'shi-ā-tėr, *n.* One who denounces or threatens publicly.

denunciatory, dē-nun'si-a-to-ri, *a.* Characterized by denunciation; ready to denounce.

deny, dē-nī', *vt.* (denying, denied). To declare not to be true; to disavow; to refuse to grant or acknowledge; not to afford or yield.

deodorize, dē-ō'dėr-īz, *vt.* (deodorizing, deodorized). To deprive of fetid odor.

deodorizer, deodorant, dē-ō'dėr-ī-zėr, dē-ō'dėr-ant, *n.* A substance which destroys fetid effluvia.

depart, dē-pärt', *vi.* To go away; to desist; to abandon; to deviate; to die.

department, dē-pärt'ment, *n.* A separate part; a division of territory; a distinct branch, as of science, &c. **departmental**, dĕ′pärt-ment′al, a. Pertaining to a department.

departure, dĕ-pär′tūr, n. Act of going away; withdrawal; abandonment; death.

depend, dĕ-pend′, vi. To hang from; to be contingent or conditioned; to rest or rely solely; to trust.

dependant, dependent, dĕ-pend′ant, dĕ-pend′ent, n. One who depends on another; a retainer. (The spelling with -ant is more common in the noun, with -ent in the adj.)

dependence, dependance, dĕ-pen′dens, dĕ-pen′dans, n. State of being dependent; connection and support; reliance; trust.

dependency, dĕ-pen′den-si, n. State of being dependent; that which is dependent; a subject territory.

dependent, dependant, dĕ-pen′dent, dĕ-pen′dant, a. Hanging down; subordinate; relying solely on another; contingent.

depict, dĕ-pikt′, vt. To paint; to delineate; to represent in words.

depilate, dep′i-lāt, vt. To strip of hair.

depilatory, dĕ-pil′a-tō′ri, n. An application to remove hair from the skin.

deplete, dĕ-plēt′, vt. (depleting, depleted). To empty, reduce, or exhaust.

depletion, dĕ-plē′shun, n. Act of depleting; act of diminishing the quantity of blood by blood-letting.

deplorable, dĕ-plōr′a-bl, a. To be deplored; lamentable; grievous; pitiable. **deplorably**, dĕ-plōr′a-bli, adv. In a manner to be deplored.

deplore, dĕ-plōr′, vt. (deploring, deplored). To feel or express deep grief for; to bewail.

deploy, dĕ-ploi′, vt. To open out; to extend, as a body of troops.—vi. To form a more extended front or line. **deployment**, dĕ-ploi′ment, n. The act of deploying.

deponent, dĕ-pō′nent, a. Laying down; that has a passive form but an active signification.—n. One who gives testimony under oath; a deponent verb.

depopulate, dĕ-pop′ū-lāt, vt. To deprive of inhabitants; to depeople. **depopulation**, dĕ-pop′ū-lā′shun, n. Act or process of depopulating; decrease of population. **depopulator**, dĕ-pop′ū-lāt-ĕr, n. One who or that which depopulates.

deport, dĕ-pōrt′, vt. To transport; to demean; to conduct (one′s self). **deportation**, dĕ-pōr-tā′shun, n. Removal from one country to another; exile.

deportment, dĕ-pōrt′ment, n. Carriage; demeanor; manner of acting.

depose, dĕ-pōz′, vt. (deposing, deposed). To dethrone; to divest of office; to degrade.—vi. To bear witness; to give testimony in writing. **deposable**, dĕ-pōz′a-bl, a. That may be deposed or deprived of office.

deposit, dĕ-poz′it, vt. To lay down; to lodge in a place; to lay in a place for preservation; to intrust; to commit as a pledge.—n. Any matter laid down or

lodged; anything entrusted to another; a thing given as security. **depositary**, dĕ-poz′i-ter-i, n. One to whom a thing is lodged in trust; a guardian. **deposition**, dep-ō-zish′un, n. Act of depositing and of deposing; attested written testimony; declaration; act of dethroning a king, or degrading an official. **depositor**, dĕ-poz′i-tĕr, n. One who makes a deposit; one who lodges money in a bank. **depository**, dĕpoz′i-tō″ri, n. A place where anything is lodged for safekeeping.

depot, dep′ō or dĕ-pō′, n. A place of deposit; headquarters of a regiment; a railway-station.

deprave, dĕ-prāv′, vt. (depraving, depraved). To make bad or worse; to impair the good qualities of; to corrupt; to vitiate. **depravation**, dep-ra-vā-shun, n. Act of depraving; deterioration; degeneracy. **depraved**, dĕ-prāvd′, a. Given to evil courses; profligate; vitiated. **depravity**, dĕ-prav′i-ti, n. Corruption of moral principles; wickedness; profligacy.

deprecate, de′prē-kāt, vt. (deprecating, deprecated). To pray for deliverance from; to plead against; to express regret or disapproval. **deprecation**, de-prē-kā′shun, n. Act of deprecating; protest; disapproval.

depreciate, dĕ-prē′shi-āt, vt. (depreciating, depreciated). To bring down the price or value of; to undervalue; disparage; to traduce.—vi. To fall in value. **depreciation**, dĕ-prē′shi-ā″shun, n. Act of depreciating; the falling of value.

depredate, dep′rē-dāt, vt. To plunder; to waste. **depredation**, de-prē-dā-shun, n. Act of plundering; pillaging. **depredator**, dep′rē-dā-tĕr, n. One who plunders or pillages; a spoiler.

depress, dĕ-pres′, vt. To press down; to lower; to humble; to deject. **depressed**, dĕ-prest′, a. Dejected; dispirited; flattened in shape. **depression**, dĕ-presh′un, n. Act of depressing; state of being depressed; a low state; a sinking of a surface; a hollow; abasement; dejection; a state of dullness. **depressive**, dĕ-pres′iv, a. Able or tending to depress or cast down.

deprive, dĕ′prīv, vi. (depriving, deprived). To take from; to dispossess; to hinder from possessing or enjoying. **deprivation**, de-pri-vā′shun, n. Act of depriving; state of being deprived; want; bereavement; disposition of a clergyman.

depth, depth, n. Deepness; a deep place; the darkest or stillest part, as of the night; the inner part; abstruseness; unsearchableness; intensity; extent of penetration.

depute, dĕ-pūt′, vt. (deputing, deputed). To appoint as a substitute; to send with authority to act for the sender; to assign to a deputy. **deputation**, de-pū-tā″shun, n. Act of deputing; the person or persons sent to transact business for another.

deputy, dep′ū-ti, n. A person appointed to act for another; a substitute; a delegate; an agent.

derange, dĕ-rānj′, *vt.* (deranging, deranged). To disturb the regular order of; to displace; to disconcert; to disorder the mind of. **deranged**, dĕ-rānjd′, *p.a.* Disordered in mind; distracted. **derangement**, dĕ-rānj′ment, *n.* A putting out of order; disorder; insanity.

derelict, der′e-likt, *a.* Abandoned.—*n.* Anything forsaken or left, especially a ship. **dereliction**, der-e-lik′shun, *n.* Act of forsaking; state of being forsaken; neglect.

deride, dĕ-rīd′, *vt.* (deriding, derided). To laugh at in contempt; to ridicule; to jeer. **derider**, dĕ-rīd′ėr, *n.* A mocker; scoffer. **deridingly**, dĕ-rīd′ing-li, *adv.* By way of derision or mockery. **derision**, dĕ-rizh′un, *n.* Act of deriding; scorn; ridicule; mockery. **derisive**, dĕ-rīs′iv, *a.* Mockery; ridiculing.

derive, dĕ-rīv′, *vt.* (deriving, derived). To draw or receive, as from a source or origin; to trace the etymology of.—*vi.* To come from. **derivable**, dĕ-rīv′a-bl, *a.* That may be drawn or derived; deducible. **derivably**, dĕ-rīv′a-bli, *adv.* By derivation. **derivation**, de-ri-vā′shun, *n.* Act of deriving; the tracing of a word from its root; deduction. **derivative**, dĕ-rīv′ăt-iv, *a.* Derived; secondary.—*n.* That which is derived; a word which takes its origin in another word. **derivatively**, dĕ-rīv′ăt-iv-li, *adv.* In a derivative manner; by derivation.

dermatology, dėr-ma-tol′o-ji, *n.* The science which treats of skin and its diseases.

derogate, der′ō-gāt, *vt.* (derogating, derogated). To detract from; to disparage.—*vi.* To detract. **derogation**, der-ō-gā′shun, *n.* Act of derogating; detraction; disparagement. **derogatory**, dēr-og′ă-tō-ri, *a.* Tending to lessen in repute, effect, &c.; disparaging.

derrick, der′ik, *n.* A kind of crane for hoisting heavy weights.

dervish, dervis, dėr′vish, dėr′vis, *n.* A poor Mohammedan priest or monk.

descant, des′kant, *n.* A discourse; discussion; a song or tune with various modulations.

descend, dĕ-send′, *vi.* To pass or move down; to invade; to derive; to pass to an heir.—*vt.* To pass or move down, on, or along. **descendant**, dĕ-sen′dant, *n.* Offspring from an ancestor; issue. **descendent**, dĕ-sen′dent, *a.* Descending; proceeding from an original or ancestor.

descent, dĕ-sent′, *n.* Act of descending; declivity; invasion; a passing from an ancestor to an heir; lineage; distance from the common ancestor; descendants; a rank in the scale of subordination.

describe, dĕ-skrīb′, *vt.* (describing, described). To mark or trace out; to represent on paper, &c.; to portray; to relate. **describable**, dĕ-skrīb′a-bl, *a.* That may be described. **description**, de-skrip′shun, *n.* Act of describing; account; relation; class, species, kind. **descriptive**, dĕ-skrip′tiv, *a.* Containing description; having the quality of representing.

descry, dĕ-skrī′, *vt.* (descrying, descried). To espy; to discover from a distance.

desecrate, des′ē-krāt, *vt.* (desecrating, desecrated). To divert from a sacred purpose; to profane. **desecrater, desecrator**, des′ē-krāt-ėr, *n.* One who desecrates. **desecration**, des-ē-krā′shun, *n.* Act of desecrating; profanation.

desert, de′zėrt, *a.* Waste; uncultivated.—*n.* An uninhabited tract; a vast sandy plain.

desert, dē-zėrt′, *vt.* To leave, as service; to abandon; to quit.—*vi.* To run away; to quit a service without permission.—*n.* That which is deserved; merit or demerit; reward. **deserter**, dē-zėrt′ėr, *n.* One who deserts; a soldier or seaman who quits the service without permission. **desertion**, dē-zėr′shun, *n.* Act of deserting; state of being deserted.

deserve, dē-zėrv′, *vt.* (deserving, deserved). To merit by qualities or services; to be worthy of.—*vi.* To merit; to be worthy of. **deservedly**, dē-zėr′ved-li, *adv.* Justly; according to desert. **deserving**, dē-zėr′ving, *a.* Worthy of reward or praise; meritorious.

desiccate, des′i-kāt, *vt.* To exhaust of moisture; to dry. **desiccant, desiccative**, des′i-kant, or dē-si′kant, dē-si′ka-tiv, *a.* Drying.—*n.* An application that dries a sore.

desiderate, dē-sid′ėr-āt, *vt.* To desire; to want; to miss. **desiderative**, dē-sid′ėr-ā-tiv, *a.* Having, implying, or denoting desire. **desideratum**, dē-sid′ėr-ā″tum, *n.;* pl. **-ata.** That which is not possessed, but is desirable; something much wanted.

design, dē-zīn′, *vt.* To delineate by drawing the outline of; to form in ideas; to plan; to propose; to mean.—*vi.* To intend.—*n.* A representation of a thing by an outline; first idea represented by lines; a plan drawn out in the mind; purpose; aim; project. **designate**, de′zig-nāt, *vt.* (designating, designated). To point out; to name; to characterize; to appoint; to allot. **designation**, de-zig-nā′shun, *n.* Act of designating; appointment; assignment; appellation. **designedly**, dē-zīn′ed-li, *adv.* By design; purposely; intentionally. **designer**, dē-zīn′ėr, *n.* One who designs; a contriver; a plotter. **designing**, dē-zīn′ing, *a.* Artful; intriguing; deceitful; treacherous.

desire, dē-zīr′, *n.* Eagerness to obtain or enjoy; aspiration; longing; a request to obtain; the object of desire; love; lust.—*vt.* (desiring, desired). To wish for the possession or enjoyment of; to covet; to ask; to petition. **desirability**, dē-zīr-a-bil″i-ti, *n.* The state or quality of being desirable. **desirable**, dē-zīr′a-bl, *a.* Worthy of desire; pleasing; agreeable. **desirably**, dē-zīr′a-bli, *adv.* In a desirable manner. **desirous**, dē-zīr′us, *a.* Full of desire; solicitous to possess and enjoy; eager.

desist, dē-sist′, *vi.* To cease to act or proceed; to forbear; to leave off. (With *from*.)

desk, desk, *n.* An inclining table to write

or read upon; a portable case for the same purpose; a lectern; a pulpit.

desolate, de'sō-lit, *a.* Destitute of inhabitants; waste; laid waste; afflicted; forlorn.—*vt.* de'sō-lāt (desolating, desolated). To deprive of inhabitants; to make desert; to ravage. **desolately,** de'sō-lit-li, *adv.* In a desolate manner. **desolation,** de-sō-lā'shun, *n.* Act of desolating; a desolate state or place; melancholy.

despair, de-spār', *n.* A hopeless state; despondency; that which causes despair; loss of hope.—*vi.* To give up all hope; to despond.

despatch, dispatch, des-pach', dis-pach', *vt.* To send away in haste; to put to death; to perform quickly; to conclude.—*n.* Act of despatching; communication on public business; speedy performance; due diligence.

desperado, des-pèr-ä'dō, *n.* A desperate fellow; a reckless ruffian.

desperate, des'pèr-it, *a.* Without care of safety; reckless; frantic; beyond hope; past cure. **desperately,** des'pèr-it-li, *adv.* In a desperate manner. **desperation,** des-pè-rä'shun, *n.* A giving up of hope; fury; disregard of danger; despair.

despicable, des'pi-ka-bl, *a.* Contemptible; vile; base; mean. **despicably,** des'pi-ka-bli, *adv.* Meanly.

despise, de-spīz', *vt.* (despising, despised). To hold in contempt; to scorn; to disdain. **despiser,** de-spīz'èr, *n.* A contemner; scorner. **despisable,** de-spīz'a-bl, *a.* That may be despised; despicable; contemptible.

despite, de-spīt', *n.* Extreme malice; defiance with contempt; an act of malice. —*vt.* To despise; to spite.—*prep.* In spite of; notwithstanding. **despiteful,** de-spīt'ful, *a.* Full of spite; malignant.

despoil, de-spoil', *vt.* To take from by force; to rob; to bereave; to rifle.

despondence, despondency, de-spon'dens, de-spon'den-si, *n.* Hopelessness; dejection. **despondent,** de-spon'dent, *a.* Depressed and inactive in despair; desponding.

despot, des'pot, *n.* An absolute ruler (generally in a bad sense); a tyrant. **despotic, despotical,** des-pot'ik, des-pot'i-kal, *a.* Belonging to a despot; absolute in power; arbitrary; tyrannical. **despotically,** des-pot'i-kal-li, *adv.* In a despotic manner; arbitrarily. **despotism,** des'pot-izm, *n.* The rule of a despot; autocracy; tyranny.

dessert, de-zèrt', *n.* That which is served at the close of a dinner, as fruits, &c.

destine, des'tin, *vt.* (destining, destined). To set or appoint to a purpose; to design; to doom; to ordain.

destination, des-tin-ā'shun, *n.* Act of destining; ultimate design; predetermined end.

destiny, des'ti-ni, *n.* State appointed or predetermined; fate; invincible necessity.

destitute, des'ti-tūt, *a.* Wanting; needy; comfortless; forlorn. **destitution,** des-ti-tū'shun, *n.* Want; poverty; indigence.

destroy, de-stroi', *vt.* To pull down; to overthrow; to devastate; to annihilate.

destroyer, de-stroi'èr, *n.* One who or that which destroys. **destructible,** de-struk'ti-bl, *a.* Liable to destruction. **destruction,** de-struk'shun, *n.* A pulling down; demolition; overthrow; death; slaughter; cause of destruction. **destructive,** de-struk'tiv, *a.* Causing destruction; pernicious; mischievous. **destructively,** de-struk'tiv-li, *adv.* With destruction; ruinously.

desuetude, des'wē-tūd, *n.* Disuse.

desultorily, de'sul-to-ri-li, *adv.* In a desultory manner; without method.

desultory, des'ul-to-ri, *a.* Passing from one subject to another, without order; unconnected; rambling.

detach, de-tach', *vt.* To separate; to disengage. **detached,** de-tacht', *p.a.* Separate. **detachment,** dē-tach'ment, *n.* Act of detaching; a body of troops, or number of ships, sent from the main army or fleet.

detail, de-tāl', To relate in particulars; to specify; in military affairs, to appoint to a particular service.—*n.* dē-tāl' or dē'tāl. An individual fact, circumstance, or portion; an item; a report of particulars. **detailed,** de-tāld', *p.a.* Related in particulars; exact.

detain, de-tān', *vt.* To keep back or from; to withhold; to arrest; to check; to retard. **detainer,** de-tān'èr, *n.* One who detains; a holding of what belongs to another. **detainment,** dē-tān'ment, *n.* Detention.

detect, de-tekt', *vt.* To discover; to bring to light. **detection,** de-tek'shun, *n.* Act of detecting; discovery of a person or thing.

detective, de-tek'tiv, *a.* Skilled or employed in detecting.—*n.* A police officer whose duty is to detect criminals; one who investigates cases for hire.

detention, de-ten'shun, *n.* Act of detaining; confinement; delay.

deter, de-tèr', *vt.* (deterring, deterred). To prevent by prohibition or danger; to discourage. **detergent,** de-tèr'jent, *a.* Cleansing; purging.—*n.* That which cleanses.

deteriorate, de-tèr'i-ō-rāt, *vi.* (deteriorating, deteriorated). To grow worse; to degenerate.—*vt.* To reduce in quality. **deterioration,** de-tèr'i-o-rā'shun, *n.* The state of process of deteriorating.

determine, de-tèr'min, *vt.* (determining, determined). To bound; to fix permanently; to decide; to establish; to give a direction to; to resolve on; to bring to an end.—*vi.* To resolve; to conclude. **determinedly,** de-tèr'mind-li, *adv.* In a determined manner. **determinable,** de-tèr'mi-na-bl, *a.* That may be decided or determined. **determinate,** de-tèr'min-āt, *a.* Fixed; positive; decisive. **determinately,** de-tèr'min-āt-li, *adv.* With certainty; resolutely. **determination,** de-tèr'mi-nā'shun, *n.* Act of determining; firm resolution; judgment; strong direction to a given point; end.

deterrent, de-tèr'ent, *a.* Tending or able to deter.—*n.* That which deters.

detest, dĕ-test', *vt.* To abhor; to loathe. **detestable,** dĕ-tes'ta-bl, *a.* Extremely hateful; abominable; odious. **detestably,** dĕ-tes'ta-bli, *adv.* Abominably. **detestation,** dĕ-tes'tā'shun, *n.* Extreme hatred; abhorrence; loathing.

dethrone, dĕ-thrōn', *vt.* (dethroning, dethroned). To divest of royal authority and dignity; to depose. **dethronement,** dĕ-thrōn'ment, *n.* Removal from a throne; deposition.

detonate, det'ō-nāt, *vt.* (detonating, detonated). To cause to explode; to cause to burn with a sudden report.—*vi.* To explode. **detonation,** det-ō-nā'shun, *n.* An explosion made by the inflammation of certain combustible bodies.

detour, dĕ-tur', *n.* Course that leaves and rejoins the direct route; turn.

detract, dĕ-trakt', *vt.* To draw away; to disparage.—*vi.* To take away from (especially reputation). **detraction,** dĕ-trak'shun, *n.* Act of detracting; depreciation; slander. **detractor,** dĕ-trak'tèr, *n.* One who detracts; a slanderer; a muscle which detracts.

detriment, det'ri-ment, *n.* Loss; damage; injury; prejudice; mischief; harm. **detrimental,** det-ri-ment'al, *a.* Causing detriment; injurious; hurtful.

detritus, dĕ-trī'tus, *n.* A mass of matter worn off from solid bodies by attrition; disintegrated materials of rocks.

deuce, dūs, *n.* A card or die with two spots; the devil; perdition.

Deuteronomy, dū-tèr-on'ō-mi, *n.* The second law, or second giving of the law by Moses; the fifth book of the Pentateuch.

devastate, dev'as-tāt, *vt.* (devastating, devastated). To lay waste; to ravage. **devastation,** dev-as-tā'shun, *n.* Act of devastating; state of being devastated; havoc.

develop, dĕ-vel'up, *vt.* To unfold; to lay open to view; to make to grow.—*vi.* To be unfolded; to become manifest; to grow or expand; to be evolved. **development,** de-vel'up-ment, *n.* Act or process of developing; expansion; growth.

deviate, dĕ'vi-āt, *vi.* (deviating, deviated). To stray; to wander; to swerve; to err. **deviation,** dĕ-vi-ā'shun, *n.* A turning aside from the right way, course, or line.

device, dĕ-vīs', *n.* That which is devised; contrivance; scheme; an emblem.

devil, dev'l, *n.* An evil spirit; Satan; a very wicked person; a machine for cutting, tearing, &c.—*vt.* (deviling, deviled). To pepper excessively and broil; to tease or cut up. **devilish,** dev'l-ish, *a.* Partaking of the qualities of the devil; diabolical; infernal. **devil-may-care,** de'vil-mā-kãr, *a.* Rollicking; reckless. **devilment,** dev'l-ment, *n.* Roguery. **devilry,** dev'l-ri, *n.* Extreme wickedness; wicked mischief.

devious, dĕ'vi-us, *a.* Out of the common way or track; erring; rambling.

devise, dĕ-vīz', *vt.* (devising, devised). To form in the mind; to contrive; to invent; to give or bequeath by will.—*n.* Act of bequeathing by will; a will; a share of estate bequeathed.

devoid, dĕ-void', *a.* Destitute; not possessing; free from.

devolve, dĕ-volv', *vt.* (devolving, devolved). To roll down; to deliver over; to transfer.—*vi.* To fall by succession.

devote, dĕ-vōt', *vt.* (devoting, devoted). To set apart by vow; to consecrate; to addict (one's self); to apply closely to; to consign. **devoted,** dĕ-vōt'ed, *a.* Ardent; zealous; strongly attached. **devotee,** dev-o-tē', *n.* One wholly devoted, particularly to religion; a votary. **devotion,** dĕ-vō'shun, *n.* Act of devoting or state of being devoted; prayer; devoutness; ardent love or affection; attachment; earnestness. **devotional,** dĕ-vō'shun-al, *a.* Pertaining to devotion; used in devotion.

devour, dĕ-vour', *vt.* To eat ravenously; to swallow up; to waste; to look on with keen delight.

devout, dĕ-vout', *a.* Pious; expressing devotion; earnest; solemn. **devoutly,** dĕ-vout'li, *adv.* Piously.

dew, dū, *n.* Moisture from the atmosphere condensed into drops on the surface of cold bodies, as grass, &c.; damp. —*vt.* To wet with dew; to moisten; to damp. **dewiness,** dū'i-nes, *n.* State of being dewy.

dewlap, dū'lap, *n.* The fold of skin that hangs from the throat of oxen, &c.

dewpoint, dū'point, *n.* The temperature at which dew begins to form.

dexterity, deks-ter'i-ti, *n.* Right-handedness; adroitness; expertness; skill. **dexterous,** dek'stèr-us, *a.* Expert in manual acts; adroit; done with dexterity. **dexterously,** dek'stèr-us-li, *adv.* With dexterity; expertly; skillfully; artfully.

dextrose, deks'trōs, *n.* Grapesugar.

diabetes, dī-a-bē'tèz, *n.* Disease characterized by a morbid discharge of urine.

diabolic, diabolical, dī-a-bol'ik, dī-a-bol'i-kal, *a.* Devilish; atrocious. **diabolically,** dī-a-bol'i-kal-li, *adv.* In a diabolical manner; very wickedly.

diacritical, dī-a-krit'i-kal, *a.* Separating; distinctive; applied to a mark used to distinguish letters similar in form.

diadem, dī'a-dem, *n.* A badge of royalty worn on the head; a crown; a coronet.

diagnose, dī'ag-nōs', *vt.* To ascertain from symptoms the true nature of. **diagnosis,** dī'ag-nō'sis, *n.* The ascertaining from symptoms the true nature of diseases. **diagnostic,** dī-ag-nōs'tik, *a.* Pertaining to diagnosis.—*n.* A symptom.

diagonal, dī-ag'ō-nal, *a.* Extending from one angle to another of a quadrilateral figure; lying in an oblique direction.—*n.* A straight line drawn between opposite angles of a quadrilateral figure. **diagonally,** dī-ag-ō'nal-li, *adv.* In a diagonal direction.

diagram, dī'a-gram, *n.* A drawing to demonstrate the properties of any figure; an illustrative figure in outline.

dial, dī'al, *n.* An instrument for showing the hour by the sun's shadow; face of a clock, &c.

dialect, dī'a-lekt, *n.* The idiom of a language peculiar to a province; language; manner of speaking. **dialectal,**

dī-a-lek'tal, *a.* Pertaining to a dialect. **dialectic, dialectical,** dī-a-lek'tik, dī-a-lek'ti-kal, *a.* Relating to dialectics; pertaining to a dialect or dialects. **dialectician,** dī'a-lek-tish"an, *n.* One skilled in dialectics; a logician; a reasoner. **dialectics,** dī-a-lek'tiks, *n.sing.* The art of reasoning; that branch of logic which teaches the rules and modes of reasoning; word-fence. Also **dialectic** in same sense.

dialogue, dī'a-log, *n.* A conversation between two or more persons.

diameter, dī-am'e-tèr, *n.* A straight line passing through the center of a circle, and terminated by the circumference; the distance through the center of any object. **diametric, diametrical,** dī'a-met"rik, dī-a-met'ri-kal, *a.* Of or pertaining to a diameter. **diametrically,** dī'a-met"ri-kal-li, *adv.* In a diametrical direction; directly.

diamond, dī'a-mund, *n.* A valuable gem, remarkable for its hardness and transparency; a rhombus; a card of the suit marked with such figures in red; a very small printing type.—*a.* Resembling a diamond; set with diamonds.

diapason, dī'a-pā"zun, *n.* The entire compass of a voice or instrument; an organ stop.

diaper, dī'a-pèr, *n.* A figured linen or cotton cloth.—*vt.* To variegate or diversify with figures.—*vi.* To draw flowers or figures on.

diaphanous, dī-af'a-nus, *a.* Having power to transmit rays of light; transparent.

diaphragm, dī'a-fram, *n.* The midriff, a muscle separating the thorax from the abdomen.

diarrhea, dī'a-rē"a, *n.* A morbidly frequent evacuation of the intestines.

diary, dī'a-ri, *n.* A register of daily events or transactions; a journal.

diastole, dī-as'to-lē, *n.* Dilatation of the heart in beating.

diathermal, diathermous, dī'a-thèr"mal, dī'a-thèr"mus, *a.* Freely permeable by heat.

diatonic, dī'a-ton"ik, *a.* In *music,* applied to the major or minor scales.

diatribe, dī'a-trīb, *n.* A continued disputation; a lengthy invective.

dibble, dib'l, *n.* A pointed instrument to make holes for planting seeds, &c.—*vt.* (dibbling, dibbled). To make holes for planting seeds, &c.

dice, dīs, *n.*; pl. of **die,** for gambling.—*vi.* (dicing, diced). To play with dice.

dichotomous, dī-kot'ō-mus, *a.* In *botany,* regularly dividing by pairs from top to bottom.

dickey, dicky, dik'i, *n.* An article of dress like the front of a dress shirt, and worn instead; the driver's seat in a carriage.

dicotyledon, dī-kot'i-lē"dun, *n.* A plant whose seeds contain a pair of cotyledons.

dictate, dik'tāt, *vt.* (dictating, dictated). To deliver, as an order or direction; to prescribe; to tell what to say or to write; to instigate.—*n.* An order delivered; an authoritative precept or maxim; an impulse. **dictation,** dik-tā'shun, *n.* Act of

dictating; the act or practice of speaking that another may write down what is spoken. **dictator,** dik'tā-tèr, *n.* One invested with absolute authority. **dictatorial,** dik-ta-tō'ri-al, *a.* Pertaining to a dictator; absolute; overbearing. **dictatorship,** dik-tā'tèr-ship, *n.* The office of a dictator.—**diction,** dik'shun, *n.* Choice of words; mode of expression; style.

dictionary, dik"shun-er'i, *n.* A book containing the words of a language arranged alphabetically, with their meanings, &c.; a work explaining the terms, &c., of any subject under heads alphabetically arranged.

dictum, dik'tum, *n.*; pl. **dicta,** An authoritative saying or assertion.

did, did, *pret.* of *do.*

didactic, didactical, dī-dak'tik, dī-dak'ti-kal, *a.* Adapted to teach; instructive; containing doctrines, precepts, &c. **didactics,** dī-dak'tiks, *n.* The art or science of teaching.

diddle, did'l, *vt.* To cheat or trick.

die, dī, *vi.* (dying, died). To cease to live; to expire, to sink gradually; to vanish.—*n.*; pl. **dice,** dīs, in first sense, in the others **dies,** dīz. A small cube with numbers from one to six; any cubic body; the dado of a pedestal; a stamp used in coining money; an implement for turning out things of a regular shape.

dielectric, dī'é-lek"trik, *n.* Any medium through or across which electric induction takes place between two conductors.

diet, dī'et, *n.* A person's regular food; food prescribed medically; a meeting of dignitaries or delegates for legislative or other purposes.—*vt.* To furnish provisions for.—*vi.* To eat according to rules prescribed. **dietary,** dī"e-ter'i, *a.* Pertaining to diet.—*n.* A system of diet; allowance of food. **dietetic, dietetical,** dī'e-tet"ik, dī'e-tet"i-kal, *a.* Pertaining to diet, or the rules for regulating diet. **dietetics,** dī'e-tet"iks, *n.* Principles for regulating the diet.

differ, dif'èr, *vi.* To be unlike or distinct; to disagree; to be at variance. **difference,** dif'èr-ens, *n.* State of being different; dissimilarity; that which distinguishes; dispute; point in dispute; remainder after a sum is subtracted. **different,** dif'èr-ent, *a.* Distinct; dissimilar. (With *from.*)—**differential,** dif-èr-en'shal, *a.* Creating a difference; discriminating.—*n.* An infinitesimal difference between two states of a variable quantity. **differentiate,** dif-èr-en'shi-āt, *vt.* To mark or distinguish by a difference.—*vi.* To acquire a distinct character. **differently,** dif'èr-ent-li, *adv.* In a different manner; variously.

difficult, dif'i-kult, *a.* Not easy to be done, &c.; perplexed; hard to please; unyielding. **difficulty,** dif'i-kul-ti, *n.* Hardness to be done; obstacle; perplexity; objection. **diffident,** dif'i-dent, *a.* Wanting confidence; bashful. **diffidence,** dif'i-dens, *n.* Want of confidence; modest reserve; bashfulness.

diffidently, dif'i-dent-li, *adv.* In a diffident manner; modestly.

diffract, di-frakt', *vt.* To bend from a straight line; to deflect. **diffraction,** di-frak'shun, *n.* The modifications which light undergoes when it passes by the edge of an opaque body; deflection.

diffuse, di-fūz', *vt.* (diffusing, diffused). To pour out and spread; to circulate; to proclaim.—*a.* di-fūs'. Widely spread; prolix; verbose. **diffusely,** di-fūs'li, *adv.* In a diffuse manner; copiously; with too many words. **diffusible,** di-fūz'i-bl, *a.* That may be diffused or dispersed. **diffusion,** di-fū'zhun, *n.* A spreading or scattering; dispersion; circulation. **diffusive,** di-fū'siv, *a.* Having the quality of diffusing; spread widely; verbose. **diffusively,** di-fū-siv-li, *adv.* Widely.

dig, dig, *vt.* (digging, digged or dug). To open and turn up with a spade; to excavate.—*vi.* To work with a spade.

digest, di-jest', *vt.* To arrange under proper heads; to think out; to dissolve in the stomach; to soften by a heated liquid; to bear with patience.—*vi.* To undergo digestion, as food.—*n.* di'jest. A collection of laws; systematic summary. **digester,** di-jes'tėr, *n.* That which assists the digestion of food. **digestible,** di-jes'ti-bl, *a.* Capable of being digested. **digestion,** di-jes'chun, *n.* Act of digesting; process of dissolving aliment in the stomach; operation of heating with some solvent. **digestive,** di-jes'tiv, *a.* Having the power to cause digestion in the stomach.—*n.* A medicine which aids digestion.

digging, dig'ing, *n.* The act of one who digs; *pl.* localities where gold is mined.

digit, dij'it, *n.* A finger; three-fourths of an inch; the twelfth part of the diameter of the sun or moon; any integer under 10.

digitalis, dij-i-tal'is, *n.* A medicine made from the leaves of the foxglove plant; used as a heart stimulant.

dignity, dig'ni-ti, *n.* Nobleness or elevation of mind; honorable place; degree of excellence; grandeur of mien; an elevated office; one who holds high rank. **dignified,** dig'ni-fīd, *a.* Marked with dignity; stately; grave. **dignify,** dig'ni-fī, *vt.* (dignifying, dignified). To invest with dignity; to exalt in rank or office; to make illustrious. **dignitary,** dig"ni-ter'i, *n.* One of exalted rank or office; an ecclesiastic who has pre-eminence over priests and canons.

digress, di-gres' or dī'gres, *vi.* To depart from the main subject; to deviate. **digression,** di-gresh'un or dī-, *n.* Act of digressing; departure from the main subject; the part of a discourse which digresses.

dike, dyke, dīk, *n.* A ditch; an embankment; a wall; a vein of igneous rock.—*vt.* (diking, diked). To surround with a dike; to secure by a bank; to drain by ditches.

dilapidate, di-lap'i-dāt, *vt.* To make ruinous; to squander.—*vi.* To go to ruin; to fall by decay. **dilapidated,**

vi-lap"i-dat'ed, *p.a.* In a ruinous condition. **dilapidation,** di-la'pi-dā'shun, *n.* Decay; ruin; destruction; ruining or suffering to decay of a church building.

dilate, dī-lāt', *vt.* (dilating, dilated). To expand; to distend.—*vi.* To swell or extend in all directions; to speak copiously; to dwell on in narration (with *on* or *upon*). **dilatability,** dī-lāt'a-bil"i-ti, *n.* Quality of being dilatable. **dilatable,** dī-lāt'a-bl, *a.* Capable of expansion; possessing elasticity; elastic. **dilatation, dilation,** dil-a-tā'shun, di-lā'shun, *n.* Act of dilating; expansion; state of being expanded or distended.

dilatorily, dil'a-tō'ri-li, *adv.* With delay.

dilatory, dil'a-tō'ri, *a.* Tardy; given to procrastination; making delay; sluggish.

dilemma, di-lem'a, *n.* An argument with two alternatives, each conclusive against an opponent; a difficult or doubtful choice.

dilettante, dil-e-tan'tē, *n.*; pl. **dilettanti,** dil-e-tan'tē. An amateur or trifler in art.

diligence, dil'i-jens, *n.* Steady application; assiduity; a four-wheeled stagecoach. **diligent,** dil'i-jent, *a.* Steady in application; industrious; persevering; prosecuted with care and constant effort. **diligently,** dil'i-jent-li, *adv.* In a diligent manner.

dill, dil, *n.* Herb with scented seeds.

dillydally, dil'i-dal-i, *vi.* To loiter, trifle.

dilute, di-lūt', *vt.* (diluting, diluted). To render liquid or more liquid; to weaken by admixture of water.—*vi.* To become attenuated or diluted.—*a.* Thin; reduced in strength. **dilution,** di-lū'shun, *n.* Act of diluting.

dim, dim, *a.* Not seeing clearly; not clearly seen; mysterious; tarnished.—*vt.* (dimming, dimmed). To dull; to obscure; to sully.

dime, dīm, *n.* A silver coin the tenth of a dollar.

dimension, di-men'shun, *n.* Extension in a single direction; measure of a thing, its size, extent, capacity (usually in *pl.*).

diminish, di-min'ish, *vt.* To reduce; to abate; to degrade.—*vi.* To become less. **diminution,** dim-i-nū'shun, *n.* Act of diminishing; state of becoming less. **diminutive,** di-min'ū-tiv, *a.* Small; little.—*n.* A word formed from another word to express a little thing of the kind.

dimity, dim'i-ti, *n.* A stout cotton fabric woven with raised stripes or figures.

dimly, dim'li, *adv.* Obscurely.

dimple, dim'pl, *n.* A small natural depression in the cheek or chin.—*vi.* (dimpling, dimpled). To form dimples. **dimpled,** dim'pld, *a.* Set with dimples.

din, din, *n.* A loud sound long continued.—*vt.* (dinning, dinned). To stun with noise; to harass with clamor.

dine, dīn, *vi.* (dining, dined). To eat a dinner.—*vt.* To give a dinner to.

dinner, din'ér, *n.* The chief meal of the day.

ding, ding, *vt.* (pret. and pp. dung or dinged). To strike; to drive; to thrust or dash.

dingdong, ding"dong', *n.* The sound of bells, &c.

dinghy, **dingey**, ding'gi, *n.* A small boat used by a ship.

dingy, din'ji, *a.* Of a dusky color; soiled.

dinner, din'ér, *n.* The principal meal of the day.

dinosaur, **dinothere**, dī'nō-sor, dī'nō-thēr, *n.* Large extinct reptile, quadruped with trunk and tusks.

dint, dint, *n.* The mark made by a blow; dent; power exerted.—*vt.* To make a mark on by a blow or by pressure.

diocese, dī'ō-sēs, *n.* An ecclesiastical division of a state, subject to a bishop. **diocesan**, dī-os'e-san or dī'ō-sē-zan, *a.* Pertaining to a diocese.—*n.* A bishop; one in possession of a diocese.

dip, dip, *vt.* (dipping, dipped, or dipt.) To plunge in a liquid; to baptize by immersion.—*vi.* To dive into a liquid and emerge; to engage in a desultory way; to look cursorily; to choose by chance; to incline.—*n.* Act of dipping; a bath; candle; downward slope.

diphtheria, dif-thēr'i-a, *n.* An epidemic inflammatory disease of the throat.

diphthong, dif'thong, *n.* A union of two vowels pronounced in one syllable. **diphthongal**, dif-thong'gal, *a.* Belonging to a diphthong.

diploma, di-plō'ma, *n.* A document conferring some power, privilege, or honor.

diplomacy, di-plō'ma-si, *n.* The art or practice of conducting international negotiations; skill in securing advantages. **diplomat**, dip'lō-mat, *n.* A diplomatist. **diplomatic**, **diplomatical**, dip-lō-mat'ik, dip-lō-mat'i-kal, *a.* Pertaining to diplomacy; skillful in gaining one's ends by tact; relating to diplomatics.

dipper, dip'ér, *n.* He or that which dips; a ladle; a bird, the waterouzel.

dipsomania, dip-sō-mā'ni-a, *n.* An uncontrollable craving for stimulants.

dire, dīr, *a.* Dreadful; dismal; terrible.

direct, di-rekt', *a.* Straight; right; in the line of father and son; not ambiguous; express.—*vt.* To point or aim at; to show the right course to; to conduct; to order; to instruct. **direction**, di-rek'shun, *n.* Act of directing; a pointing toward; course; guidance; command; address on a letter; a body of directors. **directive**, di-rek'tiv, *a.* Giving direction. **directly**, di-rekt'li, *adv.* In a direct manner; without delay; expressly. **director**, di-rek'tér, *n.* One who or that which directs; a superintendent; an instructor; a counselor; one appointed to transact the affairs of a company. **directorate**, di-rek'tōr-it, *n.* Office of a director; body of directors. **directorship**, di-rek'tér-ship, *n.* Condition or office of a director. **directory**, di-rek'tō-ri, *n.* A rule to direct; a book containing directions for public worship; a book containing a list of the inhabitants of a place, with their addresses; a board of directors.

direful, dīr'ful, *a.* Dire; dreadful; calamitous.

dirge, dérj, *n.* A song or tune intended to express grief, sorrow, and mourning.

dirigible, dir'i-ji-bl, *a.* That which may be steered or directed.—*n.* A steerable balloon.

dirt, dért, *n.* Any foul or filthy substance. —*vt.* To make foul; to defile. **dirty**, dér'ti, *a.* Soiled with dirt; mean; despicable; rainy, squally, &c.—*vt.* (dirtying, dirtied). To soil; to sully.

disability, dis-a-bil"i-ti, *n.* Want of ability; incompetence; want of legal qualification.

disable, dis-ā'bl, *vt.* (disabling, disabled). To deprive of power; to disqualify; to incapacitate.

disabuse, dis-a-būz', *vt.* To undeceive.

disadvantage, dis-ad-van'tij, *n.* Want of advantage; unfavorable; state; detriment. **disadvantageous**, dis-ad'van-tā"jus, *p.a.* Unfavorable to success or prosperity.

disaffect, dis-a-fekt', *vt.* To make less faithful or friendly; to make discontented. **disaffected**, dis-a-fek'ted, *a.* Indisposed to favor or support; unfriendly. **Disaffection**, dis-a-fek'shun, *n.* Alienation of affection; disloyalty; hostility.

disagree, dis'a-grē", *vi.* To be of a different opinion; to dissent; to be unfriendly; to be unsuitable. **disagreeable**, dis'a-grē'a-bl, *a.* Not agreeable; offensive; displeasing. **disagreeably**, dis'a-grē'a-bli, *adv.* Unpleasantly.

disagreement, dis'a-grē'ment, *n.* Difference; unsuitableness; discrepancy; discord.

disallow, dis-a-lou', *vt.* To refuse to allow; to disapprove of; to reject. **disallowable**, dis-a-lou'a-bl, *a.* Not allowable. **disallowance**, dis-a-lou'ans, *n.* Refusal to allow; disapprobation; rejection.

disappear, dis'a-pér", *vi.* To vanish from sight; to cease, or seem to cease, to be. **disappearance**, dis'a-pér"ans, *n.* Act of disappearing; removal from sight.

disappoint, dis'-a-point", *vt.* To defeat of expectation or intention; to frustrate. **disappointed**, dis'a-point"ed, *a.* Balked; soured in life. **disappointment**, dis'a-point"ment, *n.* Failure of expectation or intention.

disapprobation, dis-ap'rō-ba"shun, *n.* Disapproval; censure, expressed or unexpressed.

disapprove, dis'a-pröv", *vt.* To censure as wrong; to regard with dislike; to reject.

disapproval, dis'a-pröv'al, *n.* The act of disapproving; dislike.

disapprovingly, dis'a-pröv"ing-li, *adv.* By disapprobation.

disarm, dis-ärm', *vt.* To take the arms or weapons from; to render harmless.— *vi.* To lay down arms; to disband. **disarmament**, dis-är'ma-ment, *n.* Act of disarming.

disarrange, dis-a-rānj', *vt.* To put out of arrangement or order; to derange. **disarrangement**, dis-a-ranj'ment, *n.* Act of disturbing order; disorder.

disarray, dis-a-rā', *vt.* To undress; to

throw into disorder.—*n.* Disorder; undress.

disaster, di-zas'tèr, *n.* An unfortunate event; mishap; catastrophe; reverse. **disastrous**, di-zas'trus, *a.* Occasioning, accompanied by, or threatening disaster; calamitous; dismal. **disastrously**, di-zas'trus-li, *adv.* In a disastrous manner.

disavow, dis'a-vou", *vt.* To deny to be true; to reject; to dissent from. **disavowal**, dis'a-vou"al, *n.* Denial; repudiation.

disband, dis-band', *vt.* To dismiss from military service; to disperse.—*vi.* To retire from military service; to dissolve connection.

disbar, dis-bär', *vt.* (disbarring, disbarred). To expel from being a member of the bar.

disbelief, dis'bē-lēf", *n.* Refusal of credit or faith; distrust; unbelief. **disbelieve**, dis'bē-lēv", *vi.* To refuse to believe or credit; to have no belief in.

disburse, dis-bèrs', *vt.* (disbursing, disbursed). To pay out, as money; to expend. **disbursement**, dis-bèrs'ment, *n.* Act of disbursing; the sum paid out.

disc. See **disk**.

discard, dis-kärd', *vt.* To throw away; to cast off; to dismiss; to discharge.

discern, dis-sèrn' or di-zèrn', *vt.* To distinguish; to discriminate; to descry.—*vi.* To see or understand differences; to have clearness of mental sight. **discerner**, dis-sèrn'èr, *n.* One who discerns; a clear-sighted observer. **discernible**, dis-sèrn'i-bl, *a.* That may be discerned; perceptible. **discerning**, dis-sèrn'ing, *p.a.* Having power to discern; sharp-sighted; acute. **discerningly**, dis-sèrn'ing-li, *adv.* With discernment; acutely; with judgment. **discernment**, dis-sèrn'ment, *n.* Act or power of discerning; judgment; sagacity.

discharge, dis-chärj', *vt.* To unload; to let fly or go, as a missile; to fire off; to give vent to; to clear off by payment; to perform; to acquit; to dismiss; to release.—*vi.* To get rid of or let out a charge or contents.—*n.* Act of discharging; unloading; a firing off; emission; dismissal; release from obligation, debt, or penalty; absolution from a crime; ransom; performance; release; payment, as of a debt.

disciple, di-sī'pl, *n.* A learner; a pupil; an adherent to the doctrines of another. **discipleship**, di-sī'pl-ship, *n.* The state or position of a disciple.

discipline, dis-i-plin, *n.* Training; method of government; order; subjection to laws; punishment; correction; execution of ecclesiastical laws.—*vt.* (disciplining, disciplined). To subject to discipline; to train up well; to chastise. **disciplinable**, dis'i-plin-a-bl, *a.* Capable of discipline, or of instruction. **disciplinarian**, dis'i-pli-när"i-an, *a.* Pertaining to discipline.—*n.* One who enforces discipline; a martinet. **disciplinary**, dis"i-pli-ner'i, *a.* Pertaining to discipline; intended for discipline.

disclaim, dis-klām', *vt.* To deny all claim to; to reject; to disown. **disclaimer**, dis-klām'èr, *n.* One who disclaims; formal disavowal; renunciation.

disclose, dis-klōz', *vt.* To open; to uncover; to reveal; to divulge. **disclosure**, dis-klō'zhèr, *n.* Act of disclosing; utterance of what was secret; that which is disclosed.

discoloration, dis-kul'èr-ā"shun, *n.* Act of discoloring; alteration of color; stain. **discolor**, **discolour**, dis-kul'èr, *vt.* To alter the color of; to stain; to tinge.

discomfit, dis-kum'fit, *vt.* To rout; to defeat. *n.* Rout; overthrow. **discomfiture**, dis-kum'fi-tür, *n.* Rout; overthrow; frustration; disappointment.

discomfort, dis-kum'fèrt, *n.* Want of comfort; uneasiness; inquietude.—*vt.* To deprive of comfort; to grieve.

discompose, dis-kom-pōz', *vt.* To disturb. **discomposure**, dis-kom-pō'zhèr, *n.* Disorder; agitation; disturbance; perturbation.

disconcert, dis'kon-sèrt", *vt.* To disturb; to unsettle; to confuse; to ruffle.

disconnect, dis-ko-nekt', *vt.* To separate; to disunite. **disconnection**, dis-ko-nek'shun, *n.* Separation; want of union.

disconsolate, dis-kon'sō-lit, *a.* Comfortless; hopeless; gloomy; cheerless.

discontent, dis'kon-tent", *n.* Want of content; uneasiness of mind; dissatisfaction. **discontented**, dis-kon-ten'ted, *a.* Dissatisfied; given to grumble. **discontentedly**, dis'kon-ten"ted-li, *adv.* In a discontented manner or mood. **discontentment**, dis'kon-tent"ment, *n.* Discontent; uneasiness; inquietude.

discontinue, dis'kon-tin"ū, *vt.* To leave off; to cause to cease; to cease to take or receive.—*vi.* To cease. **discontinuance**, dis'kon-tin"ū-ans, *n.* A breaking off; cessation. **discontinuation**, dis'-kon-tin'ū-ā"shun, *n.* Act of discontinuing; discontinuance. **discontinuity**, dis-kon'tin-ū"i-ti, *n.* State of being discontinuous. **discontinuous**, dis-kon-tin"ū-us, *a.* Not continuous; broken off; interrupted.

discord, dis'kord, *n.* Want of concord; disagreement; disagreement of sounds. **discordance**, **discordancy**, dis-kor'dans, dis-kor'dan-si, *n.* Want of concord, disagreement; inconsistency; discord. **discordant**, dis-kor'dant, *a.* Wanting agreement; incongruous; dissonant; jarring.

discount, dis'kount, *n.* A sum deducted for prompt or advanced payment.—*vt.* dis-kount'. To advance the amount of, as a bill, deducting a certain rate per cent; to make an allowance for supposed exaggeration; to disregard.

discourage, dis-kur'ij, *vt.* (discouraging, discouraged). To dishearten; to dissuade. **discouragement**, dis-kur'rij-ment, *n.* Act of discouraging; that which discourages. **discouraging**, dis-kur'ij-ing, *a.* Tending to discourage.

discourse, dis-kōrs', *n.* A speech; treatise; sermon; conversation.—*vi.* (discoursing, discoursed). To talk; to converse; to treat of formally; expatiate.—*vt.* To utter.

discourteous, dis-kur'tē-us, *a.* Void of courtesy; rude. **discourtesy,** dis-kur'-tē-si, *n.* Incivility; rudeness; act of disrespect.

discover, dis-kuv'èr, *vt.* To lay open to view; to reveal; to have the first sight of; to find out; to detect. **discoverable,** dis-kuv'èr-a-bl, *a.* That may be discovered. **discoverer,** dis-kuv'èr-èr, *n.* One who discovers; an explorer. **discovery,** dis-kuv'é-ri, *n.* Act of discovering; disclosure; that which is discovered.

discredit, dis-kred'it, *n.* Want of credit; disrepute; disbelief; distrust.—*vt.* To give no credit to; to deprive of credit; to make less reputable; to bring into disesteem. **discreditable,** dis-kred'it-a-bl, *a.* Tending to discredit; injurious to reputation. **discreditably,** dis-kred'it-a-bli, *adv.* In a discreditable manner.

discreet, dis-krēt', *a.* Prudent; wary; judicious. **discreetly,** dis-krēt'li, *adv.* In a discreet manner.

discrepance, discrepancy, dis-krep'-ans, dis-krep'an-si, *n.* Discordance; disagreement.

discrete, dis'krēt, *a.* Separate; distinct. **discretion,** dis-kresh'un, *n.* Quality of being discreet; prudence; discernment; judgment; freedom of choice or action. **discretionary,** dis-kresh"un-er'i, *a.* Unrestrained except by discretion.

discriminate, dis-krim'i-nāt, *vt.* (discriminating, discriminated). To distinguish; to select from.—*vi.* To make a distinction.—*a.* dis-krim'i-nit. Having the difference marked; distinct. **discriminately,** dis-krim'i-nit-li, *adv.* In a discriminate manner. **discriminating,** dis-krim'i-nāt-ing, *p.a.* Distinguishing; able to make nice distinctions. **discrimination,** dis-krim'i-nā"shun, *n.* Discernment; judgment; distinction. **discriminative,** dis-krim'i-nā-tiv, *s.* That discriminates or distinguishes.

discursive, dis-kèr'siv, *a.* Passing from one subject to another; desultory; rambling.

discus, dis'kus, *n.* A round, flat piece of iron, &c., thrown in play; a quoit.

discuss, dis-kus', *vt.* To drive away or dissolve (a tumor, &c.); to debate; to examine by disputation; to make a trial of, as food; to consume. **discussion,** dis-kush'un, *n.* Dispersion; debate; examination.

disdain, dis-dān', *vt.* To think unworthy; to deem worthless; to scorn; to contemn.—*n.* Contempt; scorn; haughtiness; pride. **disdainful,** dis-dān'ful, *a.* Contemptuous; scornful; haughty; indignant. **disdainfully,** dis-dān'ful-li, *adv.* With scorn.

disease, di-zēz', *n.* Any state of a living body in which the natural functions are disturbed; illness; disorder.—*vt.* (diseasing, diseased). To afflict with disease; to infect; to derange.

disembark, dis'em-bärk", *vt.* To remove from a vessel to the land.—*vi.* To go ashore. **disembarkation, disembarkment,** dis-em'bär-kā"shun, dis-em-bärk'ment, *n.* Act of disembarking.

disembody, dis'em-bod"i, *vt.* To divest of body; to free from connection with the human body; to disband (troops).

disembowel, dis'em-bou"el, *vt.* (disemboweling, disemboweled). To take out the bowels of.

disenchant, dis'en-chant", *vt.* To free from enchantment.

disengage, dis'en-gāj", *vt.* To free from engagement; to detach; to release; to extricate. **disengaged,** dis'en-gājd", *p.a.* At leisure; not particularly occupied. **disengagement,** dis'en-gāj"-ment, *n.* Release from engagement; separation; extrication, leisure.

disentangle, dis'en-tang"gl, *vt.* To free from entanglement; to clear.

disfavor, dis-fā'vèr, *n.* Want of favor; unfavorable regard.—*vt.* To withhold favor from; to discountenance.

disfigure, dis-fig'ūr, *vt.* (disfiguring, disfigured). To mar the figure of; to impair the beauty, symmetry, or excellence of.

disfigurement, dis-fig'ūr-ment, *n.* Act of disfiguring; that which disfigures.

disfranchise, dis-fran'chiz, *vt.* To deprive of the rights of a free citizen. **disfranchisement,** dis-fran'chiz-ment, *n.* Act of disfranchising.

disgorge, dis-gorj', *vt.* To vomit; to discharge violently; to surrender.

disgrace, dis-grās', *n.* State of being deprived of grace or favor; cause of shame; dishonor.—*vt.* (disgracing, disgraced). To bring to shame; to degrade; to dishonor. **disgraceful,** dis-grās'ful, *a.* Shameful; causing shame; sinking reputation. **disgracefully,** dis-grās'ful-li, *adv.* In a disgraceful manner.

disguise, dis-gīz', *vt.* (disguising, disguised). To conceal by an unusual habit or mask; to dissemble; to give an unusual appearance to.—*n.* A dress intended to conceal; an assumed appearance, intended to deceive.

disgust, dis-gust', *n.* Distaste; loathing; repugnance.—*vt.* To cause distaste in; to offend the mind or moral taste of. **disgustful,** dis-gust'ful, *a.* Exciting aversion in the natural or moral taste. **disgusting,** dis-gust'ing, *a.* Provoking disgust; loathsome; nasty.

dish, dish, *n.* A broad open vessel for serving up meat at table; the meat served; any particular kind of food.—*vt.* To put in a dish; to make (a wheel) hollow or concave.

dishearten, dis-här'tn, *vt.* To discourage; to depress.

dishevel, di-shev'el, *vt.* (disheveling, disheveled). To put out of order, or spread loosely, as the hair.

dishonest, dis-on'est, *a.* Void of honesty; fraudulent; knavish; perfidious. **dishonestly,** dis-on'est-li, *adv.* In a dishonest manner. **dishonesty,** dis-on'-est-i, *n.* Want of honesty or integrity.

dishonor, dis-on'èr, *n.* Want of honor; disgrace; ignominy.—*vt.* To deprive of honor; to treat with indignity; to violate the chastity of; to decline to accept or pay, as a draft. **dishonorable,** dis-on'èr-a-bl, *a.* Destitute of honor; base;

vile. **dishonorably,** dis-on'ẽr-a-bli, *adv.* In a dishonorable manner.

disillusionize, dis'i-lū"zhun-īz, *vt.* To free from illusion.

disinclination, dis-in'kli-nā"shun, *n.* Want of propensity, desire, or affection.

disinfect, dis'in-fekt", *vt.* To cleanse from infection. **disinfectant,** dis'in-fek"tant, *n.* An agent for removing the causes of infection. **disinfection,** dis'-in-fek"shun, *n.* Purification from infecting matter.

disingenuous, dis'in-jen"ū-us, *a.* Not open, frank, and candid; crafty; cunning. **disingenuously,** dis'in-jen"ū-us-li, *adv.* In a disingenuous manner; artfully.

disinherit, dis'in-her"it, *vt.* To cut off from hereditary right.

disintegrable, dis-in'tē-gra-bl, *a.* That may be disintegrated. **disintegrate,** dis-in'tē-grāt, *vt.* To separate, as the integral parts of a body. **disintegration,** dis-in'tē-grā"shun, *n.* Act of separating integral parts of a substance.

disinterested, dis-in'tẽr-es-ted, *a.* Not interested; free from self-interest; not dictated by private advantage; impartial. **disinterestedly,** dis-in'tẽr-est-ed-li, *adv.* In a disinterested manner.

disinterment, dis'in-tẽr"ment, *n.* Act of disinterring or taking out of the earth.

disjoint, dis-joint', *vt.* To separate, as parts united by joints; to put out of joint; to make incoherent. **disjointed,** dis-join'ted, *p.a.* Unconnected; incoherent; out of joint.

disk, disk, *n.* A flat circular plate; the face of a heavenly body; center of a composite flower.

dislike, dis-līk', *n.* The opposite of liking; aversion; antipathy.—*vt.* To regard with some aversion.

dislocate, dis'lō-kāt, *vt.* To displace; to put out of joint. **dislocation,** dis-lō-kā"shun, *n.* Act of dislocating; displacement.

dislodge, dis-loj', *vt.* To remove or drive from a place of rest or a station.—*vi.* To go from a place of rest. **dislodgment,** dis-loj'ment, *n.* Act of dislodging; displacement.

disloyal, dis-loi'al, *a.* Void of loyalty; false to a sovereign; faithless. **disloyally,** dis-loi'al-li, *adv.* In a disloyal manner; perfidiously. **disloyalty,** dis-loi'al-ti, *n.* Want of loyalty or fidelity; violation of allegiance.

dismal, diz'mal, *a.* Dark; gloomy; doleful; calamitous; sorrowful. **dismally,** diz'mal-li, *adv.* Gloomily.

dismantle, dis-man'tl, *vt.* To strip; to divest; to unrig; to deprive or strip, as of military equipment or defenses; to break down.

dismay, dis-mā', *vt.* To produce terror in; to appall; to dishearten.—*n.* Loss of courage; consternation; fright.

dismember, dis-mem'bẽr, *vt.* To sever limb from limb; to separate; to mutilate. **dismemberment,** dis-mem'bẽr-ment, *n.* The act of dismembering.

dismiss, dis-mis', *vt.* To send away; to permit to depart; to discharge. **dismissal,** dis-mis'al, *n.* Dismission. **dismission,** dis-mish'un, *n.* Act of sending away; leave to depart; discharge.

dismount, dis-mount', *vi.* To descend from a horse, &c.—*vt.* To unhorse; to throw cannon from their carriages or fixed positions.

disobedience, dis-ō-bē'di-ens, *n.* Neglect or refusal to obey.

disobedient, dis-ō-bē'di-ent, *a.* Neglecting or refusing to obey; refractory.

disobey, dis-ō-bā', *vt.* To neglect or refuse to obey; to violate an order.

disorder, dis-or'dẽr, *n.* Want of order; confusion; disease. —*vt.* To put out of order; to disturb; to produce indisposition; to craze. **disordered,** dis-or'dẽrd, *p.a.* Deranged. **disorderly,** dis-or'dẽr-li, *a.* Being without proper order; confused; unruly.

disorganization, dis-or'gan-ī-zā"shun, *n.* Act of disorganizing; state of being disorganized. **disorganize,** dis-or'gan-īz, *vt.* To destroy organic structure or connected system in; to throw into confusion.

disown, dis-ōn', *vt.* To refuse to acknowledge; to renounce; to repudiate.

disparage, dis-par'ij, *vt.* (disparaging, disparaged). To dishonor by comparison with something inferior; to derogate from; to decry. **disparagement,** dis-par'ij-ment, *n.* Injury by union or comparison with something inferior; indignity; detraction.

disparate, dis'pa-rāt, *a.* Unequal; unlike.

disparity, dis-par'i-ti, *n.* Inequality; difference in degree, age, rank, &c.

dispassionate, dis-pash'un-it, *a.* Free from passion; cool; impartial. **dispassionately,** dis-pash'un-it-li, *adv.* Without passion; calmly; coolly.

dispatch, dis-pach'. *See* **despatch.**

dispel, dis-pel', *vt.* (dispelling, dispelled). To scatter; to banish.—*vi.* To fly different ways; to disappear.

dispense, dis-pens', *vt.* (dispensing, dispensed). To deal out in portions; to administer; to apply; to exempt; to grant dispensation for.—*vi.* To do without (with *with*). **dispensable,** dis-pens'a-bl, *a.* That may be dispensed with. **dispensary,** dis-pens'a-ri *n.* A place where medicines are dispensed to the poor, and medical advice is given gratis; a place where medicines are compounded. **dispensation,** dis-pen-sā'shun, *n.* Act of dispensing; distribution; good or evil dealt out by providence; exemption. **dispensatory,** dis-pen'sa-tō-ri, *a.* Having power to grant dispensations.—*n.* A book containing the method of preparing the various kinds of medicines. **dispenser,** dis-pen'sẽr, *n.* One who dispenses, distributes, or administers.

disperse, dis-pẽrs', *vt.* To scatter; to dispel; to diffuse; to distribute.—*vi.* To be scattered; to vanish. **dispersion,** dis-pẽr'shun, *n.* Act of dispersing; diffusion; dissipation.

dispirit, dis-pir'it, *vt.* To deprive of spirit; to discourage; to daunt. **dispirited,** dis-pir'it-ed, *p.a.* Dejected; tame. **dispiriting,** dis-pir'it-ing, *p.a.* Discouraging.

displace, dis-plās', *vt.* To remove from its place; to derange; to dismiss. **displacement**, dis-plās'ment, *n.* Act of displacing; quantity of water displaced by a floating body.

display, dis-plā', *vt.* To unfold; to spread before the eyes or mind; to show; to parade.—*vi.* To make a show; to talk without restraint.—*n.* An opening or unfolding; exhibition; parade.

displease, dis-plēz', *vt.* To offend; to dissatisfy; to provoke.—*vi.* To disgust. **displeased**, dis-plēzd', *p.a.* Annoyed. **displeasing**, dis-plēz'ing, *p.a.* Disgusting; disagreeable. **displeasure**, dis-plezh'er, *n.* Dissatisfaction; resentment.

disport, dis-pōrt', *n.* Sport; pastime.—*vi.* To sport; to play; to wanton.

dispose, dis-pōz', *vt.* (disposing, disposed). To arrange; to apply to a particular purpose; to incline.—*vi.* To regulate; (with *of*) to part with, to employ. **disposable**, dis-pōz'a-bl, *a.* Subject to disposal; free to be used or employed. **disposal**, dis-pōz'al, *n.* Act or power of disposing; disposition; control. **disposed**, dis-pōzd', *p.a.* Inclined. **disposition**, dis-pō-zish'un, *n.* Act of disposing; state of being disposed; arrangement; natural fitness; frame of mind; inclination.

dispossess, dis-po-zes', *vt.* To deprive of possession. **dispossession**, dis'po-zesh"un, *n.* Act of putting out of possession.

disproof, dis-prōf', *n.* Refutation.

disproportion, dis'prō-pōr"shun, *n.* Want of proportion or symmetry.—*vt.* To violate proportion; to join unfitly. **disproportional**, dis'prō-pōr"shun-al, *a.* Showing disproportion; inadequate. **disproportionate**, dis'prō-pōr"shun-āt, *a.* Not proportioned; unsymmetrical; inadequate.

disprove, dis-prōv', *vt.* To prove to be false; to confute. **disproval**, dis-prōv'-al, *n.* Act of disproving; disproof.

dispute, dis-pūt', *vi.* (disputing, disputed). To contend in argument; to debate; to strive with.—*vt.* To attempt to prove to be false; to impugn; to contest; to strive to maintain.—*n.* Controversy in words; strife.

disputable, dis-pū'ta-bl, *or* dis'pū-ta-bl, *a.* That may be disputed; controvertible. **disputant**, dis'pū-tant, *n.* One who argues in opposition to another. **disputation**, dis'pū-tā"shun, *n.* Act of disputing; controversy in words; debate.

disqualification, dis-kwol'i-fi-kā"shun, *n.* Act of disqualifying; that which disqualifies. **disqualify**, dis-kwol'i-fī, *vt.* To divest of qualifications; to incapacitate.

disquiet, dis-kwī'et, *n.* Uneasiness; anxiety.—*vt.* To make uneasy or restless. **disquieting**, dis-kwī'et-ing, *p.a.* Tending to disturb the mind. **disquietude**, dis-kwī'e-tūd, *n.* Uneasiness; anxiety.

disquisition, dis'kwi-zish"un, *n.* A systematic inquiry into any subject, by arguments; a treatise or dissertation.

disregard, dis'rē-gärd", *n.* Neglect; slight.—*vt.* To omit to take notice of; to slight. **disregardful**, dis'rē-gärd"ful, *a.* Neglectful; negligent; heedless.

disrepair, dis'rē-pār", *n.* A state of being not in repair.

disreputable, dis-rep'ū-ta-bl, *a.* Discreditable; low; mean. **disrepute**, dis-rē-pūt', *n.* Loss or want of reputation; disesteem; disgrace.

disrespect, dis-rē-spekt', *n.* Want of respect; incivility.—*vt.* To show disrespect to. **disrespectful**, dis-rē-spekt'-ful, *a.* Irreverent; discourteous; rude.

disrobe, dis-rōb', *vt.* To undress; to uncover; to divest of any surrounding appendage.

disruption, dis-rup'shun, *n.* Act of rending asunder; breach; rent; rupture. **disruptive**, dis-rup'tiv, *a.* Causing, or produced by, disruption.

dissatisfaction, dis'sat-is-fak"shun, *n.* Want of satisfaction; discontent. **dissatisfactory**, dis'sat-is-fak"tō-ri, *a.* Not satisfactory; displeasing. **dissatisfied**, dis-sa'tis-fīd, *p.a.* Discontented; offended. **dissatisfy**, dis-sat'is-fī, *vt.* To fail to satisfy; to render discontented.

dissect, dis-sekt', *vt.* To cut up; to anatomize; to divide and examine minutely. **dissecting**, dis-sek'ting, *p.a.* Used in dissection. **dissection**, dis-sek'shun, *n.* Act of cutting up anatomically; act of separating into parts for the purpose of critical examination.

dissemble, di-sem'bl, *vt. and i.* (dissembling, dissembled). To hide under a false appearance; to conceal under some pretense. **dissembler**, di-sem'blèr, *n.* One who dissembles.

disseminate, di-sem'i-nāt, *vt.* (disseminating, disseminated). To scatter; to spread. **dissemination**, di-sem'i-nā"shun, *n.* Act of disseminating; propagation. **disseminator**, di-sem'i-nā"ter, *n.* One who disseminates.

dissension, di-sen'shun, *n.* Disagreement in opinion; discord; strife.

dissent, di-sent', *vi.* To disagree in opinion; to separate from an established church, in doctrines, rites, or government.—*n.* Disagreement; separation from an established church. **dissenter**, di-sen'tèr, *n.* One who withdraws from an established church; a nonconformist. **dissentient**, di-sen'shent, *a.* Declaring dissent; disagreeing.—*n.* One who declares his dissent. **dissenting**, di-sen'ting, *p.a.* Disagreeing; connected with a body of dissenters.

dissertation, dis'er-tā"shun, *n.* A formal discourse; treatise; disquisition.

disservice, dis-sèr'vis, *n.* An ill-service; injury; harm; mischief.

dissident, dis'i-dent, *a.* Dissenting.—*n.* A dissenter.

dissimilar, dis-sim'i-lèr, *a.* Unlike. **dissimilarity**, dis-si'mi-la"ri-ti, *n.* Unlikeness; want of resemblance.

dissimilitude, dis'si-mil"i-tūd, *n.* Unlikeness; want of resemblance.

dissimulate, di-sim'ū-lāt, *vt. and i.* To dissemble. **dissimulation**, dis-si'-

mū-lā″shun, *n.* Act of dissembling; false pretension; hypocrisy.

dissipate, dis′i-pāt, *vt.* (dissipating, dissipated). To scatter; to spend; to squander.—*vi.* To scatter; disperse; to vanish. **dissipated**, dis′i-pāted, *p.a.* Dissolute; devoted to pleasure and vice. **dissipation**, dis′i-pa″shun, *n.* Dispersion; waste; dissolute conduct; diversion. **dissociate**, di-sō′shi-āt, *vt.* (dissociating, dissociated). To separate, as from society; to disunite; to part. **dissociation**, di-sō′si-ā″shon, *n.* Act of dissociating; state of separation; disunion. **dissolute**, dis′ō-lūt, *a.* Loose in behavior and morals; licentious; debauched. **dissolutely**, dis′ō-lūt-li, *adv.* In a dissolute manner. **dissolution**, dis-ō-lū″shun, *n.* Act of dissolving; a melting or liquefaction; separation of parts; decomposition; death; destruction; the breaking up of an assembly. **dissolve**, di-zolv′, *vt.* To melt; to break up; to put an end to; to cause to vanish.—*vi.* To be melted; to become soft or languid; to waste away; to perish; to break up.

dissonance, dis′ō-nans, *n.* Disagreement in sound; discord.

dissonant, dis′ō-nant, *a.* Discordant in sound; harsh; jarring; incongruous.

dissuade, di-swād′, *vt.* (dissuading, dissuaded). To exhort against; to turn from a purpose by argument. **dissuasion**, di-swā′shun, *n.* Act of dissuading; advice in opposition to something. **dissuasive**, di-swā′siv, *a.* Tending to dissuade.—*n.* Argument or motive that deters.

distaff, dis′taf, *n.* The staff to which a bunch of flax or tow is tied, and from which the thread is drawn in spinning.

distance, dis′tans, *n.* Remoteness in place or time; extent of interval between two things; the remoteness which respect requires; reserve; coldness.—*vt.* (distancing, distanced). To leave behind in a race; to outdo or excel.

distant, dis′tant, *a.* Remote in place, time, relationship, &c.; implying haughtiness, indifference, &c.; cool; shy. **distantly**, dis′tant-li, *adv.* Remotely; at a distance; with reserve.

distaste, dis-tāst′, *n.* Aversion of the taste or mind; dislike.—*vt.* To dislike. **distasteful**, dis-tāst′ful, *a.* Unpleasant to the taste; nauseous; displeasing. **distastefully**, dis-tāst′ful-li, *adv.* In a distasteful manner.

distemper, dis-tem′pėr, *n.* Any morbid state of the body; disorder; a disease of young dogs; bad constitution of the mind; a kind of painting in which the pigments are mixed with size; a pigment so mixed.

distend, dis-tend′, *vt.* To stretch by force from within; to swell.—*vi.* To swell; to dilate.

distention, dis-ten′shun, *n.* Act of distending; state of being distended.

distill, dis-til′, *vi.* (distilling, distilled). To fall in drops; to practice distillation. —*vt.* To let fall in drops; to extract spirit from, by evaporation and conden-

sation. **distillation**, dis-ti-lā′shun, *n.* Act or process of distilling. **distillery**, dis-til′ėr-i, *n.* The building where distilling is carried on.

distinct, dis-tingkt′, *a.* Separated by some mark; not the same in number or kind; separate in place; clear; definite. **distinction**, dis-tingk′shun, *n.* Act of distinguishing; that which distinguishes; difference; elevation of rank in society; eminence; a title or honor. **distinctive**, dis-tingk′tiv, *a.* Marking distinction; having power to distinguish. **distinctively**, dis-tiugk′tiv-li, *adv.* In a distinctive manner; with distinction; plainly. **distinctly**, dis-tingkt′li, *adv.* In a distinct manner; clearly; plainly; obviously.

distinguish, dis-ting′gwish, *vt.* To mark out by some peculiarity; to perceive; to make eminent; to signalize.— *vi.* To make a distinction; to find or show the difference. **distinguishable**, dis-ting′gwish-a-bl, *a.* Capable of being distinguished; worthy of note. **distinguished**, dis-ting′gwisht, *p.a.* Eminent. **distinguishing**, dis-ting′gwish-ing, *p.a.* Constituting distinction; characteristic.

distort, dis-tort′, *vt.* To twist; to pervert. **distortion**, dis-tor′shun, *n.* Act of distorting; a writhing motion; deformity; perversion of the true meaning of words.

distract, dis-trakt′, *vt.* To draw towards different objects; to perplex; to disorder the reason of; to render furious. **distracted**, dis-trak′ted, *p.a.* Disordered in intellect; crazy; frantic; insane. **distractedly**, dis-trak′ted-li, *adv.* Madly; furiously; wildly. **distracting**, dis-trak′ting, *p.a.* Perplexing. **distraction**, dis-trak′shun, *n.* Derangement; frenzy; diversion.

distrait, dis-trā′, *a.* Absent-minded.

distraught, dis-trat′, *a.* Distracted.

distress, dis-tres′, *n.* Anguish of body or mind; affliction; state of danger or destitution; act of distraining.—*vt.* To afflict with pain or anguish; to perplex. **distressed**, dis-trest′, *p.a.* Afflicted; oppressed with calamity or misfortune. **distressful**, dis-tres′ful, *a.* Full of distress; proceeding from pain or anguish; calamitous; indicating distress. **distressfully**, dis-tres′ful-li, *adv.* In a distressful or painful manner. **distressing**, dis-tres′ing, *p.a.* Afflicting; grievous.

distribute, dis-trib′ūt, *vt.* (distributing, distributed). To divide among two or more; to apportion; . to administer, as justice; to classify. **distributable**, dis-trib′ū-ta-bl, *a.* That may be distributed. **distributer**, dis-trib′u-ter, *n.* One who distributes. **distribution**, dis′tri-bū″shun, *n.* Act of distributing; apportionment.

district, dis′trikt, *n.* A limited extent of country; a circuit; a region.

distrust, dis-trust′, *vt.* To have no trust in; to doubt; to suspect.—*n.* Want of trust; doubt; suspicion; discredit. **dis-**

trustful, dis-trust'ful, *a.* Apt to distrust; suspicious; not confident.

disturb, dis-tèrb', *vt.* To throw into disorder; to agitate; to hinder; to move. **disturbance**, dis-tèr'bans, *n.* State of being disturbed; commotion; excitement; interruption of a right. **disturber**, dis-tèr'bèr, *n.* One who or that which disturbs.

disunion, dis-ūn'yun, *n.* A severing of union; disjunction; breach of concord. **disunite**, dis-ū-nīt', *vt.* To separate.—*vi.* To part; to become separate. **disuse**, dis-ūs', *n.* Cessation of use; desuetude.—*vt.* dis-ūz'. To cease to use; to neglect or omit to practice; to disaccustom.

ditch, dich, *n.* A trench in the earth for drainage or defense.—*vi.* To dig a ditch. —*vt.* To dig a ditch in; to drain by a ditch; to surround with a ditch.

ditto, dit'ō, *n.* A word used in lists, &c. meaning same as above; often written *do.*

ditty, dit'i, *n.* A song; a poem to be sung.

diuretic, dī-ū-ret"ik, *a.* Tending to produce discharges of urine.—*n.* A medicine that has this effect.

diurnal, dī-èr'nal, *a.* Relating to day; daily.—*n.* In the Roman Catholic Church, a book containing the office of each day. **diurnally**, dī-èr'nal-li, *adv.* Daily.

divan, di-van', *n.* Among the Turks, a court of justice; a council or council-chamber; a cushioned seat standing against the wall of a room.

dive, dīv, *vi.* (diving, dived). To plunge into water head-foremost; to go under water to execute some work; to go deep. **diver**, dīv'èr, *n.* One who dives; one who works under water; a bird which dives.

diverge, di-vèrj', *vi.* (diverging, diverged). To proceed from a point in different directions; to deviate; to vary. **divergence, divergency**, di-vèr'jens, di-vèr'jen-si, *n.* Act of diverging; a receding from each other. **divergent**, di-vèr'jent, *a.* Diverging; receding from each other.

divers, dī'vèrz, *a.* Different; various; sundry; more than one, but not many. **diverse**, di-vèrs', *a.* Different; unlike; various. **diversely**, di-vèrs'li, *adv.* In a diverse manner; variously. **diversifiable**, di-vèrs'i-fī"a-bl, *a.* Capable of being diversified. **diversification**, di-vèr'si-fi-kā"shun, *n.* Act of diversifying; variation; variegation. **diversified**, di-vèr'si-fīd, *p.a.* Distinguished by various forms; variegated. **diversify**, di-vèr'si-fī, *vt.* (diversifying, diversified). To make diverse in form or qualities; to variegate; to give diversity to. **diversion**, di-vèr'shun, *n.* Act of diverting; that which diverts; amusement; a feigned attack. **diversity**, di-vèr'si-ti, *n.* State of being diverse; contrariety; variety.

divert, di-vèrt', *vt.* To turn aside; to amuse.

divest, di-vest', *vt.* To strip of clothes; to deprive.

dividable, di-vīd'a-bl, *a.* Divisible.

divide, di-vīd', *vt.* (dividing, divided). To part asunder; to separate; to keep apart; to distribute, allot; to set at variance.—*vi.* To part; to be of different opinions; to vote by the division of a legislative house into parties.

dividend, div'i-dend, *n.* A number which is to be divided; share of profit; share divided to creditors.

divider, di-vīd'èr, *n.* One who or that which divides; a distributor; *pl.* compasses.

divination, div'i-nā"shun, *n.* Act of divining; a foretelling future events, or discovering things secret, by magical means.

divine, di-vīn', *a.* Of or belonging to God; excellent in the highest degree.—*n.* One versed in divinity; a clergyman. —*vt.* (divining, divined). To foretell; to presage; to guess.—*vi.* To practice divination; to have or utter presages; to guess. **divine right**, esp., the right of kings to reign regarded as given by God and indefeasible; **divine service**, public worship; **divining-rod**, switch balanced in dowser's hand to betray, by dipping, the presence of underground water or minerals.

diving bell, dīv'ing bel, *n.* An apparatus by means of which persons may descend below water to execute various operations.

divinity, di-vin'i-ti, *n.* The state of being divine; God; a deity; the science of divine things; theology.

divisibility, di-viz'i-bil"i-ti, *n.* Quality of being divisible.

divisible, di-viz'i-bl, *a.* Capable of division; separable.

division, di-vizh'un, *n.* Act of dividing; state of being divided; separation; partition; portion; a separate body of men; a process or rule in arithmetic. **divisional**, di-vizh'un-al, *a.* Creating division or discord. **divisor**, di-vī'zer, *n.* In *arithmetic*, the number by which the dividend is divided.

divorce, di-vōrs', *n.* A legal dissolution of marriage; disunion of things closely united.—*vt.* (divorcing, divorced). To dissolve the marriage contract between; to separate. **divorcee**, di-vor-sē', *n.* Divorced person. **divorcement**, di-vōrs'ment, *n.* The act of divorcing.

divot, div'ut, *n.* Turf torn from earth by a golf stroke.

divulge, di-vulj', *vt.* (divulging, divulged). To make public; to disclose.

Dixie, dik'si, *n.* The Southern states of the United States; the Confederacy.

dizziness, diz'i-nes, *n.* Giddiness; vertigo.

dizzy, diz'i, *a.* Having a sensation of whirling in the head; giddy; causing giddiness.—*vt.* (dizzying, dizzied). To make giddy.

do, dö, *vt.* or *auxiliary* (doing, pret. did, pp. done). To perform; to bring about; to pay (as honor, &c.); to transact; to finish; to prepare; to cook.—*vi.* To act or behave; to fare in health; to succeed; to suffice; to avail.

docile, dos'il, *a.* Easily taught; ready to learn; tractable; pliant. **docility**, dō-sil'i-ti, *n.* Quality of being docile.

dock, dok, *n.* A troublesome weed; the tail of a beast cut short; the stump of a tail; an enclosed area on the side of a harbor or bank of a river for ships; the place where the accused stands in court. —*vt.* To cut off; to curtail; to deduct from; to put a ship in dock.

dockage, dok'ij, *n.* Pay for using a dock.

dockyard, dok'yärd, *n.* A yard near a dock for naval stores.

docket, dok'et, *n.* A summary; a bill tied to goods; a list of cases in a court. —*vt.* To make an abstract of; to mark the contents of papers on the back; to attach a docket to.

doctor, dok'tẽr, *n.* A person who has received the highest degree in a university faculty; one licensed to practice medicine; a physician.—*vt.* To treat medically; to adulterate. **doctorate**, dok'-tẽr-it, *n.* The degree of a doctor.

doctrine, dok'trin, *n.* Instruction; whatever is taught; a principle in any science; dogma; a truth of the gospel. **doctrinaire**, dok'tri-nãr", *n.* A political theorist. **doctrinal**, dok'tri-nal, *a.* Pertaining to doctrine; containing a doctrine.

document, dok'ū-ment, *n.* Written evidence or proof; any authoritative paper containing instructions or proof.—*vt.* To furnish with documents. **documentary**, dok-ū-men'ta-ri, *a.* Pertaining to or consisting in documents.

dodder, dod'ẽr, *n.* Parasitic plant resembling tangled red twine.—*vi.* Shake with palsy; totter or potter with senility.

dodge, doj, *vi.* (dodging, dodged). To start aside; to quibble.—*vt.* To evade by a sudden shift of place.—*n.* An artifice; an evasion.

dodo, dō'dō, *n.* An extinct bird of Mauritius, having a massive, clumsy body, short strong legs, and wings useless for flight.

doe, dō, *n.* A female deer.

doeskin, dō'skin, *n.* The skin of a doe; a compact twilled woolen cloth.

dog, dog, *n.* A domestic quadruped of many varieties; a mean fellow; a gay young man.—*vt.* (dogging, dogged). To follow insidiously; to worry with importunity.

dogcart, dogkärt", *n.* A carriage with a box for holding sportsmen's dogs; a sort of double-seated gig.

doge, dōj, *n.* The chief magistrate in republican Venice.

dog-eared, dog'ērd, *a.* Having the corners of the leaves turned down (said of a book).

dogfish, dog'fish, *n.* A species of shark.

dog tag, dog tag, *n.* License tag for dogs; identification tag worn by American soldiers. *Slang.*

dogged, dog'ed, *a.* Determined, pertinacious. **doggedly**, dog'ed-li, *adv.* With obstinate resolution.

doggerel, dog'ẽr-el, *n.* A loose irregular kind of versification; wretched verse.

dogma, dog'ma, *n.* A settled opinion or belief; tenet; a doctrinal point. **dogmatic, dogmatical**, dog-mat'ik, dog-mat'i-kal, *a.* Pertaining to a dogma; asserting, or asserted, with authority or arrogance; positive. **dogmatically**, dog-mat'i-kal-li, *adv.* In a dogmatic manner. **dogmatics**, dog-mat'iks, *n.* Doctrinal theology; essential doctrines of Christianity. **dogmatism**, dog'matizm, *n.* Positiveness in assertion; arrogance in opinion. **dogmatist**, dog'matist, *n.* A dogmatic asserter; an arrogant advancer of principles.

dogtooth, dog'tōth, *n.* An eye-tooth.

doldrums, dol'drumz, *n.pl.* The dumps.

dole, dōl, *n.* That which is dealt out; share; gratuity; grief; sorrow.—*vt.* (doling, doled). To deal out; to distribute.

doleful, dōl'fyl, *a.* Full of pain, grief, &c.; expressing or causing grief; gloomy. **dolefully**, dōl'fyl-li, *adv.* In a doleful manner; sorrowfully; dismally; sadly. **dolesome**, dōl'sum, *a.* Doleful.

doll, dol, *n.* A child's puppet in human form.

dollar, dol'ẽr, *n.* A coin of the United States, Canada, Mexico, &c.

dolly, dol'i, *n.* A doll; a low, flat, wheeled frame used for moving heavy loads.

dolor, dolour, dō'lẽr, *n.* Sorrow; lamentation. **dolorous**, dō'lẽr-us, *a.* Sorrowful; doleful. **dolorously**, dō'lẽr-us-li, *adv.* Sorrowfully.

dolphin, dol'fin, *n.* A small species of whale remarkable for gamboling in the water; a fish celebrated for its changes of color when dying.

dolt, dōlt, *n.* A blockhead. **doltish**, dōlt'ish, *a.* Dull in intellect.

domain, dō-mān', *n.* Territory governed; estate; a demesne.

dome, dōm, *n.* A hemispherical roof of a building; a large cupola.

domestic, dō-mes'tik, *a.* Belonging to the house or home; tame; not foreign.— *n.* A household servant. **domesticate**, dō-mes'ti-kāt, *vt.* To accustom to remain much at home; to tame. **domestication**, dō-mes'ti-kā"shun, *n.* Act of domesticating; state of being domesticated.

domicile, dom'i-sil, *n.* A habitation; family residence.—*vt.* (domiciling, domiciled). To establish in a residence. **domiciliary**, dom'i-sil"i-er'i, *a.* Pertaining to a domicile.

dominate, dom'i-nāt, *vt.* (dominating, dominated). To rule; to predominate over. **domination**, dom-i-nā'shun, *n.* Rule; tyranny. **dominant**, dom'i-nant, *a.* Governing; predominant; ascendant. **domineer**, dom-i-nēr', *vi.* To rule tyrannically or with insolence (with *over*). **domineering**, dom-i-nēr'ing, *p.a.* Overbearing; insolent.

dominie, dom'i-ni, *n.* A pedagogue.

dominion, dō-min'yun, *n.* Sovereign authority; district governed; region.

domino, dom'i-nō, *n.* A masquerade dress; a half-mask; a person wearing a domino; *pl.* (**dominoes**), a game played with pieces of ivory or bone dotted like disk.

don, don, *n.* A Spanish title, corresponding to Eng. Mr.; an important personage; a fellow, &c., of an English college. —*vt.* (donning, donned). To put on; to invest with.

donation, dō-nā'shun, *n.* Act of giving; that which is given; a gift; a present.

done, dun, *a.* Completed.

donkey, dong'ki, *n.* An ass.

donor, dō'nèr, *n.* One who gives.

doom, döm, *n.* Judicial sentence; fate; ruin.—*vt.* To condemn to punishment; to destine. **doomed,** dömd, *p.a.* Having the doom or fate settled; destined to speedy destruction. **doomsday,** dömz'dā, *n.* The day of judgment.

door, dör, *n.* The entrance of a house or room; the frame of boards that shuts such an entrance; avenue; means of approach.

dope, döp, *n.* A pasty medicinal preparation, as of opium; any preparation of opium used to stupefy; the forecast of the result of a horse race.

Doric, dor'ik, *a.* Pertaining to Doris in Greece; denoting the earliest and plainest of the Grecian orders of architecture.

dormer, dormer window, dor'mèr, *n.* A window in a sloping roof, the frame being placed vertically.

domitory, dor'mi-tō'ri, *n.* A place to sleep in; a room in which a number sleep.

dormouse, dor'mous, *n.*; *pl.* **dormice,** dor'mīs. A small rodent which passes the winter in a lethargic or torpid state.

dorsal, dor'sal, *a.* Pertaining to the back.

dory, dō'ri, *n.* A European yellow fish, with a protrusible mouth; a small boat.

dose, dos, *n.* The quantity of medicine given at one time; something given to be swallowed.—*vt.* (dosing, dosed). To give in doses; to give medicine to.

dossier, dos'i-ā, *n.* A file of information on a subject.

dost, dust. The second sing. present of *do*.

dot, dot, *n.* A small point, as made with a pen, &c.; a speck.—*vt.* (dotting, dotted). To mark with a dot; to diversify with small objects.—*vi.* To make dots.

dotage, dōt'ij, *n.* Feebleness of mind, particularly in old age; excessive fondness.

dotard, dō'tèrd, *n.* One whose mind is impaired by age; one foolishly fond.

dote, dōt, *vi.* (doting, doted). To have the intellect impaired by age; to be foolishly fond. **doting,** dōt'ing, *p.a.* Having the mind impaired by age; foolishly fond.

doth, duth. The third sing. present of *do*.

double, dub'l, *a.* Twofold; forming a pair; of extra size, quality, &c.; deceitful.—*vt.* (doubling, doubled). To make twofold; to fold; to increase by adding an equal amount; to sail round (a cape, &c.).—*vi.* To increase twofold; to turn

or wind in running; to use sleights.—*n.* Twice as much; a turn in running; a sift; a duplicate; a wraith.

double bass, dub'l bäs, *n.* The lowest-toned instrument of the violin class.

double-dealing, du'bl-dēl'ing, *n.* Deceitful practice; duplicity.

double entry, du'bl en'tri, *n.* A mode of bookkeeping in which every transaction is entered on the debit side of one account and the credit side of another.

doublet, dub'let, *n.* A close-fitting body garment; one of a pair; one of two words really the same but different in form.

double-take, dub'l-tāk', *n.* A delayed reaction.

double-talk, du'bl-tawk, *n.* Studied form of gibberish meant to confuse.

doubloon, dub-lön', *n.* A Spanish gold coin, worth about five dollars.

doubly, dub'li, *adv.* In twice the quantity; to twice the degree.

doubt, dout, *vi.* To waver in opinion or judgment; to question; to suspect.—*vt.* To deem uncertain; to distract.—*n.* A wavering in opinion; uncertainty; suspicion. **doubter,** dout'èr, *n.* One who doubts. **doubtful,** dout'ful, *a.* Full of doubt or doubts; hesitating; ambiguous; precarious; suspicious. **doubtfully,** dout'ful-li, *adv.* In a doubtful manner; dubiously. **doubtless,** dout'les, *adv.* Without doubt; unquestionably. **doubtlessly,** dout'les-li, *adv.* Doubtless.

dough, dō, *n.* Flour or meal moistened and kneaded, but not baked; paste of bread; money.

doughty, dou'ti, *a.* Noble; brave; valiant.

doughy, dō'i, *a.* Like dough; soft; pale.

dour, dör, *a.* Grim, stubborn.

douse, dowse, dous, *vt.* and *i.* To plunge into water; to drench.

dove, duv, *n.* A pigeon; a word of endearment.

dovecot, dovecote, duv'kot', duv'kōt', *n.* A place for pigeons.

dovetail, duv'tāl', *n.* A mode of joining boards by letting one piece into another in the form of a dove's tail spread, or wedge reversed.—*vt.* and *i.* To unite by the above method; to fit exactly.

dowager, dou'ā-jèr, *n.* A title given to the widow of a person of title.

dowdy, dou'di, *n.* An awkward, ill-dressed woman.—*a.* Ill-dressed; vulgar-looking.

dowel, dou'el, *n.* A pin of wood or iron to join boards, &c.—*vt.* (doweling, doweled). To fasten by dowels.

dower, dou'èr, *n.* That portion of the property of a man which his widow enjoys during her life; the property which a woman brings to her husband in marriage; dowry. **dowered,** dou'èrd, *p.a.* Furnished with dower, or a portion. **dowerless,** dou'èr-les, *a.* Destitute of dower.

down, doun, *n.* The fine soft feathers of birds; fine hair; the pubescence of plants; a hill; a dune; a tract of naked, hilly land.—*adv.* In a descending direction; on the ground; into less bulk; paid in ready money.—*prep.* Along in descent; toward the mouth of.—*a.* Down-cast; dejected.

downcast, doun′kast, *a.* Cast downward; dejected.

downfall, doun′fal, *n.* A falling down; loss of wealth or high position; ruin.

downhill, doun′hil′, *a.* Descending; easy.—*adv.* Down a hill or slope.

downpour, doun″pōr′, *n.* A pouring down; especially, a heavy or continuous shower.

downright, doun″rīt′, *adv.* Right down; in plain terms; utterly.—*a.* Directly to the point; plain; blunt; utter.

downstairs, doun′stārz′, *a.* or *adv.* Descending the stairs; on a lower flat.

downthrow, doun″thrō, *n.* A throwing down; a falling or sinking of strata.

downtrodden, doun′trod′n, *a.* Trodden down; oppressed.

downward, downwards, doun′wẹrd, doun′wẹrdz, *adv.* From a higher place or state to a lower; in direction from a head or source.

downy, doun′i, *a.* Covered with, or pertaining to, down; soft; soothing.

dowry, dou′ri, *n.* The property which a woman brings to her husband in marriage; a dower; a gift.

doxology, doks-ol′o-ji, *n.* A hymn or form of giving glory to God.

doze, dōz, *vi.* (dozing, dozed). To sleep lightly; to be half asleep.—*vt.* To pass or spend in drowsiness.—*n.* A slight sleep; a slumber.

dozen, duz′n, *n.* Twelve things regarded collectively.

drab, drab, *n.* A sluttish woman; a strumpet; a thick woolen cloth of a dun color; a dull brownish color.—*a.* Of a dull brown color.

draconic, draconian, drā-kon′ik, drā-kō′ni-an, *a.* Relating to Draco, the Athenian law-giver; extremely severe.

draft, draft, *n.* A detachment of men or things; an order for money; the first sketch of any writing; a sketch.—*vt.* To make a draft of; to sketch; to select.

draftee, draf′tē″, *n.* A person drafted for military service.

draftsman, dräfts′man, *n.* See **draughtsman**.

drag, drag, *vt.* (dragging, dragged). To draw along the ground by main force; to haul; to explore with a drag.—*vi.* To hang so as to trail on the ground; to move slowly.—*n.* A net drawn along the bottom of the water; an instrument to catch hold of things under water; a machine for dredging; a low cart; a long coach; a contrivance to stop a wheel of a carriage; whatever serves to retard.

dragnet, drag′net, *n.* A net to be drawn along the bottom of a river or pond.

dragon, drag′un, *n.* A fabulous winged monster; a fierce person; a kind of small lizard.

dragonfly, dra″gn-flī′, *n.* A fly that preys upon other insects.

dragonish, dra′gu-nish, *a.* In the form of a dragon; dragon-like.

dragon's blood, drag′unz blud, *n.* The red juice of certain tropical plants, used for coloring varnishes, staining marble, &c.

dragoon, dra-gön′, *n.* A heavy cavalry soldier.—*vt.* To harass; to compel by force.

drain, drān, *vt.* To draw off; to filter; to make dry; to exhaust.—*vi.* To flow off gradually.—*n.* A channel for liquid; a sewer; gradual or continuous withdrawal. **drainage**, drān′ij, *n.* The act or art of draining; the system of drains; that which flows out of drains. **drainer**, drān′ẹr, *n.* A utensil on which articles are placed to drain; one who or that which drains.

drake, drāk, *n.* The male of ducks.

dram, dram, *n.* The eighth part of an ounce, or sixty grains apothecaries' measure; the sixteenth part of an ounce avoirdupois; as much spirituous liquor as is drunk at once.

drama, drä′ma, *n.* A representation on a stage; a play; dramatic literature. **dramatic, dramatical**, dra-mat′ik, dra-mat′i-kal, *a.* Pertaining to the drama; represented by action; theatrical. **dramatist**, dram′a-tist, *n.* The author of a dramatic composition. **dramatize**, dram′a-tīz, *vi.* To compose in the form of the drama.

drape, drāp, *vt.* (draping, draped). To cover with cloth or drapery.

draper, drāp′ẹr, *n.* One who sells cloth. **drapery**, drā″per-i, *n.* The occupation of a draper; fabrics of wool or linen; clothes or hangings.

drastic, dras′tik, *a.* Acting with strength or violence.—*n.* A strong purgative.

draught, draft, *n.* The act of drawing; quantity drunk at once; a sketch or outline; the depth a ship sinks in water; a current of air; *pl.* a game played on a checkered board.—*vt.* To draw out; to draft.—*a.* Used for drawing; drawn from the barrel, &c. **draughtsman**, drafts′man, *n.* One who draws plans or designs. **draughty**, draf′ti, *a.* Of or pertaining to draughts of air; exposed to draughts.

draw, dra, *vt.* (drawing, pret. drew, pp. drawn). To pull along or towards; to cause to come; to unsheathe; to suck; to attract; to inhale; to stretch; to lead, as a motive; to represent by lines drawn on a surface; to describe; to infer; to derive; to draft; to require a certain depth of water; bend (a bow); to end indecisively.—*vi.* To pull; to shrink; to advance; to practice drawing; to make a written demand for money.—*n.* Act of drawing; the lot or chance drawn; a drawn game.

drawback, dra″bak′, *n.* What detracts from profit or pleasure; duties on goods paid back when exported.

drawbridge, dra″brij″, *n.* A bridge which may be raised or drawn aside.

drawer, dra′ẹr, *n.* One who or that which draws; he who draws a bill; a sliding box in a case, &c.; *pl.* an undergarment for the lower limbs.

drawing, dra′ing, *n.* Act of one who draws; representation of objects by lines and shades; delineation.

drawing room, dra′ing röm, *n.* A room for receiving company in; formal reception of company at a court.

drawl, drạl, *vi.* To speak with slow, prolonged utterance.—*vt.* To utter in a slow tone.—*n.* A lengthened utterance.

dread, dred, *n.* Fear, united with respect; terror; the person or the thing dreaded.—*a.* Exciting great fear; terrible; venerable.—*vt.* and *i.* To fear in a great degree. **dreadful**, dred'fụl, *a.* Awful; terrible. **dreadfully**, dred'fụl-li, *adv.* Terribly.

dreadnought, **dreadnaught**, dred'nạt, *n.* A person that fears nothing; a thick cloth with a long pile; a garment made of such cloth; a new type of powerful war-ship.

dream, drēm, *n.* The thought of a person in sleep; a vain fancy.—*vi.* To have images in the mind, in sleep; to imagine; to think idly.—*vt.* To see in a dream; to spend idly. **dreamer**, drēm'ẽr, *n.* One who dreams; a fanciful man; a visionary. **dreamless**, drēm'les, *a.* Free from dreams. **dreamy**, drēm'i, *a.* Full of dreams; visionary.

drear, drēr, *a.* Dismal; gloomy. **drearily**, drē'ri-li, *adv.* Gloomily. **dreary**, drē'ri, *a.* Dismal; gloomy; oppressively monotonous.

dredge, drej, *n.* An oyster net; a dredging-machine.—*vt.* (dredging, dredged). To take with a dredge; to deepen with a dredging-machine; to powder; to sprinkle flour on meat while roasting. **dredger**, drej'ẽr, *n.* One who uses a dredge; a utensil for scattering flour on meat while roasting; a dredging-machine.

dregs, dregz, *n.pl.* Lees; grounds; the most vile and despicable part.

drench, drench, *vt.* To wet thoroughly; to soak; to purge violently.—*n.* A draught; a large dose of liquid medicine for an animal.

dress, dres, *vt.* To make straight; to put in good order; to cleanse and cover a wound; to prepare; to curry, rub, and comb; to clothe; to array; to trim.—*vi.* To arrange in a line; to put on clothes; to pay regard to dress.—*n.* Apparel; attire; a lady's gown.

dresser, dres'ẽr, *n.* One who dresses; a table on which food is dressed; a low cupboard for dishes.

dressing, dres'ing, *n.* Act of one who dresses; manure; application to a sore; stuffing of fowls, pigs, &c.; starch, &c., used in finishing silk, linen, &c.; molding round doors, windows, &c.

dressing room, dres'ing rōm, *n.* A room for dressing in.

dribble, drib'l, *vi.* (dribbling, dribbled). To fall in a quick succession of drops; to trickle.—*vt.* To throw down in drops.

driblet, **dribblet**, drib'let, *n.* A small drop; a small sum, as one of a series.

drift, drift, *n.* That which is driven by wind or water; impulse; tendency; aim; velocity of a current; the distance a vessel is driven by a current; rocks conveyed by glaciers and deposited over a country while submerged; in S. Africa, a ford.—*vi.* To move along like anything driven; to accumulate in heaps; to float or be driven by a current.—*vt.* To drive into heaps.—*a.* Drifted by wind or currents.

driftless, drift'les, *a.* Aimless.

drill, dril, *vt.* To pierce with a drill; to teach soldiers their proper movements, &c.; to teach by repeated exercise; to sow in rows; to furrow.—*vi.* To sow in drills; to muster for exercise.—*n.* A pointed instrument for boring holes; act of training soldiers; a row of seeds; a furrow.

drill, drilling, dril, dril'ing, *n.* A kind of coarse cotton cloth.

drink, dringk, *vi.* (drinking; pret. drank; pp. drunk or drunken). To swallow liquor; to take spirituous liquors to excess.—*vt.* To swallow, as liquids; to absorb.—*n.* Liquor to be swallowed; any beverage; potion. **drinkable**, dringk'a-bl, *a.* That may be drunk; fit or suitable for drink.

drinker, dringk'ẽr, *n.* One who drinks; a tippler.

drip, drip, *vi.* (dripping, dripped). To fall in drops.—*vt.* To let fall in drops.—*n.* A falling in drops; the eaves; a projecting molding. **dripping**, drip'ing, *n.* A falling in drops; the fat which falls from meat in roasting.

drive, drīv, *vt.* (driving, pret. drove, pp. driven). To impel; to hurry on; to impel and guide; to convey in a carriage; to carry on.—*vi.* To be impelled along; to aim at; to strike with force.—*n.* A journey in a vehicle; a road for driving on; a sweeping blow.

drivel, driv'l, *vi.* (driveling, driveled). To slaver; to dote; to talk rubbish.—*n.* Slaver; senseless twaddle.

driver, drīv'ẽr, *n.* One who or that which drives; a large quadrilateral sail; a main wheel; a golf club for long strokes.

drizzle, driz'l, *vi.* (drizzling, drizzled). To rain in small drops.—*vt.* To shed in small drops or particles.—*n.* A small or fine rain. **drizzly**, driz'li, *a.* Shedding small rain.

droll, drōl, *a.* Comic; queer; facetious.—*n.* A jester; a farce. **drollery**, drōl'ẽr-i, *n.* Buffoonery; comical stories.

dromedary, drom"e-der'i, *n.* A swift camel, usually the Arabian, with one hump, in distinction from the Bactrian, which has two.

drone, drōn, *n.* The male or non-working bee; an idler; a low humming sound; a large tube of the bagpipe.—*vi.* (droning, droned). To give a low dull sound; to hum.

droop, dröp, *vi.* To hang down; to languish; to fail; to be dispirited.—*vt.* To let sink or hang down.—*n.* A drooping position or state.

drop, drop, *n.* A globule of any liquid; an earring; a small quantity; part of a gallows; a distance to fall.—*vt.* (dropping, dropped). To pour or let fall in drops; to let fall; to let down; to quit; to utter casually.—*vi.* To fall in drops; to fall; to cease; to come unexpectedly.

dropout, drop'out, *n.* One who leaves school prematurely.

dropping, drop'ing, *n.* A falling in drops; that which drops; *pl.* the dung of animals.

dropsy, drop'si, *n.* An unnatural collec-

tion of water in any part of the body.
dross, dros, *n.* The scum of metals; waste matter; refuse.

drought, drout, *n.* Dry weather; want of rain; aridness; thirst; lack.

droughty, drou'ti, *a.* Dry; wanting rain.

drove, drōv, *n.* A collection of cattle driven; a crowd of people in motion.

drover, drō'vėr, *n.* One who drives cattle or sheep to market.

drown, droun, *vt.* To deprive of life by immersion in water, &c.; to inundate; to overwhelm.—*vi.* To be suffocated in water, &c.

drowse, drouz, *vi.* (drowsing, drowsed). To nod in slumber; to doze; to look heavy.—*vt.* To make heavy with sleep, or stupid. **drowsily**, drou'zi-li, *adv.* Sleepily. **drowsy**, drou'zi, *a.* Inclined to sleep; dull; sluggish; lulling.

drub, drub, *vt.* (drubbing, drubbed). To cudgel; to thrash.—*n.* A blow; a thump. **drubbing**, drub'ing, *n.* A sound beating.

drudge, druj, *vi.* (drudging, drudged). To labor at mean work.—*n.* One who labors hard in servile employments; a slave. **drudgery**, druj'ėr-i, *n.* Hard labor; toilsome work; ignoble toil.

drug, drug, *n.* Any substance used in medicine; an article of slow sale.—*vt.* (drugging, drugged). To mix with drugs; to introduce a narcotic into; to dose to excess with drugs.

druggist, drug'ist, *n.* One who deals in drugs.

druid, drö'id, *n.* A priest and judge among the ancient Celtic nations. **druidic, druidical**, drö-id'ik, drö-id'i-kal, *a.* Pertaining to the Druids. **druidism**, drö'id-izm, *n.* The doctrines, rites, and ceremonies of the Druids.

drum major, drum mā'jėr, *n.* The chief drummer of a regiment.

drum, drum, *n.* A hollow cylindrical instrument of music beaten with sticks; something in the form of a drum; the tympanum of the ear.—*vi.* (drumming, drummed). To beat a drum; to beat with the fingers, as with drumsticks; to beat rapidly.—*vt.* To expel or summon by beat of drum.

drummer, drum'ėr, *n.* One whose office is to beat the drum in military exercises.

drunk, drungk, *a.* Overcome with alcoholic liquor; intoxicated. **drunkard**, drungk'ėrd, *n.* A person who is habitually or frequently drunk. **drunken**, drungk'en, *p.a.* Inebriated; given to drunkenness; proceeding from intoxication. **drunkenness**, drungk'en-nes, *n.* Intoxication; inebriety.

dry, drī, *a.* Destitute of moisture; arid; free from juice; thirsty; uninteresting; sarcastic; harsh; cold.—*vt.* (drying, dried). To free from moisture; to deprive of natural juice; to drain.—*vi.* To lose moisture; to evaporate wholly.

dryad, drī'ad, *n.* A nymph of the woods.

dryer, drier, drī'ėr, *n.* One who or that which dries; that which exhausts moisture.

Dry Ice, drī Is, *n.* Carbon dioxide in solid state; used in refrigeration.

dryly, **drily**, drī'li, *adv.* In a dry manner; coldly; sarcastically.

dryness, drī'nes, *n.* State or quality of being dry; jejuneness; causticity.

dry rot, drī rot, *n.* A decay of timber occasioned by various species of fungi.

dual, dū'al, *a.* Expressing the number two; existing as two; twofold. **dualism**, dū'al-izm, *n.* A twofold division; the belief in two gods, the one good, the other evil; the doctrine of the existence of spirit and matter as distinct entities. **dualist**, dū'al-ist, *n.* One who holds the doctrine of dualism. **duality**, dū-al'i-ti, *n.* The state of being dual or twofold.

dub, dub, *vt.* (dubbing, dubbed). To tap with a sword and make a knight; to speak of as; to smooth; to trim.

dubious, dū'bi-us, *a.* Wavering in opinion; doubtful; uncertain. **dubiously**, dū'bi-us-li, *adv.* Doubtfully.

ducal, dū'kal, *a.* Pertaining to a duke.

ducat, duk'at, *n.* A coin formerly common in Europe, either of silver (value about $1) or gold (value about $2.28).

duchess, duch'es, *n.* The wife of a duke; a lady who has the sovereignty of a duchy.

duchy, duch'i, *n.* The dominion of a duke.

duck, duk, *vt.* and *i.* To plunge in water; to bow, stoop, or nod.—*n.* A waterfowl; a term of endearment; an inclination of the head; a canvas or coarse cloth.

duckling, duk'ling, *n.* A young duck.

duct, dukt, *n.* A canal or tube, especially in animal bodies and plants.

ductile, duk'til, *a.* That may be drawn out; docile; tractable; flexible. **ductility**, duk-til'i-ti, *n.* The property of metals which renders them capable of being drawn out without breaking; obsequiousness; ready compliance.

dude, dūd, *n.* A dandy of the first water; a brainless exquisite.

dudgeon, duj'un, *n.* A small dagger, or the handle of a dagger; ill-will; sullenness.

due, dū, *a.* Owed; owing; suitable; proper; attributable; that ought to have arrived by the time specified.—*adv.* Directly.—*n.* That which law, office, rank, &c., require to be paid or done; fee; right, just title.

duel, dū'el, *n.* A premeditated combat between two persons; single combat; contest. **duelist, duellist**, dū'el-ist, *n.* One who fights duels.

dues, dōz, *n.* Periodic membership fee.

duet, dū'et, *n.* A piece of music for two performers, vocal or instrumental.

duffer, duf'ėr, *n.* A useless fellow; poor golfer.

dug, dug, *n.* The pap or nipple; now applied only to beasts, unless in contempt.

dugout, dug'out', *n.* An excavation made in a hillside for protection from gunfire, &c.

duke, dūk, *n.* One of the highest order of nobility; a sovereign prince. **dukedom**, dūk'dum, *n.* The jurisdiction, possessions, title, or quality of a duke.

dulcet, dul'set, *a.* Sweet; harmonious.

dull, dul, *a.* Stupid; slow; blunt; drowsy;

cheerless; not bright or clear; tarnished; uninteresting.—*vt.* To make dull; to stupefy; to blunt; to make sad; to sully. —*vi.* To become dull, blunt, or stupid.

dullard, dul'ėrd, *n.* A stupid person; dolt. **dullness**, dul'nes, *n.* Stupidity; heaviness; slowness; dimness. **dully**, du'li, *adv.* Stupidly; sluggishly.

duly, dū'li, *adv.* Properly; fitly.

dumb, dum, *a.* Incapable of speech; mute; silent; not accompanied with speech.

dumbbell, dum"bel', *n.* One of a pair of weights used for exercise.

dumfound, **dumbfound**, dum'found", *vt.* To strike dumb; to confuse. Also *dumfounder*.

dummy, dum'i, *n.* One who is dumb; the exposed hand when three persons play at whist; a sham article.

dump, dump, *n.* A dull state of the mind; sadness; a thud; a clumsy piece; *pl.* low spirits; gloom; supply center.

dumpling, dump'ling, *n.* A pudding of boiled suet paste, with or without fruit.

dumpy, dump'i, *a.* Short and thick.

dun, dun, *a.* Of a dark, dull color; swarthy.—*vt.* (dunning, dunned). To demand a debt from; to urge importunately.—*n.* An importunate creditor; urgent demand for payment.

dunce, duns, *n.* One slow at learning; a dullard; a dolt.

dune, dūn, *n.* A sand hill.

dung, dung, *n.* The excrement of animals.—*vt.* To manure; to immerse (calico) in cow dung and water.—*vi.* To void excrement.

dungaree, dun'ga-rē", *n.* A coarse cotton fabric used for sails, tents, work clothes, etc. **dungarees**, *n.pl.* Trousers made from this cloth.

dungeon, dun'jun, *n.* A strong tower in the middle of a castle; a deep, dark place of confinement.

dunghill, dung'hil, *n.* A heap of dung. —*a.* Sprung from the dunghill; mean; low.

duodenum, dū'ō-dē"num, *n.* The first portion of the small intestines.

duotone, dū'ō-tōn, *n.* Any picture printed in two shades of the same color.

dupe, dūp, *n.* One who is cheated; one easily deceived.—*vt.* (duping, duped). To impose on.

duplex, dū'pleks, *a.* Double; twofold.

duplicate, dū'pli-kāt, *a.* Double; twofold.—*n.* A copy; a transcript.—*vt.* To double. **duplication**, dū'pli-kā"shun, *n.* Act of doubling; a fold; multiplication by 2.

duplicity, dū-plis'i-ti, *n.* Doubleness of heart or speech; guile; deception.

durable, dū'ra-bl, *a.* Having the quality of lasting long; permanent; firm. **durability**, dū-ra-bil'i-ti, *n.* Quality of being durable.

durance, dūr'ans, *n.* Imprisonment; custody.

duration, dū-rā'shun, *n.* Continuance in time; power of continuance; permanency.

durbar, dėr'bär, *n.* An Indian state levee or audience.

duress, dū'res, *n.* Constraint; imprisonment.

during, dūr'ing, *prep.* For the time of the continuance of.

dusk, dusk, *a.* Tending to darkness; moderately black.—*n.* A middle degree between light and darkness; twilight. **duskily**, dusk'i-li, *adv.* In a dusky manner; with partial darkness. **duskish**, dusk'ish, *a.* Moderately dusky. **dusky**, dus'ki, *a.* Partially dark; dark colored; not bright.

dust, dust, *n.* Fine dry particles of earth, &c.; powder; earth as symbolic of mortality; a low condition.—*vt.* To free from dust; to sprinkle, as with dust. **duster**, dus'tėr, *n.* A cloth, &c., for removing dust; a sieve. **dusty**, dus'ti, *a.* Covered with dust; like dust.

Dutch, duch, *a.* Pertaining to Holland, or to its inhabitants.—*n.pl.* The people of Holland; *sing.* their language.

duty, dū'ti, *n.* That which a person is bound to perform; obligation; act of reverence or respect; business, service, or office; tax; impost or customs. **duteous**, dū'tē-us, *a.* Pertaining to duty; dutiful. **duteously**, dū'tē-us-li, *adv.* In a duteous manner. **dutiful**, dū'ti-ful, *a.* Regularly performing duties required toward superiors; respectful. **dutifully**, dū'ti-ful-li, *adv.* In a dutiful manner.

dwarf, dwarf, *n.* A person or plant much below the ordinary size.—*vt.* To stunt; to make or keep small; to cause to appear small by comparison.—*a.* Below the common size; stunted. **dwarfish**, dwar'fish, *a.* Like a dwarf; very small; petty.

dwell, dwel, *vi.* (pret. and pp. dwelled or dwelt). To live in a place; to reside; to hang on with fondness; to continue. **dweller**, dwel'ėr, *n.* An inhabitant. **dwelling**, dwel'ing, *n.* Habitation; abode.

dwindle, dwin'dl, *vi.* (dwindling, dwindled). To diminish gradually; to shrink; to sink.

dye, dī, *vt.* (dyeing, dyed). To stain; to give a new and permanent color to.—*n.* A coloring liquid or matter; tinge.

dyer, dī'ėr, *n.* One whose occupation is to dye cloth and the like.

dying, dī'ing, *a.* Mortal; destined to death; uttered, given, &c., just before death; pertaining to death; fading away.

dyke, dīk. See *dike*.

dynamic, **dynamical**, dī-nam'ik, dī-nam'i-kal, *a.* Pertaining to strength, or to dynamics. **dynamics**, dī-nam'iks, *n.* The science which investigates the action of force.

dynamite, dī'na-mīt, *n.* An explosive substance consisting of some powdery matter impregnated with nitroglycerine.

dynamo, dī'na-mō, *n.* A machine for producing an electric current by mechanical power.

dynasty, dī'nas-ti, *n.* A race of kings of the same family.

dyne, dīn, *n.* A unit of force, being that force which, acting on a gram for one second, generates a velocity of a centimeter per second.

dysentery, dis"en-ter'i, *n.* A disorder of

the intestines; a flux in which the stools consist chiefly of blood and mucus.

dyspepsia, dyspepsy, dis-pep'si-a, dis-pep'si, n. Indigestion; difficulty of digestion. **dyspeptic,** dis-pep'tik, a. Afflicted with dyspepsia; pertaining dyspepsia.—n. A person afflicted with bad digestion.

E

each, ĕch, a. and pron. Every one of any number considered individually.

eager, ē'gėr, a. Sharp; ardent; keenly desirous; impetuous; earnest; intense. **eagerly,** ē'gėr-li, adv. With great ardor of desire; ardently; earnestly. **eagerness,** ē'gėr-nes, n. Ardent desire; vehemence; fervor; avidity.

eagle, ē'gl, n. A large bird of prey, of great power of flight and vision; a military standard. **eaglet,** ē'glet, n. A young eagle.

eagle-wood, ē'gl-wud, n. A fragrant wood, burned by Asiatics as incense.

eagre, eager, ā'gėr, ē'gėr, n. A tidal wave; a bore.

ear, ėr, n. The organ of hearing; power of distinguishing musical sounds; heed; regard; anything resembling an ear or ears; a spike, as of corn.—vi. To form ears, as corn.—vt. To plow or till.

earache, ēr'āk, n. Pain in the ear.

ear-drum, ēr''drum', n. The tympanum or middle ear.

earl, ėrl, n. A British title of nobility, below a marquis and above a viscount. **earldom,** ėrl'dum, n. The domain, title, or dignity of an earl.

early, ėr'li, adv. and a. In good time or season; before the usual time; prior in time.

earn, ėrn, vt. To gain by labor; to deserve.

earnest, ėr'nest, a. Ardent in the pursuit of an object; eager; zealous; serious.—n. Seriousness; a reality; first-fruits; a part given beforehand as a pledge for the whole; indication; token. **earnestly,** ėr'nest-li, adv. Warmly; zealously; importunately; eagerly.

earnings, ėr'ningz, n.pl. That which is gained or merited by labor or performance; wages; reward.

earring, ēr''ring', n. A jewel or ornament worn in the ear; a pendant.

earshot, ēr''shot', n. The distance at which words may be heard.

earth, ėrth, n. The globe we inhabit; the world; the fine mold on the surface of the globe; dry land; the ground; the hiding hole of a fox, &c.—vt. To cover with earth.—vi. To retire underground; to burrow.

earthen, ėr'then, a. Made of earth.

earthenware, ėr'then-wār, n. Ware made of clay; crockery; pottery.

earthling, ėrth'ling, n. An inhabitant of the earth; a mortal; a frail creature.

earthly, ėrth'li, a. Pertaining to the earth; sordid; worldly; sensual; conceivable.

earthquake, ėrth'kwāk, n. A shaking, trembling, or concussion of the earth.

earthward, ėrth'wėrd, adv. Toward the earth.

earthwork, ėrth'wėrk, n. A rampart or fortification of earth.

earthworm, ėrth'wėrm, n. The common worm; a mean, sordid wretch.

earthy, ėr'thi, a. Consisting of or resembling earth; gross; not refined.

ease, ēz, n. Freedom from toil, pain, anxiety, &c.; freedom from difficulty; freedom from stiffness or formality; unaffectedness.—vt. (easing, eased). To give ease to; to relieve; to calm; to alleviate; to shift a little.

easel, ē'zl, n. The frame on which pictures are placed while being painted.

easement, ēz'ment, n. That which gives ease; accommodation; privilege.

easily, ēz'i-li, adv. In an easy manner.

east, ēst, n. That part of the heavens where the sun rises; the countries east of Europe.—a. In or toward the east. **easterly,**—adv. Eastwards.

Easter, ēs'tėr, n. A festival of the Christian church in March or April, in commemoration of Christ's resurrection.

easterly, ēs'tėr-li, a. Coming from the east, as wind; situated or moving toward the east.—adv. On the east; in the direction of east.

Eastern, ēs'tėrn, a. Belonging to the east; toward the east; oriental.

Eastertide, ēs'tėr-tīd, n. The time at which Easter is celebrated.

easy, ēz'i, a. Being at ease; free from pain or anxiety; not difficult; gentle; complying; affluent; not stiff or formal.

eat, ēt, vt. (pret. ate; pp. eaten or eat). To chew and swallow, as food; to wear away; to gnaw; to consume.—vi. To take food; to taste or relish; to corrode.

eatable, ēt'a-bl, a. That may be eaten; proper for food.—n. That which is fit for, or used as food.

eaves, ēvz, n.pl. That part of the roof of a building which overhangs the walls.

eavesdrop, ēvz'drop, n. The water which drops from the eaves.—vi. To listen to what is said within doors; to watch for opportunities of hearing private conversation. **eavesdropper,** ēvz'drop'ėr, n. One who tries to hear private conversation.

ebb, eb, n. The flowing back of the tide; decline; decay.—vi. To flow back; to decay; to decline.

ebony, eb'un-i, n. A hard, heavy, dark wood admitting of a fine polish.

ebullient, ē-bul'yent, a. Boiling over, as

a liquor; over enthusiastic. **ebullition**, ē'bul-li"shun, *n*. The operation of boiling; a sudden burst, as of passion; an overflowing; outbreak.

eccentric, ek-sen'trik, *a*. Not having its axis in the center; not having the same center; deviating from usual practice, &c.; anomalous; whimsical.—*n*. An eccentric person; mechanical contrivance for converting circular into reciprocating rectilinear motion. **eccentrically**, ek-sen'trik-al-li, *adv*. In an eccentric manner. **eccentricity**, ek'sen-tris"i-ti, *n*. State or quality of being eccentric; distance ot the center of a planet's orbit from the center of the sun; singularity; oddness.

ecclesiastes, e-klē'zi-as"tez, *n*. A canonical book of the Old Testament. **ecclesiastic**, e-klē'zi-as"tik, *a*. Ecclesiastical.—*n*. A priest; a clergyman. **ecclesiastical**, e-klē'zi-as"ti-kal, *a*. Pertaining to the church; not civil or secular.

echelon, esh'e-lon, *n*. The position of troops in parallel lines, each line being a little to the right or left of the preceding one.

echo, ek'ō, *n*. A sound repeated or reverberated.—*vi*. To give out an echo.—*vt*. To reverberate or send back, as sound; to repeat with assent.

eclat, ā-klā', *n*. A burst of applause; renown; splendor.

eclectic, ek-lek'tik, *a*. Proceeding by the method of selection; applied to certain philosophers who selected from the principles of various schools what they thought sound.—*n*. One who follows an eclectic method in philosophy, &c. **eclecticism**, ek-lek'ti-sizm, *n*. The doctrine or practice of an eclectic.

eclipse, ē-klips', *n*. An interception of the light of the sun, moon, &c., by some other body; darkness; obscuration.—*vt*. (eclipsing, eclipsed). To cause an eclipse of; to excel. **ecliptic**, ē-klip'tik, *n*. The apparent path of the sun round the earth.—*a*. Pertaining to the ecliptic or an eclipse; suffering an eclipse.

eclogue, ek'log, *n*. A pastoral poem.

economic, economical, ē'ko-nom"ik, ē'ko-nom"i-kal, *a*. Pertaining to economy or economics; frugal; careful. **economically**, ē'ko-nom"i-kal-li, *adv*. With economy. **economics**, ē'ko-nom"-iks, *n*. The science of the application of wealth; political economy. **economist**, ē-kon'o-mist, *n*. One who practices economy; one versed in economics. **economize**, ē-kon'o-miz, *vt*. and *i*. (economizing, economized). To manage with prudence or frugality. **economy**, ē-kon'o-mi, *n*. Frugal use of money; the regular operations of nature; due order of things; judicious management.

ecstasy, ek'sta-si, *n*. A trance; excessive joy; rapture; enthusiasm. **ecstatic, ecstatical**, ek-stat'ik, ek-stat'i-kal, *a*. Causing or pertaining to ecstasy; entrancing; delightful beyond measure.

ecumenical, eoumenic, ek'ū-men"i-kal, ek'ū-men"ik, *a*. General; universal; applied to church councils.

eczema, ek'se-ma, *n*. A skin disease.

eddy, ed'i, *n*. A circular current of water or air.—*a*. Whirling.—*vi*. (eddying, eddied). To move circularly, or as an eddy.

edelweiss, ā'dl-vīs, *n*. An Alpine plant.

Eden, ē'den, *n*. The garden of Adam and Eve; a delightful region or residence.

edge, ej, *n*. The cutting side of an instrument; an abrupt border or margin; sharpness; keenness.—*vt*. (edging, edged). To bring to an edge; to sharpen; to fringe; to exasperate; to move by little and little.—*vi*. To move sideways or gradually. **edged**, ejd, *a*. Sharp; keen. **edge tool**, ej tōl, *n*. An instrument with a sharp edge. **edgeways, edgewise**, ej"wāz', ej"wiz', *adv*. With the edge forward or towards; sideways. **edging**, ej'ing, *n*. A border; fringe.

edible, ed'i-bl, *a*. Eatable.

edict, ē'dikt, *n*. An order issued by a prince; a decree; manifesto.

edify, ed'i-fī, *vt*. (edifying, edified). To build up, in a moral sense; to instruct or improve generally. **edifying**, ed"i-fī'ing. *p.a*. Improving; adapted to instruct. **edification**, ed'i-fi-kā"shun, *n*. A building up; improvement in knowledge, morals, &c.; instruction. **edifice**, ed'i-fis, *n*. A structure; a fabric; a large or splendid building.

edit, ed'it, *vt*. To prepare for publication; to conduct, as regards literary contents. **edition**, ē-dish'un, *n*. A published book as characterized by form or editorial labors; the whole number of copies of a work published at once. **editor**, ed'i-tèr, *n*. One who prepares or superintends for publication. **editorial**, ed'i-tō"ri-al, *a*. Pertaining to or written by an editor.—*n*. A leading article in a newspaper.

educate, ed'ū-kāt, *vt*. (educating, educated). To teach; to cultivate and train; to enlighten. **education**, ed'ū-kā"shun, *n*. Act of educating; instruction and discipline; schooling. **educational**, ed'ū-kā"shun-al, *a*. Pertaining to education. **educative**, ed"-ū-kā'tiv, *a*. Tending or able to educate; imparting education. **educator**, ed"ū-kā'ter, *n*. One who educates.

educe, ē-dūs', *vt*. (educing, educed). To draw out; to elicit; to extract. **educible**, ē-dūs'i-bl, *a*. That may be educed. **eduction**, ē-duk'shun, *n*. Act of drawing out or bringing into view.

eel, ēl, *n*. A slimy serpent-like fish.

e'er, ār. A contraction for *ever*.

eerie, ē'ri, *a*. Inspiring superstitious fear; weird.

efface, e-fās', *vt*. To remove from the face or surface of anything; to render illegible; to blot out; to wear away. **effacement**, e-fās'ment, *n*. Act of effacing.

effect, e-fekt', *n*. That which is produced; result; purpose; validity; striking appearance; impression produced by a work of art, &c.; *pl*. goods; movables; personal estate.—*vt*. To produce; to cause; to fulfill; execute. **effective**, e-fek'tiv, *a*. Having the power to produce; efficacious; efficient; effectual; fit for duty or service. **effectively**, e-fek'tiv-li, *adv*. With effect, **effectual**, e-fek'tū-al, a. Producing the effect desired or intended; valid. **effectuate**, e-fek'tū-āt, vt. To carry into effect; to bring to pass; to fulfill.

effeminate, e-fem'i-nit, a. Womanish; unmanly; weak; voluptuous.—vt. To unman; to weaken.—vi. To grow womanish or weak, **effeminately**, e-fem'i-nit-li, adv. In an effeminate manner; womanishly; weakly. **effeminacy**, e-fem'i-na-si, n. State or character of being effeminate.

effervesce, ef'ėr-ves', vi. To bubble or sparkle, as any fluid when part escapes in gas; to exhibit signs of excitement. **effervescence**, ef'ėr-ves''ens, n. Act of effervescing; strong excitement. **effervescent**, ef'ėr-ves''ent, a. Boiling or bubbling, by means of the disengagement of gas.

effete, e-fēt', a. Worn out; exhausted; barren. **efficacious**, ef'i-kā''shus, a. Producing the effect intended; having adequate power. **efficacy**, ef'i-ka-si, n. Power to produce effect; production of the effect intended; virtue; force; energy. **efficient**, e-fish'ent, a. Effecting; capable; qualified for duty. **efficiency**, e-fish'en-si, n. The state or character of being efficient; effectual agency.

effigy, ef'i-ji, n. The image or likeness of a person; portrait; figure.

effloresce, ef'lo-res'', vt. To bloom; to show a powdery substance on the surface. **efflorescence**, ef'lo-res''ens, n. The time, act, or process of flowering; a redness of the skin; mealy powder or minute crystals forming on a surface. **efflorescent**, ef'lo-res''ent, a. Showing efflorescence; liable to effloresce.

effluent, ef'flu-ent, a. Flowing out.—n. A stream that flows out of another, or out of a lake. **effluence**, ef'lū-ens, n. A flowing out; that which issues from any body or substance. **effluvial**, e-flū'vi-al, a. Pertaining to effluvia; containing effluvia. **effluvium**, e-flū'vi-um, n.; pl. **via**. Something flowing out invisibly; a disagreeable odor; a noxious exhalation.

effort, ef'ėrt, n. An exertion of strength; strenuous endeavor; struggle. **effrontery**, e-frun'te-ri, n. Audacious impudence; shameless boldness.

effulgent, e-ful'jent, a. Sending out a flood of light; gleaming; splendid. **effulgence**, e-ful'jens, n. A flood of light; great luster; splendor.

effuse, e-fūz', vt. (effusing, effused). To pour out; to shed.—vi. To emanate. **effusion**, e-fū'zhun, n. Act of pouring out; that which is poured out; in pathology, the escape of fluid out of its proper vessel into another part; cordiality of manner; a literary production. **effusive**, e-fū'siv, a. Pouring out; showing overflowing kindness.

egg, eg, n. A roundish body produced by many female animals besides birds from which their young is produced; something resembling an egg.—vt. To urge on; to instigate.

egocentric, ē-gō-sen'trik, a. Self-centered.

egoism, eg'ō-izm or ē', n. The doctrine

which refers all knowledge to the phenomena of personal existence; egotism. **egoist**, eg'ō-ist or ē', n. An egotist; one holding the doctrine of egoism. **egotism**, eg'ō-tizm or ē', n. The practice of too frequently using the word I; an exaggerated love of self; self-exaltation. **egotist**, eg'ō-tist or ē', n. One always talking of himself; one who magnifies his own achievements. **egotistic, egotistical**, eg-ō-tis'tik, eg-ō-tis'ti-kal, ē-, a. Addicted to egotism; vain.

egregious, e-grē'jus, a. Remarkable; extraordinary; enormous.

egress, ē'gres, n. Act of going out; power of departing from any confined place; exit.—vi. To go out.

egret, eg'ret or ē'gret, n. A species of heron; an aigret.

Egyptian, ē-jip'shan, a. Pertaining to Egypt.—n. A native of Egypt; a gipsy. **Egyptology**, ē'jip-tol''o-ji, n. The science of Egyptian antiquities.

eh, eh, exclam. Denoting inquiry or slight surprise.

eider, eider duck, ī'dėr, ī'der duk, n. A species of sea duck, producing down of the finest and softest kind. **eider down**, ī'dėr doun, n. Down or soft feathers of the eider-duck.

eight, āt, a. One more than seven and less than nine.—n. This number; the symbol representing this number.

eighteen, ā'tēn, a. and n. Eight and ten united.

eighteenth, ā'tēnth, a. and n. Next in order after the seventeenth; one of eighteen parts.

eighth, āth, a. and n. Next after the seventh; one of eight parts; an octave.

eighthly, āth'li, adv. In the eighth place.

eightieth, ā'ti-eth, a. and n. The ordinal of eighty.

eighty, ā'ti, a. Eight times ten.

Einstein theory, īn'stīn thē'o-ri, n. The theory of relativity, often so called because first developed by Albert Einstein.

either, ē'THėr, or ī'THėr, a. or pron. One or the other; one or two; each.—conj. or adv. Used disjunctively as correlative to or.

ejaculate, ē-jak'ū-lāt, vt. To exclaim; to utter suddenly and briefly. **ejaculation**, ē-jak'ū-lā''shun, n. Exclamation; short prayer. **ejaculatory**, ē-jak''ū-la-tō'ri, a. Of the nature of an ejaculation.

eject, ē'jekt, vt. To throw out; to dismiss; to dispossess of land or estate; to expel. **ejection**, ē-jek'shun, n. Act of casting out; expulsion; dismission. **ejectment**, ē-jekt'ment, n. Act or process of ejecting removal of a person from the wrongful possession of land or tenements. **ejector**, ē-jek'tėr, n. One who or that which ejects.

eke, ēk, vt. (eking, eked). To add to; to lengthen; to prolong.—n. An addition. —adv. Also; in addition.

elaborate, e-lab'o-rāt, vt. (elaborating, elaborated). To produce with labor; to refine by successive operations.—a. e-lab'o-rit. Wrought with labor; studied;

high-wrought. **elaborately**, ē-lab′o-rāt-li, adv. In an elaborate manner. **elaboration**, ē-lab′o-rā″shun, n. Refinement by successive operations; the process in animal and vegetable organs by which something is produced.

elapse, ē-laps′, vi. (elapsing, elapsed). To slip or glide away.

elastic, ē-las′tik, a. Having the power of returning to the form from which it is bent or distorted; rebounding. **elastically**, ē-las′ti-kal-li, adv. In an elastic manner; with a spring. **elasticity**, ē-las′tis′i-ti, n. State or property of being elastic.

elate, ē-lāt′, a. Elevated in mind; flushed, as with success.—vt. (elating, elated). To exalt; to puff up; to make proud. **elated**, ē-lāt′ed, p.a. Elate. **elation**, ē-lā′shun, n. Elevation of mind or spirits; buoyancy.

elbow, el′bō, n. The bend or joint of the arm; an angle.—vt. To push with the elbow; to push, as through a crowd.—vi. To project; to push one's way.

elder, el′dèr, a. Older; having lived a longer time; senior.—n. One who is older; an office-bearer in the Presbyterian church; a small tree with a spongy pith and dark purple or red berries. **elderly**, el′dèr-li, a. Somewhat old; beyond middle age.

eldest, el′dest, a. Oldest; most aged.

elect, ē-lekt′, vt. To pick or choose; to select for an office.—a. Chosen; chosen to an office, but not yet in office.—n. sing. or pl. One or several chosen; those favored by God. **election**, ē-lek′shun, n. Act of choosing; choice; voluntary preference; divine choice; predestination. **electioneer**, ē-lek′shun-ēr″, vi. To work for a candidate at an election. **electioneering**, ē-lek′shun-ēr″ing, n. The arts used to secure the selection of a candidate.

elective, ē-lek′tiv, a. Pertaining to or consisting in choice; exerting the power of choice.

elector, ē-lek′tèr, n. One who elects or has the right of voting. **electoral**, ē-lek′tèr-al, a. Pertaining to election or electors. **electorate**, ē-lek′tèr-it, n. A body of electors.

electric, electrical, ē-lek′trik, ē-lek′-tri-kal, a. Containing, conveying, or produced by electricity; full of fire or spirit, and capable of communicating it. **electrically**, ē-lek′tri-kal-li, adv. In the manner of electricity; by electricity. **electrician**, ē-lek′trish″an, n. One versed in the science of electricity. **electricity**, ē-lek-tris′i-ti, n. The force that manifests itself in lightning and in many other phenomena; the science which deals with these phenomena. **electrify**, ē-lek′tri-fī, vt. (electrifying, electrified). To communicate electricity to; to thrill.—vi. To become electric.

electro, ē-lek′trō, n. An electrotype. **electrode**, ē-lek′trōd, n. One of the terminals or poles of the voltaic circle. **electrodynamics**, ē-lek′trō-dī-nam″iks, n. The science of mechanical actions exerted on one another by electric cur-

rents. **electrolysis**, ē-lek′trol″i-sis, n. Decomposition by means of electricity. **electrolyte**, ē-lek′trō-līt, n. A compound decomposable by electricity. **electrometer**, ē-lek′trom″e-tèr, n. An instrument for measuring electricity. **electrotype**, ē-lek′trō-tīp, n. The art of producing copies of types, woodcuts, &c., by the electric deposition of copper on a cast from the original; a copy thus produced. **electron**, ē-lek′tron, n. Physics. An electrically charged particle which is a component of the atom and of matter; a corpuscle; a particle of negative electricity.

eleemosynary, el′ē-mos″i-ner′i, a. Given in or relating to charity; founded to dispense some gratuity.—n. One who subsists on charity.

elegant, el′ē-gant, a. Pleasing to good taste; graceful; polished; refined; symmetrical. **elegantly**, el′ē-gant-li, adv. In an elegant manner. **elegance, elegancy**, el′ē-gans, el′ē-gan-si, n. Quality of being elegant; beauty resulting from propriety; refinement.

elegiac, el′ē-jī′ak, a. Belonging to elegy; plaintive.—n. Elegiac verse.

elegy, el′ē-ji, a. A poem or a song expressive of sorrow and lamentation.

element, el′ē-ment, n. A fundamental part or principle; an ingredient; proper sphere; suitable state of things; pl. first principles of an art or science; data employed in a calculation; the bread and wine used in the Lord's supper. **elemental**, el-ē-men′tal, a. Pertaining to or produced by elements. **elementary**, el-ē-men′ta-ri, a. Primary; uncompounded; teaching first principles or rudiments.

elephant, el′ē-fant, n. A huge quadruped, having a long trunk and tusks, **elephantine**, el′ē-fan″tin, a. Pertaining to the elephant; huge; clumsy. **elevate**, el′ē-vāt, vt. (elevating, elevated). To raise; to refine or dignify; to elate; to cheer. **elevation**, el-ē-vā′shun, n. Act of elevating; state of being elevated; an elevated station; a hill; representation of a building in vertical section. **elevator**, el′ē-vāt′èr, n. One who or that which elevates; a hoist.

eleven, ē-lev′en, a. Ten and one added.—n. The sum of ten and one; the symbol representing this number; a side of players in football, cricket, &c. **eleventh**, ē-lev′enth, a. and n. Next after the tenth; one of eleven parts.

elf, elf, n.; pl. **elves**, elvz. A fairy; a goblin; a mischievous person. **elfin**, el′-fin, a. Relating to elves.—n. An elf; a little urchin. **elfish**, el′fish, a. Resembling or pertaining to elves.

elicit, ē-lis′it, vt. To draw out by reasoning, discussion, &c.; to educe.

elide, ē-līd′, vt. (eliding, elided). To strike out; to cut off or suppress (a syllable).

eligible, el′i-ji-bl, a. Fit to be chosen; suitable; legally qualified. **eligibly**, el′i-ji-bli, adv. In a manner to be worthy of choice; suitably. **eligibility**, el′i-ji-bil″i-ti, *n.* Worthiness or fitness to be chosen.

eliminate, ē-lim′i-nāt, *vt.* (eliminating, eliminated). To throw off; to cancel; to leave out of consideration. **elimination,** ē-lim′i-nā″shun, *n.* Act of eliminating.

elision, ē-lizh″un, *n.* Act of eliding; suppression of a vowel or syllable.

elite, ā-lēt′, *n. pl.* A select body; the best.

elixir, ē-lik′sėr, *n.* A liquor sought by the alchemists to transmute metals into gold or to prolong life; quintessence; a cordial.

Elizabethan, ē-liz′a-bē″than, *a.* Pertaining to Queen Elizabeth or her times.

elk, elk, *n.* The largest species of deer.

ell, el, *n.* A measure of different lengths in different countries, the English ell being 45 inches.

ellipse, e-lips′, *n.* An oval figure. **ellipsis,** e-lips′is, *n.* pl. -**ses.** A figure of syntax by which words are omitted; suppression of letters or words in printing. **elliptic, elliptical,** e-lip′tik, e-lip′ti-kal, *a.* Pertaining to an ellipse or ellipsis; having a part omitted.

elm, elm, *n.* A tree valuable for its timber.

elocution, el-ō-kū′shun, *n.* Management of the voice and gesture in speaking; pronunciation; delivery. **elocutionary,** el′ō-kū″shun-er′i, *a.* Pertaining to elocution. **elocutionist,** el′ō-kū″shun-ist, *n.* One who is versed in, or teaches, elocution.

elongate, ē-long′gāt, *vt.* (elongating, elongated). To lengthen.—*vi.* To recede apparently from the sun.—*a.* Long and slender. **elongation,** ē-long-gā′shun, *n.* Act of lengthening; state of being extended; continuation; apparent distance of a planet from the sun.

elope, ē-lōp′, *vi.* (eloping, eloped). To escape privately; to run away with a lover. **elopement,** ē-lōp′ment, *n.* Act of eloping; running away of a woman with a lover.

eloquence, el′ō-kwens, *n.* The quality or faculty of being eloquent; oratory. **eloquent,** el′ō-kwent, *a.* Having the power of fluent, elegant, or forcible speech; characterized by eloquence. **eloquently,** el′ō-kwent-li, *adv.* With eloquence; in an eloquent manner.

else, els, *a.* or *adv.* Other; besides; in addition.—*conj.* Otherwise; in the other case.

elsewhere, els′whār, *adv.* In any other place; in some other place.

elucidate, ē-lū′si-dāt, *vt.* To make clear; to free from obscurity; to explain. **elucidation,** ē-lū′si-dā″shun, *n.* Act of elucidating; illustration; explanation.

elude, ē-lūd′, *vt.* (eluding, eluded). To avoid by artifice or dexterity; to baffle; to evade. **elusion,** ē-lū′zhun, *n.* Act of eluding; evasion. **elusive,** ē-lū′siv, *a.* Practicing elusion; evasive. **elusory,** ē-lū′sō-ri, *a.* Tending to elude; evasive; fallacious.

Elysian, ē-lizh′an, *a.* Pertaining to Elysium; exceedingly delightful.

Elysium, ē-lizh′i-um, *n.* The place of future happiness; any delightful plac[e]

emaciate, ē-mā′shi-āt, *vi.* and *t.* (ema[-] ciating, emaciated). To become or mak[e] lean. **emaciation,** ē-mā′si-ā″shun, [*n.*] Act of emaciating; leanness.

emanate, em′a-nāt, *vi.* (emanating[,] emanated). To flow out; to issue; t[o] spring. **emanation,** em′a-nā″shun, [*n.*] Act of emanating; that which issues fro[m] any source or substance; effluvium. **emanant,** em′a-nant, *a.* Emanating.

emancipate, ē-man′si-pāt, *vt.* (emanc[i-] pating, emancipated). To set free fro[m] slavery; to liberate. **emancipation,** ē-man′si-pā″shun, *n.* Liberation; free[-] dom; enfranchisement. **emancipator,** e-man″si-pā′tėr, *n.* One who emancipate[s] from bondage or restraint.

emasculate, ē-mas′kū-lāt, *vt.* To cas[-] trate; to render effeminate; to expur[-] gate. **emasculation,** ē-mas′kū-lā″shun[,] *n.* Castration; effeminacy.

embalm, em-bäm′, *vt.* To preserve [a] dead body by aromatics; to cherish th[e] memory of.

embank, em-bangk′, *vt.* To enclose o[r] defend with a bank, mounds, or dikes. **embankment,** em-bangk′ment, *n.* Ac[t] of embanking; a bank raised for pro[-] tecting against inundation, or for a rail[-] way, &c.

embargo, em-bär′gō, *n.* Prohibition o[n] ships from sailing; restraint or hindrance[.] —*vt.* To put an embargo on.

embark, em-bärk′, *vt.* To put on boar[d] a ship; to engage in.—*vi.* To go o[r] board of a ship; to engage in; to tak[e] a share. **embarkation,** em-bär-kā′shun[,] *n.* Act of embarking; that which is em[-] barked.

embarrass, em-bar′as, *vt.* To involv[e] in difficulties; to entangle; to discon[-] cert. **embarrassed,** em-bar′ast, *p.a.* Entangled; confused; disconcerted; un[-] able to pay. **embarrassment,** em[-] bar′as-ment, *n.* Entanglement; trouble[;] abashment.

embassy, em′ba.si, *n.* The mission [or] charge, or residence of an ambassador[;] an important message.

embattle, em-bat′l, *vt.* To arrange in or[-] der of battle; to furnish with battle[-] ments.—*vi.* To be ranged in order of bat[-] tle.

embellish, em-bel′ish, *vt.* To mak[e] beautiful; to adorn. **embellishment,** em-bel′ish-ment, *n.* Act of embellish[-] ing; that which embellishes.

ember, em′bėr, *n.* A glowing cinder[;] chiefly in *pl.*

embezzle, em-bez′l, *vt.* (embezzling[,] embezzled). To appropriate by breach o[f] trust. **embezzlement,** em-bez′l-ment[,] *n.* Act of fraudulently appropriatin[g] money, &c., entrusted to one's care. **em[-] bezzler,** em-bez′lėr, *n.* One who em[-] bezzles.

embitter, em-bit′ėr, *vt.* To make bitte[r] or more bitter; to exasperate.

emblaze, em-blāz′, *vt.* To kindle; t[o] blazon.

emblazon, em-blā′zn, *vt.* To ador[n] with figures of heraldry; to sing th[e] praises of. **emblazonment,** em-blā″zn[-] ment, *n.* Act of emblazoning; that which is emblazoned.

emblem, em'blem, *n.* A picture representing one thing and suggesting another; a symbol; type; device. **emblematic, emblematical**, em'ble-mat"ik, em'ble-mat'i-kal, *a.* Pertaining to or comprising an emblem; symbolic.

embody, em-bod'i, *vt.* (embodying, embodied). To invest with a body; to form into a body (as troops), or into a system; to collect. **embodiment**, em-bod'i-ment, *n.* Act of embodying; state of being embodied; that in which something is embodied; incarnation.

embolden, em-bōl'den, *vt.* To give boldness to; to encourage.

embolism, em'bo-lizm, *n.* Obstruction of a blood vessel by a clot of blood.

emboss, em-bos', *vt.* To form bosses on; to fashion in relievo or raised work. **embossment**, em-bos'ment, *n.* Act of embossing; figures in relievo; raised work.

embower, em-bou'ėr, *vt.* To enclose in or cover with a bower; to shade.

embrace, em-brās', *vt.* (embracing, embraced). To take within the arms; to press to the bosom; to seize ardently; to include; to accept.—*vi.* To join in an embrace.—*n.* Clasp with the arms; a hug; conjugal endearment.

embrasure, em-brā'zhėr, *n.* An opening in a wall or parapet through which cannon are fired.

embroider, em-broi'dėr, *vt.* To adorn with ornamental needlework or figures. **embroidery**, em-broi'dėr-i, *n.* Embroidered work; variegated needlework.

embroil, em-broil', *vt.* To confuse; to disorder; to involve in troubles; to disturb. **embroilment**, em-broil'ment, *n.* The act of embroiling; state of contention, perplexity, or confusion; disturbance.

embryo, em'bri-ō, *n.* The first rudiments of an animal in the womb or of a plant in the seed; the first state of anything.—*a.* Pertaining to anything in its first rudiments. **embryology**, em'bri-ol"o-ji, *n.* The doctrine of the development of embryos. **embryonic**, em'bri-on"ik, *a.* Pertaining to an embryo, or the embryo stage.

emend, ē-mend', *vt.* To remove faults from; to improve the text or reading of. **emendation**, ē-men-dā'shun, *n.* Correction in a text, writing, &c., alteration for the better.

emerald, em'ėr-ald, *n.* A precious stone, akin to the beryl, usually green; a small printing type.—*a.* Of a bright-green colour.

emerge, ē-mėrj', *vi.* (emerging, emerged). To rise out of a fluid or other substance; to issue; to rise into view; to reappear. **emergence**, ē-mėr'jens, *n.* Act of emerging. **emergency**, ē-mėr'jen-si, *n.* Act of emerging; unforeseen occurrence; pressing necessity. **emergent**, ē-mėr'jent, *a.* Rising out of; issuing from; sudden; casual; pressing.

emeritus, ē-mer'i-tus, *a.* Discharged from duty with honor on account of infirmity, age, or long service.

emersion, ē-mėr'shun, *n.* Act of rising out of a fluid or other substance; reappearance of a heavenly body after eclipse, &c.

emery, em'er-i, *n.* A hard mineral used in cutting gems and for polishing.

emetic, ē-met'ik, *a.* Causing vomiting. —*n.* A medicine that provokes vomiting.

emigrant, em'i-grant, *a.* Emigrating; pertaining to emigration or emigrants.— *n.* One who emigrates. **emigrate**, em'i-grāt, *vi.* (emigrating, emigrated). To remove from one country or state to another for the purpose of residence. **emigration**, em-i-grā'shun, *n.* Act of emigrating; a body of emigrants.

eminent, em'i-nent, *a.* Exalted; high in office; distinguished; illustrious. **eminently**, em'i-nent-li, *adv.* In an eminent manner or position. **eminence**, em'i-nens, *n.* A rising ground; elevation; top; distinction; fame; a title of honor given to cardinals, &c.

emissary, em"i-ser'i, *n.* One sent on private business; a secret agent; a spy. **emission**, ē-mish'un, *n.* Act of emitting; that which is emitted. **emissive**, ē-mis'iv, *a.* Sending out; emitting. **emissory**, ē-mis'o-ri, *a.* Sending out; excretory.

emit, ē-mit', *vt.* (emitting, emitted). To send out; to discharge; to vent.

emollient, ē-mol'i-ent, *a.* Softening; making supple.—*n.* A substance which softens or allays irritation.

emolument, ē-mol'ū-ment, *n.* Profit arising from office or employment; salary; gain.

emotion, ē-mō'shun, *n.* Any agitation of mind; feeling. **emotional**, ē-mō'shun-al, *a.* Pertaining to or characterized by emotion.

emperor, em'pėr-ėr, *n.* The sovereign of an empire.

emphasis, em'fa-sis, *n.* A stress laid on a word or clause to enforce a meaning; impressiveness; weight. **emphasize**, em'fa-sīz, *vt.* (emphasizing, emphasized). To place emphasis on. **emphatic, emphatical**, em-fat'ik, em-fat'ik-al, *a.* Characterized by emphasis; expressive; strong; energetic. **emphatically**, em-fat'i-kal-i, *adv.* With emphasis; strongly; forcibly.

empire, em'pīr, *n.* Supreme power in governing; sway; dominion of an emperor; region over which dominion is extended.

empiric, em-pir'ik, *n.* One whose knowledge is founded exclusively on experience; a quack; a charlatan. **empirical**, em-pir'i-kal, *a.* Pertaining to or derived from experience; relying on experience without due regard to theory. **empiricism**, em-pir'i-sizm, *n.* Methods or practice of an empiric; quackery; doctrine that knowledge comes solely from experience.

employ, em-ploi', *vt.* To occupy; to engage in one's service; to keep at work; to make use of.—*n.* Business; occupation; engagement. **employee**, em-ploi'ē, *n.* One who works for an employer. **employer**, em-ploi'ėr, *n.* One who employs; one who keeps men in service. **employment**, em-ploi'ment, *n.* Act of employing; office; trade; profession; function.

emporium, em-pō′ri-um, *n.*; pl. **-ia** or **-iums**. A commercial center; a warehouse or store.

empower, em-pou′ér, *vt.* To give legal or moral power to; to authorize.

empress, em′pres, *n.* The consort of an emperor; a female invested with imperial power.

empty, emp′ti, *a.* Containing nothing, or nothing but air; void; unsatisfactory; unburdened; hungry; vacant of head.— *vt.* (emptying, emptied). To make empty.—*vi.* To become empty.—*n.* An empty packing case, &c.

empyreal, em-pir′ē-al, or em′pi-rē″al, *a.* Formed of pure fire or light; pertaining to the highest region of heaven. **empyrean**, em′pi-rē″an, em′pi-rē″an, *a.* The highest heaven.

emu, emen, ē-mū′, *n.* A large Australian bird, allied to the ostrich and cassowary.

emulate, em′ū-lāt, *vt.* (emulating, emulated). To strive to equal or excel; to vie with. **emulation**, em′ū-lā″shun, *n.* Act of emulating; rivalry; envy.

emulsion, ē-mul′shun, *n.* A soft liquid remedy resembling milk; any milk-like mixture. **emulsive**, ē-mul′siv, *a.* Milk-like; softening; yielding a milk-like substance.

enable, en-ā′bl, *vt.* (enabling, enabled). To make able; to empower; to authorize.

enact, en-akt′, *vt.* To establish by law; to decree; to perform; to act. **enactive**, en-ak′tiv, *a.* Having power to enact or establish as a law. **enactment**, en-akt′ment, *n.* The passing of a bill into a law; a decree; an act.

enamel, en-am′el, *n.* A substance of the nature of glass, used as a coating; that which is enamelled; a smooth glossy surface of various colors; the smooth substance on a tooth.—*vt.* (enameling, enameled). To lay enamel on; to paint in enamel; to form a surface like enamel; to adorn with different colors.—*vi.* To practice the art of enameling.

enamor, en-am′ér, *vt.* To inspire with love; to charm; to fill with delight.

encamp, en-kamp′, *vi.* To take up position in a camp; to make a camp.—*vt.* To form into or place in a camp. **encampment**, en-kamp′ment, *n.* Act of encamping; a camp.

encephalic, en′sē-fal″ik, *a.* Belonging to the encephalon or brain. **encephalon**, en-sef′a-lon, *n.* The contents of the skull, the brain.

enchain, en-chān′, *vt.* To fasten with a chain; to hold in bondage; to confine.

enchant, en-chant′, *vt.* To practice sorcery on; to charm; to enrapture; to fascinate. **enchanted**, en-chan′ted, *p.a.* Affected by sorcery; delighted beyond measure. **enchanter**, en-chan′tér, *n.* A sorcerer; one who charms or delights. **enchanting**, en-chan′ting, *p.a.* Charming; delighting; ravishing. **enchantment**, en-chant′ment, *n.* Act of enchanting; incantation; magic; overpowering influence of delight; fascination.

enchantress, en-chan′tres, *a.* A female enchanter; a sorceress.

encircle, en-sér′kl, *vt.* To enclose with a circle; to encompass; to embrace.

enclave, en′klāv or äng-kläv′, *n.* A place surrounded entirely by the territories of another power.

enclose, en-klōz′, *vt.* To inclose. **enclosure**, en-klō′zhér, *n.* Inclosure.

encomium, en-kō′mi-um, *n.*; pl. **-iums**. Panegyric; eulogy; praise. **encomiast**, en-kō′mi-ast, *n.* One who praises another; a panegyrist. **encomiastic, encomiastical**, en-kō′mi-as″tik, en-kō′mi-as″tik-al, *a.* Containing encomium; bestowing praise; laudatory.

encompass, en-kum′pas, *vt.* To encircle; to hem in; to go or sail round.

encore, äng′kōr, *n.* Again; once more; a call for a repetition of a performance. —*vt.* (encoring, encored). To call for a repetition of a.

encounter, en-koun′tér, *n.* A meeting in contest; a conflict; a meeting; controversy; debate.—*vt.* To meet face to face; to meet suddenly; to strive against. —*vi.* To meet unexpectedly; to conflict.

encourage, en-kur′ij, *vt.* (encouraging, encouraged). To give courage to; to stimulate; to embolden; to countenance. **encouragement**, en-kur′ij-ment, *n.* Act of encouraging; incentive; favor. **encouraging**, en-kur′ij-ing, *p.a.* Furnishing ground to hope for success.

encroach, en-krōch′, *vi.* To trespass on the rights and possessions of another; to intrude; to infringe; with *on* or *upon*. **encroacher**, en-krōch′ér, *n.* One who encroaches. **encroachment**, en-krōch′ment, *n.* Act of encroaching.

encrust, en-krust′, *vt.* To cover with a crust.

encumber, en-kum′bér, *vt.* To impede the motion of with a load; to embarrass; to load with debts or legal claims. **encumbrance**, en-kum′brans, *n.* That which encumbers; burden; hindrance; legal claims or liabilities; mortgage.

encyclic, encyclical, en-sik′lik, en-sik′li-kal, *a.* Sent to many persons or places; circular.—*n.* A letter on some important occasion sent by the pope to the bishops.

encyclopædia, encyclopedia, en-sī′klō-pē″di-a, *n.* A collection, usually alphabetical, of articles on one or more branches of knowledge.

encyclopædic, encyclopedic, en-sī′klō-pē″dik, *a.* Pertaining to an encyclopædia; universal as regards information.

end, end, *n.* The extreme point; the last part; final state; completion; close of life; death; issue; result; aim; drift.— *vt.* To bring to an end; to conclude; to destroy.—*vi.* To come to an end; to close; to cease.

endanger, en-dān′jér, *vt.* To bring into danger; to expose to loss or injury.

endear, en-dēr′, *vt.* To make dear; to make more beloved. **endearing**, en-dēr′ing, *p.a.* Making dear or more beloved; exciting affection. **endearment**, en-dēr′ment, *n.* The act of endearing; tender affection; a caress.

endeavor, endeavour, en-dev'ẽr, *n.* Effort; attempt; exertion; essay; aim.—*vi.* To try; to strive; to aim.—*vt.* To try to effect; to strive after.

endemic, endemical, en-dem'ik, en-dem'ik-al, *a.* Peculiar to a people or region, as a disease.—*n.* A disease of endemic nature.

ending, en'ding, *n.* Termination.

endive, en'div, *n.* A plant allied to chicory; garden succory.

endless, end'les, *a.* Without end; everlasting; infinite; incessant. **endlessly,** end'les-li, *adv.* Incessantly. **endlong,** end'long, *adv.* With the end forward; lengthwise.

endorse, en-dors', *vt.* (endorsing, endorsed). To write on the back of, as one's name on a bill; to assign by endorsement; to ratify. **endorsement,** en-dors'ment, *n.* The act of endorsing; a docket; signature of one who endorses; sanction or approval.

endow, en-dou', *vt.* To settle a dower on; to enrich or furnish, as with any gift, quality, or faculty; to endue; to invest. **endowment,** en-dou'ment, *n.* Act of endowing; revenue permanently appropriated to any object; natural capacity.

endure, en-dūr', *vi.* (enduring, endured). To continue in the same state; to last; to abide; to submit.—*vt.* To sustain; to bear; to undergo; to tolerate. **enduring,** en-dūr'ing, *p.a.* Lasting long; permanent. **endurable,** en-dūr'a-bl, *a.* That can be endured. **endurance,** en-dūr'ans, *n.* State of enduring; continuance; patience; fortitude.

endwise, end'wīz, *adv.* In an upright position; with the end forward.

enema, en'e-ma, *n.* A liquid or gaseous medicine injected into the rectum; a clyster.

enemy, en'e-mi, *n.* One who is unfriendly; an antagonist; a hostile army.

energy, en'ẽr-ji, *n.* Inherent power to operate or act; power exerted; force; vigor; strength of expression; emphasis. **energetic, energetical,** en'ẽr-jet'ik, en'ẽr-jet'i-kal, *a.* Acting with energy; forcible; potent; active; vigorous. **energetically,** en'ẽr-jet'i-kal-li, *adv.* With energy and effect.

energize, en'ẽr-jīz, *vi.* (energizing, energized). To act with energy.—*vt.* To give energy to.

enervate, en'ẽr-vāt or ē-nẽr'vāt, *vt.* (enervating, enervated). To deprive of strength or force; to unnerve; to debilitate. **enervation,** en'ẽr-vā"shun, *n.* Act of enervating; state of being enervated; effeminacy.

enfeeble, en-fē'bl, *vt.* (enfeebling, enfeebled). To make feeble; to weaken. **enfeeblement,** en-fē'bl-ment, *n.* The act of weakening; enervation.

enfilade, en-fi-lād', *vt.* (enfilading, enfiladed). To rake with shot through the whole length of a line or work; to fire in the flank of.—*n.* A firing in such a manner; the line of fire.

enforce, en-fōrs', *vt.* To urge with energy; to impress on the mind; to compel; to put in execution. **enforceable,**

enforcible, en-fōrs'a-bl, en-fōrs'i-bl, *a.* Capable of being enforced. **enforcement,** en-fōrs'ment, *n.* Act of enforcing; compulsion; a giving of force or effect to; a putting in execution, as law.

enfranchise, en-fran'chiz, *vt.* (enfranchising, enfranchised). To set free; to admit to the privileges of a citizen; to endow with the franchise. **enfranchisement,** en-fran'chiz-ment, *n.* Act of enfranchising; state of being enfranchised.

engage, en-gāj', *vt.* (engaging, engaged). To bind by pledge or contract; to attach; to attract; to attack.—*vi.* To bind one's self; to embark on any business; to begin to fight. **engaged,** en-gājd', *p.a.* Pledged; affianced; attached to a wall (said of a column). **engagement,** en-gāj'ment, *n.* Act of engaging; obligation; betrothal; avocation; business; conflict; battle. **engaging,** en-gāj'ing, *p.a.* Winning; attractive; pleasing.

engender, en-jen'dẽr, *vt.* To breed; to beget; to occasion.—*vi.* To be caused or produced.

engine, en'jin, *n.* Any instrument in some degree complicated; a machine to drive machinery, to propel vessels, railway trains, &c.—*vt.* (engining, engined). To furnish with an engine or engines. **engineer,** en'ji-nēr", *n.* One who constructs or manages engines; one who plans works for offense or defense; one who constructs roads, railways, &c.—*vt.* To direct the making of in the capacity of engineer. **engineering,** en'ji-nēr"ing, *n.* The art or business of an engineer.

engird, en-gẽrd', *vt.* To gird round; to encircle.

English, ing'glish, *a.* Belonging to England, or to its inhabitants.—*n.* The people or language of England.—*vt.* To translate into English.

engraft, en-graft', *vt.* To ingraft.

engrain, en-grān', *vt.* To dye with grain; to dye deep; to paint in imitation of wood.

engrave, en-grāv', *vt.* (engraving, engraved). To cut figures on with a burin; to represent by incisions; to imprint; to impress deeply. **engraver,** en-grāv'ẽr, *n.* One who engraves; a cutter of figures on metal, wood, &c. **engraving,** en-grāv'ing, *n.* Act or art of engraving; an engraved plate; an impression from an engraved plate.

engross, en-grōs', *vt.* To take up the whole of; to occupy, engage; to write a correct copy in legible characters; to take in undue quantities or degrees.—*vi.* To be employed in making fair copies of writings. **engrosser,** en-grōs'ẽr, *n.* One who engrosses. **engrossment,** en-grōs'ment, *n.* Act of engrossing; state of being engrossed; exorbitant acquisition; copy of a deed in clear writing.

engulf, en-gulf', *vt.* To ingulf; to swallow up.

enhance, en-hans', *vt.* (enhancing, enhanced). To raise to a higher point; to increase; to aggravate.—*vi.* To grow larger. **enhancement,** en-hans'ment, *n.* Act of enhancing; rise; augmentation.

enigma, ē-nig'ma, *n.* An obscure statement or question; riddle; anything inexplicable. **enigmatic, enigmatical**, ē-nig-mat'ik, ē-nig-mat'i-kal, *a.* Relating to or containing an enigma; obscure; ambiguous.

enjoin, en-join', *vt.* To order with urgency; to admonish; to prescribe.

enjoy, en-joi', *vt.* To feel gladness in; to have, use, or perceive with pleasure. **enjoyable**, en-joi'a-bl, *a.* Capable of being enjoyed. **enjoyment**, en-joi'ment, *n.* State of enjoying; pleasure; satisfaction; fruition.

enlarge, en-lärj', *vt.* (enlarging, enlarged). To make large or larger; to set free.—*vi.* To grow large or larger; to expatiate. **enlarged**, en-lärjd', *p.a.* Not narrow nor confined; broad; comprehensive; liberal. **enlargement**, en-lärj'ment, *n.* Act of enlarging; state of being enlarged; expansion; release; addition.

enlighten, en-lit'en, *vt.* To make clear; to enable to see more clearly; to instruct. **enlightened**, en-lit'end, *p.a.* Instructed; informed; unprejudiced. **enlightener**, en-lit'en-ėr, *n.* One who or that which enlightens or illuminates. **enlightenment**, en-lit'en-ment, *n.* Act of enlightening; state of being enlightened.

enlist, en-list', *vt.* To enter on a list; to engage in public service, especially military; to engage the services of.—*vi.* To engage voluntarily in public service; to enter heartily into a cause. **enlistment**, en-list'ment, *n.* Act of enlisting; voluntary engagement to serve as a soldier or sailor.

enliven, en-liv'en, *vt.* To give life or vivacity to; to gladden; to invigorate. **enlivener**, en-liv'en-ėr, *n.* One who or that which enlivens or animates.

en masse, en mas'. In a body; as a whole.

enmesh, en-mesh', *vt.* To entangle in the meshes of a net, &c.

enmity, en'mi-ti, *n.* Quality of being an enemy; hostility; ill-will; opposition.

ennoble, en-nō'bl, *vt.* (ennobling, ennobled). To make noble; to exalt; to dignify.

ennui, än-wē, *n.* Dullness of spirit; weariness; listlessness; tedium.

enormity, ē-nor'mi-ti, *n.* State or quality of being enormous; depravity; atrocity. **enormous**, ē-nor'mus, *a.* Great beyond the common measure; huge; outrageous. **enormously**, ē-nor'mus-li, *adv.* Excessively.

enough, ē-nuf', *a.* That satisfies desire; that may answer the purpose.—*n.* A sufficiency; that which is equal to the powers or abilities.—*adv.* Sufficiently; tolerably.

enow, ē-nou'. An old form of *enough.*

enrage, en-rāj', *vt.* To excite rage in; to incense.

enrapture, en-rap'tūr, *vt.* To transport with rapture; to delight beyond measure.

enrich, en-rich', *vt.* To make rich; to fertilize; to supply with an abundance of anything desirable; to adorn. **en-**

richment, en-rich'ment, *n.* Act of enriching; something that enriches.

enroll, enrol, en-rōl', *vt.* To write in a roll or register; to record. **enrollment**, en-rōl'ment, *n.* Act of enrolling; a register; a record.

ensconce, en-skons', *vt.* To cover, as with a sconce; to protect; to hide.

ensemble, än'som-bl, *n.* All parts of a thing considered together; general effect.

enshrine, en-shrīn', *vt.* To enclose in a shrine or chest; to cherish.

enshroud, en-shrou'd, *vt.* To cover with a shroud; to envelop.

ensign, en'sīn, *n.* A mark of distinction; the flag of a company of soldiers or a vessel; the lowest commissioned officer. **ensigncy, ensignship**, en'sīn-si, en'-sīn-ship, *n.* Rank or commission of an ensign.

ensilage, en'si-lāj, *n.* A mode of storing green fodder, vegetables, &c., by burying in pits or silos.

enslave, en-slāv', *vt.* (enslaving, enslaved). To reduce to slavery; to overpower. **enslavement**, en-slāv'ment, *n.* Act of enslaving; slavery; servitude. **enslaver**, en-slāv'ėr, *n.* One who enslaves.

ensnare, en-snār', *vt.* To entrap; to insnare.

ensue, en-sū', *vi.* (ensuing, ensued). To follow as a consequence; to succeed.

ensure, en-shōr', *vt.* To make sure.

entail, en-tāl', *vt.* To cut off an estate from the heirs general; to settle, as the descent of lands by gift to a man and to certain heirs; to devolve as a consequence or of necessity.—*n.* The act of entailing; an estate entailed; rule of descent settled for an estate. **entailment**, en-tāl'ment, *n.* Act of entailing; state of being entailed.

entangle, en-tang'gl, *vt.* To knit or interweave confusedly; to involve; to hamper. **entanglement**, en-tang'gl-ment, *n.* Act of entangling; state of being entangled.

enter, en'tėr, *vt.* To go or come into; to begin; to set down in writing; to register; to take possession of.—*vi.* To go or come in; begin; engage in; be an ingredient in.

enterprise, en'tėr-prīz, *n.* That which is undertaken; a bold or hazardous attempt; adventurous spirit; hardihood.— *vt.* To undertake. **enterprising**, en'-tėr-prīz'ing, *a.* Bold or prompt to attempt; venturesome.

entertain, en-tėr-tān', *vt.* To receive as a guest; to cherish; to treat with conversation; to please; to admit, with a view to consider.—*vi.* To give entertainments. **entertaining**, en-tėr-tān'ing, *p.a.* Pleasing; amusing; diverting. **entertainment**, en-tėr-tān'ment, *n.* Act of entertaining; hospitable treatment; a festival; amusement.

enthrall, enthral, en-thral', *vt.* To reduce to the condition of a thrall; to enslave.

enthrone, en-thrōn', *vt.* (enthroning, enthroned). To place on a throne.

enthusiasm, en-thū'zi-azm, *n.* An ecstasy of mind, as if from divine or spiritual influence; ardent zeal; elevation of fancy. **enthusiast**, en-thū'zi-ast, *n.* One possessed of enthusiasm; a person of ardent zeal; one of elevated fancy. **enthusiastic**, en-thū'zi-as"tik, *a.* Filled with enthusiasm; ardent; devoted; visionary. **enthusiastically**, en-thū'zi-as"tik-al-li, *adv.* With enthusiasm.

entice, en-tīs', *vt.* (enticing, enticed). To draw on, by exciting hope or desire; to allure. **enticement**, en-tīs'ment, *n.* Act or means of enticing; blandishment; wile. **enticing**, en-tīs'ing, *p.a.* Having the qualities that entice; fascinating. **enticingly**, en-tīs'ing-li, *adv.* Charmingly.

entire, en-tīr', *a.* Whole; unshared; complete; sincere; hearty; in full strength. **entirely**, en-tīr'li, *adv.* Wholly; fully.

entitle, en-tī'tl, *vt.* (entitling, entitled). To give a title to; to style; to characterize; to give a claim to; to qualify.

entity, en'ti-ti, *n.* Being; essence; existence.

entomb, en-töm', *vt.* To deposit in a tomb; to bury; to inter. **entombment**, en-töm'ment, *n.* Burial.

entomologist, en-tō-mol'ō-jist, *n.* One versed in the science of insects.

entomology, en-tō-mol'ō-ji, *n.* That branch of zoology which treats of the structure, habits and classification of insects.

entourage, än'tu-räzh, *n.* Attendants; retinue.

entrail, en'trāl, *n.* One of the intestines; generally in *pl.*; the bowels.

entrance, en'trans, *n.* Act or power of entering into a place; the door or avenue by which a place may be entered; beginning; act of taking possession.

entrance, en-trans', *vt.* To put in a trance or ecstasy; to enrapture; to transport.

entrant, en'trant, *n.* One who enters.

entrap, en-trap', *vt.* To catch in a trap; to inveigle; to decoy.

entreat, en-trēt', *vt.* To beg earnestly; to beseech; to supplicate.—*vi.* To make an earnest request; to pray. **entreatingly**, en-trēt'ing-li, *adv.* In an entreating manner. **entreaty**, en-trēt'i, *n.* Urgent prayer; earnest petition; solicitation.

entrée, än-trā, *n.* Freedom of access; a dish served at a table.

entrench, en-trench', *vt.* Same as *intrench*.

entry, en'tri, *n.* Act of entering; entrance; the passage by which persons enter a house; act of taking possession of lands, &c.; act of committing to writing.

entwine, en-twīn', *vt.* To twine; to twist round; to intwine.

enumerate, ē-nū'mer-āt, *vt.* (enumerating, enumerated). To count number by number; to reckon or mention a number of things, each separately. **enumeration**, ē-nū'mer-ā"shun, *n.* Act of enumerating; detailed account; a summing up.

enunciate, e-nun'si-āt, *vt.* (enunciating, enunciated). To utter; to pronounce; to proclaim. **enunciation**, ē-nun'si-ā"shun, *n.* Act or manner of enunciating; expression; declaration; public attestation.

envelop, en-vel'up, *vt.* To cover by wrapping or folding; to lie around and conceal. **envelope**, en've-lōp, *n.* That which infolds; a wrapper; a covering for a letter, &c.; an investing integument. **envelopment**, en-vel'up-ment, *n.* The act of enveloping; that which envelops.

envenom, en-ven'um, *vt.* To poison; to taint with malice; to exasperate.

enviable, en'vi-a-bl, *a.* Exciting or capable of envy.

envious, en'vi-us, *a.* Feeling or harboring envy; tinctured with or excited by envy.

environ, en-vī'run, *vt.* To encompass; to encircle; to besiege; to invest. **environment**, en-vī'run-ment, *n.* Act of environing; state of being environed; that which environs; conditions under which one lives. **environs**, en-vī'runz, *n.pl.* Neighborhood; vicinity.

envisage, en-vis'ij, *vt.* To look in the face of; to apprehend directly or by intuition.

envoy, en'voi, *n.* One sent on a mission; a person next in rank to an ambassador; deputed to transact business with a foreign power.

envy, en'vi, *n.* Pain or discontent excited by another's superiority or success; malice; object of envy.—*vt.* (envying, envied). To feel envy towards or on account of; to begrudge.—*vi.* To be affected with envy.

epaulet, **epaulette**, e'pal-et, *n.* A shoulder knot; a badge worn on the shoulder by military men or naval officers.

ephemera, e-fem'er-a, *n.pl.* -ræ. A fly that lives one day only; a short-lived insect. **ephemeral**, e-fem'er-al, *a.* Continuing one day only; short-lived; fleeting.

epic, ep'ik, *a.* Composed in a lofty narrative style; heroic.—*n.* A poem of elevated character, describing the exploits of heroes.

epicure, ep'i-kūr, *n.* One devoted to sensual enjoyments; a voluptuary. **epicurean**, ep'i-kū-rē'an, *a.* Luxurious; given to luxury.—*n.* A follower of Epicurus; a luxurious eater; an epicure.

epidemic, **epidemical**, ep-i-dem'ik, ep-i-dem'i-kal, *a.* Affecting a whole community, as a disease; prevalent. **epidemic**, ep-i-dem'ik, *n.* A disease which attacks many people at the same period.

epidermis, ep-i-dėr'mis, *n.* The cuticle or scarf-skin of the body; the exterior coating of the leaf or stem of a plant.

epiglottis, ep-i-glot'is, *n.* The cartilage at the root of the tongue that covers the glottis during the act of swallowing.

epigram, ep'i-gram, *n.* A short poem, usually keenly satirical; a pointed or antithetical saying. **epigrammatic**, **epigrammatical**, ep'i-gra-mat"ik, ep'i-gra-mat"i-kal, *a.* Pertaining to epigrams; like an epigram; pointed.

epigraph, ep'i-graf, *n*. An inscription; quotation; motto.

epilepsy, ep'i-lep'si, *n*. The falling-sickness; a disease characterized by spasms and loss of sense. **epileptic**, ep'i-lep"tik, *a*. Pertaining to epilepsy.—*n*. One affected with epilepsy.

epilogue, ep'i-log, *n*. A speech or short poem spoken by an actor at the end of a play.

Epiphany, ē-pif'a-ni, *n*. A church festival on 6th January celebrating the Manifestation of Christ to the wise men of the East.

episcopacy, ē-pis'kō-pa-si, *n*. Ecclesiastical government by bishops; the collective body of bishops.

episcopal, ē-pis'kō-pal, *a*. Belonging to or vested in bishops. **episcopalian**, ē-pis'kō-pā"li-an, *a*. Pertaining to bishops, or government by bishops.—*n*. One who belongs to an episcopal church. **episcopate**, ē-pis'kō-pāt, *n*. A bishopric; the collective body of bishops.

episode, ep'i-sōd, *n*. A separate story introduced to give greater variety to the events related in a poem, &c.; an incident. **episodic**, **episodical**, ep'i-sod"ik, ep'i-sod"i-kal, *a*. Pertaining to an episode; contained in an episode.

epistle, ē-pis'l, *n*. A writing communicating intelligence to a distant person; a letter. **epistolary**, ē-pis'tō-ler'i, *a*. Pertaining to epistles; suitable to correspondence.

epitaph, ep'i-taf, *n*. That which is written on a tomb; an inscription, or a couplet in honor of the dead.

epithet, ep'i-thet, *n*. Any word implying a quality attached to a person or thing.

epitome, e-pit'ō-mi, *n*. A brief summary; abridgment; compendium. **epitomize**, e-pit'ō-mīz, *vt*. To make an epitome of; to abstract; to condense.

epoch, ep'ok, *n*. A fixed point of time, from which years are numbered; period; era; date.

Epsom salt, ep'sum salt, *n*. The sulphate of magnesia cathartic.

equable, ēk'wa-bl, *a*. Uniform; even; steady. **equably**, ēk'wa-bli, *adv*. In an equable or uniform manner. **equability**, ēk-wa-bil'i-ti, *n*. State or quality of being equable.

equal, ē'kwal, *a*. The same in extent, number, degree, rank, &c.; same in qualities; uniform; proportionate; adequate; just.—*n*. One not inferior or superior to another.—*vt*. (equaling, equaled). To make equal to; to become or be equal to. **equality**, ē-kwal'i-ti, *n*. State or quality of being equal; likeness; evenness; plainness. **equalization**, ē'kwal-ī-zā"shun, *n*. Act of equalizing; state of being equalized. **equalize**, ē'kwal-īz, *vt*. (equalizing, equalized). To make equal, even, or uniform. **equally**, ē'kwal-i, *adv*. In an equal manner; alike; impartially.

equanimity, ē'kwa-nim"i-ti or ek-, *n*. Evenness of mind; steadiness of temper.

equate, ē-kwāt', *vt*. (equating, equated). To make equal; to reduce to

an equation; to reduce to mean time or motion.

equation, ē-kwā'zhun, *n*. The act of equating; an expression asserting the equality of two quantities; a quantity to be taken into account in order to give a true result.

equator, e-kwā'tèr, *n*. The great circle of our globe which divides it into the northern and southern hemispheres; a circle in the heavens coinciding with the plane of the earth's equator. **equatorial**, ē'kwa-tō"ri-al, *a*. Pertaining to the equator.—*n*. An astronomical instrument.

equestrian, ē-kwes'tri-an, *a*. Pertaining to horses or horsemanship; on horseback; skilled in horsemanship.—*n*. A horseman.

equidistant, ē'kwi-dis"tant or ek-, *a*. Being at an equal distance from.

equilateral, ē'kwi-lat"ēr-al or ek-, *a*. Having all the sides equal.

equilibrium, ē'kwi-lib"ri-um or ek-, *n*. State of rest produced by the counteraction of forces; balance.

equine, ē-kwin', *a*. Pertaining to a horse; denoting the horse kind.

equinoctial, ē-kwi-nok'shal or ek-, *a*. Pertaining to the equinoxes.—*n*. The celestial equator: when the sun is on it, the days and nights are of equal length.

equinox, ē'kwi-noks or ek'-, *n*. The time when the day and night are of equal length, about 21st March and 23rd September.

equip, ē-kwip', *vt*. (equipping, equipped). To fit out or furnish, as for war; to dress; to array. **equipage**, ek'wi-pij, *n*. An equipment; retinue; carriage of state and attendants; accouterments. **equipment**, ē-kwip'ment, *n*. Act of equipping; habiliments; warlike apparatus; necessary adjuncts.

equipoise, ē'kwi-poiz or ek'-, *n*. Equality of weights or force; equilibrium.

equitable, ek'wi-ta-bl, *a*. Distributing equal justice; just; upright; impartial. **equitably**, ek'wi-ta-bli, *adv*. In an equitable manner; justly; impartially. **equity**, ek'wi-ti, *n*. The giving to each man his due; impartiality; uprightness; a system of supplemental law founded upon precedents and established principles.

equivalence, ē-kwiv'a-lens or ek-, *n*. State of being equivalent; equality of value.

equivalent, ē-kwiv'a-lent or ek-, *a*. Equal in excellence, worth, or weight; of the same inport or meaning.—*n*. That which is equal in value, &c.; compensation.

equivocal, ē-kwiv'ō-kal, *a*. Capable of a double interpretation; doubtful. **equivocate**, ē-kwiv'ō-kāt, *vi*. To use ambiguous expressions to mislead; to quibble. **equivocation**, ē-kwiv'ō-kā"shun, *n*. Act of equivocation; ambiguity.

era, ē'ra, *n*. A fixed point of time, from which years are counted; epoch; age.

eradicate, ē-ra'di-kāt, *vt*. To root out; to destroy; to exterminate. **eradication**, ē-ra'di-kā"shun, *n*. Act of eradicating; total destruction.

erase, ē-rās', *vt.* (erasing, erased). To scrape out; to efface; to expunge.

erasement, ē-rās'ment, *n.* A rubbing out.

eraser, ē-rās'ėr, *n.* One who erases; an appliance to erase writing, &c. **erasure**, ē-rā'zhėr, *n.* Act of erasing; obliteration.

ere, ār, *adv.*, *conj.*, and *prep.* Before; sooner than.

erect, ē-rekt', *a.* Upright; bold; undismayed.—*vt.* To raise and set upright; to build; to found; to cheer.

erection, ē-rek'shun, *n.* Act of erecting; formation; anything erected; structure.

erelong, ār'long, *adv.* Before long.

erenow, ār'nou, *adv.* Before this time.

ergo, ėr'gō, *adv.* Therefore.

ergot, ėr'got, *n.* A disease of rye and other grasses; this diseased growth, used in medicine.

ermine, ėr'min, *n.* An animal of the weasel kind, a native of N. Europe and America, valued for its white fur; the fur of the ermine.

erode, ē-rōd', *vt.* (eroding, eroded). To gnaw off or away; to corrode. **erosion**, ē-rō'zhon, *n.* Act of eroding; state of being eaten away; corrosion.

erotic, ē-rot'ik, *a.* Pertaining to or prompted by love; treating of love.

err, ėr, *vi.* To wander; to stray; to depart from rectitude; to blunder.

errand, er'and, *n.* A message; mandate; business to be transacted by a messenger.

errant, er'ant, *a.* Roving; wandering about in search of adventures. **errantry**, er'ant-ri, *n.* A wandering state; a roving or rambling; the employment of a knight-errant.

erratic, e-rat'ik, *a.* Wandering; irregular; eccentric.

erratum, e-rā'tum, *n.*; pl. **-ata.** An error or mistake in writing or printing.

error, er'ėr, *n.* A deviation from truth or what is right; a mistake; a blunder; fault; offense. **erroneous**, e-rō'nē-us, *a.* Characterized by or containing error; wrong; mistaken.

Erse, ėrs, *n.* The Celtic language of the Highlands of Scotland; Gaelic.

erst, ėrst, *adv.* At first; long ago; hitherto.

erudite, er'ō-dīt, *a.* Fully instructed; deeply read; learned. **erudition**, er'ō-di"shun, *n.* Learning; knowledge gained by study; scholarship.

erupt, ē-rupt', *vt.* To throw out by volcanic action. **eruption**, ē-rup'shun, *n.* A breaking forth; a violent emission; a sudden hostile excursion; a breaking out of pimples, pustules, &c.

erysipelas, er'i-sip"e-las, *n.* A disease accompanied by fever and an eruption of a fiery acrid humor, chiefly on the face.

escalator, es-kā-lā'tėr, *n.* A moving stairway on the endless chain principle.

escallop, es-kol'lup, *n.* A bivalve shell; a scallop.

escapade, es'ka-pād", *n.* A runaway adventure; a freak; a mad prank.

escape, es-kāp', *vt.* (escaping, escaped). To get out of the way of; to pass without harm; to pass unobserved; to avoid.

—*vi.* To be free; to avoid; to regain one's liberty.—*n.* Flight, to shun danger; an evasion of legal restraint or custody. **escapement**, es-kāp'ment, *n.* Means of escaping; that part of a time-piece by which the circular motion of the wheels is converted into a vibrating one.

escarp, es-kärp', *vt.* To form into a scarp; to make to slope suddenly.—*n.* A sudden slope. **escarpment**, es-kärp'ment, *n.* A steep declivity; ground cut away nearly vertically.

eschew, es-chō', *vt.* To shun; to avoid.

escort, es'kort, *n.* A guard attending an officer or baggage, &c.; persons attending as a mark of honor.—*vt.* es-kort'. To attend and guard.

escrow, es'krō", *n.* Written agreement or deed placed in custody as bond.

escutcheon, es-kuch'un, *n.* A shield; the shield on which a coat of arms is represented.

Eskimo, es'ki-mō, *n.* A mongoloid people indigenous to Arctic regions of North America, Greenland, and parts of Siberia.

esophagus, ē-sof'a-gus, *n.* The gullet; the canal through which food and drink pass to the stomach.

esoteric, es-ō-te'rik, *a.* Taught to a select few; private; select.

especial, es-pesh'al, *a.* Distinct; chief; special. **especially**, es-pesh'al-li, *adv.* In an uncommon degree; specially.

espionage, es'pi-o-nij, *n.* Practice or employment of spies; practice of watching others without being suspected.

esplanade, es'pla-nād", *n.* An open space between the glacis of a citadel and the houses of the town; any level space near a town for walks or drives; a terrace by the sea-side.

espousal, es-pouz'al, *n.* Betrothal; nuptials; in this sense generally in *pl.*; the adopting of a cause.

espouse, es-pouz', *vt.* (espousing, espoused). To give or take in marriage; to betroth; to wed; to embrace or adopt; to uphold.

esprit, es-prē, *n.* Soul; spirit; mind; wit.

espy, es-pī', *vt.* (espying, espied). To see at a distance; to descry; to discover.

esquire, es-kwīr', *n.* A shield-bearer; a title of dignity next to a knight; a title of courtesy.—*vt.* To attend; to await on.

essay, es-ā', *vt.* To try; to make experiment of.—*n.* es'sā. An endeavor or experiment; a literary composition to prove or illustrate a particular subject; a short treatise. **essayist**, es'ā-ist, *n.* A writer of an essay or essays.

essence, es'ens, *n.* The nature, substance, or being of anything; predominant qualities of a plant or drug; an extract; perfume; fundamental doctrines, facts, &c., of a statement, &c.—*vt.* To perfume; to scent. **essential**, e-sen'shal, *a.* Relating to or containing the essence; necessary to the existence of; indispensable; highly rectified; volatile; diffusible (oils).—*n.* Something necessary; the chief point; constituent principle.

establish, es-tab'lish, *vt.* To make stable; to found permanently; to institute; to enact; to sanction; to confirm; to make good. **established**, es-tab'-lisht, *p.a.* Ratified; confirmed; set up and supported by the state. **establishment**, es-tab'lish-ment, *n.* Act of establishing; state of being established; confirmation; sanction; that which is established; a civil or military force or organization; form of doctrine and church government established under state control; place of residence or business; the number of men in a regiment, &c.

estate, es-tāt', *n.* State; condition; rank; landed property; possessions; an order or class of men in the body politic.

esteem, es-tēm', *vt.* To set a value on; to regard with respect; to prize.—*n.* Judgment of merit or demerit; estimation; great regard.

esthete, **esthetic**, &c. See **æsthete**, &c.

estimate, es'ti-māt, *vt.* (estimating, estimated). To form an opinion regarding; to calculate; to appraise; to esteem. —*n.* Valuation; calculation of probable cost. **estimation**, es-ti-mā'shun, *n.* Act of estimating; valuation; opinion; esteem. **estimable**, es'ti-ma-bl, *a.* Capable of being estimated; worthy of esteem or respect.

estrange, es-trānj', *vt.* (estranging, estranged). To alienate, as the affections. **estrangement**, es-trānj'ment, *n.* Alienation of affection or friendship.

estreat, es-trēt', *n.* In *law*, a true copy of a writing, under which fines are to be levied.—*vt.* To levy (fines) under an estreat.

estuary, es''tū-er'i, *n.* The mouth of a river where the tide meets the current; a firth.

etch, ech, *vt.* To produce designs on a copper or other plate by lines drawn through a thin coating, and then eaten into the plate by a strong acid; to draw finely in ink.—*vi.* To practice etching. **etcher**, ech'ėr, *n.* One who etches. **etching**, ech'ing, *n.* The act or art of the etcher; a mode of engraving; the impression taken from an etched plate.

eternal, ē-tėr'nal, *a.* Everlasting; without beginning or end of existence; unchangeable.—*n.* An appellation of God. **eternally**, ē-tėr'nal-li, *adv.* Forever; unchangeably; without intermission. **eternity**, ē-tėr'ni-ti, *n.* Continuance without beginning or end; duration without end; the state or time after death.

ether, ē'thėr, *n.* The clear upper air; refined air; a hypothetical medium of extreme tenuity universally diffused, and the medium of the transmission of light, heat, &c.; a very light, volatile, and inflammable fluid obtained from alcohol, used as a stimulant and anæsthetic. **ethereal**, ē-thēr'ē-al, *a.* Formed of ether; heavenly; aerial; intangible.

ethic, **ethical**, eth'ik, eth'i-kal, *a.* Relating to morals; treating of morality; delivering precepts of morality. **ethically**, eth'i-kal-li, *adv.* In an ethical manner; according to morality. **ethics**,

eth'iks, *n.* The doctrine of morals; moral philosophy; a system of moral principles.

Ethiop, **Ethiopian**, ē'thi-op, ē'thi-ō''-pi-an, *n.* A native of Ethiopia. **Ethiopic**, ē'thi-op''ik, *n.* The language of Ethiopia.—*a.* Relating to Ethiopia.

ethnic, **ethnical**, eth'nik, eth'ni-kal, *a.* Pertaining to the gentiles; pagan; ethnological. **ethnologic**, **ethnological**, eth'nō-loj''ik, eth'nō-loj''i-kal, *a.* Relating to ethnology. **ethnologist**, eth-nol'o-jist, *n.* One skilled in ethnology; a student of ethnology. **ethnology**, eth-nol'-ō-ji, *n.* That branch of science which treats of the different races of men.

etiquette, et-i-ket', *n.* Forms of ceremony or decorum; social observances.

Etruscan, ē-trus'kan, *a.* Relating to Etruria, an ancient country in Italy.—*n.* A native of ancient Etruria.

etymologic, **etymological**, et'i-mō-loj''ik, et'i-mō-loj''ik-al, *a.* Pertaining to etymology. **etymologist**, et-i-mol'o-jist, *n.* One versed in etymology. **etymology**, et-i-mol'ō-ji, *n.* That part of philology which traces the origin of words; the derivation or history of any word.

eucalyptus, ū'ka-lip''tus, *n.*; pl. **-tuses** or **-ti.** The generic name of some Australian trees of the myrtle order, usually called gum trees.

Eucharist, ū'ka-rist, *n.* The sacrament of the Lord's Supper. **Eucharistic**, **Eucharistical**, ū'ka-ris''tik, ū'ka-ris''-ti-kal, *a.* Pertaining to the Lord's Supper.

euchre, ū'kėr, *n.* A game of cards played by two, three, or four players.

eulogy, ū'lo-ji, *n.* A speech or writing in commendation; praise; panegyric. **eulogist**, ū'lo-jist, *n.* One who eulogizes. **eulogistic**, ū'lo-jis''tik, *a.* Commendatory; full of praise. **eulogium**, ū-lō'ji-um, *n.* Eulogy; encomium. **eulogize**, ū'lo-jiz, *vt.* (eulogizing, eulogized). To praise; to extol.

eunuch, ū'nuk, *n.* A castrated man.

euphemism, ū'fe-mizm, *n.* A mode of speaking by which a delicate word or expression is substituted for one which is offensive; a word or expression so substituted.

euphemistic, ū-fē-mis'tik, *a.* Rendering more decent or delicate in expression.

euphonic, **euphonious**, ū-fōn'ik, ū-fō'-ni-us, *a.* Having euphony; agreeable in sound.

euphony, ū'fō-ni, *n.* An easy, smooth enunciation of sounds; harmony of sound.

Eurasian, ūr-a'zhan, *n.* One born in Hindustan of a native mother and European father.

European, ū-rō-pē'an, *a.* Pertaining to Europe.—*n.* A native of Europe.

euthanasia, ū'tha-nāz''i-a, *n.* An easy death; a putting to death by painless means.

evacuate, ē-vak'ū-āt, *vt.* (evacuating, evacuated). To make empty; to quit; to withdraw from; to discharge. **evacuation**, ē-vak'ū-ā''shun, *n.* Act of evacuating; that which is discharged.

evade, ē-vād', *vt.* (evading, evaded). To avoid by dexterity; to slip away from;

to elude; to baffle.—*vi.* To practice evasion.

evaluate, ĕ-val'ū-āt, *vt.* To value carefully; to ascertain the amount of.

evanesce, ev'a-nes", *vi.* To vanish. **evanescence,** ev'a-nes"ens, *n.* A vanishing away; state of being liable to vanish.

evanescent, ev'a-nes"ent, *a.* Vanishing; fleeting; passing away.

evangel, ĕ-van'jel, *n.* The gospel. **evangelic, evangelical,** ĕ'van-jel"ik, ĕ'van-jel"i-kal, *a.* Pertaining to or according to the gospel; sound in the doctrines of the gospel; fervent and devout. **evangelicism,** ĕ'van-jel"i-sizm, *n.* Evangelical principles. **evangelist,** ĕ-van'je-list, *n.* One of the four writers of the history of Jesus Christ; a preacher of the gospel; a missionary. **evangelize,** ĕ-van'je-līz, *vt.* and *i.* (evangelizing, evangelized). To preach the gospel to and convert.

evaporate, ĕ-vap'ō-rāt, *vi.* (evaporating, evaporated). To pass off in vapor; to exhale; to be wasted.—*vt.* To convert into vapor; to disperse in vapors. **evaporation,** ĕ-vap'ō-rā"shun, *n.* Act of evaporating; conversion of a fluid or solid into vapor.

evasion, ĕ-vā'zhun, *n.* Act of evading; artifice to elude; shift; equivocation. **evasive,** ĕ-vā'siv, *a.* That evades; shuffling; equivocating.

eve, ĕv, *n.* Evening; the evening before a church festival; the period just preceding some event.

even, ĕ'ven, *a.* Level; smooth; equable; on an equality; just; settled; balanced; capable of being divided by 2 without a remainder.—*vt.* To make even or level; to equalize; to balance.—*adv.* Just; exactly; likewise; moreover.—*n.* The evening.

evenhanded, ĕ'ven han'ded, *a.* Impartial.

evening, ĕv'ning, *n.* The close of the day; the decline of anything.—*a.* Being at the close of day.

event, ĕ-vent', *n.* That which happens; an incident; the consequence of anything; issue; result; conclusion. **eventful,** ĕ-vent'fyl, *a.* Full of incidents; producing numerous or great changes. **eventual,** ē-ven'tū-al, *a.* Pertaining to a final issue; happening as a consequence; final; ultimate. **eventuality,** e-ven'tū-al"i-ti, *n.* That which happens; a contingent result. **eventuate,** ē-ven'tū-āt, *vi.* To come to pass.

eventide, ĕ'ven-tīd, *n.* The time of evening.

ever, ev'ẽr, *adv.* At all times; at any time; continually; in any degree.

evergreen, ev'ẽr-grēn', *n.* A plant that always retains its greenness.—*a.* Always green.

everlasting, ev'ẽr-las"ting, *a.* Enduring for ever; eternal.—*n.* Eternity; the Eternal Being; a plant whose flowers endure for many months after being plucked. **everlastingly,** ev'ẽr-las"ting-li, *adv.* Eternally; perpetually; continually.

evermore, ev'ẽr-mōr, *adv.* At all times; eternally.

every, ev'ri, *a.* Each one; all taken separately.

everybody, ev'ri-bod-i, *n.* Every person. **everyday,** ev'ri-dā', *a.* Common; usual. **everyone,** ev'ri-wun', *n.* Every person. **everywhere,** ev'ri-whār', *adv.* In every place; in all places.

evict, ĕ-vikt', *vt.* To dispossess by judicial process; to expel from lands, &c., by law. **eviction,** ĕ-vik'shun, *n.* Act of evicting; expulsion of a tenant.

evidence, ev'i-dens, *n.* That which demonstrates that a fact is so; testimony; proof; witness.—*vt.* To make evident; to prove.

evident, ev'i-dent, *a.* Clear; obvious; plain.

evil, ĕ'vl, *a.* Not good; bad; wrong; unhappy; calamitous.—*n.* That which is not good; anything which produces pain, calamity, &c.; wrong; malady.—*adv.* Not well; ill.

evince, ĕ-vins', *vt.* (evincing, evinced). To show in a clear manner; to manifest. **eviscerate,** ĕ-vis'sẽr-āt, *vt.* To take out the entrails of; to disembowel. **evisceration,** ĕ-vis'sẽr-ā"shun, *n.* Act of eviscerating.

evocation, ev'ō-kā"shun, *n.* A calling forth.

evoke, ĕ-vōk', *vt.* (evoking, evoked). To call forth or out; to summon forth.

evolution, ev-o-lū'shun, *n.* An unfolding; development; extraction of roots in arithmetic and algebra; systematic movement of troops or ships in changing their position; that theory which sees in the history of all things a gradual advance from a rudimentary condition to one more complex and of higher character. **evolutional, evolutionary,** ev-o-lū'shun-al, ev-ō-lū'shun-a-ri, *a.* Pertaining to evolution; produced by or due to evolution. **evolutionist,** ev-o-lū'shun-ist, *n.* and *a.* A believer in the doctrine of evolution.

evolve, ĕ-volv', *vt.* (evolving, evolved). To unfold; to develop; to open and expand.—*vi.* To open or disclose itself.

ewe, ū, *n.* A female sheep.

ewer, ū'ẽr, *n.* A kind of pitcher or vessel for holding water.

exacerbate, eks-as'ẽr-bāt, *vt.* To exasperate; to increase the violence of. **Exacerbation,** eks-as'ẽr-bā"shon, *n.* Increase of malignity; periodical increase of violence in a disease.

exact, eg-zakt', *a.* Strictly accurate; methodical; precise; true.—*vt.* To extort by means of authority; to demand of right; to compel.—*vi.* To practice extortion. **exacting,** eg-zakt'ing, *p.a.* Disposed to exact or claim too much. **exaction,** eg-zak'shun, *n.* Act of exacting; extortion; that which is exacted. **exactitude,** eg-zak'ti-tūd, *n.* Accuracy. **exactly,** eg-zakt'li, *adv.* In an exact manner; precisely; nicely; accurately. **exaggerate,** eg-zaj'ẽr-āt, *vt.* (exaggerating, exaggerated). To increase beyond due limits; to depict extravagantly. **exaggeration,** eg-zaj'ẽr-ā"shun, *n.* Representation of things beyond the truth. **exalt,** eg-zalt', *vt.* To raise high; to raise to power or dignity; to extol. **exalta-**

tion, eg'zal-tā"shun, *n.* Elevation to power, office, &c.; elevated estate.

examine, eg-zam'in, *vt.* (examining, examined). To inspect carefully; to inquire into; to interrogate, as a witness, a student, &c.; to discuss. **examination,** eg-zam'i-nā"shun, *n.* Act of examining; inquiry into facts, &c., by interrogation; scrutiny by study. **examiner,** eg-zam'in-èr, *n.* One who examines. **examining,** eg-zam'in-ing, *p.a.* Having power to examine; appointed to examine.

example, eg-zam'pl, *n.* A sample; pattern; model; precedent; instance.

exasperate, eg-zas'pèr-āt, *vt.* (exasperating, exasperated). To irritate; to enrage; to make worse; to aggravate. **exasperation,** eg-zas'pèr-ā"shun, *n.* Irritation; rage; fury.

excavate, eks'ka-vāt, *vt.* (excavating, excavated). To hollow out. **excavation,** eks'ka-vā'shun, *n.* Act of hollowing out; a cavity. **excavator,** eks"ka-vā'tèr, *n.* One who excavates; a machine for excavating.

exceed, ek-sēd', *vt.* To go beyond, as any limit; to surpass; to outdo.—*vi.* To go too far; to bear the greater proportion. **exceeding,** ek-sēd'ing, *a.* Great in extent, quantity, or duration.—*adv.* In a great degree. **exceedingly,** ek-sēd'ing-li, *adv.* Greatly; very much.

excel, ek-sel', *vt.* (excelling, excelled). To surpass; to transcend; to outdo.—*vi.* To be eminent or distinguished. **excellence, excellency,** ek'se-lens, ek'se-len-si, *n.* Superiority; preeminence; any valuable quality; an official title of honor. **excellent,** ek'se-lent, *a.* Of great value; distinguished in attainments; exquisite.

except, ek-sept', *vt.* To take or leave out of any number specified; to exclude.—*vi.* To object; to make objection.—*prep.* Exclusively of; without.—*conj.* Unless. **excepting,** ek-sept'ing, *prep.* and *conj.* With exception of; excluding; except. **exception,** ek-sep'shun, *n.* Act of excepting; state of being excepted; that which is excepted; an objection; offense. **exceptionable,** ek-sep'shun-a-bl, *a.* Liable to objection; objectionable. **exceptional,** ek-sep'shun-al, *a.* Forming or making an exception.

excerpt, ek'sèrpt, *n.* An extract; a passage selected from an author.—*vt.* To pick out from a book, &c.; to cite.

excess, ek-ses', *n.* That which exceeds; superabundance; intemperate conduct; that by which one thing exceeds another. **excessive,** ek-ses'iv, *a.* Beyond any given degree or limit; intemperate; extreme. **excessively,** ek-ses'iv-li, *adv.* Exceedingly.

exchange, eks-chānj', *vt.* To change one thing for another; to commute; to bargain.—*n.* Act of exchanging; interchange; barter; the thing interchanged; place where merchants, &c., of a city meet to transact business; a method of finding the equivalent to a given sum in the money of another country. **exchangeability,** eks-chān'ja-bil"i-ti, *n.* Quality of being exchangeable. **ex-**

changeable, eks-chān'ja-bl, *a.* Capable, fit, or proper to be exchanged.

exchequer, eks-chek'èr, *n.* An ancient English court for the care of the royal revenues, now a division of the High Court of Justice; a state treasury; pecuniary property.

excise, ek-sīz', *n.* A tax on certain commodities of home production and consumption, as beer, &c.; also for licenses to deal in certain commodities.—*vt.* (excising, excised). To impose a duty on articles produced and consumed at home; to cut out.

excision, ek-sizh'on, *n.* A cutting out or off; amputation; extirpation.

excisable, ek-sīz'a-bl, *a.* Liable or subject to excise.

excite, ek-sīt', *vt.* (exciting, excited). To call into action; to rouse; to stimulate.

excitability, ek-sīt'a-bil"i-ti, *n.* The state or quality of being excitable. **excitable,** ek-sīt'a-bl, *a.* Capable of being excited; prone to excitement. **excitement,** ek-sīt'ment, *n.* Act of exciting; stimulation; agitation. **exciting,** ek-sīt'ing, *p.a.* Producing excitement; deeply interesting; thrilling.

exclaim, eks-klām', *vi.* To call out, to shout.—*vt.* To declare with loud vociferation. **exclamation,** eks-kla-mā"shun, *n.* A loud outcry; a passionate sentence; a note by which emphatic utterance is marked, thus, !; an interjection. **exclamatory,** eks-klam'a-tō-ri, *a.* Containing or expressing exclamation.

exclude, eks-klūd', *vt.* (excluding, excluded). To shut out; to thrust out; to debar; to prohibit; to except. **exclusion,** eks-klū'zhun, *n.* Act of excluding; state of being excluded; prohibition; ejection. **exclusive,** eks-klū'siv, *a.* Excluding; not including; debarring from fellowship; illiberal.

excommunicate, eks-ko-mū'ni-kāt, *vt.* To eject from the communion of the church; to expel from fellowship. **excommunication,** eks-ko-mū'ni-kā"-shun, *n.* Expulsion from the communion of a church.

excoriate, eks-kō'ri-āt, *vt.* To break or wear off the cuticle of; to censure harshly.

excrement, eks'krē-ment, *n.* That which is separated from the nutriment by digestion, and discharged from the body; ordure; dung. **excremental, excrementitial, excrementitious,** eks-krē-men'tal, eks'krē-men-tish"al, eks'krē-men-tish"us, *a.* Pertaining to or consisting of excrement.

excrescence, eks-kres'ens, *n.* Anything which grows out of something else and is useless or disfiguring; a troublesome superfluity.

excrescent, eks-kres'ent, *a.* Growing out of something else abnormally; superfluous.

excrete, eks-krēt', *vt.* (excreting, excreted). To separate and discharge from the body by vital action. **excretion,** eks-krē'shun, *n.* Act or process of excreting; that which is excreted. **excre-**

tive, eks-krē'tiv, *a.* Having the power of excreting; excretory. **excretory,** eks'krē-to-ri, *a.* Having the quality of throwing off excrementitious matter by the glands.—*n.* A duct or vessel to receive secreted fluids, and to excrete them.

excruciate, eks-krö'shi-āt, *vt.* To torture; to rack. **excruciating,** eks-krö''shi-āt'ing, *p.a.* Extremely painful; agonizing; distressing. **excruciation,** eks-krö'shi-ā"shun, *n.* Act of excruciating; agony; torture.

exculpate, eks'kul-pāt, *vt.* To clear from a charge of fault or guilt; to absolve. **exculpation,** eks'kul-pā"shon, *n.* Act of exculpating; excuse. **exculpatory,** eks-kul'pa-tō-ri, *a.* Serving to exculpate; clearing from blame.

excursion, eks-kėr'shun, *n.* journey for pleasure or health; a ramble; a trip. **excursionist,** eks-kėr'shun-ist, *n.* One who joins in an excursion for pleasure. **excursive,** eks-kėr'siv, *a.* Rambling; wandering; deviating.

excusable, eks-kūz'a-bl, *a.* Admitting of excuse or justification; pardonable. **excuse,** eks-kūz', *vt.* (excusing, excused). To acquit of guilt; to pardon; to free from a duty.—*n.* eks-kūs'. A plea in extenuation of a fault; apology; that which excuses.

execrable, ek'sē-kra-bl, *a.* Deserving to be execrated or cursed; hateful; detestable.

execrate, ek'sē-krāt, *vt.* (execrating, execrated). To curse; to abominate. **execration,** ek-sē-krā'shun, *n.* Act of execrating; a curse; imprecation.

execute, ek'sē-kūt, *vt.* (executing, executed). To effect; to achieve; to inflict capital punishment on; to make valid, as by signing and sealing; to perform.—*vi.* To perform. **execution,** ek-se-kū'shun, *n.* Act of executing; act of signing and sealing a legal instrument; capital punishment; mode of performing a work of art; facility of voice or finger in music. **executioner,** ek-sē-kū'shun-ėr, *n.* One wh puts to death by law. **executive,** eg-zek'ū-tiv, *a.* That executes; carrying laws into effect, or superintending their enforcement.—*n.* The person or persons who administer the government. **executor,** eg-zek'ū-tėr, *n.* One who executes or performs; the person appointed by a testator to execute his will.

exegesis, ek'sē-jē"sis, *n.* An exposition; the science or art of literary interpretation; particularly of the Bible.

exemplar, eg-zem'plėr, *n.* A pattern; copy. **exemplarily,** eg-zem'pla-ri-li, *adv.* In an exemplary manner. **exemplary,** eg-zem'pla-ri, *a.* Serving as a pattern; worthy of imitation; explanatory.

exemplify, eg-zem'pli-fī, *vt.* (exemplifying, exemplified). To show by example; to serve as an instance of. **exemplification,** eg-zem'pli-fi-ka"shun, *n.* A showing by example; instance.

exempt, eg-zemt', *vt.* To free from; to privilege; to grant immunity from.—*a.* Free by privilege; not liable. **exemption,** ek-zemp'shun, *n.* Act of exempting; state of being exempt; immunity.

exercise, ek'sėr-sīz, *n.* Practice; use; drill; act of divine worship; application; a lesson or example for practice.—*vt.* (exercising; exercised). To employ; to practice; to train; to give anxiety to; to afflict.—*vi.* To take exercise.

exert, eg-zėrt', *vt.* To put forth, as strength; to put in action; (*refl.*) to use efforts; to strive. **exertion,** eg-zėr'-shun, *n.* Act of exerting.

exhale, ekz-hāl', *vt.* (exhaling, exhaled). To breathe out; to cause to be emitted in vapor or minute particles; to evaporate.—*vi.* To fly off as vapor. **exhalation,** eks'ha-lā"shun, *n.* Act of exhaling; that which is exhaled; vapor; effluvia.

exhaust, eg-zast', *vt.* To drain of contents; to expend entirely; to treat thoroughly; to tire. **exhausted,** eg-zast'ed, *p.a.* Wholly expended; fatigued. **exhaustible,** eg-zast'i-bl, *a.* That may be exhausted. **exhausting,** eg-zast'ing, *p.a.* Tending to exhaust. **exhaustion,** eg-zast'shun, *n.* Act of exhausting; state of being exhausted. **exhaustive,** egzast'-iv, *a.* Causing exhaustion; thorough.

exhibit, eg-zib'it, *vt.* To show; to display; to administer by way of remedy. —*n.* Anything exhibited. **Exhibiter, exhibitor,** eg-zib'i-tėr, *n.* One who exhibits. **exhibition,** eks-i-bi'shun, *n.* Act of exhibiting; display; any public show; a benefaction for students in English universities. **exhibitioner,** ek'si-bi"shun-ėr, *n.* One maintained at an English university by an exhibition. **exhibitionism,** ek'si-bi"shun-izm, *n.* A tendency to show off, attract attention.

exhilarate, eg-zil'a-rāt, *vt.* (exhilarating, exhilarated). To make cheerful; to inspirit. **exhilaration,** eg-zil'a-rā"shun, *n.* Act of exhilarating; cheerfulness; gayety.

exhort, eg-zort', *vt.* To urge to a good deed; to encourage; to warn. **exhortation,** eg'zor-ta"shun, *n.* Act of exhorting; a persuasive discourse.

exhume, eks'hūm, *vt.* (exhuming, exhumed). To unbury; to disinter. **exhumation,** eks-hū-mā'shun, *n.* Act of exhuming; disinterring of a corpse.

exigence, exigency, ek'si-jens, ek'si-jen-si, *n.* Pressing necessity; urgency. **exigent,** eks'i-jent, *a.* Urgent; pressing.

exile, ek'sīl, or eg'zīl, *n.* State of being expelled from one's native country; banishment; the person banished.—*vt.* (exiling, exiled). To banish from one's country.

exist, eg-zist', *vi.* To be; to live; to endure. **existence,** eg-zis'tens, *n.* State of being; life; continuation; anything that exists. **existent,** eg-zis'tent, *a.* Being; existing.

exit, ek'sit, *n.* A going out; the departure of a player from the stage; death; a way out.

exodus, ek'sō-dus, *n.* Way out; departure; the second book of the Old Testament.

exonerate, eg-zon'ėr-āt, *vt.* To exculpate; to acquit; to justify. **exonerative,** eg-zon'ėr-ā-tiv, *a.* That exonerates; freeing from an obligation.

exorbitant, eg-zor′bi-tant, *a.* Excessive; extravagant. **exorbitantly**; eg-zor′bi-tant-li, *adv.* Enormously; excessively. **exorbitance**, **exorbitancy**, eg-zor′bi-tans, eg-zor′bi-tan-si, *n.* A going beyond fair or usual limits; enormity; extravagance.

exorcise, ek′sor-sīz, *vt.* (exorcising, exorcised). To purify from evil spirits by adjurations. **exorcism**, ek′sor-sism, *n.* The act or ceremony of exorcising.

exotic, ekz-ot′ik, *a.* Introduced from a foreign country; not native.—*n.* Anything introduced from a foreign country.

expand, eks-pand′, *vt.* and *i.* To spread out; to enlarge; to distend; to dilate.

expanse, eks-pans′, *n.* A surface widely extended; a wide extent of space or body. **expansibility**, eks-pan′si-bil″i-ti, *n.* The capacity of being expanded. **expansible**, eks-pan′si-bl, *a.* Capable of being expanded. **expansile**, eks-pan′sil, *a.* Expansible; producing expansion. **expansion**, eks-pan′shun, *n.* Act of expanding; state of being expanded; dilatation; distention; enlargement. **expansive**, eks-pan′siv, *a.* Having the power to expand; widely extended or extending.

expatiate, eks-pā′shi-āt, *vi.* (expatiating, expatiated). To move at large; to enlarge in discourse or writing.

expatriate, eks-pā′tri-āt, *vt.* (expatriating, expatriated). To exile. **expatriation**, eks-pā′tri-ā″shun, *n.* Exile; the forsaking of one's own country.

expect, eks-pekt′, *vt.* To wait for; to look for to happen; to anticipate. **expectance**, **expectancy**, eks-pek′tans, eks-pek′tan-si, *n.* Act or state of expecting; expectation; hope. **expectant**, eks-pek′tant, *a.* Expecting; awaiting.— *n.* One who expects; one who waits in expectation. **expectation**, eks-pek-tā′shun, *n.* Act or state of expecting; prospect of good to come; prospect of reaching a certain age.

expectorate, eks-pek′tō-rāt, *vt.* (expectorating, expectorated). To expel; to phlegm, by toughing; to spit out. **expectoration**, eks-pek′tō-rā″shun, *n.* Act of expectorating; matter expectorated.

expedient, eks-pē′di-ent, *a.* Tending to promote the object proposed; proper under the circumstances; advantageous.— *n.* Means to an end; shift; plan. **expediently**, eks-pē′di-ent-li, *adv.* Fitly; suitably. **expedience**, **expediency**, eks-pē′di-ens, eks-pē′di-en-si, *n.* Quality of being expedient; property; advisability.

expedite, eks′pē-dīt, *vt.* (expediting, expedited). To free from hindrance; to accelerate; to hasten by making easier. **expedition**, eks-pē-dish′un, *n.* State of being unimpeded; dispatch; a march or voyage for hostile purposes; journey by a body of men for some valuable end; such body of men. **expeditionary** eks′pē-dish″un-er′i, *a.* Consisting in or forming and expedition. **expeditious**, eks-pē-dish′us, *a.* Speedy; prompt; nimble; active.

expel, eks-pel′, *vt.* (expelling, expelled). To drive out; to eject; to banish.

expend, eks-pend′, *vt.* To spend; to use or consume; to waste. **expenditure**, eks-pen′di-tūr, *n.* Act of expending; a laying out, as of money; money expended; expense.

expense, eks-pens′, *n.* That which is expended; cost; charge; price. **expensive**, eks-pen′siv, *a.* Requiring much expense; dear; lavish. **expensively**, eks-pen′siv-li, *adv.* In an expensive manner; at great cost or charge.

experience, eks-pēr′i-ens, *n.* Personal trial; continued observation; knowledge gained by trial or observation; trial and knowledge from suffering or enjoyment; suffering itself.—*vt.* (experiencing, experienced). To try; to know by trial; to have happen; to undergo. **experienced**, eks-pēr′i-enst, *p.a.* Taught by experience; skillful by use or observation.

experiment, eks-per′i-ment, *n.* A trial; an operation designed to discover something unknown, or to establish it when discovered.—*vi.* To make trial or experiment. **experimental**, eks-per′i-men″tal, *a.* Pertaining to, known by, or derived from experiment; having personal experience. **experimentalist**, eks-per′i-men″tal-ist, *n.* One who makes experiments. **experimentally**, eks-per′i-men″tal-li, *adv.* In an experimental way; by trial.

expert, eks-pėrt′, *a.* Skillful; dexterous; adroit.—eks′pėrt, *n.* An expert person; a scientific witness. **expertly**, eks-pėrt′-li, *adv.* In a skillful or dexterous manner; adroitly.

expiate, eks′pi-āt, *vt.* (expiating, expiated). To atone for; to make reparation for. **expiable**, eks′pi-a-bl, *a.* That may be expiated or atoned for. **expiation**, eks′pi-ā″shun, *n.* Act of expiating; atonement; reparation.

expire, ek-spir′, *vt.* (expiring, expired). To breathe out; to exhale.—*vi.* To emit the last breath; to die; to terminate. **expiry**, ek′spi-ri, *n.* Termination. **expiration**, eks′pi-rā″shun, *n.* Act of breathing out; death; end; expiry.

explain, eks-plān′, *vt.* To make plain or intelligible; to expound; to elucidate. —*vi.* To give explanations. **explanation**, eks-pla-nā′shun, *n.* Act of explaining; interpretation; clearing up of matters between parties at variance. **explanatory**, eks-plan″a-to′ri, *a.* Serving to explain. **explétive**, eks′plē-tiv, *a.* Serving to fill out; superfluous.—*n.* A word or syllable inserted to fill a vacancy or for ornament; an oath or interjection. **explicable**, eks′pli-ka-bl, *a.* Capable of being explained. **explicate**, eks′pli-kāt, *vt.* To unfold the meaning of; to explain. **explicit**, eks-plis′it, *a.* Plain in language; express, not merely implied; open. **explicitly**, eks-plis′it-li, *adv.* In an explicit manner; plainly; expressly. **explode**, eks-plōd′, *vt.* (exploding, exploded). To drive out of use or belief; to cause to burst with violence and noise. —*vi.* To burst with noise; to burst into activity or passion.

exploit, eks-ploit′, *n.* A deed; a heroic act; a deed of renown.—*vt.* To make use of; to work. **exploitation**, eks-ploi-tā'shun, *n.* Successful application of industry on any object as land, mines, &c.

xplore, eks-plōr', *vt.* (exploring, explored). To travel with the view of making discovery; to search; to examine closely.

xploration, eks-plō-rā'shun, *n.* Act of exploring; strict or careful examination.

xplorer, eks-plōr'èr, *n.* One who explores; a traveler in unknown regions.

xplosion, eks-plō'zhun, *n.* Act of exploding; a bursting with noise; a violent outburst of feeling. **explosive**, eks-plō'siv, *a.* Causing explosion; readily exploding.—*n.* Anything liable to explode, as gunpowder; a mute or non-continuous consonant, as *k, t, b.*

xponent, eks-pō'nent, *n.* One who explains or illustrates; that which indicates; the index of a power in algebra.

xport, eks-pōrt', *vt.* To convey, in traffic, to another country.—*n.* eks'pōrt. Act of exporting; quantity of goods exported; a commodity exported. **exportable**, eks-pōrt'a-bl, *a.* That may be exported. **exportation**, eks-pōr-tā-shun, *n.* Act of conveying goods to another country. **exporter**, eks-pōr'tèr, *n.* One who exports.

xpose, eks-pōz', *vt.* (exposing, exposed). To put or set out; to disclose; to lay open to attack, censure, &c.; to make liable; to exhibit. **exposé**, eks'po-zā", *n.* Exposure; statement. **exposed**, eks-pōzd', *p.a.* In danger; liable; unsheltered.

exposition, eks-pō-zish'un, *n.* Act of exposing; explanation; exhibition.

xpositor, eks-poz'i-tèr, *n.* One who expounds; an interpreter.

xpository, eks-poz'i-tō-ri, *a.* Containing exposition; explanatory.

x post facto, eks pōst fak'tō, *a.* After the deed is done; retrospective.

xpostulate, eks-pos'tū-lāt, *vi.* To remonstrate; to reason earnestly with a person on some impropriety. **expostulation**, eks-pos'tū-lā"shun, *n.* Act of expostulation; remonstrance.

xposure, eks-pō'zhèr, *n.* Act of exposing; state of being exposed; situation.

xpound, eks-pound', *vt.* To explain; to interpret; to unfold. **expounder**, eks-poun'dèr, *n.* One who expounds; an explainer; an interpreter.

xpress, eks-pres', *vt.* To press out; to set forth in words; to declare; to make known by any means; (*refl.*) to say what one has got to say.—*a.* Clearly exhibited; given in direct terms; intended or sent for a particular purpose; traveling with special speed.—*n.* A messenger or vehicle sent on a particular occasion; a message specially sent; a specially fast railway train.—*adv.* For a particular purpose; with special haste. **expressible**, eks-pres'i-bl, *a.* That may be expressed. **expression**, eks-presh'un, *n.* Act of expressing; a phrase or mode of speech; manner of utterance; a natural and lively representation in painting and sculpture; musical tone, grace, or modulation; play of features; representation of a quantity in algebra. **expression-**

less, eks-presh'un-les, *a.* Destitute of expression. **expressive**, eks-pres'iv, *a.* Serving to express; representing with force; emphatical. **expressively**, eks-pres'iv-li, *adv.* In an expressive manner; with expression. **expressly**, eks-pres'li, *adv.* In direct terms; of set purpose.

expropriate, eks-prō'pri-āt, *vt.* To take for public use; to dispossess. **expropriation**, eks-prō'pri-ā"shun, *n.* Act of dispossessing of proprietary rights.

expulsion, eks-pul'shun, *n.* A driving away by violence; state of being driven away. **expulsive**, eks-pul'siv, *a.* Having the power by expelling; serving to expel.

expunge, eks-punj', *vt.* (expunging, expunged). To blot out, as with a pen; to erase; to obliterate.

expurgate, eks'pèr-gāt or eks-pèr'gāt, *vt.* (expurgating, expurgated). To render pure; to strike offensive passages out of (a book). **expurgation**, eks'pèr-gā'shun, *n.* Act of purging or cleansing; purification.

exquisite, eks'kwi-zit, *a.* Select; highly finished; excellent; extreme; matchless, as pain or pleasure keenly felt.—*n.* A fop; a dandy.

extant, eks'tant, *a.* Still existing; in being.

extempore, eks-tem'po-rē, *adv.* and *a.* Without study or preparation; extemporary. **extemporize**, eks-tem'pō-rīz, *vi.* To speak without preparation.—*vt.* To make without forethought; to prepare in haste. **extemporaneous**, eks-tem'pō-rā"nē-us, *a.* Arising out of the time or occasion; on the spur of the moment; unpremeditated. **extemporary**, eks-tem'pō-rer-i, *a.* Arising out of the time or occasion; extemporaneous.

extend, eks-tend', *vt.* To stretch out; to spread; to prolong; to bestow on.—*vi.* To stretch; to reach; to become larger. **extension**, eks-ten'shun, *n.* Act of extending; state of being extended; that property of a body by which it occupies a portion of space; enlargement; in *logic*, the objects to which a term may be applied. **extensive**, eks-ten'siv, *a.* Having great extent; large; comprehensive. **extent**, eks-tent', *n.* Space or degree to which a thing is extended; compass; size.

extenuate, eks-ten'ū-āt, *vt.* To lessen; to weaken the force of; to palliate. **extenuation**, eks-ten'ū-ā"shun, *n.* Act of extenuating; palliation; mitigation.

exterior, eks-tēr'i-èr, *a.* External; on the outside; foreign.—*n.* The outward surface; that which is external.

exterminate, eks-tèr'mi-nāt, *vt.* To destroy utterly; to extirpate; to root out. **extermination**, eks-tèr'mi-nā"shun, *n.* Act of exterminating; eradication; extirpation.

external, eks-tèr'nal, *a.* On the outside; exterior; not being within, as causes or effects; visible; foreign. **externals**, eks-tèr'nalz, *n.pl.* Outward parts; exterior form; outward ceremonies.

exterritorial, eks-ter'i-tō"ri-al, *a.* Beyond the jurisdiction of the country in which one resides.

extinct, eks-tingkt', *a.* Extinguished; abolished; having died out. **extinction**, eks-tingk'shun, *n.* Act of extinguishing; state of being extinguished; destruction; extermination.

extinguish, eks-ting'gwish, *vt.* To put out; to quench; to destroy; to eclipse. **extinguishable**, eks-ting'gwish-a-bl, *a.* That may be quenched or destroyed. **extinguisher**, eks-ting'gwish-ėr, *n.* One who or that which extinguishes; a hollow, conical utensil to extinguish a candle.

extirpate, ek'ster-pāt or ek-stėr'pāt, *vt.* To root out; to eradicate; to destroy totally. **extirpation**, ek-stėr-pā'shun, *n.* Act of rooting out; eradication; total destruction.

extol, eks-tol', *vt.* (extolling, extolled). To exalt in eulogy; to magnify; to glorify.

extort, eks-tort', *vt.* To exact by force; to wrest or wring. **extortion**, eks-tor'shun, *n.* Act of extorting; illegal or oppressive exaction. **extortionate**, eks-tor'shun-āt, *a.* Excessive in amount; oppressive in exacting money. **extortioner, extortionist**, ek-tor'shun-ėr, eks-tor'shun-ist, *n.* One who practices extortion.

extra, eks'tra, *a.* and *adv.* Additional; beyond what is usual, due, &c.—*n.* Something in addition.

extract, eks-trakt', *vt.* To draw out or forth; to select; to draw or copy out; to find the root of a number.—*n.* eks'-trakt. That which is extracted; a quotation; an essence, tincture, &c. **extraction**, eks-trak'shun, *n.* Act of extracting; lineage; operation of drawing essences, tinctures, &c.; operation of finding the roots of numbers.

extradite, eks'tra-dīt, *vt.* To deliver up (a criminal) to the authorities of the country from which he has come. **extradition**, eks-tra-di'shun, *n.* The delivery, under a treaty, of a fugitive from justice by one government to another.

extramural, eks-tra-mūr'al, *a.* Outside the walls, as of a fortified city or university.

extraneous, eks-trā'nē-us, *a.* That is without; foreign; not intrinsic; irrelevant.

extraordinary, eks-tror"di-ner'i, *a.* Beyond that which is ordinary; unusual; remarkable; special. **extraordinarily**, eks-tror"di-ner'i-li, *adv.* In an extraordinary manner; unusually.

extravagant, eks-trav'a-gant, *a.* Exceeding due bounds; fantastic; wasteful; lavish. **extravagance, extravagancy**, eks-trav'a-gans, eks-trav'a-gan-si, *n.* A going beyond due bounds; excess; wastefulness. **extravagantly**, eks-trav'a-gant-li, *adv.* Unreasonably; excessively; wastefully. **extravaganza**, eks-trav'a-gan"za, *n.* A wild literary or musical composition.

extreme, eks-trēm', *a.* Outermost; furthest; most violent; last; worst or best; most pressing.—*n.* The utmost point or verge of a thing; end; furthest or highest degree; (*pl.*) points at the greatest distance from each other. **extremely**, eks-trēm'li, *adv.* In the utmost degree; to the utmost point. **extremist**, eks-trēm'ist, *n.* A supporter of extreme doctrines or practice. **extremity**, eks-trem'i-ti, *n.* That which is extreme; utmost point, part, or degree; utmost distress or violence.

extricate, eks'tri-kāt, *vt.* (extricating, extricated). To disentangle; to set free. **extricable**, eks't-ri-ka-bl, *a.* That can be extricated. **extrication**, eks-tri-kā'shun, *n.* Act of extricating.

extrinsic, extrinsical, eks-trin'sik, eks-trin'si-kal, *a.* Being on the outside; extraneous; accessory.

extrovert, extravert, eks'tro-vėrt, eks'tra-vėrt, *n.* One who is outgoing or exuberant in manner.

extrude, eks-tröd', *vt.* (extruding, extruded). To thrust out; to expel. **extrusion**, eks-trö'shun, *n.* Act of extruding; a driving out; expulsion.

exuberant, eg-zū'ber-ant, *a.* Superabundant; overflowing; luxuriant. **exuberance, exuberancy**, eg-zū'ber-ans, eg-zū'ber-an-si, *n.* Superabundance; overflowing fullness; rankness; luxuriance.

exude, eks-ūd', *vt.* (exuding, exuded). To discharge through the pores; to let ooze out.—*vi.* To flow through pores; to ooze out like sweat. **exudation**, eks-ū-dā'shun, *n.* Act or process of exuding; something exuded.

exult, eg-zult', *vi.* To rejoice exceedingly; to triumph. **exultant**, eg-zul'tant, *a.* Rejoicing triumphantly. **exultation**, ek'sul-tā'shun, *n.* Lively joy; triumph; rapture; ecstasy.

eye, ī, *n.* The organ of vision; sight or view; power of perception; something resembling an eye in form; a small hole; a loop or ring for fastening.—*vt.* (eyeing, eyed). To fix the eye on; to observe or watch narrowly. **eyeball**, ī'bal, *n.* The ball of the eye. **eyebrow**, ī'brou, *n.* The brow or hairy arch above the eye. **eyed**, īd, *a.* Having eyes. **eyeglass**, ī'glas, *n.* A glass to assist the sight. **eyelash**, ī'lash, *n.* The line of hair that edges the eyelid. **eyeless**, ī'les, *a.* Wanting eyes; blind. **eyelet, eyelet hole**, ī'let, ī'let hōl, *n.* A small eye or hole to receive a lace. **eyelid**, ī'lid, *n.* The cover of the eye; the movable skin with which an animal covers or uncovers the eyeball. **eyesight**, ī'sīt, *n.* The sight of the eye; view; observation; the sense of seeing. **eyesore**, ī'sōr, *n.* Something offensive to the eye or sight. **eye tooth**, ī'töth, *n.* A tooth under the eye; a canine tooth; a fang. **eyewitness**, ī'wit-nes, *n.* One who sees a thing done.

eyrie, eyry, ar'i, ī'ri, *n.* An aerie; nest of a bird of prey.

F

fabian, fā'bi-an, *a.* Delaying; lingering.

fable, fā'bl, *n.* A fictitious narrative to instruct or amuse, often to enforce a precept; falsehood; an idle story; the plot in a poem or drama.—*vi.* (fabling, fabled). To tell fables or falsehoods.—*vt.* To feign; to invent. **fabled,** fā'bld, *p.a.* Told in fables.

fabliau, fab-li-ō, *n.pl.; iaux.* A kind of metrical tale common in early French literature.

fabric, fab'rik, *n.* Frame or structure of anything; a building; texture; cloth. **fabricate,** fab'ri-kāt, *vt.* (fabricating, fabricated). To make or fashion; to form by art or labor; to devise falsely. **fabrication,** fab-ri-kā'shun, *n.* Act of fabricating; that which is fabricated; fiction. **fabricator,** fab'ri-kā-tėr, *n.* One who fabricates.

fabulous, fab'ū-lus, *a.* Containing or abounding in fable; feigned; mythical; incredible.

façade, facade, fa-säd', fa-säd', *n.* Front view or elevation of an edifice.

face, fās, *n.* The front part of an animal's head, particularly of the human head; the visage; front; effrontery; assurance; dial of a watch; &c.—*vt.* (facing, faced). To meet in front; to stand opposite to; to oppose with firmness; to finish or protect with a thin external covering; to dress the face of (a stone, &c.).—*vi.* To turn the face; to look.

facet, fas'et, fas'it, *n.* A small flat portion of a surface.

facetious, fa-sē'shus, *a.* Witty; humorous; jocose; sprightly.

facial, fā'shal, *a.* Pertaining to the face.

facile, fas'il, *a.* Easy; easily persuaded; yielding; dexterous. **facilitate,** fa-sil'i-tāt, *vt.* To make easy; to lessen the labor of. **facility,** fa-sil'i-ti, *n.* Easiness to be performed; dexterity; readiness of compliance; *pl.* means to render easy; convenient advantages.

facing, fās'ing, *n.* A covering in front for ornament or defense; a mode of adulterating tea; the movement of soldiers in turning round to the left, right, &c.; *pl.* trimmings on regimental garments.

facsimile, fak-sim'i-lē, *n.* An exact copy or likeness.

fact, fakt, *n.* Anything done; a deed; event; circumstance; reality; truth.

faction, fak'shun, *n.* A party in political society in opposition to the ruling power; a party unscrupulously promoting its private ends; discord; dissension. **factious,** fak'shus, *a.* Given to faction; prone to clamor against public measures or men; pertaining to faction.

factitious, fak-tish'us, *a.* Made by art; artificial.

factor, fak'tėr, *n.* An agent, particularly a mercantile agent; one of two or more numbers, or quantities, which, when multiplied together, form a product; one of several elements which contribute to a result.

factory, fak'to-ri, *n.* An establishment where factors in foreign countries reside to transact business for their employers; buildings appropriated to the manufacture of goods; a manufactory.

factotum, fak-tō'tum, *n.* A person employed to do all kinds of work; confidential agent.

faculty, fak'ul-ti, *n.* Any mental or bodily power; capacity; special power or authority; the body of individuals constituting one of the learned professions; a department of a university, or its professors.

fad, fad, *n.* A favorite theory; crotchet; hobby. **faddist,** fad'ist, *n.* One who deals in fads.

fade, fād, *vi.* (fading, faded). To lose color, strength, or freshness; to wither; to perish; to become indistinct.—*vt.* To cause to wither. **fading,** fād'ing, *p.a.* Liable to fade; transient.

fag, fag, *vi.* (fagging, fagged). To become weary; to drudge.—*vt.* To use as a drudge; to tire by labor.—*n.* A laborious drudge.

fagot, fag'ut, *n.* A bundle of sticks or twigs; a bundle of pieces of iron or steel for remanufacture; one hired to take the place of another at the muster of a military company.

Fahrenheit, far'en-hīt, *a.* The name of the thermometer in which the freezing point is 32° and the boiling 212°.

fail, fāl, *vi.* To become deficient; to decline; to become extinct; not to produce the effect; to be unsuccessful; to be guilty of omission or neglect; to become bankrupt.—*vt.* To cease or omit to afford aid, supply, or strength to; to forsake.—*n.* Omission; failure; want. **failing,** fāl'ing, *n.* A natural weakness; foible; fault in character or disposition. **failure,** fāl'ūr, *n.* A failing; cessation of supply or total defect; non-performance; want of success; a becoming bankrupt.

fain, fān, *a.* Glad; pleased inclined; content to accept.—*adv.* Gladly.

faint, fānt, *vi.* To become feeble; to become senseless and motionless; to swoon; to lose spirit; to vanish.—*a.* Enfeebled so as to be inclined to swoon; weak; indistinct; depressed.—*n.* A fainting fit; a swoon. **faint-hearted,** fānt'härt'ed, *a.* Cowardly; timorous; dejected. **faintly,** fānt'li, *adv.* Feebly; languidly; without vigor, vividness, or distinctness.

fair, fār, *a.* Pleasing to the eye; beautiful; white or light in respect of complexion; not stormy or wet; favorable; reasonable; impartial; honorable; plain;

unspotted; moderately good; middling. —*adv.* Openly; frankly; honestly; on good terms.—*n.* A fair woman; *the fair,* the female sex; a stated market. **fairish,** fār'ish, *n.* Moderately fair. **fairly,** fār'li, *adv.* Honestly, justly, equitably, reasonably, tolerably, &c. **fair-spoken,** fār'spō'ken, *a.* Using fair speech; courteous; plausible; bland.

fairy, fār'i, *n.* An imaginary being of human form, supposed to play a variety of pranks.—*a.* Belonging to fairies; given by fairies.

faith, fāth, *n.* Belief; trust; confidence; conviction in regard to religion; system of religious beliefs; strict adherence to duty and promises; word or honor pledged. **faithful,** fāth'ful, *a.* Full of faith; firm in adherence to duty; loyal; trusty; observant of compacts, vows, &c. **faithfully,** fāth'ful-li, *adv.* In a faithful manner; loyally; sincerely. **faithless,** fāth'les, *a.* Destitute of faith; false; not observant of promises; deceptive.

fake, fāk, *vt.* To lay (a rope) in coils; to cheat.—*n.* Single coil of a rope; a cheat.

fakir, fakeer, fä-kēr', *n.* An oriental ascetic or begging monk.

falcon, fal'kon or fạ'kn, *n.* The name of various small or medium-sized raptorial birds; a hawk of any kind trained to sport.

falconer, fal'kon-ėr, *n.* A person who breeds and trains hawks, or sports with hawks.

falconry, fal'kon-ri, *n.* The art of training hawks; hawking.

fall, fạl, *vi.* (pret. fell, pp. fallen). To sink to a lower position; to drop down; to empty or disembogue; to sink into sin, weakness, or disgrace; to come to an end suddenly; to decrease; to assume an expression of dejection, &c; to happen; to pass or be transferred; to belong or appertain; to be uttered carelessly.—*n.* Descent; tumble; death; ruin; cadence; a cascade or cataract; extent of descent; declivity; autumn; that which falls; a kind of ladies' veil; lapse or declension from innocence or goodness; *naut.* the part of a tackle to which the power is applied in hoisting.

fallacy, fal'a-si, *n.* Deception; deceitfulness; a misleading or mistaken argument. **fallacious,** fa-lā'shus, *a.* Deceitful; misleading; sophistical; delusive.

fallible, fal'i-bl, *a.* Liable to mistake or be deceived. **fallibly,** fal'i-bli, *adv.* In a fallible manner. **fallibility,** fal-i-bil'i-ti, *n.* Quality or state of being fallible.

fallout, fạl'out, *n.* Radioactive particles that fall to earth following a nuclear explosion.

fallow, fal'ō, *a.* Pale red or pale yellow; plowed, but not sowed; uncultivated.—*n.* Land left unsown after being plowed. —*vt.* To plow and harrow land without seeding it.

fallow deer, fal'ō dēr, *n.* A kind of deer smaller than the stag, and common in England in parks.

false, fạls, *a.* Not true; forged; feigned; fraudulent; treacherous; inconstant; constructed for show or a subsidiary purpose. **falsehearted,** fạls'här'ted, *a.* Deceitful; treacherous; perfidious. **falsehood,** fạls'höd, *n.* Quality of being false; untruth; fiction; a lie. **falsely,** fạls'li, *adv.* In a false manner. **falsetto,** fạl-set'ō, *n.* A false or artificial voice; the tones above the natural compass of the voice. **falsification,** fạls'i-fi-kā"shun, *n.* Act of falsifying; willful misrepresentation. **falsify,** fạl'si-fi, *vt.* (falsifying, falsified). To break by falsehood.—*vi.* To violate the truth. **falsity,** fạl'si-ti, *n.* The quality of being false; that which is false; a falsehood. **falter,** fạl'tėr, *vi.* To hesitate in speech; to fail in exertion; to fail in the regular exercise of the understanding. **faltering,** fạl'tėr-ing, *p.a.* Hesitating.

fame, fām, *n.* A public report or rumor; favorable report; celebrity; reputation. **famed,** fāmd, *a.* Renowned; celebrated. **fameless,** fām'les, *a.* Without renown.

familiar, fa-mil'yer, *a.* Well acquainted; intimate; affable; well known; free; unconstrained.—*n.* An intimate; one long acquainted; a demon supposed to attend at call. **familiarity,** fa-mil'i-ar"i-ti, *n.* State of being familiar; affability; freedom from ceremony; intimacy. **familiarize,** fa-mil'yėr-iz, *vt.* To make familiar; to accustom.

family, fam'i-li, fam'li, *n.* Household; the parents and children alone; the children as distinguished from the parents; kindred; line of ancestors; honorable descent; a group of class of animals or plants.

famine, fam'in, *n.* Scarcity of food; dearth.

famish, fam'ish, *vt.* To kill or exhaust with hunger; to starve; to kill by denial of anything necessary.—*vi.* To die of hunger; to suffer extreme hunger or thirst.

famous, fā'mus, *a.* Much talked of and praised; renowned; distinguished; admirable. **famously,** fā'mus-li, *adv.* In a famous manner; capitally.

fan, fan, *n.* An instrument for winnowing grain; an instrument to agitate the air and cool the face; something by which the air is moved; a baseball enthusiast.—*vt.* (fanning, fanned). To cool by moving the air with a fan; to winnow; to stimulate.

fanatic, fanatical, fa-nat'ik, fa-nat'i-kal, *a.* Wild in opinions, particularly in religious opinions; excessively enthusiastic. **fanatic,** fa-nat'ik, *n.* A person affected by excessive enthusiasm, particularly on religious subjects; an enthusiast; a visionary. **fanatically,** fa-nat'i-kal-li, *adv.* With wild enthusiasm. **fanaticism,** fa-nat'i-sizm, *n.* Excessive enthusiasm; religious frenzy.

fancy, fan'si, *n.* A phase of the intellect of a lighter cast than the imagination; thought due to this faculty; embodiment of such in words; opinion or notion; liking; caprice; false notion.—*vi.* (fancying, fancied). To imagine; to suppose without proof.—*vt.* To imagine; to like;

to be pleased with.—*a.* Fine; ornamental; adapted to please the fancy; beyond intrinsic value. **fancy-free**, fan'si-frē, *a.* Free from the power of love. **fancied**, fan'sid, *p.a.* Imagined; fanciful. **fancier**, fan'si-ėr, *n.* One who fancies; one who has a hobby for certain things. **fanciful**, fan'si-fyl, *a.* Full of fancy; dictated by fancy; visionary; whimsical.

fanfare, fan'fār, *n.* A flourish of trumpets; an ostentatious boast; a bravado.

fang, fang, *n.* A long, pointed tooth; the tusk of an animal; the hollow poison tooth of a serpent; a prong; a claw or talon.

fanged, fangd, *p.a.* Furnished with fangs.

fantail, fan'tāl, *n.* A variety of the domestic pigeon; stern of a ship.

fantasia, fan-tä'zē-a, *n.* A species of music ranging amidst various airs and movements.

fantastic, fantastical, fan-tas'tik, fan-tas'ti-kal, *adj.* Pertaining to fantasy or fancy; whimsical, fanciful; odd; grotesque. **fantasy**, fan'ta-si, *n.* Fancy; a vagary of the imagination; a fanciful artistic production.—*vt.* To picture in fancy.

far, fär, *a.* Remote; distant.—*adv.* To a great extent or distance in space or in time; in great part; very much; to a certain point.

farce, färs, *n.* A play full of extravagant drollery; absurdity; mere show.—*vt.* To stuff with forcement or mingled ingredients. **farcical**, fär'si-kal, *a.* Belonging to a farce; droll; ludicrous; ridiculous.

fare, fār, *vi.* (faring, fared). To go; to travel; to be in any state, good or bad; to be entertained with food; to happen well or ill.—*n.* Sum charged for conveying a person; person conveyed; food; provisions of the table.

farewell, fär'wel", *interj.* May you fare or prosper well.—*n.* Good-bye; departure; final attention. *a.* Leave-taking; valedictory.

farfetched, fär'fecht, *a.* Brought from afar; not naturally introduced; forced.

farina, fa-rī'na, *n.* Meal; flour.

farm, färm, *n.* A portion of land under cultivation; ground let to a tenant for tillage, pasture, &c.—*vt.* To let out or take on lease, as lands; to cultivate; to lease, as taxes, imposts, &c.—*vi.* To cultivate the soil. **farmer**, fär'mėr, *n.* One who cultivates a farm; one who collects taxes, &c., for a certain rate per cent. **farming**, fär'ming, *a.* Pertaining to agriculture.—*n.* The business of a farmer; agriculture; husbandry; tillage of land.

farrier, far'i-ėr, *n.* A smith who shoes horses.

farrow, far'ō, *n.* A pig; a litter of pigs.—*vt.* or *i.* To bring forth pigs.

farther, fär'THėr, *a. comp.* More remote.—*adv.* At or to a greater distance; beyond.

farthermore, fär'THėr-mōr, *adv.* Furthermore; moreover; besides.

farthermost, fär'THėr-mōst, *a. superl.* Being at the greatest distance.

farthest, far'THest, *a. superl.* Most distant.—*adv.* At or to the greatest distance.

farthing, fär'THing, *n.* The fourth of a penny.

fascinate, fas'i-nāt, *vt.* (fascinating, fascinated). To bewitch; to charm; to captivate. **fascinating**, fas'i-nāt-ing. *p.a.* Bewitching; enchanting; charming. **fascination**, fas-i-nā'shun, *n.* Act of bewitching; enchantment; charm; spell.

fascism, fash'izm, *n.* A doctrine of the Fascists; a form of dictatorial government characterized by extreme nationalism.

fashion, fash'un, *n.* The make or form of anything; external appearance; form of a garment; prevailing mode; custom; genteel life.—*vt.* To give shape to; to mold; to adapt.

fashionable, fash'un-a-bl, *a.* According to the prevailing mode; established by custom; prevailing at a particular time; observant of the fashion; stylish.

fast, fast, *a.* Firmly fixed; closely adhering; steadfast; durable; swift; dissipated.—*adv.* Firmly; rapidly; durably; near; with dissipation.—*vi.* To abstain from eating and drinking, or from particular kinds of food.—*n.* Abstinence from food; a religious mortification by abstinence; the time of fasting.

fasten, fas'n, *vt.* To fix firmly, closely or tightly; to hold together; to affix.—*vi.* To become fixed; to seize and hold on. **fastener**, fas'n-ėr, *n.* One who or that which fastens. **fastening**, fas'n-ing, *n.* Anything that binds and makes fast.

fastidious, fas-tid'i-us, *a.* Squeamish; delicate to a fault; difficult to please.

fastness, fäst'nes, *n.* State of being fast; a stronghold; a fortress or fort.

fat, fat, *a.* Fleshy; plump; unctuous; heavy; stupid; rich; fertile.—*n.* A solid oily substance found in parts of animal bodies; the best or richest part of a thing.—*vt.* (fatting, fatted). To make fat.

fatal, fā'tal, *a.* Proceeding from fate; causing death; deadly; calamitous. **fatalism**, fā'tal-ism, *n.* The doctrine that all things take place by inevitable necessity. **fatalist**, fā'tal-ist, *n.* One who maintains that all things happen by inevitable necessity. **fatality**, fa-tal'i-ti, *n.* State of being fatal; invincible necessity; fatalism; fatal occurrence; calamitous accident. **fatally**, fā'tal-li, *adv.* In a fatal manner; by decree of destiny; mortally.

fate, fāt, *n.* Destiny; inevitable necessity; death; doom; lot; *pl.* the three goddesses supposed to preside over the birth and life of men. **fated**, fāt'ed, *a.* Decreed by fate; destined. **fateful**, fāt'fyl, *a.* Producing fatal events.

father, fä'THėr, *n.* A male parent; the first ancestor; the oldest member of a society or profession; the first to practice any art; creator; a name given to God; a dignitary of the church; one of the early expounders of Christianity.—*vt.* To become a father to; to adopt; to profess to be the author of; to ascribe to one as his offspring or production.

fatherhood, fä'THėr-hyd, *n.* State of being a father; character or authority of a father. **father-in-law**, fä′THĕr-in-lą, *n.* The father of one's husband or wife.

fatherland, fä′THĕr-land, *n.* One's native country. **fatherless**, fä′THĕr-les, *a.* Destitute of a living father; without a known author. **fatherly**, fä′THĕr-li, *a.* Like a father, in affection and care; tender; paternal.

fathom, faTH′um, *n.* A measure of length containing six feet.—*vt.* To try the depth of; to sound; to master; to comprehend. **fathomable**, faTH′um-a-bl, *a.* Capable of being fathomed. **fathomless**, faTH′um-les, *a.* That cannot be fathomed; bottomless; incomprehensible.

fatigue, fa-tēg′, *vt.* (fatiguing, fatigued). To employ to weariness; to tire; to harass with toil or labor.—*n.* Weariness from bodily or mental exertion; exhaustion; toil; labors of soldiers distinct from the use of arms.

fatten, fat′n, *vt.* To make fat; to feed for slaughter; to make fertile.—*vi.* To grow fat.

fatty, fat′i, *a.* Having the qualities of fat; greasy.

fatuous, fat′ū-us, *a.* Foolish; silly; feeble in mind; imbecile.

faucet, fa′set, *n.* A pipe to be inserted in a cask, for drawing liquor.

fault, falt, *n.* A slight offense; a defect; a flaw; a break or dislocation of strata. **faultily**, fal′ti-li, *adv.* In a faulty manner; defectively.

faultless, falt′les, *a.* Without fault; free from blemish; perfect. **faulty**, fal′ti, *a.* Marked by faults; defective; imperfect; blamable; bad.

faun, fan, *n.* Among the Romans, a rural deity, the protector of agriculture and of shepherds; a sylvan deity.

fauna, fa′na, *n.* A collective term for the animals peculiar to a region or epoch.

faux pas, fō′pä′′, *n.* A false step; a breach of manners or moral conduct.

favor, favour, fä′vĕr, *n.* Good-will; kindness; a kind act; leave; a yielding to another; a token of good-will; a knot of ribbons; advantage; prejudice.—*vt.* To regard with good-will or kindness; to befriend; to show partiality to; to facilitate; to resemble in features. **favorable**, fä′vĕr-a-bl, *a.* Kindly disposed; propitious; conducive; advantageous. **favored**, fä′vĕrd, *p.a.* Regarded with favor; having special facilities; featured. **favorite, favourite**, fä′vĕr-it, *n.* A person or thing regarded with peculiar favor; a darling; a minion; one unduly favored.—*a.* Regarded with particular favor. **favoritism**, fä′vĕr-it-izm, *n.* Disposition to favor one or more persons or classes, to the neglect of others having equal claims; exercise of power by favorites.

fawn, fan, *n.* A young deer; a buck or doe of the first year; a light-brown color; a servile cringe or bow; mean flattery.—*vi.* To bring forth a fawn; to show a servile attachment; to cringe to gain favor.—*a.* Light brown. **fawningly**, fan′ing-li, *adv.* In a cringing servile way; with mean flattery.

fay, fā, *n.* A fairy; an elf.—*vt.* To fit pieces of timber together.

fealty, fē′al-ti, *n.* Fidelity to a superior; loyalty.

fear, fĕr, *n.* Painful emotion excited by apprehension of impending danger; dread; the object of fear; filial regard mingled with awe; reverence.—*vt.* To feel fear; to apprehend; to dread; to reverence.—*vi.* To be in apprehension of evil; to be afraid. **fearful**, fĕr′ful, *a.* Filled with fear; apprehensive; timid; impressing fear; dreadful. **fearless**, fĕr′les, *a.* Free from fear; undaunted; courageous; bold; intrepid.

feasible, fē′zi-bl, *a.* That may be done; practicable. **feasibly**, fē′zi-bli, *adv.* Practicably. **feasibility**, fē′zi-bil′′i-ti, *n.* Quality of being feasible; practicability.

feast, fēst, *n.* A festal day; a sumptuous entertainment; a banquet; a festival; that which delights and entertains.—*vi.* To partake of a feast; to eat sumptuously; to be highly gratified.—*vt.* To entertain sumptuously.

feat, fēt, *n.* An exploit; an extraordinary act of strength, skill, or cunning.

feather, feTH′ĕr, *n.* One of the growths which form the covering of birds; a plume; projection on a board to fit into another board; kind or nature; birds collectively; a trifle.—*vt.* To cover or fit with feathers; to turn (an oar) horizontally over the water. **feathery**, feTH′ĕr-i, *a.* Clothed or covered with feathers; resembling feathers.

feature, fē′tūr, *n.* The make or cast of any part of the face; any single lineament; a prominent part or characteristic. **featured**, fē′tūrd, *a.* Having features of a certain cast. **featureless**, fē′tūr-les, *a.* Having no distinct features.

febrile, fē′bril, *a.* Pertaining to fever; indicating fever, or derived from it.

February, feb′rụ-er′i, *n.* The second month in the year.

fecund, fē′kund, *a.* Fruitful in progeny; prolific; fertile; productive. **fecundity**, fē-kun′di-ti, *n.* State or quality of being fecund; fertility; richness of invention.

federal, fed′ĕr-al, *a.* Pertaining to a league or contract; confederated; founded on alliance between states which unite for national purposes.—*n.* One who upholds federal government. **federalism**, fed′ĕr-al-izm, *n.* The principles of federal government. **federalist**, fed′ĕr-al-ist, *n.* A federal. **federalize**, fed′ĕr-al-īz, *vt.* or *i.* To unite in a federal compact.

federate, fed′ĕr-āt, *a.* Joined in confederacy. **federation**, fed-ĕr-ā′shun, *n.* Act of uniting in a league; confederacy.

fee, fē, *n.* A reward for services; recompense for professional services; a fief; a freehold estate held by one who is absolute owner.—*vt.* (feeing, feed). To pay a fee to; to engage in one's service by advancing a fee to.

feeble, fē′bl, *a.* Weak; impotent; deficient in vigor, as mental powers, sound, light, &c.

feebly, fē′bli, *adv.* Weakly; without strength.

feed, fēd, vt. (feeding, fed). To give food to; to furnish with anything of which there is constant consumption; to fatten.—vi. To take food; to eat; to prey; to graze; to grow fat.—n. That which is eaten; fodder; portion of provender given to a horse, cow, &c. **feeder**, fēd'èr, n. One who or that which feeds; an encourager; an affluent; a branch railway. **feeding**, fēd'ing, n. Act of giving food; act of eating; that which is eaten; provender.

feel, fēl, vt. (feeling, felt). To perceive by the touch; to have the sense of; to be affected by; to examine by touching.—vi. To have perception by the touch; to have the sensibility moved; to have perception mentally.—n. Act of feeling; perception caused by the touch. **feeler**, fēl'èr, n. One who feels; an observation, &c., put forth to ascertain the views of others; an organ of touch in the lower animals. **feeling**, fēl'ing, a. Possessing great sensibility; sensitive; sympathetic.—n. The sense of touch; sensation; sensibility; emotion; empathy. **feelingly**, fēl'ing-li, adv. In a feeling manner; tenderly.

feet, fēt, n.pl. of **foot**.

feign, fān, vt. To pretend; to counterfeit; to simulate.—vi. To represent falsely; to pretend. **feigned**, fānd, p.a. Simulated; assumed. **feignedly**, fān'-ed-li, adv. In pretense.

feint, fānt, n. A pretense; an appearance of aiming at one part when another is intended to be struck.—vi. To make a feigned blow or thrust.

feldspar, **felspar**, feld'spär, fel'spär, n. A mineral consisting of silica and alumina, with potash, soda, or lime, a principal constituent in granite, porphyry, &c. Called also *Felspath*.

felicitate, fē-lis'it-āt, vt. To congratulate. **felicitation**, fē-lis'it-ā″shun, n. Congratulation. **felicitous**, fē-lis'i-tus, a. Happy; extremely appropriate; managed with skill. **felicity**, fē-lis'i-ti, n. State of being in extreme enjoyment; bliss; the joys of heaven; skillfulness; appropriateness.

feline, fē'lin, a. Pertaining to cats; like a cat.

fell, fel, a. Cruel; fierce; savage.—n. A skin or hide of an animal; a seam sewed down level with the cloth; a stony or barren hill.—vt. To cause to fall; to hew down; to sew down a seam level with the cloth.

fellow, fel'ō, n. A partner; a companion; one of the same kind; an appellation of contempt; a member of a college or incorporated society. **fellowship**, fel'ō-ship, n. Companionship; joint interest; an association; an establishment in colleges for maintaining a fellow.

felon, fel'un, n. One who has committed felony; a culprit; a whitlow.—a. Fierce; malignant; malicious. **felonious**, fe-lō'ni-us, a. Villainous; done with purpose to commit a crime. **felony**, fel'on-i, n. Any crime which incurs the forfeiture of lands or goods; a heinous crime.

felt, felt, n. A fabric made of wool, or wool and fur, wrought into a compact substance by rolling, beating, &c.; an article made of felt.—vt. To make into felt; to cover with felt.

female, fē'māl, n. One of that sex which conceives and brings forth young.—a. Belonging to the sex which produces young; feminine.

feminine, fem'i-nin, a. Pertaining to females; womanly; effeminate; denoting the gender of words which signify females. **feminism**, fem'i-nizm, n. The doctrine that embraces the industrial, mental, political, social, and sexual equality of women with men.

femur, fē'mèr, n. The thigh bone.

fen, fen, n. A marsh; bog; swamp where water stagnates.

fence, fens, n. That which defends or guards; a wall, railing, &c., forming a boundary, &c.; defense; fencing; skill in fencing or argument; a purchaser or receiver of stolen goods.—vt. (fencing, fenced). To defend; to secure by an inclosure; to ward off by argument or reasoning.—vi. To practice the swordsman's art; to parry arguments; to prevaricate. **fencer**, fen'sèr, n. One who fences or practices the art of fencing. **fencing**, fen'sing, n. The art of using a sword or foil in attack or defense; material used in making fences; that which fences.

fend, fend, vt. To keep or ward off.—vi. To act on the defensive; to provide a livelihood. **fender**, fen'dèr, n. That which defends; a utensil to confine coal to the fireplace; something to protect the side of a vessel from injury.

fennel, fen'el, n. A plant cultivated for the aromatic flavor of its seeds and for its leaves.

ferment, fèr'ment, n. That which causes fermentation, as yeast, &c.; intestine motion; agitation.—vt. fèr-ment'. To produce fermentation in; to set in agitation.—vi. To undergo fermentation; to be in agitation. **fermentation**, fèr-men-tā'shun, n. Decomposition or conversion of an organic substance into new compounds by a ferment, indicated by the development of heat, bubbles, &c.; process by which grape juice is converted into wine; agitation; excitement. **fermentative**, fèr-men'ta-tiv, a. Causing fermentation; consisting in fermentation.

fern, fèrn, n. The name of many cryptogams producing leaves called fronds.

ferocious, fē-rō'shus, a. Fierce; savage; cruel. **ferocity**, fē-ros'i-ti, n. Savage wildness; fury; fierceness.

ferret, fe'ret, n. An animal allied to the weasel, employed in unearthing rabbits; a narrow tape made of woolen thread, cotton, or silk.—vt. To hunt with ferrets; to search out cunningly.

ferrous, fe'rē-us, a. Partaking of or pertaining to iron.

ferrule, fe'rūl, n. A ring of metal round the end of a stick to strengthen it.

ferry, fe'ri, vt. (ferrying, ferried). To carry over a river or other water in a boat.—n. Place where boats pass over to convey passengers; regular conveyance provided at such a place; a boat that plies at a ferry. **ferryman,** fe'ri-man, *n.* One who keeps a ferry.

fertile, fẽr'til, *a.* Fruitful; prolific; inventive; able to produce abundantly. **fertility,** fẽr-til'i-ti, *n.* Fruitfulness; richness; fertile invention. **fertilize,** fẽr'ti-liz, *vt.* To make fertile or fruitful; to enrich; to impregnate.

ferule, fer'ūl, *n.* A flat piece of wood, or rod, used to punish children.—*vt.* To punish with a ferule.

fervent, fẽr'vent, *a.* Burning; vehement; ardent; earnest. **fervency,** fẽr'ven-si, *n.* Eagerness; ardor; warmth of devotion.

fervid, fẽr'vid, *a.* Burning; zealous; eager; earnest.

fervor, fẽr'vẽr, *n.* Heat or warmth; ardor; intensity of feeling; zeal.

festal, fes'tal, *a.* Pertaining to a feast; joyous; gay; mirthful.

fester, fes'tẽr, *vi.* To suppurate; to rankle; to putrefy; to grow virulent.—*n.* A small inflammatory tumor.

festival, fes'ti-val, *a.* Festive; joyous.—*n.* The time of feasting; a feast; an anniversary day of joy, civil or religious.

festive, fes'tiv, *a.* Pertaining to or becoming a feast; mirthful. **festivity,** fes-tiv'i-ti, *n.* Festive gayety; social joy or mirth at an entertainment.

festoon, fes-tön', *n.* A string of flowers, foliage, &c., suspended in a curve or curves; carved work in the form of a wreath of flowers, &c.—*vt.* To form in festoons; to adorn with festoons.

fetch, fech, *vt.* To bring or draw; to make; to heave, as a sigh; to obtain as its price.—*vi.* To move or turn; to bring things.—*n.* A stratagem or trick; a wraith.

fête, fāt, *n.* A feast or festival; a holiday.—*vt.* To honor with a feast.

fetid, fet'id, fē'tid, *a.* Stinking; having a strong or rancid scent.

fetish, fetich, fē'tish, fet'ish, *n.* An object regarded by some savage races as having mysterious powers, or as being the representative or habitation of a deity; any object of exclusive devotion.

fetlock, fet'lok, *n.* The tuft of hair that grows behind on a horse's feet; the joint on which this hair grows; an instrument fixed to a horse's leg to prevent him from running off.

fetter, fet'ẽr, *n.* A chain for the feet; anything that confines or restrains from motion; generally in *pl.*—*vt.* To put fetters upon; to restrain.

fettle, fet'l, *vt.* (fettling, fettled). To put in right order.—*n.* Good trim, order, or condition.

fetus, foetus, fē'tus, *n.*; pl.**-uses.** The young of an animal in the womb, or in the egg, after being perfectly formed.

feud, fūd, *n.* Hostility; a hereditary quarrel; a fief.

feudal, fū'dal, *a.* Pertaining to feuds or fiefs; pertaining to the system of holdings lands by military services. **feudalism,** fū'dal-izm, *n.* The system by which land was held in return for military service; the feudal system.

fever, fē'vẽr, *n.* A disease characterized by an accelerated pulse, heat, thirst, and diminished strength; agitation; excitement.—*vt.* To put in a fever.—*vi.* To be seized with fever. **feverish,** fē'vẽr-ish, *a.* Having a slight fever; pertaining to fever; agitated; inconstant.

few, fū, *a.* Not many; small in number. **fewness,** fū'nes, *n.* Quality of being few; smallness of number; paucity.

fez, fez, *n.* A close-fitting red cap with a tassel, worn in Turkey, Egypt, &c.

fiancé, fiancée, fē-än-sā, *n.*, *masc.*, and *fem.* An affianced or betrothed person.

fiasco, fē-as'kō, *n.* An ignominious failure.

fiat, fi'at, *n.* A decree; a command.

fib, fib, *n.* A falsehood (a softer expression than *lie*)—*vi.* (fibbing, fibbed). To tell fibs.

fiber, fi'bẽr, *n.* A thread; a fine, slender body which constitutes a part of animals, plants, or minerals. **fibril,** fi'bril, *n.* A small fiber. **fibrin, fibrine,** fi'brin, *n.* An organic substance found in animals and vegetables, and readily obtained from fresh blood. **fibrous,** fi'brus, *a.* Composed or consisting of fibers; containing fibers.

fickle, fik'l, *a.* Of a changeable mind; vacillating; capricious. **fickleness,** fik'l-nes, *n.* Inconstancy.

fiction, fik'shun, *n.* A feigned story; literature in the form of novels, tales, &c.; a falsehood; fabrication. **fictitious,** fik-tish'us, *a.* Containing fiction; imaginary; counterfeit.

fiddle, fid'l, *n.* A stringed instrument of music; a violin.—*vi.* (fiddling, fiddled). To play on a fiddle; to trifle; to trifle with the hands.—*vt.* To play on a fiddle. **fiddler,** fid'lẽr, *n.* On who plays a fiddle.

fidelity, fi-del'i-ti, *n.* Faithfulness; trustiness; loyalty; integrity.

fidget, fij'et, *vi.* To move uneasily or in fits and starts.—*n.* An uneasy restless motion. **fidgety,** fij'e-ti, *a.* Restless; uneasy.

fiduciary, fi-dū'shi-er'i, *a.* Held in trust; having the nature of a trust.—*n.* One who holds a thing in trust; a trustee.

fie, fi, An exclamation denoting contempt or dislike.

fief, fēf, *n.* An estate held of a superior on condition of military service.

field, fēld, *n.* A piece of land suitable for tillage or pasture; piece of inclosed land; place of battle; battle; open space for action; sphere; blank space on which figures are drawn; those taking part in a hunt or race.—*vi.* and *t.* To watch and catch the ball as in baseball. **field book,** fēld'buk, *n.* A book used in surveying. **field day,** fēld'dā, *n.* A day when troops are drawn out for instruction in field exercises and evolutions. **field glass,** fēld'gläs, *n.* A kind of binocular telescope. **field marshal,** fēld mär'shal, *n.* A military officer of the highest rank. **field officer,** fēld of'i-sẽr, *n.* A major, lieutenant-colonel, or colonel.

fiend, fēnd, *n.* A demon; the devil; a wicked or cruel person. **fiendish,** fēnd'ish, *a.* Like a fiend; diabolic.

fierce, fērs, *a*. Wild; savage; outrageous; violent. **fiercely**, fērs'li, *adv*. Violently; with rage.

fiery, fī'ri, *a*. Consisting of fire; like fire; impetuous; irritable; fierce. **fierily**, fī'ri-li, *adv*. In a fiery manner.

fife, fīf, *n*. A small wind-instrument used chiefly in martial music.—*vi*. (fifing, fifed). To play on a fife.

fifteen, fif'tēn', *a*. and *n*. Five and ten. **fifteenth**, fif'tēnth, *a*. The ordinal of fifteen.—*n*. A fifteenth part.

fifth, fifth, *a*. The ordinal of five.—*n*. A fifth part.

fifth column. Part of a native population that secretly aid the enemy of their country.

fiftieth, fif'ti-eth, *a*. The ordinal of fifty.—*n*. A fiftieth part.

fifty, fif'ti, *a*. and *n*. Five tens; five times ten.

fig, fig, *n*. The fruit of a tree of the mulberry family; the tree itself; a mere trifle; dress.

fight, fīt, *vi*. (fighting, fought). To strive for victory; to contend in arms.—*vt*. To war against; to contend with in battle; to win by struggle.—*n*. A struggle for victory; a battle; an encounter. **fighter**, fīt'ér, *n*. One who fights; a combatant; a warrior. **fighting**, fīt'ing, *a*. Qualified for war; fit for battle; occupied in war.

figment, fig'ment, *n*. A fiction; fabrication.

figuration, fig-ū-rā'shun, *n*. Act of giving figure; configuration; form. **figurative**, fig'ūr-ā-tiv, *a*. Containing a figure or figures; representing by resemblance; typical; metaphoric; abounding in figures of speech.

figure, fig'ūr, *n*. The form of anything as expressed by the outline; appearance; representation; a statue; a character denoting a number; a diagram; type; mode of expression in which words are turned from their ordinary signification; price.—*vt*. (figuring, figured). To make a likeness of; to represent by drawing, &c.; to cover or mark with figures; to image in the mind.—*vi*. To make a figure; to be distinguished. **figured**, fig'ūrd, *a*. Adorned with figures; free and florid. **figurehead**, fig'ūr-hed', *n*. The ornamental figure on a ship under the bowsprit. **figuring**, fig'ūr-ing, *n*. Act of making figures; figures collectively.

filament, fil'a-ment, *n*. A slender thread; a fine fibre.

filbert, fil'bèrt, *n*. The fruit of the cultivated hazel.

filch, filch, *vt*. To pilfer; to steal. **filcher**, fil'chèr, *n*. A petty thief.

file, fīl, *n*. A line or wire on which papers are strung; the papers so strung; a row of soldiers one behind another; a steel instrument for cutting and smoothing iron, wood, &c.—*vt*. (filing, filed). To arrange or place on or in a file; to bring before a court by presenting the proper papers; to rub or cut with a file; to polish.—*vi*. To march in a line one after the other.

filial, fil'i-al, *a*. Pertaining to or becoming a son or daughter.

filibuster, fil'i-bus'tèr, *n*. A buccaneer; one of those lawless adventurers who in the present century have invaded a foreign country; extended speech in debate to gain time and exhaust adversary.—*vi*. To act as a filibuster.

filigree, fil'i-grē, *n*. Ornamental open work in fine gold or silver wire.

filings, fīl'ingz, *n.pl*. Fragments or particles rubbed off by the act of filing.

fill, fil, *vt*. To make full; to occupy; to pervade; to satisfy; to surfeit; to supply with an occupant; to hold; to possess and perform the duties of.—*vi*. To grow or become full.—*n*. As much as fills or supplies want. **filler**, fil'èr, *n*. One who fills; a tube for filling bottles.

fillet, fil'et, *n*. A little band to tie about the hair; the fleshy part of the thigh in veal; meat rolled together and tied round; something resembling a fillet or band.—*vt*. (filleting, filleted). To bind with a little band.

filling, fil'ing, *n*. A making full; materials for making full; woof of a fabric.

fillip, fil'ip, *vt*. To strike with the nail of the finger, forced from the thumb with a sudden spring.—*n*. A jerk of the finger; something which tends to stimulate at once.

filly, fil'i, *n*. A female colt; a wanton girl.

film, film, *n*. A thin skin; a pellicle.—*vt*. To cover with a thin skin; the photographic film, in the form of a flexible strip, used in making a moving picture. It is about an inch wide, of sensitized translucent material resembling celluloid. **filmy**, film'i, *a*. Like a film; composed of thin membranes or pellicles.

filter, fil'tèr, *n*. A strainer; any substance through which liquors are passed.—*vt*. To purify by passing through a filter.—*vi*. To percolate; to pass through a filter.

filth, filth, *n*. That which defiles; dirt; pollution. **filthy**, fil'thi, *a*. Abounding in filth; dirty; foul; nasty; obscene.

filtrate, fil'trāt, *vt*. To filter. **filtration**, fil'trā'shun, *n*. Act or process of filtering.

fin, fin, *n*. One of the organs which enable fishes to balance themselves and regulate their movements; anything resembling a fin.

final, fī'nal, *a*. Pertaining to the end; last; ultimate; conclusive; decisive. **finale**, fē-nā'lā, *n*. The last part of a piece of music; the last place or scene in a performance. **finality**, fī-nal'i-ti, *n*. Final state; state of being final; the doctrine that nothing exists except for a determinate end. **finally**, fī'nal-li, *adv*. Ultimately; lastly; completely; beyond recovery.

finance, fi-nans', *n*. The science of public revenue and expenditure; management of money matters; *pl*. public funds or resources of money; private income.—*vi*. (financing; financed). To conduct financial operations.—*vt*. To manage the financial affairs of. **financial**, fi-nan'shal, *a*. Pertaining to finance. **financier**, fi-nan'sèr, *n*. One skilled in matters of finance.

finch, finch, *n.* A small singing bird.

find, find, *vt.* (finding, found). To come upon; to discover; to recover; to get; to perceive; to supply; to declare by verdict.—*n.* A discovery; the thing found.

finding, fīn'ding, *n.* Discovery; act of discovering; that which is found; a verdict.

fine, fīn, *a.* Slender; minute; keen; delicate; refined; elegant; amiable; noble; splendid.—*n.* Payment of money imposed as a punishment; conclusion (in *fine*).—*vt.* (finding, fined). To make fine; to purify; to impose a pecuniary penalty on. **finedrawn**, fīn'dran, *p.a.* Drawn out to too great fineness, or with too much subtlety.

finely, fīn'li, *adv.* In a fine manner; gayly; handsomely; delicately.

finery, fīn'ėr-i, *n.* Fine things; showy articles of dress; a furnace where cast-iron is converted into malleable iron.

finesse, fi-nes', *n.* Artifice; stratagem.—*vi.* To use finesse or artifice.

finger, fing'gėr, *n.* One of the five members of the hand; something resembling a finger; skill in playing on a keyed instrument.—*vt.* To handle with the fingers; to touch lightly; to pilfer.—*vi.* To dispose the fingers aptly in playing on an instrument. **fingered**, fing'gėrd, *a.* Having fingers, or parts like fingers. **fingering**, fing'gėr-ing, *n.* Act of touching lightly; manner of touching an instrument of music; a loose worsted for stocking, &c.

finical, fin'ik-al, *a.* Unduly particular about trifles; idly busy. Also *finicking* and *finikin.*

finis, fī'nis, *n.* An end; conclusion.

finish, fin'ish, *vt.* To bring to an end; to perfect; to polish to a high degree.—*vi.* To come to an end; to expire.—*n.* Completion; the last touch to a work; polish.

finite, fī'nīt, *a.* Limited; bounded; circumscribed; not infinite.

Finn, fin, *n.* A native of Finland. **Finnish**, fin'ish. *a.* Relating to the Finns.—*n.* Their language.

finny, fin'i, *a.* Furnished with fins.

fiord, fjord, fyord, *n.* An inlet of the sea such as are common in Norway.

fir, fėr, *n.* A resinous coniferous tree.

fire, fīr, *n.* Heat and light emanating from a body; fuel burning; a conflagration; discharge of firearms; splendor; violence of passion; vigor of fancy; animation; ardent affection; affliction.—*vt.* (firing, fired). To set on fire; to irritate; to animate; to bake; to cause to explode; to discharge (firearms).—*vi.* To take fire; to be inflamed with passion; to discharge firearms. **firearm**, fīr'ärm, *n.* A weapon which expels its projectile by the combustion of gunpowder. **fire brand**, fīr'brand', *n.* A piece of wood kindled; an incendiary; one who inflames factions. **fire brigade**, fīr'bri-gād', *n.* A body of men organized to extinguish fires. **fire-engine**, fīr'en-jin, *n.* An engine for throwing water to extinguish fire. **fire-escape**, fīr'es-kāp, *n.* A structure to facilitate escape from a building on fire. **firefly**, fīr'flī, *n.* A winged insect which

emits a brilliant light at night. **fireman**, fīr'man, *n.* A man who extinguishes fires, or tends the fires, of an engine. **fireproof**, fīr'prōf, *a.* Incombustible. **fireside**, fīr'sīd, *n.* A place near the fire or hearth; home; domestic life. **firework**, fīr'wėrk, *n.* Preparation of gunpowder, sulphur, &c., used for making a show, a signal, &c.

firing, fīr'ing, *n.* Act of one who fires; act of discharging firearms; application of fire; fuel; process of treating articles with fire.

firing squad, fīr'ing skwäd, *n.* A number of soldiers detailed to fire a saluting volley over the grave of a dead soldier or officer.

firm, fėrm, *a.* Steady; stable; strong; dense; hard; not fluid; fixed; resolute.—*n.* A partnership or commercial house.—*vt.* To make firm or solid.—*vi.* To become firm.

firmament, fėr'ma-ment, *n.* The sky or heavens; region of the air; an expanse.

firmly, fėrm'li, *adv.* In a firm manner; steadfastly; resolutely.

first, fėrst, *a.* Foremost in time, place, rank, value, &c.; chief; highest; the ordinal of *one.*—*adv.* Before all others in time, place, &c.

first-born, fėrst'born, *a.* Eldest.

first-class, fėrst'klas', *a.* First-rate.

firsthand, fėrst'hand', *a.* Obtained direct from the first source, producer, maker, &c.

first-rate, fėrst'rāt', *a.* Of highest excellence; pre-eminent; of largest size.

firth, fėrth, *n.* An arm of the sea into which a river discharges; a channel. Also *Frith.*

fiscal, fis'kal, *a.* Pertaining to the public treasury.—*n.* A treasurer; a public prosecutor, as in Scotland.

fish, fish, *n.* An animal that lives in water; the flesh of such animals used as food.—*vi.* To attempt to catch fish; to attempt to obtain by artifice.—*vt.* To catch or try to catch fish in; to draw out or up when in water. **fisher**, fish'ėr, *n.* One employed in fishing. **fisherman**, fish'ėr-man, *n.* One whose occupation is to catch fish. **fishery**, fish'ėr-i, *n.* The business of catching fish; a place for catching fish. **fishing**, fish'ing, *a.* Used in catching fish.—*n.* Art or practice of catching fish; place to fish in. **fishmonger**, fish"mung'gėr, *n.* A dealer in fish. **fishy**, fish'i, *a.* Consisting of fish; like fish; worn out; dubious; unsafe.

fissile, fis'il, *a.* That may be split in the direction of the grain, or of natural joints.

fission, fish'un, *n.* The act of splitting into parts; reproduction in animals of a low type through the body dividing into parts.

fissure, fish'ėr, *n.* A cleft; a longitudinal opening.—*vt.* To cleave; to crack.

fist, fist, *n.* The hand clenched; the hand with the fingers doubled into the palm.—*vt.* To strike with the fist. **fistic**, fis'tik, *a.* Pertaining to boxing. **fisticuffs**, fis'-ti-kufs, *n.* A blow with the fist; commonly in *pl.* boxing.

fistula, fis'tū-la, *n.* A shepherd's pipe; a

deep, narrow, sinuous ulcer. **fistular,** fis'tū-lėr, *a.* Hollow like a pipe.

fit, fit, *n.* A sudden activity followed by a relaxation; paroxysm; convulsion; due adjustment of dress to the body.—*a.* Conformable to a standard of right, duty, taste, &c.; suitable; proper; congruous; qualified; adequate.—*vt.* (fitting, fitted). To make fit or suitable; to furnish with anything; to adapt; to qualify for.—*vi.* To be proper or becoming; to suit; to be adapted.

fitful, fit'fŭl, *a.* Full of fits; varied by sudden impulses; spasmodic; checkered.

fitly, fit'li, *adv.* Suitably; properly.

fitter, fit'ėr, *n.* One who fits; one who puts the parts of machinery together.

fitting, fit'ing, *a.* Fit; appropriate.—*n.pl.* Things fixed on; permanent appendages.

fittingly, fit'ing-li, *adv.* Suitably.

five, fiv, *a.* and *n.* Four and one added; the half of ten. **fivefold,** fiv'fōld, *a.* In fives; consisting of five in one; five times repeated.

fix, fiks, *vt.* To make fast or firm; to settle; to define; to appoint; to deprive of volatility.—*vi.* To settle or remain permanently; to cease to be fluid; to congeal.—*n.* A condition of difficulty; dilemma. **fixation,** fiks-ā'shun, *n.* Act of fixing; state in which a body resists evaporation. **fixative,** fik'sa-tiv, *a.* Tending or causing to fix.—*n.* A substance that causes something to be stable or not fleeting. **fixed,** fikst, *p.a.* Firm; fast; settled; deprived of volatility.

fixture, fiks'tūr, *n.* That which is fixed; that which is permanently attached; an appendage.

fizz, fizzle, fiz, fiz'l, *vi.* To make a hissing sound. Also used as a noun.

flabbergast, flab'ėr-gast, *vt.* To strike with astonishment or dismay.

flabby, flab'i, *a.* Soft; yielding to the touch; languid; feeble.

flaccid, flak'sid, *a.* Flabby; soft and weak; drooping; limber.

flag, flag, *n.* A cloth, usually attached to a pole, and bearing devices expressive of nationality, &c.; a banner; a flat stone for paving; an aquatic plant with sword-shaped leaves.—*vi.* (flagging, flagged). To hang loose; to droop; to languish; to slacken.—*vt.* To lay with broad flat stones.

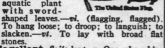

The United States Flag

flagellant, flaj'e-lant, *n.* One who whips himself in religious discipline.

flagellate, flaj'e-lāt, *vt.* To whip. **flagellation,** flaj-e-lā'shun, *n.* A flogging; the discipline of the scourge.

flagging, flag'ing, *n.* Flag-stones; a pavement or side-walk of flag-stones.

flagitious, fla-jish'us, *a.* Deeply criminal; corrupt; profligate; heinous.

flagon, fla'gun, *n.* A vessel with a narrow mouth; used for liquors.

flagrant, flā'grant, *a.* Flaming in notice; glaring; notorious; enormous. **fla-**

grancy, flā'gran-si, *n.* Quality of being flagrant; enormity. **flagrantly,** flā'-grant-li, *adv.* Glaringly; notoriously.

flail, flāl, *n.* A wooden instrument for thrashing or beating grain, &c.—*vt.* and *i.* To beat with or as if with a flail.

flake, flāk, *n.* A loose, filmy, mass of anything; a scale; a fleecy or feathery particle, as of snow; a flock, as of wool.—*vt.* (flaking, flaked). To form into flakes.—*vi.* To break in layers; to peel off. **flaky,** flāk'i, *a.* Consisting of flakes; lying in flakes; like flakes or scales.

flamboyant, flam-boi'ant, *a.* Noting that style of Gothic architecture characterized by wavy tracery in the windows; florid.

flame, flām, *n.* Light emitted from fire; a blaze; fire; heat of passion; ardor of temper or imagination; ardent love; rage; one beloved.—*vi.* (flaming, flamed). To blaze; to glow; to rage. **flaming,** flām'ing, *p.a.* Emitting a flame; violent; vehement.

flamingo, fla-ming'gō, *n.* A web-footed, long necked bird about 5 to 6 feet high.

flange, flanj, *n.* A projecting rim or edge on any substance; a raised edge on a wheel, &c.—*vt.* (flanging, flanged). To furnish with a flange.

flank, flangk, *n.* The part of the side of an animal between the ribs and the hip; the side of an army; the extreme right or left; the side of any building.—*vt.* To be situated at the side of; to place troops so as to command or attack the flank; to pass round the side of.

flannel, flan'el, *n.* A soft, nappy, woolen cloth of loose texture; garment made of flannel.

flap, flap, *n.* Something broad and flexible that hangs loose; the motion or sound of anything broad and loose, or a stroke with it; tail of a coat, &c.—*vt.* (flapping, flapped). To beat with a flap; to move, as something broad.—*vi.* To move, as wings; to wave loosely.

flapjack, flap'jak, *n.* A sort of broad pancake; an apple-puff.

flapper, flap'ėr, *n.* One who or that which flaps; a young wild duck; a flashy young woman of the 1920's.

flare, flār, *vi.* (flaring, flared). To burn with an unsteady light; to glitter with transient luster; to give out a dazzling light.—*n.* An unsteady strong light. **flaring,** flār'ing, *p.a.* Glittering; showy.

flash, flash, *n.* A sudden burst of flame and light; a gleam.—*a.* Vulgarly showy; counterfeit.—*vi.* To burst or break forth with a flash; to dart—*vt.* To throw out like a burst of light. **flashily,** flash'i-li, *adv.* Gaudily; showily. **flash point, flashing point,** flash'point, flash'ing-point, *n.* The temperature at which the vapor of oils will ignite and flash. **flashy,** flash'i, *a.* Characterized by empty show; gaudy; impulsive.

flask, flask, *n.* A kind of bottle; a bottle for the pocket; a vessel for powder.

flat, flat, *a.* Having an even surface; level; fallen; tasteless; vapid; depressed; dull; absolute; below the true pitch, as a sound.—*n.* A level; a shallow; the broad side of something; a mark in music indicating lowering of pitch; a story or floor of a house; a simpleton.

flatly, flat'li, *adv.* In a flat manner; horizontally; evenly; without spirit; positively.

flatten, flat'n, *vt.* To make flat; to level; to render less acute or sharp, as a sound. —*vi.* To grow or become flat.

flatter, flat'ėr, *vt.* To gratify by praise; to compliment; to praise falsely. **flatterer,** flat'ėr-ėr, *n.* One who flatters; a fawner; a wheedler. **flattering,** flat'ėr-ing, *a.* Bestowing flattery; agreeable to one's self-love; gratifying. **flattery,** flat'ė-ri, *n.* False praise; sycophancy; cajolery.

flattop, flat'top', *n.* Aircraft carrier.

flatulent, flat'ū-lent, *a.* Affected with gases in the stomach and intestines; generating wind in the stomach; empty; puffy. **flatulence, flatulency,** flat'ū-lens, flat'ū-len-si, *n.* State of being flatulent.

flaunt, flạnt, *vi.* and *t.* To display ostentatiously.—*n.* Bold or impudent parade. **flaunty, flaunting,** flạnt'i, flạnt'ing, *a.* Apt to flaunt; ostentatious; gaudy.

flavor, flā'vėr, *n.* The quality of a substance which affects the smell or taste; relish; zest.—*vt.* To give a flavor to. **flavored,** flā'vėrd, *p.a.* Having flavor. **flavorless,** flā'vėr-les, *a.* Without flavor; tasteless.

flaw, flạ, *n.* A crack; a defect; a speck; a gust of wind.—*vt.* To make a flaw in. **flawless,** flạ'les, *a.* Without defect; perfect.

flax, flaks, *n.* A plant, the fibers of which are formed into linen threads; the fibers prepared for manufacture.

flaxen, flak'sn, *a.* Made of or like flax; of the color of flax; fair.

flay, flā, *vt.* To strip the skin off an animal; to censure harshly.

flea, flē, *n.* An insect that leaps with great agility, and whose bite causes itch. **fleabite,** flē'bit, *n.* The bite of a flea; a thing of no moment.

fleck, flek, *n.* A spot; streak; dapple.—*vt.* To spot; to streak or stripe; to dapple.

fledgeling, flej'ling, *n.* A bird just fledged.

flee, flē, *vi.* (fleeing, fled). To run away; to hasten from.—*vt.* To shun.

fleece, flēs, *n.* The coat of wool that covers a sheep, or is shorn at one time. —*vt.* (fleecing, fleeced). To strip of the fleece; to rob or cheat heartlessly; to cover as with a fleece. **fleecy,** flēs'i, *a.* Resembling wool or a fleece; covered with wool; woolly.

fleet, flēt, *n.* A squadron or body of ships; navy.—*a.* Swift of pace; nimble. —*vi.* To fly swiftly; to flit; to be in a transient state. **fleeting,** flēt'ing, *a.* Not durable; transient; momentary. **fleetly,** flēt'li, *adv.* Rapidly; swiftly.

Fleming, flem'ing, *n.* A native of Flanders.

Flemish, flem'ish, *a.* Pertaining to Flanders.—*n.* The language of the Flemings.

flesh, flesh, *n.* The muscular part of an animal; animal food; beasts and birds used as food; the body, as distinguished from the soul; mankind; corporeal appetites; kindred; family.—*vt.* To feed with flesh; to initiate to the taste of flesh.

fleshed, flesht, *a.* Fat; fleshy; having flesh of a particular kind.

fleshy, flesh'i, *a.* Muscular; fat; corpulent; plump; pulpy.

flex, fleks, *vt.* To bend.

flexible, fleks'i-bl, *a.* That may be bent; pliant; supple; tractable; plastic. **flexibility,** fleks-i-bil'i-ti, *n.* Quality of being flexible; pliancy; readiness to comply.

flick, flik, *n.* A sharp sudden stroke, as with a whip; a flip.—*vt.* To strike with a flick; to flip.

flicker, flik'ėr, *vi.* To flutter; to wave, as an unsteady flame.—*n.* A wavering gleam.

flier, flyer, flī'ėr, *n.* One who flies or flees; a part of a machine which moves rapidly.

flight, flīt, *n.* Act of fleeing or flying; power or manner of flying; a flock of birds; a volley, as of arrows; space passed by flying; a soaring; lofty elevation, as of fancy; extravagant sally; a series of steps or stairs.

flighty, flīt'i, *a.* Full of flights or sallies of imagination, caprice, &c.; volatile; giddy.

flimsy, flim'zi, *a.* Thin; slight; weak; without force; shallow.

flinch, flinsh, *vi.* To shrink; to withdraw; to wince; to fail.

fling, fling, *vt.* (flinging, flung). To cause to fly from the hand; to hurl; to scatter; to throw to the ground.—*vi.* To fly into violent and irregular motions; to flounce; to rush away angrily.—*n.* A throw; a gibe; a lively Scottish dance.

flint, flint, *n.* A very hard siliceous stone, which strikes fire with steel; anything proverbially hard. **flintlock,** flint'lok, *n.* A musket lock in which fire is produced by a flint. **flinty,** flin'ti, *a.* Consisting of or like flint; very hard; cruel; inexorable.

flip, flip, *n.* A flick; a drink consisting of beer and spirit sweetened, and heated by a hot iron.—*vt.* To flick.

flippant, flip'ant, *a.* Speaking confidently; without knowledge; heedlessly pert; shallow. **flippancy,** flip'an-si, *n.* Quality of being flippant; heedless pertness; undue levity.

flipper, flip'ėr, *n.* The paddle of a sea-turtle; the broad fin of a fish; the arm of a seal.

flirt, flėrt, *vt.* To throw with a jerk; to make coquettish motions with (a fan).— *vi.* To run and dart about; to coquette; to play at courtship.—*n.* A sudden jerk; one who plays at courtship; a coquette. **flirtation,** flėr-tā'shun, *n.* Playing at courtship; coquetry.

flit, flit, *vi.* (flitting, flitted). To fly or dart along; to flutter; to change habitation (Scotch in this sense).

float, flōt, *n.* That which is borne on water or any fluid; a raft.—*vi.* To be borne on the surface of a fluid; to be buoyed up; to move with a light, irregular course.—*vt.* To cause to be conveyed on water; to flood; to get (a company, scheme, &c.) started. **floatboard,** flōt'-bōrd, *n.* A board of an undershot water wheel, on which the water strikes; board of a paddle-wheel. **floating,** flōt'ing, *p.a.* Circulating; fluctuating; not fixed or invested; unattached.

flock, flok, *n.* A lock of wool or hair; stuffing for mattresses, &c.; a company, as of sheep, birds, &c.; a Christian congregation in relation to their pastor.—*vi.* To gather in companies; to crowd; to move in crowds.

floe, flō, *n.* A mass of ice floating in the ocean.

flog, flog, *vt.* (flogging, flogged). To whip; to chastise with repeated blows. **flogging,** flog'ing, *n.* A whipping for punishment.

flood, flud, *n.* A great flow of water; a deluge; a river; the flowing of the tide; a great quantity; abundance.—*vt.* To overflow; to deluge; to overwhelm. **flood gate,** flud'gāt, *n.* A gate to stop or let out water. **flood mark,** flud'märk, *n.* The line to which the tide rises; high-water mark. **flood tide,** flud'tīd, *n.* The rising tide.

floor, flōr, *n.* That part of a building on which we walk; bottom of a room; story in a building; a flat, hard surface of loam; lime, &c., used in some kinds of business, as in malting.—*vt.* To lay a floor upon; to strike down.—**flooring,** flōr'ing, *n.* A floor; materials for floors.

flop, flop, *vt.* and *i.* (flopping, flopped). To clap or flap; to let down suddenly; to plump down.—*n.* A sudden sinking to the ground.

flora, flō'ra, *n.* The plants of a particular district or period; a work describing them.

floral, flō'ral, *a.* Pertaining to or made of flowers.

florid, flor'id, *a.* Flowery; bright in color; flushed with red; embellished with flowers of rhetoric; highly decorated.

florist, flō'rist, *n.* A cultivator of flowers; one who writes a flora.

floss, flos, *n.* A downy or silky substance in plants; fine untwisted silk used in embroidery. **flossy,** flos'i, *a.* Composed of or like floss.

flotilla, flō-til'a, *n.* A little fleet; or fleet of small vessels.

flotsam, flot'sam, *n.* Portion of a wreck that continues floating.

flounce, flouns, *vi.* (flouncing, flounced). To spring or turn with sudden effort; to start away in anger.—*vt.* To deck with a flounce or flounces.—*n.* A strip of cloth sewed round a gown with the lower border loose and spreading.

flounder, floun'dėr, *n.* A flat fish found in the sea near the mouths of rivers.—*vi.* To struggle, as in mire; to roll, toss, and tumble.

flour, flour, *n.* Finely ground meal of wheat or other grain; fine powder of any substance.—*vt.* To convert into flour; to sprinkle with flour. **floury,** flour'i, *a.* Resembling flour.

flourish, flur'ish; *vi.* To grow luxuriantly; to thrive; to live; to use florid language; to make ornamental strokes in writing, &c.; to move in bold and irregular figures.—*vt.* To adorn with flowers or figures; to ornament with anything showy; to brandish.—*n.* Showy splendor; parade of words and figures; fanciful stroke of the pen; decorative notes in music; brandishing. **flourishing,** flur'ish-ing, *p.a.* Prosperous; growing luxuriantly.

flout, flout, *vt.* To mock or insult; to jeer at.—*n.* A mock; an insult.

flow, flō, *vi.* To move as water; to issue; to abound; to glide smoothly; to hang loose and waving; to rise, as the tide; to circulate, as blood.—*vt.* To flow over; to flood.—*n.* A moving along, as of water; stream; current; rise of water; fullness; free expression; feeling.

flower, flou'ėr, *n.* The delicate and gaily colored leaves or petals on a plant; a bloom or blossom; youth; the prime; the best part; one most distinguished; an ornamental expression; *pl.* a powdery substance.—*vi.* To blossom; to bloom.—*vt.* To embellish with figures of flowers. **flowering,** flou'ėr-ing, *p.a.* Having flowers; blossoming. **flowery,** flou'ėr-i, *a.* Full of flowers; embellished with figurative language; florid.

flowing, flō'ing, *p.a.* Moving as a stream; abounding; fluent; undulating.

flown, flōn, pp. of *fly.*

fluctuate, fluk'tū-āt, *vi.* To move as a wave; to waver; to hesitate; to experience vicissitudes. **fluctuating,** fluk'tū-āt-ing, *p.a.* Unsteady; wavering. **fluctuation,** fluk'tū-ā"shun, *n.* A rising and falling; change; vicissitude.

flue, flō, *n.* A passage for smoke or heated air; a pipe for conveying heat; light downy matter; fluff.

fluent, flō'ent, *a.* Flowing; ready in the use of words; voluble; smooth. **fluently,** flō'ent-li, *adv.* In a fluent manner; with ready flow of words. **fluency,** flō'en-si, *n.* Quality of being fluent; facility of words; volubility.

fluff, fluf, *n.* Light down or nap such as rises from beds, cotton, &c. **fluid,** flu'id, *a.* Capable of flowing; liquid or gaseous.—*n.* Any substance whose parts easily move and change their relative position without separation; a liquid. **fluidity,** flu-id'i-ti, *n.* Quality or state of being fluid.

fluke, flōk, *n.* That part of an anchor which fastens in the ground; an accidental success; a flatfish; a parasitic worm.

flume, flōm, *n.* A channel for the water that drives a mill wheel; an artificial channel for gold-washing.

flunky, flunkey, flung'ki, *n.* A male servant in livery; a cringing flatterer; a toady.

flurry, flur'i, *n.* Bustle; hurry; a gust of wind; light things carried by the wind.—*vt.* (flurrying, flurried). To agitate or alarm.

fluorescence, flō'o-res"ens, *n.* The light emitted when certain substances are subjected to radiant energy.

fluoridation, flō'ri-dā-shun, *n.* The

treating of drinking water with fluoride to help prevent tooth decay.

flush, flush, *vi.* To become suddenly red, to blush.—*vt.* To cause to redden suddenly; to elate; to excite; to wash out by copious supplies of water; to cause to start up.—*n.* A sudden flow of blood to the face; sudden thrill; vigor; flow of water; run of cards of the same suit.—*a.* Fresh; full of vigor; affluent; even with the adjacent surface.

fluster, flus'tèr, *vt.* To agitate; to make hot with drink.—*n.* Agitation; confusion; heat.

flute, flöt, *n.* A small wind instrument with holes and keys; a channel cut along the shaft of a column; a similar channel.—*vi.* (fluting, fluted). To play on a flute.—*vt.* To play or sing in notes like those of a flute; to form flutes or channels in. **fluted**, flöt'ed, *p.a.* Channeled; furrowed.

flutter, flut'èr, *vi.* To move or flap the wings rapidly; to be in agitation; to fluctuate.—*vt.* To agitate; to throw into confusion.—*n.* Quick, confused motion; agitation; disorder.

flux, fluks, *n.* Act of flowing; any flow of matter; dysentery flow of the tide; anything used to promote fusion; fusion; liquid state from the operation of heat.—*vt.* To melt; to fuse. **fluxion**, fluk'-shun, *n.* Act of flowing; flux, a flow of blood or other fluid; an infinitely small quantity; *pl.* the analysis of infinitely small variable quantities.

fly, flī, *vi.* (flying; pret. flew; pp. flown). To move through air by wings; to move in air by the force of wind, &c.; to rise in air; to move rapidly; to pass away; to depart suddenly; to spring; to flutter.—*vt.* To flee from; to cause to float in the air.—*n.* A winged insect.

fly-fishing, flī''fish'ing, *n.* Angling for fish with flies, natural or artificial.

flying fish, flī'ing fish, *n.* A fish which can sustain itself in the air for a time by means of its long pectoral fins.

flyleaf, flī'lēf, *n.* A leaf of blank paper at the beginning and end of a book.

flypaper, flī'pā-pèr, *n.* A paper for destroying flies.

flywheel, flī'whēl, *n.* A wheel to equalize the motive power of a machine.

foal, fōl, *n.* The young of a mare, she-ass, &c.; a colt or filly.—*vt.* To bring forth, as a colt or filly.—*vi.* To bring forth a foal.

foam, fōm, *n.* Froth; spume.—*vi.* To froth; to show froth at the mouth; to rage.—*vt.* To cause to give out foam; to throw out with rage or violence. **foamy**, fōm'i, *a.* Covered with foam; frothy.

fob, fob, *n.* A little pocket for a watch in the waistband of the breeches.

focal, fō'kal, *a.* Belonging to a focus.

focus, fō'kus, *n.*; *pl.* -**cuses** or -**ci.** A point in which rays of light meet after being reflected or refracted; point of concentration.—*vt.* To bring to a focus.

fodder, fod'èr, *n.* Food for cattle, &c.—*vt.* To furnish with fodder.

foe, fō, *n.* An enemy; an opposing army; one who opposes anything.

fœtus, fē'tus, *See* **fetus.**

fog, fog, *n.* A dense vapor near the surface of the land or water; mental confusion; dimness; second growth of grass; long grass that remains in pastures till winter.

foggy, fog'i, *a.* Filled with fog; cloudy; misty; producing fogs; stupid.

fogy, fōgey, fō'gi, *n.*; *pl.* -**ies, -eys.** A stupid fellow; an old-fashioned person.

foible, foi'bl, *n.* A weak point in character; a failing; the weak part of a sword.

foil, foil, *vt.* To frustrate; to baffle; to balk.—*n.* Defeat; frustration; a sword used in fencing; a thin leaf of metal; anything which serves to set off a thing to advantage; something resembling a leaf; a curve in the tracery of Gothic windows, &c.

foist, foist, *vt.* To introduce or insert surreptitiously or without warrant; to palm off.

fold, fōld, *n.* The doubling or doubled part of any flexible substance; a plait; an inclosure for sheep; a flock of sheep; the Church.—*vt.* To double; to lay in plaits; to embrace; to confine, as sheep in a fold.—*vi.* To close together; to become folded.

folder, fōld'èr, *n.* One who folds; an instrument used in folding paper.

foliage, fō'li-ij, *n.* Leaves collectively; ornamental representation of leaves.

folio, fō'li-ō, *n.* A book of the largest size, formed by sheets of paper once doubled; a page; number appended to each page; a written page of a certain number of words.

folk, fōk, *n.* People in general; certain people discriminated from others, as old *folks.*

folklore, fōk'lōr, *n.* Rural superstitions, tales, traditions, or legends.

follicle, fol'li-kl, *n.* A little bag or vesicle in animals or plants.

follow, fol'ō, *vt.* To go or come after; to chase; to accompany; to succeed; to result from; to understand; to copy; to practice; to be occupied with; to be guided by.—*vi.* To come after another; to ensue; to result.

follower, fol'ō-èr, *n.* An adherent; disciple; imitator; attendant; dependent.

following, fol'ō-ing, *n.* A body of followers.—*p.a.* Being next after; succeeding.

folly, fol'i, *n.* Foolishness; imbecility; a weak or foolish act; criminal weakness.

foment, fō-ment', *vt.* To apply warm lotions to; to abet; to stir up (in a bad sense). **fomentation**, fō'men-tā''shun, *n.* Act of fomenting; lotion applied; instigation; encouragement.

fond, fond, *a.* Foolish; foolishly tender and loving; doting; loving; relishing. **fondle**, fon'dl, *vt.* (fondling, fondled). To treat with fondness; to caress. **fondly**, fond'li, *adv.* Foolishly; lovingly. **fondness**, fond'nes, *n.* Affection; great liking.

font, font, *n.* A large basin in which water is contained for baptizing; a complete assortment of printing types of one size.

food, fōd, *n.* Whatever supplies nourishment to animals or plants; nutriment; provisions; whatever feeds or augments.

fool, föl, *n.* One destitute of reason; a simpleton; a silly person; a buffoon.—*vi.* To play the fool; to trifle.—*vt.* To make a fool of; to deceive. **foolery,** föl'ė-ri, *n.* Habitual folly; act of folly; absurdity. **foolhardy,** föl''här'di, *a.* Daring without judgment; foolishly bold; venturesome. **foolish,** föl'ish, *a.* Void of understanding; acting without judgment or discretion; silly; ridiculous; unwise. **foolishly,** föl'ish-li, *adv.* Unwisely; absurdly.

foolscap, fölz'kap', *n.* Paper of the smallest regular size but one, about 17 inches by 14.

foot, fut, *n.;* pl. **feet,** fēt. The lower extremity of the leg; that on which a thing stands; the base; infantry; a measure of twelve inches; a measure of syllables in a verse.—*vi.* To dance; to tread to measure or music; to skip; to walk.—*vt.* To tread; to dance; trip; to add a foot to, as to a stocking. **football,** fut'bal, *n.* An inflated leather ball to be driven by the foot; a game played with such a ball. **footfall,** fut'fal, *n.* A footstep; a stumble. **foothold,** fut'hōld, *n.* That on which one may tread or rest securely; firm standing. **footing,** fut'ing, *n.* Ground for the foot; established place; basis; tread. **footlights,** fut''lits', *n.pl.* A row of lights in a theater on the front of the stage. **footman,** fut'man, *n.* A menial servant; a runner; a servant in livery. **footprint,** fut'print, *n.* The impression of the foot. **footsore,** fut'sōr, *a.* Having the feet sore or tender, as by much walking. **footstalk,** fut'stak, *n.* The stalk of a leaf. **footstep,** fut'step, *n.* A track; the mark of the foot; vestige; *pl.* example; course.

footstool, fut'stōl, *n.* A stool for the feet.

fop, fop, *n.* A coxcomb; a dandy. **foppery,** fop'ė-ri, *n.* Showy folly; idle affection. **foppish,** fop'ish, *a.* Dressing in the extreme of fashion; affected in manners.

for, for, *prep.* In the place of; because of; in favor of; toward; during; in quest of; according to; as far as; notwithstanding; proportion to.—*conj.* Because.

forage, fo'rij, *n.* Food for horses and cattle; act of providing forage.—*vi.* (foraging, foraged). To collect forage; to rove in search of food.—*vt.* To strip of provisions for horses, &c.; to supply with forage. **forager,** for'ij-ėr, *n.* One who forages.

foray, for'ā, *vt.* To ravage; to pillage.—*n.* A predatory excursion; a raid.

forbear, for-bar', *vi.* To keep away; to cease; to delay; to refrain.—*vt.* To abstain from; to avoid doing. **forbearance,** for-bar'ans, *n.* Act of forbearing; restraint of passion; long-suffering; mildness. **forbearing,** for-bar'ing, *p.a.* Patient; long-suffering.

forbid, for-bid', *vt.* To prohibit; to oppose; to obstruct.—*vi.* To utter a prohibition. **forbidden,** for-bid'n, *p.a.* Prohibited. **forbidding,** for-bid'ing,

p.a. Repelling approach; disagreeable; repulsive.

force, förs, *n.* Strength; active power; might; violence; coercion; cogency; efficacy; power for war; troops; a waterfall.—*vt.* (forcing, forced). To compel; to impel; to take by violence; to ravish; to twist or overstrain; to ripen by artificial means; to stuff; to farce.—*vi.* To use force or violence. **forced,** först, *p.a.* Affected; overstrained; unnatural. **forceful,** förs'ful, *a.* Possessing force; acting with power; impetuous.

forceps, for'seps, *n.* A surgical instrument on the principle of pincers for holding anything difficult to be held by the hand.

forcible, för'si-bl, *a.* Efficacious; potent; cogent; done by force; suffered by force.

forcing, för'sing, *n.* Art of raising plants or fruits, at an earlier season than the natural one, by artificial heat.

ford, förd, *n.* A shallow place in a river or other water, where it may be passed on foot.—*vt.* To cross by walking; to wade through.

fore, för, *a.* In front of; anterior; coming first in time; prior.—*adv.* In the part that precedes or goes first.

fore and aft, för'and-äft', *a.* In a direction from stem to stern.

forearm, för'ärm, *n.* The part of the arm between the elbow and the wrist.—*vt.* To arm for attack or resistance before the time of need.

forebode, för-bōd', *vt.* To foretell; to prognosticate; to be prescient of.

forecast, för'kast', *vt.* To foresee; to scheme beforehand.—*vi.* To foresee.—*n.* för'käst. Contrivance beforehand; foresight; estimate of what will happen.

forecastle, för'kas-l, *n.* That part of the upper deck of a vessel forward of the foremast; the forward part of a merchant vessel.

foreclose, för-klōz', *vt.* To preclude; to stop. **foreclosure,** för-klō'zhėr, *n.* Prevention.

forefather, för''fä'тнėr, *n.* A progenitor; an ancestor.

forefinger, för''fing'gėr, *n.* The finger next to the thumb.

forefoot, för'fut, *n.* One of the anterior feet of a quadruped.

forefront, för'frunt, *n.* The foremost part.

forego, för-gö', *vt.* To go before; to precede; to waive; to resign. *See* **forgo.**

foregoing, för-gö'ing, *p.a.* Preceding; antecedent.

foregone, för-gon' or för'gon, *p.a.* Past; preceding; predetermined.

foreground, för'ground, *n.* The part of a scene or picture represented as nearest the observer.

forehead, för''hed' or för'ed, *n.* The part of the face above the eyes; the brow.

foreign, for'in, *a.* Belonging to another nation or country; alien; not to the purpose; irrelevant.

foreigner, for'in-ėr, *n.* A person born in a foreign country; an alien.

foreknowledge, för-nol'ej, *n.* Knowledge of a thing before it happens.

foreleg, fōr″leg′, *n.* One of the anterior legs of an animal, chair, &c.

forelock, fōr″lok′, *n.* The lock or hair that grows from the fore part of the head.

foreman, fōr″man, *n.* The first or chief man; chief man of a jury; chief workman.

foremost, fōr″mōst, *a.* First in place, time, rank, or dignity; most advanced.

forenoon, fōr″nōn, *n.* The part of the day before noon, or from morning to noon.

forensic, fō-ren′sik, *a.* Belonging to courts of justice, or to public debate; used in court or legal proceedings.

forerunner, fōr′run-ér, *n.* One who runs before; harbinger; precursor; prognostic.

foresaid, fōr′sed, *p.a.* Aforesaid.

foresail, fōr′sāl, *n.* The lowermost square sail set on the foremast; a large fore-and-aft sail on a schooner's foremast.

foresee, fōr-sē′, *vt.* To see beforehand; to foreknow.

foreshadow, fōr-shad′ō, *vt.* To shadow or typify beforehand.

foreshorten, fōr-short′n, *vt.* To shorten, in drawing and painting, the parts of figures that stand forward.

foresight, fōr″sīt′, *n.* Foreknowledge; provident care; forethought.

forest, for′est, *n.* An extensive wood; a district devoted to the purposes of the chase; a tract once a royal forest.—*a.* Relating to a forest; sylvan; rustic.—*vt.* To convert into a forest.

forestall, fōr-stal′, *vt.* To anticipate; to hinder by preoccupation.

forester, for′es-tér, *n.* One who watches a forest and preserves the game; one who manages the timber on an estate; an inhabitant of a forest.

forestry, for′est-ri, *n.* Art of cultivating forests, or of managing growing timber.

foretaste, fōr″tāst, *n.* A taste beforehand; anticipation.—*vt.* To taste before possession; to anticipate.

foretell, fōr-tel′, *vt.* To tell beforehand; to predict.—*vi.* To utter prophecy.

forever, for-ev′ér, *adv.* At all times; through endless ages; eternally.

forewarn, fōr-warn′, *vt.* To warn beforehand; to give previous notice to.

foreword, fōr″wērd′, *n.* A preface.

forfeit, for′fit, *vt.* To lose by a misdeed.—*n.* That which is forfeited; fine; penalty. **forfeiture,** for′fi-tūr, *n.* Act of forfeiting; loss of some right, estate, honor, &c., by a crime or fault; fine; penalty.

forgather, for-gaTH′ér, *vi.* To meet.

forge, fōrj, *n.* A furnace in which iron is heated and wrought; a smithy.—*vt.* forging, forged). To frame or fabricate; to form by heating and hammering; to counterfeit.—*vi.* To commit forgery; to move on slowly and laboriously; to work one's way. **forger,** fōr′jér, *n.* One who forges; one who counterfeits. **forgery,** for′jér-i, *n.* The crime of counterfeiting; that which is forged or counterfeited.

forget, for-get′, *vt.* (forgetting; pret. forgot; pp. forgot, forgotten). To lose the remembrance of; to slight; to neglect. **forgetful,** for-get′ful, *a.* Apt to forget; neglectful; oblivious. **forgetfulness,** for-get′ful-nes, *n.* Oblivion; obliviousness; inattention. **forget-me-not,** for-get′mē-not′, *n.* A small, bright, blue flower.

forging, fōr′jing, *n.* The act of one who forges; an article of metal forged.

forgive, for-giv′, *vt.* (forgiving; pret. forgave; pp. forgiven). To pardon; to remit; to overlook. **forgiveness,** for-giv′nes, *n.* Act of forgiving; pardon; disposition to pardon; remission. **forgiving,** for-giv′ing, *p.a.* Disposed to forgive; merciful; compassionate.

forgo, for-gō′, *vt.* To forbear to enjoy or possess; to renounce; to resign.

fork, fork, *n.* An instrument with two or more prongs, used for lifting or pitching anything; a branch or division; a prong. —*vi.* To shoot into branches; to divide into two.—*vt.* To raise or pitch with a fork, as hay, &c.

forked, forkt, *a.* Opening into two or more prongs or shoots.

forlorn, for-lorn′, *a.* Deserted; abandoned; miserable. **forlorn hope,** a body of men appointed to perform some specially perilous service.

form, form, *n.* Shape; manner; pattern; order; empty show; prescribed mode; ceremony; schedule; a long seat; a bench; a class; the seat or bed of a hare. —*vt.* To shape or mold; to arrange; to invent; to make up.—*vi.* To take a form.

formal, for′mal, *a.* Relating to outward form; according to form; precise; ceremonious; having mere appearance. **formality,** for-mal′i-ti, *n.* Quality of being formal; ceremony; a mere form. **formally,** for′mal-li, *adv.* In a formal manner; precisely.

formation, for-mā′shun, *n.* Act of forming; production; manner in which a thing is formed; any assemblage of rocks or strata, referred to a common origin; arrangement.

formative, for′ma-tiv, *a.* Giving form; plastic; derivative.—*n.* That which serves to give form to a word, and is no part of the root.

former, for′mér, *n.* He who forms.— *a. comp. deg.* Before in time; long past; mentioned before another. **formerly,** for′mér-li, *adv.* In time past; of old; in days of yore.

formidable, for′mi-da-bl, *a.* Exciting fear or apprehension; difficult to deal with or undertake.

formless, form′les, *a.* Without a determinate form; shapeless.

formula, for′mū-la, *n.;* pl. **-læ.** A prescribed form; a confession of faith; expression for resolving certain problems in mathematics; expression of chemical composition. **formulate,** for′mū-lāt, *vt.* To express in a formula; to put into a precise and comprehensive statement.

fornicate, for′ni-kāt, *vi.* To have unlawful sexual intercourse. **fornication,** for′ni-kā″shun, *n.* Incontinence of unmarried persons.

forsake, for-sāk′, *vt.* (forsaking; pret.

forsook; pp. forsaken). To abandon; to renounce; to withdraw from.

orsooth, for-söth', *adv.* In very truth; in fact. (Chiefly used in irony.)

orswear, for-swâr', *vt.* To renounce upon oath; to abjure; to swear falsely; to perjure one's self.—*vi.* To swear falsely.

ort, fôrt, *n.* A fortified place; a fortress.

'orte, fôr'tā, *adv.* A direction to sing or play with force.

orte, fôrt, *n.* The strong portion of a sword blade; peculiar talent; strong point; chief excellence.

orth, fôrth, *adv.* Forward in place or order; out into public view; abroad; onward in time. **forthcoming,** fôrth'-kum"ing, *a.* Coming forth; making appearance; ready to appear. **forthright,** fôrth'rīt, *adv.* Straight forward; straightway.—*a.* Straightforward; direct. **forthwith,** fôrth'with", *adv.* Without delay. **'ortieth,** for'ti-eth, *a.* The ordinal of forty.—*n.* One of forty equal parts.

'ortify, for'ti-fī, *vt.* (fortifying, fortified). To make strong; to strengthen by forts, batteries, &c.; to invigorate; to increase the strength of. **fortification,** for'ti-fi-ka"shun, *n.* The art of science of fortifying places; the works erected in defense; a fortified place; additional strength.

'ortissimo, for-tis'i-mō, *adv.* Direction to sing or play with the utmost loudness.

'ortitude, for'ti-tūd, *n.* Firmness of mind to encounter danger, or to bear pain or adversity, resolute endurance.

'ortnight, fort'nīt, *n.* The space of fourteen days; two weeks. **fortnightly,** fort'nīt-li, *adv.* and *a.* Once a fortnight; every fortnight.

'ortress, for'tres, *n.* A fortified place; stronghold; place of security.

'ortuitous, for-tū'i-tus, *a.* Happening by chance; accidental; incidental.

'ortunate, for'tū-nit, *a.* Having good fortune; successful; coming by good luck. **fortunately,** for'tū-nit-li, *adv.* By good fortune; happily.

'ortune, for'tūn, *n.* Chance; luck; the good or ill that befalls man; means of living; estate; great wealth; destiny; the power regarded as determining the lots of life.

'ortune hunter, for'tūn hunt'ėr, *n.* A man who seeks to marry a rich woman. **'ortuneteller,** for'tūn tel'ėr, *n.* One who pretends to foretell the events of one's life.

'orty, for'ti, *a.* and *n.* Four times ten.

'orum, fō'rum, *n.* A public place in ancient Rome, where causes were tried; a tribunal; jurisdiction.

'orward, for'wėrd, *adv.* Toward a place in front; onward.—*a.* Near or towards the forepart; in advance of something; ready; bold; pert; advanced beyond the usual degree; too ready.—*vt.* To help onward; to hasten; to send forward; to transmit.

'orwardness, for'wėrd-nes, *n.* Promptness; eagerness; want of due reserve or modesty; pertness; earliness.

forwards, for'wėrdz, *adv.* Same as *forward.*

fossil, fos'il, *a.* Dug out of the earth; petrified and preserved in rocks.—*n.* Petrified remains of plants and animals found in the strata composing the surface of our globe.

foster, fos'tėr, *vt.* To nourish; to bring up; to encourage; to promote. **foster child,** fos'tėr child, *n.* A child nursed by a woman not the mother or bred by a man not the father. (Also *foster-brother, -mother, -parent,* &c.) **fostering,** fos'tėr-ling, *n.* A foster-child.

foul, foul, *a.* Covered with or containing extraneous matter which is offensive; turbid; obscene; rainy or tempestuous; unfair; loathsome; entangled or in collision.—*vt.* To defile; to dirty.—*vi.* To become dirty; to come into collision; to become clogged.—*n.* A colliding, or impending due motion; an unfair piece of play.

foulard, fö-lärd', *n.* A thin silk fabric; without twill; a silk handkerchief.

foully, foul-li, *adv.* Filthily; unfairly.

foulmouthed, foul'mouᵗʜd, *a.* Using scurrilous or abusive language.

found, found, *vt.* To lay the base of; to establish; to institute; to form by melting metal and pouring it into a mold; to cast.—*vi.* To rest or rely (with *on* or *upon*). Pret. and pp. of *find.*

foundation, foun-dā'shun, *n.* Act of founding; base of an edifice; base; endowment; endowed institution. **foundationer,** foun-dā'shun-ėr, *n.* One who derives support from the funds or foundation of a college or endowed school (Eng.).

founder, foun'dėr, *n.* One who lays a foundation; an originator; an endower; one who casts metal.—*vi.* To fill with water and sink; to miscarry; to go lame, as a horse.

foundling, found'ling, *n.* A child found without anyone to care for it.

foundry, foun'dri, *n.* An establishment for casting metals; the art of founding or casting.

fount, fount, *n.* A fountain (*poetical*); a complete stock of printing type; a font.

fountain, foun'tin, *n.* A spring or source of water; an artificial jet or shower; head of a river; original; source. **fountainhead,** foun'tin-hed, *n.* The head of a stream; primary source; origin. **fountain pen,** fount'ān pen, *n.* A pen with a reservoir for ink.

four, fôr, *a.* and *n.* Twice two; three and one. **fourfold,** fôr'fōld, *a.* and *adv.* Quadruple; four times told.—*n.* Four times as much. **four-in-hand,** fôr'in-hand', *n.* A vehicle drawn by four horses guided by one driver. **fourscore,** fôr'skôr', *a.* and *n.* Eighty. **foursquare,** fôr'skwär', *a.* Having four sides and four angles equal; quadrangular.

fourteen, fôr'tēn', *a.* and *n.* Four and ten. **fourteenth,** fôr'tēnth', *a.* The ordinal of fourteen.—*n.* One of fourteen equal parts.

fourth, fôrth, *a.* The ordinal of four.—*n.* One of four equal parts.

fowl, foul, *n.* A bird; a domestic or

barn-door bird.—*vi.* To catch wild fowls for game or food.

Fox

fox, foks, *n.* A carnivorous animal, remarkable for cunning; a sly cunning fellow.—*vt.* and *i.* To turn sour; to become marked with brown spots, as paper. **foxglove**, foks'gluv, *n.* A British plant yielding a powerful medicine, both sedative and diuretic; digitalis. **foxhound**, foks'hound, *n.* A hound for chasing foxes. **foxy**, fok'si, *a.* Pertaining to foxes; wily; cunning; stained with reddish marks; sour.

foxhole, foks'hōl, *n.* A hole dug in ground as protection in battle.

fox trot. A kind of dance; music for the dance.

fracas, frā'kas, *n.* An uproar; a brawl.

fraction, frak'shun, *n.* A fragment; a very small part; one or more of the equal parts into which a unit or number is divided. **fractional**, frak'shun-al, *a.* Belonging to a fraction; pertaining to a method of distillation by which products of different kinds are successively got from the substance treated.

fractious, frak'shus, *a.* Snappish; peevish; cross.

fracture, frak'tūr, *n.* A breach or break; breaking of a bone; manner in which a mineral breaks.—*vt.* (fracturing, fractured). To break.

fragile, fraj'il, *a.* Easily broken; frail; weak. **fragility**, fra-jil'i-ti, *n.* Quality of being fragile; delicacy of substance.

fragment, frag'ment, *n.* A part broken off; an imperfect thing. **fragmentary**, frag'men-ter'i, *a.* Composed of fragments; not complete; disconnected.

fragrance, fragrancy, frā'grans, frā'gran-si, *n.* Quality of being fragrant; sweetness of smell; perfume.

fragrant, frā'grant, *a.* Sweet-smelling; balmy; spicy; aromatic.

frail, frāl, *a.* Easily broken; weak; liable to fail and decay.—*n.* A kind of basket. **frailty**, frāl'ti, *n.* State or quality of being frail; infirmity; liableness to be deceived or seduced; failing; foible.

frame, frām, *vt.* (framing, framed). To make; to construct; to devise; to adjust; to shape; to place in a frame.—*n.* Anything composed of parts fitted together; structure; bodily structure; framework; particular state, as of the mind; mood or disposition. **framework**, frām'wėrk, *n.* A structure or fabric for supporting anything; a frame. **framing**, frām'ing, *n.* Act of constructing a frame; frame thus constructed; rough timber-work of a house.

franc, frangk, *n.* A silver coin of France, of the value of about 20 cents.

franchise, fran'chīz, *n.* Right granted by a sovereign or government; right of voting for a member of parliament.

frangible, fran'ji-bl, *a.* That may be broken; brittle; fragile. **frangibility**, fran'ji-bil''i-ti, *n.* The state or quality of being frangible.

Frank, frangk, *n.* One of the ancient German race of the Franks; a name given by Orientals to inhabitants of W. Europe.

frank, frangk, *a.* Free in uttering real sentiments; candid; outspoken.—*n.* Signature of a privileged person securing free transmission of a letter.—*vt.* To exempt from postage.

frankincense, frangk'in-sens, *n.* An odoriferous gum-resin used as a perfume.

frankly, frangk'li, *adv.* In a frank manner; openly; freely; unreservedly.

frantic, fran'tik, *a.* Mad; raving; furious; outrageous; distracted. **frantically, franticly**, fran'ti-kal-i, fran'tik-li, *adv.* Madly; outrageously.

fraternal, fra'tėr'nal, *a.* Brotherly; pertaining to brethren; becoming brothers.

fraternity, fra-tėr'ni-ti, *n.* State or relationship of a brother; brotherhood; society, class, or profession. **fraternize**, frat'ėr-nīz, *vi.* (fraternizing, fraternized). To associate as brothers, or as men of like occupation or disposition.

fratricide, frat'ri-sīd, *n.* Murder of a brother; one who murders a brother. **fratricidal**, frat-ri-sīd'al, *a.* Pertaining to fratricide.

fraud, fräd, *n.* Artifice by which the right or interest of another is injured; deception. **fraudulence, fraudulency**, fräd'ū-lens, fräd'ū-len-si, *n.* Quality of being fraudulent. **fraudulent**, fräd'ū-lent, *a.* Using fraud in bargains, &c.; founded on fraud; dishonest.

fray, frā, *n.* An affray; a broil; a fight; a frayed place in cloth.—*vt.* To rub; to fret, as cloth, by wearing.—*vi.* To become worn by rubbing.

frazzle, fraz'l, *vt.* and *i.* To fray, as a rope's end.—*n.* State of being frayed; also used figuratively.

freak, frēk, *n.* A sudden causeless turn of the mind; a caprice; a sport.—*vt.* To variegate. **freakish**, frēk'ish, *a.* Capricious; grotesque.

freckle, frek'l, *n.* A yellowish spot in the skin; any small spot or discoloration.—*vt.* or *i.* (freckling, freckled). To give or acquire freckles. **freckly**, frek'li, *a.* Sprinkled with freckles.

free, frē, *a.* Being at liberty; instituted by a free people; not arbitrary or despotic; open; clear; disjoined; licentious; candid; generous; gratuitous; guiltless. —*vt.* (freeing, freed). To set free; to liberate; to disentangle; to exempt; to absolve from some charge. **freebooter**, frē'böt'ėr, *n.* A robber; a pillager; a plunderer. **freebooting**, frē'böt'ing, *n.* Pertaining to or like freebooters. **freeborn**, frē'born, *a.* Born free; inheriting liberty. **freedman**, frēd'man, *n.* A man who has been a slave and is set free. **freedom**, frē'dum, *n.* State of being free; liberty; particular privilege; facility of doing anything; frankness; undue familiarity. **freehand**, frē'hand, *a.* Applied to drawing in which the hand is not assisted by any guiding or measuring instruments. **freehanded**, frē'han'ded, *a.* Open-handed; liberal. **freehold**, frē'hōld', *n.* An estate for which the owner owes no service except to the crown; tenure by which such an estate is held. **freeholder**, frē'hōl'dėr, *n.* The possessor of a freehold. **free lance**, frē'lans, *n*. A mercenary soldier of the middle ages; one unattached to any party. **freely**, frē'li, *adv*. In a free manner; readily; liberally. **freeman**, frē'man, *n*. One who is free; one who enjoys or is entitled to a franchise. **Freemason**, frē'mā'sn, *n*. A member of a secret friendly society or organization. **Freemasonry**, frē'mā'sn-ri, *n*. The mysteries in which freemasons are initiated. **freeness**, frē'nes, *n*. State or quality of being free; openness; frankness; liberality. **free-spoken**, frē'spō'ken, *a*. Accustomed to speak without reserve. **freestone**, frē'stōn, *n*. Any stone composed of sand or grit, easily cut. **freethinker**, frē'thingk'ėr, *n*. One who is free from the common modes of thinking in religious matters; a deist; a skeptic. **free trade**, frē trād, *n*. Commerce free from customs on foreign commodities. **free will**, frē wil, *n*. The power of directing our own actions, without restraint by necessity or fate. **freewill**, frē-wil', *a*. Spontaneous.

freeze, frēz, *vi*. (freezing; pret. froze; pp. frozen or froze). To be congealed by cold; to be hardened into ice; to be of that degree of cold at which water congeals; to stagnate; to shiver or stiffen with cold.—*vt*. To congeal; to chill. **freezing**, frēz'ing, *a*. Such as to freeze; chilling.

freight, frāt, *n*. The cargo of a ship; lading; hire of a ship; charge for the transportation of goods.—*vt*. To load with goods; to hire for carrying goods. **freightage**, frāt'ij, *n*. Act of freighting; money paid for freight. **freighter**, frāt'ėr, *n*. One who charters and loads a ship.

French, french, *a*. Pertaining to France or its inhabitants.—*n*. The language spoken by the people of France; the people of France.

frenetic, frenetical, fre-net'ik, fre-net'i-kal, *a*. Frenzied; frantic.

frenzy, fren'zi, *n*. Madness; distraction; violent agitation of the mind. **frenzied**, fren'zid, *a*. Affected with frenzy; proceeding from frenzy.

frequent, frē'kwent, *a*. That takes place repeatedly; often seen or done; doing a thing often.—*vt*. frē-kwent'. To visit often; to resort to habitually. **frequency**, frē'kwen-si, *n*. State or character of being frequent; repetition.

frequently, frē'kwent-li, *adv*. Often; many times at short intervals; commonly.

fresco, fres'kō, *n*. A method of painting with mineral and earthy pigments on walls of which the plaster is not quite dry.

fresh, fresh, *a*. Full of health and strength; vigorous; brisk; bright; not faded; in good condition; not stale; cool and agreeable; clearly remembered; new; not salt; unpracticed; unused. **freshen**, fresh'en, *vt*. To make fresh; to revive.—*vi*. To grow fresh. **freshet**, fresh'et, *n*. A small stream of fresh water; flood of a river. **freshly**, fresh'li, *adv*. In a fresh manner; with freshness; newly;

recently; anew. **freshman**, fresh'-man, *n*. A novice; a first year's student at an English university. **freshness**, fresh'nes, *n*. State or quality of being fresh, in all senses.

fret, fret, *vt*. (fretting, fretted). To eat into; to corrode; to wear away; to chafe; to vex; to ornament or furnish with frets; to variegate.—*vi*. To be vexed; to utter peevish expressions; to rankle. —*n*. Irritation; peevishness; an ornament of bands or fillets; a piece of perforated work; one of the cross-bars on the finger-board of some stringed instruments. **fretful**, fret'ful, *a*. Disposed to fret; peevish; irritable; petulant; angry.

friable, frī-a-bl, *a*. Easily rubbed down, crumbled, or pulverized.

friar, frī'ėr, *n*. A monk; a male member of a monastery.

fricassee, frik'a-sē', *n*. A dish made by cutting chickens or rabbits, &c., into pieces, and dressing them in a frying-pan, &c., with strong sauce. **fricasseed**, frik'a-sēd", *a*. Dressed in fricassee.

friction, frik'shun, *n*. A rubbing; effect of rubbing; resistance which a moving body meets with from the surface on which it moves.

Friday, frī'di, *n*. The sixth day of the week. **Good Friday**, the Friday preceding Easter, sacred as the day of Christ's crucifixion.

friend, frend, *n*. One attached to another by affection; a favorer; one who is propitious; a favorite; a Quaker. **friendless**, frend'les, *a*. Destitute of friends; wanting support; forlorn. **friendliness**, frend'li-nes, *n*. Friendly disposition. **friendly**, frend'li, *a*. Like or becoming a friend; kind; favorable; disposed to peace. **friendship**, frend'-ship, *n*. Intimacy resting on mutual esteem; kindness; aid.

frieze, frēz, *n*. A coarse woolen cloth with a map on one side; that part of the entablature of a column between the architrave and the cornice; upper part of the wall of a room and its decoration.—*vt*. (friezing, friezed). To form a nap on cloth; to frizzle; to curl.

frigate, frig'it, *n*. A ship of war less than a ship of the line.

fright, frit, *n*. Sudden and violent fear; terror; consternation; an ugly or ill-dressed person.—*vt*. To frighten. **frighten**, frit'n, *vt*. To strike with fright or fear; to terrify; to scare; to alarm. **frightful**, frit'ful, *a*. Causing fright; terrible; dreadful; fearful. **frightfully**, frit'ful-li, *adv*. In a frightful manner; dreadfully; terribly.

frigid, frij'id, *a*. Cold; wanting spirit or zeal; stiff; formal; lifeless. **frigidity**, fri-jid'i-ti, *n*. Coldness; coldness of affection; dullness.

frill, fril, *n*. A crisp or plaited edging on an article of dress; a ruffle.—*vt*. To decorate with frills. **frilling**, fril'ing, *n*. Frills, collectively; ruffles; gathers, &c.

fringe, frinj, *n*. An ornamental appendage to furniture or dress, consisting of loose threads; margin; extremely.—*vt*.

(fringing, fringed). To border with fringe or a loose edging. **fringed,** frinjd, *p.a.* Bordered with fringe; having a certain kind of border or margin.

frippery, frip'ẽr-i, *n.* Old worn-out clothes; waste matter; trifles; trumpery. —*a.* Trifling; contemptible.

Frisian, frizh'an, *a.* Belonging to Friesland.—*n.* A native or the language of Friesland.

frisk, frisk, *vi.* To dance, skip, and gambol in frolic and gayety.—*n.* A frolic; a fit of wanton gayety.

frisket, fris'ket, *n.* A frame to keep paper in position when printing.

frisky, fris'ki, *a.* Jumping with gayety; gay; frolicsome; lively.

fritter, frit'ẽr, *n.* A kind of small cake fried; a small piece of meat fried; a small piece.—*vt.* To cut into small pieces to be fried; to break into small pieces; to waste by degrees (with *away*).

frivolous, fri'vol-us, *a.* Trivial; trifling; petty. **frivolity,** fri-vol'i-ti, *n.* Acts or habit of trifling; unbecoming levity.

friz, friz, *vt.* To curl; to crisp; to form the nap of cloth into little burs.

frizzle, friz'l, *vi.* (frizzling, frizzled). To curl; to crisp, as hair; to make crisp by cooking.—*n.* A curl; a lock of hair crisped.

fro, frō, *adv.* From; away; back or backward.

frock, frok, *n.* An ecclesiastical garment; a lady's gown; a child's dress; a blouse for men.

frog, frog, *n.* An amphibious animal, remarkable for its activity in swimming and leaping; a kind of button or tassel on a coat or vestment; triangular plate in a switch.

frolic, frol'ik, *a.* Joyous; merry; frisky, *poetic.*—*n.* A merry prank; merry-making.—*vi.* To play merry pranks; to gambol. **frolicsome,** frol'ik-sum, *a.* Full of frolics; given to pranks.

from, from. *prep.* Out of the neighborhood or presence of; by reason of; denoting source, distance, absence, departure, &c.

frond, frond, *n.* The leaf of a fern or other cryptogamic plant.

front, frunt, *n.* The forehead; the whole face; the fore part; boldness; impudence.—*a.* Relating to the front or face. —*vt.* To stand with the front opposed to; to oppose; to face; to supply with a front.—*vi.* To face; to look. **frontage,** frun'tij, *n.* The front part of an edifice, quay, &c.

frontal, frun'tal, *a.* Belonging to the forehead.—*n.* An ornament for the forehead; a frontlet, a small pediment.

frontier, frun-tẽr', *n.* That part of a country which fronts another country; extreme part of a country.—*a.* Bordering; conterminous.

frontispiece, frun'tis-pēs, *n.* The principal face of a building; an illustration facing the title-page of a book.

frost, frost, *n.* That temperature of the air which causes freezing; frozen dew; rime; coldness or severity of manner.— *vt.* To injure by frost; to ornament with anything resembling hoar-frost; to fur-

nish with frost-nails. **frostbite,** frost'-bit, *n.* Insensibility or deadness in any part of the body caused by exposure to frost.—*vt.* To affect with frostbite. **frostily,** frost'i-li, *adv.* With frost or excessive cold; coldly. **frosting,** frost'-ing, *n.* The composition, resembling hoarfrost, used to cover cake, &c. **frostnail,** frost'nāl, *n.* A nail driven into a horseshoe to prevent slipping on ice. **frosty,** fros'ti, *a.* Producing or characterized by frost; chill in affection; resembling hoar-frost; gray-haired.

froth, froth, *n.* Bubbles caused by fermentation or agitation; spume; empty talk; light unsubstantial matter.—*vt.* To cause to foam.—*vi.* To foam; to throw up spume. **frothy,** froth'i, *a.* Full or consisting of froth; not firm or solid.

frouzy, frowzy, frouz'i, *a.* Fetid; musty; dingy; in disorder; slatternly.

froward, frō'wẽrd, *a.* Perverse; ungovernable; disobedient; peevish.

frown, froun, *vi.* To express displeasure by contracting the brow; to look stern; to scowl.—*n.* A wrinkling of the brow; a sour or stern look; any expression of displeasure.

frozen, frō'zn, *p.a.* Congealed by cold; frosty; chill.

fructify, fruk'ti-fī, *vt.* (fructifying, fructified). To make fruitful; to fertilize.—*vi.* To bear fruit.

frugal, frō'gal, *a.* Economical; careful; thrifty. **frugality,** frō-gal'i-ti, *n.* Prudent economy; thrift. **frugally,** frō'-gal-li, *adv.* In a frugal manner; with economy.

fruit, frōt, *n.* Whatever of a vegetable nature is of use to man or animals; the reproductive produce of a plant; such products collectively; the seed or matured ovary; that which is produced; offspring; effect; outcome.—*vi.* To produce fruit. **fruitful,** frōt'ful, *a.* Very productive; fertile; plenteous; prolific. **fruitfully,** frōt'ful-li, *adv.* In a fruitful manner; plenteously; abundantly. **fruitless,** frōt'less, *a.* Destitute of fruit; unprofitable; abortive; ineffectual. **fruity,** frō'ti, *a.* Resembling fruit; having the taste or flavor of fruit.

fruition, frō-ish'un, *n.* A using or enjoying; enjoyment; gratification; pleasure derived from use or possession.

frump, frump, *n.* A cross-tempered, old-fashioned female.

frustrate, frus'trāt, *vt.* (frustrating, frustrated). To balk; to foil; to bring to nothing; to render of no effect. **frustration,** frus-trā'shun, *n.* Disappointment; defeat.

fry, frī, (frying, fried). To cook by roasting over a fire.—*vi.* To be cooked as above; to simmer; to be in agitation. —*n.* A dish of anything fried; state of mental ferment; young fishes at an early stage; swarm of small fishes, &c.; insignificant objects.

fuchsia, fū'sha, *n.* A beautiful flowering shrub.

fuddle, fud'l, *vt.* (fuddling, fuddled). To make stupid by drink; to spend in drinking.—*vi.* To drink to excess.

fudge, fuj, *n.* or *interj.* Stuff; nonsense.

fuel, fū'el, *n.* That which serves to feed fire, or to increase excitement, &c.—*vt.* To feed or furnish with fuel.

fugitive, fū'ji-tiv, *a.* Apt to flee away; volatile; fleeting; vagabond; temporary. —*n.* One who flees from duty or danger; refugee.

fugue, fūg, *n.* A musical composition in which the parts seem to chase each other.

fulcrum, ful'krum, *n.*; pl. **-ra** or **-rums**. A support; that by which a lever is sustained, or the point about which it moves.

fulfill, fyl-fil', *vt.* To carry into effect as a prophecy, promise, &c.; to answ in execution or event; to perform; to complete. **fulfillment**, fyl-fil'ment, *n.* Accomplishment; execution; performance.

fulgency, ful'jen-si, *n.* Splendor; glitter.

fulgent, ful'jent, *a.* Glittering; shining

full, ful, *a.* Having all it can contain; abounding; crowded; entire; strong; loud; clear; mature; perfect; ample.— *n.* Complete measure; the highest state or degree (usually with *the*).—*adv.* Quite; altogether; exactly; directly.—*vt.* To scour and thicken, as woolen cloth, in a mill. **full-blown**, ful'blōn', *a.* Fully expanded, as a blossom. **fullness**, ful'nes, *n.* State of being full; abundance; extent; loudness. **fully**, ful'li, *adv.* With fullness; amply; perfectly.

fulminate, ful'mi-nāt, *vi.* (fulminating, fulminated). To lighten and thunder. to detonate; to issue threats, denunciations, &c.—*vt.* To utter or send out, as a denunciation or censure; to cause to explode.—*n.* A compound substance which explodes by percussion, friction, or heat. **fulmination**, ful-mi-nā'shun, *n.* Act of fulminating; that which is fulminated; censure; anathema; chemical explosion.

fulsome, ful'sum, *a.* Offensive from excess of praise; gross; nauseous.

fumble, fum'bl, *vi.* (fumbling, fumbled). To grope about awkwardly; to attempt or handle something bunglingly.

fume, fūm, *n.* Smoke; vapor; exhalation from the stomach, as of liquor; heat of passion.—*vi.* (fuming, fumed). To yield vapor or visible exhalations; to be hot with anger.—*vt.* To smoke; to perfume; to disperse in vapors.

fumigate, fū'mi-gāt, *vt.* (fumigating, fumigated). To smoke; to purify from infection, &c. **fumigation**, fū-mi-gā'shun, *n.* Act of fumigating; to purify from infection.

fun, fun, *n.* Sportive acts or words; merriment.

function, fungk'shun, *n.* Performance; office; duty; proper office of any organ in animals or vegetables; a ceremonial; a mathematical quantity; connected with and varying with another. **functional**, fungk'shun-al, *a.* Pertaining to functions, or to some office or function.

functionary, fungk"shun-er'i, *n.* One who holds an office or trust.

fund, fund, *n.* A stock or capital; money set apart for any object more or less permanent; store; supply.—*vt.* To pro-

vide and appropriate a fund for paying the interest of, as a debt; to place in a fund, as money.

fundament, fun'da-ment, *n.* The part of the body on which one sits; the anus.

fundamental, fun-da-men'tal, *a.* Pertaining to the foundation; essential; primary.—*n.* A leading principle which serves as the groundwork of a system; an essential.

funeral, fū'nėr-al. *n.* Burial; ceremony of burying a dead body —*a.* Used at the interment of the dead.

funereal, fū-nēr'ē al, *a.* Suiting a funeral; dark; dismal; mournful.

fungous, fung'gus, *a.* Like a mushroom or fungus; excrescent; growing suddenly, but not substantial or durable.

fungus, fung'gus, *n.*; pl. **fungi** or **funguses**, fun'jī, fung'gus-ez. A mushroom: a toadstool: spongy excrescence in animal bodies, as proud flesh formed in wounds.

funnel, fun'el, *n.* A utensil for conveying liquids into close vessels; the shaft of a chimney through which smoke ascends

funnily, fun'i-li, *adv.* In a droll manner.

funny, fun'i, *a.* Making fun; droll; comical.

fur, fėr, *n.* The short, fine, soft hair of certain animals, growing thick on the skin; furred animals collectively; something resembling fur.—*a.* Pertaining to or made of fur.—*vt.* (furring, furred). To line or cover with fur.

furbelow, fėr'bē-lō, *n.* A kind of flounce; plaited border of a petticoat or gown; any fussy trimming.

furbish, fėr'bish, *vt.* To rub or scour to brightness; to burnish. **furbisher**, fėr'bish-ėr, *n.* One who or that which furbishes.

furious, fū'ri-us, *a.* Full of rage; violent; impetuous; frantic. **furiously**, fū'ri-us-li, *adv.* With fury; vehemently; violently.

furl, fėrl, *vt.* To wrap a sail close to a yard, &c., and fasten by a cord.

furlong, fėr'long, *n.* The eighth of a mile.

furlough, fėr'lō, *n.* Leave of absence to a soldier for a limited time.—*vt.* To grant leave of absence from military service

furnace, fėr'nis, *n.* A structure in which a vehement fire may be maintained for melting ores, heating, &c.; place or occasion of torture or trial.

furnish, fėr'nish, *vt.* To supply; to equip; to yield; to provide.

furniture, fėr'ni-tūr, *n.* That with which anything is furnished; equipment; outfit; movable wooden articles in a house.

furor, fū'ror, *n.* Fury; rage.

furore, fū-rō'rā, *n.* Great enthusiasm or excitement; commotion; mania; rage.

furrier, fu'ri-ėr, *n.* A dealer in furs; one who dresses furs.

furrow, fu'rō, *n.* A trench made by a plow; a groove; a wrinkle.—*vt.* To make furrows in; to groove; to wrinkle.

furry, fėr'i, *a.* Covered or coated with fur; resembling fur.

further, fėr'THėr, *adv.* More in advance —*vt.* To help forward; to advance. **furtherance,** fėr'THėr-ans, *n.* A helping forward; promotion; advancement **furtherer,** fėr'THėr-ėr, *n.* A promoter. **furthermore,** fėr'THėr-mōr, *adv.* More in addition; moreover; besides. **furthermost,** fėr'THėr-mōst, *a.* Most remote. **furthest,** fėr'THest, *a* and *adv.* Most advanced; farthest.

furtive, fėr'tiv, *a.* Stolen; sly; stealthy. **furtively,** fėr'tiv-li, *adv.* By stealth.

fury, fū'ri, *n.* Rage; a violent rushing; frenzy; a goddess of vengeance, in mythology; a violent woman.

furze, fėrz, *n.* A prickly evergreen shrub; whin; gorse. **furzy,** fėrz'i, *a.* Overgrown with furze.

fuse, fūz, *vt.* (fusing, fused). To liquefy by heat; to dissolve; to blend or unite. —*vi.* To be melted; to become blended.

fuse, fuze, fūz, *n.* A tube or case filled with combustible matter, used in blasting or in discharging a shell, &c.

fuselage, fū'ze-lij, *n.* The elongated structure, of approximately streamline form, to which are attached the wing and tail unit of an airplane.

fusel oil, fū'zel oil, *n.* A colorless oily spirit separated in the rectification of ordinary distilled spirits.

fusillade, fū'zi-lād, *n.* A simultaneous discharge of musketry.

fusion, fū'zhun, *n.* Act or operation of fusing; state of being melted or blended; complete union.

fuss, fus, *n.* Bustle; much ado about trifles —*vi.* To make a fuss or bustle. **fussy,** fus'i, *a.* Making a fuss; bustling.

fustian, fus'chan, *n.* A coarse cotton stuff with a pile like velvet; mere stuff; bombast; an inflated style.—*a.* Made of fustian; bombastic

fusty, fus'ti, *n* Tasting or smelling of a foul or moldly cask; moldly; ill-smelling

futile, fū'tīl, *a* Serving no useful end; trivial; worthless **futility,** fū-til'i-ti, *n.* Quality of being futile; worthlessness; unimportance.

future, fū'tūr, *a.* That is to be; pertaining to time to come.—*n.* The time to come; all that is to happen; the future tense. **futurism,** fū'tūr-izm, *n.* Recent artistic and literary development esp. in Italy marked by violent departure from tradition. **futurity,** fū-tū'ri-ti, *n.* State of being future; time to come; afterages.

fuzz, fuz, *vi.* To fly off in minute particles.—*n.* Fine particles; loose, volatile matter.

fuzzy, fuz'i, *a.* Like, or covered with fuzz.

fy, fī, *interj.* Same as **fie.**

G

gab, gab, *vi.* (gabbing, gabbed). To talk much; to chatter.—*n.* Idle talk.

gabardine, gaberdine, gab'ėr-dēn", *n.* A coarse upper garment.

gabble, gab'l, *vi.* (gabbling, gabbled). To talk fast, or without meaning.—*n.* Rapid talk without meaning; inarticulate sounds rapidly uttered.

gable, gā'bl, *n.* The pointed end of a house; the triangular part of the end of a house.

gad, gad, *n.* A spike; a wedge or ingot of steel or iron.—*vi.* (gadding, gadded). To rove or ramble idly.

gadabout, gad'a-bout. *n.* One who roves about idly

gadder, gad'ėr, *n.* A gadabout.

gadfly, gad'flī, *n.* A fly which bites cattle.

Gadhelic, ga-del'ik, *a.* Pertaining to the branch of the Celtic race comprising the Erse of Ireland, the Gaels of Scotland, and the Manx.—*n.* Their language.

Gael, gāl, *n.* A Scottish Highlander. **Gaelic,** gāl'ik, *a.* Pertaining to the Celtic inhabitants of Scotland.—*n.* Their language.

gaff, gaf, *n.* A hook used by anglers in landing large fish; a spare to extend the upper edge of some fore-and-aft sails.— *vt.* To strike or secure (a salmon) by means of a gaff.

gaffer, gaf'ėr, *n.* An old rustic; a foreman.

gag, gag, *vt.* (gagging, gagged). To prevent from speaking by fixing something in the mouth; to silence by authority or force.—*n.* Something thrust into the mouth to hinder speaking; interpolations in an actor's part.

gage, gāj, *n.* A pledge; a security; a kind of plum.—*vt.* (gaging, gaged). To pledge; to bind by pledge or security; to engage. See **gauge.**

gaiety, gā'e-ti, *n.* State or quality of being gay; gayety.

gaily, gā'li, *adv.* In a gay manner; joyfully; gayly.

gain, gān, *vt* To obtain; to get, as profit or advantage; to receive, as honor; to win to one's side; to conciliate; to reach, arrive at.—*vi* To reap advantage or profit; to make progress.—*n.* Something obtained as an advantage; profit; benefit. **gainful,** gān'ful, *a.* Full of gain; profitable; advantageous; lucrative. **gaining,** gān'ing, *n.* That which one gains; usually in the *pl.* earnings. **gainless,** gān'les, *a.* Not producing gain; unprofitable.

gainsay, gān'sā, *vt.* To contradict; to oppose in words; to dispute.

gait, gāt, *n.* Walk; manner of walking or stepping; carriage.

gaiter, gā'tèr, *n.* A covering for the leg fitting over the shoe.—*vt.* To dress with gaiters.

gala, gā'la, *n.* An occasion of public festivity.

galaxy, gal'ak-si, *n.* The Milky Way; that long, luminous tract in the heavens, formed by a multitude of stars; an assemblage of splendid persons or things.

gale, gāl, *n.* A strong wind; a storm; a small shrub found in bogs.

galena, ga-lē'na, *n.* The principal ore of lead.

gall, gal, *n.* A bitter fluid secreted in the liver; bile; rancor; malignity; an excrescence produced by the egg of an insect on a plant, especially the oak; a sore place in the skin from rubbing.—*vt.* To make a sore in the skin of by rubbing; to fret; to vex; to harass.

gallant, gal'ant, *a.* Gay in attire; handsome; brave; showing politeness and attention to ladies (in this sense also pron. ga-lant')—*n.* A gay sprightly man; a daring spirit; (pron. also ga-lant') a man attentive to ladies; suitor; paramour.—*vt.* ga-lant'. To act the gallant towards; to be very attentive to (a lady). **gallantly**, gal'ant-li, *adv.* Gayly; bravely; nobly; in the manner of a wooer. **gallantry**, gal'an-tri, *n.* Show; bravery; intrepidity; polite attentions to ladies; vicious love or pretensions to love.

galleon, gal'ē-un, *n.* A large ship formerly used by the Spaniards.

gallery, gal'èr-i, *n.* A long apartment serving as a passage of communication, or for the reception of pictures, &c.; upper floor of a reception of pictures; &c.; upper floor of a church, theater, &c.; a covered passage; frame like a balcony projecting from a ship.

galley, gal'i, *n.* A low, flat-built vessel navigated with sails and oars; the cookroom of a large ship; a frame used in printing. **galley slave**, gal'i slāv, *n.* A person condemned to work on board a galley.

Gallic, gal'ik, *a.* Pertaining to Gaul, or France.

galling, gal'ing, *p.a.* Adapted to gall or chagrin; keenly annoying.

gallon, gal'lun, *n.* A liquid measure of four quarts or eight pints.

gallop, gal'up, *vi.* To move or run with leaps; to ride at this pace; to move very fast.—*n.* The pace of a horse by springs or leaps.

gallows, gal'ōz, *n.* *sing.* or *pl.*; also **gallowses**, gal'ōz-ez, in *pl.* A structure for the hanging of criminals; one of a pair of braces for the trousers.

galore, ga-lōr', *n.* Abundance; plenty.

galosh, galoche, ga-losh', *n.* A shoe worn over another shoe to keep the foot dry.

galvanism, gal'va-nizm, *n.* A species of electricity developed by the action of various metals and chemicals upon each other. **galvanic**, gal-van'ik, *a.* Pertaining to galvanism; containing or exhibiting it. **galvanize**, gal'va-nīz, *vt.* (galvanizing, galvanized). To affect with galvanism; to electroplate; to coat with tin or zinc; to restore to consciousness; to give spurious life to.

galvanometer, gal'va-nom"e-tèr, *n.* An instrument for detecting the existence and determining the strength and direction of an electric current.

gambit, gam'bit, *n.* An opening in chess incurring the sacrifice of a pawn.

gamble, gam'bl, *vi.* (gambling, gambled). To play for money. **gambler**, gam'blèr, *n.* One who plays for money or other stake. **gambling**, gam'bling, *n.* The act or practice of gaming for money or anything valuable.

gambol, gam'bul, *vi.* (gamboling, gamboled). To skip about in sport; to frisk; to frolic.—*n.* A skipping about in frolic; a prank.

game, gām, *n.* Sport of any kind; exercise for amusement, testing skill, &c.; scheme pursued; field-sports;

GAME-FISH

animals hunted.—*vi.* (gaming, gamed). To play at any sport; to play for a stake or prize; to practice gaming. **To die game**, to maintain a bold spirit to the last.

gamecock, gām'kok', *n.* A cock bred or used to fight.

gamekeeper, gām'kēp'èr, *n.* One who has the care of game on an estate.

gamesome, gām'sum, *a.* Sportive; playful.

gamester, gām'stèr, *n.* A person addicted to gaming; a gambler.

gamin, gam'in, *n.* A street arab; a neglected street-boy.

gaming, gām'ing, *n.* The act or practice of gambling.

gammon, gam'un, *n.* The thigh of a hog; pickled and smoked or dried; a smoked ham; an imposition or hoax.—*vt.* To pickle and dry in smoke; to hoax or humbug.

gamut, gam'ut, *n.* A scale on which notes in music are written, consisting of lines and spaces; range or compass.

gamy, gamey, gām'i, *a.* Having the flavor of game; courageous.

gander, gan'dèr, *n.* The male of the goose.

gang, gang, *n.* A crew or band; a squad; a vein in mining; a gangue.

ganglion, gang'gli-on, *n.*; pl. **-ia** or **ions**. An enlargement in the course of a nerve; a mass of nervous matter giving origin to nerve-fibers; a tumor on a tendon.

gangrene, gang'grēn, *n.* An eating away of the flesh; first stage of mortification.—*vt.* (gangrening, gangrened). To mortify.—*vi.* To become mortified. **gangrenous**, gang'grē-nus, *a.* Mortified; attacked by gangrene.

gangster, gang'stèr, *n.* (U.S.) A member of a gang of roughs.

gangway, gang'wā', *n.* A means of access formed of planks or boards; a passage across the House of Commons.

gannet, gan'et, *n.* The solan-goose; an aquatic bird of the pelican tribe.

gantlet, gant'let, *n.* A punishment, in

which the culprit was compelled to run between two ranks of men and receive a blow from each man; also gauntlet.

gap, gap, *n.* An opening; breach; hiatus; chasm.

gape, gāp, *vi.* (gaping, gaped). To open the mouth wide; to yawn; to open in fissures; to stand open.

garage, gä-räzh′, *n.* A building for housing automobiles.

garb, gärb, *n.* Dress; clothes; mode of dress.—*vt.* To dress.

garbage, gär′bij, *n.* Waste matter; offal; vegetable refuse.

garble, gär′bl, *vt.* (garbling, garbled). To pick out such parts as may serve a purpose; to falsify by leaving out parts; to corrupt.

garden, gär′dn, *n.* A piece of ground appropriated to the cultivation of plants; a rich, well-cultivated tract; a delightful spot.—*a.* Pertaining to or produced in a garden.—*vi.* To lay out and to cultivate a garden.— **gardener**, gär′dn-ėr, *n.* One whose occupation is to tend or keep a garden. **gardening**, gär′dn-ing, *n.* The act or art of cultivating gardens; horticulture.

gargle, gär′gl, *vt.* (gargling, gargled). To wash, as the throat.—*n.* Any liquid preparation for washing the throat.

gargoyle, gär′goil, *n.* A projecting waterspout on a building; often grotesque.

garish, gär′ish, *a.* Gaudy; showy; dazzling.

garland, gär′land, *n.* A wreath or chaplet of flowers, leaves, &c.; a collection of pieces of prose or verse.—*vt.* To deck with a garland.

garlic, gär′lik, *n.* A plant allied to the onion, with a pungent taste and strong odor.

garment, gär′ment, *n.* Any article of clothing, as a coat, a gown, &c.

garner, gär′nėr, *n.* A granary; a store.—*vt.* To store in a granary; to store up.

garnet, gär′net, *n.* A precious stone, generally of a red color.

garnish, gär′nish, *vt.* To adorn; to embellish (a dish) with something laid round.—*n.* Ornament; a embellishment round a dish. **garnishing, garnishment**, gär′nish-ing, gär′nish-ment, *n.* That which garnishes.

garniture, gär′ni-tūr, *n.* Ornamental appendages; furniture; dress.

garret, gar′et, *n.* A room in a house on the uppermost floor, immediately under the roof.

garrison, gar′i-sun, *n.* Body of troops stationed in a fort or town.—*vt.* To place a garrison in.

garrote, ga-rōt′, *vt.* To rob by seizing a person and compressing his windpipe till he becomes helpless.

garrulity, ga-ru′li-ti, *n.* Loquacity; practice or habit of talking much. **garrulous**, gar′ụ-lus, *a.* Talkative; loquacious; characterized by long prosy talk.

garter, gär′tėr, *n.* A band to hold up a stocking; the badge of the highest order of knighthood in Great Britain; the order itself.—*vt.* To bind with a garter.

gas, gas, *n.* An elastic aeriform fluid;

coal-gas, used for giving light; any similar substance; short for gasoline.

gaseous, gäs′ē-us, *a.* In the form of gas.

gash, gash, *vt.* To make a long deep incision in; to cut; to slash.—*n.* A deep and long cut, particularly in flesh.

gasket, gas′ket, *n.* A cord on the yard of a ship to tie the sail to it.

gas mask. A filter mask used to protect the lungs from irritation or poisoning.

gasoline, gasolene, gas′o-lēn, *n.* Highly inflammable petroleum liquid distillate used mainly as fuel in internal combustion engines

gasp, gasp, *vi.* To open the mouth wide to catch breath; to labor for breath; to pant.—*vt.* To emit with a gasp.—*n.* Short painful catching of the breath.

gastric, gas′trik, *a.* Belonging to the stomach.

gastronomy, gas-tron′o-mi, *n.* The art or science of good eating; epicurism.

gate, gāt, *n.* A large door or entrance; a frame of timber, iron, &c., closing an entrance, &c.; a way or passage; the frame which stops the passage of water through a dam, lock, &c. **gateway**, gāt′wā, *n.* A way through the gate of some inclosure; the gate itself.

gather, gaᴛн′ėr, *vt.* To bring together; to collect; to acquire; to pucker; to deduce by inference.—*vi.* To assemble; to increase.—*n.* A fold in cloth, made by drawing; a pucker. **gathering**, gaᴛн′-ėr-ing, *n.* The act of collecting or assembling; an assembly; a collection of pus; an abscess.

gaucherie, gō′shė-rē″, *n.* Awkwardness.

Gaucho, gou′chō, *n.* A native of the S. American Pampas of Spanish descent.

gaud, gawd, gad, *n.* A piece of showy finery, a trinket. **gaudy**, gad′i, *a.* Showy; ostentatious|; fine; tastelessly or glaringly adorned. **gaudily**, gad′i-li, *adv.* Showily; with ostentation of fine dress.

gauge, gāj′, *vt.* (gauging, gauged). To ascertain the contents of; to measure.—*n.* A measuring rod; a measure; distance between the rails in a railway; caliber; size or dimensions.

Gaul, gal, *n.* An inhabitant of Gaul, or ancient France.

gaunt, gant, *a.* Emaciated; lean; thin; famished.

gauntlet, gant′let, *n.* A large iron glove formerly worn as armor; a long glove covering the hand and wrist.

gauze, gaz, *n.* A very thin, slight, transparent stuff. **gauzy**, gaz′i, *a.* Like gauze: thin as gauze.

gavotte, ga-vot′, *n.* A sprightly dance; music for the dance.

gawk, gak, *n.* A simpleton; a booby.

gawky, gak′i, *a.* Awkward; clumsy; foolish—*n.* A stupid clumsy fellow.

gay, gā, *a.* Merry; frolicsome, showy; dressed out; dissipated. **gayety**, gā′e-ti, *n.* Feeling of being gay; mirth; jollity; festivity; showiness. **gayly**, gā′li, *adv.* Merrily; joyfully; showily.

gaze, gāz, *vi.* (gazing, gazed). To fix the eyes and look earnestly; to stare.—*n.* A fixed look; a look of eagerness, wonder, or admiration.

gazelle, ga-zel', *n.* A small, elegant species of antelope, with soft, lustrous eyes.

gazette, ga-zet', *n.* A newspaper, especially an official newspaper.—*vt.* (gazetting, gazetted). To insert in a gazette; to announce or publish officially. **gazetteer,** gaz'e-tēr', *n.* A writer or publisher of news; a dictionary of geographical information.

gear, gēr, *n.* Dress; ornaments; apparatus; harness; tackle; a train of tooth wheels.—*vt.* To put gear on; to harness. **gearing,** gēr'ing, *n.* Harness; a train of toothed wheels working into each other.

geese, gēs, *n.pl.* of goose.

Geiger counter, gī'gėr koun'tėr. A device used to detect and measure radioactivity.

gelatin, gelatine, jel'a-tin, *n.* A concrete transparent substance obtained by boiling from certain parts of animals; the principle of jelly; glue. **gelatinous,** je-lat'i-nus, *a.* Of the nature of gelatine; containing jelly.

geld, geld, *vt.* To castrate; to emasculate. **gelding,** gel'ding, *n.* Act of castrating; a castrated animal, but chiefly a horse.

gelid, jel'id, *a.* Icy cold; frosty or icy.

gem, jem, *n.* A precious stone of any kind; a jewel; anything remarkable for beauty or rarity.—*vt.* (gemming, gemmed). To adorn, as with gems; to bespangle; to embellish.

Gemini, jem'i-nī, *n.pl.* The Twins, a sign of the zodiac, containing the two stars Castor and Pollux.

gendarme, zhän-därm', *n.* A private in the armed police of France.

gender, jen'dėr, *n.* Sex, male or female; difference in words to express distinction of sex.—*vt.* To beget.—*vi.* To copulate; to breed.

genealogy, jen'ē-al"o-ji, *n.* An account of the descent of a person or family from an ancestor; pedigree; lineage. **genealogical,** jen'ē-a-loj"i-kal, *a.* Pertaining to genealogy. **genealogist,** jen'ē-al"o-jist, *n.* One who traces genealogists, or writes on genealogy.

genera, jen'ėr-a, *n.pl. See* genus.

general, jen'ėr-al, *a.* Of or belonging to a genus; not special; public; common; extensive, though not universal; usual; taken as a whole.—*n.* The whole; a comprehensive notion; a military officer of the highest rank. **generalissimo,** jen'ėr-al-is"i-mō, *n.* The supreme commander of an army. **generality,** jen'ėr-al'i-ti, *n.* State of being general; the bulk; the greatest part. **generalization,** jen'ėr-al-i-zā"shun, *n.* Act of generalizing; general inference. **generalize,** jen'ėr-al-īz, *vt.* To make general; to bring under a general law or statement.—*vi.* To classify under general heads; to reason by induction. **generally,** jen'ėr-al-i, *adv.* In general; commonly; without detail. **generalship,** jen'ėr-al-ship, *n.* The office, skill, or conduct of a general officer.

generate, jen'ėr-āt, *vt.* (generating, generated). To beget; to produce; to cause to be. **generation,** jen-ėr-ā'shun, *n.* Act of generating; single succession in natural descent; people living at the same time; race. **generative,** jen'ėr-ā-tiv, *a.* Having the power of generating; belonging to generation. **generator,** jen'ėr-ā-tėr, *n.* One who or that which generates.

generic, generical, jē-ner'ik, jē-ner'-i-kal, *a.* Pertaining to a genus. **generically,** jē-ner'i-kal-li, *adv.* With regard to a genus.

generous, jen'er-us, *a.* Noble; bountiful; liberal; full of spirit, as wine; courageous, as a steed. **generously,** jen'ėr-us-li, *adv.* Nobly; magnanimously; liberally. **generosity,** jen'ėr-os"i-ti, *n.* Nobleness of soul; liberality; munificence.

genesis, jen'e-sis, *n.* Act of producing; origin; first book of the Old Testament.

genetic, genetical, je-net'ik, je-net'-i-kal, *a.* Relating to origin or production.

genial, jēn'yal, *a.* Cordial; kindly; contributing to life and cheerfulness. **geniality,** jē'ni-al"i-ti, *n.* Sympathetic cheerfulness or cordiality. **genially,** jē'ni-al-li, *adv.* Cordially; cheerfully.

genital, jen'it-al, *a.* Pertaining to generation or birth. **genitals,** jen'it-alz, *n. pl.* The parts of generation; sexual organs.

genitive, jen'i-tiv, *a.* and *n.* Applied to a case of nouns; pronouns, &c., in English called the possessive.

genius, jēn'yus, *n.; pl.* **geniuses,** jēn'-yus-ez; in first sense **genii,** jē'ni-ī. A tutelary deity; aptitude of mind for a particular study or course of life; uncommon powers of intellect; a man with uncommon intellectual faculties; nature; peculiar character.

genre, zhän-r, *n.* A term applied to the department of painting which depicts scenes of ordinary life.

genteel, jen-tēl', *a.* Having the manners of well-bred people; refined; elegant. **genteelly,** jen-tēl'li, *adv.* In a genteel manner; politely; fashionably.

gentian, jen'shan, *n.* A bitter herbaceous plant, valued medicinally as a tonic.

gentile, jen'tīl, *a.* Pertaining to a family, race, or nation; pertaining to pagans. —*n.* (*often cap*) Any person not a Jew or a Christian; a heathen.

gentility, jen-til'i-ti, *n.* Politeness of manners; fashionable style or circumstances.

gentle, jen'tl, *a.* Well-born; refined in manners; mild; placid; not rough, violent, or wild; soothing.—*n.* A person of good birth.

gentlefolk, jen''tl-fōk', *n.* Persons of good breeding and family: more generally in *pl. gentlefolks.*

gentleman, jen'tl-man, *n.* A man of good social position; technically any man above the rank of yeoman; comprehending noblemen (Eng.); a man of good breeding or of high honor; a polite equivalent for 'man.'

gentlemanlike, gentlemanly, jen''tl-man-līk', jen'tl-man-li, *a.* Pertaining to or becoming a gentleman.

gentleness, jen'tl-nes, *n.* Quality of being gentle; tenderness; mild treatment.

gentlewoman, jen"tl-wu̇'man, *n.* A woman of good family or of good breeding.

gently, jen'tli, *adv.* Softly; meekly; mildly; with tenderness.

gentry, jen'tri, *n.* Wealthy or well-born people; people of a rank below the nobility.

genuflection, genuflexion, jen'ū-flek"shun, *n.* The act of bending the knee, particularly in worship.

genuine, jen'ū-in, *a.* Belonging to the original stock; real; pure; true. **genuinely,** jen'ū-in-li, *adv.* In a genuine manner.

genus, jē'nus, *n.*; pl. **genera,** jen'ėr-a. A kind, class, or sort; an assemblage of species having distinctive characteristics in common.

geodesic, geodetic, jē-ō-des'ik, jē-ō-det'ik, *a.* Pertaining to geodesy.

geodesy, jē-od'e-si, *n.* The geometry of the earth.

geography, jē-og'ra-fi, *n.* The science of the external features of the world; a book describing the earth or part of it. **geographer,** jē-og'ra-fėr, *n.* One versed in geography or who writes on it. **geographic, geographical,** jē-o-graf'ik, jē-o-graf'i-kal, *a.* Pertaining to geography; containing information regarding geography.

geology, jē-ol'o-ji, *n.* The science of the structure of the earth as to its rocks, strata, soil, minerals, organic remains, and changes. **geological,** jē-ō-loj'i-kal, *a.* Pertaining to geology. **geologist,** jē-ol'ō-jist, *n.* One versed in the science of geology.

geometric, geometrical, jē-ō-met'rik, jē-ō-met'rik-al, *a.* Pertaining to geometry; according to the principles of geometry.

geometry, jē-om'e-tri, *n.* The science of magnitude; that branch of mathematics which treats of the properties and relations of lines, angles, surfaces, and solids.

George, jorj, *n.* A figure of St. George on horseback, worn by knights of the Garter.

Georgian, jor'ji-an, *a.* Relating to the reigns of the four Georges, kings of Great Britain.

geranium, jē-rā'ni-um, *n.* A plant cultivated for its beautiful flowers; the crane's-bill genus of plants.

germ, jėrm, *n.* The earliest form of any animal or plant; origin; microbe; bacillus.

german, jėr'man, *a.* Come of the same parents. Cousins *german* are the sons or daughters of brothers or sisters, first cousins.

German, jėr'man, *a.* Belonging to Germany.—*n.* A native of Germany; the German language.

germane, jėr-mān', *a.* Closely allied; relevant; pertinent.

Germanic, jėr-man'ik, *a.* Pertaining to Germany; Teutonic.

germinal, jėr'mi-nal, *a.* Pertaining to a germ.

germinate, jėr'mi-nāt, *vi.* (germinating, germinated). To sprout; to bud; to begin to vegetate or grow, as seeds.

germination, jėr-mi-nā'shun, *n.* Act of germinating; first beginning of vegetation in a seed or plant.

gerrymander, ger'i-man"dėr, *vt.* To arrange so as to get an unfair result from the distribution of voters in political elections.

gerund, jer'und, *n.* A kind of verbal noun in Latin; a verbal noun, such as 'teaching' in 'fit for teaching boys.' **gerundial,** je-ruu'di-al, *a.* Pertaining to or like a gerund.

gestation, jes-tā'shun, *n.* The carrying of young in the womb from conception to delivery; pregnancy.

gesticulate, jes-tik'ū-lāt, *vi.* To make gestures or motions, as in speaking.—*vt.* To represent by gesture; to act. **gesticulation,** jes-tik'ū-lā"shun, *n.* Act of gesticulating; a gesture. **gesticulator,** jes-tik'ū-lā-tėr, *n.* One who gesticulates. **gesticulatory,** jes-tik"ū-lā-to'ri, *a.* Pertaining to gesticulation.

gesture, jes'tūr, *n.* A posture or motion of the body or limbs; action intended to express an idea or feeling, or to enforce an argument.

get, get, *vt.* (getting; pret. got; pp. got, gotten). To obtain; to gain; to reach; to beget; to learn; to induce.—*vi.* To arrive at any place or state by degrees; to become; to make gain.

getup, get"up', *n.* Equipment; dress.

gewgaw, gū'ga, *n.* A showy trifle; a toy; a splendid plaything.

geyser, gi'zėr, *n.* A hot-water spring; the water rising in a column.

ghastly, gast'li, *a.* Death-like in looks; hideous; frightful, as wounds.

gherkin, gėr'kin, *n.* A small-fruited variety of cucumber used for pickling.

ghost, gōst, *n.* The soul of man; a disembodied spirit; apparition; shadow. **ghostly,** gōst'li, *a.* Relating to the soul; spiritual; not carnal or secular; pertaining to apparitions.

ghoul, göl, *n.* An imaginary evil being which preys upon human bodies.

GI, jē' ī', *n.* Government issue; term used for enlisted military personnel and dress.

giant, jī'ant, *n.* A man of extraordinary stature; a person of extraordinary powers, bodily or intellectual.—*a.* Like a giant, extraordinary in size.

giantess, jī'ant-es, *n.* A female giant.

gibberish, gib'ėr-ish, *n.* Rapid and inarticulate talk; unmeaning words.

gibbet, jib'et, *n.* A gallows; the projecting beam of a crane, on which the pulley is fixed.—*vt.* To hang on a gibbet; to expose to scorn, infamy, &c.

gibbon, gib'un. A long-armed ape of the Indian Archipelago.

gibe, jīb, *vi.* (gibing, gibed). To utter taunting, sarcastic words; to flout; to sneer.—*vt.* To scoff at; to mock.—*n.* A scoff, taunt; reproach.

giblet, jib'let, *n.* One of those parts of poultry usually excluded in roasting, as the head, gizzard, liver, &c.; usually in *pl.*

giddy, gid'i, *a.* Having in the head a

sensation of whirling or swimming; dizzy; fickle; heedless; rendered wild by excitement.

gift, gift, *n.* Anything given; act of giving; power of giving; talent or faculty.—*vt.* To endow with any power or faculty.

gifted, gif'ted, *p.a.* Furnished with any particular talent; talented.

gig, gig, *n.* A light one-horse carriage with one pair of wheels; a ship's light boat; a long narrow rowing-boat; adapted for racing.

gigantic, ji-gan'tik, *a.* Like a giant; huge; colossal; immense.

giggle, gig'l, *n.* A kind of laugh, with short catches of the voice or breath.—*vi.* (giggling, giggled). To laugh with short catches of the breath; to titter.

gigolo, jig'ō-lō, *n.* A male paid to be a woman's escort.

gild, gild, *vt.* (pret. and pp. gilded or gilt). To overlay with gold in leaf or powder; to illuminate; to give a fair and agreeable appearance to.

gilder, gil'dèr, *n.* One who gilds; one whose occupation is to overlay things with gold.

gilding, gil'ding, *n.* The art or practice of overlaying things with gold; a thin coating of gold; fair superficial show.

gill, gil, *n.* The organ of respiration in fishes; the flap below the beak of a fowl; the flesh on the lower part of the cheeks.

gill, jil, *n.* The fourth part of a pint; a sweetheart; a wanton girl.

gilt, gilt, pp. of *gild.* Overlaid with gold; brightly adorned.—*n.* Gold laid on the surface of a thing; gilding.

gimlet, gim'let, *n.* A small borer with a pointed screw at the end.

gimp, gimp, *n.* A kind of silk twist or edging.

gin, jin, *n.* A distilled spirit flavored with juniper berries; a machine for driving piles, raising great weights, &c.; a machine for separating the seeds from cotton; a trap, snare.—*vt.* (ginning, ginned). To clear of seeds by a cotton gin; to catch in a trap.

ginger, jin'jèr, *n.* A tropical plant, the root of which has a hot, spicy quality.

gingerly, jin'jèr-li, *adv.* Cautiously; timidly; delicately; gently.

gingham, ging'am, *n.* A kind of striped cotton cloth.

gipsy, gypsy, jip'si, *n.* One of an oriental vagabond race scattered over Europe, &c., believed to have come originally from India; the language of the Gipsies; a name of slight reproach to a woman, implying roguishness.—*a.* Pertaining to or resembling the Gipsies.

giraffe, ji-raf', *n.* The cameleopard, the tallest of animals.

gird, gèrd, *vt.* (pp. girded or girt). To bind; to make fast by binding; to in-

Giraffe

vest; to encompass.—*vi.* To gibe; to sneer.—*n.* A stroke with a whip; a twitch; a sneer.

girder, gèr'dèr, *n.* One who girds; a main beam supporting a superstructure.

girdle, gèr'dl, *n.* That which girds; a band or belt; something drawn round the waist and tied or buckled.—*vt.* (girdling, girdled). To bind with a girdle, belt, or sash; to gird.

girl, gèrl, *n.* A female child; young woman.

girlhood, gèrl'hud, *n.* The state of a girl.

girlish, gèrl'ish, *a.* Like a girl; befitting a girl.

girt, gèrt, pret. and pp. of *gird.*

girt, gèrt, *vt.* To gird; to surround.

girth, gèrth, *n.* That which girds; band fastening a saddle on a horse's back; measure round a person's body or anything cylindrical.

gist, jist, *n.* The main point of a question; substance or pith of a matter.

give, giv, *vt.* (giving; pret. gave; pp. given). To bestow; to deliver; to impart; to yield; to afford; to utter; to show; to send forth; to devote (one's self); to pledge; to allow; to ascribe.—*vi.* To make gifts; to yield to pressure; to recede.

gizzard, giz'èrd, *n.* The muscular stomach of a bird.

glacial, glā'shal, *a.* Icy; frozen; relating to glaciers.

glacier, glā'shèr, *n.* An immense mass of ice formed in valleys above the snow-line, and having a slow movement downwards.

glad, glad, *a.* Affected with pleasure; pleased; cheerful; imparting pleasure.—*vt.* (gladding, gladded). To make glad; to gladden. **gladden**, glad'n, *vt.* To make glad.—*vi.* To become glad; to rejoice.

glade, glād, *n.* A green clear space or opening in a wood.

gladiator, glad"i-ā'tèr, *n.* Among the Romans, one who fought with swords, &c., for the entertainment of the people; a prize-fighter. **gladiatorial**, glad'i-a-tō'ri-al, *a.* Pertaining to gladiators.

gladiolus, glad'i-ō'lus, *n.*; pl. -li. A beautiful genus of bulbous-rooted plants, abundant in S. Africa; sword-lily.

gladly, glad'li, *adv.* With pleasure; joyfully.

gladsome, glad'sum, *a.* Joyful; cheerful; pleasing.

glamour, glam'èr, *n.* Magic influence causing a person to see objects differently from what they really are; witchery.

glance, gläns, *n.* A sudden shoot of light or splendor; a glimpse or sudden look.—*vi.* (glancing, glanced). To shine; to gleam; to dart aside; to look with a sudden rapid cast of the eye; to move quickly; to hint.—*vt.* To shoot or dart suddenly or obliquely; to cast for a moment. **glancingly**, gläns'ing-li, *adv.* By glancing; in a glancing manner; transiently.

gland, gland, *n.* An acorn; any acorn-shaped fruit; a roundish organ in many parts of the body secreting some fluid; a secreting organ in plants. **glanders,** glan'dėrz, *n.* A disease of the mucous membrane about the mouth in horses.

glandular, glan'dū-lėr, *a.* Having the character of a gland; consisting of glands.

glandule, glan'dūl, *n.* A small gland.

glare, glar, *n.* A bright dazzling light; a fierce piercing look.—*vi.* (glaring, glared). To shine with excessive luster; to look with fierce piercing eyes. **glaring,** glar'ing, *p.a.* Excessively bright; vulgarly splendid; notorious; barefaced. **glaringly,** glar'ing-li, *adv.* Openly; notoriously.

glass, glas, *n.* A hard transparent substance; a small drinking vessel of glass; a mirror; quantity of liquor that a glass vessel contains; a lens; a telescope; a barometer; *pl.* spectacles.—*a.* Made of glass; vitreous. **glass blower,** glas'blō'ėr, *n.* One who blows and fashions vessels. **glasshouse,** glas"hous', *n.* A house where glass is made; a house made of glass. **glassy,** glas'i, *a.* Made of glass; vitreous; resembling glass in its properties.

glaucoma, glaucosis, gla-kō'ma, gla-kō'sis, *n.* An opacity of the vitreous humor of the eye, giving it a bluish-green tint.

glaucous, gla'kus, *a.* Of a sea-green color; covered with a fine bluish or greenish bloom or powder.

glaze, glāz, *vt.* (glazing, glazed). To furnish with glass; to incrust with a vitreous substance; to make smooth and glossy.—*n.* A vitreous or transparent coating.

glazier, glā'zhėr, *n.* One whose business is to set window-glass.

glazing, glāz'ing, *n.* Act or art of one who glazes; enamel; glaze.

gleam, glēm, *n.* A small stream of light; brightness.—*vi.* To shoot or dart, as rays of light; to shine; to flash. **gleamy,** glēm'i, *a.* Darting beams of light; casting light in rays.

glean, glēn, *vt.* and *i.* To gather stalks and ears of grain left behind by reapers; to pick up here and there; to gather slowly and assiduously.

glee, glē, *n.* Joy; mirth; a composition for voices in three or more parts. **gleeful, gleesome,** glē'fŭl, glē'sum, *a.* Full of glee; merry; gay; joyous.

glen, glen, *n.* A narrow valley; a dale.

glib, glib, *a.* Smooth; slippery; having plausible words always ready.

glide, glīd, *vi.* (gliding, glided). To flow gently; to move or slip along with ease. —*n.* Act of moving smoothly.

glider, glīd'ėr, *n.* A motorless aeroplane.

glimmer, glim'ėr, *vi.* To shine faintly, and with frequent intermissions; to flicker.—*n.* A faint light; a twinkle. **glimmering,** glim'ėr-ing, *p.a.* Shining faintly.—*n.* A glimmer; faint view; glimpse.

glimpse, glimps, *n.* A glean or flash of light; short transitory view; faint resemblance; slight tinge.—*vi.* To appear by glimpses.

glint, glint, *vi.* To glance; to give a flash of light.—*n.* A glance, flash, gleam.

glisten, glis'n, *vi.* To glitter; to sparkle.

glitter, glit'ėr, *vi.* To sparkle with light; to be showy, specious, or striking.—*n.* Brightness; luster.

gloaming, glōm'ing, *n.* Fall of the evening; the twilight; decline.

gloat, glōt, *vi.* To gaze earnestly; to feast the eyes; to contemplate with evil satisfaction.

globe, glōb, *n.* A round solid body; a sphere; the earth; an artificial sphere on whose surface is drawn a map of the earth or heavens.—*vt.* To gather into a round mass. **globular,** glob'ū-lėr, *a.* Having the form of a ball or sphere; spherical. **globule,** glob'ūl, *n.* A little globe; a small spherical particle; one of the red particles of the blood.

globulin, glob'ū-lin, *n.* The main ingredient of blood globules and resembling albumen.

gloom, glöm, *n.* Obscurity; thick shade; sadness; aspect of sorrow; darkness of prospect or aspect.—*vi.* To shine obscurely; to be cloudy or dark; to be sullen or sad. **gloomily,** glöm'i-li, *adv.* Darkly; dismally; sullenly. **gloomy,** glöm'i, *a.* Dark; dismal; downcast; sad.

glory, glō'ri, *n.* Praise, honor, admiration, or distinction; renown; magnificence; celestial bliss; the divine presence; the divine perfections; that of which one may be proud.—*vi.* (glorying, gloried). To boast; to rejoice; to be proud with regard to something. **glorification,** glō'ri-fi-kā"shun, *n.* Act of glorifying; laudation. **glorify,** glō'ri-fī, *vt.* (glorifying, glorified). To make glorious; to ascribe glory or honor to; to extol. **glorious,** glō'ri-us, *a.* Full of glory; renowned; celebrated; grand; brilliant. **gloriously,** glō'ri-us-li, *adv.* In a glorious manner; splendidly; illustriously.

gloss, glos, *n.* Brightness from a smooth surface; sheen; specious appearance; an interpretation; comment.—*vt.* To give superficial luster to; to give a specious appearance to; to render plausible; to comment; to annotate. **glossarial,** glos-sā'ri-al, *a.* Containing explanation. **glossary,** glos'a-ri, *n.* A vocabulary explaining antiquated, or difficult words or phrases. **glosser,** glos'ėr, *n.* A writer of glosses. **glossographer,** glo-sog'ra-fėr, *n.* A writer of glosses; a scholiast.

glossy, glos'i, *a.* Smooth and shining; highly polished.

glottis, glot'is, *n.* The narrow opening at the upper part of the windpipe.

glove, gluv, *n.* A cover for the hand.— *vt.* (gloving, gloved). To cover with a glove. **glover,** gluv'ėr, *n.* One who makes or sells gloves.

glow, glō, *vi.* To burn with intense heat, especially without flame; to feel great heat of body; to be flushed; to be ardent; to rage.—*n.* White heat; brightness of color; animation. **glowing,** glō'ing, *p.a.* Exhibiting a bright color; vehement; inflamed; fervent. **glowworm,** glō'wėrm, *n.* A wingless female beetle which emits a greenish light.

glucose, glö'kōs, *n.* Grape-sugar, a sugar produced from grapes, starch, &c.

glue, glö, *n.* A tenacious, viscid matter

which serves as a cement.—vt. (gluing,
To join with glue; to unite. **gluey**,
glö'i, a. Viscous; glutinous.

glum, glum, a. Sullen; moody; dejected.

glut, glut, vt. (glutting, glutted). To
swallow greedily; to cloy; to satiate; t-
furnish beyond sufficiency.—n. Plenty,
even to loathing; supply of an article
beyond the demand.

gluten, glö'ten, n. A tough, elastic, nitrogenous substance in the flour of wheat,
&c.

glutinate, glö'tin-āt, vt. To unite with
glue. **glutinous**, glö'tin-us, a. Gluey;
viscous; viscid; tenacious; resembling
glue.

glutton, glut'n, n. One who eats to excess; one eager of anything to excess; a
carnivorous quadruped. **gluttonize**,
glut'n-īz, vi. To indulge in gluttony.
gluttonous, glut'n-us, a. Given to excessive eating; insatiable. **gluttony**,
glut'n-i, n. Excess in eating; voracity of
appetite.

glycerin, glycerine, glis'ēr-in, n. A
transparent, colorless, sweet liquid obtained from fats.

gnarl, närl, n. A protuberance on the
outside of a tree; a knot. **gnarled**,
närld, a. Knotty; perverse.

gnash, nash, vt. To strike together, as
the teeth.—vi. To strike or dash the
teeth together, as in rage or pain.

gnat, nat, n. A small two-winged fly, the
female of which bites.

gnaw, na, vt. To bite by little and little;
to bite in agony or rage; to fret; to corrode.—vi. To use the teeth in biting; to
cause steady a noying pain.

gneiss, nīs, n. A species of rock composed of quartz, feldspar, and mica, and
having a slaty structure.

gnome, nōm, n. A sprite supposed to inhabit the inner parts of the earth; a
dwarf; a maxim, aphorism.

go, gō, vi. (going; pret. went; pp. gone).
To move; to proceed; to depart; to be
about to do; to circulate; to tend; to be
guided; to be alienated or sold; to reach;
to avail; to conduce; to die; to fare; to
become.

goad, gōd, n. A pointed instrument to
make a beast move faster; anything that
stirs to action.—vt. To drive with a
goad; to instigate.

goal, gōl, n. The point set to bound a
race; a mark that players in some outdoor sport must attain; a success scored
by reaching this; final purpose; end.

goat, gōt, n. A ruminant quadruped with
long hair and horns. **goatherd**, gōt"-
hèrd', n. One whose occupation is to tend
goats. **goatskin**, gōt'skin, n. Leather
made from the skin of goats.

gobbet, gob'et, n. A mouthful; a lump.

gobble, gob'l, vt. (gobbing, gobbled).
To swallow in large pieces or hastily.—
vi. To make a noise in the throat, as a
turkey. **gobbler**, gob'lèr, n. One who
gobbles; a greedy eater; a gormandizer;
a turkey-cock.

go-between, gō"bē-twēn', n. Intermediary.

goblet, gob'let, n. A kind of cup or
drinking-vessel without a handle.

goblin, gob'lin, n. A mischievous sprite;
an elf.

go-by, gō-bī', n. A passing without notice; intentional disregard or avoidance.

God, god, n. The Supreme Being; a divinity; a deity; pl. the audience in the
gallery of a theater. **goddess**, god'es,
n. A female deity; a woman of superior
charms. **godfather**, god"fä'THèr, n. A
man who becomes sponsor for a child at
baptism. (also godmother, -son, -daugh-
ter, and child). **godhead**, god'hed, n.
Godship; divinity; divine nature or essence. **godless**, god'les, a. Having or
acknowledging no God; ungodly; atheis-
ical. **godlike**, god'lik, a. Resembling
God; divine; resembling a deity; of superior excellence. **godliness**, god'lines, n. Quality of being godly; piety;
reverence for God. **godly**, god'li, a.
Reverencing God; pious; devout; holy;
religious; righteous. **godsend**, god'-
send, n. An unexpected acquisition or
good fortune. **godship**, god'ship, n.
Deity; rank of a god. **Godspeed**, god'-
spēd, n. Success; prosperity.

goggle, gog'l, vi. (goggling, goggled).
To roll or strain the eyes.—a. Prominent; rolling, or staring (eyes).—n. A
strained or affected rolling of the eye;
pl. a kind of spectacles to protect the
eyes or cure squinting. **goggle-eyed**,
gog"l-īd', a. Having prominent, distorted,
or rolling eyes.

going, gō'ing, n. Act of one who goes;
departure; way; state of roads. **goings-
on**, actions; behavior.

goiter, goi'tèr, n. A morbid enlargement
of the thyroid gland, forming a mass on
the front of the neck.

gold, gōld, n. A precious metal of a
bright yellow color; money; something
pleasing or valuable; a bright yellow
color.—a. Made or consisting of gold.
goldbeater, gōld"bēt'èr, n. One who
beats gold into thin leaves for gilding.
golden, gōl'den, a. Made of gold; like
gold; splendid; most valuable; auspicious. **gold field**, gōld fēld', n. District
or region where gold is found. **gold-
finch**, gōld'finsh, n. A beautiful singing
bird. **goldfish**, gōld'fish, n. A fresh-
water fish of the carp family, of a bright
orange color. **gold leaf**, gōld lēf', n.
Gold beaten into a thin leaf. **gold-
smith**, gōld"smith', n. One who manufactures articles of gold and silver.
goldylocks, gōld'i-loks, n. A plant
with yellow flowers; a ranunculus.

golf, golf, n. A game played over links
with a small ball driven by clubs.—vi.
To play golf. **golfer**, gol'fèr, n. One
who plays golf. **golfing**, gol'fing, n. Act
of playing golf.

gondola, gon'dō-la, n. A long narrow
pleasure-boat, used in Venice. **gon-
dolier**, gon'dō-lèr", n. A man who rows
a gondola.

gong, gong, n. A kind of metallic drum;
a similar article used instead of a bell.

gonorrhea, gon'o-rē"a, n. A venereal
disease of the genital organs.

good, gud, a. The opposite of bad;
wholesome; useful; fit; virtuous; valuable; benevolent; clever; adequate; val-

id; able to fulfill engagements; considerable; full or complete; immaculate. —*n.* What is good or desirable; advantage; welfare; virtue; *pl.* commodities, chattels, movables. **for good,** to close the whole business; finally.—*interj.* Well; right.

good-by, good-bye, gud'bī″, *n.* or *interj.* A salutation at parting; farewell.

good-day, gud'dā″, *n.* or *interj.* A salutation at meeting or parting; farewell.

good-for-nothing, gud″for-nu′thing, *n.* An idle, worthless person.—*a.* Worthless.

good humor, gud hū′mẽr, *n.* A cheerful temper or state of mind.

good-humored, gud′hū″mẽrd, *a.* Being of a cheerful temper.

good morning, gud morn′ing, *n.* or *interj.* A form of morning salutation.

good-natured, gud′nā″tūrd, *a.* Naturally mild in temper; not easily provoked.

goodness, gud′nes, *n.* State or quality of being good; excellence, virtue, &c.; a euphemism for God.

good night, gud′ nīt′, *n.* or *interj.* A form of salutation in parting for the night.

good sense, gud′ sens′, *n.* Sound judgment.

good-tempered, gud′tem″pẽrd, *a.* Having a good temper; good-natured.

good will, gud′ wil′, *n.* Benevolence; business connection of some established business.

goody, goody-good, goody-goody, gud′i, gud′i-gud′, gud′i-gud′i, *a.* Affected with mawkish morality; squeamish in morals.

goon, gōn, *n.* Slang. A coarse, stupid person; a tough; a strikebreaker.

goose, gös, *n. pl.* **geese,** gēs. A swimming bird larger than the duck; a tailor's smoothing-iron; a silly person.

gooseberry, göz′ber-i, *n.* The fruit of a prickly shrub, and the shrub itself.

goose step, gös′ step′, *n.* Act of marking time by raising the feet alternately without advancing.

gopher, gō′fẽr, *n.* An American burrowing rodent.

Gordian knot, gor′di-an not. An inextricable difficulty‡ *to cut the Gordian knot,* to remove a difficulty by bold measures.

gore, gōr, *n.* Blood that is shed; thick or clotted blood; a wedge-shaped piece of land or cloth; a gusset.—*vt.* (goring, gored). To cut in a triangular form; to pierce with a pointed instrument, or an animal's horns.

gorge, gorj, *n.* The throat; the gullet; a narrow passage between hills or mountains; entrance into a bastion.—*vt.* and *i.* (gorging, gorged). To swallow with greediness; to glut; to satiate.

gorgeous, gor′jus, *a.* Showy; splendid; magnificent.

Gorgonzola, gor-gun-zō′la, *n.* A kind of Italian ewe-milk cheese.

gorilla, go-ril′a, *n.* The largest animal of the ape kind.

gormand, gor′mand, *n.* A glutton. **gormandize,** gor′man-dīz, *vi.* To eat

greedily or to excess.

gory, gōr′i, *a.* Covered with gore; bloody; murderous.

goshawk, gos′hok, *n.* A large bird of the hawk family.

gosling, goz′ling, *n.* A young goose.

gospel, gos′pel, *n.* The history of Jesus Christ; any of the four records of Christ's life by his apostles; scheme of salvation as taught by Christ; any general doctrine. —*a.* Relating to the gospel; accordant with the gospel.

gossamer, gos′a-mẽr, *n.* A fine, filmy substance, like cobwebs, floating in the air in calm, sunny weather; a thin fabric.

gossip, gos′ip, *n.* An idle tattler; idle talk.—*vi.* To prate; to run about and tattle. **gossipry,** gos′ip-ri, *n.* Relationship by baptismal rites; idle talk or gossip. **gossipy,** gos′ip-i, *a.* Full of gossip.

Goth, goth, *n.* One of an ancient Teutonic race; a barbarian; one defective in taste. **Gothic,** goth′ik, *a.* Pertaining to the Goths; rude; barbarous; denoting the style of architecture characterized by the pointed arch.—*n.* the languages of the Goths; the Gothic order or architecture. **Gothicism,** goth′i-sizm, *n.* Rudeness of manners; conformity to the Gothic style of architecture.

gouge, gouj, gōj, *n.* A chisel with a hollow or grooved blade.—*vt.* (gouging, gouged). To scoop out with, or as with, a gouge.

gourd, gōrd, *n.* The popular name of the family of plants represented by the melon, cucumber, &c.; a cup made from the rind of a gourd.

gourmand, gör′mänd, *n.* A glutton; a gourmet. **gourmandize,** gör′mand-īz, *vi.* To gormandize.

gourmet, gör′mä or gör′met″, *n.* A connoisseur in wines and meats; a nice feeder.

gout, gout, *n.* A painful disease, affecting generally the small joints; a drop; a clot or coagulation. **gouty,** gout′i, *a.* Diseased with or subject to gout; pertaining to gout.

govern, guv′ẽrn, *vt.* To direct and control; to regulate; to steer; to affect so as to determine the case, &c., in grammar.—*vi.* To exercise authority; to administer the laws. **governable,** guv′ẽrn-a-bl, *a.* That may be governed. **governance,** guv′ẽr-nans, *n.* Exercise of authority; control. **governess,** guv′ẽr-nes, *n.* A female who governs or instructs. **government,** guv′ẽrn-ment, *n.* Rule; control; administration of public affairs; system of policy in a state; territory ruled by a governor; executive power; the influence of a word in grammar in regard to construction. **governmental,** guv-ẽrn-men′tal, *a.* Pertaining to or sanctioned by government.

governor, guv′ẽr-nẽr, *n.* One who governs; one invested with supreme authority; a tutor; a contrivance in machinery for maintaining a uniform velocity.

governorship, guv″ẽr-nẽr-ship′, *n.* The office of a governor.

gown, goun, *n.* A woman's outer garment; a long, loose garment worn by professional men, as divines.—*vt.* To put on a gown.

grab, grab, *vt.* (grabbing, grabbed). To seize; to snatch.—*n.* A sudden grasp; implement for clutching objects.

grace, grãs, *n.* Favor; kindness; love and favor of God; state of reconciliation to God; pardon; license or privilege; expression of thanks before or after meals; title of a duke or archbishop; elegance with appropriate dignity; an embellishment; one of three ancient goddesses in whose gift were grace and beauty; in *music*, a trill, shake, &c.—*vt.* (gracing, graced). To lend grace to; to adorn; to favor. **graceful,** grãs′ful, *a.* Full of grace; beautiful with dignity; elegant. **gracefully,** grãs′ful-li, *adv.* In a graceful manner; elegantly. **graceless,** grãs′les, *a.* Void of grace; unregenerate; unsanctified; profligate.

gracious, grã′shus, *a.* Full of grace; favorable; disposed to forgive offenses and impart blessings; benignant; condescending. **graciously,** grã′shus-li, *adv.* Kindly; favorably; with kind condescension.

gradation, gra-dã′shun, *n.* Arrangement by grades; regular advance step by step; rank; series; regular process by degrees. **gradatory,** grã′da-to-ri, *a.* Proceeding step by step; marking gradation.—*n.* Steps from the cloisters into the church.

grade, grãd, *n.* A step; degree; rank; gradient.—*vt.* (grading, graded). To arrange in order of rank, &c.; to reduce to a suitable slope.

gradient, grã′di-ent, *a.* Moving by steps; rising or descending by regular degrees.—*n.* The degree of ascent or descent in a road, &c.; part of a road which slopes.

gradual, grad′ū-al, *a.* Advancing step by step; regular and slow.—*n.* An order of steps. **gradually,** grad′ū-al-li, *adv.* By degrees; step by step; regularly; graduated). To divide into regular inslowly.

graduate, grad′ū-ãt, *vt.* (graduating, tervals or degrees; to mark with such; to arrange by grades; to confer a university degree on; to reduce to a certain consistency by evaporation.—*vi.* To receive a university degree; to change gradually. —*n.* One who has received a degree of a university, &c. **graduation,** grad′ū-ã″shun, *n.* Marks to indicate degrees, &c.; regular, progression; act of conferring or receiving academical degrees.

graft, graft, *n.* A small scion of a tree inserted in another tree which is to support and nourish the scion.—*vi.* To insert a graft on; to toil; to obtain a livelihood by illegitimate gains.—*n.* Money illegitimately obtained.

grail, graal, grãl, *n.* The holy vessel containing the last drops of Christ's blood, brought to England by Joseph of Arimathea, and being afterwards lost, eagerly sought for by King Arthur's knights.

grain, grãn, *n.* A single seed of a plant; corn in general; a minute particle; a small weight; fibers of wood with regard to their arrangement; substance of a thing with respect to the size, form, or direction of the constituent particles; texture; dye.—*vt.* To paint in imitation of fibers; to granulate. **grained,** grãnd, *p.a.* Having a certain grain or texture; having a granular surface.

gram, gramme, gram, *n.* The French unit of weight, equal to 15:43 grains troy.

grammar, gram′ẽr *n.* A system of principles and rules for speaking or writing a language; propriety of speech; an outline of any subject. **grammarian,** gra-mãr′i-an, *n.* One who is versed in or who teaches grammar. **grammatical, grammatic,** gra-mat′i-kal, gra-mat′ik, *a.* Belonging to grammar; according to the rules of grammar. **grammatically,** gra-mat′i-kal-li, *adv.* According to grammar. **grammaticize,** gra-mat′i-sīz, *vt.* To render grammatical.

granary, gran′a-ri, *n.* A storehouse for grain after it is thrashed.

grand, grand, *a.* Great, figuratively; majestic; magnificent; noble.

grandam, gran′dam, *n.* An old woman; a grandmother.

grandchild, grand″child′, *n.* A son's or daughter's child.

granddaughter, grand″dg′tẽr, *n.* The daughter of a son or daughter.

grandee, gran-dē′, *n.* A man of elevated rank; a nobleman.

grandeur, gran′dūr, *n.* Greatness; sublimity; splendor; magnificence.

grandfather, grand′fä-thẽr, *n.* A father's or mother's father.

grandiloquence, gran-dil′ō-kwens, *n.* Lofty speaking; pompous language. **grandiose,** gran′di-ōs, *a.* Impressive from grandeur; bombastic; turgid.

grandly, grand′li, *adv.* In a grand or lofty manner; splendidly; sublimely.

grandmother, grand″muth′ẽr, *n.* The mother of one's father or mother.

grandsire, grand″sir′, *n.* A grandfather; any ancestor.

grandson, grand″sun′, *n.* The son of a son or daughter.

grandstand, grand″stand′, *n.* An erection on a race-course, &c., affording a good view.

grange, grãnj, *n.* A farm, with the buildings, stables, &c.

granite, gran′it, *n.* A rock composed of quartz, feldspar, and mica, or at least of two of them, confusedly crystalized. **granitic,** gra-nit′ik, *a.* Like granite; pertaining to or consisting of granite.

grant, grant, *vt.* To bestow; to confer on; to admit as true; to convey by deed or writing; to cede.—*n.* A bestowing; a gift; a conveyance in writing; the thing conveyed.

granular, gran′ū-lẽr, *a.* Consisting of or resembling grains.

granulate, gran′ū-lãt, *vt.* and *i.* (granulating, granulated). To form into grains; to make or become rough on the surface. **granulation,** gran′ū-lã″shun, *n.* Act of forming into grains; a process by which minute fleshy bodies are formed on wounds during healing; the fleshy grains themselves.

granule, gran'ŭl, *n*. A little grain.

grape, grāp, *n*. A single berry of the vine; grape-shot.

grapefruit, grāp'frōt, *n*. A large, yellow citrus fruit with a bitter rind and a mildly acid, juicy pulp; the tree bearing this fruit.

graphic, graphical, graf'ik, graf'i-kal, *a*. Pertaining to the art of writing or delineating; pictorial; vivid. **graphically**, graf'i-kal-li, *adv*. In a vivid and forcible way.

graphite, graf'īt, *n*. A form of carbon, made into pencils; plumbago; black-lead.

grapnel, grap'nel, *n*. A small anchor with four or five claws.

grapple, grap'l, *vt*. (grappling, grappled). To lay fast hold on, with hands or hooks.—*vi*. To contend in close fight, as wrestlers.—*n*. A seizing; close hug in contest; grappling-iron. **grappling-iron**, grap'ling-i'ern, *n*. An instrument of four or more iron claws for grappling and holding fast; a grapnel.

grasp, grasp, *vt*. To seize and hold by the fingers or arms; to take possession of; to comprehend.—*vi*. To make a clutch or catch.—*n*. Gripe of the hand; reach of the arms; power of seizing or comprehending.

grasping, grasp'ing, *p.a*. Avaricious; greedy.

grass, gras, *n*. Herbage; any plant of the family to which belong the grain-yielding and pasture plants.—*vt*. To cover with grass; to bleach on the grass.

grasshopper, gras"hop'er, *n*. An insect that hops among grass, allied to the locusts.

grass widow, gras'wid-ō, *n*. A wife living apart from her husband.

grassy, gras'i, *a*. Abounding with grass; resembling grass; green.

grate, grāt, *n*. A frame composed of parallel or cross bars; grating; iron frame for holding coal used as fuel.—*vt*. (grating, grated). To furnish or make fast with cross-bars; to wear away in small particles by rubbing; to offend, as by a discordant sound.—*vi*. To rub roughly on; to have an annoying effect; to sound harshly.

grateful, grāt'fyl, *a*. Pleasing; gratifying; feeling or expressing gratitude.

grater, grāt'er, *n*. An instrument for rubbing off small particles of a body.

gratify, grat'i-fī, *vt*. (gratifying, gratified). To please; to indulge, delight, humor. **gratifying**, grat"i-fī'ing, *p.a*. Giving pleasure; affording satisfaction. **gratification**, grat'i-fi-kā"shun, *n*. Act of gratifying; that which affords pleasure; satisfaction; recompense.

grating, grāt'ing, *n*. A frame or partition of bars or latticework.

gratis, grā'tis, *adv*. Without recompense; freely.—*a*. Given or done for nothing.

gratitude, grat'i-tūd, *n*. Quality of being grateful; an emotion of the heart, excited by a favor received; thankfulness.

gratuitous, gra-tū'i-tus, *a*. That is done

out of favor; free; voluntary; asserted or taken without proof. **gratuitously**, gra-tū'i-tus-li, *adv*. Freely; voluntarily.

gratuity, gra-tū'i-ti, *n*. A free ift; donation; something given in return for a favor.

grave, grāv, *vt*. (graving, pret. graved, pp. graven, graved.) To make incisions on; to engrave; to impress deeply, as on the mind; to clean, as a ship's bottom; and cover with pitch.—*n*. A pit for the dead; a tomb.—*a*. Weighty; serious; staid; thoughtful; not gay; not tawdry; in *music*, low.

grave digger, grāv' dig'er, *n*. One whose occupation is to dig graves.

gravel, grav'el, *n*. Small pebbles; a disease produced by small concretions in the kidneys and bladder.—*vt*. (graveling, graveled). To cover with gravel; to cause to stick in the sand or gravel; to puzzle. **gravelly**, grav'el-i, *a*. Abounding with gravel; consisting of gravel.

gravely, grāv'li, *adv*. In a grave, solemn manner; soberly; seriously.

gravity, grav'i-ti, *n*. The tendency of matter toward some attracting body, particularly toward the center of the earth; state or character of being grave; weight; enormity. **gravitate**, grav'i-tāt, *vi*. To be affected by gravitation; to tend towards the center. **gravitation**, grav'i-tā"shun, *n*. The force by which bodies are drawn towards the center of the earth; tendency of all matter toward all other matter.

gravy, grā'vi, *n*. The juice that comes from flesh in cooking.

gray, grey, grā, *a*. Of the color of hair whitened by age; white with a mixture of black; having gray hairs.—*n*. A gray color; a gray animal, as a horse; early morning twilight.

graybeard, greybeard, grā"bērd', *n*. An old man; an earthen jar for holding liquor (Eng.).

grayling, grā'ling, *n*. A fish of the salmon tribe.

graze, grāz, *vt*. (grazing, grazed). To rub or touch lightly in passing; to feed with growing grass as cattle; to feed on.—*vi*. To pass so as to rub lightly; to eat grass; to supply grass.—*n*. A slight rub or brush.

grazing, grāz'ing, *n*. The act of feeding on grass; pasture.

grease, grēs, *n*. Animal fat in a soft state; oily matter.—*vt*. (greasing, greased). To smear with grease. **greasy**, grēs'i, *a*. Smeared with grease; fatty; unctuous; like grease.

great, grāt, *a*. Large in bulk or number; long-continued; of vast power and excellence; eminent; majestic; pregnant; distant by one more generation, as *great*-grandfather, &c. **greathearted**, grāt"här'ted, *a*. High-spirited; magnanimous; noble. **greatly**, grāt'li, *adv*. In a great degree; much; nobly; illustriously; bravely. **greatness**, grāt'nes, *n*. Quality of being great; magnitude; nobleness; grandeur.

Grecian, grē'shan, *a*. Pertaining to Greece.—*n*. A Greek; one well versed in the Greek language.

greed, grēd, *n.* Eager desire; avarice. **greedily**, grēd'i-li, *adv.* Ravenously; eagerly. **greedy**, grēd'i, *a.* Having a keen appetite for food or drink; covetous; avaricious.

Greek, grēk, *a.* Pertaining to Greece.—*n.* A native of Greece; the language of Greece.

green, grēn, *a.* Having the color of growing plants; verdant; fresh; containing its natural juices; unripe; young; easily imposed upon.—*n.* A green color; a grassy plain or plot; *pl.* leaves and stems of young plants used in cookery. —*vt.* and *i.* To make or grow green.

greenhorn, grēn"horn', *n.* One easily imposed upon; a raw inexperienced person.

greenhouse, grēn"hous', *n.* A building in which tender plants are cultivated.

greenness, grēn'nes, *n.* Viridity; unripeness; freshness; vigor.

greensward, grēn"sward', *n.* Turf green with grass.

greet, grēt, *vt.* To salute; to meet and address with kindness.—*vi.* To meet and salute.

greeting, grēt'ing, *n.* Salutation at meeting; compliment from one absent.

gregarious, grē-gār'i-us, *a.* Assembling or being in a flock; not habitually solitary.

grenade, gre-nād', *n.* A ball of iron, &c., filled with powder, fired by a fuse. **grenadier**, gren'a-dēr', *n.* A tall footsoldier, one of a regiment of British guards.

grewsome. See **gruesome**.

greyhound, grā"hound', *n.* A tall, slender, fleet dog kept for the chase.

grid, grid, *n.* A grating; a gridiron.

griddle, grid'l, *n.* A circular plate of iron, or a shallow pan, for baking cakes. **gridiron**, grid"i'ėrn, *n.* A grated utensil for broiling flesh and fish; a frame upon which a ship rests, for inspection or repair; a football field.

grief, grēf, *n.* Pain of mind produced by loss, misfortune, &c.; sorrow; cause of sorrow; trouble. **grievance**, grēv'ans, *n.* A wrong suffered; cause of complaint; trouble. **grieve**, grēv, *vt.* (grieving, grieved). To cause grief; to deplore.— *vi.* To feel grief; to sorrow; to lament. **grievous**, grēv'us, *a.* Causing grief; hard to be borne; atrocious.

griffin, **griffon**, grif'in, grif'on, *n.* A fabled monster, in the fore part an eagle, in the hinder a lion.

grill, gril, *vt.* To broil on a gridiron; to torment, as if by broiling.—*vi.* To suffer, as if from grilling.—*n.* A grated utensil for broiling meat, &c.

grim, grim, *a.* Of a forbidding or fear-inspiring aspect; stern; sullen; surly; ugly. **grimly**, grim'li, *adv.* Fiercely; sullenly.

grimace, gri-mās', *n.* A distortion of the countenance; air of affectation.—*vi.* To make grimaces.

grime, grīm, *n.* Foul matter.—*vt.* (griming, grimed). To sully or soil deeply. **grimy**, grīm'i, *a.* Full of grime; foul.

grin, grin, *vi.* (grinning, grinned). To show the teeth, as in laughter, scorn, or anguish.—*n.* Act of showing the teeth; a forced smile or restrained laugh.

grind, grīnd, *vt.* (grinding, ground). To reduce to fine particles; to sharpen or polish by friction; to rub together; to oppress; to crush in pieces.—*vi.* To turn a mill; to be moved or rubbed together; to be pulverized by friction; to study hard.—*n.* Act of one who grinds; laborious spell of work. **grinder**, grīn'dėr, *n.* One who or that which grinds; a molar tooth. **grindstone**, grīnd"stōn', *n.* A circular stone, made to revolve, to sharpen tools.

grip, grip, *n.* The act of grasping; grasp; a fast hold; a hilt or handle.—*vt.* and *i.* (gripping, gripped). To grasp by the hand; to clutch; to hold fast.

gripe, grīp, *vt.* and *i.* (griping, griped). To grasp by the hand; to hold fast; to pinch; to give pain to the bowels.—*n.* Grasp; grip; something which grasps; *pl.* pinching pain in the bowels.

griping, grīp'ing, *p.a.* Grasping; extortionate; oppressing; distressing the bowels.

grisly, griz'li, *a.* Dreadful; fearful; ghastly.

grist, grist, *n.* Grain ground, or for grinding.

grit, grit, *n.* Sand or gravel; a hard sandstone; texture of a stone; firmness of mind; coarse part of meal. **gritty**, grit'i, *a.* Containing sand or grit; consisting of grit; sandy.

grizzle, griz'l, *n.* Gray; a gray color. **grizzled**, griz'ld, *a.* Gray; of a mixed color. **grizzly**, griz'li, *a.* Somewhat gray; gray with age; a bear.

groan, grōn, *vi.* To utter a mournful voice, as in pain or sorrow; to moan.—*n.* A deep, mournful sound, uttered in pain, sorrow, or disapprobation; any low rumbling sound.

groat, grōt, *n.* A former English coin and money of account, equal to fourpence; a small sum.

grocer, grō'sėr, *n.* A merchant who deals in tea, sugar, spices, &c. **grocery**, grō'sėr-i, *n.* A grocer's store; the commodities sold by grocers.

grog, grog, *n.* A mixture of spirit and water not sweetened. **groggy**, grog'-i, *a.* Overcome with grog; tipsy; moving in an uneasy, hobbling manner.

groin, groin, *n.* The part of the human body between the belly and thigh in front; the angular projecting curve made by the intersection of simple vaults at any angle. **groined**, groind, *a.* Having a groin or groins; formed of groins meeting in a point.

groom, gröm, *n.* A man or boy who has the charge of horses; a bridegroom.—*vt.* To feed and take care of, as a groom does horses.

groove, gröv, *n.* A channel or long hollow cut by a tool; fixed routine of life. —*vt.* (grooving, grooved). To cut a groove in; to furrow.

grope, grōp, *vt.* (groping, groped). To search in the dark by feeling; to feel one's way.—*vt.* To search out by feeling in the dark. **gropingly**, grōp'ing-li, *adv.* In a groping manner.

gross, grōs, *a.* Thick; coarse; obscene; palpable; dense; shameful; dull; whole. —*n.* Main body; bulk; the number of twelve dozen.

grossly, grōs'li, *adv.* Greatly; shamefully.

grotesque, grō-tesk', *a.* Wildly formed; extravagant; fantastic.—*n.* Whimsical figures or scenery.

grotto, grot'ō, *n.* A natural cave; an artificial ornamented cave.

ground, ground, *n.* Surface of the earth; soil; land; basis; reason; foil or background; predominating color; *pl.* dregs, sediment; ornamental land about a mansion.—*vt.* To set on the ground; to fix firmly; to instruct in first principles. —*vi.* To strike the bottom and remain fixed, as a ship. **ground floor**, ground' flōr', *n.* Floor of a house on a level with the exterior ground. **groundless**, ground'les, *a.* Wanting foundation or reason; baseless; false.

ground swell, ground' swel', *n.* Heaving of the sea caused by a distant storm. **groundwork**, ground'wèrk', *n.* Basis; fundamentals.

group, grōp, *n.* A cluster; an assemblage; an artistic combination of figures; a class.—*vt.* To form into a group or groups. **grouping**, grōp'ing, *n.* The art of arranging or mode of arrangement in a picture or work of art.

grouse, grous, *n.* The name of several wild rasorial birds, more particularly the moor-fowl or red grouse of Britain.

grove, grōv, *n.* A shady cluster of trees; a small wood.

grovel, grov'el, *vi.* (groveling, groveled). To lie prone, or creep on the earth; to be low or mean. **groveler**, grov'el-èr, *n.* One who grovels; an abject wretch. **groveling**, grov'el-ing, *p.a.* Apt to grovel; abject; base.

grow, grō, *vi.* (pret. grew, pp. grown). To be augmented by natural process; to increase; to make progress; to become; to accrue; to swell—*vt.* To raise from the soil; to produce.

growl, groul, *vi.* To murmur or snarl, as a dog; to utter an angry, grumbling sound.—*vt.* To express by growling.—*n.* Angry sound of a dog; grumbling murmur. **growler**, groul'èr, *n.* One that growls; a grumbler.

grown, grōn, *p.a.* Increased in growth; having arrived at full size or stature. **grownup**, grōn'up', *a.* Adult.

growth, grōth, *n.* Act or process of growing; product; increase; advancement.

grub, grub, *vi.* (grubbing, grubbed). To dig; to be employed meanly.—*vt.* To dig; to root out by digging.—*n.* The larva of an insect; caterpillar; maggot. Food. (slang).

grudge, gruj, *vi.* (grudging, grudged). To cherish ill-will; to be envious.—*vt.* To permit or grant with reluctance; to envy.—*n.* Reluctance in giving; secret enmity. **grudgingly**, gruj'ing-li, *adv.* In a grudging, unwilling, or envious manner.

gruel, grö'el, *n.* A light food made by boiling meal in water.

grueling, gruelling, grö'l-ing, *a.* Taxing, exhausting.

gruesome, grö'sum, *a.* Causing one to shudder; frightful; horrible; repulsive.

gruff, gruf, *a.* Of a rough or stern manner or voice; surly; harsh.

grumble, grum'bl, *vi.* (grumbling, grumbled). To murmur with discontent. **grumbler**, grum'blèr, *n.* One who grumbles; a discontented man.

grumpy, grumpish, grump'l, grump'ish, *a.* Surly; angry; gruff; *colloq.*

grunt, grunt, *vi.* To make a noise like a hog; to utter a deep guttural sound.— *n.* A deep guttural sound, as of a hog. **grunter**, grunt'èr, *n.* One who grunts; a pig.

guano, gwä'nō, *n.* A rich manure composed chiefly of the excrements of seafowls, and brought from S. America and the Pacific.

guarantee, gar'an-tē', *n.* An undertaking by a third person that a covenant shall be observed by the contracting parties or by one of them; one who binds himself to see the stipulations of another performed.—*vt.* (guaranteeing, guaranteed). To warrant; to pledge one's self for.

guarantor, gar''an-tor', *n.* One who gives a guarantee.

guard, gärd, *vt.* To keep watch over; to secure against injury, loss, or attack.—*vi.* To watch, by way of caution or defense; to be in a state of caution or defense.— *n.* Defense; protector; sentinel; escort; one who has charge of a railway train, &c. (Eng.); attention; caution; posture of defense. **guarded**, gärd'ed, *p.a.* Circumspect; framed or uttered with caution. **guardedly**, gärd'ed-li, *adv.* With circumspection. **guardhouse, guardroom**, gärd''hous', gärd''rōm', *n.* A house or room for the accommodation of a guard of soldiers, and where military defaulters are confined. **guardian**, gär'di-an, *n.* One who guards; one appointed to take charge of an orphan or ward.—*a.* Protecting.

guava, gwä'va, *n.* A small tropical tree of the myrtle family.

guerrilla, guerilla, ge-ril'a, *n.* An irregular petty war; one engaged in such.

guess, ges, *vt.* To conjecture; to form an opinion without certain means of knowledge; to surmise.—*vi.* To conjecture; to judge at random.—*n.* Conjecture; surmise.

guesswork, ges''wèrk', *n.* Work performed at hazard; only mere conjecture.

guest, gest, *n.* A visitor or friend entertained in the house or at the table of another.

guffaw, gu-fa', *n.* A loud burst of laughter.—*vi.* To burst into a loud laugh.

guide, gīd, *vt.* (guiding, guided). To lead; to direct; to influence; to regulate. —*n.* A person who guides; a director; a regulator; a guidebook. **guidance**, gīd'ans, *n.* The act of guiding; direction; government; a leading. **guidebook**, gīd''buk', *n.* A book for the guidance of travelers. **guidepost**, gīd''pōst', *n.* A

guild, gild, gild, *n.* A corporation of craftsmen, &c., for mutual aid and protection.

guilder, gil'dèr, *n.* A Dutch coin equal to 40 cents.

guile, gil, *n.* Wile; fraud; duplicity. **guileful**, gil'ful, *a.* Cunning; fraudulent. **guileless**, gil'les, *a.* Artless; sincere; honest.

guillotine, gil'ō-tēn, *n.* A machine for beheading persons; a machine for cutting paper.—*vt.* To behead by the guillotine.

guilt, gilt, *n.* Criminality; sin; wickedness. **guiltily**, gilt'i-li, *adv.* In a guilty manner. **guiltless**, gilt'les, *a.* Free from guilt. **guilty**, gil'ti, *a.* Justly chargeable with guilt; criminal; pertaining to or indicating guilt.

guinea, gin'i, *n.* A former British gold coin, or a sum of money, worth 21 shillings sterling. **guinea fowl**, gin'ē foul, *n.* A fowl allied to the peacocks and pheasants. **guinea pig**, gin'ē pig, *n.* A tailless rodent about 7 inches in length.

guise, gīz, *n.* External appearance; dress; mien; cast of behavior. **guiser**, gīz'ér, *n.* A person in disguise; a Christmas masker or mummer.

guitar, gi-tär', *n.* A musical instrument having six strings.

gulch, gulch, *n.* A gully; dry bed of a torrent.

gulf, gulf, *n.* An arm of the sea extending into the land; bay; chasm; whirlpool; anything insatiable; a wide interval.

gull, gul, *vt.* To cheat.—*n.* One easily cheated; simpleton; a marine swimming bird.

gullet, gul'et, *n.* The passage in the neck of an animal by which food and liquor are taken into the stomach.

gullible, gul'i-bl, *a.* Easily gulled or cheated.

gully, gul'i, *n.* A channel worn by water; a ravine.—*vt.* To wear into a gully.

gulp, gulp, *vt.* To swallow eagerly.—*n.* Act of taking a large swallow.

gum, gum, *n.* The fleshy substance of the jaws round the teeth; a juice which exudes from trees, &c., and thickens; a viscous substance.—*vt.* (gumming, gummed). To smear with or unite by a viscous substance.

gummy, gum'i, *a.* Of the nature of gum; productive of gum; covered with gum.

gumption, gump'shun, *n.* Understanding; capacity; shrewdness; *colloq.*

gun, gun, *n.* Any species of firearm.

gunboat, gun'bōt', *n.* A small warvessel.

guncotton, gun''kot'n, *n.* An explosive produced by soaking cotton, &c., in nitric and sulphuric acids, and leaving it to dry.

gunner, gun'ér, *n.* One who has the charge of ordnance.

gunnery, gun'ér-i, *n.* The art of firing cannon; the science of artillery.

gunpowder, gun''pou'dèr, *n.* An explo-

sive mixture of salpetre, sulphur, and charcoal.

gunshot, gun''shot', *n.* Range of a cannonshot; firing of a gun.—*a.* Made by the shot of a gun.

gunwale, **gunnel**, gun'el, *n.* The upper edge of a ship's side.

gurgle, gér'gl, *vi.* (gurgling, gurgled). To run or flow in a broken noisy current. —*n.* Sound produced by a liquid flowing from or through a narrow opening.

gush, gush, *vi.* To issue with violence and rapidity, as a fluid; to be effusively sentimental.—*n.* A sudden and violent issue of a fluid; the fluid thus emitted; effusive display of sentiment. **gushing**, gush'ing, *p.a.* Rushing forth with a gush; demonstratively affectionate.

gusset, gus'et, *n.* A piece of cloth inserted in a garment.

gust, gust, *n.* Taste; relish; a sudden blast of wind; a violent burst of passion. **gustatory**, gus'ta-tō-ri, *a.* Pertaining to taste. **gusto**, gust'ō, *n.* Relish; zest; taste. **gusty**, gus'ti, *a.* Subject to sudden blasts of wind; stormy.

gut, gut, *n.* The intestinal canal of an animal; *pl.* the entrails; a preparation of the intestines for various purposes; a channel.—*vt.* (gutting, gutted). To take out the entrails of; to plunder of contents; to destroy the interior of.

gutta-percha, gut'a-pér'cha, *n.* The hardened milky juice of a tree of E. Asia, resembling caoutchouc.

gutter, gut'èr, *n.* A channel at the side of a road, &c., for water.—*vt.* To cut or form gutters in.—*vi.* To become channeled.

guttural, gut'ér-al, *a.* Pertaining to the throat; formed in the throat.—*n.* A letter pronounced in the throat; any guttural sound.

guy, gī, *n.* A rope to steady anything; a person—*vt.* To steady or direct by means of a guy.

guzzle, guz'l, *vi.* and *t.* (guzzling, guzzled). To swallow greedily or frequently. —*n.* A debauch.

gymnasium, jim-nā'zi-um, *n.*; pl. **-ia** or **-iums**. A place for athletic exercises; a school for the higher branches of education.

gymnast, jim'nast, *n.* One who teaches or practices gymnastic exercises.

gymnastics, jim-nas'tiks, *n. pl.* The art of performing athletic exercises.

gynecology, **gynæcology**, jin- or jin'ē-kol''o-ji, *n.* The medical science of the functions and diseases peculiar to women.

gypsum, jip'sum, *n.* A mineral found as alabaster or as plaster of Paris.

gypsy, jip'si, *n.* See **gipsy**.

gyrate, jī'rāt, *vi.* (gyrating, gyrated). To move in a circle or spirally.—*a.* Moving in a circle.

gyration, jī-rā'shun, *n.* A turning or whirling round.

gyroscope, **gyrostat**, jī'rō-skōp, jī'rō-stat, *n.* An apparatus for illustrating peculiarities of rotation.

gyve, jīv, *n.* A fetter or shackle.—*vt.* (gyving, gyved). To fetter; to shackle.

H

ha, hä. An exclamation denoting surprise, joy, grief, &c.

habeas corpus, hä'be-as cor'pus, *n.* Writ requiring person to be brought before judge, &c., esp. to investigate lawfulness of his restraint.

haberdasher, hab'ĕr-dash'ĕr, *n.* A dealer in drapery goods, as woolens, silks, ribbons, &c.

haberdashery, hab'ĕr-dash'ĕr-i, *n.* The wares sold by a haberdasher.

habiliment, ha-bil'i-ment, *n.* A garment; usually in *pl.*

habilitate, ha-bil'i-tāt, *vi.* To qualify.

habit, hab'it, *n.* State of body, natural or acquired; mode of growth of a plant; aptitude acquired by practice; custom; manner; dress; outer dress worn by ladies on horseback.—*vt.* To dress; to clothe; to array.

habitable, hab'i-ta-bl, *a.* That may be inhabited.

habitat, hab'i-tat, *n.* The natural abode or locality of a plant or animal.

habitation, hab-i-tā'shun, *n.* Occupancy; abode; residence.

habitually, ha-bit'ū-al-li, *adv.* By habit; constantly.

habituate, ha-bit'ū-āt, *vt.* (habituating, habituated). To train to a habit; to make familiar by frequent use; to inure.

habitué, ha-bit'ū-ā', *n.* A habitual frequenter of any place.

hack, hak, *n.* A notch; cut; kick at football; a horse kept for hire; a worn-out horse; a literary drudge;

Hack Saw.

frame for drying fish, &c.; rack for cattle.—*vt.* To cut irregularly; to notch; to mangle; to let out for hire.—*a.* Hired; much used or worn. A taxi (slang).

hacking, hak'ing, *p.a.* Short and interrupted; as a *hacking* cough.

hackle, hak'l, *n.* A comb for dressing flax; raw silk; any flimsy substance unspun; a long pointed feather; a fly for angling.—*vt.* (hackling, hackled). To comb (flax or hemp).

hackney, hak'ni, *n.* A horse kept for hire; a coach kept for hire; nag; drudge.—*a.* Let out for hire; much used; trite.—*vt.* To use much; to make trite.

hackneyed, hak'nid, *p.a.* Much used; trite.

haddock, had'uk, *n.* A sea-fish allied to the cod.

Hades, hä'dēz, *n.* The abode of the dead.

haft, haft, *n.* A handle; that part of an instrument which is taken into the hand.—*vt.* To set in a haft.

hag, hag, *n.* An ugly old woman; a witch; an eel-shaped fish that eats into other fishes.

haggard, hag'erd, *a.* Wild; intractable; having the face worn and pale; gaunt.—*n.* An untrained or refractory hawk.

haggis, hag'is, *n.* A Scotch dish, commonly made of a sheep's stomach, with the heart, lungs, and liver minced, and mixed with suet, onions, oatmeal, salt, &c., inside.

hail, hāl, *n.* Frozen drops of rain; a wish of health; a call.—*vi.* To pour down hail; to have as one's residence, or belong to (with *from*).—*vt.* To pour down in the manner of hail; to salute; to call to; to designate as.—*interj.* A salutation expressive of well-wishing.

hailstone, hāl'stōn', *n.* A single mass of hail falling from a cloud.

hair, hār, *n.* A small filament issuing from the skin of an animal; the mass of filaments growing from the skin of an animal; anything similar; a very small distance.

hairbreadth, **hair'sbreadth**, hār'bredth, hārz'bredth, *n.* The diameter of a hair; a very small distance.—*a.* Of the breadth of a hair; very narrow.

hairdresser, hār'dres'ĕr, *n.* A barber.

hairsplitting, hār'split'ing, *n.* The making of minute distinctions in reasoning.

hairy, hār'i, *a.* Overgrown with hair; consisting of hair; resembling hair.

hake, hāk, *n.* A fish of the cod family.

halberd, hal'bĕrd, *n.* An ancient weapon consisting of a long pole ending with an ax and sharp head.

halcyon, hal'si-un, *n.* The kingfisher, fabled to have the power of producing calm weather during the period of incubation.—*a.* Calm; peaceful.

hale, hāl, *a.* Sound; healthy; robust.—*n.* A violent pull.—*vt.* (haling, haled). To take, pull, or drag by force.

half, häf, *n.*; pl. **halves**, hävz. One part of a thing divided into two equal parts.—*a.* Consisting of a half.—*adv.* In part, or in an equal part or degree.

half-brother, häf'bruth-ĕr, *n.* A brother by one parent, but not by both.

half-dead, häf-ded', *a.* Almost dead.

halfhearted, häf'härt'ed, *a.* Far from enthusiastic; lukewarm.

half pay, häf pā', *n.* Reduced allowance to an officer on retirement or when not in actual service.—*a.* Receiving half-pay.

halfpenny, hä'pen-i, *n.*; pl. **halfpence**, häf'pens or hä'pens. A copper coin, value half a penny or one cent.

halfsister, häf'sis-tĕr, *n.* A sister by one parent, but not by both.

half-witted, häf'wit-ed, *a.* Weak in intellect.

halibut, hal'i-but, *n.* A large flatfish allied to the flounder.

halitosis, hal'i-tō'sis, *n.* A malodorous condition of the breath.

hall, hạl, *n.* A large room, especially a large public room; a large room at the entrance of a house; a manor-house; the name of certain colleges at Oxford and Cambridge.

hallelujah, halleluiah, hal-ē-lụ'ya, *n.* and *interj.* A word used in sacred songs of praise, signifying *praise ye Jehovah.*

hallmark, hạl''märk', *n.* An official stamp affixed to articles of gold and silver, as a mark of their legal quality.

hallo, ha-lō', *interj.* Nearly equal to halloo.

halloo, ha-lö', *interj.* and *n.* An exclamation to invite attention; hunting cry to a dog.—*vi.* (hallooing, hallooed). To cry out.—*vt.* To encourage with shouts; to call or shout to.

hallow, hạl'ō, *vt.* To make holy; to set apart for religious use; to treat as sacred.

Hallowe'en, Hallow-even, hạl'ō-ēn, hạl'ō-ē-vn, *n.* The eve or vigil of All-Hallows or All-Saints' Day.

hallucination, ha-lū'si-nā''shun, *n.* A mistaken notion; mere dream or fancy; morbid condition in which objects are believed to be seen and sensations experienced; object or sensation thus erroneously perceived.

halo, hā'lō, *n.* A luminous ring round the sun or moon; any circle of light, as the glory round the head of saints; an ideal glory investing an object.—*vi.* To form itself into a halo:—*vt.* To surround with a halo.

halt, hạlt, *vi.* To limp; to be lame; to hesitate; to cease marching.—*vt.* To stop; to cause to cease marching.—*a.* Lame; limping.—*n.* A limp; a stopping, stoppage on march.

halter, hạl'tẽr, *n.* A rope or strap and headstall for leading or confining a horse; a rope for hanging.—*vt.* To put a halter on.

halve, häv, *vt.* (halving, halved). To divide into two equal parts.

halyard, hạl'yẽrd, *n.* Rope or tackle for raising and lowering the yards.

ham, ham, *n.* The hind part of the knee; the back of the thigh; the thigh of an animal, particularly of a hog, salted and dried in smoke.

hamlet, ham'let, *n.* A small village.

hammer, ham'ẽr, *n.* An instrument for driving nails, beating metals and the like. —*vt.* To beat or forge with a hammer; to contrive by intellectual labor.—*vi.* To work with a hammer; to labor in contrivance.

hammock, ham'uk, *n.* A kind of hanging bed.

hamper, ham'pẽr, *n.* A large basket for conveying things to market, &c.; something that encumbers; a clog.—*vt.* To put into a hamper; to hinder or impede; to embarrass.

hamstring, ham''string', *n.* One of the tendons of the ham.—*vt.* (pp. hamstrung or hamstringed). To cut the tendons of the ham, and thus to lame or disable.

hand, hand, *n.* The extremity of the arm, consisting of the palm and fingers; a measure of four inches; side or direction; skill; manner of acting; power; cards held at a game; a game; an index; a male or female in relation to an employer; person with some special faculty; style of penmanship.—*vt.* To give with the hand; to lead with the hand; to conduct; to handle.—*a.* Belonging to, or used by the hand.

handbill, hand''bil', *n.* A loose printed sheet, &c., to be circulated.

handbook, hand''bụk', *n.* A book for the hand; a manual; a guide-book.

handcuff, hand''kụf', *n.* A fetter for the hands or wrists.—*vt.* To manacle with handcuffs.

handed, han'ded, *a.* Having hands of this or that character; especially in compounds.

handful, hand'fụl, *n.* As much as the hand will grasp or hold; a small quantity or number.

handicap, han'di-kap, *n.* In racing, games, &c., an allowance to bring superior competitors to an equality with the others; a race or contest so arranged.— *vt.* To put a handicap on; to equalize by a handicap.

handicraft, han'di-kraft, *n.* Work performed by the hand; manual occupation.

handily, han'di-li, *adv.* In a handy manner.

handiwork, han''di-wẽrk', *n.* Product of manual labor; work or deed of any person.

handkerchief, hang'kẽr-chif, *n.* A cloth carried about the person for wiping the mouth, nose, &c.; a cloth worn about the neck.

handle, han'dl, *vt.* (handling, handled). To feel, use, or hold with the hand; to discuss; to deal with; to treat or use well or ill.—*n.* That part of an instrument, &c., held in the hand; instrument for effecting a purpose.

handmaid, handmaiden, hand'mād, hand'mād-n, *n.* Female servant or attendant.

handrail, hand''rāl', *n.* A rail for the hand, supported by balusters, &c., as in staircases.

handsome, hand'sum, *a.* Well formed; having a certain share of beauty along with dignity; ample; generous. **handsomely,** hand'sum-li, *adv.* In a handsome manner; ample; generously.

handwriting, hand''rit'ing, *n.* The writing peculiar to each person; any writing.

handy, han'di, *a.* Skilled in using the hands; dexterous; ready; convenient for use.

hang, hang, *vt.* (pret. and pp. hung and hanged). To suspend; to furnish with anything suspended; to cause to droop; to fit so as to allow of free motion; to put to death by suspending by the neck. —*vi.* To be suspended; to dangle; to adhere; to linger; to lean; to have a steep declivity; to be executed.

hangar, hang'ẽr, *n.* Shed for airplane &c.

hangdog, hang''dog', *n.* A degraded character.—*a.* Having a low or blackguardlike appearance.

hanger, hang'ẽr, *n.* One who or that which hangs; a short broad sword; that from which something is hung.

hanger-on, hang'ẽr-on', *n.;* pl. **hangers-on.** A servile dependant; a parasite.

hanging, hang'ing, *n.* Act of suspending; death by the halter; *pl.* linings for rooms, of tapestry, paper, &c.

hangman, hang'man, *n.* A public executioner.

hang-over, hang'ō'vẽr, *n.* The aftereffects of overindulgence in alcoholic liquids.

hank, hangk, *n.* A skein of silk, yarn, &c.; a coil.—*vt.* To form into hanks.

hanker, hang'kẽr, *vi.* To desire eagerly; to think of something longingly (with *after*).

hansom, hansom cab, han'sum, han'sum kab, *n.* A two-wheeled cab.

hap, hap, *n.* Chance; luck; fortune.—*vi.* To happen; to befall.

haphazard, hap"haz'ẽrd, *n.* Chance; accident.

hapless, hap'les, *a.* Unlucky; unhappy.

haply, hap'li, *adv.* By hap or chance; perhaps.

happen, hap'en, *vi.* To come by chance; to come about without previous design.

happy, hap'i, *a.* Being in the enjoyment of agreeable sensations from the possession of good; fortunate; propitious; well suited; apt.

happily, hap'i-li, *adv.* In a happy manner; fortunately; gracefully.

happiness, hap'i-nes, *n.* State of being happy; enjoyment of pleasure; good luck.

harangue, ha-rang', *n.* A noisy or pompous address; a declamatory public address; a tirade.—*vi.* (haranguing, harangued). To make a harangue.—*vt.* To address by a harangue.

harass, har'as, *vt.* To vex; to tire with labor; to fatigue with importunity.

harassing, har'as-ing, *p.a.* Fatiguing, tending to wear with care or anxiety.

harbinger, här'bin-jẽr, *n.* A forerunner; that which precedes and gives notice of something else.—*vt.* To precede as harbinger.

harbor, harbour, här'bẽr, *n.* A shelter; a haven for ships; an asylum.—*vt.* To shelter; to entertain in the mind.—*vi.* To take shelter; to lodge or abide for a time.

hard, härd, *a.* Not easily penetrated or separated; firm; difficult to understand; arduous; unfeeling; severe; unjust; harsh; stiff; grasping; applied to certain sounds, as sibilants contrasted with gutturals; applied to water not suitable for washing, from holding minerals.—*adv.* Close; diligently; with difficulty; fast; copiously; with force. **harden**, här'dn, *vt.* To make hard or more hard; to confirm in effrontery, obstinacy, wickedness, &c.; to make unfeeling; to inure; to render less liable to injury by exposure or use.—*vi.* To become hard or more hard; to become unfeeling; to become inured. **hardened**, här'dnd, *p.a.* Made hard or more hard; obstinate; confirmed; callous.

hard-boiled, härd'boild', *a.* Boiled to a solid, generally eggs; an unsentimental, tough person.

hardfisted, härd'fis'ted, *a.* Having hard or strong hands; covetous.

hardheaded, härd'hed'ed, *a.* Shrewd; intelligent.

hardhearted, härd'här'ted, *a.* Having an unfeeling heart; pitiless.

hardihood, här'di-hud, *n.* Quality of being hardy; boldness; intrepidity; audacity; effrontery.

hardly, härd'li, *adv.* With difficulty; scarcely; harshly.

hardness, härd'nes, *n.* State or quality of being hard in all its senses; firmness; difficulty; obduracy; rigor; niggardliness, &c.

hardship, härd'ship, *n.* Privation; affliction; oppression; injustice; grievance.

hardware, härd'wãr, *n.* Wares made of iron or other metal, as pots, knives, &c.

hardy, här'di, *a.* Bold; intrepid; full of assurance; inured to fatigue; capable of bearing exposure.

hare, här, *n.* A rodent animal allied to the rabbit, but not making burrows.

harebrained, här'bränd', *a.* Wild as a hare; giddy; volatile; heedless.

harelip, här'lip', *n.* A perpendicular division of one or both lips, but commonly the upper one, like that of a hare.

harem, hä'rem, *n.* The apartments of the female members of a Mohammedan family; the occupants.

hark, härk, *vi.* To listen; to lend the ear.

Harlequin, här'le-kwin, *n.* A performer in a pantomime, masked, dressed in tight spangled clothes and armed with a magic wand; a buffoon in general.

harlot, här'lot, *n.* A prostitute. **harlotry**, här'lot-ri, *n.* The trade or practice of prostitution.

harm, härm, *n.* Injury; hurt; evil.—*vt.* To hurt; to damage; to impair. **harmful**, härm'ful, *a.* Hurtful; injurious; noxious; mischievous. **harmless**, härm'les, *a.* Free from harm; not causing harm; inoffensive; uninjured. **harmlessly**, härm'les-li, *adv.* Without causing or receiving harm.

harmonic, harmonical, här-mon'ik, här-mon'i-kal, *a.* Pertaining to harmony; concordant; musical. **harmonic**, här-mon'ik, *n.* A less distinct tone accompanying a principal tone.

harmonica, här-mon'i-ka, *n.* A musical toy played by striking rods or plates of glass or metal with small hammers.

harmony, här'mo-ni, *n.* The just adaptation of parts to each other; musical concord; agreement; peace and friendship. **harmonics**, här-mon'iks, *n.* The doctrine of harmony or of musical sounds. **harmonious**, här-mō'-ni-us, *a.* Having harmony; having the parts adapted to each other; concordant; friendly. **harmonize**, här'mon-iz, *vi.* To be in harmony; to agree in sound or sense; to be in friendship.—*vt.* To bring into harmony; to set accompanying parts to.

harness, här'nes, *n.* Armor; furniture of

a carriage or draught horse.—*vt.* To dress in armor; to put harness on.

harp, härp, *n.* A stringed musical instrument of triangular form played with the fingers.—*vi.* To play on the harp; to dwell on tediously.

harpist, harper, här'pist, här'pėr, *n.* A player on the harp.

harpoon, här-pön', *n.* A spear or javelin, used to strike whales, &c.—*vt.* To strike, catch, or kill with a harpoon. **harpooner,** här-pön'ėr, *n.* One who uses a harpoon.

harpsichord, härp'si-kord, *n.* An obsolete stringed musical instrument something like a horizontal grand pianoforte.

Harpy, här'pi, *n.* A fabulous winged monster with the face of a woman; any rapacious animal; an extortioner.

harridan, har'i-dan, *n.* A hag; an odious old woman; a vixenish woman; a trollop.

harrow, har'ō, *n.* A frame set with spikes, to prepare plowed land for seed or to cover the seed.—*vt.* To draw a harrow over; to lacerate; to torment. **harrowing,** har'ō-ing, *p.a.* Causing acute distress to the mind.

harry, har'i, *vt.* (harrying, harried). To pillage; to plunder; to ravage.

harsh, härsh, *a.* Grating to the touch, taste or ear; jarring; rough; severe. **harshly,** härsh'li, *adv.* In a harsh manner; severely; rudely.

hart, härt, *n.* A stag or male of the red-deer.

harum-scarum, bär'um-skär'um, *a.* Harebrained; unsettled; giddy; rash.

harvest, här'vest, *n.* The season of gathering a crop, especially grain; the crop gathered; the product of labor; fruit or fruits; effects; consequences.—*vt.* To reap or gather. **harvester,** här'ves-tėr, *n.* A reaper; laborer in gathering grain; reaping-machine.

has-been, haz'bin', *n.* A person whose ability and popularity have declined.

hash, hash, *vt.* To hack; to chop; to mince and mix.—*n.* That which is chopped; cooked meat chopped up and served again; a repetition; bungle.

hasp, hasp, *n.* A clasp that passes over a staple to be fastened by a padlock.—*vt.* To fasten with a hasp.

hassock, has'ok, *n.* A thick mat or cushion used for kneeling on, &c.

haste, häst, *n.* Speed; hurry; sudden excitement of passion; precipitance.—*vt.* (hasting, hasted). To drive or urge forward; to hurry.—*vi.* To move with celerity; to be speedy. **hasten,** häs'n, *vt.* and *i.* To haste. **hastily,** häst'i-li, *adv.* In a hasty manner; speedily; rashly; precipitately; passionately. **hasty,** häs'ti, *a.* Speedy; precipitate; rash; irritable; irascible; early ripe.

hat, hat, *n.* A covering for the head.

hatch, hatch, *vt.* To produce from eggs; to contrive; to shade by crossing lines in drawing, &c.—*vi.* To produce young; to bring the young to maturity.—*n.* A brood; act of exclusion from the egg; frame of cross bars over the opening in a ship's deck; the opening itself; hatchway; trap-door.

hatchet, hach'et, *n.* A small ax with a short handle, used with one hand.

hatchway, hach"wā', *n.* An opening in a ship's deck for communication with the interior.

hate, hät, *vt.* (hating, hated). To detest; to loathe; to abhor.—*n.* Great dislike; hatred. **hateful,** hät'ful, *a.* Exciting hate; odious; loathsome; malignant. **hatefully,** hät'ful-li, *adv.* Odiously; malignantly; maliciously.

hatred, hä'tred, *n.* Great dislike or aversion; ill-will; rancor; abhorrence.

hatter, hat'ėr, *n.* A maker or seller of hats.

hauberk, ha̧'bėrk, *n.* A coat of mail.

haughty, ha̧t'i, *a.* Proud and disdainful; lofty and arrogant.

haul, ha̧l, *vt.* To pull or draw with force; to drag; to compel to go.—*n.* A violent pull; draught of fish in a net; that which is taken or gained at once. **haulage,** häl'ij, *n.* A hauling; length hauled; charged for hauling.

haunch, ha̧nch, *n.* The hip; the thigh; part of an arch between the springing and the crown; the flank.

haunt, ha̧nt, *vt.* To frequent; to resort to often; to appear in or about, as a specter.—*vi.* To be much about; to visit often.—*n.* A place much frequented; a favorite resort. **haunted,** ha̧n'ted, *p.a.* Frequently visited by apparitions; troubled by spectral visitants.

hauteur, hō-tėr', *n.* Haughty manner or spirit; pride.

have, hav, *vt.* (having, had). To possess; to accept; to enjoy; to hold in opinion; to be under necessity, or impelled by duty; to procure; to bring forth.

haven, hä'ven, *n.* A harbor; port; shelter.

haversack, hav'ėr-sak, *n.* A soldier's bag for provisions on the march.

having, hav'ing, *n.* What one has; possession; goods.

havoc, hav'uk, *n.* Devastation; wide and general destruction; slaughter.

haw, ha̧, *n.* A hedge or fence; the berry and seed of the hawthorn; hesitation of speech.—*vi.* To speak with hesitation.

hawk, ha̧k, *n.* A rapacious bird of the falcon family.—*vi.* To catch birds by means of hawks; to practice falconry; to take prey on the wing; to force up phlegm with noise.—*vt.* To carry about for sale from place to place. **hawker,** ha̧k'ėr, *n.* One who goes about selling wares; a peddler. **hawking,** ha̧k'ing, *n.* Sport of taking wild fowls by means of hawks; falconry.

hawser, ha̧'sėr, *n.* A small cable.

hawthorn, ha̧'thorn, *n.* The hedge-thorn; the white-thorn, much used for hedges.

hay, hä, *n.* Grass cut and dried for fodder.—*vt.* To make into hay. **haymaker,** hä"māk'ėr, *n.* One who cuts and dries grass for fodder; a knockout blow.

hazard, haz'ėrd, *n.* A game at dice, &c.; risk; venture; chance; fortuitous event.—*vt.* To risk; to put in danger of loss or injury. **hazardous,** haz'ėr-dus, *a.* Perilous; risky.

haze, hāz, *n.* Vapor which renders the air thick, though not so damp as in foggy weather; dimness; mental fog.

hazel, hā'zl, *n.* A small tree of the oak family that bears edible nuts.—*a.* Pertaining to the hazel; of a light-brown color.

hazy, hā'zi, *a.* Thick with haze; mentally obscure or confused.

he, hē, *pron.* of the third person, nominative. A substitute for the third person masculine, representing the man or male named before; prefixed to names of animals to specify the male.

head, hed, *n.* The anterior part of animals; uppermost part of the human body; seat of the brain, &c.; intellect; an individual; a chief; first place; top; chief part; principal source; crisis; height; promontory; division of discourse; headway.—*vt.* To form a head to; to behead; to lead; to go in front of in order to stop; to oppose.—*vi.* To form a head; to be directed, as a ship. **headache,** hed″āk′, *n.* Pain in the head. **headdress,** hed″dres′, *n.* The covering or ornaments of a woman's head. **headgear,** hed′gēr, *n.* Covering or ornaments of the head. **headily,** hed′i-li, *adv.* Hastily; rashly. **headless,** hed′les, *a.* Having no head. **headlong,** hed′long, *adv.* With the head foremost; precipitately.—*a.* Steep; precipitous; precipitate. **head money,** hed′ mu′ni, *n.* A tax levied on each individual; money paid for the heads of enemies or for prisoners caught. **headmost,** hed′mōst, *a.* Most advanced. **headpiece,** hed′pēs, *n.* Armor for the head; a helmet. **headquarters,** hed″kwar′tērz, *n.pl.* The quarters of a commander; place where one chiefly resides or carries on business. **headsman,** hedz′man, *n.* An executioner. **headstone,** hed′stōn, *n.* The chief or corner stone; stone at the head of a grave. **headstrong,** hed′strong, *a.* Resolute; obstinate; violent. **headway,** hed′wā, *n.* Progress made by a ship in motion; progress or success. **head wind,** hed′ wind, *n.* A wind that blows right against a ship, &c. **headwork,** hed′wērk, *n.* Mental or intellectual labor. **heady,** hed′i, *a.* Rash; hasty; headstrong; intoxicating.

heal, hēl, *vt.* To make hale or sound; to cure; to reconcile.—*vi.* To grow whole or sound; to recover. **healing,** hēl′ing, *p.a.* Tending to cure; mild; mollifying. —*n.* Act or process by which a cure is effected.

health, helth, *n.* A sound state of body or mind; freedom from disease; bodily conditions; wish of health and happiness (used in drinking). **healthful,** helth′ful, *a.* Full of health; healthy; wholesome; salubrious. **healthily,** helth′i-li, *adv.* Without disease; soundly. **healthy,** hel′thi, *a.* Being in health; sound; hale; salubrious; wholesome.

heap, hēp, *n.* A mass; large quantity; pile.—*vt.* To raise in a heap; to amass; to pile.

hear, hēr, *vt.* (hearing, heard). To perceive by the ear; to give audience to; to listen; to obey; to regard; to attend

favorably; to try in a court of law; to learn; to approve.—*vi.* To enjoy the faculty of perceiving sound; to listen; to be told; to receive by report. **hearer,** hēr′ēr, *n.* One who hears; an auditor. **hearing,** hēr′ing, *n.* The faculty or sense by which sound is perceived; audience; opportunity to be heard; judicial trial; reach of the ear.

hearken, harken, här′kn, *vi.* To lend the ear; to listen; to give heed.

hearsay, hēr′sā′, *n.* Report; rumor.—*a.* Given at second hand.

hearse, hērs, *n.* A carriage for conveying the dead to the grave; bier.

heart, härt, *n.* The primary organ of the blood's motion; the inner, vital, or most essential part; seat of the affections, will, &c.; disposition of mind; conscience; courage; spirit; what represents a heart; one of a suit of playing cards marked with such a figure. **heartache,** härt″āk′, *n.* Sorrow; anguish. **heartbreaking,** härt″brāk-ing, *a.* Overpowering with grief or sorrow. **heartbroken,** härt″bro′ken, *a.* Deeply afflicted or grieved. **heartburn,** härt′bern, *n.* A burning sensation in the stomach from indigestion. **hearten,** här′tn, *vt.* To give heart or courage to; to encourage; to animate. **heartfelt,** härt″felt′, *a.* Deeply felt; deeply affecting; either as joy or sorrow. **hearth,** härth, *n.* The part of a floor on which a fire is made; the house and its inmates; the fireside. **hearthstone,** härth″stōn′, *n.* Stone forming the hearth; fireside. **hearty,** här′ti, *a.* Warm; cordial; healthy; having a keen appetite; large to satisfaction. **heartily,** här′ti-li, *adv.* From the heart; sincerely; warmly; with keen relish. **heartless,** härt′les, *a.* Without heart; spiritless; without feeling or affection. **heart-rending,** härt″ren′-ding, *a.* Overpowering with anguish; deeply afflictive. **heartsick,** härt″sik′, *a.* Sick at heart; pained in mind; deeply depressed. **heart-whole,** härt″hōl′, *a.* Whole at heart; not affected with love; of good courage.

heat, hēt, *n.* The sensation produced by bodies that are hot; hot air; hot weather; high temperature; degree of temperature; a single effort; a course at a race; animal excitement; rage; ardor; animation in thought or discourse; fermentation.—*vt.* To make hot; to warm with passion or desire; to rouse into action.—*vi.* To grow warm or hot.

heater, hēt′ēr, *n.* One who or that which heats; metal for heating a smoothing-iron.

heath, hēth, *n.* A small flowering shrub growing on waste or wild places; a place overgrown with heath; waste tract.

heathen, hē′ᴛʜen, *n.* A pagan; one who worships idols; a barbarous person.—*a.* Gentile; pagan. **heathenish,** hē′ᴛʜen-ish, *a.* Belonging to pagans; idolatrous; barbarous.

heather, heᴛʜ′ēr, *n.* Common heath, a low shrub with clusters of rose-colored flowers.

heating, hēt'ing, *p.a.* Exciting action; stimulating.

heave, hēv, *vt.* (heaving; pret. and pp. heaved, hove). To lift; to move upward; to cause to swell; to raise or force from the breast, as a groan; to throw; to turn in some direction.—*vi.* To rise; to swell, as the sea; to pant; to retch; *to heave in sight*, to appear, as a ship.—*n.* A rising or swell; an effort upward; a throw; a swelling, as of the breast.

heaven, hev'en, *n.* The blue expanse surrounding the earth; the sky; the abode of God and of his angels; God or Providence; supreme felicity; bliss. **heavenly**, hev'en-li, *a.* Pertaining to heaven; divine; inhabiting heaven; enchanting.—*adv.* In a heavenly manner. **heavenward**, **heavenwards**, hev'en-werd, hev'en-werdz, *adv.* Toward heaven.

heavy, hev'i, *a.* That is heaved or lifted with difficulty; weighty; sad; grievous; burdensome; drowsy; wearisome; not easily digested; soft and miry; difficult; large in amount; dense; abundant; forcible. **heavily**, hev'i-li, *adv.* In a heavy manner; dully; gloomily; laboriously; densely. **heaviness**, hev'i-nes, *n.* Weight; gloom; dullness; oppressiveness.

Hebraic, **Hebraical**, hē-brā'ik, hē-brā'i-kal, *a.* Pertaining to the Hebrews or their language; Jewish.

Hebrew, hē'brö, *n.* An Israelite; a Jew; the Hebrew language.—*a.* Pertaining to the Hebrews.

Hebridean, heb-ri-dē'an, *a.* Pertaining to the Hebrides of Scotland.—*n.* A native of the Hebrides.

heckle, hek'l, *vt.* To badger; taunt; interrupt.

hectare, hek'tār, *n.* A French measure equal to 2.47 acres.

hectic, hek'tik, *a.* A term applied to the fever which accompanies consumption; consumptive, feverish.—*n.* A hectic fever; a flush.

hedge, hej, *n.* A fence consisting of thorns or shrubs.—*vt.* (hedging, hedged). To inclose with a hedge; to surround or restrain.—*vi.* To hide one's self; to bet on both sides; to skulk; to dodge or trim.—*a.* Pertaining to a hedge; mean; rustic.

hedgehog, hej'hog, *n.* A small insectivorous quadruped covered with prickly spines.

hedgerow, hej'rö, *n.* A row of shrubs forming a hedge.

hedonic, hē-don'ik, *a.* Pertaining to pleasure.

hedonism, hē'don-izm, *n.* The doctrine that the chief good of man lies in pursuit of pleasure.

hedonist, hē'don-ist, *n.* One who professes hedonism.

heed, hēd, *vt.* To look to or after; to regard with care; to notice.—*vi.* To mind; to consider.—*n.* Care; attention; regard.

heedful, hēd'ful, *a.* Giving heed; attentive; watchful; cautious; wary.

heedless, hēd'les, *a.* Inattentive; careless; remiss; negligent.

heel, hēl, *n.* The hind part of the foot; a cant; a low-grade person. *Slang.*—*vt.* To add a heel to; to furnish with heels, as shoes.—*vi.* To cant over from a vertical position.

heft, heft, *n.* The act of heaving; effort; weight; gist.

Hegelian, ha-gā'li-an, *a.* Pertaining to Hegel (hā'gl) or his system of philosophy.—*n.* A follower of Hegel.

hegemony, hē-jem'o-ni, or hej'e-mo'ni (or with g hard), *n.* Leadership; preponderance of one state among others.

hegira, hej'i-ra, *n.* The flight of Mohammed from Mecca (16th July, 622); the beginning of the Mohammedan era.

heifer, hef'ėr, *n.* A young cow.

heigh-ho, hā'hō. An exclamation expressing some degree of languor or uneasiness.

height, hīt, *n.* The condition of being high; distance of anything above its base or above the earth; eminence; any elevated ground; extent; degree; utmost degree. **heighten**, hīt'n, *vt.* To raise higher; to improve; to increase.

heinous, hā'nus, *a.* Hateful; characterized by great wickedness; flagrant.

heir, ār, *n.* One who succeeds or is to succeed another in the possession of property; an inheritor.—*vt.* To inherit; to succeed to. **heirdom**, ār'dum, *n.* State of an heir; succession by inheritance. **heiress**, ār'es, *n.* A female heir. **heirloom**, ār'löm, *n.* Any personal chattel which, by law, descends to the heir or has belonged to a family for a long time. **heirship**, ār'ship, *n.* The state, character, or privileges of an heir; right of inheriting.

heliotrope, hē'li-ō-tröp, *n.* Blood-stone; a heliostat; a fragrant garden plant.

helium, hē'li-um, *n.* A chemical element found in small quantities in the air and in certain minerals; first discovered in the sun in 1868.

hell, hel, *n.* The place or state of punishment for the wicked after death; the abode of the devil and his angels; the infernal powers; a gambling-house.

Hellenic, he-len'ik, or he-lē'nik, *a.* Pertaining to the inhabitants of Greece; Greek.

Hellenism, hel'en-izm, *n.* A Greek idiom; type of character peculiar to the Greeks.

hellish, hel'ish, *a.* Pertaining to hell; infernal; malignant; detestable.

helm, helm, *n.* A helmet; instrument by which a ship is steered; the rudder, tiller, &c.; place or post of management.—*vt.* To cover or furnish with a helmet.

helmet, hel'met, *n.* A covering for the head in war; head armor; a head-piece.

helmsman, helmz'man, *n.* The man at the helm of a ship.

helot, hel'ot or hē'lot, *n.* A slave.

help, help, *vt.* To lend strength or means towards effecting a purpose; to aid; to relieve; to remedy; to prevent; to avoid.—*vi.* To lend aid.—*n.* Aid; remedy; an assistant.

helper, hel'pėr, *n.* One who helps; an assistant; an auxiliary.

Helmet

helpful, help′fʉl, *a.* That gives help, aid, or assistance; useful.

helpless, help′les, *a.* Without help in one's self; needing help; affording no help; beyond help.

helpmate, help′māt, *n.* A companion who helps; an assistant; a wife.

helter-skelter, hel′tėr-skel′tėr, *adv.* A word suggestive of hurry and confusion.

helve, helv, *n.* The handle of an ax or hatchet.—*vt.* (helving, helved). To furnish with a helve, as an ax.

Helvetian, Helvetic, hel-vē′shan, hel-vet′ik, *a.* Of or pertaining to Switzerland.

hem, hem, *n.* The border of a garment, doubled and sewed to strengthen it; edge; border.—*interj.* and *n.* A sort of half cough, suggested by some feeling.—*vt.* (hemming, hemmed). To form a hem or border on; to inclose and confine; to make the sound expressed by the word *hem.*

hemisphere, hem′i-sfēr, *n.* One half of a sphere; half the celestial or terrestrial sphere. **hemispheric, hemispherical,** hem-i-sfe′rik, hem-i-sfe′ri-kal, *a.* Pertaining to or forming a hemisphere.

hemlock, hem′lok, *n.* An umbelliferous plant whose leaves and root are poisonous.

hemorrhage, hem′o-rij, *n.* A bursting forth of blood; any discharge of blood from vessels destined to contain it.

hemorrhoids, hem′o-roidz, *n. pl.* Piles.

hemp, hemp, *n.* An annual herbaceous plant of the nettle family, the fiber of which, also called hemp, is made into sail-cloth, ropes, &c.

hen, hen, *n.* The female of the domestic fowl; any female bird.

hence, hens, *adv.* From this place, time, source, reason. &c. **henceforth,** hens′fôrth″, *adv.* From this time forward. **henceforward,** hens′for″wėrd, *adv.* From this time forward; henceforth.

henchman, hench′man, *n.* A servant; a male attendant.

henpeck, hen′pek′, *vt.* To rule; said of a wife who has the upper hand of her husband. **henpecked,** hen′pekt′, *a.* Governed by his wife, as a husband.

hepatic, hē-pat′ik, *a.* Pertaining to the liver.

heptagon, hep′ta-gon, *n.* A plane figure having seven angles and seven sides.

her, hėr, *pron.* The possessive and objective case of *she:* when the possessive is used without a noun it becomes *hers.*

herald, her′ald, *n.* An officer whose business was to proclaim war or peace, bear messages, &c.; a forerunner; an officer who regulates matters relating to public ceremonies; one who records and blazons arms, &c.—*vt.* To introduce, as by a herald; to proclaim. **heraldic,** he-ral′dik, *a.* Pertaining to heralds or heraldry. **heraldry,** her′ald-ri, *n.* Art or office of a herald; art of recording genealogies and blazoning arms; heraldic figures or symbols.

herb, hėrb, *n.* Any plant with a succulent stem which dies to the root every year. **herbaceous,** hėr-bā′shus, *a.* Pertaining to herbs; having the nature of a herb.

herbivorous, her-biv′o-rus, *a.* Eating herbs; subsisting on herbaceous plants.

herculean, hėr-kū′lē-an, *a.* Belonging to or resembling Hercules; of extraordinary strength; very great or difficult.

herd, hėrd, *n.* A number of animals feeding or driven together; flock; crowd; rabble; a keeper of cattle or sheep.—*vi.* and *t.* To unite into a herd, as beasts; to congregate.

herdsman, hėrdz′man, *n.* One employed in tending herds of cattle.

here, hėr, *adv.* In this place; at this point; hither.

hereabout, hereabouts, hėr′a-bout′, hėr′a-bouts′, *adv.* About this place.

hereafter, hėr-af′tėr, *adv.* After this time; in a future state.—*n.* The time after this; a future state.

hereby, hėr-bī′, *adv.* By this; close by; near.

hereditary, he-red′i-ter′i, *a.* Relating to an inheritance; descending to an heir; that is or may be transmitted from a parent to a child.

heredity, he-red′i-ti, *n.* Hereditary transmission of qualities; the doctrine that the offspring inherits parental characteristics.

herein, hėr-in′, *adv.* In this.

hereinafter, hėr′in-äf″tėr, *adv.* In this writing or document afterwards.

hereof, hėr-ov′, *adv.* Of this; from this.

hereon, hėr-on′, *adv.* On this.

heresy, her′e-si, *n.* A fundamental error in religion; error in doctrine; heterodoxy. **heretical,** he-ret′i-kal, *a.* Containing heresy; contrary to the established faith.

hereto, hėr-tö′, *adv.* To this.

heretofore, hėr′tö-fôr″, *adv.* Before or up to the present; formerly.

hereupon, hėr′u-pon″, *adv.* On this; hereon.

herewith, hėr-with′, *adv.* With this.

heritage, her′it-ij, *n.* Inheritance; lot or portion by birth.

heritor, her′i-tėr, *n.* One who inherits; an heir: *Scots law,* a proprietor liable to pay public burdens.

hermaphrodite, hėr-maf′rō-dīt, *n.* An animal in which the characteristics of both sexes are really or apparently combined; a flower that contains both the stamen and the pistil.—*a.* Including or being of both sexes.

hermetic, hermetical, hėr-met′ik, hėr-met′i-kal, *a.* Pertaining to alchemy or to occult science; effected by fusing together the edges of the aperture, as of a bottle; perfectly close and air-tight.

hermetically, hėr-met′i-kal-li, *adv.* Chemically; by fusing the edges together.

hermit, hėr′mit, *n.* One who lives in solitude; a recluse.

hermitage, hėr′mi-tij, *n.* The habitation of a hermit.

hernia, hėr′ni-a, *n.* A protrusion of some organ of the abdomen through an interstice; a rupture. **hernial,** hėr′ni-al, *a.* Pertaining to hernia.

hero, hē′rō, *n.; pl.* **heroes,** hē′rōz. A man of distinguished valor; the person who has the principal share in some exploit, or in a play, novel, &c.

heroic, he-rō'ik, *a.* Pertaining to a hero or heroes; intrepid and noble; reciting achievements of heroes; epic.

heroically, he-rō'i-kal-li, *adv.* In a heroic manner; like a hero.

heroine, her'ō-in, *n.* A female hero.

heroism, her'ō-izm, *n.* The qualities of a hero; intrepidity; magnanimity.

heron, her'un, *n.* A wading bird with a long bill, long slender legs and neck.

hero worship, hĕr'ō wĕr'ship, *n.* Extravagant admiration of great men.

herpes, her'pēz, *n.* A skin disease characterized by eruption of inflamed vesicles.

herpetology, hĕr'pe-tol''o-ji, *n.* The natural history of reptiles.

herring, her'ing, *n.* One of those small food fishes which go in shoals in northern seas.

herringbone, he"ring-bōn', *a.* Applied to masonry, sewing, &c., which bears resemblance to the backbone of a herring.

hers, hĕrz, *pron. possessive.* See **her.**

herself, hĕr-self', *pron.* The emphatic and reflexive form of **she** and **her.**

hesitancy, hez'i-tan-si, *n.* A hesitating; vacillation.

hesitate, hez'i-tāt, *vi.* (hesitating, hesitated). To pause respecting decision or action; to stop in speaking; to stammer.

hesitation, hez-i-tā'shun, *n.* Act of hesitating; doubt; a stopping in speech.

heterodox, het'ĕr-ō-doks, *a.* Holding opinions different from those established or prevalent; not orthodox; heretical.

heterodoxy, het'er-ō-dok-si, *n.* Heresy.

heterogeneous, het'er-ō-jē"nē-us, *a.* Of a different kind or nature; composed of dissimilar parts.

hew, hū, *vt.* (pret. hewed; pp. hewed or hewn). To cut with an ax, &c.; to cut; to hack; to make smooth, as stone; to shape.

hewer, hū'ĕr, *n.* One who hews wood or stone.

hexagon, hek'sa-gon, *n.* A plane figure of six angles and six sides.

hexagonal, hek-sag'o-nal, *a.* Having six angles and six sides.

hexahedron, hek'sa-hē"-drun, *n.* A regular solid body of six sides; a cube.

hexameter, heks-am'e-tĕr, *n.* A verse of six metrical feet.—*a.* Having six metrical feet.

Hexagon.

hexangular, heks-ang'gū-lĕr, *a.* Having six angles or corners.

hey, hā, *interj.* An exclamation of joy or to call attention.

heyday, hā"dā', *interj.* An exclamation of cheerfulness.—*n.* The bloom or height; the wildness or frolicsome period of youth.

hiatus, hī-ā'tus, *n. pl.* **hiatuses.** A gap; break; lacuna; meeting of vowel sounds.

hibernate, hī-bĕr'nāt, *vt.* To pass the winter in sleep or seclusion; to winter.

hibernation, hī'bĕr-nā"shun, *n.* Act of hibernating.

Hibernian, hī-bĕr'ni-an, *a.* Pertaining to Ireland; Irish.—*n.* A native of Ireland.

hiccup, hiccough, hik'up, *n.* A spasmodic affection of the diaphragm and glottis; a convulsive catch of the respiratory muscles.—*vt.* and *i.* To have a hiccup; to utter with hiccups.

hickory, hik'ō-ri, *n.* An American tree of the walnut family, valuable for timber.

hid, hidden, hid, hid'n, *p.a.* Unseen; unknown; abstruse; profound.

hide, hīd, *vt.* (hiding, pret. hid, pp. hid, hidden). To withhold or withdraw from sight or knowledge; to screen; to secrete. —*vi.* To be or to lie concealed; to keep one's self out of view.—*n.* The skin of an animal, either raw or dressed; the human skin; an old measure of land of about 80 acres.

hidebound, hīd'bound, *a.* Having the hide abnormally tight; having the bark so close or firm as to hinder growth.

hideous, hid'ē-us, *a.* Frightful; shocking to the eye or ear. **hideously,** hid'ē-us-li, *adv.* Dreadfully; shockingly.

hiding, hīd'ing, *n.* Concealment; state of being hidden.

hie, hī, *vi.* (hying, hied). To hasten; to speed.

hierarch, hī'ĕr-ärk, *n.* One who has authority in sacred things. **hierarchical, hierarchal,** hī-ĕr-ärk'ik-al, hī-ĕr-är'kal, *a.* Pertaining to a hierarchy.

hierarchy, hī'ĕr-är-ki, *n.* Authority in sacred things; clergy in whom is confided the direction of sacred things; ecclesiastical or clerical rule.

hieroglyph, hieroglyphic, hī'ĕr-ō-glif, hī'ĕr-ō-glif"ik, *n.* A figure of an animal, plant, &c., implying a word, idea or sound, such as those in use among the ancient Egyptians; a character difficult to decipher. **hieroglyphic, hieroglyphical,** hī'ĕr-ō-glif"ik, hī'ĕr-ō-glif"ik-al, *a.* Forming a hieroglyph; relating to hieroglyphics; emblematic.

high, hī, *a.* Having a great extent from base to summit; elevated; lofty; far above the earth; elevated in rank or office; dignified; proud; violent; solemn; strong; vivid; dear; remote; sharp; far advanced; committed against the sovereign or state; tending towards putrefaction; strong-scented.—*adv.* In a high manner; to a great altitude or degree; eminently; greatly.

highborn, hī'born, *a.* Being of noble birth or extraction.

highbred, hī'bred, *a.* Bred in high life.

High-Church, hī'chĕrch, *a.* Belonging to that section of the Episcopal Church that maintains the highest notions respecting episcopacy, the priesthood, sacraments, &c.

high-flown, hī'flōn, *a.* Elevated; turgid; extravagant.

highflying, hī'flī-ing, *a.* Extravagant in claims or opinions.

high-handed, hī'hand-ed, *a.* Violent; overbearing; oppressive.

highland, hi′land, *n.* A mountainous region often in pl.—*a.* Pertaining to mountainous regions, or to the Highlands of Scotland.

Highlander, hi′land-èr, *n.* An inhabitant of the mountains; a native of the Highlands of Scotland.

highly, hi′li, *adv.* In a high manner; in a great degree; decidedly; markedly.

high-minded, hi′mind-ed, *a.* Proud; arrogant; having honorable pride.

highness, hi′nes, *n.* State or quality of being high; height; title of honor given to princes, &c.; used with poss. prons. *his, her,* &c.

high-pressure, hi′pre-shūr, *a.* Having or involving a pressure exceeding that of the atmosphere, or having a pressure greater than 50 lbs. on the square inch.

high priest, hi′prēst, *n.* A chief priest.

highroad, hi′rōd, *n.* A highway or much frequented road.

high-souled, hi′sōld, *a.* Having a high or lofty spirit; highly honorable.

high-sounding, hi′sound-ing, *a.* Making a loud sound; bombastic; ostentatious.

high-spirited, hi′spi-rit-ed, *a.* Full of spirit; bold; daring.

high-strung, hi′strung, *a.* Strung to a high pitch; high-spirited; sensitive.

high-toned, hi′tōnd, *a.* High in tone or pitch; noble; elevated.

highway, hi′wā, *n.* A public road; direct course; road; train of action.

highwayman, hi′wā-man, *n.* One who robs on the public road or highway.

hijacker, hi′jak-er, (Colloq) *n.* Originally one of a band of hoboes who preyed on harvesters of the Middle West and Northwest U. S. Recently, one who preys on bootleggers.

hilarious, hi-lā′ri-us, *a.* Full of hilarity; gay.

hilarity, hi-la′ri-ti, *n.* Cheerfulness; merriment; good humor; jollity.

hill, hil, *n.* A natural elevation of less size than a mountain; an eminence.

hillock, hil′ok, *n.* A small hill.

hilly, hil′i, *a.* Abounding with hills.

hilt, hilt, *n.* A handle, particularly of a sword.

him, him, *pron.* The objective case of *he.*

himself, him-self′, *pron.* The emphatic and reflexive form of *he* and *him.*

hind, hind, *n.* The female of the red-deer or stag; a farm servant; a rustic.—*a.* Backward; back; pertaining to the backward part. **hinder,** hind′er, *n.* Posterior; latter; after.

hinder, hin′dèr, *vt.* To prevent from moving or acting; to obstruct; to thwart; to check.—*vi.* To interpose obstacles or impediments.

hindmost, hindermost, hind′mōst, hind′èr-mōst, *a.* Farthest behind; last.

hindrance, hin′drans, *n.* Act of hindering; impediment; obstruction.

Hindu, Hindoo, hin-dö′ or hin′dö, *n.* and *a.* A member of one of the native races of India; pertaining to such.

hinge, hinj, *n.* The hook or joint on which a door, &c., hangs and turns; that on which anything depends or turns. —*vt.* (hinging, hinged). To furnish with hinges.—*vi.* To stand or turn, as on a hinge.

hint, hint, *vt.* To suggest indirectly; to insinuate.—*vi.* To make an indirect allusion.—*n.* A distant allusion; a suggestion.

hip, hip, *n.* The fleshy projecting part of the thigh; the haunch; the joint of the thigh; the fruit of the dog-rose or wild brier.—*interj.* Exclamation expressive of a call to anyone. *Hip, hip, hurrah!* the signal to cheer.

hippodrome, hip′ō-drōm, *n.* A racecourse for horses and chariots; a circus.

hippopotamus, hip-ō-pot′a-mus, *n.;* pl. **-amuses** or **-ami.** A large, hoofed, pachydermatous animal, inhabiting the Nile and other rivers in Africa.

hire, hir, *vt.* (hiring, hired). To procure for temporary use, at a certain price; to engage in service for a stipulated reward; to let; to lease (with *out*).—*n.* Price paid for temporary use of anything; recompense for personal service; wages; pay.

hireling, hir′ling, *n.* One who is hired; a mercenary.—*a.* Serving for wages; venal; mercenary.

hirsute, hèr-sūt′, *a.* Hairy; shaggy.

his, hiz, *pron.* The possessive case of *he.*

hiss, his, *vi.* To make a sound like that of the letter *s,* in contempt or disapprobation; to emit a similar sound; to whiz. —*vt.* To condemn by hissing.—*n.* The sound expressed by the verb.

hist, hist, *interj.* A word commanding silence, equivalent to hush, whist, be silent.

history, his′to-ri, *n.* An account of facts, particularly respecting nations or states; that branch of knowledge which deals with past events; narration; a story; an account of existing things, as animals or plants. **historian,** his-tō′ri-an, *n.* A writer or compiler of history. **historic, historical,** his-to′rik, his-to′rik-al. *a.* Pertaining to, connected with, contained in, or deduced from history. **historically,** his-to′rik-al-li, *adv.* In a historical manner; according to history.

histrionics, his′tri-on″iks, *n.* The art of theatrical representation.

hit, hit, *vt.* (hitting, hit). To strike or touch with some force; to give a blow to; not to miss; to reach; to light upon; to suit.—*vi.* To strike; to come in contact; to reach the intended point; to succeed. —*n.* A stroke; a blow; a lucky chance; happy thought or expression.

hitch, hich, *vi.* To move by jerks; to be entangled, hooked, or yoked.—*vt.* To fasten; to hook; to raise by jerks.—*n.* A catch; act of catching, as on a hook, &c.; knot or noose in a rope; a jerk; a temporary obstruction.

hitchhiker, hich′hik-èr, *n.* One who solicits free transportation on the highways.

hither, hiTH′èr, *adv.* To this place.—*a.* Nearer; toward the person speaking. **hithermost,** hiTH′èr-mōst, *a.* Nearest on this side. **hitherto,** hiTH′èr-tö, *adv.* To this time; till now; to this place or limit. **hitherward,** hiTH′èr-wèrd, *adv.* This way; toward this place.

hive, hiv, *n.* A box or receptacle for

honeybees; the bees inhabiting a hive; a place swarming with busy occupants.— *vt.* (hiving, hived). To collect into a hive; to lay up in store.—*vi.* To take shelter together; to reside in a collective body.

ho, hō, *interj.* A cry to excite attention, give notice, &c.

hoar, hōr, *a.* White or whitish; hoary.— *vi.* To become moldy or musty.

hoard, hōrd, *n.* A store, stock, or large quantity of anything; a hidden stock.— *vt.* To collect; to store secretly.—*vi.* To form a hoard; to lay up in store. **hoarding**, hōrd′ing, *n.* A timber inclosure round a building, &c. (Eng.)

hoar-frost, hōr′frost, *n.* The white particles of frozen dew; rime.

hoarse, hōrs, *a.* Having a grating voice, as when affected with a cold; discordant; rough; grating. **hoarsely**, hōrs′li, *adv.* With a rough, harsh, grating voice or sound.

hoary, hōr′i, *a.* White or whitish; white or gray with age.

hoax, hōks, *n.* Something done for deception or mockery; a practical joke.— *vt.* To deceive; to play a trick upon without malice.

hob, hob, *n.* The part of a grate on which things are placed to be kept warm.

hobble, bob′l, *vi.* (hobbling, hobbled). To walk lamely or awkwardly; to limp; to halt.—*vt.* To hopple.—*n.* An unequal, halting gait; perplexity.

hobby, hob′i, *n.* A small but strong British falcon; an active ambling nag; a hobby-horse; any favorite object or pursuit.

hobbyhorse, hob′i-hors, *n.* A wooden horse for children; a favorite object of pursuit.

hobgoblin, hob-gob′lin, *n.* A goblin; an imp; something that causes terror.

hobnail, hob′nāl, *n.* A nail with a thick, strong head.

hobnob, hob′nob, *vi.* (hobnobbing, hobnobbed). To drink familiarly; to be boon companions.

hock, hough, hok, *n.* The joint between the knee and fetlock; in man, the posterior part of the knee-joint.—*vt.* To hamstring.

hockey, hok′i, *n.* A game at ball played with a club curved at the lower end.

hocus-pocus, hō′kus-pō′kus, *n.* A juggler's trick; trickery used by conjurers.

hod, hod, *n.* A kind of trough for carrying mortar and brick on the shoulder.

hodge, hoj, *n.* A rustic or clown.

hodgepodge, hoj′poj, *n.* A mixed mass; a medley of ingredients; a hotchpotch.

hoe, hō, *n.* An instrument to cut up weeds and loosen the earth.—*vt.* (hoeing, hoed). To dig or clean with a hoe.—*vi.* To use a hoe.

hog, hog, *n.* A swine; a castrated boar; a sheep of a year old; a brutal or mean fellow.—*vi.* To bend, as a ship's bottom. **hoggish**, hog′ish, *a.* Brutish; filthy. **hogshead**, hogz′hed, *n.* A large cask; an old measure of capacity, containing about 52½ imperial gallons.

hogwash, hog′wosh, *n.* Refuse of a kitchen, brewery, &c., given to swine; swill.

hoist, hoist, *vt.* To heave up; to lift upward by means of tackle.—*n.* Act of raising; apparatus for raising goods, &c.; an elevator.

hoity-toity, hoi′ti-toi′ti, *a.* Frolicsome; haughty.—*n.* A romp.—*interj.* An exclamation denoting surprise, with some degree of contempt.

hokum, hō′kum, *n.* *Slang.* Nonsense.

hold, hōld, *vt.* (pret. held, pp. held, holden). To have in the grasp; to keep fast; to confine; to maintain; to consider; to contain; to possess; to withhold; to continue; to celebrate.—*vi.* To take or keep a thing in one's grasp; to stand as a fact or truth; not to give way or part; to refrain; to adhere; to derive title (with *of*).—*n.* A grasp; something which may be seized for support; power of keeping, seizing, or directing; influence; place of confinement; stronghold; interior cavity of a ship. **holder**, hōld′ėr, *n.* One who or that which holds; something by which a thing is held; one who possesses. **holdfast**, hōld′fast, *n.* That which holds fast; a catch, hook, &c. **holding**, hōld′ing, *n.* Act of keeping hold; tenure; a farm held of a superior.

hole, hōl, *n.* A hollow place in any solid body; a perforation, crevice, &c.; a den; a subterfuge.—*vt.* (holing, holed). To make a hole or holes in; to drive into a hole.

holiday, ho′li-dā, *n.* A holy or sacred day; a festival; day of exemption from labor.—*a.* Pertaining to a festival.

holiness, hō′li-nes, *n.* State or quality of being holy; moral goodness; sanctity. **His Holiness**, a title of the pope.

holla, hollo, holloa, hol-lä′, hol-lō′. An exclamation to someone at a distance, in order to call attention or in answer.

hollow, hol′ō, *a.* Containing an empty space; not solid; deep; false; deceitful. —*n.* A depression or excavation; a cavity.—*vt.* To make a hole in; to excavate.

holly, hol′i, *n.* An evergreen tree or shrub, with thorny leaves and scarlet berries.

hollyhock, hol′i-hok, *n.* A tall biennial plant of the mallow family.

holocaust, hol′o-kast, *n.* A burnt-sacrifice, of which the whole was consumed by fire; a great slaughter.

holograph, hol′o-graf, *n.* A deed or document written wholly by the person from whom it proceeds.

holster, hōl′stėr, *n.* A leathern case for a pistol, carried by a horseman.

holy, hō′li, *a.* Free from sin; immaculate; consecrated; sacred. **holy-day**, hō′li-dā. See **holiday**. **Holy Land**, Palestine.

holystone, hō′li-stōn, *n.* A soft sandstone used for cleaning the decks of ships. —*vt.* To scrub with holystone.

homage, hom′āj, *n.* An act of fealty on the part of a vassal to his lord; obeisance; reverential worship.

home, hōm, *n.* One's own abode; the abode of one's family; residence; one's own country; an establishment affording the comforts of a home.—*a.* Domestic; close; severe; poignant.—*adv.* To one's own habitation or country; to the point; effectively. **home-bred**, hōm'-bred, *a.* Native; domestic; not polished by travel. **homeless**, hōm'les, *a.* Destitute of a home. **homely**, hōm'li, *a.* Belonging to home; of plain features; plain; coarse. **Homeric**, hō-me'rik, *a.* Pertaining to or like Homer or his poetry.

home rule, hōm'rōl, *n.* Self-government for a detached part of a country. **homesick**, hōm'sik, *a.* Affected with homesickness. **home-sickness**, hōm'-sik-nes, *n.* Depression of spirits occasioned by absence from one's home or country; nostalgia. **homespun**, hōm'spun, *a.* Spun or wrought at home; plain; coarse; homely. **homestead**, hōm'sted, *n.* A house with the grounds and buildings contiguous; a home; native seat. **homeward**, hōm'wērd, *adv.* Toward one's habitation or country.—*a.* Being in the direction of home. **homicide**, hom'i-sīd, *n.* Manslaughter; a person who kills another. **homicidal**, hom'i-sīd'al, *a.* Pertaining to homicide; murderous. **homily**, hom'i-li, *n.* A sermon; a familiar religious discourse; a serious discourse or admonition. **homing**, hōm'ing, *a.* Coming home; applied to birds such as the carrier-pigeons. **hominy**, hom'i-ni, *n.* Maize hulled or coarsely ground, prepared for food by being boiled. **homogeneous**, ho'mō-jē"nē-us, *a.* Of the same kind or nature; consisting of similar parts or elements. **homogenesis**, ho'mō-jen"e-sis, *n.* Sameness of origin; reproduction of offspring similar to their parents. **homogenize**, ho-moj'n-īz, *vt.* To make homogeneous; to emulsify the fat globules in milk, using a high-temperature process. **homonym**, ho'mō-nim, *n.* A word which agrees with another in sound, and perhaps in spelling, but differs in signification. **homo sapiens**, hō'mō sā'pi-enz. Man; human beings. **homosexual**, hō-ma-sek'shō-al, *a.* Being sexually attracted to those of the same sex.—*n.* A homosexual person. **hone**, hōn, *n.* A stone of fine grit, used for sharpening instruments.—*vt.* (honing, honed). To sharpen on a hone. **honest**, on'est, *a.* Free from fraud; upright; just; sincere; candid; virtuous. **honestly**, on'est-li, *adv.* In an honest manner; with integrity; frankly. **honesty**, on'est-i, *n.* State or quality of being honest; integrity; candor; truth. **honey**, hun'i, *n.* A sweet viscous juice collected by bees from flowers; sweetness; a word of tenderness.—*vt.* To sweeten. **honeycomb**, hun'i-kōm, *n.* The waxy structure formed by bees for honey; anything having cells like a honeycomb. **honeycombed**, hun'i-kōmd, *p.a.* Having little cells resembling honeycombs.

honey-dew, hun'i-dū, *n.* A sweet substance found on certain plants in small drops. **honeyed**, hun'id, *a.* Covered with honey; sweet. **honeymoon**, hun'i-mōn, *n.* The first month after marriage; interval spent by a newly married pair before settling down at home. **honeysuckle**, hun'i-suk-l, *n.* A beautiful flowering and climbing shrub; woodbine.

honor, on'ēr, *n.* Respect; esteem; testimony of esteem; dignity; good name; a nice sense of what is right; scorn of meanness; a title of respect or distinction; one of the highest trump cards; *pl.* civilities paid; public marks of respect; academic and university distinction.—*vt.* To regard or treat with honor; to bestow honor upon; to exalt; to accept and pay when due, as a bill. **honorable**, on'ēr-a-bl, *a.* Worthy of honor; actuated by principles of honor; conferring honor; consistent with honor; performed with marks of honor; not base; honest; fair; a title of distinction. **honorably**, on'ēr-a-bli, *adv.* In an honorable manner.

honorarium, on-ēr-ā'ri-um, *n.* A fee for professional service. **honorary**, on'ēr-a-ri, *a.* Relating to honor; conferring honor; possessing a title or place without performing services or without receiving a reward.—*n.* A fee; honorarium. **hood**, hụd, *n.* A soft covering for the head; a cowl; an ornamental appendage worn at the back of an academic gown; anything resembling a hood; also hoodlum. *Slang*, criminal, ruffian.—*vt.* To dress in a hood; to cover; to blind. **hooded**, hụd'ed, *a.* Covered with a hood.

hoodwink, hụd'wingk, *vt.* To blind by covering the eyes of; to impose on. **hoof**, hōf, *n.* pl. **hoofs**, rarely **hooves**. The horny substance that covers the feet of certain animals, as the horse. **hoofed**, hōft, *a.* Furnished with hoofs. **hook**, hōk, *n.* A bent piece of iron or other metal for catching; that which catches; a sickle.—*vt.* To catch with a hook; to ensnare.—*vi.* To bend; to be curving. **hooked**, hōkt, *a.* Curved; bent; aquiline. **hoop**, hōp, *n.* A band of wood or metal confining the staves of casks, tubs, &c.; a crinoline; a ring; a loud shout.—*vt.* To bind with hoops; to encircle.—*vi.* To shout; to whoop. **hoot**, hōt, *vi.* To shout in contempt; to cry as an owl.—*vt.* To utter contemptuous cries at.—*n.* A cry or shout in contempt. **hop**, hop, *n.* A leap on one leg; a spring; a bitter plant of the hemp family used to flavor malt liquors.—*vi.* To leap or spring on one leg; to skip; to limp; to pick hops.—*vt.* To impregnate with hops. **hope**, hōp, *n.* A desire of some good, accompanied with a belief that it is attainable; trust; one in whom trust or confidence is placed; the object of hope. —*vi.* (hoping, hoped). To entertain hope; to trust.—*vt.* To desire with some expectation of attainment. **hopeful**, hōp′ful, *a.* Full of hope; having qualities which excite hope; promising. **hopeless**, hōp′les, *a.* Destitute of hope; desponding; promising nothing desirable.

hopper, hop′ėr, *n.* One who hops; a wooden trough through which grain passes into a mill; a boat to convey dredged matter.

horde, hōrd, *n.* A tribe or race of nomads; a gang; a migratory crew; rabble. —*vi.* (hording, horded). To live together like migratory tribes.

horizon, ho-ri′zon, *n.* The circle which bounds part of the earth's surface visible from a given point; the apparent junction of the earth and sky. **horizontal**, ho-ri-zon′tal, *a.* Parallel to the horizon; level; near the horizon.

hormone, hor′mōn, *n.* A secretion of endocrine glands, carried to parts of the body through the bloodstream.

horn, horn, *n.* A hard projection on the heads of certain animals; the material of such horns; wind instrument of music; extremity of the moon; drinking-cup; powder-horn; something resembling a horn; the feeler of a snail, &c. **horned**, hornd, *a.* Furnished with horns, or projections resembling horns; having two tufts of feathers on the head, as owls. **horny**, horn′i, *a.* Consisting of horn; resembling horn; hardened by labor; callous.

hornet, hor′net, *n.* A large stinging species of wasp.

hornpipe, horn′pīp, *n.* An old Welsh instrument of music; a lively air or tune, of triple time; a dance to the tune.

hornwork, horn′wėrk, *n.* An outwork in fortification, having angular points or horns.

horology, ho-rol′o-ji, *n.* The science of measuring time; art of constructing machines for measuring time, as clocks, dials. **horoscope**, hor′o-skōp, *n.* In *astrology*, a figure or scheme of the heavens from which to cast nativities and foretell events.

horror, hor′rėr, *n.* A powerful feeling of fear and abhorrence; that which may excite terror; something frightful or shocking. **horrible**, hor′ri-bl, *a.* Exciting horror; dreadful; frightful; awful; hideous. **horribly**, hor′ri-bli, *adv.* In a manner to excite horror; dreadfully; terribly. **horrid**, hor′rid, *a.* That does or may excite horror; horrible; shocking. **horridly**, hor′rid-li, *adv.* In a horrid manner; dreadfully; shockingly. **horrify**, hor′ri-fī, *vt.* (horrifying, horrified). To strike or impress with horror.

horse, hors, *n.* A well-known quadruped used for draft and carriage and in war; the male animal; cavalry; a name of various things resembling or analogous to a horse.—*vt.* (horsing, horsed). To supply with a horse; to carry on the back; to bestride.

stallion.

horseback, hors′bak, *n.* The back of a horse.

horse chestnut, hors′ches-nut, *n.* A flowering tree, the nuts of which have been used as food for animals.

horseman, hors′man, *n.* A rider on horseback; a man skilled in riding; a soldier who serves on horseback. **horsemanship**, hors′man-ship, *n.* Act of riding and of training and managing horses.

horseplay, hors′plā, *n.* Rough or rude practical jokes or the like; rude pranks.

horsepower, hors′pou-ėr, *n.* The power of a horse, or its equivalent, estimated as a power which will raise 32,000 lbs. avoirdupois one foot per minute.

horse-radish, hors′rad-ish, *n.* A perennial plant having a root of a pungent taste.

horseshoe, hors′shō, *n.* A shoe for horses, commonly of iron shaped like the letter U; anything shaped like a horseshoe.—*a.* Having the form of a horseshoe.

horsewhip, hors′whip, *n.* A whip for driving horses.—*vt.* To lash.

horsy, horsey, hor′si, *a.* Connected with, fond of, or much taken up with horses.

hortatory, hor′ta-to′ri, *a.* Giving exhortation or advice; encouraging.

horticulture, hor′ti-kul′tūr, *n.* The art of cultivating gardens. **horticulturist**, hor-ti-kul′tūr-ist, *n.* One skilled in horticulture. **horticultural**, hor-ti-kul′tūr-al, *a.* Pertaining to horticulture.

hosanna, hō-zan′na, *n.* An exclamation of praise to God, or an invocation of blessings.

hose, hōz, *n. sing.* or *pl.* A covering for the thighs, legs, or feet; close-fitting breeches; stockings; in these senses plural; a flexible pipe used for conveying water. **hosiery**, hō′zhi-ė-ri, *n.* The goods of a hosier; stockings.

hospice, hos′pis, *n.* A place of refuge and entertainment for travelers, as among the Alps

hospitable, hos′pit-a-bl, *a.* Kind to strangers and guests. **hospitably**, hos′pit-a-bli, *adv.* In a hospitable manner.

hospital, hos′pi-tal, *n.* A building for the sick, wounded, &c., or for any class of persons requiring public help. **hospitality**, hos′pi-tal″i-ti, *n.* Quality of being hospitable.

host, hōst, *n.* One who entertains a stranger or guest; an innkeeper; an army; any great number or multitude; the consecrated bread in the R. Catholic sacrament of the mass.

hostage, hos′tij, *n.* A person delivered to an enemy, as a pledge to secure the performance of conditions.

hostel, hostelry, hos′tel, hos′tel-ri, *n.* An inn; a lodging-house.

hostess, hōst′es, *n.* A female host; a woman who keeps an inn.

hostile, hos′til, *a.* Belonging to an enemy; unfriendly; antagonistic; adverse. **hostility**, hos-til′i-ti, *n.* State or quality of being hostile; state of war between nations or states; the actions of an open enemy (in *pl.*); animosity; enmity; opposition.

hostler, os'lèr, *n.* The person who has the care of horses at an inn.

hot, hot, *a.* Having sensible heat; burning; glowing; easily exasperated; vehement; eager; lustful; biting; pungent in taste.

hotbed, hot'bed, *n.* A bed of earth heated by fermenting substances, and covered with glass, used for early or exotic plants; a place which favors rapid growth.

hot-blooded, hot'blud-ed, *a.* High-spirited; irritable.

hotchpotch, hoch'poch, *n.* A mixture of miscellaneous things; jumble; in Scotland, a thick soup of vegetables boiled with meat.

hot dog, *n. Slang.* A frankfurter served in a roll.

hotel, hō-tel', *n.* A superior house for strangers or travelers; an inn; in France, a large mansion in a town.

hotheaded, hot'hed-ed, *a.* Of ardent passions; vehement; violent; rash.

hothouse, hot'hous, *n.* A house kept warm to shelter tender plants; a conservatory.

hot rod, *n.* An automobile that has been stripped down and the engine supercharged to step up its performance.

hot-tempered, hot'tem-pèrd, *a.* Of a fiery wrathful temper.

Hottentot, hot'n-tot, *n.* A member of a degraded race of S. Africa; their language.

hound, hound, *n.* A dog; a dog used in the chase; a dog-fish.—*vt.* To set on in chase; to hunt; to urge on.

hour, our, *n.* The twenty-fourth part of a day, consisting of sixty minutes; the particular time of the day; an appointed time; *pl.* certain prayers in the R. Catholic Church.

hourglass, our'glas, *n.* A glass for measuring time by the running of sand from one compartment to the other.

hourly, our'li, *a.* Happening or done every hour; often repeated; continual.—*adv.* Every hour; frequently.

house, hous, *n.;* pl. **houses,** hou'zez. A building or erection for the habitation or use of man; any building or edifice; a dwelling; a household; a family; a legislative body of men; audience or attendance; a commercial establishment.—*vt.* (housing, housed). To put or receive into a house; to shelter.—*vi.* To take shelter; to take up abode. **houseboat,** hous'bōt, *n.* A river boat supporting a wooden house. **housebreaker,** hous'brāk-èr, *n.* One who breaks into a house; a burglar. **housebreaking,** hous'brāk-ing, *n.* Burglary. **household,** hous'hōld, *n.* Those who dwell under the same roof and compose a family.—*a.* Domestic. **householder,** hous'hōld-èr, *n.* The chief of a household; one who keeps house with his family. **housekeeper,** hous'kēp-èr, *n.* A householder; a female servant who has the chief care of the house or family. **housekeeping,** hous'kēp-ing, *n.* The care or management of domestic concerns.

housemaid, hous'māld, *n.* A female servant in a house.

housewarming, hous'warm'ing, *n.* A feast on a family's entrance into a new house.

housewife, hous'wīf, *n.* The mistress of a family; a female manager of domestic affairs; a hussif (pronounced huz'if) **housewifery,** hous'wif-ri, *n.* The business of a housewife.

housing, hou'zing, *n.* A horse-cloth; *pl* the trappings of a horse.—*p.n.* Placing in houses; sheltering.

hovel, huv'l, *n.* A mean house; an open shed for cattle, &c.—*vt.* To put in a hovel.

hover, ho'vèr, *vi.* To hang fluttering in the air; to be in doubt; to linger near.

how, hou, *adv.* In what manner; to what extent; for what reason; by what means; in what state.

howbeit, bou-bē'it, *adv.* Be it as it may; nevertheless.

howdah, hou'da, *n.* A seat on an elephant's back, usually covered overhead.

however, hou-ev'èr, *adv.* In whatever manner or degree; in whatever state.—*conj.* Nevertheless; yet; still; though.

howitzer, hou'its-èr, *n.* A short piece of ordnance, designed for the horizontal firing of shells with small charges.

howl, houl, *vi.* To cry as a dog or wolf; to utter a loud mournful sound; to roar, as the wind.—*vt.* To utter or speak with outcry.—*n.* A loud protracted wail; cry of a wolf, &c

howling, houl'ing, *a.* Filled with howls or howling beasts; dreary.

howsoever, hou-sō-ev'èr, *adv.* In what manner soever; although.

hoy, hoi. An exclamation; of no definite meaning.—*n.* A small coasting vessel.

hoyden, hoi'den, *n.* A rude, bold girl; a romp.—*a.* Rude; bold; inelegant; rustic.—*vi.* To romp rudely or wildly.

hub, hub, *n.* The central cylindrical part of a wheel in which the spokes are set.

hubbub, hub'bub, *n.* A great noise of many confused voices; tumult; uproar.

huckster, huk'stèr, *n.* A retailer of small articles; a hawker.—*vi.* To deal in small articles; to higgle.—*vt.* To hawk.

huddle, hud'l, *vt.* (huddling, huddled). To crowd or press together promiscuously.—*vt.* To throw or crowd together in confusion; to put on in haste and disorder.—*n.* A confused mass; confusion.

hue, hū, *n.* Color; tint; dye; a shouting; outcry; alarm.

huff, huf, *n.* A fit of peevishness or petulance; anger.—*vt.* To treat with insolence; to bully; to make angry.—*vi.* To swell up; to bluster; to take offense. **huffy,** huf'i, *a.* Petulant; angry.

hug, hug, *vt.* (hugging, hugged). To press close in an embrace; to hold fast; to cherish; to keep close to.—*n.* A close embrace; a particular grip in wrestling.

huge, hūj, *a.* Of immense bulk; enormous; prodigious. **hugely,** hūj-li, *adv.* Very greatly; vastly.

Huguenot, hū'ge-not, *n.* A French Protestant of the period of the religious wars in France in the 16th century.

hulk, hulk, *n.* The body of an old vessel;

anything bulky or unwieldy. **hulking,** **hulky,** hul'king, hul'ki, a. Large and clumsy of body; loutish.

hull, hul, n. The outer covering of anything, particularly of a nut or of grain; husk; frame or body of a ship.—vt. To strip off the hull or hulls; to pierce the hull of a ship with a cannon-ball.

hum, hum, vi. (humming, hummed). To utter the sound of bees; to make an inarticulate, buzzing sound.—vt. To sing in a low voice; to sing or utter inarticulately.—n. The noise of bees or insects; a low, confused noise; a low, inarticulate sound.—interj. A sound with a pause, implying doubt and deliberation.

human, bū'man, a. Belonging to man or mankind; having the qualities of a man. **inhumane,** hū-mān', a. Having the feelings and dispositions proper to man; compassionate; merciful; tending to refine.

humanism, hū'man-izm, n. Human nature or disposition; polite learning.

humanist, hū'man-ist, n. One who pursues the study of polite literature; one versed in the knowledge of human nature.

humanitarian, hū-man'i-tā"ri-an, n. A philanthropist; one who believes Christ to have been a mere man; one who maintains the perfectibility of human nature without the aid of grace.

humanity, hū-man'i-ti, n. The quality of being human or humane; mankind collectively; kindness; benevolence; classical and polite literature; generally plural, the humanities.

humanize, hū'man-īz, vt. To render human or humane; to civilize; to soften.

humankind, hū'man-kind, n. The race of man; mankind.

humanly, hū'man-li, adv. After the manner of men.

humble, hum'bl, a. Of a low, mean, or unpretending character; lowly; modest; meek.—vt. (humbling, humbled). To make humble; to abase; to lower. **humbling,** hum'bl-ing, a. Adapted to abase pride and self-dependence. **humbly,** hum'bli, adv. In an humble manner; meekly; submissively.

humble pie, hum'bl-pī, n. A pie made of the humbles. to eat humble pie, to have to take a humble tone; to apologize.

humbug, hum'bug, n. A hoax; a cheat; a trickish fellow.—vt. (humbugging, humbugged). To impose on.

humdrum, hum'drum, a. Commonplace; dull.—n. A droning tone; dull monotony.

humid, hū'mid, a. Moist; damp. **humidity,** hū-mid'i-ti, n. State of being humid; moisture.

humidor, hu-mid'or, n. A box or room for keeping tobacco moist.

humiliate, hū-mil'i-āt, vt. To humble; to depress; to mortify. **humiliation,** hū-mil'i-ā"shun, n. Act of humbling; state of being humbled.

humility, hū-mil'i-ti, n. Humbleness of mind; modesty; sense of insignificance.

hummingbird, hum'ing-bėrd, n. A family of minute but richly colored birds that make a humming sound with their wings.

hummock, hum'ok, n. A rounded knoll.

humor, hū'mėr, or ū'mėr, n. Moisture or moist matter; fluid matter in an animal body, not blood; disposition; mood; a caprice; jocularity; a quality akin to wit, but depending for its effects less on point or brilliancy of expression.—vt. To comply with the inclination of; to soothe by compliance; to indulge. **humoral,** hū'mėr-al or ū', a. Pertaining to humors of the body. **humorist,** hū'-mėr-ist or ū', n. One that makes use of a humorous style in speaking or writing; a wag. **humorous,** hū'mėr-us or ū', a. Containing humor; jocular; adapted to excite laughter. **humorously,** hū'mėr-us-li, or ū', adv. In a humorous manner.

hump, hump, n. A protuberance, especially that formed by a crooked back; a hunch.

humpback, hump'bak, n. A back with a hump; a humpbacked person; a kind of whale. **humpbacked,** hump'bakt, a. Having a crooked back.

humus, hū'mus, n. Vegetable mold.

hunch, hunsh, n. A hump; a protuberance; a thick piece; a push or jerk with the fist or elbow.—vt. To bend so as to form a hump; to push with the elbow. **hunchback,** hunsh'bak, n. A humpbacked person. **hunchbacked,** hunsh'-bakt, a. Having a crooked back.

hundred, hun'dred, a. Ten times ten.—n. The sum of ten times ten; the number 100; a division or part of a county in England. **hundredfold,** hun'dred-fōld, n. A hundred times as much. **hundredth,** hun'dredth, a. The ordinal of a hundred.—n. One of a hundred equal parts. **hundredweight,** hun'dred-wāt, n. A weight of a hundred and twelve pounds avoirdupois, twenty of which make a ton.

Hungarian, hung-gā'ri-an, n. A native of Hungary; the language of the Hungarians; Magyar.—a. Pertaining to Hungary.

hunger, hung'gėr, n. An uneasy sensation occasioned by the want of food; a craving of food; a strong or eager desire. —vi. To feel the uneasiness occasioned by want of food; to desire with great eagerness. **hungry,** hung'gri, a. Feeling uneasiness from want of food; having an eager desire; lean; barren.

hunk, hungk, n. A large lump; a hunch.

hunt, hunt, vt. To chase or search for, for the purpose of catching or killing; to follow closely; to use or manage, as hounds; to pursue animals over.—vi. To follow the chase; to search.—n. The chase of wild animals for catching them; pursuit; an association of huntsmen; a pack of hounds. **hunter,** hunt'ėr, n. One who hunts; a horse used in the chase; a kind of watch. **hunting,** hunt'ing, n. The act or practice of pursuing wild animals; the chase. **huntress,** hunt'res, n. A female that hunts or follows the chase. **huntsman,** hunts'man, n. One who practices hunting; the person whose office it is to manage the chase.

hurdle, hėr'dl, n. A movable frame made of twigs or sticks, or of bars or rods.—vt.

(hurdling, hurdled). To make up, cover, or close with hurdles.

hurdy-gurdy, hėr'di-gėr-di, *n.* A stringed instrument of music, whose sounds are produced by the friction of a wheel; a barrel-organ.

hurl, hėrl, *vt.* To send whirling through the air; to throw with violence; to utter with vehemence.—*n.* Act of throwing with violence.

hurly-burly, hėr'li-bėr'li, *n.* Tumult; bustle; confusion.

hurra, hurrah, hu-rä or hu-rä', *interj.* An exclamation of joy or applause.

hurricane, hur'i-kăn, *n.* A violent storm of wind and rain.

hurry, hu'ri, *vt.* (hurrying, hurried). To drive or press forward with more rapidity; to urge to act with more celerity; to quicken.—*vi.* To move or act with haste; to hasten.—*n.* Act of hurrying; urgency; bustle. **hurried,** hu'rid, *p.a.* Characterized by hurry; done in a hurry; evidencing hurry. **hurriedly,** hu'rid-li, *adv.* In a hurried manner.

hurt, hėrt, *n.* A wound; bruise; injury; harm.—*vt.* (pret. and pp. hurt). To cause physical pain to; to bruise; to harm; to impair; to injure; to wound the feelings of. **hurtful,** hėrt'fyl, *a.* Causing hurt; tending to impair; detrimental; injurious.

hurtle, hėr'tl, *vi.* (hurtling, hurtled). To meet in shock; to clash; to fly with threatening noise; to resound.

husband, huz'band, *n.* A married man; the correlative of wife; a good manager; a steward.—*vt.* To manage with frugality; to use with economy. **husband-man,** huz'band-man, *n.* A tiller of the ground; a farmer. **husbandry,** huz'-band-ri, *n.* Farming; care of domestic affairs; thrift.

hush, hush, *a.* Silent; still; quiet.—*n.* Stillness; quiet.—*vt.* To make quiet; to repress, as noise.—*vi.* To be still; to be silent.

hush money, hush'mu-ni,, *n.* Money paid to hinder disclosure of facts.

husk, husk, *n.* The covering of certain fruits or seeds.—*vt.* To strip the husk from. **husky,** husk'i, *a.* Abounding with husks; consisting of husks; resembling husks; rough, as sound; harsh; hoarse.

hussar, hu'zär', *a.* A light-armed horse-soldier.

hussy, huz'i, *n.* A worthless woman; a jade; a pert, frolicsome wench.

hustle, hus'l, *vt.* and *i.* (hustling, hustled). To shake or shuffle together; to push or crowd; to jostle.

hut, hut, *n.* A small house, hovel, or cabin; a temporary building to lodge soldiers.—*vt.* (hutting, hutted). To place in huts, as troops.—*vi.* To take lodgings in huts.

hutch, huch, *n.* A chest or box; a corn bin; a box for rabbits; a low wagon used in coalpits; a measure of 2 bushels.

huzza, hu-zä', *n.* A shout of joy.—*vi.* To utter a loud shout of joy.

hyacinth, hi'a-sinth, *n.* A flowering, bulbous plant, of many varieties; a red variety of zircon, tinged with yellow or brown; also applied to varieties of gar-net, sapphire, and topaz. **hyacinthine** hi-a-sinth'in, *a.* Pertaining to, made of or like hyacinth.

hybrid, hib'rid, *n.* A mongrel; an ani mal or plant produced from the mixture of two species.—*a.* Mongrel.

hydra, hi'dra, *n.* A many-headed mon ster of Greek mythology.

hydrangea, hi-dran'jē-a, *n.* An Asiatic shrub with beautiful flowers, cultivated in gardens.

hydrant, hi'drant, *n.* A pipe with valves &c., by which water is drawn from a main pipe.

hydrate, hi'drāt, *n.* A chemical com pound in which water or hydrogen is a characteristic ingredient.

hydraulic, hi-dral'ik, *a.* Pertaining to fluids in motion, or the action of water utilized for mechanical purposes. **hy-draulics,** hi-dral'iks, *n.* The science of fluids in motion, and the application of water in machinery.

hydrocarbon, hi-drō-kär'bon, *n.* A chemical compound of hydrogen and carbon.

hydrocephalus, hi-drō-sef'a-lus, *n.* Water in the head.

hydrodynamic, hi'drō-di-nam"ik, *a.* Pertaining to the forces or pressure of water.

hydrodynamics, hi'drō-di-nam"iks, *n.* The dynamics of water or similar fluids.

hydrogen, hi'drō-jen, *n.* The gaseous elementary substance which combines with oxygen to form water. **hydro-genous,** hi-dro'jen-us, *a.* Pertaining to hydrogen.

hydrogen bomb, h. bomb, hi'drō-jen bom, *n.* A thermonuclear device of ex treme destructiveness.

hydrometer, hi-drom'et-ėr, *n.* An in strument for measuring the specific gravities of liquids, and strength of spir ituous liquors.

hydrophobia, hi-drō-fō'bi-a, *n.* A mor bid dread of water; a disease produced by the bite of a mad animal, especially a dog.

hydrous, hi'drus, *a.* Watery.

hydrozoon, hi-drō-zō'on, *n.*; pl. **-zoa.** A class of animals, mostly marine, in cluding the jellyfishes, &c.

hyena, hi-ē'na, *n.* A carnivorous quad ruped of Asia and Africa, feeding chiefly on carrion.

hygeian, hi-jē'an, *a.* Relating to health, or the mode of preserving health.

hygiene, hygieine, hi'ji-ēn, hi'jē-in, *n.* A system of principles designed for the promotion of health; sanitary science. **hygienic,** hi-ji-en'ik, *a.* Relating to hygiene.

hymen, hi'men, *n.* The god of marriage. **hymeneal, hymenean,** hi-men-ē'al, hi-men-ē'an, *a.* Pertaining to marriage.

hymn, him, *n.* A song of praise; a song or ode in honor of God.—*vt.* To praise or celebrate in song.—*vi.* To sing in praise.

hymnal, him'nal, *n.* A collection of hymns, generally for use in public wor ship.

hyperbola, hi-pėr'bō-la, *n.* A conic sec tion, a curve formed by a section of a cone, when the cutting plane makes a greater angle with the base than the side of the cone makes.

hyperbole, hī-pèr′bō-lē, *n.* Exaggeration; a figure of speech exceeding the truth. **hyperbolic, hyperbolical,** hī-pèr-bol′ik, hī-pèr-bol′ik-al, *a.* Belonging to the hyperbola; containing hyperbole; exceeding the truth.

hypercritic, hī-pèr-krit′ik, *n.* One critical beyond measure; a captious censor. **hypercritical,** hī-pèr-krit′ik-al, *a.* Overcritical; excessively nice or exact.

hyphen, hī′fen, *n.* A character, thus (-), implying that two words or syllables are to be connected.

hypnotic, hip-not′ik, *a.* Producing sleep. **hypnotism,** hip′no-tizm, *n.* A sleep-like condition caused by artificial means. **hypnotize,** hip′no-tīz, *vt.* To affect with hypnotism.

hypochondria, hī′pō-kon″dri-a, *n.* An ailment characterized by exaggerated anxiety, mainly as to the health; low spirits. **hypochondriac,** hī′pō-kon″dri-ak, *a.* Pertaining to or affected with hypochondria.—*n.* One affected with hypochondria.

hypocrite, hip′ō-krit, *n.* One who feigns to be what he is not; a dissembler. **hypocritical,** hip′ō-krit″i-kal, *a.* Pertaining to or characterized by hypocrisy; insincere. **hypocrisy,** hi-pok′ri-si, *n.* A feigning to be what one is not; insincerity; a counterfeiting of religion.

hypodermal, hypodermic, hī-pō-dèr′mal, hī-pō-dèr′mik, *a.* Pertaining to parts under the skin, or to the introduction of medicines under the skin.

hypotenuse, hī-pot′ē-nūs, *n.* The side of a right-angled triangle opposite the right angle.

hypothesis, hī-poth′e-sis, *n.*; pl. **-ses,** -sēz. A supposition, something assumed for the purpose of argument; a theory assumed to account for what is not understood.

hypothetic, hypothetical, hī-pō-thet″ik, hī-pō-thet″i-kal, *a.* Relating to or characterized by hypothesis; conjectural.

hysteria, hysterics, his-tēr′i-a, his-ter′iks, *n.* A nervous affection chiefly attacking women, characterized by laughing and crying, convulsive struggling, sense of suffocation, &c. **hysteric, hysterical,** his-ter′ik, his-ter′i-kal, *a.* Pertaining to hysterics or hysteria, affected by or subject to hysterics.

I

I, I, *pron.* The pronoun of the first person in the nominative case; the word by which a speaker or writer denotes himself.

iambus, ī-am′bus, *n.*; pl. **-buses** or **bi.** A poetic foot of two syllables, the first short and the last long, as in *delight.* **iamb,** ī-amb′, *n.* An iambus. **iambic,** ī-am′bik, *a.* Pertaining to the iambus; consisting of an iambus or of iambi.—*n.* An iambic foot; a verse of ambi.

iatric, iatrical, ī-at′rik, ī-at′rik-al, *a.* Relating to medicine or physicians.

Iberian, ī-bē′ri-an, *a.* Spanish.—*n.* One of the primitive inhabitants of Spain, or their language.

ibex, ī′beks, *n.* An animal of the goat family.

ibis, ī′bis, *n.*; pl. **ibises,** ī′bis-ez. A grallatorial bird allied to the stork.

ice, īs, *n.* Water or other fluid congealed; ice-cream.—*vt.* (icing, iced). To cover with ice; to convert into ice; to cover with concreted sugar; to freeze. **iceberg,** īs′bèrg, *n.* A vast body of ice floating in the ocean. **ice-bound,** īs′-bound, *a.* Totally surrounded with ice, as a ship. **ice-cream,** īs′krēm, *n.* A confection of cream, sugar, &c., frozen. **iced,** īst, *p.a.* Covered with ice; covered with concreted sugar.

ichthyology, ik-thi-ol′o-ji, *n.* That part of zoology which treats of fishes.

icicle, īs′i-kl, *n.* A pendent, conical mass of ice.

iconoclast, ī-kon′o-klast, *n.* A breaker of images; one who attacks cherished beliefs.

icy, īs′i, *a.* Abounding with ice; made of ice; resembling ice; chilling; frigid; destitute of affection or passion.

idea, ī-dē′a, *n.* That which is seen by the mind's eye; an image in the mind; object of thought; notion; conception; abstract principle; ideal view.

ideal, ī-dē′al, *a.* Existing in idea or fancy; visionary; imaginary; perfect.—*n.* imaginary model of perfection. **idealism,** ī-dē′al-izm, *n.* The system that makes everything to consist in ideas, and denies the existence of material bodies, or which denies any ground for believing in the reality of anything but percipient minds and ideas. **idealist,** ī-dē′al-ist, *n.* One who holds the doctrine of idealism; a visionary. **ideality,** ī-dē-al′i-ti, *n.* Quality of being ideal; capacity to form ideals of beauty. **idealize,** ī-dē′al-īz, *vt.* To make ideal; to embody in an ideal form. **ideally,** ī-dē′al-li, *adv.* In an ideal manner; in idea; intellectually; mentally.

identical, ī-den′tik-al, *a.* The same. **identifiable,** ī-den′ti-fī-a-bl, *a.* That may be identified. **identification,** ī-den′ti-fī-kā″shun, *n.* Act of identifying. **identify,** ī-den′ti-fī, *vt.* To make to be the same; to consider as the same in effect; to ascertain or prove to be the same. **identity,** ī-den′ti-ti, *n.* Sameness, as distinguished from similitude and diversity; sameness in every possible circumstance.

ideology, ĭ-dē-ŏl'o-jĭ, *n.* The doctrine of ideas, or operations of the understanding.

ides, ĭdz, *n. pl.* In the ancient Roman calendar the 15th day of March, May, July and October, and the 13th day of the other months.

idiocy, ĭd'ĭ-ŏ-sĭ, *n.* State of being an idiot; hopeless insanity or madness.

idiom, ĭd'ĭ-om, *n.* A mode of expression peculiar to a language; the genius or peculiar cast of a language; dialect. **idiomatic,** ĭd'ĭ-om-at"ĭk, *a.* Pertaining to the particular genius or modes of expression of a language. **idiomatically,** ĭd'ĭ-om-at"ĭk-al-lĭ, *adv.* According to the idiom of a language.

idiosyncrasy, ĭd'ĭ-o-sĭn"kra-sĭ, *n.* Peculiarity of temperament or constitution; mental or moral characteristic distinguishing an individual. **idiosyncratic,** ĭd'ĭ-o-sĭn-krat"ĭk, *a.* Of peculiar temper or disposition.

idiot, ĭd'ĭ-ot, *n.* One void of understanding; one hopelessly insane. **idiotic, idiotical,** ĭd'ĭ-ot"ĭk, ĭd'ĭ-ot"ĭ-kal, *a.* Relating to or like an idiot; absurd.

idle, ī'dl, *a.* Not engaged in any occupation; inactive; lazy; futile; affording leisure; trifling; trivial.—*vi.* (idling, idled). To be idle; to lose or spend time in inaction.—*vt.* To spend in idleness. **idleness,** ī'dl-nes, *n.* Inaction; sloth; triviality; uselessness. **idler,** ī'dl-ėr, *n.* One who idles; a lazy person; sluggard. **idly,** ī'dlĭ, *adv.* Lazily; carelessly; ineffectually; unprofitably.

idol, ī'dol, *n.* An image or symbol of a deity consecrated as an object of worship; a person honored to adoration; anything on which we set our affections inordinately.

idolater, ī-dol'at-ėr, *n.* A worshiper of idols; pagan; a great admirer. **idolatress,** ī-dol'at-res, *n.* A female idolater. **idolatrous,** ī-dol'at-rus, *a.* Pertaining to idolatry; consisting in or partaking of an excessive attachment or reverence. **idolatry,** ī-dol'at-rĭ, *n.* The worship of idols; excessive attachment to or veneration for any person or thing.

idolize, ī'dol-īz, *vt.* To worship as an idol; to love or reverence to adoration.

idyl, ī'dil, *n.* A short highly wrought descriptive poem; a short pastoral poem. **idyllic,** ī-dil'ĭk, *a.* Belonging to idyls; pastoral.

if, if, *conj.* Granting or supposing that; on condition that; whether; although.

igloo, ĭg'lö, *n.* A dome-shaped hut of packed snow, made by Eskimos.

igneous, ĭg'nē-us, *a.* Pertaining to or consisting of fire; resembling fire; proceeding from the action of fire.

ignite, ĭg-nīt', *vt.* (igniting, ignited). To set on fire.—*vi.* To take fire. **ignition,** ĭg-nĭ'shun, *n.* Act of setting on fire; act of catching fire; state of burning.

ignoble, ĭg-nō'bl, *a.* Not noble; of low birth or family; base; dishonorable. **ignobly,** ĭg-nō'blĭ, *adv.* Meanly; basely.

ignominy, ĭg'nō-mi-nĭ, *n.* Public disgrace, loss of character or reputation; infamy; shame; contempt. **ignomini-**

ous, ĭg-nō-mĭ'nĭ-us, *a.* Shameful; dishonorable; infamous; despicable.

ignoramus, ĭg-nō-rā'mus, *n. pl.* **-muses.** An ignorant person.

ignorant, ĭg'nō-rant, *a.* Wanting knowledge or information. **ignorance,** ĭg'nō-rans, *n.* State of being illiterate, uninformed, or uneducated; want of knowledge.

ignore, ĭg-nōr', *vt.* (ignoring, ignored). To pass over or overlook as if ignorant of; to disregard.

Igorrote, ē'gor-rō'ta, *n.* A native savage of Luzon, Philippine Islands.

iguana, ĭ-gwä'na, *n.* A large, edible, tropical American lizard.

Iguana.

ill, il, *a.* Bad or evil; producing evil; unfortunate; cross; crabbed; sick or indisposed; impaired; ugly; unfavorable; rude.—*n.* Evil; misfortune; calamity; disease; pain.—*adv.* Not well; badly; with pain or difficulty.

ill-bred, il'-bred', *a.* Impolite; rude.

illegal, il-lē'gal, *a.* Not legal; contrary to law; prohibited; illicit. **illegality,** il-lē-gal'ĭ-tĭ, *n.* State or quality of being illegal; unlawfulness. **illegally,** il-lē'gal-lĭ, *adv.* In an illegal or unlawful manner; unlawfully.

illegible, il-le'ji-bl, *a.* Not legible; that cannot be read. **illegibly,** il-le'ji-bli, *adv.* In an illegible manner.

illegitimate, il-lē-jit'i-māt, *a.* Not legitimate; born out of wedlock; illogical; not authorized.—*vt.* To render illegitimate. **illegitimacy,** il-lē-jit'i-ma-si, *n.* State of being illegitimate; bastardy.

ill-favored, il'fā-vėrd, *a.* Not well-favored or good-looking; plain; ugly.

illiberal, il-lib'ėr-al, *a.* Not liberal; not generous; narrow in scope; uncharitable. **illiberality,** il-lib'ėr-al"ĭ-tĭ, *n.* Quality of being illiberal; narrowness of mind.

illicit, il-lis'it, *a.* Not permitted; unlawful; lawless.

illimitable, il-lim'it-a-bl, *a.* That cannot be limited; boundless; infinite; vast.

illiterate, il-lit'ėr-āt, *a.* Unlettered; ignorant of letters or books; not educated. **illiteracy,** il-lit'ėr-a-si, *n.* State of being illiterate, want of education; ignorance.

ill-judged, il'jujd, *a.* Injudicious; unwise.

ill-mannered, il-man'ėrd, *a.* Having bad manners; rude; boorish; impolite.

ill-nature, il'nā-tūr, *n.* Bad temper; crossness; crabbedness. **ill-natured,** il'nā-tūrd, *a.* Cross; surly.

illness, il'nes, *n.* State or quality of being ill; ailment; malady; sickness.

illogical, il-lo'jik-al, *a.* Not logical; contrary to logic or sound reasoning.

ill-starred, il'stärd, *a.* Influenced by unlucky stars; fated to be unfortunate.

ill-tempered, il'tem-pėrd, *a.* Of bad temper; morose; crabbed; sour.

ill-timed, il'tīmd, *a.* Done or said at an unsuitable time.

illume, il-lūm', *vt.* To illuminate. **illuminate,** il-lūm'in-āt, *vt.* (illuminating, illuminated). To light up; to adorn with festal lamps or bonfires; to enlighten intellectually; to adorn with colored pictures, &c., as manuscripts. **illumination**, il-lūm'in-ā″shun, *n.* Act of illuminating; festive display of lights, &c.; splendor; infusion of intellectual or spiritual light; the adorning of manuscripts and books by hand with ornamental designs; such ornaments themselves.

illusion, il-lū'zhon, *n.* Deception; deceptive appearance; hallucination. **illusionist**, il-lū'zhon-ist, *n.* One given to illusion, or one who produces illusions, as by sleight of hand. **illusive**, il-lū'siv, *a.* Tending to cause illusion; deceptive; deceitful. **illusory**, il-lū'so-ri, *a.* Deceiving by false appearances; fallacious.

illustrate, il-lus'trāt or il'lus-trāt, *vt.* (illustrating, illustrated). To make clear or obvious; to explain; to explain and adorn by means of pictures, drawings, &c. **illustration**, il-lus-trā'shun, *n.* Act of illustrating; that which illustrates; an example; design to illustrate the text of a book. **illustrative**, il-lus'trāt-iv or il'lus-trāt-iv, *a.* Having the quality of illustrating or elucidating. **illustrator**, il-lus'trāt-ėr, or il'lus-trāt-ėr, *n.* One who illustrates; one who makes pictures for books.

illustrious, il-lus'tri-us, *a.* Renowned; celebrated; noble; conferring honor or renown; glorious.

ill-will, il'wil, *n.* Unkind or hostile feeling; hatred; malevolence; malice.

image, im'āj, *n.* A representation of any person or thing; a state; an idol; embodiment; a picture drawn by fancy; the appearance of any object formed by the reflection or refraction of the rays of light.—*vt.* (imaging, imaged). To represent by an image; to mirror; to form a likeness of in the mind. **imagery**, im'āj-e-ri, *n.* Images in general; forms of the fancy; rhetorical figures

imagine, im-aj'in, *vt.* (imagining, imagined). To picture to one's self; to fancy; to contrive; to think; to deem.— *vi.* To conceive; to have a notion or idea. **imaginable**, im-aj'in-a-bl, *a.* That may or can be imagined. **imaginary**, im-aj'in-a-ri, *a.* Existing only in imagination; ideal; visionary. **imagination**, im-aj'in-ā″shun, *n.* The act of imagining; the faculty by which we form a mental image, or new combinations of ideas; mental image; a mere fancy; notion. **imaginative**, im-aj'-in-at-iv, *a.* That forms imaginations; owing existence to, or characterized by imagination.

imbecile, im'be-sil, *a.* Destitute of strength; mentally feeble; fatuous; extremely foolish.—*n.* A poor, fatuous, or weak-minded creature. **imbecility**, im-be-sil'i-ti, *n.* Fatuity; silliness; helpless mental weakness.

imbed, im-bed', *vt.* To lay in a bed; to lay in surrounding matter. Also *embed.*

imbibe, im-bīb', *vt.* (imbibing, imbibed). To drink in; to absorb; to admit into the mind.

imbroglio, im-brō'lyŏ, *n.* An intricate and perplexing state of affairs; a misunderstanding of a complicated nature.

imbue, im-bū', *vt.* (imbuing, imbued). To tinge deeply; to dye; to inspire or impregnate (the mind).

imitable, im'i-ta-bl, *a.* That may be imitated; worthy of imitation. **imitate**, im'i-tāt, *vt.* (imitating, imitated). To follow as a model or example; to copy; to mimic; to counterfeit. **imitation**, im-i-tā'shon, *n.* Act of imitating; that which is made or produced as a copy; resemblance; a counterfeit. **imitative**, im'i-tāt-iv, *a.* That imitates; inclined to imitate; exhibiting an imitation. **imitator**, im'i-tāt-ėr, *n.* One who imitates; one who takes another as pattern or model.

immaculate, im-ma'kū-lāt, *a.* Without spot; undefiled; pure.

immanate, im'ma-nāt, *vi.* To flow or issue in; said of something intangible. **immanent**, im'ma-nent, *a.* Remaining in or within; inherent and indwelling.

immaterial, im-ma-tēr'i-al, *a.* Not consisting of matter; unimportant.

immature, im-ma-tūr', *a.* Not mature; not perfect or completed; premature. **immaturity**, im-ma-tūr'i-ti, *n.* State or quality of being immature; crudity.

immeasurable, im-me'zhūr-a-bl, *a.* That cannot be measured; immense.

immediate, im-mē'di-āt, *a.* Without anything intervening; acting without a medium; direct; not acting by secondary causes; present; without intervention of time. **immediately**, im-mē'di-āt-li, *adv.* Without the intervention of anything; directly; without delay; instantly; forthwith.

immemorial, im-me-mō'ri-al, *a.* Beyond memory; extending beyond the reach of record or tradition.

immense, im-mens', *a.* Immeasurable; huge; prodigious; enormous. **immensely**, im-mens'li, *adv.* To an immense extent; hugely; vastly. **immensity**, im-mens'i-ti, *n.* Condition or quality of being immense; that which is immense; infinity.

immerse, im-mėrs', *vt.* (immersing, immersed). To plunge into water or other fluid; to overwhelm; to engage deeply. **immersion**, im-mėr'shon, *n.* Act of immersing; state of being overwhelmed or deeply engaged; disappearance of a celestial body behind another or into its shadow.

immigrate, im'mi-grāt, *vi.* To come into a country for permanent residence. **immigration**, im-mi-grā'shon, *n.* Act of removing into a country for settlement. **immigrant**, im'mi-grant, *n.* A person who immigrates into a country.

imminent, im'mi-nent, *a.* Hanging over; impending; threatening; near at hand. **imminently**, im'mi-nent-li, *adv.* In an imminent manner or degree. **imminence**, im'mi-nens, *n.* Quality or condition of being imminent.

immobile, im-mōb'il, *a.* Not mobile; immovable; fixed; stable.

immobility, im-mō-bil'i-ti, *n.* State or

quality of being immobile; resistance to motion.

immoderate, im-mo'dẽr-ãt, *a.* Exceeding just or usual bounds; excessive; intemperate. **immoderately,** im-mo'dẽr-ãt-li, *adv.* Excessively; unreasonably.

immodest, im-mo'dest, *a.* Not modest; indelicate; indecent; lewd. **immodesty,** im-mo'des-ti, *n.* Want of modesty.

immolate, im'mō-lāt, *vt.* (immolating, immolated). To sacrifice; to kill, as a victim offered in sacrifice; to offer in sacrifice. **immolation,** im-mō-lā'shun, *n.* Act of immolating; a sacrifice offered.

immoral, im-mo'ral, *a.* Not moral; wicked; depraved; licentious. **immorality,** im-mō-ral'i-ti, *n.* Quality of being immoral; any immoral act or practice; vice; licentiousness; depravity.

immortal, im-mor'tal, *a.* Not mortal; everlasting; imperishable; not liable to fall into oblivion.—*n.* One who is exempt from death. **immortality,** im-mor-tal'i-ti, *n.* Condition or quality of being immortal; life destined to endure without end. **immortalize,** im-mor'tal-iz, *vt.* To render immortal; to make famous forever.

immovable, im-möv'a-bl, *a.* That cannot be moved from its place; not to be moved from a purpose; fixed; unchangeable; unfeeling.

immunity, im-mü'ni-ti, *n.* Freedom from service or obligation; particular privilege or prerogative; state of not being liable.

immure, im-mür', *vt.* (immuring, immured). To inclose within walls; to imprison.

immutable, im-mü'ta-bl, *a.* Unchangeable; unalterable; invariable. **immutably,** im-mü'ta-bli, *adv.* Unchangeably; unalterably.

imp, imp, *n.* A young or little devil; a mischievous child.

impact, im'pakt, *n.* A forcible touch; a blow; the shock of a moving body that strikes against another.

impair, impār', *vt.* To make worse; to lessen in quantity, value, excellence, or strength.

impale, im-pāl', *vt.* (impaling, impaled). To put to death by fixing on a stake; to join, as two coats of arms on one shield, with an upright line between.

impalpable, im-pal'pa-bl, *a.* Not to be felt; so fine as not to be perceived by the touch; not easily or readily apprehended by the mind.

impanel, im-pan'el, *vt.* (impaneling, impaneled). To form or enroll the list of jurors in a court of justice.

impart, im-pärt', *vt.* To give, grant, or communicate; to bestow on another; to confer; to reveal; to disclose.

impartial, im-pär'shal, *a.* Not partial; not biased; equitable; just. **impartiality,** im-pär'shi-al''i-ti, *n.* State or quality of being impartial; freedom from bias; equity. **impartially,** im-pär'shal-li, *adv.* Without bias of judgment; justly.

impassable, im-pas'a-bl, *a.* That cannot be passed or traveled over.

impasse, im'pas, *n.* A situation that defies solution; a deadlock.

impassible, im-pas'i-bl, *a.* Incapable of passion or sympathy; unmoved.

impassion, im-pa'shun, *vt.* To move or affect strongly with passion. **impassioned,** im-pa'shund, *p.a.* Actuated by passion; having the feelings warmed, as a speaker; expressive of passion, as a harangue.

impassive, im-pas'iv, *a.* Not susceptible of pain or suffering, impassible; unmoved.

impatient, im-pā'shent, *a.* Not patient; uneasy under given conditions and eager for change; not suffering quietly; not enduring delay. **impatiently,** im-pā'shent-li, *adv.* In an impatient manner. **impatience,** im-pā'shens, *n.* Condition or quality of being impatient; uneasiness under pain, suffering, &c.

impeach, im-pēch', *vt.* To charge with a crime; to bring charges of maladministration against a minister of state, &c.; to call in question; to disparage. **impeachment,** im-pēch'ment, *n.* Act of impeaching; a calling in question; accusation brought by the House of Representatives against some high official before the Senate, who act as judges.

impeccable, im-pek'a-bl, *a.* Not peccable, or liable to sin. **impeccability,** im-pek'a-bil''i-ti, *n.* Quality of being impeccable.

impecunious, im-pē-kü'ni-us, *a.* Not having money; without funds.

impede, im-pēd', *vt.* (impeding, impeded). To entangle or hamper; to obstruct. **impediment,** im-ped'i-ment, *n.* That by which one is impeded; obstruction.

impel, im-pel', *vt.* (impelling, impelled). To drive or urge forward; to press on; to instigate; to incite; to actuate.

impend, im-pend', *vi.* To hang over; to threaten; to be imminent.

impenetrable, im-pen'e-tra-bl, *a.* That cannot be penetrated; not admitting the entrance or passage of other bodies; impervious; obtuse or unsympathetic.

impenitent, im-pen'i-tent, *a.* Not penitent; not repenting of sin; obdurate.

imperative, im-per'a-tiv, *a.* Expressive of command; obligatory; designating a mood of the verb which expresses command, &c.

imperceptible, im-pẽr-sep'ti-bl, *a.* Not perceptible; not easily apprehended by the senses; fine or minute.

imperfect, im-pẽr'fekt, *a.* Not perfect; not complete; not perfect in a moral view; faulty; *imperfect tense,* a tense expressing an uncompleted action or state, especially in time past. **imperfection,** im-pẽr-fek'shun, *n.* Want of perfection; defect; fault; failing. **imperfectly,** im-pẽr'fekt-li, *adv.* In an imperfect manner; not fully.

imperial, im-pē'ri-al, *a.* Pertaining to an empire or emperor; supreme; suitable for an emperor; of superior excellence.— *n.* A tuft of hair on a man's lower lip; a size of paper measuring 30 by 22 inches. **imperialism,** im-pē'ri-al-izm, *n.* State of being imperial; imperial power or authority. **imperialist,** im-pē'ri-al-ist, *n.* A subject or soldier of an emperor; one favorable to empire or imperial government.

imperil, im-per'il, *vt.* (imperiling, imperiled). To bring into peril; to endanger.

imperious, im-pēr'i-us, *a.* Commanding; haughty; domineering; arrogant; urgent; authoritative.

imperishable, im-per'ish-a-bl, *a.* Not perishable; indestructible; everlasting.

impersonal, im-pėr'son-al, *a.* Not having personal existence; not endued with personality; not referring to any particular person; *impersonal verb,* a verb (such as *it rains*) used only with an impersonal nominative.—*n.* That which wants personality; an impersonal verb. **impersonally,** im-pėr'son-al-li, *adv.* In an impersonal manner; as an impersonal verb.

impersonate, im-pėr'son-āt, *vt.* To invest with personality; to assume the character of; to represent in character, as on the stage.

impertinent, im-pėr'ti-nent, *a.* Not pertinent; irrelevant; petulant and rude; pert; intrusive. **impertinence,** im-pėr'ti-nens, *n.* The quality of being impertinent; irrelevance; that which is impertinent; rudeness.

imperturbable, im-pėr-terb'a-bl, *a.* That cannot be agitated; unmoved; calm.

impervious, im-pėr'vi-us, *a.* Not pervious; impassable; impenetrable.

impetigo, im-pe-ti'gō, *n.* An eruption of itching pustules in clusters on the skin.

impetuous, im-pet'ū-us, *a.* Rushing with great force; forcible; precipitate; vehement of mind; hasty; passionate. **impetuously,** im-pe'tū-us-li, *adv.* Violently; with haste and force. **impetuosity,** im-pet'ū-os''i-ti, *n.* Quality of being impetuous; violence; vehemence; ardor and hurry of feelings.

impetus, im'pe-tus, *n.* The force with which any body is driven or impelled; momentum.

impiety, im-pī'e-ti, *n.* Want of piety; irreverence toward the Supreme Being; ungodliness; an act of wickedness.

impinge, im-pinj', *vi.* (impinging, impinged). To dash against; to clash.

impious, im'pi-us, *a.* Destitute of piety; irreverent toward the Supreme Being; profane; tending to dishonor God or his laws.

impish, imp'ish, *a.* Having the qualities of an imp.

implacable, im-plā'ka-bl, *a.* Not to be appeased; inexorable; unrelenting. **implacably,** im-plā'ka-bli, *adv.* In an implacable manner; inexorably.

implant, im-plant', *vt.* To set, fix, or plant; to insert; to instill; to infuse.

implausible, im-plạ'zi-bl, *a.* Not plausible.

implement, im'plē-ment, *n.* A tool, utensil, or instrument.—*vt.* To fulfill the conditions of; to perform.

implicate, im'pli-kāt, *vt.* (implicating, implicated). To involve or bring into connection with; to prove to be connected or concerned, as in an offense.

implication, im-pli-kā'shun, *n.* Act of implicating; state of being implicated; entanglement; a tacit inference; something to be understood though not expressed.

implicit, im-plis'it, *a.* Implied; fairly to be understood; though not expressed in words; trusting to another; unquestioning. **implicitly,** im-plis'it-li, *adv.* In an implicit manner; with unreserved confidence.

implore, im-plōr', *vt.* and *i.* (imploring, implored). To call upon or for, in supplication; to beseech, entreat.

imply, im-plī', *vt.* (implying, implied). To involve or contain in substance or by fair inference; to signify indirectly; to presuppose.

impolite, im-pō-līt', *a.* Not polite.

impolitic, im-pol'i-tik, *a.* Not politic; wanting policy or prudence; inexpedient.

imponderable, im-pon'dėr-a-bl, *a.* Not having weight that can be measured.

import, im-pōrt', *vt.* To bring into a place from abroad; to bear or convey, as the meaning; to signify; to imply; to be of moment or consequence to; to concern.—*n.* im'pōrt. That which is brought into a country from abroad; signification; purport; drift; importance.

importation, im-por-tā'shun, *n.* Act or practice of importing; a quantity imported.

importer, im-pōrt'ėr, *n.* One who imports; a merchant who brings goods from abroad.

important, im-por'tant, *a.* Full of import; momentous; influential; grave; consequential. **importance,** im-por'tans, *n.* Quality of being important; weight; moment; rank or standing; weight in self-estimation.

importune, im'por-tūn'', *vt.* (importuning, importuned). To press with solicitation; to urge with frequent application.—*vi.* To solicit earnestly and repeatedly. **importunity,** im'por-tū''ni-ti, *n.* Pressing or frequent solicitation; application urged with troublesome frequency. **importunate,** im-por'tu-nāt, *a.* Given to importune; troublesome ,by importuning; urgent in request or demand; persistent.

impose, im-pōz', *vt.* (imposing, imposed). To place, set, or lay on; to lay on, as a tax, penalty, duty, &c.; to lay on, as hands; to obtrude fallaciously; to palm or pass off.—*vi.* Used in phrase *to impose on* or *upon,* to deceive; to victimize. **imposing,** im-pōz'ing, *p.a.* Impressive in appearance; commanding; stately; majestic. **imposition,** im-pō-zi'shun, *n.* Act of imposing; act of laying on hands in the ceremony or ordination; that which is imposed; a tax, toll, duty, &c.; burden; imposture.

impossible, im-pos'i-bl, *a.* Not possible; that cannot be or be done. **impossibility,** im-pos'i-bil''i-ti, *n.* State or character of being impossible; that which cannot be, or cannot be done.

impost, im'pōst, *n.* That which is imposed by authority; tax or duty; point where an arch æsts on a wall or common.

impostor, im-pos'tẻr, *n.* One who imposes on others; a deceiver under a false character. **imposture,** im-pos'tūr, *n.* Imposition; fraud; deception.

impotent, im'pō-tent, *a.* Entirely wanting vigor of body or mind; feeble; destitute of the power of begetting children. **impotently,** im'pō-tent-li, *adv.* In an impotent manner; feebly; weakly. **impotence, impotency,** im'pō-tens, im'pō-ten-si, *n.* State or quality of being impotent; want of ability or power; want of the power of procreation.

impound, im-pound', *vt.* To confine in a pound or close pen; to confine; to take possession of for use when necessary.

impoverish, im-pov'ẻr-ish, *vt.* To make poor; to reduce to indigence; to exhaust the strength or fertility of, as of soil. **impoverishment,** im-pov'ẻr-ish-ment, *n.* Act of impoverishing.

impracticable, im-prak'ti-ka-bl, *a.* Not practicable; unmanageable; stubborn; incapable of being passed. **impracticability,** im-prak'ti-ka-bil"i-ti, *n.* State or quality of being impracticable.

imprecate, im'prē-kāt, *vt.* (imprecating, imprecated). To invoke, as a curse or some evil. **imprecation,** im-prē-kā'-shon, *n.* Act of imprecating; prayer that a curse or calamity may fall on anyone; malediction.

impregnable, im-preg'na-bl, *a.* That cannot be taken by force; able to resist attack; invincible, as affection. **impregnability,** im-preg'na-bil"i-ti, *n.* State of being impregnable.

impregnate, im-preg'nāt, *vt.* To make pregnant; to imbue; to saturate. **impregnation,** im-preg-nā'shun, *n.* The act of impregnating; fecundation; infusion.

impress, im-pres', *vt.* To press into; to imprint; to stamp on the mind; to inculcate; to compel to enter into public service, as seamen; to take for public use.—*n.* im'pres. That which is impressed; mark made by pressure; impression; character; act of compelling to enter into public service. **impressible,** im-pres'i-bl, *a.* That may be impressed; susceptible of impression; readily or easily affected.

impression, im-presh'un, *n.* Act of impressing; that which is impressed; mark; effect produced on the mind; an indistinct notion; idea; copy taken by pressure from type, &c.; edition; copies forming one issue of a book. **impressionable,** im-presh'un-a-bl, *a.* Susceptible of impression. **impressionism,** im-presh'un-izm, *n.* Views or practice of an impressionist. **impressionist,** im-presh'un-ist, *n.* One who lays stress on impressions; an artist who depicts scenes by their most striking characteristics as they first impress the spectator.

impressive, im-pres'iv, *a.* Making an impression; solemn; awe-inspiring. **impressively,** im-pres'iv-li, *adv.* In an impressive manner.

imprimatur, im'pri-mā"tẻr, *n.* A license to print a book, &c.; mark of approval in general.

imprint, im-print', *vt.* To impress; to stamp; to fix on the mind or memory. —*n.* im'print. The name of the printer or publisher of a book, &c., with place and time of publication.

imprison, im-priz'n, *vt.* To put into a prison; to confine; to deprive of liberty. **imprisonment,** im-priz'n-ment, *n.* Act of imprisoning; state of being imprisoned.

improbable, im-prob'a-bl, *a.* Not probable; not likely to be true; unlikely. **improbably,** im-prob'a-bli, *adv.* In an improbable manner; without probability. **improbability,** im-prob'a-bil"i-ti, *n.* Quality of being 'mprobable; unlikelihood.

impromptu, im-promp'tū, *n.* A saying, poem, &c., made off-hand; an extemporaneous composition.—*a.* Off-hand; extempore.—*adv.* Offhand.

improper, im-prop'ẻr, *a.* Not proper; unfit; not decent; erroneous; wrong. **improperly,** im-prop'ẻr-li, *adv.* In an improper manner; unsuitably; erroneously.

impropriety, im-prō-pri'e-ty, *n.* Quality of being improper; that "hich is improper; an unsuitable act, expression, &c.

improve, im-pröv', *vt.* (improving, improved). To better; to ameliorate; to mend; to rectify; to use to good purpose; to apply to practical purposes.—*vi.* To grow better. **improvement,** im-pröv'ment, *n.* Act of improving; state of being improved; a change for the better; that which improves; a beneficial or valuable addition or alteration.

improvidence, im-prov'i-dens, *n.* Want of providence or foresight; wastefulness. **improvident,** im-prov'i-dent, *a.* Not provident; wanting foresight or forethought; careless.

improvise, im'prō-vis, *vt.* To form on the spur of the moment; to compose and recite, &c., without previous preparation.

imprudent, im-prö'dent, *a.* Not prudent; indiscreet; heedless; rash. **imprudently,** im-prö'dent-li, *adv.* In an imprudent manner; indiscreetly. **imprudence,** im-prö'dens, *n.* Want of prudence; indiscretion; a rash act.

impudent, im'pū-dent, *a.* Offensively forward in behavior; bold-faced; impertinent. **impudently,** im'pū-dent-li, *adv.* In an impudent manner; impertinently. **impudence,** im'pū-dens, *n.* The quality of being impudent; impudent language or behavior; effrontery; impertinence.

impugn, im-pūn', *vt.* To attack by words or arguments; to contradict; to call in question.

impulse, im'puls, *n.* Force communicated instantaneously; effect of a sudden communication of motion; influence acting on the mind; motive; sudden determination. **impulsion,** im-pul'shun, *n.* Act of impelling; impelling force; impulse. **impulsive,** im-pul'siv, *a.* Having the power of impelling; actuated or governed by impulse. **impulsively,** im-pul'siv-li, *adv.* In an impulsive manner; by impulse.

impunity, im-pū'ni-ti, *n.* Freedom from punishment or injury, loss, &c.

impure, im-pūr', *a.* Not pure; mixed with extraneous substance; obscene; unchaste; lewd; defiled by sin or guilt; unholy. **impurity**, im-pūr'i-ti, *n.* State or quality of being impure; foul matter; obscenity.

impute, im-pūt', *vt.* (imputing, imputed). To set to the account of; to ascribe. **imputation**, im-pū-tā'shon, *n.* The act of imputing; attribution; censure; reproach.

in, in, *prep.* Within, inside of; surrounded by; indicating presence or situation within limits, whether of place, time, circumstances, &c.—*adv.* In or within some place, state, circumstances, &c.; not out.

inability, in-a-bil'i-ti, *n.* Want of ability; want of adequate means.

inaccessible, in-ak-ses'i-bl, *a.* Not accessible; not to be obtained; forbidden access.

inaccurate, in-ak'ū-rit, *a.* Not accurate; not exact or correct; erroneous. **inaccurately**, in-ak'kū-rāt-li, *adv.* In an inaccurate manner; incorrectly; erroneously. **inaccuracy**, in-ak'ū-ra-si, *n.* The state of being inaccurate; an inaccurate statement; a mistake in a statement; an error.

inactive, in-ak'tiv, *a.* Not active; not engaged in action; idle; indolent. **inactivity**, in-ak-tiv'i-ti, *n.* State or quality of being inactive. **inaction**, in-ak'-shun, *n.* Want of action; forbearance of labor; idleness; rest.

inadequate, in-ad'ē-kwit, *a.* Not equal to the purpose; disproportionate; defective. **inadequately**, in-ad'ē-kwāt-li, *adv.* In an inadequate manner; not sufficiently. **inadequacy**, in-ad'ē-kwā-si. *n.* Quality of being inadequate; insufficiency.

inadmissible, in'ad-mis''i-bl, *a.* Not admissible; not proper to be admitted, allowed, or received. **inadmissibility**, in-ad-mis'i-bil''i-ti, *n.* Quality of being inadmissible.

inadvertent, in'ad-vėr''tent, *a.* Not paying strict attention; heedless; unwary; negligent. **inadvertently**, in-ad-vėrt'ent-li, *adv.* In an inadvertent manner; from want of attention. **inadvertence, inadvertency**, in'ad-vėr''-tens, in'ad-vėr''ten-si, *n.* Quality of being inadvertent; any oversight or fault which proceeds from negligence or want of attention.

inalienable, in-āl'yen-a-bl, *a.* Incapable of being alienated or transferred to another.

inalterable, in-gl'tėr-a-bl, *a.* Unalterable.

inamorata, in-ä'mō-rä''tä, *n.* A female in love; a mistress.

inane, in-ān', *a.* Empty; void; void of sense or intelligence.—*n.* Infinite void space.

inanimate, in-an'i-māt, *a.* Not animate; destitute of animation or life; inactive; dull; spiritless.

inanity, in-an'i-ti, *n.* The quality of being inane; vacuity; mental vacuity; silliness. **inanition**, in-a-ni'shon, *n.* Vacuity; exhaustion from want of food.

inappropriate, in-ap-prō'pri-āt, *a.* Not appropriate; unsuited; not proper.

inapt, in-apt'. *a.* Unapt; unsuitable; unfit. **inaptitude**, in-apt'i-tūd, *n.* Want of aptitude; unsuitableness.

inarticulate, in-är-tik'ū-lāt, *a.* Not articulate; not jointed or articulated; not uttered distinctly. **inarticulately**, in-är-tik'ū-lāt-li, *adv.* Not with distinct syllables; indistinctly.

inasmuch, in-az-much', *adv.* Seeing; seeing that; this. being the fact.

inattention, in'a-ten''shun, *n.* Want of attention; heedlessness; neglect. **inattentive**, in'a-ten''tiv, *a.* Not attentive; regardless; thoughtless. **inattentively**, in'a-ten''tiv-li, *adv.* Without attention; heedlessly.

inaudible, in-a'di-bl, *a.* Not audible; that cannot be heard. **inaudibly**, in-a'-di-bli. *adv.* In a manner not to be heard. **inaudibility**, in-a'di-bil''i-ti, *n.* State or quality of being inaudible.

inaugurate, in-a'gū-rāt, *vt.* To induct into an office with suitable ceremonies; to perform initiatory ceremonies in connection with. **inauguration**, in-a'gū-rā''shun, *n.* Act of inaugurating; ceremonies connected with such an act. **inaugural**, in-a'gū-ral, *a.* Pertaining to inauguration.

inauspicious, in'as-pish''us, *a.* Not auspicious; ill-omened; unfavorable.

inboard, in'bōrd, *a.* Within a ship or other vessel.—*adv.* On board of a vessel.

inborn, in'born, *a.* Born in; innate; implanted by nature; natural; inherent.

inbred, in'bred, *a.* Bred within; innate.

Inca, in'ka, *n.* A king or prince of Peru before its conquest by the Spaniards.

incalculable, in-kal'kū-la-bl, *a.* Not calculable; very great. **incalculably**, in-kal'kū-la-bli, *adv.* In a degree beyond calculation.

incandescent, in-kan-des'ent, *a.* White or glowing with heat. **incandescent light**, a form of gas light; a form of electric light given forth from a filament of carbon inclosed in an airless glass globe. **incandescence**, in-kan-des'ens, *n.* Condition of being incandescent.

incantation, in-kan-tā'shon, *n.* The act of using certain words and ceremonies to raise spirits, &c.; the form of words so used; a magical charm or ceremony.

incapable, in-kā'pa-bl, *a.* Not capable; possessing inadequate power or capacity; not susceptible; incompetent; unqualified or disqualified.—*n.* One physically or mentally weak.

incapacity, in'ka-pas''i-ti, *n.* Want of capacity; incompetency; disqualification. **incapacitate**, in'ka-pas''i-tāt, *vt.* To render incapable; to deprive of competent power or ability; to disqualify.

incarcerate, in-kär'sėr-āt, *vt.* To imprison; to shut up or inclose. **incarceration**, in-kär'sėr-ā''shun, *n.* Act of incarcerating; imprisonment.

incarnadine, in-kär'na-din, *vt.* To tinge with the color of flesh; to dye red.

incarnate, in-kär'nāt, *vt.* To clothe with flesh; to embody in flesh.—*a.* Invest with flesh; embodied in flesh. **incarnation**, in'kär-nā''shun, *n.* Act of taking on a human body and the nature of man; the state of being incarnated; a vivid exemplification in person or act.

incautious, in-ka'shus. *a.* Not cautious; unwary; heedless; imprudent. **incautiously**, in-ka'shus-li, *adv.* In an incautious manner; unwarily; heedlessly.

incendiary, in-sen''dē-er'i, *n.* A person who maliciously sets fire to property; one guilty of arson; one who inflames factions; a firebrand.—*a.* Relating to arson; tending to excite sedition or quarrels. **incendiarism**, in-sen'di-a-rizm, *n.* Act or practice of maliciously setting fire to buildings

incense, in'sens, *n.* Aromatic substance burned in religious rites; odors of spices and gums, burned in religious rites; flattery or agreeable homage.—*vt.* (incensing, incensed). To perfume with incense.

incense, in-sens', *vt.* (incensing, incensed). To inflame to violent anger; to exasperate.

incentive, in-sen'tiv, *a.* Inciting; encouraging.—*n.* That which incites; that which prompts to good or ill; motive; spur.

inception, in-sep'shun, *n.* The act of beginning; first or initial state.

inceptive, in-sep'tiv. *a.* Pertaining to inception; beginning; applied to a verb which expresses the beginning of an action.—*n.* An inceptive verb.

incessant, in-ses'ant. *a.* Unceasing; unintermitted; continual; constant. **incessantly**, in-ses'ant-li, *adv.* Without ceasing; continually.

incest, in'sest, *n* Sexual commerce between near blood relations. **incestuous**, in-ses'tū-us, *a.* Guilty of incest; involving the crime of incest.

inch, inch, *n.* The twelfth part of a foot in length; a small quantity or degree.—*vt.* To drive or force by inches.

inchmeal, inch'mēl, *adv.* By inches; by little and little.

inchoate, in'kō-it, *a.* Recently begun; incipient; rudimentary.

incidence, in'si-dens, *n.* A falling or occurring; manner or direction of falling.

incident, in'si-dent, *a.* Falling or striking; happening; liable to happen; appertaining to or following another thing.—*n.* That which happens; event; an appertaining fact. **incidental**, in'si-den''tal, *a.* Casual; occasional; appertaining and subsidiary. **incidentally**, in'si-den''tal-i, *adv.* Casually; beside the main design.

incinerate, in-sin'ėr-āt, *vt.* To burn to ashes.

incipient, in-sip'i-ent, *a.* Beginning.

incise, in-sīz', *vt.* (incising, incised). To cut in or into; to carve; to engrave. **incision**, in-sizh'un, *n.* Act of cutting into; cut; gash; sharpness; trenchancy. **incisive**, in-sī'siv, *a.* Having the quality of cutting into anything; sharply and clearly expressive; trenchant.

incisor, in-sī'zėr, *n.* A front tooth which cuts or separates.

incite, in-sīt', *vt.* (inciting, incited). To move to action by impulse or influence; to instigate; to encourage. **incitement**,

in-sīt'ment, *n.* Act of inciting; that which incites; motive; impulse.

inclement, in-klem'ent, *a.* Not clement; harsh; stormy; rigorously cold. **inclemently**, in-klem'ent-li, *adv.* In an inclement manner. **inclemency**, in-klem'en-si, *n.* Want of clemency; harshness; severity of weather.

incline, in-klīn', *vi.* (inclining, inclined). To deviate from a direction regarded as normal; to slope; to be disposed; to have some wish or desire.—*vt.* To cause to lean or bend towards or away from; to give a leaning to; to dispose.—*n.* An ascent or descent; a slope. **inclined**, in-klīnd', *p.a.* Having a leaning or inclination; disposed. **inclination**, in-kli-nā'shun, *n.* The act of inclining; deviation from a normal direction; a leaning of the mind or will; tendency, bent; bias; predilection; liking.

inclose, in-klōz', *vt.* (inclosing, inclosed). To shut up or confine on all sides; to environ; to cover with a wrapper or envelope.

inclosure, in-klō'zhėr, *n.* Act of inclosing; what is inclosed; a space inclosed or fenced; something inclosed with a letter, &c.

include, in-klōd', *vt.* (including, included). To hold or contain; to comprise; to comprehend. **inclusion**, in-klō'zhun, *n.* Act of including. **inclusive**, in-klō'siv, *a.* Inclosing; comprehended in the number or sum; comprehending the stated limit. **inclusively**, in-klō'siv-li, *adv.* In an inclusive manner; so as to include something mentioned.

incognito, in-kog'ni-tō, *pred.a.* or *adv.* In disguise.—*n.* (fem. being **incognita**). One passing under an assumed name; assumption of a feigned character.

incoherent, in''kō-hēr'ent, *a.* Not coherent; wanting rational connection, as ideas, language, &c.; rambling and unintelligible. **incoherently**, in''kō-hēr''ent-li, *adv.* In an incoherent manner. **incoherence, incoherency**, in''kō-hēr''ens, in''kō-hēr'en-si, *n.* Quality of being incoherent; want of connection or agreement.

income, in'kum, *n.* Receipts or emoluments regularly coming in from property or employment; annual receipts; revenue.

income tax, in'kum taks, *n.* A tax levied on incomes according to their amount.

incoming, in'kum''ing, *p.a.* Coming in.

incommensurable, in'ko-mens''ra-bl, *a.* Not commensurable; having no common measure. **incommensurably**, in'ko-mens''ra-bli, *adv.* So at not to admit of a common measure. **incommensurability**, in'ko-mens''ra-bil''i-ti, *n.* Quality or state of being incommensurable. **incommensurate**, in'ko-mens''ūr-it, *a.* Not commensurate; incommensurable; inadequate; insufficient.

incommode, in'ko-mōd'', *vt.* (incommoding, incommoded). To give trouble;

to inconvenience; to embarrass. **incom-modious**, in'ko-mō"di-us, *a*. Not commodious; inconvenient.

incommunicable, in'ko-mū'ni-ka-bl, *a*. Not communicable; not to be communicated. **incommunicative**, in'-ko-mū'ni-kāt-iv, *a*. Not communicative; not inclined to impart information.

incomparable, in-kom'pa-ra-bl, *a*. Not comparable; that admits of no comparison with others; matchless. **incomparably**, in-kom'pa-ra-bli, *adv*. Beyond comparison.

incompatible, in'kom-pat"i-bl, *a*. Not compatible; inconsistent; irreconcilably different; that cannot be made to accord. **incompatibility**, in'kom-pat"i-bil"i-ti, *n*. State or quality of being incompatible; inconsistency; disposition or temper entirely out of harmony.

incompetent, in-kom'pet-ent, *a*. Not competent;· incapable; wanting legal qualifications; not admissible. **incompetence, incompetency**, in-kom'pet-ens, in-kom'pet-en-si, *n*. State or quality of being incompetent; want of suitable faculties, adequate means, or proper qualifications.

incomplete, in'kom-plēt", *a*. Not complete; imperfect; defective.

incomprehensible, in-kom'prē-hen"si-bl, *a*. Not comprehensible; beyond the reach of the human intellect. **incomprehensibility**, in-kom'prē-hen'si-bil"-i-ti, *n*. Quality of being incomprehensible.

inconceivable, in'kon-sē"va-bl, *a*. Incapable of being conceived or thought of. **inconceivably**, in'kon-sē"va-bli, *adv*. In a manner beyond conception.

inconclusive, in-kon-klō'siv, *a*. Not conclusive; not settling a point in debate. **inconclusively**, in-kon-klō'siv-li, *adv*. In an inconclusive manner.

incongruent, in-kon'grū-ent, *a*. Incongruous.

incongruous, in-kon'gru-us, *a*. Not congruous; not such as to mingle well or unite in harmony; inconsistent. **incongruity**, in'kon-grū"i-ti, *n*. Want of congruity; inconsistency; absurdity.

inconsequent, in-kon'se-kwent, *a*. Not consequent; not having due relevance; not following from the logical premises. **inconsequential**, in-kon'se-kwen"shal, *a*. Not consequential; not of importance.

inconsiderable, in'kon-sid"ėr-a-bl, *a*. Not considerable; unimportant; insignificant. **inconsiderably**, in'kon-sid"ėr-a-bli, *adv*. In an inconsiderable degree; very little.

inconsiderate, in'kon-sid"ėr-it, *a*. Not considerate; hasty; thoughtless; injudicious. **inconsiderately**, in'kon-sid"ėr-it-li, *adv*. Heedlessly; imprudently.

inconsistent, in'kon-sis"tent, *a*. Not consistent; incompatible; discrepant; not exhibiting consistent sentiments or conduct. **inconsistence, inconsistency**, in'kon-sis"tens, in'kon-sis"ten-si, *n*. The condition or quality of being inconsistent; opposition or disagreement of particulars; self-contradiction; incongruity; discrepancy. **inconsistently**, in'-

kon-sis'tent-li, *adv*. Incongruously; with self-contradiction.

inconsolable, in'kon-sō'la-bl, *a*. Not to be consoled; grieved beyond consolation.

inconspicuous, in'kon-spik"ū-us, *a*. Not conspicuous; unobstrusive.

inconstant, in-kon'stant, *a*. Not constant; subject to change of opinion or purpose; not firm in resolution; fickle. **inconstancy**, in-kon'stan-si, *n*. The quality of being inconstant; instability of temper or affection; fickleness.

incontestable, in'kon-tes"ta-bl, *a*. Not contestable; not to be disputed; unquestionable.

incontinent, in-kont'in-ent, *a*. Not continent; not restraining the passions or appetites; unchaste; unable to restrain discharges. **incontinence, incontinency**, in-kont'in-ens, in-kont'in-en-si, *n*. State or quality of being incontinent; indulgence of lust; inability of organs to restrain discharges.

incontrovertible, in-kon'trō-vėrt"i-bl, *a*. Not controvertible; too clear to admit of dispute.

inconvenient, in'kon-vēn"yent, *a*. Not convenient; wanting due facilities; causing embarrassment; inopportune. **inconvenience**, in'kon-vēn"yens, *n*. The quality of being inconvenient; annoyance; molestation; trouble; disadvantage. —*vt*. To put to inconvenience; to trouble.

incorporate, in-kor'pō-rāt, *vt*. To form into one body; to unite; to blend; to associate with another whole, as with a government; to form into a legal body or corporation.—*vi*. To unite; to grow into or coalesce.—*a*. Incorporated; united in one body. **incorporation**, in-kor'pō-rā"shun, *n*. Act of incorporating; state of being incorporated; union of different things; a body of individuals authorized to act as a single person.

incorrect, in'ko-rekt", *a*. Not correct; inaccurate; erroneous; faulty; untrue. **incorrectly**, in'ko-rek"li, *adv*. Not in accordance with fact; inaccurately.

incorrigible, in-kor'i-ji-bl, *a*. That cannot be corrected; bad beyond correction or reform.

incorruptible, in'ko-rup"ti-bl, *a*. Not corruptible; that cannot corrupt or decay; inflexibly just and upright.

increase, in-krēs', *vi*. (increasing, increased). To become greater; to augment; to advance in any quality, good or bad; to multiply by the production of young.—*vt*. To make greater or larger; to add to.—*n*. in'krēs. A growing larger in size, quantity, &c.; augmentation; addition; increment; profit; interest; offspring. **increasingly**, in-krē'sing-li, *adv*. In the way of increasing; by continual increase.

incredibility, in-kred'i-bil"it-i, *n*. Quality of being incredible; that which is incredible.

incredible, in-kred'i-bl, *a*. Not credible; too improbable to admit of belief. **incredibly**, in-kred'i-bli, *adv*. In a manner to preclude belief.

incredulous, in-krej'ū-lus, *a*. Not credulous; refusing or withholding belief.

incredulity, in'kre-dū"lit-i, *n.* Quality of being incredulous; skepticism.

increment, in'kre-ment, *n.* Act or process of increasing; increase; increase in the value of real property from adventitious causes.

incriminate, in-krim'i-nāt, *vt.* To bring an accusation against; to charge with a crime or fault.

incrust, in-krust', *vt.* To cover with a crust or hard coat; to form a crust on.

incrustation, in-krus-tā'shun, *n.* Act of incrusting; a crust or hard coat on the surface of a body; a covering or inlaying of marble or mosaic, &c.

incubate, in'kū-bāt, *vi.* To brood or sit on eggs for hatching. **incubation,** in'kū-bā"shun, *n.* The act of incubating; the maturation of a contagious poison in the animal system. **incubator,** in'kū-bāt-ėr, *n.* One who or that which incubates; an apparatus for hatching eggs by artificial heat.

incubus, in'kū-bus. *n.*; pl **-buses** or **bi.** A name of nightmare; something that weighs heavily on a person; burden or incumbrance; dead weight.

inculcate, in-kul'kāt, *vt.* To press or urge forcibly and repeatedly; to teach. **inculcation,** in-kul-kā'shun, *n.* The act of inculcating.

inculpate, in-kul'pāt, *vt.* To show to be in fault; to impute guilt to; to incriminate.

incult, in-kult', *a,* Uncultivated.

incumbent, in-kum'bent, *a.* Lying on; resting on a person, as duty or obligation.—*n.* One in possession of an ecclesiastical benefice or other office. **incumbency,** in-kum'ben-si, *n.* State of being incumbent; state of holding a benefice or office.

incur, in-kėr', *vt.* (incurring, incurred). To expose one's self to; to become liable to; to bring on or contract, as expense.

incurable, in-kūr'a-bl, *a.* That cannot be cured; not admitting remedy; irremediable.—*n.* A person diseased beyond cure.

incursion, in-kėr'zhun, *n.* An entering into a territory with hostile intention; inroad.

indebted, in-det'ed, *a.* Being in debt; obliged by something received. **indebtedness,** in-det'ed-nes, *n.* State of being indebted; amount of debt owed.

indecent, in-dēs'ent, *a.* Not decent; unseemly; immodest; obscene; filthy. **indecency,** in-dēs'en-si, *n.* The quality of being indecent; what is indecent in language, actions, &c.; indecorum; immodesty.

indecision, in-dē-sizh'un, *n.* Want of decision; irresolution; hesitation. **indecisive,** in-dē-sī'siv, *a.* Not decisive; wavering; vacillating.

indeed, in-dēd', *adv.* In reality; in fact; really; truly.

indefatigable, in-dē-fat'i-ga-bl, *a.* That cannot be wearied; untiring; unremitting.

indefensible, in-dē-fen'si-bl, *a.* Not defensible; untenable.

indefinable, in-dē-fī'na-bl, *a.* Incapable

of being defined; not to be clearly explained.

indefinite, in-def'i-nit, *a.* Not definite; not limited; not precise; uncertain; vague. **indefinitely,** in-def'i-nit-li, *adv.* In an indefinite manner; not precisely.

indelible, in-del'i-bl, *a.* Not to be deleted or blotted out; that cannot be obliterated. **indelibly,** in-del'i-bli. *adv.* In an indelible manner; too deeply imprinted to be effaced.

indelicacy, in-del'i-ka-si, *n.* Condition or quality of being indelicate. **indelicate,** in-del'i-kit, *a.* Wanting delicacy; offensive to modesty or nice sense of propriety; somewhat immodest.

indemnify, in-dem'ni-fī, *vt.* To make safe from loss or harm; to reimburse or compensate. **indemnity,** in-dem'ni-ti, *n.* Security given against loss, damage, or punishment; compensation for loss or injury sustained. **indemnification,** in-dem'ni-fi-kā"shun, *n.* Act of indemnifying; reparation; reimbursement of loss or damage.

indent, in-dent', *vt.* To notch; to cut into points or inequalities; to bind by indenture.—*n.* A cut or notch; an indentation. **indentation,** in-den-tā'shun, *n.* Act of indenting; a cut in the margin of something; an angular depression in any border. **indented,** in-den'ted, *p.a.* Notched; bound by indenture. **indenture,** in-den'chur, *n.* That which is indented; a deed under seal between two or more parties; each having a duplicate.—*vt.* To indent; to bind by indenture.

independent, in'dē-pen"dent, *a.* Not dependent; not subject to control; moderately wealthy; not subject to bias or influence; free; bold; separate from; irrespective.—*n.* One who is independent; (with *cap.*) one who maintains that every congregation is an independent church. **independently,** in'dē-pen"dent-li, *adv.* In an independent manner; leaving out of consideration; without bias or influence. **independence** in'dē-pen"dens, *n.* State of being independent; complete exemption from control; self-reliance; political freedom.

indescribable, in'dē-skrī"ba-bl, *a.* That cannot be described.

indestructible, in'dē-struk"ti-bl, *a.* That cannot be destroyed; imperishable.

indeterminable, in'dē-tėrm"i-na-bl, *a.* That cannot be determined, ascertained, or fixed.

indeterminate, in'dē-tėrm"i-nit, *a.* Not determinate; not settled or fixed; uncertain.

index, in'deks, *n.*; pl. **indexes** or **indices,** in'dek-sez, in'di-sēz. Something that points out; the hand ☞ used by printers, &c.; a table of contents; list of books disapproved of by R. Catholic authorities; the forefinger; the figure denoting to what power any mathematical quantity is involved.—*vt.* To provide with an index; to place in an index. **indexer,** in'deks-ėr, *n.* One who makes an index.

Indian, in'dē-an, *a.* Pertaining to India, or to the Indies, East or West; pertaining to the aborigines of America. A native of the Indies; an aboriginal native of America.

indicate, in″di-kāt′, *vt.* To point out; to show; to intimate; to suggest. **indication**, in′di-kā″shun, *n.* Act of indicating; what points out; mark; token; sign. **indicative**, in-dik′a-tiv, *a.* That serves to point out; serving as an indication; designating a mood of the verb that declares directly or asks questions. —*n.* The indicative mood. **indicator**, in″di-kāt′ėr, *n.* One who or that which indicates; a recording instrument of various kinds.

indict, in-dīt′, *vt.* To charge with a crime or misdemeanor in due form of law.

indictment, in-dīt′ment, *n.* The act of indicting; a formal charge; a written accusation of a crime or a misdemeanor.

indifference, in-dif′ėr-ens, *n.* The state or quality of being indifferent; impartiality; unconcern; apathy; mediocrity. **indifferent**, in-dif′ėr-ent, *a.* Impartial; unconcerned; apathetic; immaterial or of little moment; middling; tolerable. **indifferently**, in-dif′ėr-ent-li, *adv.* Impartially; without concern; tolerably.

indigenous, in-dij′en-us, *a.* Native, as persons; not foreign or exotic, as plants.

indigent, in′di-jent, *a.* Destitute of means of comfortable subsistence; needy.

indigested, in-dī-jes′ted, *a.* Not digested; not reduced to due form; crude. **indigestible**, in-di-jes′ti-bl, *a.* Not digestible; digested with difficulty. **indigestion**, in-di-jes′chun, *n.* Incapability of or difficulty in digesting; dyspepsia.

indignant, in-dig′nant, *a.* Affected with indignation; feeling the mingled emotions of wrath and scorn or contempt. **indignantly**, in-dig′nant-li, *adv.* In an indignant manner; with indignation. **indignation**, in-dig-nā′shun, *n.* A feeling of displeasure at what is unworthy or base; anger, mingled with contempt, disgust, or abhorrence; violent displeasure.

indignity, in-dig′nit-i, *n.* An insult; an affront; an outrage.

indigo, in′di-gō, *n.* A blue vegetable dye, from India and other places; the leguminous plant that produces the dye.

indirect, in′di-rekt″, *a.* Not direct; circuitous; not tending directly to a purpose or end; not straightforward; not resulting directly. **indirectly**, in′di-rekt″li, *adv.* In an indirect manner; not by direct means.

indiscreet, in′dis-krēt″, *a.* Not discreet; injudicious; inconsiderate. **indiscreetly**, in′dis-krēt″li, *adv.* In an indiscreet manner. **indiscretion**, in′dis-kresh″un, *n.* The condition or quality of being indiscreet; imprudence; an indiscreet act.

indiscriminate, in′dis-krim″i-nit, *a.* Without discrimination; confused.

indispensable, in-dis-pens′a-bl, *a.* Not to be dispensed with; necessary or requisite.

indispose, in′dis-pōz″, *vt.* To disincline; to disqualify; to affect with indisposition. **indisposed**, in′dis-pōzd″, *p.a.* Not disposed; disinclined; averse; somewhat ill. **indisposition**, in-dis′pō-zish″-

un, *n.* The state of being indisposed; slight ailment.

indisputable, in′dispūt″a-bl, *a.* Not to be disputed; unquestionable; certain.

indissoluble, in′dis-ol″yū-bl, *a.* Not capable of being dissolved; perpetually binding or obligatory; not to be broken.

indistinct, in′dis-tingkt″, *a.* Not distinct; faint; confused; imperfect or dim. **indistinctly**, in′dis-tingk″tli, *adv.* In an indistinct manner; dimly or obscurely. **indistinguishable**, in′dis-ting″gwish-a-bl, *a.* Incapable of being distinguished.

indite, in-dīt′, *vt.* (inditing, indited). To compose or write; to direct or dictate. **inditement**, in-dīt′ment, *n.* Act of inditing.

individual, in′di-vij″wal, *a.* Subsisting as one indivisible entity; pertaining to one only; peculiar to a single person or thing.—*n.* A being or thing forming one of its kind; a person. **individualism**, in′di-vij″wa-lizm, *n.* The quality of being individual; self-interest; a system or condition in which each individual works for his own ends. **individuality**, in′-di-vij′ū-al″it-i, *n.* Quality or condition of being individual; separate existence; the sum of the traits peculiar to an individual. **individualize**, in′di-vij″wa-liz, *vt.* To single out; to distinguish by distinctive characters. **individually**, in′di-vij″wal-i, *adv.* In an individual manner; separately.

indivisible, in′di-viz″i-bl, *a.* Not divisible; not separable into parts.—*n.* An elementary part or particle. **indivisibility**, in′di-viz′i-bil″it-i, *n.* State or quality of being indivisible.

indoctrinate, in-dok″tri-nāt, *vt.* To imbue with any doctrine; to teach; to instruct.

Indo-European, **Indo-Germanic**, in′dō-yūr″ō-pē″an, in′do-jėr-man″ik, *a.* and *n.* The root language of most of the people of Europe and some of Asia.

indolent, in′dō-lent, *a.* Habitually idle or lazy; slothful; idle; causing little or no pain. **indolence**, in′dō-lens, *n.* Habitual love of ease; laziness; idleness.

indomitable, in-dom′it-a-bl, *a.* Not to be tamed or subdued; irrepressible.

indoor, in′dōr, *a.* Being within doors; being within the house. **indoors**, in′-dōrz, *adv.* Within doors; inside a house.

indorse, &c. *See* endorse, &c.

indubitable, in-dū′bit-a-bl, *a.* Not to be doubted; too plain to admit of doubt; evident.

induce, in-dūs′, *vt.* (inducing, induced). To lead by persuasion or argument; to prevail on; to actuate; to produce or cause. **inducement**, in-dū′sment, *n.* Act of inducing; that which induces; motive; incentive.

induct, in-dukt′, *vt.* To lead or bring into; to put in possession of an ecclesiastical living or office, with customary ceremonies.

induction, in-duk′shun, *n.* The act of inducting; introduction of a clergyman into a benefice, &c.; a prologue or prelude; method of reasoning from particulars to generals; the conclusion thus arrived at; process by which one body, having electrical or magnetic properties, causes like properties in another body without direct contact. **inductive**, in-duk'tiv, a. Relating to induction; proceeding by induction; employed in drawing conclusions by induction.

indue, in-dū', vt. (induing, indued). To put on; to invest; to supply with.

indulge, in-dulj', vt. (indulging, indulged). To give free course to; to gratify by compliance; to humor to excess.—vi. To indulge one's self; to practice indulgence. **indulgence**, in-dul'jens, n. The act or practice of indulging; a favor; intemperance; gratification of desire; tolerance; remission of the penance attached to certain sins. **indulgent**, in-dul'jent, a. Prone to indulge; disposed to leniency or forbearance. **indulgently**, in-dul'jent-li, adv. In an indulgent manner.

industrial, in-dus'trē-al, a. Pertaining to industry, or to the products of industry, art or manufacture.

industry, in'dus-trē, n. Habitual diligence; steady attention to business; the industrial arts generally, or any one of them; manufacture; trade. **industrious**, in-dus'trē-us, a. Given to or characterized by industry; diligent; active. **industriously**, in-dus'trē-us-li, adv. In an industrious manner; diligently.

inebriate, in-ē'brē-āt, vt. To make drunk; to intoxicate.—n. An habitual drunkard. **inebriation**, ine'brē-ā"shun, n. Act of inebriating; state of being inebriated.

ineffable, in-ef'a-bl, a. Incapable of being expressed in words; indescribable. **ineffably**, in-ef'a-bli, adv. In an ineffable manner; unutterably; unspeakably.

ineffectual, in'e-fek"chwal, a. Not effectual; inefficient; impotent; fruitless. **inefficacy**, in-ef'i-ka-si, n. Want of efficacy; failure of effect.

inefficient, in'e-fish"ent, a. Not efficient; inefficacious; effecting nothing. **inefficiency**, in'e-fish"en-si, n. Condition or quality of being efficient; inefficacy.

ineligible, in-el'i-ji-bl, a. Not capable of being elected; not worthy to be chosen. **ineligibility**, in-el'i-ji-bil"it-i, n. State or quality of being ineligible.

inept, in-ept', a. Unsuitable; improper; foolish; silly; nonsensical. **ineptitude**, in-ep'ti-tūd', n. Condition or quality of being inept; unfitness; silliness.

inequality, in'i-kwol"it-i, n. Condition of being unequal; want of equality; an elevation or depression in a surface; diversity.

inert, in-ėrt', a. Destitute of the power of moving itself, or of active resistance to motion impressed; lifeless; sluggish; inactive. **inertia**, in-ėr'sha, n. Passiveness; inactivity; the property of matter by which it tends to retain its state of ₁est or of uniform rectilinear motion.

inestimable, in-es'ti-ma-bl, a. That cannot be estimated; invaluable; priceless. **inestimably**, in-es'ti-ma-bli, adv. In a manner not to be estimated.

inevitable, in-ev'it-a-bl, a. Not to be avoided; unavoidable; certain to befall. **inevitably**, in-ev'it-a-bli, adv. Unavoidably.

inexcusable, in'ek-skū"za-bl, a. Not to be excused; unjustifiable; indefensible. **inexcusably**, in'ek-skū"za-bli, adv. In an inexcusable manner; beyond excuse.

inexhaustible, in'eg-za"sti-bl, a. Incapable of being exhausted; unfailing.

inexorable, in-eks'ra-bl, a. Not to be persuaded by entreaty or prayer; unbending; unrelenting; implacable. **inexorably**, in-eks'ra-bli, adv. In an inexorable manner.

inexpensive, in'ek-spen"siv, a. Not expensive.

inexperience, in'ek-spir"ē-ens, n. Want of experience. **inexperienced**, in'ik-spir"ē-enst, a. Not having experience; unskilled.

inexpiable, in-ek'spē-a-bl, a. That cannot be expiated; that admits of no atonement.

inexplicable, in'ek-splik"a-bl, a. That cannot be explained or interpreted; unaccountable; mysterious. **inexplicably**, in'ek-splik-a-bli, adv. In an inexplicable manner; unaccountably.

inextinguishable, in'ek-sting"gwish-a-bl, a. That cannot be extinguished.

inextricable, in'ek-strik"a-bl, a. Not to be extricated or disentangled.

infallible, in-fal'i-bl, a. Not fallible; not liable to fail; certain. **infallibly**, in-fal'i-bli, adv. In an infallible manner; to a certainty. **infallibility**, in-fal'i-bil"it-i, n. Quality of being infallible; exemption from liability to error.

infamous, in'fa-mus, a. Notoriously vile; detestable; branded with infamy. **infamously**, in'fa-mus-li, adv. In an infamous manner; scandalously. **infamy**, in'fa-mē, n. Total loss of reputation; public disgrace; qualities detested and despised; extreme vileness.

infant, in'fant, n. A very young child; one under twenty-one years of age.—a. Pertaining to infants. **infancy**, in'fan-sē, n. State of being an infant; early childhood; period from birth to the age of twenty-one; first age of anything.

infanticide, in-fant"i-sīd', n. Child murder; a slayer of infants.

infantile, **infantine**, in'fan-tīl, in'-fan-tīn, a. Pertaining to infancy or an infant.

infantry, in-fan-trē, n. The soldiers or troops that serve on foot.

infatuate, in-fach'ū-āt, vt. To make foolish; to inspire with an extravagant passion. **infatuated**, in-fach'ū-ā-ted, p.a. Besotted; inspired with foolish passion. **infatuation**, in-fach'ū-ā"shun, n. Act of infatuating; state of being infatuated; foolish passion.

infect, in-fekt', vt. To taint with disease; to communicate bad qualities to; to corrupt. **infection**, in-fek'shun, n. Act or process of infecting; communication of disease; contagion; the thing which infects. **infectious**, **infective**, in-fek'shus, in-fek'tiv, a. Capable of infecting; contagious; easily diffused from person to person.

infer, in-fèr', *vt.* (inferring, inferred). To gather by induction or deduction; to deduce. **inferable**, in-fèr'a-bl, *a.* That may be inferred from premises; deducible; derivable. **inference**, in'fê-rens, *n.* The act of inferring; that which is inferred; deduction. **inferential**, in'fê-ren''shal, *a.* Of or pertaining to an inference.

inferior, in-fêr'ê-èr, *a.* Lower in place, station, age, value, &c.; subordinate.—*n.* A person lower in rank, importance, &c. **inferiority**, in-fêr'ê-or''it-i, *n.* State or quality of being inferior.

infernal, in-fèrn'al, *a.* Pertaining to the lower regions or hell; very wicked and detestable; diabolical.—*n.* An inhabitant of hell; a fiend; a devil. **infernal machine**, an explosive apparatus contrived for assassination or other mischief. **infernally**, in-fèrn'al-i, *adv.* In an infernal way; detestably.

infest, in-fest', *vt.* To attack; to molest; to annoy continually.

infidel, in'fid-el, *n.* A disbeliever; a skeptic; one who does not believe in God or in Christianity.—*a.* Unbelieving; skeptical. **infidelity**, in'fi-del''it-i, *n.* Want of faith or belief; skepticism; unfaithfulness in married persons; dishonesty; treachery.

infiltrate, in-fil'trāt, *vi.* To enter by the pores or interstices; to percolate. **infiltration**, in-fil-trā'shun, *n.* Act or process of infiltrating; that which infiltrates.

infinite, in'fi-nit, *a.* Not finite; without limits; not circumscribed in any way; vast.—*n.* The Infinite Being; infinite space. **infinitely**, in'fi-nit-li, *adv.* In an infinite manner; beyond all comparison. **infinitesimal**, in'fin-i-tes''i-mal, *a.* Infinitely or indefinitely small.—*n.* An infinitely small quantity.

infinitive, in-fin'it-iv, *a.* Designating a mood of the verb which expresses action without limitation of person or number, as, *to love.*—*n.* The infinitive mood.

infinitude, in-fin'i-tūd, *n.* Infinity. **infinity**, in-fin'it-i, *n.* State or quality of being infinite; unlimited extent of time, space, quantity, &c.; immensity.

infirm, in-fèrm', *a.* Not firm; weak; sickly; enfeebled; irresolute. **infirmary**, in-fèrm'a-ri, *n.* A place where the sick and injured are nursed; a hospital. **infirmity**, in-fèr'mit-i, *n.* State of being infirm; unsound state of the body; weakness of mind or resolution; failing; malady.

inflame, in-flām', *vt.* To set on fire; to kindle; to excite or increase; to incense; to make morbidly red and swollen.—*vi.* To grow hot, angry, and painful; to take fire. **inflammability**, in-flam'a-bil''it-i, *n.* State or quality of being inflammable. **inflammable**, in-flam'a-bl, *a.* That may be inflamed; easily kindled; combustible. **inflammation**, in'fla-mā''shun, *n.* Act of inflaming; state of being inflamed; a redness and swelling attended with heat, pain, and feverish symptoms. **inflammatory**, in-flam'a-tor-i, *a.* Pertaining to inflammation; tending to excite anger, animosity, tumult, or sedition.

inflate, in-flāt, *vt.* (inflating, inflated). To distend by injecting air; to puff up; to elate; to raise above the real or normal value. **inflated**, in-flāt'ed, *p.a.* Puffed up; turgid; bombastic; unduly raised in price. **inflation**, in-flā'shun, *n.* Act of inflating; state of being distended with air; state of being puffed up, as with vanity.

inflect, in-flekt', *vt.* To bend; to decline or conjugate; to modulate, as the voice. **inflection**, in-flek'shun, *n.* Act of inflecting; state of being inflected; grammatical variation of nouns, verbs, &c.; modulation of the voice; deflection or diffraction. **inflective**, in-flek'tiv, *a.* Having the power of inflecting; having grammatical inflection.

inflexed, in''flekst', *a.* Curved; bent inward.

inflexible, in-flek'si-bl, *a.* That cannot be bent; firm in purpose; pertinacious; inexorable. **inflexibility**, in-flek'si-bil''it-i, *n.* Firmness of purpose; unbending pertinacity or obstinacy. **inflexibly**, in-flek'si-bli, *adv.* In an inflexible manner; firmly; inexorably.

inflexion, in-flek'shun. See **inflection**.

inflict, in-flikt', *vt.* To cause to bear or suffer from; to impose, as pain, punishment, &c. **infliction**, in-flik'shun, *n.* Act of inflicting; punishment inflicted; calamity.

influence, in'flu-ens, *n.* Agency or power serving to affect, modify, &c.; sway; effect; acknowledged ascendency with people in power.—*vt.* To exercise influence on; to bias; to sway. **influential**, in'flu-en''shal, *a.* Exerting influence, physical or other; possessing power.

influenza, in'flō-en''za, *n.* An epidemic catarrh or cold of an aggravated kind.

influx, in'fluks, *n.* Act of flowing in; importation in abundance; point at which one stream runs into another or into the sea.

infold, in-fōld', *vt.* To fold in; to involve; to wrap up; to inclose; to embrace.

inform, in-form', *vt.* To give form to; to give life to; to communicate knowledge to; to instruct, teach, &c.—*vi.* To give information.

informal, in-for'mal, *a.* Not in the usual form or mode; not with the official or customary forms; without ceremony. **informality**, in'for-mal''i-ti, *n.* Quality of being informal; want of regular form or order. **informally**, in-for'ma-li, *adv.* In an informal manner; without the usual forms.

informant, in-for'mant, *n.* One who informs; an accuser.

information, in'for-mā''shun, *n.* The act of informing; intelligence communicated or gathered; a charge or accusation before a magistrate. **informatory**, **informative**, in-for'ma-tör'i, in-for'ma-tiv, *a.* Affording knowledge or information; instructive.

informer, in-for'mèr, *n.* One who informs; one who makes a practice of informing against others for the sake of gain.

infraction, in-frak'shun, *n.* Act of infringing; breach; violation; infringement.

infrequent, in-frē'kwent, *a.* Not frequent; seldom happening; rare. **infrequently,** in-frē'kwent-li, *adv.* Not frequently; seldom; rarely. **infrequency,** in-frē'kwen-si, *n.* State of being infrequent; rareness.

infringe, in-frinj', *vt.* (infringing, infringed). To break, as laws, agreements, &c.; to violate; to contravene.—*vi.* To encroach (with *on* or *upon*). **infringement,** in-frinj'ment, *n.* Breach; violation; encroachment.

infuriate, in-fūr'i-āt, *vt.* To madden; to enrage.—*a.* Enraged; mad; raging.

infuse, in-fūz', *vt.* (infusing, infused). To pour in, as a liquid; to instill, as principles; to steep in liquor without boiling, in order to extract solutions, &c. **infusion,** in-fū'zhun, *n.* Act or process of infusing; that which is infused; liquor obtained by infusing or steeping.

ingenious, in-jēn'yus, *a.* Possessed of cleverness, or ability; apt in contriving; contrived with ingenuity; witty or well conceived. **ingeniously,** in-jēn'yus-li, *adv.* In an ingenious manner; with ingenuity. **ingenuity,** in'je-nū''i-ti, *n.* Quality of being ingenious; ready to invention; skill in contrivance.

ingenuous, in-jen'ū-us, *a.* Open, frank, or candid; free from reserve or dissimulation. **ingenuously,** in-jen'ū-us-li, *adv.* Frankly; openly; candidly.

ingest, in-jest', *vt.* To throw into the stomach.

inglorious, in-glōr'ē-us, *a.* Not glorious; not bringing honor or glory; disgraceful. **ingloriously,** in-glōr'ē-us-li, *adv.* In an inglorious manner.

ingot, in'got, *n.* A mass of gold or silver cast in a mold; a mass of unwrought metal.

ingrain, in-grān', *vt.* To engrain.

ingrate, in'grāt, *n.* An ungrateful person.

ingratiate, in-grā''shē'āt, *vt.* To get into another's good-will or confidence; to recommend; to insinuate; always *refl.*

ingratitude, in-grat'i-tūd, *n.* Want of gratitude; unthankfulness.

ingredient, in-grēd'ē-ent, *n.* That which is a component part of any mixture; an element, component, or constituent.

ingress, in'gres, *n.* Entrance; power of entrance; means of entering.

inhabit, in-hab'it, *vt.* To live or dwell in; to occupy as a place of settled residence.—*vi.* To dwell; to live; to abide. **inhabitable,** in-hab'it-a-bl, *a.* That may be inhabited; habitable. **inhabitant, inhabiter,** in-hab'it-ant, in-hab'it-ėr, *n.* One who inhabits; one who resides permanently in a place. **inhabitation,** in-hab'i-tā''shun, *n.* The act of inhabiting; an abode.

inhale, in-hāl', *vt.* (inhaling, inhaled). To draw into the lungs; to suck in. **inhaler,** in-hā'lėr, *n.* One who or that which inhales; an apparatus for inhaling vapors and volatile substances, as steam, vapor or chloroform, &c.; a respirator.

inhalation, in'ha-lā''shun, *n.* Act of inhaling; that which is inhaled.

inhere, in-hėr', *vi.* To exist or be fixed in; to belong, as attributes or qualities, to a subject. **inherence, inherency,** in-hėr'ens, in-hėr'ens-i, *n.* State of inhering; existence in something. **inherent,** in-hir'ent, *a.* Inhering; naturally pertaining; innate. **inherently,** in-hėr'ent-li, *adv.* In an inherent manner; by inherence.

inherit, in-her'it, *vt.* To come into possession of as an heir; to receive by nature from a progenitor; to hold as belonging to one's lot.—*vi.* To take or have possession of property. **inheritance,** in-her'it-ans, *n.* Act of inheriting; that which is or may be inherited; what falls to one's lot; possession.

inhibit, in-hib'it, *vt.* To hold in or back; to restrain; to forbid; to interdict. **inhibition,** in'hi-bish''un, *n.* Act of inhibiting; a legal writ inhibiting a judge from further proceeding in a cause. **inhibitory,** in-hib'i-tōr-i, *a.* Conveying an inhibition; prohibitory.

inhuman, in-hū'man, *a.* Destitute of the kindness and tenderness that belong to a human being; cruel; merciless. **inhumanity,** in'hū-man''i-ti, *n.* Quality of being inhuman; cruelty.

inimical, in-im'i-kal, *a.* Unfriendly; hostile; adverse; hurtful; prejudicial.

inimitable, in-im'it-a-bl, *a.* That cannot be imitated or copied; surpassing imitation. **inimitably,** in-im'it-a-bli, *adv.* To a degree beyond imitation.

iniquity, in-ik'wi-ti, *n.* Want of equity; injustice; a sin or crime; wickedness. **iniquitous,** in-ik'wi-tus, *a.* Characterized by inquity; wicked; criminal.

initial, in-ish'al, *a.* Placed at the beginning; pertaining to the beginning; beginning.—*n.* The first letter of a word; *pl.* the first letter in order of the words composing a name.—*vt.* (initialing, initialed). To put one's initials to; to mark by initials.

initiate, in-ish''ē-āt', *vt.* To begin; to be the first to practice or bring in; to instruct in rudiments; to introduce into any society or set; to let into secrets; to indoctrinate. **initiation,** in-ish''ē-ā''shun, *n.* Act or process of initiating; beginning; formal introduction. **initiative,** in-ish'a-tiv, *a.* Serving to initiate.—*n.* An introductory step; first active procedure in any enterprise; power of taking the lead.

inject, in-jekt', *vt.* To throw, cast, or put in or into; to dart in; to cast or throw in. **injection,** in-jek'shun, *n.* Act of injecting; the throwing of a liquid medicine into the body by a syringe or pipe; that which is injected. **injector,** in-jek'tėr, *n.* One who or that which injects; an apparatus for supplying the boilers of steam engines with water.

injunction, in-jungk'shun, *n.* Act of enjoining; a command; precept; urgent advice; admonition.

injure, in'jėr, *vt.* (injuring, injured). To do harm to; to hurt; to damage. **injurious,** in-jėr'ē-us, *a.* Causing injury; tending to injure; hurtful; harmful.

injury, in′jėr-i, *n.* The doing of harm; harm or damage; mischief; detriment.

injustice, in-jus′tis, *n.* Want of justice or equity; iniquity; wrong.

ink, ingk, *n.* A colored liquid, usually black, for writing, printing, &c.—*vt.* To black or daub with ink.

inkling, ing′kling, *n.* A hint or whisper; a slight notion or idea.

inkstand, ingk″stand′, *n.* A vessel for holding ink.

inky, ing′ki, *a.* Consisting of or like ink; black; tarnished or blackened with ink.

inland, in″land′, *a.* Interior; remote from the sea; domestic, not foreign; confined to a country.—*adv.* In or towards the interior of a country.—*n.* The interior part of a country.

inlay, in-lā′, *vt.* (inlaying, inlaid). To lay in; to ornament by laying in thin slices of fine wood, ivory, &c., on some other surface. **inlaying**, in-lā′ing, *n.* Act or art of one who inlays; inlaid work.

inlet, in′let, *n.* A passage for entrance; place of ingress; a narrow recess in a shore.

inmate, in″māt′, *n.* One who dwells in the same house with another; one of the occupants of hospitals, asylums, prisons, &c.

inmost, in″mōst′, *a.* Furthest within; remotest from the surface or external parts.

inn, in, *n.* A house for the lodging and entertainment of travelers; a college of law professors and students.

innate, in-āt′, *a.* Inborn; natural; native; inherent. **innately**, in-āt′li, *adv.* In an innate manner; naturally.

innermost, in″ėr-mōst′, *a.* Furthest inward; most remote from the outward part.

innervate, in-ėr″vāt′, *vt.* To supply with nervous strength or stimulus. **innervation**, in′ėr-vā″shun, *n.* Act of innerving; nervous stimulation.

inning, in′ing, *n.* The ingathering of grain; *pl.* turn for using the bat in cricket, and baseball.

innkeeper, in″kē′pėr, *n.* One who keeps an inn or tavern.

innocent, in′ō-sent, *a.* Not noxious or hurtful; free from guilt; simple-hearted; guileless.—*n.* One free from guilt or harm; a natural or simpleton. **innocently**, in′ō-sent-li, *adv.* In an innocent manner. **innocence, innocency**, in′ō-sens, in′ō-sen-si, *n.* Quality of being innocent; freedom from crime or guilt; simplicity of heart.

innocuous, in-ok′ū-us, *a.* Harmless; not injurious; producing no ill effect.

innovate, in″ō-vāt′, *vi.* To introduce novelties or changes. **innovation**, in′ō-vā″shun, *n.* The act of innovating; change made in anything established. **innovator**, in′ō-vāt′ėr, *n.* One who innovates.

innuendo, in′ū-wen″dō, *n.*; pl. **innuendos or does**, dōz. An oblique hint; insinuation.

innumerable, in-ūm′e-ra-bl, *a.* Incapable of being numbered for multitude; extremely numerous; countless. **innu-**

merably, in-ūm′e-ra-bli, *adv.* Without number.

inoculate, in-ok″ū-lāt′, *vt.* To graft by inserting a bud; to communicate a disease to by morbid matter introduced into the blood; to infect; to contaminate. **inoculation**, in-ok′ū-lā″shun, *n.* The act or practice of inoculating; communication of a disease by matter introduced into the blood.

inoperative, . in-op′e-rat-iv, *a.* Not operative; not active; producing no effect.

inopportune, in-op′or-tūn″, *a.* Not opportune; inconvenient; unseasonable. **inopportunely**, in-op′or-tūn″li, *adv.* In an inopportune manner; unseasonably.

inordinate, in-ord′in-it, *a.* Excessive; immoderate. **inordinately**, in-ord′in-it-li, *adv.* In an inordinate manner; excessively.

inorganic, in′or-gan″ik, *a.* Not organic; devoid of the structure of a living being; pertaining to substances without carbon.

inquest, in″kwest′, *n.* Inquiry; a judicial inquiry before a jury; the jury itself.

inquire, in-kwīr′, *vi.* (inquiring, inquired). Often **enquire**. To ask a question; to seek for truth by discussion or investigation.—*vt.* To ask about; to seek by asking. **inquirer**, in-kwīr′ėr, *n.* One who inquires; one who seeks for knowledge or information. **inquiring**, in-kwīr′ing, *p.a.* Given to inquiry; disposed to investigation. **inquiry**, in-kwī′ri or in″kwi-ri, *n.* Often **enquiry**. The act of inquiring; a question; research; investigation; examination.

inquisition, in′kwi-zish″un, *n.* The act of inquiring; inquiry; inquest; a R. Catholic court for the examination and punishment of heretics. **inquisitional, inquisitionary**, in′kwi-zish″nal, in′kwi-zish″un-ri, *a.* Pertaining to inquisition, or to the Inquisition.

inquisitive, in-kwiz′it-iv, *a.* Addicted to inquiry; given to pry; troublesomely curious. **inquisitively**, in-kwiz′it-iv-li, *adv.* In an inquisitive manner.

inquisitor, in-kwiz′it-ėr, *n.* One whose duty it is to inquire and examine; a member of the Inquisition. **inquisitorial**, in-kwiz′i-tōr″i-al, *a.* Pertaining to an inquisitor; making searching inquiry.

inroad, in″rōd″, *n.* A hostile incursion; an invasion; attack; encroachment.

insane, in-sān′, *a.* Not sane; deranged in mind or intellect; intended for insane persons; senseless. **insanely**, in-sān′li, *adv.* In an insane manner; foolishly; without reason. **insanity**, in-san′it-i, *n.* The state of being insane;—derangement of intellect; lunacy.

insatiable, in-sā′sha-bl, *a.* Not satiable; incapable of being satisfied or appeased. **insatiate**, in-sā′shē-it, *a.* Not satisfied; insatiable. **insatiability**, in-sā-sha-bil″it-i, *n.* The quality of being insatiable.

inscribe, in-skrīb′, *vt.* (inscribing, inscribed). To write down; to imprint on, as on the memory; to address or dedicate; to mark with letters or words; to draw a figure within another. **inscrip-**

tion, in-skrip′shun, *n.* The act of inscribing; words engraved; address of a book, &c., to a person.

inscrutable, in-skrōt′a-bl, *a.* Unsearchable; that cannot be penetrated or understood by human reason. **inscrutability**, in-skrōt′a-bil″it-i, *n.* Quality of being inscrutable.

insect, in′sekt′, *n.* One of those small animals that have three divisions of the body—head, thorax, and abdomen—and usually three pairs of legs and two pairs of wings, as flies, &c.; a puny, contemptible person.—*a.* Pertaining to insects; like an insect; mean. **insecticide**, in-sek″ti-sīd′, *n.* One who or that which kills insects; the killing of insects. **insectivora**, in-sek-tiv′ō-ra, *n.pl.* An order of mammals, as the hedgehog, &c., which live greatly on insects. **insectivore**, in-sek″ti-vōr′, *n.* An animal that eats insects. **insectivorous**, in′sek′tiv′ō-rus, *a.* Feeding on insects; belonging to the Insectivora.

insecure, in′se-kūr′, *a.* Not secure; not confident of safety; unsafe. **insecurely**, in′se-kūr″li, *adv.* In an insecure manner. **insecurity**, in′se-kūr″it-i, *n.* The state of being insecure; want of security.

insensate, in-sen′sāt′, *a.* Destitute of sense or sensation; stupid; irrational.

insensible, in-sen′si-bl, *a.* Not perceived or perceptible by the senses; void of feeling; unfeeling; callous; indifferent. **insensibly**, insen′si-bli, *adv.* In an insensible manner; by slow degrees. **insensibility**, in-sen′si-bil″it-i, *n.* State or quality of being insensible; want of sensation; callousness; apathy.

insert, in-sèrt′, *vt.* To put, bring, or set in; to thrust in; to set in or among. **insertion**, in-sèr′shun, *n.* Act of inserting; thing inserted; place or mode of attachment of a part or organ to its support.

inset, in-set′, *vt.* To set in; to implant. —*n.* in′set. That which is set in; insertion.

inshore, in′shōr′, *a.* or *adv.* Near the shore.

inside, in-sīd′, *n.* The interior side or part of a thing.—*a.* Interior; internal.—*prep.* In the interior of; within.

insidious, in-sid′ē-us, *a.* Treacherous; guileful; working evil secretly.

insight, in′sīt′, *n.* Sight into; thorough knowledge; discernment; penetration.

insignia, in-sig′nē-a, *n. pl.* Badges or distinguishing marks of office or honor.

insignificance, insignificancy, in′-sig-nif″i-kans, in′sig-nif″i-kan-si, *n.* Quality or state of being insignificant; triviality.

insignificant, in′sig-nif″i-kant, *a.* Not significant; void of signification; trivial or trifling; mean; contemptible.

insincere, in″sin-sēr′, *a.* Not sincere; wanting sincerity; hypocritical; deceitful. **insincerely**, in′sin-sēr″li, *adv.* In an insincere manner; without sincerity. **insincerity**, in′sin-ser″it-i, *n.* Quality of being insincere; deceitfulness.

insinuate, in-sin′ū-wāt′, *vt.* To introduce by windings or gently; to work gradually into favor; to introduce by

gentle or artful means; to hint.—*vi.* To creep or wind; to make an insinuation; to wheedle. **insinuating**, in-sin′ū-wāt′ing, *p.a.* Given to or characterized by insinuation; insensibly winning favor and confidence. **insinuation**, in-sin′ū-wā″shun, *n.* Act of insinuating; wheedling manner; hint or innuendo.

insipid, in-sip′id, *a.* Destitute of taste; vapid; flat; dull; heavy; spiritless.

insist, in-sist′, *vi.* To rest or dilate on; to be urgent or peremptory. **insistence**, in-sis′tens, *n.* Act of insisting; persistency; urgency.

insolate, in″sō-lāt′, *vt.* To dry or prepare in the sun′s rays. **insolation**, in′-sō-lā″shun, *n.* Exposure to the rays of the sun; sunstroke.

insolent, in′sō-lent, *a.* Showing haughty disregard of others; impudent; insulting. **insolently**, in′sō-lent-li, *adv.* In an insolent manner; haughtily; rudely; saucily. **insolence**, in′sō-lens, *n.* State or quality of being insolent; insolent language or behavior.

insolvent, in-sol′vent, *a.* Not solvent; not having money, &c., sufficient to pay debts.—*n.* One unable to pay his debts. **insolvency**, in-sol′ven-si, *n.* State of being insolvent; inability to pay all debts.

insomnia, in-som′nē-a, *n.* Want of sleep; morbid or unnatural sleeplessness. **insomuch**, in′sō-much″, *adv.* To such a degree; in such wise.

inspect, in-spekt′, *vt.* To view or examine to ascertain the quality or condition, &c. **inspection**, in-spek′shun, *n.* Act of inspecting; careful survey; official examination. **inspector**, in-spek′-tèr, *n.* One who inspects; a superintendent; an overseer.

inspire, in-spīr′, *vt.* (inspiring, inspired). To breathe in; to breathe into; to communicate divine instructions to; to infuse ideas or poetic spirit into; to animate in general.—*vi.* To draw in breath; to inhale air into the lungs. **inspired**, in-spīrd′, *p.a.* Having received inspiration; produced under the influence or direction of inspiration. **inspiration**, in′spi-rā″shun, *n.* The act of inspiring; the drawing in of breath; the divine influence by which the sacred writers were instructed; influence emanating from any object; the state of being inspired; something conveyed to the mind when under extraordinary influence.

inspirit, in-spir′it, *vt.* To infuse or excite spirit in; to cheer or encourage.

instability, in′sta-bil″i-ti, *n.* Want of stability; inconstancy; fickleness.

install, in-stal′, *vt.* To place in a seat; to invest with any office with due ceremony. **installation**, in′sta-lā″shun, *n.* The act of installing. **installment**, in-stal′ment, *n.* Act of installing; a part of a whole produced or paid at various times; part payment of a debt.

instance, in′stans, *n.* Act or state of being instant or urgent; urgency; an example; an occurrence.—*vt.* To mention as an instance, example, or case.

instant, in′stant, *a.* Pressing or urgent;

immediate; making no delay; present or current.—*n.* A moment. **instantane-ous,** in'stan-tā″nē-us, *a.* Done or occurring in an instant. **instantaneously,** in'stan-tā″rē-us-li, *adv.* In an instant; in a moment. **instantly,** in'stant-li, *adv.* In an instant; immediately; with urgent importunity.

instead, in-sted', *adv.* In the place or room; in place of that.

instep, in″step', *n.* The fore part of the upper side of the foot, near its junction with the leg.

instigate, in″sti-gāt', *vt.* To spur on; to urge; to incite; to impel. **instigation,** in'sti-gā″shun, *n.* Act of instigating; incitement; temptation. **instigator,** in″sti-gāt′ẽr, *n.* One who instigates or incites another.

instill, instil, in-stil', *vt.* (instilling, instilled). To pour in, as by drops; to infuse by degrees; to insinuate imperceptibly.

instinct, in″stingkt', *n.* Spontaneous or natural impulse; the knowledge and skill which animals have without experience; intuitive feeling.—*a.* in-stingkt'. Animated or stimulated from within; inspired. **instinctive,** in-stingk′tiv, *a.* Prompted by instinct; spontaneous. **instinctively,** in-stingk′tiv-li, *adv.* In an instinctive manner; by force of instinct.

institute, in″sti-tūt', *vt.* To set up or establish; to found; to begin; to appoint to an office; to invest with a benefice.—*n.* That which is instituted; established law; principle; a literary or scientific body; an institution.—*pl.* a book of elements or principles. **institution,** in'sti-tū″shun, *n.* Act of instituting; something instituted; custom; a society for promoting any object; act of investing a clergyman with the care of souls. **institutional,** in'sti-tū″shun-al, *a.* Relating to institutions; instituted by authority; relating to elementary knowledge.

instruct, in-strukt', *vt.* To impart knowledge to; to teach; to advise or give notice to. **instruction,** in-struk′shun, *n.* Act of instructing; information; education; authoritative direction; command. **instructive,** in-struk′tiv, *a.* Conveying instruction or a useful lesson. **instructor,** in-struk′tẽr, *n.* One who instructs; a teacher.

instrument, in″stry-ment, *n.* A tool; implement; one subservient to the execution of a plan; means used; any contrivance from which music is produced; a writing instructing one in regard to something agreed upon. **instrumental,** in″stry-ment″al, *a.* Conducive to some end; pertaining to or produced by instruments, as music. **instrumentalist,** in″stry-ment″al-ist, *n.* One who plays on a musical instrument. **instrumentality,** in″stry-men-tal″it-i, *n.* State of being instrumental; agency. **instrumentation,** in″stry-men-tā″shun, *n.* The use of instruments; music for a number of instruments; art of arranging such music.

insubordinate, in′su-bord″in-it, *a.* Not

submitting to authority; riotous. **insubordination,** in′su-bord′in-ā″shun, *n.* Quality or state of being insubordinate; resistance to lawful authority.

insufferable, in-suf′ra-bl, *a.* Not to be suffered; intolerable. **insufferably,** in-suf′ra-bli, *adv.* Intolerably.

insufficient, in′su-fish″ent, *a.* Not sufficient; deficient; inadequate. **insufficiently,** in′su-fish″ent-li, *adv.* In an insufficient manner; inadequately. **insufficiency,** in′su-fish″en-si, *n.* State of being insufficient; deficiency; inadequacy.

insular, in′sū-lẽr, *a.* Pertaining to an island; forming an island; narrow-minded. **insularity,** in′sū-lar″it-i, *n.* State of being insular.

insulate, in″su-lāt', *vt.* To make into an island; to detach; to separate, as an electrified body, by interposition of non-conductors. **insulation,** in′su-lā″shun, *n.* Act of insulating; state of being insulated. **insulator,** in″su-lāt′ẽr, *n.* One who or that which insulates; a body that interrupts the communication of electricity; non-conductor.

insult, in″sult', *n.* Any gross affront or indignity; act or speech of insolence or contempt.—*vt.* in-sult'. To treat with insult or insolence.—*vi.* To behave with insolent triumph. **insulting,** in-sult′ing, *p.a.* Containing or conveying insult.

insuperable, in-sū′pra-bl, *a.* That cannot be overcome; insurmountable. **insuperability,** in-su′pra-bil″it-i, *n.* Quality of being insuperable.

insupportable, in′su-pōrt″a-bl, *a.* That cannot be supported or borne; intolerable.

insurable, in-shōr′a-bl, *a.* That may be insured against loss or damage.

insurance, in-shōr′ans, *n.* Act of insuring against loss, &c.; a system of securing, by making certain payments, a certain sum of money at death, &c. **insure,** in-shōr', *vt.* (insuring, insured). To make sure; to contract for the receipt of a certain sum in the event of loss, death, &c.

insurgent, in-sẽr′jent, *a.* Rising in opposition to lawful authority; rebellious. —*n.* One who rises in opposition to authority.

insurrection, in′sẽ-rek″shun, *n.* A rising against authority; rebellion. **insurrectional, insurrectionary,** in′-sẽ-rek″shun-al, in′sẽ-rek″shu-ner'i, *a.* Pertaining to insurrection.

intact, in-takt', *a.* Untouched; unimpaired.

intaglio, in-tal′yō, *n.* Any figure engraved or cut into a substance; a gem with a figure or device sunk below the surface.

intangible, in-tan′ji-bl, *a.* That cannot be touched; not perceptible to the touch.

integer, in″te-jẽr, *n.* A whole; whole number, in contradistinction to a fraction. **integral,** in′te-gral, *a.* Whole; forming a necessary part of a whole; not fractional.—*n.* A whole; an entire thing. **integrate,** in′te-grāt, *vt.* To make or form into one whole; to give the sum or total of. **integration**, in'te-grā"shun, *n.* The act of integrating.

integrity, in-teg'rit-i, *n.* State of being entire; an unimpaired state; honesty; probity.

integument, in-teg'ū-ment, *n.* A covering, especially a skin, membrane, or shell.

intellect, int'el-ekt, *n.* That mental faculty which receives ideas; the understanding; mental power; mind. **intellectual**, int'el-ek"chwal, *a.* Relating or appealing to the intellect; having intellect.

intelligence, in-tel'i-jens, *n.* The capacity to know; knowledge imparted or acquired; notice; an intelligent or spiritual being. **intelligent**, in-tel'i-jent, *a.* Endowed with the faculty of understanding or reason; endowed with a good intellect; well informed. **intelligently**, in-tel'i-jent-li, *adv.* In an intelligent manner. **intelligible**, in-tel'i-ji-bl, *a.* Capable of being understood; clear. **intelligentsia**, in-tel'i-jent"sē-a, *n.pl.* (Rus.) The intelligent classes as distinguished from the ignorant.

intemperate, in-tem'pe-rit, *a.* Not temperate; addicted to an excessive use of alcoholic liquors; excessive or immoderate.—*n.* One not temperate. **intemperately**, in-tem'pe-rit-li, *adv.* In an intemperate manner. **intemperance**, in-tem'pe-rans, *n.* Want of temperance; excess of any kind; habitual indulgence in alcoholic liquors.

intend, in-tend', *vt.* To design; to purpose; to mean.

intended, in-tend'ed, *p.a.* Purposed; betrothed.—*n.* An affianced lover.

intense, in-tens', *a.* Closely strained; strict; extreme in degree; violent; severe. **intensely**, in-tens'li, *adv.* In an intense manner or degree. **intensify**, in-ten"si-fī', *vt.* To render intense or more intense; to aggravate.—*vi.* To become intense. **intensity**, in-ten'sit-i, *n.* State of being intense; keenness; extreme degree; amount of energy. **intensive**, in-ten'siv, *a.* Serving to give emphasis.—*n.* Something giving emphasis.

intent, in-tent', *a.* Having the mind bent on an object; sedulously applied.—*n.* Design or purpose; meaning; drift. **intention**, in-ten'shun, *n.* Act of intending; purpose; design; intension; method of treatment in surgery; a general concept. **intentional**, in-ten'shun-al, *a.* Done with design or purpose; intended. **intentionally**, in-ten'shun-al-i, *adv.* In an intentional manner; on purpose. **intently**, in-tent'li, *adv.* In an intent manner.

inter, in-tèr', *vt.* (interring, interred). To bury; to inhume.

interact, int'e-rakt", *n.* Interval between two acts of a drama; any intermediate employment of time.—*vi.* To act reciprocally. **interaction**, int'e-rak"shun, *n.* Mutual or reciprocal action.

intercede, int'ėr-sēd", *vi.* (interceding, interceded). To mediate; to plead in favor of one; to make intercession.

intercept, int'ėr-sept", *v* To take or seize on by the way; t stop on its

passage; to obstruct the progress of; to cut or shut off. **interception**, int-ėr-sep"shun, *n.* Act of intercepting.

intercession, int'ėr-sesh"un, *n.* Act of interceding; mediation; prayer or solicitation to one party in favor of another. **intercessor**, int'ėr-ses"ėr, *n.* One who intercedes; a mediator.

interchange, int'ėr-chānj", *vt.* To change, as one with the other; to exchange; to reciprocate.—*n.* int"ėr-chānj'. Mutual change; exchange; alternate succession. **interchangeable**, int'ėr-chān"ja-bl, *a.* That may be interchanged.

intercommunicate, int'ėr-ko-mū"ni-kāt', *vi.* To communicate mutually. **intercommunication**, int'ėr-ko-mū"ni-kā"shun, *n.* Reciprocal communication.

intercourse, int'ėr-kōrs, *n.* Reciprocal dealings between persons or nations; fellowship; familiarity; sexual connection.

interdict, int'ėr-dikt", *vt.* To forbid; to place under an interdict or prohibition. —*n.* int'ėr-dikt. A prohibition; a papal prohibition of the administration of religious rites. **interdiction**, int'ėr-dik"-shun, *n.* Act of interdicting; prohibition.

interest, in'trest, *vt.* To concern; to engage the attention of.—*n.* Concern or regard; advantage; profit; profit per cent from money lent or invested; influence with a person. **interested**, in'trest-ed, *p.a.* Having an interest; liable to be affected; chiefly concerned for one's private advantage. **interesting**, in'trest-ing, *p.a.* Engaging the attention or curiosity.

interfere, int'ėr-fēr", *vi.* (interfering, interfered). To clash; to interpose; to take a part in the concerns of others. **interference**, int'ėr-fēr"ens, *n.* Act of interfering; clashing or collision. **interim**, in'te-rim, *n.* The meantime; time intervening.—*a.* Belonging to an intervening time; temporary.

interior, in-ter'ē-ėr, *a.* Internal; being within; inland.—*n.* The inner part of a thing; the inside; the inland part of a country, &c.

interject, int'ėr-jekt", *vt.* To throw in between; to insert. **interjection**, int'ėr-jek"shun, *n.* Act of throwing between; a word thrown in between words to express some emotion; an exclamation.

interlace, int'ėr-lās", *vt.* To weave together.—*vi.* To have parts intercrossing.

interlard, int'ėr-lärd", *vt.* To mix; to diversify by mixture.

interleave, int'ėr-lēv", *vt.* To insert, as blank leaves in a book between other leaves.

interline, int'ėr-līn", *vt.* To put a line or lines between; to write or print in alternate lines or between lines.

interlock, int'ėr-lok", *vi.* and *t.* To unite or lock together by a series of connections.

interlocution, int'ėr-lō-kū"shun, *n.* Dialogue; interchange of speech; an intermediate act or decree before final decision. **interlocutor**, int'ėr-lok"ūt-ėr, *n.* One who speaks in dialogue; *Scots law*, a judgment or order of any court of record. **interlocutory**, int'ėr-lok"ūtŏr′i, *a.* Consisting of dialogue; not final or definitive.

nterlope, int′ĕr-lōp″, *vi.* To traffic without proper license; to intrude. **interloper,** int′ĕr-lōp″ĕr, *n.* An intruder.

nterlude, int″ĕr-lūd′, *n.* A short entertainment between the acts of a play, or between the play and the afterpiece; a piece of music between certain more important passages.

ntermarry, int′ĕr-mar′i, *vi.* To become connected by marriage, as families. **intermarriage,** int′ĕr-mar′ij, *n.* Marriage between two families, tribes, &c.

ntermediate, int′ĕr-mēd″ē-it, *a.* Being between two extremes; intervening. **intermediary,** int′ĕr-mēd″ē-er′i, *a.* Intermediate.—*n.* An intermediate agent.

nterment, in-tĕr′ment, *n.* Burial.

ntermezzo, int′ĕr-met″sō, *n.* A short musical composition, generally of a light sparkling character; an interlude.

nterminable, in-tĕrm′i-na-bl, *a.* Admitting no limit; boundless; endless. **interminate,** in-tĕrm′i-nāt, *a.* Unbounded; unlimited; endless.

ntermission, int′ĕr-mish″un, *n.* Act or state of intermitting; pause; rest.

ntermit, int′ĕr-mit″, *vt.* (intermitting, intermitted). To cause to cease for a time; to suspend.—*vi.* To cease for a time. **intermittent,** int′ĕr-mit″ent, *a.* Ceasing at intervals; ceasing and then returning, as certain fevers.—*n.* A fever which intermits.

ntern, in-tĕrn′, *vt.* To send to and cause to remain in the interior of a country; to disarm and quarter in some place, as defeated troops.

nternal, in-tĕrn′al, *a.* Inward; not external; domestic; not foreign. **internally,** in-tĕrn′al-i, *adv.* Inwardly; mentally; spiritually.

nternational, int′ĕr-nash″un-al, *a.* Relating to or mutually affecting nations; regulating the mutual intercourse between nations.

nternecine, int′ĕr-nes″ēn, *a.* Marked by destructive hostilities; causing great slaughter.

nterpolate, in-tĕr′po-lāt, *vt.* To foist in; to add a spurious word or passage to. **interpolation,** in-tĕr′po-lā″shun, *n.* Act of interpolating; spurious word or passage inserted.

nterposal, int′ĕr-pōz″al, *n.* Act of interposing; interposition.

nterpose, int′ĕr-pōz″, *vt.* (interposing, interposed). To place between.—*vi.* To mediate; to put in or make a remark. **interposition,** int′ĕr-pō-zish″un, *n.* Act of interposing; intervention; mediation.

nterpret, in-tĕr′pret, *vt.* To explain the meaning of; to expound; to construe; to represent artistically (as an actor). **interpretation,** in-tĕr′pre-tā″shun, *n.* Act of interpreting; explanation; representation of a character on the stage. **interpreter,** in-tĕr′pret-ĕr, *n.* One who interprets; a translator.

nterrelation, int′ĕr-ri-lā″shun, *n.* Mutual or corresponding relation; correlation.

interrogate, in-ter″-o-gāt, *vt.* To question; to examine by asking questions. **interrogation,** in-ter′o-gā″shun, *n.* Act of interrogating; question put; a sign that marks a question, thus (?). **interrogator,** in-ter″o-gāt′ĕr, *n.* One who interrogates or asks questions.

interrupt, in-te-rupt″, *vt.* To break in upon the progress of; to cause to stop in speaking. **interrupted,** int′e-rupt″ed, *p.a.* Having interruptions; broken; intermitted. **interruption,** int′e-rup″shun, *n.* Act of interrupting; a break or breach; obstruction or hindrance; cause of stoppage. **intersect,** int′ĕr-sekt″, *vt.* To cut in between; to divide; to cut or cross mutually.—*vi.* To meet and cut or cross each other. **intersection,** int′ĕr-sek″shun, *n.* Act or state of intersecting; the point or line in which two lines or two planes cut each other.

intersperse, int′ĕr-spĕrs″, *vt.* To scatter or set here and there among other things. **interspersion,** int′ĕr-sper″zhun, *n.* Act of interspersing.

interstice, in-tĕr′stis, *n.* A narrow space between things closely set; a chink.

intertwine, int′ĕr-twīn″, *vt.* To unite by twining or twisting.—*vi.* To be interwoven.

interval, int′ĕr-val, *n.* A space between things; amount of separation between ranks, degrees, &c.; difference in gravity or acuteness between sounds.

intervene, int′ĕr-vēn″, *vi.* (intervening, intervened). To come or be between; to interpose or interfere. **intervention,** int′ĕr-ven″shun, *n.* Act of intervening; interposition; agency of persons between persons.

interview, int″ĕr-vū′, *n.* A meeting between persons; a conference.—*vt.* To have an interview with to get information for publication.

interweave, int′ĕr-wēv″, *vt.* To weave together; to unite intimately; to interlace.

intestate, in-tes′tāt, *a.* Dying without having made a will; not disposed of by will.—*n.* A person who dies without making a will.

intestine, in-tes′tin, *a.* Internal; domestic; not foreign.—*n.* The canal extending from the stomach to the anus; *pl.* entrails or viscera in general. **intestinal,** in-tes′tin-al, *a.* Pertaining to the intestines.

intimate, int′i-mit, *a.* Inward or internal; close in friendship; familiar; close.—*n.* An intimate or familiar friend. *vt.* int″i-māt′ (intimating, intimated). To hint or indicate; to announce. **intimately,** int′i-mit-li, *adv.* In an intimate manner; familiarly. **intimacy,** int′i-ma-si, *n.* State of being intimate; close friendship. **intimation,** int′i-mā″shun, *n.* Act of intimating; a hint; announcement.

intimidate, in-tim″i-dāt′, *vt.* To put in fear or dread; to cow; to deter with threats. **intimidation,** in-tim′i-dā″-shun, *n.* Act of intimidating.

into, in′tö, *prep.* In and to; expressing motion or direction towards the inside of, or a change of condition.

intolerable, in-tol'ra-bl, *a.* That cannot be borne; unendurable; insufferable. **intolerably,** in-tol'ra-bli, *adv.* To a degree beyond endurance. **intolerance,** in-tol'rans, *n.* Quality of being intolerant; want of toleration. **intolerant,** in-tol'rant, *a.* That cannot bear; not enduring difference of opinion or worship; refusing to tolerate others.

intonate, in''tō-nāt', *vi.* To sound the notes of the musical scale; to modulate the voice.—*vt.* To pronounce with a certain modulation. **intonation,** in'tō-nā''shun, *n.* Act or manner of intonating; modulation of the voice; utterance with a special tone.

intone, in-tōn', *vi.* To use a musical monotone in pronouncing.—*vt.* To pronounce with a musical tone; to chant.

intoxicate, in-tok''si-kāt', *vt.* To make drunk; to elate to enthusiasm or madness.—*vi.* To cause intoxication. **intoxicating,** in-tok''si-kāt'ing, *p.a.* Causing intoxication. **intoxication,** in-tok'si-kā''shun, *n.* Act of intoxicating; state of being drunk; delirious excitement; frenzy. **intoxicant,** in-tok'si-kant, *n.* That which intoxicates; an intoxicating liquor.

intractable, in-trak'ta-bl, *a.* Not tractable; not to be governed or managed; refractory.

intramural, in''tra-mūr'al, *a.* Being within the walls, as of a town or university.

intransigent, in-trans'i-jent, *a.* Irreconcilable.—*n.* An irreconcilable person.

intransitive, in-trans'it-iv, *a.* Designating a verb which expresses an action or state limited to the subject.

intrench, in-trench', *vt.* To dig a trench around, as in fortification; to fortify with a ditch and parapet; to lodge within an intrenchment.—*vi.* To invade; to encroach. **intrenchment,** in-trench'ment, *n.* Act of intrenching; a trench; any protection; encroachment.

intrepid, in-trep'id, *a.* Undaunted; fearless; bold; daring; courageous. **intrepidity,** in'tre-pid''it-i, *n.* Quality of being intrepid; undaunted courage.

intricate, in''tri-kit, *a.* Involved; complicated. **intricacy,** in''tri-ka-si, *n.* State of being intricate; complication; complexity.

intrigue, in-trēg', *n.* An underhand plot or scheme; plot of a play, &c.; an illicit intimacy between a man and woman.—*vi.* (intriguing, intrigued). To engage in an intrigue; to carry on forbidden love. **intriguing,** in-trēg'ing, *p.a.* Addicted to intrigue; given to secret machinations.

intrinsic, intrinsical, in-trin'zik, in-trin'zi-kal, *a.* Being within; inherent; essential. **intrinsically,** in-trin'zik-li, *adv.* In its nature; essentially; inherently.

introduce, in''tro-dūs'', *vt.* To lead or bring in; to insert; to bring to be acquainted; to present; to make known; to import; to bring before the public. **introduction,** in''tro-duk''shun, *n.* Act of introducing; act of making persons known to each other; act of bringing something into notice; a preliminary discourse.—**introductory,** in''tro-duk''ri, *a.* Serving to introduce; prefatory; preliminary.

introspect, in''tro-spekt'', *vt.* To look into or within. **introspection,** in-tr spek'shon, *n.* The act of looking inwardly; examination of one's o thoughts or feelings.

introvert, in''tro-vèrt'', *vt.* To turn ward.

intrude, in-trōd', *vi.* (intruding, truded). To thrust one's self in; to fo an entry or way in without permissi right, or invitation; to encroach.—*vt.* thrust in. **intrusion,** in-trö'zhun, Action of intruding; encroachment. **trusive,** in-trö'siv, *a.* Apt to intrud characterized by intrusion.

intrust, in-trust', *vt.* To deliver in trus to confide to the care of. Also *entrust.*

intuition, in''tū-ish''un, *n.* A looking o direct apprehension of a truth witho reasoning. **intuitive,** in-tū'it-iv, *a.* P ceived by the mind immediately witho reasoning; based on intuition; self-e dent. **intuitively,** in-tū'it-iv-li, *adv.* an intuitive manner; by intuition.

inundate, in'un-dāt'', *vt.* To spread flow over; to flood; to overwhelm. **undation,** in'un-dā''shun, *n.* Act inundating; a flood.

inure, in-ūr', *vt.* (inuring, inured). accustom; to harden by use.—*vi.* To applied.

invade, in-vād', *vt.* (invading, invaded To enter with hostile intentions; to ma an inroad on; to encroach on; to viola **invader,** in-vād'ér, *n.* One who vades; an assailant; an encroacher.

invalid, in-val'id, *a.* Not valid.

invalid, in''va-lid, *a.* Sick, disabled.— A person who is sick or diabled.

invaluable, in-val'ū-bl, *a.* Preci above estimation; inestimable; pricele **invaluably,** in-val'ū-bli, *adv.* Ines mably.

invariable, in-ver'ē-a-bl, *a.* Not va able; unchangeable; always uniform. **i variably,** in-ver'ē-a-bli, *adv.* Unifor ly.

invasion, in-vā'zhun, *n.* Act of inva ing; hostile entrance; infringement; vi lation.

invasive, in-vā'siv, *a.* Making invasio aggressive.

invective, in-vek'tiv, *n.* Violent utte ance of censure; railing language; tuperation.—*a.* Containing invective abusive.

inveigh, in-vā', *vi.* To attack w vectives; to rail against; to reproach; upbraid.

inveigle, in-vē'gl, *vt.* To persuade something evil; to entice; to seduce. **i veiglement,** in-vē'gl-ment, *n.* Act inveigling; seduction to evil; enticeme

invent, in-vent', *vt.* To devise or pr duce; as something new; to fabricate; conceot. **invention,** in-ven'shun, *n.* A of inventing; contrivance of that whi did not before exist; device; power of venting; ingenuity; faculty by which author produces plots, &c. **inventiv** in-ven'tiv, *a.* Able to invent; quick contrivance; ready at expedients.

ventor, in-ven'ter, *n.* One who invents; a contriver.

aventory, in"ven-tō'ri, *n.* An account or catalogue of the goods and chattels of a deceased person; a catalogue of particular things.—*vt.* To make an inventory of.

averse, in-vèrs' or in'vèrs, *a.* Opposite in order or relation; inverted. **inversely,** in-vèrs'li, *adv.* In an inverse order or manner; in inverse proportion.

aversion, in-vèr'shun, *n.* Act of inverting; state of being inverted; change of order so that the last becomes first, and the first last; a turning backward.

avert, in-vèrt', *vt.* To turn upside down; to place in a contrary position; to reverse.

avertebrate, in-vèr'tē-brāt, *a.* Destitute of a backbone or vertebral column. —*n.* An animal (one of the Invertebrata) in which there is no backbone.

averted, in-vèr'ted, *p.a.* Turned upside down; changed in order.

avest, in-vest', *vt.* To clothe; to array; to clothe with office or authority; to endow; to besiege; to lay out as money in some species of property.—*vi.* To make an investment.

avestigate, in-ves'ti-gāt, *vt.* To search into; to make careful examination of. **investigation,** in-ves'ti-gā"shun, *n.* Act of investigating; examination; search; scrutiny. **investigator,** in-ves"ti-gā'ter, *n.* One who investigates.

avestiture, in-ves'ti-tūr, *n.* Act of investing or giving possession of any manor, office, or benefice; clothing; covering.

avestment, in-vest'ment, *n.* Act of investing; act of besieging; money laid out for profit; that in which money is invested.

avestor, in-ves'ter, *n.* One who invests.

aveterate, in-vet'ér-it, *a.* Long established; deep-rooted; obstinate; confirmed. **inveteracy,** in-vet'ér-a-si, *n.* State or quality of being inveterate; obstinacy of any quality or state acquired by time.

avidious, in-vid'i-us, *a.* Envious; malignant; likely to incur hatred or to provoke envy.

avigorate, in-vig'ér-āt, *vt.* To give vigor to; to give life and energy to. **invigoration,** in-vig'or-ā"shun, *n.* Act of invigorating; state of being invigorated.

avincible, in-vin'si-bl, *a.* Not to be conquered or overcome; insurmountable. —*n.* One who is invincible. **invincibly,** in-vin'si-bli, *adv.* Unconquerably.

aviolable, in-vī'ō-la-bl, *a.* Not to be violated; that ought not to be injured or treated irreverently; not susceptible of hurt.

aviolably, in-vī'ō-la-bli, *adv.* In an inviolable manner; without profanation.

aviolate, in-vī'ō-lit, *a.* Not violated; uninjured; unprofaned; unbroken.

avisible, in-viz'i-bl, *a.* Not visible; that cannot be seen; imperceptible.

avisibly, in-viz'i-bli, *adv.* In an invisible manner; imperceptible to the eye.

avisibility, in-viz'i-bil"i-ti, *n.* State of being invisible.

avitation, in"vi-tā"shun, *n.* Act of inviting; bidding to an entertainment, &c.

invite, in-vīt', *vt.* (inviting, invited). To ask to do something; to ask to an entertainment, &c.; to allure or attract. —*vi.* To give invitation; to allure.—*n.* An invitation. **inviting,** in-vīt'ing, *p.a.* Attractive.

invocation, in'vō-kā"shun, *n.* Act of invoking; the form or act of calling for the assistance of any being, particularly a divinity.

invoice, in'vois, *n.* A written account of the merchandise sent to a person, with the prices annexed.—*vt.* (invoicing, invoiced). To make an invoice of; to enter in an invoice.

invoke, in-vōk', *vt.* (invoking, invoked). To call upon; to address in prayer; to call on for assistance and protection.

involuntary, in-vol"un-ter'i, *a.* Not voluntary; independent of will or choice. **involuntarily,** in-vol"un-ter'i-li, *adv.* In an involuntary manner.

involve, in-volv', *vt.* (involving, involved). To roll up; to envelop; to imply; to include; to implicate; to complicate; in algebra, &c., to raise a quantity to any assigned power.

invulnerable, in-vul'nèr-a-bl, *a.* That cannot be wounded; incapable of receiving injury.

inward, in'wèrd, *a.* Internal; being within; intimate; in the mind, soul, or feelings.—*adv.* Toward the inside; into the mind.—*n.pl.* The inner parts of an animal; the viscera. **inwardly,** in'wèrd-li, *adv.* In the inner parts; internally; privately.

iodine, I'ō-dīn, *n.* A non-metallic element chiefly extracted from the ashes of sea-weeds, and much used in medicine.

Ionian, ī-ō'ni-an, *a.* Pertaining to Ionia; Ionic.—*n.* One of an ancient Greek race.

Ionic, I-on'ik, *a.* Relating to Ionia, or to the Ionian Greeks; denoting an order of architecture distinguished by the volutes of its capital.

iota, I-ō'ta, *n.* The name of the Greek letter *i*; a tittle; a jot.

I O U, I' ō' ū', *n.* A signed paper having on it these letters and a sum of money borrowed, serving as an acknowledgment of a debt.

Iranian, i-rā'ni-an, *a.* Pertaining to Iran, the native name of Persia; applied to the Persian, Zend, and cognate tongues.

irascible, I-ras'i-bl, *a.* Readily made angry; easily provoked; irritable.

irate, I'rāt, *a.* Angry; enraged; incensed.

ire, Ir, *n.* Anger; wrath; rage.

iridescence, ir'i-des"ens, *n.* Property of being iridescent; exhibition of colors like those of the rainbow.

iridescent, ir'i-des"ent, *a.* Exhibiting colors like the rainbow; shimmering with rainbow colors.

iris, I'ris, *n.*; pl. **irises,** I'ris-ez. The rainbow; an appearance resembling the rainbow; the colored circle round the pupil of the eye; the flag-flower.

Irish, I'rish, *a.* Pertaining to Ireland or its inhabitants.—*n.* Natives of Ireland; the Celtic language of the natives of Ireland.

irk, ẽrk, *vt*. To weary; to annoy; to vex. (Used impersonally.) **irksome**, ẽrk'-sum, *a*. Wearisome; vexatious.

iron, ĩ'ẽrn, *n*. The most common and useful metal; an instrument made of iron; a utensil for smoothing cloth; *pl*. fetters; chains; handcuffs.—*a*. Made of iron; consisting of or like iron; harsh; severe; binding fast; vigorous; inflexible. —*vt*. To smooth with an iron; to fetter; to furnish or arm with iron.

ironbound, ĩ'ẽrn-bound', *a*. Bound with iron; surrounded with rocks; rugged.

ironclad, ĩ'ẽrn-klad', *a*. Covered with iron plates; armor-plated.—*n*. A warship covered with thick iron plates.

iron curtain. A wall of secrecy between Communist countries and free Western nations.

ironical, ĩ-ron'i-kal, *a*. Containing irony; given to irony; expressing one thing and meaning the opposite. **ironically**, ĩ-ron'i-kal-li, *adv*. By way of irony; by the use of irony.

iron lung. A device which provides the body with artificial respiration.

ironware, ĩ'ẽrn-wãr, *n*. Iron worked up into utensils, tools, &c.

irony, ĩ'ro-ni, *a*. A mode of speech which expresses a sense contrary to that conveyed by the words; a subtle kind of sarcasm.

irradiate, i-rã'di-āt, *vt*. To send forth rays of light upon; to enlighten.—*vi*. To emit rays. **irradiation**, i-rã'di-ā"-shun, *n*. Act of irradiating; illumination; apparent enlargement of an object strongly illuminated.

irrational, ir-rash'un-al, *a*. Not rational; void of reason or understanding; foolish; in *mathematics*, surd. **irrationally**, ir-rash'un-al-li, *adv*. In an irrational manner; without reason; absurdly.

irreconcilable, ir-rek'on-sīl"a-bl, *a*. Not reconcilable; inconsistent; incompatible.—*n*. One who is not to be reconciled; one who will not work in harmony with associates.

irrecoverable, ir'rē-kuv'ẽr-a-bl, *a*. Not to be recovered or regained.

irredeemable, ir'rē-dēm"a-bl, *a*. Not redeemable; not subject to be paid at its nominal value.

irreducible, ir'rē-dūs"i-bl, *a*. Not reducible; that cannot be reduced.

irrefutable, ir-ref'ū-ta-bl, or ir-ref'ūt-a-bl, *a*. That cannot be refuted; unanswerable.

irregular, ir-reg'ū-lẽr, *a*. Not regular; not according to rule or custom; anomalous; vicious; crooked; variable; deviating from the common rules in its inflections.—*n*. A soldier not in regular service. **irregularity**, ir-reg'ū-lar"i-ti, *n*. State or character of being irregular; want of regularity; that which is irregular; immoral action or behavior.

irrelevant, ir-rel'ē-vant, *a*. Not relevant; not applicable; not to the purpose. **irrelevance, irrelevancy**, ir-rel'ē-vance, ir-rel'ē-van-si, *n*. State or quality of being irrelevant.

irreligious, ir'rē-lij"us, *a*. Not religious;

contrary to religion; impious; ungod. profane.

irremediable, ir'rē-mē"di-a-bl, *a*. to be remedied; incurable; irreparab

irreparable, i-rep'a-ra-bl, *a*. Not parable; irretrievable; irremediable.

irrepressible, ir'rē-pres"i-bl, *a*. Not pressible; incapable of being repressed.

irreproachable, ir'rē-prōch"a-bl, *a*. capable of being reproached; uprig faultless.

irresistible, ir'rē-zis"ti-bl, *a*. Not sistible; that cannot be resisted; resi less

irresolute, i-rez'ō-lūt, *a*. Not resolu not firm in purpose; undecided; wav ing. **irresolution**, i-rez'ō-lū"shun, Want of resolution or decision; vacil tion.

irrespective, ir'rē-spek"tiv, *a*. Havi no respect to particular circumstan (with *of*).

irresponsible, ir'rē-spon"si-bl, *a*. responsible; not liable to answer for c sequences.

irretrievable, ir'rē-trēv"a-bl, *a*. Th cannot be retrieved; irreparable.

irreverent, i-rev'ẽr-ent, *a*. Exhibit or marked by irreverence; wanting in spect. **irreverence**, i-rev'ẽr-ens, Want of reverence; want of venerati for the deity or for things sacred; wa of due regard to a superior; irrevere conduct or action.

irreversible, ir'rē-vẽr"si-bl, *a*. Not versible; not to be annulled.

irrevocable, ir-rev'ok-a-bl, *a*. Not to recalled, revoked, or annulled; irreves ble.

irrigate, ir'i-gāt, *vt*. To bedew or spr kle; to water by means of channels streams. **irrigation**, ir'i-gā"shun, Act or operation of irrigating.

irritate, ir'i-tāt, *vt*. To rouse to ang to provoke; to inflame. **irritatin** ir'rit-āt-ing *p.a*. Causing irritation; noying. **irritability**, ir'i-ta-bil"i-ti, Quality or state of being irritable. **irritable**, ir'i-ta-bl, *a*. Susceptible of ritation; very liable to anger; easily p voked. **irritant**, ir'i-tant, *a*. Irri ing; producing inflammation.—*n*. T which irritates; a medical applicat that causes pain or heat. **irritation**, i-tā'"shun, *n*. Act of irritating; exaspe tion; annoyance; vital action in mus or organs caused by some stimulus.

irruption, i-rup'shun, *n*. A burst in; a sudden invasion or incursion.

is, iz, The third pers. sing. of the v *to be*.

isinglass, ĩ"zing-glas', *n*. Fish glue gelatinous substance prepared from airbladders of certain fishes.

Islam, is'lam, *n*. The religion of M hammed; the whole body of those w profess it. **Islamism**, is'lam-izm, Mohammedism. **Islamite**, is'lam-It, A Mohammedan.

island, ĩ'land, *n*. A piece of land s rounded by water; anything resembl an island.—*vt*. To cause to become appear like an island; to dot, as w islands. **islander**, ĩ'lan-dẽr, *n*. habitant of an island.

isle, il, *n.* An island.—*vt.* To island.

islet, ī'let, *n.* A little isle.

isobar, ī'sō-bär, *n.* A line on a map connecting places at which the mean height of the barometer at sealevel is the same.

isolate, ī'sō-lāt or is'-, *vt.* To place in or as in an island; to place by itself; to insulate. **isolation,** ī'sō-lā"shun or is'-, *n.* State of being isolated; insulation.

isometric, isometrical, ī'sō-met"rik, ī'sō-met"rik-al, *a.* Pertaining to or characterized by equality of measure.

isosceles, ī-sos'e-lēz, *a.* Having two legs or sides only that are equal (an *isosceles* triangle)

isotherm, ī'sō-thėrm, *n.* A line on a map connecting places with a like temperature. **isothermal,** ī'sō-thėr"mal, *a.* Pertaining to isotherms.

Israelite, iz'ri-el-īt, *n.* A descendant of *Israel* or Jacob; a Jew.

issue, ish'ū, *n.* The act of passing or flowing out; delivery; quantity issued at one time; event; consequence; progeny; offspring; an artificial ulcer to promote a secretion of pus; matter depending in a lawsuit.—*vi.* (issuing, issued). To pass or flow out; to proceed; to spring; to grow or accrue; to come to an issue in law; to terminate.—*vt.* To send out; to put into circulation; to deliver for use.

isthmus, is'mus or isth'mus, *n.* A neck of land connecting two much larger portions.

it, it, *pron.* A pronoun of the neuter gender, third person, nominative or objective case.

Italian, i-tal'yan, *a.* Pertaining to Italy.

—*n.* A native of Italy; the language of Italy.

Italic, i-tal'ik, *a.* Pertaining to Italy; the name of a printing type sloping towards the right.—*n.* An italic letter or type.

italicize, i-tal'i-sīz, *vt.* To print in italics.

itch, ich, *n.* A sensation in the skin causing a desire to scratch; a constant teasing desire.—*vi.* To feel an itch; to have a teasing sensation impelling to something. **itchy,** ich'i, *a.* Affected with itch.

item, ī'tem, *adv.* Also.—*n.* A separate particular; a scrap of news.—*vt.* To make a note of.

iterate, it'ėr-āt, *vt.* To repeat; to utter or do a second time. **iteration,** it'ėr-ā"shun, *n.* Act of repeating; recital or performance a second time.

itinerant, i- or ī-tin'ėr-ant, *a.* Passing or traveling from place to place; not settled.—*n.* One who travels from place to place. **itinerary,** ī-tin"ėr-er'i or i-, *n.* A work containing notices of places on a particular line of road; a travel route; plan of a tour.—*a.* Traveling; pertaining to a journey. **itinerate,** i- or ī-tin'ėr-āt, *vi.* To travel from place to place.

its, its, *pron.* The possessive case (singular of *it.*

itself, it-self', *pron.* The neuter reflexive pronoun corresponding to *himself.*

ivory, ī'vō-ri, *n.* The substance composing the tusks of the elephant, &c.; something made of ivory.—*a.* Consisting or made of ivory.

ivy, ī'vi, *n.* A plant which creeps along the ground, or climbs walls, trees, &c.

J

jab, jab, *n.* A short, quick thrust or blow.

jabber, jab'ėr, *vi.* To gabble; to talk rapidly or indistinctly; to chatter.—*vt.* To utter rapidly with confused sounds.—*s.* Rapid and indistinct talk.

jack, jak, *n.* A name of various implements; a bootjack; a contrivance for raising great weights by the action of screws; a contrivance for turning a spit; a coat serving as mail; a pitcher of waxed leather; a ball used for a mark in bowls; a flag on a bowsprit; the union flag; the male of certain animals; a young pike; the knave in a pack of cards.

jackal, jak'al, *n.* An animal resembling a fox, and closely akin to the dog.

jackass, jak"as', *n.* The male of the ass; a dolt; a blockhead.

jackdaw, jak'da, *n.* A small species of crow.

jacket, jak'et, *n.* A short outer garment; a casing of cloth, felt, wood, &c.

jackpot. The prize of accumulated takes in games of chance.

jade, jād, *n.* A mean or poor horse; a low woman; a hussy; a hard, tenacious,

green stone of a resinous aspect when polished.—*vt.* (jading, jaded). To ride or drive severely; to weary or fatigue.—*vi.* To become weary; to sink.

jag, jag, *vt.* (jagging, jagged). To cut into notches or teeth; to notch.—*n.* A notch; a ragged protuberance.

jagged, jag'd, *p.a.* Having notches or teeth; cleft; divided.

jaguar, jag'wär, *n.* The American tiger, a spotted carnivorous animal, the most formidable feline quadruped of the New World.

jail, jāl, *n.* A prison; place of confinement.

jailer, jailor, jāl'ėr, *n.* The keeper of a jail.

jalopy, ja-lop'i, *n.* An old dilapidated automobile.

jam, jam, *n.* A conserve of fruits boiled with sugar and water.—*vt.* (jamming, jammed). To crowd; to squeeze tight; to wedge in.

jamb, jam, *n.* The side-post or vertical side-piece of a door, window, &c.

jangle, jang'gl, *vi.* (jangling, jangled).

To sound harshly; to wrangle; to bicker.
—*vt.* To cause to sound discordantly.—
n. Prate; discordant sound.

janitor, jan'i-tėr, *n.* A doorkeeper; one who looks after a public building.

January, jan'ū-er'i, *n.* The first month of the year.

jape, jāp, *n.* A jest; a gibe.—*vi.* (japing, japed). To jest or joke.

jar, jär, *vi.* (jarring, jarred). To strike together discordantly; to clash; to interfere; to be inconsistent.—*vt.* To shake; to cause a short tremulous motion in.—*n.* A rattling vibration of sound; a harsh sound; contention; clash of interests or opinions; a vessel or earthenware or glass.

jardinière, jär-di-nēr', *n.* An ornamental stand for plants and flowers.

jargon, jär'gon, *n.* Confused, unintelligible talk; gibberish; phraseology peculiar to a sect, profession, &c.; a variety of zircon.

jasmine, jaz'min, *n.* A fragrant shrub, bearing white or yellow flowers.

jasper, jas'pėr, *n.* A variety of quartz, of red, yellow, and some dull colors.

jaundice, jan'dis, *n.* A disease characterized by yellowness of the eyes and skin, loss of appetite, and general lassitude.—*vt.* To affect with jaundice, or with prejudice, envy, &c.

jaunt, jant, *vi.* To ramble here and there; to make an excursion.—*n.* A trip; a tour; an excursion; a ramble.

jaunty, jän'ti, *a.* Gay and easy in manner or actions; airy; sprightly; showy.

javelin, jav'lin, *n.* A light spear thrown from the hand.

jaw, ja, *n.* The bones of the mouth in which the teeth are fixed.

jay, jā, *n.* A bird allied to the crows.

jazz, jaz, *v.* To play or dance to jazz-music.—*n.* A form of syncopated music played in discordant tones on various instruments, as the banjo, saxophone, trombone, clarinet, piano, &c.

jealous, jel'us, *a.* Uneasy through fear of, or on account of, preference given to another; suspicious love; apprehensive of rivalry; anxiously fearful or careful.

jealousy, jel'us-i, *n.* Quality of being jealous; painful suspicion of rivalry; suspicious fear or apprehension; solicitude for others.

jeep, jēp, *n.* A small, rugged automobile originally developed for the military.

jeer, jēr, *vi.* To flout; to mock; to utter severe, sarcastic reflections.—*vt.* To treat with scoffs or derision.—*n.* A scoff; biting jest, gibe.

jeeringly, jēr'ing-li, *adv.* With raillery; scornfully; contemptuously.

Jehovah, jė-hō'va, *n.* An old Hebrew name of the Supreme Being.

jejune, jė-jön', *a.* Devoid of interesting matter; meager; barren.

jelly, jel'i, *n.* Matter in a glutinous state; the thickened juice of fruit boiled with sugar; transparent matter obtained from animal substances by boiling.—*vi.* To become a jelly.

jellyfish, jel''i-fish', *n.* A gelatinous marine animal.

jeopardy, jep'ėr-di, *n.* Hazard; risk;

exposure to death, loss, or injury. **jeo**
ard, jep'ėrd, *vt.* To put in danger; hazard. **jeopardize,** jep'ėr-dīz, *vt.* To jeopard. **jeopardous,** jep'ėr-dus, *a.* Hazardous.

jerk, jėrk, *vt.* To give a sudden p thrust, or push to; to throw with a qu motion.—*vi.* To make a sudden moti —*n.* A sudden thrust, push, or twite a sudden spring; a spasmodic mo ment; a person held in low rega *Slang.*

jerked, jėrkt, *p.a.* Cut into thin sli and dried, as beef.

jerky, jėr'ki, *a.* Moving by jerks.

jersey, jėr'zi, *n.* A kind of close-fitti knitted woolen shirt; *Cap.* An island the s. coast of Britain.

jest, jest, *n.* A joke; pleasantry; obj of laughter; a laughingstock.—*vi.* make merriment; to joke. **jester,** j tėr, *n.* One who jests; a buffoon; a mer andrew. **jestingly,** jes'ting-li, *adv.* a jesting manner; not in earnest.

Jesuit, je'zū-it, *n.* One of the Society Jesus, so called, founded by Ignat Loyola, in 1534; a crafty person; an i triguer.

Jesus, jē'zus, *n.* The Saviour of me Christ.

jet, jet, *n.* A shooting forth or spouti what issues from an orifice, as wat gas, &c.; a compact and very bla species of coal, used for ornaments.— (jetting, jetted). To emit in a jet.—
To issue in a jet.

jet-black, jet'blak', *a.* Of the deepe black; of the color of jet.

jet-propelled, jet''pro-peld', *a.* P pelled by expanding gas expelled und pressure.

jetsam, jet'sam, *n.* The throwing goods overboard to lighten a ship in d tress; goods so thrown away.

jettison, jet'i-sun, *n.* The throwing goods overboard to relieve a ship; je sam.—*vt.* To throw overboard.

jetty, jet'i, *n.* A kind of pier.—*a.* Ma of jet, or black as jet.

Jew, jö, *n.* A Hebrew or Israelite.

jewel, jö'el, *n.* A personal orname containing precious stones; a preci stone.—*vt.* (jeweling, jeweled). adorn with jewels. **jeweler,** jö'el-ėr, One who makes or deals in jewels a other ornaments. **jewelry,** jö'el-ri, Jewels in general.

Jewish, jö'ish, *a.* Pertaining to t Jews.

jib, jib, *n.* The triangular foremost sa of a ship; the projecting arm of a cra **jib, jibe,** jib, jīb, *vt.* and *i.* (jibbe jibed, jibd, jībd; jibbing, jibing, jib'in jib'ing). To shift (as a fore-and-aft sai from one side to the other; to pu against the bit, as a horse; to move re tively.

jiffy, jif'i, *n.* A moment; an instar (Colloq.)

jig, jig, *n.* A quick tune; a light live dance; a mechanical contrivance of va ious kinds.—*vt.* (jigging, jigged). dance a jig; to jolt.—*vt.* To jerk; jolt.

jilt, jilt, *n.* A woman who gives her lo

hopes, and capriciously disappoints him. —*vt.* To deceive in love.—*vi.* To play the jilt.

ingle, jing'gl, *vi.* and *t.* (jingling, jingled). To sound with a tinkling metallic sound; to clink.—*n.* A rattling or clinking sound.

ingo, jing'go, *n.* An expletive used as a mild oath; a bellicose patriot; a Chauvinist.

inrikisha, jinricksha, jin-rik'shä, *n.* A small two-wheeled carriage drawn by one or more men, used in Japan, &c.

inx, jinks, *n.* An affliction of bad luck.— *vt.* To cause bad luck.

ob, job, *n.* A piece of work undertaken; a public transaction done for private profit.—*vt.* (jobbing, jobbed). To let out in separate portions or jobs; to let out for hire, as horses; to engage for hire; to peck or stab with something sharp.— *vi.* To work at chance jobs; to buy and sell as a broker; to let or hire horses.

obber, job'èr, *n.* One who jobs or works at jobs; one who lets or hires out carriages or horses; one who deals or dabbles in stocks.

ockey, jok'i, *n.* A man who rides horses in a race; a dealer in horses; one who takes undue advantage in trade.—*vt.* To play the jockey to; to ride in a race; to jostle by riding against.

ocose, jō-kōs', *a.* Given to jokes and jesting; facetious; merry; waggish.

ocular, jok'ū-lèr, *a.* Given to jesting; jocose; humorous; sportive. **jocularity,** jok'ū-lar"i-ti, *n.* Quality of being jocular; merriment; jesting. **jocund,** jō'kund or jok'und, *a.* Blithe; merry.

og, jog, *vt.* (jogging, jogged). To push with the elbow or hand; to excite attension by a slight push.—*vi.* To move at a slow trot; to walk or travel idly or slowly.—*n.* A push; a shake or push to awaken attention.

oggle, jog'l, *vt.* (joggling, joggled). To shake slightly.—*vi.* To shake; to totter. —*n.* A kind of joint in masonry and carpentry.

oin, join, *vt.* To bind, unite, or connect; to unite in league or marriage; to associate; to add; to couple.—*vi.* To unite; to be close, or in contact; to unite with in marriage, league, &c.—*n.* Place, act, &c., of joining.

oiner, join'ér, *n.* A mechanic who does the wood-work of houses; a carpenter. **joining,** join'ing, *n.* A joint junction.

oint, joint, *n.* A joining; joining of two or more bones; articulation; a fissure in strata; part of an animal cut off by a butcher.—*a.* joined; united; shared; acting in concert.—*vt.* To form with joints; to fit together; to divide into joints or pieces.—*vi.* To coalesce as by joints, or as parts fitted to each other. **jointed,** joint'ed, *p.a.* Having joints or articulations; formed with joints or nodes. **jointly,** joint'li, *adv.* In a joint manner; together; unitedly; in concert.

oist, joist, *n.* One of the pieces of timber to which the boards of a floor or the laths of a ceiling are nailed.—*vt.* To fit with joists.

oke, jōk, *n.* A jest; something said to

excite a laugh; raillery; what is not in earnest.—*vi.* (joking, joked). To jest; to sport.—*vt.* To cast jokes at; to rally.

joker, jōk'ér, *n.* One who jokes; a merry fellow. **jokingly,** jōk'ing-li, *adv.* In a joking way.

jolly, jol'i, *a.* Merry; gay; mirthful; jovial; festive; plump and agreeable in appearance. **jollity,** jol'i-ti, *n.* Quality of being jolly; mirth; merriment; gayety; joviality.

jolt, jōlt, *vi.* and *t.* To shake with sudden jerks.—*n.* A shake by a sudden jerk.

jonquil, jong'kwil, *n.* A species of narcissus or daffodil.

jostle, jos'l, *vt.* (jostling, jostled). To push or knock against.—*vi.* To hustle.

jot, jot, *n.* An iota; a tittle.—*vt.* (jotting, jotted). To set down in writing. **jotting,** jot'ing, *n.* A memorandum.

journal, jér'nal, *n.* A diary; an account of daily transactions, or the book containing such; a daily or periodical paper; a narrative of the transactions of a society, &c.; that part of an axle which moves in the bearings. **journalism,** jér'nal-izm, *n.* Occupation of writing in, or conducting a journal. **journalist,** jér'nal-ist, *n.* The writer of a journal; a newspaper editor or contributor.

journey, jér'ni, *n.* A traveling from one place to another; tour; excursion; distance traveled.—*vi.* To travel from place to place.

journeyman, jér'ni-man, *n.* A workman who has fully learned his trade.

joust, jöst, *n.* A fight on horseback man to man with lances.—*vi.* To engage in fight with lances on horseback; to tilt.

jovial, jō'vi-al, *a.* Gay; merry; jolly. **joviality,** jō'vi-al"i-ti, *n.* Festivity; merriment. **jovially,** jō'vi-al-li, *adv.* In a jovial manner.

jowl, joul, *n.* The cheek. **cheek by jowl,** with heads close together; side by side.

joy, joi, *n.* Pleasure caused by the acquisition or expectation of good; delight; exultation; cause of joy or happiness.— *vi.* To rejoice; to be glad.—*vt.* To gladden. **joyful,** joi'ful, *a.* Full of joy; blithe; gleeful; joyous; happy; blissful; exulting. **joyfully,** joi'ful'li, *adv.* In a joyful manner; gladly; delightful. **joyous,** joi'us, *a.* Experiencing joy; causing joy; glad; gay; happy; delightful.

jubilant, jō'bi-lant, *a.* Uttering songs of triumph; rejoicing; shouting with joy. **jubilation,** jō'bi-lä"shun, *n.* A rejoicing; exultation; feeling of triumph.

jubilee, jō'bi-lē, *n.* Among the Jews, every fiftieth year; a season of great public joy; a celebration of a reign, marriage, &c., after it has lasted fifty years.

Judaism, jō'dā-izm, *n.* The religious doctrines and rites of the Jews; conformity to the Jewish rites and ceremonies.

judas, jō'das, *n.* A treacherous person.

judge, juj, *n.* A civil officer who hears and determines causes in courts; one who has skill to decide on anything; a critic; a connoisseur.—*vi.* (judging, judged). To act as a judge; to pass sentence; to form an opinion; to estimate.—*vt.* To hear and determine; to examine into and

decide; to try; to esteem. judgment, juj'ment, *n.* Act of judging; good sense; discernment; opinion or estimate; mental faculty by which man ascertains the relations between ideas; sentence pronounced; a calamity regarded as a punishment of sin; final trial of the human race.

judicial, jö-dish'al, *a.* Pertaining to courts of justice; inflicted as a penalty or in judgment; enacted by law or statute.

judiciary, jö-dish"i-er'i, *a.* Relating to courts of justice.—*n.* The system of courts of justice in a government; the judges taken collectively.

judicious, jö-dish'us, *a.* Prudent; sagacious.

judiciously, jö-dish'us-li, *adv.* Discreetly.

judicature, jö'di-kā-tūr, *n.* Power of distributing justice; a court of justice; extent of jurisdiction of a judge or court.

jug, jug, *n.* A vessel for liquors, generally with a handle; a mug; a pitcher. —*vt.* (jugging, jugged). To put in a jug; to cook by putting into a jug, and thus into boiling water.

Juggernaut, jug'ėr-nat, *n.* Any idea, custom, &c., to which one devotes himself or is ruthlessly sacrificed. (*Often not caps.*)

juggle, jug'l, *vi.* (juggling, juggled). To play tricks by sleight of hand; to practice imposture.—*vt.* To deceive by artifice.—*n.* A trick by legerdemain; an imposture. **juggler,** jug'lėr, *n.* One who juggles.

jugular, jug'ū-lėr, *a.* Pertaining to the throat or neck.

juice, jös, *n.* Sap of vegetables, especially fruit; fluid part of animal substances. **juicy,** jös'i, *a.* Abounding with juice.

jujitsu, jö-jit'sö, *n.* A method of wrestling originating in Japan; judo.

julep, jö'lep, *n.* A sweet drink.

Julian, jöl'yan, *a.* Pertaining to or derived from Julius Cæsar.

July, jö-lī', *n.* The seventh month of the year.

jumble, jum'bl, *vt.* (jumbling, jumbled). To mix in a confused mass.—*vi.* To meet, mix, or unite in a confused manner.—*n.* Confused mass; disorder; confusion.

jump, jump, *vi.* To leap; to skip; to spring; to agree, tally, coincide.—*vt.* To pass over by a leap; to pass over hastily.—*n.* Act of jumping; leap; spring; bound.

jumper, jump'ėr, *n.* One who or that which jumps; a long iron chisel; a loose blouse.

junction, jungk'shun, *n.* Act or operation of joining; state of being joined; point of union; place where railways meet.

juncture, jungk'tūr, *n.* A joining or uniting; line or point of joining; point of time; point rendered critical by circumstances.

June, jön, *n.* The sixth month of the year.

jungle, jung'gl, *n.* Land covered with trees, brushwood, &c., or course, re vegetation.

junior, jön'yėr, *a.* Younger; later lower in office or rank.—*n.* A per younger than another or lower in sta ing

juniper, jö'ni-pėr, *n.* A coniferous shr the berries of which are used to fla gin.

junk, jungk, *n.* Pieces of old rope; s beef supplied to vessels; a large flat-b tomed sea-going vessel used in Chi a chunk.

junket, jung'ket, *n.* Curds mixed w cream, sweetened and flavored; a swe meat; a feast.—*vi.* and *t.* To feast.

junta, jun'ta, *n.* A meeting; a junto; grand Spanish council of state.

junto, jun'tö, *n.* A select council whi deliberates in secret on any affair of go ernment; a faction; a cabal.

Jupiter, jö'pi-tėr, *n.* The chief deity the Romans; the largest and bright planet.

jurisdiction, jör'is-dik"shun, *n.* Judic power; right of exercising authority; d trict within which power may be ex cised.

jurisprudence, jör'is-prö"dens, *n.* T science of law; the knowledge of t laws, customs, and rights of men nec sary for the due administration of j tice.

jurist, jör'ist, *n.* A man who profes the science of law; one versed in t law, or more particularly, in the ci law.

juror, jör'ėr, *n.* One who serves on jury.

jury, jör'i, *n.* A number of men select according to law and sworn to decla the truth on the evidence; a body w jointly decides as to prizes.—*a.* In sh applied to a temporary substitute, as *jury-mast.*

juryman, jör'i-man, *n.* A juror.

just, just, *a.* Right; acting rightly; u right; impartial; fair; due; merite exact.—*adv.* Exactly; precisely; near nearly; almost; merely; barely.

justice, jus'tis, *n.* Quality of being jus rectitude; propriety; impartiality; fa ness; just treatment; merited reward punishment; a judge holding a spec office.

justify, jus'ti-fī, *vt.* (justifying, j tified). To prove or show to be just; defend or maintain; to excuse; to juc rightly of; to adjust. **justifiabl** jus"ti-fī'a-bl, *a.* That may be justifie warrantable; excusable. **justifiabl** jus"ti-fī'a-bli, *adv.* In a justifiable ma ner; rightly. **justification,** jus'ti kā"shun, *n.* Act of justifying; state being justified; vindication; defense; mission of sin.

jut, jut, *vi.* (jutting, jutted). To proje beyond the main body.—*n.* A projectio

jute, jöt, *n.* A fibrous substance from plant of India of the linden family, us for carpets, bagging, &c.; the plant self.

juvenile, jö've-nil, *a.* Young; youthfu pertaining to youth.—*n.* A young pers

juxtapose, juks'ta-pöz", *vt.* To pla

near or next. Also **juxtaposit**, jux-ta-poz′it.

juxtaposition, juks′ta-pō-zish″un, *n.* A placing or being placed near.

K

Kaffr, Kafir, kaf′ér, *n.* A member of the most important dark race in S. Africa.

kale, kāl, *n.* A kind of cabbage; colewort; cabbage or greens in general.

kaiser, ki′zér, *n.* An emperor.

kaleidoscope, ka-li′dŏs-kōp, *n.* An optical instrument which exhibits an endless variety of colored figures.

kangaroo, kang′ga-rö, *n.* An Australian marsupial quadruped that moves forward by leaps.

keel, kēl, *n.* The principal timber in a ship; extending from stem to stern at the bottom; the corresponding part in iron vessels; the whole ship; somethng resembling a keel; a coalbarge.—*vi.* To capsize.

keen, kēn, *a.* Acute of mind; shrewd; sharp; eager; piercing; severe; bitter.

keenly, kēn′li, *adv.* In a keen manner; eagerly; acutely; sharply; severely; bitterly.

keep, kēp, *vt.* (keeping, kept). To hold; to preserve; to guard; to detain; to attend to; to continue any state, course, or action; to obey; to perform; to observe or solemnize; to confine to one's own knowledge; not to betray; to have in pay.—*vi.* To endure; not to perish or be impaired.—*n.* Care; guard; sustenance; a donjon or strong tower. **keeper,** kēp′ér, *n.* One who has the care or custody of persons or things; a gamekeeper; a ring which keeps another on the finger.

keeping, kēp′ing, *n.* A holding; custody; support; conformity; harmony.

keepsake, kēp′sāk, *n.* Anything kept or given to be kept for the sake of the giver.

keg, keg, *n.* A small cask or barrel.

kelp, kelp, *n.* Large sea-weeds; alkaline substance yielded by sea-weeds when burned.

Kelt, Keltic, kelt. kel′tik. *See* **Celt, Celtic.**

ken, ken, *vt.* To know; to descry.—*n.* View; reach of sight; cognizance.

kennel, ken′el, *n.* A house or cot for dogs; a pack of hounds; hole of a fox, &c.; a haunt; a gutter.—*vi.* and *t.* (kenneling, kenneled). To lodge in a kennel.

kerchief, kér′chif, *n.* A cloth to cover the head; any loose cloth used in dress.

kernel kér′nel, *n.* The edible substance contained in the shell of a nut; the core; the gist.—*vi.* (kerneling, kerneled). To harden or ripen into kernels, as the seeds of plants.

kerosene, ker′ŏ-sēn′, *n.* A lamp-oil from petroleum, extensively used in America.

kestrel, kes′trel, *n.* A small British falcon.

ketch, kech, *n.* A strongly built vessel, usually two-masted.

ketchup, kech′up, *n.* A sauce made from mushrooms, tomatoes, &c.

kettle, ket′l, *n.* A vessel of iron or other metal, used for heating and boiling water, &c.

kettledrum, ket′l-drum′, *n.* A drum made of a copper vessel covered with parchment.

key, kē, *n.* An instrument for shutting or opening a lock; a little lever by which certain musical instruments are played on by the fingers; fundamental tone in a piece of music; that which serves to explain a cipher, &c.—*vt.* To furnish or fasten with a key.

keyboard, kē″bōrd′, *n.* The series of levers in a keyed musical instrument upon which the fingers press.

keyed, kēd, *a.* Furnished with keys; set to a key, as a tune.

keystone, kē″stōn′, *n.* The top stone of an arch which being the last put in, enters like a wedge, and fastens the work together.

khaki, kak′i, *a.* Of a brownish-yellow earthy color.—*n.* A brownish-yellow earthy color; cloth of this color worn by soldiers.

khan, kän, *n.* In Asia, a governor, a prince; a chief; an eastern inn; a caravansary.

kick, kik, *vt.* To strike with the foot; to strike in recoiling, as a gun.—*vi.* To strike with the foot or feet; to manifest opposition; to restrain; to recoil.—*n.* A blow with the foot or feet; recoil of a firearm.

kid, kid, *n.* A young goat; leather made from its skin; a small wooden tub; child *slang.*—*vt.* (kidding, kidded). To bring forth a kid.—*vt.* and *vi.* To tease.

kidnap, kid′nap, *vt.* (kidnaping, kidnaped). To steal or forcibly abduct a human being.

kidney, kid′ni, *n.* Either of the two glands which secrete the urine; sort or character.

kill, kil, *vt.* To deprive of life; to slay; to slaughter for food; to deaden (pain); to overpower. **killing,** kil′ing, *p.a.* Depriving of life; overpowering; dangerous.

kiln, kil, *n.* A fabric of brick or stone, which may be heated to harden or dry anything.

kilo, kē″lö *or* kil′ō, *n.* Short for kilogram or kilometer.

kilo-, kil'o. Prefix meaning one thousand.

kilogram, kilogramme, kĕ'lō-gram, *n.* A French measure of weight, being 1000 grams or 2.2 lbs. avoir.

kilometer, kil'ō-mē'tẽr, *n.* A French measure, 1000 meters, about ⅝ of a mile or 1093.633 yards.

kilt, kilt, *n.* A kind of short petticoat worn by the Highlanders of Scotland in lieu of trousers.—*vt.* To tuck up or plait like a kilt.

kilted, kilt'ed.—Wearing a kilt.

kin, kin, *n.* Race; family; consanguinity or affinity; kindred.—*a.* Kindred; congenial.

kind, kīnd, *n.* Race; genus; variety; nature; character. **in kind**, with produce or commodities.—*a.* Humane; having tenderness, or goodness of nature; benevolent; friendly.

kindergarten, kin'dẽr-gär'tn, *n.* An infants' school in which amusements are systematically combined with instruction.

kindle, kin'dl, *vt.* (kindling, kindled). To set on fire; to light; to rouse; to excite to action, *vi.* To take fire; to be roused or exasperated.

kindly, kīnd'li, *a.* Of a kind disposition; congenial; benevolent; mild.—*adv.* In a kind manner; favorably.

kindred, kin'dred, *n.* Relationship by birth; affinity; relatives by blood.—*a.* Related; of like nature; cognate.

kine, kīn, old *pl.* of cow.

kinetic, ki-net'ik, *a.* Causing motion; applied to force actually exerted.

king, king, *n.* The sovereign of a nation; monarch; a playing card having the picture of a king; chief piece in the game of chess. **kingdom**, king'dum, *n.* The dominion of a king; realm; a primary division of natural objects (*e.g.* the mineral kingdom); place where anything prevails and holds sway. **kingfisher**, king'fish'ẽr, *n.* A bird having splendid plumage which preys on fish. **kingly**, king'li, *a.* Like a king; belonging to a king; royal; regal; splendid.

kink, kingk, *n.* A twist in a rope or thread; a crotchet.—*vi.* To twist or run into knots.

kinsfolk, kinz'fōk, *n.* People of the same kin; kindred; relations.

kinsman, kinz'man, *n.* A man of the same kin; a relative.

kipper, kip'ẽr, *n.* A salmon at the spawning season; a fish split open, salted, and dried or smoked.—*vt.* To cure (fish) by splitting open, salting, and drying.

kirk, kẽrk, *n.* A church (Scot.).

kismet, kis'met, *n.* Fate or destiny.

kiss, kis, *vt.* To touch with the lips; to caress by joining lips; to touch gently. —*vi.* To join lips; to come in slight contact.—*n.* A salute given with the lips.

kit, kit, *n.* A wooden tub for fish, butter, &c.; an outfit.

kitchen, kich'en, *n.* The room of a house appropriated to cooking. **kitchenette**, kich'e-net, *n.* A room combining a small kitchen and a pantry.

kite, kīt, *n.* A bird of the falcon family; a light frame of wood and paper constructed for flying in the air.

kith, kith, *n.* Relatives or friends collectively.

kitten, kit'n. A young cat.—*vi.* To bring forth young, as a cat.

kleptomania, klep'tō-mā'ni-a, *n.* An irresistible mania for pilfering.

knack, nak, *n.* Facility of performance; dexterity.

knapsack, nap'sak, *n.* A bag for necessaries borne on the back by soldiers, &c.

knave, nāv, *n.* A petty rascal; a dishonest man; a card with a soldier on it (the jack).—**knavery**, nāv'ẽr-i, *n.* The practices of a knave; dishonesty; roguery. **knavish**, nāv'ish, *a.* Partaking of knavery; dishonest; roguish.

knead, nēd, *vt.* To work into a mass or suitable consistency for bread, &c.

knee, nē, *n.* The joint connecting the two principal parts of the leg; a similar joint; piece of bent timber or iron used in a ship, &c.

kneecap, nē'kap', *n.* The movable bone covering the knee-joint in front.

kneel, nēl, *vi.* (pret. and pp., kneeled or knelt). To bend the knee; to rest on the bended knees.

knell, nel, *n.* The sound of a bell rung at a funeral; a death signal.—*vi.* To sound, as a funeral bell; to toil; to sound as a bad omen.

knickerbockers, nik'ẽr-bok'ẽrz, *n.pl.* A kind of loose knee-breeches. Also **knickers.**

knickknack, nik'nak, *n.* A trinket; nicknack.

knife, nif, *n.*; pl. **knives**, nīvz. A cutting instrument consisting of a blade attached to a handle; cutting part of a machine.

knight, nit, *n.* Formerly one admitted to a certain military rank; now one who holds a dignity entitling him to have Sir prefixed to his name, but not hereditary; a champion; a piece in chess.—*vt.* To dub or create a knight. **knight-errant**, nit-e'rant, *n.* A knight who traveled in search of adventures. **knighthood**, nit'hŏd, *n.* The character, rank, or dignity of a knight; knightage. **knightly**, nit'li, *a.* Pertaining to a knight.—*adv.* In a manner becoming a knight.

knit, nit, *vt.* (knitting, knitted or knit). To tie in a knot; to form in a fabric by looping a continuous thread; to unite closely; to draw together; to contract.—*vi.* To interweave a continuous thread; to grow together. **knitting**, nit'ing, *n.* Formation of a fabric by knitting-needles; fabric thus formed.

knob, nob, *n.* A hard protuberance; a boss; a round ball at the end of anything. **knobby**, nob'i, *a.* Full of knobs; hard.

knock, nok, *vt.* To strike with something thick or heavy; to strike against; to clash.—*vi.* To strike.—*n.* A stroke; a blow; a rap.

knocker, nok'ẽr, *n.* One who knocks; something on a door for knocking.

knoll, nōl, *n.* A little round hill; ringing of a bell; knell.—*vt.* and *i.* To sound, as a bell.

knot, not, *n.* A complication of threads or cords; a tie; ornamental bunch of ribbon, &c.; hard protuberant joint of a plant; a knob; bunch; group; a difficult question; a nautical mile (= 1.511 ordinary mile). —*vt.* (knotting, knotted). To tie in a knot; to unite closely.—*vi.* To become knotted; to knit knots. **knotted**, not'ed, *p.a.* Full of knots. **knotty**, not'i, *a.* Full of knots; difficult; intricate.

KNOT.

know, nō, *vt.* (pret. knew; pp. known). To perceive with certainty; to understand; to be aware of; to distinguish; to be acquainted with; to have experience of.—*vi.* To have knowledge; not to be doubtful. **knowing**, nō'ing, *p.a.* Well informed; intelligent; significant; cunning. **knowingly**, nō'ing-li, *adv.* In a knowing manner; with knowledge; intentionally. **knowledge**, nol'ej, *n.* The result or condition of knowing; clear perception; learning; information; skill; acquaintance. **known**, nōn, *p.a.* Understood; familiar.

knuckle, nuk'l, *n.* The joint of a finger, particularly at its base; knee-joint of a calf or pig.—*vt.* (knuckling, knuckled). To strike with the knuckles. **to knuckle down**, or **under**, to yield.

kohlrabi, kōl'rä'bi, *n.* A vegetable of the cabbage family, with edible beetlike stem.

Koran, kō-ran', *n.* The book regulating the faith and practice of Mohammedans, written by Mohammed.

kosher, kōsh'ėr, *a.* Fit to eat according to Judaic dietary laws.

kraal, kräl, *n.* A S. African native village.

kriegspiel, krēg"spēl', *n.* A game played with pieces representing troops.

kudos, kö'dös, *n.* Glory; fame; renown.

L

label, lā'bel, *n.* A slip of paper, &c., affixed to something and stating name, contents, &c.; a slip affixed to deeds to hold the seal.—*vt.* (labeling, labeled). To affix a label to.

labial, lā'bi-al, *a.* Pertaining to the lips. —A vowel or consonant formed chiefly by the lips, as *b*, *m*, *p*, *o*.

labium, lā'bi-um, *n.* A lip, especially the lower lip of insects.

labor, labour, lā'bėr, *n.* Exertion, physical or mental toil; work done or to be done; laborers in the aggregate; the pangs and efforts of childbirth.—*vi.* To engage in labor; to work; to proceed with difficulty; to be burdened.—*vt.* To cultivate; to prosecute with effort. **labored, laboured**, lā'bėrd, *p.a.* Produced with labor; bearing the marks of effort. **laborer, labourer**, lā'bėr-ėr, *n.* One who labors; a man who does work that requires little skill, as distinguished from an artisan. **laborious**, la-bō'ri-us, *a.* Full of labor; arduous; diligent; assiduous. **laboriously**, la-bō'ri-us-li, *adv.* In a laborious manner; with toil or difficulty.

laboratory, lab"o-ra-tō'ri, *n.* A building or room for experiment in chemistry, physics, &c.; a chemist's work-room.

laburnum, la-bėr'num, *n.* A leguminous tree, with clusters of yellow flowers.

labyrinth, lab'i-rinth, *n.* A place full of intricacies; a maze; an inexplicable difficulty; a part of the internal ear. **labyrinthian, labyrinthine**, lab"i-rin"thi-an, lab"i-rin"thin, *a.* Pertaining to a labyrinth; winding; intricate; mazy.

lac, lak, *n.* A resinous substance produced by insects on trees in Asia; in the East Indies, 100,000 (a *lac* of rupees).

lace, lās, *n.* A cord used for fastening shoes, &c.; ornamental cord or braid; a delicate fabric of interlacing threads.—*vt.* (lacing, laced). To fasten with a lace; to adorn with lace; to interlace; to mingle in small quantity.

lacerate, las'ėr-āt, *vi.* To tear; to rend; to torture; to harrow. **laceration**, las-ėr-ā'shon, *n.* Act of lacerating; the breach made by rending.

lachrymal, lak'ri-mal, *a.* Generating or secreting tears; pertaining to tears. **lachrymose**, lak'ri-mōs, *a.* Full of tears; tearful in a sentimental way; lugubrious.

lack, lak, *vt.* To want; to be without; to need; to require.—*vi.* To be in want. —*n.* Want; deficiency; need; failure.

lackadaisical, lak-a-dā'zi-kal, *a.* Affectedly pensive; weakly sentimental.

lackey, lak'i, *n.* A footboy or footman. —*vt.* and *i.* To attend as a lackey, or servilely.

lackluster, lacklustre, lak"lus'tėr, *a.* Wanting luster.

laconic, laconical, la-kon'ik, la-kon'ik-al, *a.* Expressing much in a few words; brief; sententious; pithy.

lacquer, lak'ėr, *n.* A varnish containing lac, &c.; ware coated with lacquer.—*vt.* To varnish or coat with lacquer.

lacrosse, la-kros', *n.* A game at ball, played with a large battledore or *crosse.*

lactic, lak'tik, *a.* Procured from milk. **lactation**, lak-tā'shun, *n.* Act or time of giving suck; function of secreting milk. **lacteal**, lak'tē-al, *a.* Pertaining to milk; conveying chyle.—*n.* A vessel in animal bodies for conveying the chyle from the alimentary canal.

lactine, lactose, lak'tin, lak'tōs, *n.* Sugar of milk.

lacuna, la-kū'na, *n.*; pl. **-næ.** A small depression; a blank space; gap; hiatus.

lacy, lās'i, *a.* Resembling lace.

lad, lad, *n.* A stripling; a young man.

ladder, lad'ėr, *n.* An article of wood, rope, &c., consisting of two long side-pieces connected by cross-pieces forming steps; means of rising to eminence.

lade, lād, *vt.* (lading, pret. laded, pp. laded, laden). To load; to throw in or out (a fluid) with some utensil.

laden, lād'n, *p.a.* Loaded; burdened.

lading, lād'ing, *n.* That which constitutes a load or cargo; freight; burden.

ladle, lā'dl, *n.* A utensil with a long handle for serving out liquor from a vessel.—*vt.* (ladling, ladled). To serve with a ladle.

lady, lā'di, *n.* A woman of rank or distinction, or of good breeding; a title given to a woman whose husband is not of lower rank than a knight, or whose father was not lower than an earl; the mistress of an estate. (Eng.). **lady-bird, lady-fly,** lā"di-bėrd', lā"di-flī', *n.* A small British beetle, the larva of which feeds on plant-lice. **ladylike,** lā"di-līk', *a.* Like a lady in manners. **ladyship,** lā'di-ship, *n.* Condition or rank of a lady; used as a title.

lag, lag, *a.* Coming behind; sluggish; tardy.—*n.* Quantity of retardation of some movement.—*vi.* (lagging, lagged). To loiter, tarry.

lager beer, lä'gėr bēr, *n.* A German beer stored for some months before use.

laggard, lag'ėrd, *a.* Slow; sluggish; backward.—*n.* One who lags; a loiterer.

lagoon, la-gön', *n.* A shallow lake connected with the sea or a river.

lair, lār, *n.* A place to lie or rest; the restingplace of a wild beast, &c.

laird, lārd, *n.* In Scotland, a landowner or house-proprietor.

laissez faire, le-sä-fār', *n.* A letting alone; non-interference.

laity, lā'i-ti, *n.* The people, as distinguished from the clergy; non-professional people.

lake, lāk, *n.* A body of water wholly surrounded by land; a pigment of earthy substance with red (or other) coloring matter.

lama, lä'ma, *n.* A priest of the variety of Buddhism in Tibet and Mongolia.

lamb, lam, *n.* The young of the sheep; one as gentle or innocent as a lamb.—*vi.* To bring forth young, as sheep.

lambent, lam'bent, *a.* Touching lightly, as with the lips or tongue; playing about; gliding over; twinkling.

lambkin, lam'kin, *n.* A little lamb.

lame, lām, *a.* Crippled in a limb or limbs; disabled; limping; defective; not satisfactory; not smooth.—*vt.* (laming, lamed). To make lame; to render imperfect and unsound. **lamely,** lām'li, *adv.* In a lame manner; poorly; feebly.

lament, la-ment', *vi.* To express sorrow; to weep; to grieve.—*vt.* To bewail; to deplore.—*n.* A lamentation; an elegy or mournful ballad. **lamentable,** lam'en-ta-bl, *a.* To be lamented; doleful; miserable; wretched. **lamentably,** lam'en-ta-bli, *adv.* In a lamentable manner. **lamentation,** lam'en-ta"shun, *n.* Act of lamenting; expression of sorrow; complaint.

lamina, lam'i-na, *n.* pl.; -næ. A thin plate or scale; a layer lying over another; the blade of a leaf.

lamination, lam'i-nā"shun, *n.* State of being laminated; arrangement in laminæ.

lamp, lamp, *n.* A vessel for containing oil to be burned by means of a wick; any contrivance for supplying artificial light.

lampblack, lamp"blak', *n.* A pigment made from the fine soot of gas, oil, &c.

lampoon, lam-pön', *n.* A scurrilous or personal satire in writing; a satiric attack.—*vt.* To write a lampoon against.

lamprey, lam'pri, *n.* The name of eel-like, scaleless fishes with suctorial mouths, inhabiting fresh and salt waters.

lance, lans, *n.* A weapon consisting of a long shaft with a sharp-pointed head; a long spear.—*vt.* (lancing, lanced). To pierce with a lance; to open with a lancet.

lancer, lan'sėr, *n.* One who lances; a cavalry soldier armed with a lance.

lancet, lan'set, *n.* A sharp-pointed and two-edged instrument used in letting blood, &c.

land, land, *n.* The solid matter which constitutes the fixed part of the surface of the globe; soil; estate; country; people of a country or region.—*vt.* and *i.* To set or go on the land; to disembark.

landed, land'ed, *p.a.* Having an estate in land; consisting in real estate or land.

landholder, land"höl'dėr, *n.* A holder or proprietor of land.

landing, land'ing, *n.* Act of or place for going or setting on shore; level part of a staircase between the flights.

landlady, land"lā'di, *n.* A woman who has property in land, and tenants holding from her; mistress of an inn, &c.

landlocked, land"lokt', *a.* Inclosed by land, or nearly so, as a part of the sea.

landlord, land"lord', *n.* The lord of land; owner of land or houses who has tenants under him; master of an inn, &c.

landlubber, land"lub'ėr, *n.* A seaman's term of contempt for one not a sailor.

landmark, land"märk', *n.* A mark to designate the boundary of land; an object on land that serves as a guide to seamen.

landscape, land'skāp, *n.* A portion of land which the eye can comprehend in a single view; a country scene; picture representing a piece of country.

landslip, landslide, land"slip', land"slid', *n.* A portion of a hill which slips down; the sliding down of a piece of land; victory by a large margin.

landward, land'wėrd, *adv.* Toward the land.—*a.* Inward.

lane, lān, *n.* A narrow way or street; a passage between lines of men.

language, lang'gwij, *n.* Human speech; speech peculiar to a nation; words especially used in any branch of knowledge; general style of expression; expression of thought or feeling in any way.

languid, lang'gwid, *a.* Wanting energy; listless; dull or heavy; sluggish. **languidly,** lang'gwid-li, *adv.* Weakly; feebly. **languish,** lang'gwish, *vi.* To be or become faint, feeble, or spiritless; to fade; to sink under sorrow or any continued passion; to look with tenderness. **languor,** lang'gėr, lang'gwėr, *n.* Languidness; lassitude; a listless or dreamy state. **languorous,** lang'gėr-us, *a.* Characterized by languor.

lank, langk, *a.* Loose or lax; not plump; gaunt. **lanky,** langk'i, *a.* Somewhat lank; lean.

lanolin, lanoline, lan'ō-lin, *n.* A greasy substance obtained from unwashed wool, used as an ointment.

lantern, lan'tėrn, *n.* A case in which a light is carried; part of a lighthouse in which is the light; erection on the top of a dome, &c., to give light; a tower with the interior open to view.—*vt.* To provide with a lantern.

lanyard, laniard, lan'yėrd, *n.* A short piece of rope or line, used in ships.

lap, lap, *n.* The loose lower part of a garment; the clothes on the knees of a person when sitting; the knees in this position; part of a thing that covers another; single round of a course in races; a lick, as with the tongue; sound as of water rippling on the beach.—*vt.* (lapping, lapped). To lap; to infold; to lick up; to wash gently against.—*vi.* To lie or be turned over; to lick up food; to ripple gently.

lapel, la-pel', *n.* That part of the coat which laps over the facing, &c.

lapidary, lap'i-der'i, *n.* One who cuts and engraves precious stones—*a.* Pertaining to the art of cutting stones.

lapse, laps, *n.* A slipping or gradual falling; unnoticed passing; a slip; a failing in duty; deviation from rectitude. —*vi.* (lapsing, lapsed). To pass slowly; to glide; to slip in moral conduct; to fail in duty; to pass from one to another by some omission.

larboard, lär'bŏrd, *n.* The left-hand side of a ship; port.—*a.* Pertaining to the left-hand side of a ship.

larceny, lär'se-ni, *n.* Theft of goods or personal property.

larch, lärch, *n.* A tall cone-bearing tree.

lard, lärd, *n.* The fat of swine, after being melted and separated from the flesh. —*vt.* To apply lard to; to fatten; to stuff with bacon; to interlard.

larder, lär'dėr, *n.* A room, box, &c., where meat is kept before eating.

large, lärj, *a.* Great in size, number, &c.; not small; copious; big; bulky; wide. **At large,** without restraint; with all details. **largehearted,** lärj'härt'ed, *a.* Liberal; munificent; generous. **largely,** lärj'li, *adv.* Widely; copiously; amply.

largess, largesse, lärj'es, *n.* A present; a bounty bestowed.

largo, lär'gŏ, *a.* and *adv.* In *music,* slow; slow with breadth and dignity.

lark, lärk, *n.* A small song-bird; a frolic.

larva, lär'va, *n.*; pl. **larvæ.** An insect in the caterpillar or grub state.

laryngitis, lar'in-jī''tis, *n.* Inflammation of the larynx, causing hoarseness.

larynx, lar'ingks, *n.*; pl. **larynxes, larynges,** lar'ingk-sez, la-rin'jēz. The upper part of the windpipe, a cartilaginous cavity serving to modulate the sound of the voice.

lascivious, la-siv'i-us, *a.* Wanton; lewd; lustful.

lash, lash, *n.* The thong of a whip; a whip; a stroke with a whip; a stroke of satire; a cutting remark.—*vt.* To strike with a lash; to satirize; to dash against, as waves; to tie with a rope or cord.—*vi.* To ply the whip; to strike at.

lass, las, *n.* A young woman; a girl.

lassitude, las'i-tūd, *n.* Faintness; languor of body or mind.

lasso, las'ŏ, *n.* A rope with a running noose, used for catching wild horses, &c. —*vt.* To catch with a lasso.

last, last, *a.* That comes after all the others; latest; final; next before the present; utmost.—*adv.* The last time; in conclusion.—*vi.* To continue in time; to endure; not to decay or perish.—*vt.* To form on or by a last.—*n.* A mold of the foot on which shoes are formed; a weight of 4000 lbs. **lasting,** last'ing, *p.a.* Durable; permanent.—*n.* A species of stiff woolen stuff. **lastingly,** last'-ing-li, *adv.* Durably.

latch, lach, *n.* A catch for fastening a door.—*vt.* To fasten with a latch.

late, lāt, *a.* Coming after the usual time; slow; not early; existing not long ago, but not now; deceased; recent; modern; last or recently in any place, office, &c. —*adv.* At a late time or period; recently.

lately, lāt'li, *adv.* Not long ago; recently.

latent, lā'tent, *a.* Not apparent; under the surface. **latency,** lā'ten-si, *n.* State of being latent.

lateral, lat'ėr-al, *a.* Pertaining to or on the side; proceeding from the side.

lath, lath, *n.* A long piece of wood nailed to the rafters to support tiles or plaster. —*vt.* To cover or line with laths.

lathe, lar͟H, *n.* A machine by which articles of wood &c., are turned and cut into a smooth round form.

lather, lar͟H'ėr, *n.* Foam or froth made by soap and water; foam or froth from profuse sweat, as of a horse.—*vt.* To spread over with the foam of soap.—*vi.* To become frothy.

lathing, lāth'ing, *n.* A covering made of laths; laths collectively.

Latin, lat'in, *a.* Pertaining to the Latins, a people of Latium, in Italy; Roman. —*n.* The language of the ancient Romans.

latitude, lat'i-tūd, *n.* Breadth; width; extent from side to side; scope; laxity; distance north or south of the equator, measured on a meridian; distance of a star north or south of the ecliptic.

latter, lat'ėr, *a.* Later; opposed to former; mentioned the last of two; modern; lately done or past. **latterly,** lat'-ėr-li, *adv.* Lately.

lattice, lat'is, *n.* A structure of crossed laths or bars forming small openings like net-work; a window made of laths crossing like net-work.—*a.* Furnished with a lattice.—*vt.* To form with cross bars and open work.

laud, lad, *n.* Praise; a hymn of praise; *pl.* a service of the church comprising psalms of praise.—*vt.* To praise; to celebrate. **laudable,** lad'a-bl, *a.* Deserving praise; praiseworthy; commendable. **laudatory,** lạd´a-tō-ri, *a.* Containing praise; tending to praise.—*n.* That which contains praise.

laudanum, lạ´da-num, *n.* Opium prepared in spirit of wine; tincture of opium.

laugh, lȧf, *vi.* To make the involuntary noise which sudden merriment excites; to treat with some contempt; to appear gay, bright, or brilliant.—*vt.* To express by laughing; to affect or effect by laughter.—*n.* The act of laughing; short fit of laughing. **laughable,** lȧf´a-bl, *a.* That may justly excite laughter; ridiculous; comical. **laughingly,** lȧf´ing-li, *adv.* In a merry way; with laughter. **laughingstock,** lȧf´ing-stok´, *n.* An object of ridicule. **laughter,** lȧf´tėr, *n.* Act or sound of laughing, expression of mirth peculiar to man.

launch, lȧnsh or länsh, *vt.* To throw; to cause to slide into the water; to put out into another sphere of duty, &c.—*vi.* To glide, as a ship into the water; to enter on a new field of activity; to expatiate in language.—*n.* Act of launching; the largest boat carried by a man-of-war.

laundress, lạn´dres or län´dres, *n.* A female who washes and dresses linen, &c.

laundry, lạn´dri or län´dri, *n.* Place where clothes are washed and dressed.

laureate, lạ´rē-āt, *a.* Decked or invested with laurel. **poet laureate,** in Great Britain, a poet specially appointed as the poet of the sovereign.—*n.* One crowned with a laurel; a poet laureate.—*vt.* To crown with laurel; to honor with a degree, &c.

laurel, lạ´rel, *n.* The bay-tree, a fragrant tree or shrub used in ancient times in making wreaths for victors, &c.; *pl.* a crown of laurel; honor; distinction. **laureled,** lạ´reld, *a.* Crowned with laurel, or with laurel wreath; laureate.

lava, lä´va, *n.* Rock matter that flows in a molten state from volcanoes.

lavatory, lav´a-tō-ri, *n.* A room or place for personal ablutions; a lotion.

lave, lāv, *vt.* (laving, laved). To wash; to bathe; to throw out, as water; to bale.—*vi.* To bathe; to wash one's self; to wash, as the sea on the beach.

lavender, lav´en-dėr, *n.* An aromatic plant of the mint family, which yields an essential oil and a perfume; a pale blue color with a slight mixture of gray.

lavish, lav´ish, *a.* Profuse; liberal to a fault; extravagant; superabundant.—*vt.* To expend with profusion; to squander. **lavishly,** lav´ish-li, *adv.* Profusely; wastefully.

law, lạ, *n.* A rule prescribed by authority; a statute; a precept; such rules or statutes collectively; legal procedure; litigation; a principle deduced from practice or observation; a formal statement of facts observed in natural phenomena. **lawful,** lạ´ful, *a.* Agreeable to law; allowed by law; legal; rightful. **lawfully,** lạ´ful-li, *adv.* In a lawful manner; legally. **lawless,** lạ´les, *a.* Not subject to law; contrary to law; illegal; capricious.

lawn, lạn, *n.* An open space between woods; a space of smooth level ground covered with grass; a fine linen or cambric.

lawn tennis, lạn ten´is, *n.* A game played with balls and rackets on a lawn.

lawsuit, lạ´sūt, *n.* A suit in law for the recovery of a supposed right.

lawyer, lạ´yer, *n.* One versed in the laws, or a practitioner of law.

lax, laks, *a.* Loose; flabby; soft; slack; vague; equivocal; not strict; remiss; having too frequent discharges from the bowels. **laxative,** lak´sa-tiv, *a.* Having the power of relieving from constipation.—*n.* A gentle purgative. **laxity,** lak´si-ti, *n.* State or quality of being lax; want of strictness; looseness.

lay, lā, *vt.* (pret. and pp., laid). To place in a lying position; to set or place in general; to impose; to bring into a certain state; to settle; to allay; to place at hazard; to wager; to contrive.—*vi.* To bring forth eggs; to wager.—*n.* A stratum; a layer; one rank in a series reckoned upward; a song; a narrative poem.—*a.* Not clerical; not professional.

layer, lā´ėr, *n.* One who or that which lays; a stratum; a cost, as of paint; a row of masonry, &c.; a shoot of a plant, not detached from the stalk, partly laid underground for growth.—*vt.* To propagate by bending a shoot into the soil.

layman, lā´man, *n.* One not a clergyman.

layoff, lā´of´, *n.* A period of being off or laid off work.

layout, lā´out´, *n.* Physical planning of or makeup of newspapers and advertisements.

lazy, lā´zi, *a.* Disinclined to exertion; slothful; indolent; slow. **lazily,** lā´zi-li, *adv.* Sluggishly. **laziness,** lā´zi-nes, *n.* State or quality of being lazy; indolence; sloth.

lead, led, *n.* A soft and heavy metal; a plummet; a thin plate of type-metal, used to separate lines in printing; plumbago in pencils; *pl.* the leaden covering of a roof.—*a.* Made of lead; produced by lead.—*vt.* To cover with lead; to fit with lead.

lead, lēd, *vt.* (pret. and pp., led). To guide or conduct; to direct and govern; to precede; to entice; to influence; to spend; to begin.—*vi.* To go before and show the way; to be chief or commander; to draw; to have a tendency.—*n.* Guidance; precedence.

leaden, led´n, *a.* Made of lead; like lead; heavy; inert; dull.

leader, lēd´ėr, *n.* One who leads; a guide; captain; head of a party; editorial article in a newspaper.

leadership, lēd´ėr-ship, *n.* State or condition of a leader.

leading, lēd´ing, *p.a.* Chief; principal. **leading question,** a question which suggests an answer that the questioner desires.

leaf, lēf, *n.*; *pl.* **leaves,** lēvz. One of the thin, expanded, deciduous growths of a plant; a part of a book containing two pages; a very thin plate; the movable side of a table; one side of a double door.—*vi.* To shoot out leaves; to produce leaves. **leafless**, lēf'les, *a.* Destitute of leaves. **leaflet**, lēf'let, *n.* A little leaf. **leafy**, lēf'i, *a.* Full of leaves.

league, lēg, *n.* A combination between states for their mutual aid; an alliance; a compact; a measure of three miles or knots.—*vi.* (leaguing, leagued). To form a league; to confederate.

leak, lēk, *n.* A fissure in a vessel that admits water, or permits it to escape; the passing of fluid through an aperture. —*vi.* To let water in or out of a vessel through a crevice. **leakage**, lēk'ij, *n.* A leaking; quantity of a liquid that enters or issues by leaking; an allowance for the leaking of casks. **leaky**, lēk'i, *a.* Having a leak.

lean, lēn, *vi.* (pret. and pp. leaned, leant). To slope or slant; to incline; to tend; to bend so as to rest on something; to depend.—*vt.* To cause to lean; to support or rest.

lean, lēn, *a.* Wanting flesh or fat on the body; meager; not fat; barren.—*n.* That part of flesh which consists of muscle without fat.

leap, lēp, *vi.* (pret. and pp. leaped, leapt). To spring from the ground; to jump; to rush with violence; to bound. —*vt.* To pass over by leaping.—*n.* A jump; a spring; space passed by leaping; a sudden transition.

leapfrog, lēp"frog', *n.* A game in which one stoops down and others leap over him.

leap year, lēp'yēr, *n.* A year containing 366 days; every fourth year.

learn, lèrn, *vt.* (pret. and pp. learned, learnt). To gain knowledge of or skill in; to acquire by study.—*vi.* To gain knowledge; to receive instruction. **learned**, lèr'ned, *a.* Having much knowledge: erudite; scholarly. **learnedly**, lèr'ned-li *adv.* In a learned manner: with much knowledge or erudition. **learner**, lèrn'er, *n.* One who learns; a pupil **learning**, lèrn'ing, *n.* Acquired knowledge; erudition; scholarship; education.

lease, lēs, *n.* A letting of lands, &c., for a rent; written contract for such letting; any tenure by grant or permission.—*vt.* (leasing, leased). To let; to grant by lease.

leash, lēsh, *n.* A thong or line by which a dog or hawk is held: three creatures of any kind.—*vt.* To bind by a leash.

least, lēst, *a.* Smallest.—*adv.* In the smallest or lowest degree. **at least, at the least**, to say no more; at the lowest degree.

leather, leᴛн'er, *n.* The skin of an animal prepared for use; tanned hides in general.—*a.* Leathern. **leathery**, leᴛн'ėr-i, *a.* Like leather; tough.

leave, lēv, *n.* Permission; liberty granted; a formal parting of friends.— *vt.* (leaving, left). To let remain: to have remaining at death; to bequeath; to quit; to abandon; to refer.—*vi.* To depart; to desist.

leave, lēv, *vi.* (leaving, leaved). To leaf. **leaved**, lēvd, *a.* Furnished with leaves or foliage; made with leaves or folds.

leaven, lev'en, *n.* A substance that produces fermentation, as in dough; yeast; barm.—*vt.* To mix with leaven; to excite fermentation in; to imbue.

leavings, lēv'ingz, *n.pl.* Things left; relics; refuse; offal.

lecher, lech'er, *n.* A man given to lewdness.—*vi.* To practice lewdness; to indulge lust. **lecherous**, lech'ėr-us, *a.* Addicted to lewdness or lust; lustful; lewd. **lechery**, lech'ėr-i, *n.* Free indulgence of lust.

lectern, lek'tèrn, *n.* A reading-desk in a church.

lecture, lek'tūr, *n.* A discourse on any subject; a reprimand; a formal reproof. —*vi.* (lecturing, lectured). To deliver a lecture or lectures.—*vt.* To reprimand; to reprove. **lecturer**, lek'tūr-ėr, *n.* One who lectures; one who delivers discourses to students

ledge, lej, *n.* A narrow shelf; a ridge or shelf of rocks.

edger, lej'èr. *n.* The principal book of accounts among merchants and others.

lee, lē, *n.* The quarter toward which the wind blows; shelter caused by an object keeping off the wind.—*a.* Pertaining to the side towards which the wind blows.

leech, lēch, *n.* A physician or doctor; a bloodsucking wormlike animal.—*vt.* To treat or heal; to bleed by the use of leeches.

leek, lēk, *n.* A culinary vegetable allied to the onion.

leer, lēr, *n.* A side glance; an arch or affected glance.—*vi.* To give a leer; to look meaningly.—*vt.* To turn with a leer; to affect with a leer.

lees, lēz, *n.pl.* The slime of liquor; dregs sediment.

leeward, lē'wèrd, *a.* Pertaining to the lee —*adv.* Toward the lee.

leeway, lē"wā'. *n.* The drifting of a ship to the leeward. **to make up leeway**, to overtake work in arrear.

left, left, *a* Denoting the part opposed to the right of the body.—*n.* The side opposite to the right

left-hand, left"hand', *a.* Relating to the left hand; on the left side.

left-handed, left"han'ded, *a.* Using the left hand and arm with more dexterity than the right; sinister; insincere; awkward.

leg, leg, *n* The limb of an animal; a lower or posterior limb; the long or slender support of anything.

legacy, leg'a-si, *n.* A bequest; a particular thing given by last will.

legal, lē'gal, *a.* According to, pertaining to, or permitted by law; lawful; judicial. **legality**, lē-gal'i-ti, *n.* Condition or character of being legal; conformity to law. **legalize**, lē'gal-iz, *vt.* To make legal or lawful; to authorize; to sanction. **legally**, lē'gal-li, *adv.* In a legal manner; lawfully; according to law.

legate, leg'it, *n.* An ambassador; the pope's ambassador to a foreign state. **legatee**, leg'a-tē", *n.* One to whom a legacy is bequeathed.

legation, lē-gā'shun, *n.* An embassy; a

diplomatic minister and his suite.

legato, le-gä′tō, *a.* and *adv.* Played or sung in an even, smooth, gliding manner.

legend, lej′end or lē′jend, *n.* A marvelous story handed down from early times; a non-historical narrative; an inscription. **legendary,** lej″en-der′i, or lē′jend-a-ri, *a.* Fabulous; traditional; mythical.

legerdemain, lej′ér-dē-mān″, *n.* Sleight of hand; an adroit trick.

legging, leg′ing, *n.* A covering for the leg; a long gaiter; generally in *pl.*

leghorn, leg′horn, *n.* A kind of straw plait imported from Leghorn; a hat made of it.

legible, lej′i-bl, *a.* That may be read. **legibly,** lej′i-bli, *adv.* So as to be read. **legibility,** lej′i-bil″i-ti, *n.* Quality or state of being legible.

legion, lē′jun, *n.* A Roman body of infantry soldiers, in number from 3000 to above 6000; a military force; a great number.

legislate, lej′is-lāt, *vi.* To make or enact a law or laws. **legislation,** lej′is-lā″shun, *n.* Act of making a law or laws; laws or statutes enacted. **legislativ**, lej″is-lā′tiv, *a.* Capable of or pertainin to the enacting of laws. **legislator,** lej″is-lāt-ér, *n.* A lawgiver; one who makes laws. **legislature,** lej″is-lā′tūr, *n.* The body of men invested with power to make laws.

legitimacy, lē-jit′i-ma-si *n* State of quality of being legitimate; legality **legitimate,** lē-jit′i-mit, *a.* Accordant with law; born in wedlock genuine; following by logical or natural sequence; allowable; valid.—*vt* To make legitimate. **legitimize,** lē-jit′i-mīz, *vt* To legitimate.

legume, leg′ūm, lē-gūm′, *n* A seed-vessel of two valves; a pod; *pl* pulse, pease, beans, &c **leguminous,** le-gū′mi-nus, *a.* Pertaining to legumes; consisting of pulse.

lei, lā′ē, *n.* (Hawaiian) A garland of flowers.

leisure, lē′zhér or lezh′ér, *n.* Freedom from occupation; vacant time.—*a* Not spent in labor; vacant time. **leisurely,** lē′zhér-li, *a.* Done at leisure; deliberate; slow.—*adv.* Slowly; at leisure

lemon, lem′on, *n.* An acid fruit of the orange kind; the tree that produces thi fruit.

lemonade, lem′un-ād″, *n* A beverage, usually aerated, consisting of lemou juice mixed with water and sweetened

lemur, lē′mér, *n.* A quadrumanous mammal, allied to monkeys and rodents.

lend, lend, *vt.* (lending, lent). To furnish on condition of the thing being returned; to afford or grant; *refl.* to accommodate.

lender, lend′ér, *n.* One who lends.

length, length, *n.* State or quality of being long; extent from end to end; extension; long duration; extent or degree. **at length,** at full extent; at last. **lengthen,** leng′then, *vt.* To make long or longer; to extend.—*vi.* To grow longer. **lengthily,** leng′thi-li, *adv.* In a lengthy manner. **lengthwise,** length″-

wiz′, *adv.* In the direction of the length; longitudinally. **lengthy,** leng′thi, *a.* Somewhat long.

lenient, lē′ni-ent, *a.* Acting without rigor; gentle; clement. **leniently,** lē′ni-ent-li, *adv.* In a lenient manner; mercifully; mildly. **lenience, leniency,** lē′ni-ens, lē′ni-en-si, *n.* Quality of being lenient; lenity; mildness.

lens, lenz, *n.*; pl. **lenses,** A transparent substance, usually glass, by which objects appear magnified or diminished; one of the glasses of a telescope, &c.

Lent, lent, *n.* A fast of forty days, from Ash-Wednesday till Easter. **Lenten,** lent′en, *a.* Pertaining to Lent; used in Lent; sparing; plain.

lentil, len′til, *n.* A pea-like plant, having seeds forming a very nutritious diet.

Leo, lē′ō, *n.* The Lion, the fifth sign of the zodiac.

leonine, lē′ō-nīn, *a.* Belonging to a lion; resembling a lion; applied to a rhyming Latin measure of hexameter and pentameter verses.

leopard, lep′érd, *n.* A large carnivorous animal of the cat genus, with a spotted skin.

leper, lep′ér, *n.* One affected with leprosy.

leprechaun, lep′re-kon, *n.* An Irish fairy, supposed to reveal hidden gold treasure to his captor.

leprosy, lep′rō-si, *n.* A foul cutaneous disease, characterized by dusky red or livid tubercles on the face or extremities. **leprous,** lep′rus, *a.* Infected with leprosy.

lesion, lē′zhun, *n.* Injury; wound; derangement.

less, les, *a.* Smaller; not so large or great.—*adv.* In a smaller or lower degree.—*n.* A smaller quantity.

lesson, les′n, *n.* Portion which a pupil learns at one time; portion of Scripture read in divine service; something to be learned; severe lecture; truth taught by experience.

lest, lest, *conj.* For fear that; in case.

let, let, *vt.* (letting, let). To permit; to allow; to lease.—*vi.* To be leased or let.

let, let, *vt.* To hinder; to impede.—*n.* A hindrance; impediment.

lethal, lē′thal, *a.* Deadly; mortal; fatal.

lethargy, leth′ér-ji, *n.* Morbid drowsiness; profound sleep; dullness. **lethargic,** le-thär′jik, *a.* Drowsy; morbidly inclined to sleep; dull.

letter, let′ér, *n.* A mark used as the representative of a sound; a written message; an epistle; the literal meaning; in *printing,* a single type; *pl.* learning; erudition.—*vt.* To impress or form letters on. **lettered,** let′érd, *a.* Versed in literature or science; belonging to learning. **lettering,** let′ér-ing, *n.* The act of impressing letters; the letters impressed.

letter press, let′ér pres, *n.* Letters printed by types; print.

lettuce, let′is, *n.* An annual composite plant, used in salads.

leukemia, lū-kē′mi-a, *n.* A form of cancer in which white blood cells increase abnormally.

Levant, lĕ-vant', *n.* The eastern coasts of the Mediterranean.—*vi.* To run away without paying debts.

Levantine, lĕ-van'tin, *a.* Pertaining to the Levant; designating a kind of silk cloth.

levee, lev'ē, *n.* A morning reception of visitors held by a prince; a river embankment.

level, lev'el, *n.* An instrument for detecting variation from a horizontal surface; an instrument by which to find a horizontal line; a horizontal line or plane; a surface without inequalities; usual elevation; equal elevation with something else; horizontal gallery in a mine.—*a.* Horizontal; even; flat; having no degree of superiority.—*vt.* (leveling, leveled). To make level; to lay flat on the ground; to reduce to equality; to point, in taking aim.—*vt.* To point a gun, &c.; to aim.

leveling, lev'el-ing, *n.* Act of one who levels; the art or practice of ascertaining the different elevations of objects.

lever, lē'vėr, *n.* A bar used for raising weights, &c.; a kind of watch.

leverage, lē'vėr-ij, *n.* Action or power of a lever; mechanical advantage gained by using a lever.

leviathan, lē-vī'a-than, *n.* An immense sea-monster.

levity, lev'i-ti, *n.* Lightness; inconstancy; giddiness; want of seriousness.

levy, lev'i, *vt.* (levying, levied). To raise (troops); to collect (taxes); to begin (war).—*n.* Act of raising troops or taxes; the troops or taxes raised.

lewd, lūd, *a.* Lustful; sensual; vile.

lewdly, lūd'li, *adv.* In a lewd manner.

lexicon, lek'si-kon, *n.* A word-book; a dictionary; a vocabulary containing an alphabetical arrangement of the words in a language, with the definition of each.

lexicographer, lek'si-kog"ra-fėr, *n.* The author or compiler of a dictionary.

lexicography, lek'si-kog"ra-fy, *n.* The act or art of compiling a dictionary.

leze-majesty, lēz'maj-es-ti, *n.* Any crime against the sovereign power in a state.

liable, lī'a-bl, *a.* Answerable for consequences; responsible; subject; exposed; with *to.* **liability,** lī'a-bil"i-ti, *n.* State of being liable; that for which one is liable; *pl.* debts.

liaison, lē'ā-zōn", *n.* A bond of union; an illicit intimacy between a man and woman.

liar, lī'ėr, *n.* One who utters falsehood.

libation, lī-bā'shun, *n.* Act of pouring a liquor, usually wine, on the ground or on a victim in sacrifice, in honor of some deity; the wine or other liquor so poured.

libel, lī'bel, *n.* A defamatory writing; a malicious publication; the written statement of a plaintiff's ground of complaint against a defendant.—*vt.* (libeling, libeled). To frame a libel against; to lampoon; to exhibit a charge against in court. **libeler,** lī'bel-ėr, *n.* One who libels. **libelous,** lī-bel-us, *a.* Containing a libel; defamatory.

liberal, lib'ėr-al, *a.* Generous; ample; profuse; favorable to reform or progress; not too literal or strict; free.—*n.* One who advocates greater political freedom.

liberalism, lib'ėr-al-izm, *n.* Liberal principles; the principles or practice of liberals. **liberality,** lib'ėr-al"i-ti, *n.* Largeness of mind; width of sympathy; generosity. **liberalize,** lib'ėr-al-iz, *vt.* To render liberal; to free from narrow views. **liberally,** lib'ėr-al-li, *adv.* In a liberal manner; bountifully; freely; not strictly.

liberate, lib'ėr-āt, *vt.* To free; to deliver; to set at liberty; to disengage. **liberation,** lib'ėr-ā"shun, *n.* Act of liberating. **liberator,** li'bėr-āt-ėr, *n.* One who liberates.

libertine, lib'ėr-tēn, *n.* A freedman; one who indulges his lust without restraint; a debauchee.—*a.* Licentious; dissolute.

liberty, lib'ėr-ti, *n.* State or condition of one who is free; privilege; immunity; license; district within which certain exclusive privileges may be exercised; freedom of action or speech beyond civility or decorum; state of being disengaged.

libidinous, li-bid'i-nus, *a.* Characterized by lust; lascivious; lewd.

libido, li-bī'dō, *n.* The sex drive, craving, and impulse behind all human action.

Libra, lī'bra, *n.* The Balance, the seventh sign in the zodiac.

library, lī'brer'i, *n.* A collection of books; edifice or apartment for holding books. **librarian,** li-brā'ri-an, *n.* The keeper of a library or collection of books.

libretto, li-bret'ō, *n.* The book of words of an opera, &c.

lice, lis, *n.pl.* of **louse.**

license, licence, lī'sens, *n.* Authority or liberty given to do any act; a certificate giving permission; excess of liberty; deviation from an artistic standard. **license,** *vt.* (licensing, licensed). To grant a license to; to authorize to act in a particular character. **licensee,** lī'sen-sē", *n.* One to whom a license is granted.

licentiate, li-sen'shi-āt, *n.* One who has a license to practice any art or to exercise a profession, as medicine or theology.

licentious, li-sen'shus, *a.* Characterized by license; profligate; libidinous. **licentiously,** li-sen'shus-li, *adv.* In a licentious manner; dissolutely.

lichen, lī'ken, *n.* A plant without stem and leaves, growing on the bark of trees, on rocks, &c.; an eruption of small red or white pimples.

lick, lik, *vt.* To draw the tongue over the surface of; to lap; to take in by the tongue; to beat.—*n.* A drawing of the tongue over anything; a slight smear or coat; a blow.

licorice, lik'ō-ris, *n.* A plant of the bean family, the roots of which yield a sweet juice.

lid, lid, *n.* A movable cover of a vessel or box; eyelid.

lie, lī, *vi.* (lying, lied). To utter falsehood with deceitful intention.—*n.* A falsehood; an intentional violation of truth.

lie, lī, *vi.* (lying; pret. lay; pp. lain). To

occupy a horizontal position; to rest on anything lengthwise;. to be situated; to remain; to be incumbent; to exist; to depend; to be sustainable in law. **to lie in**, to be in childbed. **to lie to**, to stop and remain stationary.—*n.* Relative position of objects; general bearing or direction.

lief, lēf, *a.* Beloved; agreeable; *poetical.* —*adv.* Gladly; willingly; readily.

liege, lēj, *a.* Bound by a feudal tenure; subject; loyal; faithful.—*n.* A vassal; a lord or superior; a sovereign; a citizen in general; generally in *pl.*

lien, lē'en or lēn, *n.* A legal claim; a right over the property of another until some claim or due is satisfied.

lieu, lū, *n.* Place; stead; preceded by *in.*

lieutenant, lū-ten'ant, *n.* An officer who supplies the place of a superior in his absence; a commissioned officer next in rank below a captain. **lieutenancy**, lū-ten'an-si, *n.* Office or commission of a lieutenant; the collective body of lieutenants.

life, līf, *n.*; pl. **lives**, līvz. State of animals and plants in which the natural functions are performed; vitality; present state of existence; time from birth to death; manner of living; animal being; spirit; vivacity; the living form; exact resemblance; rank in society; human affairs; a person; narrative of a life; eternal felicity.

life belt, līf'belt, *n.* A buoyant belt used to support the body in the water.

lifeblood, līf''blud', *n.* The blood necessary to life; vital blood.

lifeboat, līf''bōt', *n.* A boat for saving men in cases of shipwreck.

life buoy, līf'boi, *n.* A buoy to be thrown to a person in danger of drowning.

life-giving, līf''giv'ing, *a.* Giving life; inspiriting; invigorating.

lifeguard, līf'gärd, *n.* A man employed on a bathing beach to protect swimmers from drowning.

lifeless, līf''les, *a.* Deprived of life; dead; inanimate; dull; heavy; inactive.

lifelike, līf''līk', *a.* Like a living person; true to the life.

lifelong, līf''long', *a.* Lasting through life.

life-size, līf''sīz', *a.* Of the size of the person or object represented.

lifetime, līf''tīm', *n.* The time that life continues; duration of life.

lift, lift, *vt.* To raise to a higher position; to hoist; to elevate; to raise in spirit; to collect when due.—*vi.* To raise; to rise.—*n.* Act of lifting; assistance; that which is to be raised; an elevator or hoist.

ligament, lig'a-ment, *n.* That which unites one thing to another; a band; a substance serving to bind one bone to another.

ligature, lig'a-tūr, *n.* Anything that binds; a band or bandage.

light, līt, *n.* That by which objects are rendered visible; day; that which gives or admits light; illumination of mind; knowledge; open view; explanation; point of view; situation; spiritual illu-

mination.—*a.* Bright; clear; not deep, as color; not heavy; not difficult; easy to be digested; active; not laden; slight; moderate; unsteady; gay; trifling; wanton; sandy; having a sensation of giddiness; employed in light work.—*adv.* Lightly; cheaply.—*vt.* (pret. and pp. lighted or lit). To give light to; to enlighten; to ignite.—*vi.* To brighten; to descend, as from a horse, &c.; to alight; to come by chance.

lighten, līt'n, *vi.* To become brighter; to shine; to flash, as lightning.—*vt.* To illuminate; to enlighten; to flash forth; to make less heavy; alleviate; to cheer; to gladden.

lighter, līt'ėr, *n.* One who or that which lights or kindles; a large flat-bottomed boat used in loading and unloading ships.

light-fingered, līt''fing'gėrd, *a.* Thievish; addicted to petty thefts.

light-footed, līt''fut'ed, *a.* Nimble; active.

light-headed, līt'hed'ed, *a.* Thoughtless; unsteady; delirious; dizzy.

light-hearted, līt'här'ted, *a.* Free from grief or anxiety; gay; cheerful; merry.

lighthouse, līt''hous', *n.* A tower with a light on the top to direct seamen at night.

lightly, līt'li, *adv.* With little weight; easily; cheerfully; nimbly; airily.

lightning, līt'ning, *n.* The sudden and vivid flash that precedes thunder, produced by a discharge of atmospheric electricity.

lightning rod, līt'ning rod, *n.* A metallic rod to protect buildings or vessels from lightning. Also **lightning-conductor.**

lightweight, līt''wāt', *n.* Boxer weighing between 127 and 135 pounds; a person of low ability. *Slang.*

lignite, lig'nīt, *n.* Fossil wood or browncoal.

like, līk, *a.* Equal; similar; resembling; likely; feeling disposed.—*adv.* or *prep.* In the same manner; similarly; likely. —*vt.* (liking, liked). To be pleased with; to approve.—*vi.* To be pleased; to choose.—*n.* Some person or thing resembling another; a counterpart; a liking; a fancy. **likeable**, līk'a-bl, *a.* Such as to attract liking; lovable. **likelihood**, līk'li-hōd, *n.* Probability; appearance of truth or reality. **likely**, līk'li, *a.* Probable; credible; suitable.—*adv.* Probably.

liken, līk'n, *vt.* To compare; to represent as resembling or similar. **likeness**, līk'nes, *n.* Quality or state of being like; resemblance; similarity; one who resembles another; a portrait. **likewise**, līk'wīz, *adv.* In like manner; also; moreover; too. **liking**, līk'ing, *n.* Inclination; desire; preference; satisfaction.

lilac, lī'lak, *n.* A shrub with flowers generally bluish or white.

Lilliputian, lil'i-pū''shan, *n.* A person of very small size.—*a.* Very small.

lilt, lilt, *vt.* and *i.* To sing cheerfully; to give musical utterance.—*n.* A song; a tune.

lily, lil'i, *n.* A bulbous plant with showy and fragrant flowers.

limb, lim, *n.* The arm or leg, especially

the latter; a branch of a tree; graduated edge of a quadrant, &c.; border of the disk of the sun, moon, &c.—*vt.* To supply with limbs; to tear off the limbs of.

limber, lim'bér, *a.* Flexible; pliant—*n.* A carriage with ammunition boxes attached to the gun-carriage.—*vt.* and *i.* To attach the limber to the gun-carriage.

limbo, lim'bo, *n.* A supposed region beyond this world for souls of innocent persons ignorant of Christianity; any similar region; a prison of confinement.

lime, lim, *n.* Any viscous substance; calcareous earth used in cement; mortar made with lime; the linden-tree; a tree producing an inferior sort of lemon.—*vt.* (liming, limed). To smear or manure with lime; to ensnare; to cement.

limelight, lim'lit, *n.* Strong spotlight; center of attention; being in the public eye.

limestone, lim'ston, *n.* A kind of stone consisting of varieties of carbonate of lime.

limit, lim'it, *n.* Boundary; border; utmost extent; restraint; restriction.—*vt.* To bound; to circumscribe; to restrain; to restrict. **limitation**, lim'i-tā'shun, *n.* Act of limiting; state of being limited; restriction. **limitless**, lim'it-les, *a.* Having no limits; boundless; infinite; vast.

limn, lim, *vt.* To draw or paint, especially a portrait.

limousine, lim'ö-zēn″, *n.* A kind of automobile body.

limp, limp, *vi.* To halt; to walk lamely. —*n.* A halt; act of limping.—*a.* Easily bent; pliant; flaccid.

limpet, lim'pet, *n.* A marine mollusk, adhering to rocks.

limpid, lim'pid, *a.* Clear; crystal; pellucid. **limpidity**, lim-pid'i-ti, *n.* Clearness; purity; transparency.

linden, lin'den, *n.* The lime-tree.

line, lin, *n.* A small rope or cord; a threadlike marking; a stroke or score; a row of soldiers, ships, words, &c.; a verse; an outline; a short written communication; course of procedure, &c.; connected series, as of descendants; series of public conveyances, as steamers; the twelfth part of an inch; the equator; the regular infantry of an army; *pl.* works covering extended positions, and presenting a front in only one direction to the enemy.—*vt.* (lining, lined). To draw lines upon; to set with men or things in lines; to cover on the inside; to put in the inside.

lineage, lin'ē-ij, *n.* Descendants in a line from a common progenitor; race.

lineal, lin'ē-al, *a.* Composed of or pertaining to lines; in a direct line from an ancestor; hereditary.

lineament, lin'ē-a-ment, *n.* One of the lines which mark the features; feature; form.

linear, lin'ē-ér, *a.* Pertaining to a line; like a line; slender.

linen, lin'en, *n.* Cloth made of flax; underclothing.—*a.* Made of flax; resembling linen cloth.

liner, lin'ér, *n.* A vessel of a line of ocean-going steamships.

linesman, linz'man, *n.* An infantryman; one who works on power lines.

linger, ling'gér, *vi.* To delay; to loiter; to hesitate: to remain long.—*vt.* To spend wearily. **lingering**, ling'gér-ing, *a.* Protracted; given to linger.

lingerie, län'zhé-rē, *n.* Women's undergarments.

lingo, ling'gō, *n.* Language; speech; contemptuous term for a peculiar language.

lingual, ling'gwal, *a.* Pertaining to the tongue.—*n.* A sound pronounced with the tongue, as *l.* **linguist**, ling'gwist, *n.* A person skilled in languages. **linguistic**, ling-gwist'ik, *a.* Relating to language; philological.

liniment, lin'i-ment, *n.* A species of soft ointment; an embrocation.

lining, lin'ing, *n.* The covering of the inner surface of anything.

link, lingk, *n.* A single ring of a chain; anything closed like a link; anything connecting; a measure of 7·92 inches; a torch.—*vt.* To be connected.—*vt.* To join or connect, as by links; to unite.

links, lingks, *n.pl.* A stretch of uncultivated flat or undulating ground. A golf course.

linseed, lin'sēd, *n.* Flax-seed.

lint, lint, *n.* Flax; linen scraped into a soft substance and used for dressing wounds.

lintel, lin'tel, *n.* The horizontal part of the door or window frame.

lion, li'on, *n.* A carnivorous animal of the cat family; a sign in the zodiac, Leo; an object of interest and curiosity. **lioness**, li'un-es, *n.* The female of the lion. **lionhearted**, li'un-härt'ed, *a.* Having a lion's courage; brave and magnanimous. **lionize**, li'un-iz, *vt.* To treat as an object of curiosity and interest.

lip, lip, *n.* One of the two fleshy parts covering the front teeth in man, &c.; edge or border.—*vt.* (lipping, lipped). To touch as with the lip.

lipstick, lip'stik, *n.* A cartridge holding a stick of rouge for coloring the lips.

liquid, lik'wid, *a.* Fluid; not solid; soft; smooth; devoid of harshness.—*n.* A fluid; a letter with a smooth flowing sound, as *l* and *r.* **liquate**, li'kwāt, *vi.* and *t.* To melt; to separate by melting. **liqueur**, lē-kèr' or li-kör', *n.* An alcoholic beverage sweetened and containing some infusion of fruits or aromatic substances. **liquidate**, lik'wi-dāt, *vt.* To clear from obscurity; to adjust; to settle, adjust, and apportion, as a bankrupt's affairs. **liquidation**, lik'wi-dā'shun, *n.* Act of liquidating. **liquidity**, li-kwid'i-ti, *n.* State or quality of being liquid.

liquor, lik'ér, *n.* A liquid; spirituous fluids; drink.

lira, lē'rä, *n.*; pl. **lire**, lē'ra. An Italian silver coin.

lisp, lisp, *vi.* To pronounce the sibilant letters imperfectly, as in pronouncing *th* for *s*; to speak imperfectly, as a child.—*vt.* To pronounce with a lisp, or imperfectly.—*n.* The habit or act of lisping.

lissom, lis'um, **lissome**, lis'um, *a.* Supple; flexible; lithe; nimble; active.

list, list, *n.* The selvedge of cloth; a

limit or border; a roll or catalogue; inclination to one side; *pl.* a field inclosed for a combat.—*vt.* To enroll; to enlist.—*vi.* To enlist, as in the army; to desire; to be disposed; to hearken.

listen, lis'n, *vi.* To hearken; to give heed.—*vt.* To hear; to attend.

listless, list'les, *a.* Having no wish; indifferent; uninterested; languid; weary.

listlessly, list'les-li, *adv.* Without attention; heedlessly.

litany, lit'a-ni, *n.* A solemn supplication; a collection of short supplications.

liter, lē'tėr. See litre.

literal, lit'ėr-al, *a.* According to the exact meaning; not figurative; expressed by letters. **literally**, lit'ėr-al-li, *adv.* In a literal manner; not figuratively; word by word.

literary, lit"ėr-er'i, *a.* Pertaining to letters or literature; versed in letters.

literate, li'tėr-āt, *a.* Learned; literary.

literature, lit'ėr-a-tūr, *n.* Learning; literary knowledge; collective writings of a country or period; belles-lettres; the literary profession.

lithe, līᴛʜ, *a.* Pliant; flexible; limber.

lithesome, līᴛʜ'sum, *a.* Pliant; nimble.

lithium, lith'i-um, *n.* The lightest of all known solids.

lithograph, lith'ō-graf, *vt.* To engrave on stone, and transfer to paper, &c., by printing.—*n.* A print from a drawing on stone. **lithographer**, li-thog'ra-fėr, *n.* One who practices lithography. **lithographic**, lith'ō-graf"ik, *a.* Pertaining to lithography; printed from stone. **lithography**, li-thog'ra-fi, *n.* The art of drawing with special pigments on a peculiar kind of stone, and of producing impressions of the designs on paper.

Lithuanian, lith'ū-ā"ni-an, *n.* A native or citizen of Lithuania, now a republic of the U.S.S.R.

litigate, lit'i-gāt, *vt.* To contest in law.—*vi.* To carry on a suit by judicial process.

litigant, lit'i-gant, *a.* Disposed to litigate; engaged in a lawsuit.—*n.* One engaged in a lawsuit.

litigation, lit'i-gā"shun, *n.* Act or process of litigating; a lawsuit.

litmus, lit'mus, *n.* A coloring matter procured from certain lichens, used as a chemical test.

litre, lē'tėr, *n.* The French standard measure of capacity, equal to 61.028 cubic inches; the English imperial gallon being fully 4½ litres.

litter, lit'ėr, *n.* A frame supporting a bed in which a person may be borne; straw used as a bed for animals; the young produced at a birth by a quadruped; scattered rubbish; a condition of disorder.—*vt.* To furnish with bedding; to scatter in a slovenly manner; to bring forth.—*vi.* To lie in litter; to give birth to a litter.

little, lit'l, *a.* Small in size or extent; short in duration; slight; mean.—*n.* A small quantity, space, &c. **a little**, somewhat.—*adv.* In a small degree or quantity.

liturgy, lit'ėr-ji, *n.* A ritual or established formulas for public worship. **liturgic, liturgical**, li-tėr'jik, li-tė-ji-kal, *a.* Pertaining to a liturgy.

live, liv, *vi.* (living, lived). To exis to be alive; to dwell; to conduct one self in life; to feed or subsist; to acqui a livelihood; to be exempt from spiritu death.—*vt.* To lead, pass, or spen **live**, liv, *a.* Having life; not dea ignited; vivid, as color. **lived**, liv or livd, *a.* Having a life; as long-*live* **livelihood**, liv'li-hŏd, *n.* Means of li ing; maintenance; sustenance. **live long**, liv"- or liv'long', *a.* That lives endures long; lasting; tedious. **livel** liv'li, *a.* Vivacious; active; gay; viv *adv.* Briskly; vigorously.

liver, liv'ėr, *n.* One who lives; the org in animals which secretes the bile.

livery, liv'ėr-i, *n.* State of a horse th is kept and fed at a certain rate; d tinctive dress of male servants; distin tive garb worn by anybody; the body guild wearing such a garb.—*vt.* (liver ing, liveried). To clothe in, or as livery.—*a.* Resembling the liver.

livid, liv'id, *a.* Black and blue; of a le color; discolored, as flesh by contusio

living, liv'ing, *p.a.* Having life; existi in action or use.—*n.* Means of subsis ence; manner of life; the benefice of clergyman.

lizard, liz'ėrd, *n.* A four-footed, tail reptile.

llama, lä'ma, *n.* A S. American r minating animal allied to the camel, b smaller and without a hump.

llanos, lä'noz, *n.pl.* Vast grassy plai in S. America.

lo, lō, *exclam.* Look; see; behold.

loach, lōch, *n.* A small fish inhabitin clear swift streams in England.

load, lōd, *vt.* To charge with a load; burden; to encumber; to bestow in gre abundance; to charge, as a gun.—*n.* burden; cargo; a grievous weight; som thing that oppresses. **loading**, lōd'in *n.* A cargo; a burden; something add to give weight.

load line, lōd līn, *n.* A line on the si of a vessel to show the depth to whi she sinks when not overloaded.

loadstone, lodestone, lōd'stōn', *n.* ore of iron; the magnetic oxide of iro which can attract iron; a magnet.

loaf, lōf, *n.* pl. **loaves**, lōvz. A mass bread formed by the baker; a conic lump of sugar.—*vi.* To lounge.—*vt.* spend idly.

loafer, lōf'ėr, *n.* A lounger; a low idle

loam, lōm, *n.* A rich species of earth mold.—*vt.* To cover with loam. **loam** lōm'i, *a.* Consisting of or like loam.

loan, lōn, *n.* Lending; that which is len a sum of money lent at interest.—*vt.* an *i.* To lend.

loath, loth, lŏth, *a.* Disliking; unwi ing; averse; not inclined; reluctan **loathe**, lōᴛʜ, *vt.* (loathing, loathed To feel disgust at; to abhor; to abom nate.—*vi.* To feel nausea or abhorrenc **loathing**, lōᴛʜ'ing, *n.* Extreme disgu or aversion; abhorrence; detestatio **loathsome**, lōᴛʜ'sum, *a.* Exciting d gust; disgusting; detestable; abhorre

lob, lob, *n.* A dolt; a lout.—*vt.* (lobbing, lobbed). To throw or toss slowly.

lobar, lō'bėr, *a.* Pertaining to a lobe.

lobby, lob'i, *n.* An apartment giving admission to others; an entrance-hall.

lobe, lōb, *n.* A round projecting part of something; such a part of the liver, lungs, brain, &c.; the lower soft part of the ear.

lobster, lob'stėr, *n.* A ten-footed crustacean with large claws, allied to the crab.

local, lō'kal, *a.* Pertaining to a particular place; confined to a spot or definite district.—*n.* A local item of news; a local railway train. **locale,** lō-kāl', *n.* A locality. **localize,** lō'kal-īz, *vt.* To make local; to discover or detect the place of. **locally,** lō'kal-li, *adv.* In a local manner; with respect to place; in place.

locate, lō'kāt, *vt.* (locating, located). To place; to settle.—*vi.* To reside. **location,** lō-kā'shun, *n.* Act of locating; situation with respect to place; place.

loch, loch, *n.* A lake; a landlocked arm of the sea.

lock, lok, *n.* An appliance for fastening doors, &c.; mechanism by which a firearm is discharged; a fastening together; inclosure in a canal, with gates at either end; a tuft or ringlet of hair.—*vt.* To fasten with a lock and key; to shut up or confine; to join firmly; to embrace closely.—*vi.* To become fast; to unite closely by mutual insertion.

locker, lok'ėr, *n.* A close receptacle, as a drawer in a ship, closed with a lock.

locket, lok'et, *n.* A little case worn as an ornament, often containing a lock of hair.

lockjaw, lok"ja', *n.* A spasmodic rigidity of the under jaw.

locksmith, lok"smith', *n.* An artificer who makes or mends locks.

lockup, lok"up', *n.* A place in which persons under arrest are temporarily confined.

locomotion, lō'kō-mō"shun, *n.* Act or power of moving from place to place. **locomotive,** lō'kō-mō"tiv, *a.* Moving from place to place.—*n.* A steam-engine placed on wheels, and employed in moving a train of cars on a railway.

locust, lō'kust, *n.* A large insect allied to the grasshopper; the locust-tree.

locution, lō-kū'shun, *n.* A phrase; a mode of speech.

lode, lōd, *n.* An open ditch; a metallic vein, or any regular mineral vein.

lodge, loj, *n.* A small country house; a temporary abode; place where members of a society, as freemasons, meet; the society itself.—*vt.* (lodging, lodged). To furnish with temporary accommodation; to set or deposit for keeping; to beat down (growing crops).—*vi.* To have a temporary abode; to settle; to reside. **lodger,** loj'ėr, *n.* One who lodges; one who lives in a hired room or rooms. **lodging,** loj'ing, *n.* A temporary habitation; rooms let to another; usually in *pl.*

loft, loft, *n.* The space below and between the rafters; a gallery raised within a larger apartment or in a church. **loft-**

ily, lof'ti-li, *adv.* In a lofty manner or position; proudly; haughtily. **lofty,** lof'ti, *a.* Elevated in place; rising to a great height; proud; haughty; sublime; stately.

log, log, *n.* A bulky piece of timber unhewed; a floating contrivance for measuring the rate of a ship's velocity; a logbook.

logarithm, log'a-riᴛʜm, *n.* In *mathematics,* the exponent of the power to which a given invariable number must be raised in order to produce another given number. **logarithmic, logarithmical,** log'a-riᴛʜ"mik, log'a-riᴛʜ"mi-kal, *a.* Pertaining to logarithms; consisting of logarithms.

logbook, log"bŏk', *n.* Register of a ship's way, and of the incidents of the voyage.

log cabin, log house, log hut, log'-ka-bin, log'hous, log'hut, *n.* A house made of logs laid on each other.

loggerhead, log'ėr-hed', *n.* A blockhead; a dunce. **at loggerheads,** quarreling.

logic, lo'jik, *n.* The science or art of reasoning; mode of arguing. **logical,** lo'ji-kal, *a.* Pertaining to logic; skilled in logic; according to reason. **logically,** lo'ji-kal-li, *adv.* In a logical manner.

logistic, lō-jis'tik, *a.* Pertaining to judging, estimating, or calculating.

logrolling, log"rōl'ing, *n.* The joining of a number of persons to collect logs; union for mutual assistance or praise.

loin, loin, *n.* The part of an animal on either side between the ribs and the haunch-bone.

loiter, loi'tėr, *vi.* To be slow in moving; to spend time idly; to hang about.—*vt.* To waste carelessly; with *away.* **loiterer,** loi'tėr-ėr, *n.* One who loiters; a lingerer; an idler.

loll, lol, *vi.* (lolling, lolled). To lean idly; to lie at ease; to hang out, as the tongue of a dog.—*vt.* To suffer to hang out.

lollipop, lol'i-pop, *n.* A sugar confection which dissolves easily in the mouth. (Eng.)

lone, lōn, *a.* Solitary; unfrequented; single. **lonely,** lōn'li, *a.* Unfrequented by men; retired; solitary. **lonesome,** lōn'-sum, *a.* Solitary; secluded from society; lonely.

long, long, *a.* Drawn out in a line; drawn out in time; tedious; protracted; late; containing much verbal matter.—*n.* Something that is long.—*adv.* To a great extent in space or in time; at a point of duration far distant.—*vi.* To desire eagerly; with *for.*

longevity, lon-jev'i-ti, *n.* Great length of life.

longhair, *n.* A person of intellectual and sophisticated taste in the arts.

longhand, long'hand, *n.* Ordinary written characters, as distinguished from shorthand, &c.

longheaded, long"hed'ed, *a.* Having a long head; shrewd; far-sighted.

longing, long'ing, *p.a.* Earnestly desiring; manifesting desire.—*n.* An eager desire. **longingly,** long'ing-li, *adv.* With longing; eager wishes or appetite.

longitude, lon'ji-tūd, *n.* Length; distance on the surface of the globe east or west, measured by meridians. **longitudinal,** lon'ji-tū''di-nal, *a.* Pertaining to longitude; running lengthwise.

long shot. Great odds.

long-lived, long'livd', *a.* Having a long life or existence; lasting long.

long-suffering, long'suf'èr-ing, *a.* Patient; not easily provoked.—*n.* Patience of offense.

longways, longwise, long'wāz, long'wīz, *adv.* In the direction of length; lengthwise.

long-winded, long'win'ded, *a.* Not easily exhausted of breath; tedious.

look, lṳk, *vi.* To direct the eye so as to see; to gaze; to consider; to expect; to heed; to face; to appear.—*vt.* To see; to express by a look.—*n.* Act of looking; sight; gaze; glance; mien; aspect.

looking glass, lṳk'ing gläs, *n.* A mirror.

look-out, lṳk"out', *n.* A careful watching for any object; place from which such observation is made; person watching.

loom, lōm, *n.* A frame or machine by which thread is worked into cloth; that part of an oar within the boat in rowing.—*vi.* To appear larger than the real dimensions, and indistinctly; to appear to the mind faintly.

loon, lōn, *n.* A worthless fellow; a rogue; a bird, the great northern diver.

loop, lōp, *n.* A noose; a doubling of a string, &c.; a small narrow opening.—*vt.* To form into or fasten with a loop.

Loon.

loophole, lōp'hōl, *n.* A small opening in a fortification through which small-arms are discharged; a hole that affords means of escape; underhand method of evasion.

loose, lös, *a.* Not attached; untied; not dense or compact; vague; careless; having lax bowels, unchaste.—*vt.* (loosing, loosed). To untie or bind; to detach; to set free; to relax; to loosen. **loosely,** lös'li, *adv.* In a loose manner; laxly; slackly; carelessly; dissolutely. **loosen,** lös'n, *vt.* Tó make loose —*vi.* To become loose.

loot, löt, *n.* Booty; plunder, especially such as is taken in a sacked city.—*vt.* To plunder.

lop, lop, *vt.* (lopping, lopped). To cut off; to trim by cutting.—*n.* That which is cut from trees. **lop-sided,** lop'sid'ed, *a.* Heavier at one side than the other; inclining to one side.

loquacious, lo-kwā'shus, *a.* Talkative; garrulous; babbling. **loquacity,** lo-kwas'i-ti, *n.* Quality of being loquacious; garrulity.

lord, lord, *n.* A master; a ruler; proprietor of a manor; a nobleman; a British title applied to peers, sons of dukes and marquises, and the eldest sons of earls; honorary title of certain high officials; (with *cap.*) the Supreme Being.—*vi.* To act as a lord; to rule with arbitrary or despotic sway. **lordly,** lord'li, *a.* Be-coming a lord; large; ample; proud; haughty. **lordship,** lord'ship, *n.* State or quality of being a lord; a title given to a lord; dominion; sovereignty.

lore, lōr, *n.* Learning; erudition; space between the bills and the eye of a bird.

lorgnette, lor-nyet', *n.* An opera-glass.

lorn, lorn, *a.* Undone; forsaken; lonely.

lorry, lorrie, lor'i, *n.* A long four-wheeled wagon without sides. A British truck.

lose, löz, *vt.* (losing, lost). To cease to possess, as through accident; to fail to keep; to forfeit; not to gain or win; to miss; to cease or fail to see or hear; to misuse.—*vi.* To suffer loss; not to win. **losing,** löz'ing, *p.a.* Bringing or causing loss. **loss,** los, *n.* Act of losing; failure to gain; that which is lost; failure to utilize. **lost,** lost, *p.a.* Gone from our hold, view, &c.; not to be found; ruined; wasted; forfeited; perplexed; alienated.

lot, lot, *n.* A person's part or share; fate which falls to one; part in life allotted to a person; a distinct portion; a considerable quantity or number; something used to decide what is yet undecided.—*vt.* (lotting, lotted). To assign by lot; to sort; to portion.

Lothario, lō-thär'i-ō, *n.* A gay libertine.

lotion, lō'shun, *n.* A wash for the complexion; a fluid applied externally in ailments.

lottery, lot'èr-i, *n.* A scheme for the distribution of prizes by lot or chance; the distribution itself.

lotus, lō'tus, *n.* A tree, the fruit of which was fabled to cause forgetfulness of the past; applied also to the Egyptian water-lily and other plants.

loud, loud, *a.* Having a great sound; noisy; showy.—*adv.* Loudly. **loudly,** loud'li, *adv.* With great sound or noise; noisily; clamorously. **loud-speaker,** loud'spēk'èr, *n.* Any of the various receiving devices for reproducing speech, signals, &c. loud enough to be heard without the usual telephone headpieces.

lounge, lounj, *vi.* (lounging, lounged). To loiter; to loll.—*n.* An idle gait or stroll; act of reclining at ease; a place for lounging.

louse, lous, *n.*; pl. **lice,** līs. A wingless insect, parasitic on man and other animals. **lousy,** louz'i, *a.* Infested with lice.

lout, lout, *n.* A mean, awkward fellow. —*vt.* To bend or stoop down. **loutish,** lout'ish, *a.* Like a lout; clownish.

love, luv, *vt.* (loving, loved). To regard with affection; to like; to delight in.— *vi.* To be in love; to be tenderly attached.—*n.* Warm affection; fond attachment; the passion between the sexes; the object beloved; a word of endearment; Cupid, the god of love. **lovable,** luv'a-bl, *a.* Worthy of love; amiable. **love-bird,** luv'bèrd, *n.* A small species of parrot. **loveless,** luv'les, *a.* Void of love; void of tenderness. **lovelorn,** luv'lorn, *a.* Forsaken by one's love; pining from love. **lovely,** luv'li, *a.* That may excite love; beautiful; charming; delightful. **lover,** luv'èr, *n.* One who loves; a suitor; a wooer; one who likes strongly. **loving,** luv'ing, *p.a.* Fond; kind; affectionate; expressing love or kindness. **lovingly,** luv'ing-li, *adv.* With love; affectionate.

low, lō, *vi.* To bellow, as an ox or cow. **lowing,** lō'ing, *n.* The bellowing of cattle.

low, lō, *a.* Depressed below any given surface or place; not high; deep; below the usual rate; not loud; wanting strength; mean; dishonorable; not sublime; plain.—*adv.* Not aloft; under the usual price; near the ground; not loudly. **lower,** lō'ẽr, *vt.* To make lower; to let down; to abase; to reduce. **lower,** lou'ẽr, *vi.* To frown; to look sullen; to threaten a storm. **lowering,** lou'ẽr-ing, *p.a.* Threatening a storm; cloudy; overcast.

lowland, lō'land, *n.* Land which is low with respect to the neighboring country; a low or level country. **The lowlands,** the southern or lower parts of Scotland.

lowly, lō'li, *a.* Humble in position or life; meek; free from pride.—*adv.* In a low manner or condition.

low water, lō'wa'tẽr, *n.* The lowest point of the ebb or receding tide.

loyal, loi'al, *a.* Faithful to a government, plighted love, duty, &c.; constant to friends or associates. **loyalist,** loi'al-ist, *n.* One who adheres to his sovereign or constituted authority. **loyally,** loi'al-li, *adv.* In a loyal manner. **loyalty,** loi'al-ti, *n.* State or quality of being loyal; fidelity; constancy.

lozenge, loz'enj, *n.* A figure with four equal sides, having two acute and two obtuse angles; a small cake of sugar, &c.; a small diamond-shaped pane of glass.

lubber, lub'ẽr, *n.* A heavy, clumsy fellow.

lubricate, lū'bri-kāt, *vt.* To make smooth; to smear with oil, to diminish friction. **lubrication,** lū-bri-kā'shun, *n.* Act or process of lubricating. **lubricant,** lū'bri-kant, *n.* A substance for oiling or greasing. **lubricator,** lu''bri-kā-tẽr, *n.* One who or that which lubricates; an oil cup attached to a machine.

lucid, lū'sid, *a.* Full of light; shining; bright; clear; not darkened or confused by delirium; easily understood. **lucidity,** lū-sid'i-ti, *n.* The state or quality of being lucid; clearness; intelligibility. **lucidly,** lū'sid-li, *adv.* In a lucid manner.

Lucifer, lū'si-fẽr, *n.* The morning star; Satan; a match ignitible by friction.

luck, luk, *n.* That which happens to a person; chance; hap; fortune; success. **luckily,** luk'i-li, *adv.* In a lucky manner; fortunately; by good fortune. **luckless,** luk'les, *a.* Without luck; unlucky; hapless; unfortunate; ill-fated. **lucky,** luk'i, *a.* Meeting with good luck or success; fortunate; auspicious.

lucrative, lū'krat-iv, *a.* Pertaining to gain; gainful; profitable.

lucre, lū'kẽr, *n.* Gain in money or goods; profit; emolument; pelf.

lucubrate, lū'kū-brāt, *vi.* To work by lamplight; to study laboriously; to med-

itate. **lucubration,** lū'kū-brā''shun, *n.* Act of lucubrating; what is composed by night; a literary composition.

ludicrous, lū'di-krus, *a.* That serves for sport, laughable; droll; ridiculous.

luff, luf, *n.* The weather part of a fore-and-aft sail.—*vi.* To put the helm so as to turn the ship toward the wind.

lug, lug, *vt.* (lugging, lugged). To haul; to drag.—*n.* The ear; object resembling the ear, as the handle of a vessel.

luggage, lug'ij, *n.* Anything cumbersome and heavy; a traveler's baggage.

lugubrious, lū-gū'bri-us, *a.* Mournful; indicating sorrow; doleful.

lukewarm, lūk''warm', *a.* Moderately warm; tepid; not zealous; indifferent.

lull, lul, *vt.* To sing to, as a child; to soothe.—*vi.* To subside; to become calm.—*n.* A season of quiet or cessation.

lullaby, lul''a-bī', *n.* A song to lull or quiet babes; that which quiets.

lumbago, lum-bā'gō, *n.* A rheumatic affection of the muscles about the loins.

lumbar, lum'bẽr, *n.* Pertaining to or near the loins.

lumber, lum'bẽr, *n.* Anything useless and cumbersome; timber sawed or split into planks, boards, beams, joists, &c. —*vt.* To fill with lumber; to heap together in disorder.—*vi.* To move heavily, as a vehicle; to cut and prepare timber. **lumberjack,** lum''bẽr-jak', *n.* One employed in cutting timber.

luminary, lū'mi-ner'i, *n.* Any body that gives light.

luminous, lū'mi-nus, *a.* Shining; bright; giving light; clear; lucid. **luminosity,** lū'mi-nos''i-ti, *n.* The quality of being luminous; brightness; clearness.

lump, lump, *n.* A small mass of matter; a mass of things.—*vt.* To throw into a mass; to take in the gross. **lumpy,** lump'i, *a.* Full of lumps; showing small irregular waves.

lunacy, lū'na-si, *n.* Mental derangement; madness; insanity; craziness; mania. **lunatic,** lū'na-tik, *a.* Affected with lunacy; mad; insane.—*n.* A madman.

lunar, lū'nẽr, *a.* Pertaining to the moon; measured by the revolutions of the moon.

lunch, luncheon, lunch, lun'chun, *n.* A slight repast between breakfast and dinner.—*vi.* To take a lunch.

lung, lung, *n.* Either of the two organs of respiration in air-breathing animals.

lunge, lunj, *n.* A sudden thrust or pass, as with a sword.—*vi.* (lunging, lunged). To make a thrust.

lupine, lū'pin, *n.* A leguminous flowering plant.—*a.* lū'pin. Like a wolf; wolfish.

lurch, lẽrch, *vi.* To lurk; to roll or sway to one side.—*n.* A sudden roll or stagger; a difficult or helpless position.

lure, lūr, *n.* Something held out to call a trained hawk; a bait; any enticement.—*vt.* (luring, lured). To attract by a lure or bait; to entice.

lurid, lū'rid, *a.* Pale yellow, as flame; ghastly pale; wan; gloomy; dismal.

lurk, lẽrk, *vi.* To lie hid; to lie in wait.

luscious, lŭs'hus, a. Very sweet; delicious; sweet to excess.

lush, lush, a. Fresh; succulent.

lust, lust, n. Longing desire; carnal appetite; depraved affections.—vi. To desire eagerly; to have carnal desire. **lustful**, lust'ful, a. Inspired by lust or the sexual appetite; lewd; libidinous. **lustily**, lust'i-li, adv. In a lusty manner; with vigor of body; stoutly.

luster, lustre, lus'tér, n. Brightness; brilliancy; renown; a branched chandelier ornamented with cut glass; a glossy fabric for dress.

lustrous, lus'trus, a. Full of luster; bright; shining; luminous.

lusty, lust'i, a. Vigorous; robust; healthful; bulky; large; lustful.

lute, lūt, n. A stringed instrument of the guitar kind; a composition of clay, &c.—vt. (luting, luted) To play on the lute; to close or coat with lute.

Lutheran, lū'thér-an, a. Pertaining to Martin Luther, the reformer.—n. A follower of Luther **Lutheranism**, lū'thér-an-izm, n. The doctrines of the Protestant church in Germany.

luxury, luk'shö-ri, n. Extravagant indulgence; that which gratifies a fastidious appetite; anything delightful to the senses. **luxurious**, luks-ū'ri-us, a. Given to luxury; voluptuous; furnished with luxuries. **luxuriously**, luks-ū'ri-us-li, adv. In a luxurious manner; voluptuously. **luxuriant**, luks-ū'ri-ant, a. Exuberant in growth; abundant. **luxuriate**, luks-ū'ri-āt, vi. To grow exuberantly; to feed or live luxuriously; to indulge without restraint.

lyceum, li-sē'um, n. A literary institute; a higher school.

lye, li, n. Water impregnated with alkaline salt imbibed from the ashes of wood; solution of an alkali.

lying-in, li'ing-in', n. and a. Childbirth.

lymph, limf, n. Water; a watery fluid; a colorless fluid in animal bodies. **lymphatic**, lim-fat'ik, a. Pertaining to lymph; phlegmatics, sluggish.—n. A vessel in animal bodies which contains or conveys lymph.

lynch, linch, vt. To inflict punishment upon, without the forms of law, as by a mob.

lynx, lingks, n. A carnivorous animal resembling the cat, noted for its keen sight.

lyre, lir, n. A stringed instrument of the harp kind much used by the ancients.

lyric, lyrical, lir'ik, lir'i-kal, a. Pertaining to a lyre; designating that species of poetry which has reference to the individual emotions of the poet, such as songs. **lyric**, lir'ik, n. A lyric poem; an author of lyric poems.

Lyre.

lyrist, lir'ist, n. One who plays on the lyre; a writer of lyrics or lyric poetry.

M

macabre, ma-kä'br, a. Deathly; gruesome.

macadamize, mak-ad'am-īz, vt. To cover, as a road, with small broken stones, which, when consolidated, form a firm surface.

macaroni, mak-a-rō'ni, n. A paste of fine wheat flour made into small tubes; a kind of dandy in fashion in London about 1760.

macaroon, ma-ka-rön', n. A small sweetcake, containing almonds.

macaw, ma-ka', n. A bird of the parrot tribe with long tail feathers.

mace, mās, n. A staff with a heavy metal head; an ensign of authority borne before magistrates; a spice, the dried covering of the seed of the nutmeg.

macerate, mas'ér-āt, vt. To steep almost to solution; to make lean or cause to waste away. **maceration**, ma-se-rā'shon, n. Act or process of macerating.

Machiavelian, mak'i-a-vel"i-an, a. Pertaining to Machiavelli, or denoting his principles; cunning in political management.

machinate, mak'i-nāt, vt. and i. To plot or plan; to form, as a plot or scheme. **machination**, mak'i-nā"shun, n. A plot: an artful design or scheme.

machine, ma-shēn', n. Any contrivance which serves to regulate the effect of a given force or to produce or change motion; an organized system; a person who acts as the tool of another.—vt. To apply machinery to; to produce by machinery. **machine gun**, ma-shēn' gun, n. A piece of ordnance loaded and fired mechanically. **machinery**, ma-shēn'ér-i, n. The component parts of a complex machine; machines in general. **machinist**, ma-shēn'ist, n. A constructor of machines; one who works a machine.

mackerel, mak'ér-el, n. An edible sea fish.

macintosh, mak'in-tosh, n. A waterproof overcoat.

Mackerel.

macrocosm, mak'ro-koz-m, n. The universe.

mad, mad, a. Disordered in intellect; insane; crazy; frantic; furious; infatuated. vt. (madding, madded). To make mad.

madam, mad'am, n. My lady; a complimentary title given to ladies.

madcap, mad"kap', n. and a. A flighty or hare-brained person; one who indulges in frolics.

madden, mad'n, vt. To make mad.— vi. To become mad; to act as if mad.

madder, mad′ĕr, *n.* A climbing perennial plant, the root of which furnishes dyes and pigments.

madding, mad′ing, *a.* Acting madly; wild.

made, mād, pret. and pp. of *make.*

mademoiselle, mad′mwä″zel″, *n.* Miss; a title given to young unmarried ladies.

madhouse, mad″hous′, *n.* A house where mad or insane persons are confined.

madly, mad′li, *adv.* In a mad manner; frantically; furiously; rashly; wildly.

madman, mad′man, *n.* A man who is mad; a maniac; a lunatic.

madness, mad′nes, *n.* Lunacy; frenzy; extreme folly.

Madonna, ma-don′a, *n.* The Virgin Mary; a picture representing the Virgin.

madrigal, mad′ri-gal, *n.* A pastoral song; vocal composition in five or six parts.

maestro, mä-e′strō, *n.* A master of any art; a musical composer.

magazine, mag′a-zēn″, *n.* A storehouse; a repository for ammunition or provisions; a serial publication.

magenta, ma-jen′ta, *n.* A brilliant blue-red color derived from coal-tar.

maggot, mag′ut, *n.* The larva of a fly or other insect; a grub; an odd fancy.

Magi, mā′jī, *n.pl.* The caste of priests among the ancient Medes and Persians; holy men or sages of the East.

magic, maj′ik, *n.* The art of producing effects by superhuman means; sorcery; enchantment; power similar to that of enchantment.—*a.* Pertaining to magic; working or worked by or as if by magic. **magical,** maj′i-kal, *a.* Magic. **magician,** ma-jish′an, *n.* One skilled in magic; an enchanter.

magistrate, maj′is-trāt, *n.* A public civil officer, with executive or judicial authority. **magisterial,** maj′is-tēr″i-al, *a.* Pertaining to a master or magistrate; imperious; haughty; authoritative. **magistracy,** maj′is-tra-si, *n.* The office or dignity of a magistrate; the body of magistrates.

magnanimous, mag-nan′i-mus, *a.* Great of soul or mind; elevated in sentiment; liberal and honorable; not selfish. **magnanimity,** mag-na-nim′i-ti, *n.* Quality of being magnanimous; greatness of soul or mind.

magnate, mag′nāt, *n.* A great man; a person of rank or wealth.

magnesia, mag-nē′sha, *n.* Oxide of magnesium, a white slightly alkaline powder.

magnesian, mag-nē′shan, *a.* Pertaining to, containing or resembling magnesia.

magnesium, mag-nē′shi-um, *n.* Metallic base of magnesia, a white malleable metal.

magnet, mag′net, *n.* The loadstone, which has the property of attracting iron; a bar of iron or steel to which the properties of the loadstone have been imparted. **magnetic,** mag-net′ik, *a.* Pertaining to the magnet; possessing the properties of the magnet; attractive. **magnetism,** mag′ne-tizm, *n.* A property of certain bodies whereby they naturally attract or repel one another;

that branch of science which treats of magnetic phenomena; power of attraction. **magnetize,** mag′ne-tiz, *vt.* To give magne′ic properties to.—*vi.* To acquire magnetic properties.

magneto, mag-ne′tō, *n.* A rotor coil of wire within permanent magnets, rotation of which produces spark for ignition in combustion engines.

magnific, magnifical, mag-nif′ik, mag-nif′i-kal, *a.* Grand; splendid; illustrious.

magnificent, mag-nif′i-sent, *a.* Grand in appearance; splendid; showy. **magnificence,** mag-nif′i-sens, *n.* Grandeur of appearance; splendor; pomp.

magnify, mag′ni-fī, *vt.* To make great or greater; to increase the apparent dimensions of; to extol; to exaggerate. —*vi.* To possess the quality of causing objects to appear larger. **magnifier,** mag′ni-fī-ĕr, *n.* One who or that which magnifies.

magnitude, mag′ni-tūd, *n.* Greatness; size; bulk; importance; consequence.

magpie, mag′pī, *n.* A chattering bird of the crow tribe with black and white plumage.

Magyar, mag′yär, *n.* A Hungarian; the language of Hungary.

maharaja, maharajah, mä-hä′rä′ja, *n.* The title assumed by some Indian princes ruling over a considerable extent of territory.

mahogany, ma-hog′a-ni, *n.* A tree of tropical America; its wood, reddish in color; used for cabinet work.

maid, mād, *n.* A young unmarried woman; a girl; a virgin; a female servant. **maiden,** mād′n, *n.* A maid or virgin; an old Scottish instrument of capital punishment resembling the guillotine.—*a.* Pertaining to maidens; unpolluted; unused; first. **maidenhair,** mād″n-hār′, *n.* An elegant fern found growing on rocks and walls. **maidenhead,** mād′n-hed, *n.* Virginity; the hymen. **maidenhood,** mād′n-hud, *n.* The state of being a maid; virginity. **maidenly,** mād′n-li, *a.* Like a maid; gentle; modest.

mail, māl, *n.* A bag for conveying letters, &c.; letters conveyed; person or conveyance carrying the mail; armor of chain-work, &c.—*vt.* (mailing, mailed). To send by mail; to post; to arm with mail.

maim, mām, *vt.* To mutilate; to disable. —*n.* An injury by which a person is maimed.

main, mān, *a.* Chief, or most important; mighty; vast; directly applied; used with all one's might.—*n.* Strength; great effort; chief or main portion; the ocean; a principal gas or water pipe in a street.

mainland, mān″land′, *n.* The principal land, as opposed to an isle; the continent.

mainly, mān′li, *adv.* In the main; chiefly.

mainspring, mān″spring′, *n.* The principal spring of any piece of mechanism; the main cause of any action.

mainstay, mān″stā′, *n.* The stay extending from the top of a vessel's main-mast to the deck; chief support.

maintain, mān-tān', *vt.* To hold or keep in any particular state; to sustain; to continue; to uphold; to vindicate; to assert.—*vi.* To affirm a position; to assert. **maintenance**, mān'ten-ans, *n.* Act of maintaining; means of support or livelihood; continuance.

maize, māz, *n.* Indian corn.

majesty, maj'es-ti, *n.* Grandeur or dignity; a title of emperors, kings, and queens. **majestic**, ma-jes'tik, *a.* Having majesty; august; sublime; lofty; stately.

major, mā'jēr, *a.* The greater in number quantity, or extent; the more important. —*n.* A military officer next above a captain; a person aged twenty-one years complete.

major-domo, mā'jēr-dō"mō, *n.* A man who takes charge of a large household; a great officer of a palace.

majority, ma-jor'i-ti, *n.* The greater number; excess of one number over another; full age; rank or commission of a major.

make, māk, *vt.* (making, made). To produce or effect; to cause to be; to compose; to constitute; to perform; to cause to have any quality; to force; to gain; to complete; to arrive at; to have within sight.—*vi.* To act or do; to tend; to contribute; texture. **make-believe**, māk"bē-lēv', *n.* Pretense; sham.—*a.* Unreal; sham. **maker**, māk'ēr, *n.* One who makes; the Creator. **makeshift**, māk"shift', *n.* An expedient to serve a present purpose. **make-up**, māk'up, *n.* The manner in which one is dressed for a part in a play. **making**, māk'ing, *n.* Workmanship; what is made at one time; material; means of bringing success in life; state of being made; composition.

maladjustment, mal'a-just"ment, *n.* A bad or wrong adjustment.

maladministration, mal-ad-min'is-trā"shun, *n.* Bad management of affairs. **maladroit**, mal'a-droit", *a.* Awkward.

malady, mal'a-di, *n.* Any disease of the human body; moral or mental disorder.

malapert, mal'a-pėrt, *a.* Pert; saucy; impudent.—*n.* A pert, saucy person.

malapropos, mal'ap-rō-pō", *a.* and *adv.* The opposite of apropos; ill to the purpose.

malaria, ma-lār'i-a, *n.* Noxious exhalation causing fever; fever produced by this cause. **malarial, malarious,** ma-lār'i-al, ma-lār'i-us, *a.* Infected by malaria.

Malay, Malayan, ma-lā', ma-lā'an, *n.* A native of the Malay Peninsula; their language.—*a.* Belonging to the Malays.

malcontent, mal"kon-tent', *n.* A discontented person.—*a.* Discontented with the rule under which ones lives.

male, māl, *a.* Pertaining to the sex that begets young; masculine.—*n.* One of the sex that begets young; a plant which has stamens only.

malediction, mal'e-dik"shun, *n.* Evil speaking; a curse; execration.

malefactor, mal"e-fak'tēr, *n.* A criminal; a culprit; a felon.

malevolent, ma-lev'ō-lent, *a.* Having ill-will; evil-minded; spiteful; malicious. **malevolence**, ma-lev'ō-lens, *n.* Ill-will; personal hatred.

malformation, mal'for-mā"shun, *n.* Ill or wrong formation; deformity.

malice, mal'is, *n.* A disposition to injure others; spite; ill will; rancor. **malicious**, ma-lish'us, *a.* Evil-disposed; evil-minded; spiteful; rancorous.

malign, ma-līn', *a.* Of an evil nature or disposition; malicious; pernicious.—*vt.* To defame; to vilify. **malignance, malignancy,** ma-lig'nans, ma-lig'nan-si, *n.* Extreme malevolence; virulence. **malignant**, ma-lig'nant, *a.* Having extreme malevolence; unpropitious; virulent; dangerous to life; extremely heinous.—*n.* A man of extreme enmity. **malignity**, ma-lig'ni-ti, *n.* Evil disposition of heart; rancor; virulence.

malinger, ma-ling'gėr, *vi.* To feign illness in order to avoid military duty. **malingerer**, ma-ling'gėr-ėr, *n.* One who feigns himself ill.

mall, mal, *n.* A heavy wooden beetle or hammer; a public walk; a level shaded walk.

mallard, mal'ėrd, *n.* The common wild duck.

malleable, mal'ē-a-bl, *a.* Capable of being beaten out with the hammer. **malleability**, mal'ē-a-bil"i-ti, *n.* Quality of being malleable.

mallet, mal'et, *n.* A wooden hammer for beating, driving pins, chisels, &c.

malpractice, mal-prak'tis, *n.* Evil practice.

malt, malt, *n.* Barley or other grain steeped in water till it germinates, then dried in a kiln and used in brewing.—*vt.* To make into malt.—*vi.* To become malt.

Maltese, mal-tēz', *n.sing.* and *pl.* A native or natives of Malta.—*a.* Belonging to Malta.

maltreat, mal-trēt', *vt.* To treat ill or roughly; to abuse. **maltreatment**, mal-trēt'ment, *n.* Ill-usage.

mama, mamma, ma-mä', *n.* Mother.

mammal, mam'al, *n.* An animal of the class Mammalia.

mammalia, mam-mā'li-a, *n. pl.* The highest class in the animal kingdom, whose distinctive characteristic is that the female suckles the young. **mammalian**, mam-mā'li-an, *a.* Pertaining to the mammalia.

mammon, mam'un, *n.* A Syrian god of riches; riches; wealth.

mammoth, mam'uth, *n.* An extinct species of elephant.—*a.* Very large; gigantic.

man, man, *n.*; pl. **men**, men. A human being; a male adult of the human race; mankind; the male sex; a male servant; a piece in a game, as chess, &c.—*vt.* (manning, manned). To furnish with men; to guard with men; *refl.* to infuse courage into.

manacle, man'a-kl, *n.* An instrument of iron for fastening the hands; a handcuff; used chiefly in the *plural.*—*vt.* (manacling, manacled). To put manacles on; to fetter.

manage, man'ij, vt. (managing, managed). To wield; to direct in riding; to conduct or administer; to have under command; to treat with judgment.—vi. To conduct affairs. **manageable**, man'ij-a-bl, a. That may be managed; tractable. **management**, man'ij-ment, n. Act of managing; administration; manner of treating; body directing a business, &c. **manager**, man'āj-ėr, n. One who manages; one at the head of a business; a good economist.

mandarin, man-da-rin. A Chinese public official; the court-language of China.

mandate, man'dāt, n. A command; written authority to act for a person. **mandatory**, man"da-tō'ri, a. Containing a command; preceptive; directory. **mandatary**, **mandatory**, man'da-tėr-i, man"da-tō'ri, n. One to whom a mandate is given.

mandible, man'di-bl, n. An animal's jaw.

mandoline, **mandolin**, man'dō-lin, n. A musical instrument of the guitar kind.

mandrake, man'drāk, n. A narcotic plant with large thick roots.

mane, mān, n. The long hair on the neck of a hôrse, lion, &c.

maneuver, **manoeuvre**, ma-nö'vėr, n. A regulated movement, particularly of troops or ships; management with address; stratagem.—vt. (maneuvering, maneuvered). To perform military or naval maneuvers; to employ stratagem; to manage with address.—vt. To cause to perform maneuvers.

manful, man'ful, a. Having the spirit of a man; bold; honorable; energetic. **manfully**, man'ful-li, adv. Courageously.

manganese, man'ga-nēz, n. A metal resembling iron.

mange, mānj, n. A skin disease of horses, cattle, dogs, &c.

manger, man'jėr, n. A trough in which food is placed for cattle and horses.

mangle, mang'gl, vt. (mangling, mangled). To mutilate; to lacerate; to smooth, as linen.—n. A rolling press, or small calender, for smoothing cotton or linen.

mango, mang'gō, n. The fruit of the mango-tree, a native of Asia.

mangrove, mang'grōv, n. A tropical tree growing on shores.

mangy, mān'ji, a. Infected with the mange; scabby.

manhole, man"hōl', n. A hole for admitting a man into a drain, steam-boiler, &c.

manhood, man"hōd, a. State of one who is a man; humanity; virility; manliness.

mania, mā'ni-a, n. Insanity; madness; eager desire for anything; morbid craving.

maniac, mā'ni-ak, a. Affected with mania; mad.—n. A madman.

manicure, man'i-kūr, n. One whose occupation is to trim the nails, &c., of the hand.

manifest, man'i-fest, a. Clearly visible; evident; obvious.—vt. To make manifest; to display or exhibit.—n. A document stating a ship's cargo, destination, &c. **manifestation**, man'i-fes-tā"shun, n. Act of manifesting; exhibition; revelation; what serves to make manifest. **manifestly**, man'i-fest-li, adv. Evidently.

manifesto, man'i-fes"tō, n. A public declaration; a proclamation.

manifold, man'i-fōld, a. Numerous and various; of divers kinds.—vt. To multiply impressions of, as by a copying apparatus.

manikin, man'i-kin, n. A little man; a dwarf; model of the human body.

manila, ma-nil'a, n. A kind of cheroot manufactured in Manila.

manipulate, ma-nip'ū-lāt, vt. To treat with the hands; to handle; to operate upon so as to disguise. **manipulation**, ma-nip'ū-lā"shon, n. Act, art, or mode of manipulating. **manipulator**, ma-nip'ū-lāt-ėr, n. One who manipulates.

mankind, man-kind', n. The species of human beings; the males of the human race.

manlike, man'līk, a. Like a man; masculine; manly.

manliness, man'li-nes, n. The best qualities of a man; manhood; bravery.

manly, man'li, a. Having the qualities that best become a man; brave; resolute, &c.

manna, man'na, n. A substance furnished as food for the Israelites in the wilderness; the sweet juice of a species of ash.

mannequin, **manikin**, man'i-kin, n. An artist's model of wood or wax.

manner, man'ėr, n. The mode in which anything is done; method; bearing or conduct; pl. carriage or behavior; civility in society; sort or kind. **mannered**, man'ėrd. a. Having manners of this or that kind. **mannerism**, man'ėr-izm, n. Adherence to the same manner; tasteless uniformity of style; peculiarity of personal manner. **mannerly**, man'ėr-li, a. Showing good manners; polite, respectful.

mannish, man'ish, a. Characteristic of or resembling a man; bold or masculine.

man-of-war, man'ov-war', n.; pl. **men-of-war.** A war-vessel.

manor, man'ėr, n. The land belonging to a lord; a lordship. **manor-house,** ma'nor-hous, n. The mansion belonging to a manor. **manorial**, ma-nō'ri-al, a. Pertaining to a manor.

manse, mans, n. In Scotland, the dwelling-house of a Presbyterian minister.

mansion, man'shun, n. A large dwelling-house; abode; house of the lord of a manor.

manslaughter, man"sla'tėr, n. Murder; the unlawful killing of a man without malice.

mantel, **mantelpiece**, man'tl, man"-tel-pēs', n. The ornamental work above a fireplace; a narrow shelf or slab there.

mantilla, man-til'a, n. A mantle or hood; a Spanish lady's-veil.

mantle, man'tl, n. A kind of cloak worn over other garments; something that covers and conceals.—vt. (man-tling, mantled). To cloak; to cover as with a mantle.—*vi.* To become covered with a coating; to cream; to display superficial changes of hue.

mantua, man'tū-a, *n.* A lady's gown or mantle.

manual, man'ū-al, *a.* Performed by the hand; used or made by the hand.—*n.* A small book; a compendium; the servicebook of the R. Catholic Church; keyboard of an organ.

manufacture, man'ū-fak"tūr, *n.* The process of making anything by hand or machinery; something made from raw materials.—*vt.* (manufacturing, manufactured). To fabricate from raw materials; to fabricate without real grounds. —*vi.* To be occupied in manufactures. **manufacturer,** man'ū-fak"tūr-ėr, *n.* One who manufactures; owner of a manufactory. **manufacturing,** man'ū-fak"tūr-ing, *p.a.* Pertaining to or occupied in manufactures.

manumit, man'ū-mit", *vt.* (manumitting, manumitted). To release from slavery. **manumission,** man'ū-mish"-un, *n.* Emancipation.

manure, ma-nūr', *vt.* (manuring, manured). To fertilize with nutritive substances.—*n.* Any substance added to soil to accelerate or increase the production of the crops.

manuscript, man'ū-skript, *n.* A paper written with the hand; often contracted to *MS.,* pl. *MSS.*—*a.* Written with the hand.

Manx, mangks, *n.* The native language of the Isle of Man; *pl.* the natives of Man.—*a.* Belonging to the Isle of Man.

many, me'ni, *a.* Forming or comprising a number; numerous. **the many,** the great majority of people; the crowd. **so many,** the same number of; a certain number indefinitely.

map, map, *n.* A representation of the surface of the earth or any part of it.— *vt.* (mapping, mapped). To draw in a map; to plan.

maple, mā'pl, *n.* A tree of the sycamore kind.

mar, mär, *vt.* (marring, marred). To injure in any manner; to hurt, impair, disfigure, &c.

marabou, mar'a-bō, *n.* A large stork yielding valuable white feathers.

marathon race, mar'a-thon rās, *n.* An ancient Greek footrace of 26 miles 385 yards.

maraud, ma-rad', *vi.* To rove in quest of plunder; to make an excursion for booty.

marble, mär'bl, *n.* A calcareous stone of compact texture; a little, hard ball used by boys in play; an inscribed or sculptured marble stone.—*a.* Made of or like marble.—*vt.* (marbling, marbled). To stain like marble.

march, märch, *vi.* To move by steps and in order, as soldiers; to walk in a stately manner; to progress; to be situated next.—*vt.* To cause to march.— *n.* The measured walk of a body of men; a stately walk; distance passed over; a musical composition to regulate the march of troops, &c.; a frontier or

boundary (usually in *pl.*); the third month of the year.

marchioness, mär'shun-es, *n.* The wife of a marquis; a lady of the rank of a marquis.

mare, mār, *n.* The female of the horse.

margarine, mär'ja-rēn, *n.* An imitation of butter, made from animal fat.

margin, mär'jin, *n.* An edge, border, brink; edge of a page left blank; difference between the cost and selling price. —*vt.* To furnish with a margin; to enter in the margin. **marginal,** mär'jin-al, *a.* Pertaining to a margin; written or printed in the margin.

marigold, mar'i-gōld, *n.* A composite plant bearing golden-yellow flowers.

marine, ma-rēn', *a.* Pertaining to the sea; found in the sea; used at sea; naval; maritime.—*n.* A soldier who serves on board of a man-of-war; collective shipping of a country; whole economy of naval affairs.

marital, mar'i-tal, *a.* Pertaining to a husband.

maritime, mar'i-tīm, *a.* Relating to the sea; naval; bordering on the sea; having a navy and commerce by sea.

marjoram, mär'jō-ram, *n.* A plant of the mint family.

mark, märk, *n.* A visible sign or impression on something; a distinguishing sign; indication or evidence; pre-eminence or importance; a characteristic; heed or regard; object aimed at; proper standard; extreme estimate; a silver coin of Germany worth about 24 c.—*vt.* To make a mark or marks on; to denote (often with *out*); to regard, observe, heed.— *vi.* To note; to observe critically; to remark. **marked,** märkt, *p.a.* Pre-eminent; outstanding; prominent; remarkable. **marker,** mär'kėr, *n.* One who marks; a counter used in card-playing.

market, mär'ket, *n.* An occasion on which goods are publicly exposed for sale; place in which goods are exposed for sale; rate of purchase and sale; demand for commodities; privilege of keeping a public market.—*vi.* To deal in a market.—*vt.* To offer for sale in a market. **marketable,** mär'ket-a-bl, *a.* Fit for the market; that may be sold.

marksman, märks'man, *n.* One who is skillful to hit a mark; one who shoots well.

marline, mär'lin, *n.* A small line of two strands, used for winding round ships' ropes.—*vi.* To wind marline round. **marlinespike,** mär'lin-spīk', *n.* An iron tool for opening the strands of rope.

marmalade, mär'ma-lād, *n.* A preserve made from various fruits, especially acid fruits, such as the orange.

marmot, mär'mut, *n.* A hibernating rodent animal of northern latitudes.

maroon, ma-rön', *n.* A fugitive slave in the W. Indies; a brownish crimson or claret color.—*vt.* To land and leave on a desolate island.

marquee, mär-kē', *n.* A large tent erected for a temporary purpose; an officer's field tent.

marquetry, mär'ke-tri, *n.* Inlaid work.

marquis, marquess, mär'kwis, mär'-

kwes, n. A title of honor next below that of duke.

marriage, mar'ij, n. The act or ceremony of marrying; matrimony; wedlock. **marriageable,** mar'ij-a-bl, a. Of an age suitable for marriage; fit to be married. **married,** mar'id, p.a. Joined in marriage; conjugal; connubial.

marrow, mar'ō, n. A soft substance in the cavities of bones; the best part; a kind of gourd, also called *vegetable marrow.*

marry, mar'i, vt. (marrying, married). To unite in wedlock; to dispose of in wedlock; to take for husband or wife.— vi. To take a husband or a wife.

Mars, märz, n. The god of war; a planet.

marsh, märsh, n. A swamp; a tract of low wet land.—a. Pertaining to boggy places.

marshal, mär'shal, n. One who regulates rank and order at a feast, procession, &c.; a military officer of the highest rank, generally called *field-marshal.* —vt. (marshaling, marshaled). To dispose in order; to array.

marshmallow, märsh"mal'ō, n. A plant of the hollyhock genus.

marshy, mär'shi, a. Abounding in marshes; boggy; fenny; produced in marshes.

marsupial, mär-sū'pi-al, n. and a. One of a large group of mammalians whose young are born in an imperfect condition and nourished in an external abdominal pouch.

mart, märt, n. A market.

marten, mär'ten, n. A fierce kind of weasel, valued for its fur.

martial, mär'shal, a. Pertaining to war; warlike.

martin, mär'tin, n. A species of swallow.

martinet, mär'ti-net", n. A precise, punctilious, or strict disciplinarian.

martyr, mär'tèr, n. One who suffers death or persecution on account of his belief; one greatly afflicted.—vt. To put to death for adhering to one's belief. **martyrdom,** mär'tèr-dom, n. The doom or death of a martyr.

marvel, mär'vel, n. A wonder; something very astonishing.—vi. (marveling, marveled). To feel admiration or astonishment. **marvelous,** mär'vel-us, a. Exciting wonder or surprise; wonderful; astonishing.

Marxism, märk'sizm, n. A social philosophy developed by Friedrich Engels and Karl Marx.

mascot, mas'kot, n. A thing supposed to bring good luck to its owner.

masculine, mas'kū-lin, a. Male; manly; robust; bold or unwomanly; designating nouns which are the names of male animals, &c.

mash, mash, n. A mixture of ingredients beaten or blended together; a mixture of ground malt and warm water yielding wort.—vt. To mix; to beat into a confused mass.

mask, mask, n. A cover for the face; a masquerade; a sort of play common in the 16th and 17th centuries; pretense or subterfuge.—vt. To cover with a mask; to disguise; to hide.

mason, mā'sn, n. One who prepares stone, and constructs buildings; a freemason. **masonic,** ma-son'ik, a. Pertaining to the craft or mysteries of freemasons. **masonry,** mā'sn-ri, n. The art or occupation of a mason; stonework; the doctrines and practices of freemasons.

masque, mask, n. See **mask. masquerade,** mas'kèr-ād", n. An assembly of persons wearing masks; a disguise.— vi. To assemble in masks; to go in disguise.

mass, mas, n. A body of matter; a lump; magnitude; an assemblage; collection; the generality; the communion service in the R. Catholic Church. **the masses,** the populace.—vt. and i. To form into a mass; to assemble in crowds.

massacre, mas'a-kèr, n. Ruthless, unnecessary, or indiscriminate slaughter.— vt. (massacring, massacred). To kill with indiscriminate violence; to slaughter.

massage, ma-säzh' or mas'äch, n. A process of kneading, rubbing, pressing, &c., parts of person's body to effect a cure.—vt. (massaging, massage). To treat by this process. **massageuse,** ma-säzh', **masseuse,** mas'a-zhuz", ma-suz', n. A female who practices massage. **massagist, masseur,** ma-säzh'ist, ma-sür', n. Ane who practices massage.

massive, mas'iv, a. Bulky and heavy; ponderous; pertaining to a mass; not local or special.

mast, mast, n. A long upright timber in a vessel, supporting the yards, sails, and rigging; the fruit of the oak, beech, &c. (no *pl.*).—vt. To supply with a mast or masts.

master, mas'tèr, n. One who rules or directs; an employer; owner; captain of a merchant ship; teacher in a school; a man eminently skilled in some art; a word of address for men (written *Mr.* and pron. mis'tèr) and boys (written in full); a vessel having masts.—vt. To bring under control; to make one's self master of.—a. Belonging to a master; chief. **masterful,** mas'tèr-fyl, a. Inclined to exercise mastery; imperious; headstrong.

master key, mäs'tèr kè, n. The key that opens many locks.

masterly, mas'tèr-li, a. Suitable to a master; most excellent; skillful.

masterpiece, mas"tèr-pēs', n. Chief performance; anything done with superior skill.

master stroke, mas'tèr strōk, n. A masterly act or achievement.

mastery, mas'tèr-i, n. Command; preeminence; victory; superior dexterity.

masticate, mas'ti-kāt, vt. To chew and prepare for swallowing. **mastication,** mas'ti-kā"shun, n. Act of masticating.

mastiff, mas'tif, n. A large heavy dog with deep and pendulous lips.

mastodon, mas'tō-don, n. An extinct quadruped like the elephant, but larger.

mat, mat, n. An article of interwoven rushes, twine, &c., used for cleaning or protecting; anything growing thickly or closely interwoven.—*vt.* (matting, matted). To cover with mats; to entangle.—*vi.* To grow thickly together.

matador, mat'a-dôr, *n.* The man appointed to kill the bull in bull-fights.

match, mach, *n.* A person or thing equal to another; union by marriage; one to be married; a contest; a small body that catches fire readily or ignites by friction. —*vt.* To equal; to show an equal to; to set against as equal in contest; to suit; to marry.—*vi.* To be united in marriage; to suit; to tally. **matchless**, mach'les, *a.* That cannot be matched; having no equal; unrivaled.

mate, māt, *n.* A companion; a match; a husband or wife; second officer in a ship.—*vt.* (mating, mated). To equal; to match; to marry; to checkmate.

material, ma-tēr'i-al, *a.* Consisting of matter; not spiritual; important; essential; substantial.—*n.* Anything composed of matter; substance of which anything is made. **materialism**, ma-tēr'i-al-izm, *n.* The doctrine of materialists. **materialist**, ma-tēr'i-al-ist, *n.* One who asserts that all existence is material. **materialize**, ma-tēr'i-al-īz, *vt.* To reduce to a state of matter; to regard as matter.

maternal, ma-tèr'nal, *a.* Motherly; pertaining to a mother; becoming a mother. **maternity**, ma-tèr'ni-ti, *n.* The state, character, or relation of a mother.

mathematical, **mathematic**, math'ē-mat'i-kal, math'ē-mat'ik, *a.* Pertaining to mathematics.

mathematics, math'ē-mat'iks, *n.* The science of magnitude and number, comprising arithmetic, geometry, algebra, &c. **mathematician**, math'ē-ma-tish'-an, *n.* One versed in mathematics.

matin, mat'in, *n.* Morning; *pl.* morning prayers or songs; time of morning service.

matinée, mat'i-nā", *n.* An entertainment or reception held early in the day.

matricide, mā'tri-sīd, *n.* The killing of a mother; the murderer of his or her mother.

matriculate, ma-trik'ū-lāt, *vt.* To enroll; to admit to membership, particularly in a university.—*vi.* To be entered as a member. **matriculation**, ma-trik'ū-lā'shun, *n.* Act of matriculating.

matrimony, mat''ri-mō'ni, *n.* Marriage; wedlock; the married or nuptial state. **matrimonial**, mat''ri-mō'ni-al, *a.* Pertaining to matrimony; nuptial.

matrix, mā'triks, *n.*; *pl.* **matrices** (māt'ri-sēz.) The womb; a mold; substance in which a mineral, &c., is embedded.

matron, mā'trun, *n.* An elderly married woman, or an elderly lady; head nurse or superintendent of a hospital, &c. **matronly**, mā'trun-li, *a.* Like or becoming a matron; elderly; sedate.

matted, mat'ed, *p.a.* Laid with mats; entangled.

matter, mat'èr, *n.* Not mind; body; that of which anything is made; substance as distinct from form; subject; business; circumstance; import; mo-

ment; pus.—*vi.* To be of importance; to signify; to form pus.

matter-of-fact, mat'èr-ov-fakt', Treating of facts; precise; prosaic.

matting, mat'ing, *n.* Material for mats; mats collectively; coarse fabric for packing.

mattock, mat'uk, *n.* A pick-ax with one or both of its ends broad.

mattress, mat'res, *n.* A bed stuffed with hair, or other soft material, and quilted.

mature, ma-tūr', *a.* Ripe; perfect; completed; ready; having become payable.—*vt.* (maturing, matured). To make mature; to advance toward perfection.—*vi.* To become ripe or perfect; to become payable. **maturity**, ma-tū'ri-ti, *n.* State of being mature; ripeness; time when a bill of exchange becomes due.

matzoth, mat'sōth, *n.* Thin pieces of unleavened bread eaten during the Jewish Passover.

maudlin, mad'lin, *a.* Over-emotional; sickly sentimental; approaching to intoxication.

maul, mal, *n.* A large hammer or mallet. —*vt.* To beat with a maul; to maltreat severely.

maunder, man'dèr, *vi.* To speak with a beggar's whine; to drivel.

mausoleum, ma'sō-lē'um, *n.* A magnificent tomb or sepulchral monument.

mauve, mōv, *n.* A purple dye obtained from aniline.

maverick, mav'èr-ik, *n.* Wild unbranded cattle; a person whose action is not controlled by an organized group.

maw, mä, *n.* The stomach; especially of animals; paunch; crop of fowls.

mawkish, mak'ish, *a.* Apt to cause satiety or loathing, insipid; sickly.

maxilla, mak-sil'a, *n.*; *pl.* **æ.** A jawbone; a jaw. **maxillar**, **maxillary**, mak-sil'lar, mak'si-ler'i, *a.* Pertaining to the jaw or jaw-bone.

maxim, mak'sim, *n.* An established principle; axiom; aphorism; a light machine-gun.

maximum, mak'si-mum, *n.* The greatest decree or quantity.—*a.* Greatest.

May, mā, *n.* The fifth month of the year; hawthorn blossom.—*vi.* To celebrate the festivities of May-day.—*v. aux.* (pret. might, mīt). Used to imply possibility, opportunity, permission, desire, &c.

mayonnaise, **mayonaise**, mā'o-nāz", *n.* A sauce of yolks of eggs, oil, &c.

mayor, mā'èr, *n.* The chief magistrate of a city or borough. **mayoral**, mā'èr-al, *a.* Pertaining to a mayor. **mayoralty**, mā'èr-al-ti, *n.* Office of a mayor.

Maypole, mā'pōl', *n.* A pole to dance around on May-day.

maze, māz, *vt.* (mazing, mazed). To bewilder; to amaze.—*n.* Perplexed state of things; bewilderment; a labyrinth; a confusing network of paths or passages.

me, mē, *pron. pers.* The objective of *I*.

mead, mēd, *n.* A fermented liquor made from honey and water; a meadow; *poet.*

meadow, med'ō, *n.* A low level tract of

land under grass.—*a.* Belonging to a meadow.

meager, mē'gėr, *a.* Thin; lean; poor; scanty.

meal, mēl, *n.* Portion of food taken at one time; a repast; ground grain; flour.

mealy, mēl'i, *a.* Having the qualities of meal; powdery; farinaceous. **mealy-mouthed,** mēl'i-mouтнd', *a.* Unwilling to tell the truth in plain language; soft-spoken; inclined to hypocrisy.

mean, mēn, *a.* Low in rank or birth; humble; base; contemptible; occupying a middle position; middle; intermediate. —*n.* What is intermediate; average rate or degree; medium; *pl.* measure or measures adopted; agency (generally used as *sing.*); income or resources.—*vt.* (pret. and pp. meant). To have in the mind; to intend; to signify; to import. —*vi.* To have thought or ideas, or to have meaning.

meander, mē-an'dėr, *n.* A winding course; a bend in a course; a labyrinth. —*vi.* To wind about; to be intricate.

meaning, mēn'ing, *p.a.* Significant.—*n.* Design; signification; purport; force. **meaningless,** mēn'ing-les, *a.* Having no meaning.

meaningly, mēn'ing-li, *adv.* Significantly.

meantime, mēn'tīm, *adv.* During the interval; in the intervening time.—*n.* The interval between one period and another.

meanwhile, mēn'whīl, *adv.* and *n.* Meantime.

measles, mē'zlz, *n.* A contagious disease in man, characterized by a crimson rash. **measly,** mē'zli, *a.* Infected with measles; slight; worthless.

measure, mezh'ėr, *n.* The extent or magnitude of a thing; a standard of size; a measuring rod or line; that which is allotted; moderation; just degree; course of action; legislative proposal; musical time; meter; a grave solemn dance; *pl.* beds or strata.—*vt.* (measuring, measured). To ascertain the extent or capacity of; to estimate; value; to pass through or over; to proportion; to allot.—*vi.* To have a certain extent. **measurable,** mezh'ėr-a-bl. *a.* That may be measured; not very great; moderate. **measured,** mezh'ėrd, *p.a.* Deliberate and uniform; stately; restricted; moderate. **measureless,** mezh'ėr-les, *a.* Without measure; boundless; vast; infinite. **measurement,** mezh'ėr-ment, *n.* Act of measuring; amount ascertained.

meat, mēt, *n.* Food in general; the flesh of animals used as food; the edible portion of something (the *meat* of an egg).

mechanic, me-kan'ik, *a.* Mechanical.—*n.* An artisan; an artisan employed in making and repairing machinery. **mechanical,** me-kan'i-kal, *a.* Pertaining to mechanism or machinery; resembling a machine; done by the mere force of habit; pertaining to material forces; physical. **mechanics,** me-kan'iks, *n.* The science which treats of motion and force. **mechanism,** mek'a-nizm, *n.* A

mechanical contrivance; structure of a machine.

medal, med'l, *n.* A piece of metal in the form of a coin, stamped with some figure or device, as a memento or reward. **medalist,** med'l-ist, *n.* An engraver or stamper of medals; one skilled in medals; one who has gained a medal.

medallion, me-dal'yun, *n.* A large antique medal; a circular or oval tablet.

meddle, med'l, *vi.* (meddling, meddled). To interfere; to intervene officiously. **meddler,** med'lėr, *n.* One who meddles; an officious person; a busybody. **meddlesome,** med'l-sum, *a.* Given to interfering; meddling; officiously intrusive.

medial, mē'di-al, *a.* Middle; mean; pertaining to a mean or average.

median, mē'di-an, *a.* Situated in the middle; passing through or along the middle.

mediate, mē'di-āt, *a.* Middle; intervening; acting as a means; not direct.—*vi.* (mediating, mediated). To negotiate between contending parties, with a view to reconciliation; to intercede. **mediation,** mē'di-ā"shun, *n.* Act of mediating; intercession; entreaty for another. **mediator,** mē'di-ā'tėr, *n.* One who mediates; an intercessor; an advocate.

medical, med'i-kal, *a.* Pertaining to the art of curing diseases; tending to cure. **medically,** med'i-kal-li, *adv.* According to the rules of medicine.

medicate, med'i-kāt, *vt.* (medicating, medicated). To treat with medicine; to impregnate with anything medicinal. **medicine,** med'i-sin, *n.* Any substance used as a remedy in treating diseases; the science and art of curing.

medicinal, me-dis'i-nal, *a.* Pertaining to medicine; containing healing ingredients.

medieval, mediæval, mē'di-ē"val, *a.* Pertaining to the middle ages.

mediocre, mē"di-ō'kėr, *a.* Of moderate degree; middling. **mediocrity,** mē'di-ok"ri-ti, *n.* State of being mediocre; a moderate degree or rate; a person of mediocre talents or abilities.

meditate, med'i-tāt, *vi.* (meditating, meditated). To dwell on anything in thought; to cogitate.—*vt.* To think on; to scheme; to intend. **meditation,** med'i-tā"shun, *n.* Act of meditating; serious contemplation. **meditative,** med'i-tāt-iv, *a.* Addicted to meditation; expressing meditation.

Mediterranean, med'i-te-rā"nē-an, *a.* Surrounded by land; now applied exclusively to the *Mediterranean* Sea.

medium, mē'di-um, *n.*; *pl.* **-ia, iums.** Something holding a middle position; a mean; means of motion or action; agency of transmission; instrumentality. —*a.* Middle; middling.

medley, med'li, *n.* A mingled mass of ingredients; a miscellany; a jumble.

medulla, me-dul'a, *n.* Marrow. **medullary, medular,** med"u-ler'i, med'u-ler, *a.* Pertaining to, consisting of, or resembling marrow.

meek, mēk, *a.* Soft, gentle, or mild of temper; forbearing; humble; submissive.

meerschaum, mēr'shum, *n.* A silicate of magnesium, used for tobacco pipes; a tobacco pipe made of this.

meet, mēt, *vi.* (meeting, met). To come face to face with; to come in contact with; to encounter; to light on; to receive; to satisfy.—*vi.* To come together; to encounter; to assemble.—*n.* A meeting, as of huntsmen.—*a.* Fit; suitable; proper. **meeting,** mēt'ing, *n.* A coming together; an interview; an assembly; encounter.

meetly, mēt'li, *adv.* Fitly; suitably.

megaphone, meg'a-fōn, *n.* A device enabling persons to converse at a great distance.

melancholia, mel'an-kō''li-a, *n.* Morbid melancholy.

melancholy, mel''an-kol'i, *n.* Mental alienation characterized by gloom and depression; hypochondria; dejection; sadness.—*a.* Gloomy; dejected; calamitous; somber.

mêlée, mā-lā', *n.* A confused fight; an affray.

meliorate, mēl-yo-rāt, *vt.* To make better; to improve.—*vi.* To grow better. **melioration,** mēl'yo-rā''shun, *n.* Improvement.

mellifluent, mellifluous, me-lif'lō-ent, me-lif'lō-us, *a.* Flowing with honey or sweetness; smooth; sweetly flowing. **mellifluence,** me-lif'lō-ens, *n.* A flow of honey or sweetness; a sweet smooth flow.

mellow, mel'ō, *a.* Soft with ripeness; soft to the ear, eye, or taste; toned down by time; half-tipsy.—*vt.* To make mellow; to soften.—*vi.* To become mellow.

melodrama, mel'ō-drä'ma, *n.* Properly a musical drama; a serious play, with startling incidents, exaggerated sentiments, and splendid decoration. **melodramatic,** mel'ō-dra-mat''ik, *a.* Pertaining to melodrama; sensational.

melody, mel'ō-di, *n.* An agreeable succession of sounds; sweetness of sound; the particular air or tune of a musical piece. **melodic,** me-lod'ik, *a.* Of the nature of melody; relating to melody. **melodious,** me-lō'di-us, *a.* Containing melody; musical; agreeable to the ear. **melodist,** me'lō-dist, *n.* A composer or singer of melodies.

melon, mel'un, *n.* A kind of cucumber and its large, fleshy fruit.

melt, melt, *vt.* To reduce from a solid to a liquid state by heat; to soften; to overcome with tender emotion.—*vi.* To become liquid; to dissolve; to be softened to love, pity, &c.; to pass by imperceptible degrees. **melting,** melt'ing, *p.a.* Tending to soften; affecting; feeling or showing tenderness.

member, mem'bėr, *n.* An organ or limb of an animal body; part of an aggregate; one of the persons composing a society, &c.; a representative in a legislative body. **membership,** mem'bėr-ship, *n.* State of being a member; the members of a body.

membrane, mem'brān, *n.* A thin flexible texture in animal bodies; a similar texture in plants. **membranous,** mem'bra-nus, *a.* Belonging to or like a membrane; consisting of membranes.

memento, me-men'tō, *n.* That which reminds; a souvenir; a keepsake.

memoir, mem'wär, *n.* A written account of events or transactions; a biographical notice; recollections of one's life (usually in the *pl.*)

memorable, mem'ō-ra-bl, *a.* Worthy to be remembered; signal; remarkable; famous. **memorably,** mem'ō-ra-bli, *adv.* In a memorable manner. **memorandum,** mem'ō-ran''dum, *n.*; pl. **-dums,** or **da.** A note to help the memory; brief entry in a diary; formal statement.

memory, mem'ō-ri, *n.* The faculty of the mind by which it retains knowledge or ideas; remembrance; recollection; the time within which a person may remember what is past; something remembered. **memorial,** me-mō'ri-al, *a.* Pertaining to memory or remembrance; serving to commemorate.—*n.* That which preserves the memory of something; a monument; memorandum; a written representation of facts, made as the ground of a petition. **memorize,** mem'ō-rīz, *vt.* To cause to be remembered; to record.

menace, men'is, *n.* A threat; indication of probable evil.—*vt.* (menacing, menaced). To threaten. **menacingly,** men'i-sing-li, *adv.* In a menacing or threatening manner.

menage, mā-näzh', *n.* A household; housekeeping; household management.

menagerie, me-naj'ėr-i, *n.* A collection of wild animals kept for exhibition.

mend, mend, *vt.* To repair; to restore to a sound state; to amend.—*vi.* To advance to a better state; to improve.

mendacious, men-dā'shus, *a.* Lying; false; given to telling untruths. **mendacity,** men-das'i-ti, *n.* Quality of being mendacious; deceit; untruth.

mendicity, men-dis'i-ti, *n.* State of being a mendicant; the life of a beggar. **mendicant,** men'di-kant, *a.* Begging. —*n.* A beggar; one who makes it his business to beg alms; a begging friar.

menial, mē'ni-al, *a.* Belonging to household servants; low with regard to employment.—*n.* A domestic servant (used mostly disparagingly).

meningitis, men'in-ji''tis, *n.* Inflammation of the membranes of the brain or spinal cord.

menses, men'sēz, *n.pl.* The monthly discharge of a woman. **menstrual,** men'strō-al, *a.* Monthly; pertaining to the menses of females. **menstruate,** men'strō-āt, *vi.* To discharge the menses. **menstruation,** men'strō-ā''shun, *n.* Act of menstruating; period of menstruating.

mensuration, men'sūr-ā''shun, *n.* The act, process, or art of measuring. **mensurable,** men'sūr-a-bl, *a.* Measurable.

mental, men'tal, *a.* Pertaining to the mind; performed by the mind; intellectual. **mentally,** men'tal-li, *adv.* In a mental manner; intellectually; in thought.

menthol, men'thol, *n.* A white crystalline substance obtained from oil of peppermint.

ention, men'shun, *n.* A brief notice or remark about something.—*vt.* To make mention of; to name.

entor, men'tor, *n.* A friend and sage adviser.

enu, měn'ū, *n.* A list of dishes to be served at a dinner, &c.; a bill of fare.

ercantile, mèr'kan-til, *a.* Pertaining to merchandise; trading; commercial.

ercenary, mèr'sē-ner'i, *a.* Hired; venal; that may be hired; greedy of gain; sordid.—*n.* One who is hired; a soldier hired into foreign service.

erchandise, mèr'chan-dīz, *n.* The goods of a merchant; objects of commerce; trade.

erchant, mèr'chant, *n.* One who carries on trade on a large scale; a man who exports and imports goods.—*a.* Relating to trade; commercial. **merchantman**, mèr'chant-man, *n.* A ship engaged in commerce, a trading vessel.

ercury, mèr'kū-ri, *n.* Quicksilver, a heavy metal, liquid at all ordinary temperatures; the planet nearest the sun. **mercurial**, mèr-kū'ri-al, *a.* Like the god Mercury; flighty; fickle; pertaining to or containing quicksilver.

Mercury

ercy, mèr'si, *n.* Willingness to spare or forgive; clemency; pity; a blessing; benevolence; unrestrained exercise of authority. **merciful**, mèr'si-ful, *a.* Full of mercy; compassionate; tender; clement; mild.

erciless, mèr'si-les, *a.* Destitute of mercy; pitiless; cruel; hard-hearted.

ere, mēr, *a.* This or that and nothing else; simple, absolute, entire, utter.—*n.* A pool or small lake; a boundary.

erely, mēr-li, *adv.* For this and no other purpose; solely; simply; only.

eretricious, mer'ē-trish'us, *a.* Pertaining to prostitutes; alluring by false show; gaudy.

erge, mèrj, *vt.* (merging, merged). To cause to be swallowed up or incorporated.—*vi.* To be sunk, swallowed, or lost.

eridian, mē-rid'i-an, *n.* Pertaining to mid-day or noon; pertaining to the acme or culmination.—*n.* Mid-day; point of greatest splendor; any imaginary circle passing through both poles, used in marking longitude; a similar imaginary line in the heavens passing through the zenith of any place.

erino, me-rē'nō, *a.* Belonging to a Spanish variety of sheep with long and fine wool; made of the wool of the merino sheep.—*n.* A merino sheep.

erit, mer'it, *n.* What one deserves; desert; value; good quality.—*vt.* To deserve; to have a just title to; to incur. **meritorious**, mer'i-tō''ri-us, *a.* Having merit; praiseworthy.

ermaid, mèr''mād', *n.* A fabled marine creature, having the upper part like a woman and the lower like a fish.

erry, mer'i, *a.* Joyous; jovial; hilarious, gay and noisy; mirthful; sportive. **merrily**, mer'i-li, *adv.* In a merry manner; with mirth; with gaiety and laughter. **merriment**, mer'i-ment, *n.* Mirth; noisy gayety; hilarity.

mesa, mā'sa, *n.* A high tableland with steeply sloped sides.

mésalliance, mā'zal'yäns'', *n.* A misalliance; an unequal marriage.

mesh, mesh, *n.* The space between the threads of a net; something that entangles; implement for making nets.—*vt.* To catch in a net.

mesmerist, mez'mèr-ist, *n.* One who practices or believes in mesmerism. **mesmerism**, mez'mèr-izm, *n.* The doctrine that some persons can exercise influence over the will and nervous system of others; animal magnetism; hypnotism. **mesmerize**, mez'mèr-īz, *vt.* To bring into a state of mesmeric or hypnotic sleep.

mess, mes, *n.* A dish of food; food for a person at one meal; a number of persons who eat together, especially in the army or navy; a disorderly mixture; muddle.—*vi.* To take meals in common with others.

message, mes'ij, *n.* A communication, written or verbal; an official written communication.

messenger, mes'en-jèr, *n.* One who bears a message; a harbinger.

Messiah, me-sī'a, *n.* The Anointed One; Christ, the Anointed.

messieurs, mes'èrz, *n.* Sirs; gentlemen; the plural of *Mr.*, generally contracted into *Messrs.* (mes'èrz).

metabolism, me-tab'ō-lizm, *n.* Change or metamorphosis; chemical change of nutriment taken into the body. **metabolic**, met'a-bol''ik, *a.* Pertaining to change or metamorphosis.

metal, met'l, *n.* An elementary substance, such as gold, iron, &c., having a peculiar luster and generally fusible by heat; the broken stone for covering roads. **metallic**, me-tal'ik, *a.* Pertaining to, consisting of, or resembling metal.

metallurgic, met'l-èr''jik, *a.* Pertaining to metallurgy. **metallurgy**, met''l-èr'ji, *n.* Art of working metals; art or operation of separating metals from their ores by smelting.

metamorphosis, met'a-mor''fō-sis, *n.*; *pl.* **-ses.** Change of form or shape; transformation. **metamorphic**, met'a-mor''fik, *a.* Pertaining to metamorphosis or metamorphism. **metamorphose**, met'a-mor''fōz, *vt.* To change into a different form; to transform.

metaphor, met'a-fōr, *n.* A figure of speech founded on resemblance, as 'that man is a fox'. **metaphoric, metaphorical**, met'a-fōr''ik, met'a-fōr''i-kal, *a.* Pertaining to metaphor; not literal; figurative.

metaphysics, met'a-fiz''iks, *n.* The science of the principles and causes of all things existing; the philosophy of mind as distinguished from that of matter. **metaphysic**, met'a-fiz''ik, *a.* Metaphysical.—*n.* Metaphysics. **meta-**

physical, met'a-fiz"i-kal, *a.* Pertaining to metaphysics; according to rules or principles of metaphysics.

mete, mēt, *vt.* (meting, meted). To measure; to measure out; to dole.

meteor, mē'tē-ėr, *n.* An atmospheric phenomenon; a transient luminous body; something that transiently dazzles. **meteoric**, mē'tē-or"ik, *a.* Pertaining to or consisting of meteors; proceeding from a meteor; transiently or irregularly brilliant. **meteorite**, mē'tē-ėr-īt, *n.* A meteorolite. **meteorolite**, mē'tē-ėr"ō-līt, *n.* A meteoric stone; an aerolite. **meteorological**, mē'tē-ėr-ō-loj"i-kal, *a.* Pertaining to meteorology. **meteorologist**, mē'tē-ėr-ol"o-jist, *n.* One versed or skilled in meteorology. **meteorology**, mē'tē-ėr-ol"o-ji, *n.* The science of atmospheric phenomena.

meter, mē'tėr, *n.* One who or that which measures; a measuring instrument for gas or water; arrangement of syllables in poetry; verse; rhythm; a French measure of length 39·37 inches; a metre.

methinks, mē-thingks', *v. impers.* (pret. methought). It seems to me; I think.

method, meth'ud, *n.* Mode or manner of procedure; system; classification. **methodic, methodical**, me-thod'ik, me-thod'i-kal, *a.* Systematic; orderly. **methodism**, meth'od-izm, *n.* Observance of method or system; (with *cap.*) the doctrines and worship of the Methodists. **methodist**, meth'ud-ist, *n.* One who observes method; (with *cap.*) one of a sect of Christians founded by John Wesley.

methyl, meth'il, *n.* The hypothetical radical of wood-spirit and its combinations. **methylated**, meth"i-lāt'ed, *a.* Impregnated or mixed with methyl; containing wood-naphtha.

metre, mètre, mē'tėr, me-tr, *n.* A French measure of length, a meter. **metric**, met'rik, *a.* Pertaining to the decimal system. **metric, metrical**, met'rik, met'ri-kal, *a.* Pertaining to rhythm; consisting of verse.

metropolis, me-trop'ō-lis, *n.* The capital of a country; see of a metropolitan bishop. **metropolitan**, met'rō-pol"-i-tan, *a.* Belonging to a metropolis, or to a mother-church.—*n.* An archbishop.

mettle, met'l, *n.* Moral or physical constitution; spirit; courage; fire. **mettled**, met'ld, *a.* High-spirited; ardent. **mettlesome**, met'l-sum, *a.* Full of spirit; brisk; fiery.

mew, mū, *n.* The cry of a cat.—*vt.* To cry as a cat.

mews, mūz, *n.* Place where carriage-horses are kept in large towns; a lane in which stables are situated.

Mexican, mek'si-kan, *n.* A native or inhabitant of Mexico.

mezzo, med'zō, *a.* In *music*, middle; mean.

mezzo-soprano, a treble voice between soprano, and contralto.

miasma, mi-az'ma, *n.*; pl. **miasmata**, mi-az'ma-ta. The effluvia of any putrefying bodies; noxious emanation; malaria.

mica, mī'ka, *n.* A mineral cleavable in thin shining elastic plates.

mice, mīs, *n.pl.* of *mouse.*

microbe, mī'krōb, *n.* A microscopic organism such as a bacillus or bacterium; verse in miniature.

microcosm, mī'krō-koz-m, *n.* The universe in miniature.

micrometer, mī-krom'e-tėr, *n.* An instrument for measuring small objects, spaces, or angles.

microphone, mī'krō-fōn, *n.* An instrument to augment small sounds by means of electricity.

microphyte, mī'krō-fīt, *n.* A microscopic plant, especially one that is parasitic.

microscope, mī'krō-skōp, *n.* An optical instrument for magnifying. **microscopic, microscopical**, mī'krō-skop"ik, mī'krō-skop"i-kal, *a.* Pertaining to a microscope; visible only by the aid of a microscope; very minute.

mid, mid, *a.*; no compar.; superl., midmost. Middle; intervening.

mid-air, mid'ār, *n.* The middle of the sky; a lofty position in the air.

midday, mid'dā', *n.* The middle of the day; noon.—*a.* Pertaining to noon.

middle, mid'l, *a.*; no compar.; superl. middlemost. Equally distant from the extremes; intermediate; intervening. **middle ages**, the period from the fall of the Roman Empire to about 1450.—*n.* Point or part equally distant from the extremities; something intermediate. **middle-aged**, mid'l-ājd', *a.* Being about the middle of the ordinary age of man. **middle class**, mid'l klās', *n.* The class of people holding a social position between the working-classes and the aristocracy of Britain.—*a.* mid'l-klas' or relating to the middle classes. **middleman**, mid"l-man', *n.* An intermediary between two parties; an agent between producers and consumers.

middling, mid'ling, *a.* Of middle rank, state, size, or quality; medium; mediocre.

midge, mij, *n.* A small gnat or fly.

midland, mid'land, *a.* Being in the interior country; inland.

midnight, mid"nīt', *n.* The middle of the night; twelve o'clock at night.—*a.* Pertaining to midnight; dark as midnight.

midriff, mid'rif, *n.* The diaphragm.

midshipman, mid"ship'man, *n.* A young officer in the navy, below a sub-lieutenant.

midst, midst, *n.* The middle.—*prep.* Amidst; *poet.*

midsummer, mid'sum'ėr, *n.* The middle of summer; the summer solstice, about June 21.

midway, mid'wā', *n.* The middle of the way or distance.—*a.* and *adv.* In the middle of the way; half-way.

midwife, mid"wīf', *n.* A woman that assists other women in childbirth. **midwifery**, mid"wif'ri, *n.* Obstetrics.

midwinter, mid'win'tėr, *n.* The middle of winter; the winter solstice, December 21.

mien, mēn, *n.* Look; bearing; carriage.

miff, mif, *n.* A slight quarrel.

might, mīt, *n.* Great power or ability to act; strength; force.—*v. aux.* Pret. of *may.* **mightily**, mīt'i-li, *adv.* In a mighty manner; with might; powerfully; greatly. **mighty**, mīt'i, *a.* Having might; strong; powerful; potent; very great; vast.

mignonette, min'yun-et" or min', *n.* A fragrant annual plant.

migrate, mī'grāt, *vi.* (migrating, migrated). To remove to a distant place or country. **migration**, mī'grā-shun, *n.* Act of migrating; removal from one place to another. **migratory**, mī"gra-tō'ri, *a.* Disposed to migrate; roving; passing from one climate to another, as birds. **migrant**, mī'grant, *n.* One who migrates; a migratory bird or other animal.

mikado, mi-kä'dō, *n.* The emperor of Japan.

milch, milch, *a.* Giving milk, as cows. **mild**, mīld, *a.* Gentle in temper or disposition; merciful; soft; bland; mellow. **mildness**, mīld'nes, *n.* State or quality of being mild; gentleness; clemency. **mildew**, mil'dū, *n.* A minute parasitic fungus that causes decay in vegetable matter; condition so caused.—*vt.* and *i.* To taint with mildew.

mile, mil, *n.* A measure of length or distance equal to 1760 yards. **mileage**, mil'ij, *n.* Fees paid for travel by the mile; aggregate of miles traveled, &c. **milestone**, mil"stōn', *n.* A stone or block set up to mark the miles on a road.

military, mil'i-ter'i, *a.* Pertaining to soldiers or war; martial; soldierly; belligerent.—*n.* The whole body of soldiers; the army. **militancy**, mil'i-tan-si, *n.* Warfare; combativeness. **militant**, mil'i-tant, *a.* Serving as a soldier; fighting; combative. **militarism**, mil'i-ta-izm, *n.* The system that leads a nation to pay excessive attention to military affairs.

militate, mil'i-tāt, *vi.* (militating, militated). To stand arrayed; to have weight or influence.

militia, mi-lish'a, *n.* A body of soldiers not permanently organized in time of peace.

militiaman, mi-li'sha-man, *n.* One who belongs to the militia.

milk, milk, *n.* A whitish fluid secreted in female animals, serving as nourishment for their young; what resembles milk; white juice of plants.—*vt.* To draw milk from. **milker**, mil'kėr, *n.* One who milks; a cow giving milk. **milkmaid**, milk"mād', *n.* A woman who milks or is employed in the dairy. **milkman**, milk"man', *n.* A man that sells milk or carries milk to market. **milky**, mil'ki, *a.* Pertaining to, resembling, yielding, or containing milk.

mill, mil, *n.* A machine for making meal or flour; a machine for grinding, &c.; a building that contains the machinery for grinding, &c.—*vt.* To pass through a mill; to stamp in a coining press; to throw, as silk; to full, as cloth.

milled, mild, *p.a.* Passed through a mill; having the edge transversely grooved, as a coin.

millennium, mi-len'i-um, *n.* An aggregate of a thousand years; the thousand years of Christ's reign on earth.

miller, mil'ėr, *n.* One who keeps or attends a mill for grinding grain.

millet, mil'et, *n.* A kind of small grain of various species used for food.

milligram, mil'i-gram, *n.* The thousandth part of a gram.

millimeter, mil"i-mē'tėr, *n.* The thousandth part of a meter.

milliner, mil'i-nėr, *n.* One who makes headdresses, hats, &c., for females. **millinery**, mil"i-ner'i, *n.* Articles made or sold by milliners; occupation of a milliner.

million, mil'yun, *n.* A thousand thousands; a very great number, indefinitely. **millionaire**, mil'yun-ār", *n.* One worth a million of dollars, &c.; a very rich person. **millionth**, mil'yunth, *a.* The ten hundred thousandth.

millpond, mil"pond", *n.* A pond furnishing water for driving a mill-wheel.

millrace, mil"rās', *n.* The stream of water driving a mill-wheel; channel in which it runs.

millstone, mil"stōn', *n.* One of the stones used in a mill for grinding grain.

millwheel, mil"whēl', *n.* A wheel used to drive a mill; a water-wheel.

millwright, mil"rīt', *n.* A mechanic who constructs the machinery of mills.

mime, mīm, *n.* A species of ancient drama in which gestures predominated; an actor in such performances. A mimic.

mimeograph, mim"ē-ō-graf, *n.* A machine that reproduces copies from a stencil.

mimic, mim'ik, *a.* Imitative; consisting of imitation.—*n.* One who imitates or mimics.—*vt.* (mimicking, mimicked). To imitate, especially for sport; to ridicule by imitation. **mimicry**, mim'ik-ri, *n.* Imitation, often for sport or ridicule.

mimosa, mī-mō'sa, *n.* A leguminous plant.

minaret, min'a-ret", *n.* A slender lofty turret on Mohammedan mosques, with one or more balconies; a small spire.

minatory, min'a-tō'ri, *a.* Threatening; menacing.

mince, mins, *vt.* (mincing, minced). To cut or chop into very small pieces; to extenuate or palliate; to utter with affected softness; to clip, as words.—*vi.* To walk with short steps; to speak with affected nicety.—*n.* Mince-meat. **mincemeat**, mins"mēt', *n.* Meat chopped or minced small. **mince pie**, mins'pī, *n.* A pie made with minced meat and other ingredients. **mincing**, min'sing, *p.a.* Speaking or walking affectedly; affectedly elegant.

mind, mīnd, *n.* The intellectual power in man; understanding; cast of thought and feeling; inclination; opinion; memory.—*vt.* To attend to; to observe; to regard. **minded**, mīnd'ed, *a.* Disposed; inclined. **mindful**, mīnd'ful, *a.* Bearing in mind; attentive; regarding with

care; heedful. **mindless,** mīnd′les, *a.*
Destitute of mind; unthinking; stupid;
negligent; careless.

mine, mīn, *adv. pron.* My, belonging to
me.—*n.* A pit from which coal, ores,
&c., are taken; an underground passage
in which explosives may be lodged for
destructive purposes; a rich source or
store of wealth.—*vi.* (mining, mined).
To undermine; to sap. **miner,** mīn′ėr,
n. One who works in a mine.

mineral, min′ėr-al, *n.* An inorganic
body existing on or in the earth.—*a.*
Pertaining to or consisting of minerals;
impregnated with mineral matter. **min-
eralogist,** min′ėr-al″ō-jist, *n.* One who
is versed in the science of minerals.
mineralogy, min′ėr-al″ō-ji, *n.* The
science of the properties of mineral substances.

mingle, ming′gl, *vt.* (mingling, mingled). To mix up together; to blend; to
debase by mixture.—*vi.* To be mixed; to
join.

miniature, min′i-a-tūr, *n.* A painting of
very small dimensions, usually in water-
colors on ivory, vellum, &c.; anything
represented in a greatly reduced scale;
a small scale.—*a.* On a small scale;
diminutive.

minim, min′im, *n.* Something exceedingly small; a dwarf; a note in music
equal to two crochets; the smallest
liquid measure; a single drop.

minimize, min′i-mīz, *vt.* (minimizing,
minimized). To reduce to a minimum;
to represent as of little moment; to depreciate.

minimum, min′i-mum, *n.* The least
quantity assignable; the smallest amount
or degree.

mining, mīn′ing, *a.* Pertaining to mines.
—*n.* The art or employment of digging
mines.

minion, min′yun, *n.* An unworthy favorite; a servile dependant; a minx; a
small kind of printing type.

minister, min′is-tėr, *n.* A servant; attendant; agent; a member of a government; a political representative or ambassador; the pastor of a church.—*vt.*
To give; to supply.—*vi.* To perform
service; to afford supplies; to contribute.
ministerial, min′is-tėr″i-al, *a.* Pertaining to ministry, ministers of state,
or ministers of the gospel. **ministrant,**
min′is-trant, *a.* Performing service;
acting as minister or attendant. **minis-
tration,** min′is-trā″shun, *n.* Act of
ministering; service; ecclesiastical function.

minor, mī′nėr, *a.* Lesser; smaller; of
ministering; service; instrumentality;
state of being a minister; profession of a
minister of the gospel; the clergy; the
administration.

mink, mingk, *n.* A quadruped allied to
the polecat and weasel.

minnow, min′ō, *n.* A very small fish
inhabiting fresh-water streams.

minor, mī′nėr, *a.* Lesser; smaller; of
little importance; petty; in *music,* less
by a lesser semitone.—*n.* A person not
yet 21 years of age.

minority, mi-nor′i-ti, *n.* State of being

a minor; period from birth until 21 yea[rs]
of age; the smaller number or a numb[er]
less than half; the party that has th[e]
fewest votes.

minster, min′stėr, *n.* A monastery; th[e]
church of a monastery; a cathed[ral]
church.

minstrel, min′strel, *n.* A musician;
bard; a singer. **minstrelsy,** min′stre[l]-
si, *n.* The art or occupation of a mi[n]-
strel; instrumental music; music; son[g];
a body of songs or ballads.

mint, mint, *n.* The place where mone[y]
is coined; a source of abundant suppl[y];
a herbaceous aromatic plant.—*vt.* [To]
coin; to invent; to forge; to fabricat[e].
mintage, min′tij, *n.* That which [is]
coined or stamped; duty paid for coinin[g].

minuend, min′ū-end, *n.* The numb[er]
from which another is to be subtracted.

minuet, min′ū-et″, *n.* A slow, gracef[ul]
dance; the tune or air for it.

minus, mī′nus, *a.* Less; less by [so]
much; wanting; the sign (—).

minuscule, mi-nus′kūl, *n.* A small so[rt]
of letter used in MSS. in the midd[le]
ages.

minute, mi-nūt′, *a.* Very small; precise[;]
particular; exact.

minute, min′it, *a.* The sixtieth part [of]
an hour or degree; short sketch of [an]
agreement, &c., in writing; a note [to]
preserve the memory of anything.—*v[t.]*
(minuting, minuted). To write down [a]
concise statement or note of.

minutely, mi-nūt′li, *adv.* With minut[e]-
ness; exactly; nicely.

minutiae, mi-nū′shi-ē, *n.pl.* Small [or]
minute things; minor or unimportant d[e]-
tails.

minx, mingks, *n.* A pert, forward girl.

miracle, mir′a-kl, *n.* A marvel; a supernatural event; a miracle-play. **miraculous,** mi-rak′ū-lus, *a.* Performed supernaturally; wonderful; extraordinary.

mirage, mi-räzh′, *n.* An optical illusio[n]
causing remote objects to be seen doubl[e]
or to appear as if suspended in the air.

mire, mīr, *n.* Wet, muddy soil; mud.—
vt. and *i.* (miring, mired). To sink [in]
mire; to soil with mud.

mirror, mir′ėr, *n.* A lookingglass; an[y]
polished substance that reflects image[s];
an exemplar.—*vt.* To reflect, as in [a]
mirror.

mirth, mėrth, *n.* The feeling of bein[g]
merry; merriment; glee; hilarit[y].
mirthful, mėrth′ful, *a.* Full of mirth[;]
merry; jovial; amusing. **mirthles[s],**
mėrth′les, *a.* Without mirth; joyless.

misadventure, mis′ad-ven″tūr, *n.* A[n]
unlucky accident; misfortune; ill-luck[.]

misanthrope, misanthropist, mis′-
an-thrōp, mis-an′thro-pist, *n.* A hater [of]
mankind. **misanthropic, misan-
thropical,** mis-an-throp′ik, mis-an-
throp′i-kal, *a.* Pertaining to a misanthrope; hating mankind. **misanthropy[,]**
mis-an′thro-pi, *n.* Hatred or dislike [of]
mankind.

misapply, mis′a-pli″, *vt.* To appl[y]
amiss; to apply to a wrong purpos[e].
misapplication, mis′ap-li-kā″shun, [n.]
The act of misapplying; a wrong ap[-]
plication.

isapprehend, mis'ap-rē-hend", *vt.* To misunderstand; to take in a wrong ense. misapprehension, mis'ap-rē-en"shun, *n.* Act of misapprehending; mistake.

isappropriate, mis'a-prō'pri-āt, *vt.* To appropriate wrongly.

isarrange, mis'a-rānj", *vt.* To arange improperly.

isbegotten, mis'bē-got"n, *p.a.* Unlawfully or irregularly begotten.

isbehave, mis'bē-hāv", *vi.* To behave ll; to conduct one's self improperly. isbehavior, mis'bē-hāv"yėr, *n.* Ill ehavior; misconduct.

isbelief, mis'bē-lēf", *n.* Erroneous beief; false religion. misbelieve, mis'-ē-lēv", *vt.* To believe erroneously.

iscalculate, mis'kal"kū-lāt, *vt.* To miscalculate erroneously. miscalculation, mis'kal-kū-lā"shun, *n.* Erroneous alculation.

iscall, mis-kal', *vt.* To call by a wrong ame; to revile or abuse.

iscarry, mis-kar'i, *vi.* To fail to reach ts destination; to fail of the intended ffect; to bring forth young before the roper time. miscarriage, mis-kar'ij, *n.* Act of miscarrying; failure; act of ringing forth young before the time; bortion.

iscellany, mis"e-lā'ni, *n.* A mixture f various kinds; a collection of various iterary productions. miscellaneous, ais"e-lā"nē-us, *a.* Consisting of several inds; promiscuous; producing written ompositions of various sorts.

ischance, mis-chans', *n.* Ill-luck; aisfortune; mishap; disaster.

ischief, mis'chif, *n.* Harm; injury; amage; vexatious affair; annoying conuct. mischievous, mis'chi-vus, *a.* Causing mischief; harmful; fond of nischief; troublesome in conduct.

iscible, mis'i-bl, *a.* That may be nixed.

isconceive, mis'kon-sēv", *vt.* and *i.* Co conceive erroneously; to misappreend. misconception, mis'kon-sep"-hun, *n.* An erroneous conception; misapprehension.

isconduct, mis-kon'dukt, *n.* Misbeavior; mismanagement.—*vt.* mis-konlukt'. To conduct amiss; *refl.* to mis-ehave.

isconstruction, mis'kon-struk"shun, *n.* Wrong construction or interpretation.

isconstrue, mis'kon-strō", *vt.* To contrue or interpret erroneously.

iscount, mis-kount', *vt.* and *i.* To nistake in counting.—*n.* An erroneous ounting.

iscreant, mis'krē-ant, *n.* A vile retch; an unprincipled scoundrel.

isdeed, mis-dēd', *n.* An evil action; ransgression.

isdemeanor, mis'dē-mēn"ėr, *n.* Ill ehavior; an offense inferior to felony.

isdirect, mis'di-rekt", *vt.* To direct to wrong person or place. misdirecion, mis'di-rek"shun, *n.* Act of misirecting; wrong direction; error of a udge in charging a jury, in matters of aw or of fact.

iser, mī'zėr, *n.* A niggard; one who in

wealth acts as if suffering from poverty.

miserable, miz'ėr-a-bl, *a.* Very unhappy; wretched; worthless; despicable. miserably, miz'ėr-a-bli, *adv.* In a miserable manner.

miserly, mī'zėr-li, *a.* Like a miser in habits; penurious; sordid; niggardly.

misery, miz'er-i, *n.* Great unhappiness; extreme distress; wretchedness.

misfeasance, mis-fē'zans, *n.* In *law*, a wrong done; wrong-doing in office.

misfit, mis-fit', *n.* A bad fit.—*vt.* To make (a garment, &c.) of a wrong size; to supply with something not suitable.

misfortune, mis-fōr'tūn, *n.* Ill fortune; calamity; mishap.

misgive, mis-giv', *vt.* To fill with doubt; to deprive of confidence; to fail. misgiving, mis-giv'ing, *n.* A failing of confidence; doubt; distrust.

misgovern, mis-guv'ėrn, *vt.* To govern ill. misgovernment, mis-guv'ėrn-ment, *n.* Act of misgoverning; bad administration.

misguide, mis-gīd', *vt.* To guide into error; to direct to a wrong purpose or end.

mishap, mis-hap', *n.* A mischance; an unfortunate accident.

misinform, mis'in-form", *vt.* To give erroneous information to.

misinterpret, mis'in-tėr'pret, *vt.* To interpret erroneously. misinterpretation, mis'in-tėr'pre-tā"shun, *n.* Act of interpreting erroneously.

misjudge, mis-juj', *vt.* To judge erroneously.—*vi.* To err in judgment.

mislay, mis-lā', *vt.* To lay in a wrong place; to lay in a place not recollected.

mislead, mis-lēd', *vt.* To lead astray; to cause to mistake; to deceive.

mismanage, mis-man'ij, *vt.* To manage ill; to administer improperly. mismanagement, mis-man'ij-ment, *n.* Bad management.

misnomer, mis-nō'mėr, *n.* A mistaken or inapplicable name or designation.

misogamy, mis-sog'a-mi, *n.* Hatred of marriage. misogamist, mi-sog'a-mist, *n.* A hater of marriage.

misplace, mis-plās', *vt.* To put in a wrong place; to set on an improper object.

misprint, mis-print', *vt.* To print wrongly.—*n.* A mistake in printing.

misquote, mis-kwōt', *vt.* To quote erroneously; to cite incorrectly.

misrepresent, mis'rep-rē-zent", *vt.* To represent falsely. misrepresentation, mis'rep-re-zen-tā"shun, *n.* False or incorrect account.

misrule, mis-rōl', *n.* Bad rule; misgovernment.—*vt.* To govern badly or oppressively.

miss, mis, *vt.* To fail in hitting; obtaining, finding, &c.; to feel the loss of; to omit; to let slip.—*vi.* To fail to strike what is aimed at; to miscarry.—*n.* A failure to hit, obtain, &c.; loss; want; an unmarried woman.

missal, mis'al, *n.* The R. Catholic massbook.

misshape, mis-shāp', *n.* A bad or incorrect form.—*vt.* To shape ill. mis-

shapen, mis-shāp'n, *a.* Ill-formed; ugly.

missile, mis'il, *a.* Capable of being thrown.—*n.* A weapon or projectile thrown with hostile intention, as an arrow, a bullet.

missing, mis'ing, *p.a.* Not to be found; wanting, lost.

mission, mish'un, *n.* A sending or delegating; duty on which one is sent; destined end or function; persons sent on some political business or to propagate religion; a station of missionaries.

missionary, mish"un-er'i, *n.* One sent to propagate religion.—*a.* Pertaining to missions.

missive, mis'iv, *a.* Such as is sent; proceeding from some authoritative source.—*n.* A message; a letter or writing sent.

misspell, mis-spel', *vt.* To spell wrongly. **misspelling,** mis-spel'ing, *n.* A wrong spelling.

misspent, mis-spent', *p.a.* Ill-spent; wasted.

misstate, mis-stāt', *vt.* To state wrongly; to misrepresent. **misstatement,** mis-stāt'ment, *n.* A wrong statement.

mist, mist, *n.* Visible watery vapor; aqueous vapor falling in numerous but almost imperceptible drops; something which dims or darkens.

mistake, mis-tāk', *vt.* To misunderstand or misapprehend; to regard as one when really another.—*vi.* To err in opinion or judgment.—*n.* An error in opinion or judgment; blunder; fault. **mistaken,** mis-tāk'n, *p.a.* Erroneous; incorrect.

mister, mis'tèr, *n. See* **master.**

mistletoe, mis'l-tō or miz'l-tō, *n.* A plant that grows parasitically on various trees, and was held in veneration by the Druids.

mistreat, mis-trēt', *vt.* To treat badly; to abuse.

mistress, mis'tres, *n.* The female appellation corresponding to *master;* a woman who has authority, ownership; a concubine; a title of address applied to married women (written *Mrs.* and pronounced mis'iz).

mistrust, mis-trust', *n.* Want of confidence or trust; suspicion.—*vt.* To distrust; to suspect; to doubt. **mistrustful,** mis-trust'ful, *a.* Full of mistrust; suspicious; wanting confidence.

misty, mis'ti, *a.* Overspread with mist; dim; obscure; clouded; hazy.

misunderstand, mis'un-dèr-stand", *vt.* To understand wrongly; to mistake. **misunderstanding,** mis'un-dèr-stand"ing, *n.* Misconception; difference; dissension.

misuse, mis-ūz', *vt.* To use to a bad purpose, to abuse.—*n.* mis-ūs'. Improper use; misapplication.

mite, mīt, *n.* A minute animal of the class Arachnida (cheese *mite,* &c.); a very small coin formerly current; a very little creature.

miter, mī'tèr, *n.* A high pointed cap worn by bishops.—*vt.* (mitering, mitered). To adorn with a miter. **mitered,**

mi'tèrd, *p.a.* Wearing a miter; having the privilege of wearing a miter.

mitigate, mit'i-gāt, *vt.* To make soft or mild; to assuage, lessen, abate, moderate. **mitigation,** mit'i-gā"shun, *n.* Act of mitigating; alleviation. **mitigant,** mit'i-gant, *a.* Softening; soothing.

mitt, mit, *n.* A mitten.

mitten, mit'n, *n.* A covering for the hand without fingers, or without a separate covering for each finger.

mix, miks, *vt.* (mixing, mixed or mixt). To unite or blend promiscuously; to mingle; to associate.—*vi.* To become united or blended; to join; to associate. **mixed,** mikst, *p.a.* Promiscuous; indiscriminate; miscellaneous.

mixture, miks'tūr, *n.* Act of mixing; state of being mixed; a compound; liquid medicine of different ingredients.

moan, mōn, *vi.* To utter a low dull sound through grief or pain.—*vt.* To bewail or deplore.—*n.* A low, dull sound due to grief or pain; a sound resembling this.

moat, mōt, *n.* A deep trench round a castle or other fortified place.—*vt.* To surround with a ditch for defense.

mob, mob, *n.* A crowd; disorderly assembly; rabble.—*vt.* (mobbing, mobbed). To attack in a disorderly crowd; to crowd round and annoy.

mobile, mō'bil, *a.* Capable of being easily moved; changeable; fickle. **mobility,** mō-bil'i-ti, *n.* State of being mobile; susceptibility of motion; inconstancy. **mobilization,** mō'bi-li-za"shun or mob-i, *n.* The act of mobilizing. **mobilize,** mō'bi-liz, *vt.* To put (troops, &c.) in a state of readiness for active service.

moccasin, mok'a-sin, *n.* A shoe of deerskin or soft leather, worn by North American Indians; a venomous serpent of the United States.

mock, mok, *vt.* To mimic in contempt or derision; to flout; to ridicule; to set at naught; to defy.—*vi.* To use ridicule to gibe or jeer.—*n.* A derisive word or gesture; ridicule; derision.—*a.* Counterfeit; assumed; derision. **mockery,** mok'èr-i, *n.* Derision; sportive insult; counterfeit appearance; vain effort. **mock-heroic,** mok'he-rō'ik, *a.* Burlesquing the heroic in poetry, action, &c. **mockingbird,** mok'ing-bèrd", *n.* An American bird of the thrush family.

mode, mōd, *n.* Manner; method; fashion; custom.

model, mod'el, *n.* A pattern; an image, copy, facsimile; standard, plan, or type; a person from whom an artist studies his proportions, postures, &c.—*vt.* (modeling, modeled). To plan after some model; to form in order to serve as a model; to mold.—*vi.* To make a model. **moderate,** mod'èr-āt, *vt.* To restrain from excess; to temper, lessen, allay.—*vi.* To become less violent or intense; to preside as a moderator.—*a.* Not going to extremes; temperate; medium; mediocre. —*n.* One not extreme in opinions. **moderation,** mod'èr-ā"shun, *n.* Act of moderating; state or quality of being moderate; act of presiding as a moderator.

moderator, mod'ẽr-ā"tẽr, *n.* One who or that which moderates; a president, especially of courts in Presbyterian churches.

modern, mod'ẽrn, *a.* Pertaining to the present time; of recent origin; late; recent.—*n.* A person of modern times. **modernism,** mod'ẽr-nizm, *n.* Modern practice, character, phrase, or mode of expression. **modernize,** mod'ẽr-nīz, *vt.* To adapt to modern ideas, style, or language.

modest, mod'est, *a.* Restrained by a sense of propriety; bashful; diffident; chaste; moderate; not excessive. **modesty,** mod'es-ti, *n.* Quality of being modest; bashful reserve; chastity; freedom from excess.

modicum, mod'i-kum, *n.* A little; a small quantity; small allowance or share.

modify, mod'i-fī, *vt.* (modifying, modified). To qualify; to change or alter; to vary. **modification,** mod'i-fi-kā"shun, *n.* Act of modifying; state of being modified; change.

modish, mod'ish, *a.* According to the mode of fashion; affectedly fashionable. **modiste,** mō-dēst', *n.* A woman who deals in articles of ladies' dress; dressmaker.

modulate, mod'ū-lāt, *vt.* To proportion; to adjust; to vary (the voice) in tone; to transfer from one key to another.—*vi.* To pass from one key into another. **modulation,** mod'ū-lā"shun, *n.* Act of modulating; act of inflecting the voice; melodious sound; change from one scale to another. **modulator,** mod'ū-lā"tẽr, *n.* One who or that which modulates.

Mogul, mō-gul', *n.* A Mongolian. **The Great Mogul,** the ruler of the Mongolian empire in Hindustan.

mohair, mō"hār', *n.* The hair of the Angora goat; cloth made of this hair; an imitation wool and cotton cloth.

Mohammedan, mō-ham'e-dan, *a.* Pertaining to Mohammed, or the religion founded by him.—*n.* A follower of Mohammed.

Mohammedanism, mō-ham'e-dan-izm, *n.* The religion of Mohammed.

moiety, moi'e-ti, *n.* The half; a portion.

moire, mō'rā, mwä'rā", *n.* A watered appearance on metals or cloths; watered silk.

moist, moist, *a.* Moderately wet; damp. **moisten,** mois'n, *vt.* To make moist or damp; to wet in a small degree. **moisture,** mois'tūr, *n.* A moderate degree of wetness; humidity.

molar, mō'lẽr, *a.* Serving to grind the food in eating.—*n.* A grinding or double tooth.

molasses, mō-las'ez, *n.sing.* A syrup from sugar in the process of making; treacle.

mold, mōld, *n.* Fine soft earth; mustiness or mildew; dust from incipient decay; form in which a thing is cast; model; shape; character.—*vt.* To cause to contract mold; to cover with mold or soil; to model; to shape; to fashion.—*vi.* To become moldy.

molder, mōl'dẽr, *n.* One who molds or is employed making castings in a foundry.

—*vi.* To turn to mold or dust by natural decay.—*vt.* To convert into mold or dust.

molding, mōld'ing, *n.* Anything cast in a mold; ornamental contour or form in wood or stone along an edge or a surface.

moldy, mōl'di, *a.* Overgrown with mold; musty; decaying.

mole, mōl, *n.* A small discolored protuberance on the human body; a mound or breakwater to protect a harbor from the waves; a small burrowing insectivorous animal.

molecule, mol'e-kūl, *n.* A very minute particle of matter. **molecular,** mō-lek'-ū-lẽr, *a.* Belonging to or consisting of molecules.

molehill, mōl"hil", *n.* A little hillock of earth thrown up by moles; a very small hill.

moleskin, mōl"skin", *n.* A strong twilled fustian or cotton cloth.

molest, mō-lest', *vt.* To annoy; to disturb; to harass; to vex. **molestation,** mō"les-tā"shun, *n.* Act of molesting; disturbance; annoyance.

mollify, mol'i-fī, *vt.* (mollifying, mollified). To soften; to assuage; to appease; to reduce in harshness; to tone down.

mollusk, mol'usk, *n.* An animal whose body is soft, as mussels, snails, cuttlefish, &c.; one of the *Mollusca*.

mollycoddle, mol"i-kod'l, *n.* A timid, effeminate male; a milksop.

molt, mōlt, *vi.* and *t.* To shed or cast the hair, feathers, skin, horns, &c., as birds and other animals.—*n.* Act or process of changing the feathers, &c.; time of molting.

molten, mōl'ten, old pp. of *melt.* Melted; made of melted metal.

moment, mō'ment, *n.* A minute portion of time; a second; momentum; importance; gravity. **momentarily,** mō"-men-tẽr'i-li, *adv.* Every moment; for a moment. **momentary,** mō"men-tẽr-i, *a.* Done in a moment; continuing only a moment. **momentous,** mō-men'tus, *a.* Of moment; important; weighty.

momentum, mō-men'tum, *n.* pl.; **-ta.** The force possessed by a body in motion; impetus.

monarch, mon'ẽrk, *n.* A supreme governor of a state; a sovereign; one who or that which is chief of its kind.—*a.* Supreme; ruling. **monarchic, monarchical,** mō-när'kik, mō-när'ki-kal, *a.* Pertaining to monarchy; vested in a single ruler. **monarchist,** mon'ẽr-kist, *n.* An advocate of monarchy. **monarchy,** mon'ẽr-ki, *n.* Government in which the supreme power is lodged in a single person, actually or nominally; a kingdom.

monastery, mon"as-tẽr-i, *n.* A house for monks, sometimes for nuns; abbey; priory; convent. **monastic,** mō-nas'tik, *a.* Pertaining to monasteries or monks; recluse.—*n.* A monk. **monasticism,** mō-nas'ti-sizm, *n.* Monastic life; the monastic system or condition.

Monday, mun'di, *n.* The second day of the week.

money, mun'i, *n.* Coin; pieces of gold, silver, or other metal, stamped by public

monger, mung'gẽr, *n.* A trader; now only in composition, as in iron*monger.*

Mongol, Mongolian, mong'gol, mong-gō'li-an, *n.* A native of Mongolia.—*a.* Belonging to Mongolia.

mongoose, mong'gös, *n.* A common ichneumon of India.

mongrel, mung'grel, *a.* Of a mixed breed; hybrid.—*n.* An animal of a mixed breed.

monition, mō-nish'un, *n.* Admonition; warning; intimation.

monitor, mon'i-tẽr, *n.* One who admonishes; one who warns of faults or informs of duty; a senior pupil in a school appointed to instruct and look after juniors; a lizard; a type of war-vessel.

monk, mungk, *n.* A male inhabitant of a monastery, bound to celibacy.

monkey, mung'ki, *n.* A long-tailed quadrumanous animal; a playful or mischievous youngster.

monkish, mungk'-ish, *a.* Like a monk, or pertaining to monks; monastic.

Monkey Wrench.

monkshood, mungks'hud', *n.* A plant of the crowfoot family.

monocle, mon'o-k'l, *n.* An eyeglass having one lens.

monogamy, mō-nog'a-mi, *n.* The practice or principle of marrying only once; the marrying of only one at a time. **monogamist,** mō-nog'a-mist, *n.* One who practices or upholds monogamy. **monogamous,** mō-nog'a-mus, *a.* Upholding or practicing monogamy.

monogram, mon'ō-gram, *n.* A cipher composed of several letters interwoven.

monograph, mon'ō-graf, *n.* An account of a single person, thing, or class of things.

monolith, mon'ō-lith, *n.* A pillar, column, &c., consisting of a single stone.

monologue, mon'ō-log, *n.* A speech uttered by one person alone; a soliloquy.

monomania, mon'ō-mā"ni-a, *n.* Insanity in regard to a single subject or class of subjects; a craze.

monopoly, mō-nop'o-li, *n.* An exclusive trading privilege; assumption of anything to the exclusion of others. **monopolist,** mō-nop'o-list, *n.* One that monopolizes or possesses a monopoly. **monopolize,** mō-nop'o-liz, *vt.* To obtain a monopoly of; to engross entirely.

monosyllable, mon'ō-sil'a-bl, *n.* A word of one syllable. **monosyllabic,** mon'ō-si-lab"ik, *a.* Consisting of one syllable, or of words of one syllable.

monotheism, mon'ō-thē-izm, *n.* The doctrine of the existence of one God only.

monotone, mon'ō-tōn, *n.* A single tone; unvaried pitch of the voice. **monotonous,** mō-not'o-nus, *a.* Exhibiting monotony; wanting variety; unvaried.

monotony, mō-not'o-ni, *n.* Uniformity of sound; a dull uniformity; an irksome sameness or want of variety.

monsoon, mon-sön', *n.* The trade-wind of the Indian seas, blowing from N.E. from November to March, and S.W. from April to October.

monster, mon'stẽr, *n.* An animal of unnatural form or of great size; one unnaturally wicked or evil.—*a.* Of inordinate size. **monstrosity,** mon-stros'i-ti, *n.* State or quality of being monstrous; that which is monstrous. **monstrous,** mon'strus, *a.* Unnatural in form; enormous; huge; horrible.—*adv.* Exceedingly.

month, munth, *n.* The period measured by the moon's revolution (the lunar month, about 29½ days); one of the twelve parts of the year (the calendar month, 30 or 31 days). **monthly,** munth'li, *a.* Done or happening once a month, or every month.—*n.* A publication appearing once a month.—*adv.* Once a month; in every month.

monument, mon'ū-ment, *n.* Anything by which the memory of a person or of an event is preserved; a memorial: a singular or notable instance. **monumental,** mon'ū-men"tal, *a.* Pertaining to or serving as a monument; preserving memory; great and conspicuous.

moo, mö, *vi.* (mooing, mooed). To low, as a cow.—*n.* The low of a cow.

mood, möd, *n.* Temper of mind; disposition; a fit of sullenness; a form of verbs expressive of certainty, contingency, &c.; a form of syllogism. **moody,** möd'i, *a.* Subject to moods or humors; out of humor; gloomy; sullen.

moon, mön, *n.* The changing luminary of the night; the heavenly body next to the earth, revolving round it in about 29½ days; a satellite of any planet; a month. **moonbeam,** mön"bēm', *n.* A ray of light from the moon. **moonlight,** mön"lit', *n.* The light afforded by the moon.—*a.* Illuminated by the moon; occurring during moonlight. **moonlit,** mön"lit', *a.* Illuminated by the moon.

moonshine, mön"shin', *n.* The light of the moon; show without substance; pretense.

moonstone, mön"stön', *n.* A translucent variety of felspar used in trinkets, &c.

moon-struck, mön"struk', *a.* Affected by the influence of the moon; lunatic.

moony, mön'i, *a.* Pertaining to or like the moon or moonlight; bewildered or silly.

moor, mŭr, *n.* A tract of waste land, or of hilly ground on which game is preserved; a native of the northern coast of Africa.—*vt.* To secure a ship in a particular station, as by cables and anchors.—*vi.* To be confined by cables.

moorage, mŭr'ij, *n.* A place for mooring.

mooring, mŭr'ing, *n.* Act of one who moors; *pl.* the anchor, &c. by which a ship is moored; the place where a ship is moored.

Moorish, mŭr'ish, *a.* Pertaining to the Moors.

moose, mōs, *n*. The American variety of the elk.

moot, mōt, *vt*. To debate; to discuss.—*a*. Debatable; subject to discussion.

mootpoint, mōt'point', *n*. A point debated or liable to be debated.

mop, mop, *n*. A cloth or collection of yarns fastened to a handle, and used for cleaning; a grimace.—*vt*. (mopping, mopped). To rub with a mop; to wipe.—*vi*. To grimace.

mope, mōp, *vi*. (moping, moped). To show a downcast air; to be spiritless or gloomy.—*n*. One who mopes.

moraine, mō-rān', *n*. An accumulation of debris on glaciers or in the valleys at their foot.

moral, mor'al, *a*. Relating to morality or morals; ethical; virtuous; supported by reason and probability.—*n*. The practical lesson inculcated by any story; *pl*. general conduct as right or wrong; mode of life; ethics. **morale**, mō-ral', *n*. Mental condition of soldiers, &c., as regards courage, zeal, hope. **moralist**, mo'ral-ist, *n*. One who teaches morals; a writer or lecturer on ethics; one who inculcates or practices moral duties. **morality**, mō-ral'i-ti, *n*. The doctrine of moral duties; ethics; moral character or quality; quality of an action in regard to right and wrong; an old form of drama in which the personages were allegorical representations of virtues, vices, &c. **moralize**, mor'al-īz, *vt*. To apply to a moral purpose; to draw a moral from.—*vi*. To make moral reflections; to draw practical lessons from the facts of life.

morass, mō-ras', *n*. A tract of low, soft, wet ground; a marsh; a swamp; a fen.

morbid, mor'bid, *a*. Diseased; sickly; not sound and healthful. **morbific**, mor-bif'ik, *a*. Causing disease.

mordant, mor'dant, *n*. A substance, such as alum, which fixes colors; matter by which gold-leaf is made to adhere.—*a*. Biting; severe.

more, mōr, *a. comp*. of *much* and *many*. Greater in amount, extent, degree, &c.; greater in number.—*adv*. In a greater degree, extent, or quantity; in addition. —*n*. A greater quantity or number; something further.

moreover, mōr-ō'vèr, *adv*. Further; besides; likewise.

mores, mō'rēz, *n.pl*. Customs; basic ways.

morgue, marg, *n*. A place where dead bodies are kept for identification; a reference file kept by newspapers.

moribund, mor'i-bund, *a*. In a dying state.

Mormon, mor'mun, *n*. A member of a sect founded in the United States in 1830, who practice polygamy; a Latterday Saint.

morn, morn, *n*. The morning; *poetic*.

morning, mor'ning, *n*. The first part of the day; the time between dawn and the middle of the forenoon; the first or early part. Often used as an *adj*.

morning star, mor'ning stär, *n*. The planet Venus when it rises before the sun.

morocco, mō-rok'ō, *n*. A fine kind of leather prepared from goat skin. The country.

moron, mō'ron, *n*. A mentally deficient person.—*a*. Moronic.

morose, mō-rōs', *a*. Of a sour or sullen temper; gloomy; churlish; surly. **morosely**, mō-rōs'li, *adv*. In a morose manner; with sullenness.

morphia, morphine, mor'fi-a, mor'fēn, *n*. The narcotic principle of opium, a powerful anodyne.

morrow, mo'rō, *n*. The day next after the present, or a specified day.

morse, mors, *n*. The walrus; a telegraph code.

morsel, mor'sel, *n*. A bite; a mouthful; a fragment; a little piece in general.

mortal, mor'tal, *a*. Subject to death; deadly; fatal; human.—*n*. A being subject to death; a human being. **mortality**, mor-tal'i-ti, *n*. State of being mortal; actual death of great numbers of men or beasts; death-rate.

mortar, mor'tèr, *n*. A vessel, in which substances are pounded with a pestle; a short piece of ordnance, thick and wide, for throwing shells, &c.; a mixture of lime and sand with water, used as a cement for building.

mortgage, mor'gij, *n*. A conveyance of land or house property as security for a debt; the deed effecting this conveyance. *vt*. (mortgaging, mortgaged). To grant or assign on mortgage; to pledge. **mortgagee**, mor-gi-jē', *n*. The person to whom an estate is mortgaged.

mortify, mor'ti-fī, *vt*. (mortifying, mortified). To affect with gangrene or mortification; to subdue by abstinence or rigorous severities; to humiliate; to chagrin.—*vi*. To lose vitality while yet a portion of a living body. **mortification**, mor'ti-fi-kā"shun, *n*. Act of mortifying; condition of being mortified; death of a part of an animal body while the rest is alive; the subduing of the passions by penance, abstinence, &c.; chagrin.

mortise, mor'tis, *n*. A hole cut in one piece of material to receive the tenon of another piece.—*vt*. To cut a mortise in; to join by a tenon and mortise.

mortuary, mor'tū-er'i, *n*. A place for the temporary reception of the dead.—*a*. Pertaining to the burial of the dead.

mosaic, mō'zā'ik, *n*. Inlaid work of marble, precious stones, &c., disposed on a ground of cement so as to form designs.—*a*. Pertaining to or composed of mosaic.

Moslem, moz'lem, *n*. An orthodox Mohammedan.

mosque, mosk, *n*. A Mohammedan place of worship.

mosquito, mos-kē'tō, *n*. A stinging gnat or fly.

moss, mos, *n*. A small plant with simple branching stems and numerous small leaves; a bog; a place where peat is found.—*vt*. To cover with moss by natural growth.

mossy, mos'i, *a*. Overgrown or abounding with moss; covered or bordered with moss.

most, mŏst, *a.* superl. of *more*. Greatest in any way.—*adv.* In the greatest degree, quantity, or extent; mostly; chiefly.—*n.* The greatest number; the majority; greatest amount; utmost extent, degree, &c. **mostly**, mŏst′li, *adv.* For the most part; mainly; chiefly; generally speaking.

mote, mŏt, *n.* A small particle; anything proverbially small.

motel, mō-tel′, *n.* A hotel for motorists.

moth, moth, *n.* The name of numerous nocturnal insects allied to the butterflies.

mother, muTH′ẽr, *n.* A female parent; a woman who has borne a child; source or origin; an abbess or other female at the head of a religious institution; a slimy substance that gathers in vinegar, &c.—*a.* Native; natural; inborn; vernacular. **mother church**, muTH′ẽr chẽrch, *n.* An original church; a metropolitan church. **mother country**, muTH′ẽr kun′tri, *n.* A country which has sent out colonies; a country as the producer of anything. **motherhood**, muTH′ẽr-hŏd, *n.* State of being a mother. **mother-in-law**, muTH′ẽr-in-lạ, *n.* The mother of one's husband or wife. **motherly**, muTH′ẽr-li, *a.* Like or becoming a mother; maternal; affectionate. **mother-of-pearl**, muTH′ẽr-ov-pẽrl′, *n.* The hard silvery brilliant internal layer of several kinds of shells.

motif, mō-tēf′, *n.* The main theme or design.

motile, mō′til, *a.* Having inherent power of motion.

motion, mō′shun, *n.* Act or process of moving; power of moving; movement; internal impulse; proposal made; evacuation of the intestines.—*vi.* To make a significant gesture with the hand. **motionless**, mō′shun-les, *a.* Wanting motion; being at rest.

motive, mō′tiv, *n.* That which incites to action; cause; inducement; purpose; theme in a piece of music; prevailing idea of an artist.—*a.* Causing motion.—*vt.* To supply a motive to or for; to prompt.

motor, mō′tẽr, *n.* A moving power; force or agency that sets machinery in motion; a motor-car.—*a.* Imparting motion.

motorboat, mō′tẽr-bŏt′, *n.* A boat propelled by a motor.

motorcar, mō′tẽr-kär′, *n.* A self propelling conveyance for passengers.

motor-cycle, mō′tẽr-sī′kl, *n.* A bicycle having a motor.

mottle, mot′l, *n.* A blotched or spotted character of surface.—*vt.* (mottling, mottled). To mark with spots or blotches as if mottled. **mottled**, mot′ld, *p.a.* Spotted; marked with spots of different colors.

motto, mot′ō, *n.*; pl. **-oes**, or **-os**. A short sentence or phrase, or a single word, adopted as expressive of one's guiding idea.

mound, mound, *n.* An artificial elevation of earth; a bulwark; a rampart; the globe which forms part of the regalia.

mount, mount, *n.* A hill; a mountain; that with which something is fitted; a setting, frame, &c.; opportunity or means of riding on horseback; a horse.—*vi.* To rise; to get on horseback or upon any animal; to amount.—*vt.* To raise aloft; to climb; to place one's self upon, as on horseback; to furnish with horses; to set in or cover with something; to set off to advantage.

mountain, moun′tin, *n.* An elevated mass larger than a hill; anything very large.—*a.* Pertaining to a mountain; found on mountains.

mountaineer, moun′ti-nẽr′, *n.* An inhabitant of a mountainous district; a climber of mountains.—*vi.* To practice the climbing of mountains.

mountainous, moun′ti-nus, *a.* Full of mountains; large, as a mountain; huge.

mountebank, moun′tē-bangk, *n.* One who mounts a bench or stage in a public place, and vends medicines or nostrums; a quack; any boastful and false pretender.

mourn, mōrn, *vi.* To sorrow; to lament; to wear the customary habit of sorrow.—*vt.* To grieve for; to deplore. **mourner**, mōrn′ẽr, *n.* One who mourns; one who attends a funeral. **mournful**, mōrn′fụl, *a.* Expressing sorrow; sad; calamitous; sorrowful.

mouse, mous, *n.*; pl. **mice**, mīs. A small rodent quadruped that infests houses, fields, &c.—*vi.* mouz. (mousing, moused). To hunt for or catch mice. **mouser**, mouz′ẽr, *n.* A cat good at catching mice.

moustache, mus-tash′, *n. See* **mustache.**

mouth, mouth, *n.*; pl. **mouths**, mouTHz. The opening in the head of an animal into which food is received, and from which voice is uttered; opening of anything hollow, as of a pitcher, or of a cave, pit, &c.; the part of a river, &c., by which it joins with the ocean.—*vt.* mouth. To take into the mouth; to utter with a voice affectedly big.—*vi.* To speak with a loud, affected voice; to vociferate. **mouthful**, mouth′fụl, *n.* As much as the mouth contains at once; a small quantity. **mouthpiece**, mouth′pēs, *n.* The part of a wind-instrument to which the mouth is applied; a tube by which a cigar, &c., is held in the mouth; one who delivers the opinions of others.

move, mōv, *vt.* (moving, moved). To cause to change place, posture, or position; to set in motion; to affect; to rouse; to prevail on; to propose, as a resolution.—*vi.* To change place or posture; to stir; to begin to act; to shake; to change residence; to make a proposal to a meeting.—*n.* The act of moving; a movement; proceeding; action taken. **movable**, mōv′a-bl, *a.* Capable of being moved; changing from one time to another.—*n.* Any part of a man's goods capable of being moved; *pl.* goods, commodities, furniture. **movement**, mōv′ment, *n.* Act of moving; motion; change of position; manner of moving; gesture; an agitation to bring about some result desired; wheel-work of a clock. **moving**, mōv′ing, *p.a.* Causing to move or act; pathetic; affecting.

mow, mō or mou, *n.* A pile of hay or sheaves of grain deposited in a barn; part of a barn where they are packed; a wry face.—*vt.* To lay in a mow.—*vi.* To make mouths.

mow, mō, *vt.* (pret. mowed, pp. mowed or mown). To cut down, as grass, &c.; to cut the grass from; to cut down in great numbers.—*vi.* To cut grass; to use the scythe. **mower**, mō'èr, *n.* One who mows; a mowing-machine. **mowing machine**, mō'ing ma-shēn, *n.* A machine to cut down grass, grain, &c.

much, much, *a.* comp. *more*, superl. *most.* Great in quantity or amount; abundant.—*adv.* In a great degree; by far; greatly.—*n.* A great quantity; something strange or serious.

mucilage, mū'si-lij, *n.* A solution in water of gummy matter; a gummy substance found in certain plants.

muck, muk, *n.* Dung in a moist state; something mean, vile, or filthy.—*vt.* To manure with muck; to remove muck from. **mucky**, muk'i, *a.* Filthy; nasty.

mucous, **mucose**, mū'kus, *a.* Pertaining to mucus, or resembling it; slimy. **mucous membrane**, a membrane that lines all the cavities of the body which open externally, and secretes mucus.

mucus, mū'kus, *n.* A viscid fluid secreted by the mucous membrane.

mud, mud, *n.* Moist and soft earth; sediment from turbid waters; mire.—*vt.* (mudding, mudded). To soil with mud; to make turbid.

muddle, mud'l, *vt.* (muddling, muddled). To make muddy; to intoxicate partially; to confuse; to make a mess of.—*vi.* To become muddy; to act in a confused manner.—*n.* A mess; confusion; bewilderment. **muddleheaded**, mud'l-hed'ed, *a.* Stupidly confused or dull; doltish.

muddy, mud'i, *a.* Abounding in mud; miry; stupid; obscure.—*vt.* (muddying, muddied). To soil with mud; to cloud.

muezzin, mū-ez'in, *n.* A Mohammedan crier who proclaims from a minaret the summons to prayers.

muff, muf, *n.* A warm cover for receiving both hands; a soft, useless fellow.

muffin, muf'in, *n.* A light spongy cake.

muffle, muf'l, *vt.* (muffling, muffled). To cover close, particularly the neck and face; to conceal; to deaden the sound of by wrapping cloth, &c., round. —*n.* The tumid and naked portion of the upper lip and nose of ruminants and rodents. **muffler**, muf'lèr, *n.* A cover for the face or neck; a silencer for motor-cars.

mufti, **muftee**, muf'ti, muf'tē, *n.* A doctor of Mohammedan law; civilian dress.

mug, mug, *n.* A small vessel of earthenware or metal for containing liquor; a jug. **muggy**, **muggish**, mug'i, mug'ish, *a.* Damp and close; moist; moldy.

mulatto, mū-lat'ō, *n.* A person who is the offspring of a white and a negro.

mulberry, mul'ber'i, *n.* The berry of a tree, and the tree itself, cultivated to supply food for silk-worms.

mulch, mulch, *n.* Dungy material protecting the roots of newly-planted shrubs, &c.

mulct, mulkt, *n.* A fine.—*vt.* To fine; to deprive.

mule, mūl, *n.* The offspring of an ass and mare, or a horse and she-ass; a hybrid animal. **muleteer**, mū'le-tēr', *n.* One who drives mules. **mulish**, mūl'ish, *a.* Like a mule; stubborn.

mull, mul, *vt.* To heat, sweeten, and flavor with spices, as ale or wine.

mulligatawny, mul'i-ga-tạ"ni, *n.* An E. Indian curry soup.

mullet, mul'et, *n.* A name for fishes of two different families, the gray mullets and the red mullets.

multifarious, mul'ti-far"i-us, *a.* Having great diversity or variety.

multiple, mul'ti-pl, *a.* Manifold; having many parts or divisions.—*n.* A number which contains another an exact number of times. **multiplicand**, mul'ti-pli-kând", *n.* A number to be multiplied by another. **multiplication**, mul'ti-pli-kā"shun, *n.* Act or process of multiplying; state of being multiplied; reproduction of animals. **multiplicative**, mul'ti-pli-kā'tiv, *a.* Tending to multiply. **multiplier**, mul'ti-pli-èr, *n.* One who or that which multiplies; the number by which another is multiplied. **multiply**, mul'ti-plī, *vt.* (multiplying, multiplied). To increase in number; to add to itself any given number of times. —*vi.* To increase in number, or to become more numerous by reproduction; to extend.

multitude, mul'ti-tūd, *n.* State of being many; a great number, collectively or indefinitely; a crowd. **the multitude**, the populace. **multitudinous**, mul'ti-tū"di-nus, *a.* Consisting of or pertaining to a multitude.

mum, mum, *a.* Silent.—*n.* A species of ale brewed from wheaten malt, &c.

mumble, mum'bl, *vi.* (mumbling, mumbled). To mutter; to speak with mouth partly closed; to eat with the lips close. —*vt.* To utter with a low, inarticulate voice.

mummer, mum'èr, *n.* A masker; a masked buffoon; a play-actor. **mummery**, mum'èr-i, *n.* A masquerade; buffoonery; hypocritical parade.

mummy, mum'i, *n.* A dead human body embalmed after the manner of the ancient Egyptians, with wax, balsams, &c. **mummify**, mum'i-fī, *vt.* To make into a mummy; to embalm as a mummy.

mumps, mumps, *n.* Silent displeasure; sullenness; a disease consisting in an inflammation of the salivary glands.

munch, munch, *vt.* and *i.* To chew audibly.

mundane, mun'dān, *a.* Belonging to this world; worldly; earthly.

municipal, mū-nis'i-pal, *a.* Belonging to a corporation or city. **municipality**, mū-nis'i-pal"i-ti, *n.* A town possessed of local self-government; community under municipal jurisdiction.

munificent, mū-nif'i-sent, *a.* Liberal in giving; bountiful; liberal; generous. **munificence**, mū-nif'i-sens, *n.* A bestowing liberally; liberality; generosity.

munition, mū-nish'un, *n.* Military stores; ammunition; material for any enterprise.

mural, mū'ral, *a.* Pertaining to a wall; resembling a wall; perpendicular or steep.

murder, mèr'dèr, *n.* Act of killing a human being with premeditated malice. —*vt.* To kill (a human being) with premeditated malice; to mar by bad execution. **murderer,** mer'dèr-èr, *n.* One who murders, or is guilty of murder. **murderess,** mèr'dèr-es, *n.* A female who commits murder. **murderous,** mèr'dèr-us, *a.* Pertaining to murder; guilty of murder; meditating murder; bloody.

murk, mèrk, *n.* Darkness; gloom. **murky,** mèr'ki, *a.* Dark; obscure; gloomy.

murmur, mèr'mèr, *n.* A low continued or repeated sound; a hum; a grumble or mutter.—*vi.* To utter a murmur or hum; to grumble.—*vt.* To utter indistinctly; to mutter.

murrain, mur'in, *n.* A deadly and infectious disease among cattle, &c.

muscat, mus'kat, *n.* A kind of grape, and the wine made from it.

muscle, mus'l, *n.* A definite portion of an animal body consisting of fibers susceptible of contraction and relaxation, and thus effecting motion; a mussel. **muscled,** mus'ld, *a.* Having muscles. **muscular,** mus'kū-lèr, *a.* Pertaining to or consisting of muscle; performed by a muscle; strong; brawny; vigorous. **muscularity,** mus"kū-lar'i-ti, *n.* State of being muscular.

muse, mūz, *n.* One of the nine sister goddesses of the Greeks and Romans presiding over the arts; poetic inspiration; a fit of abstraction.—*vi.* (musing, mused). To ponder; to meditate in silence; to be absent in mind.—*vt.* To meditate on.

museum, mū-zē'um, *n.* A repository of interesting objects connected with literature, art, or science.

mushroom, mush'röm, *n.* An edible fungus; an upstart.—*a.* Pertaining to mushrooms; resembling mushrooms in rapidity of growth.

music, mū'zik, *n.* Melody or harmony; the science of harmonious sounds; the written or printed score of a composition. **musical,** mū'zi-kal, *a.* Belonging to music; producing music; melodious; harmonious; fond of or skilled in music. **music hall,** mū'zik hal, *n.* A place of public entertainment in which the spectators are treated to singing, dancing, &c. **musician,** mū-zish'an, *n.* One skilled in music.

musing, mūz'ing, *n.* Meditation.

musk, musk, *n.* A strong-scented substance obtained from the musk-deer; the animal itself; a musky smell; a plant giving out such a smell.—*vt.* To perfume with musk.

musk deer, musk dēr, *n.* A deer of Central Asia, the male of which yields the perfume musk.

musket, mus'ket, *n.* A general term for any hand-gun used for military purposes; a sparrow-hawk or hawk of inferior kind. **musketeer,** mus-ke-tēr', *n.* A soldier armed with a musket. **musketry,** mus'-ket-ri, *n.* The fire of muskets; troops armed with muskets; the art or science of firing small-arms.

muskrat, musk'rat, *n.* An American rodent having a musky odor and prized for its fur.

musky, musk'i, *a.* Having the odor of musk; fragrant.

muslin, muz'lin, *n.* A fine thin cotton cloth.—*a.* Made of muslin.

mussel, mus'l, *n.* The common name of a genus of bivalve shell-fish.

must, must, *vi.* without inflection, and present or past. A defective or auxiliary verb expressing obligation or necessity. —*n.* New wine unfermented.

mustache, mus-tash', *n.* The long hair on the upper lip.

mustard, mus'tèrd, *n.* An annual plant cultivated for its pungent seeds; the condiment obtained from its seeds.

muster, mus'tèr, *vt.* To collect, as troops; to assemble or bring together.— *vi.* To assemble; to meet in one place.— *n.* An assembling of troops; register of troops mustered; an array.

musty, mus'ti, *a.* Moldy; sour; stale.

mutable, mū'ta-bl, *a.* Changeable; inconstant; unstable; variable; fickle. **mutability,** mū'ta-bil"i-ti, *n.* Quality or state of being mutable; inconstancy.

mutation, mū-tā'shun, *n.* Act or process of changing; change; alteration, either in form or qualities; modification.

mute, mūt, *a.* Silent; incapable of speaking; dumb; not pronounced, or having its sound checked by a contact of the vocal organs, as certain consonants (*t, p, k,* &c.).—*n.* A dumb person; a hired attendant at a funeral; a mute consonant.—*vi.* (muting, muted).

mutilate, mū'ti-lāt, *vt.* To injure or disfigure by cutting a piece from; to maim; to render imperfect. **mutilation,** mū'ti-lā"shun, *n.* Act of mutilating; state of being mutilated; removal of some essential part.

mutiny, mū'ti-ni, *n.* An insurrection of soldiers or seamen; revolt against constituted authority.—*vi.* (mutinying, mutinied). To rise against lawful authority. **mutineer,** mū-ti-nēr', *n.* One guilty of mutiny. **mutinous,** mū'ti-nus, *a.* Exciting or engaging in mutiny; seditious.

mutter, mut'èr, *vi.* To utter words with compressed lips; to mumble; to murmur. —*vt.* To utter with a low murmuring voice.—*n.* Murmur; obscure utterance.

mutton, mut'n, *n.* The flesh of sheep, raw or dressed for food.

mutual, mū'tū-al, *a.* Reciprocal; interchanged; given and received on both sides. **mutually,** mū'tū-al-li, *adv.* In a mutual manner; reciprocally.

muzzle, muz'l, *n.* The projecting mouth and nose of an animal; the open end of a gun or pistol, &c.; a cover for the mouth which hinders an animal from biting.—*vt.* (muzzling, muzzled). To cover the mouth of to prevent biting or eating; to gag.

my, mī, *pron.* The possessive case sing. of *I*; belonging to me.

myopia, mī-ō'pi-a, *n.* Short-sightedness; near-sightedness.

myriad, mir'i-ad, *n.* A countless number; the number of ten thousand collectively.—*a.* Innumerable

myrrh, mêr, *n.* An aromatic gum resin exuded by a spiny Arabian shrub.

myrtle, mêr'tl, *n.* An evergreen shrub

myself, mī-self', *compd. pron.*; pl. **ourselves**, our-selvz'. As a nominative it is used, generally after I to express emphasis—I, and not another; in the objective often used reflexively and without any emphasis.

mystery, mis'tèr-i, *n.* Something above human intelligence; a secret; an old form of drama in which the characters and events were drawn from sacred history; a trade, craft, or calling. **mysterious**, mis-tēr'i-us, *a.* Containing mystery; beyond human comprehension; unintelligible; enigmatical. **mysteriously**, mis-tē'ri-us-li, *adv.* In a mysterious manner.

mystic, mystical, mis'tik, mis'ti-kal. *a.* Obscure to human comprehension; involving some secret meaning or import; ti-fi-kā"shur, *n.* The act of mystifying **mystic**, *n.* One who holds the doctrines of mysticism. **mysticism**, mis'ti-sizm, *n.* Views in religion based on communication between man and God through spiritual perception; obscurity of doctrine.

mystify, mis'ti-fī, *vt.* (mystifying, mystified). To perplex intentionally; to bewilder; to befog. **mystification**, mis'-ti-fi-kā"shun, *n.* The act of mystifying or state of being mystified.

myth, mith, *n.* A tradition or fable embodying the notions of a people as to their gods, origin, early history, &c.; an invented story. **mythic, mythical**, mith'ik, mith'i-kal, *a.* Relating to myth; described in a myth; fabulous; fabled. **mythologist, mythologer**, mi-thol'-o-jist, mi-thol'o-jèr, *n.* One versed in mythology. **mythology**, mi-thol'o-ji, *n.* The science or doctrine of myths; the myths of a people collectively.

N

nab, nab, *vt.* (nabbing, nabbed). To catch or seize suddenly or unexpectedly.

nabob, nā'bob, *n.* A provincial governor under a viceroy in the Mogul empire; a European who has enriched himself in the East.

nacre, nā'kèr, *n.* Mother-of-pearl. **nacreous**, nā'krē-us, *a.* Consisting of or resembling nacre.

nadir, nā'dèr, *n.* That point of the lower hemisphere of the heavens directly opposite to the zenith; the lowest point.

nag, nag, *n.* A small horse; a horse in general.—*vt.* and *i.* (nagging, nagged). To find fault constantly.

naiad, nā'ad, *n.* A water nymph; a female deity that presides over rivers and springs.

nail, nāl, *n.* The horny substance at the end of the human fingers and toes; a claw; a small pointed piece of metal, to be driven into timber, &c.; a stud or boss; a measure of 2¼ inches.—*vt.* To fasten or stud—with nails; to hold fast or make secure

naive, nä-ēv', *a.* Ingenuous; simple; artless. **naiveté**, nä-ēv'tā, *n* Native simplicity; unaffected ingenuousness.

naked, nā'ked, *a.* Not having clothes on; bare; nude; open to view; mere, bare, simple; destitute; unassisted. **nakedness**, nā'ked-nes, *n.* State of being naked; nudity; bareness.

namby-pamby, nam'bi-pam'bi, *a.* Affectedly pretty; insipid; vapid.

name, nām, *n.* That by which a person or thing is designated; appellation; title; reputation; eminence; sound only; not reality; authority; behalf; a family.—*vt.* (naming, named). To give a name

to; to-designate; to style; to nominate; to speak of or mention as.

nameless, nām'les, *a.* Without a name; not known to fame; inexpressible.

namely, nām'li, *adv.* By name; particularly; that is to say.

namesake, nām'sāk, *n.* One whose name has been given to him for the sake of another; one of the same name as another.

nap, nap, *n.* The woolly substance of the surface of cloth, &c.; the downy substance on plants; a short sleep.—*vi.* (napping, napped). To have a short sleep; to drowse.

nape, nāp, *n.* The prominent joint of the neck behind; the back part of the neck.

naphtha, naf'tha or nap', *n.* A volatile, limpid, bituminous liquid, of a strong peculiar odor and very inflammable.

napkin, nap'kin, *n.* A sort of towel used at table; a handkerchief.

narcissus, nār-sis'us, *n.* An extensive genus of bulbous flowering plants.

narcotic, när-kot'ik, *n.* A substance which relieves pain and produces sleep. —*a.* Having the properties of a narcotic.

narrate, na-rāt', or nar', *vt.* (narrating, narrated) To tell or relate, orally or in writing. **narration**, na-rā'shun, *n.* Act of narrating; a narrative; relation; story. **narrative**, nar'a-tiv, *a.* Pertaining to narration.—*n.* That which is narrated or related; a relation orally or in writing. **narrator**, na-rāt'èr, or nar'rāt-èr, *n.* One who narrates.

narrow, na'rō, *a.* Of little breadth; not wide or broad; very limited; straitened; not liberal; bigoted; near; close; scrutinizing.—*n.* A narrow channel; a strait; usually in *pl.*—*vt.* To make narrow.—*vi.* To become narrow; to contract in breadth. **narrow-minded,** na'rō-mīn'-ded, *a.* Illiberal; of confined views or sentiments.

nasal, nā'zal, *a.* Pertaining to the nose; formed or affected by the nose, as speech.—*n.* An elementary sound uttered partly through the nose. **nascent,** nas'ent, *a.* Arising; coming into being; springing up.

nastily, nas'ti-li, *adv.* In a nasty manner.

nasturtium, nas'tèr'shum, *n.* A genus of herbs, including the common water-cress.

nasty, nas'ti, *a.* Filthy; dirty; indecent; disagreeable in taste or smell; troublesome.

natal, nā'tal, *a.* Pertaining to birth; dating from one's birth; pertaining to the buttocks.

nation, nā'shon, *n.* A body of people inhabiting the same country, or united under the same government; great number. **national,** nash'on-al, *a.* Pertaining to a nation; public; attached to one's own country. **nationality,** nash'un-al''i-ti, *n.* Quality of being national; national character; strong attachment to one's own nation; a nation. **nationalize,** nash'un-al-īz, *vt.* To make the common property of the nation as a whole.

native, nā'tiv, *a.* Pertaining to the place or circumstances of one's birth; indigenous; inborn; occurring in nature pure or unmixed.—*n.* One born in a place or country; an indigenous animal or plant; an oyster raised in an artificial bed.

nativity, na-tiv'i-ti, *n.* Birth; time, place and manner of birth.

nattily, nat'i-li, *adv.* Sprucely; tidily.

natty, nat'i, *a.* Neat; tidy; spruce.

natural, nat'ū-ral, *a.* Pertaining to nature; produced or effected by nature; consistent with nature; not artificial; according to the life; not revealed; bastard; unregenerated.—*n.* An idiot; a fool. **naturalism,** nat'ū-ral-izm, *n.* The doctrine that there is no interference of any supernatural power in the universe; realism in art. **naturalist,** nat'-ū-ral-ist, *n.* One versed in natural science or natural history. **naturalization,** nat'ū-ral-i-zā''shun, *n.* Act of investing an alien with the privileges of a native citizen.

naturalize, nat'ū-ral-īz, *vt.* To make natural; to confer the privileges of a native subject upon; to acclimatize.

nature, nā'tūr, *n.* The universe; the total of all agencies and forces in the creation; the inherent or essential qualities of anything; individual constitution; sort; natural human instincts; reality as distinct from that which is artificial.

naught, nat, *n.* Nothing. **to set at naught,** to slight or disregard; a cipher.—*a.* Worthless.

naughty, na'ti, *a.* Bad; mischievous. **naughtily,** na'ti-li, *adv.* In a naughty manner; mischievously.

nausea, na'shē-a, *n.* Sickness.

nauseate, na'shē-āt, *vi.* To feel nausea. —*vt.* To loathe; to affect with disgust.

nauseous, na'shus, *a.* Loathsome; disgusting.

nautical, na'tik-al, *a.* Pertaining to ships, seamen, or navigation; naval; marine.

nautilus, na'ti-lus, *n.* A mollusk with a many-chambered shell in the form of a flat spiral.

naval, nā'val, *a.* Pertaining to ships; pertaining to a navy; nautical; maritime.

nave, nāv, *n.* The central block or hub of a wheel; middle part, lengthwise, of a church.

navel, nā'vel, *n.* A depression in the center of the abdomen, the end of the umbilical cord.

navigate, nav'i-gāt, *vi.* To conduct or guide a ship; to sail.—*vt.* To manage in sailing, as a vessel; to sail or guide a ship over. **navigation,** nav'i-ga''shun, *n.* Act of navigating; science or art of managing ships. **navigator,** na'vi-gāt-èr, *n.* One who directs the course of a ship. **navigable,** nav'i-ga-bl, *a.* That may be navigated; affording passage to ships.

navy, nā'vi, *n.* All the ships of a certain class belonging to a country; the whole of the ships of war belonging to a nation.

nay, nā, *adv.* No; not only so.—*n.* Denial; refusal.

Nazi, na'tsē, *a.* Of or having to do with the Nazis.—*n.* A member of the National Socialist Workers' Party in Germany under Adolf Hitler (1933-1945).

neap, nēp, *a.* Low, or not rising high; applied to the lowest tides.

near, nēr, *a.* Not distant in place, time, or degree; intimate; affecting one's interest or feelings; parsimonious; narrow; on the left of a horse; not circuitous.—*prep.* Close to; nigh.—*adv.* Almost; within a little; close to the wind.—*vt.* and *i.* To approach; to come near. **nearly,** nēr'li, *adv.* Closely; intimately; almost.

nearsighted, nēr'sīt'ed, *a.* Shortsighted.

neat, nēt, *n.* Cattle of the bovine genus. —*a.* Pure; clean; trim; tidy; clever; smart; without water added. **neatly,** nēt'li, *adv.* Tidily; smartly; cleverly.

nebula, neb'ū-la, *n.*; pl. *æ.* Celestial objects like white clouds, generally clusters of stars. **nebular,** neb'ū-lèr, *a.* Pertaining to nebulæ. **nebulous,** neb'ū-lus, *a.* Cloudy; hazy.

necessary, nes''e-ser'i, *a.* Such as must be; inevitable; essential; acting from necessity.—*n.* Anything indispensably requisite. **necessarily,** nes''e-ser'i-li, *adv.* In a necessary manner; by necessity; indispensably. **necessitate,** nē-ses'i-tāt, *vt.* To make necessary; to render unavoidable; to compel. **necessity,** nē-ses'i-ti, *n.* Condition of being necessary; need; irresistible compulsion; what is absolutely requisite; extreme indigence.

neck, nek, *n.* The part of an animal's body between the head and the trunk; a narrow tract of land; the slender part of a vessel, as a bottle.

neckerchief, nek'ėr-chif, *n.* A kerchief for the neck.

necklace, nek'lis, *n.* A string of beads, precious stones, &c., worn round the neck.

necktie, nek"tī', *n.* A tie worn round the neck.

necrology, ne-krol'o-ji, *n.* A register of deaths; a collection of obituary notices.

necromancy, nek"rō-man'si, *n.* The revealing of future events through pretended communication with the dead; sorcery.

necrosis, ne-krō'sis, *n.* Death or mortification of a bone; a disease of plants.

nectar, nek'tėr, *n.* The fabled drink of the gods; any very sweet and pleasant drink; the honey of a flower.

nee, née, nā, *pp.* Born; a term indicating a married woman's maiden name.

need, nēd, *n.* A state that requires supply or relief; urgent want; necessity; poverty; destitution.—*vt.* To have necessity or need for; to lack, require.—*vi.* To be necessary; used impersonally. **needful**, nēd'ful, *a.* Needy; necessary; requisite. **needless**, nēd'les, *a.* Not needed or wanted; unnecessary; not requisite; useless. **needlessly**, nēd'les-li, *adv.* In a needless manner; without necessity.

needle, nē'dl, *n.* An instrument for inter-weaving thread; a small steel instrument for sewing; a magnetized piece of steel in a compass attracted to the pole; anything in the form of a needle. **needlework**, nē"dl-wėrk', *n.* Work done with a needle; business of a seamstress.

needs, nēdz, *adv.* Of necessity; necessarily; indispensably; generally with *must.*

needy, nēd'i, *a.* Being in need; necessitous; indigent; very poor.

ne'er, nār. A contraction of *never.*

nefarious, nē-fār'i-us, *a.* Wicked in the extreme; infamous; atrocious.

negation, nē-gā'shun, *n.* A denial; contradiction or contradictory condition.

negative, neg'a-tiv, *a.* That denies; implying denial or negation; implying absence; the opposite of positive.—*n.* A word which denies, as *not, no*; a proposition by which something is denied; a veto; a photographic picture on glass, in which the lights and shades are the opposite of those in nature.—*vt.* To prove the contrary of; to reject by vote. **negatively**, neg'a-tiv-li, *adv.* In a negative manner; with or by denial.

neglect, neg-lekt', *vt.* To treat with no regard; to slight; to set at naught; to overlook.—*n.* Omission; slight; negligence. **neglectful**, neg-lekt'ful, *a.* Showing neglect; heedless; careless; inattentive.

negligé, neg'li-zhā, *n.* Easy or unceremonious dress; a loose gown. *a.* Carelessly arrayed; careless. Also *negligee.*

negligence, neg'li-jens, *n.* Quality of being negligent; neglect; carelessness.

negligent, neg'li-jent, *a.* Characterized by neglect; apt to neglect; careless; neglectful.

negotiate, nē-gō'shi-āt, *vi.* To treat with another respecting purchase and sale; to hold diplomatic intercourse; to conduct communications in general.—*vt.* To procure or bring about by negotiation; to pass into circulation (as a bill of exchange). **negotiation**, nē-gō'shi-ā"shun, *n.* A negotiating; the treating with another regarding sale or purchase; diplomatic bargaining. **negotiator**, ne-gō"shi-ā'tėr, *n.* One who negotiates. **negotiability**, nē-gō'shi-a-bil"i-ti, *n.* Quality of being negotiable. **negotiable**, nē-gō'shi-a-bl, *a.* That may be negotiated; that may be transferred by assignment or indorsement.

Negro, nē'grō, *n.* A member of the black race.

neigh, nā, *vi.* To utter the cry of a horse; to whinny.—*n.* The voice of a horse.

neighbor, neighbour, nā'bėr, *n.* One who lives or dwells near, or on friendly terms with another; a fellow-being.—*vt.* To be near to; to adjoin. **neighborhood, neighbourhood**, nā'bėr-hud, *n.* Condition of being neighbors; neighbors collectively; vicinity; locality.

neither, nē'THėr, or nī'THėr, *pron.* and *pron. adj.* Not either; not the one or the other. *conj.* Not either; nor.

Nemesis, nem'e-sis, *n.* A female Greek divinity personifying retributive justice; just retribution or punishment.

neolithic, nē-ō-lith'ik, *a.* Belonging to a period in which implements of polished stone were used, the more recent of the two stone periods.

neon light, nē'on līt. A glass tube filled with neon, a chemical element, which lights up when an electric current is passed through it.

neophyte, nē'ō-fit, *n.* One newly implanted in the church; proselyte; novice; tyro.—*a.* Newly entered on some state.

nephew, nef'ū, *n.* The son of a brother or sister.

nephritic, ne-frit'ik, *a.* Pertaining to the kidneys. **nephritis**, nē-frī'tis, *n.* Inflammation of the kidneys.

nepotism, nep'o-tizm, *n.* Undue patronage of relations; favoritism shown to nephews and other relatives.

Neptune, nep'tūn, *n.* The God of the sea; a planet, the eighth in order from the sun.

Nereid, nēr'ē-id, *n.* A sea nymph; a marine annelid; a sea-centipede.

nerve, nėrv, *n.* One of the fibrous threads in animal bodies whose function is to convey sensation and originate motion; fortitude; courage; energy; something resembling a nerve.—*vt.* (nerving, nerved). To give strength or vigor to; to steel. **nerveless**, nėrv'les, *a.* Destitute of nerve or strength; weak; wanting strength of will.

nervous, nėr'vus, *a.* Pertaining to the nerves; affecting the nerves; having the nerves easily affected; easily agitated; having nerve or bodily strength; vigorous; sinewy, **nervousness**, nėr'vus-nes, *n.* State or quality of being nervous.

nest, nest, *n.* The place or bed formed by a bird for laying and hatching her eggs; a number of persons frequenting the same haunt; a snug abode.—*vi.* To build a nest, to nestle. **nestle**, nes'l, *vi.* (nestling, nestled). To make or occupy a nest; to lie close and snug.—*vt.* To shelter, as in a nest; to cherish. **nestling**, nest'ling, *n.* A young bird in the nest, or just taken from the nest.

net, net, *n.* A texture of twine, &c., with meshes, commonly used to catch fish, birds, &c.; a snare.—*vt.* (netting, netted). To make into a net; to take in a net; to capture by wile.

net, nett, net, *a.* Being clear of all deductions; estimated apart from all expenses.—*vt.* (netting, netted). To gain as clear profit.

nether, neTH'ėr, *a.* Lower.

nethermost, neTH'ėr-mōst, *a.* Lowest.

netting, net'ing, *n.* A piece of net-work.

nettle, net'l, *n.* A weed with stinging hairs.—*vt.* ʻ(nettling, nettled.) To irritate or annoy somewhat; to pique.

network, net'wėrk, *n.* Work formed like a net; an interlacement.

neural, nū'ral, *a.* Pertaining to the nerves or nervous system. **neuralgia**, nū-ral'ja, *n.* Pain in a nerve. **neuralgic**, nū-ral'jik, *a.* Pertaining to neuralgia. **neurology**, nū-rol'o-ji, *n.* That branch of science which treats of the nerves.

neurotic, nū-rot'ik, *a.* Relating to the nerves; liable to nervous diseases; hysterical.

neuter, nū'tėr, *a.* Neutral; neither masculine nor feminine; neither active nor passive, as a verb.—*n.* An animal of neither sex; a plant with neither stamens nor pistils; a noun of the neuter gender.

neutral, nū'tral, *a.* Not siding with any party in a dispute; indifferent; neither acid nor alkaline.—*n.* A person or nation that takes no part in a contest between others. **neutrality**, nū-tral'i-ti, *n.* State of being neutral. **neutralization**, nū'tral-ī-zā'shun, *n.* Act of neutralizing. **neutralize**, nū'tral-īz, *vt.* To render neutral or inoperative; to counteract.

neutron, nū'tron, *n.* One of the particles in the make-up of the atom.

never, nev'ėr, *adv.* Not ever; at no time; in no degree; not at all.

nevermore, nev'ėr-mōr'', *adv.* Never again; at no future time.

nevertheless, nev'ėr-THĒ-les'', *adv.* Not the less; notwithstanding; yet; however.

new, nū, *a.* Recent in origin; novel; not before known; different; unaccustomed; fresh after any event; not second-hand. —*adv.* Newly; recently.

new-fangled, nū-fang'gld, *a.* Fond of novelty; of new and unfamiliar fashion.

Newfoundland, nū-found'land or nū'found-land, *n.* A large dog, remarkable for sagacity and swimming powers.

newness, nū'nes, *n.* State or quality of being new; novelty; unfamiliarity.

news, nūz, *n.* Recent intelligence or information; tidings; a newspaper.

newspaper, nūz''pā'pėr, *n.* A sheet of paper printed periodically for circulating news.

newt, nūt, *n.* A small amphibian of lizardlike appearance.

next, nekst, *a.* superl. of *nigh*. Nearest in place, time, rank, or degree.—*adv.* At the time or turn nearest.

nib, nib, *n.* The bill or beak of a bird; the point of anything, particularly of a pen.—*vt.* (nibbing, nibbed). To furnish with a nib; to mend the nib of, as a pen.

nibble, nib'l, *vt.* and *i.* (nibbling, nibbled). To bite a little at a time; to bite at; to carp at.—*n.* A little bite.

niblick, nib'lik, *n.* A golf-club with a small heavy iron head.

nice, nīs, *a.* Fastidious; punctilious; accurate; pleasant; delicate; dainty. **nicety**, nī'se-ti, *n.* State or quality of being nice; precision; a minute difference; *pl.* delicacies or dainties.

niche, nich, *n.* A recess in a wall for a statue, a vase, &c.

nick, nik, *n.* The exact point of time; the critical time; a notch; a score.—*vt.* To hit upon exactly; to make a nick in; to mark with nicks.

nickel, nik'el, *n.* A valuable metal of a white color and great hardness, magnetic, and when pure malleable and ductile. Five cents.

nickname, nik'nām, *n.* A name given in contempt or jest.—*vt.* To give a nickname to.

nicotine, nik'ō-tēn, *n.* A volatile alkaloid from tobacco, highly poisonous.

niece, nēs, *n.* The daughter of one's brother or sister.

niggard, nig'ėrd, *n.* A miser; a stingy person; a sordid, parsimonious wretch. —*a.* Miserly; sordidly parsimonious.

nigh, nī, *a.* Near; ready to aid.—*adv.* Near; almost.—*prep.* Near to.

night, nīt, *n.* The daily period of darkness; the time from sunset to sunrise; a state or time of darkness, depression, &c.; ignorance; obscurity; death.

nightcap, nīt''kap', *n.* A cap worn in bed; liquor taken before going to bed.

nightfall, nīt''fal', *n.* The close of the day; evening.

nightingale, nīt'in-gāl, *n.* A small insectivorous migratory bird that sings at night.

nightjar, nīt'jär', *n.* The goat-sucker.

nightly, nīt'li, *a.* Done by night or every night; nocturnal.—*adv.* By night; every night.

nightmare, nīt''mär', *n.* A feeling of suffocation during sleep, accompanied by intense anxiety or horror; some oppressive or stupefying influence.

nightshade, nīt''shad', *n.* A plant of the potato genus, &c., which possesses narcotic or poisonous properties.

night watch, nīt''woch, *n.* A guard in the night; a distinct period in the night.

nil, nil, *n.* Nothing.

nimble, nim'bl, *a.* Quick in motion; moving with ease and celerity; agile; prompt.

nimbus, nim'bus, *n.* A rain-cloud; a halo surrounding the head in representations of divine or sacred personages.

nincompoop, nin'kom-pōp, *n.* A fool; a blockhead; a simpleton.

nine, nīn, *a.* One more than eight.

ninepins, nīn"pinz', *n.pl.* A game with nine pins of wood at which a ball is rolled.

nineteen, nīn'tēn', *a.* and *n.* Nine and ten.

nineteenth, nīn'tēnth', *a.* The ordinal of nineteen.—*n.* A nineteenth part.

ninetieth, nīn'ti-eth, *a.* The ordinal of ninety.—*n.* A ninetieth part.

ninety, nīn'ti, *a.* and *n.* Nine times ten.

ninny, nin'i, *n.* A fool; a simpleton.

ninth, nīnth, *a.* The ordinal of nine.—*n.* A ninth part.

nip, nip, *vt.* (nipping, nipped). To catch and compress sharply; to snip or bite off; to blast, as by frost; to benumb.—*n.* A pinch, as with the fingers; a blast by frost; a small drink.

nippers, nip'ėrz, *n.pl.* Small pincers.

nipple, nip'l, *n.* A teat; pap; something like a nipple; nozzle.

nit, nit, *n.* The egg of a louse, &c.

niter, nitre, nī'tėr, *n.* Nitrate of potassium or saltpeter, used for making gunpowder, in dyeing, medicine, &c.

nitrate, nī'trāt, *n.* A salt of nitric acid.

nitric, nī'trik, *a.* Pertaining to niter; containing nitrogen and oxygen.

nitrogen, nī'tro-jen, *n.* The elementary uninflammable gas constituting about four-fifths of the atmospheric air. **nitrogenous**, nī-troj'e-nus, *a.* Pertaining to or containing nitrogen.

nitroglycerin, nitroglycerine, nī'trō-glis'ėr-in, *n.* A powerful explosive produced by the action of nitric and sulphuric acids on glycerine.

nitrous, nī'trus, *a.* Pertaining to niter; applied to compounds containing less oxygen than those called *nitric*.

no, nō, *adv.* A word of denial or refusal; not in any degree; not.—*n.* A denial; a negative vote.—*a.* Not any; none.

noble, nōb'l, *a.* Of lofty lineage; belonging to the peerage; illustrious; lofty in character; magnanimous; magnificent; stately.—*n.* A person of rank; a peer; an old English gold coin, value, 6s. 8d. sterling. **nobility**, nō-bil'i-ti, *n.* State or quality of being noble; the peerage. **nobleman**, nō'bl-man, *n.* A noble; a peer. **noblesse**, nō-bles', *n.* The nobility.

nobody, nō'bo-di, *n.* No person; no one; a person of no standing or position.

nocturn, nok'tėrn, *n.* A religious service formerly used in the R. Catholic Church at midnight, now a part of matins. **nocturnal**, nok-tėr'nal, *a.* Done or happening at night; nightly. **nocturne**, nok'tėrn, *n.* A painting or piece of music expressing some of the characteristic effects of night.

nod, nod, *vi.* (nodding, nodded). To make a slight bow; to let the head sink from sleep; to incline the head, as in assent or salutation, &c.—*vt.* To incline; to signify by a nod.—*n.* A quick inclination of the head.

node, nōd, *n.* A knot; a protuberance; a sort of knot on a stem where leaves arise; one of the two points in which two great circles of the celestial sphere intersect. **nodose**, nō'dōs, *a.* Knotted; jointed.

nodule, nod'ūl, *n.* A little knot or lump.

noggin, nog'in, *n.* A small wooden cup.

noise, noiz, *n.* A sound of any kind; a din; clamor; frequent talk.—*vt.* (noising, noised). To spread by rumor or report. **noiseless**, noiz'les, *a.* Making no noise; silent. **noisily**, noiz'i-li, *adv.* In a noisy manner.

noisome, noi'sum, *a.* Noxious to health; offensive; disgusting; fetid.

noisy, noiz'i, *a.* Making a loud noise; turbulent; obstreperous.

nomad, nō'mad, *n.* One who leads a wandering or pastoral life. **nomadic**, nō-mad'ik, *a.* Pertaining to nomads; wandering for pasturage; pastoral.

nomenclature, nō"men-klā'tūr, *n.* A system of names; vocabulary of terms appropriated to any branch of science.

nominal, nom'i-nal, *a.* Pertaining to a name; titular; not real; merely so called.

nominate, nom'i-nāt, *vt.* To name; to designate or propose for an office. **nomination**, nom-i-nā'shun, *n.* Act of nominating; power of appointing to office; state of being nominated. **nominative**, nom'i-nā-tiv, *a.* A term applied to the case of a noun or pronoun when subject of a sentence.—*n.* The nominative case; a nominative word. **nominator**, nom'i-nā-tėr, *n.* One who nominates. **nominee**, no-mi-nē', *n.* A person nominated; one proposed to fill a place or office.

nonce, nons, *adv.* Present occasion or purpose.

nonchalant, non'sha-lant, *a.* Indifferent; careless; cool. **nonchalance**, non'sha-lans, *n.* Indifference.

noncommissioned, non'ko-mish"und, *a.* Not having a commission; noting officers below the rank of lieutenant.

nonconductor, non'kon-duk"tėr, *n.* A substance which does not conduct, or transmits with difficulty, heat, electricity, &c.

nonconforming, non'kon-for"ming, *a.* Not conforming to the established church. **nonconformist**, non'kon-for"mist, *n.* One who does not conform to the established church. **nonconformity**, non'kon-for"mi-ti, *n.* Neglect or failure of conformity; refusal to unite with an established church.

nondescript, non'dē-skript, *a.* That has not been described; abnormal; odd; indescribable.—*n.* A person or thing not easily described or classed.

none, nun, *n.* or *pron.* Not one; not any; not a part; not the least portion.

nonentity, non-en'ti-ti, *n.* Non-existence; a thing not existing; a person utterly without consequence or importance.

nonpareil, non'pa-rel", *n.* A person or thing having no equal; a nonesuch; a sort of apple; a very small printing type.

nonpartisan, non-pär'ti-zan, *a.* Not committed to any party or view; neutral.

nonplus, non'plus, *n.* A state in which one can say or do no more.—*vt.* (nonplussing, nonplussed). To bring to a stand; to puzzle.

nonresidence, non-rez'i-dens, *n.* Failure to reside where official duties require one to reside, or on one's own lands; residence by clergymen away from their cures.

nonsense, non'sens, *n.* Words without meaning; absurdity; things of no importance. **nonsensical**, non-sen'si-kal, *a.* Destitute of sense; unmeaning; absurd; foolish.

nonunion, non-ūn'yun, *a.* Not of union make; pertaining to an establishment operating as an open shop.

noodle, nö'dl, *n.* A simpleton; a mixture of flour and water, or flour and eggs, made into thin, flat strips; the head. *Slang.*

nook, nök, *n.* A corner; a secluded retreat.

noon, nön, *n.* The middle of the day; twelve o'clock; the prime. **noonday**, nön'dā', *n.* Mid-day; noon.—*a.* Pertaining to mid-day; meridional. **noontide**, nön'tīd', *n.* The time of noon; mid-day. —*a.* Pertaining to noon.

noose, nös, *n.* A running knot, which binds the closer the more it is drawn.—*vt.* (noosing, noosed). To tie or catch in a noose; to entrap.

nor, nor, *conj.* A word used to render negative a subsequent member of a clause or sentence; correlative to *neither* or *other negative*; also equivalent to *and not.*

norm, norm, *n.* A rule; a pattern; a type.

normal, nor'mal, *a.* According to a rule; conforming with a certain type or standard; regular; perpendicular. **normal school**, a training-college for teachers. —*n.* A perpendicular.

Norman, nor'man, *n.* A native of Normandy.—*a.* Pertaining to Normandy or the Normans; denoting the round-arched style of architecture.

Norse, nors, *n.* The language of Norway and Iceland.—*a.* Belonging to ancient Scandinavia.

Norseman, nors'man, *n.* A native of ancient Scandinavia.

north, north, *n.* One of the cardinal points, the opposite of *south*; a region opposite to the south.—*a.* Being in the north.

northeast, north'ēst", *n.* The point midway between the north and east.—*a.* Northeastern. — *adv.* Northeastward. **northeaster**, north'ēs"tėr, *n.* A wind from the northeast. **northeastern**, north'ēs"tėrn, *a.* Pertaining to, from, toward, or in the northeast. **northeastward**, north'ēst"wėrd, *adv.* Toward the northeast.

northerly, north'ėr-li, *a.* Pertaining to the north; northern; proceeding from the north.—*adv.* Toward the north. **northern**, nor'THėrn, *a.* Being in the north; toward the north; proceeding from the north.—*n.* An inhabitant of the north. **northerner**, nor'THėr-nėr, *n.* A native or inhabitant of a northern

part. **northernmost**, north'ėrn-möst, *a.* Situated at the point farthest north. **northward**, **northwards**, north'-wėrd, north'wėrdz, *adv.* and *a.* Toward the north.

North Pole. The northern end of the earth's axis.

North Star. The star, Polaris, that is almost directly over the North Pole.

northwest, north'west", *n.* The point mid-way between the north and west.— *a.* Northwestern.—*adv.* Northwestward. **northwesterly**, north'west"ėr-li, *a.* Toward or from the northwest. **northwestern**, north'west"ėrn, *a.* Pertaining to, from, toward, or in the northwest. **northwestward**, north'west"wėrd, *adv.* Towards the northwest.

Northwest Territories. A division of northern Canada, east of the Yukon Territory.

Norwegian, nor-wē'jan, *a.* Belonging to Norway.—*n.* A native of Norway.

nose, nöz, *n.* The organ of smell, employed also in respiration and speech; the power of smelling; scent; sagacity; a nozzle.—*vt.* and *i.* (nosing, nosed). To smell; to twang through the nose; to pry officiously.

nosegay, nöz'gā', *n.* A bunch of flowers used to regale the sense of smell; a bouquet.

nostalgia, nos-tal'ji-a, *n.* Vehement desire to revisit one's native country; home-sickness.

nostril, nos'tril, *n.* One of the two apertures of the nose.

nostrum, nos'trum, *n.* A quack medicine, the ingredients of which are kept secret.

not, not, *adv.* A word that expresses negation, denial, or refusal.

notable, nö'ta-bl, *a.* Worthy of note; remarkable; conspicuous.—*n.* A person or thing of note or distinction.

notably, nö'ta-bli, *adv.* In a notable manner; remarkably; especially.

notary, nö'ta-ri, *n.* An officer authorized to attest documents, to protest bills of exchange, &c.; called also *Notary Public.*

notation, nö-tā'shun, *n.* Act of recording anything by marks, or the marks employed, as in algebra, music, &c.

notch, noch, *n.* An incision; nick; indentation.—*vt.* To cut a notch in; to indent.

note, nöt, *n.* A mark, sign, or token; an explanatory or critical comment; a memorandum; a bill, account; a paper promising payment; a communication in writing; notice; reputation; distinction; a character representing a musical sound, or the sound itself.—*vt.* (noting, noted). To observe carefully; to mark; to set down in writing. **notebook**, nöt'buk', *n.* A book in which notes or memoranda are written. **noted**, nöt'ed, *p.a.* Celebrated; famous. **noteworthy**, nöt'wėr"THi, *a.* Deserving notice; worthy of observation or notice.

nothing, nuth'ing, *n.* Not anything; non-existence; a trifle; a cipher.—*adv.* In no degree.

notice, nö'tis, *n.* Act of noting; regard;

information; order; intimation; civility; a brief critical review.—*vt.* (noticing, noticed). To take note of; to perceive; to make observations on, to treat with attention. **noticeable**, nō'tis-a-bl, *a.* That may be noticed; worthy of observation.

notify, nō'ti-fī, *vt.* To make known; to declare; to give notice to; to inform. **notification**, nō'ti-fi-kā'shun, *n.* Act of notifying; intimation; the writing which communicates information.

notion, nō'shun, *n.* A mental conception; idea; opinion; slight feeling or inclination.

notorious, nō-tō'ri-us. *a.* Publicly known and spoken of; known to disadvantage. **notoriety**, nō'tō-rī"e-ti, *n.* State of being notorious; discreditable publicity; one who is notorious.

notwithstanding, not'wiTH-stan"ding, *prep.* and *conj.* In spite of; nevertheless.

nought, nat, *n.* Naught; not anything; nothing; a cipher.

noun, noun, *n.* A word that denotes any object of which we speak.

nourish, nur'ish, *vt.* To feed; to supply with nutriment; to encourage; to foster. **nourisher**, nu'rish-ėr, *n.* A person or thing that nourishes. **nourishing**, nur'ish-ing, *p.a.* Helping to nourish; promoting growth; nutritious. **nourishment**, nur'ish-ment, *n.* Act of nourishing; nutrition; food; nutriment.

novel, nov'el, *a.* Of recent origin or introduction; new and striking; unusual. —*n.* A fictitious prose narrative picturing real life. **novelist**, nov'el-ist, *n.* A writer of novels. **novelty**, nov'l-ti, *n.* Quality of being novel; a new or strange thing.

November, nō-vem'bėr, *n.* The eleventh month of the year.

novice, nov'is, *n.* One who is new in any business; a beginner; a tyro; a probationer. **novitiate**, nō-vish'i-āt, *n.* State of being a novice; time of probation of a novice.

now, nou, *adv.* and *conj.* At the present time; at that time; after this; things being so.—*n.* The present time.

nowadays, nou"a-dāz', *adv.* In these days; in this age.

noway, **noways**, nō'wā, nō'wāz, *adv.* In no manner or degree; nowise.

nowhere, nō'hwar, *adv.* Not in any place or state.

nowise, nō'wīz, *adv.* Not in any manner or degree.

noxious, nok'shus, *a.* Hurtful; pernicious; unwholesome; corrupting to morals.

nozzle, noz'l, *n.* The projecting spout of something; terminal part of a pipe.

nuance, nụ-äns', *n.* A gradation of color; delicate degree in transitions.

nubile, nū'bil, *a.* Marriageable.

nuclear, nū'klē-ėr, *a.* Pertaining to or resembling a nucleus. **nuclear physics**. Branch of physics that deals with the structure of the atomic nucleus. **nucleus**, nū'klē-us, *n.;* pl. **-lei**. A kernel or something similar; a mass about which matter is collected; body of a comet.

nude, nūd, *a.* Naked; bare; undraped. **nudity**, nū'di-ti, *n.* State of being nude.

nudge, nuj, *n.* A jog with the elbow.—*vt.* (nudging, nudged). To give a jog with the elbow.

nugget, nug'et, *n.* A lump, as of gold.

nuisance, nū'sans, *n.* That which annoys or is offensive; a plague or pest; a bore.

null, nul, *a.* Of no force or validity; of no importance or account.—*n.* A cipher. **nullify**, nul'i-fī, *vt.* (nullifying, nullified). To render null; to deprive of force.

numb, num, *a.* Benumbed; without sensation and motion; torpid.—*vt.* To make numb or torpid; to deaden.

number, num'bėr, *n.* An aggregate of units, or a single unit; a numeral; many; one of a numbered series of things; part of a periodical; metrical arrangement of syllables; difference of form in a word to express unity or plurality.—*vt.* To reckon; to enumerate; to put a number on; to reach the number of. **numberless**, num'bėr-les, *a.* That cannot be numbered; countless; innumerable.

numeral, nū'mėr-al, *a.* Pertaining to number; consisting of or representing number.—*n.* A figure used to express a number.

numerate, nū'mėr-āt, *vt.* (numerating, numerated). To count; to enumerate. **numeration**, nū'mėr-ā"shun, *n.* Act or art of numbering. **numerator**, nū'mėr-āt-ėr, *n.* One who numbers; the number (above the line) in vulgar fractions which shows how many parts of a unit are taken. **numerical**, nū-mer'i-kal, *a.* Belonging to number; consisting in numbers.

numerous, nū'mėr-us, *a.* Consisting of a great number of individuals; many.

numskull, num'skul, *n.* A blockhead; a dunce; a dolt; a stupid fellow.

nun, nun, *n.* A woman devoted to religion who lives in a convent; a female monk.

nuncio, nun'shi-o, *n.* An ambassador of the pope at the court of a sovereign.

nunnery, nun'ėr-i, *n.* A house in which nuns reside.

nuptial, nup'shal, *a.* Pertaining to marriage. **nuptials**, nup'shalz, *n. pl.* Marriage.

nurse, nėrs, *n.* One who suckles or nourishes a child; one who tends the young, sick, or infirm; an attendant in a hospital; one who or that which nurtures or protects.—*vt.* (nursing, nursed). To act as nurse to; to suckle; to rear; to tend in sickness or infirmity; to foment; to foster. **nursery**, nėr'sėr-i, *n.* The place in which children are nursed and taken care of; a place where trees, plants, &c., are propagated.

nurture, nėr'tūr, *n.* Upbringing; education; nourishment.—*vt.* (nurturing, nurtured). To nourish; to educate; to bring or train up.

nut, nut, *n.* A fruit containing a seed or kernel within a hard covering; a small block of metal or wood with a grooved hole, to be screwed on the end of a bolt; a demented or eccentric person. *Slang.*

nutcracker, nut″krak′ẽr, *n.* An instrument for cracking nuts; also pl. *nutcrackers.*

nutmeg, nut″meg, *n.* The aromatic kernel of the fruit of a tree of the Malay Archipelago.

nutrient, nū′tri-ent, *a.* Nutritious.—*n.* Any substance which nourishes. **nutriment**, nū′tri-ment, *n.* That which nourishes; nourishment; food; aliment. **nutrition**, nū-tri′shon, *n.* Act or process of nourishing; that which nourishes; nutriment. **nutritious**, nū-trish′us, *a.* Serving to nourish; containing or supplying nutriment. **nutritive**, nū′tri-tiv, *a.* Pertaining to nutrition; nutritious.

nutshell, nut′shel, *n.* The hard shell in closing the kernel of a nut.

nutty, nut′i, *a.* Abounding in nuts; flavored like a nut; resembling a nut demented or eccentric.

nuzzle, nuz′l, *vi.* and *t.* (nuzzling, nuzzled). To rub or work with the nose; to put a ring into the nose of; to lie snug to nestle.

nylon, nī′lon, *n.* A synthetic of great toughness and elasticity, used in cloth or bristles; NYLON—a trade name.

nymph, nimf, *n.* A goddess of the mountains, forests, meadows, or waters a young and attractive woman; maiden; the chrysalis of an insect.

nymphomania, nim″fō-ma″ni-a, *n.* A strong, ungovernable sexual desire in women.

O

O, ō. An exclamation used in earnest or solemn address; often distinguished from *Oh*, which is more strictly expressive of emotion.

oaf, ōf, *n.* A fairy changeling; a dolt. **oafish**, ōf′ish, *a.* Stupid; dull; doltish.

oak, ōk, *n.* A valuable tree of many species. **oaken**, ōk′n, *a.* Made or consisting of oak.

oakum, ō′kum, *n.* Old ropes untwisted into loose fibers employed for calking, &c.

oar, ōr, *n.* A long piece of timber used to propel a boat.—*vt.* To impel by rowing. **oared**, ōrd, *a.* Furnished with oars. **oarsman**, ōrz′man, *n.* One who rows at the oar.

oasis, ō-ā′sis, *n.*; pl. **-ses**, -sēz. A fertile spot where there is water in a desert.

oat, ōt, *n.* A cereal plant valuable for its grain.

oath, ōth, *n.* An appeal to God for the truth of what is affirmed; an imprecation.

oatmeal, ōt′mēl′, *n.* Meal of oats produced by grinding or pounding.

obdurate, ob′dū-rāt, *a.* Hardened in heart; hardened against good; stubborn; inflexible. **obduracy**, ob′dū-ra-si, *n.* State or quality of being obdurate; impenitence; obstinacy.

obedient, ō-bē′di-ent, *a.* Submissive to authority; dutiful; compliant. **obedience**, o-bē′di-ens, *n.* Act of obeying; quality of being obedient; submission to authority.

obeisance, ō-bā′sans, *n.* A bow or courtesy; act of reverence, deference, or respect.

obelisk, ob′e-lisk, *n.* A tall four-sided pillar, tapering as it rises, and terminating in a small pyramid; a mark (†) used in printing.

obese, ō-bēs′, *a.* Excessively corpulent; fat. **obesity**, ō-bēs′i-ti, *n.* State or

quality of being obese; excessive corpulency.

obey, ō-bā′, *vt.* To comply with, as commands or requirements; to be ruled by; to yield to.—*vi.* To submit to authority

obituary, ō-bit″ū-er′i, *n.* An account of a person or persons deceased; list of the dead.—*a.* Relating to the decease of a person.

object, ob′jekt, *n.* That about which any faculty of the mind is employed; end; purpose; a concrete reality; the word clause, &c., governed by a transitive verb or by a preposition.—*vt.* ob-jekt′ To oppose in words or arguments. **objection**, ob-jek′shun, *n.* Act of objecting adverse reason; fault found. **objectionable**, ob-jek′shun-a-bl, *a.* Justly liable to objections; reprehensible. **objective** ob-jek′tiv, *a.* Pertaining to an object relating to whatever is exterior to the mind (also pron. ob′jek-tiv); belonging to the case which follows a transitive verb or preposition.—*n.* The objective case; object, place, &c., aimed at. **objectivity**, ob′jek-tiv″i-ti, *n.* State or quality of being objective.

object lesson, ob′jekt-les″n, *n.* A lesson from actual examples. **objector**, ob-jek′tẽr, *n.* One who objects.

objurgate, ob-jẽr′gāt, *vt.* and *i.* To chide, reprove, or reprehend. **objurgation**, ob′jẽr-gā″shun, *n.* Act of objurgating; reproof

oblate, ob-lāt′, *a.* Flattened or depressed at the poles, as a sphere or globe. **oblation**, ob-lā′shun, *n.* Anything offered in sacred worship; a sacrifice.

obligate, ob′li-gāt, *vt.* To bring under some obligation; to oblige. **obligation** ob′li-gā″shun, *n.* That which morally obliges; binding power of a promise contract, or law; a favor bestowed and binding to gratitude; a bond with a condition annexed, and a penalty for non-fulfillment. **obligatory**, ob-lig″

tŏ'ri, *a.* Imposing an obligation; binding; requiring performance.

oblige, ŏ-blīj', *vt.* (obliging, obliged). To constrain; to bind by any restraint; to lay under obligation of gratitude; to render service or kindness to. **obliging,** ŏ-blīj'ing, *p.a.* Having the disposition to oblige; civil; courteous; kind.

oblique, ob-lēk', *a.* Neither perpendicular nor parallel; slanting; indirect; sinister.

obliterate, ob-lit'ēr-āt, *vt.* To blot out; to efface; to cause to be forgotten. **obliteration,** ob-lit'ēr-ā'shun, *n.* Act of obliterating; effacement; extinction.

oblivion, ob-liv'i-on, *n.* State of being forgotten; forgetfulness; act of forgetting. **oblivious,** ob-liv'i-us, *a.* That easily forgets; forgetful; causing forgetfulness.

oblong, ob'long, *a.* Rectangular, and longer than broad.—*n.* An oblong figure.

obloquy, ob'lō-kwi, *n.* Censorious speech; contumely; odium; infamy.

obnoxious, ob-nok'shus, *a.* Odious; offensive; hateful; unpopular.

oboe, ō'bō, *n.* A musical wind-instrument made of wood; a hautboy.

obscene, ob-sēn', *a.* Indecent; offensive to chastity and delicacy; inauspicious. **obscenity,** ob-sen'i-ti, *n.* State or quality of being obscene; ribaldry; lewdness.

obscure, ob-skūr', *a.* Darkened; dim; not easily understood; abstruse; unknown to fame; indistinct.—*vt.* (obscuring, obscured). To darken; to make less visible, legible, or intelligible; to tarnish. **obscurity,** ob-skū'ri-ti, *n.* State or quality of being obscure; darkness.

obsequies, ob'se-kwiz, *n.pl.* Funeral rites and solemnities. **obsequious,** ob-sē'kwi-us, *a.* Promptly obedient or submissive; compliant; fawning.

observe, ob-zērv', *vt.* (observing, observed). To take notice of; to behold with attention; to remark; to keep religiously; to celebrate; to comply with; to practice.—*vi.* To remark; to be attentive. **observer,** ob-zēr'ver, *n.* One who observes; a spectator; one who observes phenomena for scientific purposes. **observing,** ob-sēr'ving, *p.a.* Given to observation; attentive. **observably,** ob-zēr'va-bli, *adv.* In a manner worthy of observation. **observance,** ob-zēr'vans, *n.* Act of observing; respect; performance of rites, &c; rule of practice; thing to be observed. **observant,** ob-zēr'vant, *a.* Observing; regardful; carefully attentive. **observation,** ob'zēr-vā'shun, *n.* The act, power, or habit of observing; information or notion gained by observing; a remark; due performance. **observatory,** ob-zēr'va-tō'ri, *n.* A place for astronomical observations; place of outlook. **observable,** ob-zēr'va-bl, *a.* That may be observed; worthy of notice; remarkable.

obsession, ob-sesh'un, *n.* Act of besieging; persistent attack; state of being beset.

obsolete, ob'sō-lēt, *a.* Antiquated; out of date; rudimentary. **obsolescent,** ob'sō-les''ent, *a.* Becoming obsolete; passing into desuetude.

obstacle, ob'sta-kl, *n.* A stoppage; hindrance; obstruction; impediment.

obstetric, obstetrical, ob-stet'rik, ob-stet'ri-kal, *a.* Pertaining to midwifery. **obstetrician,** ob'ste-trish''an, *n.* One skilled in obstetrics; an accoucheur. **obstetrics,** ob-stet'riks, *n* The science or art of midwifery.

obstinate, ob'sti-nit, *a.* Inflexible; stubborn; fixed firmly in opinion or resolution. **obstinacy,** ob'sti-na-si, *n.* State or quality of being obstinate; inflexibility; pertinacity.

obstreperous, ob-strep'ēr-us, *a.* Making a tumultuous noise; loud; noisy; clamorous.

obstruct, ob-strukt', *vt.* To block up, as a way or passage; to impede; to hinder in passing; to retard; to interrupt. **obstruction,** ob-struk'shun, *n.* Act of obstructing; that which impedes progress; obstacle; impediment; check. **obstructionist,** ob-struk'shun-ist, *n.* One who practices obstruction; an obstructive. **obstructive,** ob-struk'tiv, *a.* Hindering; causing impediment.—*n.* One who hinders the transaction of business.

obtain, ob-tān', *vt.* To get possession of; to acquire; to earn.—*vi.* To be received in common use; to prevail; to hold good. **obtainable,** ob-tān'a-bl, *a.* That may be obtained, procured, or gained.

obtrude, ob-tröd', *vt.* (obtruding, obtruded). To thrust prominently forward; to offer with unreasonable importunity. —*vi.* To enter when not desired. **obtruder,** ob-tröd'ēr, *n.* One who obtrudes. **obtrusion,** ob-trö'zhun, *n.* Act of obtruding; a thrusting upon others by force or unsolicited. **obtrusive,** ob-trö'siv, *a.* Disposed to obtrude; forward.

obtuse, ob-tūs', *a.* Not pointed or acute; greater than a right angle; dull; stupid.

obverse, ob-vèrs', *n.* and *a.* That side of a coin which has the face or head on it.

obviate, ob'vi-āt, *vt.* (obviating, obviated). To meet, as difficulties or objections; to get over; to remove.

obvious, ob'vi-us, *a.* Easily discovered, seen, or understood; evident; manifest.

occasion, o-kā'zhun, *n.* Occurrence; incident; opportunity; cause; need; juncture.—*vt.* To cause; to produce. **occasional,** o-kā'zhun-al, *a.* Occurring at times; made as opportunity admits; incidental.

Occident, ok'si-dent, *n.* The West. **occidental,** ok'si-den''tal, *a.* Western.

occult, o-kult', *a.* Hidden; invisible and mysterious.—*vt.* To conceal by way of eclipse.

occupy, ok'ū-pī, *vt.* (occupying, occupied). To take possession of; to hold and use; to cover or fill; to employ; to engage; often *refl.*—*vi.* To be an occupant. **occupancy,** ok'ū-pan-si, *n.* Act of occupying; a holding in possession; term during which one is occupant. **occupant,** ok'ū-pant, *n.* An occupier. **occupation,** ok-ū-pā'shun, *n.* Act of occupying; act of taking possession; tenure; business; employment; vocation.

occur, o-kèr', *vi.* (occurring, occurred).

To come to the mind; to happen; to be met with; to be found here and there.

occurrence, o-kur'ens, *n*. The act of occurring or taking place; any incident or accidental event; an observed instance.

ocean, ō'shan, *n*. The vast body of water which covers more than three-fifths of the globe; the sea; one of the great areas into which the sea is divided; any immense expanse.—*a*. Pertaining to the great sea. **oceanic**, ō-shē-an'ik, *a*. Pertaining to the ocean; found or formed in the ocean.

ocher, ochre, ō'kèr, *n*. A clay used as a pigment, of a pale-yellow or brownish-red color. **ochery, ocherous**, ō'kèr-i, ō'kèr-us, *a*. Consisting of, resembling, or containing ocher.

octagon, ok'ta-gon, *n*. A plane figure having eight angles and sides. **octagonal**, ok-tag'on-al, *a*. Having eight angles and eight sides.

octane rating, ok'tān rāt'ing. Rating based on measurement of antiknock properties of gasoline.

octave, ok'tāv, *a*. Eighth; denoting eight.—*n*. An eighth; the eighth day or the eight days after a church festival; a stanza of eight lines; in *music*, an interval of seven degrees or twelve semitones.

octavo, ok-tā'vō, *n*. A book in which the sheets are folded into eight leaves. —*a*. Having eight leaves to the sheet; written 8vo.

October, ok-tō'bèr, *n*. The tenth month of the year.

octogenarian, ok'tō-je-nâr'i-an, *n*. One between eighty and ninety years of age.

octopus, ok'tō-pus, *n*.; pl. **-puses**. A two-gilled cuttle-fish, having eight arms furnished with suckers.

ocular, ok'ū-lèr, *a*. Pertaining to or depending on the eye; received by actual sight.

oculist, ok'ū-list, *n*. One skilled in diseases of the eyes.

odd, od, *a*. Not even; not exactly divisible by 2; not included with others; incidental; casual; belonging to a broken set; queer. **oddfellow**, od'fel-ō, *n*. A member of a friendly society, modeled on freemasonry. **oddity**, od'i-ti, *n*. Singularity; a singular person or thing. **odds**, odz, *n. sing.* or *pl*. Inequality; excess; difference in favor of one; advantage; amount by which one bet exceeds another.

ode, ōd, *n*. A song; a short poem; a lyric poem of a lofty cast.

odious, ō'di-us, *a*. Hateful; offensive; disgusting. **odium**, ō'di-um, *n*. Hatred; dislike; the quality that provokes hatred, blame, &c.

odor, odour, ō'dèr, *n*. Any scent or smell; fragrance; reputation. **odoriferous**, ō-dor-if'èr-us, *a*. Diffusing smell; perfumed; fragrant. **odorless**, ō'dèr-les, *a*. Free from odor. **odorous**, ō'dèr-us, *a*. Emitting a scent or odor; sweet of scent; fragrant.

o'er, ō'èr, contracted from *over*.

of, ov, *prep*. Denoting source, cause, motive, possession, quality, condition,

material; concerning, relating to, about.

off, of, *adv*. Away; distant; not on; from; not toward. **well off, ill off**, in good or bad circumstances.—*a*. Distant; farther away; as applied to horses, right hand.—*prep*. Not on; away from; to seaward from.—*interj*. Begone!

offal, of'al, *n*. The parts of an animal butchered which are unfit for use; refuse.

offend, o-fend', *vt*. To displease; to shock; to cause to sin or neglect duty.—*vi*. To sin; to commit a fault; to cause dislike or anger. **offender**, o-fend'èr, *n*. One who offends; a transgressor; a delinquent; a trespasser.

offense, offence, o-fens', *n*. Injury; an affront, insult, or wrong; displeasure; transgression of law; misdemeanor. **offensive**, o-fens'iv, *a*. Causing offense; causing displeasure or annoyance; disgusting; impertinent; used in attack; aggressive.—*n*. Act or posture of attack. **offensively**, o-fens'iv-li, *adv*. In an offensive manner; disagreeably; aggressively.

offer, of'èr, *vt*. To present for acceptance or rejection; to tender; to bid, as a price or wages.—*vi*. To present itself; to declare a willingness; to make an attempt.—*n*. Act of offering; act of bidding a price; the sum bid. **offering**, of'èr-ing, *n*. Act of one who offers; that which is offered; a gift; oblation.

offertory, of'èr-tō-ri, *n*. Sentences read or repeated in church while the alms or gifts are collecting; the alms collected.

offhand, of'hand″, *a*. Done without thinking or hesitation; unpremeditated. —*adv*. On the spur of the moment; promptly.

office, of'is, *n*. Special duty or business; high employment or position under government; function; service; a formulary of devotion; a place where official or professional business is done; persons intrusted with certain duties; persons who transact business in an office; *pl*. kitchens, outhouses, &c., of a mansion or farm.

officer, of'i-sèr, *n*. A person invested with an office; one who holds a commission in the army or navy.—*vt*. To furnish with officers.

official, o-fish'al, *a*. Pertaining to an office or public duty; made by virtue of authority.—*n*. One invested with an office of a public nature. **officialism**, o-fi'shal-izm, *n*. Excessive official routine.

officiate, of-fish'i-āt, *vi*. To perform official duties; to act in an official capacity.

officious, of-fish'us, *a*. Troublesome in trying to serve; intermeddling.

offing, of'ing, *n*. That part of the sea nearer to the horizon than to the shore.

offset, of'set, *n*. A shoot or scion; a sum or amount set off against another as an equivalent; a contrast or foil.—*vt*. To set off, as one account against another.

offshoot, of'shōt', *n*. A shoot of a plant; anything growing out of another.

offspring, of'spring', *n. sing.* or *pl*. That which springs from a stock or parent; a child or children; progeny; issue.

oft, oft, *adv*. Often; *poet*.

often, of'n, *adv.* Frequently; many times.

oftentimes, of'n-tīmz', *adv.* Often.

ofttimes, oft'tīmz, *adv.* Frequently; often.

ogle, ō'gl, *vt.* (ogling, ogled). To view with side glances.—*n.* A side glance or look. **ogler**, ō'glėr, *n.* One who ogles.

ogre, ō'gėr, *n.* A monster in fairy tales, who lived on human flesh; one like an ogre. **ogress**, ō'gres, *n.* A female ogre.

oh, ō, *exclam.* (See O.) Denoting surprise, pain, sorrow, or anxiety.

ohm, ōm, *n.* The unit of electric resistance.

oil, oil, *n.* An unctuous inflammable liquid drawn from various animal and vegetable substances; a similar substance of animal origin; an oil-color.—*vi.* To smear or rub over with oil.

oilcloth, oil''kloth', *n.* Painted canvas for floor-covering, &c.; floor-cloth.

oilcolor, oil'kul'ėr, *n.* A pigment made by grinding a coloring substance in oil.

oil painting, oil' pān'ting, *n.* Art of painting with oil-colors; picture painted in oil-colors.

oilskin, oil''skin', *n.* Waterproof cloth.

oily, oil'i, *a.* Consisting of, containing, or resembling oil; unctuous; hypocritically pious.

ointment, oint'ment, *n.* Any soft, unctuous substance used for smearing the body or a diseased part; an unguent.

o.k. or okay, ō'kā', *a.* and *adv.* A term of approval; correct; all right.

okra, ō'kra, *n.* A plant bearing an edible vegetable having sticky green pods.

old, ōld, *a.* Grown up to maturity and strength; aged; of some particular age; long made or used; not new or fresh; ancient; antiquated. **of old**, long ago; in ancient times. **olden**, ōl'den, *a.* old; ancient. **old-fashioned**, ōld'fash'und, *a.* Characterized by antiquated fashion; aping old people.

oleaginous, ō-lē-aj'i-nus, *a.* Oily; unctuous.

oleander, ō-lē-an'dėr, *n.* An evergreen flowering shrub.

olfactory, ol-fak'tō-ri, *a.* Pertaining to smelling; having the sense of smelling.—*n.* An organ of smelling.

oligarch, ol'i-gärk, *n.* One of a few persons in power; an aristocrat. **oligarchy**, ol'i-gär'ki, *n.* Government in which the supreme power is in a few hands; those who form such a class or body.

olive, ol'iv, *n.* An evergreen tree; its fruit, from which a valuable oil is expressed; the color of the olive; the emblem of peace.—*a.* Relating to, or of the color of the olive.

Olympiad, ō-lim'pi-ad, *n.* A period of four years reckoned from one celebration of the Olympic games to another, the first Olympiad beginning 776 B.C.

Olympian, Olympic, ō-lim'pi-an, ō-lim'pik, *a.* Pertaining to Olympus, or to Olympia, in Greece; relating to the Greek games celebrated at Olympia.

omega, ō-mē'ga; ō'me-ga, *n.* The last letter of the Greek alphabet, long *o*; the last, or the ending.

omelet, om'e-let, *n.* A kind of pancake or fritter made with eggs, &c.

omen, ō'men, *n.* An event thought to portend good or evil; an augury; presage.—*vi.* To augur; to betoken.—*vt.* To predict.

ominous, om'i-nus, *a.* Containing an omen, and especially an ill omen; inauspicious. **ominously**, om'i-nus-li, *adv.* In an ominous manner; with ill omen.

omit, ō-mit', *vt.* (omitting, omitted). To pass over or neglect; not to insert or mention. **omission**, ō-mish'un, *n.* Act of omitting; neglect or failure to do something required; failure to insert or mention; something omitted.

omnibus, om'ni-bus, *n.* A large vehicle for conveying passengers.

omnipotent, om-nip'ō-tent, *a.* All-powerful; almighty; possessing unlimited power. **omnipotence**, om-nip'ō-tens, *n.* Almighty or unlimited power; an attribute of God.

omnipresent, om'ni-prez''ent, *a.* Present in all places at the same time; ubiquitous. **omnipresence**, om'ni-prez''ens, *n.* Presence in every place at the same time.

omniscient, om-nish'ent, *a.* Knowing all things; having universal knowledge. **omniscience, omnisciency**, om-nish'ens, om-nish'en-si, *n.* The faculty of knowing all things; universal knowledge.

omnivorous, om-niv'ō-rus, *a.* All-devouring; eating food of every kind.

on, on, *prep.* Above and touching; by contact with the surface or upper part; in addition to; at or near; immediately after and as a result; in reference or relation to; toward or so as to affect; at the peril of; among the staff of; pointing to a state, occupation, &c.—*adv.* Onward; in continuance; adhering; not off.

once, wuns, *adv.* One time; formerly; immediately after; as soon as. **at once**, all together; suddenly forthwith.

oncoming, on''kum'ing, *a.* Approaching; nearing.—*n.* Approach.

one, wun, *a.* Being but a single thing or a unit; closely united; forming a whole; single.—*n.* The first of the simple units; the symbol representing this (= 1). **at one**, in union or concord.—*pron.* Any single person; any man; any person; a thing; particular thing. **oneness**, wun'nes, *n.* State or quality of being one; singleness; individuality; unity.

onerous, on'ėr-us, *a.* Burdensome; heavy.

oneself, wun-self', *pron.* One's self; one's own person.

one-sided, wun''sīd'ed, *a.* Having one side only; limited to one side; partial; unfair.

onion, un'yun, *n.* A plant with a bulbous root, used as an article of food.

onlooker, on''luk'ėr, *n.* A spectator.

only, ōn'li, *a.* Single; sole; alone.—*adv.* For one purpose alone; simply; merely; solely.—*conj.* But; excepting that.

onrush, on''rush', *n.* A rapid onset.

onset, on″set′, *n.* A violent attack; assault.

onslaught, on″slat′, *n.* An attack; onset.

onus, ō′nus, *n.* A burden.

onward, onwards, on′wĕrd, on′wĕrdz, *adv.* Forward; on; in advance.

onward, on′wĕrd, *a.* Advanced or advancing; progressive; improved.

onyx, on′iks, *n.* A semi-pellucid gem with variously-colored veins, a variety of quartz; an agate with layers of chalcedony.

ooze, ōz, *n.* A soft flow, as of water; soft mud or slime; liquor of a tan-vat.—*vi.* (oozing, oozed). To flow or issue forth gently; to percolate.—*vt.* To emit in the shape of moisture. **oozy**, ō′zi, *a.* Miry; containing soft mud.

opacity, ō-pas′i-ti, *n.* State or quality of being opaque.

opal, ō′pal, *n.* A precious stone, which exhibits changeable reflections of green, blue, yellow, and red. **opalescent**, ō′pal-es″ent, *a.* Resembling opal; having the irridescent tints of opal. **opaline**, ō′pal-in, *a.* Pertaining to or like opal.— *n.* A semi-translucent glass.

opaque, ō-pāk′, *a.* Not transparent.

open, ō′pen, *a.* Not shut, covered, or blocked; not restricted; accessible; public; spread out; free, liberal, bounteous; candid; clear; exposed; fully prepared; attentive; amenable; not settled; enunciated with a full utterance.—*n.* An open or clear space.—*vt.* To make open; to unclose; to cut into; to spread out; to begin; to make public; to declare open; to reveal.—*vi.* To unclose itself; to be parted; to begin. **open door**, ō′pen-dōr′, *n.* The policy of the dominant country of giving to other nations equal commercial privileges in a dependency. **opener**, ō′pen-ĕr, *n.* One who or that which opens. **open-handed**, ō′pen-han′ded, *a.* Having an open hand; generous; liberal. **open-hearted**, ō′pen-här′ted, *a.* Candid; frank; generous. **opening**, ō′pen-ing, *a.* First in order; beginning.—*n.* Act of one who or that which opens; an open place; aperture; beginning; vacancy; opportunity of commencing a business, &c.

opera, op′ĕr-a, *n.* A dramatic composition set to music and sung and acted on the stage; a theater where operas are performed.

operate, op′ĕr-āt, *vi.* (operating, operated). To work; to act; to produce effect; to exert moral power or influence. —*vt.* To act; to effect; to drive, as a machine.

operation, op′ĕr-ā″shun, *n.* Act or process of operating; agency; action; process; surgical proceeding to which the human body is subjected; movements of troops or war-ships. **operative**, op′ĕr-ā″tiv, *a.* That operates; producing the effect; having to do with manual or other operations.—*n.* One who works or labors; an artisan. **operator**, op′ĕr-ā″tĕr, *n.* One who operates.

operetta, op′ĕr-et″a, *n.* A short musical drama of a light character.

ophthalmia, of-thal′mi-a, *n.* Inflamma-

tion of the eye or its appendages. **ophthalmic**, of-thal′mik, *a.* Pertaining to the eye or to ophthalmia. **ophthalmist**, of-thal′mist, *n.* An oculist.

opiate, ō′pi-āt, *n.* Any medicine that contains opium; a narcotic.

opine, ō-pin′, *vi.* and *t.* To think; to suppose.

opinion, ō-pin′yun, *n.* A judgment or belief; notion; persuasion; estimation. **opinionated**, ō-pin″yūn-āt′ed, *a.* Stiff or obstinate in opinion; conceited.

opium, ō′pi-um, *n.* The inspissated juice of a kind of poppy, one of the most energetic of narcotics.

opossum, ō-pos′um, *n.* The name of several marsupial mammals of America.

opponent, o-pō′nent, *a.* Opposing; antagonistic; opposite.—*n.* One who opposes; an adversary; an antagonist.

opportune, op-or-tūn′, *a.* Seasonable; timely; well-timed; convenient. **opportunist**, op″or-tūn′ist, *n.* One who waits upon favorable opportunities; a politician more influenced by place and power than principle. **opportunity**, op′-or-tū″ni-ti, *n.* A fit or convenient time; favorable conjuncture.

oppose, o-pōz′, *vt.* (opposing, opposed). To place over against; to place as an obstacle; to act against; to resist; to check. —*vi.* To make objections; to act obstructively. **opposed**, o-pōzd′, *p.a.* Adverse; hostile.

opposite, op′ō-zit, *a.* Facing; adverse; contrary; inconsistent.—*n.* An adversary. **opposition**, op′ō-zish″un, *n.* Act of opposing; attempt to check or defeat; contradiction; inconsistency; the collective body of opponents of a ministry.

oppress, ō-pres′, *vt.* To press or weigh down unduly; to harass; to overpower; to overburden. **oppression**, ō-presh″un, *n.* Act of oppressing; severity; hardship; dullness of spirits. **oppressive**, ō-pres′iv, *a.* Burdensome; unjustly severe; tyrannical. **oppressor**, ō-pres′ĕr, *n.* One who oppresses; a cruel governor or taskmaster.

opprobrious, ō-prō′bri-us, *a.* Containing opprobrium; scurrilous; abusive.

opprobrium, ō-prō′bri-um, *n.* Scurrilous language; disgrace; scurrility; infamy.

optic, op′tik, *a.* Pertaining to sight; relating to the science of optics.—*n.* An organ of sight; an eye. **optical**, op′tikal, *a.* Relating to the science of optics; optic. **optician**, op-tish′an, *n.* A person skilled in optics; one who makes or sells optical instruments.

optics, op′tiks, *n.* The science which treats of the nature and properties of light and vision, optical instruments, &c.

optimism, op′ti-mizm, *n.* The opinion or doctrine that everything is for the best; tendency to take the most hopeful view. **optimist**, op′ti-mist, *n.* One who believes in optimism. **optimistic**, op′-ti-mis″tik, *a.* Relating to or characterized by optimism.

option, op′shun, *n.* Choice; free choice; power of choosing. **optional**, op′shunal, *a.* Left to one's own option or choice; depending on choice.

opulent, op′ū-lent, *a.* Wealthy; rich.
opulence, op′ū-lens, *n.* Wealth; riches.
or, or, *conj.* A particle that marks an alternative, and frequently corresponds with *either* and *whether.*—*adv.* Ere; before.—*n.* Heraldic name for gold.

oracle, or′a-kl, *n.* Among the Greeks and Romans, the answer of a god to an inquiry respecting some future event; place where the answers were given; the sanctuary of the ancient Jews; any person reputed uncommonly wise; a wise or authoritative utterance. **oracular**, ŏ-rak′ū-lėr, *a.* Pertaining to or like an oracle; uttering oracles; authoritative; sententious; ambiguous.

oral, ō′ral, *a.* Pertaining to the mouth; spoken, not written.

orange, or′enj, *n.* An evergreen fruit-tree, and also its fruit; the color of this fruit; a reddish yellow.—*a.* Belonging to an orange; colored as an orange; **orange peel**, or′enj-pēl′, *n.* The rind of an orange separated from the fruit; the peel of the bitter orange dried and candied.

orangutan, orangoutang, o-rang′ŏ-tan′, o-rang′ŏ-tang′, *n.* One of the largest of the anthropoid or manlike apes.

orate, ō-rāt′, *vi.* (orating, orated). To make an oration; to talk loftily; to harangue. **oration**, ō-rā′shun, *n.* A formal public speech; an eloquent speech or address. **orator**, or′a-tėr, *n.* A public speaker; a skilled or eloquent speaker. **oratorical**, or′a-tor″i-kal, *a.* Pertaining to an orator or to oratory; rhetorical. **oratorio**, or′a-tō″ri-ō, *n.* A sacred musical composition. **oratory**, or″a-tō′ri, *n.* A small chapel; a religious place of speaking; eloquence.

orb, ōrb, *n.* A sphere; a heavenly body; a circular disk; a hollow globe.—*vt.* To encircle.

orbit, ōr′bit, *n.* The path of a planet or comet; cavity in which the eye is situated. **orbital**, ōr′bi-tal, *a.* Pertaining to an orbit.

orchard, ōr′chėrd, *n.* An inclosure devoted to the culture of fruit-trees.

orchestra, ōr′kes-tra, *n.* That part of the Greek theater allotted to the chorus; that part of a theater, &c., appropriated to the musicians; a body of musicians. **orchestral**, ōr-kes′tral, *a.* Pertaining to an orchestra; suitable for or performed in the orchestra. **orchestration**, ōr′kes-trā″shun, *n.* Arrangement of music for an orchestra; instrumentation.

orchid, orchis, or′kid, or′kis, *n.* A perennial plant with tuberous fleshy root and beautiful flowers.

ordain, or-dān′, *vt.* To establish authoritatively; to decree; to invest with ministerial or sacerdotal functions.

ordeal, ōr′dē-al, *n.* A trial by fire and water; severe trial or strict test.

order, or′dėr, *n.* Regular disposition; proper state; established method; public tranquillity; command; instruction to supply foods or to pay money; rank, class, division, or dignity; a religious fraternity; division of natural objects; *pl.* clerical character, specially called

holy orders. **in order**, for the purpose.—*vt.* To place in order; to direct; to command; to give an order or commission for.—*vi.* To give command. **orderly**, or′dėr-li, *a.* In accordance with good order; well ordered; regular; on duty.—*n.* A private soldier or non-commissioned officer, who attends on a superior officer.—*adv.* According to due order.

ordinal, or′di-nal, *a.* Expressing order or succession.—*n.* A number denoting order (as *first*); a book containing an ordination service.

ordinance, or′di-nans, *n.* That which is ordained; law, statute, edict, decree.

ordinary, or′di-nėr′i, *a.* Conformable to order; regular; customary; common; of little merit.—*n.* An ecclesiastical judge; a judge who takes cognizance of causes in his own right; an eating-house where the prices are settled. **ordinarily**, or′di-nėr′i-li, *adv.* In an ordinary manner; usually; generally.

ordinate, or′di-nāt, *a.* Regular; methodical.—*n.* In *geometry*, a line of reference determining the position of a point. **ordination**, or′di-nā″shun, *n.* Act of ordaining; act of conferring sacerdotal power; act of settling a Presbyterian clergyman in a charge. **ordnance**, ord′nans, *n.* Cannon or great guns collectively; artillery.

ordure, or′dūr, *n.* Dung; excrement.

ore, ōr, *n.* A mineral substance from which metals are obtained by smelting; metal.

organ, or′gan, *n.* An instrument or means; a part of an animal or vegetable by which some function is carried on; a medium of conveying certain opinions; a newspaper; the largest wind-instrument of music. **organic**, or-gan′ik, *a.* Pertaining to or acting as an organ; pertaining to the animal and vegetable worlds; organized; systematized. **organism**, or′gan-izm, *n.* Organic structure; a body exhibiting organic life. **organist**, or′gan-ist, *n.* One who plays on the organ. **organize**, or′gan-īz, *vt.* To give an organic structure to; to establish and systematize; to so arrange as to be ready for service. **organizer**, or′gan-īz-ėr, *n.* One who organizes, establishes or systematizes. **organization**, or′gan-i-zā″shun, *n.* Act or process of organizing; suitable disposition of parts for performance of vital functions.

orgy, or′ji, *n.* A wild or frantic revel; a drunken party.

orient, ō′ri-ent, *a.* Rising, as the sun; eastern; oriental; bright.—*n.* The East; luster as that of a pearl.—*vt.* To define the position of; to cause to lie from east to west. **oriental**, ō′ri-ent″al, *a.* Eastern; from the east.—*n.* A native of some eastern country. **orientation**, ō′ri-en-tā″shun, *n.* A turning towards the east; position east and west.

orifice, or′i-fis, *n.* The mouth or aperture of a tube, pipe, &c.; an opening; a vent.

origin, or′i-jin, *n.* Source; beginning; derivation; cause; root; foundation.

original, ō-rij′i-nal, *a.* Pertaining to origin; primitive; first in order; having the power to originate; not copied.—*n*. Origin; source; first copy; model; that from which anything is translated or copied; a person of marked individuality. **originality**, ō-rij′i-nal″i-ti, *n*. Quality or state of being original; power of producing new thoughts, &c. **originally**, ō-rij′i-nal-i, *adv*. In an original manner; primarily; at first.

originate, ō-rij′i-nāt, *vt*. (originating, originated). To give origin to; to produce.—*vi*. To have origin; to be begun. **origination**, ō-rij′i-nā″shun, *n*. Act or mode of originating; first production. **originator**, ō-rij″i-nā′tèr, *n*. One who or that which originates.

oriole, ō′ri-ōl, *n*. A bird with golden plumage.

Orion, ō-rī′on, *n*. A constellation of the southern hemisphere.

orison, or′i-zun, *n*. A prayer.

ornament, or′na-ment, *n*. That which adorns or embellishes; decoration.—*vt*. To decorate; to adorn. **ornamental**, or′na-men″tal, *a*. Serving to ornament; pertaining to ornament. **ornamentation**, or′na-men-tā″shun, *n*. Act of ornamenting; ornaments or decorations.

ornate, or-nāt′, *a*. Richly ornamented; adorned; of a florid character.

ornithology, or′ni-thol″ō-ji, *n*. The science which treats of birds. **ornithological**, or′ni-thō-loj″i-kal, *a*. Pertaining to ornithology. **ornithologist**, or′ni-thol″ō-jist, *n*. A person who is skilled in ornithology.

orotund, ō′rō-tund, *a*. Characterized by fullness and clearness; rich and musical.

orphan, or′fan, *n*. A child bereaved of father or mother, or of both.—*a*. Bereaved of parents.—*vt*. To reduce to being an orphan. **orphanage**, or′fan-ij, *n*. The state of an orphan; a home for orphans.

orthodox, or′thō-doks, *a*. Sound in opinion or doctrine; sound in religious doctrines; in accordance with sound doctrine.

orthography, or-thog′ra-fi, *n*. The art of writing words with the proper letters; spelling.

oscillate, os′i-lāt, *vi*. To swing; to vibrate; to vary or fluctuate. **oscillation**, os′i-lā″shun, *n*. Act or state of oscillating; vibration. **oscillatory**, os′sil-la-to-ri, *a*. Oscillating; swinging; vibrating.

osculate, os′kū-lāt, *vt*. and *i*. To kiss; to touch; as curves. **osculation**, os′kū-lā″shun, *n*. Act of kissing; a kiss; a coming in contact.

osier, ō′zhèr, *n*. The name of various species of willow, employed in basket-making.—*a*. Made of osier or twigs; like osier.

osmose, os′mōs, *n*. The tendency of fluids to pass through porous partitions and mix.

osprey, os′pri, *n*. A kind of hawk or eagle which feeds on fish; one of its feathers.

ossification, os′i-fi-kā″shun, *n*. The process of changing into a bony substance.

ossify, os′i-fī, *vt*. and *i*. To change into bone, or into a substance of the hardness of bone.

ostensible, os-ten′si-bl, *a*. Put forth as having a certain character; apparent and not real; pretended; professed. **ostensibly**, os-ten′si-bli, *adv*. In an ostensible manner; professedly.

ostensive, os-ten′siv, *a*. Showing; exhibiting.

ostentation, os′ten-tā″shun, *n*. Ambitious display; vain show; parade; pomp. **ostentatious**, os-ten-tā″shus, *a*. Characterized by ostentation; showy.

osteology, os′tē-ol″ō-ji, *n*. The science which treats of the bones and bone-tissue.

ostracize, os′tra-sīz, *vt*. To banish by ostracism; to expel; to banish from society. **ostracism**, os′tra-sizm, *n*. A mode of political banishment in ancient Athens effected by public vote; expulsion.

ostrich, os′trich, *n*. A large running bird of Africa, Arabia, and S. America, the largest of existing birds.

other, uTH′ėr, *a*. and *pron*. Not the same; second of two; not this; opposite; often used reciprocally with *each*.

otherwise, uTH′ėr-wiz′, *adv*. In a different manner; not so; by other causes; in other respects.—*conj*. Else; but for this.

otter, ot′ėr, *n*. An aquatic carnivorous animal resembling the weasel, but larger.

Ottoman, ot′ō-man, *a*. Pertaining to or derived from the Turks.—*n*. A Turk; a kind of couch introduced from Turkey.

ouch, ouch, *n*. The socket in which a precious stone is set; a brooch; an exclamation of pain.

ought, at, *n*. Aught.—*v*. To be held or bound in duty or moral obligation.

ounce, ouns, *n*. The twelfth part of a pound troy, and the sixteenth of a pound avoirdupois; an Asiatic animal like a small leopard.

our, our, *a*. or *pron*. Pertaining or belonging to us. **ours** is used when no noun follows.

ourself, our-self′, *pron*. Used for *myself*; as a more dignified word, in the regal style.

ourselves, our-selvz′, *pron. pl*. We or us, not others; added to *we* by way of emphasis, but in the objective often without emphasis and reflexively.

oust, oust, *vt*. To eject; to turn out.

out, out, *adv*. On or towards the outside; not in or within; forth; beyond usual limits; not in proper place; public; exhausted; deficient; not in employment; loudly; in error; at a loss; having taken her place as a woman in society.—*n*. One who is out; a nook or corner.—*vt*. To put out.—*interj*. Away! begone!

out-and-out, out′and-out′, *a*. Thorough; thorough-paced; absolute; complete.

outbid, out-bid′, *vt*. To bid more than another.

outbreak, out″brāk′, *n*. A breaking forth; eruption; sudden manifestation as of anger, disease, &c.

outburst, out″bėrst′, *n*. A bursting or breaking out; an outbreak.

outcast, out″kast′, *p.a*. Cast out; rejected.—*n.* An exile; one driven from home or country.

outcome, out″kum′, *n.* The issue; result; consequence.

outcrop, out″krop′, *n.* Exposure of strata at the surface of the ground.

outcry, out″kri′, *n.* A loud cry; exclamation; clamor; noisy opposition.

outdistance, out-dis′tans, *vt.* To excel or leave behind in any competition.

outdo, out-dō′, *vt.* To excel; to surpass.

outdoor, out″dōr′, *a.* In the open air; not required to reside in a poorhouse.

outdoors, out′dōrz″, *adv.* Abroad; in the open air.

outer, out′ĕr, *a.* Being on the outside; external.—*n.* That part of a target beyond the circles surrounding the bull's-eye; a shot which hits this part.

outermost, out′ĕr-mōst, *a.* Being farthest out; being on the extreme external part.

outfit, out′fit, *n.* A fitting out, as for a voyage; equipment of one going abroad.

outfitter, out″fit′ĕr, *n.* One who makes an outfit; clothier, &c.

outflank, out-flangk′, *vt.* To maneuver so as to attack in the flank; to get the better of.

outflow, out″flō′, *n.* Act of flowing out; efflux.

outgeneral, out-jen′ĕr-al, *vt.* To gain advantage over by superior military skill.

outgo, out-gō′, *vt.* To go beyond; to excel.—*n.* out′gō. Expenditure.

outgoing, out″gō′ing, *n.* Act of going out; expenditure; outlay.—*a.* Going out.

outgrow, out-grō′, *vt.* To surpass in growth; to grow too great or old for anything. **outgrowth,** out″grōth′, *n.* Excrescence; result.

outing, out′ing, *n.* A short excursion; an airing; short time spent out-of-doors.

outlandish, out-lan′dish, *a.* Foreign; strange; uncouth; bizarre.

outlast, out-läst′, *vt.* To last longer than.

outlaw, out″lạ, *n.* A person excluded from the benefit of the law.—*vt.* To deprive of the benefit and protection of law; to proscribe. **outlawry,** out″lạ′ri, *n.* The putting of a man out of the protection of law.

outlay, out′lā, *n.* Expenditure.

outlet, out′let, *n.* Place by which anything is discharged; exit; a vent.

outline, out′lin, *n.* The line by which a figure is defined; contour; general scheme.—*vt.* To draw the exterior line of; to sketch.

outlive, out-liv′, *vt.* To survive.

outlook, out″lōk′, *n.* A looking out; vigilant watch; place of watch; prospect.

outlying, out′li-ing, *a.* Lying at a distance from the main body; being on the frontier.

outmaneuver, outmanoeuvre, out′-ma-nö″vĕr, or -nü″vĕr, *vt.* To surpass in maneuvering.

outnumber, out-num′bĕr, *vt.* To exceed in number.

out-of-door, out′ov-dōr′, *a.* Open-air.

out-of-doors, out′ov-dōrz′, *adv.* Out of the house.

out-of-the-way, out′ov-the-wā′, *a.* Se-

cluded; unusual; uncommon.

out-patient, out″pā′shent, *n.* A patient not residing in a hospital, but who receives medical advice, &c., from the institution.

outpost, out″pōst′, *n.* A station at a distance from the main body of an army; troops placed as such a station.

outpour, out″pōr′, *vt.* To pour out.

output, out″pŏt′, *n.* Quality of material produced within a specified time.

outrage, out″rāj, *vt.* (outraging, outraged). To do extreme violence or injury to; to abuse, to commit a rape upon.—*n.* Excessive abuse; injurious violence. **outrageous,** out-rā′jus, *a.* Characterized by outrage; furious; exorbitant; atrocious. **outrageously,** out-rā′jus-li, *adv.* In an outrageous manner; furiously; excessively.

outrigger, out″rig′ĕr, *n.* A structure of spars, &c., rigged out from the side of a sailing-boat; a projecting bracket on a boat, with the row lock at the extremity; a light boat provided with such apparatus.

outright, out″rit′, *adv.* Completely; utterly.

outrun, out-run′, *vt.* To exceed in running; to leave behind; to go beyond.

outset, out″set′, *n.* Beginning.

outshine, out-shin′, *vi.* To shine out or forth.—*vt.* To excel in luster.

outside, out′sid′, *n.* The external surface or superficies; exterior; the utmost; extreme estimate.—*a.* Exterior; superficial.—*prep.* On the outside of. **outsider,** out′sid″ĕr, *n.* One not belonging to a party, association, or set.

outskirt, out″skĕrt′, *n.* Parts near the edge of an area; border; purlieu; generally in *pl.*

outspoken, out″spō′kn, *a.* Free or bold of speech; candid; frank.

outstanding, out-stan′ding, *a.* Projecting outward; prominent; unpaid; undelivered.

outstrip, out-strip′, *vt.* To outgo; to outrun; to advance beyond; to exceed.

outvote, out-vōt′, *vt.* To exceed in the number of votes; to defeat by plurality of votes.

outward, out′wĕrd, *a.* External; exterior; visible; adventitious.—*adv.* Tending toward the exterior; from a port or country. **outward bound,** out′wĕrd bound, *a.* Bound to some foreign port; going seaward. **outwardly,** out′wĕrd-li, *adv.* Externally; in appearance; not sincerely.

outwear, out-wār′, *vt.* To wear out; to last longer than.

outweigh, out-wā′, *vt.* To exceed in weight, value, &c.; to overbalance.

outwit, out-wit′, *vt.* (outwitting, outwitted). To overreach; to defeat by superior ingenuity.

ova, ō′va, *n.*; plural of *ovum*.

oval, ō′val, *a.* Shaped like an egg; elliptical.—*n.* A figure shaped like an egg or ellipse.

ovarian, ō-vār′i-an, *a.* Belonging to the ovary.

ovary, ō′va-ri, *n.* The female organ in which ova are formed.

ovate, ō'vāt, *a.* Egg-shaped; oval.

ovation, ō-vā'shun, *n.* A lesser triumph among the ancient Romans; triumphal reception; public marks of respect.

oven, uv'n, *n.* A place built in closely for baking, heating, or drying.

over, ō'vėr, *prep.* Above; denoting motive, occasion, or superiority; across; throughout; upwards of.—*adv.* From side to side; in width; on all the surface; above the top or edge; in excess; completely; too.—*a.* Upper; covering.

overact, ō-vėr-akt', *vt.* To perform to excess.

overalls, ō"vėr-alz', *n. pl.* Loose trousers worn over the others to protect them.

overawe, ō'vėr-s", *vt.* To restrain by awe.

overbalance, ō'vėr-bal"ans, *vt.* To weigh down; to exceed in importance; to destroy the equilibrium of.—*n.* Excess.

overbear, ō'vėr-bār', *vt.* To bear down; to overpower; to domineer over. **overbearing,** ō'vėr-bār"ing, *a.* Haughty and dogmatical; imperious; domineering.

overboard, ō"vėr-bōrd', *adv.* Over the side of a ship; out of a ship.

overburden, ō'vėr-bėr"dn, *vt.* To load with too great weight; to overload.

overcast, ō'vėr-kāst', *vt.* To cloud; to darken; to sew coarsely over a rough edge.

overcharge, ō"vėr-chärj', *vt.* To charge or burden to excess; to fill too numerously.—*n.* ō'vėr-chärj. An excessive charge.

overcoat, ō"vėr-kōt', *n.* An upper coat; topcoat.

overcome, ō'vėr-kum', *vt.* To be victorious over; to master; to get the better of.—*vi.* To gain the superiority.

overcrowd, ō'vėr-kroud", *vt.* To crowd to excess, especially with human beings.

overdo, ō'vėr-dō", *vt.* To do to excess; to fatigue; to boil, bake, or roast too much.

overdose, ō'vėr-dōs", *n.* Too great a dose.—*vt.* ō-ver-dōs'. To dose excessively.

overdraw, ō'vėr-dra", *vt.* To draw upon for a larger sum than is standing at one's credit; to exaggerate.

overdue, ō'vėr-dū", *a.* Past the time of payment or arrival.

overflow, ō'vėr-flō', *vt.* (pp. overflowed and overflown). To flow or spread over; to flood; to overwhelm.—*vi.* To be so full that the contents run over; to abound.—*n.* ō'vėr-flō. An inundation; superabundance. **overflowing,** ō'vėr-flō"ing, *p.a.* Abundant; copious; exuberant.

overgrow, ō'vėr-grō', *vt.* To grow beyond; to cover with growth or herbage.—*vi.* To grow beyond the fit or natural size. **overgrowth,** ō"vėr-grōth', *n.* Exuberant or excessive growth.

overhand, ō'vėr-hand', *a.* and *adv.* With the hand over the object.

overhang, ō"vėr-hang', *vt.* and *i.* To hang, impend, jut, or project over.

overhaul, ō'vėr-hal", *vt.* To examine thoroughly with a view to repairs; to re-examine; to gain upon or overtake.—

n. ō"vėr-hal'. Examination; inspection; repair.

overhead, ō'vėr-hed", *adv.* Above; aloft.

overhear, ō'vėr-hēr", *vt.* To hear by accident or stratagem.

overheat, ō'vėr-hēt", *vt.* To heat to excess.

overhung, ō'vėr-hung", *p.a.* Hung or covered over; adorned with hangings.

overjoy, ō-vėr-joi', *vt.* To give excessive joy to.—*n.* ō'vėr-joi". Joy to excess.

overland, ō'vėr-land', *a.* Passing by land; made upon or across the land.

overlap, ō'vėr-lap", *vt.* To lap or fold over.—*n.* ō"vėr-lap', The lapping of one thing over another.

overlay, ō"vėr-lā', *vt.* To lay over; to coat or cover; to smother.

overload, ō"vėr-lōd', *vt.* To load too much; to overburden.

overlook, ō'vėr-lōk", *vt.* To oversee; to superintend; to view from a higher place; to pass by indulgently.

overlord, ō"vėr-lord', *n.* One who is lord over another; a feudal superior.

overmuch, ō"vėr-much', *a.* and *adv.* Too much.—*n.* More than sufficient.

overnight, ō"vėr-nīt', *adv.* Through or during the night; in the night before.

overpass, ō'vėr-päs", *vt.* To pass over; to overlook; to omit; to surpass.

overpay, ō'vėr-pā", *vt.* To pay too highly.

overpower, ō'vėr-pou"ėr, *vt.* To be too powerful for; to bear down by force; to overcome; to subdue; to crush. **overpowering,** ō'vėr-pou"ėr-ing, *p.a.* Excessive in degree or amount; irresistible.

overproduction, ō'vėr-prō-duk"shun, *n.* Production in excess of demand.

overrate, ō'vėr-rāt", *vt.* To rate at too much; to regard too highly.

overreach, ō'vėr-rēch", *vt.* To reach over or beyond; to deceive by artifice; to outwit.

override, ō'vėr-rīd", *vt.* To ride over; to supersede; to set at naught.

overrule, ō'vėr-rōl", *vt.* To control; to govern with high authority; to disallow.

overrun, ō'vėr-run", *vt.* To run or spread over; to ravage; to outrun.—*vi.* To overflow; to run over.

oversea, ō'vėr-sē', *a.* Foreign; from beyond sea. **overseas,** ō'vėr-sēz', *adv.* Abroad.

oversee, ō-vėr-sē', *vt.* To see or look over; to overlook; to superintend.

overseer, ō'vėr-sēr", *n.* One who oversees or overlooks; a superintendent; an inspector.

overshadow, ō'vėr-shad"ō, *vt.* To throw a shadow over; to shelter.

overshoe, ō"vėr-shō', *n.* A shoe worn over another; an outer waterproof shoe.

overshoot, ō-vėr-shōt', *vt.* To shoot over; to shoot beyond.

overshot, ō"vėr-shot', *p.a.* Shot beyond; having the water flowing on to the top as a water wheel.

oversight, ō"vėr-sīt', *n.* Superintendence; a mistake, error, omission, neglect.

overspread, ō'vėr-spred", *vt.* To spread over; to cover over; to scatter over.

overstate, ō′vėr-stāt″, *vt.* To state in too strong terms; to exaggerate in statement.

overstep, ō′vėr-step″, *vt.* To step over or beyond; to exceed.

overstock, ō′vėr-stok″, *vt.* To stock to excess; to fill too full.

overstrain, ō′vėr-strān″, *vt.* To strain or stretch too much; to exaggerate.—*vi.* To make too violent efforts.—*n.* ō′vėr-strān. Excessive strain; injurious effort.

overt, ō′vėrt, *a.* Open to view; manifest; not hidden; public; apparent.

overtake, ō′vėr-tāk″, *vt.* To come up with; to catch; to take by surprise

overtax, ō′vėr-taks″, *vt.* To tax too heavily; to make too severe demands upon.

overthrow, ō′vėr-thrō′, *vt.* To throw or turn over; to overset; to defeat; to destroy.—*n.* ō′vėr-thrō. Ruin defeat.

overtime, ō′vėr-tīm′, *n.* Time during which one works beyond the regular hours.

overtly, ō′vėrt-li, *adv.* Openly; publicly.

overture, ō′vėr-tūr, *n.* A proposal; offer; a musical introduction to oratorios, operas, &c.

overturn, ō′vėr-tėrn″, *vt.* To overset or overthrow; to capsize; to subvert; to ruin.

overweening, ō′vėr-wēn″ing, *a.* Haughty; arrogant; proud; conceited.

overweight, ō′vėr-wāt″, *vt.* To overburden.—*n.* Excess of weight; preponderance.

overwhelm, ō′vėr-hwelm″, *vt.* To whelm entirely; to swallow up; to submerge; to crush.

overwork, ō′vėr-wėrk″, *vt.* To work beyond strength; to tire with labor.—*n.* ō′vėr-wėrk. Work done beyond one's strength or beyond the amount required.

overwrought, ō′vėr-rat″, *p.a.* Wrought to excess; excited to excess; tasked beyond strength.

oviparous, ō-vip′a-rus, *a.* Bringing forth eggs; producing young from eggs.

ovoid, ō′void, *a.* Egg-shaped.

ovoviviparous, ō′vō-vī-vip″a-rus, *a.* Producing eggs which are hatched within the body (as is the case with vipers): opposed to *oviparous.*

ovum, ō-vum, *n.*; pl. **-ova.** A small vesicle within the ovary of a female, when impregnated becoming the embryo.

owe, ō, *vt.* (owing, owed). To be indebted in; to be obliged or bound to pay; to be obliged for. **owing**, ō′ing, *p. pr.* Required by obligation to be paid; ascribable; due.

owl, oul, *n.* A nocturnal bird of prey. **owlet**, oul′et, *n.* An owl; a young owl. **owlish**, oul′ish, *a.* Resembling an owl.

own, ōn, *a.* Belonging to; used distinctively and emphatically, after a possessive pronoun, or a noun in the possessive.—*vt.* To hold or possess by right; to acknowledge or avow; to concede. **owner**, ōn′ėr, *n.* One who owns; the rightful possessor or proprietor. **ownership**, ōn′ėr-ship, *n.* State of being an owner; legal or just claim or title.

ox, oks, *n.*: pl. **oxen**, ok′sen. Any animal of the bovine genus; a male of the bovine genus castrated.

oxide, ok′sīd, *n.* A compound of oxygen with another element. **oxidize**, ok′si-dīz, *vt.* To convert into an oxide; to cause to combine with oxygen.—*vi.* To change into an oxide. **oxidate**, ok′si-dāt, *vt.* To oxidize. **oxidation**, ok′si-dā″shun, *n.* The operation or process of converting into an oxide.

oxygen, ok′si-jen, *n.* A gaseous element, a component of atmospheric air and water, and essential to animal and vegetable life and combustion. **oxygenate**, ok′si-jen-āt, *vt.* To unite or cause to combine with oxygen. **oxygenize**, ok′si-jen-īz, *vt.* To oxygenate. **oxygenous**, oks-ij′en-us, *a.* Pertaining to, obtained from, or containing oxygen.

oyer, ō′yėr, *n.* A hearing or trial of causes in law.—*Court of oyer and terminer*, an English court for determining felonies and misdemeanors.

oyez, ō′yes. The introduction to a proclamation by a public crier, repeated three times.

oyster, ois′tėr, *n.* A bivalve shellfish or mollusk. **oyster bed**, ois′tėr bed, *n.* A bed or breeding-place of oysters.

ozone, ō′zōn, *n.* A kind of gas with a peculiar odor, a modification of oxygen existing in the atmosphere.

P

pabulum, pab′ū-lum, *n.* Food; that which feeds either mind or body. **pabular**, pab′ū-lėr, *a.* Pertaining to food. **pace**, pās, *n.* A step; space between the two feet in walking; distance of 2½ feet or 5 feet; gait; rate of progress.—*vi.* (pacing, paced). To step; to walk slowly; to move by lifting the legs on the same side together, as a horse.—*vt.*

To measure by steps; to accompany and set a proper rate of motion; to race. **pacer**, pās′ėr, *n.* One who paces; a horse trained to pace.

pachydermatous, pak′i-dėr″ma-tus, *a.* Thick-skinned; not sensitive to ridicule, sarcasm, &c.

pacify, pa′si-fī, *vt.* (pacifying, pacified). To give peace to; to appease; to allay. **pacific**, pa-sif′ik, *a.* Suited to make peace; pacifying; calm. **the Pacific Ocean**, the ocean between America, Asia, and Australia. **pacification**, pas′i-fi-kā″shun, *n.* Act of making peace; appeasement. **pacifier**, pa′si-fi-ér, *n.* One who pacifies.

pack, pak, *n.* A bundle; a bale; a set of playing-cards; a set of hounds or dogs; a gang.—*vt.* To make up into a bundle; to fill methodically with contents; to manipulate with fraudulent design; to dismiss without ceremony; to stuff.—*vi.* To make up bundles; to depart in haste (with *off* or *away*). **package**, pak′ij-*n.* A bundle or bale; a packet; charge for packing goods. **packer**, pak′ér, *n.* One who packs or prepares merchandise for transit.

packet, pak′et, *n.* A small pack; a parcel; a vessel employed regularly in carrying mail, goods, and passengers.

packhorse, pak′hors′, *n.* A horse employed in carrying goods and baggage on its back.

pack-ice, pak′īs′, *n.* An assemblage of large floating pieces of ice.

packing, pak′ing, *n.* Act of one who packs; material used in packing; stuffing.

pact, pakt, *n.* A contract; an agreement or covenant.

pad, pad, *n.* An easy-paced horse; a robber who invests the road on foot; a soft saddle; a cushion; a quantity of blotting-paper.—*vi.* (padding, padded). To walk or go on foot; to rob on foot.—*vt.* To furnish with padding. **padding**, pad′ing, *n.* Act of stuffing; material used in stuffing; literary matter inserted in a book, &c., merely to increase the bulk.

paddle, pad′l, *vi.* (paddling, paddled). To play in water with hands or feet; to row.—*vt.* To propel by an oar or paddle.—*n.* A broad short oar; a floatboard of a paddle-wheel. **paddle box**, pad′l boks, *n.* The wooden covering of the paddle-wheel of a steamer. **paddler**, pad′lér, *n.* One who paddles. **paddle wheel**, pad′l whēl, *n.* A wheel with boards on its circumference, propelling a steamship.

paddock, pad′uk, *n.* A toad or frog; an inclosure under pasture, usually adjoining a house.

paddy, pad′i, *n.* Rice in the husk, whether in the field or gathered.

padlock, pad″lok′, *n.* A lock with a link to be fastened through a staple.—*vt.* To fasten or provide with a padlock.

pæan, pē′an, *n.* A war song; song of triumph.

pagan, pā′gan, *n.* A heathen.—*a.* Heathenish; idolatrous. **paganism**, pā′gan-izm, *n.* Religious worship of pagans; heathenism.

page, pāj, *n.* A young male attendant on persons of distinction; one side of a leaf of a book; a written record.—*vt.* (paging, paged). To number the pages of.

pageant, paj′ent, *n.* Something intended for pomp; a show, as at a public rejoicing.—*a.* Showy; pompous. **pageantry**,

paj′ent-ri, *n.* Pageants collectively; show; pompous spectacle.

pagination, paj-i-nā″shun, *n.* Act of paging; figures indicating the number of pages.

pagoda, pa-gō′da, *n.* A Hindu or Buddhist temple.

paid, pād, *a.* No longer owed; recompensed.—*vt.* *past tense and past participle of* pay.

pail, pāl, *n.* An open vessel for carrying liquids. **pailful**, pāl′ful, *n.* The quantity that a pail will hold.

pain, pān, *n.* A penalty; bodily suffering; distress; anguish; *pl.* the throes of childbirth; labor; diligent effort.—*vt.* To cause pain to; to afflict; to distress. **painful**, pān′ful, *a.* Full of pain; distressing; grievous; difficult. **painless**, pān′les, *a.* Free from pain. **painstaking**, pānz″tāk′ing, *a.* Giving close application; laborious and careful.—*n.* The taking of pains; careful labor.

paint, pānt, *vt.* To represent by colors and figures; to cover with color; to portray; to delineate.—*vi.* To practice painting.—*n.* A substance used in painting; a pigment; rouge. **painter**, pān′tér, *n.* One whose occupation is to paint; one skilled in representing things in colors; a rope to fasten a boat. **painting**, pān′ting, *n.* Art or employment of laying on colors; art of representing objects by colors; a picture; colors laid on.

pair, pār, *n.* Two things of like kind, suited, or used together; a couple; a man and his wife; two members on opposite sides in parliament, &c., who agree not to vote for a time.—*vi.* To join in pairs; to mate.—*vt.* To unite in pairs.

Pakistani, pak′i-stan″i, *n.* A citizen of Pakistan, a republic of two separated provinces, northeast and northwest of India.

palace, pa′lis, *n.* The house in which an emperor, king, bishop, &c., resides; a splendid residence.

palanquin, palankeen, pal′an-kēn″, *n.* A covered conveyance used in India, China, &c.; borne on the shoulders of men.

palatable, pal′it-a-bl, *a.* Agreeable to the palate or taste; savory.

palate, pal′it, *n.* The roof of the mouth; taste; relish; intellectual taste. **palatal**, pal′a-tal, *a.* Pertaining to the palate; uttered by the aid of the palate.—*n.* A sound pronounced by the aid of the palate, as that of j.

palatial, pa-lā′shal, *a.* Pertaining to a palace; becoming a palace; magnificent.

palatinate, pa-lat′i-nāt, *n.* The province or seignory of a palatine.

palatine, pal′a-tīn, *a.* Pertaining to a palace; possessing royal privileges.— *County palatine*, a county over which an earl, bishop, or duke ruled with royal powers.—*n.* One invested with royal privileges and rights.

palaver, pa-läv′ér, *n.* A long or serious conference; idle talk.—*vt.* To flatter or humbug.—*vi.* To talk idly; to engage in a palaver.

pale, pāl, *n.* A pointed stake; an inclosure; sphere or scope.—*vt.* (paling, paled). To inclose with pales; to fence in.—*vi.* To turn pale.—*a.* Whitish; wan; deficient in color; not bright; dim.

Palestine, pal-es-tīn, *n.* The country of the Jews in Biblical times; now divided between Arab states and Israel.

palette, pal'et, *n.* A thin oval board on which a painter lays his pigments.

palfrey, pal'fri, *n.* A riding horse; a small horse fit for ladies.

palinode, pal'i-nōd, *n.* A recantation.

palisade, pa-li-sād', *n.* A fence or fortification of pales or posts.—*vt.* (palisading, palisaded). To surround or fortify with stakes.

pall, pal', *n.* An outer mantle of dignity; a cloth thrown over a coffin at a funeral; a linen cloth to cover a chalice; a covering.—*vt.* To cover with a pall; to shroud; to make vapid; to cloy.—*vt.* To become vapid or cloying.

palladium, pal-lā'di-um, *n.* A statue of the goddess Pallas; bulwark; safeguard; a grayish white hard malleable metal.

pallbearer, pal"bar'ēr, *n.* One who carries and attends casket at funerals.

pallet, pal'et, *n.* A palette; a tool used by potters, &c.; a small rude bed.

palliate, pal'i-āt, *vt.* To extenuate; to mitigate; to lessen, abate, alleviate. **palliation**, pal'i-ā'shon, *n.* Act of palliating; what serves to palliate. **palliative**, pal'i-ā-tiv, *a.* Serving to palliate. —*n.* That which palliates.

pallid, pal'id, *a.* Pale; wan.

pallor, pal'ēr, *n.* Paleness.

palm, pām, *n.* The inner part of the hand; a measure of 3 or 4 inches; a name of plants constituting an order of endogens; a branch or leaf of such a plant; victory; triumph.—*vt.* To conceal in the palm of the hand; to impose by fraud.

palmer, pām'ēr, *n.* A pilgrim that returned from the Holy Land with a branch of palm; one who palms or cheats.

palmistry, pālm'is-tri, *n.* The art of telling fortunes by the hand.

palm oil, pām'oil, *n.* A fatty substance resembling butter, obtained from palms.

Palm Sunday, pām' sun'dā, *n.* The Sunday before Easter.

palpable, pal'pa-bl, *a.* Perceptible by the touch; plain; obvious. **palpably**, pal'pa-bli, *adv.* Plainly; obviously.

palpitate, pal'pi-tāt, *vi.* (palpitating, palpitated). To pulsate rapidly; to throb; to tremble. **palpitation**, pal'pi-tā"shun, *n.* Act of palpitating; violent pulsation of the heart.

palsy, pal'zi, *n.* Paralysis, especially of a minor kind.—*vt.* (palsying, palsied). To affect with palsy; to paralyze.

paltry, pal'tri, *a.* Mean and trivial; trifling; worthless; contemptible.

pampas, pam'paz, *n.pl.* The immense grassy treeless plains of South America.

pamper, pam'pēr, *vt.* To gratify to the full; to furnish with that which delights.

pamphlet, pam'flet, *n.* A small book, stitched but not bound; a short treatise.

pamphleteer, pam'flet-ēr", *n.* A writer of pamphlets; a scribbler.

pan, pan, *n.* A broad and shallow vessel, of metal or earthenware; a pond for evaporating salt water to make salt; part of a gunlock holding the priming; the skull; the Greek and Roman god of flocks and herds.

panacea, pan'a-sē"a, *n.* A remedy for all diseases; a universal medicine.

Panama Canal, pan'a-mä ca-nal'. A canal across the Central American republic of Panama, connecting the Atlantic and Pacific oceans.

pancake, pan"kāk', *n.* A thin cake fried in a pan or baked on an iron plate.

pancreas, pan'krē-as, *n.* A fleshy gland or organ between the bottom of the stomach and the vertebræ; the sweetbread in cattle. **pancreatic**, pang'-krē-at"ik, *a.* Pertaining to the pancreas.

panda, pan'da, *n.* A black and white, bearlike animal of the Himalayas.

pandemonium, pan'dē-mō"ni-um, *n.* The abode of the evil spirits; any lawless, disorderly place or assemblage.

pander, pan'dēr, *n.* A pimp; a male bawd.—*vi.* To act as agent for the lusts of others; to be subservient to lust or desire. Also *pandar.*

pane, pān, *n.* A plate of glass inserted in a window, door, &c.; a panel.

panegyric, pan'ē-jir"ik, *n.* A laudatory speech; eulogy; encomium; laudation. **panegyric, panegyrical**, pan'ē-jir"-ik, pan'ē-jir"i-kal, *a.* Containing panegyric, praise, or eulogy; encomiastic.

panel, pan'el, *n.* A surface distinct from others adjoining in a piece of work; a sunk portion in a door, &c.; a piece of wood on which a picture is painted; list of those summoned to serve on a jury; in Scotland, the accused.—*vt.* (paneling, paneled). To form with panels. **paneling**, pan'el-ing, *n.* Paneled work.

pang, pang, *n.* A sharp and sudden pain; painful spasm; throe.

panic, pan'ik, *n.* A sudden fright; terror inspired by a trifling cause.—*a.* Extreme, sudden, or causeless; said of fright.

pannier, pan'yēr, *n.* A wicket-basket; a basket for a person's or beast's back.

panoply, pan'ō-pli, *n.* Complete armor of defense; a full suit of armor. **panoplied**, pan'ō-plid, *a.* Wearing a panoply.

panorama, pan'ō-rä"ma, *n.* A picture presenting from a central point a view of objects in every direction. **panoramic**, pan'ō-ram"ik, *a.* Belonging to or like a panorama.

pansy, pan'zi, *n.* A garden variety of violet; heart's-ease.

pant, pant, *vi.* To breathe quickly; to gasp; to desire ardently.—*n.* A gasp; a throb.

pantaloon, pan'ta-lön", *n.* A character in the old Italian comedy; in harlequinades, a fatuous old man, the butt of the clown. **pantaloons**, pan't'a-lönz", *n.pl.* Tightly fitting trousers; trousers in general.

pantheism, pan'thē-izm, *n.* The doctrine that the universe is God, or that all things are manifestations of God. **pantheist**, pan'thē-ist, *n.* One who believes in pantheism. **pantheistic**, pan'-

thē-is"tik, *a.* Pertaining to pantheism.

pantheon, pan'thē-on, *n.* A temple dedicated to all the gods; all the divinities collectively worshipped by a people.

panther, pan'thėr, *n.* A spotted carnivorous animal, otherwise called the leopard.

pantomime, pan'tō-mīm, *n.* A representation in dumb-show; a Christmas stage entertainment of the burlesque kind. **pantomimic,** pan'tō-mim"ik, *a.* Pertaining to pantomime or dumb-show.

pantry, pan'tri, *n.* An apartment in which provisions are kept, or where plate and knives, &c., are cleaned.

pants, pants, *n. pl.* Trousers.

panzer, pan'zėr, *a.* The German term for armor, referring to armored troops (tanks).

pap, pap, *n.* A kind of soft food for infants; the pulp of fruit; a teat; a round hill.

papa, pa-pä', *n.* A childish name for father.

papacy, pā'pa-si, *n.* The office and dignity of the pope; the popes collectively; papal authority or jurisdiction; popedom.

papal, pā'pal, *a.* Belonging to the pope.

papaw, pawpaw, pa-pạ', *n.* A tropical tree and its fruit, whose juice makes tough meat tender; papaya.

paper, pā'pėr, *n.* A substance formed into thin sheets used for writing, printing, &c.; a leaf, or sheet of this; a journal; an essay or article; promissory notes, bills of exchange, &c.—*a.* Made or consisting of paper; appearing merely in documents without really existing; slight.—*vt.* To cover with paper; to inclose in paper.

paper hanger, pā-pėr hang'ėr, *n.* One who lines walls with paper-hangings.

papier-mâché, pā'pėr-ma-shā', *n.* A material prepared by pulping different kinds of paper into a mass, which is molded into various articles, dried, and japanned.

papillary, pap'i-lėr-i, *a.* Pertaining to or resembling the nipple. Also *papillose.*

papist, pā'pist, *n.* A Roman Catholic.

papoose, pa-pōs', *n.* A North American Indian baby.

papyrus, pa-pī'rus, *n.*; pl. **-ri.** An Egyptian sedge, the stems of which afforded an ancient writing material; a written scroll of papyrus.

par, pär, *n.* State of equality; equality in condition or value; state of shares or stocks when they may be purchased at the original price.

parable, par'a-bl, *n.* An allegorical representation of something real in life or nature, embodying a moral.

parabola, pa-rab'ō-la, *n.* A conic section shown when a cone is cut by a plane parallel to one of its sides; the curve described theoretically by a projectile.

parabolic, parabolical, par'a-bol"ik, par'a-bol"i-kal, *a.* Expressed by or pertaining to parable; belonging to a parabola.

parachute, par'a-shöt, *n.* An apparatus like a large umbrella, enabling an aëro-

naut to drop to the ground without injury.

parade, pa-rād', *n.* Ostentation; show; military display; place where such display is held.—*vt.* (parading, paraded). To exhibit in ostentatious manner; to marshal in military order.—*vi.* To walk about for show; to go about in military procession.

paradigm, par'a-dim, *n.* A pattern, model, or example.

paradise, par'a-dīs, *n.* The garden of Eden; a place of bliss; heaven.

paradox, pa'ra-doks, *n.* An assertion or proposition seemingly absurd, yet true in fact; a seeming contradiction. **paradoxical,** par'a-dok"si-kal, *a.* Having the nature of a paradox; inclined to paradox.

paraffin, paraffine, par'a-fin, *n.* A solid white substance obtained from the distillation of wood, bituminous coal or shale, &c.

paragon, par'a-gon, *n.* A model; a perfect example of excellence.

paragraph, par'a-graf, *n.* The character ¶ used as a reference, &c.; a distinct section of a writing, distinguished by a break in the lines; a brief notice.

parakeet, par'a-kēt, *n. See* **parrakeet.**

parallax, par'a-laks, *n.* The apparent change of position of an object when viewed from different points; the difference between the place of a heavenly body as seen from the earth's surface and its center at the same time.

parallel, par'a-lel, *a.* Extended in the same direction, and in all parts equally distant, as lines or surfaces; running in accordance with something; equal in all essential parts.—*n.* A line which throughout its whole length is equidistant from another line; conformity in all essentials; likeness; comparison; counterpart.—*vt.* To place so as to be parallel; to correspond to; to compare.

parallelism, par'a-lel-izm, *n.* State of being parallel; resemblance; comparison.

parallelogram, par'a-lel"ō-gram, *n.* A quadrilateral, whose opposite sides are parallel and equal.

Parallelogram.

paralysis, pa-ral'i-sis, *n.* A diseased state of nerves by which the power of action or sensation is lost. **paralytic,** par'a-lit"ik, *a.* Pertaining to or affected with paralysis.—*n.* A person affected with palsy. **paralyze,** par'a-līz, *vt.* (paralyzing, paralyzed). To affect with paralysis; to reduce to a helpless state.

paramount, par'a-mount, *a.* Chief; superior.

paramour, par'a-mōr, *n.* A lover; one who wrongfully holds the place of a spouse.

paranoia, par'a-noi"a, *n.* A mental disorder characterized by delusions, as of grandeur or persecution.

parapet, par'a-pet, *n.* A wall or rampart breast-high; a wall on the edge of a bridge, quay, &c.

paraphernalia, par'a-fėr-nā"li-a, *n.pl.* That which a bride brings besides her dowry, as clothing, jewels, &c.; personal attire; trappings.

paraphrase, par'a-frāz, *n*. A statement giving the meaning of another statement; a loose or free translation; a sacred song based on a portion of Scripture.—*vt*. To make a paraphrase of; to explain or translate with latitude.

parasite, par'a-sīt, *n*. One who frequents the rich, and earns his welcome by flattery; a sycophant; an animal that lives upon or in another; a plant which grows on another. **parasitic, parasitical**, par'a-sit"-ik, par'a-sit"i-kal, *a*. Belonging to a parasite; living on some other body.

parasol, par'a-sol, *n*. A small umbrella used to keep off the sun's rays.

parboil, pär"boil', *vt*. To boil partly.

parcel, pär'sel, *n*. A portion of anything; a small bundle or package; a collection.—*vt*. (parceling, parceled.) To divide into portions; to make up into packages.

parcel post, pär'sel-pōst', *n*. Department of a post-office by which parcels are sent.

parch, pärch, *vt*. To dry to extremity; to scorch.—*vi*. To become very dry; to be scorched.

parchment, pärch'ment, *n*. The skin of a sheep or goat dressed for writing on; a document written on this substance.

pardon, pär'dn, *vt*. To forgive; to forbear to exact a penalty for; to overlook; to excuse. *n*. Forgiveness; remission of a penalty. **pardonable**, pär'dn-a-bl, *a*. That may be pardoned; venial; excusable. **pardoner**, pär'dun-ėr, *n*. One who pardons; formerly a seller of the pope's indulgences.

pare, pār, *vt*. (paring, pared). To trim by cutting; to dress; to cut away by little and little; to diminish.

paregoric, par'e-gor"ik, *a*. Encouraging; soothing; assuaging pain.—*n*. An anodyne.

parent, par'ent, *n*. One who brings forth or begets; a father or mother; a progenitor; cause; origin. **parentage**, par'en-tij, *n*. Extraction; birth **parental**, pa-rent'al, *a*. Pertaining to or becoming parents; tender; affectionate.

parenthesis, pa-ren'the-sis, *n*.; pl. **-theses**. A sentence or words inserted in another sentence, usually in curves, thus, ( ). **parenthetic, parenthetical**, par'en-thet"ik, par'en-thet"i-kal, *a*. Pertaining to or of the nature of a parenthesis.

pariah, pā'ri-a, *n*. One of the lowest class of people in Hindustan; an outcast.

paring, pār'ing, *n*. That which is pared off; rind; act of slicing off and burning the surface of grass-land.

parish, par'ish, *n*. An ecclesiastical division under the care of a priest or parson; a subdivision of a county for civil purposes.—*a*. Belonging to a parish; parochial. **parishioner**, pa-rish'un-ėr, *n*. One who belongs to a parish; a member of the parish church.

Parisian, par-rizh'an, *a*. Pertaining to Paris.—*n*. A native or resident of Paris.

parity, par'i-ti, *n*. Equality; likeness; like state or degree; analogy.

park, pärk, *n*. A piece of ground inclosed; ornamental ground adjoining a house; ground in a town for recreation; an assemblage of heavy ordnance.—*vt*. To inclose in a park; leave in a particular place for a while, as a car.

parlance, pär'lans, *n*. Conversation; talk; idiom.

parley, pär'li, *vi*. To confer; to discuss orally.—*n*. Mutual discourse; conference with an enemy in war.

parliament, pär'li-ment, *n*. An assembly of persons for deliberation, &c.; the legislature of Great Britain and Ireland; any similar legislative assembly. **parliamentarian**, pär'li-men-tār"i-an, *n*. An adherent of parliament; one of those who adhered to the parliament in the time of Charles I. **parliamentary**, pär'li-men"ta-ri, *a*. Pertaining to, done by, or according to the rules and usages of parliament.

parlor, pär'lėr, *n*. The sitting-room in a house which the family usually occupy.

parochial, pa-rō'ki-al, *a*. Belonging to a parish; narrow in views; provincial.

parody, par'o-di, *n*. An adaptation of the words of an author, &c., to a different purpose; a burlesque imitation.—*vt*. (parodying, parodied). To imitate in parody.

parole, pa-rōl', *n*. Words or oral declarations; word of honor; a promise by a prisoner of war not to bear arms against his captors for a certain period, or the like; a military countersign.—*a*. Oral; not written.

paroxysm, par'ok-sizm, *n*. A violent access of feeling (as of rage); convulsion; spasm.

parquetry, pär'ket-ri, *n*. Inlaid woodwork, principally used for floors.

parrakeet, par'a-kēt, *n*. A small parrot of the eastern hemisphere.

parricide, par'i-sīd, *n*. A person who murders his father or mother; the murder of a parent.

parrot, par'ut, *n*. A family of birds, including parrakeets, macaws, cockatoos, &c.; a bird which can imitate the human voice.

parry, par'i, *vt*. and *i*. (parrying, parried). To ward off.

parse, pärs, *vt*. (parsing, parsed). To tell the relation of the parts of speech in a sentence.

parsimony, pär'si-mō'ni, *n*. The habit of being sparing in expenditure of money; excessive frugality; miserliness; closeness. **parsimonious**, pär'si-mō"ni-us, *a*. Niggardly; miserly; penurious.

parsley, pärs'li, *n*. A garden vegetable, used for flavoring in cooking.

parsnip, pärs'nip, *n*. An umbelliferous plant with a fleshy esculent root.

parson, pär'sn, *n*. The priest or incumbent of a parish; a clergyman. **parsonage**, pär'sn-ij, *n*. The official dwelling-house of a parson.

part, pärt, *n*. A portion or piece of a whole; a section; a constituent or organic portion; share; lot; party; duty;

business; character assigned to an actor in a play; *pl.* faculties; superior endowments; regions; locality.—*vt.* To divide; to sever; to share; to distribute; to intervene.—*vi.* To become separated, broken, or detached; to quit each other; to depart.

partake, pär-tāk', *vi.* (partaking; pret. partook; pp. partaken). To take or have a part with others; to share; to have something of the nature, claim, or right. —*vt.* To share. **partaker**, pär-tāk'ėr, *n.* One who partakes; a sharer; accomplice; associate.

parterre, pär-tār', *n.* A piece of ground with flower-beds; the pit of a theater.

partial, pär'shal, *a.* Belonging to or affecting a part only; not general; biased to one party; having a fondness **partiality**, pär'shi-al"i-ti, *n.* Unfair bias; undue favor shown; a liking or fondness.

participate, par-tis'i-pāt, *vi.* and *t.* To partake, share. **participation**, pär-tis'-i-pā"shun, *n.* Act of participating; a sharing with others. **participator**, pär-tis"i-pā-tėr, *n.* One who participates or partakes; a partaker.

participle, par'ti-si-pl, *n.* A word having the properties of both an adjective and verb.

particle, pär'ti-kl, *n.* An atom; a jot; a very small portion; a word not inflected.

particular, pėr-tik'ū-lėr, *a.* Pertaining to a single person or thing; private; special; exact; precise; circumstantial; notable; fastidious.—*n.* A single instance; detail; distinct circumstance. **particularity**, pėr-tik"ū-lar"i-ti, *a.* State or quality of being particular; minuteness of detail; that which is particular. **particularize**, pėr-tik'ū-lėr-īz, *vt.* To make particular mention of; to specify in detail.—*vi.* To be particular to details.

parting, pär'ting, *p.a.* Serving to part or divide; given at separation; departing.—*n.* Division; separation; leave-taking.

partisan, partizan, pär'ti-zan, *n.* An adherent of a party or faction; a party man.—*a.* Adhering to a faction.

partition, pär-tish'un, *n.* Act of parting or dividing; division; a division-wall; part where separation is made.—*vt.* To divide by partitions; to divide into shares.

partly, pärt'li, *adv.* In part; in some measure.

partner, pärt'nėr, *n.* One who shares with another; an associate in business; a husband or wife. **partnership**, pärt'-nėr-ship, *n.* Fellowship; the association of two or more persons in any business; joint interest or property.

partridge, pär'trij, *n.* A game bird of the grouse family.

parturition, pär'tū-rish"un, *n.* The act of bringing forth young.

party, pär'ti, *n.* A body of individuals; one of two litigants; a company made up for an occasion; a single person; a detachment of troops.—*a.* Of or pertaining to a party.

parvenu, pär've-nū, *n.* An upstart; a

person who has newly risen to eminence.

paschal, pas'kal, *a.* Pertaining to the passover or to Easter.

pasha, pa-shä', pä'sha, *n.* A Turkish governor of a province, or military commander.

pass, pas, *vi.* (pret. and pp., passed or past). To go by or past; to change; to die; to elapse; to be enacted; to be current; to thrust in fencing or fighting; to go successfully through an examination.—*vt.* To go past, beyond, or over; to cross; to live through; to undergo with success (as an examination); to circulate; to utter; to take no notice of; to enact; to thrust; to void, as fæces.—*n.* A passage; a defile; a license to pass; a thrust; manipulation; condition; extremity. **passable**, pas'a-bl, *a.* That may be passed, traveled, or navigated; current; tolerable; allowable; pretty fair.

passage, pas'ij, *n.* Act of passing; transit; a journey, especially by a ship; a road; channel; a gallery or corridor; access; episode; part of a book, &c., referred to; enactment; an encounter.

passbook, pas'buk, *n.* A book in which to enter articles bought on credit; bankbook.

passé, passée, pa-sä', *a.* Past; faded; past the heyday of life.

passenger, pas'en-jėr, *n.* A traveler; one who travels in a public conveyance.

passible, pas'i-bl, *a.* Capable of feeling; susceptible of impressions.

passion, pash'un, *n.* A suffering or enduring; the last suffering of Christ; a strong feeling or emotion; violent anger; ardor; vehement desire; love. **passionate**, pa'shun-it, *a.* Moved by passion; vehement; animated; irascible; hasty. **passionless**, pa'shun-les, *a.* Void of passion; calm of temper.

Passion play, pa'shun-plā', *n.* A play representing scenes in the passion of Christ.

passive, pas'iv, *a.* Capable of feeling; suffering; not acting; unresisting; inert; in *grammar*, expressing that the nominative is the object of some action or feeling.

passkey, pas"kē', *n.* A key for several locks, a master key; a latch key.

passover, pas"ō'vėr, *n.* A feast of the Jews commemorative of the deliverance in Egypt, when the destroying angel passed over the houses of the Israelites; the sacrifice offered.

passport, pas'pōrt, *n.* A license empowering a person to travel; that which enables one to reach some desired object.

password, pas'wėrd, *n.* A secret word to distinguish a friend from a stranger.

past, past, *p.a.* Gone by or beyond; belonging to an earlier period; spent; ended.—*n.* Former time.—*prep.* Beyond; out of reach of; after.—*adv.* By; so as to pass.

paste, pāst, *n.* A mass in a semi-fluid state; a mixture of flour, &c., used in cookery, or to cause substances to adhere; a mixture of clay for pottery; a brilliant glassy substance, used in making imitations of gems.—*vt.* (pasting, pasted). To unite or fasten with paste.

pasteboard, pāst″bŏrd′, *n.* A thick paper formed of sheets pasted together; cardboard.

pastel, pas-tel′, *n.* A colored crayon; a drawing made with colored crayons; the art of drawing with colored crayons.

pasteurize, pas′tẽr-īz, *vt.* To sterilize milk after the manner of Pasteur.

pastime, pas″tim′, *n.* Recreation; diversion; sport; play.

pastor, pas′tẽr, *n.* A minister of a church. **pastoral,** pas′to-ral, *a.* Pertaining to shepherds; rustic; rural; relating to the care of souls, or to a pastor.—*n.* A poem dealing with shepherds; a poem of rural life; a letter addressed by a bishop to the clergy and people of his diocese. **pastorate,** pas′tẽr-it, *n.* Office or jurisdiction of a pastor; the body of pastors.

pastry, pās′tri, *n.* Eatables made of paste; crust of pies, tarts, &c.

pasture, pas′tūr, *n.* Grass for the food of cattle; grazing ground; grass land.—*vt.* (pasturing, pastured). To feed on growing grass.—*vi.* To graze. **pasturage,** pas′tūr-ij, *n,* Grazing ground; growing grass for cattle.

pasty, pās′ti, *a.* Like paste.—*n.* A meat pie covered with paste.

pat, pat, *n.* A light stroke with the fingers or hand; a tap; a small lump of butter beat into shape.—*vt.* (patting, patted). To strike gently; to tap.—*a.* Hitting the mark; apt; convenient.—*adv.* Fitly; just in the nick.

patch, pach, *n.* A piece of cloth sewed on a garment to repair it; a small piece of silk stuck on the face for adornment; a small piece of ground.—*vt.* To mend by sewing on a patch; to repair clumsily; to make hastily without regard to forms (with *up*).

patchwork, pach″wẽrk′, *n.* Work composed of varied pieces sewed together; work composed of pieces clumsily put together.

patchy, pach′i, *a.* Full of patches.

pate, pāt, *n.* The head, or rather the top of the head.

patella, pa-tel′a, *n.* A small pan, vase, or dish; the knee-pan.

patent, pat′ent; pā′tent, *n.* A writing (called *letters patent*) granting a privilege, as a title of nobility; a similar writing, securing exclusive right to an invention or discovery.—*a.* Open; manifest; secured by patent; lacquered (leather).—*vt.* To secure, as the exclusive right of a thing to a person.

patentee, pat′en-tē″; pā′ten-tē″, *n.* One to whom a patent is granted.

paternal, pa-tẽr′nal, *a.* Fatherly; derived from the father; hereditary. **paternity,** pa-tẽr′ni-ti, *n.* Fathership, relationship of a father to his offspring; origin; authorship.

paternoster, pā′tẽr-nos′tẽr, *n.* The Lord's prayer; a rosary; every tenth bead in a rosary.

path, path, *n.* A way beaten by the feet of man or beast; a footway; course or track; way or passage; course of life.

pathetic, pa-thet′ik, *a.* Full of pathos; affecting; exciting pity, sorrow, &c.

pathologic, pathological, path′ō-loj″ik, path′ō-loj″i-kal, *a.* Pertaining to pathology.

pathologist, pa-thol′ō-jist, *n.* One who is versed in or who treats of pathology.

pathology, pa-thol′ō-ji, *n.* That part of medicine which explains the nature of diseases, their causes and symptoms.

pathos, pā′thos, *n.* Expression of strong or deep feeling; that quality which excites tender emotions, as pity, sympathy, &c.

pathway, path″wā′, *n.* A path; course of life.

patient, pā′shent, *a.* Enduring without murmuring; not easily provoked; persevering; not hasty.—*n.* A person or thing passively affected; a person under medical treatment. **patience,** pā′shens, *n.* Quality of being patient; endurance; composure; forbearance.

patina, pat′i-na, *n.* The fine green rust on ancient bronzes, copper coins, &c.

patois, pat′wä, *n.* A rustic or provincial form of speech.

patriarch, pā′tri-ärk, *n.* The chief of a race, tribe, or family; a dignitary above an archbishop in the Greek Church. **patriarchal,** pā′tri-är″kal, *a.* Belonging to a patriarch; subject to a patriarch.

patrician, pa-trish′an, *n.* Belonging to the senators of ancient Rome; of noble birth.—*n.* A person of noble birth.

patrimony, pat′ri-mō′ni, *n.* A paternal inheritance; a church estate or revenue. **patrimonial,** pat′ri-mō′ni-al, *a.* Pertaining to a patrimony; inherited.

patriot, pā′tri-ut, or pat′, *n.* A person who loves his country, and zealously defends its interest.—*a.* Patriotic. **patriotism,** pā′tri-ut-izm or pat′, *n.* The qualities of a patriot; love of one's country. **patriotic,** pā′tri-ot″ik, or pat-, *a.* Actuated or inspired by the love of one's country; directed to the public welfare.

patrol, pa-trōl′, *n.* The marching round by a guard at night to secure the safety of a camp; the guards who go such rounds.—*vi.* (patrolling, patrolled). To go the rounds as a patrol.—*vt.* To pass round, as a guard.

patron, pā′trun, *n.* A protector; one who supports or protects a person or a work; one who has the disposition of a church-living, professorship, or other appointment; a guardian saint. **patronage,** pā′trun-ij; pat′, *n.* Act of patronizing; special support; guardianship, as of a saint; right of presentation to an ecclesiastical benefice. **patroness,** pā′trun-es, *n.* A female patron. **patronize,** pā′trun-īz; pat′, *vt.* To act as patron of; to countenance or favor; to assume the air of a superior to. **patronizing,** pā′trun-īz′ing; pat″, *p.a.* Assuming the airs of a patron; acting like one who condescends to patronize or favor.

patronymic, pat′rō-nim″ik, *n.* A name derived from that of parents or ancestors.

patter, pat′ẽr, *vi.* To make a sound like that of falling drops; to move with quick steps; to mumble; to talk in a glib way.—*n.* A quick succession of small sounds; chatter; prattle.

pattern, pat'ērn, *n.* A model proposed for imitation; a sample; an ornamental design.

patty, pat'i, *n.* A little pie; a pasty.

paucity, pa̤'si-ti, *n.* Fewness; scarcity; smallness of quantity.

Pauline, pal'īn, *a.* Pertaining to St. *Paul*, or to his writings.

paunch, pansh, *n.* The belly, and its contents; the abdomen. **paunchy**, pan-chi, *a.* Big-bellied.

pauper, pa̤'pėr, *n.* A poor person; one dependent on the public for maintenance. **pauperism**, pa̤'pėr-izm, *n.* State of indigent persons requiring public support. **pauperize**, pa̤'pėr-iz, *vt.* To reduce to pauperism.

pause, pa̤z, *n.* A temporary cessation; cessation proceeding from doubt; suspense.—*vi.* (pausing, paused). To make a short stop: to delay; to deliberate; to hesitate.

pave, pāv, *vt.* (paving, paved). To cover with stone, brick, &c., so as to make a level and solid surface for carriages or foot passengers. **pavement**, pāv'ment, *n.* The solid floor of a street, courtyard, &c.; paved part of a road used by foot passengers; material with which anything is paved.

pavilion, pa-vil'yun, *n.* A tent; a small building having a tent-formed roof; a building of ornamental character for entertainments; the outer ear.—*vt.* To furnish with pavilions; to shelter with a tent.

paving, pāv'ing, *n.* Pavement.—*a.* Used for pavements.

paw, pa̤, *n.* The foot of animals having claws.—*vi.* To draw the forefoot along the ground.—*vt.* To scrape with the forefoot; to handle roughly.

pawl, pa̤l, *n.* A short bar preventing a capstan, &c., from rolling back.

pawn, pan, *n.* Something given as security for money borrowed; a pledge; state of being pledged; a pawnshop; a piece of the lowest rank in chess.—*vt.* To give in pledge; to pledge with a pawnbroker. **pawnbroker**, pan'brō'kėr, *n.* A person licensed to lend money at a legally fixed rate of interest on goods deposited with him.

pay, pā, *vt.* (paying, paid). To give money, &c., for goods received or service rendered; to reward; to discharge, as a debt; to give; to cover with tar or pitch. —*vi.* To make a payment; to be profitable or remunerative.—*n.* An equivalent for money due, goods, or services; salary; wages; reward. **payable**, pā'a-bl, *a.* That may or ought to be paid; justly due.

payee, pā'ē̄, *n.* One to whom money is to be paid.

paymaster, pā'mas'tėr, *n.* An officer whose duty is to pay the men their wages.

payment, pā'ment, *n.* Act of paying; what is given for service done; reward.

pea, pē, *n.*; pl. **peas**, **pease**. A well-known flowering plant cultivated for its seeds; one of the seeds of the plant.

peace, pēs, *n.* A state of quiet; calm; repose; public tranquillity; freedom from war; concord. **peaceable**, pēs'a-bl, *a.* Disposed to peace; peaceful; pacific; calm. **peaceful**, pēs'ful, *a.* Free from war, noise, or disturbance; quiet; mild.

peacemaker, pēs'māk'ėr, *n.* One who reconciles parties at variance.

peace offering, pēs' of'ėr-ing, *n.* Something offered to procure reconciliation.

peach, pēch, *n.* A well-known tree and its fruit, allied to the almond.—*vi.* To betray one's accomplice.

peacock, pē'kok', *n.* A large gallinaceous bird with rich plumage; properly the male bird.

pea jacket, pē' jak'et, *n.* A thick woolen jacket worn by seamen, fishermen, &c.

peak, pēk, *n.* A projecting point; the top of a mountain ending in a point; the upper corner of a sail extended by a yard; also, the extremity of the yard or gaff.—*vi.* To look sickly; to be emaciated. **peaked**, pēkt, *a.* Ending in a peak or point.

peal, pēl, *n.* A series of loud sounds, as of bells, thunder, &c.; a set of bells tuned to each other; chime.—*vi.* To give out a peal.—*vt.* To cause to ring or sound.

peanut, pē'nut, *n.* A Brazilian herb (*Arachis hypogaea*) whose flowers push themselves into the ground and ripen to form pods with nutlike seeds. The seed, when roasted, can be crushed into paste as peanut butter.

pear, pār, *n.* A well-known fruit-tree; one of the fruits of the tree.

pearl, pėrl, *n.* A smooth lustrous whitish gem produced by certain mollusks; something resembling a pearl; a small printing type; what is choicest and best.—*a.* Relating to or made of pearl or mother-of-pearl.—*vt.* To set or adorn with pearls.

pearly, pėr'li, *a.* Containing pearls; like a pearl or mother-of-pearl; clear; pure.

peasant, pez'ant, *n.* A rustic; one whose business is rural labor.—*a.* Rustic. **peasantry**, pez'an-tri, *n.* Peasants; rustics; the body of country people.

peat, pēt, *n.* A kind of turf used as fuel; a small block of this cut and dried for fuel.

pebble, peb'l, *n.* A stone rounded by the action of water; agate and rock-crystal used for glass in spectacles. **pebbly**, peb'li, *a.* Full of pebbles.

pecan, pē-kan', -kän', *n.* A species of hickory and its fruit.

peccable, pek'a-bl, *a.* Liable to sin; apt to transgress the divine law.

peccadillo, pek'a-dil'ō, *n.* A slight trespass or offense; a petty crime or fault.

peccary, pek'a-ri, *n.* A quadruped of America, allied to the swine.

peck, pek, *n.* A dry measure of eight quarts.—*vt.* and *i.* To strike with the beak, or something pointed; to pick up, as food, with the beak.

pecker, pek'ėr, *n.* One who or that which pecks; a woodpecker.

pectic, pek'tik, *a.* Having the property of forming a jelly.

pectoral, pek'to-ral, *a.* Pertaining to the breast.—*n.* A breastplate; a medicine for the chest and lungs.

peculate, pek'ū-lāt, *vi.* To appropriate money or goods intrusted to one's care. **peculation,** pe-kū-lā'shon, *n.* Act of peculating; embezzlement. **peculator,** pek"ū-lātèr, *n.* One who peculates.

peculiar, pě-kūl'yèr, *a.* One's own; characteristic; particular; unusual; odd. **peculiarity,** pě-kū'li-ar"i-ti, *n.* Quality of being peculiar, something peculiar to a person or thing.

pecuniary, pě-kū'ni-er'i, *a.* Relating to or connected with money; consisting of money.

pedagogue, ped'a-gog, *n.* A teacher of children, a schoolmaster. **pedagogic,** ped'a-goj"ik, *a.* Resembling or belonging to a pedagogue. **pedagogics,** ped'a-goj"iks, *n.* The science or art of teaching. **pedagogy,** ped'a-gō-ji, *n.* The art or office of a pedagogue; the teaching profession.

pedal, pěd'al, *a.* Pertaining to a foot or to a pedal.—*n.* pe'dal. A lever to be pressed by the foot; a part of a musical instrument acted on by the feet.

pedant, ped'ant, *n.* One who makes a vain display of his learning; a narrow-minded scholar. **pedantic,** pe-dan'tik, *a.* Pertaining to or characteristic of a pedant. **pedantry,** ped'ant-ri, *n.* The qualities or character of a pedant; boastful display of learning; obstinate adherence to rules.

peddle, ped'l, *vi.* and *t.* (peddling, peddled). To travel and sell small-wares; to trifle. **peddler,** ped'lèr, *n.* One who peddles; a pedlar.

pedestal, pe'des-tal, *n.* The base or support of a column, pillar, statue, vase, &c.

pedestrian, pe-des'tri-an, *a.* Going on foot; performed on foot.—*n.* One who journeys on foot.

pediatrics, pē-di-at'riks, *n.* Branch of medicine dealing in the treatment of children. **pediatrician,** pē'di-a-trish"-an, *n.* Doctor specializing in treatment of children.

pedigree, ped'i-grē, *n.* Lineage; line of ancestors; genealogy.

pediment, ped'i-ment, *n.* The triangular mass resembling a gable at the end of buildings in the Greek style; a triangular decoration over a window, a door, &c.

pedlar, pedler, ped'lèr, *n.* A petty dealer who carries his wares with him.

pedometer, pe-dom'ē-tèr, *n.* An instrument which measures how far a person walks.

peel, pēl, *vt.* To strip off, as bark or rind; to flay; to pare; to pillage.—*vi.* To lose the skin, bark, or rind; to fall off, as bark or skin.—*n.* The skin or rind; a baker's wooden shovel.

peep, pēp, *vi.* To chirp as a chicken; to begin to appear; to look through a crevice.—*n.* A chirp; a look through a small opening; first appearance.

peer, pèr, *n.* One of the same rank; an equal; an associate; a nobleman (duke, marquis, earl, viscount, or baron).—*vi.* To appear; to peep out; to look narrowly. **peerage,** pèr'ij, *n.* The rank or dignity of a peer; the body of peers. **peeress,** pèr'es, *n.* A woman ennobled

by descent, by creation, or by marriage.

peerless, pèr'les, *a.* Matchless.

peevish, pē'vish, *a.* Fretful; querulous; hard to please; forward.

peg, peg, *n.* A piece of wood used in fastening things together; the pin of a musical instrument; a pin on which to hang anything.—*vt.* (pegging, pegged). To fasten with pegs.—*vi.* To work diligently.

pekoe, pē'kō, *n.* A fine black tea.

pelagic, pe-laj'ik, *a.* Belonging to the ocean; inhabiting the open ocean.

pelican, pel'i-kan, *n.* A large web-footed bird with a very large bill.

pellagra, pe-la'gra, *n.* A disease characterized by skin eruptions and nervous gastric disorders, caused by dietary deficiencies.

pellet, pel'et, *n.* A little ball; one of the globules of small shot.

pell-mell, pellmeel, pel'mel', *adv.* With confused violence; in utter confusion.

pellucid, pe-lū'sid, *a.* Transparent; not opaque; translucent.

pelt, pelt, *n.* A raw hide; a blow; a heavy shower.—*vt.* To strike with something thrown.—*vi.* To throw missiles; to fall in a heavy shower.

pelvis, pel'vis, *n.* The bony cavity forming the framework of the lower part of the abdomen. **pelvic,** pel'vik, *a.* Pertaining to the pelvis.

pen, pen, *n.* An instrument for writing with ink; style or quality of writing; a small inclosure for cows, &c.; a fold.—*vt.* (penning, penned). To write; to compose; to coop or shut up.

penal, pē'nal, *a.* Relating to, enacting, or incurring punishment. **penalty,** pen'al-ti, *n.* Punishment for a crime or offense; forfeit for non-fulfillment of conditions; sum to be forfeited; a fine.

penance, pen'ans, *n.* An ecclesiastical punishment imposed for sin; voluntary suffering as an expression of penitence.

pence, pens, *n.* The plural of *penny.*

penchant, pen'chant, *n.* Strong inclination; bias.

pencil, pen'sil, *n.* A small brush used by painters; an instrument of black-lead, &c., for writing and drawing; a converging or diverging aggregate of rays of light.—*vt.* (penciling, penciled). To write or mark with a pencil.

pend, pend, *vi.* To impend; to wait for settlement.

pendant, pen'dant, *n.* Anything hanging down by way of ornament; a hanging apparatus for giving light, &c.; an appendix or addition; a flag borne at the mast-head.

pendent, pen'dent, *a.* Hanging; pendulous; projecting.—*n.* Something hanging.

pending, pend'ing, *p.a.* Hanging in suspense; undecided.—*pret.* During.

pendulous, pen'dū-lus, *a.* Hanging; hanging so as to swing; swinging.

pendulum, pen'dū-lum, *n.* A body suspended and swinging; the swinging piece in a clock which regulates its motion.

penetrate, pen'e-trāt, *vt.* and *i.* To enter or pierce, as into another body; to affect, as the mind; to cause to feel; to understand. **penetration**, pen'e-trā"-shun, *n.* Act of penetrating; sagacity; discernment. **penetrative**, pe'ne-trăt-iv, *a.* Piercing; sharp; subtle; acute; discerning. **penetrable**, pen'e-tra-bl, *a.* That may be entered or pierced; susceptible of moral or intellectual impression.

penguin, pen'gwin, *n.* A web-footed sea bird having rudimentary wings useless for flight but effective in swimming.

penicillin, pen'i-sil'in, *n.* An antibiotic derived from a mold similar to the green mold that grows on bread.

peninsula, pen-in'sū-la, *n.* A portion of land almost surrounded by water. **peninsular**, pen-in'sū-lẽr *a.* In the form of, pertaining to, or inhabiting a peninsula.

penis, pē'nis, *n.* The male organ of generation.

penitent, pen'i-tent, *a.* Suffering sorrow on account of one's own sins; contrite.—*n.* One who repents of sin. **penitence**, pen'i-tens, *n.* State of being penitent; repentance; contrition. **penitential**, pen-i-ten'shal, *a.* Pertaining to or expressing penitence.—*n.* A Roman Catholic book of rules for penitents.

penitentiary, pen-i-ten'sha-ri, *a.* Relating to penance.—*n.* One who does penance; an office or official of the R. Catholic church connected with the granting of dispensations, &c.; a house of correction.

penknife, pen'nīf', *n.* A small pocketknife.

penman, pen'man, *n.*; pl. **-men.** A man who teaches writing; a writer. **penmanship**, pen'man-ship, *n.* The use of the pen; art or manner of writing.

pennant, pen'ant, *n.* A small flag; a pennon; a pendant.

penniless, pen'i-les, *a.* Without money.

pennon, pen'ūn, *n.* A small pointed flag carried on spears or lances.

penny, pen'i, *n.*; pl. **pennies** or **pence**, pen'iz, pens. (*Pennies* denotes the number of coins; *pence* the value.) A bronze English coin, the twelfth of a shilling; money.

pennyweight, pen''i-wāt', *n.* A troy weight containing twenty-four grains.

penny-wise, pen'i-wīz', *a.* Wise in saving small sums at the hazard of larger.

pension, pen'shun, *n.* A stated yearly allowance in consideration of past services; a boarding-house on the Continent (pronounced päng-syong).—*vt.* To grant a pension to. **pensionary**, pen'shun-er-i, *a.* Receiving a pension; consisting in a pension.—*n.* A pensioner. **pensioner** pen'shun-ẽr, *n.* One in receipt of a pension; a student at Cambridge (Eng.), who pays for his board and other charges.

pensive, pen'siv, *a.* Thoughtful; expressing thoughtfulness with sadness.

pent, pent, *p.a.* Shut up; confined (often with *up*).

pentagon, pen'ta-gon, *n.* A plane figure having five angles and five sides. **pen-**

tagonal, pen-tag'o-nal, *a.* Having five corners or angles.

pentahedron, pen'ta-hē"drun, *n.* A solid figure having five equal faces.

pentameter, pen-tam'e-tẽr, *n.* A poetic verse of five feet.

Pentateuch, pen'ta-tūk, *n.* The first five books of the Old Testament.

Pentecost, pen'tē-kost, *n.* A festival of the Jews on the fiftieth day after the Passover; Whitsuntide.

penthouse, pent'hous, *n.* A luxury apartment on top of a building.

penury, pen'ū-ri, *n.* Poverty; indigence; want of the necessaries of life. **penurious**, pe-nū'ri-us, *a.* Pertaining to penury; parsimonious; niggardly.

peon, pē'on, *n.* An attendant; a native constable; a day-laborer; a kind of serf.

peony, pē'o-ni, *n.* A genus of plants of the ranunculus family, with large flowers.

people, pē'pl, *n.* The body of persons who compose a community, race, or nation; persons indefinitely.—*vt.* (peopling, peopled). To stock with inhabitants; to populate.

pepper, pep'ẽr, *n.* A plant and its aromatic pungent seed, much used in seasoning, &c.—*vt.* To sprinkle with pepper; to pelt with shot or missiles; to drub thoroughly.

peppercorn, pep'ẽr-korn', *n.* The berry or fruit of the pepper plant.

peppermint, pep'ẽr-mint, *n.* A plant of the mint genus having a penetrating aromatic smell and a strong pungent taste.

peppery, pep'ẽr-i, *a.* Having the qualities of pepper; choleric; irascible.

pepsin, **pepsine**, pep'sin, *n.* The active principle of gastric juice.

peptic, pep'tik, *a.* Promoting digestion; relating to digestion; digestive.

per, pẽr, *prep.* A Latin preposition used in the sense of *by* or *for*, chiefly in certain Latin phrases, as *per annum*, by or for the year.

peradventure, pẽr'ad-ven"tūr, *adv.* Perhaps.

perambulate, pẽr-am'bū-lāt, *vt.* To walk through or over; to traverse; to survey. **perambulation**, pẽr-am'bū-lā"shun, *n.* Act of perambulating; survey or inspection. **perambulator**, pẽr-am'bū-lā'ter, *n.* One who perambulates; a child's carriage propelled by hand from behind.

perceive, pẽr-sēv', *vt.* (perceiving, perceived). To apprehend by the organs of sense or by the mind; to observe; to discern. **perceivable**, pẽr-sēv'a-bl, *a.* That may be perceived; perceptible.

percentage, pẽr-sen'tij, *n.* The allowance, duty, rate of interest, proportion, &c., reckoned on each hundred.

perceptible, pẽr-sep'ti-bl, *a.* Perceivable. **perception**, pẽr-sep'shun, *n.* Act, process, or faculty of perceiving; discernment. **perceptive**, pẽr-sep'tiv, *a.* Relating to perception; having the faculty of perceiving.

perch, pẽrch, *n.* A spiny fresh-water fish; a roost for fowls; an elevated place or position; 5½ yards, also called a rod or pole; 30¼ square yards, a square rod.—*vi.* To sit on a perch; to light, as a bird.—*vt.* To place on a perch.

perchance, pėr-chans', *adv.* Perhaps.

percolate, pėr'kō-lāt, *vt.* and *i.* To strain through; to filter. **percolation**, pėr'kō-lā"shun, *n.* Act of percolating; passing of liquid through a porous body. **percolator**, pėr'kō-lā-tėr, *n.* One who or that which filters.

percussion, pėr-kush'un, *n.* Collision; impact; the act of striking the surface of the body to determine by sound the condition of the organs subjacent.

perdition, pėr-dish'un, *n.* Entire ruin; utter destruction; eternal death.

peregrinate, per'ē-gri-nāt, *vi.* To travel from place to place; to wander. **peregrination**, per'e-gri-nā"shun, *n.* A traveling; a wandering.

peremptory, per'emp-tō-ri, *a.* Such as to preclude debate; decisive; absolute. **peremptorily**, per'emp-tō-ri-li, *adv.* In a peremptory manner; absolutely; positively.

perennial, per-en'i-al, *a.* Lasting through the year; perpetual; unceasing. —*n.* A plant whose root remains alive more years than two.

perfect, pėr'fekt, *a.* Finished; complete; fully informed; completely skilled; faultless; in *grammar*, denoting a tense which expresses an act completed.—*vt.* To accomplish; to make perfect; to make fully skillful. **perfection**, pėr-fek'shun, *n.* State of being perfect; an excellence perfect in its kind.

perfidy, pėr'fi-di, *n.* Act of breaking faith or allegiance; the violation of a trust reposed; treachery; disloyalty. **perfidious**, pėr-fid'i-us, *a.* Guilty of or involving perfidy; treacherous; faithless.

perforate, pėr'fō-rāt, *vt.* To bore or penetrate through; to pierce with a pointed instrument. **perforator**, pėr'fō-rā'tėr, *n.* One who or that which perforates. **perforation**, pėr-fo-rā'shon, *n.* Act of perforating; a hole bored.

perforce, pėr-fōrs', *adv.* By force or violence; of necessity.

perform, pėr-form', *vt.* To accomplish; to effect; to do; to act.—*vi.* To act a part; to play on a musical instrument, &c. **performance**, pėr-for'mans, *n.* Act of performing; deed; achievement; a literary work; exhibition on the stage; entertainment at a place of amusement. **performer**, pėr-form'ėr, *n.* One who performs, as an actor, musician, &c.

perfume, pėr'fūm, *n.* A pleasant scent or smell; fragrance.—*vt.* (perfuming, perfumed). To scent with perfume; to impregnate with a grateful odor. **perfumer**, pėr-fūm'ėr, *n.* One who or that which perfumes; one who sells perfumes. **perfumery**, pėr-fūm'ėr-i, *n.* Perfumes in general; the art of preparing perfumes.

perfunctory, pėr-fungk'tō-ri, *a.* Done carelessly or in a half-hearted manner; negligent.

perhaps, pėr-haps', *adv.* It may be; peradventure; perchance; possibly.

perigee, per'i-jē, *n.* That point in the moon's orbit nearest the earth.

peril, per'il, *n.* Risk; hazard; danger.—

vt. (periling, periled). To hazard; to expose to danger. **perilous**, per'il-lus, *a.* Dangerous; hazardous; full of risk.

perimeter, pe-rim'e-tėr, *n.* The outer boundary of a body or figure.

period, pėr'i-ud, *n.* The time taken up by a heavenly body in revolving round the sun; the time at which anything ends; end; an indefinite portion of any continued state or existence; a complete sentence; the point that marks the end of a sentence, thus (.). **periodic**, pėr'i-od"ik, *a.* Pertaining to period or revolution; happening by recurrence, at a stated time. **periodical**, pėr'i-od"i-kal, *n.* A magazine, newspaper, &c., published at regular periods.—*s.* Periodic.

peripatetic, pe'ri-pa-tet"ik, *a.* Walking about; itinerant; pertaining to Aristotle's system of philosophy, taught while walking.—*n.* One who walks; a follower of Aristotle.

periphery, pe-rif'ėr-i, *n.* The boundary line of a figure.

periphrasis, pe-rif'ra-sis, *n.* A roundabout form of expression; circumlocution.

periscopic, per-i-skop'ik, *a.* Viewing on all sides; applied to spectacles having concavo-convex lenses.

perish, per'ish, *vi.* To die; to wither and decay; to be destroyed; to come to nothing. **perishable**, per'ish-a-bl, *a.* Liable to perish; subject to decay or destruction.

peritoneum, peritonæum, per'i-tō-nē"um, *n.* A membrane investing the internal surface of the abdomen, and the viscera contained in it.

peritonitis, per'i-tō-nī"tis, *n.* Inflammation of the peritoneum.

periwig, per'i-wig, *n.* A small wig; a peruke.

periwinkle, per-i-wing'kl, *n.* A univalve mollusk found abundantly on British rocks.

perjure, pėr'jėr, *vt.* (perjuring, perjured). To forswear; willfully to make a false oath when administered legally. **perjurer**, pėr'jėr-ėr, *n.* One who perjures himself. **perjury**, pėr'jėr-i, *n.* Act or crime of forswearing; act of violating an oath or solemn promise.

perk, pėrk, *a.* Trim; spruce; pert.—*vi.* To hold up the head pertly.—*vt.* To make trim; to prank; to hold up (the head) pertly.

permanent, pėr'ma-nent, *a.* Lasting; durable; not decaying; abiding; fixed. **permanence, permanency**, pėr'ma-nens, pėr'ma-nen-si, *n.* State or quality of being permanent; duration; fixedness.

permeate, pėr'mē-āt, *vt.* (permeating, permeated). To pass through the pores or interstices of; to penetrate without rupture or displacement of parts. **permeation**, pėr'mē-ā"shun, *n.* Act of permeating.

permit, pėr-mit', *vt.* and *i.* (permitting, permitted). To allow; to grant; to suffer; to concede.—*n.* per'mit. A written permission or license given by competent authority. **permissible**, pėr-mis'i-bl, *a.* Allowable. **permission**, pėr-mish'un, *n.* Act of permitting; allowance; authorization.

permutation, pĕr'mŭ-tā"shun, *n.* Interchange; in *mathematics,* any of the ways in which a set of quantities can be arranged.

pernicious, pĕr-nish'us, *a.* Having the quality of destroying or injuring; destructive; deadly; noxious.

perorate, per'ō-rāt, *vi.* To make a peroration; to speechify; to spout.

peroration, per'ō-rā"shun, *n.* A rhetorical passage at the conclusion of a speech.

peroxide, pĕr-ok'sĭd, *n.* That oxide of a given base which contains the greatest quantity of oxygen.

perpend, per-pend', *vt.* To weigh in the mind; to consider; to ponder.

perpendicular, pĕr'pen-dik"ū-lĕr, *a.* Perfectly upright or vertical; being at right angles to a given line or surface.— *n.* A line at right angles to the plane of the horizon or to another line.

perpetrate, pĕr'pe-trāt, *vt.* To do in a bad sense; to be guilty of; to commit.

perpetration, pĕr'pe-trā"shun, *n.* The act of perpetrating; commission.

perpetual, pĕr-pet'ū-al *a.* Continuing without end; permanent; everlasting.

perpetuate, pĕr-pet'ū-āt, *vt.* To make perpetual; to preserve from oblivion.

perpetuation, pĕr-pet'ū-ā"shun, *n.* Act of perpetuating or making perpetual.

perpetuity, pĕr'pe-tū"i-ti, *n.* State or quality of being perpetual; endless duration; something of which there will be no end.

perplex, pĕr-pleks', *vt.* To entangle or involve; to embarrass; to distract. **perplexity,** pĕr-plek'si-ti, *n.* State of being puzzled or at a loss; bewilderment; state of being intricate or involved.

perquisite, pĕr'kwi-zit, *n.* Something in addition to regular wages or salary.

persecute, pĕr'se-kūt, *vt.* (persecuting, persecuted). To harass with unjust punishment; to afflict for adherence to a particular creed. **persecution,** pĕr'se-kū"shun, *n.* Act or practice of persecuting; state of being persecuted; continued annoyance. **persecutor,** per"se-kū'tĕr, *n.* One who persecutes.

persevere, pĕr-se-vēr', *vi.* (persevering, persevered). To continue steadfastly in any business; to pursue steadily any design. **perseverance,** per'sē-vēr"ans, *n.* Act or habit of persevering; continued diligence.

Persian, pĕr'zhan, *a.* Pertaining to Persia, the Persians or their language.— *n.* A native of Persia; language spoken in Persia.

persiflage, pĕr'si-fläzh, *n.* Idle bantering talk.

persist, pĕr-sist', *vi.* To continue steadily in any business or course; to persevere; to continue in a certain state. **persistence, persistency,** pĕr-sis'tens, pĕr-sis'ten-si, *n.* Act or state of persisting; perseverance; continuance; obstinacy. **persistent,** pĕr-sis'tent, *a.* Persisting; steady; tenacious.

person, pĕr'sun, *n.* An individual human being; each of the three beings of

the Godhead; bodily form; one of the three inflections of a verb. **in person,** by one's self; not by representatives.

personable, pĕr'sun-a-bl, *a.* Having a well-formed body; of good appearance.

personage, pĕr'sun-ij, *n.* A person of importance; a man or woman of distinction.

personal, pĕr'sun-al, *a.* Pertaining to a person; peculiar or proper to him or her; belonging to face and figure; denoting the person in a grammatical sense. **personality,** per'su-nal"i-ti, *n.* State of being personal; that which constitutes an individual a distinct person; disparaging remark on one's conduct and character; in *law,* personal estate.

personify, pĕr-son'i-fī, *vt.* To represent with the attributes of a person; to impersonate. **personification,** pĕr-son'i-fi-kā"shun, *n.* Act of personifying; embodiment; a metaphor which represents inanimate objects as possessing the attributes of persons.

personnel, pĕr'so-nel", *n.* The body of persons employed in any occupation.

perspective, pĕr-spek'tiv, *n.* The art of representing objects on a flat surface so that they appear to have their natural dimensions and relations; a representation of objects in perspective; view. —*a.* Pertaining to the art of perspective.

perspicacity, pĕr'spi-kas"i-ti, *n.* Acuteness of discernment; penetration; sagacity. **perspicacious,** pĕr'spi-kā"shus, *a.* Quick-sighted; of acute discernment.

perspicuity, pĕr'spi-kū"i-ti, *n.* The quality of being perspicuous; easiness to be understood; plainness; distinctness. **perspicuous,** pĕr-spik'ū-us, *a.* Clear to the understanding; lucid.

perspire, per-spīr', *vi.* (perspiring, perspired). To emit the moisture of the body through the skin; to sweat; to exude.—*vt.* To emit through pores. **perspiration,** pĕr'spi-rā"shun, *n.* Act of perspiring; exudation of sweat; sweat.

persuade, pĕr-swād', *vt.* (persuading, persuaded). To influence by argument, advice, &c.; to induce; to prevail on. **persuasion,** pĕr-swā'zhun, *n.* Act of persuading; settled opinion or conviction; a creed or belief; a sect or party. **persuasive,** pĕr-swā'siv, *a.* Having the power of persuading; calculated to persuade.—*n.* That which persuades; an incitement.

pert, pĕrt, *a.* Lively; brisk; saucy; bold.

pertain, pĕr-tān', *vi.* To belong; to relate; to concern; to regard.

pertinacity, pĕr-ti-nas'i-ti, *n.* Obstinacy; resolution; constancy. **pertinacious,** pĕr'ti-nā"shus, *a.* Obstinate; inflexible; determined; persistent.

pertinent, pĕr'ti-nent, *a.* Related to the subject or matter in hand; apposite; fit. **pertinence, pertinency,** pĕr'ti-nens, pĕr'ti-nen-si, *n.* Quality or state of being pertinent; fitness; appositeness.

perturb, pĕr-tĕrb', *vt.* To disturb; to agitate; to disquiet; to confuse. **perturbation,** pĕr'tĕr-bāsh"un, *n.* Act of perturbing; disorder; uneasiness; cause of disquiet.

peruse, pe-rūz', *vt.* (perusing, perused).

To read through; to read with attention; to examine carefully. **perusal,** pe-röz'al, *n.* Act of perusing or reading.

Peruvian, pe-rö'vi-an, *a.* Pertaining to Peru.—*n.* A native of Peru.

pervade, pėr-vād', *vt.* (pervading, pervaded). To pass or flow through; to permeate; to be diffused through. **pervasion,** pėr-vā'zhun, *n.* Act of pervading. **perverse,** pėr-vėrs', *a.* Obstinate in the wrong; stubborn; untractable; petulant. **perversion,** pėr-vėr'zhun, *n.* A diverting from the true intent or object; misapplication. **perversity,** pėr-vėr'si-ti, *n.* State or quality of being perverse; disposition to thwart. **perversive,** pėr-vėr'siv, *a.* Tending to pervert. **pervert,** pėr-vėrt', *vt.* To turn from truth or proper purpose; to corrupt; to misinterpret; to misapply.—*n.* pėr'vėrt. One who has been perverted.

pessimism, pes'i-mizm, *n.* The doctrine that the present state of things tends only to evil; the tendency always to look at the dark side of things. **pessimist,** pes'i-mist, *n.* One who believes in pessimism, or takes an unfavorable view of affairs. **pessimistic,** pes'i-mis''tik, *a.* Pertaining to pessimism.

pest, pest, *n.* A deadly epidemic disease; plague; pestilence; a mischievous person. **pester,** pes'tėr, *vt.* To plague; to trouble; to annoy with little vexations. **pestiferous,** pes-tif'ėr-us, *a.* Pestilential; noxious; infectious; contagious. **pestilence,** pes'ti-lens, *n.* Any contagious disease that is epidemic and fatal; something morally evil or destructive. **pestilent,** pes'ti-lent, *a.* Pestilential; michievous; pernicious; troublesome. **pestilential,** pes'ti-len''shal, *a.* Partaking of the nature of a pestilence or the plague; destructive; pernicious.

pestle, pes'l, *n.* An instrument for pounding substances in a mortar.—*vt.* and *i.* (pestling, pestled). To pound with a pestle.

Pestle and Mortar.

pet, pet, *n.* A darling; any little animal fondled and indulged; fit of peevishness.—*vt.* (petting, petted). To fondle; to indulge.

petal, pet'l, *n.* A flower leaf.

petite, pė-tēt', *a.* Small in figure; tiny.

petition, pė-tish'un, *n.* An entreaty, supplication, or prayer; a written application in legal proceedings.—*vt.* To supplicate; to solicit. **petitionary,** pė-tish'un-er'i, *a.* Supplicatory; containing a petition. **petitioner,** pė-ti'shun-ėr, *n.* One who petitions or presents a petition.

petrel, pet'rel, *n.* A web-footed sea-bird often found far from land.

petrify, pet'ri-fī, *vt.* To turn into stone or a fossil; to paralyze or stupefy.—*vi.* To become stone, or of a stony hardness. **petrifaction,** pet'ri-fak''shun, *n.* The process of changing into stone; a fossil. **petroleum,** pe-trō'lē-um, *n.* Rock-oil; an inflammable liquid found in the earth.

petticoat, pet'i-kōt, *n.* A loose undergarment worn by females.

pettifog, pet'i-fog, *vi.* (pettifogging, pettifogged). To act in petty cases, as a lawyer. **pettifogger,** pet'i-fog'ėr, *n.* A lawyer employed in small or mean business.

pettish, pet'ish, *a.* In a pet; peevish.

petty, pet'i, *a.* Small; little; trifling; trivial.

petulant, pet'ū-lant, *a.* Irritable; peevish; fretful; saucy; pert; capricious. **petulance, petulancy,** pet'ū-lans, pet'ū-lan-si, *n.* Quality of being petulant; peevishness; pettiness; forwardness.

pew, pū, *n.* An inclosed seat in a church.

pewter, pū'tėr, *n.* An alloy mainly of tin and lead; a vessel made of pewter.—*a.* Relating to or made of pewter.

phaeton, fā'e-tn, *n.* An open carriage on four wheels.

phalanx, fā'langks, *n.*; pl. **-anges, -anxes.** The heavy-armed infantry of an ancient Greek army; a body of troops in close array; a small bone of the fingers or toes.

phallus, fal'us, *n.* The emblem of the generative power in nature, especially in certain religious usages. **phallic,** fal'ik, *a.* Pertaining to the phallus.

phantasm, fan'tazm, *n.* An apparition; a phantom; an idea; notion, or fancy. **phantasmagoria,** fan-taz'ma-gō''ri-a, *n.* An exhibition of figures by shadows, as by the magic lantern; illusive images. **phantasmal,** fan-taz'mal, *a.* Spectral; illusive.

phantasy, fan'ta-si, *n. See* **fantasy.**

phantom, fan'tom, *n.* An apparition; a specter; a fancied vision; a phantasm.

Pharisee, far'i-sē, *n.* A Jew strict in religious observances; a hypocrite.

pharmacy, fär'ma-si, *n.* The art or practice of preparing medicines; a drug store. **pharmaceutic, pharmaceutical,** fär'ma-sū''tik, fär'ma-sū''ti-kal, *n.* Pertaining to the knowledge or art of pharmacy. **pharmacology,** fär'ma-kol''o-ji, *n.* The science of drugs; the art of preparing medicines.

pharynx, far'ingks, *n.* The muscular sac between the mouth and the œsophagus.

phase, fāz, *n.* A particular stage of the moon or a planet in respect to illumination; state of a varying phenomenon; one of the various aspects of a question.

pheasant, fez'ant, *n.* A bird commonly reared and preserved for sport and food.

phenix, phoenix, fē'niks, *n.* A female bird of ancient legend, said to live 500 years, when she burnt herself, and rose again from her ashes; an emblem of immortality; a paragon.

phenomenon, fē-nom'ē-non, *n.*; pl. **-mena.** An appearance; anything visible; an appearance whose cause is not immediately obvious; something extraordinary. **phenomenal,** fē-nom'e-nal, *a.* Pertaining to or constituted by a phenomenon; extremely remarkable; astounding.

phial, fī'al, *n.* A small glass bottle. *See* **vial.**

philander, fi-lan'dėr, *vi.* To make love sentimentally to a lady; to flirt.

philanthropy, fil-an'thro-pi, *n.* The love of man or of mankind; benevolence toward the whole human family. **philanthropist**, fil-an'thrŏ-pist, *n.* One devoted to philanthropy; one who exerts himself in doing good to his fellowmen. **philanthropic**, **philanthropical**, fi'lan-throp''ik, fi'lan-throp''i-kal, *a.* Relating to philanthropy; entertaining good-will towards all men; benevolent.

philately, fi-lat'e-li, *n.* The practice of collecting postage-stamps.

philharmonic, fil-här-mon'ik, *a.* Loving harmony; musical.

Philippine, fil'i-pēn, *a.* Pertaining to the Philippine Islands or the people who live there.

Philistine, fi-lis'tin or fil'is-tin, *n.* A person deficient in culture, and wanting in taste; a person of narrow views.

philology, fi-lol'o-ji, *n.* The study of language; linguistic science. **philological**, **philologic**, fil'ŏ-loj''i-kal, fil'-ŏ-loj''ik, *a.* Pertaining to philology.

philosophy, fi-los'o-fi, *n.* The science which tries to account for the phenomena of the universe; metaphysics; the general principles underlying some branch of knowledge; practical wisdom. **philosopher**, fi-los'ŏ-fėr, *n.* A person versed in philosophy; one who studies moral or mental science. **philosophic**, **philosophical**, fil'ŏ-sof''ik, fil'ŏ-sof''i-kal, *a.* Pertaining or according to philosophy; given to philosophy; calm; cool; temperate; rational. **philosophize**, fi-los''-ŏ-fiz, *vi.* To act the philosopher; to reason like a philosopher; to formulate a philosophical theory.

philter, **philtre**, fil'tėr, *n.* A love-charm; a potion supposed to excite love.

phlebotomy, flē-bot'ŏ-mi, *n.* The act or practice of opening a vein; blood-letting.

phlegm, flem, *n.* The viscid matter of the digestive and respiratory passages; bronchial mucus; coldness; indifference. **phlegmatic**, fleg-mat'ik, *a.* Abounding in or generating phlegm; cold; sluggish.

phobia, fō'bi-a, *n.* An ingrained fear or aversion to an object or situation.

phoenix, fī'niks. See **phenix**.

phonetic, fō-net'ik, *a.* Pertaining to the voice; representing sounds. **phonetics**, fō-net'iks, *n.pl.* The doctrine or science of sounds, especially of the human voice; the representation of sounds.

phonograph, fō'nŏ-graf, *n.* An instrument for registering and reproducing sounds. **phonography**, fō-nog'ra-fi, *n.* The description of sounds; the representation of sounds by characters; phonetic shorthand.

phosphate, fos'fāt, *n.* A salt of phosphoric acid.

phosphorus, fos'for-us, *n.* An elementary substance which undergoes slow combustion at common temperatures. **phosphorate**, fos'for-āt, *vt.* To combine or impregnate with phosphorus. **phosphoresce**, fos-fō-res', *vi.* To give out a phosphoric light. **phosphorescence**, fos'fō-res''ens, *n.* State or quality of being phosphorescent. **phosphorescent**, fos'fō-res''ent, *a.* Shining with a faint light like that of phosphorus; luminous without sensible heat. **phosphoric**, fos-fo'rik, *a.* Pertaining to, or obtained from, or resembling phosphorus. **phosphorous**, fos'fō-rus, *a.* Pertaining to or obtained from phosphorus.

photoengraving, fō'tō-en-grāv''ing, *n.* A method of reproduction in which printing relief is achieved by photography and etching of metal plate; the product of this process.

photogenic, fō'tō-jen''ik, *a.* Ideally suited for being photographed.

photograph, fō'tŭ-graf, *n.* A picture obtained by photography.—*vt.* To produce a representation of by photographic means. **photographer**, fō-tog'ra-fėr *n.* One who takes pictures by means of photography. **photographic**, **photographical**, fō'tō-graf''ik, fō'tō-graf''i-kal, *a.* Pertaining to photography. **photography**, fō-tog'ra-fi, *n.* The art or practice of producing representations of scenes and objects by the action of light on chemically-prepared surfaces.

photosynthesis, fō'tō-sin''thē-sis, *n.* Process in plant cells of capturing radiant energy from the sun and transforming it into chemical energy as food.

phrase, frāz, *n.* A short sentence or expression; an idiom; style; diction.—*vt* and *i.* (phrasing, phrased). To style; to express. **phraseology**, frā'zē-ol''o-ji, *n.* Manner of expression; peculiar words used in a sentence; diction; style.

phrenetic, fre-net'ik, *a.* Having the mind disordered; frantic.—*n.* A frenzied person.

phrenologist, fre-nol'o-jist, *n.* One versed in phrenology. **phrenology**, fre-nol'o-ji, *n.* The doctrine that a person's endowments may be discovered by the configuration of the skull.

physic, fiz'ik, *n.* The science of medicine; the art of healing; a medicine; a cathartic.—*vt.* (physicking, physicked). To treat with physic; to remedy.

physical, fiz'i-kal, *a.* Pertaining to nature or natural productions; bodily; as opposed to mental or moral; material; pertaining to physics.

physician, fi-zish'an, *n.* A person skilled in the art of healing; a doctor.

physics, fiz'iks, *n.* That branch of science which deals with mechanics, dynamics, light, heat, sound, electricity, and magnetism; natural philosophy. **physicist**, fiz'i-sist, *n.* One skilled in physics; a natural philosopher.

physiognomy, fiz'i-og''nŏ-mi, *n.* The art of perceiving a person's character by his countenance; particular cast or expression of countenance.

physiography, fiz'i-og''ra-fi, *n.* The science of the earth's physical features and phenomena; physical geography.

physiology, fiz'i-ol'ŏ-ji, *n.* The science of the phenomena of life; the study of the functions of living beings. **physiologist**, fiz'i-ol'ŏ-jist, *n.* One who is versed in physiology. **physiologic**, **physiological**, fiz'i-ŏ-loj''ik, fiz'i-ŏ-loj''i-kal, *a.* Pertaining to physiology.

physique, fi-zēk', *n.* A person's physical or bodily structure or constitution.

pianist, pi-an'ist, *n.* A performer on the pianoforte.

piano, pi-ä'nō, *a.* In *music*, soft.

piano, pi-an'o, *n.* A pianoforte.

pianoforte, pi-an'ō-fōr"tā, *n.* A musical metal-stringed instrument with a keyboard, sounded by hammers acting on the strings.

piazza, pi-az'a, *n.* A rectangular open space surrounded by colonnades.

pica, pī'ka, *n.* A printing type having six lines in an inch, used as the standard size.

picador, pik'a-dōr, *n.* A horseman with a lance who excites the bull in a bull-fight.

picaresque, pik'a-resk", *a.* Pertaining to rogues; describing the fortunes of adventurers.

piccolo, pik'o-lō, *n.* A small flute with shrill tones; an octave flute.

pick, pik, *vt.* To strike at with something pointed; to peck at; to clean by the teeth, fingers, &c.; to select; to pluck; to gather.—*vi.* To eat slowly; to nibble; to pilfer.—*n.* A pointed tool; a pickax; choice; selection.

pickax, pickaxe, pik"aks', *n.* A sharp-pointed iron tool used in digging, mining, &c.

pickerel, pik'ėr-el, *n.* A fresh-water fish of the pike family.

picket, pik'et, *n.* A pointed stake used in fortification; a pale; an advanced guard or outpost; a game at cards.—*vt.* To fortify with pickets; to post as a guard of observation.

pickle, pik'l, *n.* Brine; a solution of salt and water for preserving flesh, fish, &c.; vegetables preserved in vinegar; a state of difficulty or disorder; a troublesome child.—*vt.* (pickling, pickled). To preserve in or treat with pickle.

pickpocket, pik"pok'et, *n.* One who steals from the pocket of another.

picnic, pik'nik, *n.* and *a.* A pleasure-party the members of which carry provisions with them.—*vi.* (picnicking, picnicked). To take part in a picnic party.

pictorial, pik-tō'ri-al, *a.* Pertaining to or forming pictures; illustrated by pictures.

picture, pik'tūr, *n.* A painting, drawing, &c., exhibiting the resemblance of anything; any resemblance or representation.—*vt.* To represent pictorially; to present an ideal likeness of; to describe in a vivid manner. **picturesque,** pik'tūr-esk", *a.* Forming, or fitted to form, a pleasing picture; abounding with vivid imagery; graphic.

pie, pī, *n.* A paste baked with something in or under it; a mass of types unsorted; the magpie.

piebald, pī"bald', *a.* Having spots or patches of various colors; pied; mongrel.

piece, pēs, *n.* A portion of anything; a distinct part; a composition or writing of no great length; a separate performance; a picture; a coin; a single firearm.—*vt.* (piecing, pieced). To patch; to join.—*vi.* To unite or join on.

piecemeal, pēs"mēl', *adv.* In or by pieces; in fragments; by little and little.

piecework, pēs"wėrk', *n.* Work done by the piece or job; work paid by quantity.

pied, pīd, *a.* Party-colored; spotted.

pier, pēr, *n.* A mass of solid stonework for supporting an arch, bridge, &c.; a projecting wharf or landing-place.

pierce, pērs, *vt.* (piercing, pierced). To stab or perforate with a pointed instrument; to penetrate; to move deeply.—*vi.* To enter; to penetrate. **piercer,** pėr'sėr, *n.* One who or that which pierces; an instrument that bores; that organ of an insect with which it pierces.

piety, pī'e-ti, *n.* Reverence or veneration towards God; godl:ness; devotion; religion.

pig, pig, *n.* A young swine; a swine in general; an oblong mass of unforged metal.—*vt.* or *i.* (pigging, pigged). To bring forth pigs; to act like pigs.

pigeon, pij'un, *n.* A well-known bird of many varieties; a dove; a simpleton; a gull.

pigeonhole, pij"un-hōl', *n.* A hole for pigeons to enter their dwelling; a division in a desk or case for holding papers.

pigheaded, pig'hed'ed, *a.* Having a head like a pig; stupidly obstinate.

pig iron, pig' i'ėrn, *n.* Iron in pigs, as it comes from the blast-furnace.

pigment, pig'ment, *n.* Paint; any preparation used by painters, dyers, &c., to impart colors to bodies; coloring matter.

pigmy. *See* **pygmy.**

pigskin, pig'skin', *n.* The skin of a pig especially when prepared for saddlery; a football.

pigtail, pig"tāl', *n.* The tail of a pig; the hair of the head tied behind in a tail.

pike, pīk, *n.* A spike or pointed piece; a fork used in husbandry; a fresh-water fish with a pointed snout.

pilaster, pi-las'tėr, *n.* A square pillar, slightly projecting from a wall.

pile, pīl, *n.* A heap; a large mass of buildings; a galvanic or voltaic battery; hair; nap on cloth; a beam driven into the ground to support some superstructure; a heraldic figure like a wedge.—*vt.* (piling, piled). To heap; to amass; to drive piles into; to support with piles.

piles, pīlz, *n.pl.* A disease of the rectum near the anus; hemorrhoids.

pilfer, pil'fėr, *vi.* To steal in small quantities; to practice petty theft.—*vt.* To filch. **pilferer,** pil'fėr-ėr, *n.* One who pilfers.

pilgrim, pil'grim, *n.* A wanderer; one who travels to visit a holy place or relics. **pilgrimage,** pil'gri-mij, *n.* A journey to some holy place; the journey of human life.

piker, pīk'ėr, *n. Slang.* A petty or niggardly person.

pill, pil, *n.* A medicine in the form of a little ball; anything nauseous to be accepted.—*vt.* To dose with pills; to form into pills; to rob; to plunder.

pillage, pil'ij, *n.* Act of plundering; plunder; spoil.—*vt.* (pillaging, pillaged). To rob by open violence; to plunder.

pillar, pil'ėr, *n.* A column; a perpendicular support; a supporter.

pillion, pil'yun, *n.* A cushion for a

woman to ride on behind a person on horseback; the pad of a saddle.

pillory, pil'ō-ri, *n.* A frame of wood with movable boards and holes, through which were put the head and hands of an offender.—*vt.* (pillorying, pilloried). To punish with the pillory; to expose to ridicule, abuse, &c.

pillow, pil'ō, *n.* A long soft cushion; something that bears or supports.—*vt.* To rest or lay on for support.

pillowcase, **pillowslip**, pil"ō-kās', pil"ō-slip', *n.* The movable case or sack which is drawn over a pillow.

pilot, pī'lot, *n.* One whose occupation is to steer ships; a guide; a director of one's course.—*vt.* To act as pilot of; to guide through dangers or difficulties.

pimp, pimp, *n.* A man who provides gratifications for others' lusts; a procurer.—*vi.* To pander; to procure women for others.

pimpernel, pim'pėr-nel, *n.* A little red-flowered annual found in British cornfields.

pimple, pim'pl, *n.* A small elevation of the skin, with an inflamed base. **pimpled**, pim'pld, *a.* Having pimples; full of pimples. **pimply**, pim'pli, *a.* Pimpled.

pin, pin, *n.* A longish piece of metal, wood, &c., used for a fastening, or as a support; a peg; a bolt.—*vt.* (pinning, pinned). To fasten with a pin or pins; to hold fast.—*vt.* To inclose; to pen or pound.

pinafore, pin"a-fōr', *n.* A little apron.

pincers, pin'serz, *n.pl.* An instrument for gripping anything; nippers; prehensile claws. Also *Pinchers*.

pinch, pinch, *vt.* To press hard or squeeze; to nip; to afflict.—*vt.* To press painfully; to be sparing.—*n.* A close compression, as with the fingers; a nip; a pang; straits; a strong iron lever; as much as is taken by the finger and thumb; a small quantity.

pin-cushion, pin"kŏsh'un, *n.* A small cushion in which pins are kept.

pine, pīn, *n.* A valuable evergreen coniferous tree, furnishing timber, turpentine, pitch, and resin; the pineapple.—*vi.* (pining, pined). To languish; to grow weakly with pain, grief, &c.

pineapple, pīn'ap-l, *n.* A fruit like the cone of a pine-tree but different in character; the plant itself.

piney, **piny**, pīn'i, *a.* Pertaining to pines; abounding with pines.

ping, ping, *n.* The sound made by a flying bullet.

pinion, pin'yun, *n.* A bird's wing; the joint of a wing remotest from the body; a large wing-feather; a small toothed wheel; a fetter for the arms.—*vt.* To bind the wings of; to cut off, as the first joint of the wing; to fetter.

pink, pingk, *n.* A garden flower; a light rose-color or pigment; the flower or something supremely excellent.—*a.* Of a fine light rose-color.—*vt.* To work in eyelet-holes; to scallop; to stab.—*vi.* To wink or blink.

pinkeye, pingk'ī, *n.* A disease attacking horses, a kind of influenza.

pinmoney, pin'mun-i, *n.* A sum of money settled on a wife for her private expenses.

pinnace, pin'is, *n.* A small vessel navigated with oars and sails usually with two masts; a boat with eight oars.

pinnacle, pin'a-kl, *n.* A rocky peak; a sharp top; a turret above a building.

pinnate, pin'āt, *a.* Shaped like a feather.

pint, pint, *n.* The eighth part of a gallon.

pioneer, pī-o-nēr', *n.* One whose business is to prepare the road for an army; make entrenchments, &c.; one who leads the way.—*vt.* To prepare a way for.—*vi.* To act as pioneer.

pious, pī'us, *a.* Devout; godly; holy; proceeding from piety.

pip, pip, *n.* The kernel or seed of fruit; a spot on cards; a disease of fowls.

pipe, pīp, *n.* A wind-instrument of music; a long tube; a tube with a bowl at one end for tobacco; the windpipe; a call of a bird; a wine measure containing about 105 imperial gallons.—*vi.* (piping, piped). To play on a pipe; to whistle.—*vt.* To utter in a high tone; to call by a pipe or whistle.

piper, pīp'ėr, *n.* One who plays on a pipe; a bagpiper; a sea-urchin.

pippin, pip'in, *n.* An apple of various kinds.

piquant, pē'kant, *a.* Making a lively impression; sharp; lively; interesting; pungent. **piquancy**, pē'kan-si, *n.* Quality of being piquant; sharpness; pungency.

pique, pēk, *n.* Irritation; offense taken; slight anger.—*vt.* (piquing, piqued). To nettle; to touch with envy, jealousy, &c.; to pride or value (one's self).—*vi.* To cause irritation.

pirate, pī'rit, *n.* A robber on the high seas; a ship engaged in piracy; one who publishes others' writings without permission.—*vi.* (pirating, pirated). To rob on the high-seas.—*vt.* To take without right, as writings. **piratical**, pī-rat'i-kal, *a.* Having the character of a pirate; pertaining to piracy. **piracy**, pī'ra-si, *n.* The act or practice of robbing on the high seas; infringement of the law of copyright.

pironette, pir'ō-et", *n.* A turning about on the toes in dancing.—*vi.* To make a pirouette; to whirl about on the toes.

piscatorial, **piscatory**, pis'kā-tō"ri-al, pis'kā-tō-ri, *a.* Relating to fishing.

Pisces, pis'ēz, *n. pl.* The Fishes, a sign in the zodiac; the vertebrate animals of the class fishes.

pish, pish, *exclam.* A word expressing contempt.—*vi.* To express contempt by uttering *pish!*

pismire, pis'mīr', *n.* The ant or emmet.

pistachio, pis-tä'shi-ō, *n.* The nut of a small tree cultivated in S. Europe for its fruit; the tree itself, also called *pistacia*.

pistil, pis'til, *n.* The seed-bearing organ of a flower.

pistol, pis'tl, *n.* A small firearm fired with one hand—*vt.* (pistoling, pistoled). To shoot with a pistol.

piston, pis'tun, *n.* A cylindrical piece of metal which fits exactly into a hollow cylinder, and works alternately in two directions.

piston rod, pis'ton rod, *n*. A rod which connects a piston to some other piece, and either moved by the piston or moving it.

pit, pit, *n*. A hollow in the earth; the shaft of a mine; a vat in tanning, dyeing, &c.; a concealed hole for catching wild beasts; a small cavity or depression; part of the floor of a theater.—*vt*. (pitting, pitted). To lay in a pit or hole; to mark with little hollows; to set in competition.

pit-a-pat, pit'a-pat', *adv*. In a flutter; with palpitation or quick succession of beats.

pitch, pich, *vt*. To thrust, as a pointed object; to fix; to set; to throw; to set the key-note of; to set in array; to smear or cover with pitch.—*vi*. To settle; to fall headlong; to fix choice; to encamp; to rise and fall, as a ship.—*n*. A throw; degree of elevation; highest rise; descent; elevation of a note; a thick dark resinous substance obtained from tar.

pitch-dark, pich'därk', *a*. Dark as pitch; very dark.

pitcher, pich'ėr, *n*. A vessel with a spout, for holding liquors.

pitchfork, pich''fork', *n*. A fork used in throwing hay, &c.; a tuning-fork.—*vt*. To lift or throw with a pitch-fork; to put suddenly into any position.

piteous, pit'ē-us, *a*. That may excite pity; sorrowful; sad; miserable; pitiful.

pitfall, pit'fal, *n*. A pit slightly covered over, forming a kind of trap.

pith, pith, *n*. The spongy substance in the center of exogenous plants; the spinal cord or marrow of an animal; strength or force; energy; cogency; essence.

pithily, pith'i-li, *adv*. In a pithy manner; cogently; with energy. **pithy**, pith'i, *a*. Consisting of pith; terse and forcible; energetic; sententious.

pitiable, pit'i-a-bl, *a*. Deserving pity or compassion; lamentable; miserable.

pitiful, pit'i-fyl, *a*. Full of pity; compassionate; woeful; to be pitied; paltry; despicable.

pitiless, pit'i-les, *a*. Feeling no pity; hardhearted; merciless; relentless; unmerciful.

pittance, pit'ans, *n*. A very small portion allowed or assigned; a charity gift.

pity, pit'i-, *n*. Sympathy or compassion; ground of pity; thing to be regretted.—*vt*. (pitying, pitied). To feel pain or grief for; to sympathize with.—*vi*. To be compassionate.

pivot, piv'ut, *n*. A pin on which something turns; a turning-point; that on which important results depend.—*vt*. To place on or furnish with a pivot.

pixy, pixie, pik'si, *n*. A sort of English fairy.

placable, pla'ka-bl, *a*. Readily appeased or pacified; willing to forgive.

placard, pla-kärd', or plak'ärd, *n*. A written or printed bill posted in a public place; a poster.—*vt*. To post placards.

place, plās, *n*. An open space in a town; a locality, spot, or site; position; room; en edifice; quarters; a passage in a book; rank; office; calling; ground or occasion; stead.—*vt*. (placing, placed). To put or set; to locate; to appoint or set in an office, rank or condition; to invest; to lend.

placenta, pla-sen'ta, *n*. The after-birth; an organ developed in mammals during pregnancy, connecting the mother and fœtus; the part of the seed-vessel to which the seeds are attached.

placid, plas'id, *a*. Gentle; quiet; mild; unruffled; calm. **placidity**, pla-sid'i-ti, *n*. State or quality of being placid.

placket, plak'et, *n*. A petticoat; the opening or slit in a petticoat or skirt.

plagiarize, plā'ji-a-riz, *vt*. To purloin the published thoughts or words of another. **plagiarism**, plā'ji-a-rizm, *n*. The act of plagiarizing; literary theft. **plagiarist**, plā'ji-a-rist, *n*. One who plagiarizes the writings of another.

plague, plāg, *n*. A stroke or calamity; severe trouble; a pestilential disease; a person who annoys or troubles.—*vt*. (plaguing, plagued). To vex; to scourge as with disease or any evil.

plaid, plad, *n*. A large woolen cloth, frequently of tartan, worn as a wrap.

plain, plān, *a*. Without elevations and depressions; smooth; level; clear; undisguised; artless; sincere; simple; mere; bare; evident; obvious.—*n*. A piece of level land.—*adv*. Distinctly.

plain-dealing, plān'dēl'ing, *n*. Conduct free from stratagem or disguise; sincerity.—*a*. Dealing with sincerity.

plain-spoken, plān'spō'ken, *a*. Speaking plainly or with bluntness.

plaint, plānt, *n*. A complaint or lamentation; representation made of injury or wrong done.

plaintiff, plān'tif, *n*. In *law*, the person who commences a suit before a tribunal for the recovery of a claim; opposed to *defendant*.

plaintive, plān'tiv, *a*. Expressive of sorrow or grief; repining; mournful; sad.

plait, plāt, *n*. A fold; a doubling of cloth, &c.; a braid, as of hair, &c.—*vt*. To fold; to double in narrow strips; to braid. **plaited**, plāt'ed, *p.a*. Folded; braided.

plan, plan, *n*. The representation of anything on a flat surface; sketch; scheme; project; method; process.—*vt*. (planning, planned). To form a plan or representation of; to scheme.—*vi*. To form a scheme.

plane, plān, *a*. Without elevations or depressions; perfectly level; even; flat. —*n*. A smooth or perfectly level surface; a joiner's tool, used in paring or smoothing wood.—*vt*. To make level or smooth; to smooth by the use of a plane.

planet, plan'et, *n*. A celestial body which revolves about the sun or other center.

planetary, plan''e-ter'i, *a*. Pertaining to or produced by planets.

plankton, plang'ton, *n*. Small, microscopic life found in large bodies of water.

plank, plangk, *n*. A flat broad piece of

sawed timber.—*vt.* To cover or lay with planks.

plant, plant, *n.* One of the living organisms of the vegetable kingdom; an herb; a shoot or slip; the machinery, &c., necessary to carry on a business.—*vt.* To set in the ground for growth; to set firmly; to establish; to furnish with plants; to set and direct, as cannon.—*vi.* To set plants in the ground.

plantain, plan'tin, *n.* A species of herbs and common weeds found in various temperate regions.

plantain, plantain tree, plan'tin, plan'tin trē, *n.* A tropical plant of the same genus as the banana.

plantation, plan-tā'shun, *n.* The act of planting; the place planted; a wood or grove; a colony; an estate cultivated for the crops suited to warm regions.

planter, plan'tėr, *n.* One who plants; one who owns a plantation abroad.

plaque, plak, *n.* An ornamental plate; a flat plate on which enamels are painted; a brooch; the plate of a clasp.

plash, plash, *n.* A puddle; a pool; a splash.—*vi.* To make a noise in water; to splash.—*vt.* To bend down and interweave the branches or twigs of.

plasma, plaz'ma, *n.* Formless matter; the simplest form of organized matter in the vegetable and animal body. **plasmic, plasmatic**, plaz'mik, plaz-mat'ik, *a.* Pertaining to a plasma.

plaster, plas'tėr, *n.* An adhesive substance used in medical practice; a mixture of lime, water, sand, &c., for coating walls; calcined gypsum, used with water for finishing walls, for casts, cement, &c.—*vt.* To overlay with plaster; to lay on coarsely.

plastic, plas'tik, *a.* Having the power to give form to matter; capable of being molded; applied to sculpture, as distinguished from painting, &c. **plasticity**, plas-tis'i-ti, *n.* The state or quality of being plastic.

plat, plat, *vt.* (platting, platted). To plait; to weave; to make a ground-plan of.—*n.* A plot of ground devoted to some special purpose.

plate, plāt, *n.* A flat piece of metal; gold and silver wrought into utensils; a shallow flattish dish for eatables; an engraved piece of metal for printing; a page of stereotype for printing—*vt.* (plating, plated). To cover with a thin coating of metal, as of silver.

plateau, pla-tō', *n.*; pl. **-teaux** or **teaus** (-tōz). An elevated, broad, flat area of land; a table-land.

plate glass, plāt gläs, *n.* A superior kind of thick glass used for mirrors, windows, &c.

platform, plat"form', *n.* A raised structure with a flat surface; the place where guns are mounted on a battery; the raised walk at a railway-station; a structure for speakers at public meetings; a declared system of policy.

plating, plāt'ing, *n.* The art of covering articles with gold or silver; the coating itself.

platinum, pla'tin-um, *n.* The heaviest of all metals, hard, ductile, malleable, and of a silvery color.

platitude, plat'i-tūd, *n.* A trite or stupid remark; a truism. **platitudinous**, plat'i-tū"di-nus, *a.* Of the nature of platitude.

Platonic, plā-ton'ik, *a.* Pertaining to Plato, or his philosophy, school, or opinions; not sensual; purely spiritual.

platoon, pla-tön', *n.* Two files of soldiers, forming a subdivision of a company.

platter, plat'ėr, *n.* A large flat dish.

platypus, plat'i-pus, *n.* The duckbill.

plaudit, plã'dit, *n.* Applause; acclamation; usually in *pl.* **plauditory**, plã'-di-to-ri, *a.* Applauding; commending.

plausible, plã'zi-bl, *a.* Apparently worthy of praise; apparently right; specious; fair-spoken. **plausibility**, plã'zi-bil"i-ti, *n.* Quality of being plausible; speciousness.

play, plā, *vi.* To do something for amusement; to sport; to gamble; to perform on an instrument of music; to act with free motion; to personate a character.—*vt.* To put in action or motion; to use, as an instrument of music; to act; to contend against; to perform.—*n.* Any exercise for diversion; sport; gaming; action; use; practice; a drama; motion; scope; swing.

play-bill, plā'bil, *n.* A bill exhibited as an advertisement of a play.

player, plā'ėr, *n.* An actor; musician; gamester.

playground, plā"ground', *n.* A piece of ground set apart for open-air recreation.

playhouse, plā"hous', *n.* A theater.

playmate, plā"māt', *n.* A play-fellow.

plaything, plā"thing', *n.* a toy.

playwright, plā"rīt', *n.* A maker of plays.

plea, plē, *n.* A suit or action at law; that which is alleged in support, justification, or defense; an excuse; a pleading.

plead, plēd, *vi.* (pleading, pleaded or pled). To argue in support of or against a claim; to present an answer to the declaration of a plaintiff; to supplicate with earnestness; to urge.—*vt.* To discuss and defend; to argue; to offer in excuse; to allege in a legal defense.

pleader, plēd'ėr, *n.* One who pleads; a lawyer who argues in a court of justice.

pleading, plēd'ing, *n.* The act of one who pleads; one of the written statements in a litigant's demand or defense.

pleasant, plez'ant, *a.* Pleasing; agreeable; grateful; humorous; sportive.

pleasantry, plez'an-tri, *n.* Gayety; humor; raillery; a jest; a frolic.

please, plēz, *vt.* (pleasing, pleased). To excite agreeable sensations or emotions in; to delight; to gratify; to seem good to.—*vi.* To give pleasure; to be kind enough. **pleasurable**, plezh'ėr-a-bl, *a.* Pleasing; giving pleasure; affording gratification. **pleasure**, plezh'ėr, *n.* The gratification of the senses or of the mind; agreeable emotion; delight; joy; approbation; choice; will; purpose; command; arbitrary will or choice.

plebeian, ple-bē'yan, *a.* Pertaining to the common people; vulgar; common.—

n. One of the lower ranks of men; one of the common people of ancient Rome.

plebiscite, pleb'i-sit, or pleb'i-sit, *n.* A vote of a whole people or community.

pledge, plej, *n.* Personal property given in security of a debt; a pawn; a surety; a hostage; the drinking of another's health.—*vt.* (pledging, pledged). To deposit as a security; to engage solemnly; to drink a health to.

plenary, plē'na-ri, *a.* Full; complete.

plenipotentiary, plen'i-pō-ten"shi-er'i, *n.* A person with full power to act for another; an ambassador with full power.—*a.* Containing or invested with full power.

plenty, plen'ti, *n.* Abundance; copiousness; sufficiency.—*a.* Plentiful; abundant. **plenitude**, plen'i-tūd, *n.* The state of being full or complete; plenty; abundance. **plenteous**, plen'tē-us, *a.* Abundant; copious; ample. **plentiful**, plen'ti-fōl, *a.* Being in plenty or abundance; copious; ample; abundant.

plethora, pleth'ō-ra, *n.* Excess of blood; repletion; superabundance; a glut.

pleura, plō'ra, *n.*; pl. **-ae.** A thin membrane which covers the inside of the thorax, and invests either lung. **pleural**, plōr'al, *a.* Pertaining to the pleura. **pleurisy**, **pleuritis**, plōr'i-si, plōr-ī'tis, *n.* An inflammation of the pleura.

plexus, plek'sus, *n.* A network of vessels, nerves, or fibers.

pliable, plī'a-bl, *a.* Easy to be bent; flexible; supple; pliant; easily persuaded. **pliancy**, plī'an-si, *n.* The state or quality of being pliant or pliable. **pliant**, plī'ant, *a.* Pliable; readily yielding to force or pressure without breaking; plastic; limber.

pliers, plī'ėrz, *n.pl.* A small pair of pincers for bending wire, &c.

plight, plīt, *vt.* To pledge, as one's word or honor; to give as a security; never applied to property or goods.—*n.* A pledge; a solemn promise; predicament; risky or dangerous state.

plod, plod, *vi.* (plodding, plodded). To trudge or walk heavily; to toil; to drudge.—*vt.* To accomplish by toilsome exertion. **plodder**, plod'ėr, *n.* One who plods; a dull, heavy, laborious person.

plot, plot, *n.* A small piece of ground; a plan, as of a field, &c., on paper; a scheme; a conspiracy; the story of a play, novel, &c.—*vt.* (plotting, plotted). To make a plan of; to devise.—*vi.* To conspire; to contrive a plan. **plotter**, plot'ėr, *n.* One who plots; a conspirator.

plover, pluv'ėr, *n.* A grallatorial bird, as the golden plover, lapwing, &c.

plow, **plough**, plou, *n.* An instrument for turning up the soil.—*vt.* To turn up with the plow; to make grooves in; to run through, as in sailing.—*vi.* To turn up the soil with a plow; to use a plow.

plowman, **ploughman**, plou"man', *n.* One who holds a plow; a farm laborer.

plowshare, **ploughshare**, plou"shār', *n.* The part of a plow which cuts the ground at the bottom of the furrow.

pluck, pluk, *vt.* To pick or gather; to pull sharply; to twitch; to strip by plucking; to reject as failing in an ex-amination.—*n.* The heart, liver, and lights of a sheep, ox, &c.; courage or spirit. **pluckily**, pluk'i-li, *adv.* In a plucky manner; spiritedly. **plucky**, pluk'i, *a.* Spirited; courageous.

plug, plug, *n.* A stopple or stopper; a bung; a peg; a cake of tobacco.—*vt.* (plugging, plugged). To stop with a plug; to make tight by stopping a hole.

plum, plum, *n.* A fleshy fruit containing a kernel; the tree producing it; a raisin; a handsome sum or fortune generally.

plumage, plöm'ij, *n.* The feathers of a bird.

plumb, plum, *n.* A plummet; a perpendicular position.—*a.* Perpendicular.—*adv.* In a perpendicular direction.—*vt.* To set perpendicularly; to sound with a plummet; to ascertain the capacity of; to sound.

plumber, plum'ėr, *n.* One who works in lead, especially pipes, tanks, &c.

plumb line, plum lin, *n.* A line with a weight attached, used to determine a perpendicular; a plummet.

plume, plöm, *n.* The feather of a bird; a feather or feathers worn as an ornament; an ostrich's feather.—*vt.* (pluming, plumed). To pick and adjust, as feathers; to strip of feathers; to adorn with feathers; *refl.* to pride.

plummet, plum'et, *n.* A piece of lead, &c., attached to a line used in sounding the depth of water; a plumb-line.

plump, plump, *a.* Fat; stout; chubby.—*vt.* To make plump; to dilate.—*vi.* To plunge or fall like a heavy mass; to fall suddenly; to vote for only one candidate.—*adv.* Suddenly; at once; flatly.

plunder, plun'dėr, *vt.* To deprive of goods or valuables; to pillage; to spoil.—*n.* Robbery; pillage; spoil; booty. **plunderer**, plun'dėr-ėr, *n.* One who plunders.

plunge, plunj, *vt.* (plunging, plunged). To thrust into water or other fluid; to immerse; to thrust or push; to cast or involve.—*vi.* To dive or rush into water, &c.; to pitch or throw one's self headlong; to throw the body forward and the hind-legs up, as a horse.—*n.* Act of plunging into water, &c.; act of throwing one's self headlong, like an unruly horse. **plunger**, plun'jėr, *n.* One who or that which plunges; a diver; a solid cylinder used as a piston in pumps.

plunk, plungk, *vt.* To strum (a stringed instrument); to put down forcefully.

plural, plö'ral, *a.* Relating to, containing, or expressing more than one.—*n.* The number which designates more than one.

plurality, plö-ral'i-ti, *n.* State of being plural; two or more; majority; more than one benefice held by the same clergyman.

plus, plus, *n.* A character (+) noting addition.

plush, plush, *n.* A textile fabric with a velvet nap on one side.

plutocrat, plö'tō-krat, *n.* A person possessing power on account of his riches. **plutocracy**, plö-tok'ra-si, *n.* The power or rule of wealth.

plutonic, plö-ton'ik, *a.* Pertaining to Pluto or to the regions of fire; volcanic; subterranean; dark.

plutonium, plö-tō'ni-um, *n.* A radio-active chemical element; symbol *Pu.*

ply, plī, *vt.* (plying, plied). To employ with diligence; to work at; to assail briskly; to beset; to press.—*vi.* To work steadily; to go in haste; to run regularly between any two ports, as a vessel.—*n.* A fold; a plait.

pneumatic, nū-mat'ik, *a.* Pertaining to air; moved or played by means of air; filled with or fitted to contain air.

pneumonia, nū-mō'ni-a, *n.* An inflammation of the lungs.

poach, pōch, *vt.* To cook (eggs) by breaking and pouring among boiling water; to pierce; to tread or stamp.—*vi.* To encroach on another's ground to steal game; to kill game contrary to law; to be or become swampy. **poacher**, pōch'èr, *n.* One who steals game; one who kills game unlawfully.

pock, pok, *n.* A pustule raised on the skin in disease, especially in small-pox.

pocket, pok'et, *n.* A small bag or pouch in a garment, &c.; a certain quantity, from 1½ to 2 cwts., as of hops; a mass of rich ore.—*vt.* To put in the pocket; to take clandestinely.

pocketbook, pok'et-buk', *n.* A small book for carrying papers in the pocket.

pod, pod, *n.* The seed-vessel of certain plants, as peas, &c.—*vi.* (podding, podded). To produce pods; to swell and appear like a pod.

podium, pō'di-om, *n.* A small, raised platform for an orchestra conductor or a public speaker.

poem, pō'em, *n.* A piece of poetry; a composition in verse.

poesy, pō'e-si, *n.* The art of making or composing poems; poetry.

poet, pō'et, *n.* The author of a poem; a person distinguished for poetic talents.

poetaster, pō"et-as'tèr, *n.* A petty poet; a pitiful rhymer or writer of verses.

poetic, poetical, pō-et'ik, pō-et'i-kal, *a.* Pertaining or suitable to poetry; expressed in poetry or measure; possessing the peculiar beauties of poetry.

poetics, pō-et'iks, *n.* That branch of criticism which treats of the nature of poetry.

poetry, pō'et-ri, *n.* The language of the imagination or emotions expressed rhythmically; the artistic expression of thought in emotional language; whatever appeals to the sense of ideal beauty; verse; poems.

poignant, poin'yant, *a.* Sharp to the taste; pointed; keen; bitter; severe; piercing. **poignancy**, poin'yan-si, *n.* Quality of being poignant; severity; acuteness.

point, point, *n.* The sharp end of anything; a small headland; sting of an epigram; telling force of expression; exact spot; verge; stage; degree; a mark of punctuation; a mark or dot; end or purpose; characteristic; argument; *pl.* the movable guiding rails at junctions on railways.—*vt.* To make pointed; to aim; to indicate; to punctuate; to fill the joints of with mortar.—*vi.* To direct the finger to an object; to indicate the presence of game, as dogs do; to show distinctly.

point-blank, point'blangk', *a.* and *adv.* Having a horizontal direction; direct; express.

pointed, point'ed, *p.a.* Having a sharp point; sharp; personal; epigrammatic.

pointer, poin'tèr, *n.* One who or that which points; a kind of dog trained to point out game.

pointless, point'les, *a.* Having no point; blunt; without wit or application.

poise, pois, *n.* Weight; balance; that which balances.—*vt.* (posing, poised). To balance in weight; to hold in equilibrium.—*vi.* To be balanced or suspended; to depend.

poison, poi'zn, *n.* Any agent capable of producing a morbid effect on anything endowed with life.—*vt.* To infect with poison; to taint, impair, or corrupt. **poisonous**, poi'zn-us, *a.* Having the qualities of poison; venomous; deadly.

poke, pōk, *n.* A bag or sack; a pouch; a gentle thrust.—*vt.* (poking, poked). To thrust or push against with something pointed; to stir; to jog.—*vi.* To grope; to search. **poker**, pō'kèr, *n.* One who or that which pokes; an iron bar used in poking a fire; a game at cards.

polar, pō'lèr, *a.* Pertaining to the pole or poles; situated near or proceeding from one of the poles; pertaining to the magnetic pole. **polarity**, pō-lar'i-ti, *n.* State of being polar; property of pointing towards the poles. **polarization**, pō'lèr-ī-zā'shon, *n.* Act of polarizing; state of having polarity. **polarize**, pō'lèr-iz, *vt.* To communicate polarity or polarization to.

Polaris, pō-lär'is, *n.* The North Star.

pole, pōl, *n.* A long piece of wood; a measure of 5½ yards or 30¼ square yards; one of the extremities of the axis of the celestial sphere or the earth; the pole-star; one of the two points in a magnet in which the power seems concentrated; (with cap.) a native of Poland.—*vt.* (poling, poled). To furnish with poles; to impel by poles.

poleax, poleaxe, pōl"aks', *n.* A battle-ax; an ax used in killing cattle.

pole-cat, pōl'kat, *n.* A carnivorous animal, nearly allied to the weasel, distinguished by its offensive smell.

polemic, pō-lem'ik, *a.* Pertaining to controversy; disputative.—*n.* A disputant. **polemical**, pō-lem'i-kal, *a.* Polemic. **polemics**, pō-lem'iks, *n.* Disputation; controversial writings.

police, pō'lēs', *n.* The internal government of a community; a body of civil officers for enforcing order, cleanliness, &c.—*vt.* (policing, policed). To guard or regulate by police. **policeman**, pō-lēs'man, *n.* An ordinary member of a body of police.

policy, pol'i-si, *n.* The governing a city, state, or nation; line of conduct with respect to foreign or internal affairs; dexterity of management; pleasure-grounds around a mansion; contract of insurance.

Polish, pŏl'ish, *a.* Of Poland.—*n.* Language of Poland.

polish, pŏl'ish, *vt.* To make smooth and glossy; to make elegant and polite.—*vt.* To become smooth; to receive a gloss.—*n.* Gloss; elegance of manners.

polite, pō-līt', *a.* Polished in manners; refined; urbane; elegant; well-bred.

politic, po'li-tik, *a.* Showing policy; adapted to the public prosperity; sagacious; subtle; well devised. **body politic,** the citizens of a state. **political,** pō-lit'i-kal, *a.* Belonging or pertaining to a nation or state; public; derived from connection with government; politic; treating of politics. **politician,** pol-i-tish'an, *n.* One versed in or occupying himself with politics. **politics,** pol'i-tiks, *n.* The science of government; political affairs, or the contests of parties for power.

polka, pōl'ka, *n.* A dance of Bohemian origin; the air played to the dance.

poll, pōl, *n.* The head or the back part of the head; a register of persons; the voting of electors; an election.—*vt.* To lop or clip; to enroll or register; to receive or give, as votes.

pollen, pol'en, *n.* The fecundating dust or male element of flowers. **pollenize,** pol'en-īz, *vt.* To supply or impregnate with pollen. **pollinate,** pol'i-nāt, *vt.* To pollenize.

poll tax, pōl taks, *n.* A tax levied by the poll or head; a capitation-tax.

pollute, po-lūt', *vt.* (polluting, polluted). To defile; to profane; to taint morally; to debauch. **pollution,** po-lū'shun, *n.* Act of polluting; defilement; uncleanness.

polo, pō'lō, *n.* A game at ball resembling hockey, played on horseback.

poltroon, pol-trön' or pol', *n.* An arrant coward; a dastard.—*a.* Base; vile.

polyandry, pol''i-an'dri, *n.* The practice of having more husbands than one at the same time.

polygamy, po-lig'a-mi, *n.* The practice of having more wives or husbands than one at the same time. **polygamist,** po-lig'a-mist, *n.* A person who practices polygamy.

polyglot, pol'i-glot, *a.* Many-tongued; containing, speaking, or knowing several languages.—*n.* A book (as a Bible) printed in several languages in parallel columns.

polygon, pol'i-gon, *n.* A plane figure of many angles and sides.

polyhedron, pol''i-hē''drun, *n.* A body or solid contained by many sides or planes.

Polynesian, pol''i-nē''shan, *n.* A native of Polynesia, a group of islands in the South Pacific.

polyp, polype, pol'ip, *n.* The sea-anemone, or some allied animal.

polysyllable, pol''i-sil'a-bl, *n.* A word of more syllables than three.

polytechnic, pol''i-tek'nik, *a.* Comprehending many arts; designating a school teaching many branches of art or science.—*n.* A school of instruction in arts.

pomade, pō-mād', *n.* Perfumed ointment; pomatum.

pomegranate, pŏm''gran'it, *n.* A fruit of the size of an orange, containing numerous seeds; the tree producing the fruit.

pommel, pum'el, *n.* A knob or ball; the knob on the hilt of a sword; the protuberant part of a saddle-bow.—*vt.* (pommeling, pommeled). To beat; to belabor.

pomp, pomp, *n.* A showy procession; display; pageantry; splendor; parade. **pomposity,** pom-pos'i-ti, *n.* Ostentation; vainglorious show. **pompous,** pomp'us, *a.* Displaying pomp; showy; ostentatious; high-flown.

pond, pond, *n.* A body of water less than a lake, artificial or natural.

ponder, pon'dėr, *vt.* To weigh in the mind; to consider.—*vi.* To deliberate. **ponderable,** pon'dėr-a-bl, *a.* That may be weighed. **ponderous,** pon'dėr-us, *a.* Heavy; weighty; massive.

pongee, pon'jē, *n.* A soft unbleached silk.

poniard, pon'yėrd, *n.* A small dagger.—*vt.* To pierce with a poniard; to stab.

pontiff, pon'tif, *n.* A high priest; applied particularly to the pope. **pontifical,** pon'tif'i-kal, *a.* Belonging to a high-priest or to the pope.—*n.* A book containing rites performable by a bishop; *pl.* the dress of a priest or bishop. **pontificate,** pon-tif'i-kāt, *n.* The dignity of a high-priest; papacy.

pontoon, pon-tön', *n.* A kind of boat for supporting temporary bridges; a water-tight structure to assist in raising submerged vessels.

pony, pō'ni, *n.* A small horse.

poodle, pö'dl, *n.* A small dog with long silky curling hair.

pooh, pö, *interj.* An exclamation of contempt or disdain; poh.

pooh-pooh, pö'pö', *vt.* To sneer at.

pool, pöl, *n.* A small pond; a puddle; a hole in the course of a stream; the stakes at cards, &c.; a variety of play at billiards.

poop, pöp, *vt.* The stern of a ship; the highest and aftmost deck of a ship.

poor, pör, *a.* Needy; indigent; destitute of value or merit; infertile; mean; paltry; lean; weak; impotent; unhappy; wretched.

pop, pop, *n.* A small, smart sound.—*vi.* (popping, popped). To make a small, smart sound; to enter or issue forth suddenly.—*vt.* To offer with a quick sudden motion; to thrust or push suddenly.—*adv.* Suddenly.

popcorn, pop'korn, *n.* Parched maize.

pope, pöp, *n.* The head of the Roman Catholic church.

popinjay, pop'in-jā, *n.* A parrot; the green woodpecker; a fop.

poplar, pop'lėr, *n.* A tree of numerous species.

poplin, pop'lin, *n.* A fabric made of silk and wool, of many varieties.

poppy, pop'i, *a.* A plant with showy flowers and yielding opium.

populace, pop'ū-lis, *n.* The common people; the multitude; the mob.

popular, pop'ū-lėr, *a.* Pertaining to the common people; familiar; plain; liked by people in general; prevalent. **popu-**

larity, pop'ŭ-lar"i-ti, *n.* State or quality of being popular; favor of the people. **popularize**, pop'ŭ-lẽr-īz, *vt.* To make popular or suitable to the common mind; to spread among the people.

populate, pop'ŭ-lāt, *vt.* To people; to furnish with inhabitants. **population**, pop'ū-lā"shun, *n.* Act or process of populating; number of people in a country, &c.; the inhabitants. **populous**, pop'ŭ-lus, *a.* Abounding in people; full of inhabitants.

porcelain, pōr'se-lin, *n.* The finest species of pottery ware.

porch, pōrch, *n.* A portico; covered approach at the entrance of buildings.

porcine, pōr'sīn, *a.* Pertaining to swine; like a swine; hog-like.

porcupine, pôr'kū-pīn, *n.* A rodent animal, about 2 feet long, with erectile spines.

pore, pōr, *n.* A minute opening in the skin, through which the perspirable matter passes; a small interstice.—*vi.* (poring, pored). To look with steady attention; to read or examine with perseverance.

porgie, porgy pōr'gi, *n.* A kind of fish.

pork, pōrk, *n.* The flesh of swine, fresh or salted, used for food. **porker**, pōr'kẽr, *n.* A hog; a young pig for roasting.

pornography, por-nog'ra-fi, *n.* Literature in which prostitutes figure.

porous, pō'rus, *a.* Having pores. **porosity**, pō-ros'i-ti, *n.* Quality or state of being porous.

porphyry, por'fi-ri, *n.* A reddish Egyptian stone like granite; a hard igneous rock containing crystals of feldspar, &c.

porpoise, por'pus, *n.* A small cetaceous mammal of the Northern Seas.

porridge, por'ij, *n.* A kind of soup or broth; a dish of oatmeal boiled in water till thickened.

porringer, por'in-jẽr, *n.* A small dish for porridge.

port, pōrt, *n.* A harbor or haven; a gate; an opening in the side of a ship; a porthole; the left side of a ship; mien; demeanor.—*vt.* To carry (as a rifle) slanting upwards towards the left; to turn to the left, as the helm.

port, port wine, pōrt, pōrt wīn, *n.* A kind of wine made in Portugal.

portable, pōr'ta-bl, *a.* That may be carried; not bulky or heavy.

portage, pōr'tij, *n.* Act of carrying; carriage; freight.

portal, pōr'tal, *n.* A door or gate; the main entrance of a cathedral, &c.—*a.* Belonging to a vein connected with the liver.

portcullis, pōrt-kul'is, *n.* A sliding or falling grating of timber or iron at the gateway of a fortified place.

portend, por-tend', *vt.* To foretoken; to presage; to threaten. **portent**, por'tent or por-tent', *n.* That which foretokens; an omen of ill. **portentous**, por-ten'tus, *a.* Ominous; fore-showing ill; monstrous; wonderful.

porter, pōr'tẽr, *n.* A doorkeeper; a carrier; a dark brown malt liquor.

portfolio, pōrt-fō'li-ō, *n.* A case for drawings, papers, &c.; office and functions of a minister of state.

porthole, pōrt'hōl', *n.* The embrasure of a ship of war.

portico, pōr'ti-kō, *n.* A colonnade or covered walk; a porch.

portion, pōr'shun, *n.* A part; a share or allotment; fate; final state.—*vt.* To parcel; to divide.

portly, pōrt'li, *a.* Of noble carriage or bearing; stately; rather tall, and inclining to stoutness.

portmanteau, pōrt-man'tō, *n.* A bag for carrying clothes, &c., in traveling:

portrait, pōr'trāt, *n.* A picture of a person; a vivid description. **portraiture**, pōr'trā-tūr, *n.* A portrait; the art or practice of making portraits, or describing vividly in words.

portray, pōr-trā', *vt.* To delineate; to depict; to describe in words. **portrayal**, pōr-trā'al, *n.* The act of portraying; delineation; representation.

Portuguese, por'tū-gēz, *a.* Pertaining to Portugal.—*n.* The language of Portugal; the people of Portugal.

pose, pōz, *n.* Attitude or position; an artistic posture.—*vi.* (posing, posed). To attitudinize; to assume characteristic airs.—*vt.* To cause to assume a certain posture; to state or lay down; to perplex or puzzle. **poser**, pōz'ẽr, *n.* One who poses; something that poses, puzzles, or puts to silence.

position, pō-zish'un, *n.* State of being placed; place; posture; rank; state; principle laid down; thesis.

positive, poz'i-tiv, *a.* Definitely laid down; explicit; absolute; actual; confident; dogmatic; affirmative; noting the simple state of an adjective; applied to the philosophical system of Auguste Comte, which limits itself to human experience; applied to electricity produced by rubbing a vitreous substance.—*n.* That which is positive; the positive degree.

posse, pos'ē, *n.* A small body of men; possibility.

possess, po-zes', *vt.* To have and hold; to own; to affect by some power or influence; to pervade; to put in possession; to furnish or fill. **possession**, po-zesh'un, *n.* Act or state of possessing; ownership; occupancy; land, estate, or goods owned. **possessive**, po-zes'iv, *a.* Pertaining to possession; expressing or denoting possession.—*n.* The possessive case; a pronoun or other word denoting possession. **possessor**, po-zes'ẽr, *n.* One who possesses; owner; master; occupant.

possible, pos'i-bl, *a.* That may be or exist; that may be done; practicable; not impossible, though improbable. **possibility**, pos'i-bil"i-ti, *n.* State or condition of being possible.

post, pōst, *n.* A piece of timber, &c., set up-right; a place assigned; a military or other station; office or employment; a carrier of letters, messages, &c.; a system for the public conveyance of letters, &c.; a post-office; a size of paper, about 18 or 19 inches by 15.—*vi.* To travel with post-horses; to hasten on.—

vt. To place; to place in the post-office; to transfer (accounts or items) to the ledger; to make master of full details; to fix up in some public place.—*a.* Used in traveling quickly.

postage, post'ij, *n.* The charge for conveying letters or other articles by post.

postal, pos'tal, *a.* Relating to posts, or the carrying of mails.

post card, post'kärd', *n.* A card sent by post as a means of correspondence.

post chaise, post' shäz' *n.* A chaise for travelers who travel with post-horses.

post-date, post'dät", *vt.* To inscribe with a later date than the real one.

poster, pos'tėr, *n.* One who posts; a courier; a large printed bill for advertising.

posterior, pos-tēr-i-ėr, *a.* Later or subsequent; hinder.—*n.* A hinder part; *pl.* the hinder parts of an animal.

posterity, pos-te'ri-ti, *n.* Descendants; succeeding generations.

postern, post'ėrn, *n.* A back door; private entrance; a covered passage under a rampart.

posthaste, post-häst', *n.* Haste or speed.—*adv.* With speed or expedition.

post horse, post'hors, *n.* A horse for the rapid conveyance of passengers, &c.

posthumous, pos'tū-mus, *a.* Born after the death of the father; published after the death of the author; existing after one's decease.

postilion, (or -lI-), post-til'yun, *n.* One who rides the near leading horse of a carriage and four, or the near horse of a pair.

postman, post-man, *n.* A post or courier; letter-carrier.

postmaster, post"mas'tėr, *n.* The officer who superintends a post-office.

post meridian, post me-rid'i-an, *a.* After the meridian; being in the afternoon. P.M.

post-mortem, post'mor"tem, *a.* After death.—*n.* An examination or inquiry after death.

post office, post of'is, *n.* An office where letters are received for transmission; a government department that has the duty of conveying letters, &c.

postpone, post-pōn', *vt.* (postponing, postponed). To put off to a later time; to set below something else in value.

postponement, post-pōn'ment, *n.* Act of postponing.

postscript, post'skript, *n.* A paragraph added to a letter after it is signed; something added on to a book, &c., by way of supplement.

postulate, pos'tū-lāt, *n.* Something assumed for the purpose of future reasoning; enunciation of a self-evident problem.—*vt.* To assume or take for granted.

posture, pos'tūr, *n.* Attitude; relative position of parts; situation; condition.

posy, pō'zi, *n.* A verse or motto inscribed on a ring, &c., or sent with a nosegay; a bouquet.

pot, pot, *n.* A metallic or earthenware vessel more deep than broad; the quantity contained in a pot; a sort of paper of small-sized sheets.—*vt.* (potting,

potted). To put in a pot; to preserve in pots; to plant in a pot of earth.

potable, pō'ta-bl, *a.* Drinkable.

potash, pot'ash, *n.* Vegetable alkali in an impure state, procured from the ashes of plants.

potassium, pō-tas'i-um, *n.* The metallic basis of potash, a soft, white, light metal.

potato, pō-tā'tō, *n.*; *pl.* -oes. A well-known plant and its esculent tuber.

potboiler, pot"boil'ėr, *n.* A work of art executed merely to earn money.

potency, pō'ten-si, *n.* State or quality of being potent; might; force. **potent**, pō'tent, *a.* Mighty; strong; powerful; efficacious. **potentate**, pō'ten-tāt, *n.* One who possesses great power or sway; a monarch. **potential**, pō-ten'shal, *a.* Possible; latent; that may be manifested. **potentiality**, pō-ten'shi-al"i-ti, *n.* Quality of being potential; possibility; not actuality.

pother, pothʼėr, *n.* Bustle; confusion; flutter.—*vi.* To make a pother or stir.—*vt.* To harass; to puzzle.

potion, pō'shun, *n.* A draught; a liquid medicine; a dose to be drunk.

potluck, pot"luk', *n.* What may be for a meal without special preparation.

potpourri, pō'pö-rē", *n.* A mixed dish of meat and vegetables; a medley.

potsherd, pot"shėrd', *n.* A piece or fragment of an earthenware pot.

pottage, pot'ij, *n.* A food of meat boiled to softness in water; porridge.

potter, pot'ėr, *n.* One who makes earthenware vessels or crockery.—*vi.* To busy one's self about trifles; to move slowly. **pottery**, pot'ėr-i, *n.* The ware made by potters; place where earthen vessels are made.

pouch, pouch, *n.* A pocket; a small bag.—*vt.* To put into a couch; to pocket.

poultice, pōl'tis, *n.* A soft composition applied to sores.—*vt.* (poulticing, poulticed). To apply a poultice to.

poultry, pōl'tri, *n.* Domestic fowls.

pounce, pouns, *n.* A fine powder to prevent ink from spreading on paper; the claw or talon of a bird.—*vt.* (pouncing, pounced). To sprinkle or rub with pounce.—*vi.* To fall on and seize with the pounces or talons; to fall on suddenly.

pound, pound, *n.* A standard weight of 12 ounces troy or 16 ounces avoirdupois; an English money of account, equal to twenty shillings; an inclosure for cattle.—*vt.* To confine in a pound; to beat; to pulverize. **poundage**, poun'dij, *n.* A rate per pound; payment rated by the weight of a commodity; confinement of cattle in a pound.

pour, pōr, *vi.* To flow or issue forth in a stream.—*vt.* To let flow out or in; to emit; to throw in profusion.

pout, pout, *vi.* To thrust out the lips; to look sullen; to be prominent.—*n.* Protrusion of the lips. **pouter**, pou'tėr, *n.* One who pouts; a kind of pigeon with a prominent breast.

poverty, pov-ėr-ti, *n.* State of being poor; indigence; want; defect; insufficiency.

powder, pou'dèr, *n.* A dry substance of minute particles; dust; gunpowder.—*vt.* To reduce to fine particles; to sprinkle with powder; to corn as meat.—*vi.* To fall to dust; to use powder for the hair or face. **powdery,** pou'dèr-i, *a.* Dusty; friable.

power, pou'èr, *n.* Ability to act or do; strength; influence; talent; command; authority; one who exercises authority; a state or government; warrant; a mechanical advantage or effect; product of the multiplication of a number by itself. **powerful,** pou'èr-ful, *a.* Having great power; strong; potent; cogent; influential. **powerless,** pou'èr-les, *a.* Destitute of power; weak; impotent.

pox, poks, *n.* A disease characterized by pecks or pustules.

practice, practise, prak'tis, *n.* A doing or effecting; custom; habit; actual performance; exercise of any profession; medical treatment; training; drill; dexterity.—*vt.* practicing, practiced). To put in practice; to do or perform frequently or habitually; to exercise, as any profession; to commit; to teach by practice.—*vi.* To perform certain acts frequently for instruction or amusement; to exercise some profession. **practicability,** prak'ti-ka-bil"i-ti, *n.* Quality or state of being practicable. **practicable,** prak'ti-ka-bl, *a.* That may be done or effected; feasible; passable. **practical,** prak'ti-kal, *a.* Pertaining to practice, action, or use; not merely theoretical; skilled in actual work.

practitioner, prak-tish'un-èr, *n.* One engaged in some profession, particularly law or medicine.

pragmatic, pragmatical, prag-mat'ik, prag-mat'i-kal, *a.* Meddling; impertinently busy or officious.

prairie, prår'i, *n.* An extensive tract of grassy land, generally destitute of trees.

praise, prāz, *n.* Approbation or admiration expressed; eulogy; honor; gratitude or homage to God, often in song; the object, ground, or reason of praise.—*vt.* (praising, praised). To extol; to commend; to honor. **praiseworthy,** prāz"wèr'THi, *a.* Deserving of praise; commendable; laudable.

prance, prans, *vi.* (prancing, pranced). To spring, leap, or caper, as a horse; to strut about ostentatiously.

prank, prangk, *vt.* To adorn in a showy manner; to dress up.—*vi.* To have a showy appearance.—*n.* A merry trick; a caper.

prate, prāt, *vi.* (prating, prated). To babble, chatter, tattle.—*vt.* To utter foolishly.—*n.* Trifling talk; unmeaning loquacity.

prattle, prat'l, *vi.* (prattling, prattled). To talk much and idly, like a child; to prate.—*n.* Trifling or puerile talk.

prawn, pran, *n.* A small crustaceous animal of the shrimp family.

pray, prā, *vi.* and *t.* To beg, supplicate, or implore; to address God.

prayer, prar, *n.* One who prays; the act of praying; a petition; a solemn petition to God; a formula of worship, public or private; that part of a written petition which specifies the thing desired to be granted.

preach, prēch, *vi.* To deliver a sermon; to give earnest advice.—*vt.* To proclaim; to publish in religious discourses; to deliver in public, as a discourse. **preacher,** prēch'èr, *n.* One who preaches; a person who delivers a sermon. **preachment,** prēch'ment, *n.* A sermon; a discourse affectedly solemn (in contempt).

preamble, prē-am'bl, or prē', *n.* An introduction; introductory part of a statute.

precarious, prē-kā̇r'i-us, *a.* Depending on the will of another; uncertain; insecure.

precaution, prē-kạ'shun, *n.* Previous care; caution to prevent evil or secure good.—*vt.* To caution beforehand.

precede, prē-sēd', *vt.* (preceding, preceded). To go before in time, rank, or importance; to preface. **precedence, precedency,** prē-sēd'ens, prē-sēd'en-si, *n.* Act or state of preceding; priority; order according to rank; superior importance. **precedent,** prē-sēd'ent, *a.* Preceding; going before in time; anterior. **precedent,** prē' or pre'sē-dent, *n.* Something done or said, serving as an example or rule.

precept, prē'sept, *n.* Anything enjoined as an authoritative rule of action; injunction; doctrine; maxim. **preceptive,** prē-sep'tiv, *a.* Containing precepts; didactic. **preceptor,** prē-sep'tèr, *n.* A teacher; an instructor; the teacher of a school.

precession, prē-sesh'un, *n.* Act of going before; advance.

precinct, prē'singt, *n.* A bounding line; a part near a border; a minor territorial division.

precious, presh'us, *a.* Of great worth or value; costly; cherished; affected.

precipice, pres'i-pis, *n.* A headless declivity; a steep or overhanging cliff.

precipitance, precipitancy, prē-sip'i-tans, prē-sip'i-tan-si, *n.* Headlong hurry; rash or excessive haste.

precipitant, prē-sip'i-tant, *a.* Falling or rushing headlong; precipitate.

precipitate, prē-sip'i-tāt, *vt.* and *i.* To throw or hurl headlong; to hasten excessively; to cause to sink or to fall to the bottom of a vessel, as a substance in solution.—*a.* Headlong; overhasty.—*n.* A substance deposited from a liquid in which it has been dissolved.

precipitous, prē-sip'i-tus, *a.* Very steep; headlong in descent.

précis, prā-sē', *n.* A concise or abridged statement; a summary; an abstract.

precise, prē-sīs', *a.* Sharply or exactly defined; exact; strictly accurate or correct; particular; formal; punctilious. **precisian,** prē-sizh'an, *n.* One rigidly exact in the observance of rules. **precision,** prē-sizh'on, *n.* State of being precise; exactness; accuracy.

preclude, prē-klöd', *vt.* (precluding, precluded). To shut out; to hinder; to render inoperative by anticipative action. **preclusive,** prē-klö'siv, *a.* Tending to preclude; hindering by previous obstacles.

precocious, prē-kō'shus, *a.* Ripe before the natural time; acting like an adult though not grown up. **precocity**, prē-kos'i-ti, *n.* State or quality of being precocious; early development of the mental powers.

preconceive, prē'kon-sēv", *vt.* To form a conception or opinion of beforehand. **preconception**, prē'kon-sep"shun, *n.* Act of preconceiving; conception previously formed.

precursory, prē-kėr'sō-ri, *a.* Forerunning. **precursor**, prē-kėr'sėr, *n.* A forerunner; a harbinger.

predacious, prē-dā'shus, *a.* Living by prey; given to prey on other animals. **predatory**, pred'a-tō-ri, *a.* Plundering; practicing rapine.

predecessor, pred'ē-ses"ėr, *n.* One who has preceded another in any state, office, &c.

predestination, prē-des'ti-nā"shon, *n.* The act of foredaining events; the doctrine that God has from eternity determined whatever comes to pass, and has preordained men to everlasting happiness or misery.

predetermine, prē'dē-tėr"min, *vt.* and *i.* To determine beforehand.

predicament, prē-dik'a-ment, *n.* Class or kind; condition; dangerous or trying state.

predicate, pred'i-kāt, *vt.* and *i.* To affirm one thing of another; to assert.—*n.* In *logic*, that which is affirmed or denied of the subject; in *grammar*, the word or words which express what is affirmed or denied of the subject. **predication**, pred'i-kā"shun, *n.* The act of predicating; affirmation; assertion. **predicative**, pred"i-kā'tiv, *a.* Expressing predication; not used before a noun.

predict, prē-dikt', *vt.* To foretell; to prophesy. **prediction**, prē-dik'shun, *n.* The act of predicting; a prophecy. **predictor**, prēdik'tėr, *n.* One who predicts.

predilection, prē'di-lek"shun, *n.* A previous liking or preference; a prepossession of mind in favor of a person or thing.

predispose, prē'dis-pōz", *vt.* To dispose beforehand; to fit or adapt previously.

predominate, prē-dom'i-nāt, *vi.* and *i.* To have surpassing power or authority; to rule. **predominant**, prē-dom'i-nant, *a.* Predominating; prevalent; ruling; controlling. **predominance, predominancy**, prē-dom'i-nans, prē-dom'i-nan-si, *n.* Prevalence over others; superiority; ascendancy.

pre-eminent, prē-em'i-nent, *a.* Eminent above others; surpassing or distinguished. **pre-eminence**, prē-em'i-nens, *n.* State of being pre-eminent; superiority.

pre-emption, prē-emp'shun, *n.* The act or right of purchasing before others.

preen, prēn, *vt.* To trim with the beak; said of birds dressing their feathers.

preface, pref'ās, *n.* Something introductory to a discourse or book, &c.—*vt.* (prefacing, prefaced). To introduce by preliminary remarks. **prefatory**, pref"-a-tō'ri, *a.* Pertaining to or having the nature of a preface.

prefect, praefect, prē'fekt, *n.* One placed over others; a governor, chief magistrate. **prefecture**, prē'fek-tūr, *n.* Office, jurisdiction, or official residence of a prefect.

prefer, prē-fėr', *vt.* (preferring, preferred). To bring or lay before; to present, as a petition, &c.; to exalt; to set higher in estimation; to choose rather. **preferable**, pref'ėr-a-bl, *a.* Worthy to be preferred; more desirable. **preference**, pref'ėr-ens, *n.* Act of preferring; state of being preferred; choice. **preferential**, pref'ėr-en"shal, *a.* Implying preference. **preferment**, prē-fėr'ment, *n.* Act of preferring; promotion; a superior office.

prefix, prē-fiks', *vt.* To put before or at the beginning of something.—*n.* prē'fiks. A letter, syllable, or word added at the beginning of a word.

pregnant, preg'nant, *a.* Being with young; full of meaning or consequence. **pregnancy**, preg'nan-si, *n.* State of being pregnant; time of going with child. **prehensile**, prē-hen'sīl, *a.* Fitted for seizing or laying hold; grasping.

prehistoric, prē'his-tor"ik, *a.* Relating to a time anterior to written records.

prejudge, prē-juj', *vt.* To judge beforehand; to condemn unheard. **prejudgment**, prē-juj'ment, *n.* Judgment without full examination. **prejudicate**, prē-jū'di-kāt, *vt.* and *i.* To prejudge; to judge with prejudice.

prejudice, prej'ō-dis, *n.* An unwarranted bias; prepossession; detriment; injury.—*vt.* To bias the mind of; to do harm to. **prejudicial**, prej'ō-dish"al, *a.* Causing prejudice; hurtful; detrimental.

prelate, prel'it, *n.* An ecclesiastic of high rank, as an archbishop, bishop, &c.

preliminary, prē-lim"i-ner'i, *a.* Introductory; preparatory; prefatory.—*n.* Something introductory; preface; prelude.

prelude, prel'ūd or prē-lūd', *vt.* (preluding, preluded). To introduce; to preface. —*vi.* To form a prelude.—*n.* prel'ūd or prē'lūd. Something preparatory; a musical introduction.

premature, prē'ma-tūr", *a.* Happening; performed, &c., too early; untimely.

premeditate, prē-med'i-tāt, *vt.* and *i.* To meditate upon beforehand; to contrive previously; to deliberate. **premeditation**, prē'med-i-tā"shun, *n.* Act of premeditating; previous deliberation.

premier, prē'mi-ėr, *a.* First; chief.—*n.* The first minister of state; prime minister.

premise, prē'mīz', *vt.* (premising, premised). To put forward by way of preface; to lay down, as antecedent to another statement.—*vi.* To make an introductory statement.

premise, premiss, pre'mis, *n.* A proposition laid down as a base of argument; *pl.* the portion of a legal document where articles of property to be transferred are described; a house and its adjuncts.

premium, prē'mi-um, *n.* A reward or prize; a bonus; a bounty; sum paid for insurance; increase in value.

premonition, pre'mō-nish"un, *n.* Previous warning, notice, or information. **premonitory**, prē-mon"i-tō'ri, a. Giving previous warning or notice.

preoccupy, prē-ok'ū-pī, vt. To occupy before another; to engross before another; to engross beforehand. **preoccupancy**, prē-ok'ū-pan-si, n. Preoccupation; previous occupancy. **preoccupation**, prē-ok'ū-pā"shun, n. Act of preoccupying; prior possession; state of being preoccupied. **preoccupied**, prē-ok'ū-pid, p.a. Occupied beforehand; absorbed; abstracted.

preordain, prē'or-dān', vt. To appoint beforehand; to foreordain.

prepare, prē-pār', vt. and i. (preparing, prepared). To make ready; to adjust; to provide; to procure as suitable. **preparation**, prep'a-rā"shun, n. Act or operation of preparing; that which is prepared; state of being prepared. **preparatory**, prē-par"a-tō'ri, a. Serving to prepare; introductory; preliminary.

prepay, prē-pā', vt. To pay in advance. **prepayment**, prē-pā'ment, n. Act of prepaying; payment in advance.

preponderant, prē-pon'dėr-ant, a. Superior in power, influence, or the like. **preponderance**, prē-pon'dėr-ans, n. State of being preponderant. **preponderate**, prē-pon'dėr-āt, vt. To outweigh; to exceed in influence or power.

preposition, prep'ō-zish"un, n. A word governing a noun, pronoun, or clause. **prepositional**, pre-pö-zi'shon-al, a. Pertaining to a preposition.

prepossess, prē'po-zes", vt. To take possession of beforehand; to preoccupy; to prejudice. **prepossession**, prē'po-zesh"un, n. Preconceived opinion; prejudice; bias.

preposterous, prē-pos'tėr-us, a. Absurd; irrational; monstrous; utterly ridiculous.

prerogative, prē-rog'a-tiv, n. A prior claim or title; an exclusive privilege; an official and hereditary right.

presage, pres'ij, or prē'sāj, n. A presentiment; a prognostic, omen, or sign.—vt. and i. prē-sāj', (presaging, presaged). To betoken; to forebode; to predict.

Presbyterian, prez'bi-tēr"i-an, a. Pertaining to presbyters; pertaining to ecclesiastical government by presbyteries. —n. A member of one of the Christian churches who vest church governments in presbyteries.

prescient, prē'shi-ent, a. Foreknowing. **prescience**, prē'shi-ens, n. Foreknowledge.

prescribe, prē-skrib', vt. (prescribing, prescribed). To lay down authoritatively for direction; to appoint; to direct to be used as a remedy.—vi. To give directions; to give medical directions; to become of no validity through lapse of time. **prescription**, prē-skrip'shun, n. Act of prescribing; that which is prescribed; a claim or title based on long use; the loss of a legal right by lapse of time. **prescriptive**, prē-skrip'tiv, a. Consisting in or acquired by long use.

present, prez'ent, a. Being at hand, in view, or in a certain place; not existing; ready at hand: quick in emergency.—n. Present time; pl. term used in a legal document for the document itself. **presence**, prē'zens, n. State of being present; existence in a certain place; company; sight; port; mien; the person of a great personage; an appearance or apparition; readiness.

present, prē-zent', vt. To introduce to or bring before a superior; to show; to give or bestow; to nominate to an ecclesiastical benefice; to lay before a public body for consideration; to point or aim, as a weapon.—n. prē'zent. A donation; a gift.

presentable, prē-zen'ta-bl, a. That may be presented; in such trim as to be able to present one's self. **presentation**, prez'en-tā"shun, n. Act of presenting; thing presented; the act or right of presenting a clergyman to a parish.

presentiment, prē-sen'ti-ment, n. Previous apprehension; anticipation of impending evil; foreboding.

presentment, prē-zent'ment, n. Act of presenting; appearance; representation.

preserve, prē-zėrv', vt. (preserving, preserved). To save from injury; to keep in a sound state; to maintain; to restrict the hunting of, as game.—n. Something that is preserved, as fruit, vegetables, &c.; ground set apart for animals intended for sport or food. **preservation**, prez'ėr-vā"shun, n. Act of preserving; state of being preserved; safety. **preservative**, prē-zėr'vā-tiv, a. Tending to preserve.—n. That which preserves; a preventive of injury or decay.

preside, prē-zīd', vi. (presiding, presided). To exercise authority or superintendence; to have the post of chairman. **presidency**, prez'i-den-si, n. Act of presiding; the office, jurisdiction, or term of office of a president. **president**, prez'i-dent, n. One who presides; the head of a province or state; the highest officer of state in a republic. **presidential**, prez-i-den'shal, a. Pertaining to a president. **presidentship**, prez'i-dent-ship, n. The office of president.

press, pres, vt. To bear or weigh heavily upon; to squeeze; to urge; to enforce; to emphasize; to solicit earnestly; to force into service.—vi. To bear heavily or with force; to crowd; to push with force.—n. A pressing; a crowd; an instrument for squeezing or crushing; a machine for printing; the art or business of printing; periodical literature; an upright cupboard; urgency.

pressing, pres'ing, p.a. Urgent.

pressman, pres'man, n. One who attends to a printing-press; a journalist.

pressure, presh'ėr, n. The act of pressing; the force of one body acting on another; moral force; distress or difficulty; urgency.

prestidigitation, pres'ti-di'ji-tā"shon, n. Skill in legerdemain; juggling.

prestige, pres-tēzh' or pres'tij, n. Influence based on high character or conduct.

presto, pres'tō, adv. Quickly; in a trice.

presume, prē-zūm', vt. (presuming, presumed). To take for granted; to take the liberty; to make bold.—*vi.* To infer; to act in a forward way. **presumption,** prē-zump'shun, *n.* Act of presuming; supposition; forwardness; arrogance. **presumptive,** prē-zump'tiv, *a.* Based on presumption or probability. **presumptuous,** prē-zump'tū-us, *a.* Taking undue liberties; arrogant; overweening.

presuppose, prē'su-pōz", *vt.* To suppose or imply as previous; to necessitate as prior.

pretend, prē-tend', *vt.* To feign; to simulate; to assume or profess to feel; use as a pretext.—*vi.* To assume a false character; to sham; to put in a claim. **pretense, pretence,** pre-tens', *n.* Act of pretending; simulation; feint; pretext. **pretentious,** prē-ten'shus, *a.* Full of pretension; showy.

preterit, preterite, pret'ėr-it, *a.* Past.—*n.* The past tense.

preternatural, prē'tėr-nat''ūr-al, *a.* Beyond what is natural; abnormal; anomalous.

pretext, prē'tekst or prē-tekst', *n.* An ostensible reason or motive; a pretense.

pretty, prit'i, *a.* Having diminutive beauty; of a pleasing form without dignity; comely; neatly arranged; affectedly nice; foppish.—*adv.* Moderately. **prettily,** prit'i-li, *adv.* In a pretty manner.

pretzel, pret'sel, *n.* A salted biscuit baked in the form of a loose knot.

prevail, prē-vāl', *vi.* To gain the victory or superiority; to be in force; to succeed; to gain over by persuasion. **prevalence, prevalency,** prev'a-lens, prev'a-len-si, *n.* State or quality of being prevalent; superiority. **prevalent,** prev'alent, *a.* Prevailing; predominant; extensively existing.

prevaricate, prē-var'i-kāt, *vi.* To act or speak evasively; to shuffle; to quibble. **prevarication,** prē-var'i-kā"shun, *n.* Act of prevaricating; a shuffling or quibbling; misrepresentation by giving evasive evidence. **prevaricator,** prē-var'i-kā-tėr, *n.* One who prevaricates.

prevent, prē-vent', *vt.* To stop or intercept; to impede; to thwart. **prevention,** prē-ven'shun, *n.* The act of preventing; a hindering by previous action; measure of precaution. **preventive,** prē-ven'tiv, *a.* Tending to prevent.—*n.* That which prevents; an antidote previously taken. Also *Preventitive.*

previous, prē'vi-us, *a.* Antecedent; prior.

prey, prā, *n.* Property taken from an enemy; spoil; booty; a victim.—*vi.* To take prey or booty; to get food by rapine; to cause to pine away; with *on.*

price, prīs, *n.* The value which a seller sets on his goods; cost; value; worth.— *vt.* (pricing, priced). To set a price on; to ask the price of. **priceless,** prīs'les, *a.* Too valuable to admit of a price; invaluable; inestimable.

prick, prik, *n.* A slender pointed thing that can pierce; a thorn; a puncture by a prick; a sting; tormenting thought.— *vt.* To pierce with a prick; to erect, as ears; to spur; to sting with remorse; to

trace by puncturing.—*vi.* To spur on; to ride rapidly; to feel a prickly sensation.

prickle, prik'l, *n.* A small sharp-pointed shoot; a thorn; a small spine.—*vt.* To prick; to cause a prickly feeling in.

prickly, prik'li, *a.* Full of small sharp points or prickles; pricking or stinging.

pride, prīd, *n.* State or quality of being proud; inordinate self-esteem; a cause of pride; glory or delight; highest pitch; splendid show.—*vt.* To indulge pride; to value (one's self).

priest, prēst, *n.* A man who officiates in sacred offices; a clergyman above a deacon and below a bishop. **priesthood,** prēst'hud, *n.* The office or character of a priest; the order of priests. **priestly,** prēst'li,- *a.* Resembling a priest; pertaining to a priest; sacerdotal.

prig, prig, *n.* A conceited, narrow-minded fellow; one who affects superiority; a thief.—*vt.* (prigging, prigged). To steal. **priggish,** prig'ish, *a.* Conceited; affected.

prim, prim, *a.* Formal; affectedly nice; demure.—*vt.* (primming, primmed). To deck with nicety.

primacy, prī'ma-si, *n.* Position of chief rank; the office or dignity of primate or archbishop.

prima donna, prē'ma don'a. The first or chief female singer in an opera.

prima facie, prī'ma fā'shi-ē. At first view or appearance.

primal, prī'mal, *a.* Primary; primitive.

primarily, prī'mer-i-li, *adv.* In a primary manner; originally; in the first place. **primary,** prī'mer-i, *a.* First; chief; first in time; original; elementary; radical.—*n.* That which stands first or highest in importance; a large feather of a bird's wing.

primate, prī'mit, *n.* A chief ecclesiastic; an archbishop.

prime, prīm, *a.* Foremost; first; original; first in rank, excellence, or importance; not divisible by any smaller number.—*n.* The earliest stage; full health, strength, or beauty; the best part.—*vt.* (priming, primed). To make ready for action; to supply with powder for communicating fire to a charge; to instruct or prepare beforehand; to lay on the first color in painting.

primer, prim'ėr, *n.* An elementary educational book; a size of printing-type.

primeval, prī-mē'val, *a.* Being of the earliest age or time; original; primitive.

priming, prīm'ing, *n.* The powder used to ignite a charge; a first layer of paint; water carried over with the steam into the cylinder.

primitive, prim'i-tiv, *a.* Being the first or earliest of its kind; original; antiquated; primary; radical; not derived.— *n.* That which is original; an original word.

primogeniture, prī'mō-jen"i-tūr, *n.* Seniority among children; right by which the eldest son succeeds to his father's real estate.

primordial, prī-mor'di-al, *a.* First of all; first in order; original; earliest formed.—*n.* First principle or element.

primrose, prim"rōz', *n.* An early flowering plant.—*a.* Resembling a yellow primrose in color; abounding with primroses.

prince, prins, *n.* A chief ruler; the son of a king or emperor; the chief of any body of men.

princess, prin'ses, *n.* A female of the rank of a prince; the consort of a prince.

principal, prin'si-pal, *a.* First; chief; most important or considerable.—*n.* A chief or head; the president, governor, or chief in authority; one primarily engaged; a capital sum lent on interest.

principality, prin-si-pal'i-ti, *n.* Sovereignty; territory of a prince.

principia, prin-sip'i-a, *n.pl.* First principles; elements.

principle, prin'si-pl, *n.* Cause or origin; a general truth; a fundamental law; a rule of action; uprightness; an element.

principled, prin'si-pld, *a.* Holding certain principles; fixed in certain principles.

prink, pringk, *vt.* To deck.—*vi.* To dress for show; to strut.

print, print, *vt.* To mark by pressure; to stamp; to form or copy by pressure, as from types, &c.—*vi.* To use or practice typography; to publish.—*n.* A mark made by pressure; an engraving, &c.; state of being printed; a newspaper; printed calico.

printer, prin'tėr, *n.* One who prints; more especially, the printer of letter-press.

printing press, print'ing pres, *n.* A press for the printing of books, &c.

prior, prī'ėr, *a.* Preceding; earlier.—*adv.* Previously.—*n.* A monk next in dignity to an abbot. **prioress**, prī'ėr-es, *n.* A female prior. **priority**, prī-or'i-ti, *n.* State of being prior; pre-eminence; preference. **priory**, prī'ō-ri, *n.* A convent of which a prior is the superior.

prism, prizm, *n.* A solid whose ends are any similar, equal, and parallel plane figures and whose sides are parallelograms. **prismatic**, priz-mat'ik, *a.* Pertaining to a prism; formed or exhibited by a prism.

prison, priz'n, *n.* A place of confinement; a jail.—*vt.* To imprison. **prisoner**, priz'nėr, *n.* One shut up in a prison; a captive.

pristine, pris'tēn, *a.* Original; first; earliest.

prithee, pri'тнē. A colloquial corruption of pray thee, I pray thee.

private, prī'vit, *a.* Separate from others; solitary; personal; secret; not having a public or official character. **in private**, secretly.—*n.* A common soldier. **privacy**, prī'va-si, *n.* A state of being private; seclusion; secrecy. **privateer**, prī'va-tēr', *n.* A private vessel licensed to seize or plunder the ships of an enemy.—*vi.* To engage in privateering.

privation, prī-vā'shun, *n.* Act of depriving; state of being deprived; destitution; want; hardship.

privet, priv'et, *n.* A shrub much used for ornamental hedges.

privilege, priv'i-lij, *n.* A separate and personal advantage; a prerogative, immunity, or exemption.—*vt.* To grant some right or exemption to; to authorize.

privy, priv'i, *a.* Private; assigned to private uses; secret; privately knowing (with *to*).—*n.* A water-closet. **privy council**, pri'vi koun'sil, *n.* The council of state of the British sovereign. **privily**, priv'i-li, *adv.* Privately; secretly.

prize, prīz, *n.* That which is seized; that which is deemed a valuable acquisition; a reward.—*vt.* (prizing, prized). To value highly.

prize fight, prīz fīt, *n.* A boxing match for a prize.

prize ring, prīz ring, *n.* An inclosed place for prize-fights; boxers collectively.

probability, prob'a-bil"i-ti, *n.* Likelihood; appearance of truth.

probable, prob'a-bl, *a.* Likely; credible.

probably, prob'a-bli, *adv.* In a probable manner; as is probable; likely.

probate, prō'bāt, *n.* The proceeding by which a person's will is established and registered; official proof of a will. **probation**, pro-bā'shun, *n.* Act of proving; proof; trial; period of trial; novitiate. **probationary**, pro-bā'shun-er'i, *a.* Serving for probation or trial. **probationer**, pro-bā'shun-ėr, *n.* One who is on probation; a novice; in Scotland, a student in divinity licensed to preach.

probe, prōb, *n.* A surgeon's instrument for examining a wound, ulcer, or cavity.—*vt.* (probing, probed). To apply a probe to; to examine thoroughly.

probity, prōb'i-ti, *n.* Uprightness; honesty; rectitude; integrity.

problem, prob'lem, *n.* A question proposed for solution; a knotty point to be cleared up. **problematic, problematical**, prob'lem-at"ik, prob'lem-at"i-kal, *a.* Of the nature of a problem; questionable; doubtful.

proboscis, prō-bos'is, *n.*; pl. **proboscides**, prō-bos'i-dēz. The snout or trunk of an elephant, &c.; the sucking-tube of insects.

procedure, prō-sē'dūr, *n.* Act or manner of proceeding; conduct; management.

proceed, prō-sēd', *vi.* To go forth or forward; to issue, arise, emanate; to prosecute any design; to carry on a legal action; to take a university degree. **proceeds**, prō'sēdz, *n. pl.* Money brought in by some pieces of business.

process, pros'es, *n.* A proceeding or moving forward; gradual progress; course; method of manipulation; lapse; course of legal proceedings; a projecting portion.

procession, prō-sesh'un, *n.* A marching forward; a train of persons moving with ceremonious solemnity. **processional**, prō-sesh'un-al, *a.* Pertaining to a procession.—*n.* A service-book containing prayers, hymns, &c.

proclaim, prō-klām', *vt.* To announce publicly; to promulgate; to publish. **proclamation**, prok'la-mā"shun, *n.* Act of proclaiming; an official public announcement.

proclivity, prō-kliv'i-ti, *n.* Inclination; propensity; tendency. **proclivous**, prō-kli'vus, *a.* Inclining forward; tending by nature.

procrastinate, prō-kras'ti-nāt, *vt.* and *i.* To put off from day to day; to postpone. **procrastination**, prō-kras'ti-nā"shun, *n.* Act or habit of procrastinating; dilatoriness.

procreate, prō'krē-āt, *vt.* To beget; to generate; to engender. **procreation**, prō'krē-ā"shun, *n.* Act of procreating or begetting.

proctor, prok'tėr, *n.* A legal practitioner in a civil or ecclesiastical court; an official in a university who sees that good order is kept.

procure, prō-kūr', *vt.* (procuring, procured). To obtain; to cause, effect, contrive.—*vi.* To pimp. **procurement**, prō-kūr'ment, *n.* The act of procuring or obtaining. **procurer**, prō-kūr'ėr, *n.* A pimp. **procuress**, prō-kū'res or prok'ū-res, *n.* Female pimp.

prod, prod, *n.* A pointed instrument, as a goad; a stab.—*vt.* (prodding, prodded). To prick with a pointed instrument; to goad.

prodigal, prod'i-gal, *a.* Lavish; wasteful.—*n.* A waster; a spendthrift. **prodigality**, prod'i-gal"i-ti, *n.* Extravagance in expenditure; profusion; waste.

prodigy, prod'i-ji, *n.* A portent; a wonder or miracle; a monster. **prodigious**, prō-dij'us, *a.* Portentous; extraordinary; huge; enormous.

produce, prō-dūs', *vt.* (producing, produced). To bring forward; to exhibit; to bring forth, bear, yield; to supply; to cause; to extend, as a line.—*n.* prō'dūs. What is produced; outcome; yield; agricultural products. **producer**, prō-dūs'-ėr, *n.* One who produces. **product**, pro'dukt, *n.* That which is produced; result; effect; number resulting from multiplication. **production**, prō-duk'-shun, *n.* Act or process of producing; product; performance; literary composition. **productive**, prō-duk'tiv, *a.* Having the power of producing; fertile; causing to exist; producing commodities of value. **productivity**, prō'duk-tiv"i-ti, *n.* Power of producing.

profane, prō-fān', *a.* Not sacred; secular; irreverent; blasphemous; impure. —*vt.* (profaning, profaned). To treat with irreverence; to desecrate. **profanity**, prō-fan'i-ti, *n.* Quality of being profane; profane language or conduct. **profanation**, prof'a-nā"shun, *n.* Act of violating sacred things; desecration.

profess, prō-fes', *vt.* To avow; to acknowledge; to declare belief in; to pretend; to declare one's self versed in.— *vi.* To declare openly. **professedly**, prō-fes'ed-li, *adv.* By profession or avowal; avowedly. **profession**, prō-fesh'un, *n.* Act of professing; declaration; vocation, such as medicine, law, &c.; the body of persons engaged in such calling. **professional**, prō-fesh'un-al, *a.* Pertaining to a profession.— *n.* A member of any profession; one who makes a living by arts, sports, &c., in which amateurs engage.

professor, prō-fes'ėr, *n.* One who professes; a teacher of the highest rank in a university, &c. **professorial**, prō'fe-sō"ri-al, *a.* Pertaining to a professor. **professorship**, prō-fes'ėr-ship, *n.* The office or post of a professor.

proffer, prof'ėr, *vt.* (proffering, proffered). To offer for acceptance.—*n.* An offer made.

proficiency, proficience, prō-fish'en-si, prō-fish'ens, *n.* State of being proficient; skill and knowledge acquired.

proficient, prō-fish'ent, *a.* Fully versed; competent.—*n.* An adept or expert.

profile, prō'fīl, *n.* An outline; an outline of the human face seen sideways; the side face.—*vt.* To draw in profile.

profit, prof'it, *n.* Any advantage, benefit or gain; pecuniary gain.—*vt.* To benefit; to advance.—*vi.* To derive profit; to prove; to be made better or wiser. **profitable**, prof'it-a-bl, *a.* Bringing profit or gain; lucrative; beneficial; useful. **profiteer**, prof-i-tēr', *n.* One who makes what is considered an unreasonable profit, as by taking advantage of a public need in time of war. **profitless**, prof'it-les. Void of profit, gain, or advantage.

profligate, prof'li-gāt, *a.* Abandoned to vice; utterly dissolute.—*n.* A depraved man. **profligacy**, prof'li-ga-si, *n.* A profligate course of life; depravity; debauchery.

profound, prō-found', *a.* Deep; deep in skill or knowledge; far-reaching; bending low; humble.—*n.* The ocean; the abyss. **profundity**, prō-fun'di-ti, *n.* State or quality of being profound; depth.

profuse, prō-fūs', *a.* Lavish; exuberant. **profusion**, prō-fū'zhun, *n.* State or quality of being profuse; exuberant; plenty.

progenitor, prō-jen'i-tor, *n.* A forefather. **progeny**, pro'je-ni, *n.* Offspring; descendants.

prognosis, prog-nō'sis, *n.* A forecast of the course of a disease. **prognostic**, prog-nos'tik, *a.* Foreshowing.—*n.* Omen; presage; token. **prognosticate**, prog-nos'ti-kāt, *vt.* To foretell; to predict; to foreshow.—*vi.* To judge or pronounce from prognostics. **prognostication**, prog-nos'ti-kā"shun, *n.* Act of prognosticating; presage.

program, programme, prō'gram, *n.* A plan of proceedings; statement of the order of proceedings in any entertainment.

progress, prog'res, prō'res, *n.* A going forward; a journey of state; a circuit; advance; development.—*vi.* prō-gres', To advance; to improve. **progression**, prō-gresh'un, *n.* Act of progressing; progress; regular or proportional advance. **progressive**, prō-gres'iv, *a.* Making steady progress; advancing; advocating progress.

prohibit, prō-hib'it, *vt.* To forbid; to interdict by authority; to prevent. **prohibition**, prō-i-bish'un, *n.* Act of prohibiting; an interdict; inhibition. **prohibitive, prohibitory**, prō-hib'-i-tiv, prō-hib"i-tō'ri, *a.* Implying prohibition; forbidding.

project, prō-jekt', *vt.* To throw out or forth; to scheme; to delineate.—*vi.* To shoot forward; to jut.—*n*. pro'jekt. A scheme, plan. **projectile**, prŏ-jek'til, *a*. Throwing forward.—*n*. A body impelled forward; a missile from a gun. **projection**, prŏ-jek'shun, *n*. Act of projecting; a prominence; representation of something by lines, &c., drawn on a surface. **projector**, prŏ-jek'tẽr, *n*. One who plans; that which casts something forward.

prolapse, **prolapsus**, prŏ-laps', prŏ-lap'sus, *n*. A falling down of some internal organ from its proper position.

prolate, prŏ'lat, *a*. Applied to a sphere projecting too much at the poles.

proletariat, prŏ-le-tar″i-at, *n*. Proletarians collectively; the lower classes. **proletarian**, prŏ-le-tar″i-an, *n*. and *a*. Applied to a member of the poorest class.

prolific, prŏ-lif'ik, *a*. Fruitful; productive.

prolix, prŏ'liks, *a*. Long and wordy; diffuse. **prolixity**, prŏ-lik'si-ti, *n*. State or quality of being prolix.

prologue, prŏ'log, *n*. A preface or introduction; address spoken before a dramatic performance.—*vt*. To preface.

prolong, prŏ-long', *vt*. To lengthen out; to protract; to postpone. **prolongation**, prŏ'long-gā″shun, *n*. Act of prolonging; part prolonged; extension.

promenade, prom'e-näd', *n*. A walk for pleasure; a place set apart for walking. —*vi*. (promenading, promenaded). To walk for pleasure.

prominent, prom'i-nent, *a*. Jutting out; protuberant; eminent. **prominence**, prom'i-nens, *n*. State of being prominent; projection; protuberance.

promiscuous, prŏ-mis'kū-us, *a*. Confused; indiscriminate; miscellaneous.

promise, prom'is, *n*. A statement binding the person who makes it; ground or basis of expectation; pledge.—*vt*. (promising, promised). To make a promise of; to afford reason to expect.—*vi*. To make a promise; to afford expectations. **promissory**, prom″i-sō'ri, *a*. Containing a promise or binding declaration.

promontory, prom″un-tō'ri, *n*. A headland; a cape.

promote, prŏ-mōt', *vt*. (promoting, promoted). To forward or further; to advance; to encourage; to exalt; to form (a company). **promoter**, prŏ-mōt'ẽr, *n*. One who or that which promotes; an encourager; one engaged in getting up a joint-stock company. **promotion**, prŏ-mō'shun, *n*. Act of promoting; advancement; encouragement.

prompt, prompt, *a*. Ready; unhesitating; done without delay.—*vt*. To incite to action; to tell a speaker words he forgets; to suggest. **prompter**, promp'tẽr, **prudé**, promp'ti-tūd, *n*. State or quality of being prompt; cheerful alacrity.

promulgate, prŏ-mul'gāt, *vt*. (promulgating, promulgated). To publish; to proclaim. **promulgation**, prŏ'mul-gā″shun, *n*. Act of promulgating, publication.

prone, prŏn, *a*. Bending forward; lying with the face downward; sloping; apt. **prong**, prong, *n*. A spike, as of a fork. **pronominal**, prŏ-nom'i-nal, *a*. Belonging to or of the nature of a pronoun. **pronoun**, prŏ'noun, *n*. A word used instead of a noun.

pronounce, prŏ-nouns', *vt*. and *i*. (pronouncing, pronounced). To articulate by the organs of speech; to utter formally; to declare or affirm. **pronounceable**, prŏ-nouns'a-bl, *a*. That may be pronounced or uttered. **pronounced**, prŏ-nounst', *p.a*. Strongly marked or defined; decided; glaring.

pronunciation, prŏ-nun'si-ā″shun, *n*. Act or mode of pronouncing; utterance.

proof, prŏf, *n*. Something which tests; trial; what serves to convince; evidence; firmness; a certain standard of strength in spirit; an impression in printing for correction; early impression of an engraving.—*a*. Impenetrable; able to resist.

prop, prop, *n*. A body that supports a weight; a support.—*vt*. (propping, propped). To support by a prop; to sustain generally.

propagate, prop'a-gāt, *vt*. To multiply by generation or reproduction; to diffuse; to increase.—*vi*. To have young or issue; to be multiplied by generation, &c. **propagation**, prop'a-gā″shun, *n*. Act of propagating; diffusion. **propaganda**, prop'a-gan″da, *n*. An institution or system for propagating any doctrine. **propagandist**, prop'a-gan″dist, *n*. One who labors in spreading any doctrines.

propel, prŏ-pel', *vt*. (propelling, propelled). To drive, push, or thrust forward. **propeller**, prŏ-pel'ẽr, *n*. One who or that which propels; a screw for propelling.

propense, prŏ-pens', *a*. Naturally inclined; disposed; prone. **propensity**, prŏ-pen'si-ti, *n*. Bent of mind; natural tendency; disposition.

proper, prop'ẽr, *a*. One's own; peculiar; used as the name of a particular person or thing; adapted; correct; real. **property**, prop'ẽr-ti, *n*. A peculiar quality or attribute; characteristic; ownership; the thing owned; estate; a stage requisite.

prophecy, prof'e-si, *n*. A foretelling; a prediction; inspired prediction or utterance. **prophesy**, prof'e-sī, *vt*. To foretell; to predict.—*vi*. To utter prophecies. **prophet**, prof'et, *n*. One who foretells future events. **prophetess**, prof'et-es, *n*. A female prophet. **prophetic**, **prophetical**, prŏ-fet'ik, prŏ-fet'i-kal, *a*. Pertaining to a prophet or prophecy; unfolding future events.

prophylactic, prŏ-fi-lak'tik, *a*. Preventive of disease.—*n*. A medicine which preserves against disease.

propinquity, prŏ-ping'kwi-ti, *n*. Nearness; vicinity; kindred.

propitiate, prŏ-pish'i-āt, *vt*. To make propitious; to appease. **propitiation**, prŏ-pish'i-ā″shun, *n*. Act of propitiating or what propitiates; atonement. **propitiatory**, prŏ-pish'i-a-tō'ri, *a*. Having the power to make propitious; conciliatory.—*n*. Among the Jews, the mercyseat. **propitious**, prŏ-pish'us, *a*. Favorable; disposed to be gracious or merciful. **proponent**, prŏ-pō'nent, *n*. One who advocates or supports a cause or idea.

proportion, pro-pōr'shun, *n.* Comparative relation; relative size and arrangement; symmetry; just or equal share; lot; that rule which enables us to find a fourth proportional to three numbers. —*vt.* To adjust in due proportion; to form with symmetry. **proportionable,** pro-pōr'shun-a-bl, *a.* That may be proportioned; in proportion; corresponding; symmetrical. **proportional,** pro-pōr'shun-al, *a.* Having a due proportion; relating to proportion.—*n.* A number or quantity proportioned. **proportionate,** pro-pōr'shun-it, *a.* Proportional.—*vt.* To make proportional.

propose, pro-pōz', *vt.* (proposing, proposed). To offer for consideration.—*vi.* To make a proposal; to purpose; to offer one's self in marriage. **proposal,** pro-pōz'al, *n.* That which is proposed; offer; proposition. **proposition,** prop'ō-zish'-un, *n.* That which is proposed; a proposal; offer of terms; a form of speech in which something is affirmed or denied.

propound, pro-pound', *vt.* To propose; to offer for consideration; to put, as a question.

proprietor, pro-prī'e-tėr, *n.* An owner; one who has legal right to anything. **proprietress,** pro-prī'e-tres, *n.* A female proprietor. **proprietary,** pro-prī'e-ter'i, *a.* Belonging to a proprietor.—*n.* A proprietor; a body of proprietors.

propriety, pro-prī'e-ti, *n.* State of being proper; fitness; consonance with established principles or customs; justness.

propulsion, pro-pul'shun, *n.* Act of propelling or of driving forward.

prosaic, pro-zā'ik, *a.* Pertaining to prose; dull; commonplace.

proscribe, pro-skrib', *vt.* To outlaw; to condemn as dangerous; to interdict. **proscription,** pro-skrip'shun, *n.* Act of proscribing; outlawry; utter rejection. **proscriptive,** pro-skrip'tiv, *a.* Pertaining to or consisting in proscription; proscribing.

prose, prōz, *n.* Speech or language not in verse.—*vi.* (prosing, prosed). To write or speak in a dull, tedious, style.—*a.* Relating to prose; prosaic.

prosecute, pros'e-kūt, *vt.* and *i.* (prosecuting, prosecuted). To persist in; to carry on; to pursue at law. **prosecution,** pros'e-kū''shun, *n.* Act of prosecuting; the carrying on of a suit at law; the party by whom criminal proceedings are instituted. **prosecutor,** pros''e-kū'-tėr, *n.* One who prosecutes, especially in a criminal suit.

proselyte, pros'e-līt, *n.* A convert to the Jewish faith; a new convert.—*vt.* To make a convert of. **proselytism,** pros'-e-lit-izm, *n.* The making of proselytes; conversion. **proselytize,** pros'e-lit-īz *vt.* To make a proselyte of.—*vi.* To engage in making proselytes.

prosody, pros'o-di, *n.* The rules of meter or versification.

prospect, pros'pekt, *n.* A distant view; sight; scene; outlook; exposure; expectation.—*vt.* and *i.* To make search for precious stones or metals. **prospective,** pro-spek'tiv, *a.* Looking forward; regard-

ing the future. **prospectus,** pro-spek'-tus, *n.* A statement of some enterprise proposed, as a literary work, a new company, &c.

prosper, pros'pėr, *vi.* To increase in wealth or any good; to thrive.—*vt.* To make to succeed. **prosperity,** pros-per'-i-ti, *n.* Flourishing state; satisfactory progress; success. **prosperous,** pros'-pėr-us, *a.* Successful; flourishing; fortunate; thriving.

prostitute, pros'ti-tūt, *vt.* (prostituting, prostituted). To offer publicly for lewd purposes for hire; to devote to anything base.—*a.* Openly devoted to lewdness.—*n.* A female given to indiscriminate lewdness. **prostitution,** pros'ti-tū''shun, *n.* Practice of offering the body to indiscriminate intercourse with man; debasement.

prostrate, pros'trāt, *a.* Lying with the body flat; lying at mercy.—*vt.* (prostrating, prostrated). To lay flat or prostrate; to bow in reverence; to overthrow; to ruin. **prostration,** pros-trā'shun, *n.* Act of prostrating; great depression of strength or spirits.

protect, pro-tekt', *vt.* To shield from danger, injury, &c.; to guard against foreign competition by tariff regulations. **protection,** pro-tek'shun, *n.* Act of protecting; shelter; defense; the system of favoring articles of home production by duties on foreign articles. **protectionist,** pro-tek'shun-ist, *n.* One who favors the protection of some branch of industry; one opposed to free-trade. **protective,** pro-tek'tiv, *a.* Affording protection; sheltering; defensive. **protector,** pro-tek'tor, *n.* One who protects; a defender; a guardian; a preserver. **protectorate,** pro-tek'tėr-it, *n.* Government by a protector; a country protected by another.

protégé, prō'te-zhā; fem. **protégée,** prō'te-zhā, *n.* One under the care of another.

proteide, prō'tē-īd, *n.* A name of certain nitrogenous substances forming the soft tissues of the body, and found also in plants; protein.

protest, pro-test', *vi.* To affirm with solemnity; to make a formal declaration of opposition.—*vt.* To assert; to mark for non-payment, as a bill.—*n.* pro'-test, A formal declaration of dissent; a declaration that payment of a bill has been refused.

protestant, prot'est-ant, *n.* One of the party who adhered to Luther at the Reformation; a member of a reformed church.—*a.* Belonging to the religion of the Protestants. **protestation,** prot'es-tā''shun, *n.* The act of protesting; a protest.

protocol, prō'to-kol, *n.* A diplomatic document serving as a preliminary to diplomatic transactions.

proton, prō'ton, *n.* Physics. An electrically charged particle that is a component of the atom and of matter and carries a positive charge of electricity. Its mass varies; it is much smaller than the atom. It is complementary to the electron.

protoplasm, prō'tō-plazm, *n*. A substance constituting the basis of living matter in animals and plants.

prototype, prō'tō-tīp, *n*. An original type or model; a pattern.

protract, prō-trakt', *vt*. To prolong; to delay; to defer; to draw to a scale. **protraction**, prō-trak'shun, *n*. Act of protracting; act of laying down on paper the dimensions of a field, &c. **protractor**, prō-trak'tėr, *n*. One who or that which protracts; an instrument for surveying; a muscle which draws forward a part.

protrude, prō-trōd', *vt*. and *i*. (protruding, protruded). To thrust forward; to project. **protrusion**, prō-trō'zhun, *n*. A thrusting forth. **protrusive**, prō-trō'siv, *a*. Protruding.

protuberance, prō-tū'bėr-ans, *n*. A swelling or tumor; a prominence; a knob. **protuberant**, prō-tū'bėr-ant, *a*. Swelling; bulging out.

proud, proud, *a*. Having a high opinion of one's self; haughty; of fearless spirit; ostentatious; magnificent. **proud flesh**, an excessive granulation in wounds or ulcers.

prove, prōv, *vt*. (proving, proved). To try by experiment; to test; to establish the truth or reality of; to demonstrate; to obtain probate of.—*vi*. To be found by experience or trial; to turn out to be. **provable**, prōv'a-bl, *a*. That may be proved.

proven, prōv'en, *pp*. Proved.

provender, prov'en-dėr, *n*. Dry food or fodder for beasts; provisions; food.

proverb, prov'ėrb, *n*. A popular saying, expressing a truth or common fact; an adage; a maxim; a by-word; a dark saying. **proverbial**, prō-vėr'bi-al, *a*. Pertaining to or like a proverb; commonly spoken of.

provide, prō-vīd', *vt*. and *i*. (providing, provided). To procure beforehand; to prepare; to supply; to stipulate previously. **provided**, prō-vīd'ed, *conj*. On condition. **providence**, prov'i-dens, *n*. Foresight; the care which God exercises over his creatures; God; a providential circumstance. **provident**, prov'i-dent, *a*. Foreseeing and providing for wants; prudent; frugal. **providential**, prov'i-den'shal, *a*. Effected by providence.

province, prov'ins, *n*. A territory at some distance from the metropolis; a large political division; sphere of action; department. **provincial**, prō-vin'shal, *a*. Pertaining to or forming a province; characteristic of the people of a province; rustic.—*n*. A person belonging to a province. **provincialism**, prō-vin'shal-izm, *n*. A rustic idiom or word.

provision, prō-vizh'un, *n*. Act of providing; preparation; stores provided; victuals; stipulation; proviso.—*vt*. To supply with provisions. **provisional**, prō-vizh'un-al, *a*. Provided for present need; temporary.

proviso, prō-vī'zō, *n*. An article or clause in any statute or contract; stipulation. **provisory**, prō-vī'zo-ri, *a*. Making temporary provision; temporary; conditional.

provoke, prō-vōk', *vt*. (provoking, provoked). To incite; to stimulate; to incense; to irritate.—*vi*. To produce anger. **provoking**, prō-vōk'ing, *p.a*. Exciting resentment; annoying; vexatious. **provocation**, prov'ō-kā''-shun, *n*. Act of provoking; cause of resentment; incitement. **provocative**, prō-vok'a-tiv, *a*. Serving to provoke; exciting.—*n*. A stimulant.

provost, prov'ust, *n*. The head of certain bodies, as colleges; chief dignitary of a cathedral; chief magistrate of a Scotch burgh. **provost marshal**, prō'vō-mär'shal, *n*. A military officer who attends to offenses against discipline.

prow, prou, *n*. The forepart of a ship.

prowess, prou'es, *n*. Bravery; boldness and dexterity in war; gallantry.

prowl, proul, *vi*. and *t*. To roam or wander stealthily.—*n*. Act of one who prowls.

proximate, prok'si-mit, *a*. Nearest; next; in closest relationship; immediate.

proximity, proks-im'i-ti, *n*. State of being proximate; immediate nearness.

proxy, prok'si, *n*. Agency of a substitute; a deputy; a writing by which one authorizes another to vote in his stead.

prude, prōd, *n*. A woman affecting great reserve and excessive delicacy. **prudence**, prō'dens, *n*. Quality of being prudent; caution; discretion. **prudent**, prō'dent, *a*. Provident; careful; discreet; judicious. **prudential**, prō-den-shal, *a*. Proceeding from or dictated by prudence; politic.

prudery, prōd'ėr-i, *n*. The conduct of a prude; affected delicacy of feeling. **prudish**, prōd'ish, *a*. Like a prude; affecting excessive modesty or virtue.

prune, prōn, *vt*. (pruning, pruned). To trim; to cut or lop off; to clear from superfluities.—*n*. A plum, particularly a dried plum.

prurient, prōr'i-ent, *a*. Itching after something; inclined to lascivious thoughts. **prurience**, **pruriency**, prōr'i-ens, prōr'i-en-si, *n*. An itching desire for anything; tendency to lascivious thoughts.

pry, prī, *vi*. (prying, pried). To peep narrowly; to look closely; to peer.—*n*. A keen glance.

psalm, säm, *n*. A sacred song or hymn.

psalmist, säm'ist or sal'mist, *n*. A writer or composer of psalms.

pseudo-, sū'dō. A prefix signifying false or spurious.

pseudonym, sū'dō-nim, *n*. A false or feigned name; a name assumed by a writer.

pshaw, sha, *interj*. An expression of contempt, disdain, or impatience.

psychiatry, sī-kī-a-tri, *n*. Medical treatment of diseases of the mind.

psychic, **psychical**, sī'kik, sī'ki-kal, *a*. Belonging to the soul; psychological; pertaining to that force by which spiritualists aver they produce "spiritual" phenomena. **psychologic**, **psychological**, sī-ko-loj'ik, sī-ko-loj'ik-al, *a*. Pertaining to psychology or science of mind. **psychologist**, sī-kol'o-jist, *n*. One who is conversant with psychology.

psychology, si-kol'o-ji, *n.* That branch of knowledge which deals with the mind; mental science.

ptarmigan, tär'mi-gan, *n.* The white grouse.

Ptolemaic, tol-ē-mā'ik, *a.* Pertaining to Ptolemy, or to his system of the universe, in which the sun revolved round the earth.

ptomaine, tō'mān, *n.* A name of certain substances generated during putrefaction or morbid conditions prior to death.

puberty, pū'bèr-ti, *n.* The age at which persons can beget or bear children. **pubescence,** pū-bes'ens, *n.* Puberty; the downy substance on plants. **pubescent,** pū-bes'ent, *a.* Arriving at puberty, covered with fine soft hairs.

public, pub'lik, *a.* Not private; pertaining to a whole community; open or free to all; common; notorious.—*n.* The people, indefinitely. **In public,** in open view.

publican, pub'li-kan, *n.* A collector of public revenues; keeper of a public-house (Eng.).

publication, pub'li-kä'shun, *n.* Act of publishing; announcement; promulgation; act of offering a book, &c., to the public by sale; any book, &c., published. **publicity,** pub-lis'i-ti, *n.* State of being made public; notoriety; currency.

publish, pub'lish, *vt.* To make public; to proclaim; promulgate; to cause to be printed and offered for sale. **publisher,** pub'lish-èr, *n.* One who publishes, especially books.

pucker, puk'èr, *vt.* and *i.* To gather into small folds; to wrinkle.—*n.* A fold or wrinkle, or a collection of folds.

pudding, pud'ing, *n.* An intestine; a sausage; a dish variously compounded, of flour, milk, eggs, fruit, &c.

puddle, pud'l, *n.* A small pool of dirty water; clay worked into a mass impervious to water.—*vt.* (puddling, puddled). To make muddy; to make water-tight with clay; to convert pig-iron into wrought-iron. **puddling,** pud'ling, *n.* The operation of working clay so as to resist water; clay thus used; process of converting cast-iron into malleable iron.

pudgy, puj'i, *a.* Fat and short.

pueblo, pweb'lō, *n.* A village or type of building of the early Indians of south-western U.S.; an Indian of one of the pueblos.

puerile, pū'èr-il, *a.* Boyish; childish. **puerility,** pū-èr-il''i-ti, *n.* State of being puerile; boyishness; that which is puerile.

puff, puf, *n.* A sudden emission of breath; a whiff; a short blast of wind; a puff-ball; piece of light pastry; a consciously exaggerated commendation.—*vi.* To give a quick blast with the mouth; to breathe hard after exertion.—*vt.* To drive with a blast; to inflate; to praise extravagantly.

puffin, puf'in, *n.* A diving bird of the auk family.

pug, pug, *n.* A monkey; a dwarf variety of dog.

pugilism, pū'ji-lizm, *n.* The practice of boxing or fighting with the fist. **pugil-**

ist, pū'ji-list, *n.* One who fights with his fists. **pugilistic,** pū-ji-lis'tik, *a.* Pertaining to pugilism.

pugnacious, pug-nā'shus, *a.* Disposed to fight; quarrelsome. **pugnacity,** pug-nas'i-ti, *n.* Quality of being pugnacious; inclination to fight.

pug nose, pug'nōz', *n.* A nose turned up at the end; a snub-nose.

puke, pūk, *vi.* and *t.* (puking, puked). To vomit.

pulchritude, pul'kri-tūd, *n.* Beauty; comeliness.

pule, pūl, *vi.* (puling, puled). To cry like a chicken; to whine; to whimper.

pull, pul, *vt.* To draw towards one; to tug; to rend; to pluck; to gather.—*vi.* To draw; to tug. To tug.—*n.* Act of pulling; a twitch; act of rowing a boat; a drink; a struggle.

pullet, pul'et, *n.* A young hen.

pulley, pul'i, *n.* A small wheel in a block, used in raising weights.

Pullman car, pul'man kär, *n.* A luxuriously fitted up railway-coach.

pulmonary, pul'mō-ner'i, *a.* Pertaining to or affecting the lungs.

Pulmotor, pul'mō'tèr, *n.* An apparatus for producing artificial respiration by pumping oxygen or air into or out of the lungs, as of a person who has been asphyxiated.

pulp, pulp, *n.* Moist, soft animal or vegetable matter.—*vt.* To make into pulp; to deprive of the pulp.

pulpit, pul'pit, *n.* An elevated place for a preacher; preachers generally.

pulsate, pul'sāt, *vi.* To beat or throb. **pulsation,** pul-sā'shun, *n.* The beating of the heart or an artery; a throb.

pulse, puls, *n.* The beating of the heart or an artery; vibration; leguminous plants or their seeds, as beans, &c.—*vi.* (pulsing, pulsed). To beat or throb.

pulverize, pul'vèr-īz, *vt.* To reduce to dust or fine powder.

puma, pū'ma, *n.* A carnivorous quadruped of the cat kind; the cougar.

pumice, pūm'is or pum'is, *n.* A light and spongy stone, used for polishing.

pump, pump, *n.* A machine for raising water or extracting air; a shoe used in dancing.—*vi.* To work a pump.—*vt.* To raise with a pump; to free from liquid by a pump; to put artful questions to extract information.

pumpkin, pump'kin, *n.* A plant and its fruit; a kind of gourd or vegetable marrow.

pun, pun, *n.* A play on words like in sound, but different in meaning; a kind of quibble. *vi.* (punning, punned). To make a pun or puns.

punch, punch, *n.* An instrument for driving holes in metal, &c.; a blow or thrust; a beverage of spirits, lemonjuice, water, &c.; a buffoon; a short-legged, barrel-bodied horse; a short fat fellow.—*vt.* To stamp or perforate with a punch; to hit with the fist.

puncheon, pun'chun, *n.* A perforating or stamping tool; a punch; a cask containing from 84 to 120 gallons.

punctilio, pungk-til'i-ō, *n.* A nice point of exactness in conduct or ceremony.

punctilious, pungk-til'i-us, *a.* Very exact in forms of behavior or ceremony.

punctual, pungk'tū-al, *a.* Exact; made or done at the exact time. **punctuality,** pungk'tū-al"i-ti, *n.* Quality of being punctual; scrupulous exactness.

punctuate, pungk'tū-āt, *vt.* To mark with the points necessary in writings. **punctuation,** pungk'tū-ā"shun, *n.* The act, art, or system of punctuating a writing.

puncture, pungk'tūr, *n.* The act of pricking; a small hole thus made.—*vt.* (puncturing, punctured). To pierce with a small point.

pungent, pun'jent, *a.* Biting; acrid; caustic; keen; stinging. **pungency,** pun'jen-si, *n.* State or quality of being pungent; sharpness; keenness.

punish, pun'ish, *vt.* To inflict pain or any evil on, as a penalty; to chastise; to hurt. **punishable,** pun'ish-a-bl, *a.* Liable to punishment; capable of being punished. **punishment,** pun'ish-ment, *n.* Act of punishing; penalty. **punitive,** pū'ni-tiv, *a.* Pertaining to, awarding, or involving punishment.

punster, pun'stėr, *n.* One skilled in punning.

punt, punt, *n.* A square flat-bottomed boat.—*vt.* To convey in a punt; to propel (a boat) with a pole.

puny, pū'ni, *a.* Small and weak; petty.

pup, pup, *n.* A puppy.—*vi.* (pupping, pupped). To bring forth whelps.

pupa, pū'pa, *n.*; pl. **-æ.** The chrysalis form of an insect.

pupil, pū'pl, *n.* A young person under the care of a tutor; the aperture in the iris through which the rays of light pass.

puppet, pup'et, *n.* A small figure in the human form mechanically worked; a person who is a mere tool.

puppy, pup'i, *n.* A whelp; a young dog; a conceited, foppish fellow.

purblind, pėr'blīnd', *a.* Dim-sighted.

purchase, pėr'chis, *vt.* (purchasing, purchased). To buy; to obtain by labor, danger, &c.—*n.* Acquisition of anything by money; what is bought; mechanical advantage. **purchasable,** pėr'chis-a-bl, *a.* That may be purchased or bought. **purchaser,** pėr'chis-ėr, *n.* A buyer.

pure, pūr, *a.* Clean; clear; unmixed; spotless; chaste; genuine; sincere; absolute.

purge, pėrj, *vt.* and *i.* (purging, purged). To make pure or clean; to clear from accusation; to evacuate the bowels of.—*n.* The act of purging; a cathartic medicine. **purgation,** pėr-gā"shun, *n.* Act or operation of purging. **purgative,** pėr'ga-tiv, *a.* Having the power of purging.—*n.* A medicine that purges. **purgatory,** pėr"ga-tō'ri, *a.* Tending to purge or cleanse.—*n.* In the R. Catholic religion, a place in which souls after death are purified from sins; any place or state of temporary suffering.

purify, pū'ri-fī, *vt.* (purifying, purified). To make pure or clear; to free from admixture; to free from guilt.—*vi.* To become pure or clear. **purification,** pū'ri-fi-kā"shun, *n.* Act of purifying; a cleansing from guilt or sin. **purifier,** pū'ri-fī'ėr, *n.* One who or that which purifies or cleanses.

purism, pūr'izm, *n.* Practice of rigid purity; fastidious niceness in the use of words. **purist,** pūr'ist, *n.* One excessively nice in the use of words, &c.

Puritan, pū'ri-tan, *n.* One very strict in religious matters or in conduct; an early Protestant dissenter from the Church of England.—*a.* Pertaining to the Puritans. **puritanic, puritanical,** pū'ri-tan"ik, pū'ri-tan"i-kal, *a.* Puritan; over-rigid in religion.

purity, pū'ri-ti, *n.* State or quality of being pure; cleanness; innocence; chastity.

purl, pėrl, *n.* Spiced malt liquor; gentle murmur of a stream.—*vi.* To murmur, as a stream; to reverse a stitch in knitting.

purlieu, pėr'lū, *n.* Part lying adjacent; outskirts; generally in *pl.*

purloin, pėr-loin', *vt.* To steal or pilfer; to filch; to take by theft or plagiarism.

purple, pėr'pl, *n.* A color produced by mixing red and blue; a purple robe, the badge of the Roman emperors; regal power.—*a.* Of a color made of red and blue; dyed with blood.—*vt.* (purpling, purpled). To make purple.

purport, pėr-pōrt', *n.* Meaning; import. —*vt.* To signify; to profess.

purpose, pėr'pus, *n.* End or aim; design; intention matter in question.—*vt.* and *i.* (purposing, purposed). To propose; to intend.

purr, pėr, *vi.* To murmur, as a cat when pleased.—*n.* The sound of a cat when pleased.

purse, pėrs, *n.* A small bag or receptacle for money; money collected as a prize or a present; finances.—*vt.* (pursing, pursed). put in a purse; to pucker.

purser, pėr'sėr, *n.* A person belonging to a ship, who keeps accounts.

pursue, pėr-sū', *vt.* (pursuing, pursued). To follow with a view to overtake; to chase; to use measures to obtain; to carry on.—*vi.* To go in pursuit; to act as prosecutor. **pursuer,** pėr-sū'ėr, *n.* One who pursues; the plaintiff. **pursuit,** pėr-sūt', *n.* Act of pursuing; chase; quest; business occupation. **pursuant,** pėr-sū'ant, *a.* Done in prosecution of anything; conformable.

purvey, pėr-vā', *vt.* To provide.—*vi.* To supply provisions, especially for a number. **purveyor,** pėr-vā'ėr, *n.* One who purveys; a caterer.

pus, pus, *n.* The soft yellowish substance formed in suppuration; matter of a sore.

push, push, *vt.* To press against with force; to thrust or shove; to enforce; to urge; to prosecute energetically.—*vi.* To make a thrust or effort; to force one's way.—*n.* Act of pushing; vigorous effort; emergency; enterprise.

pusillanimous, pū'si-lan"i-mus, *a.* Without strength of mind; timid; cowardly. **pusillanimity,** pū'si-la-nim"i-ti, *n.* Weakness of spirit; cowardice; timidity.

puss, pụs, *n.* A cat; a hare. **pussy**, pụs'i, *n.* A diminutive of puss.

pustule, pus'tūl, *n.* A small blister; small elevation of the cuticle, containing pus.

put, pụt, *vt.* (putting, put). To place in any position or situation; to apply; to propose or propound; to state in words.

put, putt, put, *vt.* (putting, putted). To throw (a heavy stone) from the shoulder; in golf, to play the ball into the hole.

putrid, pū'trid, *a.* In a state of decay; rotten; corrupt. **putridity**, pū-trid'i-ti, *n.* State of being putrid; corruption. **putrefaction**, pū"trē-fak"shun, *n.* Process or state of putrefying; decomposition. **putrefy**, pū'trē-fī, *vi.* (putrefying, putrefied). To render putrid.—*vt.* To decay; to rot. **putrescence**, pū-tres'ens, *n.* State of becoming rotten; a putrid state. **putrescent**, pū-tres'ent, *a.* Growing putrid.

putter, pụt'ẽr, *n.* One who puts, sets, or places; a kind of golfing club (pron. put'ẽr).

putting green, put'ing grēn', *n.* A smooth piece of sward round a hole in a golf course.

putty, put'i, *n.* A paste made of whiting and linseed-oil.—*vt.* To cement or fill with putty.

puzzle, puz'l, *vt.* (puzzling, puzzled). To perplex; to entangle.—*vi.* To be bewildered.—*n.* Perplexity; something to try ingenuity.

pygmy, pig'mi, *n.* A dwarf; anything little.—*a.* Dwarfish; little.

pyjamas, pī-jä'maz, *n. pl.* A sleeping-suit.

pylorus, pī-lō'rus, *n.* The lower orifice of the stomach.

pyorrhea, pī'o-rē"a, *n.* An infection of the gums, causing the teeth to loosen in the sockets.

pyramid, pir'a-mid, *n.* A solid body having triangular sides meeting in a point at the top. **pyramidal**, pi-ram'-i-dal, *a.* Formed like a pyramid; relating to a pyramid. **pyramidic, pyramidical**, pir'a-mid"ik, pir'a-mid"i-kal, *a.* Having the form of a pyramid; relating to a pyramid.

pyre, pīr, *n.* A heap of combustibles for burning a dead body; a funeral pile.

pyrites, pi-rī'tēz, *n.* A mineral combining sulphur with iron, copper, cobalt, &c.

pyromania, pī"rō-mā'ni-a, *n.* .Psychotic impulse to start fires.

pyrotechnic, pī"rō-tek'nik, *a.* Pertaining to pyrotechny or fireworks. Also *pyrotechnical*. **pyrotechnics, pyrotechny**, pī'rō-tek"niks, pī'rō-tek'ni, *n.* The art of making fireworks; the use of fireworks.

Pythagorean, pi-thag'o-rē"an, *a.* Having to do with the ideas and theories of the Greek philosopher and mathematician Pythagoras.

python, pī'thon, *n.* A large non-venomous serpent.

Q

qua, kwä, *adv.* In the quality or character of; as being; as.

quack, kwak, *vt.* To cry like a duck; to boast; to practice quackery.—*n.* The cry of a duck; a pretender to skill or knowledge, especially medical.—*a.* Pertaining to quackery. **quackery**, kwak'ẽr-i, *n.* Practice or boastful pretenses of a quack, particularly in medicine. **quackish**, kwak'ish, *a.* Like a quack.

quadrangle, kwod"rang'gl, *n.* A plane figure, having four angles and sides; an inner square of a building. **quadrangular**, kwod-rang'gū-lẽr, *a.* Having four angles and four sides.

quadrant, kwod'rant, *n.* The fourth part of a circle or its circumference; an old instrument for taking altitudes and angles; an old form of sextant.

quadratic, kwod-rat'ik, *a.* In *algebra*, involving the square of an unknown quantity.

quadrennial, kwod-ren'i-al, *a.* Comprising four years; occurring once in four years.

quadrilateral, kwod"ri-lat"ẽr-al, *a.* Having four sides and four angles.—*n.*

A plane figure having four sides and angles.

quadrille, kwo-dril' or ka-dril', *n.* A game at cards for four; a dance for four couples, each forming the side of a square; music for such a dance.

quadrillion, kwod-ril'yun, *n.* The fifth power of a thousand; a number represented by a unit and 15 ciphers.

quadruped, kwod'rụ-ped, *n.* An animal with four legs or feet.

quadruple, kwod'rụ-pl, *a.* Fourfold.—*n.* Four times the sum or number.—*vt.* To make fourfold.—*vi.* kwod-rö'p'l To become fourfold.

quadruplicate, kwod-rö'pli-kāt, *a.* Fourfold.—*vt.* To make fourfold.

quaff, kwaf, *vt.* and *i.* To drain to the bottom; to drink copiously.

quagmire, kwag"mir', *n.* A piece of soft, wet, boggy land; a bog; a fen.

quail, kwāl, *vi.* To shrink; to flinch; to cower.—*n.* A small bird allied to the partridge.

quaint, kwänt, *a.* Fanciful; curious; old and antique; singular; whimsical.

quake, kwäk, *vi.* (quaking, quaked). To

shake; to tremble; to quiver.—*n.* A shake; tremulous agitation.

quaker, kwāk'ėr, *n.* One who quakes; one of the religious sect called the *Society of Friends* (*cap.*).

qualify, kwol'i-fī, *vt.* (qualifying, qualified). To give proper or suitable qualities to; to furnish with the knowledge, skill, &c., necessary; to modify or limit; to soften or moderate; to dilute.—*vi.* To become qualified or fit. **qualification,** kwol'i-fi-kā"shun, *n.* Act of qualifying; state of being qualified; suitable quality or characteristic; legal power; ability; modification; restriction. **qualified,** kwol'i-fīd, *p.a.* Having qualification; competent; limited; modified.

quality, kwol'i-ti, *n.* Sort, kind, or character; a distinguished property or characteristic; degree of excellence; high rank. **qualitative,** kwol"i-tā'tiv, *a.* Relating to quality; estimable according to quality.

qualm, kwäm, *n.* A sudden fit of nausea; a twinge of conscience; compunction.

quandary, kwon'da-ri, *n.* A state of perplexity; a predicament.

quantify, kwon'ti-fī, *vt.* To determine the quantity of; to modify with regard to quantity.

quantity, kwon'ti-ti, *n.* That property in virtue of which a thing is measurable; bulk; measure; amount; metrical value of syllables.

quantum, kwon'tum, *n.* A quantity; an amount; a sufficient amount.

quarantine, kwor'an-tēn, *n.* The period during which a ship suspected of being infected is obliged to forbear all intercourse with a port.—*vt.* To cause to perform quarantine.

quarrel, kwor'el, *n.* An angry dispute; a brawl; cause of dispute; a dart for a cross-bow; a glazier's diamond.—*vi.* (quarreling, quarreled). To dispute violently; to disagree. **quarrelsome,** kwor'el-sum, *a.* Apt to quarrel; contentious; irascible; choleric.

quarry, kwor'i, *n.* A place where stones are dug from the earth; an animal pursued for prey; game killed.—*vt.* (quarrying, quarried). To dig or take from a quarry.

quart, kwōrt, *n.* The fourth part of a gallon; two pints.

quarter, kwôr'tėr, *n.* The fourth part of anything; 28 lbs.; 8 bushels; any direction or point of the compass; a district; locality; division of a heraldic shield; proper position; mercy to a beaten foe; *pl.* shelter or lodging; encampment.—*vt.* To divide into four equal parts; to cut to pieces; to furnish with lodgings or shelter; to add to other arms on a heraldic shield.—*vi.* To lodge. **quarter-deck,** kwôr'tėr-dek', *n.* The upper deck of a ship abaft the mainmast. **quarterly,** kwôr'tėr-li, *a.* Recurring each quarter of the year.—*adv.* Once in a quarter of a year.—*n.* A periodical published quarterly. **quartermaster,** kwôr"tėr-mas'tėr, *n.* An officer who has charge of the barracks, tents, stores, &c., of a regiment.

quartet, quartette, kwôr-tet', *n.* A musical composition in four parts; the performers of such a composition.

quarto, kwôr'tō, *n.* A book in which the sheets are folded into four leaves.—*a.* Having four leaves to the sheet.

quartz, kwôrts, *n.* A pure variety of silica, a constituent of granite and other rocks.

quash, kwosh, *vt.* To subdue or quell; to suppress; to annul or make void.

quasi, kwä'sī. A prefix implying appearance without reality; sort of; sham.

quatrain, kwot'rān, *n.* A stanza of four lines rhyming alternately.

quaver, kwā'vėr, *vi.* To have a tremulous motion; to vibrate.—*vt.* To utter with a tremulous sound.—*n.* A shake or rapid vibration of the voice, or on a musical instrument; a musical note equal to half a crotchet.

quay, kē, *n.* A built landing-place for vessels; a wharf.

queasy, kwē'zi, *a.* Sick at the stomach; inclined to vomit; fastidious; squeamish.

queen, kwēn, *n.* The wife of a king; a female sovereign; a pre-eminent woman; the sovereign of a swarm of bees; a playing-card; a piece at chess.

queenly, kwēn'li, *a.* Like a queen; becoming a queen; suitable to a queen.

queer, kwēr, *a.* Odd; droll; peculiar.

quell, kwel, *vt.* To subdue; to quiet; to allay.

quench, kwench, *vt.* To put out, as fire; to allay or slake, as thirst; to repress.—*vi.* To be extinguished; to lose zeal.

querulous, kwer'ū-lus, *a.* Complaining; murmuring; peevish.

query, kwēr'i, *n.* A question; the mark of interrogation (?).—*vi.* (querying, queried). To ask a question or questions. —*vi.* To question; to mark with a query.

quest, kwest, *n.* Act of seeking; search; pursuit; inquiry; solicitation.

question, kwes'chun, *n.* Act of asking; an interrogation; inquiry; discussion; subject of discussion.—*vi.* To ask a question; to doubt.—*vt.* To interrogate; to doubt; to challenge. **questionable,** kwes'chun-a-bl, *a.* That may be questioned; doubtful.

queue, kū, *n.* The tail of a wig; a pigtail; a number of persons waiting in a row.

quibble, kwib'l, *n.* A turn of language to evade the point in question; a pun.—*vi.* (quibbling, quibbled). To evade the question of truth by artifice; to prevaricate; to pun.

quick, kwik, *a.* Alive; brisk; swift; keen; sensitive; irritable.—*n.* A growing plant, usually hawthorn, for hedges; the living flesh; sensitiveness.—*adv.* Quickly; soon. **quicken,** kwik'en, *vt.* To revive or resuscitate; to cheer; to increase the speed of; to sharpen; to stimulate.—*vi.* To become alive; to move quickly or more quickly.

quicklime, kwik"lim', *n.* Lime burned but not yet slaked with water.

quicksand, kwik"sand', *n.* A movable sandbank under water; sand yielding under the feet; something treacherous.

quicksilver, kwik"sil'vėr, *n.* Mercury.

quid, kwid, *n.* A piece of tobacco chewed and rolled about in the mouth.

quiescence, kwĭ-es'ens, *n.* Rest; repose. **quiescent**, kwĭ-es'ent, *a.* Resting; still; tranquil; silent.—*n.* A silent letter.

quiet, kwī'et, *a.* At rest; calm; still; peaceful; patient; secluded; not glaring or showy.—*n.* Rest; repose; peace; security.—*vt.* To make quiet; to calm; to full; to allay. **quietude**, kwī'e-tūd, *n.* Rest; quiet.

quietus, kwī-ē'tus, *n.* A final discharge of an account; a finishing stroke.

quill, kwil, *n.* The strong feather of a goose, &c.; a feather made into a pen; the spine of a porcupine; a piece of reed used by weavers; a plait of a ruffle. —*vt.* I plait.

quilt, kwilt, *n.* A padded bed-cover.— *vt.* To form into a quilt; to sew pieces of cloth with soft substance between. **quilting**, kwilt'ing, *n.* The act of making a quilt; the material used for quilts.

quince, kwins, *n.* The fruit of a tree allied to the pear and apple; the tree itself.

quinine, kwī'nīn; kwi-nēn', *n.* An alkaline substance obtained from the bark of trees of the cinchona genus.

quinsy, kwin'zi, *n.* An inflammation of the tonsils or throat.

quintessence, kwint-es'ens, *n.* The fifth or highest essence of a natural body; the purest or most essential part of a thing.

quintet, quintette, kwin-tet', *n.* A musical composition in five parts; the performers of such a composition.

quintuple, kwin'tu-pl, *a.* Fivefold.—*vt.* To make fivefold.

quip, kwip, *n.* A sharp sarcastic turn; a severe retort; a gibe.

quire, kwīr, *n.* A chorus; a choir; part of a church where the singers sit; twenty-four sheets of paper.

quirk, kwėrk, *n.* An artful turn for evasion; a shift; a quibble.

quit, kwit, *a.* Discharged; released; free; clear.—*vt.* (quitting, quitted). To discharge; to rid; to acquit; to leave; to abandon.

quite, kwīt, *adv.* Completely; wholly; entirely; altogether; very.

quittance, kwit'ans, *n.* Acquittance; recompense; return; payment.

quiver, kwiv'ėr, *n.* A case or sheath for arrows.—*vi.* To shake with small rapid movements; to tremble; to shiver.

quixotic, kwiks-ot'ik, *a.* Chivalrous to extravagance; aiming at visionary ends.

quiz, kwiz, *n.* A hoax; a jest; one who quizzes; one liable to be quizzed.—*vt.* (quizzing, quizzed). To make fun of, as by obscure questions; to look at inquisitively. **quizzical**, kwiz'i-kal, *a.* Partaking of the nature of a quiz; addicted to quizzing.

quoin, koin, *n.* An external solid angle as of a building; a wedge.

quoit, kwoit, *n.* A flattish ring of iron, thrown at a mark.—*vi.* To throw or play at quoits.

quondam, kwon'dam, *a.* Former.

quorum, kwō'rum, *n.* A number of the members of any body competent to transact business.

quota, kwō'ta, *n.* A share or proportion assigned to each.

quote, kwōt, *vt.* (quoting, quoted). To adduce or cite, as from some author; to name as the price of an article. **quotation**, kwō-tā'shun, *n.* Act of quoting; passage quoted; the naming of the price of commodities or the price specified.

quoth, kwōth, *vt.* Said; spoke; used only in the first and third persons preterite, and before its nominative.

quotient, kwō'shent, *n.* The number resulting from the division of one number by another, showing how often the one contains the other.

R

rabbet, rab'et, *vt.* To cut so as to make a joint along an edge.—*n.* The cut so made on an edge to form a joint.

rabbi, rab'ī, *n.* A Jewish teacher or expounder of the law. **Rabbinic, Rabbinical**, ra-bin'ik, ra-bin'i-kal, *a.* Pertaining to the Hebrew learning and teachers after Christ.

rabbit, rab'it, *n.* A burrowing rodent allied to the hare.

rabble, rab'l, *n.* A crowd of vulgar, noisy people; the mob; the lower class of people.

rabid, rab'id, *a.* Raving; furious; mad.

rabies, rā'bi-ēz, *n.* A disease affecting certain animals, especially dogs, from which hydrophobia is communicated.

raccoon, racoon, ra-kön', *n.* An American carnivorous animal.

race, rās, *n.* A body of individuals sprung from a common stock; a breed or stock; a running; a contest in speed; a course or career; a rapid current or channel.— *vi.* (racing, raced). To run swiftly; to contend in running.—*vt.* To cause to contend in speed.

race horse, rās hors, *n.* A horse bred or kept for racing.

racial, rā'shal, *a.* Pertaining to race or lineage; pertaining to the races of man.

racing, rās'ing, *n.* Act of running in a race; the business of joining in horse-races.

rack, rak, *vt.* To stretch unduly; to distort; to punish on the rack; to torture; to strain.—*n.* Something used for stretching; an instrument of torture; torment; anguish; a frame for fodder, &c.; a bar with teeth on one of its edges; flying broken clouds; wreck.

racket, rak'et, *n.* A confused din; clamor; the bat used in tennis, &c.; *pl.* a game like tennis.—*vi.* To make a racket; to frolic.

racketeer, rak'e-tēr", *n.* One who preys on and obtains money from organized society by unlawful means.

racy, rās'i, *a.* Strong and well-flavored.

radar, rā'dār, *n.* A device for detecting the distance and location of unseen objects by the reflection of radio waves.

radial, rā'di-al, *a.* Relating to a radius; grouped or appearing like radii or rays.

radiant, rā'di-ant, *a.* Emitting rays of light or heat; issuing in rays; beaming. **radiance**, rā'di-ans, *n.* Brightness shooting in rays; luster; brilliancy; splendor.

radiation, rā'di-ā"shun, *n.* Act of radiating; emission of rays; beamy brightness. **radiate**, rā'di-āt, *vi.* To emit rays of light; to shine; to spread abroad as in rays.—*vt.* To emit in divergent lines; to enlighten.—*a.* Having rays or lines resembling radii.

radiator, rā'di-ā-tėr, *n.* An apparatus used either to heat externally or to cool internally.

radical, rad'i-kal, *a.* Pertaining to the root; original; thorough-going; native; underived; relating to radicals in politics.—*n.* A root; a simple, underived word; one who advocates extreme political reform.

radicle, ra'di-kl, *n.* A small root; that part of the seed which becomes the root.

radio, rā'di-ō, *a.* Of or pertaining to, employing, or operated by radiant energy, specifically that of electric waves.

radish, rad'ish, *n.* A plant, the young root of which is eaten raw, as a salad.

radium, rā'di-um, *n.* A rare radio-active substance; supposed a metal, obtained from pitchblende.

radius, rā'di-us, *n.* pl. **-ii, -iuses.** A straight line from the center of a circle to the circumference; a bone of the forearm.

raffle, raf'l, *n.* A kind of lottery.—*vi.* raffling, raffled). To engage in a raffle.—*vt.* To dispose of by raffle.

raft, raft, *n.* Logs fastened together and floated; a floating structure.

rafter, räf'tėr, *n.* A large sloping piece of timber supporting a roof.

rag, rag, *n.* A rough separate fragment; tattered cloth; a shred; a tatter.

ragamuffin, rag"a-muf'in, *n.* A paltry fellow; a mean wretch.

rage, rāj, *n.* Violent anger; fury; enthusiasm; rapture.—*vi.* (raging, raged). To be furious with anger; to be violently agitated.

ragged, rag'ed, *a.* Rent or worn into rags; tattered; rugged; wearing tattered clothes.

ragout, ra-gö', *n.* A dish of stewed and highly seasoned meat and vegetables.

ragtime, rag"tīm', *n.* A form of jazz; the rhythm of ragtime.

ragweed, rag"wēd', *n.* A common weed whose pollen causes hay fever.

raid, rād, *n.* A hostile incursion; a foray. —*vi.* To engage in a raid.—*vt.* To make a raid on.

rail, rāl, *n.* A horizontal bar of wood or metal; a connected series of posts; a railing; one of the parallel iron bars forming a track for locomotives, &c.; a railway; a grallatorial bird.—*vt.* To inclose with rails; to furnish with rails.—*vi.* To use abusive language; to scold; to inveigh.

railing, rāl-ing, *n.* A fence; rails in general.

raillery, rāl'ėr-i, *n.* Light ridicule or satire; banter; jesting language.

railroad, rāl"rōd', *n.* A railway.

railway, rāl"wā', *n.* A road having iron rails laid in parallel lines, on which locomotives draw cars; all the land, buildings, and machinery required for traffic on the road.

raiment, rā'ment, *n.* Clothing; vestments.

rain, rān, *n.* The moisture of the atmosphere falling in drops; a shower of anything.—*vi.* To fall in drops from the clouds; to fall like rain.—*vt.* To pour or shower down.

rainbow, rān"bō', *n.* An arc of a circle consisting of all the prismatic colors appearing in the heavens opposite the sun.

rainfall, rān"fal', *n.* A fall of rain; the amount of water that falls as rain.

raise, rāz, *vt.* (raising, raised). To cause to rise; to lift upward; to excite; to recall from death; to stir up; to construct; to levy; to breed; to originate; to give vent to; to inflate; to cause to be relinquished (a siege).

raisin, rā'zn, *n.* A dried grape.

rajah, rä'jä, *n.* A Hindu king or ruler; a title of Hindus of rank.

rake, rāk, *n.* An implement for collecting hay or straw, smoothing earth, &c.; a dissolute, lewd man; slope.—*vt.* (raking, raked). To apply a rake to; to gather with a rake; to ransack; to enfilade.—*vi.* To use a rake; to search minutely; to incline; to slope aft, as masts. **raking**, rāk'ing, *n.* Act of using a rake; severe scrutiny. **rakish**, rāk'ish, *a.* Like a rake; dissolute; debauched; sloping, as masts.

rally, ral'i, *vt.* (rallying, rallied). To reunite, as disordered troops; to collect, as things scattered; to attack with raillery; to banter.—*vi.* To recover strength or vigor.—*n.* A stand made by retreating troops; recovery of strength.

ram, ram, *n.* The male of the sheep; a battering-ram; the loose hammer of a pile-driving machine; a heavy steel beak of a war-vessel; an iron-clad ship with such a beak; one of the signs of the zodiac.—*vt.* (ramming, rammed). To strike with a ram; to batter; to cram.

ramble, ram'bl, *vi.* (rambling, rambled). To roam carelessly about; to talk incoherently; to have parts stretching irregularly.—*n.* An irregular excursion; a maze.

ramify, ram'i-fī, *vt.* To divide into branches.—*vi.* To be divided; to branch out.

ramp, ramp, *vi.* To climb, as a plant; to rear on the hind-legs; to spring.—*n.* A spring or leap; a slope.

rampage, ram'pāj or ram-pāj', *vi.* To

prance about; to rage and storm.—*n.* Violent conduct.

rampant, rampant, *a.* Rank in growth; exuberant; unrestrained; in *heraldry,* standing up on the hind-legs.

rampart, ram'pärt, *n.* A mound of earth round a place, capable of resisting cannon-shot; a bulwark; a defense.

ramrod, ram''rod', *n.* A rod used in ramming down the charge in a gun, pistol, &c.

ramshackle, ram''shak'-l, *a.* Dilapidated; rickety.

ranch, ranche, ranch, *n.* An extensive farming establishment for rearing cattle and horses.

rancid, ran'sid, *a.* Having a rank or stinking smell; strong-scented; sour; musty. **rancidity,** ran-sid'i-ti, *n.* Quality of being rancid.

rancor, rancour, rang'kėr, *n.* Deepseated enmity; malice; malignity. **rancorous,** rang'kėr-us, *a.* Characterized by rancor; malignant; malicious; virulent.

random, ran'dum, *n.* Action without definite object; chance; caprice. **at random,** in a haphazard manner.—*a.* Left to chance; done without previous calculation.

range, rānj, *vt.* (ranging, ranged). To set in a row; to dispose systematically; to wander through or scour.—*vi.* To rank; to rove about; to fluctuate.—*n.* A row; a rank; compass or extent; a kitchen stove; distance to which a projectile is carried; a place for gun practice. **ranger,** rān'jèr, *n.* One who ranges, an official connected with a forest or park.

rank, rangk, *n.* A row; a line; a social class; comparative station; titled dignity.—*vt.* To place in a line; to classify. —*vi.* To belong to a class; to put in a claim against a bankrupt.—*a.* Luxuriant in growth; strong-scented; utter; coarse; disgusting.

rankle, rang'kl, *vi.* (rankling, rankled). To fester painfully; to continue to irritate.—*vt.* To irritate; to inflame.

ransack, ran'sak, *vt.* To plunder; to search thoroughly.

ransom, ran'sum, *n.* Release from captivity by payment; price paid for redemption or pardon.—*vt.* To pay a ransom for; to buy off; to deliver.

rant, rant, *vi.* To speak in extravagant language.—*n.* Boisterous, empty declamation; bombast.

rap, rap, *n.* A quick smart blow; a knock.—*vi.* (rapping, rapped). To strike a quick, sharp blow.—*vt.* To strike with a quick blow.

rapacious, ra-pā'shus, *a.* Greedy of plunder; subsisting on prey; extortionate. **rapacity,** ra-pas'i-ti, *n.* Exorbitant greediness; extortionate practices.

rape, rāp, *n.* A seizing by violence; carnal knowledge of a woman against her will; a plant of the cabbage kind, whose seeds yield an oil.—*vt.* (raping, raped). To carry off violently; to ravish.

rapid, rap'id, *a.* Very swift; speedy; hurried.—*n.* A swift current in a river.

rapidity, ra-pid'i-ti, *n.* State or quality of being rapid; celerity; velocity.

rapier, rā'pi-ėr, *n.* A long narrow sword; a sword used only in thrusting.

rapine, rap'in, *n.* Act of plundering; violent seizure of goods; pillage.

rapport, ra-pōrt', *n.* Complete understanding and harmony.

rapt, rapt, *a.* Transported; enraptured.

rapture, rap'tūr, *n.* Extreme joy or pleasure; ecstasy; transport; enthusiasm. **rapturous,** rap'tūr-us, *a.* Marked with rapture; ecstatic; ravishing.

rare, rār, *a.* Not dense or compact; sparse; not frequent; uncommon; very valuable; underdone, as meat.

rarebit, rar'bit, *n.* A dainty morsel.

rarefy, rār'ē-fī, *vt.* and *i.* (rarefying, rarefied). To make or become less dense. **rarefaction,** rār'ē-fak''shun, *n.* Act or process of rarefying; state of being rarefied.

rarity, rār'i-ti, *n.* State of being rare; a thing valued for its scarcity; tenuity.

rascal, ras'kal, *n.* A scoundrel; a rogue. —*a.* Worthless; mean; low; base. **rascality,** ras-kal'i-ti, *n.* Act of a rascal; mean dishonesty; base fraud. **rascallion,** ras-kal'yun, *n.* A low, mean person; a rascally wretch. Also *Rapscallion.*

rash, rash, *a.* Precipitate; hasty; overbold; incautious.—*n.* An eruption on the skin.

rasp, rasp, *vt.* To rub with something rough; to grate; to utter harshly.—*vi.* To rub or grate.—*n.* A coarse file; a raspberry.

raspberry, raz''bėr'i, *n.* The fruit of a plant allied to the bramble; the plant itself.

rat, rat, *n.* A small rodent; one who deserts his party.—*vi.* (ratting, ratted). To catch or kill rats; to desert one's party.

ratchet, rach'et, *n.* A catch which abuts against the teeth of a wheel to prevent it running back.

rate, rāt, *n.* Proportion, standard; degree; degree of speed; price; a tax; assessment.—*vt.* (rated, rated). To fix the value, rank, or degree of; to appraise; to reprove; to scold.—*vi.* To be classed in a certain order.

rather, räᴛʜ'ėr, *adv.* More readily; preferably; more properly; somewhat.

ratify, rat'i-fī, *vt.* (ratifying, ratified). To confirm; to approve and sanction. **ratification,** rat'i-fi-kā''shun, *n.* Act of ratifying; confirmation; act of giving sanction.

ratio, rā'shō, *n.* Relation or proportion; rate.

ration, rā'shun, *n.* A daily allowance of provisions; allowance.—*vt.* To supply with rations.

rational, rash'un-al, *a.* Endowed with reason; agreeable to reason; judicious. **rationale,** rash'un-ā''lē, *n.* Exposition of the principles of some process, action, &c. **rationalist,** rash'un-al-ist, *n.* An adherent of rationalism; one who rejects the supernatural element in Scripture. **rationality,** rash'un-al'i-ti, *n.* The quality of being rational; the power of reasoning.

ratline, ratlin, rat'lin, *n.* One of the ropes forming ladders in a ship's shrouds.

ratsbane, rats''bān', *n.* Poison for rats.

rattle, rat'l, *vi.* and *i.* (rattling, rattled). To clatter; to chatter fluently.—*n.* A rapid succession of clattering sounds; an instrument or toy which makes a clattering sound; one who talks much and rapidly.

rattlesnake, rat''l-snāk', *n.* A venomous American snake, with horny pieces at the point of the tail which rattle.

raucous, ra'kus, *a.* Hoarse; harsh.

ravage, rav'ij, *n.* Devastation; havoc.—*vt.* (ravaging, ravaged). To lay waste; to pillage.

rave, rāv, *vi.* (raving, raved). To be delirious; to speak enthusiastically; to dote.

ravel, rav'el, *vt.* (raveling, raveled). To disentangle; to make intricate; to involve.

raven, rāv'en, *n.* A bird of prey of the crow kind, of a black color.

ravenous, rav'en-us, *a.* Furiously voracious; hungry even to rage.

ravine, ra-vēn', *n.* A long hollow formed by a torrent; a gorge or pass.

raving, rāv'ing, *n.* Irrational, incoherent talk; delirious utterances.

ravish, rav'ish, *vt.* To carry away by violence; to enrapture; to commit a rape upon.

raw, ra, *a.* Not cooked or dressed; not manufactured; unfinished; not diluted; bare, as flesh; galled; sensitive; inexperienced; cold and damp.

ray, rā, *n.* A line of light; a gleam of intellectual light; one of a number of diverging radii; a flat-fish.—*vt.* and *i.* (raying, rayed). To shine forth; to radiate; to streak.

rayon, rā'on, *n.* A synthetic fiber; fabric made from rayon fiber.

raze, rāz, *vt.* (razing, razed). To graze; to lay level with the ground; to efface.

razor, rā'zėr, *n.* A knife for shaving off hair.

reach, rēch, *vt.* To extend; to hand; to extend or stretch from a distance; to arrive at; to gain.—*vi.* To extend; to stretch out the hand in order to touch; to make efforts at attainment.—*n.* Act or power of extending to; straight course of a river; scope.

react, rē-akt', *vi.* To act in return; to return an impulse; to act reciprocally upon each other.—*vt.* To perform anew.

reaction, rē-ak'shun, *n.* A reacting; reciprocal action; tendency to revert to a previous condition; exhaustion consequent on activity, and *vice versa.* **reactionary,** rē-ak''shun-er'i, *a.* Pertaining to or favoring reaction.—*n.* One who attempts to reverse political progress.

reactive, rē-ak'tiv, *a.* Having power to react; tending to reaction.

read, rēd, *vt.* (reading, read). To peruse; to utter aloud, following something written or printed; to explain.—*vi.* To peruse; to study; to stand written or printed; to make sense.—*a.* red. Instructed by reading; learned. **readable,** rēd'a-bl, *a.* That may be read; legible; fit or deserving to be read.

reader, rēd'ėr, *n.* One who reads; one who reads aloud prayers, lectures, &c.; one who corrects printers' errors; a reading-book.

ready, re'di, *a.* Prepared; in order; prompt; willing; inclined; at hand; opportune. **readily,** re'di-li, *adv.* In a ready manner; quickly; promptly; easily; cheerfully. **readiness,** re'di-nes *n.* Quickness; promptitude; facility; aptitude; alacrity.

ready-made, red'i-mād', *a.* Made beforehand; kept in stock ready for use or sale.

real, rē'al, *a.* Actual; true; genuine; in *law,* pertaining to things fixed or immovable, as lands and houses. **realism,** rē'al-izm, *n.* The endeavor in art or literature to reproduce nature or describe life as it actually appears. **realist,** rē'al-ist, *n.* One who practices or believes in realism. **reality,** rē-al'i-ti, *n.* State or quality of being real; actuality; fact; truth. **realize,** rē'al-īz, *vt.* (realizing, realized). To make real; to convert into money; to impress on the mind as a reality; to render tangible or effective; to acquire; to gain.

realm, relm, *n.* The dominions of a sovereign; a region, sphere, or domain.

realty, rē'al-ti, *n.* The fixed nature of property termed *real*; real property.

ream, rēm, *n.* A package of paper, consisting generally of 20 quires, or 480 sheets.

reap, rēp, *vt.* and *i.* To cut with a scythe, &c., as grain; to gather; to clear of a grain crop; to receive as a reward of labor, &c.

rear, rēr, *n.* The part behind; the part of an army behind the rest; the background.—*vt.* To raise; to bring up, as young; to breed, as cattle; to build up.—*vi.* To rise on the hind legs, as a horse; to become erect.

rear-guard, rēr'gärd', *n.* The part of an army that marches in the rear.

rearrange, rē'a-rānj'', *vt.* To arrange again; to put in different order.

reason, rē'zn, *n.* A motive or cause; explanation; faculty for logical operations; justice; equity; moderate demands.—*vi.* To exercise the faculty of reason; to argue; to discuss.—*vt.* To examine or discuss by arguments; to persuade by reasoning. **reasonable,** rē'zn-a-bl, *a.* Having the faculty of reason; rational; conformable to reason; moderate; fair; tolerable.

reassemble, rē'-a-sem''bl, *vt.* and *i.* To assemble again.

reassert, rē'a-sėrt'', *vt.* To assert again.

reassure, rē'a-shōr'', *vt.* To assure anew; to free from fear or terror; to reinsure.

rebate, rē'bāt, *vt.* (rebating, rebated). To blunt; to diminish; to make a discount from.

rebate, rebatement, rē'bāt, rē-bāt'ment, *n.* Abatement in price; deduction.

rebel, re'bel, *n.* One who makes war against or opposes constituted authorities.—*a.* Rebellious; acting in revolt.—*vi.* rē-bel' (rebeling, rebelled.) To oppose lawful authority; to revolt; to conceive a loathing. **rebellion**, re-bel'yun, *n.* Act of rebelling; an armed rising against a government. **rebellious**, re-bel'yus, *a.* Pertaining to rebellion; mutinous; insubordinate.

rebound, rē-bound', *vi.* To spring or bound back; to recoil.—*n.* The act of flying back on collision; resilience.

rebuff, rē-buf', *n.* A sudden check; a repulse; refusal.—*vt.* To beat back; to check; to repel the advances of.

rebuild, rē-bild', *vt.* To build again.

rebuke, rē-būk', *vt.* (rebuking, rebuked). To reprimand; to reprove sharply.—*n.* A direct and severe reprimand; reproof.

rebus, rē'bus, *n.* A set of words represented by pictures of objects; a kind of puzzle made up of such pictures.

rebut, rē-but', *vt.* (rebutting, rebutted). To repel; to refute; in *law*, to oppose by argument, plea, or countervailing proof. **rebuttal**, rē-but'al, *n.* Refutation.

recalcitrant, rē-kal'si-trant, *a.* Not submissive; refractory.

recall, rē-kal', *vt.* To call or bring back; to revive in memory.—*n.* A calling back.

recant, rē-kant', *vt.* To retract, as a declaration.—*vi.* To retract one's words. **recantation**, rē'kan-tā'shun, *n.* Act of recanting; retraction.

recapitulate, rē'ka-pit''ū-lāt, *vt.* To give a summary of.—*vi.* To repeat briefly. **recapitulation**, rē'ka-pit''ū-lā''-shun, *n.* Act of recapitulating; summary.

recapture, rē-kap'tūr, *n.* Act of retaking; a prize retaken.—*vt.* To retake.

recast, rē-kast', *vt.* To throw again; to mold anew.

recede, rē-sēd', *vi.* (receding, receded). To go back; to withdraw.—*vt.* To cede back.

receipt, rē-sēt', *n.* Act of receiving; that which is received; a written acknowledgment of something received; a recipe.—*vt.* To give a receipt for; to discharge, as an account.

receive, rē-sēv', *vt.* (receiving, received). To take, as a thing offered; to admit; to entertain; to contain; to be the object of; to take stolen goods. **receiver**, rē-sēv'ėr, *n.* One who or that which receives; one who takes stolen goods from a thief. **receivable**, rē-sēv'a-bl, *a.* That may be received.

recent, rē'sent, *a.* New; late; fresh.

receptacle, rē-sep'ta-kl, *n.* A place or vessel in which anything is received; repository.

reception, rē-sep'shun, *n.* Act or manner of receiving; welcome; a formal receiving of guests; admission or acceptance.

receptive, rē-sep'tiv, *a.* Such as to receive readily; able to take in or contain. **receptivity**, rē'sep-tiv''i-ti, *n.* The state or quality of being receptive.

recess, rē-ses', *n.* A withdrawing; place or period of retirement; time during which business is suspended; a niche in a wall; an alcove. **recession**, rē-sesh'-un, *n.* Act of receding; withdrawal; a granting back.

recipe, res'i-pē, *n.* A medical prescrip-

tion; a statement of ingredients for a mixture.

recipient, rē-si'pi-ent, *n.* One who or that which receives; a receiver.

reciprocal, re-sip'rō-kal, *a.* Reciprocating; alternate; done by each to the other; mutual; interchangeable. **reciprocate**, rē-sip'rō-kāt, *vi.* To move backward and forward; to alternate.—*vt.* To exchange; to give in requital. **reciprocation**, rē-sip'rō-kā''shun, *n.* Act of reciprocating; a mutual giving. **reciprocity**, re-si-pros'i-ti, *n.* Reciprocation; interchange; reciprocal obligation; equal commercial rights mutually enjoyed.

recite, rē-sīt', *vt.* and *i.* (reciting, recited). To repeat aloud, as a writing committed to memory; to relate; to recapitulate. **recital**, rē-sīt'al, *n.* Act of reciting; narration; a musical entertainment. **recitation**, re-si-tā'shun. *n.* Recital; the delivery before an audience of the composition of others.

reck, rek, *vt.* To heed; to regard. **reckless**, rek'les, *a.* Heedless, careless; rash.

reckon, rek'n, *vt.* and *i.* To count; to estimate; to account, consider. **reckoner**, rek'un-ėr, *n.* One who or that which reckons or computes. **reckoning**, rek'un-ing. *n.* Calculation: a statement of accounts with another; landlord's bill; calculation of a ship's position.

reclaim, rē-klām', *vt.* To claim back; to reform; to tame; to recover; to reduce to a state fit for cultivation. **reclaimable**, rē-klām'a-bl, *a.* That may be reclaimed, reformed or tamed. **reclamation**, re-kla-mā'shun, *n.* Act of reclaiming; a claim made.

recline, rē-klīn', *vt.* and *i.* (reclining, reclined). To lean; to rest or repose.

recluse, rē-klōs', *a.* Retired; solitary.— *n.* A person who lives in seclusion; a hermit.

recognize, rek'og-nīz, *vt.* (recognizing, recognized). To know again; to admit a knowledge of; to acknowledge formally; to indicate one's notice by a bow, &c.; to indicate appreciation of. **recognition**, rek'og-nish''un. *n.* Act of recognizing; avowal; acknowledgment. **recognisance**. rē-kog'ni-zans or rē-kon'i-zans, *n.* Recognition; an obligation, as to appear at the assizes, keep the peace, &c.

recoil, rē-koil', *vi.* To move or start back; to retreat; to shrink; to rebound. —*n.* A starting or falling back; rebound, as of a gun.

recollect, rek'o-lekt'', *vt.* To remember; to recover composure of mind (with refl. pron.). **re-collect**, rē'ko-lekt'', *vt.* To collect again. **recollection**, re-ko-lek'shon, *n.* Act of recollecting; remembrance; something recalled to mind.

recommend, rek'o-mend'', *vt.* To praise to another; to make acceptable; to commit with prayers; to advise. **recommendation**, rek'o-men-dā''shun, *n.* The act of recommending; a favorable representation; that which procures favor.

recompense, rek'om-pens, *vt.* (recompensing, recompensed). To compensate;

to requite; to make amends for.—*n.* Compensation; reward; amends.

reconcile, rĕk'on-sīl, *vt.* (reconciling, reconciled). To make friendly again; to adjust or settle; to harmonize. **reconcilement**, rek-on-sīl'ment, *n.* Reconciliation; renewal of friendship. **reconciliation**, rĕk'on-sil'i-ā''shun, *n.* Act of reconciling; renewal of friendship.

recondite, rĕk'un-dīt, or rē-kon'dīt, *a.* Abstruse; profound.

recondition, rē'kon-dish''un, *vt.* To restore to a good condition by repairing or rebuilding.

reconnoiter, reconnoitre, rĕk'o-noi''tẽr, *vt.* and *i.* (reconnoitering, reconnoitered). To make a preliminary survey of; to survey for military purposes. **reconnaissance**, re-kon'i-sans, *n.* The act or operation of reconnoitering.

reconsider, rē'kon-sid''ẽr, *vt.* To consider again. **reconsideration**, rē-kon-si'dẽr-ā''shon, *n.* Act of reconsidering; renewed consideration.

reconstruct, rē'kon-strukt'', *vt.* To construct again; to rebuild.

record, rē-kord', *vt.* To preserve in writing; to register; to chronicle.—*n.* rek'ord. A written memorial; a register; a public document; memory; one's personal history; best result in contests.

recorder, rē-kor'dẽr, *n.* One who records; an official registrar; an old musical instrument; a registering apparatus.

recount, rē-kount', *vt.* To relate in detail; to count again.—*n.* A second counting.

recoup, rē-köp', *vt.* To recompense or compensate; to indemnify.

recourse, rē-kōrs', *n.* A going to with a request, as for aid; resort in perplexity.

recover, rē-kuv'ẽr, *vt.* To get back; to regain; to revive; to rescue; to obtain in return for injury or debt.—*vi.* To grow well; to regain a former condition. **recovery**, rē-kuv'ẽr-i, *n.* Act of recovering; restoration from sickness, &c.; the obtaining of something by legal procedure.

recreant, rek'rē-ant, *a.* Craven; cowardly; apostate.—*n.* One who basely yields in combat; a cowardly wretch.

recreate, rek'rē-āt, *vt.* To revive; to enliven; to amuse.—*vi.* To take recreation. **re-create**, rē'krē-āt'', *vt.* To create anew. **recreation**, rek'rē-ā''shun, *n.* Refreshment of the strength and spirits after toil; amusement; entertainment.

recriminate, rē-krim'i-nāt, *vi.* To return one accusation with another.—*vt.* To accuse in return. **recrimination**, rē-krim'i-nā''shun, *n.* Act of recriminating; a counter-accusation. **recriminative, recriminatory**, re-krim''i-nā'tiv, re-krim''i-na-tō'ri, *a.* Recriminating or retorting accusation.

recruit, rē-kröt', *vt.* To repair; to supply with new soldiers.—*vi.* To gain new supplies of anything; to raise new soldiers.—*n.* A soldier newly enlisted.

rectangle, rek'tang'gl, *n.* A quadrilateral having all its angles right angles. **rectangular**, rek-tang'gū-lẽr, *a.* Right-angled.

rectify, rek'ti-fī, *vt.* (rectifying, recti-

fied). To correct; to refine by repeated distillation. **rectification**, rek'ti-fi-kā''shun, *n.* Act or operation of rectifying; process of refining by repeated distillation. **rectifier**, rek''ti-fī'ẽr, *n.* One who or that which rectifies; a refiner of alcohol.

rectitude, rek'ti-tūd, *n.* Integrity; probity; uprightness; honesty.

rector, rek'tẽr, *n.* A ruler; an Episcopal clergyman who has the cure of a parish; a head of certain institutions, chiefly academical. **rectory**, rek'tō-ri, *n.* A church or living held by a rector; a rector's house.

rectum, rek'tum, *n.* The lowest part of the large intestine opening at the anus.

recumbent, rē-kum'bent, *a.* Leaning; reclining; reposing; inactive.

recuperate, rē-kū'pẽr-āt, *vt.* and *i.* (recuperating, recuperated). To recover. **recuperation**, rē-kū'pẽr-ā''shun, *n.* Recovery. **recuperative**, rē-kū''pẽr-ā'tiv, *a.* Tending or pertaining to recovery.

recur, rē-kẽr', *vi.* (recurring, recurred). To return; to be repeated at a stated interval. **recurrence**, rē-kẽr'ens, *n.* Act of recurring; return; recourse. **recurrent**, rē-kẽr'ent, *a.* Recurring from time to time.

red, red, *a.* Of a color resembling that of arterial blood.—*n.* A color resembling that of arterial blood; a red pigment.

redact, rē-dakt', *vt.* To edit; to give a presentable literary form to. **redaction**, rē-dak'shun, *n.* Act of preparing for publication; the work thus prepared.

redactor, rē-dak'tẽr, *n.* An editor.

redbreast, red'brest', *n.* A British bird; the robin.

redcoat, red'kō't, *n.* A familiar name for a British soldier.

red deer, red dēr, *n.* The common stag.

redden, red'n, *vt.* To make red.—*vi.* To become red; to blush.

redeem, rē-dēm', *vt.* To buy back; to ransom; to rescue; to save; to atone for; to employ to the best purpose; to perform, as what has been promised. **redeemable**, rē-dēm'a-bl, *a.* That may be redeemed. **redeemer**, rē-dēm'ẽr, *n.* One who redeems; Jesus Christ.

redemption, rē-demp'shun, *n.* The act of redeeming; state of being redeemed; ransom; release; deliverance.

red-handed, red'hand'ed, *a.* With red or bloody hands; in the act.

red-hot, red'hot', *a.* Red with heat; very hot.

red-letter, red''let'ẽr, *a.* Having red letters; fortunate or auspicious.

redolent, red'ō-lent, *a.* Emitting an odor; having or diffusing a sweet scent. **redolence**, red'ō-lens, *n.* Quality of being redolent; fragrance; perfume; scent.

redouble, rē-dub'l, *vt.* To double again. —*vi.* To become twice as much.

redoubt, rē-dout', *n.* See **redout**. **redoubtable**, rē-dout'a-bl, *a.* Such as to cause dread; formidable; valiant.

redress, rē-dres', *vt.* To set right; to adjust; to repair; to relieve.—*n.* Relief; deliverance; reparation.

redskin, red''skin', *n.* A Red Indian, or Indian of North America.

red tape, red tāp, *n.* Excessive official routine and formality.—*a.* Characterized by excessive routine or formality.

reduce, rē-dūs', *vt.* (reducing, reduced). To bring down; to decrease; to degrade; to subdue; to bring under rules or within categories; to restore to its proper place. **reducible**, rē-dūs'i-bl, *a.* That may be reduced. **reduction**, re-duk'shun, *n.* Act of reducing; diminution; conversion into another state or form; subjugation.

redundant, rē-dun'dant, *a.* Superfluous; having more words than necessary. **redundancy**, **redundance**, rē-dun'dan-si, rē-dun'dans, *n.* Superfluity.

redwood, red'wöd', *n.* The giant sequoia; a large coniferous timber tree of the Pacific Coast.

re-echo, rē-ek'ō, *vt.* and *i.* To echo back; to reverberate.—*n.* The echo of an echo.

reed, rēd, *n.* A tall broad-leaved grass growing in marshy places, or its hollow stems; a musical instrument; a rustic pipe.

reef, rēf, *n.* The part of a sail which can be drawn together to expose a smaller area; a range of rocks in the sea near the surface; a vein containing gold.—*vt.* To take in a reef; to reduce the extent of a sail.

reek, rēk, *n.* Vapor; steam; exhalation; smoke.—*vi.* To smoke; to exhale.

reel, rēl, *n.* A bobbin for thread; a revolving appliance for winding a fishing-line; a staggering motion; a lively Scottish dance; a spool on which a photographic film is wound; hence, a strip of moving picture film about 1,000 feet in length wound on a spool.—*vt.* To wind upon a reel; to stagger.

refection, rē-fek'shun, *n.* Refreshment after hunger or fatigue; a repast.

refectory, rē-fek'tō-ri, *n.* A room for refreshment or meals.

refer, rē-fėr', *vt.* (referring, referred). To trace or carry back; to attribute; to appeal; to assign.—*vi.* To respect or have relation; to appeal; to apply; to allude. **referable**, ref'ėr-a-bl, *a.* That may be referred, assigned, attributed, &c. **referee**, ref'ėr-ē'', *n.* One to whom a matter in dispute is referred for decision; an umpire.

reference, ref'ėr-ens, *n.* Act of referring; allusion; relation; one of whom inquiries may be made.

referendum, ref'ėr-en''dum, *n.* The referring of a measure passed by a legislature to the people for final approval.

refill, rē-fil', *vt.* To fill again.

refine, rē-fīn', *vt.* (refining, refined). To increase the fineness of; to purify; to make elegant; to give culture to.—*vi.* To become purer; to indulge in hair-splitting. **refinement**, rē-fīn'ment, *n.* Act of refining; elegance; culture; nicety. **refiner**, rē-fīn'ėr, *n.* One who refines, specially metals, liquors, sugars, &c. **refinery**, rē-fīn'ėr-i, *n.* A place and apparatus for refining sugar, metals, &c.

refit, rē-fit', *vt.* and *i.* (refitting, refitted). To fit anew, to repair.—*n.* Repair.

reflect, rē-flekt', *vt.* To cast back; to throw off, as light or heat, after striking the surface; to mirror.—*vi.* To throw back light or heat; to meditate; to bring reproach. **reflection**, rē-flek'shun, *n.* Act of reflecting; that which is produced by being reflected; meditation; a censorious remark; reproach. **reflective**, rē-flekt'iv, *a.* Throwing back rays; meditating. **reflector**, rē-flek'tėr, *n.* One who reflects; a polished surface for reflecting light, &c.

reflex, rē'fleks, *a.* Bent or directed back; done involuntarily or unconsciously.—*n.* A reflection.

reflexive, rē-flek'siv, *a.* Reflective; having respect to something past; in *grammar*, having for its object a pronoun which stands for the subject; also applied to such pronouns.

reform, rē-form', *vt.* and *i.* To change from worse to better; to amend; to form anew.—*n.* A beneficial change; amendment; a change in the regulations of parliamentary representation. **reformation**, re-for-mā'shon, *n.* Act of reforming; amendment; the Protestant revolution of the sixteenth century. **reformation**, ref'or-mā''shun, *n.* The act of forming anew; a second forming. **reformatory**, rē-for''ma-tō''ri, *n.* An institution for reclaiming young criminals. **reformed**, rē-formd', *a.* Restored to a good state; amended; having accepted the principles of the Reformation. **reformer**, rē-form'ėr, *n.* One who reforms; one who took a part in the Reformation; one who promotes political reform.

refract, rē-frakt', *vt.* To bend back sharply; to deflect (a ray of light) on passing from one medium into another. **refraction**, rē-frak'shun, *n.* Act of refracting; a change of direction in rays on passing from one medium into another. **refractive**, rē-frak'tiv, *a.* Pertaining to refraction; having power to refract. **refractory**, rē-frak'tō-ri, *a.* Sullen in disobedience; stubborn; unmanageable; resisting ordinary treatment.

refrain, rē-frān', *vt.* To restrain; to keep (one's self) from action.—*vi.* To forbear; to abstain.—*n.* The burden of a song; part repeated at the end of every stanza.

refresh, rē-fresh', *vt.* To revive; to reanimate; to freshen. **refreshing**, rē-fresh'ing, *a.* Invigorating; reanimating; enlivening. **refreshment**, rē-fresh'ment, *n.* Act of refreshing; that which refreshes; *pl.* food and drink.

refrigerate, rē-frij'ē-rāt, *vt.* To cool. **refrigeration**, rē-frij'je-rā''shon, *n.* Act of refrigerating; abatement of heat. **refrigerator**, rē-frij''ėr-ā'tėr, *n.* That which refrigerates; an apparatus for cooling or for making ice; an ice-box; ice-chest.

refuge, ref'ūj, *n.* Protection from danger or distress; a retreat; a shelter; a device; contrivance; shift.—*vt.* and *i.* To shelter. **refugee**, ref-ū-jē', *n.* One who flees for refuge; one who flees to another country or place for safety.

refulgent, rē-ful'jent, *a.* Casting a

bright light; shining; splendid. **reful-gence, refulgency,** rē-ful'jens, rē-ful'jen-si, *n.* Splendor; brilliancy.

refund, rē-fund', *vt.* To pay back; to repay; to reimburse.

refurnish, rē-fēr'nish, *vt.* To furnish anew.

refuse, re'fūz, *a.* Rejected; worthless.—*n.* Waste matter; dregs.

refuse, rē-fūz', *vt.* (refusing, refused). To deny, as a request or demand; to decline; to reject.—*vi.* To decline a request or offer. **refusal,** rē-fūz'al, *n.* Act of refusing; choice of taking or refusing.

refute, rē-fūt', *vt.* (refuting, refuted). To disprove; to overthrow by argument. **refutable,** ref'ū-ta-bl, *a.* That may be refuted or disproved. **refutation,** ref'ū-ta''shun, *n.* Act or process of refuting; disproof.

regain, rē-gān', *vt.* To gain anew; to recover; to retrieve; to reach again.

regal, rē'gal, *a.* Kingly; royal.

regale, rē-gāl', *vt.* and i. (regaling, regaled). To refresh sumptuously; to feast.—*n.* A splendid feast; a treat.

regalia, rē-gā'li-a, *n. pl.* Ensigns of royalty, as the crown, scepter, &c.

regality, rē-gal'i-ti, *n.* Royalty; kingship.

regard, rē-gärd', *vt.* To notice carefully; to observe; to respect; to heed; to view in the light of; to relate to.—*n.* Look or gaze; respect; notice; heed; esteem; deference; *pl.* good wishes. **regarding,** rē-gärd'ing, *prep.* Respecting; concerning; relating to. **regardless,** rē-gärd'les, *a.* Without regard or heed; heedless; negligent; careless.

regatta, rē-gat'a, *n.* A race in which yachts or boats contend for prizes.

regent, rē'jent, *a.* Ruling.—*n.* A ruler; one who governs during the minority or disability of the king. **regency,** rē'jen-si, *n.* Government of a regent; men intrusted with the power of a regent.

regenerate, rē-jen'ėr-āt, *vt.* To generate anew; to bring into a better state.—*n.* Born anew; changed to a spiritual state. **regeneration,** re-jen'ėr-a''shun, *n.* Act of regenerating; that change by which love to God is implanted in the heart.

regime, rā-zhēm', *n.* Mode of management; administration; rule. **regimen,** rej'i-men, *n.* Orderly government; regulation of diet, exercise, &c. **regiment,** rej'i-ment, *n.* A body of troops under the command of a colonel. **regimental,** rej'i-men''tal, *a.* Belonging to a regiment.

region, rē'jun, *n.* A tract of land; country; territory; portion of the body.

register, rē'jis-tėr, *n.* An official record; a roll; a book for special entries of facts; device for indicating work done by machinery; musical compass; a stop in an organ.—*vt.* To record; to insure (a letter). *vi.* To enter one's name. **registered,** re'jis-tėrd, *p.a.* Enrolled; protected by enrollment; insured. **registrar,** rē'jis-trär, *n.* An officer who keeps a public register or record. **registration,** rej'is-tra''shun, *n.* Act of registering; enrollment. **registry,** re'jis-tri, *n.*

Registration; place where a register is kept; an entry.

regress, rē'gres, *n.* Return; power of returning.—*vi.* rē-gres'. To go back. **regression,** rē-gresh'un, *n.* The act of passing back or returning; retrogression.

regret, rē-gret', *n.* Grief at something done or undone; remorse; penitence.—*vt.* (regretting, regretted). To be sorry for; to lament. **regretful,** rē-gret'ful, *a.* Full of regret. **regrettable,** rē-gret'a-bl, *a.* Admitting of or calling for regret.

regular, reg'ū-lėr, *a.* Conformed to a rule, law or principle; normal; methodical; uniform; having the parts symmetrical; thorough.—*n.* A monk who has taken the vows in some order; a soldier of a permanent army. **regularity,** reg'ū-lar''i-ti, *n.* State or character of being regular; steadiness or uniformity.

regulate, reg'ū-lāt, *vt.* (regulating, regulated). To adjust by rule; to put or keep in good order; to direct. **regulation,** reg'ū-lā''shun, *n.* Act of regulating; a rule; a precept. **regulator,** reg'ū-lāt-ėr, *n.* One who or that which regulates.

regurgitate, rē-gėr'ji-tāt, *vt.* and *i.* To pour or cause to surge back.

rehabilitate, rē'ha-bil''i-tāt, *vt.* To restore to a former capacity or position; to re-establish in esteem.

rehearse, rē-hėrs', *vt.* (rehearsing, rehearsed). To repeat; to recite; to relate; to repeat in private for trial. **rehearsal,** rē-hėr'sal, *n.* Act of rehearsing; recital; a trial performance.

Reich, rīk', *n.* Formerly Germany or its government.

reign, rān, *vi.* To be sovereign; to rule; to prevail.—*n.* Royal authority; supremacy; time of a sovereign's supreme authority.

reimburse, rē'im-bėrs'', *vt.* To refund; to pay back. **reimbursement,** rē'im-bėrs''ment, *n.* Act of reimbursing; payment.

rein, rān, *n.* The strap of a bridle, by which a horse is governed; an instrument for restraining; restraint.—*vt.* To govern by a bridle; to restrain.—*vi.* To obey the reins.

reincarnation, rē'in-kär-nā''shun, *n.* Rebirth.

reindeer, rān'dēr, *n.* A deer of northern parts, with broad branched antlers.

reinforce, rē'in-fōrs'', *vt.* To strengthen by new assistance, as troops.—*n.* An additional thickness given to an object to strengthen it. **reinforcement,** rē'in-fors''ment, *n.* Act of reinforcing; additional troops or ships.

reins, rānz, *n.pl.* The kidneys; lower part of the back; seat of the affections and passions.

reinstate, rē'in-stāt'', *vt.* To instate anew; to restore to a former position.

reissue, rē-ish'ū, *vt.* To issue a second time.—*n.* A second or repeated issue.

reiterate, rē-it'ėr-āt, *vt.* To repeat again and again; to do or say repeatedly. **reiteration,** rē-it'ėr-ā''shun, *n.* Repetition.

reject, rē-jekt', *vt.* To cast off; to discard; to repel. to forsake; to decline. **rejection**, rē-jek'shun, *n.* Act of rejecting. refusal to accept or grant.

rejoice, rē-jois', *vi.* (rejoicing, rejoiced) To be glad; to exult.—*vt.* To gladden; to cheer.

rejoicing, rē-jois'ing, *n.* Act of expressing joy; festivity.

rejoin, re-join', *vt.* To join again; to answer.—*vi.* To answer to a reply. **rejoinder**, rē-join'dėr, *n.* An answer to a reply.

rejuvenate, rē-jö've-nāt, *vt.* To restore to youth; to make young again. **rejuvenescence**, rē-jö've-nes'ens, *n.* A renewing of youth.

relapse, rē-laps', *vi.* (relapsing, relapsed). To slip back; to return to a former state.- *n.* A falling back, either in health or morals.

relate, rē-lāt', *vt.* (relating, related). To tell; to narrate; to ally by kindred. —*vi.* To refer; to stand in some relation. **related**, rē-lāt'ed, *p.a.* Connected by blood; standing in some relation. **relation**, rē-lā'shun, *n.* Act of relating; account; reference; connection; kindred; a relative; proportion.

relationship, rē-lā'shun-ship, *n.* The state of being related; kinship.

relative, rel'a-tiv, *a.* Having relation or reference; not absolute or existing by itself; relevant.—*n.* Something considered in its relation to something else; one allied by blood; a word which relates to or represents another word or sentence.

relax, rē-laks', *vt.* To slacken; to loosen or weaken; to unbend.—*vi.* To become loose, feeble, or languid; to abate in severity. **relaxation**, re'lak-sā"shun, *n.* Act of relaxing; abatement of rigor; recreation.

relay, rē-lā', *n.* A supply of horses placed on the road to relieve others; a squad of men to relieve others; a supply stored up.—*vt.* To lay again; to lay a second time.

release, rē-lēs', *vt.* (releasing, released). To liberate; to disengage; to acquit.— *n.* Liberation; discharge; acquittance.

relegate, rel'e-gāt, *vt.* To consign to some remote destination; to banish.

relent, rē-lent', *vi.* To soften in temper; to yield or become less severe. **relentless**, rē-lent'les, *a.* Unmerciful; implacable: pitiless.

relevant, rel'e-vant, *a.* Applicable; pertinent; to the purpose. **relevance**, **relevancy**, rel'e-vans, rel'e-van-si, *n.* State or quality of being relevant; pertinence.

reliable, rē-lī'a-bl, *a.* That may be relied on; trustworthy.

reliant, rē-lī'ant, *a.* Confident; self-reliant. **reliance**, rē-lī'ans, *n.* Act of relying; trust; confidence; dependence.

relic, rel'ik, *n.* A remaining fragment; the body of a deceased person (usually in *pl.*); a memento or keepsake.

relict, rel'ikt, *n.* A widow.

relief, rē-lēf', *n.* Ease or mitigation of pain; succor; remedy; redress; assistance given to a pauper; one who relieves another by taking duty; prominence of figures above a plane surface in sculp-

ture, carving, &c.; prominence or distinctness.

relieve, rē-lēv', *vt.* (relieving, relieved). To remove or lessen, as anything that pains; to ease; to succor; to release from duty; to give variety to; to set off by contrast; to give the appearance of projection to.

religion, rē-lij'un, *n.* An acknowledgment of our obligation to God; practical piety; devotion; any system of faith and worship. **religious**, rē-lij'us, *a.* Pertaining to religion; teaching religion; used in worship; devout; scrupulously faithful.

relinquish, rē-ling'kwish, *vt.* To give up; to leave; to resign; to renounce.

relish, rel'ish, *vt.* To enjoy the taste of; to have a pleasing taste.—*n.* Taste, usually pleasing; fondness; flavor; something to increase the pleasure of eating.

relive, rē-liv', *vi.* To live again.

reluctant, rē-luk'tant, *a.* Loath; averse; acting with slight repugnance. **reluctance**, **reluctancy**, rē-luk'tans, rē-luk'tan-si, *n.* Aversion; unwillingness.

rely, rē-lī', *vi.* (relying, relied). To rest with confidence; to trust; with *on* or *upon*.

remain, rē-mān', *vi.* To continue in a place or condition; to abide; to be left; to last.—*n.* That which is left; *pl.* a dead body; literary works of one who is dead. **remainder**, rē-mān'dėr, *n.* That which remains; residue; remnant; an estate limited so as to be enjoyed after the death of the present possessor or otherwise.—*a.* Left over.

remand, rē-mand', *vt.* To call or send back; to send back to jail.

remark, rē-märk', *n.* Notice; an observation in words; a comment.—*vt.*, To observe; to utter by way of comment. **remarkable**, re-mär'ka-bl, *a.* Worthy of remark; conspicuous; unusual; extraordinary.

remarry, rē-mar'i, *vt.* and *i.* To marry again.

remediable, re-mē'di-a-bl, *a.* Curable. **remedy**, rem'e-di, *n.* That which cures a disease; that which counteracts an evil; redress.—*vt.* (remedying, remedied). To cure; to repair; to redress; to counteract. **remedial**, re-mē'di-al, *a.* Affording a remedy; healing; intended for a remedy.

remember, rē-mem'bėr, *vt.* To have in the memory; to think of; to observe; to give a gratuity for service done.—*vi.* To have something in remembrance. **remembrance**, rē-mem'brans, *n.* The keeping of a thing in mind; memory; what is remembered; a memorial; a keepsake.

remind, rē-mīnd', *vt.* To put in mind; to cause to remember. **reminder**, rē-mīn'dėr, *n.* One who reminds; a hint that awakens remembrance.

reminiscent, rem'i-nis"ent, *a.* Having remembrance; calling to mind. **reminiscence**, rem'i-nis"ens, *n.* Recollection; what is recalled to mind; account of past incidents within one's knowledge.

remiss, rē-mis', *a.* Careless; negligent; heedless; slack. **remission**, rē-mish'un, *n.* Act of remitting; relinquishment; abatement; pardon.

remit, rĕ-mit', *vt.* (remitting, remitted). To relax; to abate; to relinquish; to forgive; to transmit or send.—*vi.* To slacken; to abate in violence for a time. **remittance**, rĕ-mit'ans, *n.* Act of remitting; the sum or thing remitted.

remnant, rem'nant, *n.* That which is left; a scrap, fragment.—*a.* Remaining.

remodel, rĕ-mod'l, *vt.* To model anew.

remold, rĕ-mōld', *vt.* To mold anew.

remonstrate, rĕ-mon'strāt, *vi.* To present strong reasons against an act; to expostulate. **remonstrant**, rĕ-mon'strant, *a.* Remonstrating. **remonstrance**, rĕ-mon'strans, *n.* Act of remonstrating; expostulation; strong representation against something.

remorse, rĕ-mors', *n.* Reproach of conscience; compunction for wrong committed. **remorseful**, rĕ-mors'ful, *a.* Full of remorse; impressed with a sense of guilt. **remorseless**, rĕ-mors'les, *a.* Without remorse; ruthless; relentless; merciless.

remote, rĕ-mōt', *a.* Distant in place or time; not immediate or direct; slight; inconsiderable.

removable, rĕ-möv'a-bl, *a.* That may be removed. **removal**, rĕ-möv'al, *n.* Act of removing; a moving to another place. **remove**, rĕ-möv', *vt.* (removing, removed). To move from its place; to take away; to displace from an office; to banish or destroy.—*vi.* To be moved from its place; to change the place of residence.—*n.* A removal; departure.

remunerate, rĕ-mū'nér-āt, *vt.* To reward for service; to recompense. **remuneration**, rĕ-mū'nér-ā"shun, *n.* Act of remunerating; reward; compensation. **remunerative**, rĕ-mū'nér-ā'tiv, *a.* Affording remuneration; profitable.

renaissance, ren'e-sáns", *n.* Revival; the revival of letters and arts in the fifteenth century.

renascent, rĕ-nas'ent, *a.* Springing into being again; reappearing; rejuvenated. **renascence**, rĕ-nas'ens, *n.* The state of being renascent; also same as *Renaissance.*

rend, rend, *vt.* (rending, rent). To force asunder; to tear away; to sever.—*vi.* To be or become torn; to split.

render, ren'dér, *vt.* To give in return; to give back; to present; to afford; to invest with qualities; to translate; to interpret; to clarify, as tallow. **rendering**, ren'dér-ing, *n.* Version; translation; interpretation.

rendezvous, rän'de-vö, *n.* A place of meeting.—*vi.* To meet at a particular place.

rendition, ren-dish'un, *n.* A rendering; interpretation; translation; surrender.

renegade, ren'ē-gād, *n.* An apostate; a deserter.

renew, rĕ-nū', *vt.* To make new again; to repair; to repeat; to grant anew; to transform.—*vi.* To grow or begin again. **renewal**, rĕ-nū'al, *n.* Act of renewing; a new loan on a new bill or note.

renounce, rĕ-nouns', *vt.* (renouncing, renounced). To disown; to reject; to forsake.—*vi.* To revoke.

renovate, ren'ō-vāt, *vt.* To renew; to restore to freshness. **renovator**, ren'ō-vāt-ér, *n.* One who or that which renovates. **renovation**, ren'ō-vā'shun, *n.* Act of renovating; renewal.

renown, rĕ-noun', *n.* Fame; glory; reputation.—*vt.* To make famous. **renowned**, rĕ-nound', *a.* Famous; celebrated; eminent; remarkable.

rent, rent, *n.* Money, &c.; payable yearly for the use of lands or tenements; a tear; a schism.—*vt.* To let on lease; to hold on condition of paying rent.—*vi.* To be leased or let for rent.

rental, ren'tal, *n.* A roll or account of rents; gross amount of rents from an estate.

renunciation, rĕ-nun'si-ā"shun, *n.* Act of renouncing; disavowal; abandonment.

reoccupy, rĕ-ok'ū-pī, *vt.* To occupy anew.

reopen, rĕ-ō'pen, *vt.* and *i.* To open again.

reorganize, rĕ-or'gan-īz, *vt.* To organize anew.

repair, rĕ-pār', *vt.* To restore; to refit; to mend; to retrieve.—*vi.* To betake one's self; to resort.—*n.* Restoration; supply of loss; state as regards repairing; a resorting; abode. **reparable**, rep'a-ra-bl, *a.* That may be repaired. **reparation**, rep'a-rā"shun, *n.* Act of repairing; restoration; satisfaction for injury; amends.

repartee, rep'ér-tē", *n.* A smart, ready, and witty reply.

repast, rĕ-past', *n.* Act of taking food; food taken; a meal.—*vt.* and *i.* To feed.

repatriate, rē-pā'tri-āt, *vt.* To restore to one's own country.

repay, rē-pā', *vt.* To pay back or again; to refund; to requite. **repayable**, rē-pā'a-bl, *a.* That is to be or may be repaid. **repayment**, rē-pā'ment, *n.* Act of repaying; money repaid.

repeal, rĕ-pēl', *vt.* To recall; to revoke; to abrogate; as a law.—*n.* Act of repealing; abrogation.

repeat, rĕ-pēt', *vt.* To do or utter again; to recite; to recapitulate.—*n.* Repetition. **repeatedly**, rĕ-pēt'ed-li, *adv.* With repetition; again and again; indefinitely. **repeater**, rĕ-pēt'ér, *n.* One who repeats; a watch that strikes the hours; an indeterminate decimal.

repel, rĕ-pel', *vt.* (repelling, repelled). To drive back; to resist successfully.—*vi.* To cause repugnance; to shock. **repellent**, rĕ-pel'ent, *a.* Having the effect of repelling; repulsive; deterring.

repent, rĕ-pent', *vi.* To feel regret for something done or left undone; to be penitent.—*vt.* To remember with self-reproach or sorrow. **repent**, rē'pent, *a.* Creeping. **repentance**, rĕ-pen'tans, *n.* Act of repenting; sorrow for sin; penitence; contrition. **repentant**, rĕ-pen'tant, *a.* Repenting.

repercuss, rē'pér-kus", *vt.* To drive back (as sound or air); to make rebound. **repercussion**, re'pér-kush"un, *n.* Act of driving back; reverberation.

répertoire, rep'ér-twär, *n.* The aggregate of pieces that an actor or company performs. **repertory,** rep''ér-tō'ri, *n.* A treasury; a magazine; a repository.

repetition. rep'ē-tish''un, *n.* Act of repeating; recital: that which is repeated.

repine, rē-pīn', *vi.* (repining, repined). To fret one's self; to complain discontentedly: to murmur.

replace, rē-plãs', *vt.* (replacing, replaced). To put again in the former place; to put in the place of another; to take the place of.

replenish, rē-plen'ish, *vt.* To fill again; to fill completely; to stock abundantly.

replete, rē-plēt', *a.* Filled up; full; abounding: thoroughly imbued. **repletion,** rē-plē'shun, *n.* State of being replete; superabundant fullness; surfeit.

replica, rep'li-ka, *n.* A copy of a picture or a piece of sculpture made by the hand that executed the original.

reply, rē-plī', *vi.* and *t.* (replying, replied). To answer; to respond; to do something in return.—*n.* An answer; a response; a rejoinder.

report, rē-pōrt', *vt.* and *i.* To bring back, as an answer; to relate; to give an official statement of: to take down from the lips of a speaker, &c.; to lay a charge against.—*n.* An account; rumor; repute; noise of explosion; official statement; account of proceedings. **reporter,** rē-pōr'tėr, *n.* One who reports; one of a newspaper staff who gives accounts of public meetings, events, &c.

reposal, rē-pōz'al, *n.* The act of reposing or resting with reliance.

repose, rē-pōz', *vt.* (reposing, reposed). To lay at rest.—*vi.* To lie at rest; to rely.—*n.* A lying at rest; tranquillity; composure: absence of show of feeling. **reposeful,** rē-pōz'ful, *a.* Full of repose; affording repose or rest; trustful.

reposit, rē-poz'it, *vt.* To lay up; to lodge, as for safety. **repository,** rē-poz''i-tō'ri, *n.* A place where things are stored; warehouse.

reprehend, rep'rē-hend'', *vt.* To charge with a fault; to reprove; to censure. **reprehensible,** rep'rē-hen''si-bl, *a.* Deserving reprehension; blamable. **reprehension,** rep'rē-hen''shun, *n.* Act of reprehending; reproof; censure; blame.

represent, rep'rē-zent'', *vt.* To exhibit by a likeness of; to typify; to act the part of; to describe; to be a substitute for; to exemplify. **representation,** rep'rē-zen-tā''shun, *n.* The act of representing; an image or likeness; dramatic performance; a remonstrance; the representing of a constituency. **representative,** rep'rē-zen''ta-tiv, *a.* Fitted or serving to represent; conducted by the agency of delegates; typical.—*n.* One who or that which represents; a person elected to represent a constituency.

repress, rē-pres', *vt.* To press back; to check; to quell. **repression,** rē-presh'un, *n.* Act of repressing or subduing; check; restraint. **repressive,** rē-pres'iv, *a.* Having power or tending to repress.

reprieve, rē-prēv', *vt.* (reprieving, reprieved). To grant a respite to; to relieve temporarily.—*n.* Suspension of the execution of a criminal's sentence; respite.

reprimand, rep'ri-mand, *n.* A severe reproof for a fault.—*vt.* rep-ri-mand'. To administer a sharp rebuke to.

reprint, rē-print', *vt.* To print again.—*n.* rē'print. A second or new edition.

reprisal, rē-prīz'al, *n.* Seizure from an enemy by way of retaliation; retaliation.

reproach, rē-prōch', *vt.* To charge severely with a fault; to censure.—*n.* Censure; blame; source of blame; disgrace. **reproachable,** rē-prōch'a-bl, *a.* Deserving reproach. **reproachful,** rē-prōch'ful, *a.* Containing or expressing reproach; opprobrious.

reprobate, rep'rō-bāt, *a.* Morally abandoned; profligate.—*n.* A wicked; depraved wretch.—*vt.* To disapprove strongly; to reject.

reproduce, rē'prō-dūs'', *vt.* To produce again; to generate, as offspring; to portray or represent. **reproduction,** rē'prō-duk''shun, *n.* Act or process of reproducing; that which is produced anew; an accurate copy. **reproductive,** rē'prō-duk''tiv, *a.* Pertaining to or used in reproduction.

reproof, rē-prōf', *n.* Words intended to reprove; rebuke.

reprove, rē-prōv', *vt.* (reproving, reproved). To charge with a fault orally; to chide; to rebuke. **reproval,** rē-prōv'al, *n.* Reproof.

reptile, rep'til, *a.* Creeping; groveling. *n.*—An animal that moves on its belly, or by means of small short legs. **reptilian,** rep-til'i-an, *a.* Belonging to the class of reptiles.—*n.* A reptile.

republic, rē-pub'lik, *n.* A commonwealth; a state in which the supreme power is vested in elected representatives. **republican,** rē-pub'li-kan, *a.* Pertaining to or consisting of a republic.—*n.* One who favors republican government. **republicanism,** rē-pub'li-kan-izm, *n.* A republican form of government; republican principles.

repudiate, rē-pū'di-āt, *vt.* (repudiating, repudiated). To divorce; to reject; to disavow. **repudiation,** rē-pū'di-ā''shun, *n.* Act of repudiating; rejection; disavowal.

repugnant, rē-pug'nant, *a.* Opposed; inconsistent; inimical; offensive. **repugnance,** rē-pug'nans, *n.* Aversion; reluctance; dislike; inconsistency.

repulse, rē-puls', *n.* Act of repelling; a check or defeat; refusal; denial.—*vt.* (repulsing, repulsed). To repel. **repulsion,** rē-pul'shun, *n.* Act of repelling; feeling of aversion. **repulsive,** rē-pul'siv, *a.* That repulses or repels; repellent; forbidding.

reputable, rep''ū-ta-bl, *a.* Held in esteem; estimable.

reputation, rep'ū-tā''shun, *n.* Character derived from public opinion; repute; good name; honor; fame.

repute, rē-pūt', *vt.* (reputing, reputed). To estimate; to deem.—*n.* Reputation; character; good character.

reputedly, rē-pūt'ed-li, *adv.* In common repute.

request, rė-kwest', *n.* An expressed desire; a petition; thing asked for; a state of being asked for.—*vt.* To ask; to beg.

requiem, rē'kwi-em, *n.* A mass for the dead in the R. Catholic Church; music for this mass.

require, rė-kwīr', *vt.* (requiring, required). To ask as of right; to demand; to have need for; to find it necessary.

requirement, rė-kwīr'ment, *n.* Act of requiring; demand; an essential condition; something necessary.

requisite, rek'wi-zit, *a.* Necessary; essential.—*n.* Something indispensable.

requisition, rek'wi-zish"un, *n.* Act of requiring; demand; a written call or invitation.—*vt.* To make a demand upon or for.

requite, rė-kwīt', *vt.* To repay; to reward; to retaliate on. **requital**, rė-kwīt'al, *n.* Act of requiting; reward; recompense; retribution.

rescind, rė-sind', *vt.* To abrogate; to annul; to repeal; to revoke.

rescue, res'kū, *vt.* (rescuing, rescued). To deliver from confinement, danger, or evil.—*n.* Act of rescuing; deliverance. **rescuer**, res'kū-ėr, *n.* One that rescues.

research, rė-sėrch', *n.* A diligent seeking of facts or principles; investigation. —*vt.* To search again.

resemble, rė-zem'bl, *vt.* (resembling, resembled). To be like; to liken; to compare. **resemblance**, rė-zem'blans, *n.* Likeness; similarity; something similar; similitude.

resent, rė-zent', *vt.* To take ill; to consider as an affront; to be angry at.—*vi.* To feel resentment. **resentful**, rė-zent'ful, *a.* Full of resentment; of a vindictive temper. **resentment**, rė-zent'ment, *n.* Deep sense of injury; indignation; revengeful feeling.

reservation, rez'ėr-vā"shun, *n.* Act of reserving; reserve; concealment; state of being treasured up; proviso. **reserve**, rė-zėrv', *vt.* (reserving, reserved). To keep in store; to retain.—*n.* Act of reserving; that which is retained; retention; habit of restraining the feelings; coldness towards others; shyness; troops kept for an exigency. **reserved**, rė-zėrvd', *a.* Showing reserve; not free or frank; restrained; cautious.

reservoir, res'ėr-vwar, *n.* A place where anything is kept in store; an artificial lake to supply a town with water.

reside, rė-zīd', *vi.* (residing, resided). To have one's abode; to dwell; to inhere. **residence**, rez'i-dens, *n.* Act or state of residing; abode; home; dwelling. **residency**, rez'i-den-si, *n.* Residence; official residence of a British resident in India. **resident**, rez'i-dent, *a.* Residing. —*n.* One who resides; a dweller; a public minister at a foreign court. **residential**, rez'i-den"shal, *a.* Pertaining to or suitable for residence.

residue, rez'i-dū, *n.* That which remains after a part is taken; remainder. **residual**, rė-zid'ū-al, *a.* Left after a part is taken. **residuary**, rė-zid'ū-er-i, *a.* Pertaining to the residue.

resign, rė-zīn', *vt.* To give up; to renounce; to submit, as to Providence. **resignation**, rez'ig-nā"shun, *n.* Act of resigning; state of being resigned; habitual submission to Providence. **resigned**, rė-zīnd', *a.* Submissive; patient.

resilience, resiliency, rė-sil'i-ens, rė-sil'i-en-si, *n.* Act of resiling or rebounding; rebound from being elastic. **resilient**, rė-sil'i-ent, *a.* Inclined to resile; rebounding.

resin, rez'in, *n.* An inflammable vegetable substance; the hardened juice of pines. **resinous**, rez'i-nus, *a.* Pertaining to, like, or obtained from resin.

resist, rė-zist', *vt.* and *i.* To withstand; to oppose; to struggle against. **resistance**, rė-zis'tans, *n.* Act of resisting; check; quality of not yielding to force. **resistant, resistent**, rė-zis'tant, *a.* Making resistance.—*n.* One who or that which resists. **resistible**, rė-zist'i-bl, *a.* That may be resisted. **resistless**, rė-zist'les, *a.* That cannot be resisted; that cannot resist.

resolute, rez'ō-lūt, *a.* Having fixedness of purpose; determined; steadfast. **resolution**, rez'ō-lū"shun, *n.* Character of being resolute; determination; a formal decision; operation of separating the component parts; solution.

resolve, rė-zolv', *vt.* (resolving, resolved). To separate the component parts of; to analyze; to solve; to determine; to decide.—*vi.* To separate into component parts; to melt; to determine; to decide.—*n.* Fixed purpose of mind; resolution. **resolvent**, rė-zol'vent, *a.* Having power to resolve or to dissolve; causing solution.

resonant, rez'ō-nant, *a.* Resounding; full of sounds. **resonance**, rez'ō-nans, *n.* State or quality of being resonant; act of resounding.

resort, rė-zort', *vi.* To have recourse; to go; to repair frequently.—*n.* Recourse; concourse; a haunt.

resound, rė-zound', *vt.* To give back the sound of; to echo; to praise.—*vi.* To sound again; to echo; to be much praised.

resource, rė-sōrs', *n.* Any source of aid or support; expedient; *pl.* funds; means.

respect, rė-spekt', *vt.* To regard; to relate to; to honor; to have consideration for.—*n.* Regard; attention; due deference; bias; a point or particular; reference. **respectability**, rė-spek'ta-bil"i-ti, *n.* State or quality of being respectable. **respectable**, rė-spek'ta-bl, *a.* Worthy of respect; held in good repute; moderately good. **respectably**, rė-spek'ta-bli, *adv.* In a respectable manner; moderately; pretty well. **respectful**, rė-spekt'ful, *a.* Marked by respect; civil; dutiful; courteous. **respecting**, rė-spekt'ing, *prep.* In regard to; regarding; concerning.

respective, rė-spek'tiv, *a.* Relating severally each to each; relative. **respectively**, rė-spek'tiv-li, *adv.* In their respective relations; as each belongs to each.

respire, rė-spīr', *vi.* and *t.* (respiring, respired). To breathe; to recover one's breath. **respiration,** res′pi-rā″shun, *n.* Act of respiring or breathing.

respirator, res′′pi-rā″tẽr, *n.* An appliance covering the mouth, and serving to exclude cold air, dust, &c. **respiratory,** rē-spir′′a-tō′ri, *a.* Serving for respiration; pertaining to respiration.

respite, res′pit, *n.* Temporary intermission; interval; a reprieve.—*vt.* (respiting, respited). To grant a respite to; to reprieve.

resplendent, rē-splen′dent, *a.* Very bright; shining with brilliant luster.

respond, rē-spond′, *vi.* To answer; to suit.—*n.* A short anthem; response. **respondent,** rē-spon′dent, *a.* Answering; corresponding.—*n.* One who responds; one who answers in a lawsuit.

response, rē-spons′, *n.* An answer; reply. **responsibility,** rē-spon′si-bil′′i-ti, *n.* State of being responsible; that for which one is responsible; ability to answer in payment. **responsible,** rē-spon′si-bl, *a.* Answerable; accountable; important. **responsive,** rē-spon′siv, *a.* Making reply; answering; correspondent; suited.

rest, rest, *n.* Cessation of action; peace; sleep; an appliance for support; a pause; remainder; the others.—*vi.* To cease from action; to lie for repose; to be supported; to be in a certain state; remain; to be left.—*vt.* To lay at rest; to place, as on a support. **restful,** rest′ful, *a.* Giving rest; quiet.

restaurant, res′tō-rant, *n.* An establishment for the sale of refreshments.

restitution, res′ti-tū″shun, *n.* Act of restoring; reparation; amends.

restive, res′tiv, *a.* Stubborn; fidgeting; impatient under restraint or opposition.

restless, rest′les, *a.* Without rest; disturbed; uneasy; anxious.

restore, re-stōr′, *vt.* (restoring, restored). To make strong again; to repair; to cure; to reestablish; to give back. **restorable,** rē-stōr′a-bl, *a.* Capable of being restored. **restoration,** res′tō-rā″shun, *n.* Act of restoring; replacement; recovery; the re-establishment of the English monarchy in 1660. **restorative,** rē-stōr′a-tiv, *a.* Having power to renew strength.—*n.* A medicine which restores strength.

restrain, rē-strān′, *vt.* To hold back; to curb; to check; to repress; to restrict. **restraint,** rē-strānt′, *n.* Act of restraining; hindrance; curb; limitation.

restrict, rē-strikt′, *vt.* To limit; to curb. **restriction,** rē-strik′shun, *n.* Act of restricting; limitation; a reservation. **restrictive,** rē-strik′tiv, *a.* Having the quality of restricting; imposing restraint.

result, rē-zult′, *vi.* To rise as a consequence; to issue; to ensue; to end.—*n.* Consequence; effect; issue; outcome.

resultant, rē-zul′tant, *a.* Following as a result or consequence.

resume, rē-zūm′, *vt.* (resuming, resumed). To take up again; to begin again. **resumption,** rē-sump′shun, *n.* Act of resuming. **resumptive,** rē-zump′tiv, *a.* Resuming.

résumé, rā′zū-mā″, *n.* A recapitulation; a summary.

resurgent, rē-sẽr′jent, *a.* Rising again.

resurrection, rez′u-rek″shun, *n.* A rising again; the rising of the dead at the general judgment.

resuscitate, rē-sus′i-tāt, *vt. and i.* To revive. **resuscitation,** rē-sus′i-tā″-shun, *n.* Act of resuscitating; restoration to life.

retail, rē-tāl′, *vt.* To sell in small quantities; to tell to many.—*n.* rē′tāl. The sale of commodities in small quantities; used also as *adj.* **retailer,** re′tāl-ẽr, *n.* One who retails.

retain, rē-tān′, *vt.* To hold back; to keep in possession; to detain; to hire; to engage. **retainer,** rē-tān′ẽr, *n.* One who retains; an adherent or dependent; a fee to engage a counsel.

retake, rē-tāk′, *vt.* To take again or back.

retaliate, rē-tal′i-āt, *vi. and t.* To return like for like; to repay; to take revenge. **retaliation,** rē-tal′i-ā″shun, *n.* The return of like for like; requital; reprisal. **retaliative, retaliatory,** rē-tal′′i-ā″-tiv, rē-tal′′i-ā tō′ri, *a.* Returning like for like.

retard, rē-tärd′, *vt.* To render slower; to impede; to delay; to postpone. **retardation,** rē′tär-dā″shun, *n.* Act of retarding; diminution in speed; obstruction.

retch, rech, *vi.* To make an effort to vomit; to strain, as in vomiting.

retention, rē-ten′shun, *n.* Act or power of retaining; maintenance; memory.

retentive, rē-ten′tiv, *a.* Characterized by retention; having power to retain ideas.

reticent, ret′i-sent, *a.* Having a disposition to be silent; reserved. **reticence,** ret′i-sens, *n.* Act or character of keeping silence; keeping of one's own counsel.

retina, ret′i-na, *n.* One of the coats of the eye where visual impressions are received.

retinue, ret′i-nū, *n.* A train of attendants; a suite.

retire, rē-tīr′, *vi.* (retiring, retired). To go back; to withdraw from business or active life; to go to bed.—*vt.* To remove from service; to pay when due, as a bill of exchange. **retired,** rē-tīrd′, *a.* Secluded; private; having given up business. **retirement,** rē-tīr′ment, *n.* Act of retiring; retired life; seclusion. **retiring,** rē-tīr′ing, *a.* Reserved; unobtrusive; granted to one who retires from service.

retort, rē-tõrt′, *vt.* To retaliate; to throw back.—*vi.* To return an argument or charge.—*n.* A severe reply; a repartee; a chemical vessel for distilling.

retouch, rē-tuch′, *vt.* To improve by new touches, as a picture, &c.

retrace, rē-trās′, *vt.* To trace back; to trace over again.

retract, rē-trakt′, *vt.* To draw back; to recall.—*vi.* To unsay one's words. **retractable,** rē-trakt′a-bl, *a.* Capable of being retracted. **retraction,** rē-trak′-shun, *n.* Act of drawing back; recantation; retractation. **retractor**, rē-trak'-tẽr, *n*. One who retracts; a muscle that draws back some part.

retreat, rē-trēt', *n*. Act of retiring; seclusion; a shelter; the retiring of an army from an enemy.—*vi*. To draw back; to retire from an enemy.

retrench, rē-trench', *vt*. To lessen; to limit or restrict.—*vi*. To economize. **retrenchment**, rē-trench'ment, *n*. Act of curtailing; economy; an interior rampart.

retribution, ret'ri-bū''shun, *n*. Act of rewarding; a requital for evil done. **retributive, retributory**, rē-trib'ū-tiv, rē-trib'ū-tō'ri, *a*. Making retribution; entailing justly deserved punishment.

retrieve, rē-trēv', *vt*. (retrieving, retrieved). To recover; to regain; to repair. **retrievable**, rē-trēv'a-bl, *a*. That may be retrieved or recovered. **retrieval**, rē-trēv'al, *n*. Act of retrieving. **retriever**, rē-trēv'ẽr, *n*. A dog that brings in game which a sportsman has shot.

retroact, ret'rō-akt'', *vi*. To act backward, in opposition, or in return.

retrocede, ret'rō-sēd'', *vi*. To go back; to retire.—*vt*. To cede back.

retrograde, ret'rō-grād or rē', *a*. Going backward; appearing to move from east to west in the sky.—*vi*. To go backward. **retrogression**, ret'rō-gresh''un; rē'trō- *n*. Act of going backward. **retrogressive**, ret'rō-gres''iv; rē'trō-, *a*. Going or moving backwards; declining.

retrospect, ret'rō-spekt or rē', *n*. A view of things past; backward survey. **retrospection**, ret'rō-spek''shun or rē', *n*. Act or faculty of looking on things past. **retrospective**, ret'rō-spek''tiv or rē-, *a*. Looking back; affecting things past.

return, rē-tẽrn', *vi*. To come or go back; to recur.—*vt*. To send back; to repay; to report officially; to elect; to yield.—*n*. Act of returning; repayment; election of a representative; profit; an official statement; *pl*. tabulated statistics; a light tobacco.

reunion, rē-ūn'yun. *n*. Union after separation; a meeting for social purposes. **reunite**, rē'ū-nīt'', *vt*. and *i*. To unite again; to reconcile after variance.

reveal, rē-vēl', *vt*. To disclose; to divulge; to make known by divine means.

reveille, rev'e-lē'', re-vāl'yi, *n*. The morning beat of drum or bugle sound to awaken soldiers.

revelation, rev'e-lā''shun, *n*. Act of revealing; that which is revealed; divine communication; the Apocalypse.

revel, rev'el, *n*. A feast with noisy jollity.—*vi*. (reveling, reveled). To carouse; to delight.

reveler, rev'el-ẽr, *n*. One who revels.

revelry, rev'el-ri, *n*. Noisy festivity; jollity.

revenge, rē-venj', *vt*. and *i*. (revenging, revenged). To take vengeance for; to avenge.—*n*. Act of revenging; retaliation; deliberate infliction of injury in return for injury; vindictive feeling. **revengeful**, rē-venj'ful, *a*. Full of revenge; vindictive; resentful.

revenue, rev'e-nū, *n*. Income; the annual income of a state.

reverberate, rē-vẽr'bẽr-āt, *vt*. and *i*. To return, as sound; to echo; to reflect, as heat or light. **reverberation**, rē-vẽr'bẽr-ā''shun, *n*. Act of reverberating; an echo.

revere, rē-vēr', *vt*. (revering, revered). To regard with awe and respect; to venerate. **reverence**, rev'ẽr-ens, *n*. Awe combined with respect; veneration; an obeisance; a reverend personage; a title of the clergy.—*vt*. To revere; to pay reverence to. **reverend**, rev'ẽr-end, *a*. Worthy of reverence; a title given to clergymen. **reverent**, rev'ẽr-ent, *a*. Expressing reverence; humble; impressed with reverence. **reverential**, rev'ẽr-en''shal, *a*. Proceeding from reverence, or expressing it.

reverie, rev'ẽr-i, *n*. A loose train of thoughts; a day-dream; a visionary project.

reversal, rē-vẽr'sal, *n*. Act of reversing; a change or overthrowing.

reverse, rē-vẽrs', *vt*. (reversing, reversed). To alter to the opposite; to annul.—*n*. A reversal; a complete change or turn; a check; a defeat; the contrary; the back or under-surface.—*a*. Turned backward; opposite. **reversible**, rē-vẽr'si-bl, *a*. That may be reversed. turned outside in, or the like. **reversion**, rē-vẽr'shun, *n*. A reverting or returning; succession to an office after the present holder's term; a return towards some ancestral type; return of an estate to the grantor or his heirs.

revert, rē-vẽrt', *vt*. To reverse.—*vi*. To return to a former position, habit, statement, &c.; to return to the donor. **revertible**, rē-vẽr'ti-bl, *a*. That may revert, as an estate.

review, rē-vū', *vt*. To view again; to reconsider; to write a critical notice of; to inspect.—*vi*. To write reviews.—*n*. A re-examination; a criticism; a periodical containing criticisms; official inspection of troops. **reviewer**, rē-vū'ẽr, *n*. One who writes reviews.

revile, rē-vīl', *vt*. (reviling, reviled). To vilify; to upbraid; to abuse.

revise, rē-vīz', *vt*. (revising, revised). To go over with care for correction.—*n*. A revision; a second proof-sheet in printing. **reviser**, rē-vī'zer, *n*. One who revises. **revision**, rē-vizh'un, *n*. Act of revising; revisal; what is revised.

revive, rē-vīv', *vi*. (reviving, revived). To return to life; to recover new vigor.—*vt*. To bring again to life; to refresh; to bring again into use or notice. **revival**, rē-vīv'al, *n*. Act of reviving; restoration from neglect or depression; religious awakening.

revoke, rē-vōk', *vt*. (revoking, revoked). To repeal; to annul.—*vi*. In *card playing*, to neglect to follow suit. **revocable**, rev'ō-ka-bl, *a*. That may be revoked. **revocation**, rev'ō-kā''shun, *n*. Act of revoking; annulment; repeal.

revolt, rē-vōlt', *vi*. To renounce allegiance; to rebel; to be disgusted; with *at*.—*vi*. To shock.—*n*. Rebellion; mutiny. **revolting**, rē-vōl'ting, a. Exciting extreme disgust; shocking.

revolution, rev'ō-lū''shun, n. Act of revolving; rotation; a turn; circuit; a cycle of time; a radical change; overthrow of existing political institutions. **revolutionary**, rev'ō-lū''shun-er'-i, a. Pertaining to or tending to produce a revolution.—n. A revolutionist. **revolutionist**, rev'ō-lū''shun-ist, n. The favorer of revolution. **revolutionize**, rev'ō-lū''shun-īz, vt. To bring about a complete change in.

revolve, rē-volv', vi. (revolving, revolved). To turn round an axis or center.—vt. To cause to turn round; to consider attentively.

revolver, rē-vol'vėr, n. A pistol with several chambers, each containing a charge fired by means of a revolving motion.

revulsion, rē-vul'shun, n. A violent drawing away; a violent change, especially of feeling.

reward, rē-ward', n. What is given in return for good done; recompense; punishment.—vt. To repay; to requite.

rewrite, rē-rīt', vt. To write over again.

rhapsody, rap'so-di, n. A short epic poem, or portion of an epic; a confused series of extravagantly enthusiastic statements. **rhapsodic**, **rhapsodical**, rap-sod'ik, rap-sod'i-kal, a. Pertaining to rhapsody.

rhetoric ret'ō-rik, n. The art of using language effectively; the art which teaches oratory; eloquence; flashy oratory; declamation. **rhetorical**, rē-tor'i-kal, a. Pertaining to, exhibiting, or involving rhetoric. **rhetorician**, ret'ō-rish''an, n. One who teaches or is versed in rhetoric; a declaimer.

rheum, rōm, n. A thin serous fluid secreted by the mucous glands, &c. **rheumatic**, rō-mat'ik, a. Pertaining to or like rheumatism; subject to rheumatism. **rheumatism**, rō'ma-tizm, n. A painful disease of the muscles and joints. **rheumy**, rōm'i, a. Pertaining to, like, or affected with rheum.

rhinoceros, ri-nos'ėr-os, n. A large hoofed animal, allied to the hippopotamus, with one or two horns on the nose.

rhododendron, rō'dō-den''dron, n. An evergreen shrub with large brilliant flowers.

rhomb, rhombus, romb, rom'bus, n. A quadrilateral whose sides are equal, but the angles not right angles. **rhombic**, rom'bik, a. Having the figure of a rhomb.

Rhomboid.

rhomboid, rom'boid, n. A quadrilateral whose opposite sides only are equal, and whose angles are not right angles. **rhomboidal**, rom-boi'dal, a. Having the shape of a rhomboid.

rhubarb, rō'bärb, n. A plant of which the leaf-stalks are used in cookery, and the roots of some species in medicine.

rhyme, rime, rīm, n. A correspondence of sound in the ends of words or verses; a short poem; a word rhyming with another.—vi. (rhyming, rhymed). To make verses; to accord in sound.—vt. To put into rhyme. **rhymer, rhymester,**

rīm'ėr, rīm'stėr, n. One who makes rhymes; a poor poet.

rhythm, rithm, n. Periodical emphasis in verse or music; metrical movement; harmony; rhyme; meter; verse. **rhythmic, rhythmical**, rith'mik, rith'mi-kal, a. Pertaining to or having rhythm.

rib, rib, n. One of the curved bones springing from the backbone; something resembling a rib; a long ridge on cloth.—vt. (ribbing, ribbed). To furnish with ribs; to inclose with ribs.

ribald, rib'ald, n. A low, lewd fellow.—a. Low; obscene. **ribaldry**, rib'ald-ri, n. Obscene language; indecency.

ribbon, rib'un, n. A narrow band of silk, satin, &c.

rice, rīs, n. A cereal plant, whose seed forms a light nutritious food.

rich, rich, a. Having abundant possessions; wealthy; costly; valuable; fertile; plentiful; bright; mellow; highly flavored; highly provocative of amusement. **riches**, rich'ez, n. Wealth; opulence; affluence. **richness**, rich'nes, n. Wealth; fertility; brilliancy; sweetness.

rick, rik', n. A stack or pile of grain or hay.—vt. To pile up in ricks, as hay.

rickets, rik'ets, n. pl. A disease of children in which there is usually some distortion of the bones. **rickety**, rik'e-ti, a. Affected with rickets; feeble; shaky.

ricochet, rik'ō-shā'', n. A rebounding from a flat, horizontal surface.—vt. and i. rik'ō-shet''. To operate upon by ricochet firing; to rebound.

rid, rid, vt. (ridding, rid). To make free; to clear; to disencumber.—a. Free; clear. **riddance**, rid'ans, n. Act of ridding; disencumbrance.

riddle, rid'l, n. A puzzling question; an enigma; a coarse sieve.—vt. (riddling, riddled). To solve; to sift; to make many holes in.

ride, rid, vi. (riding, pret. rode, pp. ridden). To be borne on horseback, in a vehicle, &c.; to have ability as an equestrian; to be at anchor.—vt. To sit on, so as to be carried; to go over in riding; to domineer over.—n. An excursion on horseback, or in a vehicle; a road for the amusement of riding. **rider**, rīd'ėr, n. One who rides; one who manages a horse; a supplement or amendment; subsidiary problem.

ridge, rij, n. A long narrow prominence; strip thrown up by a plow; a long crest of hills; upper angle of a roof.—vt. (ridging, ridged). To form into ridges.

ridicule, rid'i-kūl, n. Laughter with contempt; mockery; satire.—vt. To treat with ridicule; to make sport of. **ridiculous**, ri-dik'ū-lus, a. Worthy of or fitted to excite ridicule; droll; absurd.

rife, rif, a. Abundant; prevalent; replete.

riffraff, rif''raf', n. Refuse; the rabble.

rifle, rī'f'l, n. A gun the inside of whose barrel is grooved; pl. a body of troops with rifles.—vt. (rifling, rifled). To groove spirally the bore of; to rob; to plunder.

rifleman, rī'fl-man, n. One of a body of troops armed with rifles.

rift, rift, n. An opening; a cleft; a fissure.—vt. and i. To cleave; to split.

rig, rig, *vt.* (rigging, rigged). To clothe; to accouter; to fit with tackling.—*n.* Dress; style of the sails and masts of a ship. **rigger**, rig'ér, *n.* One whose occupation is to fit up the rigging of a ship. **rigging**, rig'ing, *n.* The ropes which support the masts, extend the sails, &c., of a ship.

right, rit, *a.* Straight; upright; just; suitable; proper; real; correct; belonging to that side of the body farther from the heart; to be worn outward; perpendicular; formed by one line perpendicular to another.—*adv.* Justly; correctly; very; directly; to the right hand.—*n.* What is right; rectitude; a just claim; authority; side opposite to the left.—*vt.* To put right; to do justice to; to restore to an upright position.—*vi.* To resume a vertical position. **righteous**, ri'chus, *a.* Upright; pious; just; honest; virtuous; equitable. **righteousness**, ri-chus-nes, *n.* Integrity; purity of heart and rectitude of life; justice. **rightful**, rit'ful, *a.* Having a just or legal claim; just; lawful. **right-hand**, rit''hand', *a.* Belonging to or on the side next the right hand; essentially needful or serviceable. **right-handed**, rit''han'ded, *a.* Using the right hand more easily than the left. **rightly**, rit'li, *adv.* In a right manner; properly; fitly; justly; correctly.

rigid, rij'id, *a.* Stiff; unyielding; not pliant; strict; stern; rigorous. **rigidity**, ri-jid'i-ti, *n.* State or quality of being rigid; stiffness; severity; harshness.

rigmarole, rig'ma-rōl, *n.* A succession of confused statements.

rigor, rig'ér, *n.* A sudden coldness attended by shivering; stiffness; strictness; austerity; severity; intense cold. **rigorous**, rig'ér-us, *a.* Characterized by rigor; severe; stringent.

rill, ril, *n.* A small brook.

rim, rim, *n.* The border or edge of a thing; brim.—*vt.* (rimming, rimmed). To put a rim round.

rime, rīm, *n.* White or hoar frost; a chink; rhyme.

rind, rīnd, *n.* The outward coat of trees, fruits, &c.; bark; peel.

rinderpest, rin'der-pest, *n.* A virulent contagious disease affecting cattle.

ring, ring, *n.* Anything in the form of a circle; a circle of gold, &c., worn on the finger; an area in which games, &c., are performed; a group of persons; sound of a bell; a metallic sound.—*vt.* To encircle; to cause to sound; to repeat often or loudly.—*vi.* To sound; to resound; to tingle.

ringleader, ring''lēd'ér, *n.* The leader of a circle of persons engaged in any evil course.

ringlet, ring'let, *n.* A small ring; a curl.

ringworm, ring''wérm', *n.* A contagious skin disease forming discolored rings.

rink, ringk, *n.* A portion of a sheet of ice marked off for curling; a smooth flooring for skating on with roller-skates.

rinse, rins, *vt.* (rinsing, rinsed). To wash by laving water over; to cleanse the interior by the introduction of any liquid.

riot, rī'ut, *n.* An uproar; a tumult; wild and loose festivity; revelry.—*vi.* To engage in a riot; to revel. **rioter**, rī'ut-ér, *n.* One who engages in a riot. **riotous**, rī'ut-us, *a.* Indulging in riot or revelry; tumultuous; seditious; excessive.

rip, rip, *vt.* (ripping, ripped). To tear or cut open; to take out by cutting or tearing.—*n.* A rent; a scamp.

riparian, rī-pā'ri-an, *a.* Pertaining to the bank of a river.

ripe, rīp, *a.* Brought to perfection in growth; mature; complete; ready for action or effect.—*vt.* and *i.* (riping, riped). To mature. **ripen**, rīp'en, *vi.* To grow or become ripe; to become ready.—*vt.* To mature.

ripple, rip'l, *vi.* (rippling, rippled). To show a ruffled surface, as water; to make a gentle sound, as running water.—*vt.* To clean the seeds from, as flax.—*n.* A ruffle of the surface of water; a comb for separating the seeds from flax.

rise, rīz, *vi.* (rising, pret. rose, pp. risen). To pass to a higher position; to stand up; to bring a session to an end; to arise; to swell by fermentation; to slope upwards; to become apparent; to come into existence; to rebel.—*n.* Act of rising; ascent; elevation. **rising**, rīz'ing, *p.a.* Increasing in power, &c.; advancing to adult years.—*n.* Act of one who or that which rises; appearance above the horizon; resurrection; an insurrection; a prominence.

risible, riz'i-bl, *a.* Having the faculty of laughing; ludicrous; ridiculous.

risk, risk, *n.* Hazard; peril; jeopardy.—*vt.* To hazard; to dare to undertake. **risky**, ris'ki, *a.* Dangerous; full of risk.

risqué, rēs'kā'', *a.* Suggestive; off color.

rissole, rē'sōl'', *n.* A dish of minced meat or fish covered with a paste and fried.

rite, rīt, *n.* A formal act of religion, &c.; form; ceremony; observance; usage. **ritual**, rit'ū-al, *a.* Pertaining to rites.—*n.* A book containing the rites of a church; a system of rights; ceremonial.

rival, rī'val, *n.* One who pursues the same object as another; a competitor.—*a.* Having the same pretensions or claims; competing.—*vt.* (rivaling, rivaled). To strive to excel; to compete with. **rivalry**, rī'val-ri, *n.* Act of rivaling; competition; emulation.

rive, rīv, *vt.* and *i.* (riving, rived, pp. rived and riven). To tear or rend; to split; to cleave.

river, riv'ér, *n.* A large stream of water on land; a copious flow; abundance.

rivet, riv'et, *n.* A metallic bolt whose end is hammered broad after insertion.—*vt.* (riveting, riveted). To fasten with rivets; to clinch; to make firm. **riveter**, riv'et-ér, *n.* One who rivets; a workman employed in fixing rivets.

rivulet, riv'ū-let, *n.* A small stream.

roach, rōch, *n.* A fresh-water fish of the carp family.

road, rōd, *n.* An open way or public passage; a highway; a means of approach; a roadstead (usually in *plural*).

roadster, rōd'stér, *n.* A sports-type automobile with a convertible top and one cross seat; a horse well fitted for the road or employed in traveling.

roadway, rōd"wā', *n*. The part of a road traveled by horses and carriages; highway.

roam, rōm, *vi*. To wander; to rove; to ramble.

roan, rōn, *a*. Of a mixed color with a shade of red predominant.—*n*. A roan color, or horse of this color; a leather prepared from sheepskin.

roar, rōr, *vi*. To cry with a full, loud sound; to bellow; to bawl or squall.—*vt*. To cry out aloud.—*n*. A full, loud sound of some continuance; cry of a beast. **roaring**, rōr'ing, *n*. Loud, continued sound; a bronchial disease in horses.—*a*. Characterized by noise; disorderly; very brisk.

roast, rōst, *vt*. To cook by exposure to a fire; to parch by heat; to banter severely.—*vi*. To become roasted.—*n*. Roasted meat; part selected for roasting. —*a*. Roasted.

rob, rob, *vt*. (robbing, robbed). To strip unlawfully and by force; to deprive by stealing; to deprive. **robber**, rob'ėr, *n*. One who robs. **robbery**, rob'ėr-i, *n*. Act or practice of robbing; theft.

robe, rōb, *n*. A gown, or long, loose garment, worn over other dress; an elegant dress.—*vt*. (robing, robed). To put a robe upon; to invest.

robin, rob'in, *n*. The European bird called also redbreast.

robot, rō'bot, *n*. A mechanical device that simulates actions of human beings; one who works mechanically.

robust, rō-bust', *a*. Sturdy; vigorous; muscular.

rock, rok, *vt*. To move backwards and forwards without displacing; to swing.— *vi*. To sway; to reel.—*n*. A large mass of stone; defense; source of peril or disaster; a kind of solid sweetmeat.

rock crystal, rok'kris'tal, *n*. Crystallized quartz.

rocker, rok'ėr, *n*. One who rocks; a curving piece on which a cradle, &c., rocks; a trough for washing ore by agitation.

rockery, rok'ėr-i, *n*. An ornamented mound formed of fragments of rock, for ferns, &c.

rocket, rok'et, *n*. A projectile; firework; a garden plant.

rocking horse, rok'ing-hōrs', *n*. A wooden horse mounted on rockers; a hobby-horse.

rock salt, rok'sạlt', *n*. Mineral salt; common salt found in masses in the earth.

rocky, rok'i, *a*. Full of rocks; resembling a rock; stony; obdurate.

rococo, rō-kō'kō, *n*. and *a*. A meaninglessly decorative style of ornamentation of the time of Louis XIV and XV.

rod, rod, *n*. A straight slender stick; a badge of office; an enchanter's wand; a fishing-rod; a measure of 5½ lineal yards.

rodent, rō'dent, *a*. Gnawing; belonging to the gnawing animals (Rodentia).—*n*. An animal that gnaws, as the squirrel.

rodeo, rō'dĕ-ō, *n*. (*Sp. Am.*) The driving

of cattle together to be branded. A round-up.

roe, rō, *n*. The spawn of fishes; female of the hart.

roebuck, roe deer, rō"buk', rō dēr, *n*. A small species of European deer of elegant shape and remarkably nimble.

Roentgen rays, rėnt'gen. X rays (named after Wilhelm Conrad Röntgen, their discoverer).

rogue, rōg, *n*. A knave; a wag; a sly fellow.

roguery, rō'gėr-i, *n*. Knavish tricks; fraud; waggery; mischievousness. **roguish**, rō'gish, *a*. Pertaining to or like a rogue; knavish; waggish.

roil, roil, *vt*. To render turbid by stirring.

roister, 'rois'tėr, *vi*. To bluster; to swagger. **roisterer**, rois'tėr-ėr, *n*. A blustering or turbulent fellow.

rôle, rōl, *n*. A part represented by an actor; any conspicuous part or function.

roll, rōl, *vt*. To turn on its surface; to wrap on itself by turning; to involve in a bandage or the like; to press with a roller.—*vi*. To turn over and over; to run on wheels; to be tossed about; to sound with a deep prolonged sound.—*n*. Act of rolling; something rolled up; an official document; a catalogue; a cake of bread; a roller; a prolonged deep sound.

roll call, rōl'kạl', *n*. The calling over a list of names, as of soldiers.

roller, rōl'ėr, *n*. One who or that which rolls; a cylinder for smoothing, crushing, &c.; that on which something may be rolled up; a long, heavy, swelling wave.

roller skate, rōl'ėr skāt, *n*. A skate mounted on small wheels or rollers.

rollick, rol'ik, *vi*. To move with a careless swagger; to be jovial.

rolling, rōl'ing, *p.a*. Revolving; making a continuous noise; undulating.

rolling pin, rōl'ing pin, *n*. A round piece of wood with which dough is rolled out.

rolling stock, rōl'ing stok, *n*. The cars, engines, &c., of a railway.

rolypoly, rō'li-pō'li, *n*. Paste spread with jam and rolled into a pudding.

Roman, rō'man, *a*. Pertaining to Rome or its people and to the Roman Catholic religion; applied to the common upright letter in printing.

romance, rō-mans', *n*. A tale in verse in a Romance dialect; a popular epic or tale in prose or verse of some length; a tale of extraordinary adventures; tendency to the wonderful or mysterious; a fiction.—*a*. (with *cap.*) A term applied to the languages sprung from the Latin. —*vi*. To tell fictitious stories. **romancer**, rō-man'sėr, *n*. One who romances; a writer of romance. **romancist**, rō-man'sist, *n*. A romancer. **romantic**, rō-man'tik, *a*. Pertaining to romance; fanciful; extravagant; wildly picturesque. **romanticism**, rō-man'ti-sizm, *n*. State or quality of being romantic; a reaction in literature or art from classical to medieval or modern qualities; romantic feeling. **romanticist**, rō-man'ti-sist, *n*. One imbued with romanticism.

romp, romp, *n*. Rude play or frolic; a

boisterous girl.—*vi.* To play boisterously; to frisk about.

rood, rōd, *n.* A cross or crucifix; the fourth part of an acre; a measure of 5½ lineal yards.

roof, rōf, *n.* The cover of any building; a canopy; the palate; a house.—*vi.* To cover with a roof; to shelter. **roofing,** rōf'ing, *n.* Act of covering with a roof; materials of a roof; the roof itself.

rooftree, rōf''trē', *n.* A main beam in a roof.

rook, ruk, *n.* A kind of crow; a cheat; a piece in chess.—*vi.* and *t.* To cheat; to rob. **rookery,** ruk'ėr-i, *n.* A grove used for nesting-place by rooks; a resort of thieves, &c.

rookie, rooky, rok'i, *n. Slang.* Novice; beginner; new recruit in the armed forces.

room, rōm, *n.* Space; scope; opportunity; stead; apartment in a house; chamber. **roomy,** rōm'i, *a.* Spacious; wide; large.

roost, rōst, *n.* The pole on which birds rest at night; a collection of fowls resting together.—*vi.* To occupy a roost; to settle.

rooster, rōs'tėr, *n.* The male of the domestic fowl; a cock.

root, rōt, *n.* That part of a plant which fixes itself in the earth; lower part of anything; origin; a form from which words are derived.—*vi.* To fix the root; to be firmly fixed.—*vt.* To plant deeply; to impress durably; to tear up or out; to eradicate.

rooted, rōt'ed, *a.* Fixed; deep radical.

rootlet, rōt'let, *n.* A little root.

rope, rōp, *n.* A cord or line of some thickness; a row or string of things united.—*vi.* (roping, roped). To draw out in threads.—*vt.* To pull by a rope; to fasten or inclose with a rope.

ropery, rōp'ėr-i, *n.* A place where ropes are made.

rosary, rō'za-ri, *n.* A garland of roses; an anthology; a string of beads on which R. Catholics number their prayers.

rose, rōz, *n.* A plant and its flower, of many species; an ornamental knot of ribbon; a perforated nozzle of a spout, &c.—*a.* Of a purplish-red color.

roseate, rōz'ē-āt, *a.* Rosy; blooming.

rosemary, rōz''mär'i, *n.* An ever-green shrub, yielding a fragrant essential oil.

rosery, rōz'ėr-i, *n.* A place where roses grow; a nursery of rose bushes.

rosette, rō-zet', *n.* An ornamental knot of ribbons; an architectural ornament.

rose water, rōz'wa'tėr, *n.* Water tinctured with roses by distillation.

rosewood, rōz''wud', *n.* The wood of a tree used in cabinet-work, when freshly cut having a faint smell of roses.

Rosh Hashana, rosh ha-shä'na. The Jewish New Year.

rosin, roz'in, *n.* The resin left after distilling off the volatile oil from turpentine; resin in a solid state.—*vt.* To rub with rosin.

roster, ros'tėr, *n.* A list showing the rotation in which individuals, regiments, &c., are called on to serve.

rostrum, ros'trum, *n.;* pl. **-tra.** The

beak or bill of a bird; the ram of an ancient ship; *pl.* a platform or pulpit.

rosy, rōz'i, *a.* Like a red rose in color; blooming; blushing; cheering; hopeful.

rot, rot, *vi.* (rotting, rotted). To become rotten; to decay.—*vt.* To make rotten.—*n.* Putrid decay; a fatal distemper of sheep; a disease injurious to plants; nonsense.

rotate, rō'tāt, *vi.* (rotating, rotated). To revolve round a center or axis, like a wheel; to act in turn.—*vt.* To cause to turn like a wheel. **rotary,** rō'ta-ri, *a.* Turning, as a wheel on its axis. **rotation,** rō-tā'shun, *n.* Act of rotating; the turning of a wheel or solid body on its axis; succession in a series.

rote, rōt, *n.* Repetition of words by memory; mere effort of memory.

rotten, rot'n, *a.* Decomposed; decaying; putrid; unsound; corrupt; fetid.

rotund, rō-tund', *a.* Round; spherical.

rotunda, rō-tun'da, *n.* A round building.

rotundity, rō-tund'i-ti, *n.* Roundness.

roué, rö-ā', *n.* A man devoted to pleasure and sensuality; a licentious man; a rake.

rouge, rözh, *n.* A cosmetic to impart ruddiness to the complexion.—*vt.* and *i.* (rouging, rouged). To paint with rouge.

rough, ruf, *a.* Not smooth; rugged; boisterous; harsh; rude; cruel; vague; hasty.—*vt.* To make rough; to roughhew. **to rough it,** to submit to hardships.—*n.* State of being rough or unfinished; a rowdy. **roughcast,** ruf''kast', *vt.* To form roughly; to cover with a coarse plaster.—*n.* A first plan or model; a coarse plastering. **roughen,** ruf'en, *vt.* To make rough.—*vi.* To become rough. **roughhew,** ruf'hū'', *vt.* To hew without smoothing; to give the first form to a thing. **roughly,** ruf'li, *adv.* Coarsely; without finish; harshly; approximately.

roughshod, ruf'shod', *a.* Shod with shoes armed with points.

roulette, rö-let', *n.* A game of chance; an engraver's tool with a toothed wheel.

round, round, *a.* Circular; spherical; large; open; candid; brisk, as a trot; not minutely accurate, as a number.—*n.* That which is round; rung of a ladder; a circular course or series; circuit made by one on duty; a vocal composition in parts; ammunition for firing once; a turn or bout.—*vt.* To make round; to encircle; to make full and flowing; to pass round.—*vi.* To become round or full; to make a circuit.—*adv.* In a circle; around; not directly.—*prep.* About; around.

roundabout, round''a-bout', *a.* Indirect; circuitous.—*n.* A revolving structure on which children ride.

roundly, round'li, *adv.* In a round manner; openly; plainly; vigorously.

round robin, round rob'in, *n.* A written petition signed by names in a circle.

rouse, rouz, *vt.* (rousing, roused). To arouse; to awaken; to stir up.—*vi.* To awake; to arise.—*n.* A carousal; a drinking frolic. **rousing,** rouz'ing, *a.* Having power to rouse or excite; very active or busy.

rout, rout, *n.* A crowd; a rabble; a fashionable evening assembly; total defeat of troops; confusion of troops defeated.—*vt.* To defeat and throw into confusion; to overthrow; to rouse or drive out.

route, rōt, *n.* A course or way.

routine, rō-tēn', *n.* A round of business or pleasure; regular course.

rove, rōv, *vi.* (roving, roved). To move about aimlessly; to roam; to ramble.—*vt.* To wander over; to card into flakes, as wool.

rover, rōv'ėr, *n.* One who roves; a pirate;

row, rō, *n.* A series in a line; a rank; a line of houses; an excursion in a boat with oars.—*vt.* To impel by oars, as a boat; to transport by rowing.—*vi.* To work with the oar.

row, rou, *n.* A noisy disturbance; a riot.—*vt.* To scold.

rowdy, rou'di, *n.* A turbulent fellow; a rough.—*a.* Disreputable; blackguardly.

rowdyism, rou'di-izm, *n.* The conduct of a rowdy; turbulent blackguardism.

rowel, rou'el, *n.* The little wheel of a spur, formed with sharp points.

rowlock, rō'lok, *n.* A contrivance on a boat's gunwale to support the oar.

royal, roi'al, *a.* Pertaining to a king; regal; kingly; august.—*n.* A large kind of paper; a shoot of a stag's antlers.

royalist, roi'al-ist, *n.* An adherent to a king or kingly government. **royally**, roi'al-i, *adv.* In a royal or kingly manner; like a king; as becomes a king.

royalty, roi'al-ti, *n.* State or character of being royal; a royal personage; share paid to a superior, inventor, or author.

rub, rub, *vt.* (rubbing, rubbed). To move something along the surface of with pressure; to scour; to remove by friction; to chafe.—*vi.* To move along with pressure; to fret.—*n.* Act of rubbing; friction; obstruction; difficulty; a gibe.

rubber, rub'ėr, *n.* One who rubs; thing used in polishing or cleaning; obstruction or difficulty; contest of three games in whist.

rubber, rub'ėr, *n.* An elastic substance made from the sap of certain tropical trees, or by various chemical processes.

rubbish, rub'ish, *n.* Refuse; debris; trash.

rubble, rub'l, *n.* Broken stones of irregular shapes; masonry of such stones.

rube, rōb, *n.* Slang. Country bumpkin.

rubicund, rō'bi-kund, *a.* Red or highly colored, as the face; ruddy.

ruble, rō'bl, *n.* The monetary unit of the U.S.S.R.

rubric, rō'brik, *n.* Important words in a manuscript, &c., colored red; a heading or title; direction in a prayer-book.

ruby, rō'bi, *n.* A valuable gem, a variety of corundum of various shades of red; a fine red color; a blotch on the face; a small printing type.—*vt.* To make red.—*a.* Red.

rudder, rud'ėr, *n.* The instrument by which a ship is steered.

ruddy, rud'i, *a.* Of a red color; reddish; of a lively flesh color.—*vt.* (ruddying, ruddied). To make red or ruddy.

rude, rōd, *a.* Unformed by art or skill; rough; uncivilized; uncivil; impudent; violent.

rudiment, rō'di-ment, *n.* The original of anything; a first principle; an undeveloped organ; *pl.* first elements of a science or art. **rudimentary**, rō'di-men''ta-ri, *a.* Pertaining to rudiments consisting in first principles; initial; in an undeveloped state.

rue, rō, *vt.* (ruing, rued). To repent of; to regret.—*vi.* To become sorrowful or repentant.—*n.* An acrid ill-smelling plant. **rueful**, rō'ful, *a.* Woeful; mournful; piteous; expressing or suggesting sorrow.

ruff, ruf, *n.* A plaited color or frill; a ruffle; act of trumping at cards.—*vt.* To trump instead of following suit at cards.

ruffian, ruf'i-an, *n.* A boisterous brutal fellow.—*a.* Like a ruffian; brutal.

ruffle, ruf'l, *vt.* (ruffling, ruffled). To rumple; to derange; to disturb.—*vi.* To bluster.—*n.* A plaited cambric, &c., attached to one's dress; frill; state of being agitated; low vibrating beat of a drum.

rug, rug, *n.* A heavy fabric used to cover a bed, protect a carpet, &c.; a mat.

rugged, rug'ed, *a.* Full of rough projections; rough; harsh; crabbed.

ruin, rō'in, *n.* Destruction; fall; overthrow; anything in a state of decay; that which destroys; *pl.* remains of a city, house, &c.; state of being destroyed.—*vt.* To bring to ruin; to destroy; to impoverish. **ruination**, rō'i-nā''shun, *n.* Act of ruinating; overthrow; demolition. **ruinous**, rō'i-nus, *a.* Fallen to ruin; dilapidated; destructive; baneful.

rule, rōl, *n.* A ruler or measure; a guiding principle or formula; a precept, law, maxim; government; control; regulation; order; method.—*vt.* (ruling, ruled). To govern; to manage; to decide; to mark with lines by a ruler.—*vi.* To exercise supreme authority; to maintain a level, as the market price; to settle, as a rule of court. **ruler**, rōl'ėr, *n.* One who rules or governs; an instrument by which lines are drawn.

ruling, rōl'ing, *a.* Having control; reigning; predominant.—*n.* A point settled by a judge, chairman, &c.

rum, rum, *n.* Spirit distilled from cane-juice or molasses.—*a.* Odd; queer. (Eng.).

rumble, rum'bl, *vi.* (rumbling, rumbled). To make a dull, continued sound.

ruminant, rō'mi-nant, *a.* Chewing the cud.—*n.* An animal that chews the cud; a hoofed ruminating animal.

ruminate, rō'mi-nāt, *vi.* To chew the cud; to meditate.—*vt.* To meditate on. **rumination**, rō'mi-nā''shun, *n.* Act of ruminating; meditation or reflection.

rummage, rum'ij, *vt.* (rummaging, rummaged). To search narrowly but roughly; to ransack.—*n.* A careful search; turning about of things.

rummy, rum'i, *a.* Pertaining to rum.—*n.* A card game.

rumor, rō'mėr, *n.* A current story; a mere report.—*vt.* To report; to spread abroad.

rump, rump, *n.* End of an animal's

backbone; buttocks; fag-end of something.

rumple, rum'pl, *vt.* (rumpling, rumpled). To wrinkle; to ruffle.—*n.* A fold or plait.

rumpus, rum'pus, *n.* A great noise; disturbance.

run, run, *vi.* (running, pret. ran, pp. run). To move by using the legs more quickly than in walking; to take part in a race; to flee; to spread; to ply; to move or pass; to become fluid; to continue in operation; to have a certain direction; to have a certain purport; to be current; to continue in time.—*vt.* To cause to run; to pursue, as a course; to incur; to break through (a blockade); to smuggle; to pierce; to melt; to carry on.—*n.* Act of running; course or distance run; a trip; course, tenor, &c.; general demand, as on a bank; place where animals may run; generality.

runaway, run'a-wā, *n.* One who flies from danger or restraint; deserter; fugitive.—*a.* Effected by running away or eloping.

rune, rön, *n.* One of a set of alphabetic characters peculiar to the ancient northern nations of Europe. **rung,** rung, *n.* A heavy staff; the round or step of a ladder.

runic, rö'nik, *a.* Pertaining to runes.

runner, run'ėr, *n.* One who runs; a messenger; a bird of the order Cursores; a stem running along the ground and taking root; that on which something runs or slides.

running, run'ing, *a.* Kept for the race; continuous; in succession; discharging pus.

runt, runt, *n.* A dwarfed animal; a variety of pigeon; stalk of a cabbage.

rupee, rö-pē', *n.* A silver coin the unit of value in India.

rupture, rup'tūr, *n.* Act of breaking or bursting; fracture; breach; open hostility; hernia.—*vt.* (rupturing, ruptured). To cause a rupture in; to break.

rural, rur'al, *a.* Pertaining to the country; rustic.

ruse, röz, *n.* Artifice; trick; deceit.

rush, rush, *vi.* To move with great speed; to enter over-hastily.—*n.* A violent motion or course; an eager demand; a plant found in damp places; a reed.

rusk, rusk, *n.* A light hard cake browned in the oven.

russet, rus'et, *a.* Of a reddish-brown color; coarse; homespun; rustic.—*n.* A reddish-brown color; coarse country cloth; a kind of winter apple.

Russian, rush'an, *a.* Pertaining to Russia.—*n.* A native of Russia; the language of Russia.

rust, rust, *n.* The red coating formed on iron exposed to moisture; a parasitic fungus; loss of power by inactivity.—*vi.* To contract rust; to degenerate in idleness.—*vt.* To make rusty.

rustic, rus'tik, *a.* Pertaining to the country; rural; homely; unpolished.—*n.* A countryman; a peasant; a clown.

rusticate, rus'ti-kāt, *vi.* To dwell in the country.—*vt.* To banish from a university for a time. **rustication,** rus'ti-kā"shun, *n.* Act of rusticating; state of being rusticated. **rusticity,** rus-tis'i-ti, *n.* State or quality of being rustic; simplicity; artlessness.

rustle, rus'l, *vi.* and *t.* (rustling, rustled). To make the noise of things agitated, as straw, leaves, &c.—*n.* The noise of things that rustle; a slight sibilant sound.

rusty, rus'ti, *a.* Covered with rust; impaired by inaction; rough; grating.

rut, rut, *n.* The track of a wheel; a line cut with a spade; line of routine; time during which certain animals are under sexual excitement.—*vt.* (rutting, rutted). To cut in ruts.—*vi.* To be in heat, as deer.

ruthless, röth'les, *a.* Cruel; pitiless.

rye, ri, *n.* A cereal plant and its seed.

rye grass, ri'gras', *n.* A kind of grass much cultivated for cattle and horses.

S

Sabbath, sab'ath, *n.* The day of rest; Sunday.

sabbatic, sabbatical, sa-bat'ik, sa-bat'i-kal, *a.* Pertaining to the Sabbath; pertaining to a recurrence by sevens.

saber, sā'bėr, *n.* A sword with one edge; a cavalry sword.—*vt.* (sabering, sabered). To strike or kill with a saber.

sable, sā'bl, *n.* A small animal of the weasel family; the fur of the sable; black.—*a.* Black; dark.

sabot, sa-bō', *n.* A wooden shoe worn by continental peasants.

sabotage, sab'ō-täzh", *n.* A deliberate, covert destruction by internal enemy agents.

Saber.

saboteur, sab'ō-tėr", *n.* A person engaging in sabotage.

sac, sak, *n.* A bag; receptacle for a liquid.

saccharin, sak'a-rin, *n.* A substance of great sweetness obtained from coal tar.

saccharine, sak'ka-rin, *a.* Pertaining to or of the nature of sugar; sugary.

sacerdotal, sas'ėr-dō"tal, *a.* Pertaining to priests or the priesthood; priestly.

sachem, sā'chem, *n.* A chief among some of the American Indian tribes.

sachet, sa-shā', *n.* A small bag for odorous substances.

sack, sak, *n.* A bag for flour, wool, &c.; that which a sack holds; a sort of jacket; a dry wine; pillage of a town.—*vt.* To put in sacks; to pillage, as a town.

sacrament, sak′ra-ment, *n.* A solemn religious ordinance observed by Christians, as baptism or the Lord's Supper. **sacramental,** sak′ra-men″tal, *a.* Constituting or pertaining to a sacrament.

sacred, sā′kred, *a.* Set apart for a holy purpose; consecrated; religious; set apart to some one in honor; venerable. **sacredly,** sā′kred-li, *adv.* In a sacred manner; religiously; inviolably; strictly.

sacrifice, sak′ri-fis, *n.* The offering of anything to God; anything offered to a divinity; surrender made in order to gain something else.—*vt.* (sacrificing, sacrificed). To make an offering or sacrifice of.—*vi.* To offer up a sacrifice to some deity. **sacrificial,** sak′ri-fish″al, *a.* Pertaining to sacrifice; performing sacrifices.

sacrilege, sak′ri-lej, *n.* Violation of sacred thing. **sacrilegious,** sak′ri-lē″jus, *a.* Relating to or implying sacrilege; profane; impious.

sacrosanct, sak′rō-sangkt, *a.* Sacred and inviolable; holy and venerable.

sad, sad, *a.* Sorrowful; affected with grief; gloomy; distressing; calamitous. **sadden,** sad′n, *vt.* To make sad.—*vi.* To become sad.

saddle, sad′l, *n.* A seat for a rider on a horse's back; something like a saddle in shape or use.—*vt.* (saddling, saddled). To put a saddle on; to burden.

saddlecloth, sad′l-klath″, *n.* A cloth to be placed under a saddle; a housing.

saddler, sad′lėr, *n.* One whose occupation is to make saddles or harness in general.

sadism, sad′iz′m. *n.* Deriving vicarious pleasure from inflicting pain on others.— *a.* **sadistic,** sa-dis′tik.

safe, sāf, *a.* Secure; free from danger; unharmed; no longer dangerous; trustworthy.—*n.* A strong box or chamber for securing valuables; a cool receptacle for meat. **safeguard,** sāf″gärd′, *n.* One who or that which guards; a defense; protection; a passport.—*vt.* To guard. **safety,** sāf′ti, *n.* State of being safe; freedom from danger, hurt, or loss. **safety match,** sāf′ti-mach′, *n.* A match which lights only on a special substance. **safety valve,** sāf′ti-valv′, *n.* A valve on a boiler, which lets the steam escape when the pressure becomes too great.

saffron, saf′run, *n.* A bulbous plant allied to the crocus, with flowers of a rich orange color.—*a.* Of a deep yellow.

sag, sag, *vi.* (sagging, sagged). To sink in the middle; to yield under care, difficulties, &c.

saga, sä′ga, *n.* An ancient Scandinavian legend of some length.

sagacious, sa-gā′shus, *a.* Quick of perception; shrewd; sage. **sagacity,** sa-gas′i-ti, *n.* Quickness of discernment; shrewdness; high intelligence.

sage, sāj, *a.* Wise; sagacious; well-judged; grave.—*n.* A wise man; a man venerable for years, and of sound judgment; a labiate plant.

sagittal, saj′i-tal, *a.* Pertaining to an arrow; resembling an arrow.

Sagittarius, saj′i-tā″ri-us, *n.* The archer, a sign of the zodiac.

sago, sā′gō, *n.* A starchy substance much used as food, prepared from the pith of several species of palms.

sahib, sä′ib, *n.* An Eastern term of respect, much the same as "Sir" or "Mr."

sail, sāl, *n.* A piece of cloth to catch the wind and so move a ship; a ship; a passage in a ship.—*vi.* To be carried over the water by sails or steam, &c.; to begin a voyage; to glide.—*vt.* To pass over by means of sails; to navigate. **sailcloth,** sāl″klath′, *n.* Canvas used in making sails for ships. **sailer,** sāl′ėr, *n.* One who sails; a ship, with reference to her speed. **sailing,** sāl′ing, *p.a.* Moved by sails and not by steam.—*n.* Act of setting sail; art or rules of navigation. **sailor,** sāl′ėr, *n.* A seaman; a mariner.

saint, sānt, *n.* One eminent for piety and virtue; one of the blessed; a person canonized.—*vt.* To canonize. **sainted,** sän′ted, *a.* Holy; sacred; canonized; gone to heaven; dead.

sake, sāk, *n.* Cause; purpose; regard.

salaam, sa-läm′, *n.* A ceremonious salutation or obeisance among orientals.— *vt.* and *i.* To salute with a salaam.

salacious, sa-lā′shus, *a.* Lustful. **salacity,** sa-las′i-ti, *n.* Lust; lecherousness.

salad, sal′ad, *n.* A dish of certain vegetables, as lettuce, cress, &c., dressed and eaten raw.

salamander, sal″a-man′dėr, *n.* A small harmless amphibian; a kind of lizard formerly believed able to live in fire.

salary, sal′a-ri, *n.* A stipulated recompense for services; stipend; wages. **salaried,** sal′a-rid, *p.a.* Having a salary.

sale, sāl, *n.* Act of selling; power or opportunity of selling; market; auction; state of being to be sold. **saleable,** sāl′a-bl, *a.* That may be sold; being in demand.

salesman, sālz′man, *n.* One employed to sell goods.

salicylic, sal′i-sil″ik, *n.* An acid used as an antiseptic, &c.

salient, sā′li-ent, *a.* Springing; darting; projecting; conspicuous. **salience,** sā′li-ens, *n.* Projection; protrusion.

saline, sā′līn, *a.* Consisting of salt; salt.—*n.* A salt spring.

saliva, sa-lī′va, *n.* The fluid secreted by certain glands, which moistens the mouth and assists digestion. **salivant,** sal′i-vant, *a.* Exciting salivation.—*n.* That which produces salivation. **salivary,** sal′i-ver′i, *a.* Pertaining to the saliva; secreting or conveying saliva. **salivate,** sal′i-vāt, *vt.* To produce an unusual secretion and discharge of saliva. **salivation,** sal′i-vā″shun, *n.* Act of salivating; excessive secretion of saliva.

sallow, sal′ō, *a.* Having a pale, sickly, yellowish color.—*n.* A kind of willow.

sally, sal′i, *n.* A leaping forth; a rush of troops from a besieged place; a dart of intellect, fancy, &c.; frolic.—*vi.* (sallying, sallied). To leap forth; to issue suddenly.

salmagundi, salmagundy, sal′ma-

gun"di, *n.* A dish of chopped meat, eggs, anchovies, cabbage, &c.; a miscellany.

salmi, salmis, sal'mi, *n.* A ragout of woodcocks, larks, thrushes, &c.

salmon, sạm'un, *n.* A large fish highly valued as food. **salmon trout,** sam'un-trout', *n.* The sea-trout, like the salmon in form and color.

salon, sa'lon", *n.* An apartment for the reception of company; a saloon.

saloon, sa-lōn', *n.* A spacious apartment; a large public room; main cabin of a steamer; a public place where alcoholic drinks are sold.

salt, sạlt, *n.* A substance for seasoning and preserving food; a compound produced by the combination of a base with an acid; taste; savor; piquancy; an old sailor.—*a.* Impregnated with salt; pungent.—*vt.* To sprinkle or season with salt.

saltcellar, salt"sel'ẽr, *n.* A small vessel used at table for holding salt.

saltpeter, sạlt"pē"'tẽr, *n.* Niter.

saltwater, sạlt"wạ'tẽr, *n.* Water impregnated with salt; sea-water.

salubrious, sa-lū'bri-us, *a.* Healthful. **salubrity,** sa-lū'bri-ti, *n.* Healthfulness.

salute, sa-lūt', *vt.* (saluting, saluted). To greet; to greet by a bow, &c.; to kiss; to honor.—*vi.* To perform a salutation; to greet each other.—*n.* Act of saluting; greeting; a kiss; a bow; discharge of artillery, &c. **salutary,** sal"ū-ter'i, *a.* Healthful; wholesome; beneficial; profitable. **salutation,** sal'u-tā"shun, *n.* Act of saluting; a greeting; a salute.

salve, salv, *vt.* (salving, salved). To save a ship or goods from wreck, fire, &c. **salvable,** sal'va-bl, *a.* That may be saved; admitting of salvation. **salvage,** sal'vij, *n.* Act of saving a ship or goods from shipwreck, fire, &c.; an allowance for the saving of property; goods thus saved. **salvation,** sal-vā"shun, *n.* Act of saving; redemption of man from sin; that which saves.

salve, säv, sav, *n.* A healing ointment; remedy.—*vt.* (salving, salved). To apply salve to; to remedy.

salver, sal'vẽr, *n.* A tray on which articles are presented.

salvo, sal'vō, *n.* A reservation; excuse; salute of guns; a shouting or cheering.

same, sām, *a.* Identical; not different or other; of like kind; just mentioned. **all the same,** nevertheless. **sameness,** sām'nes, *n.* Similarity; identity; monotony.

samovar, sam'o-vär, *n.* A Russian tea-making urn.

sample, sam'pl, *n.* A specimen; a part presented as typical of the whole.—*vt.* (sampling, sampled). To take a sample of.

sampler, sam'plẽr, *n.* One who samples; one who exhibits samples of goods; a piece of fancy sewed or embroidered work.

samurai, sam'ụ-rī, *n.* A military class, or member of this class, of feudal Japan; the gentry or lesser nobility.

sanatorium, san'a-tō"ri-um, *n.* A place to which people go for the sake of their health.

sanctify, sangk'ti-fī, *vt.* (sanctifying, sanctified). To make holy; to hallow; to make pure from sin. **sanctimonious,** sangk'ti-mō"'ni-us, *a.* Making a show of sanctity; hypocritical. **sanctification,** sangk'ti-fi-kā"shun, *n.* Act of sanctifying; consecration. **sanctified,** sangk'ti-fīd, *p.a.* Made holy; consecrated; sanctimonious.

sanction, sangk'shun, *n.* Confirmation; ratification; authority.—*vt.* To ratify; to authorize; to countenance.

sanctity, sangk'ti-ti, *n.* State of being sacred; holiness; inviolability.

sanctuary, sangk"tū-er'i, *n.* A sacred place; a place of worship; part of a church where the altar is placed; a place of protection to criminals, debtors, &c.; shelter.

sanctum, sangk'tum, *n.* A sacred place; a private room.

sand, sand, *n.* Fine particles of stone; *pl.* tracts of sand on the sea-shore, &c. —*vt.* To sprinkle or cover with sand. **sandy,** san'di, *a.* Abounding with sand; like sand; yellowish red; arid or dry.

sandal, san'dal, *n.* A kind of shoe consisting of a sole fastened to the foot.

sandalwood, san''dal-wụd', *n.* The fragrant wood of certain E. Indian trees.

sandblast, sand''blast', *n.* Sand driven by a blast of steam or air.

sandpaper, sand''pā'pẽr, *n.* Paper coated with fine sand, used to smooth and polish.

sandpiper, sand''pip'ẽr, *n.* A grallatorial bird allied to the snipe, plover, &c.

sandstone, sand''stōn', *n.* A stone composed of agglutinated grains of sand.

sandwich, sand'wich, *n.* Slices of bread, with meat or something savory between. —*vt.* To insert like the meat in a sandwich; to fit between two other pieces. **sandwichman,** sand'wich-man', *n.* A man carrying two advertising boards, one before and one behind.

sane, sān, *a.* Sound in mind; discreet.

sang-froid, sän-frwä, *n.* Coolness; imperturbable calmness.

sanguinary, sang''gwi-ner'i, *a.* Bloody; murderous; savage; cruel. **sanguine,** sang'gwin, *a.* Consisting of blood; full of blood; of the color of blood; cheerful; confident. **sanguineous,** sang-gwin'ē-us, *a.* Bloody; abounding with blood; sanguine.

sanitary, san''i-ter'i, *a.* Pertaining to or designed to secure health; hygienic. **sanitation,** san'i-tā"shun, *n.* The adoption of sanitary measures for the health of a community.

sanity, san'i-ti, *n.* State of being sane; soundness of mind.

sans, sanz, *prep.* Without; deprived of.

Sanskrit, Sanscrit, san'skrit, *n.* and *a.* The ancient language of the Hindus.

Santa Claus, san'ta klạs. A corruption of St. Nicholas of folklore, who distributed gifts at Christmastime.

sap, sap, *vt.* (sapping, sapped). To undermine; to destroy by some invisible process.—*vi.* To proceed by undermining. —*n.* A trench; vital juice of plants.

sapient, sā'pi-ent, *a.* Wise; sage; discerning; now generally ironic. **sapience**, sā'pi-ens, *n.* Wisdom; often used ironically.

sapling, sap'ling, *n.* A young tree.

sapor, sā'pŏr, *n.* Taste; savor; relish.

sapper, sap'ėr, *n.* One who saps; a soldier employed to dig saps or trenches.

sapphire, saf'īr, *n.* A precious stone of very great hardness, and of various shades of blue; a rich blue color; blue.

sappy, sap'i, *a.* Abounding with sap; juicy; succulent; young and soft. Silly.

saraband, sar'a-band, *n.* A slow Spanish dance; a piece of music for the dance.

Saracen, sar'a-sen, *n.* A Mussulman of the early and proselytizing period.

sarcasm, sär'kazm, *n.* A bitter cutting jest; a severe gibe; keen irony. **sarcastic**, sär-kas'tik, *a.* Containing sarcasm; scornfully severe; taunting.

sarcoma, sär-kō'ma, *n.* A malignant, cancerous tumor.

sarcophagus, sär-kof'a-gus, *n.*; pl. -**gi** and **guses**. A coffin of stone.

sardine, sär-dēn', *n.* A small fish allied to the herring and pilchard.

sardonic, sär-don'ik, *a.* Forced, as a laugh; bitterly ironical; sarcastic.

sarong, sa-rong', *n.* A brightly printed square of cloth worn as a skirt by the women of the East Indies.

sarsaparilla, sär'sa-pa-ril''a, *n.* The rhizome of several tropical plants yielding a demulcent medicine.

sartorial, sär-tō'ri-al, *a.* Pertaining to a tailor.

sash, sash, *n.* A long band or scarf worn for ornament; the frame of a window; a frame for a saw.—*vt.* To furnish with sashes or sash windows.

sassafras, sas'a-fras, *n.* A kind of laurel, the root of which has medicinal virtues.

Satan, sā'tan, *n.* The devil or prince of darkness; the chief of the fallen angels. **satanic**, sā-tan'ik, *a.* Having the qualities of Satan; devilish; infernal.

satchel, sach'el, *n.* A little sack or bag; a bag for a schoolboy's books.

sate, sāt, *vt.* (sating, sated). To satiate; to satisfy the appetite of; to glut.

sateen, sa-tēn', *n.* A glossy fabric like satin, but with a woolen or cotton face.

satellite, sat'e-līt, *n.* An attendant; an obsequious dependant; a small planet revolving round another.

satiety, sa-tī'e-ti, *n.* State of being satiated; repletion; surfeit.

satin, sat'in, *n.* A glossy close-woven silk cloth.—*a.* Belonging to or made of satin. **satinet**, sat'i-net'', *n.* A thin species of satin; a cloth made in imitation of satin, having a cotton warp and woolen filling. **satinwood**, sat''in-wud', *n.* The wood of an Indian tree, heavy and durable. **satiny**, sat'in-i, *a.* Resembling satin.

satire, sat'īr, *n.* A writing ridiculing vice or folly; an invective poem; sarcastic or contemptuous ridicule. **satirio**, sa-tir'ik, **satirical**, sa-tir'i-kal, *a.* Belonging to satire; given to satire; sarcastic. **satirist**, sat'i-rist, *n.* One who satirizes. **satirize**, sat'i-rīz, *vt.* To ex-

pose by satire; to censure in a satiric manner.

satisfaction, sat'is-fak''shun, *n.* Act of satisfying; gratification of desire; contentment; payment; compensation.

satisfactory, sat'is-fak''to-ri, *a.* Giving satisfaction; making amends.

satisfy, sat'is-fī, *vt.* and *i.* (satisfying, satisfied). To gratify fully; to content; to fulfill the claims of; to answer; to free from doubt.

satrap, sā'trap or sat'rap, *n.* A governor of a province of ancient Persia; a viceroy.

saturate, sat'ū-rāt, *vt.* To imbue till no more can be received; to soak thoroughly. **saturation**, sat'ū-rā''shun, *n.* Act of saturating; complete impregnation.

Saturday, sat'ėr-di, *n.* The seventh day of the week.

Saturn, sat'ėrn, *n.* An ancient Roman deity; a planet.

saturnine, sat'ėr-nīn, *a.* Morose; gloomy; phlegmatic.

satyr, sat'ėr, *n.* A sylvan deity of the ancient Greeks and Romans, part man and part goat, and extremely wanton.

sauce, sąs, *n.* A liquid to be eaten with food to give it relish; pertness.—*vt.* To make savory with sauce; to be pert to. **saucepan**, sąs''pan', *n.* A small metallic vessel for boiling or stewing.

saucer, są'sėr, *n.* A piece of china, &c., in which a cup is set.

saucy, są'si, *a.* Showing impertinent boldness; pert; impudent; rude. **saucily**, są'si-li, *adv.* Pertly; petulantly.

saunter, sạn'tėr, *vi.* To stroll about idly; to loiter.—*n.* A stroll; a leisurely pace.

sausage, są'sij, *n.* The prepared intestine of an ox, &c., stuffed with minced meat.

savage, sav'ij, *a.* Wild; uncultivated; barbarous; brutal.—*n.* One who is uncivilized; a barbarian. **savagery**, sav'ij-ri, *n.* State of being savage; cruelty; barbarity.

savant, sa-vän', *n.* A man of learning; a man eminent for his scientific acquirements.

save, sāv, *vt.* (saving, saved). To preserve; to protect; to rescue; to spare; to keep from doing or suffering; to reserve; to obviate.—*vi.* To be economical. —*prep.* Except. **saving**, sāv'ing, *a.* Thrifty; that secures from evil; containing some reservation.—*n.* What is saved; sums accumulated by economy; generally *pl.*—*prep.* Excepting.

savior, **saviour**, sāv'yėr, *n.* One who saves from evil, destruction, or danger; Christ.

savor, **savour**, sā'vėr, *n.* Taste; flavor; odor; distinctive quality.—*vi.* To have a particular taste; to partake of some characteristic of something else.—*vt.* To taste or smell with pleasure; to like. **savorless**, sā'vėr-les, *a.* Destitute of savor; insipid. **savory**, sā'vėr-i, *n.* A labiate plant used to flavor dishes, &c.— *a.* Having a good savor; agreeable to the taste; palatable.

saw, są, *n.* A cutting instrument, consisting of a thin blade of steel with a toothed edge; a saying or maxim.—*vt.* and *i.* To cut with a saw.

sawdust, sa̤"dust', *n.* Small fragments of wood produced by the action of a saw.

sawfish, sa̤"fish', *n.* A fish allied to the sharks with a long serrated bony snout.

sawmill, sa̤"mil', *n.* A mill for sawing timber, driven by water, steam, &c.

sawyer, sä'yèr, *n.* One who saws timber.

saxhorn, saks"horn', *n.* A brass wind-instrument.

saxifrage, sak'si-frij, *n.* A plant which grows among rocks.

Saxon, sak'sun, *n.* An Anglo-Saxon; one of English race; a native of modern Saxony.—*a.* Pertaining to the Saxons or to modern Saxony; Anglo-Saxon.

saxophone, sak'so-fōn, *n.* A wind instrument with a reed mouthpiece and finger keys.

say, sā, *vt.* (saying, said). To utter in words; to speak; to declare; to assume. —*vi.* To speak; to relate.—*n.* A speech; statement. **saying,** sā'ing, *n.* Something said; speech; an adage; a maxim; a proverb.

scab, skab, *n.* An incrusted substance over a sore in healing; a disease of sheep; the mange in horses; one who takes the place of a striking union worker. **scabby,** skab'i, *a.* Affected with scab or scabs; mangy; mean; worthless.

scabbard, skab'èrd, *n.* The sheath of a sword.

scabies, skā'bi-ēz, *n.* Scab; mange; itch.

scaffold, skaf'ōld, *n.* A temporary platform for workmen; an elevated platform for the execution of a criminal.—*vt.* To furnish with a scaffold. **scaffolding,** skaf'ōld-ing, *n.* A structure for support of workmen in building.

scald, skạld, *vt.* To burn or injure with hot liquor; to expose to a boiling or violent heat.—*n.* An injury caused by a hot liquid.—*a.* Covered with scurf; scabby; paltry.

scale, skāl, *n.* A thin flake on the skin of an animal; dish of a balance; balance itself (generally *pl.*); anything graduated used as a measure; series of steps or ranks; relative dimensions; succession of notes; gamut.—*vt.* (scaling, scaled). To weigh, as in scales; to strip of scales; to clean; to climb, as by a ladder.—*vi.* To come off in thin layers.

scallion, skal'yun, *n.* A shallot.

scallop, skol'up; skal'-, *n.* An edible bivalve of the oyster family; a curving on the edge of anything.—*vt.* To cut the edge of into scallops or segments of circles. **scalloped,** skol'upt, *p.a.* Cut at the edge into segments of circles.

scalp, skalp, *n.* The skin of the top of the head, with the hair on it.—*vt.* To deprive of the scalp.

scalpel, skal'pel, *n.* A knife used in anatomical dissections.

scaly, skāl'i, *a.* Covered with scales; resembling scales, laminæ, or layers.

scamp, skamp, *n.* A knave; swindler; rogue.—*vt.* To do in a perfunctory manner.

scamper, skam'pèr, *vi.* To run with speed; to scurry.—*n.* A hurried run.

scan, skan, *vt.* (scanning, scanned). To measure by the metrical feet, as a verse; to scrutinize; to eye.

scandal, skan'dal, *n.* Public reproach; shame; defamatory talk; slander. **scandalize,** skan'dal-īz, *vt.* To offend by some action deemed disgraceful; to shock. **scandalmonger,** skan"dal-mung'gèr, *n.* One who deals in or retails scandals. **scandalous,** skan'dal-us, *a.* Causing scandal; shameful; defamatory; slanderous.

Scandinavian, skan'di-nā"vi-an, *n.* Native or inhabitant of Norway, Sweden, Denmark, or Iceland; the languages of these countries.

scansion, skan'shun, *n.* The act of scanning; metrical structure of verse.

scant, skant, *a.* Not full; scarcely sufficient; scarce.—*vt.* To limit; to stint; to grudge.—*adv.* Scarcely; hardly. **scantily, scantly,** skan'ti-li, skant'li, *adv.* In a scant or scantily manner. **scanty,** skan'ti, *a.* Scant, insufficient.

scape, skāp, *n.* A stem rising directly from a root and bearing the fructification without leaves; the shaft of a feather or column.—*vt.* and *i.* To escape.

scapegoat, skāp"gōt', *n.* One made to bear the blame of others.

scapegrace, skāp"grās', *n.* A graceless fellow; a careless, hare-brained fellow.

scapula, skap'ū-la, *n.* The shoulder-blade.

scar, skär, *n.* The mark of a wound or ulcer; a cicatrix; a cliff; a bare place on the side of a hill.—*vt.* (scarring, scarred). To mark with a scar; to wound.

scarab, scarabee, skar'ab, skar'a-bē, *n.* The sacred beetle of the Egyptians.

Scaramouch, skar"a-mouch', *n.* A buffoon; a poltroon or braggadocio.

scarce, skärs, *n.* Not plentiful; deficient; uncommon. **scarce, scarcely,** skärs, skärs'li, *adv.* Hardly; scantly; barely; with difficulty. **scarcity,** skär'si-ti, *n.* State or condition of being scarce; deficiency; dearth.

scare, skär, *vt.* (scaring, scared). To strike with sudden terror; to frighten.— *n.* A sudden fright; a causeless alarm. **scarecrow,** skär"krō', *n.* Anything set up to scare birds from crops; anything terrifying without danger; a ragged or very odd-looking person.

scarf, skärf, *n.*; pl. **scarfs,** skärfs, and **scarves,** skärvz. A light article of dress worn round the neck, &c.; a joint in timber.—*vt.* To unite (timber) by means of a scarf.

scarlet, skär'let, *n.* A bright-red color. —*a.* Of a bright-red color. **scarlet fever,** skär'let fē'vèr, *n.* Same as *Scarlatina.*

scathe, skāth, *n.* Damage; injury.—*vt.* (scathing, scathed). To injure; to harm. **scatheful,** skāth'ful, *a.* Harmful. **scatheless,** skāth'les, *a.* Without harm.

scathing, skāth'ing, *p.a.* Injuring; harming; blasting.

scatter, skat'èr, *vt.* To disperse; to spread; to strew; to disunite.—To be dispersed; to straggle apart. **scatter-brain**, skat″ẽr-brān′, n. A thoughtless person. **scattered**, skat′ẽrd, p.a. Thinly spread; loose and irregular in arrangement.

scavenger, skav′en-jẽr, n. One employed to clean the streets.

scenario, se-nä′ri-ō, n. The complete story of the plot of a photoplay.

scene, sēn, n. A stage; a distinct part of a play; a painted device on the stage; place of action or exhibition; general appearance of any action; a view; display of emotion. **scenery**, sēn′ẽr-i, n. The painted representations on the stage; pictorial features; landscape characteristics. **scenic**, **scenical**, sē′nik, sē′ni-kal, a. Pertaining to the stage; dramatic; theatrical.

scent, sent, n. That which causes the sensation of smell; odor; fragrance; power of smelling; chase followed by the scent; tract.—vt. To perceive by the sense of smell; to imbue with odor.

scepter, **sceptre**, sep′tẽr, n. A staff or baton worn by a ruler as a symbol of authority. **sceptered**, sep′tẽrd, a. Invested with a scepter; having royal power; regal.

sceptic, **skeptic**, skep′tik, n. One who doubts or disbelieves.—a. Skeptical. **sceptical**, **skeptical**, skep′ti-kal, a. Doubting; doubting the truth of revelation. **scepticism**, **skepticism**, skep′ti-sizm, n. Doubt; incredulity.

schedule, sked′ūl, n. A paper containing a list, and annexed to a larger writing, as to a will, deed, &c.; an inventory.—vt. (scheduling, scheduled). To place in a schedule.

scheme, skēm, n. A combination of things adjusted by design; a system; project; diagram.—vt. and i. (scheming, schemed). To plan, contrive, project.

scherzo, sker′tso, n. A passage of a sportive character in musical pieces.

schism, sizm, n. A separation; breach among people of the same religious faith. **schismatic**, **schismatical**, siz-mat′ik, siz-mat′i-kal, a. Pertaining to schism; implying schism; tending to schism.

schist, shist, n. A rock of a slaty structure.

schizophrenia, skiz′ō-frē″ni-a, n. A mental disorder characterized by withdrawal from reality, and delusions. **schizoid**, skiz′oid, a. **schizophrenic**, skiz′ō-fren″ik, a. and n.

scholar, skol′ẽr, n. One who attends a school; a pupil; a learned person; an undergraduate in an English university who is aided by college revenues. **scholarship**, skol′ẽr-ship, n. Erudition; a foundation for the support of a student. **scholastic**, skō-las′tik, a. Pertaining to a scholar or school; pertaining to the schoolmen; pedantic; needlessly subtle. **school**, skōl, n. A place of instruction; a body of pupils; disciples; sect or body; a system or custom; a shoal (of fishes). —a. Relating to a school; scholastic.— vt. To instruct; to reprove. **schoolboard**, skōl′bõrd′, n. A body elected by taxpayers to provide adequate instruction

for the district. **schoolhouse**, skōl′-hous′, n. A house used as a school; a schoolmaster's house. **schooling**, skōl′-ing, n. Instruction in school; tuition; reproof; reprimand. **schoolmaster**, skōl′mäs′tẽr, n. He who teaches a school, or in a school.

schooner, skōn′ẽr, n. A vessel with two or more masts, her chief sails fore-and-aft.

sciatic, **sciatical**, sī-at′ik, sī-at′i-kal, a. Pertaining to the hip or to sciatica. **sciatica**, sī-at′i-ka, n. Neuralgia or inflammation of the sciatic nerve or great nerve of the thigh.

science, sī′ens, n. Knowledge; knowledge reduced to a system; the facts pertaining to any department of mind or matter in their due connections; skill resulting from training. **scientific**, sī′en-tif″ik, a. Pertaining to science; versed in science; according to the rules or principles of science. **scientifically**, sī′en-tif″i-kal-i, adv. In a scientific manner. **scientist**, sī′en-tist, n. One versed in science; a scientific man.

scimitar, sim′i-tẽr, n. A short curved sword.

scintilla, sin-til′a, n. A spark; glimmer; trace. **scintillate**, sin′ti-lāt, vi. To emit sparks; to sparkle, as the fixed stars. **scintillation**, sin′ti-lā″shun, n. Twinkling; coruscation.

scion, sī′un, n. A cutting or twig; a young shoot; a descendant; an heir.

scissors, siz′ẽrs, n.pl. A cutting instrument consisting of two blades.

scleroma, **sclerosis**, sklē-rō′ma, sklē-rō′sis, n. Induration of the cellular tissue.

scoff, skąf, n. An expression of derision or scorn; a gibe.—vi. To utter contemptuous language; to jeer; to mock.— vt. To mock at.

scold, skōld, vi. To find fault with rude clamor; to utter harsh, rude rebuke.— vt. To reprimand loudly; to chide.—n. A clamorous, foul-mouthed woman.

sconce, skons, n. A case or socket for a candle; a projecting candlestick; a detached fort; a head-piece; the skull. —vt. To ensconce.

scoop, skōp, n. An implement for lifting things; an instrument for hollowing out; the act of scooping.—vt. To take out with a scoop; to lade out; to hollow out.

scope, skōp, n. An aim or end; intention; amplitude of range; space; sweep.

scorbutic, skōr-bū′tik, a. Pertaining to or diseased with scurvy.

scorch, skōrch, vt. To burn superficially; to singe; to parch.—vi. To be so hot as to burn a surface; to be dried up; to ride a cycle at excessive speed.

score, skōr, n. A notch; a long scratch or mark; an account or reckoning; the number twenty; a debt; the number of points made in certain games; motive; ground; draught of a musical composition.—vt. (scoring, scored). To make scores or scratches on; to record; to get for one's self, as points, &c., in games. **scorer**, skōr′ẽr, n. One who keeps the scores of competitors, or the like; an instrument to mark numbers, &c., on trees.

scorn, skôrn, *n.* Extreme contempt; subject of contempt.—*vt.* To hold in extreme contempt; to despise.—*vi.* To feel or show scorn. **scorner,** skôrn'ér, *n.* One who scorns; a scoffer. **scornful,** skorn'ful, *a.* Filled with or expressing scorn; contemptuous.

scorpion, skôr'pi-un, *n.* An animal of the class Arachnida, with a jointed tail terminating with a venomous sting; a sign of the zodiac.

Scot, skot, *n.* A native of Scotland; a tax or contribution.

Scotch, skoch, *a.* Pertaining to Scotland or its inhabitants; Scottish.—*n.* The dialect of Scotland; the people of Scotland; Scotch whiskey.

scotch, skoch, *vt.* To cut with shallow incisions; to notch.—*n.* A slight cut.

Scotchman, skoch'man, *n.* A native of Scotland.

scot-free, skot'frē', *a.* Free from payment of scot; untaxed; unhurt; clear; safe.

Scots, skots, *a.* Scottish.—*n.* The Scottish language. **Scotsman,** skots'man, *n.* A native of Scotland. **Scottish,** skot'ish, *a.* Pertaining to Scotland, its inhabitants, or language.

scoundrel, skoun'drel, *n.* A mean, worthless fellow; a rascal.—*a.* Base; unprincipled.

scour, skour, *vt.* and *i.* To clean by rubbing; to purge violently; to range for the purpose of finding something; to pass swiftly over.

scourge, skêrj, *n.* A lash; a whip; an affliction sent for punishment; one who harasses.—*vt.* (scourging, scourged). To lash; to chastise; to harass.

scout, skout, *n.* A person sent to obtain intelligence regarding an enemy; a college servant.—*vi.* To act as a scout.—*vt.* To watch closely; to treat with disdain.

scow, skou, *n.* A flat-bottomed boat.

scowl, skoul, *vi.* To wrinkle the brows, as in displeasure; to frown.—*n.* A deep angry frown; gloom.

scrabble, skrab'l, *vi.* and *t.* To scrawl; to scribble.—*n.* A scribble.

scrag, skrag, *n.* Something dry, or lean with roughness. **scragged,** skrag'ed, *a.* Like a scrag; scraggy. **scraggy,** skrag'i, *a.* Rough or rugged; scragged; lean and bony.

scramble, skram'bl, *vi.* (scrambling, scrambled). To move or climb on all-fours; to push rudely in eagerness for something.—*n.* Act of scrambling; eager contest. **scrambling,** skram'bling, *a.* Irregular; straggling.

scrap, skrap, *n.* A small piece; a fragment; a little picture for ornamenting screens, &c.—*n.* and *vi.* Slang. To fight; quarrel.

scrapbook, skrap'buk, *n.* A book for preserving extracts, drawings, prints, &c.

scrape, skrāp, *vt.* (scraping, scraped). To rub with something hard; to clean by a sharp edge; to act on with a grating noise; to erase; to collect laboriously.—*vi.* To roughen or remove a surface by rubbing; to make a grating noise.—*n.* Act of scraping; an awkward bow; an awkward predicament. **scraper,** skrāp'-ér, *n.* One who or that which scrapes; an instrument for scraping or cleaning.

scraping, skrāp'ing, *n.* What is scraped from a substance, or is collected by scraping.

scrappy, skrap'i, *a.* Consisting of scraps; incomplete; disjointed.

scratch, skrach, *vt.* and *i.* To mark or wound with something sharp; to tear with the nails; to withdraw from the list of competitors.—*n.* A score in a surface; a slight wound; a line from which runners start, &c.; one most heavily handicapped in a contest.—*a.* Taken at random; hastily collected. **scratcher,** skrach'ér, *n.* One who or that which scratches; a gallinaceous bird.

scrawl, skral, *vt.* and *i.* To write or draw carelessly or awkwardly.—*n.* Inelegant or hasty writing.

scream, skrēm, *vi.* To shriek; to utter a shrill cry.—*n.* A sharp, shrill cry. **screamer,** skrēm'ér, *n.* One that screams; a name of certain birds.

screech, skrēch, *vi.* To scream; to shriek.—*n.* A sharp, shrill cry.

screech owl, skrēch'oul', *n.* An owl that screeches in opposition to one that hoots.

screen, skrēn, *n.* An article to intercept heat, cold, &c.; a shelter; a kind of sieve; an ornamental partition in a church.—*vt.* To shelter; to conceal; to sift. **screenings,** skrēn'ingz, *n.pl.* The refuse matter left after sifting coal, &c.

screw, skrō, *n.* A cylinder with a spiral ridge which enables it when turned to enter another body; a screw-propeller; a twist or turn; a niggard.—*vt.* To fasten by a screw; to twist; to oppress. **screw driver,** skrō'driv'ér, *n.* An instrument for turning screw-nails.

scribble, skrib'l, *vt.* and *i.* (scribbling, scribbled). To write with haste or without care; to tease coarsely, as cotton or wool.—*n.* Careless writing; a scrawl. **scribbler,** skrib'lér, *n.* One who writes carelessly or badly; a machine which teases cotton or wool.

scribe, skrib, *n.* A writer; notary; copyist; doctor of the law among the Jews.

scrimmage, skrim'ij, *n.* A tussle; a confused, close struggle in football.

scrimp, skrimp, *vt.* To make too small or short; to scant; to limit.—*a.* Scanty.

scrip, skrip, *n.* A small bag; a wallet; a small writing; a certificate of stock.

script, skript, *n.* Handwriting; printing type resembling handwriting.

Scripture, skrip'tūr, *n.* The Old and New Testaments; the Bible; often *pl.* —*a.* Scriptural. **scriptural,** skrip'tūr-al, *a.* Contained in or according to the Scriptures; biblical.

scrivener, skriv'nér, *n.* An old name for a notary; a money-broker; a writer; a poor author.

scrofula, skrof'ū-la, *n.* A disease, a variety of consumption, often showing itself by glandular tumors in the neck which suppurate. **scrofulous,** skrof'ū-lus, *a.* Pertaining to scrofula; diseased or affected with scrofula.

scroll, skrōl, *n.* A roll of paper or parchment; a draft or first copy; a spiral ornament; a flourish added to a person's name.

scrotum, skrō'tum, *n.* The bag which contains the testicles.

scrub, skrub, *vt.* (scrubbing, scrubbed). To rub hard with something rough, to make clean or bright.—*vi.* To be diligent and penurious.—*n.* One who labors hard and lives sparingly; a mean fellow; a worn-out brush; low underwood.—*a.* Mean. **scrubby**, skrub'i, *a.* Small and mean; stunted in growth; niggardly; shabby.

scruple, skrö'pl, *n.* A weight of 20 grains; doubt; hesitation; backwardness. —*vi.* (scrupling, scrupled). To doubt; to hesitate. **scrupulous**, skrö'pū-lus, *a.* Having scruples; cautious; conscientious; exact.

scrutiny, skrö'ti-ni, *n.* Close search; careful investigation; an authoritative examination of votes given at an election. **scrutinize**, skrö'ti-nīz, *vt.* and *i.* To examine closely; to investigate.

scud, skud, *vi.* (scudding, scudded). To run quickly; to run before a strong wind with little or no sail.—*vt.* To pass over quickly.—*n.* Act of scudding; loose, vapory clouds.

scuffle, skuf'l, *n.* A confused struggle.— *vi.* (scuffling, scuffled). To strive confusedly at close quarters.

scull, skul, *n.* A short oar, used in pairs. —*vt.* To propel by sculls, or by moving an oar at the stern.

scullery, skul'ér-i, *n.* A place where culinary utensils are cleaned and kept.

scullion, skul'yun, *n.* A servant of the scullery; a low, worthless fellow.

sculptor, skulp'tèr, *n.* One who works in sculpture; an artist who carves or models figures.

sculptural, skulp'tūr-al, *a.* Pertaining to sculpture.

sculpture, skulp'tūr, *n.* The art of carving wood or stone into images; an image in stone, &c.—*vt.* (sculpturing, sculptured). To carve; to form, as images on stone, &c.

scum, skum, *n.* Impurities which rise to the surface of liquors; refuse.—*vt.* (scumming, scummed). To take the scum from.—*vi.* To throw up scum.

scummy, skum'i, *a.* Covered with scum.

scupper, skup'ér, *n.* A hole for carrying off water from the deck of a ship.

scurf, skèrf, *n.* Dry scales or flakes on the skin; matter adhering to a surface.

scurrile, skèr'il, *a.* Scurrilous. **scurrility**, sku-ril'i-ti, *n.* Scurrilous language; low abuse; insolence. **scurrilous**, skèr'i-lus, *a.* Foulmouthed; abusive; obscenely jocular.

scurry, skèr-i, *vt.* (scurrying, scurried). To run rapidly; to hurry.—*n.* Hurry; haste.

scurvy, skèr'vi, *n.* A disease caused by insufficiency of vegetable food.—*a.* Vile; mean; malicious. **scurvily**, skèr'vi-li, *adv.* In a scurvy manner; basely; meanly; shabbily.

scutcheon, skuch'un, *a.* A shield for armorial bearings; an escutcheon.

scuttle, skut'l, *n.* A broad basket; a pail for coal; a hatchway in a ship's deck; a short run; a quick pace.—*vt.* (scuttling, scuttled). To sink by making holes in (a ship).—*vi.* To scurry.

scythe, sīтн, *n.* An implement for mowing grass, &c.—*vt.* To cut with a scythe.

sea, sē, *n.* The mass of salt water covering most of the earth; some portion of this; a name of certain lakes; a large wave; a surge; a flood.

seaboard, sē'bōrd', *n.* The seacoast.

sea breeze, sē'brēz', *n.* A wind or current of air blowing from the sea upon land.

seacoast, sē'kōst', *n.* The land adjacent to the sea or ocean.

sea dog, sē'dag', *n.* The dog-fish; the common seal; a sailor who has been long afloat.

seafarer, sē'fār'èr, *n.* One who fares or travels by sea; a mariner; a seaman.

seafaring, sē'fār'ing, *a.* Going to sea; employed in seamanship.

seagoing, sē'gō'ing, *a.* Traveling by sea, as a vessel which trades with foreign ports.

sea green, sē'grēn', *a.* Having the greenish color of sea-water.

sea horse, sē'hōrs', *n.* The walrus; a small fish with head shaped like a horse's.

seal, sēl, *n.* A hard substance bearing some device, used to make impressions; the wax stamped with a seal; assurance; that which makes fast; a carnivorous marine mammal.— *vt.* To set a seal to; to confirm; to fasten; to shut or keep close.

sea legs, sē legz, *n.pl.* The ability to walk on a ship's deck when pitching or rolling.

Sea Horse.

sealer, sēl'ér, *n.* One who seals; an officer in Chancery who seals writs, &c.; one engaged in the seal-fishery.

sea level, sē'lev'el, *n.* The level of the surface of the sea.

sealing, sēl'ing, *n.* The operation of taking seals and curing their skins.

sealing wax, sēl'ing-waks', *n.* A resinous compound used for sealing letters, &c.

sea lion, sē'lī'un, *n.* The name of several large seals.

seam, sēm, *n.* The joining of two edges of cloth; a line of juncture; a vein of metal, coal, &c.; a scar.—*vt.* To unite by a seam; to scar.

seaman, sē'man, *n.* A sailor; a mariner.

seamanship, sē'man-ship, *n.* The art or skill of a seaman; art of managing a ship.

seamstress, sēm'stres, *n.* A woman whose occupation is sewing; a sempstress.

seamy, sēm'i, *a.* Having a seam; showing seams; showing the worst side; disagreeable.

séance, sā'äns", *n.* A session, as of some public body; a sitting with the view of evoking spiritual manifestations.

seaplane, sē''plān', *n.* An airplane designed to rise from and land on water.

seaport, sē''pōrt', *n.* A harbor on the seacoast; a town on or near the sea.

sear, sēr, *vt.* To wither; to dry; to cauterize; to deaden.—*a.* Dry; withered.

search, sèrch, *vt.* To look through to find something; to examine.—*vi.* To seek diligently; to inquire.—*n.* Act of searching; examination; inquiry. **searcher**, sèrch'èr, *n.* One who or that which searches; an investigator. **searching**, sèrch'ing, *a.* Penetrating; trying; closely scrutinizing.

sea room, sē''rōm', *n.* Ample distance from land, shoals, or rocks, for a vessel.

sea rover, sē''rōv'èr, *n.* A pirate.

seascape, sē''skāp, *n.* A picture representing a scene at sea; a sea-piece.

sea serpent, sē''sèr'pent, *n.* An enormous marine animal resembling a serpent, the existence of which is doubtful.

seashore, sē''shōr', *n.* The shore of the sea; ground between high and low water mark.

seasick, sē''sik', *a.* Affected with sickness caused by the motion of a vessel at sea. **seasickness**, sē''sik'nes, *n.* Sickness produced by the motion of a vessel at sea.

seaside, sē''sīd', *n.* The sea-coast.

season, sē'zn, *n.* A division of the year; a suitable time; a time; time of the year marked by special activity; seasoning.—*vt.* To accustom; to acclimatize; to flavor.—*vi.* To become suitable by time. **seasonable**, sē'zn-a-bl, *a.* Natural to the season; opportune; timely. **seasoning**, sē'zn-ing, *n.* Something added to food to give it relish; relish; condiment.

seat, sēt, *n.* That on which one sits; a chair, stool, &c.; place of sitting; a right to sit; residence; station.—*vt.* To place on a seat; to settle; to locate; to assign seats to; to fit up with seats.

seaward, sē'wèrd, *a.* and *adv.* Toward the sea.

seaweed, sē''wēd', *n.* A marine plant.

seaworthy, sē''wèr'тні, *a.* Fit to go to sea; fit for a voyage.

sebaceous, sē-bā'shus, *a.* Made of, containing, or secreting fatty matter.

secede, sē-sēd', *vi.* (seceding, seceded). To withdraw from fellowship or association.

secession, sē-sesh'un, *n.* Act of seceding. **secessionist**, sē-sesh'un-ist, *n.* One who advocates or engages in a secession.

seclude, sē-klöd', *vt.* (secluding, secluded). To shut up apart; to separate; *refl.* to withdraw into solitude. **secluded**, sē-klöd'ed, *a.* Separated from others; retired; sequestered. **seclusion**, sē-klö'zhun, *n.* Act of secluding; retired mode of life; privacy.

second, sek'und, *a.* Next after the first; repeated again; inferior; other.—*n.* One who or that which comes next a first; one who supports another; attendant in a duel; sixtieth part of a minute; a lower part in music; *pl.* a coarse kind of flour.—*vt.* To follow in the next place; to support; to join with in proposing some measure.

secondary, sek''un-der'i, *a.* Of second place; subordinate; not elementary place; subordinate; not elementary

secondarily, sek''un-der'i-li, *adv.* In a secondary manner; secondly.

second cousin, sek'und kuz'n, *n.* The son or daughter of a cousin-german.

secondhand, sek'und-hand', *a.* Received not from the original possessor; not new.

secondly, sek'und-li, *adv.* In the second place.

second-rate, sek'und-rāt', *a.* Of the second order in size, dignity, or value.

second sight, sek'und sīt, *n.* The power of seeing things future; prophetic vision.

secret, sē'kret, *a.* Hidden; concealed; private; unseen.—*n.* Something hidden or not to be revealed; a mystery. **secrecy**, sē'kre-si, *n.* State or character of being secret; seclusion; fidelity to a secret. **secretly**, sē'kret-li, *adv.* In a secret manner; privately; privily; not openly.

secretary, sek''rē-ter'i, *n.* A person employed to write orders, letters, &c.; an escritoire; one who manages the affairs of a department of government. **secretaryship**, sek''rē-ter'i-ship, *n.* The office or employment of a secretary. **secretarial**, sek'rē-tār''i-al, *a.* Pertaining to a secretary. **secretariate**, sek'rē-tār''i-at, *n.* The position or business of a secretary.

secrete, sē-krēt', *vt.* (secreting, secreted). To hide; to separate from the blood in animals, or from the sap in vegetables. **secretion**, sē-krē'shun, *n.* Act or process of secreting; matter secreted, as bile, &c. **secretive**, sē-krē'tiv, *a.* Causing secretion; secretory; given to secrecy; reticent.

sect, sekt, *n.* A body of persons united in tenets, chiefly in religion or philosophy; a school; a denomination. **sectarian**, sek-tār'i-an, *a.* Pertaining to a sect or sectary.—*n.* One of a sect.

section, sek'shun, *n.* Act of cutting; a distinct part; subdivision of a chapter &c.; representation of an object as if cut asunder by an intersecting plane. **sectional**, sek'shun-al, *a.* Pertaining to a section; composed of independent sections.

sector, sek'tèr, *n.* A part of a circle between two radii; a mathematical instrument useful in making diagrams.

secular, sek'ū-lèr, *a.* Pertaining to things not spiritual or sacred; worldly; temporal; coming once in a century. **secularism**, sek'ū-lèr-izm, *n.* The elimination of the religious element from life.

Sector.

secure, sē-kūr', *a.* Free from care or danger; heedless; undisturbed; safe; confident.—*vt.* (securing, secured). To make safe or certain; to seize and confine; to guarantee; to fasten. **securely**, sē-kūr'li, *adv.* In a secure manner; in security; safely. **security**, sē-kū'ri-ti, *n.* Safety; confidence; protection; guarantee; a surety; an evidence of property, as a bond, a certificate of stock, &c.

sedan, sĕ-dan′, n. A kind of covered chair for a single person, borne on poles by two men; a type or model of an automobile.

sedate, sĕ-dāt′, a. Composed in manner; staid; placid; sober; serious.

sedative, sed′a-tiv, a. Tending to soothe; assuaging pain.—n. A medicine which assuages pain, &c.

sedentary, sed′′en-ter′i, a. Accustomed to sit much; requiring much sitting.

sedge, sej, n. A coarse grass-like plant growing mostly in marshes and swamps.

sedgy, sej′i, a. Abounding in sedge.

sediment, sedi-ment, n. That which settles at the bottom of liquor; lees.

sedimentary, sed′i-men′′ta-ri, a. Pertaining to sediment; formed of sediment.

sedition, sĕ-dish′un, n. A commotion in a state; insurrection; civic discord. **seditious**, sĕ-dish′us, a. Pertaining to sedition; stirring up sedition; inflammatory.

seduce, sĕ-dūs′, vt. (seducing, seduced). To lead astray; to corrupt; to entice to a surrender of chastity. **seducer**, sĕ-dūs′ėr, n. One who seduces. **seduction**, sĕ-duk′shun, n. Act of seducing; allurement; the persuading of a female to surrender her chastity. **seductive**, sĕ-duk′tiv, a. Tending to seduce; enticing; alluring.

sedulous, sed′ū-lus, a. Assiduous; diligent; industrious.

see, sĕ, vt. (seeing, pret. saw. pp. seen). To perceive by the eye; to notice; to discover; to understand; to receive; to experience; to attend.—vi. To have the power of sight; to understand; to consider.—interj. Lo! look!—n. A seat of episcopal power; a diocese.

seed, sĕd, n. That product of a plant which may produce a similar plant; seeds collectively; the semen; first principle; offspring.—vi. To produce seed; to shed the seed.—vt. To sow; to supply with seed. **seeded**, sĕd′ed, a. Sown; sprinkled or covered with seed; bearing seed. **seedling**, sĕd′ling, n. A plant reared from the seed. **seedy**, sĕd′i, a. Abounding with seeds; run to seed; shabby; feeling or appearing wretched.

seeing, sĕ′ing, conj. Since; inasmuch as.

seek, sĕk, vt. and i. (seeking, sought). To search for; to solicit; to have recourse to.

seem, sĕm, vi. To appear; to look as if; to imagine; to feel as if. **seeming**, sĕm′ing, p.a. Appearing; specious.—n. Appearance; semblance. **seemingly**, sĕm′ing-li, adv. Apparently. **seemly**, sĕm′li, a. Becoming; suitable; decorous. —adv. In a suitable manner.

seer, sēr, n. One who sees into futurity; a prophet.

seesaw, sē′′sa′, n. A swinging movement up and down; a game in which children swing up and down on the two ends of a balanced piece of timber.—vi. and t. To move up and down or to and fro.

seethe, sēth, vt. (seething, seethed). To boil; to soak.—vi. To be in a state of ebullition; to be hot.

segment, seg′ment, n. A part cut off; a section; a natural division of a body (as an orange).

segregate, seg′rē-gāt, vt. To set apart or separate. **segregation**, seg′rē-gā′′shun, n. Act of segregating; separation.

seine, sein, sān, sēn, n. A large fishing net.—vt. (seining, seined). To catch with a seine.

seismic, **seismal**, sīz′mik, sīz′mal, a. Pertaining to earthquakes. **seismograph**, sīz′mō-graf, n. An instrument to register shocks of earthquakes.

seize, sēz, vt. (seizing, seized). To lay hold of suddenly; to take by force or legal authority; to attack, as a disease, fear, &c.; to comprehend; to put in possession.—vi. To take hold or possession. **seizure**, sē′zhėr, n. Act of seizing; thing taken or seized; a sudden attack.

seldom, sel′dum, adv. Rarely; not often.

select, sĕ-lekt′, vt. To choose; to pick out; to cull.—a. Chosen; choice; exclusive. **selection**, sĕ-lek′shun, n. Act of selecting; a collection of things selected. **selective**, sĕ-lek′tiv, a. Pertaining to selecting; tending to select.

self, self, n.; pl. **selves**, selvz. One's individual person; personal interest; a blossom of a uniform color (with pl. **selfs**).—a. or pron. Same. Affixed to pronouns and adjectives to express emphasis or distinction, or reflexive usage.

self-acting, self′-ak′′ting, a. Acting of itself; automatic.

self-command, self′-ko-mand′′, a. Command of one's powers or feelings; coolness.

self-conceit, self′-kon-sēt′′, n. A high opinion of one's self; vanity; self-sufficiency.

self-confident, self′-kon′′fi-dent, a. Confident of one's own strength or abilities.

self-conscious, self′-kon′′shus, a. Conscious of one's personal states or acts; apt to think of how one's self appears.

self-contained, self′-kon-tānd′′, a. Wrapped up in one's self; reserved.

self-control, self′-kon-trōl′′, n. Control exercised over one's self; self-command.

self-denial, self′-dē-nī′′al, n. The forbearing to gratify one's own desires.

self-educated, self′-ed′′ū-kāt′ed, a. Educated by one's own efforts.

self-esteem, self′-es-tēm′′, n. The esteem or good opinion of one's self; vanity.

self-evident, self′-ev′′i-dent, a. Evident in its own nature; evident without proof.

self-government, self′-guv′′ėrn-ment, n. The government of one's self; government by rulers appointed by the people.

self-important, self′-im-pōr′′tant, a. Important in one's own esteem; pompous.

self-imposed, self′im-pōzd′′, a. Imposed or voluntarily taken on one's self.

selfish, self′fish, a. Devoted unduly to self; influenced by a view to private advantage.

self-made, self′-mād′′, a. Made by one's self; risen in the world by one's exertions.

self-possessed, self′-po-zest′′, a. Cool

and composed; not excited or flustered.

self-possession, self'-po-zesh"un, *n.* The possession of one's faculties; self-command.

self-respect, self'-rē-spekt", *n.* Respect for one's self; proper pride.

self-righteous, self'-rī"chus, *a.* Righteous in one's own esteem; sanctimonious.

self-same, self"-sām', *a.* Exactly the same; the very same; identical.

self-satisfied, self'-sat"is-fīd, *a.* Satisfied with one's self; showing complacency.

self-seeking, self'-sēk"ing, *a.* Selfish.

self-sufficient, self'-su-fish"ent, *a.* Having too much confidence in one's self; conceited; assuming; overbearing.

self-willed, self'-wild", *a.* Willful; obstinate.

sell, sel, *vt.* (selling, sold). To give in exchange for money, &c.; to betray.— *vi.* To practice selling; to be sold.

seller, sel'ėr, *n.* The person who sells.

Seltzer, selt'sėr, *n.* A carbonated water.

semaphore, sem'a-fōr, *n.* An apparatus for signalling at a distance, usually a pole supporting a movable arm.

semblance, sem'blans, *n.* Similarity; resemblance; image; appearance.

semen, sē'men, *n.* The seed or fecundating fluid of male animals; sperm.

semester, sē-mes'tėr, *n.* A school term usually of eighteen weeks' duration.

semicircle, sem"i-sėr'k'l, *n.* The half of a circle. **semicircular**, sem'i-sėr"kū-lėr, *a.* Forming a semicircle.

semicolon, sem'i-kō'lon, *n.* The point (;), marking a greater break than a comma.

semidetached, sem'i-dē-tacht", *a.* Partly separated; joined on to another house, but the two detached from other buildings.

seminal, sem'i-nal, *a.* Pertaining to seed; germinal; rudimental.

seminar, sem'i-när, *n.* A group of students doing advanced work; course of study for such a group.

seminary, sem"i-ner'i, *n.* A school or academy; a place for educating for the priesthood.

semination, sem'i-nā"shun, *n.* Act of sowing; the natural dispersion of seeds.

Semite, sem'īt, *n.* A descendant of Shem; one of the Semitic race; a Shemite. **Semitic**, se-mit'ik, *a.* Pertaining to the Semites; Hebrew.

senate, sen'it, *n.* The legislative body in ancient Rome; the upper branch of a legislature; the governing body of a university, &c. **senator**, sen'a-tėr, *n.* A member of a senate. **senatorial**, sen'a-tō"ri-al *a.* Pertaining to a senate. **senatus**, sē-nā'tus, *n.* A senate; the governing body in certain universities.

send, send, *vt.* (sending, sent). To cause to go or be carried; to transmit; to direct to go and act; to make befall.— *vi.* To despatch an agent or message.

sender, sen'dėr, *n.*

senile, sē'nīl, *a.* Pertaining to old age; characterized by the failings of old age. **senility**, sē-nil'i-ti, *n.* State of being old; dotage.

senior, sēn'yėr, *a.* Older; older or more advanced in office.—*n.* One older in age or office. **seniority**, sēn-yor'i-ti, *n.* State of being senior; superiority in office.

senna, sen'a, *n.* The dried leaves of certain plants used as a purgative; the plant itself.

sennight, sen'īt, *n.* A week.

sennit, sen'it, *n.* A sort of flat braided cordage used on ships.

señor, sā-nyōr', *n.* A Spanish form of address, corresponding to "Mr." or "Sir"; a gentleman.

señora, sā-nyō'rä, *n.* Madame or Mrs.; a lady.

señorita, sen-yō-rē'tä, *n.* Miss; a young lady.

sensation, sen-sā'shun, *n.* Impression made through the senses; feeling; power of feeling; what produces excited interest. **sensational**, sen-sā'shun-al, *a.* Relating to sensation; producing excited interest. **sensationalism**, sen-sā'shun-al-izm, *n.* The doctrine that all ideas are derived through our senses; sensational writing.

sense, sens, *n.* The faculty of receiving impressions; a separate faculty of perception; sight, hearing, taste, smell, or touch; consciousness; discernment; understanding; good judgment; meaning. **senseless**, sens'les, *a.* Wanting sense; unfeeling; unreasonable; foolish.

sensibility, sen'si-bil"i-ti, *n.* State or quality of being sensible; acuteness of perception; delicacy of feeling. **sensible**, sen'si-bl, *a.* That may be perceived by the senses; perceptible; sensitive; easily affected; cognizant; reasonable.

sensitive, sen'si-tiv, *a.* Having the capacity of receiving impressions; easily affected; having the feelings easily hurt. **sensitize**, sen'si-tiz, *vt.* To render sensitive; to make capable of being acted on by the rays of the sun.

sensory, sen'sō-ri, *a.* Relating to the sensorium; conveying sensation.

sensual, sen'shu-al, *a.* Pertaining to the senses, as distinct from the mind; carnal; voluptuous; indulging in lust. **sensualism**, sen'shu-al-izm, *n.* Sensuality; sensationalism. **sensualist**, sen'shu-al-ist, *n.* A person given to sensuality; a voluptuary.

sensuous, sen'shu-us *a.* Pertaining to the senses; readily affected through the senses.

sentence, sen'tens, *n.* Opinion; a maxim; a judgment; a number of words containing complete sense.—*vt.* (sentencing, sentenced). To pass sentence upon; to condemn. **sententious**, sen-ten'shus, *a.* Abounding in maxims; terse; gravely judicial.

sentient, sen'shent, *a.* Having the capacity of sensation; perceptive; sensible.

sentiment, sen'ti-ment, *n.* Thought prompted by emotion; tenderness of feeling; sensibility; a thought or opinion. **sentimental**, sen'ti-men"tal, *a.* Having sentiment; apt to be swayed by emotional feelings; mawkishly tender. **sentimentalist**, sen'ti-men"tal-ist, *n.* One who affects sentiment. **sentimentality**, sen'ti-men-tal"i-ti, *n.* State or quality of being sentimental.

sentinel, sen'ti-nel, *n.* One who is set to keep watch; a sentry.

sentry, sen'tri, *n.* A soldier placed on guard; guard; watch; sentinel's duty.

sepal, sē'pal or sep'al, *n.* The leaf of a calyx.

separate, sep'a-rāt, *vt.* (separating, separated). To put or set apart; to disjoin.—*vi.* To go apart; to cleave or split.—*a.* Detached; distinct; individual. **separation**, sep'a-rā″shun, *n.* Act of separating; disunion; incomplete divorce. **separator**, sep″a-rā'tèr, One who or that which separates.

sepia, sē'pi-a, *n.* The cuttle-fish; a brown pigment obtained from the cuttle-fish.

September, sep-tem'bèr, *n.* The ninth month of the year.

septic, sep'tik, *a.* Promoting or causing putrefaction.—*n.* A substance causing putrefaction.

septuagenarian, sep'tū-a-je-nār″i-an, *n.* A person seventy years of age.

Septuagint, sep'tū-a-jint, *n.* A Greek version of the Old Testament, finished about 200 B. C.

septum, sep'tum, *n.*; *pl.* -ta. A wall separating cavities, as in animals and plants.

sepulcher, sep'ul-kèr, *n.* A tomb.—*vt.* To bury.

sepulchral, sē-pul'kral, *a.* Pertaining to a sepulcher; grave; hollow, as a voice.

sequel, sē'kwel, *n.* That which follows; a succeeding part; result; issue.

sequence, sē'kwens, *n.* A coming after; succession; arrangement; series.

sequent, **sequential**, sē'kwent, sē-kwen'shal, *a.* Following; succeeding.

sequester, sē-kwes'tèr, *vt.* To set apart; *refl.* to retire into seclusion; in *law*, to separate from the owner until claims of creditors be satisfied; to appropriate. **sequestration**, sē-kwes-trā″shun, *n.* Act of sequestering; separation.

seraglio, sē-ral'yō, *n.* The palace of the Turkish sultan at Constantinople; a harem.

seraph, ser'af, *n.*; *pl.* -phs or -phim. An angel of the highest rank or order. **seraphic**, sē-raf'ik, *a.* Pertaining to a seraph; celestial; pure.

Serb, sèrb, *n.* A native or inhabitant of Serbia; the language of Serbia.

serenade, ser'e-nād″, *n.* Music played at night under the windows of ladies.—*vt.* (serenading, serenaded). To entertain with a serenade.—*vi.* To perform a serenade.

serene, sē-rēn', *a.* Clear; bright; calm; unruffled; a form of address for princes, &c., in Germany and Austria.—*n.* Serenity; what is serene. **serenity**, sē-ren'i-ti, *n.* State of being serene; peace; calmness; coolness.

serf, sèrf, *n.* A villein; a forced laborer attached to an estate; a bondman. **serfdom**, sèrf'dum, *n.* The state or condition of serfs.

serge, sèrj, *n.* A tough twilled worsted cloth; a twilled silken fabric.

sergeant, **serjeant**, sär'jent, *n.* A non-

commissioned officer above corporal; a police-officer.

serial, sēr'i-al, *a.* Pertaining to a series; forming a series.—*n.* A written composition issued in numbers.

series, sēr'ēz, *n.pl.* the same. A succession of things; sequence; course.

seriocomic, sēr'i-ō-kom″ik, *a.* Having a mixture of seriousness and comicality.

serious, sēr'i-us, *a.* Grave; earnest; momentous; attended with danger.

sermon, sèr'mun, *n.* A religious discourse by a clergyman; a homily.—*vt.* To tutor; to lecture. **sermonize**, sèr'mun-īz, *vi.* To preach; to inculcate rigid rules; to harangue.

serous, sēr'us, *a.* Pertaining to serum; thin; watery; like whey; secreting serum. **serosity**, sē-ros'i-ti, *n.* State of being serous.

serpent, sèr'pent, *n.* A scaly reptile without feet; a bass musical instrument of wood; a firework.—*a.* Pertaining to a serpent. **serpentine**, sèr'pen-tēn, *a.* Resembling or pertaining to a serpent; spiral.—*n.* A rock resembling a serpent's skin in appearance, used for decoration.—*vi.* To wind like a serpent.

serrate, **serrated**, ser'āt, ser'āt-ed, *a.* Notched on the edge like a saw; toothed. **serration**, se-rā'shun, *n.* Formation in the shape of a saw.

serried, ser'id, *a.* Crowded; in close order.

serum, sēr'um, *n.* The watery part of curdled milk; whey; the thin part of the blood, &c.

servant, sèr'vant, *n.* One who serves; an attendant in a household; a drudge.

serve, sèrv, *vt.* (serving, served). To work for and obey; to minister to; to set on a table for a meal; to conduce to; to be sufficient for; to manage or work; to deliver or transmit to; to perform the conditions of.—*vi.* To perform offices for another; to perform duties; to suffice; to suit.

server, sèr'vèr, *n.* One who or that which serves; a salver.

service, sèr'vis, *n.* Act of one who serves; employment; kind office; military or naval duty; period of such duty; usefulness; public religious worship; liturgy; set of dishes for the table; supply of things regularly provided. **serviceable**, sèr'vis-a-bl, *a.* That renders service; useful; beneficial.

servicebook, sèr'vis-buk′, *n.* A book used in church service; a prayer-book. **service station**, A gas station.

serviette, sèr'vi-et″, *n.* A table-napkin.

servile, sèr'vil, *a.* Slavish; mean; dependent; fawning; meanly submissive. **servility**, sèr-vil'i-ti, *n.* State of being servile; mean submission. **servitor**, sèr'vi-tèr, *n.* A male servant. **servitude**, sèr'vi-tūd, *n.* State of a slave; slavery; compulsory labor.

sesame, ses'a-mē, *n.* An annual herbaceous plant, the seeds of which yield a fine oil.

session, sesh'un, *n.* The sitting of a court, &c.; for business; time or term of sitting. **court of session**, the highest civil court of Scotland.

set, set, *vt.* (setting, set). To put or dispose in a certain place or position; to fix; to appoint; to estimate; to regulate or adjust; to fit to music; to adorn; to interpose; to incite.—*vi.* To disappear below the horizon; to solidify; to tend; to point out game; to apply one's self.—*p.a.* Placed, fixed, &c.; determined; established.—*n.* The descent of the sun, &c.; attitude, position; turn or bent; number of things combining to form a whole; a complete assortment; a clique.

seton, set"af, *n.* Any counterbalance; an equivalent; a counter claim.

settee, se-tē', *n.* A long seat with a back to it; a kind of sofa.

setter, set'èr, *n.* One who or that which sets; a sporting dog.

setting, set'ing, *n.* Act of sinking below the horizon; that in which something, as a jewel, is set; music set for certain words.

settle, set'l, *n.* A bench with a high back and arms.—*vt.* (settling, settled). To place in a more or less permanent position; to establish; to quiet; to determine; to reconcile; to pay; to square or adjust; to colonize.—*vi.* To become fixed; to fix one's abode; to subside; to become calm; to adjust differences or accounts. **settled**, set'ld, *p.a.* Established; steadfast; stable; methodical. **settlement**, set'l-ment, *n.* Act of settling; establishment in life; colonization; a colony; adjustment; liquidation; arrangement; settling of property on a wife. **settler**, set'lèr, *n.* One who settles; a colonist; that which decides anything. **settling**, set'ling, *n.* Act of one who settles; payment, as of an account; *pl.* dregs.

set-to, set" tō', *n.* A sharp contest.

seven, sev'en, *a.* and *n.* One more than six. **sevenfold**, sev'en-fōld', *a.* Repeated seven times.—*adv.* Seven times as much or often. **seventeen**, sev'en-tēn' *a.* and *n.* Seven and ten. **seventeenth**, sev'en-tēnth' *a.* and *n.* The next in order after the sixteenth; one of seventeen equal parts. **seventh**, sev'enth, *a.* Next after the sixth; containing or being one part of seven.—*n.* One part in seven. **seventhly**, sev'enth-li, *adv.* In the seventh place. **seventieth**, sev'en-ti-eth, *a.* and *n.* The next after sixty-ninth; one of seventy equal parts. **seventy**, sev'en-ti, *a.* and *n.* Seven times ten.

sever, sev'èr, *vt.* To separate by violence; to keep distinct.—*vi.* To separate. **severable**, sev'èr-a-bl, *a.* Capable of being severed.

several, sev'èr-al, *a.* Separate; distinct; more than two, but not very many. **severally**, sev'èr-al-i, *adv.* Separately. **severance**, se'vèr-ans, *n.* Act of severing; separation.

severe, sē-vēr', *a.* Serious; grave; harsh; stern; austere; rigidly exact; keen. **severity**, sē-ver'i-ti, *n.* State or quality of being severe; rigor; intensity; austerity.

sew, sō, *vt.* and *i.* To unite or make by needle and thread. **sewer**, sō'èr, *n.* One who sews.

sewage, sū'ij, *n.* The filthy matter which passes through sewers. **sewer**, sū'èr, *n.* A subterranean drain, as in a city, to carry off water, filth, &c. **sewerage**, sū'èr-ij, *n.* The system of sewers as in a city; sewage.

sewing, sō'ing, *n.* Act of using a needle; that which is sewed; stitches made.

sex, seks, *n.* That character by which an animal is male or female.

sextant, seks'tant, *n.* The sixth part of a circle; an instrument for measuring the angular distances of objects by reflection.

sexton, seks'tun, *n.* An under officer of a church who takes care of the sacred vessels, acts as janitor, &c.

sextuple, seks'tū-pl, *a.* Sixfold.

sexual, seks'shu-al; seks'ū-al, *a.* Pertaining to, proceeding from, characterized by sex. **sexuality**, sek'shu-al"i-ti, *n.* State of being sexual. **sexually**, sek'shu-a-li, *adv.* In a sexual manner.

shabby, shab'i, *a.* Poor in appearance; threadbare; mean; paltry; stingy. **shabbily**, shab'i-li, *adv.* In a shabby manner; with shabby clothes; meanly.

shack, shak, *n.* A small cabin of poor appearance and construction.

shackle, shak'l, *n.* A fetter; a manacle; that which obstructs free action.—*vt.* (shackling, shackled). To bind with shackles; to hamper.

shad, shad, *n. sing.* and *pl.* A fish of the herring family.

shade, shād, *n.* Obscurity caused by the interception of light; obscure retreat; twilight dimness; a screen; darker part of a picture; gradation of light; a scarcely perceptible degree or amount; a ghost. —*vt.* (shading, shaded). To screen from light; to obscure; to protect; to darken; to mark with gradations of color. **shading**, shād'ing, *n.* Act of making shade; light and shade in a picture.

shadow, shad'ō, *a.* A figure projected by the interception of light; shade; an inseparable companion; an imperfect representation; a spirit; protection.—*vt.* To shade; to cloud; to screen; to represent faintly; to follow closely. **shadowy**, shad'ō-i, *a.* Full of shadow; shady; dark; dim; unsubstantial.

shady, shād'i, *a.* Abounding in shade; affording shade; of dubious morality.

shaft, shaft, *n.* The long part of a spear or arrow; body of a column; spire of a steeple, &c.; pole of a carriage; a line of large axle; a narrow passage, as into a mine.

shag, shag, *n.* Coarse hair or nap; cloth with a coarse nap; tobacco leaves shredded for smoking (Eng.).—(shagging, shagged). To make shaggy. **shaggy**, shag'i, *a.* Covered with shag; rough; rugged.

shah, shä, *n.* A title given by Europeans to the monarch of Persia.

shake, shāk, *vt.* (shaking; pret. shook; pp. shaken). To cause to move with quick vibrations; to agitate; to move from firmness; to cause to waver; to trill.—*vi.* To tremble; to shiver; to quake.—*n.* A wavering or rapid motion;

tremor; shock; a trill in music; a crack in timber.

hakedown, shăk″doun′, *n.* A temporary substitute for a bed formed on the floor.

haker, shāk′ẽr, *n.* A person or thing that shakes; a member of a religious sect.

haky, shāk′ĭ, *a.* Apt to shake or tremble; unsteady; feeble.

hale, shāl, *n.* A fine-grained rock; a clay rock having a slaty structure.

hall, shal, *verb auxiliary*; pret. *should*, shŏd. In the first person it forms part of the future tense; in the second and third persons it implies authority.

hallop, shal′up, *n.* A small light boat.

hallot, sha-lot′, *n.* A species of onion.

hallow, shal′ō, *a.* Not deep; superficial; simple; silly.—*n.* A place where the water is not deep; a shoal.

ham, sham, *n.* That which appears to be what it is not; imposture; humbug. —*a.* False; counterfeit.—*vt* and *i.* (shamming, shammed). To feign, pretend.

hamble, sham′bl, *vi.* (shambling, shambled). To walk awkwardly, as if the knees were weak.—*n.* The gait of one who shambles.

hambles, sham′blz, *n.pl.* A flesh-market; a slaughter-house; a place of butchery.

hambling, sham′bling, *p.a.* Walking with an irregular, clumsy pace.

hame, shām, *n.* A painful sensation excited by guilt, disgrace, &c.; reproach; disgrace.—*vt.* (shaming, shamed). To make ashamed; to disgrace. **shamefaced**, shām″fāst′, *a.* Easily put out of countenance; modest; bashful. **shameful**, shām′ful, *a.* Full of shame; disgraceful; scandalous; infamous. **shameless**, shām′les, *a.* Destitute of shame; immodest; unblushing.

hammy, shamois, sham′i, sha′mwä″, *n.* A soft leather for polishing, prepared originally from the skin of the chamois.

hampoo, sham-pö′, *vt.* (shampooing, shampooed). To press and rub the body after a hot bath; to wash and rub thoroughly the head.

hamrock, sham′rok, *n.* A trefoil plant, the national emblem of Ireland.

hank, shangk, *n.* The leg; the shinbone; the part of a tool connecting the acting part with a handle; the stem of an anchor.

ha'nt, shänt. A colloquial contraction of *shall not.*

hanty, shan′ti, *n.* A hut or mean dwelling; song sung by sailors working together.

hape, shāp, *vt.* (shaping, shaped). To form; to mold; to adjust.—*vi.* To suit. —*n.* Form or figure; make; a model; a dish of blancmange, &c. **shapeless**, shāp′les, *a.* Destitute of any regular form; deformed. **shapely**, shāp′li, *a.* Well-formed; symmetrical; handsome.

hard, shärd, *n.* A fragment of an earthen vessel; the wing-case of a beetle.

hare, shâr, *n.* A part bestowed or contributed; lot or portion; a plow-share.— *vt.* (sharing, shared). To part among

two or more; to participate in.—*vi.* To have part.

shareholder, shär″hōl′dẽr, *n.* One who holds shares in a joint property.

sharer, shär′ẽr, *n.* One who shares.

shark, shärk, *n.* A voracious sea fish; an unscrupulous person; a sharper.

sharp, shärp, *a.* Having a very thin edge or fine point; keen; abrupt; not blurred; shrewd; acid; shrill; fierce; short and rapid; biting; barely honest; in *music*, raised a semitone.—*n.* A note raised a semitone, marked by the sign (♯); the sign itself; *pl.* the hard part of wheat.—*vt.* To sharpen.—*adv.* Sharply; exactly; rapidly. **sharpen**, shär′pen, *vt.* To make sharp or sharper; to whet. —*vi.* To become sharp. **sharpener**, shär′pen-ẽr, *n.* One who or that which sharpens; a tool for sharpening. **sharper**, shär′pẽr, *n.* One who lives by sharp practices; a tricky fellow; a cheat; a sharpener. **sharply**, shärp′li, *adv.* In a sharp manner; severely; keenly; acutely; abruptly. **sharpness**, shärp′nes, *n.* Keenness; pungency; acuteness. **sharpshooter**, shärp″shŏt′ẽr, *n.* A soldier skilled in shooting with exactness.

shatter, shat′ẽr, *vt.* To break into many pieces; to overthrow, destroy.—*vt.* To be broken into fragments.—*n.* A fragment.

shave, shāv, *vt.* (shaving, shaved). To cut off the hair from the skin with a razor; to cut off thin slices from; to skim along; to fleece.—*vi.* To cut off the beard with a razor.—*n.* A cutting off of the beard; a thin slice; an exceedingly narrow escape.

shaveling, shāv′ling, *n.* A man shaved; a monk or friar, in contempt.

shaver, shāv′ẽr, *n.* A barber; one who fleeces; a fellow; a wag.

shavetail, shāv″tāl′, *n. Slang.* A newly commissioned second lieutenant.

shaving, shāv′ing, *n.* Act of one who shaves; a thin slice pared off.

shawl, shal, *n.* An article of dress, used mostly as a loose covering for the shoulders.

she, shē, *pron. nominative.* The feminine pronoun of the third person.

sheaf, shēf, *n.*; pl. **sheaves**, shēvz. A bundle of the stalks of wheat, oats, &c.; any similar bundle.—*vt.* To make into sheaves.—*vi.* To make sheaves.

shear, shēr, *vt.* and *i.* (pret. sheared or shore, pp. sheared or shorn). To cut with shears; to clip the wool from; to cut from a surface; to fleece.

shears, shērz, *n.pl.* An instrument of two blades for cutting.

shearwater, shẽr″wa′tẽr, *n.* A marine bird of the petrel family.

sheath, shēth, *n.* A case for a sword, &c.; a scabbard; wing-case of an insect. **sheathe**, shĒTH, *vt.* (sheathing, sheathed). To put into a sheath; to protect by a casing. **sheathed**, shĒthd, *p.a.* Put in or having a sheath; covered with sheathing. **sheathing**, shĒTH′ing, *n.* Act of one who sheathes; that which sheathes; covering of metal to protect a ship's bottom.

shed, shed, *vt.* (shedding, shed). To cast

or throw off; to emit or diffuse; to let fall in drops; to spill.—*vi.* To let fall seed, a covering, &c.—*n.* A watershed; the opening between the threads in a loom through which the shuttle passes; a penthouse; a hut; a large open structure.

sheen, shēn, *n.* Brightness; splendor.—*a.* Bright; shining; *poetical.*

sheep, shēp, *sing.* and *pl.* A ruminant animal valued for its wool and flesh; a silly or timid fellow. **sheep's eye,** a loving or wistful glance. **sheepfold,** shēp″fōld′, *n.* A fold or pen in which sheep are collected or confined. **sheepish,** shēp′ish, *a.* Like a sheep; foolish; bashful; over-modest or diffident. **sheeprun,** shēp′run′, *n.* A large tract of grazing country for pasturing sheep. **sheepskin,** shēp″skin′, *n.* The skin of a sheep prepared with the wool on; leather prepared from it.

sheer, shēr, *a.* Mere; downright; precipitous.—*vi.* To deviate from the proper course.—*n.* The upward bend of a ship at stem or stern.

sheet, shēt, *n.* A broad, thin piece of anything; broad expanse; piece of linen or cotton spread on a bed; piece of paper; a rope fastened to the lower corner of a sail.—*vt.* To furnish with sheets; to shroud.

sheet anchor, shēt′ang′kėr, *n.* A large anchor used only in danger; last refuge.

sheeting, shēt′ing, *n.* Linen or cotton cloth for making bed-sheets.

sheet iron, shēt′ī′ėrn, *n.* Iron in broad plates.

sheik, shēk, *n.* An Arab chief; a title of dignity among the Arabs.

shekel, shek′el, *n.* An ancient Jewish weight of about half an ounce, and silver coin worth about 60 cents.

shelf, shelf, *n.*; *pl.* **shelves,** shelvz. A board fixed along a wall to support articles; a ledge; a ledge of rocks in the sea. **shelfy,** shelf′i, *a.* Full of rocky shelves.

shell, shel, *n.* A hard outside covering; an outside crust; framework; any slight hollow structure; a projectile containing a bursting charge.—*vt.* To strip off the shell of; to throw bomb-shells into or among.—*vi.* To cast the exterior covering.

shellac, she-lak′, *n.* Lac melted and formed into thin cakes.

shellfish, shel″fish′, *n. sing.* and *pl.* A mollusk or a crustacean whose external covering consists of a shell.

shelly, shel′i, *a.* Abounding with shells; consisting of shells.

shell shock, combat fatigue.

shelter, shel′tėr, *n.* A protection; asylum; refuge; security.—*vt.* To protect; to screen.—*vi.* To take shelter.

shelve, shelv. *vt.* (shelving, shelved). To place on a shelf; to dismiss from use or attention; to furnish with shelves.—*vi.* To slope. **shelving,** shelv′ing, *n.* The operation of fixing up shelves; shelves collectively.

shepherd, shep′ėrd, *n.* One who tends sheep. **shepherdess,** shep′ėrd-es, *n.* A woman who tends sheep; a rural lass.

sherbet, shėr′bet, *n.* An Eastern drink of water, the juice of fruits, and sugar.

sheriff, sher′if, *n.* An officer in each county to whom is entrusted the administration of the law.

sherry, sher′i, *n.* A wine of southern Spain.

sibbleth, shib′ō-leth, *n.* The watch word of a party; a cry or motto.

shield, shēld, *n.* A broad piece of armor carried on the arm; protection; an escutcheon with a coat of arms.—*vt.* To cover, as with a shield; to protect.

shift, shift, *vi.* To change; to change place or direction; to manage; to practice indirect methods.—*vt.* To remove to alter; to dress in fresh clothes.—*n.* A change; expedient; evasion; an under garment; a squad of workmen; the working time of a relay of men; the spell of work. **shiftless,** shift′less, *a.* Destitute of expedients; wanting in energy or effort. **shifty,** shif′ti, *a.* Full of shifts; fertile in expedients or evasions; tricky.

shilling, shil′ing, *n.* An English silver coin equal to twelve pence.

shilly-shally, shil″i-shal′i, *vi.* To hesitate.—*n.* Foolish trifling; irresolution.

shimmer, shim′ėr. *vi.* To emit a faint or tremulous light; to glisten.—*n.* A glistening.

shin, shin, *n.* The fore-part of the leg between the ankle and the knee.

shine, shīn, *vi.* (shining, shone). To give out a steady brilliant light; to be lively, bright, or conspicuous.—*vt.* To cause to shine.—*n.* Brightness; fair weather.

shingle, shing′gl, *n.* A thin piece of wood used in covering roofs; loose gravel and pebbles.—*vt.* To cover with shingles; to hammer so as to expel slag or scoria from in puddling iron.

shingles, shing′glz, *n.* An eruptive disease which spreads around the body.

shingling, shing′gling, *n.* A covering of shingles; a process in reducing iron from the cast to the malleable state.

shining, shīn′ing, *a.* Bright; illustrious. **shiny,** shīn′i, *a.* Bright; brilliant; clear.

ship, ship, *n.* A vessel of some size adapted to navigation; a three-masted square-rigged vessel.—*vt.* (shipping shipped). To put on board of a ship; to transport in a ship; to hire for service in a ship; to fix in its place.—*vi.* To engage for service on a ship; to embark. **shipboard,** ship″bōrd′, *n.* The deck or interior of a ship; used in *on shipboard*. **shipbuilder,** ship″bil′dėr, *n.* One who builds ships; a naval architect; a ship wright.

shipbuilding, ship″bil′ding, *n.* The art of constructing vessels for navigation.

shipmate, ship″māt′, *n.* One who serves in the same ship; a fellow-sailor.

shipment, ship′ment, *n.* Act of putting goods on board of a ship; goods shipped.

shipper, ship′ėr, *n.* One who sends good on board a ship for transportation.

shipping, ship′ing, *n.* Ships in general aggregate tonnage.

shipshape, ship″shāp′, *a.* Having a sea manlike trim; well arranged.

hipwreck, ship″rek′, *n*. The wreck or loss of a ship; destruction; ruin.—*vt*. To wreck; to cast away; to ruin.

hipyard, ship″yärd′, *n*. A yard or place in which ships are constructed.

hire, shīr (but shir in county names). *n*. A county.

hirk, shèrk, *vt*. and *i*. To avoid unfairly; to seek to avoid duty.

hirt, shèrt, *n*. A man's loose under garment of linen, &c.; a lady's blouse.—*vt*. To clothe with a shirt.

hiver, shiv′ėr, *vt*. To shatter.—*vi*. To fall into many small pieces; to tremble, as from cold; to shudder.—*n*. A small fragment; a shaking fit; shudder.

hivery, shiv′ėr-i, *a*. Pertaining to shivering; characterized by shivering.

hoal, shōl, *n*. A multitude; a crowd; a sandbank or bar; a shallow.—*vi*. To become more shallow.—*a*. Shallow.

hoaly, shōl′i, *a*. Full of shoals.

hock, shok, *n*. A violent striking against; violent onset; a sudden disturbing emotion; a stook; a thick mass of hair.—*vt*. To give a shock to; to encounter violently; to disgust; to make hok′ing, *a*. Serving to shock; dreadful; disgusting; offensive.

hock troops. Troops who lead the attack.

hod, shod, pret. and pp. of *shoe*.

hoddy, shod′i, *n*. Fiber obtained from old woolen fabrics mixed with fresh wool and manufactured anew; inferior cloth made from this.—*a*. Made of shoddy; rashy.

hoe, shö, *n*. A covering for the foot; a plate of iron nailed to the hoof of a horse, &c.—*vt*. (shoeing, shoed). To furnish with shoes.

hoeblack, shö″blak′, *n*. A person that cleans shoes.

hoehorn, shoeing-horn, shö″hörn′, shö″ing-hörn′, *n*. A curved implement used to aid in putting on shoes.

hoemaker, shö″māk′ėr, *n*. One who makes shoes.

hone, shōn, pret. and pp. of *shine*.

hook, shuk, pret. and pp. of *shake*.— *n*. The staves for a single barrel made into a package.

hoot, shöt, *vt*. (shooting, shot). To cause to fly forth; to discharge; to hit or kill with a missile; to empty out suddenly; to thrust forward; to pass rapidly under, over, &c.—*vi*. To charge a missile; to dart along; to sprout; to project.—*n*. A shooting; a young branch; a sloping trough; a race for shooting rubbish. **shooting**, shöt′ing, *n*. Sport of killing game with firearms; tract over which game is shot; sensation of a darting pain.—*a*. Pertaining to one who shoots.

hop, shop, *n*. A place where goods are sold by retail (Eng.); a building in which mechanics work; one's special business.—*vi*. (shopping, shopped). To visit shops for purchasing goods.

hopkeeper, shop″kēp′ėr, *n*. One who keeps a store; one who sells goods by retail (Eng.).

shoplifter, shop″lif′tèr, *n*. One who steals in a store on pretense of buying.

shore, shōr, *n*. Land along the edge of the sea; the coast; a prop.—*vt*. To support by props; pret. of *shear*.

shorn, shörn, pp. of *shear*.

short, shört, *a*. Not long or tall; scanty; deficient; concise; snappish; severe; brittle.—*adv*. Abruptly; insufficiently.—*n*. Something short; *pl*. knee-breeches. **in short**, in few words; briefly.

shortage, shōr′tij, *n*. Amount short or deficient; deficit.

shortcoming, shört″kum′ing, *n*. A failing of the usual quantity; a delinquency.

shorten, shört′n, *vt*. To make short or shorter; to deprive.—*vi*. To contract.

shorthand, shört″hand′, *n*. A shorter mode of writing than is usually employed.

shorthanded, shört′han′ded, *a*. Not having the usual number of assistants.

Shorthorn, shört″hörn′, *n*. One of a breed of cattle with very short horns.

short-lived, shört′livd′, *a*. Not living or lasting long; of short continuance.

shortly, shört′li, *adv*. Quickly; soon; briefly.

shortsighted, shört′sīt′ed, *a*. Unable to see far; myopic; wanting foresight.

short-winded, shört′win′ded, *a*. Affected with shortness of breath.

shot, shot, *n*. Act of shooting; a projectile; a bullet; bullets collectively; range or reach; a marksman; the number of fish caught in one haul; a reckoning.— *vt*. (shotting, shotted). To load with shot.

should, shud, the pret. of *shall*, denoting present or past duty or obligation, or expressing a hypothetical case.

shoulder, shōl′dèr, *n*. The joint by which the arm or the fore-leg is connected with the body; a projection; support.—*vt*. To push with the shoulder; to put upon the shoulder.—*vi*. To push forward.

shoulderblade, shōl′dèr-blād′, *n*. The bone of the shoulder; scapula.

shoulderstrap, shōl′dèr-strap′, *n*. A strap worn on the shoulder, either to support dress, or as a badge of distinction.

shout, shout, *vi*. To utter a loud and sudden cry.—*vt*. To utter with a shout. —*n*. A loud sudden cry.

shove, shuv, *vt*. and *i*. (shoving, shoved). To push forward; to press against; to jostle.—*n*. Act of shoving; a push.

shovel, shuv′l, *n*. An instrument with a broad shallow blade, for lifting earth, &c.—*vt*. (shoveling, shoveled). To throw with a shovel. **shovelful**, shuv″l-ful, *n*. As much as a shovel will hold.

show, shō, *vt*. (pret. showed, pp. shown or showed). To display to the view of others; to let be seen; to make known; to prove; to bestow, afford.—*vi*. To appear.—*n*. Act of showing; exhibition; appearance; pretense; pageant; things exhibited for money.

shower, shou′ėr, *n*. A fall of rain, &c.; a copious supply.—*vt*. To water with a shower; to bestow liberally.—*vi*. To rain in showers.—*n.* A party given for a prospective bride.

showily, shō'i-li, *adv.* In a showy manner.

showman, shō'man, *n.* One who exhibits a show; the owner of a traveling show.

showroom, shō'rōm', *n.* A room in which a show is exhibited; an apartment where goods are displayed.

showy, shō'i, *a.* Making a great show; ostentatious; gorgeous; gaudy.

shrapnel, shrap'nel, *n.* A shell filled with bullets, timed to burst at any given point.

shred, shred, *vt.* (shredding, shred or shredded). To tear into small pieces.—*n.* A long, narrow piece cut off; a tatter.

shrew, shrō, *n.* A peevish, ill-tempered woman; a scold; a shrew-mouse.

shrewish, shrō'ish, *a.* Having the qualities of a shrew; peevish; vixenish.

shrewd, shrōd, *a.* Astute; sagacious; discerning; sharp. **shrewdly,** shrōd'li, *adv.* Astutely.

shrewmouse, shrō"mous', *n.* A small insectivorous animal resembling a mouse.

shriek, shrēk, *vi.* To cry out shrilly; to scream.—*n.* A shrill cry; a scream.

shrift, shrift, *n.* The act of shriving or being shriven; confession to a priest; absolution.

shrike, shrīk, *n.* An insessorial bird which feeds on insects, small birds, &c.; a butcherbird.

shrill, shril, *a.* Sharp or piercing in sound; uttering an acute sound.—*vi.* and *t.* To utter an acute piercing sound. **shrilly,** shril'li, *adv.* In a shrill manner; acutely.—*a.* shril'li. Somewhat shrill.

shrimp, shrimp, *n.* A small crustacean allied to the lobster; a mannikin.

shrine, shrīn, *n.* A case, as for sacred relics; a tomb; altar; a place hallowed from its associations.—*vt.* (shrining, shrined). To enshrine.

shrink, shringk, *vi.* (pret. shrank or shrunk, pp. shrunk or shrunken). To contract spontaneously; to shrivel; to withdraw, as from danger; to flinch.—*vt.* To cause to contract.—*n.* Contraction. **shrinkage,** shringk'ij, *n.* A shrinking; diminution in bulk or quantity; reduction.

shrive, shrīv, *vt.* (shriving, pret. shrove or shrived, pp. shriven or shrived). To hear the confession of; to confess and absolve.

shrivel, shriv''l, *vi.* and *t.* (shriveling, shriveled). To shrink into wrinkles; to shrink and form corrugations.

shroud, shroud, *n.* That which clothes or covers; a winding-sheet; one of the large ropes in a ship supporting the mast. —*vt.* To cover; to dress for the grave; to screen.

Shrove Tuesday, shrōv'tūz'di, *n.* The Tuesday before the first day of Lent.

shrub, shrub, *n.* A woody plant less than a tree; a plant with several woody stems from the same root; a beverage containing the juice of fruit, &c. **shrubbery,** shrub'ẽr-i, *n.* An ornamental plantation of shrubs; shrubs collectively. **shrubby,** shrub'i, *a.* Full of shrubs; resembling a shrub; consisting of brushwood.

shrug, shrug, *vt.* and *i.* (shrugging, shrugged). To draw up or to contract, the shoulders.—*n.* A drawing up of the shoulders.

shrunken, shrungk'en, *p.a.* Having shrunk; shriveled; contracted.

shuck, shuk, *n.* A shell or husk.

shudder, shud'ẽr, *vi.* To tremble with fear, horror, &c.; to quake.—*n.* A tremor.

shuffle, shuf'l, *vt.* (shuffling, shuffled). To shove one way and the other; to confuse; to change the position of cards.—*vi.* To change position; to quibble; to move with a dragging gait; to scrape the floor in dancing.—*n.* An evasion; mixing of cards; scraping movement in dancing. **shuffler,** shuf'lẽr, *n.* One who shuffles; one who prevaricates; one who plays tricks. **shuffling,** shuf'ling, *a.* Moving with irregular gait; evasive; prevaricating.

shun, shun, *vt.* (shunning, shunned). To avoid; to refrain from; to neglect.

shunt, shunt, *vi.* and *t.* In railways, to turn from one line of rails into another; to free one's self of.

shut, shut, *vt.* (shutting, shut). To close or stop up; to bar; to preclude; to exclude; to confine.—*vi.* To close itself; to be closed.—*a.* Made close; closed; not resonant.

shutter, shut'ẽr, *n.* One who shuts; movable covering for a window or aperture.

shuttle, shut'l, *n.* An instrument used by weavers for shooting the thread of the woof between the threads of the warp.

shuttlecock, shut"l-kok', *n.* A cork stuck with feathers, and struck by a battledore.—*vt.* To throw backwards and forwards.

shy, shī, *a.* Timid; retiring; reserved; coy; cautious; wary.—*vi.* (shying, shied). To start suddenly aside, as a horse.—*vt.* To throw.—*n.* The starting suddenly aside of a horse. **shyness,** shī'nes, *n.* Quality or state of being shy; reserve; coyness.

Siamese, sī'a-mēz', *n.sing.* and *pl.* A native of Siam; the language of Siam.

sibilant, sib'i-lant, *a.* Hissing.—*n.* letter uttered with a hissing, as *s* and *z*.

sibyl, sib'il, *n.* A prophetess; sorceress.

sic, sik, *adv.* Thus; it is so; often used within brackets in quoting, to note that a peculiarity in the quotation is literally exact.

sick, sik, *a.* Affected with disease of any kind; ill; inclined to vomit; disgusted or weary; pertaining to those who are sick. **sickbay,** sik'bā', *n.* A place in a ship partitioned off for invalids. **sicken,** sik'en, *vt.* To make sick; to disgust.—*vi.* To become sick; to be disgusted; to languish. **sickening,** sik'en-ing, *a.* Making sick; disgusting. **sickish,** sik'ish, *a.* Somewhat sick. **sickly,** sik'li, *a.* Affected with sickness; not healthy; ailing; languid; faint.—*adv.* In a sick manner or condition. **sickness**, sik'nes, *n*. Disease; ill-health; illness; nausea.

sickle, sik'l, *n*. An instrument for cutting grain, used with one hand; a reaping-hook.

side, sīd, *n*. The broad or long surface of a body; edge, border; right or left half of the body; part between the top and bottom; any party or interest opposed to another.—*a*. Being on, from, or toward the side; indirect.—*vi*. (siding, sided). To embrace the opinions of one party.

side arms, sīd'ärmz', *n.pl*. Arms carried by the side, as sword, bayonet, &c.

sideboard, sīd'bōrd', *n*. A piece of furniture used to hold dining utensils, &c.

sided, sīd'ed, *p.a*. Having a side or sides; used in composition.

side light, sīd'līt', *n*. A light at a side; information thrown indirectly on a subject.

sidelong, sīd'lang', *adv*. Laterally; obliquely.—*a*. Lateral; oblique.

sidereal, sī-dēr'ē-al, *a*. Pertaining to stars; measured by the motion of the stars.

sidesaddle, sīd'sad'l, *n*. A saddle for a woman.

sidewalk, sīd'wak', *n*. A raised walk for foot-passengers by the side of a street or road.

sideways, sīd'wāz', *adv. See* **sidewise.**

siding, sīd'ing, *n*. A short additional line of rails laid for the purpose of shunting.

sidle, sī'dl, *vi*. (sidling, sidled). To go or move side foremost; to move to one side.

siege, sēj, *n*. A regular attack of a fortified place; continued endeavor to gain possession.

sienna, sē-en'a, *n*. An earth of a fine yellow color, used as a pigment.

siesta, sē-es'ta, *n*. A sleep or rest in the hottest part of the day.

sieve, siv, *n*. A utensil for separating the smaller particles of a loose substance.

sift, sift, *vt*. To separate by a sieve; to examine minutely.—*vi*. To pass as if through a sieve. **sifter,** sift'ér, *n*. One who sifts; a sieve.

sigh, sī, *vi*. To make a long breath audibly, as from grief; to make a melancholy sound.—*n*. A long breath made audibly, as in grief.

sight, sīt, *n*. Act or power of seeing; view; vision; visibility; estimation; a show; an appliance for guiding the eye. —*vt*. To see; to descry; to give the proper elevation and direction to, as a cannon. **sighted**, sīt'ed, *a*. Having sight; seeing in a particular manner; having sights, as a rifle. **sightless**, sīt'les, *a*. Wanting sight; blind. **sightly**, sīt'li, *a*. Pleasing to the sight or eye; agreeable to look on. **sight-seeing,** sīt'sē'ing, *n*. The act of seeing sights or visiting scenes of interest. **sight-seer**, sīt'sē'ér, *n*. One who goes to see sights or curiosities.

sign, sīn, *n*. A mark or stamp indicative of something; a token; indication; emblem; a symbol or character.—*vt*. To

express by a sign; to affix a signature to. —*vi*. To make a sign or signal.

signal, sig'nal, *n*. A sign to communicate intelligence, orders, &c., at a distance.— *a*. Worthy of note; remarkable.—*vt*. or *i*. (signaling, signaled). To communicate by signals. **signalize**, sig'nal-īz, *vt*. To make remarkable; to distinguish by some fact or exploit. **signally**, sig'nal-i, *adv*. In a signal manner; eminently; remarkably; memorably.

signature, sig'na-tūr, *n*. A mark impressed; the name of a person written by himself; in *printing*, a distinctive letter or mark at the bottom of the first page of each sheet. **signatory, signatary,** sig'na-tō-ri, sig'na-ter-i, *a*. Relating to the signing of documents.—*n*. One who signs; a state representative who signs a public document.

signboard, sīn'bōrd', *n*. A board on which one sets a notice of his occupation or of articles for sale.

signer, sīn'ér, *n*. One who signs.

signet, sig'net, *n*. A seal; seal used by the sovereign in sealing private letters. **signet ring**, sig'net ring, *n*. A ring containing a signet or private seal.

signify, sig'ni-fī, *vt*. (signifying, signified). To make known either by signs or words; to betoken; to mean; to imply; to import. **significance, significancy,** sig-nif'i-kans, sig-nif'i-kan-si, *n*. Meaning; import. **significant**, sig-nif'i-kant, *a*. Signifying something; indicative; important. **signification**, sig'ni-fi-kā''shun, *n*. Act of signifying; meaning; import; sense.

signor, signior, sē'nyōr; sēn'yōr, *n*. An English form of Italian *Signore*, Spanish *Senor*, equivalent to *Sir* or *Mr*.; a gentleman.

signora, sē-nyō'rä, *n. Madam* or *Mrs.*; a lady.

signorina, sē'nyō-rē''nä, *n. Miss;* a young lady.

signpost, sīn''pōst', *n*. A post on which a sign hangs; a finger-post.

silent, sī'lent, *a*. Not speaking; mute; dumb; taciturn; making no noise.

silence, sī'lens, *n*. State of being silent; quiet; secrecy; absence of mention.—*vt*. To put to silence; to quiet; to cause to cease firing.

silhouette, sil'u-et'', *n*. A profile portrait filled in with a dark color.

silica, silex, sil'i-ka, sī'leks, *n*. Oxide of silicon, the chief constituent of quartz, flint, &c. **silicate**, sil'i-kāt, *n*. A compound of silica with certain bases. **siliceous, silicious**, si-lish'us, *a*. Pertaining to, containing, or like silica. **silicon, silicium**, sil'i-kon, si-lish'i-um, *n*. The non-metallic element of which silica is the oxide.

silk, silk, *n*. The fine thread produced by various caterpillars, particularly the silkworm; cloth made of silk; garment made of this cloth.—*a*. Pertaining to silk; silken. **silken**, sil'ken, *a*. Made of silk; silky. **silkworm**, silk'wèrm', *n*. A worm which produces silk; the larva of various moths which spin a silken cocoon for the chrysalis. **silky**, sil'ki, *a*.

Made of silk; like silk; soft and smooth to the touch.

sill, sil, *n*. The timber or stone at the foot of a door or window; the threshold; the floor of a gallery in a mine.

silly, sil'i, *a*. Weak in intellect; foolish; unwise.

silo, sī'lō, *n*. The pit in which green fodder is preserved in the method of ensilage.

silt, silt, *n*. A deposit of fine earth from running or standing water.—*vt*. To fill with silt.

silver, sil'vėr, *n*. A precious metal of a white color; money; plate made of silver. —*a*. Made of silver; silvery.—*vt*. and *i*. To cover with a coat of silver; to tinge with gray. **silversmith**, sil'vėr-smith', *n*. One whose occupation is to work in silver. **silver-tongued**, sil'vėr-tungd', *a*. Having a smooth tongue or speech. **silvery**, sil'vėr-i, *a*. Like silver; covered with silver; clear as the sound of a silver bell.

simian, simious, sim'i-an, sim'i-us, *a*. Pertaining to apes or monkeys; ape-like.

similar, sim'i-lėr, *a*. Like; resembling; having like parts and relations but not of the same magnitude. **similarity**, sim'i-lar″i-ti, *n*. State of being similar; likeness; resemblance.

simile, sim'i-lē, *n*. A figure of speech consisting in likening one thing to another.

similitude, si-mil'i-tūd, *n*. Likeness; resemblance; comparison.

simmer, sim'ėr, *vi*. To boil gently.

simper, sim'pėr, *vi*. To smile in a silly manner.—*n*. A silly or affected smile.

simple, sim'pl, *a*. Not complex; single; not involved; clear; artless; mere; plain; sincere; silly.—*n*. Something not mixed; a medicinal herb. **simpleton**, sim'pl-tun. *n*. A simple or silly person; one easily deceived. **simplicity**, sim-plis'i-ti, *n*. State or quality of being simple; singleness; artlessness; sincerity; plainness; foolishness. **simplify**, sim'pli-fī, *vt*. To make simple; to make plain or easy. **simply**, sim'pli, *adv*. In a simple manner; artlessly; plainly; merely; foolishly.

simulate, sim'ū-lāt, *vt*. To counterfeit; to feign. **simulation**, sim'ū-lā″shun, *n*. Act of simulating; pretense.

simultaneous, sī-mul-tā'nē-us, *a*. Taking place or done at the same time.

sin, sin, *n*. A transgression of the divine law; moral depravity; an offense in general.—*vi*. (sinning, sinned). To violate the divine law or any rule of duty.

since, sins, *adv*. From that time; from then till now; ago.—*prep*. Ever from the time of; after.—*conj*. From the time when; because that.

sincere, sin'sēr', *a*. Pure; unmixed; real; genuine; guileless; frank; true. **sincerity**, sin-ser'i-ti, *n*. Honesty of mind or intention; freedom from hypocrisy.

sinecure, sī'nē-kūr, *n*. An ecclesiastical benefice without cure of souls; a paid office without employment.

sinew, sin'ū, *n*. The fibrous cord which unites a muscle to a bone; a tendon;

strength.—*vt*. To bind, as by sinews; to strengthen. **sinewy**, sin'ū-i, *a*. Consisting of a sinew or sinews; brawny; vigorous; firm.

sinful, sin'ful, *a*. Full of sin; wicked; iniquitous; wrong.

sing, sing, *vi*. (pret. sang, sung, pp. sung). To utter sounds with melodious modulations of voice; to have a ringing sensation.—*vt*. To utter with musical modulations of voice; to celebrate in song; to tell.

singe, sinj, *vt*. (singeing, singed). To burn slightly; to burn the surface of.—*n*. A burning of the surface.

singer, sing'ėr, *n*. One who sings; a bird that sings.

Singhalese, sing'ga-lēz, *a*. Pertaining to Ceylon.

single, sing'gl, *a*. Being one or a unit; individual; unmarried; performed by one person; simple; sincere.—*vt*. (singling, singled). To select individually with *out*. **singlehanded**, sing'gl hand'ed, *a*. Unassisted; by one's own efforts. **single-minded**, sing'gl-mīn'ded, *a*. Free from guile; honest; straightforward. **singly**, sing'gli, *adv*. In a single manner; individually; separately; sincerely.

singsong, sing'sang', *n*. A drawling tone; repetition of similar words or tones.

singular, sing'gū-lėr, *a*. That is single, expressing one person or thing; remarkable; rare; odd.—*n*. The singular number. **singularity**, sing'gū-lar″i-ti, *n*. Peculiarity; eccentricity.

sinister, sin'is-tėr, *a*. Left; evil; baneful; malign; unlucky.

sink, singk, *vi*. (pret. sank, or sunk, pp. sunk). To descend in a liquid; to subside; to enter; to decline in worth, strength, &c.—*vt*. To immerse; to submerge; to make by digging; to depress; to degrade.—*n*. A receptacle for liquid filth; a sewer; place where iniquity is gathered. **sinker**, singk'ėr, *n*. One who sinks; a weight on some body to sink it. **sinking**, singk'ing, *a*. Causing to sink; depressing; set apart for the reduction of a debt.

sinner, sin'ėr, *n*. One who sins; a transgressor; offender; criminal.

sinuous, sin'ū-us, *a*. Bending or curving in and out; crooked. **sinuosity**, sin'ū-os″i-ti, *n*. Quality of being sinuous; a curving; a wavy line.

sinus, sī'nus, *n*. A curved opening; a bay; a cavity containing pus; a fistula.

sip, sip, *vt*. (sipping, sipped). To drink in small quantities; to drink out of.—*vi*. To take a fluid with the lips.—*n*. A small quantity of liquid taken with the lips.

siphon, sī'fon, *n*. A bent tube used for drawing off liquids, as from a cask, &c.

sir, sėr, *n*. A word of respect used to men; title distinctive of knights and baronets.

sire, sīr, *n*. A respectful word of address to a king; a father; male parent of a horse, &c.

siren, sī'ren, *n*. A sea-nymph who enticed seamen by songs, and then slew them; a woman dangerous from her fascinations; a fog-signal.—*a.* Bewitching.

Sirius, sir′i-us, *n.* The Dog-star.

sirloin, sêr′loin, *n.* The upper part of a loin of beef; a loin of beef.

sirocco, si-rok′ō, *n.* An oppressive south or south-east wind in Italy.

sissy, sis′i, *n.* A shy, retiring, effeminate boy or man.

sister, sis′tėr, *n.* A female born of the same parents; a female of the same kind, society, &c. **sisterhood**, sis′tėr-hŭd, *n.* State or condition of a sister; a society of females.

sister-in-law, sis″tėr-in-lg′, *n.* A husband or wife's sister. **sisterly**, sis′tėr-li, *a.* Becoming a sister; affectionate.

sit, sit, *vi.* (sitting, sat). To rest on the lower extremity of the body; to incubate; to remain; to be placed; to suit; to have a seat in Parliament, &c.; to hold a session.—*vt.* To keep the seat upon (a horse, &c.).

site, sit, *n.* Situation; a plot of ground for building on.

sitter, sit′ėr, *n.* One who sits; one who sits for his portrait; a bird that incubates.

sitting, sit′ing, *n.* Act of one who sits; occasion on which one sits for a portrait; a session; seat in a church pew.

situate, sit′ū-āt, *a.* Placed with respect to any other object. **situated**, sit″ū-āt′ed, *a.* Having a site or position; situate; circumstanced. **situation**, sit″ū-ā″shun, *n.* Position; station; plight; post or engagement.

six, siks, *a.* and *n.* One more than five. **sixfold**, siks′fōld′, *a.* and *adv.* Six times. **sixpence**, siks′pens, *n.* An English silver coin worth twelve cents; value of twelve cents. **sixpenny**, siks″pen′i, *a.* Worth sixpence. **sixteen**, siks′tēn′, *a.* and *n.* Six and ten. **sixteenmo**, siks′tēn″mō, *n.* Sexto-decimo. **sixteenth**, siks′tēnth′, *a.* The sixth after the tenth.—*n.* One of sixteen equal parts. **sixth**, siksth, *a.* Next after the fifth.—*n.* One part in six. **sixthly**, siksth′li, *adv.* In the sixth place. **sixtieth**, siks′ti-eth, *a.* and *n.* The next after fifty-ninth; one of sixty equal parts. **sixty**, siks′ti, *a.* and *n.* Six times ten.

sizable, **sizeable**, sīz′a-bl, *a.* Of considerable bulk; of reasonable size.

size, sīz, *n.* Comparative magnitude; bigness; bulk; a glutinous substance used by painters, &c.—*vt.* (sizing, sized). To arrange according to size; to take the size of; to cover with size. **sized**, sīzd, *a.* Having a particular size. **sizer**, sīz′ėr, *n.* One who or that which sizes; a kind of gauge. **sizing**, sīz′ing, *n.* Size or weak glue; act of covering with size.

sizzle, siz′l, *vi.* To burn with a hissing sound.—*n.* A hissing noise.

skate, skāt, *n.* A narrow steel bar fastened under the foot, for moving rapidly on ice; a flat fish.—*vi.* (skating, skated). To slide on skates.

skating rink, skāt′ing ringk, *n.* A rink or prepared area for skating.

skein, skān, *a.* A small hank of thread.

skeleton, skel′e-tun, *n.* The bony framework of an animal; general structure or frame; outline.—*a.* Resembling a skeleton. **skeleton key**, a thin light key that opens various locks.

skeptic. *See* **sceptic**.

sketch, skech, *n.* An outline or general delineation; a first rough draft.—*vt.* To draw a sketch of; to give the chief points of; to plan.—*vi.* To practice sketching. **sketchy**, skech′i, *a.* Having the nature of a sketch; unfinished; incomplete.

skew, skū, *a.* Oblique.—*adv.* Awry; obliquely.—*vt.* To put askew.

skewer, skū′ėr, *n.* A pin for fastening meat.—*vt.* To fasten with skewers.

ski, skē, *n.* One of two wooden runners attached to the feet for gliding over snow or water.—*vi.* (skiing, skied). To glide over snow or water with skis.

skid, skid, *n.* A drag for the wheels of a vehicle.—*vt.* (skidding, skidded). To check with a skid.—*vi.* To slip sideways on mud, ice, &c., as a cycle.

skiff, skif, *n.* A small light boat.

skill, skil, *n.* Ability; knowledge united with dexterity; aptitude. **skilled**, skild, *a.* Having skill; expert. **skilful**, **skilful**, skil′fụl, *a.* Skilled; dexterous; expert; clever.

skillet, skil′et, *n.* A small vessel of metal, with a long handle, for heating water, &c.

skim, skim, *vt.* (skimming, skimmed). To remove the scum from; to take off from a surface; to pass lightly over; to glance over superficially.—*vi.* To glide along. **skimmer**, skim′ėr, *n.* A utensil for skimming liquors; an aquatic swimming bird. **skim milk**, skim milk, *n.* Milk from which the cream has been taken. **skimming**, skim′ing, *n.* Act of one who skims a liquid; scum removed.

skin, skin, *n.* The natural outer coating of animals; a hide; bark; rind.—*vt.* (skinning, skinned). To strip the skin from; to cover superficially.—*vi.* To be covered with skin.

skin-deep, skin′dēp′, *a.* Superficial; slight.

skin diving. Underwater swimming or diving with portable, compressed-air equipment.

skinflint, skin″flint′, *n.* A niggard.

skinner, skin′ėr, *n.* One who skins; one who deals in skins, pelts, or hides; a furrier.

skinny, skin′i, *a.* Consisting of skin or nearly so; wanting flesh.

skip, skip, *vi.* (skipping, skipped). To leap lightly; to bound; to spring.—*vt.* To pass with a bound; to omit.—*n.* A light leap; a large basket on wheels, used in mines.

skipper, skip′ėr, *n.* The master of a merchant vessel; a sea-captain.

skipping rope, skip′ing rōp′, *n.* A small rope swung by young persons under their feet and over their heads in play.

skirmish, skėr′mish, *n.* A slight battle; a brief contest.—*vi.* To fight in short contests or in small parties.

skirt, skėrt, *n.* The lower and loose part of a garment; border; a woman's garment like a petticoat.—*vt.* To border.—*vi.* To be on the border.

skit, skit, *n.* A satirical or sarcastic attack.

skittish, skit'ish, *a.* Timorous; wanton; frisky; hasty; fickle.

skulk, skulk, *vi.* To lurk; to sneak out of the way; to shun doing one's duty.

skulk, skulker, skulk, skulk'ėr, *n.* A person who skulks or avoids duties.

skull, skul, *n.* The bony case which contains the brain.

skullcap, skul''kap', *n.* A cap fitting closely to the head.

skunk, skungk, *n.* An animal of the weasel family, with glands that emit a fetid fluid.

sky, skī, *n.* The apparent arch of the heavens; the region of clouds; climate.

skylark, skī''lärk' *n.* The common lark that mounts and sings as it flies. **skylarking,** skī''lärk'ing, *n.* Gambols in the rigging of a ship; frolicking of any kind.

skylight, skī''līt', *n.* A window in the roof of a building.

skyward, skī'wėrd, *a.* and *adv.* Toward the sky.

slab, slab, *n.* A thin flat piece of anything, as marble.—*a.* Thick and slimy.

slabber, slab'ėr, *vi.* To slaver; to drivel. —*vt.* To sup up hastily; to besmear.—*n.* Slaver.

slabby, slab'i, *a.* Viscous; slimy.

slack, slak, *a.* Not tight or tense; loose; remiss; backward; not busy.—*adv.* In a slack manner; partially; insufficiently. —*n.* The part of a rope that hangs loose; small broken coal.—*vt.* and *i.* To slacken; to slake. **slacken,** slak'n, *vi.* To become slack; to abate; to flag.—*vt.* To lessen the tension of; to relax. **slacker,** slak'ėr, *n.* One who avoids or neglects a duty or responsibility; especially to his country in time of war.

slacks, slaks, *n.pl.* Trousers, generally for informal wear.

slag, slag, *n.* The scoria from a smelting furnace or volcano; fused dross of metal. **slaggy,** slag'i, *a.* Pertaining to or like slag.

slake, slāk, *vt.* (slaking, slaked). To quench, as thirst or rage; to extinguish. —*vi.* To abate; to become extinct.—*n.* A muddy tract adjoining the sea.

slam, slam, *vt.* and *i.* (slamming, slammed). To shut with violence; to bang.—*n.* A violent shutting of a door; grand slam; winning thirteen tricks in the card game of bridge.

slander, slan'dėr, *n.* A false report maliciously uttered; defamation.—*vt.* To defame; to calumniate. **slanderer,** slan'dėr-ėr, *n.* One who slanders; a defamer; a calumniator. **slanderous,** slan'dėr-us, *a.* Containing slander; that utters slander; defamatory.

slang, slang, *n.* and *a.* A class of expressions not generally approved of, as being inelegant or undignified.—*vt.* To address with slang; to abuse vulgarly. **slangey, slangy,** slang'i, *a.* Of the nature of slang; addicted to the use of slang.

slant, slant, *a.* Sloping.—*vt.* and *i.* To turn from a direct line; to slope; to incline.—*n.* A slope. **slantly, slantwise,** slant'li, slant'wīz', *adv.* So as to slant; obliquely.

slap, slap, *n.* A blow with the open hand, or something broad.—*vt.* (slapping, slapped). To strike with the open hand.—*adv.* With a sudden and violent blow.

slapdash, slap''dash', *adv.* All at once; offhand; at random.

slash, slash, *vt.* To cut by striking violently and at random.—*vi.* To strike violently and at random with a cutting instrument.—*n.* A long cut; a cut made at random. **slashed,** slasht, *p.a.* Cut with a slash; having long narrow openings, as a sleeve.

slat, slat, *n.* A narrow strip of wood.

slate, slāt, *n.* Rock which splits into thin layers; a slab or smooth stone for covering buildings; a tablet for writing upon; a roster of candidates of a political party.—*vt.* (slating, slated). To cover with slates.

slate pencil, slāt' pen'sil, *n.* A pencil of soft slate, used for writing on slates.

slating, slāt'ing, *n.* Act of covering with slates; the cover thus put on; severe criticism.

slattern, slat'ėrn, *n.* A female who is not tidy; a slut.—*a.* Slatternly.

slaughter, slạ'tėr, *n.* A slaying; carnage; massacre; a killing of beasts for market. **slaughterhouse,** slạ'tėr-hous', *n.* A house where beasts are killed for the market.

Slav, Slavonian, släv, sla-vō'ni-an, *n.* One of a race of Eastern Europe, comprising the Russians, Poles, Bohemians, Bulgarians, &c.

slave, slāv, *n.* A person wholly subject to another; a bondman; drudge.—*vi.* (slaving, slaved). To labor as a slave. **slave driver,** slāv' driv'ėr, *n.* An overseer of slaves; a severe or cruel master. **slaver,** slāv'ėr, *n.* A person or vessel engaged in the slave-trade. **slavery,** slāv'ėr-i, *n.* State of a slave; bondage; servitude; drudgery. **slave trade,** slāv' trād', *n.* The business of purchasing or kidnaping men and women, and selling them for slaves. **slavish,** slāv'ish, *a.* Pertaining to slaves; servile; mean; oppressively laborious. **slavishly,** slāv'ish-li, *adv.* In a slavish manner; servilely; meanly.

slaver, slav'ėr, *n.* Saliva driveling from the mouth; drivel.—*vi.* To suffer the saliva to issue from the mouth.—*vt.* To smear with saliva.

Slavic, Slavonic, Slavonian, släv'ik, sla-von'ik, sla-vō'ni-an, *a.* Pertaining to the Slavs, or to their language.

slay, slā, *vt.* (pret. slew, pp. slain). To kill by violence; to murder; to destroy. **slayer,** slā'ėr, *n.* One who slays; murderer.

sleazy, slāzi, *a.* Thin; flimsy; wanting firmness of texture, as silk. Also *sleesy.*

sled, sled, *n.* A sledge.—*vt.* (sledding, sledded). To convey on a sled.

sledge, sledge hammer, slej, slej' ham'ėr, *n.* A large, heavy hammer.

sledge, slej, *n.* A vehicle on runners used over snow or ice; a sledge.—*vt.* and *i.* To convey or travel in a sledge.

sleek, slēk, *a.* Smooth and glossy.—*vt.* To make smooth and glossy.

sleep, slēp, *vi.* (sleeping, slept). To take

rest by a suspension of voluntary exercise of the powers of body and mind; to be dormant or inactive.—*vt.* To pass in sleeping; to get rid of by sleeping; with *off.*—*n.* That state in which volition is suspended; slumber; death; dormant state. **sleeper,** slēp'ér, *n.* One that sleeps; a timber supporting a weight; in railways, a beam of wood supporting the rails. **sleeping,** slēp'ing, *a.* Reposing in sleep; pertaining to sleep; causing sleep. **sleeping sickness,** slēp'ing sik'nes, *n.* A fatal African disease whose first symptom is prolonged sleeping. **sleeplessness,** slēp'les-nes, *n.* State of being sleepless; persistent inability to sleep. **sleepy,** slēp'i, *a.* Inclined to sleep; drowsy; lazy; sluggish.

sleet, slēt, *n.* Hail or snow mingled with rain.—*vi.* To snow or hail with rain. **sleeve,** slēv, *n.* That part of a garment covering the arm.—*vt.* (sleeving, sleeved). To furnish with sleeves. **sleeveless,** slēv'les, *a.* Having no sleeves; wanting a pretext; bootless.

sleigh, slā, *n.* A vehicle on runners for transporting persons on snow or ice.

sleight, slīt, *n.* A sly artifice; an artful trick; dexterity.

slender, slen'dér, *a.* Thin; slim; slight; feeble; meager; scanty.

sleuth, slōth, *n.* A detective.

slew, slō, *vt.* To slue. Pret. of *slay.*

slice, slīs, *vt.* (slicing, sliced). To cut into thin pieces; to divide.—*n.* A thin, broad piece cut off.

slide, slīd, *vi.* (sliding, pret. slid, pp. slid, slidden). To move along a surface by slipping; to pass smoothly or gradually.—*vt.* To thrust smoothly along a surface.—*n.* A smooth and easy passage; that part of an apparatus which slides into place. **slider,** slīd'ér, *n.* One who slides; part of an instrument that slides. **sliding,** slīd'ing, *a.* Made so as to slide freely; fitted for sliding.—*n.* The act of one who slides; lapse; backsliding. **sliding scale,** slīd'ing skāl', *n.* A sliding-rule; a varying rate of payment.

slight, slīt, *a.* Small; trifling; not thorough; slender; frail.—*n.* Intentional disregard.—*vt.* To disregard; to treat with disrespect. **slightly,** slīt'li, *adv.* In a slight manner or measure; but little; somewhat; slenderly.

slim, slim, *a.* Slight; slender; thin; flimsy; cunning.

slime, slīm, *n.* A soft or glutinous substance; moist earth or mud; viscous substance exuded by certain animals.—*vt.* (sliming, slimed). To cover with slime; to make slimy. **slimy,** slīm'i, *a.* Abounding with slime; consisting of slime; viscous; glutinous.

sling, sling, *vt.* (slinging, slung). To throw; to hang so as to swing; to place in a sling.—*n.* An instrument for throwing stones; a bandage to support a wounded limb; a rope for raising heavy articles.

slink, slingk, *vi.* (slinking, slunk). To sneak; to steal away.—*vt.* To cast prematurely.—*n.* A premature calf.

slip, slip, *vi.* (slipping, slipped). To move smoothly along; to glide; to de-

part secretly; to have the feet slide; to err; to escape insensibly.—*vt.* To put or thrust secretly; to omit; to disengage one's self from; to make a slip of for planting.—*n.* A sliding of the feet; an unintentional error; a twig cut for planting or grafting; a long narrow piece; a leash by which a dog is held; a long strip of printed matter; a loose covering; an inclined plane upon which a ship is built. **slipper,** slip'ér, *n.* One who slips or lets slip; a loose, light shoe for household wear. **slippery,** slip'ér-i, *a.* So smooth as to cause slipping; untrustworthy; uncertain.

slipshod, slip'shod', *a.* Shod with slippers; having shoes down at heel; slovenly.

slit, slit, *vt.* (slitting, slit or slitted). To cut lengthwise; to cut into long strips. —*n.* A long cut or opening.

sliver, sliv'ér or slī'vér, *vt.* To cleave; to cut into long thin pieces.—*n.* A long piece cut off; a splinter.

slobber, slob'ér, *vi.* and *t.* To slaver; to slabber.—*n.* Slaver; liquor spilled. **slobbery,** slob'ér-i, *a.* Moist; sloppy.

sloe, slō, *n.* A British shrub of the plum genus, the blackthorn; also its fruit.

slogan, slō'gan, *n.* A war-cry; a watchword.

sloop, slōp, *n.* A vessel with one mast, hardly different from a cutter.

slop, slop, *vt.* (slopping, slopped). To soil by liquid; to spill.—*n.* Water carelessly thrown about; a smock-frock; *pl.* mean liquid food; waste dirty water; wide breeches; ready-made clothing.

slope, slōp, *n.* An oblique direction; a declivity.—*vt.* and *i.* (sloping, sloped). To form with a slope; to incline.

sloppy, slop'i, *a.* Muddy; plashy; slovenly.

slot, slot, *n.* A bolt or bar; an oblong hole; track of a deer.—*vt.* (slotting, slotted). To make a slot in.

sloth, slōth or sloth, *n.* Indolence; laziness; idleness; a South American mammal. **slothful,** slōth'ful, or sloth', *a.* Addicted to sloth; sluggish; lazy; indolent.

slouch, slouch, *n.* A stoop in walking; an ungainly gait; a droop.—*vi.* To hang down; to have a drooping gait.—*vt.* To cause to hang down. **slouching,** slouch'ing, *a.* Drooping downward; walking heavily and awkwardly.

slough, slou, *n.* A place of deep mud; a hole full of mire.

slough, sluf, *n.* The cast-off skin of a serpent, &c.; the dead flesh that separates from living parts in a wound.

sloven, sluv'en, *n.* A man habitually negligent of neatness and order. **slovenly,** sluv'en-li, *a.* Disorderly; not neat or tidy.—*adv.* In a negligent manner.

slow, slō, *a.* Moving little in a long time; not rapid; dilatory; heavy in wit; dull; behind in time.—*vt.* and *i.* To delay; to slacken in speed.

sludge, sluj, *n.* Mire; soft mud. **sludgy,** sluj'i, *a.* Miry; slushy.

slug, slug, *n.* A sluggard; a shell-less snail injurious to plants; a piece of metal used for the charge of a gun.

sluggard, slug'ẽrd, *n.* A person habitually lazy; a drone.—*a.* Sluggish.

sluggish, slug'ish, *a.* Lazy; slothful; inert; not quick.

sluice, slös, *n.* A contrivance to control the flow of water in a river, dam, &c.; a trough to separate gold from sand, &c.; flood-gate.—*vt.* (sluicing, sluiced). To wet abundantly; to cleanse by means of sluices.

slum, slum, *n.* A low, dirty street of a city.—*vi.* (slumming, slummed). To visit slums from benevolent motives.

slumber, slum'bẽr, *vi.* To sleep; to be inert or inactive.—*n.* Light sleep; repose. **slumberous, slumbrous,** slum'bẽr-us, slum'brus, *a.* Inviting or causing sleep.

slump, slump, *n.* The whole number taken in one lot.—*vt.* To throw into one lot.—*vi.* To sink in walking, as in snow.

slung, slung, pret. & pp. of *sling.*

slunk, slungk, pret. & pp. of *slink.*

slur, slẽr, *vt.* (slurring, slurred). To soil; to traduce; to pass lightly over; to pronounce in a careless indistinct manner.—*n.* A slight reproach; a stain or stigma.

slush, slush, *n.* Sludge or soft mud; wet, half-melted snow. **slushy,** slush'i, *a.* Consisting of slush; resembling slush.

slut, slut, *n.* A woman negligent of tidiness and dress; a slattern. **sluttish,** slut'ish, *a.* Not neat or cleanly.

sly, slī, *a.* Cunning; crafty; wily; shrewd. **slyly,** slī'li, *adv.* Cunningly; craftily. **slyness,** slī'nes, *n.* Artful secrecy; cunning; craftiness.

smack, smak, *vi.* To make a sharp noise with the lips; to taste; to savor.—*vt.* To make a sharp noise with; to slap.—*n.* A loud kiss; a sharp noise; a smart blow; a slap; a slight taste; a smattering; a fishing vessel.

small, smal, *a.* Little; petty; short; weak; gentle; not loud; narrow-minded; mean.—*n.* The small part of a thing; *pl.* small-clothes.

small arms, smal' ärmz' *n. pl.* A general name for rifles, pistols, &c., as distinguished from cannon.

smallpox, smal'poks', *n.* A contagious eruptive disease.

smart, smärt, *n.* A quick, keen pain; pungent grief.—*a.* Keen; quick; sharp; brisk; witty; spruce; well dressed.—*vi.* To feel a sharp pain; to be acutely painful; to be punished. **smartly,** smärt'li, *adv.* Keenly; briskly; sharply; wittily; sprucely.

smash, smash, *vt.* To dash to pieces.—*vi.* To go to pieces.—*n.* A breaking to pieces; ruin; bankruptcy.

smatter, smat'ẽr, *vi.* To have a slight knowledge; to talk superficially.—*n.* A superficial knowledge. **smattering,** smat'ẽr-ing, *n.* A superficial knowledge.

smear, smēr, *vt.* To overspread with anything adhesive; to daub; to soil.

smell, smel, *vt.* (smelling, smelled or smelt). To perceive by the nose; to perceive the scent of; to detect.—*vi.* To give out an odor.—*n.* The faculty by which odors are perceived; scent; perfume. **smelling,** smel'ing, *n.* The sense

of smell. **smelling salts,** smel'ing salts, *n. pl.* Volatile salts used as a stimulant.

smelt, smelt, *vt.* To melt, as ore, to separate the metal.—*n.* A small fish allied to the salmon. **smelter,** smel'tẽr, *n.* One who smelts ore.

smile, smil, *vi.* (smiling, smiled). To show pleasure, sarcasm, pity, &c.; by a look; to appear propitious.—*vt.* To express by a smile; to affect by smiling.—*n.* A set of the features expressing pleasure, scorn, &c.; favor.

smirch, smẽrch, *vt.* To stain; to smudge.

smirk, smẽrk, *vi.* To smile affectedly or pertly.—*n.* An affected smile.

smite, smīt, *vt.* (smiting, pret. smote, pp. smitten). To strike; to slay; to blast; to afflict; to affect with love, &c.—*vi.* To strike; to clash together.

smith, smith, *n.* One who works in metals. **smithy,** smith'i, *n.* The shop of a smith.

smock, smok, *n.* A chemise; a smock-frock.—*vt.* To clothe with a smock; to pucker diagonally.

smog, smog, *n.* Overhang of smoke and fog.

smoke, smōk, *n.* The exhalation from a burning substance; vapor; idle talk; nothingness; a drawing in and puffing out of tobacco fumes.—*vi.* (smoking, smoked). To emit smoke; to use tobacco.—*vt.* To apply smoke to; to befoul by smoke; to fumigate; to use in smoking. **smokeless,** smōk'les, *a.* Having no smoke. **smoker,** smōk'ẽr, *n.* One who smokes; one who uses tobacco. **smoking,** smōk'ing, *n.* Act of one who or that which smokes; the use of tobacco.—*a.* Pertaining to smoking. **smoky,** smōk'i, *a.* Emitting smoke; filled or tarnished with smoke; like smoke.

smoke screen. Heavy smoke to screen movements of troops or ships.

smolder, smōl'dẽr, *vi.* To burn and smoke without flame; to exist in a suppressed state.

smooth, smōTH, *a.* Even on the surface; glossy; moving equably; not harsh; bland.—*n.* Smooth part of anything.—*vt.* To make smooth; to level; to make easy; to palliate; to soothe.

smote, smōt, pret. of *smite.*

smother, smuTH'ẽr, *n.* Stifling smoke; suffocating dust.—*vt.* To stifle; to suffocate; to suppress.—*vi.* To be suffocated or suppressed; to smother.

smudge, smuj, *vt.* (smudging, smudged). To stain with dirt or filth; to smear.—*n.* A stain; a smear.

smug, smug, *a.* Neat; spruce; affectedly nice.—*vt.* (smugging, smugged). To make smug.

smuggle, smug'l, *vt.* (smuggling, smuggled). To import or export secretly and in defiance of law; to convey clandestinely. **smuggler,** smug'lẽr, *n.* One who smuggles; a vessel employed in smuggling goods.

smut, smut, *n.* A spot or stain; a spot of soot, &c.; a disease in grain; obscene language.—*vt.* and *i.* (smutting, smutted). To stain with smut; to tarnish.

smutty, smut'i, *a.* Soiled with smut; affected with mildew; obscene.

snack, snak, *n.* A small portion of food; a hasty repast; a bite; a share.

snaffle, snaf'l, *n.* A bridle consisting of a slender bit without a curb.—*vt.* To bridle; to manage with a snaffle.

snag, snag, *n.* A short projecting stump; a shoot; the time of a deer's antler; a tree in a river dangerous to vessels.

snail, snāl, *n.* A slimy, slow-creeping mollusk; a slug; a sluggard.

snake, snāk, *n.* A serpent. **snaky**, snāk'i, *a.* Pertaining to a snake; cunning; insinuating; infested with snakes.

snap, snap, *vt.* (snapping, snapped). To bite or seize suddenly; to break with a sharp sound; to break short.—*vt.* To try to seize with the teeth; to break suddenly or without bending.—*n.* A quick eager bite; a sudden breaking; a sharp noise; a kind of cake or cracker. **snappish**, snap'ish, *a.* Apt to snap; peevish; tart; crabbed.

snapshot, snap'shot', *n.* A hasty shot at a moving animal; snap'shot', a photograph taken hastily with a hand camera.

snare, snār, *n.* A line with a noose for catching animals; anything that entraps. —*vt.* (snaring, snared). To catch with a snare; to ensnare.

snarl, snärl, *vi.* To growl, as an angry dog; to talk in rude murmuring terms. —*vt.* To entangle.—*A* sharp angry growl; a knot; embarrassment. **snarling**, snärl'ing, *a.* Given to snarl; growling; snappish; peevish.

snatch, snach, *vt.* To seize hastily or abruptly.—*vi.* To make a grasp.—*n.* A hasty catch; a short fit or turn; a small portion; a snack.

sneak, snēk, *vt.* To creep privately; to go furtively; to crouch.—*n.* A mean fellow; one guilty of underhand work. **sneaky**, snēk'i, *a.* Mean; underhand.

sneer, snēr, *vi.* To show contempt by a look; to jeer; to speak derisively.—*n.* A look or grin of contempt; a scoff, a jeer.

sneeze, snēz, *vi.* (sneezing, sneezed). To emit air through the nose, &c., by a kind of involuntary convulsive effort.— *n.* A single act of sneezing.

sniff, snif, *vi.* To draw air audibly up the nose; to snuff.—*n.* A slight smell; snuff.

snigger, snig'ėr, *vi.* To laugh in a suppressed manner.—*n.* A suppressed laugh; a giggle.

snip, snip, *vt.* (snipping, snipped). To cut off at a stroke with shears; to clip. —*n.* A single cut with shears; a bit cut off.

snipe, snīp, *n.* A grallatorial bird with a long bill; a simpleton.

snippet, snip'et, *n.* A small part or share.

snivel, sniv'l, *vi.* (sniveling, sniveled). To run at the nose; to whimper.—*n.* Whimpering; maudlin sentiment.

snob, snob, *n.* A shoemaker; one who apes gentility; a would-be aristocrat. **snobbery**, snob'ėr-i, *n.* The quality of being snobbish. **snobbish**, **snobby**, snob'ish, snob'i, *a.* Like a snob; pretending to gentility.

snood, snōd, *n.* A fillet or ribbon for the hair.

snooze, snöz, *n.* A nap or short sleep.— *vi.* (snoozing, snoozed). To take a short nap.

snore, snōr, *vi.* (snoring, snored). To breathe with a rough, hoarse noise in sleep.—*n.* A breathing with a hoarse noise in sleep.

snort, snört, *vi.* To force air with violence through the nose.—*n.* A loud sound produced by forcing the air through the nostrils.

snot, snot, *n.* The mucus of the nose.

snout, snout, *n.* The projecting nose of a beast; muzzle; nozzle.

snow, snō, *n.* Watery particles congealed in the air and falling in flakes.—*vi.* To fall in snow; used impersonally.—*vt.* To scatter like snow. **snowball**, snō'bal', *n.* A ball of snow.—*vt.* To pelt with snowballs.—*vi.* To throw snowballs. **snowplow**, snō'plou', *n.* An implement for clearing away the snow from roads, &c. **snowshoe**, snō'shō', *n.* A light frame worn on the feet to keep the wearer from sinking in snow; a snowboot. **snow-white**, snō'whīt', *a.* White as snow. **snowy**, snō'i, *a.* White like snow; abounding with snow; pure white.

snub, snub, *vt.* (snubbing, snubbed). To stop or rebuke with a tart, sarcastic remark; to slight designedly.—*n.* A check; a rebuke.

snub-nose, snub'nōz', *n.* A flat nose.

snuff, snuf, *vt.* To draw up through the nose; to smell; to crop, as the snuff of a candle.—*vi.* To draw up air or tobacco through the nose; to take offense.—*n.* A drawing up through the nose; resentment; burned wick of a candle; pulverized tobacco. **snuffle**, snuf'l, *vi.* (snuffling, snuffled). To speak through the nose; to breathe hard through the nose. —*n.* A sound made by air drawn through the nostrils; nasal twang; *pl.* an ailment accompanied by snuffling with the nose.

snug, snug, *a.* Neat; trim; cozy. **snuggle**, snug'l, *vi.* (snuggling, snuggled). To lie close for convenience or warmth; to nestle.

so, sō, *adv.* In this or that manner; to that degree; thus; extremely; very; the case being such; thereby.—*conj.* Provided that; in case that; therefore; accordingly.

soak, sōk, *vt.* To let lie in a fluid till the substance has imbibed all that it can; to steep; to wet thoroughly.—*vi.* To steep; to enter by pores; to tipple. **soaker**, sōk'ėr, *n.* One who soaks; a hard drinker. **soaking**, sōk'ing, *p.a.* Such as to soak; that wets thoroughly; drenching. **soaky**, sōk'i, *a.* Moist on the surface; steeped in or drenched with water.

so-and-so, sō'and-sō', *n.* A certain person not named; an indefinite person or thing.

soap, sōp, *n.* A compound of oil or fat with an alkali, used in washing.—*vt.* To rub or cover with soap. **soapy**, sōp'i, *a.* Resembling soap; smeared with soap; unctuous.

soar, sōr, *vi.* To mount upon the wing;

to rise high; to tower.—*n.* A towering flight; a lofty ascent.

sob, sob, *vi.* (sobbing, sobbed). To sigh or weep convulsively; to make a similar sound.—*n.* A convulsive catching of the breath in weeping or sorrow.

sober, sō'bėr, *a.* Temperate; not drunk; calm; cool; staid; grave; dull-looking.—*vt.* To make sober.—*vi.* To become sober.

sobriety, sō-brī'e-ti, *n.* Temperance; abstemiousness; moderation; saneness; sedateness; gravity.

sobriquet, sō'bri-kā, *n.* A nickname.

soccer, sok'ėr, *a.* Association or Rugby style of play in football.

sociable, sō'sha-bl, *a.* Fond of companions; inclined to mix in society; social. **sociability**, sō'sha-bil"i-ti, *n.* Quality of being sociable.

social, sō'shal, *a.* Pertaining to society; sociable; consisting in union or mutual converse; living in communities. **socialism**, sō'shal-izm, *n.* A theory of social organization aiming at co-operative action and community of property. **socialist**, sō'shal-ist, *n.* One who advocates socialism; a collectivist. **socialistic**, sō'shal-is"tik, *a.* Pertaining to socialism. **socialize**, sō'shal-īz, *vt.* To render social; to regulate according to socialism.

society, sō-sī'e-ti, *n.* Fellowship; company; a body of persons united for some object; persons living in the same circle; those who take the lead in social life.

sociology, sō'si-ol"ō-ji, *n.* The science which treats of society, its development, the progress of civilization, &c. **sociologist**, sō'si-ol"ō-jist, *n.* One versed in sociology.

sock, sok, *n.* The shoe of the ancient actors of comedy; a short woven covering for the foot.

socket, sok'et, *n.* A cavity into which anything is fitted.

sod, sod, *n.* That layer of earth which is covered with grass; piece of turf.

soda, sō'da, *n.* The alkali carbonate of sodium used in washing, glass-making, &c., and extensively made from salt.

sodality, sō-dal'i-ti, *n.* A fellowship or fraternity.

soda water, sō'da-wa̤'tėr, *n.* An effervescent drink generally consisting of water into which carbonic acid has been forced.

sodden, sod'n, *a.* Seethed; saturated; soaked and soft; not well baked; doughy.

sodium, sō'di-um, *n.* A soft light silvery metallic element.

sodomy, sod'um-i, *n.* A carnal copulation against nature. **sodomite**, sod'um-īt, *n.* One guilty of sodomy.

sofa, sō'fa, *n.* A long seat with a stuffed bottom, back, and ends.

soft, soft, *a.* Easily yielding to pressure; delicate; mild; effeminate; not loud or harsh; not strong or glaring.—*adv.* Softly.—*interj.* Be soft; stop; not so fast. **soften**, sof'en, *vt.* To make soft or more soft; to mollify; to alleviate; to tone down.—*vi.* To become soft; to relent; to become milder. **softening**, sof'en-ing, *n.* Act of making or becoming more soft or softer. **soft-spoken**, soft'spō'ken, *a.* Speaking softly; mild; affable.

soft-pedal, soft-ped'l, *vt.* To tone down.

soft-soap, *vt.* To flatter or gush over.

soil, soil, *vt.* To sully; to tarnish; to manure; to feed (cattle) indoors with green fodder.—*vi.* To tarnish.—*n.* Dirt; ordure; tarnish; the upper stratum of the earth; mold; loam; earth; land; country.

soiree, swa̤-rā', *n.* A meeting of some body at which there are tea and other refreshments, with music, speeches, &c.

sojourn, sōj-ėrn', *vi.* To reside for a time.—*n.* A temporary residence or stay. **sojourner**, sōjėrn'ėr, *n.* One who sojourns; a temporary resident.

solace, sol'is, *vt.* (solacing, solaced). To cheer or console; to allay.—*n.* Consolation; comfort; relief; recreation.

solar, sō'lėr, *a.* Pertaining to the sun, or proceeding from it; sunny; measured by the progress of the sun.

solder, sod'ėr, *vt.* To unite metals by a fused metallic substance; to patch up.—*n.* A metallic cement.

soldier, sōl'jėr, *n.* A man in military service; a man of distinguished valor. **soldiering**, sōl'jėr-ing, *n.* The occupation of a soldier. **soldier-like**, **soldierly**, sōl"jėr-līk', sōl'jėr-li, *a.* Like or becoming a soldier; brave.

sole, sōl, *n.* The under side of the foot; the bottom of a shoe; a marine fish allied to the flounder.—*vt.* (soling, soled). To furnish with a sole, as a shoe.—*a.* Single; individual; only; alone.

solecism, sol'e-sizm, *n.* A grammatical error; deviation from correct idiom. **solecize**, sol'e-sīz, *vi.* To commit solecism.

solemn, sol'em, *a.* Marked with religious gravity or sanctity; impressive; earnest; affectedly grave. **solemnity**, so-lem'ni-ti, *n.* Gravity; impressiveness; a solemn ceremony. **solemnize**, sol'em-nīz, *vt.* To honor by solemn ceremonies; to celebrate; to make grave.

solicit, sō-lis'it, *vt.* and *i.* To ask earnestly; to beg; to invite; to disquiet; to incite. **solicitant**, sō-lis'i-tant, *n.* One who solicits. **solicitation**, sō-lis'i-tā"shun, *n.* Earnest request; supplication; entreaty. **solicitor**, sō-lis'i-tėr, *n.* One who solicits; an attorney; a law-agent. **solicitous**, sō-lis'i-tus, *a.* Anxious; very desirous; concerned; apprehensive. **solicitude**, sō-lis'i-tūd, *n.* State of being solicitous; carefulness; concern; anxiety.

solid, sol'id, *a.* Resisting pressure; not liquid or gaseous; not hollow; cubic; sound; not frivolous.—*n.* A body that naturally retains the same shape. **solidarity**, sol'i-dar"i-ti, *n.* Unity or communion of interests and responsibilities. **solidification**, sō-lid'i-fi-kā"shun, *n.* Act or process of solidifying. **solidify**, sō-lid'i-fī, *vt.* (solidifying, solidified). To make solid.—*vi.* To become solid. **solidity**, sō-lid'i-ti, *n.* State or quality of being solid; density; firmness; soundness. **solidly**, sol'id-li, *adv.* In a solid manner; firmly; compactly; on firm grounds.

soliloquy, sō-lil′ō-kwi, *n.* A speaking to one's self; discourse of a person alone. **soliloquize**, sō-lil′ō-kwiz, *vi.* To utter a soliloquy.

solitaire, sol′i-tār′, *n.* A solitary; an article of jewelry in which a single gem is set; a game for a single person.

solitary, sol′i-ter′i, *a.* Being alone; lonely; retired; not much frequented; shared by no companions; single; sole.— *n.* A hermit; a recluse. **solitarily**, sol′-i-ter′i-li, *adv.* In a solitary manner; in solitude; alone.

solitude, sol′i-tūd, *n.* State of being alone; a lonely life; a lonely place.

solo, sō′lō, *n.* A tune or air for a single instrument or voice. **soloist**, sō′lō-ist, *n.* A solo singer or performer.

solstice, sol′stis, *n.* The time when the sun arrives at the point farthest north or south of the equator, namely 21st June and 22nd Dec.; either of the two points in the ecliptic where the sun then appears to be. **solstitial**, sol-stish′al, *a.* Pertaining to a solstice; happening at a solstice.

soluble, sol′ū-bl, *a.* Susceptible of being dissolved in a fluid; capable of being solved, as a problem. **solubility**, sol′ū-bil″i-ti, *n.* Quality of being soluble.

solution, sō-lū′shun, *n.* A dissolving; preparation made by dissolving a solid in a liquid; act of solving; explanation; termination or crisis of a disease.

solve, solv, *vt.* (solving, solved). To explain; to make clear; to unravel; to work out. **solvable**, sol′va-bl, *a.* Soluble.

solvent, sol′vent, *a.* Having the power of dissolving; able to pay all debts.—*n.* A fluid that dissolves any substance. **solvency**, sol′ven-si, *n.* Ability to pay debts.

somber, som′bėr, *a.* Dark; gloomy; dismal.—*vt.* (sombering, sombered). To make somber.

sombrero, som-brā′rō, *n.* A broad-brimmed hat.

some, sum, *a.* A certain; a; a little; indefinite and perhaps considerable; about or near.—*pron.* An indefinite part, quantity, or number; certain individuals.

somebody, sum′bod′i, *n.* A person indeterminate; a person of consideration.

somehow, sum′hou, *adv.* In some way not yet known; one way or another.

somersault, **somerset**, sum′ėr-salt, sum′ėr-set, *n.* A leap in which the heels turn over the head; a turn of the body in the air.

something, sum′thing, *n.* A thing, quantity, or degree indefinitely; a person or thing of importance.—*adv.* Somewhat.

sometime, sum′tīm′, *adv.* Once; formerly; by and by.—*a.* Former; whilom.

sometimes, sum′tīmz′, *adv.* At some or certain times; not always; now and then.

somewhat, sum′whot′, *n.* Something; more or less.—*adv.* In some degree; a little.

somewhere, sum′whār′, *adv.* In some place; to some place.

somnambulate, som-nam′bū-lāt, *vi.* and *t.* To walk or walk over in sleep. **somnambulism**, som-nam′bū-lizm, *n.* The act or practice of walking in sleep. **somnambulist**, som-nam′bū-list, *n.* One who walks in his sleep.

somnolent, som′nō-lent, *a.* Sleepy; drowsy. **somnolence**, som′nō-lens, *n.* Sleepiness.

son, sun, *n.* A male child.

sonar, sō′när, *n.* An underwater detecting device.

sonata, sō-nä′ta, *n.* A musical composition of several movements for a solo instrument.

song, song, *n.* That which is sung; vocal music or melody; a poem to be sung; a lyric; poetry; a trifle.

songbird, song′bėrd′, *n.* A bird that sings.

songster, song′stėr, *n.* A singer. **songstress**, song′stres, *n.* A female singer.

son-in-law, sun″in-la′, *n.* A man married to one's daughter.

sonnet, son′et, *n.* A poem of fourteen pentameter lines.

sonorous, sō-nō′rus, *a.* Giving sound when struck; resonant; high-sounding.

soon, sön, *adv.* In a short time; shortly; early; quickly; promptly; readily; gladly.

soot, sut, *n.* A black substance formed from burning matter.—*vt.* To cover or foul with soot. **sooty**, sut′i, *a.* Producing soot; consisting of soot; foul with soot; dusky; dark.

sooth, söth, *a.* True. *n.* Truth, reality.

soothe, sōTH, *vt.* (soothing, soothed). To please with soft words; to flatter; to pacify, to assuage; to soften. **soothing**, sōTH′ing, *p.a.* Serving to soothe, calm, or assuage, mollifying. **soothsayer**, sōth′sā′ėr, *n.* One who foretells or predicts; a prophet.

sop, sop, *n.* Something dipped in broth or liquid food; anything given to pacify. —*vt.* (sopping, sopped). To steep in liquor.

sophist, sof′ist, *n.* A captious or fallacious reasoner. **sophism**, sof′izm, *n.* A specious but fallacious argument; a subtlety in reasoning. **sophisticate**, sō-fis′ti-kāt, *vt.* To pervert by sophistry; to adulterate. **sophistication**, sō-fis′ti-kā″shun, *n.* Adulteration; act or art of quibbling; a quibble. **sophistry**, sof′-is-tri, *n.* Fallacious reasoning.

sophomore, sof′o-mōr, *n.* A second-year student in college.

soporific, sō′pō-rif″ik, *a.* Causing sleep. —*n.* A drug or anything that induces sleep.

soprano, sō-prä′nō, *n.* The highest female voice; a singer with such a voice.

sorcerer, sōr′sėr-ėr, *n.* A wizard; an enchanter; a magician. **sorceress**, sōr′sėr-es, *n.* A female sorcerer. **sorcery**, sōr′sėr-i, *n.* Magic; enchantment; witchcraft.

sordid, sor′did, *a.* Dirty; foul; vile; base; niggardly; covetous.

sore, sōr, *a.* Painful; severe; distressing;

tender; galled.—*n.* An ulcer, wound, &c.—*adv.* Severely; sorely.

sorghum, sor'gum, *n.* A kind of millet.

sorrel, sor'el, *n.* A plant allied to the docks; a reddish or yellow-brown color.—*a.* Of a reddish color.

sorrily, sor'i-li, *adv.* In a sorry manner; meanly; pitiably; wretchedly.

sorrow, sor'ō, *n.* Affliction or distress of mind; grief; regret.—*vi.* To feel sorrow; to grieve. **sorrowful,** sor'ō-ful, *a.* Full of sorrow; sad; mournful; dejected.

sorry, sor'i, *a.* Feeling sorrow; grieved; sorrowful; wretched; pitiful.

sort, sort, *n.* Nature or character; kind; species; manner; a set.—*vt.* To assort; to arrange; to reduce to order.—*vi.* To consort; to agree.

sortie, sor'tē, *n.* The issuing of troops from a besieged place; a sally.

S O S. Letters in the telegraph code denoting distress.

so-so, sō"s', *a.* Middling.

sot, sot, *n.* A dolt or blockhead; a habitual drunkard. **sottish,** sot'ish, *a.* Like a sot; foolish; given to drunkenness.

sou, sö, *n.* A French copper coin, worth about a cent.

soufflé, sö'flä" *n.* A light dish, partly composed of white of eggs.

soul, sōl, *n.* The spiritual principle in man; the moral and emotional part of man's nature; elevation of mind; fervor; essence; an inspirer or leader; a person. **souled,** sōld, *a.* Instinct with soul or feeling. **soulless,** sōl'les, *a.* Without a soul; without nobleness of mind; mean; spiritless.

sound, sound, *a.* Not in any way defective; healthy; valid; free from error; orthodox; just; heavy.—*n.* A narrow channel of water; a strait; air-bladder of a fish; that which is heard; noise.—*vt.* To measure the depth of; to examine medically; to try to discover the opinion, &c., of; to cause to give out a sound; to pronounce.—*vi.* To give out a sound; to appear on narration; to be spread or published. **sounding,** sound'ing, *a.* Causing sound; sonorous; having a lofty sound; bombastic. **sounding board,** sound'ing-bōrd', *n.* A canopy over a platform, &c., to direct the sound of a speaker's voice to the audience. **soundings,** sound'ingz, *n.pl.* The depths of water in rivers, harbors, &c. **soundless,** sound'les, *a.* That cannot be fathomed; noiseless. **soundly,** sound'li, *adv.* Healthily; validly; thoroughly; with heavy blows. **soundness,** sound'nes, *n.* Healthiness; solidity; validity; orthodoxy.

soup, söp, *n.* A liquid food made generally from flesh and vegetables.

soup kitchen, söp' kich'en, *n.* An establishment for supplying soup to the poor.

sour, sour, *a.* Acid or sharp to the taste; tart; peevish; morose.—*vt.* To make sour; to make cross or discontented; to embitter.—*vi.* To become sour or peevish. **sourly,** sour'li, *adv.* Acidly; peevishly.

source, sörs, *n.* That from which any-

thing rises; the spring, &c., from which a stream proceeds; first cause; origin.

souse, sous, *n.* Pickle; the ears, feet, &c., of swine pickled; a swoop.—*vt.* (sousing, soused). To steep in pickle; to plunge into water.—*vi.* To swoop.—*adv.* With sudden descent or plunge.

south, south, *n.* The region in which the sun is at mid-day.—*a.* Being in or toward the south; pertaining to or from the south.—*adv.* Toward the south.

southeast, south'ēst", *n.* The point midway between the south and east.—*a.* Pertaining to or from the southeast.—*adv.* Toward the southeast. **southeaster,** south'ēs"tėr, *n.* A wind from the southeast. **southeasterly,** south'ēs"tėr-li, *a.* In the direction of southeast; from the southeast. **southeastern,** south'ēst"ėrn, *a.* Pertaining to or toward the southeast.

southerly, suTH'ėr-li, *a.* Lying at or toward the south; coming from the south.

southern, suTH'ėrn, *a.* Belonging to the south; southerly. **southerner,** suTH'ėr-nėr, *n.* An inhabitant or native of the south. **southernmost,** suTH'ėrn-mōst, *a.* Farthest toward the south.

southing, souTH'ing, *n.* Motion to the south; difference of latitude in sailing southward.

southpaw, south"pạ', *n.* A left-handed baseball pitcher.

southward, south'wėrd, *adv.* and *a.* Toward the south.

southwest, south'west", *n.* The point midway between the south and the west.—*a.* Pertaining to or from the southwest.—*adv.* Toward the southwest.

southwester, south'wes"tėr, *n.* A strong southwest wind; a waterproof hat with a flap hanging over the neck, often Sou'wester.

souvenir, sö'vė-nėr", *n.* A keepsake.

sovereign, sov'ėr-in, *a.* Supreme in power; chief.—*n.* A monarch; the standard British gold coin, value 20s., or £1 sterling, $2.80. **sovereignty,** sov'ėr-in-ti, *n.* Supreme power.

soviet, sō'vi-et", *n.* In Russia (lit.) a council; specifically, any of the various elected governing bodies of the Soviet Republic established by the Revolution of 1917 and following Bolshevistic régime.

sow, sou, *n.* The female of the swine.

sow, sō, *vt.* (pret. sowed, pp. sowed or sown). To scatter seed over; to spread abroad.—*vi.* To scatter seed for growth. **sower,** sō'ėr, *n.* One who sows.

soy, soi, *n.* A sauce prepared in China and Japan from a bean; the plant producing the bean.

spa, spä, *n.* A place to which people go on account of a spring of mineral water.

space, spās, *n.* Extension; room; interval between points or objects; quantity of time; a while.—*vt.* (spacing, spaced). To arrange at proper intervals; to arrange the spaces in. **spacial,** Same as Spatial. **spacious,** spā'shus, *a.* Roomy; widely extended; ample; capacious.

spade, spād, *n.* An instrument for digging; a playing card of a black suit.—*vt.* (spading, spaded). To dig with a spade;

to use a spade on. **spadeful**, spād′fụl, *n.* As much as a spade will hold.

spake, spāk. A preterit of *speak*.

span, span, *n.* Reach or extent in general; space between the thumb and little finger; nine inches; a short space of time; the stretch of an arch; a yoke of animals.—*vt.* (spanning, spanned). To extend across; to measure with the hand with the fingers extended.

spangle, spang′gl, *n.* A small glittering metal ornament; a small sparkling object.—*vt.* (spangling, spangled). To adorn with spangles.

Spaniard, span′yėrd, *n.* A native of Spain.

spaniel, span′yel, *n.* A dog of several breeds; a cringing, fawning person.

Spanish, span′ish, *a.* Pertaining to Spain.—*n.* The language of Spain.

spank, spangk, *vt.* To move or run along quickly.—*vt.* To slap or smack. **spanker**, spangk′ėr, *n.* One that spanks; a large fore-and-aft sail on the mizzenmast. **spanking**, spangk′ing, *a.* Moving quickly; dashing; free-going.

spar, spär, *n.* A long piece of timber; a pole; a crystalline mineral; boxing-match; flourish of the fists.—*vi.* (sparring, sparred). To fight in show; to box; to bandy words.

spare, spär, *a.* Scanty; thin; sparing or chary; superfluous; held in reserve.—*vt.* (sparing, spared). To use frugally; to dispense with; to omit; to use tenderly; to withhold from.—*vi.* To be frugal; to use mercy or forbearance.

sparing, spär′ing, *a.* Saving; economical. **sparingly**, spär′ing-li, *adv.* Frugally; not lavishly; seldom; not frequently.

spark, spärk, *n.* A particle of ignited substance, which flies off from burning bodies; a small transient light; a gay man; a lover.—*vi.* To emit particles of fire; to sparkle.

sparkle, spär′kl, *n.* A little spark; luster.—*vi.* (sparkling, sparkled). To emit sparks; to glitter; to be animated. **sparkling**, spärk′ling, *a.* Emitting sparks; glittering; lively.

sparrow, spar′ō, *n.* A bird of the finch family.

sparse, spärs, *a.* Thinly scattered; not thick; or close together. **sparsely**, spärs′li, *adv.* Thinly.

Spartan, spär′tan, *a.* Pertaining to ancient Sparta; hardy; undaunted; enduring.

spasm, spazm, *n.* A violent contraction of a muscle; a convulsive fit. **spasmodic**, spaz-mod′ik, *a.* Relating to spasm; convulsive; overstrained in expression or style.

spastic, spas′tik, *a.* Spasmodic.

spat, spat, *n.* The spawn of shell-fish.—*vi.* (spatting, spatted). To emit spawn or spat.

spate, spait, spāt, *n.* A sudden heavy flood, especially in mountain streams.

spatial, spā′shal, *a.* Pertaining to space; existing in space.

spatter, spat′ėr, *vt.* To scatter a liquid substance on; to sprinkle; to asperse.—*n.* Act of spattering; something sprinkled.

spatula, spat′ū-la, *n.* A broad thin flexible blade, used by painters, apothecaries, &c.

spavin, spav′in, *n.* A disease of horses affecting the joint of the hind-leg between the knee and the fetlock, and causing lameness.

spawn, span, *n.* The eggs or ova of fish, frogs, &c., when ejected; offspring, in contempt.—*vt.* and *i.* To eject or deposit, as spawn.

spay, spā, *vt.* To destroy the ovaries of, as is done to female animals.

speak, spēk, *vi.* (p:et, spoke, spake, pp. spoken). To utter words; to talk; to deliver a speech; to argue; to plead; to be expressive.—*vt.* To utter with the mouth; to pronounce; to accost; to express. **speaker**, spēk′ėr, *n.* One who speaks; the person who presides in a deliberative assembly, as the Senate. **speaking**, spēk′ing, *p.a.* Used to convey speech; forcibly expressive; vivid in resemblance; extending to phrases of civility.

spear, spēr, *n.* A long, pointed weapon; a lance.—*vt.* To pierce or kill with a spear.

spearman, spēr′man, *n.* One armed with a spear.

special, spesh′al, *a.* Pertaining to a species; particular; distinctive; having a particular purpose or scope. **specialist**, spesh′al-ist, *n.* One who devotes himself to some particular subject. **speciality**, spesh′i-al″i-ti, *n.* Special characteristic; that in which a person is specially versed. **specialize**, spesh′al-īz. *vt.* To assign a specific use to.—*vi.* To apply one's self to a particular subject. **specially**, spesh′al-i, *adv.* Especially; for a particular purpose or occasion. **specialty**, spesh′al-ti, *n.* Special characteristic; a special pursuit; a special product.

specie, spē′shi, *n.* Metallic money; coin. **species**, spē′shēz, *n. sing.* and *pl.* Outward appearance; a kind, sort, or variety; a class.

specific, spe-sif′ik, *a.* Pertaining to, designating or constituting a species; definite; precise.—*n.* A remedy which exerts a special action in the cure of disease; an infallible remedy. **specifically**, spe-sif′ik-al-i, *adv.* In a specific manner; definitely; particularly.

specify, spes′i-fī, *vt.* (specifying, specified). To make specific; to state in detail. **specification**, spes′i-fi-kā″shun, *n.* The act of specifying; deails of particulars; particular mention; statement. **specimen**, spes′i-men, *n.* A sample; a part intended to typify the whole.

specious, spē′shus, *a.* Superficially correct; appearing well at first view; plausible. **speciously**, spē′shus-li, *adv.* Plausibly.

speck, spek, *n.* A small spot; a stain; a flaw; an atom.—*vt.* To spot. **speckle**, spek′l, *n.* A speck; a small colored marking.—*vt.* (speckling, speckled). To mark with small specks. **speckled**, spek′ld, *p.a.* Marked with specks; spotted.

spectacle, spek′ta-kl, *n.* A show; a sight; an exhibition; a pageant; *pl.* glasses to assist or correct defective vision. **spectacular**, spek-tak'ū-lèr, *a.* Pertaining to or of the nature of a show.

spectator, spek-tā'tèr, *n.* A looker-on; a beholder; an eye-witness.

specter, spek'tèr, *n.* An apparition; a ghost; a phantom.

spectral, spek'tral, *a.* Pertaining to a specter; ghostly; pertaining to spectra.

spectroscope, spek'trō-skōp, *n.* The instrument employed in spectrum analysis.

spectrum, spek'trum, *n.*; pl. **-tra.** An image seen after the eyes are closed; a specially-colored band of light, showing prismatic colors produced when light is subjected to analysis by a spectroscope.

speculate, spek'ū-lāt, *vi.* (speculating, speculated). To meditate; to engage in risky financial transactions with a view to profit. **speculation**, spek'ū-lā"shun, *n.* Act of speculating; contemplation; theory; hazardous financial transactions. **speculative**, spek"ū-lā'tiv, *a.* Given to speculation; theoretical; pertaining to speculation in trade. **speculator**, spek"-ū-lā'tèr, *n.* A theorizer; one who speculates in business.

speech, spēch, *n.* The faculty of speaking; language; talk; what is spoken; a saying; a formal discourse; oration. **speechify**, spēch'i-fī, *vi.* To make a speech; to harangue. **speechless**, spēch'les, *a.* Destitute of the faculty of speech; dumb; mute; silent.

speed, spēd, *n.* Success; velocity; haste. —*vi.* (speeding, sped). To make haste; to prosper.—*vt.* To despatch in haste; to help forward; to dismiss with good wishes. **speedily**, spēd'i-li, *adv.* In a speedy manner; quickly; with haste; soon. **speedy**, spēd'i, *a.* Having speed; quick; nimble; not dilatory.

spell, spel, *n.* An incantation; a charm; fascination; a turn of work; a period.— *vt.* (pret. and pp. spelled or spelt). To give the letters of in order; to read; to import.—*vi.* To form words with the proper letters. **spelling**, spel'ing, *n.* Act of one who spells; orthography; letters that form a word. **spelling book**, spel'ing buk', *n.* A book for teaching children to spell and read.

spend, spend, *vt.* (spending, spent). To lay out as money; to squander; to pass, as time; to exhaust of force.—*vi.* To spend money; to be dissipated.

spendthrift, spend"thrift', *n.* and *a.* One who spends improvidently; a prodigal.

spent, spent, *p.a.* Wearied; exhausted; having deposited spawn.

sperm, spèrm, *n.* The seminal fluid of animals.

spermaceti, spèr'ma-sē"ti, *n.* A fatty material obtained from a species of whale.

spermatic, spèr-mat'ik, *a.* Seminal.

spermatozoon, spèr'ma-tō-zō"on, *n.*; pl. **-oa.** One of the microscopic bodies in the semen of animals essential to impregnation.

sperm whale, spèrm' whāl', *n.* The spermaceti whale or cachalot.

spew, spū, *vt.* To vomit; to cast out with abhorrence.—*vi.* To vomit.

sphenoid, sfē'noid, *a.* Resembling a wedge.—*n.* A wedge-shaped body.

sphere, sfēr, *n.* An orb; a ball; a globe; a sun, star, or planet; circuit of motion; action, &c.; range; province; rank.— *vt.* (sphering, sphered). To place in a sphere or among the spheres. **spheral**, sfēr'al, *a.* Pertaining to the spheres; rounded like a sphere. **spheric, spherical**, sfer'ik, sfer'i-kal, *a.* Pertaining to a sphere; globular. **spherically**, sfer'-i-kal-i, *adv.* In the form of a sphere. **spheroid**, sfēr'oid, *n.* A body like a sphere, but not perfectly spherical. **spheroidal**, sfē-roi'dal, *a.* Having the form of a spheroid.

sphincter, sfingk'tèr, *n.* A ring-like muscle closing the external orifices of organs, as the mouth or anus.

sphinx, sfingks, *n.* A monster or figure with the bust of a woman on the body of a lioness, said to have proposed a riddle; a person who puts puzzling questions.

spicate, spī'kāt, *a.* Eared like corn.

spice, spīs, *n.* A vegetable production, aromatic to the smell and pungent to the taste; something piquant; flavor; smack. —*vt.* (spicing, spiced). To season with spice; to flavor. **spicily**, spīs'i-li, *adv.* In a spicy manner; pungently; with flavor.

spick-and-span, spik'and-span', *a.* Trim; flawless.—*adv.* Quite (with *new*).

spicy, spīs'i, *a.* Producing or abounding with spice; pungent; piquant; racy.

spider, spī'dèr, *n.* An animal that spins webs for taking its prey.

spiel, spēl, *n. Slang. U.S.* Glib speech or talk.

spigot, spig'ut, *n.* A peg to stop a faucet or cask.

spike, spīk, *n.* A piece of pointed iron; an ear of corn, &c.—*vt.* (spiking, spiked). To fasten or set with spikes; to stop the vent of a cannon) with a nail, &c.; to fix upon a spike.

spill, spil, *vt.* (pret. and pp. spilled or spilt). To suffer to fall, flow over, &c.; to shed.—*vi.* To be shed; to be suffered to fall, be lost, or wasted.

spilth, spilth, *n.* That which is spilled or wasted lavishly.

spin, spin, *vt.* (spinning, spun). To draw out and twist into threads; to protract; to whirl; to make threads, as a spider.— *vi.* To work at drawing and twisting threads; to rotate; to go quickly.—*n.* Act of spinning; a rapid run.

spinach, spin'ich, **spinage**, spin'āj, *n.* A culinary vegetable.

spinal, spī'nal, *a.* Pertaining to the spine.

spindle, spin'dl, *n.* A pin carrying a bobbin in a spinning machine; a small axis; a long, slender stalk; a measure of yarn.—*vi.* To grow in a long slender stalk.

spindle-legs, spindle-shanks, spin"-dl-legz', spin"dl-shangks', *n.* Long slender legs, or a person having such.

spine, spīn, *n.* A prickle; a thorn; a thin, pointed spike in animals; the backbone or spinal column. **spined**, spīnd, *a.* Having spines.

spinnaker, spin'a-kėr, *n.* A triangular sail carried by yachts on the opposite side to the main-sail in running before the wind.

spinner, spin'ėr, *n.* One who spins; a contrivance for spinning; a spider.

spinster, spin'stėr, *n.* A woman who spins; an unmarried woman; an old maid.

spiny, spīn'i, *a.* Thorny; difficult.

spiræa, spī-rē'a, *n.* A genus of flowering plants.

spire, spīr, *n.* A winding line like a screw, a spiral; a wreath; a convolution; a steeple; a stalk or blade of grass, &c.—*vi.* (spiring, spired). To taper up. **spiral**, spī'ral, *a.* Pertaining to a spire; winding like a screw.—*n.* A curve winding like a screw. **spirally**, spī'ral-i, *adv.* In a spiral form or direction; in the manner of a screw.

Spiral.

spirit, spir'it, *n.* The breath of life; the soul; a specter; vivacity; courage; mood; essence; real meaning; intent; a liquid obtained by distillation; *pl.* alcoholic liquor.—*vt.* To infuse spirit into; to encourage. **spirited**, spir'i-ted, *p.a.* Showing spirit; animated; lively; bold; courageous. **spiritless**, spir'it-les, *a.* Destitute of life or spirit; dejected; depressed.

spirit level, spir'it lev'el, *n.* A glass tube nearly filled with spirit, for determining when a thing is horizontal by the central position of an air-bubble.

spiritual, spir'it-ū-al, *a.* Pertaining to spirit; not material; mental; intellectual; divine; pure; ecclesiastical. **spiritualism**, spir'it-ū-al-izm, *n.* State of being spiritual; doctrine of the existence of spirit distinct from matter; belief that communication can be held with departed spirits. **spiritualist**, spir'it-ū-al-ist, *n.* One who professes a regard for spiritual things only; one who believes in spiritualism. **spiritualistic**, spir'it-ū-al-is"tik, *a.* Relating to spiritualism. **spirituality**, spir'it-ū-al"i-ti, *n.* Quality or state of being spiritual; spiritual nature or character. **spiritualize**, spir'it-ū-al-īz, *vt.* To render spiritual; to convert to a spiritual meaning. **spiritually**, spir'it-ū-al-i, *adv.* In a spiritual manner.

spit, spit, *n.* A prong on which meat is roasted; low land running into the sea.—*vt.* (spitting, spitted). To put on a spit; to pierce.

spit, spit, *vt.* and *i.* (spitting, spat). To eject from the mouth, as saliva.—*n.* What is ejected from the mouth; spittle.

spite, spit, *n.* A feeling of ill-will; malice; rancor. **in spite of**, notwithstanding.—*vt.* (spiting, spited). To mortify or chagrin; to thwart. **spiteful**, spit'fyl, *a.* Having a desire to annoy or injure; malignant; malicious.

spitfire, spit'fīr, *n.* A violent or passionate person; one who is irascible or fiery.

spittle, spit'l, *n.* Saliva; the moist matter ejected from the mouth.

spittoon, spi-tön', *n.* A vessel to receive discharges of spittle.

splash, splash, *vt.* and *i.* To bespatter with liquid matter.—*n.* A quantity of wet matter thrown on anything; a noise from water dashed about; a spot of dirt.

splay, splā, *vt.* To slope or form with an angle.—*n.* A sloped surface.—*a.* Turned outward, as a person's feet.

splayfooted, splā"fyt'ed, *a.* Having the feet turned outward; having flat feet.

spleen, splēn, *n.* The milt, an organ in the abdomen connected with digestion; spite; ill-humor; low spirits. **spleeny**, splēn'i, *a.* Affected with or characterized by spleen; splenetic.

splendid, splen'did, *a.* Brilliant; magnificent; famous; celebrated. **splendidly**, splen'did-li, *adv.* Brilliantly; magnificently; richly.

splendor, splen'dėr, *n.* Brilliancy; magnificence; display; pomp; grandeur.

splenetic, sple-net'ik, *a.* Affected with spleen; morose; sullen; spiteful.—*n.* One affected with spleen.

splice, splīs, *vt.* (splicing, spliced). To unite, as two ropes, by interweaving the strands; to unite by overlapping, as timber.—*n.* Union of ropes by interweaving; piece added by splicing.

splint, splint, *n.* A splinter; piece of wood to confine a broken bone when set. **splinter**, splin'tėr, *n.* A piece of wood or other solid substance, split off.—*vi.* To split into splinters; to shiver, **splintery**, splin'tėr-i, *a.* Liable to splinter; consisting of splinters.

split, split, *vt.* (splitting, split). To divide lengthwise; to cleave; to rend; to burst.—*vi.* To part asunder; to burst; to crack; to differ in opinion.—*n.* A rent; fissure; breach or separation.—*a.* Divided; rent; deeply cleft.

splotch, sploch, *n.* A spot; smear.

spoil, spoil, *n.* Pillage; booty; plunder.—*vt.* To plunder; to impair; to ruin; to injure by over-indulgence.—*vi.* To grow useless; to decay.

spoiler, spoil'ėr, *n.* One who spoils; a plunderer.

spoke, spōk, *n.* A bar of a wheel; the round of a ladder; a bar.—*vt.* (spoking, spoked). To furnish with spokes. Pret. of *speak.* **spoken**, spō'ken, *p.a.* Oral; speaking (as in fair-spoken).

spokesman, spōks'man, *n.* One who speaks for another.

spoliate, spō'li-āt, *vt.* To spoil; to plunder. **spoliation**, spō'li-ā"shun, *n.* Pillage.

sponge, spunj, *n.* A soft porous marine substance which readily imbibes liquids; a mean parasite.—*vt.* (sponging, sponged). To wipe with a sponge; to wipe out completely; to harass by extortion; to get by mean arts.—*vi.* To imbibe; to act as a hanger-on. **sponger**, spun'jėr, *n.* One who sponges, **spongy**, spun'ji, *a.* Soft and full of cavities; soaked and soft.

sponsor, spon'sėr, *n.* A surety or guarantor; a godfather or godmother.

spontaneous, spon-tā'nē-us, *a.* Voluntary; self-originated; acting by its own impulse. **spontaneity**, spon'ta-nē"i-ti, *n.* Self-originated activity; readiness.

spoof, spöf, *n.* A joke; a parody.—*vt.* and *i.* To fool; to hoax.

spook, spök, *n.* A ghost; an apparition.

spool, spöl, *n.* A reel to wind thread or yarn on.

spoon, spön, *n.* A domestic utensil for taking up liquids, &c., at table.—*vt.* To take up with a spoon. **spoonful**, spön'-ful, *n.* As much as a spoon contains.

spoor, spur, *n.* The track or trail of an animal.

sporadic, spö-rad'ik, *a.* Scattered; occurring here and there in a scattered manner.

spore, spör, *n.* The reproductive germ of a cryptogamic plant; a germ of certain animal organisms.

sporran, **sporan**, spor'an, *n.* The fur pouch worn in front of the kilt.

sport, spört, *n.* A game; a merry-making; out-of-door recreation, as shooting, horse-racing, &c.; jest; object of mockery; a plant or animal that differs from the normal type.—*vt.* To divert (one's self); to wear in public.—*vi.* To play; to frolic; to practice the diversions of the field. **sportful**, spört'ful, *a.* Sportive. **sporting**, spört'ing, *a.* Indulging in sport; belonging to sport. **sportive**, spör'tiv, *a.* Full of sport; gay; playful; frolicsome; jocular. **sportsman**, spörts'man, *n.* One who engages in shooting, fishing, &c.

spot, spot, *n.* A place discolored; a speck; a blemish; a flaw; a locality.—*vt.* (spotting, spotted). To make a spot on; to stain; to catch with the eye. **spotless**, spot'les, *a.* Free from spots; unblemished; pure; immaculate. **spotted**, spot'ed, *a.* Marked with spots; speckled. **spotty**, spot'i, *a.* Full of spots; spotted.

spouse, spouz, *n.* A husband or wife.

spout, spout, *n.* A nozzle, or projecting mouth of a vessel; a water-spout; a jet or gush of water.—*vt.* and *i.* To discharge in a jet and with some force; to mouth or utter pompously.

sprain, sprän, *vt.* To overstrain, as the muscles or ligaments of a joint.—*n.* A violent strain of a joint without dislocation.

sprawl, spral, *vi.* To struggle or show convulsive motions; to lie or crawl with the limbs stretched.

spray, sprā, *n.* A twig; collection of small branches; water or any liquid flying in small drops or particles.—*vt.* To cause to take the form of spray; to treat with spray.

spread, spred, *vt.* (spreading, spread). To stretch or expand; to overspread; to disseminate; to emit; to diffuse.—*vi.* To stretch out; to be diffused.—*n.* Extent; diffusion; a meal or banquet.

spread eagle, spred' ē'gl, *n.* The figure of an eagle with the wings and legs extended.—**spread-eagle**, spred"ē'gl, *a.* Pretentious; defiantly bombastic.

spree, sprē, *n.* A merry frolic; a carousal.

sprig, sprig, *n.* A small shoot or twig; a spray; a scion; a small square brad. **spriggy**, sprig'i, *a.* Full of sprigs or small branches.

sprightly, sprīt'li, *a.* Full of spirit; lively; brisk; gay; vivacious.

spring, spring, *vi.* (pret, sprang or sprung, pp. sprung). To leap; to start up; to dart; to warp; to become cracked; to originate.—*vt.* To start or rouse; to propose on a sudden; to crack; to jump over.—*n.* A leap; resilience; an elastic body, made of various materials, especially steel; cause; an issue of water; source of supply; season of the year when plants begin to grow; a crack in timber. **springboard**, spring"börd', *n.* An elastic board used in vaulting, &c.

spring tide, spring' tīd', *n.* The high tide which happens at the new and full moon.

springtime, spring"tīm', *n.* The spring.

spring water, spring' wa'tèr, *n.* Water issuing from a spring.

springy, spring'i, *a.* Elastic; light of foot; abounding with springs; wet; spongy.

sprinkle, spring'kl, *vt.* and *i.* (sprinkling, sprinkled). To scatter in small drops; to bedew.—*n.* A small quantity scattered in drops. **sprinkling**, spring'kling, *n.* Act of one who sprinkles; a sprinkle; a small quantity distributed in a scattered manner.

sprint, sprint, *n.* A short swift foot-race; a spurt.

sprit, sprit, *n.* A small spar which crosses a sail to extend and elevate it.

sprite, sprit, *n.* A spirit; a kind of goblin.

sprout, sprout, *vi.* To bud; to push out new shoots.—*n.* A shoot of a plant; *pl.* young coleworts; Brussels sprouts.

spruce, sprös, *a.* Neat in dress; trim; smug.—*n.* A pine-tree yielding valuable timber.

spry, sprī, *a.* Nimble; active; lively.

spud, spud, *n.* A small spade for cutting the roots of weeds. A potato.

spume, spūm, *n.* Froth; foam.—*vi.* To froth.

spun, spun, pret. & pp. of *spin.*

spunk, spungk, *n.* Touchwood; tinder; nettle; pluck; courage.

spur, spèr, *n.* An instrument with sharp points, worn on horsemen's heels; incitement; stimulus; a sharp outgrowth; a moutain mass that shoots from another.—*vt.* (spurring, spurred). To prick with a spur; to incite; to put spurs on.—*vi.* To travel with great expedition.

spurious, spū'ri-us, *a.* Bastard; not genuine; counterfeit; false.

spurn, spèrn, *vt.* To drive away, as with the foot; to reject with disdain; to treat with contempt.—*vt.* To kick up the heels; to manifest disdain.

spurred, spèrd, *a.* Wearing spurs.

spurt, spèrt, *vt.* and *i.* To spirt.—*n.* A gush of liquid; sudden effort for an emergency; sudden increase of speed.

sputter, sput'èr, *vi.* To emit saliva in speaking: to throw out moisture; to speak hastily and indistinctly.

sputum, spū'tum, *n.* Spittle.

spy, spī, *vt.* (spying, spied). To gain sight of; to gain knowledge of by artifice; to explore.—*vi.* To pry.—*n.* One who keeps watch on the actions of others;

a secret emissary.

spyglass, spī'glass', *n*. A small telescope.

squab, skwob, *a*. Short; fat; plump; unfeathered.—*n*. A short, fat person; an unfledged bird; a kind of couch.

squabble, skwob'l, *vi*. (squabbling, squabbled). To dispute noisily; to wrangle.—*n*. A scuffle; a brawl.

squad, skwod, *n*. A small party of men assembled for drill; any small party.

squadron, skwod'run, *n*. The principal division of a regiment of cavalry, usually from 100 to 200 men; a division of a fleet.

squalid, skwol'id, *a*. Foul; filthy.

squall, skwal', *vi*. To cry out; to scream violently.—*n*. A long scream; a violent gust of wind; a brief storm of wind.

squally, skwal'i, *a*. Abounding with squalls.

squalor, skwol'ėr, *n*. Foulness; filthiness.

squander, skwon'dėr, *vt*. To waste; to spend money foolishly.

square, skwär, *a*. Having four equal sides and four right angles; forming a right angle; just; honest; even; suitable.—*n*. A figure having four equal sides and right angles; any similar figure or area; an instrument having one edge at right angles to another; product of a number multiplied by itself; level; equality.—*vt*. (squaring, squared). To make square; to form to right angles; to adjust; to fit; to settle (accounts); to multiply a number by itself.—*vi*. To suit; to spar (colloq.).

squash, skwosh, *vt*. To crush; to beat or press into pulp or a flat mass.—*n*. Something easily crushed; a kind of gourd; a game played indoors with ball and rackets.

squat, skwot, *vi*. (squatting, squatted). To sit upon the hams or heels; to cower; to settle on land without any title.—*a*. Cowering; short and thick.—*n*. The posture of one who squats.

squatter, skwot'ėr, *n*. One that settles on unoccupied land without a title.

squaw, skwa, *n*. Among American Indians, a female or wife.

squawk, skwak, *vi*. To cry with a harsh voice.

squeak, skwēk, *vi*. To utter a sharp, shrill sound.—*n*. A sharp, shrill sound.

squeal, skwēl, *vi*. To cry with a sharp, shrill voice; to act as an informer. *Slang*.—*n*. A shrill, sharp cry.

squeamish, skwēm'ish, *a*. Having a stomach easily turned; fastidious.

squeeze, skwēz, *vt*. (squeezing, squeezed). To subject to pressure; to harass by extortion; to hug.—*vi*. To press; to crowd.—*n*. An application of pressure; compression.

squelch, skwelch, *vt*. To crush; destroy.—*vi*. To be crushed.—*n*. A flat heavy fall.

squib, skwib, *n*. A small firework; a lampoon; a skit.—*vi*. (squibbling, squibbled). To throw squibs; to utter sarcastic reflections.

squid, skwid, *n*. A cuttle-fish.

squint, skwint, *a*. Looking obliquely or different ways.—*n*. An oblique look; an affection in which the optic axes do not coincide.—*vi*. To have a squint; to look obliquely.

squire, skwīr, *n*. A gentleman next in rank to a knight; a country gentleman; a beau.—*vt*. (squiring, squired). To attend as a squire or beau; to escort.

squirm, skwėrm, *vi*. To wriggle; to writhe.—*n*. A wriggling motion.

squirrel, skwėr'el, *n*. A rodent with a long bushy tail, living in trees.

squirt, skwėrt, *vt*. To eject out of an orifice in a stream.—*vi*. To spurt.—*n*. An instrument which ejects a liquid in a stream; a syringe; a small jet; a spurt.

stab, stab, *vt*. and *i*. (stabbing, stabbed). To pierce or kill with a pointed weapon; to wound figuratively; to injure secretly.—*n*. A thrust or wound with a pointed weapon; underhand injury; poignant pain.

stable, stā'bl, *a*. Firm; firmly established; steadfast.—*n*. A house for horses, &c.—*vt*. (stabling, stabled). To put or keep in a stable.—*vi*. To dwell in a stable. **stability**, sta-bil'i-ti, *n*. State or quality of being stable; steadfastness; firmness. **stabling**, stā'bling, *n*. Act of keeping in a stable; accommodation for horses.

staccato, sta-kä'tō, *a*. In *music*, a direction to perform notes in a detached or pointed manner.

stack, stak, *n*. A large, regularly built pile of hay, grain, &c.; a number of chimneys standing together; a single tall chimney; a high rock detached.—*vt*. To build into a stack; to pile together.

stadium, stā'di-um, *n*. A Greek measure equal to 606 feet 9 inches; a place where outdoor events or games are held.

staff, staf, *n*.; pl. **staves** or **staffs**, stävz, stafs. A stick or rod; a prop or support; a baton; the five parallel lines on which musical characters are written; a body of officers attached to an army as a whole (pl. *staffs*); a body of persons assisting in any undertaking.

staff officer, staf' of'i-sėr, *n*. An officer upon the staff of an army or regiment.

stag, stag, *n*. A male animal, especially the male red-deer; a hart.

stage, stāj, *n*. An elevated platform; the platform on which theatrical performances are exhibited; place of action; a halting-place; distance between two stopping-places; degree of progression; point reached.—*vt*. (staging, staged). To put upon the theatrical stage.

stagecoach, stāj"kōch', *n*. A coach that runs regularly for the conveyance of passengers.

stagestruck, stāj"struk', *a*. Seized by a passionate desire to become an actor.

stagger, stag'ėr, *vi*. To reel; to totter; to waver.—*vt*. To cause to waver; to amaze.—*n*. A sudden swaying of the body; *pl*. a disease of cattle, &c., attended with giddiness.

staging, stāj'ing, *n*. A temporary structure for support; scaffolding.

stagnate, stag'nāt, *vi*. (stagnating, stagnated). To cease to flow; to become motionless or dull. **stagnant**, stag'nant, *a.* Not flowing; motionless; still; dull; not brisk. **stagnation**, stag-nā'shun, *n.* State of being or becoming stagnant.

staid, stād, *a.* Sober; grave; sedate. **staidly**, stād'li, *adv.* Gravely; sedately.

stain, stān, *vt.* To mark or spot; to discolor; to soil; to disgrace; to tinge with color.—*vi.* To take stains; to become stained.—*n.* A discoloration; a spot; disgrace; a color. **stainless**, stān'les, *a.* Free from stains; untarnished; unblemished.

stair, stār, *n.* One of a set of steps to go up or down by; a series of connected steps.

staircase, stār'kās', *n.* The part of a building which contains the stairs.

stake, stāk, *n.* A sharpened piece of wood; a post; that which is pledged or wagered; hazard (preceded by *at*).—*vt.* (staking, staked). To support, defend, or mark with stakes; to pledge; to wager.

stalactite, sta-lak'tīt, *n.* A mass of calcareous matter attached, like an icicle, to the roof of a cavern.

stalagmite, sta-lag'mit, *n.* A deposit of stalactite matter on the floor of a cavern.

stale, stāl, *a.* Vapid; tasteless; not new; musty; trite.—*vt.* (staling, staled). To make stale.—*vi.* To discharge urine, as cattle.—*n.* Urine of horses and cattle.

stalk, stak, *n.* The stem of a plant; part that supports a flower, leaf, fruit, &c.; a stately step or walk.—*vi.* To walk in a dignified manner.—*vt.* To watch and follow warily, as game, for the purpose of killing.

stalker, stak'ėr, *n.* One who stalks; a kind of fishing-net.

stalking-horse, stak''ing-hōrs', *n.* A horse behind which a fowler conceals himself; a mask; a pretense.

stall, stal, *n.* A place where a horse or ox is kept and fed; division of a stable; a bench or shed where anything is exposed to sale, &c.; the seat of a clerical dignitary in the choir; a seat in a theater. —*vt.* To put into a stall; to plunge into mire. To stop.

stallion, stal'yun, *n.* A horse not castrated.

stalwart, **stalworth**, stōl'wėrt, stōl'wurth, *a.* Stout-hearted; tall and strong.

stamen, stā'men, *n.* The male organ of fructification in plants.

stamina, stam'i-na, *n.pl.* Whatever constitutes the principal strength; robustness; power of endurance.

stammer, stam'ėr, *vi.* and *t.* To make involuntary breaks in utterance; to stutter.—*n.* Defective utterance; a stutter.

stamp, stamp, *vt.* To strike by thrusting the foot down; to impress; to imprint; to affix a postage-stamp to; to coin; to form.—*vi.* To strike the foot forcibly downward.—*n.* Act of stamping; an instrument for crushing or for making impressions; mark imprinted; a postage-stamp; character; sort.

stampede, stam-pēd', *n.* A sudden fright and flight, as of horses.—*vt.* (stampeding, stampeded). To take sudden flight.—*vt.* To cause to break off in a stampede.

stance, stans, *n.* Position; posture.

stanch, **staunch**, stänch, stanch, *vt.* To stop from running, as blood; to stop the flow of blood from.—*vi.* To cease to flow.—*a.* Strong and tight; constant and zealous; loyal.

stanchion, stan'shun, *n.* A prop or support; a post of timber or iron.

stand, stand, *vi.* (standing, stood). To be upon the feet in an upright position; to be on end; to have locality; to stop; to endure; to persevere; to be as regards circumstances; to be equivalent; to become a candidate; to hold a certain course; to be valid.—*vt.* To set on end; to endure.—*n.* Act of standing; a stop; a halt; a station; a small table or frame; platform for spectators at gatherings.

standard, stan'dėrd, *n.* A flag of war; a banner; a rule or measure; criterion; test; a certain grade in schools; an upright support.—*a.* Serving as a standard; satisfying certain legal conditions; not trained on a wall, &c., but standing by itself.

standard-bearer, stan''dėrd-bār'ėr, *n.* An officer who bears a standard.

standing, stand'ing, *a.* Upright; erect; established; permanent; stagnant.—*n.* Act of one who stands; duration; place to stand in; power to stand; rank.

standpoint, stand''point', *n.* A fixed point or station; point of view from which a matter is considered.

standstill, stand''stil', *n.* A stop.

stand-up, stand''up', *a.* Erect; fought by combatants standing boldly up.

stanza, stan'za, *n.* A verse or connected number of lines of poetry.

staple, stā'pl, *n.* An emporium; a principal commodity; chief constituent thread or pile of wool, cotton, or flax; raw material; an iron loop with two points.—*a.* Chief; principal; established in commerce.—*vt.* (stapling, stapled) To adjust the staples of, as wool. **stapler**, stā'plėr, *n.* A dealer in staple commodities; one who assorts wool.

star, stär, *n.* Any celestial body except the sun and moon; a heavenly body similar to our sun; a figure with radiating points; a badge of honor; an asterisk thus (*); a brilliant theatrical performer.—*vt.* (starring, starred). To adorn with stars; to bespangle.—*vi.* To shine as a star; to appear as an eminent actor among inferior players.

starboard, stär'bōrd, *n.* and *a.* The righthand side of a ship.

starch, stärch, *n.* A vegetable substance employed for stiffening linen, &c.; stiffness of behavior.—*vt.* To stiffen with starch. **starched**, stärcht, *p.a.* Stiffened with starch; precise; formal. **starchy** stärch'i. *a.* Consisting of starch; resembling starch; stiff; precise.

stare, stär, *vi.* (staring, stared). To look with fixed eyes wide open; to gaze; to stand out stiffly.—*vt.* To effect or abash by staring.—*n.* A fixed look with the eyes; a starling.

starfish, stär''fish', *n.* A marine animal like a star with five or more rays.

stargazer, stär"gäz'ér, *n.* One who gazes at the stars; an astrologer.

stark, stärk, *a.* Stiff; rigid; strong; mere; downright.—*adv.* Wholly.

starless, stär'les, *a.* Having no stars visible.

starlight, stär"lit', *n.* The light proceeding from the stars.

starlike, stär'lik', *a.* Like a star; lustrous.

starling, stär'ling, *n.* A bird allied to the crows, capable of being taught to whistle.

starlit, stär"lit', *a.* Lighted by stars.

starred, stärd, *p.a.* Adorned with stars; influenced in fortune by the stars.

starry, stär'i, *a.* Abounding or adorned with stars; like stars.

Stars and Stripes. The flag of the U.S. with fifty stars and thirteen stripes.

Star-Spangled Banner. The U.S. national anthem; the U.S. flag.

start, stärt, *vi.* To move with sudden quickness; to wince; to deviate; to set out; to begin; to move from its place.—*vt.* To rouse suddenly; to startle; to originate; to dislocate.—*n.* A sudden motion; a twitch; outset; a handicap.

starter, stär'tér, *n.* One who starts; one who sets persons or things in motion.

startle, stär'tl, *vi.* (startling, startled). To move suddenly.—*vt.* To cause to start; to frighten.—*n.* A start, as from fear. **startling,** stär'tling, *a.* Such as to startle; surprising; alarming.

starve, stärv, *vi.* (starving, starved). To perish with cold; to suffer from hunger; to be very indigent.—*vt.* To kill or distress with hunger or cold; to make inefficient through insufficient expenditure.

starvation, stär-vä'shun, *n.* Act of starving; keen suffering from hunger or cold.

starveling, stärv'ling, *n.* A person, animal, or plant weak through want of nutriment.—*a.* Pining with want.

state, stät, *n.* Condition; situation; rank; pomp; grandeur; an estate (of the realm); a commonwealth; a nation; civil power.—*a.* National; public; governmental.—*vt.* (stating, stated). To express the particulars of; to narrate.

statecraft, stät"kraft', *n.* The art of conducting state affairs; statesmanship.

stated, stät'ed, *p.a.* Established; regular.

statehouse, stät"hous', *n.* The building in which a state legislature meets.

stately, stät'li, *a.* Such as pertains to state; august; grand; lofty; dignified.

statement, stät'ment, *n.* Expression of a fact or opinion; narrative.

stateroom, stät"röm', *n.* A magnificent room; separate cabin in a steamer.

statesman, stäts'man, *n.* A man versed in state affairs or in the arts of government.

static, stat'ik, *a.* Statical. **statical,** stat'i-kal, *a.* Pertaining to bodies at rest or in equilibrium.

statics, stat'iks, *n.* That branch of dynamics which treats of forces in equilibrium, the body on which they act being at rest.

station, stä'shun, *n.* Place where anything stands; post assigned; situation;

social position; a regular stopping-place, as on railways, &c.—*vt.* To assign a position to; to post.

stationary, stä'shun-er'i, *a.* Fixed; not moving; not appearing to move.

stationer, stä'shun-ér, *n.* One who sells paper, pens, ink, pencils, &c.

stationery, stä'shun-er'i, *n.* and *a.* Articles sold by stationers, as paper, ink, &c.

station master, stä'shun mas'tér, *n.* The official in charge of a railway-station.

statistician, stat'is-tish"an, *n.* One versed in statistics.

statistics, sta-tis'tiks, *n.* A collection of facts, tabulated numerically; the science of subjects as elucidated by facts.

statuary, stat"ū-er'i, *n.* One who carves statues; the art of carving statues; statues regarded collectively.

statue, stat'ū, *n.* An image of a human figure or animal in marble, bronze, or other solid substance. **statuesque,** stat'ū-esk", *a.* Partaking of or having the character of a statue. **statuette,** stat'ū-et", *n.* A small statue.

stature, stat'ūr, *n.* The height of any-one standing; bodily tallness.

status, stä'tus, *n.* Social position; rank; condition; position of affairs.

statute, stat'ūt, *n.* A law passed by the legislature of a state; an enactment; a fundamental or permanent rule or law. **statute book,** stat'ūt bụk', *n.* A book of statutes; the whole statutes of a country. **statutory,** stat"ū-tö'ri, *n.* Enacted by statute.

staunch, stanch, *See* **stanch.**

stave, stäv, *n.* A pole; one of the pieces of timber of casks, &c.; a stanza; in *music,* the staff.—*vt.* (staving, staved). To break in a stave of; to break a hole in (pret. & pp. also *stove*). **to stave off,** to put off; to delay.

stay, stä, *vt.* (pret. & pp. stayed or staid). To prop; to stop; to delay; to await.—*vi.* To remain; to reside; to delay; to forbear to act; to stop.—*n.* Sojourn; stop; obstacle; a prop; a rope to support a mast; *pl.* a stiffened bodice worn by females; a corset.

stead, sted, *n.* Place or room which another had or might have; assistance; preceded by *in.*—*vt.* To be of use to.

steadfast, sted'fast, *a.* Firm, constant; resolute; steady.

steady, sted'i, *a.* Firm; stable; constant; regular; equable.—*vt.* (steadying, steadied). To make or keep firm. **steadily,** sted'i-li, *adv.* In a steady manner; without shaking or tottering; assiduously. **steady-going,** sted"i-gō'-ing, *a.* Of steady or regular habits.

steak, stäk, *n.* A slice of beef, &c., broiled or cut for broiling.

steal, stēl, *vt.* (pret. stole, pp. stolen). To take feloniously; to pilfer; to gain by address or imperceptibly; to perform secretly.—*vi.* To pass silently or privily; to practice theft. **stealing,** stēl'ing, *n.* Theft.

stealth, stelth, *n.* A secret method or procedure; a proceeding by secrecy. **stealthily,** stel'thi-li, *adv.* By stealth.

stealthy, stel'thi, *a.* Done by stealth; furtive; sly.

steam, stēm, *n.* The vapor of water; aeriform fluid generated by the boiling of water.—*vi.* To give out steam; to rise in vaporous form; to sail by means of steam.—*vt.* To expose tc steam; to apply steam to.

steamboat, steam vessel, stēm″bōt′, stēm′ ves'el, *n.* A vessel propelled by steam.

steam engine, stēm′ en'jin, *n.* An engine worked by steam.

steamer, stēm'ėr, *n.* A steamboat; a fire-engine with pumps worked by steam; a vessel in which articles are subjected to steam.

steam power, stēm′ pou'ėr, *n.* The power of steam mechanically applied.

steamship, stēm″ship′, *n.* A steamboat.

steed, stēd, *n.* A horse; a horse of high mettle, for state or war.

steel, stēl, *n.* A very hard form of iron, produced by addition of carbon; weapons, swords, &c.; a knife-sharpener; sternness; rigor.—*a.* Made of or like steel; unfeeling; rigorous.—*vt.* To furnish with steel; to harden. **steely**, stēl'i, *a.* Made of or like steel; hard.

steelyard, stēl′yärd, *n.* A kind of balance for weighing, with unequal arms.

steep, stēp, *a.* Sloping greatly; precipitous.—*n.* A precipitous place; a cliff; process of steeping; liquid in which something is steeped.—*vt.* To soak; to imbue.

steeple, stē′p'l, *n.* A lofty erection attached to a church, &c.; spire.

steeplechase, stē′pl-chās′, *n.* A horse-race across country and over obstacles.

steer, stēr, *vt.* and *i.* To direct and govern, as a ship; to guide; to pursue a course in life.—*n.* A young ox; a bullock.

steerage, stēr'ij, *n.* The steering of a ship; part of a ship allotted to inferior passengers, usually in the fore part.

steersman, stērz′man, *n.* One who steers a ship.

stellar, stellary, stel'ėr, stel'ėr-i, *a.* Pertaining to stars; astral; starry.

stem, stem, *n.* The principal body of a tree, shrub, &c.; the stalk; stock or branch of a family; the prow of a vessel. —*vt.* (stemming, stemmed). To make way against; to press forward through; to dam up; to check.

stench, stench, *n.* An ill smell; stink.

stencil, sten'sil, *n.* A thin plate with a pattern cut through it, brushed over with color to mark a surface below.—*vt.* (stenciling, stenciled). To form by a stencil; to color with stencils.

stenographer, stenographist, ste-nog′ra-fėr, ste-nog′ra-fist, *n.* One who is skilled in stenography or shorthand. **stenographic, stenographical**, sten-ō-graf'ik, sten-ō-graf'i-kal, *a.* Pertaining to or expressed in shorthand. **stenography**, ste-nog′ra-fi, *n.* The art of writing in shorthand; shorthand.

stentorian, sten-tō′ri-an, *a.* Extremely loud; able to utter a loud and deep sound.

step, step, *vi.* (stepping, stepped). To move the leg and foot in walking; to walk.—*vt.* To set (the foot); to fix the foot, as of a mast.—*n.* A pace; a small space; a grade; a rise; footprint; gait; footfall; action adopted; something to support the feet in ascending round of a ladder; *pl.* a step-ladder.

stepbrother, step″brᴜᴛн′ėr, *n.* A father's or mother's son by another marriage.—Also *stepsister*.

stepfather, step″fä′ᴛнėr, *n.* A mother's second or subsequent husband.—Also *stepmother*.

stepladder, step'lad-ėr, *n.* A portable self-supporting ladder.

steppe, step, *n.* An extensive treeless plain in Russia and Siberia.

steppingstone, step″ing-stōn′, *n.* A stone to raise the feet above a stream or mud; a means of progress or advancement.

stepson, step″sun′, *n.* The son of a husband or wife by a former marriage.—Also *stepdaughter, stepchild*.

stereoscope, ster″ē-ō-skōp′, *n.* An optical instrument by which two pictures taken under a small difference of angular view and placed side by side appear as one, the objects seeming solid and real. **stereotype**, ster″ē-ō-tīp′, *n.* and *a.* A metal plate presenting a facsimile of a page of type; an electrotype plate.—*vt.* To make stereotype of; to fix unchangeably. **stereotyped**, ster″ē-ō-tīp′, *p.a.* Made or printed from stereotype plates; fixed.

sterile, ster'il, *a.* Barren; unfruitful; incapable of reproduction; barren of ideas. **sterility**, ste-ril'i-ti, *n.* Quality or state of being sterile; unproductiveness. **sterilize**, ster″i-līz, *vt.* To make sterile; to render free from bacteria or germs. **sterilizer**, ster″i-līz′ėr, *n.* One who sterilizes; an apparatus to destroy bacilli, &c.

sterling, stėr'ling, *a.* An epithet distinctive of English money; genuine; of excellent quality.

stern, stėrn, *a.* Austere; harsh; rigid; stringent.—*n.* The hind part of a ship.

sternum, stėr′num, *n.* The breast-bone.

stethoscope, steth′ō-skōp, *n.* An instrument for sounding the chest, lungs, &c.

stevedore, stē″ve-dōr′, *n.* One who loads or unloads vessels.

stew, stū, *vt.* To boil slowly in a closed vessel.—*vi.* To be cooked slowly.—*n.* Meat stewed; a bathing house with hot baths; a brothel; a state of excitement.

steward, stū′ėrd, *n.* One who manages affairs for another; one who helps to manage a public function; an officer on a vessel who attends to passengers, &c. **stewardess**, stū′ärd-es, *n.* A female steward.

stick, stik, *vi.* (sticking, stuck). To pierce or stab; to fasten by piercing, gluing, &c.; to fix; to set.—*vi.* To adhere; to abide firmly; to be brought to a stop; to scruple.—*n.* A rod or wand; a staff; a stiff awkward person.

stickler, stik'lėr, *n.* One who stickles; an obstinate contender about trifles.

sticky, stik'i, *a.* Adhesive; gluey; viscid.

stiff, stif, *a.* Rigid; tense; not moving

easily; thick; not natural and easy; formal in manner; stubborn; difficult; strong. **stiffen,** stif'en, *vt.* To become stiff or stiffer.

stiffening, stif'en-ing, *n.* Something used to make a substance more stiff; starch, &c. **stiffly,** stif'li, *adv.* In a stiff manner; firmly; rigidly; obstinately; formally. **stiff-necked,** stif'nekt', *a.* Stubborn; inflexibly obstinate; contumacious. **stiffness,** stif'nes, *n.* Want of pliancy; rigidity; viscidness; stubbornness; formality.

stifle, stī'fl, *vt.* and *i.* (stifling, stifled). To suffocate; to smother; to suppress.—*n.* The joint of a horse next to the buttock.

stigma, stig'ma, *n.*; pl. **-mas** or **-mata.** A brand made with a red-hot iron; any mark of infamy; part of a flower pistil which receives the pollen; *pl.* stigmata, bodily marks like Christ's wounds impressed supernaturally. **stigmatic,** stig-mat'ik, *a.* Pertaining to stigmas or stigmata.—*n.* A person marked with stigmata. **stigmatize,** stig'ma-tīz, *vt.* To characterize by some opprobrious epithet.

stile, stīl, *n.* A step or steps to aid persons in getting over a fence or wall.

stiletto, sti-let'ō, *n.* A small strong dagger; a pointed instrument for making eyelet-holes.—*vt.* (stilettoing, stilettoed). To stab or pierce with a stiletto.

still, stil, *a.* At rest; calm; silent; not loud; soft; not effervescing.—*vt.* To make still; to check; to appease or allay. —*adv.* To this time; always; nevertheless; yet.—*n.* A vessel or apparatus for distilling; a distillery. **stillborn,** stil'born', *a.* Dead at the birth; abortive; produced unsuccessfully. **still life,** stil' līf, *n.* Objects such as dead game, vegetables, &c., represented in painting. **stillness,** stil'nes, *n.* Calmness; quiet. **stilly,** stil'i, *a.* Still; quiet; *poet.*—*adv.* stil'li. Silently; calmly; quietly.

stilt, stilt, *n.* Either of a pair of poles, with a rest for the foot, used for raising the feet in walking. **stilted,** stilt'ed, *a.* Elevated as if on stilts; stiff and bombastic; jerky.

stimulate, stim'ū-lāt, *vt.* To rouse up; to incite; to excite greater vitality in. **stimulant,** stim'ū-lant, *a.* Serving to stimulate.—*n.* An agent which produces an increase of vital energy; an intoxicant. **stimulating,** stim'ū-lāt-ing, *p.a.* Serving to stimulate or rouse; rousing; stirring. **stimulation,** stim'ū-lā''shun, *n.* Act of stimulating; incitement; use of a stimulus.

stimulus, stim'ū-lus, *n.*; pl. **-li.** Something that stimulates; an incitement.

sting, sting, *vt.* (stinging, stung). To pierce, as wasps, &c.; to prick, as a nettle; to pain acutely.—*n.* A sharp-pointed defensive organ of certain animals; the thrust of a sting into the flesh; something that gives acute pain; the biting effect of words.

stinging, sting'ing, *p.a.* Furnished with a sting; goading; sharp; keen.

stingy, stin'ji, *a.* Very niggardly; meanly avaricious; scanty.

stink, stingk, *vi.* (stinking, stunk). To emit a strong offensive smell; to be in disrepute.—*n.* A strong offensive smell.

stint, stint, *vt.* To restrict; to make scanty.—*vi.* To cease; to desist from.— *n.* Limit; restraint; restriction.

stipend, stī'pend, *n.* Yearly allowance; salary.

stipple, stip'l, *vt.* (stippling, stippled). To engrave by means of dots.—*n.* A process of engraving by means of dots.

stipulate, stip'ū-lāt, *vi.* (stipulating, stipulated). To make an agreement; to contract; to settle terms. **stipulation,** stip'ū-lā''shun, *n.* Act of stipulating; a contract; item in a contract.

stir, stėr, *vt.* (stirring, stirred). To put into motion; to agitate; to rouse; to provoke; to disturb.—*vi.* To move one's self; not to be still; to be awake or out of bed.—*n.* Commotion; bustle; disorder. **stirring,** stėr'ing, *p.a.* Active in business; bustling; rousing; exciting.

stirrup, stī'rup, *n.* A metal loop, suspended by a strap, to support the foot in riding.

stitch, stich, *n.* A sharp pain; one complete movement of a needle in sewing; a complete turn or link in knitting, netting, &c.—*vt.* and *i.* To sew by making stitches in; to unite by stitches.

stoat, stōt, *n.* The ermine in its summer fur.

stock, stok, *a.* A post; a lifeless mass; stem of a tree; wooden piece of a rifle; a stiff cravat; an original progenitor; lineage; capital invested in any business; money funded in government securities; stone; animals belonging to a farm; liquor used to form a foundation for soups and gravies; a sweet-smelling garden plant; *pl.* an instrument of punishment confining the offenders' ankles or wrists; timbers on which a ship is supported while building.—*vt.* To provide with a stock; to lay up in store.—*a.* Kept in stock; standing; permanent.

stockade, stok-ād', *n.* A defense of strong posts stuck close to each other; an inclosure made with posts.—*vt.* (stockading, stockaded). To fortify with posts fixed in the ground.

stockbroker, stok''brō'kėr, *n.* A broker who buys and sells stocks or shares for others.

stock exchange, stok'eks-chānj', *n.* The place where stocks or shares are bought and sold; an organized association of stockbrokers.

stockholder, stok''hōl'dėr, *n.* A shareholder or proprietor of stock.

stocking, stok'ing, *n.* A close-fitting knitted covering for the foot and leg.

stock list, stok list, *n.* A list showing the price of stocks, the transactions in them, &c.

stockpile, stok''pīl', *n.* An accumulation of commodities or atomic weapons.

stock-still, stok'stil', *a.* Still as a stock or fixed post; perfectly still.

stock-taking, stok'tāk-ing, *n.* A periodical examination and valuation of the goods in a shop, &c.

stodge, stoj, *vt.* (stodging, stodged). To stuff or cram.—*n.* A jumbled mass.

stodgy, stoj'i, *a.* Crammed together roughly; crude and indigestible.

Stoic, stō'ik, *n.* One of an Athenian sect of philosophers, who held that men should strive to be unmoved by joy or grief, regarding virtue alone as the highest good; an apathetic person; one indifferent to pleasure or pain. **stoical**, stō'i-kal, *a.* Like a stoic; manifesting indifference to pleasure or pain. **Stoicism**, stō'i-sizm, *n.* Indifference to pleasure or pain.

stoke, stōk, *vt.* (stoking, stoked). To keep supplied with fuel, as a fire. **stoker**, stōk'ėr, *n.* One who attends to a furnace or large fire.

stole, stōl, *n.* A long and narrow scarf worn round the neck, with the ends hanging down, by clergymen of the Anglican and Roman Catholic churches.

stolid, stol'id, *a.* Dull; foolish; stupid. **stolidity**, stō-lid'i-ti, *n.* Dullness of intellect; stupidity.

stomach, stum'ak, *n.* A membranous sac, the principal organ of digestion; appetite; inclination.—*vt.* To brook; to put up with. **stomacher**, stum'a-kėr, *n.* An ornamental article of dress worn by females on the breast.

stone, stōn, *n.* A hard mass of earthy or mineral matter; a pebble; a precious stone; concretion in the kidneys or bladder; the nut of a fruit; a measure of 14 lbs. avoirdupois.—*a.* Made of stone; like stone.—*vt.* (stoning, stoned). To pelt with stones; to free from stones; to provide with stones.

Stone Age. The earliest known period of human culture, characterized by the use of stone tools and preceding the Bronze Age.

stonecutter, stōn″kut'ėr, *n.* One whose occupation is to cut or hew stones.

stone-dead, stōn'ded', *a.* As lifeless as a stone.

stone-deaf, stōn'def', *a.* Totally deaf.

stonework, stōn″wėrk', *n.* Work consisting of stone; masons; work of stone.

stony, stōn'i, *a.* Pertaining to, abounding in or like stone; hard; pitiless; frigid.

stonyhearted, stōn'i-här'ted, *a.* Hardhearted; cruel; pitiless; unfeeling.

stool, stōl, *n.* A portable seat without a back for one person; the seat used in evacuating the bowels; a discharge from the bowels.

stool pigeon. A spy; an informer.

stoop, stöp, *vi.* To bend the body forward and downward; to yield; to deign; to pounce.—*n.* Act of stooping; bend of the back or shoulders; a condescension; swoop. **stooping**, stöp'ing, *p.a.* Having a stoop; in act to stoop; bowed, as the shoulders.

stop, stop, *vt.* (stopping, stopped). To stuff up; to close; to arrest the progress of; to put an end to; to regulate the sounds of musical strings by the fingers, &c.—*vi.* To cease from any motion; to come to an end; to stay; to remain.—*n.* Obstruction; interruption; pause; a series of pipes in an organ giving distinctive sounds; a point in writing.

stopgap, stop″gap', *n.* That which fills up a gap; a temporary expedient.

stoppage, stop'ij, *n.* Act of stopping; a halt.

stopper, stop'ėr, *n.* One who or that which stops; a stopple.—*vt.* To close with a stopper.

stopping, stop'ing, *n.* Act of one who stops; that which stops or fills up.

stop watch, stop'woch, *n.* A watch one of the hands of which can be stopped instantaneously so as to mark with accuracy any point of time.

store, stōr, *n.* A large quantity for supply; abundance; a place where goods are kept; a shop; *pl.* necessary articles laid up for use.—*a.* Pertaining to a store; kept in store.—*vt.* (storing, stored). To amass; to supply; to reposit in a store for preservation. **storage**, stōr'ij, *n.* Act of storing; charge for keeping goods in a store. **storehouse**, stōr″hous', *n.* A place in which things are stored; a repository. **storekeeper**, stōr″kēp'ėr, *n.* One who has the care of a store or stores. **store-room**, stōr″-rōm', *n.* A room for the reception of stores.

storied, stō'rid, *a.* Having stories or tales associated with it; celebrated in story.

stork, stork, *n.* A large grallatorial or wading bird resembling the heron.

storm, storm, *n.* A violent disturbance of the atmosphere; a tempest; an outbreak; assault on a strong position.—*vt.* To take by assault; to attack.—*vi.* To be in violent agitation; to rage. **stormy**, stor'mi, *a.* Abounding with storms; boisterous; passionate; angry.

story, stō'ri, *n.* A narrative; an account; a tale; a fiction; a falsehood.

story, storey, stō'ri, *n.* A stage or floor of a building.

stoup, stöp, or stoup, *n.* A basin for holy water in a R. Catholic church; a flagon.

stout, stout, *a.* Bold; valiant; sturdy; bulky; corpulent.—*n.* A dark-brown malt liquor. **stoutly**, stout'li, *adv.* Boldly; lustily.

stove, stōv, *n.* An apparatus for warming a room, cooking, &c.—*vt.* (stoving, stoved). To heat in a stove. Pret. of *stave.*

stow, stō, *vt.* To put in a suitable place; to pack; to compactly arrange anything in. **stowage**, stō'ij, *n.* Act of stowing; room for things to be packed away; charge for stowing goods. **stowaway**, stō″a-wā', *n.* One who hides himself on a ship to obtain a free passage.

strabismus, stra-biz'mus, *n.* A squint in a person's eyes.

straddle, strad'l, *vi.* and *t.* (straddling, straddled). To spread the legs wide; to sit astride; to stride across.

strafe, sträf, *vt.* To spray with machine-gun fire from aircraft.

straggle, strag'l, *vi.* (straggling, straggled). To rove; to wander in a scattered way; to occur at intervals. **straggler**, strag'lėr, *n.* One who straggles; a vagabond.

straight, strāt, *a.* Stretched tight; direct; correct; upright.—*n.* A straight part or piece; straight direction.—*adv.*

Immediately; directly.—*vt.* To straighten.

straightedge, strāt″ej′, *n.* An implement with a perfectly straight edge for testing surfaces or drawing straight lines.

straighten, strāt′n, *vt.* To make straight.

straightforward, strāt′for″wĕrd, *a.* Proceeding in a straight course; candid; honest; frank; open.—*adv.* Directly forward. **straightforwardly**, strāt″for″wĕrd-li, *adv.* In a straightforward manner.

straightway, strāt′wā′, *adv.* Directly; immediately; forthwith; without delay.

strain, strān, *vt.* To stretch tightly; to exert to the utmost; to overtask; to sprain; to carry too far; to wrest; to filter.—*vi.* To exert one's self; to filter.—*n.* Violent effort; excessive stretching or exertion; tenor; theme; a lay; tune; race; family blood; tendency. **strained**, strānd, *a.* Stretched to the utmost; forced or unnatural. **strainer**, strān′ĕr, *n.* One who strains; an instrument for filtration.

strait, strāt, *a.* Confined; narrow; close; strict.—*n.* A narrow passage; a narrow stretch of water (often *pl.*); a position of hardship or difficulty.

straiten, strāt′n, *vt.* To make strait; to distress; to hamper.

strait-laced, strāt′lāst′, *a.* Laced tightly; excessively strict or scrupulous.

straitjacket, strāt′jak-et, *n.* A strong garment used to restrain lunatics.

strand, strand, *n.* The shore of a sea or lake; one of the twists of rope.—*vt.* and *i.* To drive or be driven ashore.

strange, strānj, *a.* Foreign; wonderful; odd; not familiar. **strangely**, strānj′li, *adv.* In a strange manner; wonderfully; remarkably. **stranger**, strān′jĕr, *n.* A foreigner; an alien; one unknown; a visitor.

strangle, strang′gl, *vt.* (strangling, strangled). To choke; to throttle; to suppress or stifle.

strangulate, strang′gū-lāt, *vt.* To strangle; to stop vital action in by compression. **strangulation**, strang′gū-lā″shon, *n.* Act of strangling; compression of the windpipe, constriction.

strap, strap, *n.* A long narrow slip of leather, &c.; a plate or strip of metal.—*vt.* (strapping, strapped). To beat with a strap; to fasten with a strap.

strapping, strap′ing, *a.* Tall and well made; handsome.

stratagem, strat′a-jem, *n.* A piece of generalship; an artifice in war; a wile.

strategic, **strategical**, stra-tē′jik, stra-tē′ji-kal, *a.* Pertaining to strategy; effected by strategy. **strategist**, strat′te-jist, *n.* One skilled in strategy. **strategy**, stra′te-ji, *n.* The science of military operations; generalship.

stratify, strat′i-fī, *vt.* To form into a stratum or strata; to lay in strata. **stratification**, strat′i-fi-kā″shun, *n.* Arrangement in strata or layers.

stratum, strā′tum, *n.*; *pl.* **-ta**. A layer of any substance, as sand, clay, &c., especially when one of a number. Strata.

stratus, strā′tus, *n.* A low, dense, horizontal cloud.

straw, strą, *n.* The stalk of grain, pulse, &c.—*a.* Made of straw.

strawberry, strą′ber′i, *n.* A herbaceous plant and its succulent fruit.

stray, strā, *vi.* To go astray; to err; to roam.—*a.* Having gone astray; straggling.—*n.* Any domestic animal that wanders at large.

streak, strēk, *n.* A long mark; a stripe; appearance of a mineral when scratched.—*vt.* To form streaks in. **streaky**, strēk′i, *a.* Striped; variegated with streaks.

stream, strēm, *n.* A river or brook; a current; drift.—*vi.* and *t.* To move in a stream; to stretch in a long line; to float at full length in the air.

streamer, strēm′ĕr, *n.* That which streams out; a long pennon; a luminous beam or column.

street, strēt, *n.* A road in a tower or village; the roadway and houses together.

strength, strength, *n.* Property of being strong; force or energy; power; support; vigor; intensity; amount or numbers of an army, fleet, or the like. **on the strength of**, in reliance upon, on the faith of. **strengthen**, streng′then, *vt.* and *i.* To make or become strong or stronger.

strenuous, stren′ū-us, *a.* Energetic; vigorous; zealous; ardent; earnest.

streptococcus, strep′tō-kok″us, *n.* A species of bacteria which multiplies in chainlike formations and causes many diseases.

streptomycin, strep′tō-mī″sin, *n.* A powerful antibiotic derived from a mold organism.

stress, stres, *vt.* To put in difficulties; to subject to emphasis.—*n.* Constraint; pressure; weight; violence; as of weather; emphasis.

stretch, strech, *vt.* To draw out tight; to extend; to straighten; to strain; to exaggerate.—*vi.* To reach or extend; to spread; to have elasticity.—*n.* Strain; extent; scope; expanse; a turn or spell.

stretcher, strech′ĕr, *n.* One who stretches; a contrivance for stretching things; a litter for carrying persons.

strew, strö or strō, *vt.* (pp. strewed or strewn). To scatter or sprinkle; to cover by scattering; to besprinkle.

stricken, strik′en, pp. of *strike*. Struck; smitten; advanced in age.

strict, strikt, *a.* Tight; tense; exact; severe; rigorous; not loose or vague. **strictly**, strikt′li, *adv.* In a strict manner; correctly; definitely; rigorously; severely.

stricture, strik′tūr, *n.* A contraction of any canal of the body; a critical remark; censure.

stride, strīd, *vi.* (striding, pret. strode, pp. stridden). To walk with long steps; to straddle.—*vt.* To pass over at a step.—*n.* A long step; a measured tread.

strident, strī′dent, *a.* Harsh; grating.

strife, strīf, *n.* Act of striving; struggle; contest; discord; conflict; quarrel or war.

strike, strīk, *vi.* (striking, pret. struck,

pp. struck, stricken). To move or turn aside rapidly; to light (upon); to make a blow; to hit; to be stranded; to yield; to quit work to compel better terms. —*vt.* To smite; to mint; to thrust in; to notify by sound; to occur to; to impress strongly; to effect at once; to lower, as the flag or sails of a vessel.— *n.* Act of workmen who quit work to force their employer to give better terms; a strickle. **striker**, strik′ėr, n. One who or that which strikes; one who engages in a strike. **striking**, strik′ing, *p.a.* Surprising; remarkable; notable.

string, string, *n.* A small cord; a piece of twine; a line with the things on it; chord of a musical instrument; a series. —*vt.* (stringing, strung). To furnish with string; to put on a string; to make tense.

stringent, strin′jent, *a.* Strict; rigorous; rigid. **stringency**, strin′jen-si, *n.* State of being stringent.

stringy, string′i, *a.* Consisting of strings; fibrous; ropy; viscid; sinewy.

strip, strip, *vt.* (stripping, stripped). To deprive of a covering; to skin; to deprive; to pillage.—*vi.* To take off the covering or clothes.—*n.* A long narrow piece.

stripe, strīp, *n.* A long narrow division or marking; a streak; a strip; a stroke with a lash; a wale or weal.—*vt.* (striping, striped). To form or variegate with stripes.

stripling, strip′ling, *n.* A tall slender youth; a lad.

strive, strīv, *vi.* (striving, pret. strove, pp. striven). To endeavor; to make efforts; to struggle; to vie.

stroke, strōk, *n.* A blow; calamity; attack; striking of a clock; touch; a masterly effort; a dash in writing or printing; a touch of the pen; a line; a gentle rub; the sweep of an oar; a stroke-oar.—*vt.* (stroking, stroked). To rub gently with the hand.

stroke oar, strōk ōr, *n.* The aftmost oar of a boat; the man that uses it.

stroll, strōl, *vi.* To ramble; to rove; to roam.—*n.* A short leisurely walk.

stroller, strōl′ėr, *n.* One who strolls; a vagabond; a vagrant; an itinerant player.

strong, strong, *a.* Having power or force; robust; not easily broken; firm; effectual; earnest; containing much alcohol; glaring; forcible; tending upwards in price; effecting inflection by internal vowel change. **stronghold**, strong″- hōld′, *n.* A place of strength or security; a fortified place. **strongly**, strong′li, *adv.* With strength or power; forcibly; firmly; greatly. **strong room**, strong rōm, *n.* A room in which valuables are kept.

strontium, stron′shi-um, *n.* A metal of a yellow color, somewhat harder than lead.

strop, strop, *n.* A strip of leather, &c., for sharpening razors.—*vt.* (stropping, stropped). To sharpen on a strop.

strove, strōv, pret. of *strive.*

struck, struk, pret. and pp. of *strike.*

structure, struk′tūr, *n.* A building of

any kind; manner of building; make organization. **structural**, struk′tūr-al, *a.* Pertaining to structure.

struggle, strug′l, *vi.* (struggling, struggled). To make great efforts; to strive; to contend.—*n.* A violent effort of the body; forcible effort; contest; strife.

strum, strum, *vi.* and *t.* (strumming, strummed). To play unskillfully on a stringed instrument; to thrum.

strumpet, strum′pet, *n.* A prostitute.

strut, strut, *vi.* (strutting, strutted). To walk with affected dignity.—*n.* A lofty, proud step or walk; a strengthening piece placed diagonally in a framework.

strychnia, **strychnine**, strik′ni-a, strik′nin, *n.* A vegetable alkaloid poison obtained from the seeds of nux-vomica.

stub, stub, *n.* The stump of a tree; a remaining part of anything.—*vt.* (stubbing, stubbed). To grub up by the roots.

stubble, stub′l, *n.* The stumps of a grain crop left in the ground after reaping.

stubborn, stub′ėrn, *a.* Not to be moved or persuaded; obstinate; intractable. **stubbornly**, stub′ėrn-li, *adv.* Obstinately.

stubby, stub′i, *a.* Abounding with stubs; short and thick.

stucco, stuk′kō, *n.* A fine plaster; work made of stucco; plaster of Paris or gypsum.—*vt.* (stuccoing, stuccoed). To overlay with stucco.

stuck-up, stuk′up′, *a.* Giving one's self airs of importance; proud; pompous.

stud, stud, *n.* A post; a prop; a nail with a large head; an ornamental button; a set of breeding horses; a person's horses collectively.—*vt.* (studding, studded). To adorn with studs; to set thickly, as with studs.

student, stū′dent, *n.* One who studies; a scholar; a bookish man.

studied, stu′did, *a.* Made the object of study; qualified by study; premeditated.

studio, stū′di-ō, *n.* The work place of a painter or sculptor.

studious, stū′di-us, *a.* Given to study; mindful; earnest; careful; deliberate. **studiously**, stū′di-us-li, *adv.* Diligently; carefully; deliberately.

study, stud′i, *n.* Earnest endeavor; application to books, &c.; subject which one studies; apartment devoted to study; a reverie; a preparatory sketch.—*vt.* and *i.* (studying, studied). To apply the mind to; to investigate; to have careful regard to.

stuff, stuf, *n.* Substance indefinitely; material; cloth; a light woolen fabric; goods; trash.—*vt.* To pack; to thrust in; to fill, as meat with seasoning; to fill, as an animal's skin to preserve the form.—*vi.* To cram; to feed gluttonously.

stuffing, stuf′ing, *n.* That which is used to fill anything, as a cushion; substance put into a fowl for cooking.

stuffy, stuf′i, *a.* Difficult to breathe in; close; stifling.

stultify, stul′ti-fī, *vt.* To prove foolish; to cause to seem absurd; to make a fool of.

stumble, stum′bl, *vi.* (stumbling, stumbled). To trip in moving; to walk unsteadily; to fall into error; to light by chance (with *on*).—*n.* A trip in walking or running; a blunder. **stumbling block, stumbling stone,** stum'bling blok, stum'bling stōn, *n.* Any cause of stumbling or erring.

stump, stump, *n.* The part of a tree, limb, &c., left after the rest is cut off or destroyed; a worn-down tooth; a wicket in cricket.—*vt.* To lop, as trees; to make a tour through, delivering speeches; to put out of play in cricket by knocking down a stump.—*vi.* To walk stiffly or noisily.

stump speech, stump spēch, *n.* A speech made from an improvised platform; a frothy harangue.

stumpy, stump'i, *a.* Full of stumps; short and thick.

stun, stun, *vt.* (stunning, stunned). To overpower the sense of hearing of; to stupefy; to make senseless with a blow; to surprise completely. **stunner,** stun'ẽr, *n.* Something that stuns; a person or thing of showy appearance. **stunning,** stun'ing, *p.a.* Such as to stun; first-rate; excellent.

stunt, stunt, *vt.* To stop the growth of; to dwarf.—*n.* A check in growth. **stunted,** stunt'ed, *a.* Hindered from growth; dwarfish in growth or size.

stupefy, stū'pē-fī, *vt.* (stupefying, stupefied). To deprive of sensibility. **stupefaction,** stū'pē-fak"shun, *n.* State of being stupefied; insensibility; stupidity.

stupendous, stū-pen'dus, *a.* Of astonishing magnitude; grand or awe-inspiring.

stupid, stū'pid, *a.* Struck senseless; foolish; dull in intellect; nonsensical. **stupidity,** stū-pid'i-ti, *n.* Extreme intellectual dullness; senselessness.

stupor, stū'pẽr, *n.* A condition in which the faculties are deadened; torpor; insensibility.

sturdy, stẽr'di, *a.* Stout; strong; hardy; firm; robust; vigorous. **sturdily,** stẽr'di-li, *adv.* Hardily; stoutly; lustily.

sturgeon, stẽr'jun, *n.* A genus of large fishes having flesh valuable as food.

stutter, stut'ẽr, *vi.* To stammer.—*n.* A stammer; broken utterance of words.

sty, stī, *n.* An inclosure for swine; any filthy hovel or place.—*vt.* (stying, stied). To shut up in a sty.

sty, stye, stī *n.* A small inflammatory tumor on the edge of the eyelid.

Stygian, stij'i-an, *a.* Pertaining to Styx, a fabled river of hell over which the shades of the dead passed; dark and gloomy; infernal.

style, stīl. *n.* A burn; pin of a sundial; manner of writing with regard to language; a characteristic mode in the fine arts; type; external manner, mode, or fashion; title; in *botany*, a slender prolongation of the ovary supporting the stigma.—*vt.* (styling, styled). To term; to designate.

stylish, stīl'ish, *a.* In the mode; fashionable.

stylist, stīl'ist, *n.* A writer or speaker careful of his style; a master of style.

stylus, stī'lus, *n.* A style or pointed instrument.

styptic, stip'tik, *a.* Able to stop bleeding.—*n.* A substance which stops a flow of blood.

suave, swäv, *a.* Gracious in manner; blandly polite; pleasant. **suavity,** swä-vi-ti, *n.* Graciousness of manner; blandness; urbanity.

sub, sub, *n.* A contraction for *subordinate.*

subaltern, su-bal'tẽrn or sub'l-tẽrn, *a.* Holding a subordinate position.—*n.* A commissioned military officer below the rank of captain.

subcommittee, sub"ko-mit'ē, *n.* An under committee; a division of a committee.

subcutaneous, sub'kū-tā"nē-us, *a.* Situated immediately under the skin.

subdivide, sub'di-vīd", *vt.* To divine part of into more parts.—*vi.* To be subdivided; to separate.—**subdivision,** sub'di-vizh"un, *n.* Act of subdividing; a part of a larger part.

subdue, sub-dū', *vt.* (subduing, subdued). To subjugate; to overpower; to tame; to soften; to tone down. **subdued,** sub-dūd', *a.* Toned down; reduced in intensity; low in tone.

subject, sub'jekt, *a.* Ruled by another; liable; prone; submissive.—*n.* One who owes allegiance to a ruler or government; matter dealt with; theme; topic; the nominative of a verb; the thinking agent or principle.—*vt.* sub-jekt', To subdue; to make liable; to cause to undergo. **subjection,** sub-jek'shun, *n.* Act of subjecting; subjugation; enthrallment.

subjective, sub-jek'tiv, or sub'jek-tiv, *a.* Relating to the subject; belonging to ourselves, the conscious subject; exhibiting strongly the personality of the author. **subjectivity,** sub'jek-tiv"i-ti, *n.* State or quality of being subjective; character of exhibiting the individuality of an author. **subject matter,** sub'jekt mat'ẽr, *n.* The matter or theme presented for consideration.

subjoin, sub-join', *vt.* To add at the end: to affix, to annex; to attach. **subjoinder,** sub-join'dẽr, *n.* A rejoinder.

subjugate, sub'jō-gāt, *vt.* To subdue; to conquer and compel to submit. **subjugation,** sub'jō-gā"shun, *n.* Act of subjugating or subduing; subdual; subjection.

subjunctive, sub-jungk'tiv, *a.* and *n.* Applied to a mood of verbs that expresses condition. hypothesis, or contingency.

sublease, sub"lēs', *n.* A lease granted to a subtenant.

sublet, sub'let', *vt.* To let to another person, the party letting being himself a lessee.

sublimate, sub'li-māt, *vt.* To raise by heat into vapor, as a solid, which on cooling returns again to the solid state; to refine; to elevate.—*n.* The product of sublimation. **sublimation,** sub'li-mā"shun, *n.* The process or operation of sublimating; exaltation; a highly refined product.

sublime, sub-līm', *a.* High in place of excellence; affecting the mind with a sense of grandeur; noble; majestic. **the**

sublime, the grand in the works of nature or of art; grandeur of style; highest degree.—*vt.* (subliming, sublimed). To render sublime; to sublimate.—*vi.* To be susceptible of sublimation. **sublimely**, sub-līm'li, *adv.* In a sublime manner; grandly; majestically; loftily. **sublimity**, sub-lim'i-ti, *n.* State or quality of being sublime; grandeur; majesty.

submachine gun, sub'ma-shēn" gun. A small, portable machine gun.

submarine, sub'ma-rēn", *a.* Being under the surface of the sea; a kind of ship.

submerge, sub-mèrj', *vt.* and *i.* (submerging, submerged). To put under or cover with water; to drown; to sink.

submerse, **submersed**, sub-mèrs', submèrst', *a.* Being or growing under water. **submersion**, sub-mér'shun, *n.* Act of submerging; state of being under fluid; a dipping or plunging.

submit, sub-mit', *vt.* (submitting, submitted). To yield or surrender; to refer; to state, as a claim.—*vi.* To surrender; to acquiesce; to suffer without complaint. **submission**, sub-mish'un, *n.* Act of submitting; surrender; humble behavior; obedience; resignation.

submissive, sub-mis'iv, *a.* Yielding; obedient; compliant; humble; modest. **submissively**, sub-mis'iv-li, *adv.* In a submissive manner; obediently; humbly.

subordinate, su-bor'di-nit, *a.* Inferior; occupying a lower position.—*n.* One who stands in rank, power, &c., below another.—*vt.* To place in a lower order or rank. **subordination**, su-bor'di-nā"shun, *n.* The act of subordinating; inferiority of rank; subjection.

suborn, sub-orn', *vt.* To bribe to commit perjury; to bribe to some wickedness. **subornation**, sub'or-nā"shun, *n.* Act of suborning.

subpœna, sub-pē'na, *n.* A writ summoning a witness under a penalty.—*vt.* (subpœnaing, subpœaed). To serve with a writ of subpœna.

subscribe, sub-skrib', *vt.* and *i.* (subscribing, subscribed). To append one's own signature to; to promise to contribute (money) by writing one's name; to assent. **subscriber**, sub-skrib'ér, *n.* One who subscribes. **subscript**, sub'skript, *a.* Underwritten; written below something. **subscription**, sub-skrip'shun, *n.* Act of subscribing; signature; attestation; a sum subscribed.

subsequent, sub'sē-kwent, *a.* Following in time; succeeding; next. **subsequence**, sub'sē-kwens, *n.* The state of being subsequent.

subserve, sub-sérve', *vt.* and *i.* (subserving, subserved). To serve; to be instrumental to; to promote. **subservience**, **subserviency**, sub-sér'vi-ens, sub-sér'vi-en-si, *n.* State of being subservient. **subservient**, sub-sér'vi-ent, *a.* Acting as a tool; serving to promote some end.

subside, sub-sid', *vt.* (subsiding, subsided). To sink or fall to the bottom; to settle down; to abate. **subsidence**, sub-sid'ens or sub'si-dens, *n.* Act or process of subsiding.

subsidy, sub'si-di, *n.* A sum of money granted for a purpose; a sum given by a government to meet expenses. **subsidiary**, sub-sid"i-er'i, *a.* Pertaining to a subsidy; aiding; assistant; subordinate. —*n.* An assistant. **subsidize**, sub'si-diz, *vt.* (subsidizing, subsidized). To furnish with a subsidy; to purchase the assistance of another by a subsidy.

subsist, sub-sist', *vi.* To have existence; to live; to inhere. **subsistence**, sub-sis'tens, *n.* Existence; real being; livelihood; sustenance. **subsistent**, sub-sis'tent, *a.* Having being or existence; inherent.

subsoil, sub'soil, *n.* The bed or stratum of earth below the surface soil.

subspecies, sub'spē-shiz, *n.* A subdivision of species.

substance, sub'stans, *n.* That of which a thing consists; material; a body; essence; purport; means and resources. **substantial**, sub-stan'shal, *a.* Actually existing; real; solid; strong; moderately wealthy. **substantiality**, sub-stan'shi-al"i-ti, *n.* State of being substantial. **substantially**, sub-stan'shal-li, *adv.* With reality of existence; strongly; in substance; in the main. **substantiate**, sub-stan'shi-āt, *vt.* To give substance to; to prove. **substantiation**, sub-stan'shi-ā"shun, *n.* Act of substantiating; evidence; proof. **substantive**, sub'stan-tiv, *a.* Expressing existence; independent; real; of the nature of a noun.—*n.* A noun.

substitute, sub'sti-tūt, *vt.* (substituting, substituted). To put in the place of another; to exchange.—*n.* A person or thing in the place of another; a deputy. **substitution**, sub'sti-tū"shun, *n.* Act of substituting; state of being substituted.

substratum, sub-strā'tum, *n.;* pl. **-ta**. A layer or stratum under another.

substructure, sub-struk'tūr, *n.* An under structure; a foundation.

subterfuge, sub'tér-fūj, *n.* An artifice to escape or justify; evasion; a dishonest shift.

subterranean, **subterraneous**, sub'te-rā"nē-an, sub'te-rā"nē-us, *a.* Being under the surface of the earth.

subtle, sut'l, *a.* Thin or tenuous; acute; sly; cunning; artful. **subtlety**, sut'l-ti, *n.* Quality of being subtle; delicacy; craft; cunning; acuteness; nicety of distinction; something subtle. **subtly**, sut'li, *adv.* Artfully; cunningly; nicely.

subtract, sub-trakt', *vt.* To withdraw or take from; to deduct. **subtraction**, sub-trak'shun, *n.* The taking of a number or quantity from a greater.

subtrahend, sub"tra-hend', *n.* A sum or number to be subtracted.

suburb, sub'érb, *n.* An outlying part of a city or town. **suburban**, sub-ér'ban, *a.* Relating to the suburbs; being in the suburbs of a city.

subversion, sub-vér'shun, *n.* Act of subverting; overthrow; destruction; ruin. **subversive**, sub-vér'siv, *a.* Tending to subvert, overthrow, or ruin; with *of.* **subvert**, sub-vért', *vt.* To ruin utterly; to overturn; to pervert.

subway, sub'wā, *n.* An underground passage; an underground railway.

succeed, suk-sēd', *vt.* To follow in order; to take the place of; to come after. —*vi.* To follow in order; to ensue; to become heir; to obtain the end or object desired; to prosper. **success,** suk-ses', *n.* Issue; favorable result; good fortune; prosperity; something that succeeds. **successful,** suk-ses'fōl, *a.* Accompanied by or attaining success; having the desired effect; prosperous; fortunate. **successfully,** suk-ses'fōl-li, *adv.* Prosperously; fortunately; favorably. **succession,** suk-sesh'un, *n.* /. following of things in order; series of things; lineage; right of inheriting; act or right of succeeding to an office, rank, &c. **successional,** suk-sesh'un-al, *a.* Pertaining to succession; consecutive. **successive,** suk-ses'iv, *a.* Coming in succession; consecutive. **successively,** suk-ses'iv-li, *adv.* In succession; in a series or order. **successor,** suk-ses'er, *n.* One who succeeds or follows another.

succinct, suk-singkt', *a.* Compressed into few words; brief; concise. **succinctly,** suk-singkt'li, *adv.* Concisely.

succor, succour, suk-ėr, *vt.* To help when in difficulty; to aid; to relieve.—*n.* Aid; help; assistance given in distress; the person or thing that brings relief.

succulent, suk'ū-lent, *a.* Full of sap or juice; sappy; juicy. **succulence, succulency,** suk'ū-lens, suk'ū-len-si, *n.* Juiciness.

succumb, su-kum', *vi.* To yield; to submit; to sink unresistingly.

such, such, *a.* Of like kind or degree; similar; like; the same as mentioned.

suck, suk, *vt.* and *i.* To draw with the mouth; to draw milk from with the mouth; to imbibe; to absorb.—*n.* Act of sucking; milk drawn from the breast.

sucker, suk'ėr, *n.* One who or that which sucks; an organ in animals for sucking; piston of a pump; shoot of a plant; the sucking fish; one who is easily deceived or cheated.

suckle, suk'l, *vt.* (suckling, suckled). To give suck to; to nurse at the breast. **suckling,** suk'ling, *n.* A young child or animal nursed by the mother's milk.

sucrose, sū'krōs, *n.* A name for the sugars identical with cane-sugar.

suction, suk'shun, *n.* Act of sucking; the sucking up of a fluid by the pressure of the external air.

sudden, sud'en, *a.* Happening without warning; abrupt; quick; hasty; violent. **suddenly,** sud'en-li, *adv.* Unexpectedly; without preparation; all at once.

suds, sudz, *n.pl.* Water impregnated with soap and forming a frothy mass.

sue, sū, *vt.* (suing, sued). To seek justice from by legal process; to seek in marriage.—*vi.* To prosecute a suit at law; to petition.

suet, sū'et, *n.* The harder fat of an animal about the kidneys and loins.

suffer, suf'ėr, *vt.* To endure; to undergo; to be affected by; to permit.—*vi.* To undergo pain; to be injured. **sufferable,** suf'ėr-a-bl, *a.* That may be tolerated, permitted, endured, or borne. **sufferance,** suf'ėr-ans, *n.* Endurance; pain endured; passive consent; allowance. **sufferer,** suf'ėr-ėr, *n.* One who endures pain; one who permits or allows. **suffering,** suf'ėr-ing, *n.* The bearing of pain; pain endured; distress.

suffice, su'fis, *vi.* (sufficing, sufficed). To be sufficient.—*vt.* To satisfy; to content. **sufficiency,** suf-fish-en-si, *n.* State of being sufficient; competence; ability; conceit. **sufficient,** suf-fish'ent, *a.* Adequate; enough; competent; fit; able. **sufficiently,** suf-fish'ent-li, *adv.* To a sufficient degree; enough.

suffix, suf'fiks, *n.* A letter or syllable added to the end of a word.—*vt.* To add a letter or syllable to a word.

suffocate, suf'ō-kāt, *vt.* (suffocating, suffocated). To stifle; to choke by stopping respiration; to kill by depriving of oxygen. **suffocation,** suf'ō-kā"shun, *n.* Act of suffocating; condition of being suffocated.

suffrage, suf'rij, *n.* A vote; assent; right of voting for a representative.

suffuse, su'fūz', *vt.* (suffusing, suffused). To overspread, as with a fluid or a color. **suffusion,** su-fū'zhun, *n.* Act of suffusing; state of being suffused; that which is suffused.

sugar, shög'ér, *n.* A sweet granular substance, manufactured from sugar-cane, maple, beet, &c.; something sweet like sugar.—*a.* Belonging to or made of sugar. —*vt.* To season, mix, &c., with sugar; to sweeten.

sugar cane, shög'ér kän, *n.* The cane or plant from whose juice much sugar is obtained.

sugar plum, shög'ér plum', *n.* A comfit made of boiled sugar; a bon-bon.

sugary, shy'gér-i, *a.* Like sugar; containing sugar; sweet; flattering.

suggest, sug-jest' or su-jest', *vt.* To hint; to insinuate; to propose; to intimate. **suggestion,** sug-jes'chun, *n.* A hint; a tentative proposal; insinuation; intimation. **suggestive,** sug-jes'tiv, *a.* Containing a suggestion; suggesting what does not appear on the surface. **suggestively,** sug-jes'tiv-li, *adv.* In a suggestive manner; by way of suggestion.

suicide, sū'i-sid, *n.* Self-murder; one guilty of self-murder. **suicidal,** sū'i-sid"al, *a.* Pertaining to or partaking of the crime of suicide.

suit, sūt, *n.* Act of suing; a request; courtship; a suing at law; a set of things.—*vt.* and *i.* To adapt; to fit; to be agreeable to; to agree. **suitable,** sūt'a-bl, *a.* That suits; fitting; proper; appropriate; becoming. **suitability,** sūt'a-bil"i-ti, *n.* State or quality of being suitable; fitness.

suite, swēt, *n.* A company of attendants; a retinue; a connected series, as of apartments.

suitor, sūt'ér, *n.* One who sues; one who prosecutes a suit at law; a wooer.

sulfanilamide, sul'fa-nil"a-mid, *n.* A substance derived from coal tar and used in treating many infections.

sulk, sulk, *vi.* To indulge in a sulky or sullen fit or mood. **sulkily,** sul'ki-li, *adv.* In a sulky manner. **sulks,** sulks, *n.pl.* Sulky fit or mood. **sulky,** sul'ki, *a.* Sullen; morose.—*n.* A light two-wheeled carriage for one person.

sullen, sul'en, *a.* Gloomily angry and silent; morose; sour; dismal; somber.

sullenly, sul'en-li, *adv.* In a sullen manner; gloomily; with sulky moroseness.

sully, sul'i, *vt.* (sullying, sullied). To soil; to tarnish; to stain or pollute.—*vi.* To be soiled.—*n.* Soil; tarnish; spot.

sulphate, sul'fāt, *n.* A salt of sulphuric acid.

sulphide, sul'fīd, *n.* A combination of sulphur with another element.

sulphite, sul'fīt, *n.* A salt composed of sulphurous acid with a base.

sulphur, sul'fėr, *n.* Brimstone; a simple mineral substance of a yellow color which burns with a pale-blue flame. **sulphureous,** sul-fū'rē-us, *a.* Sulphurous. **sulphuret,** sul'fū-ret, *n.* A sulphide. **sulphureted,** sul'fū-ret-ed, *a.* Having sulphur in combination. **sulphuric,** sul-fū'rik, *a.* Pertaining to sulphur. **sulphurous,** sul'fūr-us, *a.* Impregnated with or containing sulphur; like sulphur.

sultan, sul'tan, *n.* A Mohammedan sovereign; the ruler of Turkey. **sultana,** sul-tan'a, *n.* The queen of a sultan; a kind of raisin.

sultry, sul'tri, *a.* Very hot; oppressive; close and heavy.

sum, sum, *n.* The whole aggregate; essence or substance; a quantity of money; an arithmetical problem.—*vt.* (summing, summed). To add into one whole; to reckon up; to recapitulate.

sumac, sumach, shō'mak, *n.* A shrub the leaves of which are used for tanning.

summary, sum'a-ri, *a.* Concise; brief; intended to facilitate despatch.—*n.* An abridged account; an abstract. **summarily,** sum'a-ri-li, *adv.* In a summary manner; briefly; promptly. **summarize,** sum'a-rīz, *vt.* To make a summary, abstract, or abridgment of.

summation, sum-ā'shun, *n.* Act or process of summing; addition; aggregate.

summer, sum'ėr, *n.* The warmest season of the year; a lintel; a girder.—*a.* Relating to summer.—*vi.* To pass the summer.—*vt.* To keep or carry through the summer.

summit, sum'it, *n.* The top; highest point; highest degree; acme.

summon, sum'un, *vt.* To call by authority to appear at a place, especially a court of justice; to send for; to call up. **summons,** sum'unz, *n.* A call by authority to appear; a citation; document containing such citation; an earnest call.

sump, sump, *n.* A pond of water for use in salt-works; a reservoir.

sumptuous, sump'tū-us, *a.* Very expensive or costly; splendid; magnificent.

sun, sun, *n.* The self-luminous orb which gives light and heat to all the planets; sunshine or sunlight; sunny position; chief source of light, glory, &c.; a year.—*vt.* (sunning, sunned). To expose to the sun's rays.

sunbeam, sun"bēm', *n.* A ray of the sun.

sunbonnet, sun"bon'et, *n.* A bonnet for protecting the face and neck from the sun.

sunburn, sun"bėrn', *vt.* To discolor or scorch by the sun; to tan.

Sunday, sun'di, *n.* The Christian Sabbath; the first day of the week.—*a.* Belonging to the Christian Sabbath.

sunder, sun'dėr, *vt.* To part; to separate; to disunite in any manner.

sun-dial, sun"dī'al, *n.* An instrument to show the time by a shadow cast by the sun.

sundown, sun"doun', *n.* Sunset.

sundry, sun'dri, *a.* Several; divers; various; a few.

sunflower, sun"flou'ėr, *n.* A plant with a large yellow flower.

sunken, sungk'en, *p.a.* Sunk; covered with water; below the general surface; shaded.

sunless, sun'les, *a.* Destitute of the sun; shaded.

sunlight, sun"līt', *n.* The light of the sun.

sunlit, sun'lit, *a.* Lit by the sun.

sunny, sun'i, *a.* Like the sun; brilliant; exposed to the sun; having much sunshine; bright or cheerful.

sunrise, sunrising, sun"rīz', sun"rīz'ing, *n.* The first appearance of the sun in the morning; time of such appearance; the east.

sunset, sunsetting, sun"set', sun"set'ing, *n.* The descent of the sun below the horizon; evening; close or decline; the west.

sunshade, sun"shād', *n.* A shade from the rays of the sun; a small umbrella.

sunshine, sun"shīn', *n.* The light of the sun; warmth; brightness; cheerfulness.

sunshiny, sun"shīn'i, *a.* Sunny.

sunstroke, sun"strok', *n.* A bodily affection produced by exposure to the sun.

sup, sup, *vt.* (supping, supped). To take into the mouth with the lips, as a liquid.—*vi.* To take supper.—*n.* A sip; a small mouthful.

superabound, sū"pėr-a-bound", *vi.* To abound to excess; to be superabundant.

superabundance, sū"pėr-a-bun"dans, *n.* Excessive abundance; more than enough. **superabundant,** sū"pėr-a-bun"dant, *a.* Abounding to excess; more than sufficient.

superannuate, sū"pėr-an"ū-āt, *vt.* To pension off on account of old age.—*vi.* To retire on a pension. **superannuated,** sū"pėr-an"ū-āt-ed, *a.* Impaired or disabled by old age; having received a retiring allowance for long service. **superannuation,** sū"pėr-an"ū-ā"shun, *n.* Act of superannuating; a senile state.

superb, sū-pėrb', *a.* Magnificent; sumptuous; splendid; august; grand. **superbly,** sū-pėrb'li, *adv.* In a superb, magnificent, or splendid manner.

supercargo, sū"pėr-kär"gō, *n.* A person in a merchant ship who superintends the commercial concerns of the voyage.

supercharge, sū"pėr-chärj", *vt.* To increase in power.

supercilious, sū"pėr-sil"i-us, *a.* Lofty with pride; haughty; overbearing.

superficial, sū"pėr-fish"al, *a.* Being on the surface; shallow; not thorough. **superficiality,** sū"pėr-fish"i-al"i-ti, *n.*

Quality of being superficial; shallowness. **superficially,** sū'pėr-fish"al-li, *adv.* Without going deep; slightly; not thoroughly.

superfluous, sū-pėr'flō-us, *a.* Being more than is wanted; redundant; unnecessary. **superfluity,** sū'pėr-flō"i-ti, *n.* Superabundance; something beyond what is necessary.

superhuman, sū'pėr-hū"man, *a.* Above or beyond what is human; divine.

superimpose, sū'pėr-im-pōz", *vt.* To lay or impose on something else.

superintend, sū'pėr-in-tend", *vt.* To have the charge and oversight of; to direct or manage; to take care of with authority. **superintendence,** sū'pėr-in-ten"dens, *n.* Oversight; direction; management. **superintendent,** sū'pėr-in-ten"dent, *n.* One who manages and directs; an overseer.—*a.* Overlooking others with authority.

superior, sū-pėr'i-ėr, *a.* Higher; higher in rank or dignity; greater in excellence. —*n.* One who is superior to another; chief of a monastery, convent, or abbey. **superiority,** sū-pėr'i-or"i-ti, *n.* Quality of being superior; pre-eminence; advantage.

superlative, sū-pėr'la-tiv, *a.* Highest in degree; supreme.—*n.* That which is superlative: the highest degree of adjectives or adverbs. **superlatively,** sū-pėr'la-tiv-li, *adv.* In a superlative manner; in the highest degree.

supernal, sū-pėr'nal, *a.* Relating to things above; celestial; heavenly.

supernatural, sū'pėr-nat'ū-ral, *a.* Being above or beyond nature; miraculous.

supernumerary, sū'pėr-nū"mėr-er-i, *a.* Exceeding the number stated, necessary, or usual.—*n.* A person or thing beyond a number stated, but required in an emergency.

superscribe, sū-pėr-skrīb', *vt.* To write upon or over; to put an inscription on. **superscription,** sū'pėr-skrip"shun, *n.* Act of superscribing; that which is written or engraved above or on the outside; address on a letter, &c.

supersede, sū'pėr-sēd", *vt.* (superseding, superseded). To set aside; to take the place of; to supplant.

supersensitive, sū-pėr-sen'si-tiv, *a.* Excessively sensitive.

supersonic, sū'pėr-son"ik, *a.* Faster than the speed of sound; pertaining to sound waves above the limit of human hearing.

superstition, sū-pėr-stish'un, *n.* Groundless belief in supernatural agencies; a popular belief held without reason. **superstitious,** sū'pėr-stish"us, *a.* Addicted to superstition; proceeding from or manifesting superstition.

superstructure, sū'pėr-struk"tūr, *n.* Any structure raised on something else.

supervene, sū'pėr-vēn", *vi.* (supervening, supervened). To come, as something extraneous; to happen. **supervention,** sū'pėr-ven"shun, *n.* Act of supervening.

supervise, sū'pėr-vīz", *vt.* (supervising, supervised). To oversee and direct; to superintend; to inspect. **supervision,**

su'pėr-vizh"un, *n.* Act of supervising; superintendence; direction. **supervisor,** sū'pėr-vī"zėr, *n.* One who supervises; a superintendent; an overseer. **supervisory,** sū'pėr-vī"zo-ri, *a.* Pertaining to or having supervision.

supine, sū-pīn', *a.* Lying on the back; indolent; careless.—*n.* sū'pīn. A part of the Latin verb. **supinely,** sū-pīn'li, *adv.* In a supine manner; carelessly indolent; listlessly.

supper, sup'ėr, *n.* The last meal of the day; the evening meal.

supplant, su-plant', *vt.* To take the place of, usually by stratagem.

supple, sup'l, *a.* Pliant; flexible; yielding.—*vt.* (suppling, suppled). To make supple.—*vi.* To become supple.

supplement, sup'lē-ment, *n.* An addition; an appendix.—*vt.* sup-lē-ment'. To increase or complete by a supplement. **supplemental, supplementary,** sup'lē-men"tal, sup'lē-men"ta-ri, *a.* Of the nature of a supplement; serving to supplement.

suppliant, sup'li-ant, *a.* Supplicating; entreating earnestly; beseeching.—*n.* A supplicant; a humble petitioner. **supplicant,** sup'li-kant, *a.* Suppliant.—*n.* One who supplicates; a suppliant. **supplicate,** sup'li-kāt, *vt.* (supplicating, supplicated). To beg humbly for; to entreat; to address in prayer.—*vi.* To beg; to petition; to beseech. **supplication,** sup'li-kā"shun, *n.* Humble and earnest prayer; entreaty.

supply, su-plī', *vt.* (supplying, supplied). To furnish; to provide; to satisfy.—*n.* Act of supplying; quantity supplied; store; *pl.* stores or articles necessary; money provided for government expenses.

support, su-pōrt', *vt.* To rest under and bear; to prop; to endure; to assist; to second; to maintain; to provide for. —*n.* Act of supporting; a prop; help; sustenance; maintenance. **supportable,** su-pōr'ta-bl, *a.* That may be supported; endurable; bearable. **supporter,** su-pōr'tėr, *n.* One who or that which supports; a defender; adherent; prop; figure on each side of a heraldic shield.

suppose, su-pōz', *vt.* (supposing, supposed). To lay down or regard as matter of fact; to take for granted; to imply; to imply.—*vi.* To think; to imagine. **supposition,** sup'ō-zish"un, *n.* Act of supposing; hypothesis; assumption; surmise.

suppress, su-pres', *vt.* To put down; to crush; to quell; to check; to conceal. **suppression,** su-presh'un, *n.* Act of suppressing; concealment; morbid retention of discharges; ellipsis. **suppressive,** su-pres'iv, *a.* Suppressing or tending to suppress. **suppressor,** su-pres'or, *n.* One who suppresses.

suppurate, sup'ū-rāt, *vi.* (suppurating, suppurated). To form or generate pus; to fester. **suppuration,** su-pū-rā"shun, *n.* Process or state of suppurating.

supramundane, su'pra-mun"dān, *a.* Being above the world; celestial.

supreme, sū-prēm', *a.* Highest in authority; utmost; greatest possible. **supremely**, sū-prēm'li, *adv.* In a supreme manner or degree; to the utmost extent. **supremacy**, sū-prem'a-si, *n.* State or character of being supreme; supreme authority.

surcease, sėr-sēs, *vi.* To cease; to leave off.—*n.* Cessation; stop; *poetical.*

surcharge, sėr-chärj', *vt.* To overload. —*n.* An excessive load; an overcharge.

surcingle, sėr''sing'gl, *n.* A belt, band, or girth for a horse.

sure, shör, *a.* Certain; positive; unfailing; stable; secure.—*adv.* Certainly. **surely**, shör'li, *adv.* In a sure manner; firmly; stably; certainly; presumably. **surety**, shör'ti, *n.* State of being sure; certainty; security; one who gives security; a bail.

surf, sėrf, *n.* The swell of the sea which breaks on the shore, rocks, &c.

surface, sėr'fis, *n.* The exterior part of anything that has length and breadth; outside; external appearance.—*a.* Pertaining to the surface; superficial.

surfboard, sėrf''bōrd', *n.* A long, narrow board used in riding the surf.

surfeit, sėr'fit, *n.* An overloading of the stomach; disgust caused by excess; satiety.—*vt.* and *i.* To feed to excess; to nauseate; to cloy.

surge, sėrj, *n.* The swelling of a wave; a large wave; a rolling swell of water.— *vi.* (surging, surged). To swell; to rise high and roll, as waves.

surgeon, sėr'jon, *n.* A medical man who treats diseases or injuries of the body by manual operation. **surgery**, sėr'jėr-i, *n.* The operative branch of medical practice; a doctor's consulting room and dispensary. **surgical**, sėr'ji-kal, *a.* Pertaining to surgeons or surgery.

surly, sėr'li, *a.* Gloomily sour or morose; churlish; boisterous; dismal.

surmise, sėr-mīz', *n.* A supposition; conjecture; speculation.—*vt.* (surmising, surmised). To guess; to imagine; to suspect.

surmount, sėr-mount', *vt.* To mount or rise above; to overcome.

surname, sėr''nām', *n.* The family name of an individual.—*vt.* To give a surname to.

surpass, sėr-päs', *vt.* To go beyond; to excel; to outdo. **surpassing**, sėr-pas'ing, *a.* Excellent in an eminent degree; exceeding others.

surplice, sėr'plis, *n.* A white garment worn by clergy and choristers.

surplus, sėr'plus, *n.* and *a.* Excess beyond what is required; balance. **surplusage**, sėr'plus-ij, *n.* Surplus matter.

surprise, sėr-prīz', *n.* Act of coming upon unawares, or of taking suddenly; emotion excited by something unexpected; astonishment.—*vt.* (surprising, surprised). To fall upon unexpectedly; to take unawares; to astonish. **surprising**, sėr-prīz'ing, *a.* Exciting surprise; wonderful; extraordinary. **surprisingly**, sėr-prīz'ing-li, *adv.* In a surprising manner; astonishingly; remarkably.

surrealism, su-rē'al-izm, *n.* A modern movement in art and literature that delves into the subconscious for its material and mode of expression.

surrender, sur-ren'dėr, *vt.* To deliver up; to yield to another; to resign; to relinquish.—*vi.* To yield.—*n.* Act of surrendering; a yielding or giving up.

surreptitious, sėr'ep-tish''us, *a.* Done by stealth; clandestine; underhand.

surrogate, sėr'rō-gāt, *n.* The deputy of a bishop or his chancellor.

surround, sė-round', *vt.* To be round about; to encompass; to invest. **surrounding**, sė-round'ing, *n.* An environment; generally in *pl.*

surtax, sėr'taks', *n.* A tax heightened for a particular purpose; an extra tax.

surveillance, sėr-vāl'ans, *n.* A keeping watch over; superintendence; oversight.

survey, sėr-vā', *vt.* To oversee; to examine; to measure and value, as land, &c.; to determine the boundaries, natural features, &c., of.—*n.* sėr'vā or sėr-vā'. A general view; examination; determination or account of topographical particulars. **surveying**, sėr-vā'ing, *n.* The art or practice of measuring and delineating portions of the earth's surface. **surveyor**, ser-vā'ėr, *n.* One who surveys; an overseer; inspector.

survive, sėr-vīv', *vt.* (surviving, survived). To outlive; to live beyond the life of; to outlast.—*vi.* To live after another or after anything else. **survivor**, sėr-vī'ver, *n.* One who survives; the longer liver of two persons. **survival**, sėr-vī'al, *n.* A living beyond the life of another person, thing, or event; old habit, belief, &c., existing merely from custom.

susceptible, su-sep'ti-bl, *a.* Capable of admitting any change or influence; impressible; sensitive. **susceptibility**, su-sep'ti-bil''i-ti, *n.* Quality of being susceptible.

suspect, sus-pekt', *vt.* To imagine as existing; to mistrust; to imagine to be guilty; to doubt.—*vi.* To have suspicion. —*n.* sus'pekt. A suspected person.

suspend, sus-pend', *vt.* To hang; to cause to cease for a time; to debar temporarily; to stay.

suspender, sus-pen'dėr, *n.* One who suspends; *pl.* braces.

suspense, sus-pens', *n.* State of being uncertain; indecision; cessation for a time. **suspension**, sus-pen'shun, *n.* Act of suspending; intermission; abeyance; deprivation of office or privileges for a time. **suspension bridge**, suspen'shun brij, *n.* A bridge of chains, wire-ropes, or the like.

suspicion, sus-pish'un, *n.* Act of suspecting; fear of something wrong; mistrust. **suspicious**, sus-pish''us, *a.* Mistrustful; inclined to suspect; apt to raise suspicion; doubtful. **suspiciously**, sus-pish'us-li, *adv.* With suspicion; so as to excite suspicion.

sustain, sus-tān', *vt.* To rest under and bear up; to support; to aid effectually; to undergo; to endure; to hold valid; to confirm; to continue. **sustenance**, sus'tē-nans, *n.* Act of sustaining; support; maintenance; food.

uture, sū'tŭr, *n.* A sewing together; a seam; the uniting of the parts of a wound by stitching; seam or joint of the skill.

wab, swob, *n.* A mop for cleaning floors, decks, &c.—*vt.* (swabbing, swabbed). To clean with a swab.

waddle, swod'l, *vt.* (swaddling, swaddled). To swathe; to bind tight with clothes.—*n.* A swaddling-band. **swaddling band,** swod'ling band, *n.* A band of cloth to swaddle an infant.

wag, swag, *vi.* (swagging, swagged). To sway, as something heavy and pendent; to sag.—*n.* Slang. Loot.

wagger, swag'ėr, *vt.* To strut; to bluster.—*n.* Pretentious strut; bluster. **swaggering,** swag'ėr-ing, *p.a.* Apt to swagger; exhibiting an insolent bearing.

wain, swān, *n.* A peasant or rustic; a hind; a country gallant; a wooer.

wallow, swol'ō, *vi.* To receive through the gullet into the stomach; to ingulf; to absorb; to believe readily; to put up with.—*n.* The gullet; voracity; capacity of swallowing; a small migratory bird.

wamp, swomp, *n.* A piece of wet spongy land; a fen; a bog.—*vt.* To sink in a swamp; to overwhelm; to overset or fill, as a boat in water. **swampy,** swomp'i, *a.* Low, wet, and spongy; marshy.

wan, swon, *n.* A long-necked web-footed bird of the duck family. **swan's-down,** swonz'doun', *n.* The down of the swan; a kind of soft thick cloth.

wap, swop, *vt.* (swapping, swapped). To barter; to exchange.—*n.* An exchange.

ward, sward, *n.* The grassy surface of land; turf; sod.—*vt.* To cover with sward.

warm, swärm, *n.* A large body of small insects; a multitude.—*vi.* To depart from a hive in a body; to crowd; to abound; to climb a tree, pole, &c., by clasping it with the arms and legs.

warthy, swar'THi, *a.* Being of a dark hue or dusky complexion; tawny; black.

wash, swosh, *vi.* To splash or dash, as water; to bluster.

washbuckler, swosh'buk'lėr, *n.* A swaggering fellow; a bravo; a bully.

wastika, swastica, swos'ti-ka, *n.* A primitive symbol, much like the Greek cross, that the Nazis of Germany adopted as their party symbol.

wath, swath or swoth, *n.* A line of mown grass or grain; track formed by mowing; sweep of a scythe in mowing.

wathe, swāTH, *vt.* (swathing, swathed). To bind with a bandage; to swaddle.—*n.* A bandage.

way, swā, *vi.* To swing or vibrate; to incline; to govern.—*vt.* To swing; to wield; to bias; to influence; to rule.—*n.* Swing or sweep; preponderance; power; rule; ascendency.

wear, swär, *vi.* and *t.* (swearing; pret. swore; pp. sworn). To make a solemn declaration, with an appeal to God for its truth; to make promise upon oath; to cause to take an oath; to curse. **swearer,** swär'ėr, *n.* One who swears.

weat, swet, *n.* The moisture which comes out upon the skin; labor; moisture resembling sweat.—*vi.* (pret. and pp. sweated or sweat). To emit sweat or moisture; 'to toil.—*vt.* To exude; to cause to perspire; to employ at starvation wages. **sweater,** swet'ėr, *n.* One who sweats; a grinding employer; a heavy woolen jersey.

Swede, swēd, *n.* A native of Sweden; a Swedish turnip. **Swedish,** swēd'ish, *a.* Pertaining to Sweden.—*n.* The language used in Sweden.

sweep, swēp, *vt.* (sweeping, swept). To rub over with a brush; to carry with a long swinging motion; to drive off in numbers at a stroke.—*vi.* To pass with swiftness and violence; to pass with pomp; to move with a long reach.—*n.* Reach of a stroke, &c.; range; rapid survey; a curve; one who sweeps chimneys. **sweeping,** swēp'ing, *a.* Wide and comprehensive in scope. **sweepings,** swēp'ingz, *n.pl.* Things collected by sweeping; rubbish. **sweepstake, sweepstakes,** swēp'stāk, swēp'stāks, *n.* A prize made up of several stakes.

sweet, swēt, *a.* Agreeable to the taste or senses; having the taste of honey or sugar; fragrant; melodious; beautiful; not salt or sour; gentle.—*n.* A sweet substance; a bonbon; a word of endearment. **sweetbread,** swēt'bred', *n.* The pancreas of an animal used as food. **sweetbrier,** swēt'brī'ėr, *n.* A shrubby plant cultivated for its fragrant smell. **sweeten,** swēt'n, *vt.* To make sweet.—*vi.* To become sweet. **sweetening,** swēt'n-ing, *n.* Act of making sweet; that which sweetens. **sweetheart,** swēt'-härt', *n.* A lover, male or female. **sweetish,** swēt'ish, *a.* Somewhat sweet. **sweetly,** swēt'li, *adv.* In a sweet manner; gratefully; harmoniously. **sweetmeat,** swēt'mēt', *n.* A confection made of sugar; fruit preserved with sugar. **sweet pea,** swēt pē, *n.* A pea-like plant with showy sweet-scented flowers.

swell, swel, *vi.* (pp. swelled or swollen). To grow larger; to heave; to bulge out; to increase.—*vt.* To expand or increase; to puff up.—*n.* Act of swelling; gradual increase; a rise of ground; a wave or surge; an arrangement in an organ for regulating the intensity of the sound; an important person; a dandy. **swelling,** swel'ing, *a.* Tumid; turgid.—*n.* A tumor; a protuberance.

swelter, swel'tėr, *vi.* To be overcome with heat; to perspire.—*vt.* To oppress with heat.

swerve, swėrv, *vi.* (swerving, swerved). To deviate; to turn aside; to waver.

swift, swift, *a.* Speedy; rapid; fleet; ready; prompt.—*n.* A bird like the swallow. **swiftly,** swift'li, *adv.* Speedily; fleetly.

swig, swig, *vt.* and *i.* (swigging, swigged). To drink in large gulps.—*n.* A large draught.

swill, swil, *vi.* To swallow large draughts; to drink greedily.—*n.* Drink taken in large quantities; liquid food given to swine.

swim, swim, *vi.* (swimming; pret. swam, swum; pp. swum). To float; to move through water by the motion of the limbs or fins; to be flooded; to be dizzy.—*vt.* To pass by swimming.—*n.* Act of swimming; distance swum; air-bladder of fishes. **swimmer,** swim'ēr, *n.* One who swims; a bird or other animal that swims. **swimming,** swim'ing, *n.* The act or art of moving on the water by means of the limbs; a dizziness or giddiness in the head. **swimmingly,** swim'ing-li, *adv.* Smoothly; without obstruction; with great success.

swindle, swin'dl, *vt.* (swindling, swindled). To cheat; to defraud deliberately.—*n.* A scheme to dupe people out of money; fraud. **swindler,** swin'dlēr, *n.* One who swindles; a cheat; one who defrauds people grossly.

swine, swīn, *n.sing.* and *pl.* A hog; a pig; a sow or boar; *pl.* hogs collectively.

swing, swing, *vi.* (swinging, swung). To move to and fro, as a body suspended; to turn round at anchor; to be hanged. —*vi.* To make to oscillate; to brandish. —*n.* Sweep of a body; swinging gait; apparatus for persons to swing in; free course.

swinish, swīn'ish, *a.* Like swine; gross.

swipe, swīp, *vt.* and *i.* (swiping, swiped). To strike with a sweeping blow; to steal. *Slang.*—*n.* A sweeping blow.

swirl, swērl, *vi.* To form eddies; to whirl in eddies.—*n.* An eddy.

swish, swish, *vt.* To swing or brandish; to lash.—*n.* A sound as of a switch in the air, a scythe in cutting grass, &c.

Swiss, swis, *n.sing.* or *pl.* A native of Switzerland.—*a.* Belonging to the Swiss.

switch, swich, *n.* A small flexible twig or rod; a movable rail at junctions; a device for changing the course of an electric current.—*vt.* To strike with a switch; to shunt.

swivel, swiv'l, *n.* A link in a chain partly consisting of a pivot turning in a hole in the next link; a fastening that allows the thing fastened to turn round freely.—*vi.* (swiveling, swiveled). To turn on a swivel.

swollen, swōl'en, *p.* and *a.* Swelled.

swoon, swōn, *vi.* To faint.—*n.* A fainting fit; a faint; syncope.

swoop, swōp, *vi.* To dart upon prey suddenly; to stoop.—*vt.* To take with a swoop.—*n.* The pouncing of a bird on its prey; a falling on and seizing.

sword, sōrd, *n.* A military weapon consisting of a long steel blade and a hilt, used for thrusting or cutting; the emblem of justice, authority, war, or destruction; the military profession. **swordfish,** sōrd'fish', *n.* A large fish allied to the mackerel having the upper jaw elongated so as to somewhat resemble a sword. **swordplay,** sōrd'plā', *n.* Fencing or fighting with swords. **swordsman,** sōrdz'man, *n.* A man who carries a sword; a man skilled in the use of the sword.

sworn, swōrn, *p.a.* Bound by oath; having taken an oath; closely bound.

sybarite, sib'a-rīt, *n.* A person devoted to luxury and pleasure.

sycamore, sik'a-mōr, *n.* A fruit tree of the fig family; a maple naturalized Britain; the plane tree of America.

sycophant, sik'ō-fant, *n.* A servile ha ger-on of great people; a parasite; me flatterer. **sycophantic,** sik'ō-fan''t *a.* Obsequiously flattering; meanly par sitic.

syllabic, syllabical, si-lab'ik, si-lab i-kal, *a.* Pertaining to a syllable or sy lables. **syllable,** sil'a-ble, *n.* A sou or combination of sounds uttered wi one effort; the smallest expressive el ment of language.—*vt.* To articulate.

syllabus, sil'a-bus, *n.* An abstrac compendium; a summary statement pr ceeding from a pope.

syllogism, sil'ō-jizm, *n.* A form of re soning or argument, consisting of tw premises and a conclusion.

sylph, silf, *n.* A fabulous aerial spiri a woman of graceful and slender propo tions. **sylphid,** sil'fid, *n.* A diminuti sylph. **sylphidine,** sil'fi-din, *a.* Like relating to a sylph.

sylva, sil'va, *n.* The forest trees of an region or country collectively. **sylva silvan,** sil'van, *a.* Pertaining to wood; wooded; rural.

symbol, sim'bul, *n.* A sign; an emblem a type; a figure; an attribute; a cre or summary of articles of religion. **syn bolic, symbolical,** sim-bol'ik, sin bol'i-kal, *a.* Serving as a symbol; repr sentative; figurative; typical. **symbo ism,** sim'bul-izm, *n.* The attributing things a symbolic meaning; meaning e pressed by symbols; use of symbol **symbolize,** sim'bul-īz, *vt.* To represe by a symbol; to typify; to treat symbolic.—*vi.* To express or represe in symbols.

symmetry, sim'ē-tri, *n.* Due propo tion of parts or elements; harmony; cc respondence of arrangement. **symme rical,** si'met'ri-kal, *a.* Having sym metry; proportional in all its part finely or regularly made.

sympathy, sim'pa-thi, *n.* Fellow-fee ing; compassion; agreement of inclin tions; correspondence of sensations affections. **sympathetic, sympa thetical,** sim'-pa-thet''ik, sim'pa-thet i-kal, *a.* Able to participate in the sc rows and joys of others; compassionat **sympathize,** sim'pa-thiz, *vi.* (symp thizing, sympathized). To have sy pathy; to feel in consequence of wh another feels; to condole; to harmoniz

symphony, sim'fō-ni, *n.* Unison sound; a musical composition for a fu orchestra. **symphonic,** sim-fon'ik, Pertaining to a symphony.

symposium, sim-pō'zi-um, *n.*; pl. -i A merry feast; a convivial party; a di cussion by different writers in a pe odical.

symptom, simp'tom, *n.* That which i dicates the existence and character something else; a mark, sign, or toke **symptomatic,** sim'tō-mat''ik, *a.* Pe taining to symptoms; serving as a sym tom.

synagogue, sin'a-gog, *n.* A congrega tion of Jews met for worship; a Jewi place of worship.

ynchronism, sing'kro-nizm, *n.* Concurrence of events in time; tabular arrangement of history according to dates. **synchronize**, sing'kro-nīz, *vi.* To agree in time.—*vt.* To make to agree in time. **synchronous**, sing'kro-nus, *a.* Happening at the same time; simultaneous.

yncopate, sing'ko-pāt, *vt.* To contract by omission of letters from the middle; to prolong a note in music. **syncopation**, sing'ko-pā"shun, *n.* Act of syncopating; contraction of a word; interruption of the regular measure in music.

yncretism, sing'krē-tizm, *n.* The attempted blending of irreconcilable principles, as in philosophy or religion.

yndicate, sin'di-kāt, *n.* A body of syndics; office of a syndic; body of persons associated to promote some enterprise.—*vt.* To form a syndicate or body for the use of.

ynod, sin'ud, *n.* A council or meeting of ecclesiastics; an ecclesiastical court; a meeting or council in general.

ynonym, sin'ō-nim, *n.* A word having the same signification as another. **synonymous**, si-non'i-mus, *a.* Having the same meaning.

ynopsis, si-nop'sis, *n.*; pl. **-ses.** A summary; brief statement of topics; conspectus.

yntax, sin'taks, *n.* The construction of sentences in grammar; due arrangement of words in sentences. **syntactic, syntactical**, sin-tak'tik, sin-tak'ti-kal, *a.* Pertaining to syntax.

ynthesis, sin'the-sis, *n.*; *pl.* **-ses.** The putting of things together to form a whole; composition or combination. **synthetic, synthetical**, sin-thet'ik, sin-thet'i-kal, *a.* Pertaining to synthesis; consisting in synthesis.

syphilis, sif'i-lis, *n.* A contagious venereal disease. **syphilitic**, sif-i-lit'ik, *a.* Pertaining to or infected with syphilis.

Syriac, sir'i-ak, *a.* Pertaining to Syria. —*n.* The ancient language of Syria.

Syrian, sir'i-an, *a.* Pertaining to Syria. —*n.* A native of Syria.

syringe, sir'inj, *n.* A tube and piston serving to draw in and expel fluid.—*vt.* (syringing, syringed). To inject by a syringe; to cleanse by injections from a syringe.

syrup, sir'up, *n.* A strong solution of sugar in water; any sweet thick fluid; the uncrystallizable fluid separated from crystallized sugar in refining. **syrupy**, sir'u-pi, *a.* Like syrup.

system, sis'tem, *n.* An assemblage of things forming a connected whole; a complex but ordered whole; the body as a functional unity; a plan or scheme; method. **systematic, systematical**, sis'tem-at"ik, sis'tem-at"i-kal, *a.* Pertaining to system; methodical. **systematize**, sis'tem-at-īz, *vt.* To reduce to a system or regular method. **systemic**, sis-tem'ik, *a.* Pertaining to a system, or to the body as a whole.

systole, sis'to-lē, *n.* The contraction of the heart and arteries for driving onwards the blood and carrying on the circulation. **systolic**, sis-tol'ik, *a.* Relating to systole.

T

ab, tab, *n.* A small flap or projecting piece.

abby, tab'i, *n.* A rich watered silk or other stuff; a cat of a brindled color; a female cat.—*vt.* To water or cause to look wavy.

abby-cat, tab'i-kat, *n.* A tabby.

abernacle, tab'ĕr-nak'l, *n.* A booth; a temporary habitation; a place of worship; a repository for holy things.—*vi.* To sojourn.

able, tā'bl, *n.* A thing with a flat surface; an article of furniture having a flat surface; fare or eatables; persons sitting at a table; a syllabus; index; list.—*vt.* (tabling, tabled). To tabulate; to lay on a table.—*a.* Appertaining to a table.

ableau, tab'lō, *n.*; pl. **tableaux**, tab'loz. A picture; a striking group or dramatic scene.

ablecloth, tā"bl-kloth', *n.* A cloth for covering a table, particularly at meals.

able d'hôte, tā'bl dōt', *n.* A common table for guests at a hotel.

ableland, tā"bl-land', *n.* A distinct area or region of elevated flat land; a plateau.

tablet, tab'let, *n.* A small slab for writing on; a slab bearing an inscription; a small flattish cake, as of soap, &c.

tabloid, tab'loid, *n.* A newspaper of small format, usually with condensed stories and many photos.

taboo, tabu, ta-bö', *n.* The setting of something apart from human contact; prohibition of contact or intercourse.—*vt.* (tabooing, tabooed). To interdict approach to or contact with.

tabor, tabour, tā'bĕr, *n.* A small drum. —*vt.* To play on a tabor.

tabular, tab'ū-lĕr, *a.* In form of a table; having a flat surface; set in columns **tabulate**, tab'ū-lāt, *vt.* (tabulating, tabulated). To set down in a table of items.—*a.* Tabular.

tacit, tas'it, *a.* Implied, but not expressed in words; silent; unspoken. **tacitly**, tas'it-li, *adv.* In a tacit manner; silently; by implication; without words.

taciturn, tas'i-tèrn, *a.* Habitually silent; not apt to talk or speak. **taciturnity**, tas'i-tèr"ni-ti, *n.* Habitual silence or reserve in speaking.

tack, tak, *n.* A small nail; a slight fastening; a rope for certain sails; course of a ship as regards the wind; in *Scots law*, a lease.—*vt.* To fasten by tacks; to attach slightly; to append.—*vi.* To change the course of a ship so as to have the wind acting from the other side.

tackle, tak'l, *n.* Gear or apparatus; pulleys and ropes for moving weights; ropes and rigging, &c., of a ship.—*vt.* (tackling, tackled). To supply with tackle; to set vigorously to work upon; to seize. **tackling**, tak'ling, *n.* Tackle; gear; rigging; harness or the like.

tact, takt, *n.* Touch; nice perception or discernment; adroitness in words or actions. **tactic, tactical**, tak'tik, tak'ti-kal, *a.* Pertaining to tactics. **tactician**, tak-tish'an, *n.* One versed in tactics. **tactics**, tak'tiks, *n.pl.* The science and art of disposing forces in order for battle and performing evolutions. **tactless**, takt'les, *a.* Destitute of tact.

tactile, tak'til, *a.* Capable of being touched or felt; pertaining to the sense of touch.

tadpole, tad"pōl', *n.* The young of the frog in its first state from the spawn.

taffeta, taf'e-ta, *n.* A silk fabric, or a mixed fabric of silk and wool.

tag, tag, *n.* A metallic point to the end of a string; an appendage; catch-word of an actor's speech.—*vt.* (tagging, tagged). To fit with a tag; to tack or join.

tail, tāl, *n.* The projecting termination of an animal behind; the hinder or inferior part; the reverse of a coin; limited ownership.

tailor, tā'lėr, *n.* One who makes men's outer garments.—*vi.* To practice making men's clothes.

taint, tānt, *vt.* To defile; to infect; to vitiate.—*vi.* To be infected or corrupted. —*n.* Infection; corruption, a stain; a blemish on reputation.

take, tāk, *vt.* (taking; pret. took; pp. taken). To receive or accept; to capture; to captivate; to understand; to feel concerning; to employ; to need; to form or adopt; to assume; to note down; to be infected or seized with; to bear; to conduct, carry; to leap over.—*vi.* To direct one's course; to please; to have the intended effect; to admit of being made a portrait of.

take-off, tāk'of, *n.* Leaving the ground to become air-borne, particularly an airplane; a caricature or burlesque.

talc, tak, *n.* A magnesian mineral, unctuous to the touch.—*vt.* To rub with talc.

tale, tāl, *n.* Number counted; reckoning; a story; a narrative.

talent, tāl'ent, *n.* An ancient weight and denomination of money; a special faculty; general mental power; people of high abilities collectively. **talented**, tāl'en-ted, *a.* Furnished with talents or great intellectual power.

talisman, tal'is-man, *n.* A charm; a magical figure cut or engraved on stone or metal; something producing extraordinary effects.

talk, tak, *vi.* To utter words; to converse.—*vt.* To speak; to gain over by persuasion; to discuss.—*n.* Familiar conversation; report; rumor; subject of discourse; discussion. **talkative**, tak'a-tiv, *a.* Given to much talking; loquacious; garrulous; prating. **talker**, tak'ėr, *n.* One who talks; a loquacious person; prattler.

tall, tal, *a.* High in stature; lofty; remarkable; extravagant.

tallow, tal'ō, *n.* The fat of oxen, sheep, &c., melted and separated from the fibrous matter.—*vt.* To smear with tallow.

tally, tal'i, *n.* A piece of wood on which notches are cut to keep accounts; anything made to suit another.—*vt.* (tallying, tallied). To record on a tally; to make to correspond.—*vi.* To correspond or agree exactly.

tallyho, tal'i-hō", *interj.* and *n.* huntsman's cry to urge on his hounds.

Talmud, tal'mud, *n.* The Hebrew civil and canonical laws, traditions, &c.

talon, tal'un, *n.* The claw of a bird of prey.

talus, tā'lus, *n.* The ankle; slope; sloping heap of broken rocks.

tamarind, tam'a-rind, *n.* A tropical leguminous tree and its fruit.

tambourine, tam'bö-rēn", *n.* A musical instrument of the drum species played on with the hand, and having jingles attached.

tame, tām, *a.* Having lost its natural wildness; domesticated; spiritless; insipid.—*vt.* (taming, tamed). To make tame; to subdue; to depress. **tameless** tām'les, *a.* Untamable. **tamely**, tām'li *adv.* In a tame manner; submissively meanly; without spirit.

Tamil, tam'il, *n.* One of a Dravidian race of S. India; their language.

tamp, tamp, *vt.* To ram tight with clay &c.; to stamp or make firm.

tamper, tamp'ėr, *vi.* To meddle or interfere; to influence secretly.

tan, tan, *vt.* (tanning, tanned). To convert into leather, as skins; to make sun burnt; to flog.—*vi.* To become tanned —*n.* Bark used for tanning; a yellowish brown color.—*a.* Like tan in color tawny.

tandem, tan'dem, *adv.* With two horse harnessed singly one before the other.- *n.* A wheeled carriage so drawn; a cyc for two persons, one behind the other.

tang, tang, *n.* A taste; characteristic flavor or property; part of a tool which fits into the handle; tongue of a buckl

tangent, tan'jent, *n.* A straight line which touches a circle or curve, but which when produced, does not cut it **tangential**, tan-jen'shal, *a.* Pertaining to a tangent; in the direction of a tangent.

tangerine, tan'je-rēn", *n.* A kind orange with an easily removable skin.

tangible, tan'ji-bl, *a.* That may b touched; real; actual; evident.

tangle, tang'gl, *vt.* (tangling, tangled) To unite confusedly; to involve; to complicate.—*n.* A confused knot of thread

tango, tang'gō, *n.* A South American dance and its music.

tank, tangk, *n.* A storage vessel to con

ain liquids or gas; a reservoir; a kind of self-propelling land fort or engine of destruction consisting of a casement of heavy armor plates mounted on a tractor.

ankard, tangk'ĕrd, *n.* A large drinking vessel, often with a cover.

anker, tangk'ĕr, *n.* A ship equipped to transport oil or other liquids.

anner, tan'ĕr, *n.* One who tans hides, or converts them into leather by the use of tan. **tannery,** tan'ĕr-i, *n.* A place where tanning is carried on; art or process of tanning.

annic, tan'ik, *a.* Applied to an acid in oak, gali-nuts, &c., the efficient substance in tanning.

anning, tan'ing, *n.* The converting of hides into leather by the use of tan or other substances; leather manufacture.

antalize, tan'ta-līz, *vt.* (tantalizing, tantalized). To torment by presenting something desirable which cannot be attained; to excite by hopes that are never realized.

antamount, tan"ta-mount', *a.* Equal; equivalent in value, force, or effect.

antrum, tan'trum, *n.* A fit of ill-humor; display of temper; chiefly in *pl.*

ap, tap, *n.* A plug to stop a hole in a cask; a spigot; a faucet; a gentle blow; pat.—*vt.* (tapping, tapped). To broach, as a cask; to draw liquid from; to strike gently.—*vi.* To strike a gentle blow.

ape, tāp, *n.* A narrow strip of woven work, used for strings and the like.

apeline, tape measure, tāp"līn', āp' mezh'ĕr, *n.* A tape marked with feet, inches, &c., used in measuring.

aper, tā'pĕr, *n.* A long wick coated with wax; a small light; tapering form; gradual diminution of thickness.—*vi.* To become gradually smaller.—*vt.* To cause to taper.

ape recorder. A sound-recording device using sensitized tape.

apestry, tap'es-tri, *n.* A kind of rich woven hangings of wool and silk, with pictorial representations.—*vt.* To adorn with tapestry.

apeworm, tāp'wĕrm, *n.* A parasitic worm found in the intestines of animals.

aploca, tap'i-ō'ka, *n.* A farinaceous substance prepared from cassava meal.

apir, tā'pĕr, *n.* A hoofed animal allied to the rhinoceros, with a nose resembling a small proboscis.

aproom, tap'rōm', *n.* A room in which beer is served from the tap (Eng.).

aproot, tap'rōt', *n.* Main root of a plant.

ar, tar, *n.* A thick, dark, viscid substance obtained from pine or fir, coal, shale, &c.; a sailor.—*vt.* (tarring, tarred). To smear with tar.

arantula, ta-ran'tū-la, *n.* A kind of spider found in S. Italy; the dance tarantella.

ardy, tär'di, *a.* Slow; dilatory; late; backward; reluctant. **tardily,** tär'di-li, *adv.* Slowly.

are, tar, *n.* A leguminous plant; vetch; allowance for the weight of the package of a commodity.

target, tär'get, *n.* A small circular shield; a mark shot at in rifle practice.

tariff, tar'if, *n.* A list of goods with the duties to be paid; a list of charges generally.

tarnish, tär'nish, *vt.* To sully; to dim. —*vi.* To lose luster.—*n.* A spot; soiled state.

tarpaulin, tär-pa'lin, *n.* Canvas covered with tar.

tarpon, tär'pon, *n.* A large American sea fish; a game fish.

tarry, ta'ri, *vi.* (tarrying, tarried). To stay; to delay.—*vt.* To wait for.

tart, tärt, *a.* Sharp to the taste; sour; acid; severe; snappish.—*n.* A species of pastry, consisting of fruit baked in paste.

tartan, tär'tan, *n.* Cloth woven in colors in a checkered pattern; a Mediterranean vessel somewhat resembling a sloop.—*a.* Consisting of or resembling tartan.

Tartar, tär'tĕr, *n.* A native of Tartary; a very irascible or rigorous person; a shrew; a reddish crust deposited by wine on casks; a concretion formed on the teeth.

task, task, *n.* A piece of work imposed by another or requiring to be done; burdensome employment; toil.—*vt.* To impose a task upon.

taskmaster, task"mas'tĕr, *n.* One who imposes a task, or burdens with labor.

tassel, tas'l, *n.* An ornament consisting of a knob with hanging threads.—*vi.* (tasseling, tasseled). To put forth a tassel or flower, as maize.—*vt.* To adorn with tassels.

taste, tāst, *vi.* (tasting, tasted). To test by the tongue and palate; to perceive the flavor of; to experience; to partake of.— *vt.* To make trial by the tongue and palate; to have a flavor; to have experience.—*n.* Act of tasting; sense of tasting; flavor; intellectual relish or discernment; manner or style. **tasteful,** tāst'ful, *a.* Having a high taste or relish; having good taste. **tasteless,** tāst'les, *a.* Having no taste; insipid; stale; flat; void of good taste. **tastily,** tās'ti-li, *adv.* With good taste. **tasty,** tās'ti, *a.* Having or showing good taste; tasteful; palatable; nice; fine.

ta-ta, ta'ta, *n.* and *interj.* A familiar form of salutation at parting; good-by.

tatter, tat'ĕr, *n.* A rag or part torn and hanging to the thing. **tattered,** tat'ĕrd, *p.a.* Showing tatters; torn; hanging in rags.

tatting, tat'ing, *n.* A kind of crochet, made with a shuttle-shaped needle.

tattle, tat'l, *vi.* (tattling, tattled). To talk idly; to gossip.—*n.* Prate; idle talk. **tattler,** tat'lĕr, *n.* One who tattles; an idle talker; one who spreads idle gossip. **tattling,** tat'ling, *a.* Given to idle talk.

tattoo, ta-tō', *n.* A beat of drum and bugle-call at night, calling soldiers to their quarters.—*vt.* and *i.* To prick the skin and stain the punctured spot with colors.

taught, tät, *p.* & *pp.* of teach.

taunt, tạnt, *vt.* To reproach with severe or sarcastic words; to upbraid.—*n.* A bitter or sarcastic reproach.

Taurus, ta′rus, *n.* The Bull, one of the twelve signs of the zodiac.

taut, tạt, *a.* Tight; not slack.

tavern, tav′ẽrn, *n.* A house where liquors are sold; an inn.

taw, tạ, *vt.* To make into white leather for gloves, &c., by treating skins with alum, salt, and other matters.—*n.* A marble to be played with; a game at marbles.

tawny, tạ′ni, *a.* Of a yellowish-brown color, like things tanned.

tax, taks, *n.* A contribution levied by authority; a rate, duty, or impost charged on income or property; a burdensome duty; an exaction.—*vt.* To impose a tax on; to put to a certain effort; to accuse. **taxation,** taks-ā′shun, *n.* Act of levying taxes; the aggregate of taxes.

taxicab, tak″si-kab′, *n.* A motor cab having a taximeter.

taxidermy, tak″si-dẽr′mi, *n.* The art of stuffing animals, or of preserving the skins.

taximeter, tak″si-mē′tẽr, *n.* A device for measuring distance traveled by a vehicle.

taxonomy, taks-on′ō-mi, *n.* That department of natural history which treats of the laws and principles of classification.

tea, tē, *n.* The dried leaves of plants cultivated in China, Assam, Ceylon, &c.; the plant itself; a decoction of tea leaves in boiling water; any decoction of vegetables.—*n.* (teasing, teased). To take tea.

teach, tēch, *vt.* (teaching, taught). To instruct; to inform; to make familiar with.—*vi.* To practice giving instruction. **teachable,** tēch′a-bl, *a.* That may be taught; apt to learn; docile. **teacher,** tēch′ẽr, *n.* One who teaches; an instructor; a preceptor; a schoolmaster. **teaching,** tēch′ing, *n.* Act or business of instructing; instruction.

teacup, tē′kup, *n.* A small cup for drinking tea from.

teak, tēk, *n.* An E. Indian tree which furnishes hard and valuable timber.

teal, tēl, *n.* A small duck found about fresh-water lakes.

team, tēm, *n.* A brood; horses or other beasts harnessed together; a side in a game, match, &c. **teamster,** tēm′stẽr, *n.* One who drives a team.

teapot, tē″pot′, *n.* A vessel in which tea is infused.

tear, tãr, *vt.* (pret. tore; pp. torn). To pull in pieces; to rend; to wound; to drag; to pull with violence; to make by rending.—*vi.* To be rent or torn; to rage.—*n.* A rent.

tear, tẽr, *n.* A drop of the watery fluid appearing in the eyes; any transparent drop. **tear drop,** tẽr drop, *n.* A tear. **tearful,** tẽr′fûl, *a.* Abounding with tears; weeping; shedding tears. **tearless,** tẽr′les, *a.* Shedding no tears; without tears; unfeeling.

tease, tēz, *vt.* (teasing, teased). To pull apart the fibers of; to annoy; to torment.

teaspoon, tē′spön, *n.* A small spoon used in stirring tea or coffee; a measure ment in cooking.

teat, tēt, *n.* The projecting part of the female breast; pap; nipple.

technical, tek′ni-kal, *a.* Pertaining an art, science, profession, handicra &c. **technicality,** tek′ni-kal″i-ti, Quality or state of being technic **technics,** tek′niks, *n.* The arts general (used as a sing.); techni objects or terms. **technological,** tek no-loj″ik-al, *a.* Pertaining to technolog **technology,** tek-nol′ō-ji, *n.* The s ence of the industrial arts.

tedious, tē′di-us, *a.* Tiresome; wea some; irksome; fatiguing; dilator tardy. **tediously,** tē′di-us-li, *ad* Wearisomely. **tedium,** tē′di-um, *n.* Ir someness.

tee, tē, *n.* A point of aim or startin point in certain games, as quoits a golf.

teem, tēm, *vi.* To bring forth young; be prolific.—*vt.* To bring forth. **teem ing,** tēm′ing, *a.* Producing youn prolific; overflowing; exceedingly abu dant.

teens, tēnz, *n.pl.* The years of one's a having the termination *-teen.*

teeth, tēth, *n.pl.* of *tooth.* **teeth** tēтн, *vi.* (teething, teethed). To hav the teeth growing or cutting the gum **teething,** tēтн′ing, *n.* Operation, pro ess, or period of the first growth of teet

teetotal, tē′tō-tal, *a.* Totally abstainir from intoxicants. **teetotaler, teeto** **taller,** tē-tō′tal-ẽr, *n.* A total abstain from intoxicants.

tegument, teg′ū-ment, *n.* A cover covering; an integument.

telegram, tel′ē-gram, *n.* A communic tion sent by telegraph. **telegrap** tel′ē-graf, *n.* Any apparatus for transm ting messages to a distance; an apparat for transmitting messages along a wi by electricity, but now also wireless.— *vt.* To convey or announce by telegrap **telegraphic, telegraphical,** tel′ graf″ik, tel′ē-graf″i-kal, *a.* Pertaining the telegraph; communicated by a tel graph. **telegraphist,** te-leg′ra-fist, te-leg′ra-fist, *n.* One who works a tel graph. **telegraphy,** te-leg′ra-fi, *n.* Th art or practice of communicating by telegraph.

telepathy, te-lep′a-thi, or tel′ē-path— *n.* Occult communication between pe sons at some distance. **telepathic,** tel ē-path″ik, *a.* Pertaining to telepathy.

telephone, tel′ē-fōn, *n.* An instrume transmitting sound to a distance b means of electricity and telegraph wire —*vt.* (telephoning, telephoned). T transmit by means of the telephon **telephonic,** tel′ē-fon″ik, *a.* Relating the telephone; communicated by th telephone.

telescope, tel′ē-skōp, *n.* An optical i strument for viewing distant objects.— *vt.* (telescoping, telescoped). To driv the parts of into each other, like th joints of a telescope. **telescopic,** tel ē-skop″ik, *a.* Pertaining to a telescop seen only by a telescope; able to disce objects at a distance; far-seeing; far-reaching; as a *telescopic* eye.

elevision, tel"ē-vizh'un, *n.* The instantaneous transmission to a distance of images, views, or objects by telegraphy either with wires or without.

ell, tel, *vt.* (telling, told). To number; to relate; to disclose; to explain; to distinguish; to inform; to bid.—*vi.* To give an account; to take effect. **teller**, tel'èr, *n.* One who tells; an officer of a bank who receives and pays money; one appointed to count votes. **telling**, tel'ing, *p.a.* Having great effect. **telltale**, tel"tāl', *a.* Telling tales; blabbing; serving to betray; informative.—*n.* One who discloses private concerns, or what he should suppress.

emerity, tē-mer'i-ti, *n.* Contempt of danger; extreme boldness; rashness.

temerarious, tem'èr-ar"i-us, *a.* Reckless.

emper, tem"per, *vt.* To proportion duly; to moderate; to form to a proper hardness.—*n.* Due mixture; disposition of the mind; temperament; irritation; state of a metal as to its hardness; medium.

empera, tem'pèr-a, *n.* Distemper, in *painting.*

emperament, tem'pèr-a-ment, *n.* Due mixture of qualities; combined mental and physical constitution; disposition.

emperamental, tem'pèr-a-men"tal, *a.* Easily excited or upset.

emperance, tem'pèr-ans, *n.* Moderation in indulgence of the natural appetites; sobriety; abstinence from intoxicants.

emperate, tem'pèr-it, *a.* Moderate; abstemious; free from ardent passion; calm; cool; measured; sober. **temperately**, tem'pèr-it-li, *adv.* Moderately; calmly.

emperature, tem'pèr-a-tūr, *n.* State with regard to heat or cold; climatic heat.

empered, tem'pèrd, *a.* Having a certain disposition or temper; disposed.

empest, tem"pest, *n.* A violent storm; hurricane; violent tumult or commotion.

tempestuous, tem-pes'tū-us, *a.* Very stormy; turbulent; subject to storms of passion.

emple, tem'pl, *n.* A place of worship; a church; part of the head between the forehead and the ear.

emplet, template, tem'plet, tem'plāt, *n.* A board whose edge is shaped so as to serve as a guide in making an article with a corresponding contour.

empo, tem'pō, *n.* The time of a piece of music; musical time.

emporal, tem'pō-ral, *a.* Pertaining to time; pertaining to this life; not spiritual or ecclesiastical; secular; pertaining to the temples of the head.—*n.* Anything temporal or secular; a temporality.

emporary, tem'pō-rèr-i, *a.* Lasting but for a time; transient; provisional. **temporarily**, tem'pō-rer-i-li, *adv.* For a time only; provisionally.

emporize, tem'pō-rīz, *vi.* To comply with the time or occasion; to trim.

empt, temt, *vt.* To incite to an evil act;

to provoke; to entice; to put to a test. **temptation**, temp-tā'shun, *n.* Act of tempting; state of being tempted; enticement to evil[1]; an allurement. **tempter**, temp'tèr, *n.* One who tempts; the devil. **tempting**, temp'ting, *p.a.* Adapted to tempt; attractive; seductive. **temptress**, temp'res, *n.* A female; who tempts.

ten, ten, *a.* and *n.* Twice five; nine and one.

tenable, ten'a-bl, *a.* That may be held or maintained.

tenacious, te-nā'shus, *a.* Holding fast; retentive; adhesive; stubborn. **tenaciously**, te-nā'shus-li, *adv.* Obstinately; with firm adherence; toughly. **tenacity**, te-nas'i-ti, *n.* State or quality of being tenacious; adhesiveness; glutinousness; toughness; cohesiveness.

tenant, ten'ant, *n.* One who occupies lands or houses for which he pays rent. —*vt.* To hold as a tenant.—*vi.* To live as a tenant; to dwell. **tenancy**, ten'an-si, *n.* A holding lands or tenements as a tenant; tenure.

tend, tend, *vi.* To move in or have a certain direction; to conduce; to attend. —*vt.* To attend; to guard; to take care of. **tendency**, ten'den-si, *n.* Inclination; leaning; bent; proneness.

tender, ten'dèr, *n.* One who attends; a small vessel employed to attend on a larger one; a car with fuel, &c., attached to a locomotive; an offer of money or service; an estimate; thing offered.— *vt.* To present for acceptance.—*a.* Fragile; delicate; compassionate; kind. **tenderly**, ten'dèr-li, *adv.* In a tender manner; with tenderness; mildly; fondly. **tenderfoot**, ten'dèr-fut, *n.* A term originating in the American West—a newcomer or novice; greenhorn.

tendon, ten'don, *n.* A sinew; a hard, insensible cord or bundle of fibres by which a muscle is attached to a bone.

tendril, ten'dril, *n.* A slender, twining growth, by which a plant adheres to something.

tenebrous, tenebrose, ten'ē-brus, *a.* Dark; gloomy. **tenebrosity**, ten-ē-bros'i-ti, *n.* Darkness.

tenement, ten'ē-ment, *n.* An abode; a habitation; a block of buildings divided into separate houses.

tenet, ten'et, *n.* A doctrine, opinion, principle, or dogma.

tenfold, ten"fōld, *a.* Ten times more.

tennis, ten'is, *n.* A game played on a court having a net stretched across the center. The players use rackets to hit the ball back and forth over the net.

tenon, ten'un, *n.* The specially shaped end of a piece of wood, &c., to be inserted into the mortise to form a joint.

tenor, ten'èr, *n.* A prevailing course or direction; purport; substance, as of a discourse; the highest of the male adult chest voices; one who sings a tenor part. —*a.* Adapted for singing or playing the tenor.

tense, tens, *n.* Inflection of a verb to express time.—*a.* Stretched; tight; strained to stiffness; rigid; not lax.

tensile, ten'sil, *a.* Pertaining to tension; capable of tension.

tension, ten'shun, *n.* Act of stretching; state of being stretched; tightness; strain; intensity; elastic force.

tent, tent, *n.* A portable shelter consisting of some flexible covering; a roll of lint, &c., to dilate a sore.—*vi.* To lodge in a tent.—*vt.* To supply with tents; to probe; to keep open with a tent, as a tent.

tentacle, ten'ta-kl, *n. sing.* and *pl.* **A** filiform organ of various animals, used for prehension or as a feeler.

tentative, ten'ta-tiv, *a.* Experimental; empirical.—*n.* An essay; a trial. **tentatively**, ten'ta-tiv-li, *adv.* By way of experiment or trial.

tenterhook, ten''ter-hök' *n.* A hook for stretching cloth on a tenter; anything that painfully strains, racks, or tortures.

tenth, tenth, *a.* Next after the ninth.—*n.* One of ten equal parts. **tenthly**, tenth'li, *adv.* In the tenth place.

tenuous, ten'ū-us, *a.* Thin; slender. **tenuity**, ten-ū'i-ti, *n.* State of being thin or fine; thinness; slenderness; rarity.

tenure, ten'ūr, *n.* A holding or manner of holding real estate; condition of occupancy; manner of possessing in general.

tepee, tē'pē, tep'ē, *n.* A cone-shaped tent (usually of skins) used by the North American Indians, especially of the Great Plains.

tepid, tep'id, *a.* Moderately warm; lukewarm.

tercentenary, tėr-sen'te-nėr-i, *a.* Comprising three hundred years.—*n.* The three hundredth anniversary.

term, tėrm, *n.* A limit; boundary; time for which anything lasts; period of session, &c.; day on which rent or interest is paid; a word; a word having a technical meaning; *pl.* conditions; relative position or footing.—*vt.* To name; to call.

termagant, tėr'ma-gant, *n.* A brawling woman; a shrew; a scold.—*a.* Quarrelsome; shrewish.

terminal, tėr'mi-nal, *a.* Pertaining to or forming the end; terminating.—*n.* An extremity; the clamping screw at each end of a voltaic battery. **terminate**, tėr'mi-nāt, *vt.* and *i.* (terminating, terminated). To bound; to limit; to end.—*a.* Limited. **termination**, tėr'mi-nā''shun, *n.* Act of terminating; close; extremity; ending of a word; conclusion; result.

terminology, tėr'mi-nol'o-ji, *n.* The science or theory of technical or other terms; terms used in any art, science, &c:

terminus, tėr'mi-nus, *n.*; pl. **-ni.** A boundary; a limit; station at the end of a railway, &c.

termite, tėr'mīt, *n.* A neuropterous insect commonly called the white-ant.

tern, tėrn, *n.* A long-winged bird of the gull family.—*a.* Consisting of three.

Terpsichorean, tėrp'si-kō-rē''an, *a.* Relating to Terpsichore, the goddess of dancing.

terra, ter'rä, *n.* Earth; the earth. **terra firma**, dry land.

terrace, ter'is, *n.* A raised level bank of earth; a raised flat area; a row of houses; flat roof of a house.—*vt.* (terracing, terraced). To form into or furnish with a terrace.

terra cotta, ter'a kot'a, A kind of pottery, commonly of a reddish color; a work of art in terra-cotta.

terrapin, ter'a-pin, *n.* A fresh-water tortoise.

terrestrial, te-res'tri-al, *a.* Pertaining to the earth; mu:dane; pertaining to land.—*n.* An inhabitant of the earth.

terrible, ter'i-bl, *a.* Adapted to arouse terror; dreadful; fearful; extraordinary. **terribly**, ter'i-bli, *adv.* In a terrible manner; dreadfully; excessively; very greatly.

terrier, ter'i-ėr, *n.* A small variety of dog that creeps into holes in the earth, after animals that burrow.

terrify, ter'i-fi, *vt.* (terrifying, terrified). To cause or produce terror in; to alarm. **terrific**, te-rif'ik, *a.* Terrifying; dreadful. **terrifically**, te-rif'i-kal-li *adv.* In a terrific manner; terribly; frightfully.

territory, ter''i-tō'ri, *n.* A definite piece of land under any distinct administration; a dominion; region; country. **territorial**, ter'i-tō''ri-al, *a.* Pertaining to a territory; concerned with a certain district.

terror, ter'ėr, *n.* Such fear as agitates body and mind; dread; alarm; cause of fear. **terrorism**, ter'ėr-izm, *n.* A system of government by terror; intimidation. **terrorize**, ter'ėr-iz, *vt.* To impress with terror; to domineer over by means of terror.

terse, tėrs, *a.* Free from superfluities of language; concise; forcible; pithy. **tersely**, tėrs'li, *adv.* Pithily; concisely.

tertian, tėr'shan, *a.* Occurring or having its paroxysms every third day, as a fever. **tertiary**, ter''shi-er'i, *a.* Third; applied to the third great division of stratified rocks, resting on the chalk.—*n.* The tertiary system of rocks.

tessellate, tes'e-lāt, *vt.* To form with small square stones into a mosaic pattern; to lay with checkered work.

test, test, *n.* A vessel used in trying or refining gold, &c.; a cupel; examination; means of trial; a standard; oath taken before admission to privileges; a hard outer covering.—*vt.* To put to a trial; to examine; to prove.

testament, tes'ta-ment, *n.* In *law*, a person's will; (with cap.) one of the two general divisions of the Scriptures. **testamental**, tes-ta-men'tal, *a.* Testamentary. **testamentary**, tes'ta-men''ta-ri, *a.* Pertaining to a will; bequeathed or done by will.

testate, tes'tāt, *a.* Having left a will. **testator**, tes-tāt'or, *n.* A man who leaves a will or testament at death.

testicle, tes'ti-kl, *n.* One of the two glands which secrete the seminal fluid in males.

testify, tes'ti-fi, *vi.* (testifying, testified). To bear witness; to give evidence. —*vt.* To bear witness to.

testimonial, tes'ti-mō"ni-al, *n.* A certificate of qualifications; a gift in token of appreciation or esteem.

testimony, tes'ti-mo-ni, *n.* Witness; evidence; affirmation; attestation; profession; divine revelation; law of God.

testy, tes'ti, *a.* Fretful; peevish; petulant.

tetanus, tet'a-nus, *n.* Spasm with rigidity: lock-jaw.

tête-à-tête, tāt'-ä-tāt', *adv.* Face to face; in private.—*n.* A private interview or talk.

tether, teTH'ėr, *n.* A rope confining a grazing animal within certain limits; scope allowed.—*vt.* To confine with a tether.

tetrahedron, tet'ra-hē"dron, *n.* A solid body having four equal triangles as its faces.

Teuton, tū'ton, *n.* A person of Germanic race in the widest sense of the term. **Teutonic,** tū-ton'ik, *a.* Belonging to the Teutons and to the languages spoken by them.—*n.* The languages collectively of the Teutons.

text, tekst, *n.* An author's own work as distinct from annotations; a passage of Scripture selected as the subject of a discourse; a topic; a large kind of handwriting; particular kind of lettering.

textbook, tekst"bōk', *n.* A book containing the leading principles of a science. &c., arranged for the use of students.

textile, teks'til, *a.* Woven; capable of being woven.—*n.* A fabric made by weaving.

textual, teks'tū-al, *a.* Containing in the text; pertaining to the text.

texture, teks'tūr, *n.* A web; that which is woven; a fabric; manner in which constituent parts are connected; the grain or peculiar character of a solid.

thalamus, thal'a-mus, *n.;* pl. **-mi.** A large ganglion in the brain; the receptacle of a flower, or part on which the carpels are placed.

than, THan, *conj.* A particle used after certain adjectives and adverbs expressing comparison or diversity, as *more, other,* &c.

thank, thangk, *n.* Expression of gratitude; an acknowledgment of favor or kindness; almost always in *pl.*—*vt.* To give thanks to; to express gratitude to for a favor. **thankful,** thangk'fụl, *a.* Grateful; impressed with a sense of kindness received, and ready to acknowledge it. **thankfully,** thangk'fụl-li, *adv.* In a thankful manner; gratefully. **thankless,** thangk'les, *a.* Ungrateful; not obtaining or likely to gain thanks. **thank offering,** thangk of'ėr-ing, *n.* An offering made with a sense of gratitude. **thanksgiving,** thanks-giv'ing, *n.* Act of giving thanks; public celebration of divine goodness.

that, THat, *a.* and *pron.;* pl. **those,** THōz. A pronominal adjective pointing to a person or thing mentioned or understood; a demonstrative pronoun; a relative pronoun equivalent to *who* or *which.*

—*conj.* Introducing a person, purpose, or result, a noun clause, or a wish.

thatch, thach, *n.* Straw rushes used to cover a building or stacks.—*vt.* To put thatch on. **thatching,** thach'ing, *n.* Act or art of covering buildings with thatch; material so used.

thaw, thạ, *vi.* To melt, as ice or snow; to cease to freeze; to become genial.—*vt.* To melt; to make less cold or reserved.—*n.* The melting of ice or snow; warmth after frost.

the, THē or. THi, *def. art.* Used before nouns with a specifying or limiting effect; used before adjectives and adverbs in the comparative degree it means by so much.

theater, theatre, thē'a-tėr, *n.* A house for the exhibition of dramatic performances; a place of action; a room for anatomical demonstrations, &c. **theatric,** thē-at'rik, **theatrical,** thē-at'ri-kal, *a.* Pertaining to a theater; calculated for display: artificial; false. **theatricals,** thē-at'ri-kalz, *n.pl.* Dramatic performances, especially by amateurs.

thee, THē, *pron.* The objective and dative case of *thou.*

theft, theft, *n.* Act of stealing; unlawful taking of another's goods; thing stolen.

their, THār, *pronominal* or *possessive adj.* Pertaining or belonging to them. **theirs,** possessive case of *they,* used without a noun.

theism, thē'izm, *n.* Acknowledgment of the existence of a God; belief in gods. **theist,** thē'ist, *n.* One who believes in the existence of a God. **theistic, theistical,** thē-is'tik, thē-is'ti-kal, *a.* Pertaining to theism or to a theist.

them, THem, *pron.* The dative and objective case of *they;* those persons or things.

theme, thēm, *n.* A subject or topic; short dissertation by a student; leading subject in a musical composition. **thematic,** thē-mat'ik, *n.* Pertaining to a theme.

themselves, THem-selvz', *pron.* Pl. of *himself, herself, itself.*

then, THen, *adv.* At that time, past or future; soon afterward.—*conj.* In that case; therefore.

thence, THens, *adv.* From that place or time; for that reason; elsewhere. **thenceforth,** THens'fōrth", *adv.* From that time; forward. **thenceforward,** THens'for"wėrd, *adv.* From that time or place onward.

theocracy, thē-ok'ra-si, *n.* Government by the immediate direction of God; the state thus governed. **theocrasy,** thē-ok'ra-si, *n.* Intimate union of the soul with God in contemplation. **theocratic, theocratical,** thē-o-krat'ik, thē-o-krat'i-kal, *a.* Pertaining to a theocracy. **theodicy,** thē-od'i-si, *n.* A vindication of the ways of God in creation; a doctrine as to the providential government of God.

theology, thē-ol'o-ji, *n.* The science of God and divine things; divinity. **theologian,** thē'o-lō"ji-an, *n.* A person well versed in theology; a divine. **theo-**

logic, theological, thē-o-loj'ik, thē-o-loj'i-kal, a. Pertaining to theology.

theory, thē'ō-ri, n. Speculation; hypothesis to explain something; rules or knowledge of an art as distinguished from practice. **theorem,** thē'ō-rem, n. A proposition to be proved by reasoning; a speculative truth. **theoretic, theoretical,** thē'ō-ret'ik, thē'ō-ret'i-kal, a. Pertaining to theory; speculative; not practical. **theorist, theorizer,** thē'ō-rist, thē'ō-rīz''ēr, n. One who forms theories. **theorize,** thē'ō-rīz, vi. (theorizing, theorized). To form a theory or theories; to speculate.

therapeutic, ther'a-pū''tik, a. Pertaining to the healing art; curative. **therapeutics,** ther'a-pū''tiks, n. That part of medicine which deals with the application and operation of remedies.

therapy, ther'a-pi, n. Treatment of diseases.

there, thār, adv. In or at that place; at that point; thither. **thereabout, thereabouts,** thār'a-bout, thār'a-bouts, adv. About that; near that place; nearly. **thereafter,** thār-af'tēr, adv. After that; accordingly; afterward. **thereat,** thār-at', adv. At that place; at that time or event; on that account. **thereby,** thār-bī', adv. By that; in consequence of that; near that place; nearly. **therefor,** thār-for', adv. For that or this. **therefore,** thār'for, adv. or conj. For that or this reason; consequently. **therefrom,** thār-from', adv. From this or that. **therein,** thār-in', adv. In that or this place, time, thing, or respect. **thereof,** thār-ov', adv. Of that or this. **thereon,** thār-on', adv. On that or this. **thereto, thereunto,** thār-tö', thār'un-tö'', adv. To that or this. **thereunder,** thār-un'dèr, adv. Under that or this. **thereupon,** thār'up-on'', adv. Upon that or this; in consequence of that; immediately. **therewith,** thar-with', adv. With that or this. **therewithal,** thār'wiTH-al'', adv. Therewith.

thermal, thermic, thèr'mal, thèr'mik, a. Pertaining to heat; warm; hot.

thermometer, thèr'mom'ē-tèr, n. An instrument for measuring temperature.

thermostat, thèr'mō-stat, n. A device which automatically regulates a heating unit.

thesaurus, the-sa̱'rus, n. A treasury; a lexicon.

these, тнēz, pronominal adj. Pl. of this.

thesis, thē'sis, n.; pl. **-ses.** A proposition which a person advances; a theme; an essay written by a candidate for a degree.

Thespian, thes'pi-an, a. Relating to dramatic acting.

thews, thūz, n.pl. Muscles, sinews, strength.

they, тнā, pron. pl. The plural of he, she or it; sometimes used indefinitely.

thick, thik, a. Having extent measured through; dense; foggy; crowded; close; stupid; gross.—n. The thickest part.—adv. In close succession; fast or close together. **thicken,** thik'en, vt. To make thick or thicker.—vi. To become thick.

thickening, thik'en-ing, n. Something put into a liquid or mass to make it more thick. **thicket,** thik'et, n. A wood or collection of trees or shrubs closely set. **thickhead,** thik''hed', n. A stupid fellow. **thick-headed,** thik''hed'-ed, a. Stupid. **thickish,** thik'ish, a. Somewhat thick. **thickly,** thik'li, adv. Densely; closely; in quick succession. **thickness,** thik'nes, n. Measure through and through; thick part; denseness. **thickset,** thik''set', a. Thickly planted; stout; stumpy.—n. A close hedge; dense underwood. **thick-skinned,** thik'skind', a. Having a thick skin or rind; callous; insensible.

thief, thēf, n.; pl. **thieves,** thēvz. A person who steals or is guilty of theft. **thieve,** thēv, vi. and t. (thieving, thieved). To practice theft; to steal. **thievish,** thēv'ish, a. Given to stealing.

thigh, thī, n. The thick part of the leg above the knee; the femur.

thimble, thim'bl, n. A metal cover for the finger in sewing.

thin, thin, a. Not thick; rare; sparse; slim; lean; meager; faint or feeble.—vt. (thinning, thinned). To make thin.—vi. To become thin.

thine, тнīn, pronominal adj., poss. of thou. Thy; belonging to thee.

thing, thing, n. Whatever may be thought of or spoken of; any separate entity; a creature; matter, circumstance, event; pl. clothes, personal belongings, &c.

think, thingk, vi. (thinking, thought). To have the mind occupied on some subject; to judge; to intend; to imagine; to consider.—vt. To imagine; to believe; to consider. **thinker,** thingk'ēr, n. One who thinks; one who writes on speculative subjects. **thinking,** thingk'ing, p.a. Having the faculty of thought; cogitative.—n. Act or state of one who thinks; thought.

thin-skinned, thin'skind', a. Having a thin skin; unduly sensitive; irritable.

third, thèrd, a. The next after the second; being one of three equal parts.—n. The third part of anything. **thirdly,** thèrd'li, adv. In the third place.

thirst, thèrst, n. The desire or distress occasioned by want of water; eager desire after anything.—vi. To feel thirst; to desire vehemently. **thirsty,** thèrs'ti, a. Feeling thirst; having a vehement desire; dry; parched.

thirteen, thèr'tēn', a. and n. Ten and three. **thirteenth,** thèr'tēnth', a. The third after the tenth.—n. One of thirteen equal parts.

thirtieth, thèr'ti-eth, a. The next after the twenty-ninth.—n. One of thirty equal parts.

thirty, thèr'ti, a. and n. Thrice ten.

this, тнis, a. and pron.; pl. **these,** тнēz. A demonstrative, used with or without a noun, referring to something present, near, or just ended.

thistle, this'l, n. A prickly composite plant, the national emblem of Scotland.

thither, тнiтн'ēr, adv. To that place; opposed to hither; to that end or point.

tho', THŌ. A short spelling of *though*.

thong, thong, *n.* A strap of leather, used for fastening anything.

thorax, thō'raks, *n.*; pl. **-races.** That part of the human body which contains the lungs, heart, &c.; the chest.

thorn, thorn, *n.* A tree or shrub armed with spines or prickles: a prickle; anything troublesome. **thorny**, thorn'i, *a.* Full of thorns or spines; prickly; troublesome: vexatious.

thorough, thu'rō, *a.* Passing through or to the end: complete: perfect. **thoroughbred**, thru"rō-bred', *a.* Bred from pure and unmixed blood, as horses; completely bred or accomplished; high-spirited.—*n.* An animal of pure blood. **thoroughfare**, thėr"ō-far', *n.* A passage through: unobstructed way; power of passing. **thorough-going**, thėr"ō-gō'ing, *a.* Going, or ready to go, all lengths; extreme. **thoroughly**, thur'ō-li, *adv.* In a thorough manner; full; entirely; completely.

those, THŌz, *a.* and *pron.* Pl. of *that*.

thou, THou, *pron.* The second personal pronoun singular; in ordinary language supplanted by the plural form *you*.

though, THō, *conj.* Granting it to be the fact that; notwithstanding that; if. —*adv.* However.

thought, thạt, *n.* The power or act of thinking; idea: opinion; judgment; notion; purpose: contemplation; care; concern. **thoughtful**, thạt'ful, *a.* Full of thought; meditative; careful; considerate; anxious. **thoughtfully**, thạt'ful-li, *adv.* In a thoughtful manner; considerately. **thoughtless**, thạt'les, *a.* Free from thought or care; light-minded; heedless; careless.

thousand, thou'zand, *a.* and *n.* Ten hundred; a great number indefinitely. **thousandth**, thou'zandth, *a.* Completing the number a thousand.—*n.* One of a thousand equal parts.

thrall, thrạl, *n.* A slave; a bondsman. **thraldom**, thrạl'dom, *n.* Bondage.

thrash, thresh, thrash, thresh, *vt.* To beat out the grain or seeds from; to beat soundly; to drub. **thrasher, thresher**, thrash'ėr, thresh'ėr, *n.* One who thrashes grain: a species of shark. **thrashing, threshing**, thrash'ing, thresh'ing, *n.* Act of beating out grain; a sound drubbing.

thread, thred, *n.* A fine cord; any fine filament; prominent spiral part of a screw; continued course or tenor; general purpose.—*vt.* To pass a thread through: to pass or pierce through. **threadbare**, thred"bār', *a.* Having the nap worn off; worn out; trite; hackneyed. **thready**, thred'i, *a.* Like thread; consisting of or containing thread.

threat, thret, *n.* A menace; declaration of intention to punish or hurt. **threaten**, thret'n, *vt.* To use threats towards; to menace; to show to be impending.—*vi.* To use threats. **threatening**, thret'n-ing, *a.* Indicating a threat, or something impending.

three, thrē, *a.* and *n.* Two and one. **threefold**, thrē"fold', *a.* Consisting of three in one; triple.—*adv.* Trebly.

threescore, thrē"skŏr', *a.* Three times a score: sixty.

threnody, thren'ō-di, *n.* A song of lamentation; a dirge.

thresh, thresh, *vt. See* **thrash.**

threshold, thresh'ōld, *n.* The stone or piece of timber which lies under a door; a door-sill; entrance: outset.

thrice, thris, *adv.* Three times.

thrift, thrift, *n.* Frugality; economy; sea-pink. **thriftily**, thrif'ti-li, *adv.* In a thrifty manner; frugally. **thriftless**, thrift'les, *a.* Having no thrift; wasteful; profuse; extravagant. **thrifty**, thrif'ti, *a.* Characterized by thrift; frugal; economical.

thrill, thril, *vt.* To send a quiver through; to affect with a keen tingling. —*vi.* To quiver; to move tremulously. —*n.* A warbling; thrilling sensation. **thrilling**, thril'ing, *p.a.* Serving to thrill; exciting.

thrive, thrīv, *vi.* (thriving, pret. throve, pp. thriven). To prosper; to grow vigorously; to flourish. **thriving**, thrīv'ing, *p.a.* Prosperous; successful; growing; flourishing.

throat, thrŏt, *n.* The fore part of the neck of an animal; the opening downward at the back of the mouth.

throb, throb, *vi.* (throbbing, throbbed). To beat, as the heart, with unusual force or rapidity; to palpitate.—*n.* A beat or strong pulsation.

throe, thrō, *n.* Extreme pain; anguish of travail in childbirth.—*vi.* (throeing, throed). To struggle in extreme pain.

thrombosis, throm-bō'sis, *n.* The obstruction of a blood-vessel by a clot of blood.

throne, thrōn, *n.* The seat of a king or ruler; sovereign power and dignity.—*vt.* (throning, throned). To place on a royal seat; to enthrone; to exalt.

throng, throng, *n.* A crowd; a great number.—*vi.* and *t.* To crowd or press together.

throttle, throt'l, *n.* The windpipe or trachea; the throat; the gullet.—*vt.* (throttling, throttled). To choke; to strangle.

through, thrö, *prep.* From end to end of; by means of; on account of; throughout.—*adv.* From end to end; to completion.—*a.* Going with little or no interruption from one place to another. **throughout**, thrö-out', *prep.* Quite through; in every part of.—*adv.* In every part.

throw, thrō, *vt.* (pret. threw, pp. thrown). To fling or cast; to propel; to twist filaments of together; to venture at dice; to shed; to utter; to overturn. —*vi.* To cast; to cast dice.—*n.* Act of one who throws; a cast; distance to which a thing is thrown; venture.

throwback, thrō"bak', *n.* A reversion to an earlier and more primitive ancestral type.

thrum, thrum, *n.* The end of weavers' threads cut off; any coarse yarn.—*vt.* (thrumming, thrummed). To make of or cover with thrums; to drum; to tap.

thrush, thrush, *n.* A singing bird; a

disease affecting the lips and mouth; also a disease in the feet of the horse.

thrust, thrust, *vt.* (pret. and pp. thrust). To push or drive with force; to shove; to stab; to obtrude (one's self). —*vi.* To make a push; to make a lunge with a weapon; to intrude.—*n.* A violent push; a stab; a horizontal outward pressure.

thud, thud, *n.* The dull sound of a blow; a blow causing a dull sound.

thumb, thum, *n.* The short thick finger of the hand.—*vt.* To soil or handle awkwardly with the fingers.

thumbnail, thum″nāl′, *n.* Nail of the thumb.—*a.* Very brief or small.

thumbscrew, thum″skrö′, *n.* A screw to be turned by the fingers; the thumbkins.

thump, thump, *n.* A dull, heavy blow; sound made by such a blow.—*vt.* and *i.* To strike with something thick or heavy.

thunder, thun′dėr, *n.* The sound which follows lightning; any loud noise.—*vi.* To emit the sound of thunder; to make a loud noise.—*vt.* To emit with noise and terror; to publish, as any denunciation. **thunderbolt**, thun″dėr-bölt′, *n.* A shaft of lightning; a daring hero; a fulmination. **thunderclap**, thun″dėr-klap′, *n.* A clap or sudden loud burst of thunder. **thundercloud**, thun″dėr-kloud′, *n.* A cloud that produces lightning and thunder. **thundering**, thun′dėr-ing, *a.* Producing or accompanied by a noise like thunder; extraordinary or excessive. **thunderous**, thun′dėr-us, *a.* Producing thunder; thundery. **thunderstrom**, thun″dėr-storm′, *n.* A storm accompanied with thunder. **thunderstruck**, thun″dėr-struk′, *a.* Struck or blasted by lightning; amazed.

Thursday, thėrz′di, *n.* The fifth day of the week.

thus, THus, *adv.* In this manner; to this degree or extent; accordingly.

thwack, thwak, *vt.* To strike, bang, beat.—*n.* A heavy blow; a bang.

thwart, thwart, *a.* Transverse; being across.—*vt.* To cross; to frustrate or defeat.—*n.* The bench on which the rowers sit, athwart the boat.

thy, THI, *pron. poss.* of *thou.* Belonging or pertaining to thee.

thyme, tim, *n.* A small aromatic shrub of the mint family.

thyroid, thī′roid, *n.* The thyroid gland, the secretion of which controls growth.

thyself, THi-self′, *pron.* Used after *thou,* to express distinction with emphasis; also used without *thou.*

tiara, tī-ār′a, *n.* An ornament worn on the head; the pope's triple crown.

tibia, tib′i-a, *n.* A kind of ancient musical pipe; the shin-bone.

tic, tik, *n.* Facial neuralgia.

tick, tik, *vi.* To make a small noise by beating, &c.—*vt.* To mark with a tick or dot.—*n.* A small distinct noise; a small dot; a small parasitical mite; cover containing the feathers.

ticket, tik′et, *n.* A label; a card or paper enabling one to enter a place, travel in a railway, &c.—*vt.* To put a ticket on; to label.

ticking, tik′ing, *n.* A striped, closely woven cloth containing the feathers, &c., of beds.

tickle, tik′l, *vt.* (tickling, tickled). To touch and cause a peculiar thrilling sensation in; to please; to flatter; to puzzle.

tickler, tik′lėr, *n.* One who tickles or pleases; something that puzzles or perplexes.

ticklish, tik′lish, *a.* Easily tickled; touchy; liable to be overthrown; difficult; critical.

tidal, tīd′al, *a.* Pertaining to tides.

tidbit, *See* **titbit.**

tide, tīd, *n.* Time; season; the rising and falling of the sea; flow; current.—*vt.* or *i.* (tiding, tided). To drive with the tide.

tideless, tīd′les, *a.* Having no tide.

tidetable, tīd′tā-bl, *n.* A table showing the time of high-water. **tidewaiter**, tīd″wāt′ėr, *n.* An officer who watches the landing of goods, to secure the payment of customs duties. **tideway**, tīd″wā′, *n.* The channel in which the tide sets.

tidily, tī′di-li, *adv.* Neatly.

tidings, tī′dingz, *n. pl.* News; intelligence.

tidy, tī′di, *a.* Clean and orderly; neat; trim; moderately large.—*vt.* (tidying, tidied). To make tidy.—*n.* A piece of fancy work to throw over a chair, &c.

tie, tī, *vt.* (tying, tied). To bind; to fasten; to oblige; to constrain.—*n.* That which binds or fastens together; a fastening; a neck-tie; bond; obligation; an equality in numbers.

tier, tėr, *n.* A row; a rank.

tiff, tif, *n.* A fit of peevishness; a slight quarrel; small draught of liquor.—*vi.* To be in a pet.—*vt.* To sip.

tiger, tī′gėr, *n.* An Asiatic carnivorous striped mammal of the cat family as large as the lion; a boy in livery. **tigerish**, tī′gėr-ish, *a.* Like a tiger.

tight, tīt, *a.* Compact; well-knit; stanch; not loose; fitting close or too close; taut; slightly intoxicated; difficult to obtain, as money. **tighten**, tīt′n, *vt.* To make tight or tighter.—*vi.* To become tight. **tightly**, tīt′li, *adv.* In a tight manner; closely; compactly. **tights**, tīts, *n.pl.* A tight-fitting covering for the legs or whole body.

tigress, tī′gres, *n.* A female tiger.

tile, tīl, *n.* A slab of baked clay for covering roofs, floors, walls, &c.—*vt.* (tiling, tiled). To cover with tiles; to guard against the entrance of the uninitiated.

tiler, tīl′ėr, *n.* One who makes or lays tiles; the doorkeeper of a mason lodge. **tiling**, tīl′ing, *n.* The laying of tiles, tiles collectively.

till, til, *n.* A money box or drawer for money in a shop, &c.—*prep.* To the time of; until.—*vt.* To cultivate; to plow and prepare for seed. **tillage**, til′ij, *n.* Act or operation of tilling; cultivation; agriculture. **tiller**, til′ėr, *n.* One who tills; the handle of a rudder; shoot of a plant springing from the root.—*vi.* To put forth shoots from the root.

tilt, tilt, *vi.* To run or ride and thrust with a lance; to joust; to lean or slope; to heel over.—*vt.* To set in a sloping position; to cover with an awning.—*n.* Inclination forward; a military contest with lances on horseback; a tilt-hammer; an awning.

timber, tim'bėr, *n.* Wood suitable for building purposes; trees yielding such wood; one of the main beams of a fabric. —*vt.* To furnish with timber. **timbering**, tim'bėr-ing, *n.* Timber materials; the timber in a structure.

timber line. The point above which trees do not grow on the slopes of mountains or in frigid regions.

timbre, tim'bėr or tam'bėr, *n.* Characteristic quality of sound.

time, tim, *n.* The measure of duration; a particular part or point of duration; occasion; season; epoch; present life; leisure; rhythm; rate of movement.—*vt.* (timing, timed). To adapt to the time or occasion; to regulate or measure as to time. **time fuse**, tim fūz, *n.* A fuse arranged so as to explode a charge at a certain time. **time-honored**, tim'on'-ėrd, *a.* Honored for a long time. **timekeeper**, tim"kēp'ėr, *n.* A clock; one appointed to keep the workmen's time. **timeless**, tim'les, *a.* Untimely; eternal. **timely**, tim'li, *a.* Being in good time; opportune.—*adv.* Early; in good season. **timetable**, tim"tā'bl, *n.* A table of the times of starting of trains, &c.

timely, tim'li, *a.* Opportune; well-timed.

timid, tim'id, *a.* Fearful; timorous; wanting courage; faint-hearted; shy. **timidity**, ti-mid'i-ti, *n.* State or quality of being timid; habitual cowardice.

timorous, tim'ėr-us, *a.* Fearful; timid.

tin, tin, *n.* A malleable metal of a white color tinged with gray; a dish made of tin.—*vt.* (tinning, tinned). To cover with tin; to put in a tin.

tincture, tingk'tūr, *n.* A tinge, tint, or shade; slight quality added to anything; flavor; extract or solution of the active principles of some substance.—*vt.* (tincturing, tinctured). To tinge; to imbue.

tinder, tin'dėr, *n.* An inflammable substance used for obtaining fire from a spark.

tine, tin, *n.* The tooth of a fork or harrow; a prong; point of a deer's horn.

tin foil, tin'foil, *n.* Tin, alloyed with a little lead, reduced to a thin leaf.

tinge, tinj, *vt.* (tingeing, tinged). To give a certain hue or color to; to tint; to imbue.—*n.* A slight color; tint; tincture; smack.

tingle, ting'gl, *vi.* (tingling, tingled). To feel a kind of thrilling sensation.—*vt.* To cause to give a sharp, ringing sound.

tinker, tingk'ėr, *n.* A mender of kettles, pans, &c.; a botcher.—*vt.* and *i.* To mend; to cobble; to botch.

tinkle, ting'kl, *vi.* (tinkling, tinkled). To make small, sharp sounds; to tingle; to clink.—*vt.* To cause to clink.—*n.* A sharp, ringing noise. **tinkling**, ting'-kling, *n.* A small, sharp, ringing sound.

tin plate, tin plāt, *n.* Thin sheet-iron coated with tin.

tinsel, tin'sel, *n.* Thin, glittering metallic sheets; cloth overlaid with foil; something superficially showy.—*a.* Con-

sisting of tinsel; showy to excess.—*vt.* (tinseling, tinseled). To adorn with tinsel.

tinsmith, †in"smith', *n.* A tinner.

tint, tint, *n.* A tinge; a slight coloring; hue.—*vt.* To tinge. **tinting**, tint'ing, *n.* A forming of tints; a particular way of shading in engraving.

tintinnabulation, tin'ti-nab'ū-lā"-shun, *n.* A tinkling or ringing sound, as of bells.

tiny, ti'ni, *a.* Very small; little; puny.

tip, tip, *n.* A small end or point; a tap; a small present in money.—*vt.* (tipping, tipped). To form the tip of; to cant up, as a cart; to give a small money-gift to. **tip-off**, tip'of', *n.* A confidential warning or alerting.

tipple, tip'l, *vi.* (tippling, tippled). To drink spirituous liquors habitually.—*vt.* To drink or imbibe often.—*n.* Liquor. **tippler**, tip'lėr, *n.* A toper; a soaker.

tipsy, tip'si, *a.* Fuddled; affected with strong drink; intoxicated.

tiptoe, tip'tō', *n.* The tip or end of the toe.

tiptop, tip'top', *a.* Excellent; first-rate.

tirade, ti-rād', *n.* A violent declamation; an invective; a harangue.

tire, tir, *n.* A head-dress; a band or hoop round a wheel; attire.—*vt.* (tiring, tired). To fatigue; to weary; to adorn; attire.—*vi.* To become weary. **tiresome**, tir'sum, *a.* Wearisome; tedious.

'tis, tiz, a contraction of *it is*.

tissue, tish'ū, *n.* Any woven stuff; a textile fabric; a primary layer of organic substance; a fabrication. **tissue paper**, tish'ū pā'pėr, *n.* A very thin paper, used for protecting or wrapping.

tit, tit, *n.* A morsel; a small horse; a woman, in contempt; a titmouse or tomtit.

Titan, ti'tan, *n.* A giant deity in Greek mythology. **titanic**, ti-tan'ik, *a.* Pertaining to the Titans; gigantic; huge; pertaining to titanium.

titanium, ti-tā'ni-um, *n.* A metallic element somewhat resembling tin.

titbit, tidbit, tit"bit', tid'bit', *n.* A small morsel; a particularly nice piece.

tithe, tiTH, *n.* The tenth part of anything; tenth part allotted to the clergy; any small part.—*vt.* (tithing, tithed). To levy a tithe on.—*vi.* To pay tithes. **tithing**, tiTH'ing, *n.* Act of levying tithes; a tithe.

titillate, ti'til-lāt, *vi.* To tickle. **titillation**, ti-til-lā'shon, *n.* Act of tickling; state of being tickled; any slight pleasure.

title, ti'tl, *n.* An inscription put over anything; heading; name; appellation of dignity; a right; document which is evidence of a right.—*vt.* (titling, titled). To entitle; to name. **titled**, ti'tld, *a.* Having a title of nobility. **title deed**, ti'tl dēd, *n.* The writing evidencing a man's right or title to property. **title page**, ti'tl pāj, *n.* The page of a book which contains its title. **title role**, ti'tl rōl, *n.* The part in a play which gives its name to it.

titmouse, tit"mous', *n.*; pl. **-mice.** A small inessorial bird with shrill notes.

titter, tit'ẽr, *vi.* To laugh with restraint. —*n.* A restrained laugh.

tittle-tattle, tit'l-tat'l, *n.* Idle trifling talk; empty prattle.—*vi.* To prate.

titular, tit'ū-lẽr, *a.* Holding a position by title or name only; nominal.

tizzy, tiz'i, *n.* Slang. Dither; state of excitement.

TNT or **T.N.T.** *Abbr.* Trinitrotoluene. A very high explosive; an explosive situation.

to, tö or tụ, *prep.* Denoting motion towards; indicating a point reached, destination, addition, ratio, opposition, or contrast; marking an object; the sign of the infinitive mood.—*adv.* Forward; on.

toad, töd, *n.* A reptile resembling the frog but not adapted for leaping. **toadstool,** töd'stöl', *n.* A fungus. **toady,** tö'di, *n.* A base sycophant; a flatterer. —*vt.* (toadying, toadied). To fawn upon.

to-and-fro, tö'and-frö', *a.* Backward and forward; reciprocal.

toast, töst, *vt.* To scorch by the heat of a fire; to warm thoroughly; to drink in honor of.—*n.* Bread scorched by the fire; anyone or anything honored in drinking; a sentiment proposed in drinking. **toaster,** tös'tẽr, *n.* One who toasts; an instrument for toasting bread or cheese.

tobacco, tö-bak'ö, *n.* A narcotic plant of the potato family; its leaves prepared for smoking. **tobacconist,** tö-bak'ö-nist, *n.* A dealer in tobacco.

toboggan, tö-bog'an, *n.* A kind of sled used for sliding down snow-covered slopes. —*vi.* To use such a sled.

toosin, tok'sin, *n.* An alarum bell.

tod, tod, *n.* A mass of foliage; an old weight of 28 pounds for wool; a fox.

today, to-day, tö-dā', *n.* The present day; also, on this day, adverbially.

toddle, tod'l, *vi.* (toddling, toddled). To walk with short, tottering steps.—*n.* A little toddling walk.

toddy, tod'i, *n.* A sweet juice extracted from palm-trees; a mixture of spirit and hot water sweetened.

to-do, tö-dö', *n.* Ado; bustle; commotion.

toe, tö, *n.* One of the small members forming the extremity of the foot.—*vt.* (toeing, toed). To touch or reach with the toes.

toga, tö'ga, *n.* A loose robe, the principal outer garment of the ancient Romans.

together, tụ-geᴛн-ẽr, *adv.* In company; in concert; without intermission.

toil, toil, *vi.* To labor; to work; to drudge.—*n.* Labor with fatigue; a string or web for taking prey. **toilsome,** toil'sum, *a.* Attended with toil; laborious; wearisome; fatiguing.

toilet, toi'let, *n.* A cloth over a table in a dressing-room; a dressing-table; act or mode of dressing; attire; a water closet.

toilette, toi-let', *n.* A woman's dressing and grooming; her attire or costume.

Tokay, tö-kā', *n.* A rich highly prized wine produced at Tokay in Northern Hungary, made from white grapes.

token, tö'ken, *n.* A mark; sign; indication; souvenir; keepsake; a piece of money current by sufferance, not coined by authority.

tolerate, tol'ẽr-āt, *vt.* (tolerating, tolerated). To allow or permit; to treat with forbearance; to put up with; allow religious freedom to. **toleration,** tol'ẽr-ā″shon, *n.* Act of tolerating; allowance given to that which is not wholly approved; recognition of the right of private judgment in religion. **tolerable,** tol'ẽr-a-bl, *a.* That may be tolerated; passable; middling. **tolerably,** tol'ẽr-a-bli, *adv.* In a tolerable manner; moderately well; passably. **tolerance,** tol'ẽr-ans, *n.* The quality of being tolerant; toleration; endurance. **tolerant,** tol'ẽr-ant, *a.* Ready to tolerate; enduring; indulgent; favoring toleration.

toll, töl, *n.* A tax on travelers or vehicles passing along public roads, &c.; stroke of a bell.—*vi.* To pay or take toll; to sound, as a bell, with slow, measured strokes.—*vt.* To take toll from; to sound (a bell); to ring on account of. **tollgate,** töl'gāt, *n.* A gate where toll is taken. **tollhouse,** töl'hous, *n.* A house where a man who takes the toll is stationed.

tomahawk, tom'a-hak, *n.* A hatchet used in war by the N. American Indians. —*vt.* To cut or kill with a tomahawk.

tomato, tö-mā'tö, *n.*; pl. **-toes.** A tropical plant and its fruit, now widely cultivated.

tomb, töm, *n.* A grave; a sepulchral structure.—*vt.* To bury; to entomb.

tomboy, tom″boi', *n.* A wild, romping girl.

tombstone, töm″stön', *n.* A stone erected over a grave; a sepulchral monument.

tomcat, tom″kat', *n.* A full-grown male cat.

tome, töm, *n.* A volume; a large book.

tomfool, tom'föl', *n.* A silly fellow. **tomfoolery,** tom'föl″ẽr-i, *n.* Foolishness; trifling; absurd knick-knacks.

tomorrow, tö-mor'ö, *n.* The day after the present; on the day after the present, adverbially.

tomtit, tom″tit', *n.* The titmouse.

tom-tom, tom″tom', *n.* A primitive drum beaten with the hands; a monotonous, rhythmic beat.

ton, tun, *n.* A weight equal to 20 hundred-weight or 2240 pounds avoirdupois; 2000 pounds in U.S.

tone, tön, *n.* Any sound in relation to its pitch, quality, or strength; sound as expressive of sentiment; timbre; healthy activity of animal organs; mood; tenor; prevailing character.—*vt.* (toning, toned). To give a certain tone to. **to tone down,** to soften, **tonal,** tön'al, *a.* Pertaining to tone.

tongs, tongz, *n.pl.* A metal instrument for taking hold of coals, heated metals, &c.

tongue, tung, *n.* The fleshy movable organ in the mouth, of taste, speech, &c.; speech; a language; strip of land; a tapering flame; pin of a buckle.—*vt.* To utter; to scold; to modify with the tongue in playing, as in the flute. **tongue-tied,** tung'tīd, *a.* Having an impediment in the speech; unable to speak freely.

tonic, ton'ik, *a.* Increasing strength; restoring healthy functions; relating to tones or sounds.—*n.* A medicine that gives tone to the system; the key-note in music.

tonight, tō-nīt', *n.* The present night; in the present or coming night, adverbially.

tonnage, tun'ij, *n.* The number of tons carried by a ship; a duty on ships; ships estimated by their carrying capacity.

tonsil, ton'sil, *n.* One of the two oblong glands on each side of the throat.

tonsillectomy, ton'si-lek''tō-mi, *n.* Removal of the tonsils by surgery.

tonsillitis, ton'si-lī''tis, *n.* An inflammation of the tonsils.

tonsorial, ton-sō'ri-al, *a.* Pertaining to a barber or to shaving.

tonsure, ton'shėr, *n.* The act of clipping the hair; the round bare place on the heads of the Roman Catholic priests. **tonsured,** ton'shėrd, *a.* Having a tonsure; clerical.

too, tö, *adv.* Over; more than sufficiently; very; likewise; also; besides.

tool, töl, *n.* Any instrument to be used by the hands; a person used as an instrument by another.—*vt.* To shape or mark with a tool. **tooling,** töl'ing, *n.* Skilled work with a tool; carving; ornamental marking.

toot, töt, *vi.* To make a noise like that of a pipe or horn.—*vt.* To sound, as a horn.—*n.* A sound blown on a horn.

tooth, töth, *n.*; pl. **teeth,** tēth. A bony growth in the jaws for chewing; any projection resembling a tooth.—*vt.* To furnish with teeth; to indent. **toothache,** töth''āk', *n.* A pain in the teeth. **toothed,** tötht, *a.* Having teeth or cogs. **toothless,** töth'les, *a.* Having no teeth. **toothpick,** töth''pik', *n.* An instrument to pick out substances lodged among the teeth. **toothsome,** töth'sum, *a.* Grateful to the taste; palatable.

top, top, *n.* The highest part of anything; highest rank; platform in ships surrounding the head of the lower masts; a whirling toy.—*a.* Being on the top; highest.—*vi.* (topping, topped). To rise aloft; to be eminent.—*vt.* To cap; to surmount; to rise to the top of.

topaz, tō'paz, *n.* A transparent or translucent gem of various light colors.

top-coat, top''kōt', *n.* An upper or over coat.

toper, töp'ėr, *n.* A tippler.

top-heavy, top''hev'i, *a.* Having the top or upper part too heavy for the lower.

topic, top'ik, *n.* Subject of any discourse; matter treated of. **topical,** top'i-kal, *a.* Pertaining to a topic; local; pertaining to the topics of the day. **topically,** top'i-kal-li, *adv.* Locally; with application to a particular part.

topmost, top'mōst, *a.* Highest; uppermost.

topography, to-pog'ra-fi, *n.* The description of a particular place, tract of land, &c. **topographic, topographical,** top'ō-graf''ik, top'ō-graf''i-kal, *a.* Descriptive of a place.

topping, top'ing, *p.a.* Rising aloft; preeminent; fine; gallant.

topple, top'l, *vi.* (toppling, toppled). To fall, as with the top first.—*vt.* To throw forward.

topsoil, top''soil', *n.* The top layer of soil; rich soil.

topsy-turvy, top'si-tėr-vi, *adv.* Upside down.

toque, tōk, *n.* A kind of flattish hat.

Torah, Tora, tō'ra, *n.* The Pentateuch; law or precept in Jewish literature.

torch, torch, *n.* A light to be carried in the hand; a flambeau. **torch-light,** torch'lit, *n.* The light of a torch or of torches; also adjectively.

toreador, tor'e-a-dor', *n.* A Spanish bull-fighter, especially one on horseback.

torment, tor'ment, *n.* Extreme pain; torture; that which gives pain.—*vt.* tor-ment'. To torture; to distress; to tease. **tormenter,** tor-men'tėr, *n.* One who torments.

tormentor, tor-men'tėr, *n.* One who torments; a kind of harrow with wheels.

tornado, tor-nā'dō, *n.*; pl. **-oes.** A violent whirling wind; a hurricane.

torpedo, tor-pē'dō, *n.*; pl. **-oes.** A fish allied to the rays; an explosive engine propelled under water. **torpedo boat,** tor-pē'dō bōt, *n.* A small swift boat intended to discharge torpedoes.

torpid, tor'pid, *a.* Numb; stupefied; stupid; sluggish; inactive. **torpidity,** tor-pid'i-ti, *n.* State of being torpid; numbness; dullness; inactivity. **torpor,** tor'por, *n.* State of being torpid; numbness; loss of motion; sluggishness.

torrent, tor'ent, *n.* A violent rushing stream. **torrential, torrentine,** to-ren'shal, to-ren'tin, *a.* Pertaining to a torrent.

torrid, tor'id, *a.* Parched; violently hot; burning or parching.

torsion, tor'shun, *n.* The act of twisting; the force with which a body, such as a wire, resists a twist; the twisting of the cut end of an artery to stop the flow of blood.

torso, tor'sō, *n.* The trunk of a statue deprived of its head and limbs.

tort, tort, *n.* Wrong; injury. **tortious,** tor'shus, *a.* Of the nature of or implying tort or injury.

tortoise, tor'tus or tor'tis, *n.* A reptile covered with a flattened shell; a turtle.

tortoiseshell, tor'tusshel, *n.* The shell of tortoises which inhabit tropical seas.

tortuous, tor'tū-us, *a.* Twisted; circuitous and underhand; roundabout.

torture, tor'tūr, *n.* Extreme pain; agony; torment.—*vt.* (torturing, tortured). To pain to extremity; to torment; to harass.

Tory, tō'ri, *n.* An ardent supporter of established institutions in politics; a Conservative.—*a.* Pertaining to Tories.

toss, tos, *vt.* To pitch; to fling; to jerk, as the head; to agitate.—*vi.* To roll and tumble; to be in violent commotion.—*n.* A throw; pitch; throw of the head. **toss-up,** tos''up', *n.* The throwing up of a coin to decide something; an even chance.

tot, tot, *n.* Anything small or insignificant.—*vt.* (totting, totted). To sum (with *up*).

total, tō′tal, *a.* Pertaining to the whole; complete.—*n.* The whole; an aggregate. **totality,** tō-tal′i-ti, *n.* Total amount. **totally,** tō′tal-li, *adv.* Wholly; completely.

totalitarian, tō-tal′i-tār″i-an, *a.* Having to do with absolute government control.—*n.* One who favors totalitarian principles.

totem, tō′tem, *n.* A figure, as of an animal, plant, &c., used as a badge of a tribe or family among rude races.

totter, tot′ėr, *vi.* To threaten to fall; to vacillate; to shake; to reel. **tottery,** tot′ėr-i, *a.* Unsteady; shaking.

toucan, tö′kan, *n.* A scansorial bird of tropical America having an enormous beak.

touch, tuch, *vt.* To perceive by the sense of feeling; to come in contact with; to taste; to reach or arrive at; to refer to; to affect.—*vi.* To be in contact; to take effect; to make mention; to call when on a voyage.—*n.* Act of touching; contact; sense of feeling; a trait; a little; a stroke; distinctive handling. **touching,** tuch′ing, *a.* Affecting; moving; pathetic.—*prep.* Concerning; with respect to. **touchstone,** tuch″stōn′, *n.* A compact, dark-colored, siliceous stone used in testing gold and silver; a test or criterion. **touchy,** tuch′i, *a.* Irritable; irascible; apt to take offense.

touchdown, tuch″doun′, *n.* The act of scoring six points in American football by being lawfully in possession of the ball on, above, or behind the opponent's goal line; an aircraft's first contact with the ground on landing.

touch and go. A delicate and dangerous situation.

tough, tuf, *a.* Flexible and not brittle; tenacious; durable; viscous; stiff; stubborn. **toughen,** tuf′en, *vi.* To grow tough.—*vt.* To make tough. **toughish,** tuf′ish, *a.* Somewhat tough.

toupee, toupet, tö-pē′, tö′pā, *n.* A curl or artificial lock of hair; a small wig or upper part of a wig.

tour, tör, *n.* A journey; a lengthy jaunt or excursion.—*vi.* To make a tour. **tourist,** tör′ist, *n.* One who makes a tour.

tourmalin, tourmaline, tör′ma-lin, *n.* A mineral of various colors, possessing strong electrical properties.

tournament, tör′na-ment, *n.* A martial sport performed by knights on horseback; contest in which a number take part.

tourney, tör′ni, *n.* A tournament.—*vi.* To tilt; to engage in a tournament.

tourniquet, tör′ni-ket, *n.* A bandage tightened by a screw to check a flow of blood.

tousle, tou′zl, *vt.* (tousling, tousled). To dishevel.

tout, tout, *vi.* To ply or seek for customers.—*n.* One who plies for customers.

tow, tō, *vt.* To drag, as a boat, by a rope.—*n.* Act of towing; state of being towed; coarse part of flax or hemp. **to-**

ward, towards, tō′ėrd, tō′ėrdz, *prep.* In the direction of; regarding; in aid of; for; about.—*adv.* At hand; going on.

towel, tou′el, *n.* A cloth for drying the skin after washing, or for domestic purposes. **toweling,** tou′el-ling, *n.* Cloth for towels.

tower, tou′ėr, *n.* A lofty narrow building; a citadel; a fortress.—*vi.* To soar; to be lofty; to stand sublime. **towering,** tou′ėr-ing, *a.* Very high; extreme; violent.

towline, tō′lin, *n.* A rope used in towing.

town, toun, *n.* Any collection of houses larger than a village; a city; borough; inhabitants of a town; the metropolis.—*a.* Pertaining to a town. **town clerk,** toun klėrk, *n.* An officer who acts as clerk to the council of a town. **town hall,** toun hal, *n.* A building belonging to a town in which the town-council ordinarily hold their meetings. **townsfolk,** tounz″fōk′, *n.pl.* Townspeople. **township,** toun′ship, *n.* Territory of a town; division of certain parishes. **townspeople,** tounz″pē′pl, *n.pl.* The inhabitants of a town.

toxic, toxical, tok′sik, tok′si-kal, *a.* Pertaining to poisons; poisonous. **toxicology,** tok′si-kol″ō-ji, *n.* That branch of medicine which treats of poisons and their antidotes. **toxin,** toks′in, *n.* A poisonous substance generated in an animal body.

toy, toi, *n.* A plaything; a bauble; a trifle.—*vi.* To dally; to trifle.

trace, trās, *n.* A mark left by anything; footstep; vestige; track; one of the straps by which a carriage, &c., is drawn.—*vt.* (tracing, traced). To track out; to follow by marks left; to draw or copy with lines or marks. **traceable,** trās′a-bl, *a.* That may be traced. **tracery,** trās′ėr-i, *n.* A species of rich open work, seen in Gothic windows, &c. **tracing,** trās′ing, *n.* Act of one who traces; copy of a design made by following its lines through a transparent medium.

trachea, trā′kē-a, *n.* The wind-pipe. **tracheotomy,** trā-kē-ot′ō-mi, *n.* The operation of cutting into the trachea, as in suffocation.

track, trak, *n.* A footprint; rut made by a wheel; trace; beaten path; course.—*vt.* To trace; to follow step by step; to tow by a line from the shore. **tracker,** trak′ėr, *n.* One who hunts by following the track. **trackless,** trak′les, *a.* Having no track; untrodden; pathless.

tract, trakt, *n.* A region of indefinite extent; a short dissertation. **tractable,** trak′ta-bl, *a.* That may be easily managed; docile; manageable. **tractably,** trak′ta-bli, *adv.* In a tractable manner; with ready compliance.

traction, trak′shun, *n.* The act of drawing a body along a surface of land or water.

tractor, trak′tėr, *n.* An automobile used for drawing and hauling something, as a vehicle, plow, harrow, &c.

trade, trād, *n.* Employment; commerce; traffic; those engaged in any trade.—*a.*

Pertaining to trade.—*vi.* (trading, traded). To traffic; to carry on commerce; to have dealings.—*vt.* To sell or exchange in commerce. **trade-mark**, trād″märk′, *n.* A distinctive mark put by a manufacturer on his goods. **trader**, trād′ẽr, *n.* One engaged in trade. **tradesman**, trādz′man, *n.* One who practices a trade; a store-keeper; an artisan. **trades-people**, trādz″pē′pl, *n.* Tradesmen. **trade-union**, trād″ŭn′yon, *n.* A combination of workmen in a trade to secure conditions most favorable for labor. **trade-unionism**, trād″ŭn″yon-izm, *n.* The principles or practices of trade-unions. **trade-unionist**, trād″ŭn″yon-ist, *n.* A member of a trade-union. **trade-wind**, trād-wind, *n.* A periodic wind blowing for six months in one direction. **trading**, trād′ing, *p.a.* Carrying on commerce; engaged in trade; venal.

tradition, tra-dish′on, *n.* The handing down of opinions, stories, &c., from father to son, by oral communication; a statement so handed down. **traditional, traditionary**, tra-dish′un-al, tra-dish″un-er-i, *a.* Relating to or derived from tradition.

traduce, tra-dūs′, *vt.* (traducing, traduced). To calumniate; to vilify; to defame. **traducer**, tra-dūs′ẽr, *n.* One that traduces; a slanderer; a calumniator.

traffic, ″traf′ik, *n.* An interchange of commodities; commerce; goods or persons passing along a road, railway, &c.; dealings.—*vi.* (trafficking, trafficked). To trade; to deal; to trade meanly or mercenarily. **trafficker**, traf′ik-ẽr, *n.* One who traffics.

tragedy, traj′e-di, *n.* A drama representing an important event generally having a fatal issue; a fatal and mournful event; a murderous or bloody deed. **tragic, tragical**, traj′ik, traj′i-kal, *a.* Pertaining to tragedy; murderous; calamitous. **tragically**, traj′i-kal-li, *adv.* In a tragic manner. **tragedian**, tra-jē′di-an, *n.* A writer of tragedy; an actor of tragedy. **tragedienne**, tra-jē′di-en″, *n.* A female actor of tragedy.

rail, trāl, *n.* Something dragged behind; a train; the end of a field gun-carriage that rests on the ground in firing; a path; track followed by a hunter; the intestines of certain birds and fishes which are sent to the table without being extracted.—*vt.* To draw behind or along the ground; to drag.—*vi.* To be dragged along a surface; to hand down loosely; to grow along the ground. **trailer**, trāl′ẽr, *n.* One who trails; a plant which cannot grow upward without support; a van pulled by a truck. A mobile home. **rain**, trān, *vt.* To draw; to entice; to rear and instruct; to drill; to bring into proper bodily condition; to shape; to bring to bear, as a gun.—*vi.* To undergo special drill.—*n.* A trail; that part of a gown which trails; tail; a series, course; retinue; line of cars and an engine on a railway; line to conduct fire to a charge or mine. **trained**, trānd, *p.a.* Formed by training; exercised; instructed;

skilled by practice. **trainer**, trān′ẽr, *n.* One who prepares men or horses for races, &c. **training**, trān′ing, *n.* Act of one who trains; education; drill.

traipse, trapes, trāps, *vi.* (traipsing, traipsed). To gad about in an idle way.

trait, trāt or trā, *n.* A stroke; touch; feature; characteristic; peculiarity.

traitor, trā′tẽr, *n.* One who betrays his trust or allegiance; one guilty of treason. **traitorous**, trā′tẽr-us, *a.* Guilty of treason; treacherous; treasonable. **traitress**, trā′tres, *n.* A female traitor.

trajectory, tra-jck′tō-ri, *n.* The path described by a body, as a planet, projectile, &c.

tram, tram, *n.* One of the rails or tracks of a tramway; a tram-car; a tramway (Eng.); a kind of silk thread.

trammel, tram′el, *n.* A net for birds or fishes; shackles for regulating the motions of a horse; whatever hinders or confines; an iron hook.—*vt.* (trammeling, trammeled). To impede; to shackle.

tramp, tramp, *vt.* and *i.* To tread under foot; to travel on foot.—*n.* A tread; sound made by the feet in walking; journey on foot; a strolling beggar. **trample**, tram′pl, *vt.* (trampling, trampled). To tread on heavily; to tread down; to treat with pride or insult.—*vi.* To treat in contempt; to tread with force.

trance, trans, *n.* A state of insensibility; ecstasy; catalepsy.—*vt.* (trancing, tranced). To entrance; to enchant.

tranquil, trang′kwil, *a.* Quiet; calm; undisturbed; peaceful. **tranquillity**, trang-kwil′i-ti, *n.* State of being tranquil; quietness; calmness; peace. **tranquilize**, trang′kwil-īz, *vt.* To render tranquil; to quiet; to compose. **tranquilly**, trang′kwil-li, *adv.* Quietly.

tranquilizer, trang″kwil-īz′ẽr, *n.* A drug used to tranquilize, ease tension.

transact, trans-akt′, *vt.* and *i.* To carry through; to perform; to manage. **transaction**, trans-ak′shun, *n.* The doing of any business; affair; proceeding; *pl.* reports of proceedings of societies.

transatlantic, trans′at-lan″tik, *a.* Being beyond or crossing the Atlantic.

transcend, trans-send′, *vt.* To rise above; to surpass; to outgo; to excel; to exceed. **transcendence, transcendency**, trans-sen′dens, trans-sen′den-si, *n.* Transcendent state; superior excellence. **transcendent**, trans-sen′dent, *a.* Supreme in excellence; transcending human experience. **transcendental**, trans-sen-dent′al, *a.* Transcendent; transcending knowledge acquired by experience; abstrusely speculative.

transcribe, tran-skrīb′, *vt.* (transcribing, transcribed). To write over again or in the same words; to copy. **transcript**, tran′skript, *n.* That which is transcribed; a copy; an imitation. **transcription**, tran-skrip′shun, *n.* Act of transcribing; a copy; transcript.

transept, tran′sept, *n.* The transverse portion of a church built in form of a cross.

transfer, trans-fėr′, vt. (transferring, transferred). To convey from one place or person to another; to make over.—n. trans′fėr. Act of transferring; removal of a thing from one place or person to another; something transferring. **transferable**, trans-fėr′a-bl or trans′fėr-a-bl, a. Capable of being transferred. **transferee**, trans′fėr-ē″, n. The person to whom a transfer is made. **transference**, trans′fėr-ens, n. Act of transferring; passage of anything from one place to another.

transfigure, trans-fig′ūr, vt. To change in form or shape; to idealize. **transfiguration**, trans-fig′ū-rā″shun, n. A change of form or figure; the supernatural change in the appearance of Christ on the mount; a Church feast held on the 6th of August, in commemoration of this change.

transfix, trans-fiks′, vt. To pierce through; to cause to be immovable.

transform, trans-form′, vt. To change the form of; to change, as the natural disposition of.—vi. To be changed in form. **transformation**, trans′for-mā″shun, n. Act of transforming; an entire change in form, disposition, &c.

transformer, trans-for′mėr, n. One who transforms; a device that changes the potential or strength of an electric current.

transfuse, trans-fūz′, vt. (transfusing, transfused). To transfer by pouring; to cause to pass from one to another. **transfusion**, trans-fū′zhun, n. Act of transfusing, as the blood of one animal into another.

transgress, trans-gres′, vt. To break or violate; to infringe.—vi. To do wrong; to sin. **transgression**, trans′gresh′un, n. Act of tresgressing; a trespass; offense; crime. **transgressor**, trans-gres′ėr, n. One who transgresses; an offender; a criminal.

transient, tran′shent, a. Passing quickly; fleeting; momentary; fugitive.

transistor, tran-zis′tėr, n. A device which amplifies electricity by controlling the flow of electrons.

transit, tran′sit, n. Act of passing; passage; passage of a heavenly body over the disk of a larger one. **transition**, tran-zish′on, n. Passage from one place, state, or topic to another.—a. Pertaining to passage from one state, &c., to another. **transitional, transitionary**, tran-zish′un-al, tran-zi′shun-a-ri, a. Containing or denoting transition. **transitive**, tran′sit-iv, a. In grammar, taking an object after it, as a verb. **transitory**, tran′si-tō′ri, a. Passing away; fleeting; transient.

translate, trans-lāt′, vt. (translating, translated). To remove from one place to another; to transfer; to render into another language. **translation**, trans-lā′shun, n. Act of translating; removal; act of turning into another language; interpretation; a version. **translator**, trans-lā′tėr, n. One who renders one language into another.

transliterate, trans-lit′ėr-āt, vt. To

write or spell in different characters intended to express the same sound.

translucent, trans-lū′sent, a. Transmitting rays of light, but not so as to render objects distinctly visible; transparent; clear.

transmigrate, trans-mī′grāt, vi. To pass from one country or body to another. **transmigration**, trans′mi-grā″-shun, n. Act of transmigrating; the passing of a soul into another body after death. **transmigratory**, trans-mī′gra-tō′ri, a. Passing from one place or state to another.

transmit, trans-mit′, vt. (transmitting, transmitted). To send from one person or place to another; to hand down; to allow to pass through. **transmission**, trans-mish′un, n. Act of transmitting; transference; a passing through any body, as of light through glass.

transmitter, trans-mit′ėr, n. A person or thing that transmits something; the part of a telephone that changes sound waves into electric waves; the portion of a telegraph instrument that sends the message.

transmute, trans-mūt′, vt. (transmuting, transmuted). To change from one nature or substance into another. **transmutable**, trans-mūt′a-bl, a. Capable of being transmuted. **transmutation**, trans′mū-tā″shun, n. Act of transmuting; conversion into something different.

transoceanic, trans′ō-shē-an″ik, a. Beyond the ocean; crossing the ocean.

transom, tran′sum, n. A strengthening horizontal beam; a cross-bar.

transparent, trans-pār′ent, a. That can be seen through distinctly; not sufficien to hide underlying feelings. **transparently**, trans-pār′ent-li, adv. Clearly; so as to be seen through. **transparence**, trans-pār′ens, n. Transparency. **transparency**, trans-pār-en-si, n. State o quality of being transparent; something transparent; a picture painted on trans parent materials.

transpire, trans-pīr′, vt. (transpiring transpired). To emit through the pôre of the skin; to send off in vapor.—v To exhale; to escape from secrecy; t become public. **transpiration**, tran spi-rā′shun, n. Act or process of tran spiring; exhalation.

transplant, trans-plant′, vt. To remov and plant in another place. **transplantation**, trans′plan-tā″shun, n. Ac of transplanting; removal.

transport, trans-pōrt′, vt. To carr from one place to another; to carry int banishment; to carry away by violenc of passion; to ravish with pleasure.—n trans′pōrt. Transportation; a ship em ployed to carry soldiers, warlike stores &c.; passion; ecstasy. **transportation**, trans′pōr-tā″shun, n. Act of trans porting; banishment to a penal settle ment; transmission; conveyance.

transpose, trans-pōz′, vt. (transposing transposed). To change the order o things by putting each in the other place; to cause to change places. **trans**

osal, trans-pōz'al, *n.* Act of transposing; transposition.

transposition, trans'pō-zish"un, *n.* Act of transposing; state of being transposed; change of the order of words for effect.

transverse, trans-vèrs' or trans'vèrs, *a.* lying or being across or in a cross direction. **transversal,** trans-vèr'sal, *a.* Transverse; running or lying across.

trap, trap, *n.* A contrivance for catching unawares; an ambush; a contrivance in drains to prevent effluvia rising; a carriage of any kind, on springs; a kind of movable ladder; an igneous rock.—*vt.* (trapping, trapped). To catch in a trap; to insnare; to adorn.—*vi.* To set traps or game.

trap door, trap dōr, *n.* A door in a floor or roof, with which when shut it is flush.

trapeze, tra-pēz', *n.* A sort of swing, consisting of a cross-bar, suspended by cords, for gymnastic exercises.

trapezoid, trap'ē-zoid, *n.* A plane four-sided figure having two sides parallel.

trapper, trap'èr, *n.* One who traps animals for their furs.

trappings, trap'ingz, *n.pl.* Ornaments; dress; decorations; finery.

trappist, trap'ist, *n.* A member of an ascetic order of the Roman Catholic Church.

trash, trash, *n.* Loppings of trees; broken pieces; rubbish; refuse.—*vt.* To lop. **trashy,** trash'i, *a.* Worthless; useless.

trauma, tra'ma, *n.* An injury to the body; shock; the resulting state of mind.

traumatic, tra-mat'ik, *a.* Pertaining to wounds.—*n.* A medicine useful in the cure of wounds.

travail, trav'āl, *vi.* To labor; to toil; to suffer the pangs of childbirth.—*n.* Labor; severe toil; childbirth.

travel, trav'el, *n.* Act of journeying; journey to a distant country; *pl.* account of occurrences during a journey.—*vi.* (traveling, traveled). To journey; to go to a distant country; to pass; to move. **traveled,** trav'eld, *p.a.* Having made many journeys; experienced from traveling. **traveler,** trav'el-èr, *n.* One who travels; one who travels from place to place to solicit orders for goods, &c. **traveling,** trav'el-ing, *p.a.* Pertaining to, used in, or incurred by travel.

travelogue, travelog, trav'e-log, *n.* An illustrated lecture on travel; a motion picture on travel.

traverse, trav'èrs, *a.* Transverse.—*n.* something that is transverse; something that thwarts; a denial.—*vt.* (traversing, traversed). To cross; to thwart; to cross in traveling; to deny.—*adv.* Athwart; crosswise.

travesty, trav'es-ti, *vt.* (travestying, travestied). To transform so as to have a ludicrous effect; to burlesque.—*n.* A burlesque treatment; parody.

trawl, tral, *vi.* To fish with a trawl-net; to drag, as a net.—*n.* A trawl-net. **trawler,** tral'èr, *n.* One who trawls; a fishing vessel which fishes with a trawl-

net. **trawling,** tral'ing, *n.* The act of one who trawls; fishing with a trawl-net.

tray, trā, *n.* A sort of waiter or salver, of wood, metal, &c., on which dishes and the likes are presented.

treacherous, trech'èr-us, *a.* Guilty of treachery; faithless; traitorous; perfidious. **treacherously,** trech'èr-us-li, *adv.* Traitorously; faithlessly; perfidiously. **treachery,** trech'èr-i, *n.* Violation of allegiance or of faith; perfidy; treason.

treacle, trē'kl, *n.* The uncrystallizable part of sugar obtained in refineries; molasses.

tread, tred, *vi.* (pret. trod; pp. trod, trodden). To set the foot on the ground; to step; to walk with a measured step; to copulate, as fowls.—*vt.* To plant the foot on; to trample; to dance; to walk on in a formal manner; to copulate with, as a bird.—*n.* A step; gait; horizontal part of the step of a stair.

treadle, tred'l, *n.* The part of a loom or other machine moved by the foot.

treadmill, tred'mil, *n.* A mill worked by persons or animals treading on movable steps.

treason, trē'zn, *n.* A betrayal; breach of allegiance; treachery; disloyalty. **treasonable,** trē'zn-a-bl, *a.* Pertaining to, consisting of, or involving treason.

treasure, trezh'èr, *n.* Wealth accumulated; great abundance; something very much valued.—*vt.* (treasuring, treasured). To lay up or collect; to prize. **treasurer,** trezh'èr-èr, *n.* One who has the charge of a treasury or funds. **treasure-trove,** trezh'èr-trōv', *n.* Money or bullion found hidden, the owner of which is not known. **treasury,** trezh'èr-i, *n.* A place where treasure is laid up; department of government which controls the revenue; a book containing much valuable material.

treat, trēt, *vt.* To handle; to act towards; to discourse on; to entertain; to manage.—*vi.* To handle; to discourse; to negotiate.—*n.* An entertainment given as a compliment; an unusual gratification.

treatise, trē'tis, *n.* A written composition on some particular subject; a dissertation.

treatment, trēt'ment, *n.* Act or manner of treating; management; usage.

treaty, trē'ti, *n.* Negotiation; agreement between two or more nations.

treble, treb'l, *a.* Threefold; triple; in *music,* pertaining to the highest sounds. —*n.* The highest part in a concerted piece of music; a soprano.—*vt.* and *i.* (trebling, trebled). To make or become thrice as much. **trebly,** treb'li, *adv.* Triply.

tree, trē, *n.* A perennial plant having a woody trunk and branches; something resembling a tree; a cross; a wooden piece in machines, &c.—*vt.* (treeing, treed). To cause to take refuge in a tree.—*vi.* To take refuge in a tree.

trefoil, trē'foil, *n.* A three-leaved plant, as clover; an architectural ornament, consisting of three cusps.

trek, trek, *vi.* (trekking, trekked). To travel by wagon.

trellis, trel'is, *n.* A structure of cross-barred work or lattice-work.—*vt.* To furnish with a trellis; to form like a trellis.

tremble, trem'bl, *vi.* (trembling, trembled). To shake involuntarily; to quiver; to vibrate.—*n.* An involuntary shaking; a tremor. **trembling**, trem'bling, *n.* Act or state of shaking involuntarily; a tremor.

tremendous, trē-men'dus, *a.* Such as may cause trembling; terrible; extraordinary. **tremendously**, trē-men'dus-li, *adv.* In a tremendous manner; astoundingly.

tremor, trem'ėr, *n.* An involuntary trembling; a shivering; vibration.

tremulous, trem'ū-lus, *a.* Trembling; shaking; quivering; vibratory.

trench, trench, *vt.* To dig a ditch in; to turn over and mix, as soil.—*vi.* To cut a trench or trenches; to encroach (with *on* or *upon*).—*n.* A long narrow excavation; a deep ditch cut for defense.

trenchant, tren'chant, *a.* Cutting; keen; severe. **trencher**, tren'chėr, *n.* A wooden plate on which meat may be carved; food; pleasures of the table. **trencher-man**, trench'ėr-man, *n.* A great eater.

trench coat. A raincoat of military design or style.

trench mouth. An infectious inflammation of the mouth and gums.

trend, trend, *vi.* To extend in a particular direction.—*n.* Direction; tendency.

trepan, trē-pan', *n.* A surgical saw for removing a portion of the skull.—*vt.* (trepanning, trepanned). To perforate with a trepan; to insnare.

trephine, tre-fīn', *n.* An improved form of the trepan.—*vt.* (trephining, trephined). To perforate with a trephine.

trepidation, trep'i-da"shun, *n.* Confused alarm; perturbation; involuntary trembling.

trespass, tres'pas, *vi.* To enter unlawfully upon the land of another; to do wrong; to offend.—*n.* An offense; a sin; wrong done by entering on the land of another. **trespasser**, tres'pas-ėr, *n.* One who trespasses; a wrongdoer; a sinner.

tress, tres, *n.* A braid, lock or curl of hair.

trestle, tres'l, *n.* A frame for supporting things; a frame with three or four legs attached to a horizontal piece.

triad, trī'ad, *n.* A union of three; a trinity.

trial, trī'al, *n.* Act of trying; examination by a test; experience; probation; temptation; judicial examination.

trial balloon. An act designed to test public reaction.

triangle, trī"ang'gl, *n.* A figure having three sides and angles. **triangular**, trī-ang'gū-lėr, *a.* Having three angles; having the form of a triangle.

tribe, trīb, *n.* A division or class of people; a family or race; a class of animals or plants. **tribal**, trīb'al, *a.* Belonging to a tribe. **tribesman**, trība'man, *n.* A member of a tribe.

tribulation, trib'ū-lā"shun, *n.* Severe trouble or affliction; distress; trial; suffering.

tribune, trib'ūn, *n.* Among the ancient Romans, a magistrate chosen by the people, to protect them from the patricians; a platform; tribunal; throne of a bishop. **tribunal**, trī-bū'nal, *n.* The seat of a judge; a court of justice.

tribute, trib'ūt, *n.* A sum paid by one prince or nation to another; personal contribution. **tributary**, trib'ū-ter'i, *a.* Paying tribute to another; subject; contributing.—*n.* One that pays tribute; stream which falls into another.

trice, trīs, *n.* A very short time; an instant.—*vt.* (tricing, triced). To hoist by a rope.

trichina, tri-kī'na, *n.*; pl. **-næ**. A minute nematoid worm, the larva of which causes disease in the flesh of mammals. **trichiniasis, trichinosis**, trik-i-nī"a-sis, trik-i-nō'sis, *n.* The disease produced by trichinæ.

trick, trik, *n.* An artifice; a crafty device; fraud; a knack or art; a person's practice or habit; a prank; all the cards played in one round.—*vt.* To deceive; to impose on; to cheat; to draw in out of line; to dress; to adorn (often with *out*). **trickery**, trik'ėr-i, *n.* Artifice; imposture. **trickster**, trik'stėr, *n.* One who practices tricks. **tricky**, trik'i, *a.* Trickish; mischievous.

tricolor, tricolour, trī"kul'ėr, *n.* The national French banner of blue, white, and red vertically.

tricycle, trī'sik-l, *n.* A cycle with three wheels.

trident, trī'dent, *n.* Any instrument in the form of a fork with three prongs.

tried, trīd, *p.a.* Tested by trial or experience; staunch; true.

trifle, trī'fl, *n.* Something of no moment or value; a kind of fancy confection.—*vi.* (trifling, trifled). To act with levity; to play or toy; to finger lightly.—*vt.* To waste. **trifler**, trī'flėr, *n.* One who trifles or acts with levity. **trifling**, trī'fling, *a.* Apt to trifle; frivolous; trivial; insignificant.

trig, trig, *vt.* (trigging, trigged). To stop or fasten, as a wheel.—*a.* Trim; spruce; neat.

trigger, trig'ėr, *n.* The catch which, on being pulled, liberates the hammer of the lock of a gun; an act that may set something in motion.

trigonometry, trig'ō-nom'e-tri, *n.* The science of determining the sides and angles of triangles; a geometrical method of calculation. **trigonometric, trigonometrical**, trig'ō-nō-met"rik, trig'ō-nō-met"ri-kal, *a.* Pertaining to trigonometry.

trill, tril, *n.* A shake of the voice in singing; a quavering sound.—*vt.* To sing with a quavering voice; to sing sweetly or clearly.—*vi.* To sound with tremulous vibrations; to pipe; to trickle.

trillion, tril'yon, *n.* The product of a million multiplied by itself.

trilogy, tril'o-ji, *n.* A series of three

connected dramas, each complete in itself.

trim, trim, *vt.* (trimming, trimmed). To put in order; to embellish; to clip or pare; to adjust.—*vi.* To hold a middle course between parties.—*a.* Set in good order; properly adjusted; neat; tidy.—*n.* Condition; order; mood; dress. **trimly,** trim'li, *adv.* Neatly; smartly. **trimmer,** trim'ẻr, *n.* One who trims; a laborer who arranges the cargo of coal on a ship; one who fluctuates between parties. **trimming,** trim'ing, *n.* Act of one who trims; behavior of one who fluctuates between parties; ornamental appendages; *pl.* accessories.

trinity, trin'i-ti, *n.* A union of three in one; (*Cap.*) the union in one Godhead of the Father, Son, and Holy Spirit.

trinket, tring'ket, *n.* A small ornament; a trifle.—*vi.* To intrigue; to traffic.

trio, trē'ō, or trī'ō, *n.* Three united; musical composition for three voices or instruments; performers of a trio.

trip, trip, *vi.* (tripping, tripped). To run or step lightly; to skip; to stumble; to err.—*vt.* To cause to fall or stumble; to loose an anchor.—*n.* A stumble; a light short step; an excursion or jaunt; a mistake.

tripartite, trī-pär'tīt or trip'ẻr-tit, *a.* Divided into three parts; made between three parties.

tripe, trīp, *n.* The stomach of ruminating animals prepared for food.

trip hammer, trip ham'ẻr, *n.* A large hammer used in forges; a tilt-hammer.

triphthong, trif'thong or trip'thong, *n.* A union of three vowels in one syllable, as in *adieu.*

triple, trip'l, *a.* Threefold; treble.—*vt.* (tripling, tripled). To treble. **triplet,** trip'let, *n.* Three of a kind; three lines of poetry rhyming together; one of three children born at a birth. **triplicate,** trip'li-kāt, *a.* Threefold.—*n.* A third thing corresponding to two others.

tripod, trī'pod, *n.* A three-footed pot, seat, or stand.

triptych, trip'tik, *n.* A picture or carving in three compartments side by side; a treatise in three sections.

trisect, trī'sekt″, *vt.* To cut into three equal parts. **trisection,** trī-sek'shun, *n.* Act of trisecting; division of a thing into three equal parts.

trite, trīt, *a.* Hackneyed; threadbare; stale.

Triton, trī'ton, *n.* A sea deity with fishlike lower extremities.

triturate, trit'ū-rāt, *vt.* (triturating, triturated). To rub or grind to a very fine powder.

triumph, trī'umf, *n.* A magnificent procession in honor of a victorious Roman general; victory; achievement; joy for success.—*vi.* To rejoice for victory; to obtain victory; to exult insolently. **triumphal,** trī-um'fal, *a.* Pertaining to or used in a triumph. **triumphant,** trī-um'fant, *a.* Feeling triumph; victorious; celebrating victory; expressing joy for success. **triumphantly,** trī-um'fant-li, *adv.* In a triumphant manner; exultantly.

triumvir, trī-um'vẻr, *n.* One of three men united in office. **triumvirate,** trī-um'vi-rāt, *n.* A coalition of three men in office or authority.

trivet, triv'et, *n.* Anything supported by three feet; an iron frame whereon to place vessels before or over a fire.

trivial, triv'i-al, *a.* Common; commonplace; trifling; insignificant. **triviality,** triv'i-al″i-ti, *n.* State or quality of being trivial; a trifle.

trochaic, trō-kā'ik, *a.* Pertaining to or consisting of trochees.

troche, trōch, or trosh, *n.* A small lozenge containing a drug.

trochee, trō'kē, *n.* A metrical foot of two syllables, the first long and the second short.

trod, trodden. *See* tread.

troglodyte, trog'lō-dīt, *n.* A cave dweller; one living in seclusion.

Trojan, trō'jan, *a.* Pertaining to ancient Troy.—*n.* An inhabitant of ancient Troy; a jolly fellow; a plucky determined fellow.

troll, trōl, *vt.* To roll; to pass round; to sing in a full, jovial voice.—*vi.* To go round; to fish for pike by trolling.—*n.* A going round; a part-song; a reel on a fishing-rod; a dwarfish being in Scandinavian mythology, dwelling in caves and mounds.

trolley, trolly, trol'i, *n.* A kind of small truck; a streetcar; a wheel riding on a cable or metal track for the purpose of conducting electricity.

trolling, trōl'ing, *n.* Act of one who trolls; a method of rod-fishing for pike with a dead bait; trawling.

trollop, trol'up, *n.* A woman loosely dressed; a slattern; a drab.

trombone, trom'bōn, *n.* A deep-toned instrument of the trumpet kind.

troop, tröp, *n.* A collection of people; a company; a body of soldiers; *pl.* soldiers in general; a troupe.—*vi.* To collect in numbers; to march in a body.

trooper, tröp'ẻr, *n.* A horse-soldier.

troopship, tröp'ship′, *n.* A transport.

trophy, trō'fi, *n.* A memorial of some victory; an architectural ornament representing the stem of a tree, hung with military weapons.

tropic, trop'ik, *n.* Either of two circles on the celestial sphere, limiting the sun's apparent annual path; either of two corresponding parallels of latitude including the torrid zone; *pl.* the regions between or near these.—*a.* Pertaining to the tropics. **tropical,** trop'i-kal, *a.* Pertaining to the tropics or to a trope.

trot, trot, *vi.* (trotting, trotted). To run with small steps; to move fast.—*vt.* To cause to trot.—*n.* Pace of a horse more rapid than a walk.

troth, troth or trōth, *n.* Truth; faith.

trotter, trot'ẻr, *n.* One who trots; a trotting horse; foot of an animal.

troubadour, trö'ba-dör, *n.* One of a class of poets who flourished in S. Europe, especially in Provence, from the eleventh to the end of the thirteenth century.

trouble, trub'l, *vt.* (troubling, troubled). To disturb; to distress; to busy.—*n.*

Distress; agitation; affliction; labor.

troublesome, trub'l-sum, *a.* Annoying; vexatious; burdensome; tiresome.

troublous, trub'lus, *a.* Full of trouble or disorder; agitated; disquieting.

trouble shooter, trub'l shŏt'ėr, *n.* One who locates the source or cause of trouble.

trough, trof, *n.* A long vessel for holding water or food for animals; a depression between two waves.

trounce, trouns, *vt.* (trouncing, trounced). To punish or to beat severely.

troupe, trŏp, *n.* A troop; a company of performers, as acrobats.

trousers, trou'zėrz, *n.pl.* A garment for men, covering the lower part of the trunk and each leg separately.

trousseau, trŏ'sŏ'', *n.* The clothes and general outfit of a bride.

trout, trout, *n.* A fresh-water fish of the salmon tribe.

trover, trŏ'vėr, *n.* The gaining possession of goods by finding them, or otherwise than by purchase.

trow, trŏ, *vi.* To believe; to suppose.

trowel, trou'el, *n.* A hand tool for lifting and dressing mortar and plaster, &c.; a gardener's tool.—*vt.* (troweling, troweled). To dress or form with a trowel.

troy, troy weight, troi, troi wāt, *n.* A weight used for gold and silver.

truant, trŏ'ant, *n.* One who shirks duty; one who stays from school without leave. *a.* Idle; willfully absenting one's self. **truancy**, trŏ'an-si, *n.* Act of playing truant.

truce, trŏs, *n.* A temporary cessation of hostilities; armistice; short quiet.

truck, truk, *vi.* and *t.* To barter; to truck.—*n.* Exchange of commodities; barter; a small wheel; a barrow with two low wheels; an open railway wagon for baggage; a large automotive vehicle for hauling freight on the highways.

truckle, truk'l, *n.* A small wheel or castor.—*vt.* (truckling, truckled). To move on rollers; to trundle.—*vi.* To yield obsequiously; to submit.

truckle bed, truk'l bed, *n.* A low bed that runs on wheels and may be pushed under another.

truculent, truk'ū-lent, *a.* Terrible of aspect; fierce; wild; savage; fell. **truculence, truculency**, truk'ū-lens, truk'-ū-len-si, *n.* Ferocity; fierceness.

trudge, truj, *vi.* (trudging, trudged). To walk with labor or fatigue; to walk heavily.

true, trŏ, *a.* Conformable to fact; truthful; genuine; constant; faithful; loyal; honest; exact; correct; right. **true blue**, trŏ blŏ, *n.* A person of inflexible honesty or stanchness.—*a.* Stanch; inflexible. **truehearted**, trŏ'härt-ed, *a.* Being of a true or faithful heart; honest; sincere. **truelove**, trŏ'luv', *n.* One truly loved or loving; a lover; a sweetheart. **truepenny**, trŏ'pen'i, *n.* A familiar phrase for an honest fellow.

truly, trŏ'li, *adv.* In a true manner; according to truth; honestly; justly.

truism, trŏ'izm, *n.* A self-evident truth.

trump, trump, *n.* A winning card; one of a suit for the time being superior to the others; a person upon whom one can depend; a trumpet.—*vt.* To take with a trump card; to concoct or forge.

trumpery, trum'pė-ri, *n.* Worthless finery; trifles; trash.—*a.* Worthless.

trumpet, trum'pet, *n.* A metal wind-instrument of music; one who praises.—*vt.* To publish by sound of trumpet; to noise abroad; to sound the praises of.

trumpeter, trum'pet-ėr, *n.* One who sounds a trumpet; one who proclaims; a variety of the domestic pigeon.

truncate, trung'kāt, *vt.* To cut off; to lop.—*a.* Truncated. **truncated**, trung'-kāt-ed, *p.a.* Cut short abruptly. **truncation**, trung-kā'shun, *n.* Act of truncating; state of being truncated.

truncheon, trun'chun, *n.* A short staff; a club; a baton of authority; a tree the branches of which have been lopped off to produce rapid growth.—*vt.* To beat; to cudgel.

trundle, trun'dl, *vi.* (trundling, trundled). To roll, as on little wheels or as a bowl.—*vt.* To cause to roll.—*n.* A little wheel; a small truck. **trundle bed**, trun'dl bed, *n.* A truckle bed.

trunk, trungk, *n.* The woody stem of a tree; body of an animal without the limbs; main body; chest for containing clothes, &c.; proboscis of an elephant, &c.; a long wooden tube.

trunk line, trungk lïn, *n.* The main line of a railway.

truss, trus, *n.* A bundle, as of hay or straw; a bandage used in cases of rupture; a combination of timbers constituting an unyielding frame.—*vt.* To put in a bundle; to make tight or fast; to skewer.

trust, trust, *n.* Reliance; confidence; hope; credit; that which is intrusted; safe-keeping; care; management; a combination to control prices and supply of commodities.—*vt.* To rely on; to believe; to intrust; to sell to upon credit; to be confident.—*vi.* 'To have reliance; to confide readily.—*a.* Held in trust. **trustee**, trus-tē', *n.* One appointed to hold property for the benefit of those entitled to it. **trusteeship**, trus-tē'-ship, *n.* The office or functions of a trustee. **trustworthy**, trust''wėr'тні, *a.* Worthy of trust or confidence; faithful; reliable. **trusty**, trust'i, *a.* That may be trusted; trustworthy; that will not fail; strong.

truth, trŏth, *n.* Conformity to fact or reality; integrity; constancy; exactness; reality; verified fact. **truthful**, trŏth'-ful, *a.* Closely adhering to truth; veracious; correct; true. **truthfully**, trŏth'ful-li, *adv.* In a truthful manner.

try, tri, *vt.* (trying, tried). To test; to make trial of; to afflict; to endeavor.—*n.* The act of trying; a trial; experiment. **trying**, tri'ing, *a.* Severe; afflictive.

tryst, trist, *n.* An appointment to meet; a rendezvous.—*vi.* To agree to meet at any particular time or place.

tsar, tsär. Same as *czar*.

tsetse, tset'sē, *n.* An African fly whose bite is often fatal to horses and cattle.

T square, tē skwâr, *n.* A sort of ruler shaped like a T, used in drawing straight or perpendicular lines.

tub, tub, *n.* An open wooden vessel; a small cask; a clumsy boat; a vessel used as a bath.—*vt.* (tubbing, tubbed). To set in a tub.—*vi.* To make use of a bathing-tub.

tuba, tū′ba, *n.* A large musical instrument of brass, low in pitch.

tubby, tub′i, *a.* Like a tub; tub-shaped.

tube, tūb, *n.* A pipe; a hollow cylinder. —*vt.* (tubing, tubed). To furnish with a tube.

tuber, tū′bėr, *n.* An underground fleshy stem or root; a knot or swelling in any part.

tubercle, tū′bėr-kl, *n.* A small tuber; a little projecting knob; a small mass of morbid matter developed in different parts of the body. **tubercular,** tū-bėr′kū-lėr, *a.* Pertaining to or affected with tubercles; consumptive. Also **tuberculate, tuberculose, tuberculous. tuberculosis,** tū-bėr′kū-lō″sis, *n.* A disease due to the formation of tubercles; consumption.

tuberose, tuberous, tūb″rōz′, tū′bėr-ōs, *a.* Knobbed; having tubers; resembling a tuber.

tubing, tūb′ing, *n.* Act of providing with tubes; a length of tube; series of tubes.

tubular, tūb′ū-lėr, *a.* Having the form of a tube; consisting of tubes. Also **tubulose, tubulous.**

tuck, tuk, *vt.* To gather into a narrower compass; to fold in or under.—*n.* A horizontal fold in a garment to shorten it.

tucker, tuk′ėr, *n.* One who tucks; a sort of frill round the top of a woman's dress.

Tuesday, tūz′di, *n.* The third day of the week.

tuft, tuft, *n.* A cluster; clump; head of flowers.—*vt.* To adorn with tufts.

tug, tug, *vt.* and *i.* (tugging, tugged). To pull with effort; to haul along; to drag by steam-tug.—*n.* A drawing or pulling with force; a tugboat.

tugboat, tug′bōt′, *n.* A powerful steamboat used for towing other vessels.

tug of war, tug′ ov wạr′, *n.* A trial of strength between two parties of men tugging at opposite ends of a rope.

tuition, tū-ish′un, *n.* Guardianship; instruction; business of teaching.

tulip, tū′lip, *n.* A plant of the lily family with richly-colored flowers.

tulle, tyl, *n.* A thin silk fabric.

tumble, tum′bl, *vi.* (tumbling, tumbled). To roll about; to lose footing and fall.—*vt.* To throw about; to rumple; to overturn.—*n.* A fall; a somersault. **tumbler,** tum′blėr, *n.* One who tumbles; an acrobat; a large drinking glass; a variety of pigeon.

tumbleweed, tum′bl-wēd, *n.* Any plant that breaks off from its roots and is blown about by the wind.

tumbrel, tumbril, tum′brel, tum′bril, *n.* A dung-cart; a covered military cart for tools, ammunition, &c.; a kind of ducking-stool for scolds.

tumid, tū′mid, *a.* Swollen; distended; pompous; inflated; bombastic. **tumidity,** tū-mid′i-ti, *n.* A swelled state.

tumor, tumour, tū′mėr, *n.* A morbid swelling in some part of the body.

tumult, tū′mult, *n.* A commotion or disturbance; uproar; high excitement. **tumultuary,** tū-mul′tū-er′i, *a.* Tumultuous. **tumultuous,** tū-mul′tū-us, *a.* Full of tumult; disorderly; turbulent; violent.

tun, tun, *n.* Any large cask; a vat.

tuna, tō′na, *n.* A large edible sea fish of the mackerel tribe.

tundra, tön′dra, *n.* An immense stretch of flat boggy country in the arctic parts of Siberia and North America.

tune, tūn, *n.* A short air or melody; harmony; correct intonation; state of an instrument when it can give the proper sounds; frame of mind; mood.—*vt.* (tuning, tuned). To put into tune; to adapt. **tuneful,** tūn′ful, *a.* Full of tune; melodious. **tuneless,** tūn′les, *a.* Destitute of tune; unmusical. **tuner,** tūn′ėr, *n.* One who tunes musical instruments. **tuning,** tūn′ing, *n.* The art or operation of bringing musical instruments into tune. **tuning fork,** tūn′ing fork, *n.* A steel two-pronged instrument for regulating the pitch of voices or instruments.

tungsten, tung′sten, *n.* A heavy metal of grayish-white color.

tunic, tū′nik, *n.* A garment of various kinds; an ecclesiastical vestment worn over the alb; a short military coat; a covering membrane; an integument.

tunnel, tun′el, *n.* A tubular opening; a funnel; a subterranean passage cut through a hill, &c.—*vt.* (tunneling, tunneled). To form a tunnel through or under.

tunny, tun′i, *n.* A large fish of the mackerel tribe.

turban, tėr′ban, *n.* A head-dress worn by the Orientals, consisting of a fez and a sash wound round it; a kind of head-dress worn by ladies.

turbid, tėr′bid, *a.* Muddy; having the sediment disturbed; not clear.

turbine, tėr′bin, *n.* A kind of water-wheel, usually horizontal, made to revolve under the influence of pressure derived from a fall of water; a similar contrivance driven by steam.

turbot, tėr′but, *n.* A species of large flat-fish.

turbulent, tėr′bū-lent, *a.* Being in violent commotion; refractory; disorderly. **turbulence, turbulency,** tėr′bū-lens, tėr′bū-len-si, *n.* State of being turbulent; tumult; confusion; riotous behavior.

tureen, tu-rēn′, *n.* A large and deep dish for holding soup at table.

turf, tėrf, *n.* The grassy layer on the surface of the ground; a sod. **the turf,** the race-course; the business of horse-racing.—*vt.* To cover with turf or sod.

turgid, tėr′jid, *a.* Swelling; swollen; bloated; inflated; bombastic. **turgidity,** tėr-jid′i-ti, *n.* State of being turgid; bombast; inflation of style.

Turk, tėrk, *n.* A member of the ruling race of Turkey; a tyrannical man.

turkey, tėr′ki, *n.* A large gallinaceous fowl.

Turkish, tėr′kish, *a.* Pertaining to Turkey, or to the Turks, or to their language.—*n.* The language spoken by the Turks.

turmeric, tėr′mėr-ik, *n.* An E. Indian plant of the ginger family yielding a condiment, a yellow dye, and a test for alkalies.

turmoil, tėr′moil, *n.* Disturbance; trouble; disquiet.—*vt.* To harass.

turn, tėrn, *vt.* To cause to move round; to shape by a lathe; to direct; to alter in course; to blunt; to reverse; to change.—*vi.* To revolve; to depend; to change position or course; to return; to have recourse; to become; to become sour; to reel; to become nauseated; to result.—*n.* Act of turning; a revolution; a bend; a short walk; an alteration of course; occasion; occasional act of kindness or malice; purpose; character; short spell, as of work; nervous shock. **turncoat**, tėrn′kōt′, *n.* One who meanly forsakes his party or principles. **turning**, tėrn′ing, *n.* A turn; bend; place where a road diverges from another; art or operation of shaping; articles in a lathe. **turning point**, tėrn′ing point, *n.* The point on which or where a thing turns; the point at which a deciding change takes place.

turnip, tėr′nip, *n.* A plant of the cabbage genus, cultivated for its bulbous esculent root.

turnkey, tėrn′kē′, *n.* A person who has charge of the keys of a prison.

turnout, tėrn′out′, *n.* A coming forth; persons who have come out on some particular occasion; an equipage; the net quantity of produce yielded.

turnover, tėrn′ō′vėr, *n.* The amount of money turned over or drawn in a business.

turnpike, tėrn′pīk′, *n.* A turnstile; a toll-bar or toll-gate.

turnstile, tėrn′stīl′, *n.* A post at some passage surmounted by horizontal arms which move as a person pushes through.

turntable, tėrn′tā′bl, *a.* A revolving platform for reversing engines on a railway, or for shifting them from one line of rails to another.

turpentine, tėr′pen-tīn, *n.* A resinous substance flowing from trees, as the pine, larch, fir, &c.; the oil distilled from this.

turpitude, tėr′pi-tūd, *n.* Inherent baseness or vileness; moral depravity.

turquoise, tėr′koiz, *n.* A greenish-blue or blue opaque precious stone.

turret, tur′ėt, *n.* A little tower on a larger building; a strong cylindrical iron structure on an iron-clad. **turreted**, tur′et-ed, *a.* Furnished with turrets; formed like a tower.

turtle, tėr′tl, *n.* A species of small pigeon; the sea-tortoise.

turtledove, tėr′tl-duv′, *n.* The European turtle or pigeon.

Tuscan, tus′kan, *a.* Pertaining to Tuscany in Italy; designating the unornamented, unfluted order of architecture. —*n.* An inhabitant of Tuscany; the Tuscan order; the Tuscan dialect of Italian.

tush, tush, an *exclamation* indicating impatience or contempt.—*n.* A tusk; the canine tooth of a horse.

tusk, tusk, *n.* A long prominent tooth of certain animals, as the elephant. **tusker**, tus′kėr, *n.* An elephant that has its tusks developed.

tussle, tus′l, *n.* A struggle; scuffle.

tut, tut, *exclam.* Synonymous with *tush*.

tutor, tū′tėr, *n.* A guardian; a private instructor; a fellow of an English college who superintends the studies of undergraduates.—*vt.* To instruct. **tutelage**, tū′tē-lij, *n.* Guardianship; protection; state of being under a guardian. **tutoress**, tū′tor-es, *n.* A female tutor. **tutorial**, tū-tō′ri-al, *a.* Belonging to or exercised by a tutor or instructor.

tuxedo, tux, tuk-sē′dō, tuks, *n.* A short dinner coat or dinner jacket; a suit with such a jacket.

twaddle, twod′l, *vi.* (twaddling, twaddled). To prate; to chatter; to prose.— *n.* Empty, silly talk; gabble.

twain, twān, *a.* Two.—*n.* A pair.

twang, twang, *vi.* To make the sound of a string which is stretched and suddenly pulled.—*vt.* To make to sound sharply.—*n.* A sharp vibrating sound; a nasal sound.

'twas, twoz. A contraction of *It was*.

tweak, twēk, *vt.* To twitch; to pinch and pull suddenly.—*n.* A sharp pinch or jerk.

tweed, twēd, *n.* A twilled woolen fabric made in mixed colors.

tweezers, twēz′ėrz, *n.pl.* Small pincers to pluck out hairs, &c.; small forceps.

twelfth, twelfth, *a.* The second after the tenth.—*n.* One of twelve equal parts.

Twelfth-day, twelfth′′dā′. The twelfth day after Christmas; festival of the Epiphany.

Twelfth-night, twelfth′′nīt′, *n.* The evening of the festival of the Epiphany.

twelve, twelv, *a.* and *n.* Ten and two.

twelvemonth, twelv′munth′, *n.* A year.

twenty, twen′ti, *a.* and *n.* Two tens, or twice ten. **twentieth**, twen′ti-eth, *a.* The ordinal of twenty.—*n.* One of twenty equal parts.

twice, twīs, *adv.* Two times; doubly.

twiddle, twid′l, *vt.* and *i.* (twiddling, twiddled). To twirl in a small way; to fiddle with.

twig, twig, *n.* A small shoot or branch. —*vt.* and *i.* (twigging, twigged). To observe; to understand.

twilight, twī′′lit′, *n.* The faint light of the sun reflected after sunset and before sunrise; dubious view or condition.—*a.* Faint; seen or done by twilight.

twill, twil, *vt.* To weave so as to produce a kind of diagonal ribbed appearance.— *n.* A textile fabric with a kind of diagonal ribbed surface; surface of this kind.

twin, twin, *n.* One of two born together; one of a pair or couple.—Being one of two born at a birth; very similar; twofold.

twine, twīn, *n.* A strong thread com

posed of two or three strands; a twist.—
vt. and *i.* (twining, twined). To twist;
to weave; to coil; to wrap closely about.

twinge, twinj, *vt.* and *i.* (twinging,
twinged). To affect with or have a sharp,
sudden pain.—*n.* A sudden, sharp, darting pain.

twinkle, twingk'l, *vi.* (twinkling, twin-
kled). To sparkle; to shine with a
quivering light.—*n.* A gleam or sparkle.

twinkling, twingk'ling, *n.* A quick
movement of the eye; a wink; an instant; the scintillation of the stars.

twin-screw, twin'skrö', *n.* A steam vessel fitted with two propellers on separate
shafts.

twirl, twèrl, *vt.* and *i.* To turn round
with rapidity; to spin.—*n.* A rapid
whirl.

twist, twist, *n.* Something twined, as a
thread, &c.; roll of tobacco; a spiral;
contortion; mental or moral bent.—*vt.*
and *i.* To form into a cord; to twine; to
contort; to insinuate; to pervert.

twit, twit, *vt.* (twitting, twitted). To
reproach; to taunt; to upbraid.

twitch, twich, *vt.* To pull with a sudden jerk; to tug.—*vi.* To be suddenly
contracted.—*n.* A sudden pull; short
spasmodic contraction of a muscle.

twitter, twit'ér, *vi.* To utter small,
tremulous notes, as birds; to chirp.—*n.*
A chirp or continued chirping.

'twixt, twikst, a contraction of *betwixt.*

two, tö, *a.* and *n.* One and one together.

two-faced, tö'fāst', *a.* Having two faces;
insincere; given to double-dealing.

twofold, tö'föld', *a.* Double.—*adv.* Doubly; in a double degree.

two-handed, tö'hand-ed, *a.* Having two
hands; used or wielded by both hands.

twosome, tö'sum, *n.* A couple.

two-time, tö'tim, *vt.* To betray; to be
unfaithful.

tycoon, ti-kön', *n.* A wealthy indus-
trialist.

tyke, tike, tik, *n.* A small child.

tympanum, tim'pa-num, *n.*; pl. **-na.**
The drum of the ear.

type, tip, *n.* A distinguishing mark; emblem; symbol; ideal representative;
model; letter used in printing; such letters collectively.

typesetter, tip''set'ér, *n.* One who sets
up type; a compositor; a type-setting
machine.

typewriter, tip''rit'ér, *n.* A machine
used as a substitute for the pen, producing letters by inked types.

typhoid, ti'foid, *n.* A fever characterized
by abdominal pains and diarrhœa; en-
teric fever.

typhoon, ti-fön', *n.* A violent hurricane
on the coasts of China and Japan.

typhus, ti'fus, *n.* A contagious or epidemic fever characterized by a deep livid
eruption.

typical, tip'i-kal, *a.* Pertaining to a
type; emblematic; symbolic; representative. **typically**, tip'i-kal-li, *adv.* In a
typical manner; by way of image; sym-
bolically.

typify, tip'i-fi, *vt.* To serve as a type
of; to represent; to exemplify.

typography, ti-pog'ra-fi, *n.* The art
of printing; style of printing. **typo-
graphic, typographical**, ti'pö-graf''-
ik, ti'pö-graf'i-kal, *a.* Pertaining to typography or printing.

tyranny, tir'an-i, *n.* Rule of a tyrant;
despotic exercise of power; oppression.

tyrant, ti'rant, *n.* A despot; a cruel
sovereign or master; an oppressor. **ty-
rannous**, tir'a-nus, *a.* Tyrannical; unjustly severe; oppressive. **tyrannic,
tyrannical**, ti-ran'ik, ti-ran'i-kal, *a.*
Pertaining to a tyrant; despotic; cruel.

tyrannize, tir'a-niz, *vi.* To act the
tyrant; to rule with oppressive severity.

tyro, tiro, ti'rö, *n.*; pl. **-os.** A beginner; a raw hand; a novice.

Tyrolese, ti' or ti'rol-ēz, *a.* Belonging to
the Tyrol.—*n.* A native or natives of the
Tyrol.

tzar, tzarina, tsär, tsä-rē'na. Same as
czar, czarina.

U

ubiquity, ū-bik-wi-ti, *n.* Existence everywhere at the same time; omnipresence. **ubiquitous**, ū-bik'wi-tus, *a.*
Existing or being everywhere; omnipresent.

udder, ud'ér, *n.* The glandular organ of
cows, &c., in which the milk is produced.

ugh, u, an *exclamation* expressing horror
or recoil, usually accompanied by a
shudder.

ugly, ug'li, *a.* Repulsive; disagreeable in
appearance; hateful; ill-omened.

ukase, ū-kās', *n.* An edict of the Russian
government.

ulcer, ul'sér, *n.* A sore that discharges
pus. **ulcerate**, ul'sér-āt, *vt.* To affect
with an ulcer.—*vi.* To become ulcerous.

ulceration, ul'sér-ā''shun, *n.* The process of ulcerating; an ulcer. **ulcerous**,
ul'sér-us, *a.* Having the nature of an
ulcer; affected with ulcers.

ulna, ul'na, *n.* The larger of the two
bones of the forearm.

ulster, ul'stér, *n.* A long loose overcoat.

alterior, ul-tēr-i-ér, *a.* Being beyond or
on the farther side; more remote; distant; not avowed; reserved.

ultimate, ul'ti-mit, *a.* Farthest; last
or final; extreme; arrived at as a final
result. **ultimately**, ul'ti-mit-li, *adv.*
As an ultimate result; finally; at last.

ultimatum, ul'ti-mā''tum, *n.*; pl. **-ta**
or **-tums.** The last offer; a final proposition which being rejected may be followed by war.

ultimo, ul'ti-mō, *a.* The last (month): usually contracted to *ult.*

ultra, ul'tra, *prefix, a.* Beyond due limit; extreme.—*n.* An ultraist.

ultramarine, ul'tra-ma-rēn″, *a.* Being beyond the sea.—*n.* A beautiful and durable sky-blue.

ultraviolet, ul'tra-vī″ō-let, *a.* Lying beyond violet of the visible spectrum.

ululate, ul'ū-lāt, *vi.* To howl, as a dog.

umbel, um'bel, *n.* That mode of inflorescence which consists of a number of flower-stalks spreading from a common center, each bearing a single flower.

umber, um'ber, *n.* A soft earthy pigment of an olive-brown color in its raw state, but redder when burnt.

umbilicus, um-bil-i'kus, *n.* The navel.

umbilical, umbilic, um-bil'i-kal, um-bil'ik, *a.* Pertaining to the navel.

umbra, um'bra, *n.* The total shadow of the earth or moon in an eclipse.

umbrage, um'brij, *n.* Shade; obscurity; jealousy; offense; resentment. **umbrageous,** um-brā'jus, *a.* Shady.

umbrella, um-brel'la, *n.* A portable shade which opens and folds, for sheltering the person from the sun or rain.

umlaut, ōm'lout, *n.* The change of a vowel in one syllable through the influence of a different vowel in the syllable immediately following.

umpire, um'pīr, *n.* A person to whose decision a dispute is referred; a judge, arbiter, or referee.

unable, un-ā'bl, *a.* Not able; not having sufficient ability; not equal for some task.

unacceptable, un'ak-sept″a-bl, *a.* Not acceptable or pleasing; unwelcome.

unaccommodating, un'ak-kom″mō-dāt'ing, *a.* Not ready to oblige; uncompliant.

unaccomplished, un'ak-kom'plisht, *a.* Not performed completely; not having accomplishments.

unaccountable, un'ak-kount″a-bl, *a.* Not to be accounted for; not responsible.

unaccustomed, un'ak-kus″tumd, *a.* Not accustomed; not habituated; unusual.

unacknowledged, un'ak-nol″ejd, *a.* Not acknowledged; not recognized or owned.

unacquainted, un'a-kwān″ted, *a.* Not acquainted; not having familiar knowledge.

unadorned, un'a-dornd″, *a.* Not adorned; not embellished.

unadvisable, un'ad-vīz″a-bl, *a.* Not advisable; not expedient; not prudent.

unadvised, un'ad-vizd″, *a.* Not advised; not prudent; not discreet; rash.

unadvisedly, un'ad-vīz″ed-li, *adv.* Imprudently; indiscreetly; rashly.

unaffected, un'a-fek″ted, *a.* Not affected; natural; simple; sincere; not moved.

unaided, un'ād″ed, *a.* Without aid.

unalloyed, un'a-loid″, *a.* Not alloyed; entire; perfect.

unalterable, un'al″tėr-a-bl, *a.* Not alterable; unchangeable; immutable.

unamiable, un-ā'mi-a-bl, *a.* Not amiable; not adapted to gain affection.

unanimous, ū-nan'i-mus, *a.* Being of one mind; agreeing in determination; formed by unanimity. **unanimity,** ū-na-ni′mi-ti, *n.* State of being unanimous; perfect concord.

unanswerable, un-an'sėr-a-bl, *a.* Not to be satisfactorily answered; irrefutable.

unappealable, un-a-pēl′a-bl, *a.* Not appealable; admitting no appeal; that cannot be carried to a higher court by appeal.

unappeasable, un-a-pēz′a-bl, *a.* Not to be appeased or pacified; not placable.

unappreciated, un'a-prē″shi-āt-ed, *a.* Not duly estimated or valued.

unapproachable, un'a-prōch″a-bl, *a.* That cannot be approached; inaccessible.

unappropriate, un'a-prō″pri-āt, *a.* Not appropriate; inappropriate. **unappropriated,** un'a-prō″pri-āt-ed, *a.* Not appropriated; not applied to a specific object.

unarmed, un-ärmd′, *a.* Not having arms or armor; not equipped.

unasked, un-askt′, *a.* Not asked; unsolicited.

unaspiring, un'as-pīr″ing, *a.* Not ambitious.

unassailable, un'a-sāl″a-bl, *a.* Not assailable; that cannot be assaulted.

unassuming, un'a-sūm″ing, *a.* Not assuming; retiring; modest.

unassured, un'a-shōrd″, *a.* Not confident; not to be trusted; not insured.

unattended, un'a-tend″ed, *a.* Having no attendants; not medically attended.

unattractive, un'a-trak″tiv, *a.* Not attractive.

unauthorized, un-a′thor-īzd, *a.* Not authorized; not warranted.

unavailable, un'a-vāl″a-bl, *a.* Not available; vain; useless.

unavailing, un'a-vāl″ing, *a.* Of no avail; ineffectual; useless.

unavoidable, un'a-void″a-bl, *a.* Not to be shunned; inevitable.

unaware, un'a-wār″, *pred. a.* or *adv.* Not aware; unconscious; inattentive.

unawares, un'a-wārz″, *adv.* Unexpectedly; inadvertently; unconsciously.

unbearable, un-bār′a-bl, *a.* Not to be endured; intolerable.

unbecoming, un'bē-kum″ing, *a.* Not becoming; improper.

unbefitting, un'bē-fit″ing, *a.* Unsuitable.

unbelief, un'bē-lēf″, *n.* Incredulity; infidelity; disbelief of the gospel.

unbeliever, un'bē-lēv″ėr, *n.* One who does not believe; an infidel.

unbelieving, un'bē-lēv″ing, *a.* Not believing; incredulous; infidel.

unbend, un-bend′, *vi.* To become relaxed or not bent; to give up stiffness of manner.—*vt.* To free from bend or flexure; to relax.

unbiased, unbiassed, un-bī'ast, *a.* Free from any bias or prejudice; impartial.

unbid, unbidden, un-bid′, un-bid′n, *a.* Not bid; spontaneous; uninvited.

unblushing, un-blush′ing, *a.* Not blushing; shameless; impudent.

unbolt, un-bōlt′, *vt.* To remove a bolt from; to unbar.

unbolted, un-bōlt′ed. *a.* Unsifted; not having the bran separated by a bolter.

unbosom, un-bŏz′um, *vt.* To open the bosom of; to reveal in confidence.

unbound, un-bound′. *a.* Not bound; loose; not under obligation.

unbounded, un-bound′ed. *a.* Having no bound or limit; infinite; unrestrained.

unbridled, un-brī′dld. *a.* Unrestrained.

unbroken, un-brō′ken. *a.* Not broken; not tamed; not interrupted.

unburden, unburthen, un-bėr′dn, un-bėr′ᴛʜn, *vt.* To rid of a load or burden.

unbutton, un-but′n, *vt.* To undo the buttons of.

uncalled, un-kạld′, *a.* Not called; not summoned; not invited.

uncanny, un-kan′i, *a.* Not canny; mysterious; of evil and supernatural character.

uncared, un-kārd′, *a.* Not regarded; not heeded; often with *for*.

unceasing, un-sēs′ing, *a.* Not ceasing; continual.

uncertain, un-sėr′tin, *a.* Not certain; doubtful; inconstant.

uncertainty, un-sėr′tin-ti, *n.* Want of certainty; dubiety.

unchallenged, un-chal′enjd, *a.* Not objected to; not called in question.

unchangeable, un-chānj′a-bl, *a.* Not capable of change; immutable; unchanging.

unchanging, un-chānj′ing, *a.* Not changing; suffering no change.

uncharitable, un-char′it-a-bl, *a.* Not charitable; ready to think evil; harsh.

unchaste, un-chāst′, *a.* Not chaste; lewd.

unchristian, un-kris′chan, *a.* Contrary to the spirit or laws of Christianity.

uncial, un′shi-al, *n.* A letter of large size used in ancient Greek and Latin manuscripts.

unciform, un′si-form, *a.* Having a curved or hooked form.

uncivil, un-siv′il, *a.* Not civil; ill-mannered.

uncivilized, un-siv′i-līzd, *a.* Not civilized.

uncle, ung′kl, *n.* The brother of one's father or mother.

unclean, un-klēn′, *a.* Not clean; foul; dirty; morally impure; lewd. **uncleanly,** un-klen′li, *a.* Not cleanly; foul; dirty; indecent.

unclouded, un-kloud′ed, *a.* Free from clouds; clear; not obscured.

uncomfortable, un-kum′fėrt-a-bl, *a.* Not comfortable; uneasy; ill at ease.

uncommon, un-kom′mun, *a.* Not common; rare; strange; remarkable.

uncommunicative, un′ko-mū″ni-kāt-iv, *a.* Not apt to communicate; reserved.

uncompromising, un-kom″prō-mīz′-ing, *a.* Not agreeing to terms; unyielding.

unconcern, un-kon-sėrn′, *n.* Want of concern; apathy; indifference. **unconcerned,** un-kon′sėrnd′, *a.* Not concerned; not anxious; feeling no solicitude.

unconditional, un′kon-dish″un-al, *a.* Not limited by conditions; absolute.

unconfined, un′kon-fīnd″, *a.* Not confined; free from restraint or control.

unconfirmed, un′kon-fėrmd″, *a.* Not confirmed; not firmly established.

unconnected, un-ko-nekt′ed, *a.* Not connected; separate; incoherent; loose.

unconquerable, un-kong′kėr-a-bl, *a.* Not conquerable; insuperable.

unconscionable, un-kon′shun-a-bl, *a.* Not conscionable; inordinate; unreasonable.

unconscious, un-kon′shus, *a.* Not conscious; not perceiving; unaware.

unconstitutional, un′kon-sti-tū″shun-al, *a.* Not agreeable to the constitution of a country.

uncontrollable, un-kon-trōl′a-bl, *a.* That cannot be controlled or restrained.

uncontroverted, un-kon′trō-vėrt-ed, *a.* Not controverted; not called in question.

unconverted, un′kon-vėrt″ed, *a.* Not converted; not regenerated.

uncork, un-kork′, *vt.* To draw the cork from.

uncorrected, un′ko-rekt″ed, *a.* Not corrected; not revised; not reformed.

uncouple, un′kup″l, *vt.* To loose, as dogs coupled together; to disjoin.

uncouth, un-kōth′, *a.* Strange; odd in appearance; awkward.

uncover, un-kuv′ėr, *vt.* To divest of a cover; to disclose.—*vi.* To take off the hat.

unction, ungk′shun, *n.* Act of anointing; an unguent; religious fervor; sham devotional fervor; oiliness.

unctuous, ungk′tū-us, *a.* Oily; greasy; nauseously emotional; fawning.

uncultivated, un-kul″ti-vāt′ed, *a.* Not cultivated; not tilled; boorish or rude.

uncut, un-kut′, *a.* Not cut.

undated, un-dāt′ed, *a.* Not dated.

undaunted, un-dạnt′ed, *a.* Intrepid; fearless.

undeceive, un-dē-sēv′, *vt.* To free from deception or mistake.

undecided, un′dē-sīd″ed, *a.* Not decided; hesitating; irresolute.

undefinable, un′dē-fīn″a-bl, *a.* Not definable; indefinable.

undefined, un′dē-fīnd″, *a.* Not defined; lacking in clearness or definiteness.

undemonstrative, un′dē-mon″stra-tiv, *a.* Not demonstrative; reserved.

undeniable, un′dē-nī″a-bl, *a.* Incapable of being denied; indisputable.

under, un′dėr, *prep.* Below; beneath; undergoing; affected by; subject to; inferior; during the time of; included in; in accordance with.—*adv.* In a lower condition or degree.—*a.* Lower; subject; subordinate.

underbred, un′dėr-bred, *a.* Of inferior breeding or manners; ill-bred; vulgar.

underbrush, un″dėr-brush′, *n.* Shrubs growing under large trees; undergrowth.

undercharge, un′dėr-chärj″, *vt.* To charge insufficiently.—*n.* un′dėr-chärj. Too low a charge or price.

underclothes, underclothing, un″-dėr-klōᴛʜz′, un″dėr-klōᴛʜ′ing, *n.* Clothes worn under others or next the skin.

undercurrent, un″dėr-ku′rent, *n.* A current below another; some movement or influence not apparent.

undergo, un'der-gō", *vt.* To bear; to experience; to suffer.

undergraduate, un'der-grad"ū-āt, *n.* A student who has not taken his first degree.

underground, un"der-ground', *a.* and *adv.* Below the surface of the ground.

undergrowth, un"der-grōth", *n.* Shrubs or small trees growing among large ones.

underhand, un"der-hand', *a.* Working by stealth; secret; deceitful.—*adv.* In a clandestine manner.

underhung, un'der-hung", *a.* Projecting beyond the upper jaw; said of the under jaw.

underlay, un'der-lā", *vt.* To lay beneath; to support by something laid under.

underlie, un'der-lī", *vt.* To lie beneath; to be at the basis of.

underline, un'der-līn", *vt.* To mark with a line below the words.

underling, un'der-ling, *n.* An inferior person or agent; a mean sorry fellow.

undermine, un'der-mīn", *vt.* To sap; to injure by underhand means.

underneath, un'der-nēth", *adv.* Beneath; below.—*prep.* Under; beneath.

underrate, un'der-rāt", *vt.* To rate too low; to undervalue.

undersell, un'der-sel", *vt.* To sell at a lower price than.

undershot, un"der-shot', *a.* Moved by water passing under, as a wheel.

undershrub, un'der-shrub", *n.* A low shrub, the branches of which decay yearly.

undersign, un'der-sīn", *vt.* To write one's name at the foot or end of; to subscribe.

undersized, un"der-sīzd', *a.* Being of a size or stature less than common; dwarfish.

understand, un'der-stand", *vt.* To comprehend; to see through; to suppose to mean; to infer; to assume; to recognize as implied although not expressed.—*vi.* To comprehend; to learn. **understanding,** un'der-stand"ing, *a.* Intelligent.—*n.* Comprehension; discernment; knowledge; intellect; agreement of minds; anything agreed upon.

understate, un'der-stāt", *vt.* To state too low or as less than actually.

undertake, un'der-tāk", *vt.* To take in hand; to engage in; to attempt; to guarantee.—*vi.* To take upon one's self; to promise; to stand bound. **undertaker,** un'der-tāk"er, *n.* One who undertakes; one who manages funerals. **undertaking,** un'der-tāk"ing, *n.* That which is undertaken; enterprise; promise.

undertone, un'der-tōn", *n.* A low tone.

undertow, un"der-tō', *n.* An undercurrent opposite to that at the surface; the backward flow of a wave breaking on a beach.

undervalue, un'der-va"lū, *vt.* To value below the real worth; to esteem lightly.

underwear, un"der-wâr', *n.* Underclothes.

underworld, un"der-wèrld', *n.* The lower world; this world; the antipodes; the place of departed souls; Hades.

underwrite, un'der-rīt", *vt.* To write

under; to subscribe one's name and become answerable for a certain amount.

underwriter, un"der-rīt'er, *n.* One who underwrites or insures; an insurer.

underwriting, un"der-rīt'ing, *n.* The business of an underwriter.

undesirable, un'dē-zīr"a-bl, *a.* Not desirable.

undetermined, un'dē-ter"mind, *a.* Not determined; not decided, fixed, or settled.

undeterred, un'dē-tèrd", *a.* Not restrained by fear or obstacles.

undigested, un'di-jest"ed, *a.* Not digested; not properly prepared or arranged; crude.

undignified, un-dig'ni-fid, *a.* Not dignified; showing a want of dignity.

undine, un'dēn, *n.* A water-spirit of the female sex.

undisguised, un'dis-gīzd", *a.* Not disguised; open; candid; artless.

undisposed, un'dis-pōzd", *a.* Not set apart; not allocated; not sold; with *of.*

undisputed, un'dis-pūt"ed, *a.* Not disputed; not called in question; incontestable.

undistinguished, un'dis-ting"gwisht, *a.* Not having any distinguishing mark; not famous; not possessing distinction.

undisturbed, un'dis-tèrbd", *a.* Free from disturbance; calm; tranquil; not agitated.

undivided, un'di-vīd"ed, *a.* Not divided; whole; entire.

undo, un-dö', *vt.* To reverse what has been done; annul; to loose; to take to pieces; to ruin.

undoer, un-dö'er, *n.* One who reverses what has been done; one who ruins.

undoing, un-dö'ing, *n.* Reversal; ruin.

undone, un'dun, *pp.* Not done.

undone, un-dun', *pp.* Untied or unfastened; reversed; ruined.

undoubted, un-dout'ed, *a.* Not doubted; indubitable; indisputable. **undoubtedly,** un-dout'ed-li, *adv.* Without doubt; without question; indubitably.

undress, un-dres', *vt.* To divest of dress or clothes; to strip.—*n.* un'dres. A loose negligent dress; ordinary dress. **undressed,** un-drest', *a.* Not dressed; not attired; not prepared; in a raw state.

undue, un-dū', *a.* Not due; not yet demandable by right; not right; inordinate.

undulate, un'dū-lāt, *vi.* To have a wavy motion; to wave.—*vt.* To cause to wave.

undulation, un'dū-lā"shun, *n.* Act of undulating; a wavy motion; a wavy form; a gentle slope; a vibratory motion. **undulatory,** un"dū-la-to'ri, *a.* Having an undulating character; moving like waves.

unduly, un-dū'li, *adv.* In an undue manner; unlawfully; unwarrantably; excessively.

undying, un-dī'ing, *a.* Not dying; imperishable.

unearned, un-èrnd', *a.* Not merited by labor or services. **unearned increment,** the increase in the value of property not due to any expenditure on the part of the owner.

unearth, un-èrth', *vt.* To drive or bring from the earth; to uncover; to discover.

unearthly, un-êrth′li, *a.* Not earthly; weird.

uneasy, un-ēz′i, *a.* Restless; disturbed; somewhat anxious: unquiet; stiff; not graceful; unpleasing; irksome.

uneducated, un-ed″ū-kāt′ed, *a.* Not educated; illiterate; ignorant.

unemotional, un′ē-mō″shun-al, *a.* Not emotional; impassive.

unemployed, un′em-ploid′, *a.* Not employed; having no work; not being in use.

unending, un-end′ing, *a.* Not ending; perpetual; eternal.

unendurable, un′en-dūr″a-bl, *a.* Intolerable.

unengaged, un′en-gājd″, *a.* Not engaged.

unenlightened, un′en-lit″nd, *a.* Not enlightened; not illuminated, mentally or morally.

unenterprising, un-en″tèr-priz″ing, *a.* Wanting in enterprise; not adventurous.

unenviable, un-en′vi-a-bl, *a.* Not enviable; not to be envied.

unequal, un-ē′kwal, *a.* Not equal; inadequate; insufficient; not equable. **unequaled,** un-ē′kwald, *a.* Not to be equaled; unrivaled.

unequivocal, un′ē-kwiv″ō-kal, *a.* Not equivocal; not doubtful; clear; evident.

unerring, un-ēr′ing, *a.* Not erring; incapable of error; certain.

unessential, un′e-sen″shal, *a.* Not essential; not absolutely necessary.

uneven, un-ē′ven, *a.* Not even or level; rough; crooked; not fair or just; odd.

unexampled, un′eg-zam″pld, *a.* Having no example or similar case; unprecedented.

unexcelled, un′ek-seld″, *a.* Not excelled.

unexceptionable, un′ek-sep″shun-a-bl, *a.* Not liable to any exception; excellent.

unexpected, un′eks-pekt″ed, *a.* Not expected; not looked for; sudden.

unexpired, un′eks-pīrd″, *a.* Not expired; not having come to the end of its term.

unexplored, un′eks-plōrd″, *a.* Not explored; not visited by any traveler.

unfading, un-fād′ing, *a.* Not fading; not liable to wither or decay; ever fresh.

unfailing, un-fāl′ing, *a.* Not liable to fail; that does not fail; certain.

unfair, un-fār′, *a.* Not honest or impartial; ñot just; inequitable; disingenuous.

unfaithful, un-fāth′fyl, *a.* Not faithful.

unfamiliar, un′fa-mil″yèr, *a.* Not familiar; not accustomed; strange.

unfashionable, un-fash′un-a-bl, *a.* Not fashionable or according to the fashion.

unfasten, un-fäs′n, *vt.* To loose; to unfix.

unfathomable, un-faтн′um-a-bl, *a.* That cannot be fathomed; incomprehensible.

unfavorable, un-fā′vèr-a-bl, *a.* Not favorable; not propitious; discouraging.

unfeeling, un-fēl′ing, *a.* Devoid of feeling; hard-hearted; harsh; brutal.

unfeigned, un-fānd′, *a.* Not feigned; sincere.

unfermented, un′fer-ment″ed, *a.* Not having undergone fermentation.

unfetter, un-fet′êr, *vt.* To loose from fetters; to set at liberty.

unfinished, un-fin′isht, *a.* Not finished.

unfit, un-fit′, *a.* Not fit: unsuitable; not competent.—*vt.* To make unfit.

unfix, un-fiks′, *vt.* To cause to be no longer fixed; to loosen; to unsettle.

unflinching, un-flinch′ing, *a.* Not flinching; not shrinking; resolute.

unfold, un-fōld′, *vt.* To open the folds of; to display.—*vi.* To open out.

unforeseen, un′fèr-sēn″, *a.* Not foreseen.

unforgiving, un′for-giv″ing, *a.* Not forgiving; implacable.

unformed, un-formd′, *a.* Not formed or molded into regular shape.

unfortunate, un-for′tū-nit, *a.* Not fortunate; unlucky; unhappy.—*n.* One who is unfortunate; a prostitute. **unfortunately,** un-for′tū-nit-li, *adv.* In an unfortunate manner; by ill fortune.

unfounded, un-found′ed, *a.* Having no real foundation; groundless; idle.

unfrequented, un′frē-kwent″ed, *a.* Not frequented; rarely visited; solitary.

unfriendly, un-frend′li, *a.* Not friendly.

unfrock, un-frok′, *vt.* To divest of a frock; to deprive of the character of a priest.

unfruitful, un-fröt′fyl, *a.* Not fruitful; barren.

unfunded, un-fun′ded, *a.* Not funded; having no permanent fund for the payment of its interest; said of government debt when it exists in the form of exchequer bills or the like.

unfurl, un-fèrl′, *vt.* To loose from a furled state; to expand to catch the wind.

unfurnished, un-fèr′nisht, *a.* Not furnished; unsupplied; unprovided.

ungainly, un-gān′li, *a.* Not handsome; uncouth; clumsy; awkward; ill-shaped.

ungallant, un-gal′ant, *a.* Not gallant; not polite, courtly, or attentive to ladies.

ungenerous, un-jen′èr-us, *a.* Not generous; illiberal; dishonorable; mean.

ungentlemanly, un-jen′tl-man-li, *a.* Not becoming a gentleman.

ungird, un-gèrd′, *vt.* To loose from a girdle or band; to unbind.

unglazed, un-glāzd′, *a.* Not glazed; not furnished with panes of glass.

ungodly, un-god′li, *a.* Not godly; wicked.

ungovernable, un-guv′èrn-a-bl, *a.* That cannot be governed; wild; refractory.

ungraceful, un-grās′fyl, *a.* Not graceful.

ungracious, un-grā′shus, *a.* Not gracious; uncivil; rude; impolite.

ungrammatical, un′gra-mat″i-kal, *a.* Not according to grammar.

ungrateful, un-grāt′fyl, *a.* Not grateful; not thankful; unpleasing; harsh.

ungrounded, un-groun′ded, *a.* Having no foundation or support; groundless.

ungrudging, un-gruj′ing, *a.* Without a grudge; freely giving; hearty; liberal.

unguarded, un-gärd′ed, *a.* Not guarded; not cautious; negligent.

unguent, ung'gwent, *n.* An ointment.

unhallowed, un-hal'ōd, *a.* Not hallowed or sanctified; profane; unholy.

unhand, un-hand', *vt.* To loose from the hand or hands; to lose hold of.

unhandy, un-hand'i, *a.* Not handy; awkward; not convenient.

unhappily, un-hap'i-li, *adv.* In an unhappy manner; unfortunately.

unhappy, un-hap'i, *a.* Not happy; sad; unfortunate; unlucky; evil; ill-omened.

unharmed, un-härmd', *a.* Not harmed.

unharness, un-här'nes, *vt.* To strip of harness; to loose from harness; to disarm.

unhealthy, un-hel'thi, *a.* Not healthy; sickly; insalubrious; unwholesome.

unheard, un-hèrd', *a.* Not heard; not admitted to audience; not known (with *of*).

unheeded, un-hē'ded, *a.* Not heeded; disregarded; neglected.

unheeding, un-hē'ding, *a.* Not heeding; careless.

unhesitating, un-he'zi-tāt'ing, *a.* Not hesitating; not remaining in doubt; prompt.

unhinge, un-hinj', *vt.* To take from the hinges; to unfix; to loosen; to derange.

unholy, un-hō'li, *a.* Not holy; not sacred; unhallowed; profane; impious; wicked.

unhoped, un-hōpt', *a.* Not hoped for; not expected; often followed by *for*.

unhorse, un-hors', *vt.* To throw from a horse; to cause to dismount.

unhurt, un-hèrt', *a.* Not hurt; not harmed; free from wound or injury.

unicorn, ū'ni-korn, *n.* A fabulous animal like a horse, with a long single horn on the forehead.

unification, ū'ni-fi-kā"shun, *n.* The act of unifying or uniting into one.

uniform, ū'ni-form, *a.* Having always one and the same form; equable; invariable; consistent.— *n.* A distinctive dress worn by the members of the same body.

Unicorn

uniformity, ū'ni-for"mi-ti, *n.* State or character of being uniform; conformity to one type; agreement; consistency.

uniformly, ū"ni-form'li, *adv.* In a uniform manner; invariably.

unify, ū'ni-fī, *vt.* To form into one.

unilluminated, un'il-lūm"in-āt'ed, *a.* Not illuminated; dark; ignorant.

unimaginable, un'i-maj"in-a-bl, *a.* Not imaginable; inconceivable.

unimpaired, un'im-pārd", *a.* Not impaired; not diminished; uninjured.

unimpassioned, un'im-pa"shund, *a.* Not impassioned; tranquil; not violent.

unimpeachable, un'im-pēch"a-bl, *a.* Not impeachable; blameless; irreproachable.

unimportant, un'im-pōr"tant, *a.* Not important; not of great moment.

unimproved, un'im-prövd", *a.* Not improved; not cultivated.

uninhabited, un'in-hab"it-ed, *a.* Not inhabited by men; having no inhabitants.

uninjured, un-in'jèrd, *a.* Not injured.

uninstructed, un'in-strukt"ed, *a.* Not instructed; not educated.

unintelligent, un'in-tel"i-jent, *a.* Not intelligent; not showing intelligence; stupid. **unintelligible,** un'in-tel"i-ji-bl, *a.* Not intelligible; meaningless.

unintentional, un'in-ten"shun-al, *a.* Not intentional; done without design.

uninterested, un-in'tèr-est-ed, *a.* Not interested; having no interest or concern. **uninteresting,** un-in'tèr-est-ing, *n.* Not interesting; dull; tame.

uninterrupted, un-in'tèr-rupt"ed, *a.* Not interrupted; unintermitted; incessant.

uninviting, un-in-vīt'ing, *a.* Not inviting; unattractive; rather repellent.

union, ūn'yon, *n.* Act of joining; combination; agreement; harmony; marriage; confederacy; a trades-union; a mixed fabric of cotton, flax, jute, silk, or wool, &c.; a certain kind of flag.

unionist, ūn'yun-ist, *n.* One who advocates union; a trades-unionist; one who upholds the present union of the two kingdoms of Great Britain and Ireland.

union jack, ūn'yon jak, *n.* The national flag of Great Britain and Ireland, formed by the union of the cross of St. George, the saltire of St. Andrew and the saltire of St. Patrick.

uniparous, ū-nip'a-rus, *a.* Producing one at a birth.

unique, ū-nēk', *a.* Without a like or equal; unmatched; unequaled.

United States. A country of North America consisting of fifty states, the District of Columbia, Puerto Rico, and other possessions.

United Kingdom. A kingdom in northwestern Europe consisting of Great Britain and Northern Ireland.

United Nations. A world-wide organization of nations dedicated to establishing world peace.

unison, ū'ni-sun, *n.* Accordance; agreement; harmony; concord. **unisonant, unisonous,** ū-nis'ō-nant, ū-nis'ō-nus, *a.* Being in unison; concordant.

unit, ū'nit, *n.* A single thing or person; an individual; the number 1; a dimension or quantity assumed as a standard.

Unitarian, ū'ni-tār"i-an, *n.* One who ascribes divinity to God only and denies the Trinity.—*a.* Pertaining to Unitarians. **Unitarianism,** ū'ni-tār"i-an-izm, *n.* The doctrines of Unitarians.

unite, ū-nīt', *vt.* (uniting, united). To combine; to connect; to associate.—*vi.* To become one; to combine; to concur. **united,** ū-nīt'ed, *a.* Joined; combined together; made one. **unitedly,** ū-nīt'ed-li, *adv.* In a united manner; jointly; in combination. **unity,** ū'ni-ti, *n.* State of being one; concord; agreement; harmony; artistic harmony and symmetry.

univalve, ū"ni-valv', *n.* A shell having one valve only.

universe, ū'ni-vèrs, *n.* The whole system of created things; the world. **universal,** ū'ni-vèr"sal, *a.* Pertaining to all; total; whole.—*n.* A general notion or idea. **universalist,** ū'ni-vèr"sal-ist, *n.* One who holds that all men will be saved. **universality**, ū'ni-vèrs-al″i-ti. *n.* State of being universal. **universally**, ū'ni-vèr″sal-li, *adv.* With extension to the whole; without exception.

university, ū'ni-vèr″si-ti, *n.* An institution for instruction in science and literature, &c.; and having the power of conferring degrees.

univocal, ū-ni'vō-kal, *n.* Having one meaning only; having unison of sounds. —*n.* A word having only one meaning.

unjust, un-just', *a.* Not just, upright or equitable. **unjustifiable**, un-jus'ti-fī″-a-bl, *a.* Not justifiable. **unjustly**, un-just'li, *adv.* Wrongfully.

unkempt, un-kempt', *a.* Uncombed; rough.

unkind, un-kīnd', *a.* Not kind; cruel. **unkindly**, un-kīnd'li, *a.* Unkind; ungracious.—*adv.* In an unkind manner.

unknowingly, un-nō'ing-li. *adv.* Without knowledge or design; unwittingly.

unknown, un-nōn', *a.* Not known; not discovered, found out, or ascertained.

unlace, un-lās', *vt.* To loose the lacing or fastening of; to unfasten.

unlawful, un-lạ'fụl, *a.* Not lawful; illegal.

unlearn, un-lèrn', *vt.* To forget the knowledge of. **unlearned**, un-lèr'ned, *a.* Not learned or erudite; illiterate; (un-lèrnd') not known.

unless, un-les', *conj.* If it be not that; if . . . not; except; excepting.

unlettered, un-let'èrd, *a.* Unlearned.

unlicensed, un-li'senst, *a.* Not having a license; done without due license.

unlike, un-līk', *a.* Not like; dissimilar; having no resemblance; diverse. **unlikely**, un-līk-li, *a.* Not likely; improbable; likely to fail; unpromising.

unlimber, un-lim'bèr, *vt.* To take off or detach the limbers from.

unlimited, un-lim'it-ed, *a.* Not limited; boundless; indefinite.

unload, un-lōd', *vt.* To take the load from; to discharge; to empty out.

unlock, un-lok', *vt.* To unfasten; to open.

unlooked-for, un-lökt″for', *a.* Not looked for; not expected; not foreseen.

unloose, un-lös', *vt.* To loose; to untie; to undo; to set at liberty.

unlovely, un-luv'li, *a.* Not lovely; not attractive; repulsive or repellent.

unlucky, un-luk'i, *a.* Not lucky; unfortunate; not successful; ill-omened.

unmake, un-māk', *vt.* To reverse the making of; to destroy.

unman, un-man', *vt.* To deprive of the character of a man; to unnerve.

unmanageable, un-man'ij-a-bl. *a.* Not manageable; beyond control.

unmanly, un-man'li, *a.* Not manly; effeminate; childish; cowardly.

unmannerly, un-man'èr-li, *a.* Not mannerly; rude; ill-bred.

unmask, un-mask', *vt.* To strip of a mask; to expose.—*vi.* To put off a mask.

unmatched, un-macht', *a.* Matchless.

unmeaning, un-mēn'ing, *a.* Having no meaning; senseless; vacuous.

unmeasured, un'mezh″èrd, *a.* Not measured; immense; infinite; excessive.

unmentionable, un'men″shun-a-bl, *a.* Not mentionable.—*n.pl.* Trousers.

unmerciful, un-mèr'si-fụl, *a.* Not merciful; merciless.

unmerited, un-mer'it-ed, *a.* Not deserved.

unmindful, un-mīnd'fụl, *a.* Not mindful; regardless.

unmistakable, unmistakeable, un-mis-tāk'a-bl, *a.* Not capable of being mistaken; clear; obvious.

unmitigated, un-mit″i-gāt'ed, *a.* Not mitigated; thorough-paced.

unmixed, unmixt, un-mikst', *a.* Not mixed; pure; unadulterated; unalloyed.

unmoved, un-mövd', *a.* Not moved; firm; calm; cool.

unmusical, un-mū'zi-kal, *a.* Not musical.

unnatural, un-nat'ūr-al, *a.* Not natural; contrary to nature; affected; artificial.

unnavigable, un-nav'i-ga-bl, *a.* Not navigable; incapable of being navigated.

unnecessary, un-nes'e-ser″i, *a.* Not necessary; needless.

unneighborly, un-nā'bèr-li, *a.* Not neighborly; not kind and friendly.

unnerve, un-nèrv', *vt.* To deprive of nerve, strength, or composure; to enfeeble.

unnoticed, un-nō'tist, *a.* Not observed.

unnumbered, un-num'bèrd, *a.* Not numbered; innumerable; indefinitely numerous.

unobjectionable, un'ob-jek″shun-a-bl, *a.* Not liable to objection; unexceptionable.

unobservant, unobserving, un'ob-zèrv″ant, un'ob-zèrv″ing, *a.* Not observant.

unobtrusive, un'ob-trö″siv, *a.* Not obtrusive; not forward; modest; retiring.

unoccupied, un-ok'ū-pīd, *a.* Not occupied; not possessed; at leisure; leisure.

unoffending, un-o-fend'ing, *a.* Not giving offense; harmless; innocent; inoffensive.

unofficial, un-o-fish'al, *a.* Not official.

unopposed, un-o-pōzd', *a.* Not opposed; not meeting with any obstruction.

unorganized, un-ör'gan-izd, *a.* Not organized; not belonging to a group or union.

unorthodox, un-ör'tho-doks, *a.* Not orthodox; heterodox.

unostentatious, un-os'ten-tā″shus, *a.* Not ostentatious; not showy; modest.

unpack, un-pak', *vt.* To take from a package; to unload.

unpaid, un-pād', *a.* Not paid; remaining due; not receiving a salary.

unpalatable, un-pal'it-a-bl, *a.* Not palatable; disagreeable to the taste or feelings.

unparalleled, un-par'a-leld *a.* Having no parallel; unequaled; matchless.

unpardonable, un-par'dn-a-bl, *a.* Not to be forgiven; incapable of being pardoned.

unparliamentary, un-pär'li-men″ta-ri, *a.* Contrary to the usages or rules of proceeding in parliament; unseemly, as language.

unpatriotic, un-pā'tri-ot"ik, *a.* Not patriotic; wanting in patriotism.

unpin, un-pin', *vt.* To loose from pins; to unfasten.

unpleasant, un-ple'zant, *a.* Not pleasant.

unpleasing, un-plēz'ing, *a.* Unpleasant.

unplumbed, un-plumd', *a.* Not fathomed.

unpoetic, unpoetical, un'pō-e"tik, un'pō-e"ti-kal, *a.* Not poetical.

unpolished, un-po'lisht, *a.* Not polished; rude; plain.

unpopular, un-pop'ū-lèr, *a.* Not popular.

unpractical, un-prak'ti-kal, *a.* Not practical.

unpracticed, un-prak'tist, *a.* Not having been taught by practice; raw; unskilful.

unprecedented, un-pres"ē-den'ted, *a.* Having no precedent; unexampled.

unprejudiced, un-prej'ū-dist, *a.* Not prejudiced; free from bias; impartial.

unpremeditated, un'prē-med"i-tāt-ed, *a.* Not previously meditated; spontaneous.

unprepared, un'prē-pārd", *a.* Not prepared.

unpretending, un-prē-tend'ing, *a.* Not pretending to any distinction; unassuming.

unprincipled, un-prin'si-pld, *a.* Not having settled principles; immoral.

unproductive, un'prō-duk"tiv, *a.* Not productive; infertile; not returning a profit.

unprofessional, un'prō-fesh"un-al, *a.* Contrary to the customs of a profession; not belonging to a profession.

unprofitable, un-prof'it-a-bl, *a.* Not profitable; useless; profitless.

unpromising, un-prom'is-ing, *a.* Not giving promise of success, &c.

unproved, un-prövd', *a.* Not proved; not established as true by proof.

unpublished, un-pub'lisht, *a.* Not published.

unqualified, un-kwol'i-fīd, *a.* Not qualified; not having the requisite qualifications; not modified by conditions.

unquestionable, un-kwes'chun-a-bl, *a.* Not to be called in question; indubitable.

unquiet, un-kwī'et, *a.* Not quiet; disturbed.

unravel, un-rav'el, *vt.* To disentangle; to disengage or separate; to solve.

unread, un-red', *a.* Not perused; illiterate.

unreadable, un-rēd'a-bl, *a.* Incapable of being read; illegible; not worth reading.

unready, un-red'i, *a.* Not ready; not prompt to act.

unreal, un-rē'al, *a.* Not real; not substantial.

unreality, un-rē-al'i-ti, *n.* Want of real existence; that which has no reality.

unreason, un-rē'zn, *n.* Want of reason; folly; absurdity.

unreasonable, un-rē'zn-a-bl, *a.* Not reasonable; immoderate.

unrecorded, un-rē-kor'ded, *a.* Not recorded or registered; not kept in remembrance by documents or monuments.

unredeemed, un'rē-dēmd", *a.* Not redeemed; not fulfilled; unmitigated.

unrefined, un'rē-fīnd", *a.* Not refined or purified; not polished in manners, taste, &c.

unregenerate, un'rē-jen"ėr-it, *a.* Not regenerated or renewed in heart.

unregistered, un-rej'is-tėrd, *a.* Not registered or entered in a register.

unrelated, un'rē-lāt"ed, *a.* Not connected by blood; having no connection.

unrelenting, un'rē-lent"ing, *a.* Not relenting; relentless; hard; pitiless.

unreliable, un'rē-lī"a-bl, *a.* Not reliable; untrustworthy.

unrelieved, un-rē-lēvd', *a.* Not relieved; monotonous.

unremitting, un'rē-mit"ing, *a.* Not remitting or abating; incessant; continued.

unrepresented, un-re'prē-zent"ed, *a.* Not represented; not having a representative; not yet put on the stage.

unrequited, un'rē-kwīt"ed, *a.* Not requited; not recompensed.

unreserved, un'rē-zėrvd", *a.* Not reserved or restricted; full; free; open; frank.

unreservedly, un'rē-zėr"ved-li, *adv.* Without reservation; frankly.

unrest, un-rest', *n.* Disquiet; uneasiness.

unrestrained, un-rē-strānd', *a.* Not restrained; licentious; loose.

unrighteous, un-rī'chus, *a.* Not righteous; not just; wicked.

unripe, un-rīp', *a.* Not ripe; not mature; not fully prepared; not completed.

unrivaled, unrivalled, un-rī'vald, *a.* Having no rival; incomparable.

unroll, un-rōl', *vt.* and *i.* To open out from being in a roll; to unfold; to display.

unromantic, un'rō-man"tik, *a.* Not romantic; not given to romantic fancies.

unroof, un-röf', *vt.* To strip off the roof of.

unruffled, un-ruf'ld, *a.* Not ruffled; calm; tranquil; not agitated; not disturbed.

unruly, un-rö'li, *a.* Disregarding rule; turbulent; ungovernable; disorderly.

unsafe, un-sāf', *a.* Not safe; perilous.

unsaid, un-sed', *a.* Not spoken.

unsatisfactory, un'sat-is-fak"tō-ri, *a.* Not satisfactory; not satisfying.

unsavory, unsavoury, un-sā'vėr-i, *a.* Not savory; insipid; unpleasing; offensive.

unsay, un-sā', *vt.* To recant; to retract.

unscathed, un-skāᴛHd', *a.* Not scathed; uninjured.

unscrew, un-skrö', *vt.* To draw the screw from; to unfasten by screwing back.

unscrupulous, un-skrö'pū-lus, *a.* Having no scruples; regardless of principle.

unseal, un-sēl', *vt.* To remove the seal from; to open after having been sealed.

unseasonable, un-sē'zn-a-bl, *a.* Not seasonable; ill-timed; untimely.

unseat, un-sēt', *vt.* To remove from a seat; to depose from a seat in a legislature.

unseemly, un-sēm'li, *a.* Not seemly; indecorous; improper.—*adv.* Unbecomingly.

unseen, un-sēn', *a.* Not seen; invisible.

unselfish, un-sel'fish, *a.* Not selfish.

unsentimental, un-sen'ti-men"tal, *a.* Not sentimental; matter-of-fact.

unserviceable, un-sèr'vis-a-bl, *a.* Useless.

unsettle, un-set'l, *vt.* To change from a settled state; to unhinge; to derange.

unsettled, un-set'ld, *p.a.* Not settled; not calm or composed; having no fixed habitation; irregular; unpaid.

unsex, un-seks', *vt.* To deprive of the qualities of sex; to deprive of the qualities of a woman.

unshaken, un-shā'kn, *a.* Not shaken; resolute; firm.

unshapely, un-shāp'li, *a.* Not shapely; ill formed.

unsheathe, un-shēTH', *vt.* To draw from the sheath or scabbard.

unshod, un-shod', *a.* Having no shoes.

unshrinking, un-shringk'ing, *a.* Not shrinking; not recoiling; fearless.

unsightly, un-sīt'li, *a.* Not slightly; repulsive; ugly; deformed.

unsisterly, un-sis'tèr-li, *a.* Not like or becoming a sister.

unskillful, un-skil'ful, *a.* Not skillful; having no or little skill; wanting dexterity.

unsociable, un-sō'sha-bl, *a.* Not sociable.

unsocial, un-sō'shal, *a.* Not social; not caring to mix with one's fellows.

unsoiled, un-soild', *a.* Not soiled; pure.

unsold, un-sōld', *a.* Not sold.

unsolicited, un'sōl-is"it-ed, *a.* Not asked.

unsophisticated, un'sō-fis"ti-kāt'ed, *a.* Pure; natural; artless; simple.

unsought, un-sat', *a.* Not sought for.

unsound, un-sound', *a.* Not sound; erroneous; not orthodox.

unsparing, un-spär'ing, *a.* Not sparing; profuse; severe; rigorous.

unspeakable, un-spēk'a-bl, *a.* Incapable of being spoken or uttered; unutterable.

unspoken, un-spō'kn, *a.* Not spoken.

unspotted, un-spot'ed, *a.* Free from spots; free from moral stain; pure.

unstable, un-stā'bl, *a.* Not stable; inconstant; irresolute; wavering.

unstamped, un-stampt', *a.* Not having a stamp impressed or affixed.

unsteady, un-sted'i, *a.* Not steady; shaking; fickle; varying.

unstinted, un-stint'ed, *a.* Not stinted; profuse.

unstop, un-stop', *vt.* To free from a stopper, as a bottle; to free from obstruction.

unstring, un-string', *vt.* To deprive of strings; to relax; to loosen.

unstrung, un-strung', *a.* Deprived of strings; having the nerves shaken.

unstudied, un-stud'id, *a.* Not studied; not premeditated; easy; natural; ignorant.

unsubstantial, un'sub-stan"shal, *a.* Not substantial; not real; not nutritive.

unsuccessful, un'suk-ses"ful, *a.* Not successful; not fortunate in the result.

unsuitable, un-sūt'a-bl, *a.* Not suitable; ill adapted; unfit.

unsuited, un-sūt'ed, *a.* Not suited; unfit.

unsullied, un-sul'id, *a.* Not sullied; pure.

unsung, un-sung', *a.* Not sung; not celebrated in song or poetry.

unsurpassed, un-sèr-past', *a.* Not surpassed, excelled, or outdone.

unsusceptible, un'su-sep"ti-bl, *a.* Not susceptible.

unsuspecting, un-sus-pekt'ing, *a.* Not suspecting; free from suspicion.

unswerving, un-swèrv'ing, *a.* Not swerving; unwavering; firm.

unsworn, un-swōrn', *a.* Not sworn; not bound by oath.

untainted, un-tānt'ed, *a.* Not tainted.

untamable, untameable, un-tām'a-bl, *a.* Not capable of being tamed.

untasted, un-tās'ted, *a.* Not tasted; not experienced.

untaught, un-tat', *a.* Not educated; unlettered; ignorant.

untenable, un-ten'a-bl, *a.* Not to be maintained by argument; not defensible.

unthinkable, un-thingk'a-bl, *a.* That cannot be made an object of thought.

unthinking, un-thingk'ing, *a.* Not given to think; not heedful; inconsiderate.

unthought, un-that', *a.* Not thought or conceived; often followed by *of*.

unthread, un-thred', *vt.* To draw or take out a thread from.

untidy, un-tī'di, *a.* Not tidy; slovenly.

untie, un-tī', *vt.* (untying, untied). To loosen, as a knot; to undo; to unfasten.

until, un-til', *prep.* or *conj.* Till; to; till the time or point that.

untimely, un-tīm'li, *a.* Not timely; illtimed; inopportune.—*adv.* Unseasonably.

untiring, un-tīr'ing, *a.* Not tiring; unwearied.

unto, un'tö, *prep.* To.

untold, un-tōld', *a.* Not told; not revealed or counted.

untouched, un-tucht', *a.* Not touched; uninjured; not affected.

untoward, un-tō'wèrd, *a.* Not toward; forward; awkward; vexatious.

untowardly, un-tō'wèrd-li, *a.* Untoward.—*adv.* Perversely.

untraceable, un-trās'a-bl, *a.* Incapable of being traced.

untractable, un-trak'ta-bl, *a.* Not tractable; refractory.

untraveled, untravelled, un-trav'eld, *a.* Not trodden by passengers; not having traveled.

untried, un-trīd', *a.* Not tried; not attempted; not yet experienced; not determined in law.

untrod, untrodden, un-trod', un-trod'n, *a.* Not having been trod; unfrequented.

untroubled, un-tru'bld, *a.* Not troubled; not agitated or ruffled; not turbid.

untrue, un-trö', *a.* Not true; false.

untrustworthy, un-trust'wèr-THi, *a.* Not worthy of being trusted; unreliable.

untruth, un-trŏth', *n.* Falsehood.

untruthful, un-trŏth'fẏl, *a.* Not truthful.

untwist, un-twist', *vt.* and *i.* To separate, as threads twisted.

unused, un-ūzd', *a.* Not used; not put to use; not accustomed.

unusual, un-ū'zhö-al, *a.* Not usual; rare.

unutterable, un-ut'ėr-a-bl, *a.* That cannot be uttered; inexpressible.

unvalued, un-va'lūd, *a.* Not valued; not prized; neglected; inestimable.

unvaried, un-vā'rɪd, *a.* Not varied.

unvarnished, un-vär'nisht, *a.* Not varnished; not artfully embellished; plain.

unveil, un-vāl', *vt.* To remove a veil from; to uncover; to disclose to view.

unvoiced, un-voist', *a.* Not spoken; not uttered with voice as distinct from breath.

unwarranted, un-wor'an-ted, *a.* Not warranted; unjustifiable; not certain.

unwary, un-wār'i, *a.* Not cautious.

unwashed, un-wosht', *a.* Not washed; dirty.

unwavering, un-wā'vèr-ing, *a.* Not wavering; steady; steadfast.

unwed, un-wed', *a.* Unmarried.

unwelcome, un-wel'kum, *a.* Not welcome; not pleasing or grateful.

unwell, un-wel', *a.* Not well; indisposed.

unwholesome, un-hōl'sum, *a.* Not wholesome; insalubrious; causing sickness.

unwieldy, un-wēl'di, *n.* Movable with difficulty; unmanageable.

unwilling, un-wil'ing, *a.* Not willing; loath; disinclined; reluctant.

unwind, un-wind', *vt.* To wind off.—*vi.* To admit of being unwound.

unwise, un-wiz', *a.* Not wise; injudicious.

unwitting, un-wit'ing, *a.* Not knowing; unconscious; unaware.

unwomanly, un-wy'man-li, *a.* Not womanly; unbecoming a woman.

unwonted, un-wŏnt'ed, *a.* Not wonted; not common; unusual; infrequent.

unworldly, un-wėrld'li, *a.* Not worldly; not influenced by worldly or sordid motives.

unworthy, un-wèr'ᴛʜi, *a.* Not worthy; worthless; base; not becoming or suitable.

unwrap, un-rap', *vt.* To open or undo, as what is wrapped up.

unwritten, un-rit'n, *a.* Not written; blank; understood though not expressed.

unyielding, un-yēld'ing, *a.* Stiff; firm; obstinate.

unyoke, un-yōk', *vt.* To loose from a yoke.

up, up, *adv.* Aloft; in or to a higher position; upright; above the horizon; out of bed; in a state of sedition; from the country to the metropolis; quite; to or at an end.—*prep.* To a higher place or point on; towards the interior of.

up-and-coming, up'and-kum'ing, *a.* Showing promise; enterprising.

upbraid, up-brād', *vt.* To reproach; to chide; to taunt.

upbringing, up"bring'ing, *n.* Training; education; breeding.

upcast, up"kast', *a.* Cast up.—The ventilating shaft of a mine.

upheave, up-hēv', *vt.* To heave or lift up from beneath. **upheaval,** up-hēv'al, *n.* Act of upheaving; lifting of a portion of the earth's crust.

uphill, up"hil', *a.* Leading or going up a rising ground; difficulty; fatiguing.

uphold, up-hōld', *vt.* To hold up; to keep erect; to support; sustain.

upholster, up-hōl'ster, *vt.* To furnish with upholstery. **upholsterer,** up-hōl'stėr-ėr, *n.* One who furnishes houses with curtains, carpets, &c. **upholstery,** up-hōl'stėr-i, *n.* The articles supplied by upholsterers.

upkeep, up'kēp, *n.* Maintenance.

upland, up'land, *n.* Higher grounds; hill-slopes.—*a.* Pertaining to uplands. **uplander,** up'land-ėr, *n.* An inhabitant of the uplands.

uplift, up-lift', *vi.* To lift up.—*n.* up'lift. A raising; rise; exaltation.

upmost, up'mŏst, *a.* Highest; uppermost.

upon, u-pon', *prep.* Up and on; resting on; on.

upper, up'ėr, *a.* Higher in place or rank.—*n.* The upper part of a shoe.

upper hand, up'ėr hand, *n.* Superiority.

uppermost, up'ėr-mŏst, *a.* *superl.* Highest in place, rank, or power.

uppish, up'ish, *a.* Assuming lofty airs; arrogant.

upraise, up-rāz', *vt.* To raise or lift up.

uprear, up-rēr', *vt.* To rear up; to raise.

upright, up'rīt, *a.* Straight up; erect; honest; just.—*n.* A vertical piece.

uprise, up-riz', *vi.* To rise up; to slope upwards.—*n.* up'riz. Rise; elevation.

uprising, up-riz'ing, *n.* Rise; ascent or acclivity; a riot; a rebellion.

uproar, up'rŏr, *n.* A great tumult; violent disturbance; bustle and clamor. **uproarious,** up-rŏr'i-us, *a.* Making an uproar or tumult; tumultuous.

uproot, up-rŏt', *vt.* To tear up by the roots.

upset, up-set', *vt.* To overturn; to discompose completely.—*n.* up'set. Act of upsetting.—*a.* Fixed; determined.

upshot, up'shot, *n.* Final issue; end.

upside, up"sīd', *n.* The upper side.

upstage, up'stāj', *adv.* Toward the rear of the stage.—*a.* Aloof; haughty.

upstairs, up"stärz', *a.* or *adv.* Ascending the stairs; in or pertaining to the upper part of a house.

upstart, up-stärt', *vi.* To start up suddenly.—*n.* up'stärt. A parvenu.

upturn, up-tèrn', *vt.* and *i.* To turn up. —up'tèrn, *n.* An upward turn.

upward, up'wėrd, *a.* Directed to a higher place; ascending.—*adv.* Upwards.

upwards, up'wėrdz, *adv.* To a higher place; above (with *of*).

uranium, ū-rā'ni-um, *n.* A rare metal, colored like nickel or iron.

Uranus, ū'ra-nus, *n.* The most distant of all the planets except Neptune.

urban, ėr'ban, *a.* Of or belonging to a city or town.

bane, ér-bān', *a.* Courteous; polite.
rbanity, ér-ban'i-ti, *n.* Politeness; urtesy.

chin, ér'chin, *n.* A hedgehog; a sea-chin; a child or small boy.

eter, ū-rē'tér, *n.* The duct that con-ys the urine from the kidney to the adder.

ethra, ū-rē'thra, *n.* The duct by ich the urine is discharged from the adder.

ge, érj, *vt.* (urging, urged). To press do something; to incite; to solicit; to sist on.—*vi.* To press forward. **ur-ncy**, ér'jen-si, *n.* Pressure of diffi-ty or necessity; importunity. **ur-nt**, ér'jent, *a.* That urges; pressing; portunate; vehement; eager. **ur-ntly**, ér'jent-li, *adv.* In an urgent nner; with importunity; vehemently. **ne**, ū'rin, *n.* An animal fluid secreted the kidneys, and stored in the bladder fore being discharged. **uric**, ū'rik, *a.* rtaining to or obtained from urine. **'inal**, ū'rin-al, *n.* A convenience for rsons requiring to pass urine. **uri-ry**, ū"ri-ner'i, *a.* Pertaining to urine. **inate**, ū'ri-nāt, *vi.* To discharge ne.

**, érn, *n.* A vase swelling in the mid-; a vessel for water.

ine, ér'sin, *a.* Pertaining to or re-mbling a bear.

us, *pron.* The objective case of *we*.
ble, ūz'a-bl, *a.* That may be used.
ge, ūz'ij, *n.* Act or manner of using; atment; practice; custom; use.
, ūz, *n.* Act of employing anything; ployment; utility; need; practice; nt.—*vt.* ūz (using, used). To put to ; to employ; to accustom; to treat. *vi.* To be accustomed. **useful, ūs'ful, al; advantageous. **useless**, ūs'les, *a.* rthless; unavailing. **user**, ūz'ér, *n.* e who uses.

er, ush'ér, *n.* A door-keeper; an of-r who introduces strangers, &c.; a

subordinate teacher.—*vt.* To give en-trance to; to introduce.

usual, ū'zhū-al, *a.* Customary; common; frequent; ordinary; general. **usually**, ū'zhū-al-li, *adv.* Customarily.

usury, ū'zhō-ri, *n.* Extortionate interest for money; practice of taking exorbitant interest. **usurer**, ū'zhō-rér, *n.* One who takes exorbitant interest. **usurious**, ū-zhōr'i-us, *a.* Pertaining to usury.

usurp, ū-zérp', *vt.* To seize and hold without right; to appropriate wrongfully. **usurpation**, u'zér-pā"shun, *n.* Act of usurping; illegal seizure or possession. **usurper**, ū-zér'pér, *n.* One who seizes power or possessions without right.

utensil, ū-ten'sil, *n.* That which is used; an instrument; implement.

uterus, ū'tér-us, *n.*; pl. **-ri**. The womb. **uterine**, ū'tér-in, *a.* Pertaining to the uterus.

utilitarian, ū-til'i-tār"i-an, *a.* Per-taining to utility or utilitarianism.—*n.* One who holds the doctrine of utilitar-ianism.

utility, ū-til'i-ti, *n.* State or quality of being useful; usefulness; a useful thing. **utilize**, ū'ti-līz, *vt.* (utilizing, utilized). To render useful; to put to use; to make use of.

utmost, ut'mōst, *a.* Being farthest out; uttermost; extreme.—*n.* The greatest power, degree, or effort.

Utopia, ū-tō'pi-a, *n.* A place or state of ideal perfection. **utopian**, ū-tō'pi-an, *a.* Ideally perfect.—*n.* An ardent but unpractical reformer.

utter, ut'ér, *a.* Complete; total; abso-lute.—*vt.* To give vent to; to put into circulation; to declare; to speak. **ut-terance**, ut'ér-ans, *n.* Act of uttering; pronunciation; words uttered. **utterly**, ut'ér-li, *adv.* Totally; absolutely. **ut-termost**, ut'ér-mōst, *a.* Being in the furthest or greatest degree; extreme.—*n.* The utmost power or degree.

uvula, ū'vū-la, *n.* The small fleshy body which hangs over the root of the tongue.

V

cant, vā'kant, *a.* Empty; void; un-upied; leisure; thoughtless; inane. **cancy**, vā'kan-si, *n.* Empty space; cuity; an interval of leisure; listless-s; a place or office not occupied. **ate**, vā'kāt, *vt.* (vacating, vacated). make vacant; to leave unoccupied; annul. **vacation**, va-kā'shun, *n.* Act vacating; intermission; recess; holi-s.

cinate, vak'si-nāt, *vt.* To inoculate h the cow-pox, in order to ward off all-pox. **vaccination**, vak'si-nā"-n, *n.* The act, art, or practice of ccinating.

cine, vak'sēn, *a.* Pertaining to cows to cow-pox.

vacillate, vas'i-lāt, *vi.* To sway; to waver; to fluctuate. **vacillating**, va'-sil-lāt-ing, *p.a.* Inclined to vacillate; apt to waver; inconstant. **vacillation**, vas'i-lā"shun, *n.* A wavering; fluctuation of mind; unsteadiness.

vacuous, vak'ū-us, *a.* Empty; void; vacant; inane; inexpressive. **vacuity**, va-kū'i-ti, *n.* Emptiness; vacancy; in-anity; vacant expression.

vacuum, vak'ū-um, *n.* Empty space; a void; an inclosed space void of air.

vacuum cleaner. A machine using suction and brushes to clean floors, carpets, upholstery, etc.

vagabond, vag'a-bond, *a.* Wandering to

and fro; pertaining to a vagrant.—*n.* A wanderer; a vagrant; a rascal.

vagary, va-gār'i, *n.* A **wild freak;** a whim.

vagina, va-ji'na, *n.* A sheath; the canal in females leading inwards to the uterus. **vaginal,** vaj'i-nal, *a.* Pertaining to or like a sheath; pertaining to the vagina.

vagrant, vā'grant, *a.* Wandering; unsettled.—*n.* A wanderer; a vagabond; a sturdy beggar; a tramp. **vagrancy,** vā'gran-si, *n.* State or life of a vagrant.

vague, vāg, *a.* Indefinite; hazy; uncertain. **vaguely,** vāg'li, *adv.* In a vague manner.

vain, vān, *a.* Without real value; empty; worthless; ineffectual; light-minded; conceited. **in vain,** to no purpose. **vainglorious,** vān'glō"ri-us, *a.* Feeling or marked by vainglory; boastful. **vainglory,** vān'glō"ri, *n.* Empty pride; undue elation. **vainly,** vān'li, *adv.* In a vain manner; without effect; with vanity; idly.

valance, val'ans, *n.* The drapery hanging round a bed, couch, &c.

vale, vāl, *n.* A valley.

valediction, val'ē-dik"shun, *n.* A farewell. **valedictory,** val'e-dik"tō-ri, *a.* Bidding farewell; pertaining to a leave-taking.

valence, valency, vā'lens, vā'len-si, *n.* The force which determines with how many atoms of an element an atom of another element will combine chemically.

valentine, val'en-tin, *n.* A sweetheart selected or got by lot on St. *Valentine's* Day, 14th February; a missive of an amatory or satirical kind, sent on this day.

valet, val'et or val'ā, *n.* A man-servant. —*vt.* To attend on a gentleman's person.

Valhalla, val-hal'a, *n.* In Norse mythology, the great hall where Odin receives and entertains the souls of heroes fallen in battle.

valiant, val'yant, *a.* Brave; courageous; intrepid; heroic. **valiantly,** val'yant-li, *adv.* Bravely; heroically.

valid, val'id, *a.* Well based or grounded; sound; just; good or sufficient in law. **validate,** val'id-āt, *vt.* To make valid. **validity,** va-lid'i-ti, *n.* Justness; soundness; legal sufficiency.

valise, va-lēs', *n.* A small traveling bag.

Valkyrie, val-kir'i, *n.* In Norse mythology, one of the maidens who ride the air and hover over battlefields choosing those to be slain and those worthy to be led to Valhalla.

valley, val'i, *n.* A low tract of land between hills; a river-basin.

valor, valour, val'èr, *n.* Bravery; courage; intrepidity; prowess in war. **valorous,** va'lor-us, *a.* Brave; valiant.

value, va'lū, *n.* Worth; utility; importance; import; precise signification.—*vt.* (valuing, valued). To rate at a certain price; to estimate; to esteem; to prize; to regard. **valueless,** va'lū-les, *a.* Worthless. **valuable,** va'lū-a-bl, *a.* Of great worth; precious; worthy.—*n.* A thing of value; choice article of personal property; usually in *pl.* **valuation,**

val'ū-ā"shun, *n.* Act or art of valuin appraisement; estimated worth.

valve, valv, *n.* A leaf of a folding doo a lid for an orifice, opening only o way and regulating the passage of flui a separable portion of the shell of a m lusk.

vamp, vamp, *n.* The upper leather of boot; a piece added for appearance sak a flirt.—*vt.* To repair; to furbish up; patch.

vampire, vam'pīr, *n.* A dead person b lieved to have an unnatural life so as be able to leave the grave at night a suck the blood of living persons; an e tortioner; a blood-sucker; a vampire ba **vampire bat,** vam'pīr bat, *n.* A bloo sucking bat of South America; also a b that does not suck blood.

van, van, *n.* The front of an army fleet; foremost portion; a winnowi fan; a covered vehicle for goods.

vanadium, va-nā'di-um, *n.* A silve brittle metal.

Vandal, van'dal, *n.* One who willfully ignorantly destroys any work of art the like; one of the Germanic tribe w sacked Rome. **vandalism,** van'dal-iz *n.* Conduct of a vandal; hostility to or literature.

Vandyke, van-dīk', *n.* A short, point style of beard.

vane, vān, *n.* A weathercock; the bro part of a feather on either side of t shaft; blade of a windmill, &c.

vanguard, van"gärd', *n.* The troops w march in the van of an army.

vanilla, va-nil'a, *n.* A tropical orchi a fragrant substance obtained from used for seasoning.

vanish, van'ish, *vi.* To disappear; pass away.

vanity, van'i-ti, *n.* Quality or state being vain; worthlessness; vain pursu desire of indiscriminate admiration; co ceit; a trifle.

vanquish, vang'kwish, *vt.* To conque to overcome; to confute.

vantage, van'tij, *n.* Advantage; va tage-ground.

vapid, vap'id, *a.* Spiritless; flat; du **vapidity,** va-pid'i-ti, *n.* Flatness; du ness; want of life or spirit.

vapor, vapour, vā'pèr, *n.* An exha tion or fume; visible moisture or stea hazy matter; a vain imagination; *pl.* nervous hysterical affection; the blues. *vi.* To boast; to bully.

vaporize, vā'nèr-iz, *vt.* To convert in vapor.—*vi.* To pass off in vapor.

vaporous, vā'pèr-us, *a.* Like vapor; f of vapors; unreal; whimsical.

variable, vār'i-a-bl, *a.* That may va or alter; changeable; fickle; unstead **variability,** var'i-a-bil"i-ti, *n.* State being variable; liability to vary.

variant, vār'i-ant, *a.* Varying; differe —*n.* Something the same but with a other form; a different version. **vax ance,** vār'i-ans, *n.* Variation; disagre ment; dissension; discord.

variation, var'i-ā"shun, *n.* Act or pr ess of varying; alteration; amount rate of change; inflection; deviation.

varicose, var'i-kōs, *a.* Exhibiting

morbid enlargement or dilation, as the veins.

varied, vär'id, *p.a.* Characterized by variety; diverse; various.

variegate, vär'i-e-gāt, *vt.* (variegating, variegated). To diversify in appearance; to mark with different colors.

variety, va-rī'e-ti, *n.* State or quality of being varied or various; diversity; a varied assortment; a sort; a kind.

variorum, var'i-ō″rum, *a.* Applied to an edition of a work containing the notes of various editors.

various, vär'i-us, *a.* Different; several; changeable; uncertain; diverse.

varlet, vär'let, *n.* A footman; a rascal.

varnish, vär'nish, *n.* A clear solution of resinous matter, for coating surfaces and giving a gloss; outside show; gloss.— *vt.* To lay varnish on; to gloss over.

varsity, vär'si-ti, *n.* The team representing a school in any sport.

vary, vär'i, *vt.* (varying, varied). To change; to diversify.—*vi.* To alter; to change; to differ; to swerve; to disagree.

vascular, vas'kū-lėr, *a.* Pertaining to those vessels that have to do with conveying blood, chyle, &c.

vase, väs, *n.* A vessel of some size and of various materials and forms, generally ornamental rather than useful.

vaseline, vas'e-lēn, *n.* A substance obtained from petroleum, used in ointments, &c.

vassal, vas'al, *n.* A feudal tenant; a subject; a retainer; a bondman. **vassalage,** vas'al-ij, *n.* Servitude; dependence.

vast, vast, *a.* Of great extent; immense; mighty; great in importance or degree. —*n.* A boundless space; immensity. **vastly,** väst'li, *adv.* Very greatly; exceedingly.

vat, vat, *n.* A large vessel for holding liquors; a tun; a wooden tank or cistern.—*vt.* (vatting, vatted). To put in a vat.

Vatican, vat'i-kan, *n.* The palace of the Pope at Rome; the papal power or government.

vaudeville, vo'de-vil, *n.* A light, gay song; a ballad; a dramatic piece with light or comic songs.

vault, vạlt, *n.* An arched roof; a subterranean chamber; a cellar; a leap; a leap with the hand resting on something. —*vt.* To arch.—*vi.* To leap; to bound. **vaulted,** vạlt'ed, *p.a.* Arched; concave. **vaulting,** vạlt'ing, *n.* Vaulted work; vaults collectively.—*p.a.* Leaping.

vaunt, vạnt, *vi.* To brag; to exult.—*vt.* To boast of; to make a vain display of. —*n.* A boast.

veal, vēl, *n.* The flesh of a calf.

Veda, vā'dä or vē'dä, *n.* The body of ancient Sanskrit hymns on which Brahmanism is based.

veer, vēr, *vi.* To change direction; to turn round.—*vt.* To direct to a different course.

vegetable, vej'e-ta-bl, *a.* Belonging to or like plants.—*n.* A plant; a plant for culinary purposes. **vegetal,** vej'e-tal, *a.* Vegetable; pertaining to the vital phenomena common to plants and animals.

vegetarian, vej'e-tar″i-an, *n.* One who abstains from animal food and lives on vegetables. **vegetate,** vej'e-tāt, *vi.* (vegetating, vegetated). To grow as plants; to live a monotonous, useless life; to have a mere existence. **vegetation,** vej'e-tā″shun, *n.* The process of growing, as plants; plants in general. **vegetative,** vej″e-tā'tiv, *a.* Having the power to produce growth in plants.

vehement, vē'e-ment, *a.* Very eager or urgent; ardent; violent; furious. **vehemence,** vē'e-mens, *n.* Ardor; violence; force; impetuosity; fury.

vehicle, vē'i-kl, *n.* Any kind of carriage moving on land; conveyance; medium. **vehicular, vehiculary,** vē-hik'ū-lėr, vē-hik'ū-lėr-i, *a.* Pertaining to a vehicle.

veil, vāl, *n.* A screen; an article of dress shading the face; a covering or disguise; the soft palate.—*vt.* To cover with a veil; to envelop; to disguise.

vein, vān, *n.* A blood-vessel which returns impure blood to the heart and lungs; a blood-vessel; a sap tube in leaves; a crack in a rock, filled up by substances different from the rock; a streak; disposition; mood.—*vt.* To fill or variegate with veins.

veldt, veld, velt, *n.* A term in S. Africa for open uninclosed country.

vellum, ve'lum, *n.* A fine parchment made of calf's skin.

velocipede, vē-los'i-pēd, *n.* A light vehicle propelled by the rider; bicycle, &c.

velocity, vē-los'i-ti, *n.* Rate of motion; speed; rapidity.

velvet, vel'vet, *n.* A rich silk stuff with a close, fine, soft pile.—*a.* Made of or like velvet. **velveteen,** vel-ve-tēn', *n.* A cloth made of cotton in imitation of velvet; cotton velvet. **velvety,** vel'-ve-ti, *a.* Made of or resembling velvet.

venal, vē'nal, *a.* Ready to accept a bribe; mercenary. **venality,** vē-nal'i-ti, *n.* State of being venal; prostitution of talents or services.

venation, vē-nā'shun, *n.* The manner in which the veins of leaves are arranged.

vend, vend, *vt.* To sell. **vender,** ven'-dėr, *n.* One who vends; a seller.

vendetta, ven-det'a, *n.* A blood feud; the practice of the nearest of kin executing vengeance on a murderer.

vendor, vend-ėr', *n.* A vender; a seller.

veneer, ve-nēr', *n.* A thin facing of fine wood glued on a less valuable sort; any similar coating; fair outward show.—*vt.* To overlay with veneer; to put a fine superficial show on.

venerate, ven'ėr-āt, *vt.* (venerating, venerated). To reverence; to revere; to regard as sacred. **venerable,** ven'ėr-a-bl, *a.* Worthy of veneration; deserving respect from age, character, or associations. **veneration,** ven'ėr-a″shun, *n.* The highest degree of respect and reverence; respect mingled with some degree of awe.

venereal, ve-nēr'ē-al, *a.* Pertaining to sexual intercourse.

venery, ven'ė-ri, *n.* Hunting; sexual intercourse.

venesection, ven′ē-sek″shun, *n*. Blood-letting; phlebotomy.

Venetian, vē-nē′shan, *a*. Belonging to Venice; denoting a window blind made of thin slips of wood.

vengeance, ven′jans, *n*. Punishment in return for an injury; penal retribution. **vengeful**, venj′ful, *a*. Full of vengeance; vindictive; retributive; revengeful.

venial, vē′ni-al, *a*. That may be pardoned or forgiven; excusable.

venison, ven′i-zn or ven′zn, *n*. The flesh of deer.

venom, ven′um, *n*. Poison; spite; malice; malignity; virulency. **venomous**, ven′um-us, *a*. Full of venom; poisonous; noxious; spiteful.

venous, vē′nus, *a*. Pertaining to a vein; contained in veins, as blood; venose.

vent, vent, *n*. A small opening; flue or funnel; an outlet; the anus; utterance; expression; sale; market.—*vt*. To let out; to publish.

ventilate, ven′ti-lāt, *vt*. (ventilating, ventilated). To winnow; to expose to the air; to supply with fresh air; to be let freely discussed. **ventilation**, ven′ti-lā″shun, *n*. Act of ventilating; replacement of vitiated air by fresh air; a bringing forward for discussion. **ventilator**, ven′ti-lāt-ėr, *n*. A contrivance for keeping the air fresh in any close space.

ventral, ven′tral, *a*. The abdominal region.

ventricle, ven′tri-kl, *n*. A small cavity in an animal body; either of two cavities of the heart which propel the blood in the arteries.

ventriloquism, ventriloquy, ven-tril′o-kwizm, ven-tril′o-kwi, *n*. The art of uttering sounds so that the voice appears to come not from the actual speaker. **ventriloquist**, ven-tril′o-kwist, *n*. One who practices or is skilled in ventriloquism.

venture, ven′tūr, *n*. An undertaking which involves hazard or danger; a commercial speculation; thing put to hazard; chance.—*vi*. (venturing, ventured). To make a venture; to dare.—*vt*. To risk. **venturesome**, ven′tūr-sum, *a*. Apt or inclined to venture; bold; hazardous. **venturous**, ven′tūr-us, *a*. Venturesome.

venue, ven′ū, *n*. A thrust; the place where an action is laid or the trial of a cause takes place.

Venus, vē′nus, *n*. The Roman goddess of beauty and love; a planet.

veracious, ve-rā′shus, *a*. Observant of truth; truthful; true. **veracity**, ve-ras′i-ti, *n*. Truthfulness; truth; that which is true.

veranda, verandah, ve-ran′da, *n*. An open portico or light gallery along the front of a building.

verb, vėrb, *n*. The part of speech which signifies to be, to do, or to suffer. **verbal**, vėr′bal, *a*. Relating to words; spoken; literal; derived from a verb.—*n*. A noun derived from a verb. **verbally**, vėr′bal-li, *adv*. In a verbal manner; by words uttered; word for word.

verbatim, vėr-bā′tim, *n*. Word for word.

verbena, vėr-bē′na, *n*. A genus of plants (and type of an order), some of which are cultivated for the beauty of their flowers.

verbiage, vėr′bi-ij, *n*. Verbosity.

verbose, vėr-bōs′, *a*. Wordy; prolix. **verbosity**, vėr-bos′i-ti, *n*. Superabundance of words; wordiness; prolixity.

verdant, vėr′dant, *a*. Green with herbage or foliage; simple and inexperienced. **verdancy**, ver′dan-si, *n*. Greenness; inexperience.

verdict, vėr′dikt, *n*. The answer of a jury; decision in general; opinion.

verdigris, verdegris, vėr′di-gris, vėr′de-gris, *n*. Rust of copper; substance obtained by exposing copper to air and acetic acid.

verdure, vėr′dūr, *n*. Greenness; fresh green vegetation.

verge, vėrj, *n*. A rod of office; a mace; a wand; brink; margin; compass; scope. —*vi*. (verging, verged). To incline; to tend; to border.

verify, ver′i-fi, *vt*. (verifying, verified). To prove to be true; to confirm; to fulfill. **verifiable**, ver″-i-fi′a-bl, *a*. That may be verified. **verification**, ver′i-fi-kā″shun, *n*. Act of verifying; confirmation.

verily, ver′i-li, *adv*. In truth; really; truly.

verisimilar, ver′i-sim″i-lėr, *a*. Having the appearance of truth; probable; likely.

verity, ver′i-ti, *n*. Truth; reality; a truth. **veritable**, ver′i-ta-bl, *a*. True; real; actual.

vermicelli, vėr-mi-sel′li, *n*. An Italian foodstuff similar to spaghetti.

vermin, vėr′min, *n.pl.* or *sing*. Small, bothersome animals such as fleas, lice, bedbugs, rats, or mice; birds and animals which prey upon game; worthless or offensive person or persons.

vermouth, vėr-möth, *n*. A white wine flavored with herbs and used in cocktails or as a liqueur.

versatile, vėr′sa-til, *a*. Capable of doing many things well.

verse, vėrs, *n*. A measured line of poetry; short division of any composition, especially of the chapters of the Bible.

version, vėr′shun, *n*. A translation from one language into another; particular account or description; act of turning a fetus in the uterus for delivery.

versus, vėr′sus, *prep*. Against.

vertebra, vėr′te-bra, *n*. One of the bones of the spinal column.

vertebrate, vėr′te-brāt, *n*. An animal that has a backbone.

vertical, vėr′ti-kal, *a*. Upright; at right angles to the supporting surface.

vertigo, vėr′ti-gō, *n*. Dizziness, giddiness.

very, ver′i, *a*. Identical; the same.—*adv*. extremely; in a high degree.

vessel, ves′l, *n*. A utensil for holding anything, especially liquids; ship; container.

vesicle, ves′i-kl, *n*. A membranous bladder or sac; a cell; a cyst.

vest, vest, *n*. A sleeveless jacket; waistcoat; undershirt.

vestal, ves'tal, *a.* Pure; chaste.—*n.* Virgin; nun.

vested, ves'ted, *a.* Under the control of a person or persons; fixed; robed.

vestibule, ves'ti-būl, *n.* A small room or hall between the outer door and the interior of a building.

vestige, ves'tij, *n.* Remnant; trace; a body organ which, in the course of evolution, has lost its usefulness.

vestry, ves'tri, *n.* A room within or attached to a church where the vestments are kept; sacristy; such a room used for meetings; in the Church of England, a group that manages church business.

veteran, vet'ėr-an, *n.* One who has served in the armed forces; a person who has had much experience in a particular business, occupation, etc.

veterinarian, vet'ėr-i-nar"i-an, *n.* A doctor who treats animals.

veto, vē'tō, *n.* Refusal to give consent; prohibition.—*vt.* To refuse to give consent.

vex, veks, *vt.* To irritate by small annoyances or provocations; harass; tease.

vexation, veks-ā'shun, *n.* Being annoyed or troubled; cause of annoyance or trouble.

via, vi'a, *prep.* By way of.

viable, vi'a-bl, *a.* Capable of living, applied to a new-born child.

viaduct, vi'a-dukt, *n.* A long bridge for carrying a road or railway over a valley.

vial, vi'al, *n.* A phial; a small glass bottle.

viand, vi'and, *n.* Meat dressed; food; victuals; used chiefly in *pl.*

vibrate, vi'brāt, *vi.* (vibrating, vibrated). To swing; to quiver; to be unstable.—*vt.* To wave to and fro; to cause to quiver. **vibration**, vi-brā'shun, *n.* Act of vibrating; a swing; a quivering motion. **vibrant**, vi'brant, *a.* Vibrating; tremulous. **vibratory**, vi'bra-to-ri, *a.* Causing to vibrate; vibrating.

vicar, vik'ėr, *n.* A substitute in office; deputy; the priest of a parish in England who receives the smaller tithes, or a salary. **vicarage**, vik'ėr-ij, *n.* The benefice of a vicar; residence of a vicar.

vicarious, vi-kār'i-us, *a.* Pertaining to a substitute; deputed, substituted or suffered for or in the place of another.

vice, vis, *n.* A blemish; fault; moral failing; profligacy; a fault or bad trick in a horse; an iron instrument which holds fast anything worked upon; a prefix denoting position second in rank.

vice, vi'se, *prep.* In place of.

vice-admiral, vis-ad'mi-ral, *n.* Naval officer, the next in rank under the admiral.

vice-chancellor, vis'chan"sel-lor, *n.* An officer acting as deputy for a chancellor.

vice-consul, vis'kon"sul, *n.* One who acts for a consul; a consul of subordinate rank.

vicegerent, vis'jē"rent, *n.* One who acts in the place of a superior; a substitute.

vice-president, vis'prez'i-dent, *n.* An office-bearer next in rank below a president.

viceregal, vis'rē"gal, *a.* Pertaining to a viceroy or viceroyalty.

viceroy, vis'roi, *n.* One who governs in place of a king or queen.

vicinity, vi-sin'i-ti, *n.* Neighborhood; proximity.

vicious, vish'us, *a.* Characterized by vice; faulty; depraved; immoral; spiteful.

vicissitude, vi-sis'i-tūd, *n.* Change or alternation; one of the ups and downs of life.

victim, vik'tim, *n.* A living being sacrificed; a person or thing destroyed; a person who suffers; a gull. **victimize**, vik'tim-iz, *vt.* To make a victim of; to cheat; to deceive.

victor, vik'tėr, *n.* One who conquers; one who proves the winner.—*a.* Victorious.

victoria, vik-tō'ri-a, *n.* A four-wheeled carriage, with a collapsible top, seated for two persons. **victoria cross** (*cap.*); a British medal granted for valor in battle.

Victorian, vik-tō'ri-an, *a.* Having to do with the time of Queen Victoria; prudish; bigoted.—*n.* One who lived or wrote at the time of Queen Victoria.

victorious, vik-tō'ri-us, *a.* Having gained victory; conquering; indicating victory. **victory**, vik'to-ri, *n.* Conquest; a gaining of the superiority in any contest.

victual, vit'l, *n.* Food provided; provisions; generally in *pl.*—*vt.* (victualing, victualed). To supply with victuals or stores.

victualer, vit'l-ėr, *n.* One who furnishes victuals; a tavern-keeper; a ship carrying provisions for other ships.

vide, vi'dē. See; refer to.

video, vid'i-ō, *n.* Television.

vie, vi, *vi.* (vying, vied). To contend.

Viennese, vi'e-nēz", *n. sing.* and *pl.* A native of Vienna; natives of Vienna.

view, vū, *n.* A look; inspection; consideration; range of vision; power of perception; sight; scene; pictorial sketch; judgment; intention.—*vt.* To see; to survey; to consider.—*vi.* To look. **viewer**, vū'ėr, *n.* One who views, surveys, or examines; an inspector; an overseer.

vigil, vij'il, *n.* Act of keeping awake; a devotional watching; the eve or day preceding a church festival. **vigilance**, vij'i-lans, *n.* Watchfulness. **vigilant**, vij'i-lant, *n.* Watchful; circumspect; wary; on the outlook; alert.

vigilante, vij'i-lan"ti, *n.* Member of an organization or group that combats crime in absence of legal authority.

vignette, vin-yet', or vi-net', *n.* Flowers, head and tail pieces, &c., in books; a woodcut without a definite border; a small photographic portrait; a small attractive picture.

vigor, vigour, vig'ėr, *n.* Active force or strength; physical force; strength of mind. **vigorous**, vig'ėr-us, *a.* Full of vigor; strong; lusty; powerful; energetic.

viking, vi'king, *n.* An ancient Scandinavian rover or sea-robber.

vile, vil, *a.* Morally worthless; despicable; depraved; bad. **vilely**, vil'li, *adv.* Basely; meanly. **vilification**, vil'i-fi-kā"shun, *n.* The act of vilifying or defaming. **vilify**, vil'i-fī, *vt.* (vilifying, vilified). To defame; to traduce; to slander.

villa, vil'a, *n.* A country seat; a suburban house.

village, vil'ij, *n.* A collection of houses, smaller than a town and larger than a hamlet. **villager**, vil'ij-èr, *n.* An inhabitant of a village.

villain, vil'in or vil'ān, *n.* A feudal serf; a peasant; a knave or scoundrel. **villainous**, vil'in-us, *a.* Base; vile; wicked; depraved; mean. **villainy**, vil'in-i, *n.* Depravity; wickedness; a crime.

vim, vim, *n.* Vigor; energy.

vincible, vin'si-bl, *a.* Conquerable.

vindicate, vin'di-kāt, *vt.* (vindicating, vindicated). To prove to be just or valid; to maintain the rights of; to defend; to justify. **vindication**, vin'di-kā"shun, *n.* Act of vindicating; a defense or justification. **vindicative**, vin-dik'a-tiv, *a.* Tending to vindicate.

vindictive, vin-dik'tiv, *a.* Revengeful.

vine, vin, *n.* A climbing plant producing grapes; the slender stem of any climbing plant.

vinegar, vin'ē-gèr, *n.* Diluted and impure acetic acid, obtained from wine, beer, &c.; sourness of temper.

vineyard, vin'yèrd, *n.* A plantation of vines producing grapes.

vinous, vī'nus, *a.* Having the qualities of wine; pertaining to wine.

vintage, vint'ij, *n.* The gathering of the grape crop; the crop itself; the wine produced by the grapes of one season.

vintner, vint'nèr, *n.* One who deals in wine; a wine-seller; a licensed victualer.

viol, vi'ul, *n.* An ancient musical instrument like the violin.

viola, vē'ō-la, *n.* A large kind of violin.

violate, vi'ō-lāt, *vt.* (violating, violated). To injure; to outrage; to desecrate; to profane; to transgress. **violation**, vi'ō-lā"shun, *n.* Infringement; transgression; desecration; rape.

violent, vi'ō-lent, *a.* Impetuous; infurious; outrageous; fierce; severe. **violence**, vi'ō-lens, *n.* Quality of being violent; vehemence; outrage; injury.

violet, vi'ō-let, *n.* A genus of plants that includes the pansy, &c.; a plant having a bluish-purple flower with a delicious smell; a rich bluish-purple.—*a.* Of a bluish-purple color.

violin, vī-ō-lin', *n.* A musical instrument with four catgut strings, played with a bow; a fiddle. **violinist**, vī'ō-lin"ist, *n.* A player on the violin.

violist, vi'ul-ist, *n.* A player on the viola.

violoncello, vē'ō-lon-chel"ō or vi'ō-lon-sel"ō, *n.* A large and powerful bow instrument of the violin kind.

viper, vī-pèr, *n.* A venomous serpent. **viperous**, vī'pèr-us, *a.* Having the qualities of a viper.

Viola

virago, vi-rā'gō, *n.* A manlike woman; a termagant.

virgin, vèr'jin, *n.* A woman who has had no carnal knowledge of man; a maid; a sign of the zodiac.—*a.* Chaste; maidenly; unsullied. **virginal**, vèr'ji-nal, *a.* Maidenly; virgin.—*n.* An ancient keyed musical instrument resembling the spinet. **virginity**, vèr-jin'i-ti, *n.* Maidenhood; perfect chastity.

Virgo, vèr'gō, *n.* The Virgin in the zodiac.

virile, vir'il, or vī'ril, *a.* Pertaining to man; masculine; manly; strong. **virility**, vi-ril'i-ti, *n.* Manhood; the power of procreation; masculine action or vigor.

virtual, vèr'tū-al, *a.* Being in essence or effect, not in name or fact. **virtually**, vèr'tū-al-li, *adv.* In efficacy or effect, though not really.

virtue, vèr'tū, *n.* Moral goodness; rectitude; morality; chastity; merit; efficacy. **virtuous**, vèr'tū-us, *a.* Marked by virtue; morally good; pure or chaste.

virtuoso, vèr'tū-ō"sō, *n.*; pl. **-osos** or **-osi**. A man skilled in fine arts, or curiosities, &c.

virulent, vir'ū-lent, *a.* Very poisonous or noxious; bitter in enmity; malignant. **virulence**, vir'ū-lens, *n.* Acrimony; malignity; rancor.

virus, vī'rus, *n.* Contagious poisonous matter; extreme acrimony; malignity.

visage, viz'ij, *n.* The face or countenance. **visaged**, viz'ijd, *a.* Having a visage of this or that sort.

vis-à-vis, vē'zä've", *adv.* Face to face.—*n.* One placed face to face with another; a light carriage for two persons sitting face to face.

viscera, vis'èr-a, *n.* *pl.* The entrails. **visceral**, vis'er-al, *a.* Pertaining to the viscera.

viscid, vis'id, *a.* Sticky or adhesive; glutinous; tenacious. **viscidity**, vi-sid'i-ti, *n.* Glutinousness. **viscosity**, vis-kos'i-ti, *n.* Viscidity.

viscount, vī'kount, *n.* A nobleman of rank between an earl and baron. **viscountess**, vi"koun'tes, *n.* The wife of a viscount.

viscous, vis'kus, *a.* Glutinous; viscid.

visé, vē-zā, *n.* An indorsation upon a passport denoting that it has been examined and found correct.

visible, viz'i-bl, *a.* Perceivable by the eye; apparent; open; conspicuous. **visibly**, viz'i-bli, *adv.* In a visible manner; manifestly; conspicuously; obviously.

vision, vizh'un, *n.* Act of seeing; sight; that which is seen; an apparition; a fanciful view. **visionary**, vizh"un-èr'i, *a.* Pertaining to visions; imaginative; imaginary; not real.—*n.* One who is visionary; one who upholds impracticable schemes.

visit, viz'it, *vt.* To go or come to see; to view officially; to afflict.—*vi.* To practice going to see others; to make calls.—*n.* Act of visiting; a call. **visitant**, viz'i-tant, *n.* A visitor. **visitation**, viz'i-ta"shun, *n.* Act of visiting; a formal or official visit; special dispensation of divine favor or retribution. **visiter, visitor,** viz'it-ėr, viz'it-or, *n.* One who visits; a caller; an inspector. **visiting,** viz'it-ing, *a.* Pertaining to visits; authorized to visit and inspect.—*n.* The act or practice of paying visits.

visor, vizor, vī'zėr, *n.* The movable faceguard of a helmet; a mask.

vista, vis'ta, *n.* A view through an avenue; trees, &c., that form the avenue; an extended view.

visual, vizh'ū-al, *a.* Pertaining to sight or vision; used in seeing.

vital, vī'tal, *a.* Pertaining to life: necessary to life; indispensable; essential. **vitality,** vī-tal'i-ti, *n.* State or quality of having life; principle of life; animation. **vitalize,** vī'tal-īz, *vt.* To give life to; to furnish with the vital principle.

vitamin, vitamine, vī'ta-min, *n.* According to Dr. Casimir Funk, a nitrogenous substance found in some nucleic acids in the form of pyrimidine bases, minute quantities of which are essential to the diet of man, birds, and other animals as a nutritive force and for stimulating growth. It is present in beans, whole wheat, fresh vegetables and fruits, etc. The disease beri-beri is attributed to its absence.

vitiate, vish'i-āt, *vt.* (vitiating, vitiated). To make faulty; to impair; to corrupt; to invalidate. **vitiation,** vish'i-ā"shun, *n.* Act of vitiating; depravation.

vitreous, vit'rē-us, *a.* Glassy; pertaining to glass; resembling glass. **vitrify,** vit'ri-fī, *vt.* To convert into glass by heat.—*vi.* To become glass.

vitriol, vit'ri-ol, *n.* Sulphuric acid or one of its compounds. **vitriolic,** vit'ri-ol'ik, *a.* Pertaining to vitriols; like vitriol; very biting or sarcastic.

vituperate, vī-tū'pėr-āt, *vt.* To abuse; to censure offensively; to rate. **vituperation,** vī-tū'pėr-ā"shun, *n.* Act of vituperating; abuse; abusive language. **vituperative,** vī-tū'pėr-ā-tiv, *a.* Containing vituperation; abusive; railing.

vivacious, vī-vā'shus or vi-, *a.* Lively; brisk; sprightly; tenacious of life. **vivacity,** vī-vas'i-ti, or vi-, *a.* Animation; spirit; liveliness.

vivid, viv'id, *a.* Bright, clear, or lively; forcible; striking; realistic. **vividly,** viv'id-li, *adv.* In a vivid manner; with life; with striking truth. **vivify,** viv'i-fī, *vt.* (vivifying, vivified). To make alive; to endue with life; to animate.

viviparous, vī-vip'a-rus, *a.* Producing young in a living state.

vivisection, viv'i-sek"shun, *n.* Act of experimenting on a living animal. **vivisector,** viv'i-sek'ter, *n.* One who practices vivisection.

vixen, viks'n, *n.* A she-fox; a snappish, bitter woman; a termagant. **vixenish,** viks'en-ish, *a.* Pertaining to a vixen.

vizier, vī-zēr', or vi'zi-ėr, *n.* A high political officer in Turkey, &c.

vocabulary, vō-kab'ū-lėr-i, *n.* A list of words arranged alphabetically and explained briefly; range of expression.

vocal, vō'kal, *a.* Pertaining to the voice; uttered by the voice; endowed

with a voice; having a vowel character. **vocalist,** vō'kal-ist, *n.* A vocal musician; a public singer. **vocalize,** vō'kal-īz, *vt.* To form into voice; to make vocal. **vocally,** vō'kal-li. *adv.* With voice; with an audible sound; in words.

vocation, vō-kā'shun, *n.* A calling; employment; profession; business.

vocative, vok'a-tiv, *a.* Relating to calling by name.—*n.* The vocative case.

vociferate, vō-sif'ėr-āt, *vi.* and *t.* (vociferating, vociferated). To cry out with vehemence; to exclaim. **vociferation,** vō-sif'ėr-ā"shun, *n.* A violent outcry; clamor. **vociferous,** vō-sif'ėr-us, *a.* Making a loud outcry; clamorous; noisy.

vodka, vod'ka, *n.* An intoxicating spirit distilled from rye, much used in Russia.

vogue, vōg', *n.* Temporary mode or fashion.

voice, vois, *n.* The sound uttered by the mouth; articulate human utterance; state of vocal organs; speech; sound emitted; right of expressing an opinion; vote; a form of verb inflection.—*vt.* (voicing, voiced). To utter or express; to declare. **voiceless,** vois'les, *a.* Having no voice or vote.

void, void, *a.* Empty; devoid; ineffectual; null.—*n.* An empty space.—*vt.* To make vacant; to quit; to nullify; to emit; to evacuate from the bowels. **voidance,** void'ans, *n.* Act of voiding; ejection from a benefice; vacancy.

volatile, vol'a-til, *a.* Readily diffusible in the atmosphere; flighty; airy; fickle. **volatility,** vol'a-til"i-ti, *n.* Quality of being volatile; capability of evaporating; flightiness; fickleness; levity. **volatilize,** vol'a-til-īz, *vt.* To cause to exhale or evaporate.—*vi.* To become vaporous.

volcano, vol-kā'no, *n.*; pl. **-oes.** A mountain emitting clouds of vapor, gases, showers of ashes, lava, &c. **volcanic,** vol-kan'ik, *a.* Pertaining to volcanoes; produced by a volcano.

vole, vōl, *n.* A rodent animal resembling a rat or mouse; a deal at cards that draws all the tricks.

volition, vō-lish'un, *n.* Act or power of willing; will.

volley, vol'i, *n.* A discharge of a number of missile weapons, as small-arms; emission of many things at once.—*vt.* and *i.* To discharge or be discharged in a volley; to sound like a volley.

volleyball, vol"i-bal', *n.* An athletic team game played by hitting a large, inflated ball back and forth by hand over a net.

volt, vōlt, *n.* A sudden movement in fencing to avoid a thrust; the unit of electromotive force.

voltage, vōl'tij, *n.* Electromotive force expressed in volts.

voluble, vol'ū-bl, *a.* Rolling round or revolving; glib in speech; over fluent. **volubility,** vol-ū-bil'i-ti, *n.* Great readiness or fluency of speech.

volume, vol'yum, *n.* Something rolled up; a book; a coil; a convolution; mass or bulk; quantity or strength. **voluminous,** vō-lū'mi-nus, *a.* Bulky; being in many volumes; having written much; copious.

voluntary, vol'un-tēr-i, *a.* Willing; free to act; spontaneous; regulated by the will.—*n.* A volunteer; a supporter of voluntaryism; an organ solo during a church service. **voluntarily**, vol'un-tēr-i-li, *adv.* Spontaneously; of one's own free-will.

volunteer, vol'un-tēr", *n.* A person who enters into military or other service of his own free-will.—*a.* Pertaining to volunteers.—*vt.* To offer or bestow voluntarily.—*vi.* To enter into any service voluntarily.

voluptuary, vō-lup"tū-er'i, *n.* One addicted to luxury; a sensualist. **voluptuous**, vō-lup'tū-us, *a.* Pertaining to sensual pleasure; luxurious. **voluptuously**, vō-lup'tū-us-li, *adv.* Luxuriously; sensually.

volute, vō-lūt', *n.* A spiral scroll characteristic of Ionic and Corinthian capitals. **voluted**, vō-lūt'ed, *a.* Having a volute or volutes.

vomit, vo'mit, *vi.* To eject the contents of the stomach by the mouth.—*vt.* To eject from the stomach; to belch forth. —*n.* Matter ejected from the stomach; an emetic. **vomitory**, vom'i-tō-ri, *a.* Causing vomiting.—*n.* An emetic.

voodoo, vō'dō, *n.* A person among the negroes who professes to be a sorcerer; sorcery; an evil spirit.

voracious, vō-rā'shus, *a.* Eating or swallowing greedily; ravenous; rapacious. **voracity**, vō-ras'i-ti, *n.* Quality of being voracious; greediness of appetite.

vortex, vor'teks, *n.*; pl. **-tices** or **-texes**. A whirling motion in any fluid; a whirlpool or a whirlwind; an eddy.

votary, vō'ta-ri, *n.* One who is bound by a vow; one devoted to some particular service, state of life, &c. **votaress**, vō'ta-res, *n.* A female votary.

vote, vōt, *n.* Act or power of expressing opinion or choice; a suffrage; thing conferred by vote; result of voting; votes collectively.—*vi.* (voting, voted). To give a vote.—*vt.* To choose or grant by vote. **voter**, vōt'ér, *n.* One who votes; an elector.

votive, vō'tiv, *a.* Pertaining to a vow; promised or given in consequence of a vow.

vouch, vouch, *vt.* To attest; to affirm; to answer for.—*vi.* To bear witness; to stand surety. **voucher**, vouch'ér, *n.* One who vouches; a paper which serves to vouch the truth of accounts, or to confirm facts of any kind; a written evidence of the payment of money. **vouchsafe**, vouch-sāf', *vt.* (vouchsafing, vouchsafed). To condescend to grant; to concede.—*vi.* To deign.

vow, vou, *n.* A solemn promise; an oath; promise of fidelity.—*vt.* To promise solemnly; \ dedicate, as to a divine power.—*vi.* To make vows.

vowel, vou'el, *n.* A sound produced by opening the mouth and giving utterance to voice; the letter which represents such a sound.—*a.* Pertaining to a vowel; vocal.

voyage, voi'ij, *n.* A journey by water to a distance.—*vi.* (voyaging, voyaged). To pass by water. **voyager**, voi'ij-ér, *n.* One who voyages.

vulcanite, vul'kan-īt, *n.* A superior vulcanized india-rubber; ebonite. **vulcanize**, vul'kan-īz, *vt.* To harden (india-rubber) by combining with sulphur, &c.

vulgar, vul'gér, *a.* Pertaining to the common people; vernacular; common; coarse. **vulgarian**, vul-gār'i-an, *n.* A vulgar person. **vulgarism**, vul'gér-izm, *n.* A vulgar phrase or expression; vulgarity. **vulgarity**, vul-gar'i-ti, *n.* Coarseness; an act of low manners.

Vulgate, vul'gāt, *n.* The Latin version of the Scriptures used by the R. Catholic church.

vulnerable, vul'nér-a-bl, *a.* That may be wounded; liable to injury.

vulture, vul'tûr, *n.* A bird of prey which lives chiefly on carrion. **vulturine**, vul'tūr-īn, *a.* Belonging to or resembling the vulture.

W

wad, wod, *n.* A soft mass of fibrous material used for stuffing; material for stopping the charge in a gun.—*vt.* (wadding, wadded). To furnish with a wad or wadding.

wadding, wod'ing, *n.* A soft fibrous stuff used for stuffing articles of dress; wad.

waddle, wod'l, *vi.* (waddling, waddled). To walk with a rolling gait; to toddle.

wade, wād, *vi.* (wading, waded). To walk through a substance that hinders the lower limbs, as water; to move or pass with labor.—*vt.* To ford. **wader**, wād'ér, *n.* One that wades; a wading or grallatorial bird.

wafer, wā'fér, *n.* A thin cake, as of bread; a thin disk of paste for fastening letters.—*vt.* To seal with a wafer.

waft, wäft, *vt.* To impel through water or air.—*vi.* To sail or float.—*n.* A sweep, as with the arm; a breath of wind. **waftage**, wäf'tij, *n.* The act of wafting; state of being wafted.

wag, wag, *vt.* and *i.* (wagging, wagged). To swing or sway; to wave; to nod.—*n.* A wit; a joker.

wage, wāj, *vt.* (waging, waged). To carry on; to engage in, as in a contest.— *n.* Payment for work done; hire; recompense; generally in *pl.*

wager, wā'jér, *n.* A bet; stake laid; subject on which bets are laid.—*vt.* and *i.* To bet; to stake.

waggish, wag'ish, *a*. Roguish in merriment; jocular; sportive.

waggle, wag'l, *vi*. and *t*. (waggling, waggled). To sway; to wag with short movements

wagon, waggon, wag'un, *n*. A four-wheeled vehicle for heavy loads.

waif, wāf, *n*. A stray article; a neglected, homeless wretch.

wail, wāl, *vt*. To lament; to bewail.—*vi*. To weep.—*n*. A mournful cry or sound.

wailing, wāl'ing, *n*. Loud weeping.

wainscot, wān'skut, *n*. The panel-work that lines the walls of a room.—*vt*. (wainscoting, wainscoted). To line with wainscot. **wainscoting**, wān'skut-ing, *n*. Wainscot, or the material used for it.

waist, wāst, *n*. That part of the human body between the ribs and hips; middle part of a ship. **waistband**, wāst''band', *n*. The band of trousers, &c., which encompasses the waist. **waistcoat**, wāst''kōt', *n*. A short sleeveless garment worn under the coat; a vest.

wait, wāt, *vi*. To stay in expectation; to continue in patience; to attend; to serve at table.—*vt*. To await.—*n*. Act of waiting; ambush; a musician who promenades in the night about Christmas time (Eng.). **waiter**, wāt'ėr, *n*. One who waits; a male attendant; a small tray or salver. **waitress**, wāt'res, *n*. A female waiter.

waive, wāv, *vt*. (waiving, waived). To relinquish; to forego.

wake, wāk, *vi*. (waking, woke or waked). To be awake; to awake; to become active.—*vt*. To rouse from sleep; to arouse.—*n*. The feast of the dedication of a parish church (Eng.); a vigil; the watching of a dead body prior to burial; track left by a ship; track in general. **wakeful**, wāk'fụl, *a*. Keeping awake in bed; indisposed to sleep; watchful; vigilant. **waken**, wāk'en, *vi*. To wake.—*vt*. To rouse from sleep; to rouse into action.

walk, wak, *vi*. To advance by steps without running; to go about; to behave.—*vt*. To pass over or through on foot; to lead about.—*n*. A short excursion on foot; gait; an avenue, promenade, &c.; sphere; way of living; tract of ground or grazing. **walker**, wak'ėr, *n*. One who walks; a pedestrian. **walking**, wak'ing, *n*. The act or practice of moving on the feet without running; practice of taking walks; pedestrianism. **walking stick**, wak'ing stik, *n*. A staff or stick carried in the hand in walking.

walkout, wak''out', *n*. A labor strike.

wall, wal, *n*. A structure of stone or brick, inclosing a space, forming a division, supporting a weight, &c.; side of a building or room; means of protection.—*vt*. To inclose with a wall; to defend by walls.

wallet, wol'et, *n*. A bag or knapsack; sack; bundle; pocket-book.

walleye, wal''ī', *n*. An eye in which the iris is of a very light gray or whitish color.

wallflower, wal''flou'ėr, *n*. A plant with fragrant yellowish flowers; a shy and unpopular person at a dance.

Walloon, wo-lön', *n*. A people inhabiting part of Belgium and north-eastern France; their language, a French dialect.

wallop, wol'op, *vt*. To beat; to drub; to thrash.

wallow, wol'ō, *vi*. To tumble and roll in water or mire; to live in filth or gross vice.

Wall Street. The chief financial center in the U.S., located in downtown New York.

walnut, wal'nut, *n*. A valuable tree, a native of Persia; the edible nut of the tree.

walrus, wol'rus, *n*. A huge marine carnivorous mammal inhabiting the arctic seas.

waltz, walts, *n*. A kind of dance for two persons; music for the dance.—*vi*. To dance a waltz.

wampum, wom'pum, *n*. Small beads made of shells, used by the American Indians as money or ornaments.

wan, won, *a*. Dark or gloomy; languid of look; pale.

wand, wond, *n*. A long flexible stick; a rod; a staff of authority; a baton.

wander, won'dėr, *vi*. To ramble here and there; to roam; to rove; to err; to be delirious.—*vt*. To traverse. **wanderer**, won'dėr-ėr, *n*. One who wanders; a rambler; one that goes astray. **wandering**, won'dėr-ing, *a*. Given to wander; unsettled.—*n*. A traveling without a settled course; aberration.

wane, wān, *vt*. (waning, waned). To diminish; to grow less, as the moon; to fail; to decline.—*n*. Decline; decrease.

want, wont, *n*. State of not having; deficiency; lack; need; indigence.—*vt*. To be without; to lack; to require; to desire.—*vi*. To be deficient; to be in want.

wanton, won'tun, *a*. Not kept in due restraint; unprovoked; lustful; frolicsome; rank.—*n*. A lewd person; a trifler.—*vi*. To revel unrestrainedly; to sport lasciviously. **wantonly**, won'tun-li, *adv*. Without restraint or provocation; sportively; lasciviously.

wapiti, wop'i-ti, *n*. The North American stag.

war, war, *n*. A contest between nations or parties carried on by force of arms; profession of arms; art of war; hostility; enmity.—*vi*. (warring, warred). To make or carry on war; to strive.

warble, war'bl, *vt*. and *i*. (warbling, warbled). To utter musically in a quavering manner; to carol; to sing musically.—*n*. A quavering melodious sound; a song.

warbler, war'blėr, *n*. A singer; a song-bird.

war cry, war krī, *n*. A word, cry, motto, or phrase used in common by troops in battle.

ward, ward, *vt*. To guard; to fend off; to turn aside.—*n*. Guard; a defensive motion or position in fencing; custody; guardianship; a minor who is under guardianship; a division of a town or county; apartment of a hospital.

warden, war'dn, *n*. A guardian; a keeper; head of a college; superior of a conventual church.

warder, war'dèr, *n.* A guard; a keeper.

wardrobe, ward'rōb, *n.* A piece of furniture in which wearing apparel is kept; a person's wearing apparel collectively.

wardroom, ward'rōm', *n.* A room in a warship where the principal officers mess.

wardship, ward'ship, *n.* Guardianship; also pupilage.

ware, wār, *n.* Articles of merchandise; goods; generally in *pl.*; sea-weeds, employed as a manure, &c.—*a.* On one's guard; aware: *poet.*—*vt.* To beware of: *poet.*

warehouse, wār'hous', *n.* A storehouse for goods; a large store.—*vt.* To deposit or secure in a warehouse. **warehouseman**, wār'hous'man, *n.* One who keeps or is employed in a warehouse.

warfare, war'fār', *n.* Military service; war; contest; hostilities.

warily, wār'i-li, *adv.* Cautiously.

warlike, war'lik', *a.* Pertaining to war; military; fit for war; disposed for war.

warm, warm, *a.* Having moderate heat; flushed; zealous; excitable; brisk; rich. —*vt.* To make warm; to animate; to interest.—*vi.* To become warm or animated. **warmer**, war'mèr, *n.* One who or that which warms. **warmhearted**, warm"har'ted, *a.* Having warmth of heart; cordial; sincere; hearty. **warmly**, warm'li, *adv.* In a warm manner; with heat; hotly; eagerly; earnestly. **warmth**, warmth, *n.* Gentle heat; cordiality; ardor; animation; enthusiasm; slight anger or irritation.

warn, warn, *vt.* To caution against; to admonish; to advise; to inform previously. **warning**, warn'ing, *n.* Act of one who warns; caution against danger, &c.; admonition; previous notice.

warp, warp, *vt.* and *i.* To turn or twist out of shape; to contort; to pervert; to move, as a ship, by a rope attached to something.—*n.* The threads extended lengthwise in a loom; a rope used in moving a ship; deposit of rich mud; twist of wood in drying. **warped**, warpt, *a.* Twisted by shrinking; perverted.

warrant, wor'ant, *vt.* To guarantee; to authorize; to justify.—*n.* An act or instrument investing one with authority; guarantee; document authorizing an officer to seize an offender; authority; a voucher; right. **warrant officer**, wo'rant of'is-èr, *n.* An officer ranking below a commissioned officer. **warranty**, wo'ran-ti, *n.* Warrant; guarantee; authority; a legal deed of security.

warren, wor'en, *n.* Ground appropriated for rabbits; a preserve in a river for fish.

warrior, war'i-èr, *n.* A soldier; a brave or able soldier.

warship, war'ship', *n.* A ship constructed for engaging in warfare; a man-of-war.

wart, wart, *n.* A hard dry growth on the skin.

wary, wār'i, *c.* Cautious; prudent.

was, woz, *v.* The first and third person singular of the past tense of *to be.*

wash, wosh, *vt.* To apply water, &c., to, to cleanse; to flow along or dash against; to remove by ablution; to tint lightly.— *vi.* To cleanse one's self by water; to stand the operation of washing; to stand the test.—*n.* Act of washing; clothes washed on one occasion; flow or dash of water; sound made by water; a shallow; swill; lotion; thin coat of color or metal. **wash basin**, wosh bā'sn, *n.* A basin for washing the face and hands in. **washboard**, wosh"bōrd', *n.* A board with a ribbed surface for washing clothes on; a board to prevent the sea from breaking over the gunwale of a boat; a skirting-board. **washer**, wosh'èr, *n.* One who or that which washes; a ring of iron, leather, &c., used under a nut that is screwed on a bolt. **washerwoman**, wosh'èr-wu'man, *n.* A woman that washes clothes for hire. **washing**, wosh'ing, *n.* Act of cleansing with water; ablution; clothes washed. **washstand**, wosh"stand', *n.* A piece of bedroom furniture supporting a basin. **wash tub**, wosh tub, *n.* A tub in which clothes are washed. **washy**, wosh'i, *a.* Watery; highly diluted; thin; weak; feeble; worthless.

washout, wosh"out', *n.* A washing out of soil by rain or flood; a failure. *Slang.*

wasp, wosp, *n.* An active, stinging, winged insect, resembling the bee. **waspish**, wosp'ish, *a.* Like a wasp; venomous; irritable; snappish.

wassail, wos'l, *n.* A festive occasion with drinking of healths; a drinking bout; liquor used on such occasions.—*vi.* To hold a merry drinking meeting.

waste, wāst, *vt.* (wasting, wasted). To make desolate; to ravage; to wear away gradually; to squander.—*vi.* To decrease gradually.—*a.* Desolate; spoiled; refuse. —*n.* Act of wasting; prodigality; refuse matter; gradual decrease; a desert region. **wasteful**, wāst'ful, *a.* Causing waste; destructive; ruinous; lavish; prodigal. **waster**, wās'tèr, *n.* One who wastes; a prodigal; a squanderer. **wasting**, wās'ting, *a.* Such as to waste; desolating; enfeebling.

watch, woch, *n.* A keeping awake to guard, &c.; vigilance; a guard; time during which a person is on guard or duty; a small pocket time-piece.—*vi.* To keep awake; to give heed; to act as a guard, &c.; to wait.—*vt.* To look with close attention at or on; to tend; to guard. **watchdog**, woch"dog', *n.* A dog kept to guard premises and property. **watcher**, woch'èr, *n.* One who watches. **watchful**, woch'ful, *a.* Keeping on the watch; vigilant; attentive; cautious. **watchmaker**, woch"māk'èr, *n.* One who makes or repairs watches. **watchman**, woch'man, *n.* A guard; a caretaker on duty at night. **watchtower**, woch"tou'èr, *n.* A tower on which a sentinel is placed to watch. **watchword**, woch"wèrd', *n.* A word by which sentinels distinguish a friend from an enemy; a motto.

water, wa'tèr, *n.* A transparent fluid; a fluid consisting of hydrogen and oxygen; the sea; rain; saliva; urine; color or luster of a diamond, &c.—*vt.* To wet or supply with water; to give a wavy appearance to, as silk.—*vi.* To shed liquid matter; to take in water; to gather saliva; to have a longing desire.

water closet, wạ'tẽr kloz'et, *n.* A privy in which the discharges are carried away by water.

water color, wạ'tẽr kul'ẽr, *n.* A pigment ground up with water and isinglass or other mucilage instead of oil.

watercourse, wạ'tẽr-kōrs', *n.* A stream of water; a channel for water.

watered, wạ'tẽrd, *a.* Having a wavy and shiny appearance on the surface.

waterfall, wạ'tẽr-fạl', *n.* A fall or steep descent in a stream; a cascade.

water front. Land and buildings fronting on a body of water.

water hole. A small pond or drinking place used by animals; pool.

watering place, wạ'tẽr-ing plās, *n.* A place to which people resort for mineral waters, or for bathing, &c.

water level, wạ'tẽr lev'el, *n.* The level at which water stands; a leveling instrument in which water is employed.

water line, wạ'tẽr līn, *n.* The line formed by the surface of water, as on ships.

waterlogged, wạ'tẽr-logd', *a.* Floating but full of water, as a ship.

watermark, wạ'tẽr-märk', *n.* A mark indicating the rise and fall of water; a mark made in paper during manufacture.

water mill, wạ'tẽr mil, *n.* A mill whose machinery is driven by means of water.

water moccasin. A poisonous water snake of the southern United States, which reaches a length of over four feet.

water power, wạ'tẽr pou-ẽr, *n.* The power of water employed to drive machinery.

waterproof, wạ'tẽr-prōf', *a.* So compact as not to admit water.—*n.* Cloth made waterproof; a garment of such cloth.—*vt.* To render impervious to water.

watershed, wạ'tẽr-shed', *n.* A rise of land from which rivers, &c., naturally flow in opposite directions.

water skiing. A water sport in which a person on water skis is towed by a speedboat.

waterspout, wạ'tẽr-spout', *n.* A column of spray or water drawn up from the sea or a lake by a violent whirlwind.

watertight, wạ'tẽr-tīt', *a.* So tight as to retain or not to admit water; stanch.

waterway, wạ'tẽr-wā', *n.* That part of a river, the sea, &c., through which vessels sail.

waterwheel, wạ'tẽr-whēl', *n.* A wheel for raising water, or moved by water.

waterworks, wạ'tẽr-wẽrks', *n.pl.* The works and appliances for the distribution of water to communities; ornamental fountains.

watery, wạ'tẽr-i, *a.* Pertaining to or like water; thin; moist; tasteless; insipid.

wattle, wot'l, *n.* A hurdle or interlaced rods.—*vt.* (wattling, wattled). To interlace (twigs or branches); to plait.

wave, wāv, *vi.* and *t.* (waving, waved). To sway or play loosely; to undulate; to brandish; to beckon.—*n.* A swell or ridge on moving water; anything resembling a wave; an undulation; a signal made by waving the hand, a flag. **wave**

length. In physics, the distance between two successive places in the wave train that are in the same state of compression. **wavelet,** wāv'let, *n.* A small wave. **waver,** wā'vẽr, *vi.* To wave gently; to fluctuate; to be undetermined. **waverer,** wā'vẽr-ẽr, *n.* One who wavers. **wavy,** wāv'i, *a.* Rising or swelling in waves; full of waves; undulating.

wax, waks, *n.* A tenacious substance excreted by bees or in the ear; any similar substance; sealing-wax.—*vt.* To smear or rub with wax.—*vi.* To increase; to grow; to become. **wax cloth,** waks kloth, *n.* Cloth covered with a waxy coating; floor-cloth. **waxen,** waks'en, *a.* Made of wax. **waxwork,** waks'-wẽrk', *n.* Work in wax; figures of persons in wax as near reality as possible. **waxy,** waks'i, *a.* Resembling wax; made of wax; abounding in wax.

way, wā, *n.* A track, path, or road of any kind; distance traversed; progress; direction; line of business; condition; device; method; course; *pl.* the timbers on which a ship is launched.

wayfarer, wā''fār'ẽr, *n.* One who fares or travels; a traveler; a foot-passenger. **wayfaring,** wā''fār'ing, *a.* Traveling; passing; being on a journey.

waylay, wā'lā''. *vt.* To lay one's self in the way of; to beset in ambush.

wayside, wā''sīd', *n.* The side of a road. —*a.* Growing, situated, &c., by sides of roads.

wayward, wā'wẽrd, *a.* Full of troublesome whims; froward; peevish; perverse. **waywardly,** wā'wẽrd-li, *adv.* Perversely.

we, wē, *pron.* Plural of *I.*

weak, wek, *a.* Not strong; feeble; infirm; frail; silly; vacillating; wanting resolution; wanting moral courage; ineffective; denoting verbs inflected by adding a letter or syllable. **weaken,** wēk'n, *vt.* To make weak or weaker.—*vi.* To become weak or weaker. **weakling,** wēk'ling, *n.* A weak creature. **weakly,** wēk'li, *adv.* Feebly; not forcibly; injudiciously.—*a.* Infirm. **weakness,** wēk'nes, *n.* The state or quality of being weak; irresolution; want of validity; a failing.

weal, wēl, *n.* Welfare; prosperity; happiness; mark of a stripe; wale.

wealth, welth, *n.* Riches; affluence; opulence; abundance. **wealthy,** wel'thi, *a.* Possessing wealth; rich; opulent; abundant; ample.

wean, wēn, *vt.* To accustom to do without the mother's milk; to alienate; to disengage from any habit. **weanling,** wēn'ling, *n.* A child or animal newly weaned.

weapon, wep'un, *n.* Any instrument of offense or defense.

wear, wār, *vt.* (pret. wore, pp. worn). To carry as belonging to dress; to have on; to waste by rubbing; to destroy by degrees; to produce by rubbing; to exhibit.—*vi.* To last well or ill; to waste gradually; to make gradual progress.—*n.* Act of wearing; diminution by friction, use, time, &c.; fashion. **wearer,** wār'-ẽr, *n.* One who wears. **wearing,** wār'-

ing, a. Used by being worn; such as to wear; exhausting.

weary, wēr'i, a. Having the strength or patience exhausted; tired; disgusted; tiresome.—vt. (wearying, wearied). To make weary; to tire.—vi. To become weary.

weasel, wē'zl, n. A small carnivorous animal akin to the ferret, &c.

weather, weᴛн'ėr, n. The general atmospheric conditions at any particular time.—a. Turned towards the wind; windward.—vt. To affect by the weather; to sail to the windward of; to bear up against and overcome. **weatherbeaten**, weᴛн"ėr-bēt'n, a. Beaten by the weather; hardened by exposure. **weathercock**, weᴛн"ėr-kok', n. Something in the shape of a cock, &c., for showing the direction of the wind; a vane; a fickle person. **weatherglass**, weᴛн"ėr-gläs', n. A barometer. **weather-wise**, weᴛн"ėr-wiz', a. Wise or skillful in forecasting the weather. **weather-worn**, weᴛн"ėr-wōrn', a. Worn by the action of the weather.

weatherproof, weᴛн"ėr-pröf', a. Able to withstand exposure to all kinds of weather.—vt. To insulate against weather.

weave, wēv, vt. (weaving, pret. wove, pp. woven). To form by interlacing thread, yarn, &c.; to form a tissue with; to work up; to contrive.—vi. To practice weaving; to be woven. **weaver**, wēv'ėr, n. One who weaves; one whose occupation is to weave. **weaving**, wēv'ing, n. Act or art of producing cloth or other textile fabrics.

web, web, n. The whole piece of cloth woven in a loom; a large roll of paper; membrane which unites the toes of water-fowl; the threads which a spider spins; a cobweb; anything carefully contrived. **webbed**, webd, a. Having the toes united by a membrane or web. **webbing**, web'ing, n. A strong fabric of hemp, two or three inches wide.

webfoot, web"fut', n. A foot whose toes are united by a membrane.

webfooted, web"fut'ed, a. Having the toes united by a membrane.

wed, wed, vt. and i. (wedding, wedded, and wed). To marry; to unite closely. **wedded**, wed'ed, a. Pertaining to matrimony; intimately united. **wedding**, wed'ing, n. Marriage; nuptials.

wedge, wej, n. A body sloping to a thin edge at one end.—vt. (wedging, wedged). To drive as a wedge is driven; to crowd or compress; to fasten or split with a wedge.

wedlock, wed'lok, n. The wedded state; marriage.

Wednesday, wenz'di, n. The fourth day of the week.

wee, wē, a. Small; little.

weed, wēd, n. Any plant regarded as useless or troublesome; a sorry, worthless animal; a cigar; pl. mourning dress of a widow or female.—vt. To free from weeds or anything offensive. **weedy**, wēd'i, a. Consisting of weeds; abounding with weeds; worthless.

week, wēk, n. The space of seven days;

space from one Sunday to another. **weekday**, wēk'dā', n. Any day of the week except Sunday. **weekly**, wēk'li, a. Coming or done once a week; lasting for a week.—n. A periodical appearing once a week.—adv. Once a week.

ween, wēn, vi. To think; to fancy.

weep, wēp, vi. (pret and pp. wept). To manifest grief, &c., by shedding tears; to drip; to droop.—vt. To lament; to shed or drop, as tears; to get rid of by weeping. **weeper**, wēp'ėr, n. One who weeps; a sort of white linen cuff on a mourning dress. **weeping**, wēp'ing, n. Lamenting; the shedding of tears.

weever, wē'vėr, n. A spined edible fish.

weevil, wē'vl, n. An insect of the beetle family, destructive to grain, fruit, &c.

weft, weft, n. The woof of cloth.

weigh, wā, vt. To raise; to find the heaviness of; to allot or take by weight; to consider; to balance; to burden.—vi. To have weight; to amount to in weight; to bear heavily. **weight**, wāt, n. Heaviness; gravity; the amount which anything weighs; a metal standard for weighing; a heavy mass; pressure; burden; importance; moment.—vt. To add to the heaviness of. **weighty**, wāt'i, a. Heavy; important; momentous; cogent.

weir, wēr, n. A dam across a stream for supplying water to a mill, irrigation, &c.; a fence of twigs in a stream for catching fish.

weird, wērd, n. Destiny; fate.—a. Connected with fate; unearthly.

welcome, wel'kum, a. Received with gladness; grateful; pleasing.—n. Greeting or kind reception.—vt. (welcoming, welcomed). To receive kindly and hospitably.

weld, weld, vt. To hammer into union, as heated iron; to unite closely.—n. A junction by hammering of heated metals.

welfare, wel'fār, n. Well-being; prosperity; happiness.

welkin, wel'kin, n. The sky; the heavens; the firmament.

well, wel, adv. In a proper manner; rightly; commendably; considerably.—a. Being in health; comfortable; fortunate; convenient; proper.

well-being, wel'bē'ing, n. State of being well; prosperity; happiness; welfare.

wellborn, wel'born', a. Born of a good family; of good descent.

well-bred, wel'bred', a. Of good breeding; polite; refined.

well-meaning, wel'mēn'ing, a. Having a good intention.

well-spoken, wel'spōk-n, a. Spoken well; speaking well; civic; courteous.

wellspring, wel"spring', n. A fountain; a source of continual supply.

well-timed, wel'timd', a. Done at a proper time; opportune.

well-to-do, wel'tö-dö', a. Being in easy circumstances; well off; prosperous.

Welsh, welsh, a. Pertaining to Wales or to its people.—n. The language of Wales; pl. the inhabitants of Wales.

welt, welt, n. A border or edging; a strip of leather sewed round the upper of a boot to which the sole is fastened.

—*vt.* To furnish with a welt; to beat severely.

welter, wel'tẽr, *vi.* To roll; to tumble about; to wallow.—*n.* A turmoil.—*a.* Said of a borserace in which extra heavy weights are laid on some horses.

wen, wen, *n.* A harmless fatty tumor.

wench, wench, *n.* A young woman; a woman of loose character.—*vi.* To frequent the company of women of ill-fame.

wend, wend, *vt.* To go; to direct.—*vi.* To go; to travel.

went, went. Used as the pret. of *go.*

were, wer, *v.* The past tense plural indicative and the past subjunctive of *be.*

werewolf, wẽr'wulf', *n.* A man transformed into a wolf.

wert, wẽrt. The second person singular of *was* or *were.*

Wesleyan, wes'li-an, *a.* Pertaining to the religious body established by John Wesley.—*n.* A Methodist.

west, west, *n.* The point where the sun sets, opposite the east.—*a.* Being in or towards the west; coming from the west.—*adv.* To the west. **westerly,** wes'tẽr-li, *a.* Tending or being towards the west; coming from the west.—*adv.* Tending or moving towards the west. **western,** wes'tẽrn, *a.* Being in or moving towards the west; coming from the west. **westernmost,** wes'tẽrn-mōst, *a.* Farthest to the west. **westing,** wes'ting, *n.* Space or distance westward. **westmost,** west'most, *a.* Farthest to the west. **westward,** west'wẽrd, *adv.* Toward the west. **westwardly,** west'-wẽrd-li, *adv.* In a direction toward the west. **westwards,** west'wẽrdz, *adv.* Westward.

Western Hemisphere. That half of the world which includes North and South America.

West Point. The U.S. military academy located at West Point, N.Y.

wet, wet, *a.* Covered or soaked with water; moist; rainy.—*n.* Water; moisture; rain.—*vt.* (wetting, wetted). To make wet; to soak in liquor.

wether, weTH'ẽr, *n.* A ram castrated.

wet nurse, wet nẽrs, *n.* A nurse engaged to suckle an infant.

whack, whak, *vt.* and *i.* To thwack; to give a resounding blow to.—*n.* A resounding blow; a thwack.

whale, hwãl, *n.* The largest of sea animals, a mammal. **whalebone,** hwãl"bōn', *n.* An elastic horny substance obtained from the upper jaw of certain whales; baleen. **whaler,** hwãl'ẽr, *n.* A person or ship employed in the whale-fishery.

wharf, hwarf, *n.*; pl. **-fs** or **-ves.** A quay for loading or unloading ships.

what, hwot, *pron.* An interrogative pronoun used chiefly of things; employed adjectively as equivalent to how great, remarkable, &c.; substantively as equivalent to the thing (or things) which.

whatever, hwot-ev'ẽr, *pron.* Used as substantive, anything that; all that; used as an adj., of any kind.

whatnot, hwot'not, *n.* A piece of household furniture with shelves for books, &c.

whatsoever, whatsoe'er, hwot'sō-ev"ẽr, hwot'sō-ãr", *pron.* Whatever (emphatic).

wheat, hwēt, *n.* A cereal plant; its seeds, which yield a white nutritious flour. **wheatear,** hwēt"ēr', *n.* An ear of wheat. **wheaten,** whēt'n, *a.* Pertaining to wheat; made of wheat.

wheedle, hwē'dl, *vt.* and *i.* (wheedling, wheedled). To flatter; to cajole; to coax.

wheel, hwēl, *n.* A circular frame turning on an axis; an old instrument of torture; a revolution; a cycle.—*vt.* To cause to turn round.—*vi.* To turn round; to revolve; to roll forward. **wheelbarrow,** hwēl"bar'o, *n.* A barrow with one wheel. **wheeld,** hwēld, *a.* Having wheels. **wheelwright,** hwēl"rīt', *n.* A wright, whose occupation is to make wheels.

wheel base. The distance, usually in inches, between front and rear axles of automobiles, &c.

wheel chair. A chair on wheels for invalids which can be moved by the occupant.

wheeze, hwēz, *vi.* (wheezing, wheezed). To breathe hard and audibly, as persons affected with asthma. **wheezy,** whēz'i, *a.* Affected with wheezing.

whelk, hwelk, *n.* A shell-fish, a species of periwinkle or mollusk; a pustule.

whelm, hwelm, *vt.* To engulf; to swallow up; to ruin or devastate.

whelp, hwelp, *n.* A puppy; a cub; a young man.—*vi.* To bring forth whelps.—*vt.* To bring forth; to originate.

when, hwen, *adv.* and *conj.* At what or which time; while; whereas; used substantively with *since* or *till.*

whence, hwens, *adv.* and *conj.* From what place, source, &c.; how.

whencesoever, hwens'sō-ev"ẽr, *adv.* From whatever place, cause, or source.

whene'er, whenever, hwen'ãr", hwen'-ev'ẽr, *adv.* At whatever time.

where, hwãr, *adv.* and *conj.* At or in what place; at the place in which; whither.

whereabout, hwãr"a-bout', *adv.* and *conj.* About what place; concerning which.

whereabouts, hwãr"a-bouts', *adv.* and *conj.* Near what or which place; whereabout; often used substantively.

whereas, hwãr-az', *conj.* Things being so: when really or in fact.

whereat, hwãr-at', *adv.* and *conj.* At which or what.

whereby, hwãr-bī', *adv.* and *conj.* By which or what.

wherefore, hwãr'for, *adv.* and *conj.* For which reason; consequently; why.

wherein, hwãr-in', *adv.* and *conj.* In which; in which thing, time, respect, &c.

whereof, hwãr-ov', *adv.* and *conj.* Of which or what.

whereon, hwãr-on', *adv.* and *conj.* On which or on what.

whereto, hwãr-tö', *adv.* and *conj.* To which or what; to what end.

whereupon, hwar'u-pon", *adv.* Upon which or what; in consequence of which.

wherever, **where'er**, hwār'ev'èr, hwār'âr", *adv.* At whatever place.

wherewith, **wherewithal**, hwār-with', hwār'with-al', *adv.* and *conj.* With which or what.—*n.* Means or money.

wheery, hwer'i, *n.* A light river boat for passengers.

whet, bwet, *vt.* (whetting, whetted or whet). To rub to sharpen; to edge; to excite; to stimulate.—*n.* Act of sharpening; something that stimulates the appetite.

whether, hwetн'ér, *pron.* Which of two.—*conj.* or *adv.* Which of two or more, introducing alternative clauses.

whetstone, hwet'stōn', *n.* A stone used for sharpening instruments by friction.

whew, hwū, *exclam.* A sound made with the lips, expressing astonishment or contempt.—*n.* The sound thus uttered.

whey, hwā, *n.* The thin part of milk, from which the curd, &c., have been separated.

which, hwich, *pron.* An interrogative pronoun, used adjectively or substantively; a relative pronoun, the neuter of *who;* an indefinite pronoun, any one which.

whichever, **whichsoever**, hwich-ev'èr, hwich'sō-ev'èr, *pron.* No matter which; anyone.

whiff, bwif, *n.* A puff of air; a puff conveying a smell.—*vt.* and *i.* To puff; to throw out whiffs; to smoke.

Whig, hwig, *n.* A member of a political party in Britain, opposed to *Tories;* a member of the Liberal party, opposed to *Radicals;* in the Revolutionary War, a patriot.—*a.* Belonging to or composed of Whigs.

while, hwil, *n.* A time; short space of time.—*conj.* During the time that; though.—*vt.* (whiling, whiled). To cause to pass pleasantly: usually with *away.*

whilst, hwilst, *adv.* While.

whim, hwim, *n.* A sudden fancy; caprice.

whimper, hwim'pèr, *vi.* To express grief with a whining voice.—*vt.* To utter in a low, whining tone.—*n.* A peevish cry.

whimsey, **whimsy**, hwim'zi, *n.* A whim; a caprice; a capricious notion.

whimsical, hwim'zik-al, *a.* Full of whims; capricious; odd.

whine, hwin, *vi.* (whining, whined). To express distress by a plaintive drawling cry.—*n.* A drawling plaintive tone; mean or affected complaint.

whinny, hwin'i, *vi.* (whinnying, whinnied). To neigh, especially in a low tone.—*n.* Neigh of a horse.

whip, hwip, *vt.* (whipping, whipped). To put or snatch with a sudden motion; to flog; to drive with lashes; to beat into a froth.—*vi.* To start suddenly and run.—*n.* A lash; the driver of a carriage; a legislator who looks after the attendance of his party; the summons he sends out.

whip hand, hwip hand, *n.* The hand that holds the whip; control.

whipper snapper, hwip'ér snap'ér, *n.* A diminutive, insignificant person.

whipping, hwip'ing, *n.* Act of striking with a whip; flagellation.

whir, hwèr, *vi.* (whirring, whirred). To fly, revolve, &c., with a whizzing or buzzing sound; to whiz.—*n.* A buzzing sound.

whirl, hwèrl, *vt.* and *i.* To turn round rapidly; to move quickly.—*n.* A rapid turning.

whirligig, hwèrl'i-gig', *n.* A toy which children spin or whirl round.

whirlpool, hwèrl''pōl', *n.* An eddy or gulf where the water moves round in a circle.

whirlwind, hwèrl''wind', *n.* A whirling wind; a violent wind moving as if round an axis, this axis at the same time progressing.

whisk, hwisk, *vt.* To sweep or agitate with a light rapid motion.—*vi.* To move nimbly.—*n.* A rapid, sweeping motion; a small besom; an instrument for frothing cream, eggs, &c.

whisker, hwis'kèr, *n.* Long hair growing on the cheek.

whisky, **whiskey**, hwis'ki, *n.* An ardent spirit distilled generally from barley; a light one-horse chaise.

whisper, hwis'pèr, *vt.* To speak with a low sibilant voice; to converse secretly.—*vt.* To utter in a whisper.—*n.* A low soft sibilant voice; a faint utterance.

whispering, hwis'pèr-ing, *a.* Speaking in a whisper; having or giving a soft sibilant sound.—*n.* Act of one who whispers; talebearing.

whist, hwist, *interj.* Silence! hush!—*a.* Silent.—*n.* A game at cards, played by four persons.

whistle, hwis'l, *vi.* (whistling, whistled). To utter a clear shrill sound by forcing the breath through the lips; to warble; to sound shrilly.—*vt.* To utter or signal by whistling.—*n.* Sound produced by one who whistles; any similar sound; a small pipe blown with the breath; instrument sounded by steam.

whit, hwit, *n.* The smallest particle; tittle.

white, hwit, *a.* Being of the color of pure snow; pale; pallid; pure and unsullied.—*n.* The color of snow; a white pigment; white of an egg, eye, &c.—*vt.* (whiting, whited). To make white.

white lead, hwit led, *n.* A carbonate of lead much used in painting; ceruse.

white-livered, hwit'liv'èrd, *a.* Cowardly.

whiten, hwit'n, *vt.* To make white; to bleach; to blanch.—*vi.* To grow white.

whitewash, hwit'wosh', *n.* A composition of lime or whiting and water, for whitening walls, &c.—*vt.* To cover with whitewash; to restore the reputation of.

whither, hwiтн'ér, *adv.* To what or which place; where.

whiting, hwit'ing, *n.* A small fish of the cod tribe; pulverized chalk used in whitewashing, for cleaning plate, &c.

whitish, hwit'ish, *a.* Somewhat white.

Whitmonday, hwit'mun'dā, *n.* The Monday following Whitsunday.

Whitsunday, hwit'sun'dā, *n.* The seventh Sunday after Easter.

Whitsuntide, hwit″sun-tīd′, *n.* The season of Pentecost.

whittle, hwit′l, *n.* A large knife.—*vt.* (whittling, whittled). To cut or pare with a knife.

whiz, hwiz, *vi.* (whizzing, whizzed). To make a humming or hissing sound.—*n.* A hissing and humming sound.

who, hö, *pron.*; possessive **whose,** höz; objective **whom,** höm. A relative and interrogative pronoun always used substantively and with reference to persons.

whoever, hö′ev′ėr, *pron.* Any one without exception; any person whatever.

whole, hōl, *a.* Sound; healthy; healed; intact; entire.—*n.* An entire thing; total assemblage of parts.

wholesale, hōl′sāl′, *n.* Sale of goods by the entire piece or in large quantities.—*a.* Pertaining to trade in large quantities; priced for quantity sale, as to retailers or jobbers; priced lower than retail; extensive; indiscriminate.

wholesome, hōl′sum, *a.* Tending to promote health; salubrious; useful; salutary.

wholly, hōl′li, *adv.* As a whole; entirely.

whoop, höp or whöp, *vi.* To shout loudly; to hoot.—*vt.* To shout at; to hoot; to insult with shouts.—*n.* A shout; a loud clear call.

whooping cough, höp′ing kof, or höp′, *n.* A contagious ailment common in childhood, marked by a convulsive cough.

whopper, hwop′ėr, *n.* Anything uncommonly large; a manifest lie.

whore, hör, *n.* A prostitute; a harlot.—*vi.* (whoring, whored). To have to do with prostitutes.

whorl, whėrl or whorl, *n.* A ring of leaves, &c., of a plant all on the same plane.

whose, höz, *pron.* The possessive case of *who* or *which.*

whosoever, hö′sö-ev′ėr, *pron.* Any person whatever; any one.

why, whī, *adv.* and *conj.* For what reason; wherefore.

wick, wik, *n.* The loose spongy string or band in candles or lamps.

wicked, wik′ed, *a.* Evil in principle or practice; sinful; immoral; bad; roguish. **wickedly,** wik′ed-li, *adv.* In a wicked manner; viciously; immorally. **wickedness,** wik′ed-nes, *n.* Immorality; depravity; sin; a wicked act.

wicker, wik′ėr, *n.* A small pliable twig; work made of such twigs.—*a.* Made of plaited twigs.

wicket, wik′et, *n.* A small gate; in *cricket,* one of the three upright rods at which the bowler aims.

wide, wīd, *a.* Having a great extent each way; broad; extensive; liberal; remote from anything.—*adv.* At or to a distance; far from; astray. **wide-awake,** wīd′a-wāk, *a.* On the alert.—*n.* A soft felt hat with a broad brim. **widely,** wīd′li, *adv.* Extensively; far. **widen,** wīd′n, *vt.* To make wide or wider.—*vi.* To grow wide or wider.

widgeon, wigeon, wij′un, *n.* A migratory water-fowl of the duck group.

widow, wid′ō, *n.* A woman whose husband is dead.—*vt.* To bereave of a husband. **widower,** wid′ō-ėr, *n.* A man whose wife is dead.

width, width, *n.* Breadth; extent from side to side.

wield, wēld, *vt.* To manage freely in the hands; to sway; to exercise. **wieldy,** wēld′i, *a.* Manageable.

wife, wīf, *n.*; pl. **wives,** wīvz. A married woman. **wifely,** wīf′li, *a.* Like or becoming a wife.

wig, wig, *n.* An artificial covering of hair for the head.

wight, wīt, *n.* A human being; a person.—*a.* Strong and active; of warlike prowess.

wigwam, wig′wam, *n.* A tent or hut of the North American Indians.

wild, wīld, *a.* Living in a state of nature; not tame; not cultivated; desert; stormy; furious; frolicsome; rash; extravagant; excited.—*n.* An uncultivated tract.

wilderness, wil′dėr-nes, *n.* A desert; waste; irregular collection of things.

wildfire, wīld″fīr′, *n.* A kind of lightning unaccompanied by thunder; erysipelas.

wild-goose chase. A futile or useless chase or attempt.

wildly, wīld′li, *adv.* In a wild state or manner; irrationally; savagely.

wild oats. The wild oat; youthful carousing and dissipation. *Slang.*

wile, wīl, *n.* An artifice; stratagem; trick.—*vt.* (wiling, wiled). To entice; to while. **wileful,** wīl′ful, *a.* Wily; tricky.

will, wil, *v. aux.* (past, would), expresses futurity in the second and third persons, and willingness, &c., or determination in the first.—*vt.* and *i.* To determine by choice; to wish; to bequeath.—*n.* Wish; choice; determination; purpose; legal declaration of a person as to what is to be done after his death with his property; faculty by which we determine to do or not to do something; volition. **willful,** wil′ful, *a.* Under the influence of self-will; obstinate; wayward; intentional. **willfully,** wil′ful-li, *adv.* In a willful manner; obstinately; with set purpose. **willing,** wil′ing, *a.* Ready; desirous; spontaneous; voluntary; prompt. **willingly,** wil′ing-li, *adv.* In a willing manner; cheerfully; readily; gladly.

will-o′-the-wisp, wil′o-тне-wisp′, *n.* The ignis-fatuus.

willow, wil′ō, *n.* A tree or shrub, valuable for basket-making, &c. **willowy,** wil′ō-i, *a.* Abounding with willows; slender and graceful.

will power. Self-control.

willy-nilly, wil′i-nil′i, *adv.* Willing or unwilling.

wily, wīl′i, *a.* Using wiles; cunning; sly.

wimble, wim′bl, *n.* An instrument for boring holes.—*vt.* (wimbling, wimbled). To bore, as with a wimble.

wimple, wim′pl, *n.* A female head-dress still worn by nuns.—*vt.* (wimpling, wimpled). To cover with a wimple; to hoodwink.—*vi.* To ripple; to undulate.

win, win, *vt.* (winning, won). To gain; to be victorious in; to allure; to reach; to attain.—*vi.* To gain the victory.

wince, wins, *vi.* (wincing, winced). To shrink, as from pain; to start back.—*n.* A start, as from pain. **wincey,** win'si, *n.* A strong cloth with a cotton warp and a woolen weft.

winch, winch, *n.* The bent handle for turning a wheel, &c.; a kind of windlass turned by a crank handle.

wind, wind, in poetry often wīnd, *n.* Air in motion; a current of air; breath; power of respiration; empty words; flatulence.—*vt.* wind (pret. & pp. wound, sometimes winded). To blow, as a horn. —*vt.* wind (pret. & pp. winded). To follow by the scent; to render scant of wind; to let rest and recover wind.

wind, wīnd, *vt.* (pret. & pp. wound). To bend or turn; to twist; to coil.—*vi.* To twine or twist; to crook; to bend; to meander.

windage, win'dij, *n.* The difference between the diameter of a gun and that of the shell; influence of the wind in deflecting a missile; extent of deflection.

windbag, wind'bag, *n.* A bag filled with wind; a man of mere words; a noisy pretender.

windfall, wind'fal, *n.* Fruit blown down; an unexpected legacy or advantage.

winding, wīn'ding, *a.* Bending; twisting; spiral.—*n.* A turn or turning; a bend.

winding sheet, wīnd'ing-shēt, *n.* A sheet in which a corpse is wrapped.

wind instrument, wind'in-stru-ment, *n.* An instrument of music played by wind or breath, as an organ, flute, &c.

windjammer, wind'jam'ér, *n.* A sailing ship; one of its crew.

windlass, wind'las, *n.* A revolving cylinder on which a rope is wound; used for raising weights, &c., by hand or steam power.

windmill, wind'mil', *n.* A mill driven by the wind.

window, win'dō, *n.* An opening in a wall for the admission of light or air; the frame (usually fitted with glass) in this opening.

window sash, win'dō sash, *n.* The light frame in which glass is set in windows.

windpipe, wind'pīp', *n.* The cartilaginous pipe or passage for the breath; the trachea.

windup, wīnd'up', *n.* The conclusion or final settlement of any matter; the close.

windward, wind'wérd, *n.* The point from which the wind blows.—*a.* and *adv.* Towards the wind.

windy, win'di, *a.* Boisterous; exposed to the wind; empty; flatulent.

wine, wīn, *n.* An intoxicating liquor obtained from the fermented juice of grapes, &c.

wine cellar, wīn sel'ér, *n.* An apartment or cellar for storing wine.

wineglass, wīn'glas', *n.* A small glass in which wine is drunk.

wine press, wīn pres, *n.* An apparatus in which the juice is pressed out of grapes.

wine taster, wīn tas'tér, *n.* A person employed to judge of wine for purchasers.

wing, wing, *n.* One of the anterior limbs in birds; organ of flight; flight; a lateral extension; side; side division of an army, &c.—*vt.* To furnish with wings; to fly; to traverse by flying; to wound in the wing.

winged, wingd, *a.* Having wings; swift.

wink, wingk, *vi.* To shut and open one eyelid; to give a hint by the eyelids; to connive; to be willfully blind (with *at*).—*n.* Act of shutting and opening the eyelids rapidly; a twinkling; a hint given by means of the eye.

winning, win'ing, *a.* Attractive; charming.—*n.* The sum won by success in competition; chiefly in *pl.*

winnow, win'ō, *vt.* To separate the chaff from by wind; to fan; to sift; to scrutinize.—*vi.* To separate chaff from grain.

winsome, win'sum, *a.* Attractive; winning.

winter, win'tér, *n.* The cold season of the year; a year; any cheerless situation.—*a.* Belonging to winter.—*vi.* To pass the winter.—*vt.* To keep or feed during winter.

wintry, wintery, win'tri, win'tér-i, *a.* Pertaining or suitable to winter; cold; stormy.

wipe, wīp, *vt.* (wiping, wiped). To clean by gentle rubbing; to strike gently; to efface.—*n.* A rub for the purpose of cleaning; a gibe.

wire, wīr, *n.* A thread of metal; a telegraph wire; the telegraph.—*vt.* (wiring, wired). To bind with wire; to put a wire on; to send by telegraph.—*vi.* To communicate by telegraph.

wireless telegraphy, wīr'les tē-leg'-ra-fy, *n.* A system of telegraphing by means of electric waves transmitted through the air without wires.

wire-puller, wīr'pul-ér, *n.* One who pulls the wires of puppets; one who secretly controls the actions of others; an intriguer.

wire-pulling, wīr'pul-ing, *n.* The procedure of a wire-puller.

wire tapping. A process of spying on telephone or telegraph wires.

wiry, wīr'i, *a.* Made of or like wire; tough; lean and sinewy.

wisdom, wiz'dum, *n.* Sound judgment and sagacity; prudence; learning or erudition.

wisdom tooth, wiz'dom tōth, *n.* A large back double tooth, the last to come.

wise, wīz, *a.* Having wisdom; sagacious; judicious; skilled; sage.—*n.* Manner; mode. **wiseacre,** wīz'ā-kér, *n.* A pretender to wisdom; a dunce who poses as a wise man. **wisely,** wīz'li, *adv.* Sensibly; judiciously.

wisecrack, wīz'krak', *n.* Flippant remark.

wish, wish, *vi.* To have a desire; to long; with *for.*—*vt.* To desire; to long for; to invoke.—*n.* A desire; the thing desired. **wishful,** wish'ful, *a.* Desirous; eager; earnest.

shy-washy, wish'i-wosh'i, a. Very in and weak; diluted; feeble.

sp, wisp, n. A small bundle of straw,

stful, wist'fyl, a. Thoughtful; attene; earnest; pensive; longing. **wistlly**, wist'fyl-li, adv. In a wistful anner; attentively; pensively; longly.

t, wit, vt. and i. (pres. tense, wot, t. wist, pres. part. witting and wotg.) To know; to be aware. **to wit**, mely; that is to say.—n. Understand; sense; wisdom; intelligence; facty of associating ideas cleverly and apt language; a person possessing this culty; cleverness.

tch, wich, n. A woman who practices rcery.—vt. To bewitch.

tchcraft, wich"kraft', n. Sorcery; chantment; fascination.

tch hazel, See **wych-hazel**.

tching, wich'ing, a. Bewitching.

th, wiŦH, prep. Against; in the comny of; among; showing; marked by; mediately after; through; by.—n. ith or with. A withe.

thal, wiŦH-al', adv. Moreover; likese; at the same time.—prep. With; ed after relatives at the end of a use.

thdraw, wiŦH-dra', vt. To draw back away; to retract; to cause to retire. vi. To retire; to secede. **withawal**, wiŦH-dra'al, n. Act of withawing or taking back; a recalling.

the, wiŦH, with or withe, n. A willow twig; y flexible twig used to bind something. **ther**, wiŦH'ér, vi. To fade or shrivel; become dry and wrinkled; to decline. vt. To cause to fade; to prove fatal **withering**, wiŦH'ér-ing, a. Such as wither, blast, or fatally affect.

thers, wiŦH' érz, n. pl. The junction the shoulder-bones of a horse, form-the highest part of the back.

hhold, wiŦH-hōld', vt. To hold back; restrain; to retain; not to grant.

hin, wiŦH-in', prep. In the interior in the compass of.—adv. In the in-part; inwardly; indoors; at home.

hout, wiŦH-out', prep. On the oute of; out of; beyond; not having.—v. On the outside; outwardly; out-of-ors.

hstand, wiŦH-stand', vt. and i. To pose; to resist.

less, wit'les, a. Destitute of wit; ughtless; indiscreet; silly.

ness, wit'nes, n. Testimony; attesta-n of a fact or event; one who knows sees anything; one who gives evidence a trial.—vt. To attest; to see the exe-ion of a legal instrument, and sub-ibe it.—vi. To bear testimony.

ted, wit'ed, a. Having wit. **wittism**, wit'i-sizm, n. A witty remark. **ttily**, wit'i-li, adv. With wit. **witagly**, wit'ing-li, adv. Knowingly; by sign. **witty**, wit'i; a. Possessed of h; full of wit; keenly or brilliantly morous; facetious.

ve, wiv, vt. and i. (wiving, wived). provide with or take a wife.

res, wivz, pl. of **wife**.

wizard, wiz'érd, n. A wise man or sage; a sorcerer; a magician; a conjurer.

wizen, **wizened**, wiz'n, wiz'nd, a. Hard, dry, and shriveled; withered; weazen.

woad, wōd, n. A plant, the leaves of which yield a blue dye.

wobble, wob'l, vt. (wobbling, wobbled). To move unsteadily in rotating; to rock.

woe, wō, n. Grief; misery; affliction. **woebegone**, **woebegone**, wō"bē-gon', a. Overwhelmed with woe; sorrowful; melancholy. **woeful**, **woful**, wō'fyl, a. Full of woe; sorrowful; afflicted; wretched; pitiful. **woefully**, **wofully**, wō'fyl-li, adv. In a woeful manner; wretchedly; extremely.

wolf, wulf, n.; pl. **wolves**, wulvz. A carnivorous quadruped akin to the dog, crafty and rapacious; a cruel or cunning person. **wolfish**, wulf'ish, a. Like a wolf.

wolfram, wul'fram, n. An ore of the metal tungsten; the metal itself.

woman, wu'man, n.; pl. **women**, wi'-men. The female of the human race; the female sex; an adult female. **womanhood**, wu'man-hyd, n. The state, character, or qualities of a woman. **womanish**, wu'man-ish, a. Suitable to a woman; feminine; effeminate. **womankind**, wu'man-kind, n. Women collectively; the female sex. **womanlike**, wu'man-lik, a. Like a woman. **womanly**, wu'man-li, a. Becoming a woman; feminine in a praiseworthy sense.

womb, wōm, n. The uterus; place where anything is produced; any deep cavity.

wombat, wom'bat, n. A marsupial mammal about the size of a badger.

won, wun, pret. and pp. of **win**.

wonder, wun'dér, n. Something very strange; a prodigy or marvel; feeling excited by something strange.—vi. To be struck with wonder; to marvel; to entertain some doubt and curiosity. **wonderful**, wun'dér-fyl, a. Marvelous; surprising; strange; astonishing. **wonderfully**, wun'dér-fyl-li, adv. In a wonderful manner; surprisingly; very. **wonderment**, wun'dér-ment, n. Wonder; surprise; astonishment. **wondrous**, wun'drus, a. Wonderful; strange. —adv. Remarkably. **wondrously**, wun'drus-li, adv. In a wondrous or wonderful manner or degree.

won't, wōnt. A contraction for **will not**.

wont, wōnt or wunt, a. Accustomed.—n. Custom; habit; use.—vi. (pret. & pp. wont, sometimes wonted). To be accustomed to use. **wonted**, wōnt'ed or wunt'ed, a. Accustomed; usual.

woo, wö, vt. and i. (wooing, wooed). To make love to; to solicit in love; to court.

wood, wyd, n. A large collection of growing trees; the hard or solid substance of trees; timber.—vi. To take in or get supplies of wood.—vt. To supply with wood.

woodbine, wyd"bīn', n. The wild honeysuckle.

woodcock, wyd"kok', n. A bird allied to the snipe, esteemed for the table.

woodcut, wŏŏd″kut′, *n.* An engraving on wood, or a print from such engraving.

wooded, wŏŏd′ed, *a.* Abounding in or covered with wood or growing timber.

wooden, wŏŏd′n, *a.* Made of wood; clumsy; awkward; dull.

wood engraving, wŏŏd en-grāv′ing, *n.* The art of producing designs in relief on the surface of a block of wood; an impression from such a block.

woodland, wŏŏd″land′, *n.* Land covered with wood.—*a.* Relating to woods; sylvan.

woodman, wŏŏd′man. *n.* A forester.

woodpecker, wŏŏd″pek′ėr, *n.* A climbing bird which feeds on insects and their larvæ on trees.

woodwork, wŏŏd″wėrk′, *n.* The part of any structure that is made of wood.

woody, wŏŏd′i, *a.* Abounding with wood; wooded; consisting of wood; like wood.

woof, wŏŏf, *n.* The threads that cross the warp in weaving the weft; texture in general.

wool, wŏŏl, *n.* That soft species of hair on sheep; any fleecy substance resembling wool. **woolen,** wŏŏl′en, *a.* Made of or pertaining to wool.—*n.* Cloth made of wool. **woolgathering,** wŏŏl″gaᴛʜ′ėr-ing, *n.* Act of gathering wool; indulgence of idle fancies; a foolish or fruitless pursuit. **woolly,** wŏŏl′i, *a.* Consisting of wool; resembling wool; clothed with wool.

wop, wop, *vt.* (wopping, wopped). To whop.

word, wėrd, *n.* An articulate sound expressing an idea; a term; information; a saying; motto; order; assertion or promise; in *pl.,* talk; wrangle.—*vi.* To express in words. **wording,** wėr′ding, *n.* The mode of expressing in words; form of stating. **wordy,** wėr′di, *a.* Using many words; verbose.

wore, wōr, pret. of *wear.*

work, wėrk, *n.* Effort; labor; employment; a task; achievement; a literary or artistic performance; some extensive structure; establishment where labor of some kind is carried on; result of force acting.—*vi.* (pret. & pp. worked or wrought). To put forth effort; to labor; to take effect; to tend or conduce; to seethe; to ferment.—*vt.* To bestow labor upon; to bring about; to keep at work; to influence; to achieve; to fashion; to embroider; to cause to ferment. **workable,** wėr′ka-bl, *a.* That can be worked, or that is worth working. **workaday,** wėrk″a-dā′, *a.* Working-day; everyday; toiling. **worker,** wėr′kėr, *n.* One that works; a toiler; a laborer: a working bee. **workhouse,** wėrk″hous′, *n.* A house in which able-bodied paupers work; a pauper asylum. **working,** wėr′king, *a.* Engaged in bodily toil; industrious.—*n.* Act of laboring; movement; operation; fermentation; *pl.* portions of a mine; &c., worked. **working class,** wėrk′ing klas, *n.* Those who earn their bread by manual labor. **working-day,** wėrk″ing-dā′, *a.* A day on which labor is performed.—*a.* Relating to such days; laborious. **workman,** wėrk′man, *n.* An artisan; mechanic;

laborer; worker. **workmanlike,** wėrk′man-līk′, *a.* Like a proper workman; skillful; well performed. **workmanship,** wėrk′man-ship, *n.* Skill or art of a workman; style or character of execution; art; dexterity; handicraft. **workshop,** wėrk″shop′, *n.* A shop or building where any craft or work is carried on.

world, wėrld, *n.* The whole creation; the earth; any celestial orb; a large portion of our globe; sphere of existence; a domain or realm; mankind; the public; great degree or quantity. **worldling,** wėrld′ling, *n.* One devoted exclusively to worldly pleasures. **worldly,** wėrld′li, *a.* Relating to this world or this life; secular; carnal; sordid. **world-wide,** wėrld′wīd′, *a.* Wide as the world; tending over all the world.

worm, wėrm, *n.* A small creeping animal; an intestinal parasite; *pl.* the disease caused by such parasites; something vermicular or spiral.—*vi.* To wriggle; to work gradually and secretly.—*vt.* To effect by stealthy means; *refl.* to insinuate one's self; to extract cunningly. **worm-eaten,** wėrm″ēt′n, *a.* Gnawed by worms; having cavities made by worms. **wormling,** wėrm′ling, *n.* A minute worm. **wormwood,** wėrm″wŏŏd, *n.* A plant with bitter, tonic, and stimulating qualities. **wormy,** wėrm′i, *a.* Abounding with worms; eaten by worms; groveling; earthy.

worn, wōrn, pp. of *wear.*

worn-out, wōrn″out′, *a.* Useless from being worn; wearied; exhausted.

worry, wu′ri, *vt.* (worrying, worried). To tear with the teeth, as dogs; to harass; to annoy.—*vi.* To trouble one's self; to fret.—*n.* Trouble; care; anxiety.

worse, wėrs, *a.* Bad or ill in a greater degree; inferior; more unwell; more ill off. **worsen,** wėr′sn, *vi.* and *t.* To grow or make worse. **worser,** wėr′sėr, *a.* and *adv.* A redundant comparative of *worse.*

worship, wėr′ship, *n.* Dignity; honor; a title of honor; religious service; adoration; reverence.—*vt.* (worshiping, worshiped). To adore; to pay divine honor to; to idolize.—*vt.* To perform religious service. **worshiper,** wėr′ship-ėr, *n.* One who worships. **worshipful,** wėr′ship-fụl, *a.* Worthy of honor or high respect; honorable.

worst, wėrst, *a.* Bad or evil in the highest degree.—*n.* The most evil state or action.—*adv.* Most extremely.—*vt.* defeat. **worsted,** wŏŏs′ted, *n.* Yarn spun from wool, and used in knitting.—*a.* Made of worsted.

wort, wėrt, *n.* The infusion of malt before it becomes beer by fermentation; herb.

worth, wėrth, *a.* Equal in value or price to; deserving of; possessing.—*n.* Value; price; merit; excellence.—*vi.* To be; betide. **worthily,** wėr′ᴛʜi-li, *a.* In a worthy manner; suitable; deservedly; justly. **worthless,** wėrth′les, *a.* Having no worth; valueless; contemptible; not deserving. **worthy,** wėr′ᴛʜi, *a.* possessing worth; estimable; virtuous; serving; fitting.—*n.* A man of eminence

would, wụd. Pret. of *will*, mainly used in subjunctive or conditional senses.

would-be, wụd'bē, *a.* Wishing to be; vainly pretending to be.—*n.* A vain pretender.

wound, wönd, *n.* A cut or stab, &c.; injury; hurt or pain to the feelings; damage.—*vt.* or *i.* To inflict a wound on; to pain.

wove, wōv, pret. and sometimes pp. of *weave*.

wrack, rak, *n.* Sea-weed generally; wreck; a thin flying cloud.

wraith, rāth, *n.* An apparition of a person about to die or newly dead.

wrangle, rang'gl, *vi.* (wrangling, wrangled). To dispute angrily; to argue.—*n.* A dispute. **wrangler**, rang'glėr, *n.* One who wrangles; in Cambridge University, one who attains a certain rank in the examination for honors in mathematics.

wrap, rap, *vt.* (wrapping, wrapped or wrapt). To fold or roll; to cover by something wound; to envelop.—*n.* An outer article of dress for warmth. **wrap'r**, rap'ėr. One that wraps; a cover; a loose upper garment. **wrapping**, rap'ing, *a.* Used or designed to wrap.— A cover; a wrapper.

wrath, rath, *n.* Violent anger; rage; fury. **rathful**, rath'fụl, *a.* Full of wrath furious; wroth.

wreak, rēk, *vt.* To revenge or avenge; to inflict; to gratify by punishment.

wreath, rēth, *n.* Something twisted or curled; a garland; a chaplet; a snow-drift. **wreathe**, rēTH, *vt.* (wreathing, wreathed). To twist into a wreath; to entwine; to encircle; to dress in a garland.—*vi.* To be entwined.

wreck, rek, *n.* Ruin; overthrow; a ruin; destruction of a vessel at sea.—*vt.* To cause to become a wreck; to ruin. **wreckage**, rek'ij, *n.* Act of wrecking; remains of a ship or cargo that has been wrecked. **wrecker**, rek'ėr, *n.* One who causes shipwrecks or plunders wrecks; one who recovers goods from wrecked vessels.

wren, ren, *n.* A name of various small birds; a small song-bird.

wrench, rench, *n.* A violent twist; injury by twisting; an instrument for screwing a bolt or nut.—*vt.* To pull with a twist; to distort.

wrest, rest, *vt.* To twist; to take or force by violence; to distort.—*n.* Act of wresting; a wrench; an implement to tune stringed instruments with.

wrestle, res'l, *vi.* (wrestling, wrestled). To contend by grappling and trying to throw down; to struggle.—*vt.* To contend with in wrestling.—*n.* A bout at wrestling. **wrestler**, res'lėr, *a.* One who wrestles.

wretch, rech, *n.* A miserable person; a mean, base, or vile person. **wretched**, rech'ed, *a.* Very miserable; distressing; worthless; despicable. **wretchedly**, rech'ed-li, *adv.* In a wretched manner; most miserably; contemptibly.

wriggle, rig'l, *vi.* and *t.* (wriggling, wriggled). To move with writhing or twisting.—*n.* A quick twisting motion.

wright, rit, *n.* An artisan or artificer; a worker in wood; a carpenter.

wring, ring, *vt.* (wringing, wrung). To twist with the hands; to twist and compress; to torture; to extort.—*vi.* To writhe. **wringer**, ring'ėr, *n.* One who wrings; an apparatus for forcing water from clothes.

wrinkle, ring'kl, *n.* A small ridge or furrow; a crease; a hint; a notion.—*vt.* and *i.* (wrinkling, wrinkled). To form into wrinkles; to contract into furrows; to crease. **wrinkly**, ring'kli, *a.* Somewhat wrinkled; puckered.

wrist, rist, *n.* The joint by which the hand is united to the arm. **wristband**, rist"band', *n.* The band of a sleeve covering the wrist. **wristlet**, rist'let, *n.* Some small object worn round the wrist; a bracelet.

writ, rit, *n.* That which is written; the Scriptures; a legal document commanding a person to do some act.

write, rit, *vt.* (writing, pret. wrote, pp. written). To form by a pen, &c.; to set down in letters or words; to cover with letters; to send in writing; to compose. —*vi.* To trace characters with a pen, &c.; to be engaged in literary work; to conduct correspondence. **writer**, rit'ėr, *n.* One who writes; an author; a clerk; in Scotland, a law agent. **writing**, rit'ing, *n.* Act of one who writes; a book, manuscript, or document; style. **written**, rit'n, *a.* Expressed in writing.

writhe, rīTH, *vt.* (writhing, writhed). To twist or distort, as the body or limbs.—*vi.* To twist and turn; to be distorted, as from agony.

wrong, rong, *a.* Not right; not fit; not what ought to be; erroneous.—*n.* What is not right; an injustice; injury.—*adv.* In a wrong manner.—*vt.* To do wrong to; to treat with injustice. **wrongdoer**, rong"dō'ėr, *n.* One who does wrong. **wrongful**, rong'fụl, *a.* Injurious; unjust. **wrongheaded**, rong'-hed'ed, *a.* Obstinately or perversely wrong; stubborn. **wrongly**, rong'li, *adv.* In a wrong manner; mistakenly; erroneously; unjustly.

wroth, roth, *a.* Very angry; indignant.

wrought, rąt, pret. and pp. of *work*.

wry, ri. *a.* Crooked; twisted; askew.

wych-hazel, wich'hā'zel, *n.* An American shrub with yellow flowers.

X

xanthic, zan'thik, *a.* Yellowish.

xanthin, xanthine, zan'thin, *n.* A yellow coloring matter.

xanthochroi, zan-thok'ro-i, *n. pl.* The fair white group of men.

xanthous, zan'thus, *a.* Of the fair-haired type.

xebec, zē'bėk, or ze-bek', *n.* A three-masted vessel used in the Mediterranean.

xenophobia, zen'ō-fō"bi-a, *n.* Fear or hatred of strangers or foreigners, or of anything strange or foreign.

xiphoid, zif'oid, *a.* Shaped like a sword.

X ray. A ray of short wave length that can penetrate solids, used to photograph the internal body structure.

xylem, zī'lem, *n.* The woody portion of vegetable tissue.

xylograph, zī'lo-graf, *n.* A wood-engraving.

xylography, zī-log'ra-fi, *n.* Wood-engraving; a process of decorative painting on wood.

xyloid, zī'loid, *a.* Having the nature of wood; reesmbling wood.

xylophagous, zī-lof'a-gus, *a.* Feeding on wood.

xylophone, zī'lō-fōn, *n.* A musical instrument consisting of a series of wooden bars of different lengths which are struck by small, wooden hammers.

xyst, xystus, zist, zis'tus, *n.* A covered portico or open court for athletic exercises.

xyster, zis'tėr, *n.* A surgeon's instrument for scraping bones.

Y

yacht, yot, *n.* A light vessel used for racing, pleasure, &c.—*vi.* To sail in a yacht. **yachting,** yot'ing, *a.* Belonging to a yacht.—*n.* Act of sailing a yacht. **yachtsman,** yots'man, *n.* One who keeps or sails a yacht.

yahoo, yä'hö, *n.* A rude, boorish person.

yak, yak, *n.* A wild ox with long silky hair.

yam, yam, *n.* A climbing plant, cultivated in tropical climates for its large roots.

yankee, yang'kē, *n.* A citizen of New England; a native of the United States.

yap, yap, *vi.* (yapping, yapped). To yelp; to bark.—*n.* Cry of a dog; yelp.

yard, yärd, *n.* A standard measure of 3 feet; a long beam slung crosswise to a mast and supporting a sail; piece of enclosed ground.

yardarm, yärd"ärm', *n.* Either end of a ship's yard.

yardstick, yärd"stik', *n.* A stick 3 feet in length.

yarn, yärn, *n.* Thread prepared from wool or flax for weaving; a story

yaw, yạ, *vi.* To swerve suddenly in sailing.—*n.* The sudden temporary deviation of a ship.

yawl, yạl, *n.* A small ship's boat, usually rowed by four or six oars; a small two-masted yacht.—*vi.* To howl; to yell.

yawn, yạn, *vi.* To have the mouth open involuntarily while a deep breath is taken; to gape.—*n.* A gaping; act of yawning; a chasm.

ye, yē, *pron.* The nominative and objective plural of the second personal pronoun.

yea, yā, *adv.* Yes; the opposite of *nay.*

year, yėr, *n.* The period of time during which the earth makes one revolution in its orbit; twelve months; *pl.* old age; time of life. **year book,** yēr"buk', *n.* A book published every year giving fresh information regarding matters that change. **yearling,** yėr'ling, *n.* A young beast one year old.—*a.* Being a year old. **yearly,** yėr'li, *a.* Annual; happening every year.—*adv.* Once a year.

yearn, yėrn, *vi.* To feel uneasiness of mind from longing or pity; to long. **yearning,** yėrn'ing, *a.* Longing.—*n.* A feeling of longing desire.

yeast, yēst, *n.* A yellowish substance produced in alcoholic fermentation; barm. **yeasty,** yēs'ti, *a.* Like or containing yeast.

yegg, yeg, *n. Slang.* A burglar; especially one who robs safes.

yell, yel, *vi.* To cry out with a loud piercing noise; scream.—*n.* A loud, piercing outcry.

yellow, yel'ō, *a.* Being of a bright golden color.—*n.* A bright golden color. **yellow fever,** yel'ō fē'vėr, *n.* A malignant fever of warm climates, attended with yellowness of the skin.

yelp, yelp, *vi.* To utter a sharp bark or cry, as a dog.—*n.* A sharp cry of a dog.

yeoman, yō'man, *n.; pl.* **-men.** A man who owns a small estate in land; a gentleman farmer; one of the yeomanry (Eng.). **yeomanry,** yō'man-ri, *n.* The collective body of yeomen; a volunteer cavalry force.

yes, yes, *adv.* Even so; expressing affirmation or consent; opposed to *no*.

yester, yes′tèr, *a.* Pertaining to the day before the present; last. **yesterday,** yes′tèr-dā, *n.* The day before the present. —*adv.* On the day last past.

yet, yet, *adv.* In addition; still; hitherto; nevertheless. —*conj.* Nevertheless; however.

yew, yō, *n.* An evergreen tree, with poisonous leaves, and yielding a hard durable timber.

Yiddish, yid′ish, *n.* A language spoken by many European Jews.

yield, yēld, *vt.* To produce in return for labor, &c.; to afford; to grant; to give up. —*vi.* To submit; to comply; to produce. —*n.* Amount yielded; product; return. **yielding,** yēld′ing, *a.* Inclined to yield; accommodating; compliant; facile.

yodel, yodle, yō′dl, *vt.* and *i.* (yodeling, yodling, yodeled, yodled). To sing like the Swiss and Tyrolese mountaineers by changing suddenly from the natural voice to the falsetto.

yoga, yō′ga, *n.* A system of Hindu religious philosophy requiring intense concentration on the deity or other object, with the aim of identifying with it.

yoghourt, yogurt, yō′gört, *n.* A kind of thickened milk fermented by *Lactobacillus bulgaricus.*

yoke, yōk, *n.* Gear connecting draught animals by passing across their necks; a pair of draught animals; something resembling a yoke; shoulder-piece of a garment supporting the rest; servitude; burden; a bond; a tie. —*vt.* (yoking, yoked). To put a yoke on; to couple; to enslave.

yokel, yō′kl, *n.* A rustic; an ignorant peasant; a country bumpkin.

Yom Kippur, yom kip′ėr. The Day of Atonement; a holiday and day of fasting for the Jews.

yolk, yōk, *n.* The yellow part of an egg.

yon, yon, *a.* That; those; yonder.

yonder, yon′dėr, *a.* That or those away there. —*adv.* At or in that place there.

yore, yōr, *adv.* Long ago; in old time; now used only in the phrase *of yore.*

you, yō, *pron.* The nominative and objective plural of *thou:* commonly used when a single person is addressed.

young, yung, *a.* Being in the early stage of life; youthful. —*n.* The offspring of an animal. **youngish,** yung′ish, *a.* Somewhat young. **youngster,** yung′-stèr, *n.* A young person.

your, yōr, possessive corresponding to *ye, you.* Pertaining or belonging to you.

yours, yōrz, *poss. pron.* That or those which belong to you.

yourself, yōr-self′, *pron.*; pl. **-selves.** You, used distinctively or reflexively.

youth, yōth, *n.* State or quality of being young; period during which one is young; a young man; young persons collectively. **youthful,** yōth′ful, *a.* young; pertaining to youth; fresh or vigorous, as in youth.

yowl, youl, *vi.* To give a long distressful or mournful cry, as a dog. —*n.* A mournful cry.

yule, yōl, *n.* Christmas.

Z

zany, zā′ni, *n.* A buffoon or merry-andrew.

zeal, zēl, *n.* Eagerness; passionate ardor; enthusiasm. **zealot,** zel′ut, *n.* One who is zealous; a fanatical partisan; a bigot. **zealous,** zel′us, *a.* Inspired with zeal; fervent; eager; earnest. **zealously,** zel′us-li, *adv.* In a zealous manner; ardently; eagerly; fervently.

zebra, zē′bra, *n.* A striped South African animal allied to the horse and ass.

zebu, zē′bū, *n.* The humped ox of India.

zend, zend, *n.* An ancient Iranian or Persian language, closely allied to Sanskrit.

zenith, zē′nith or zen′ith, *n.* The point of the heavens right above a spectator's head; highest point.

zephyr, zef′ėr, *n.* The west wind; any soft, mild, gentle breeze.

zeppelin, zep′e-lin, *n.* A dirigible balloon of the rigid type, consisting of a cylindrical, trussed and covered frame supported by internal gas cells and provided with means of propulsion and control.

zero, zēr′ō, *n.* Number or quantity diminished to nothing; a cipher; lowest point.

zero hour. Crucial point; time set for action to begin.

zest, zest, *n.* Orange or lemon peel, used to flavor liquor; relish; charm; gusto.

Zeus, zūs, *n.* The supreme god of the ancient Greeks.

zigzag, zig′zag′, *n.* Something in the form of straight lines with sharp turns.— *a.* Having sharp turns or bends. —*vi.* (zigzagging, zigzagged). To move in a zigzag fashion; to form zigzags. **zigzaggy,** zig′zag′i, *a.* Zigzag.

zinc, zingk, *n.* A metal of bluish-white color, used for roofing, to form alloys, &c. —*vt.* (zincking, zincked). To cover with zinc.

zinc oxide. Powder used in making glass, paints, ointments, etc.

zing, zing, *n. Slang.* A high-pitched sound; energy.

Zion, zī′un, *n.* A hill in Jerusalem which in ancient Jewish times was the center of Hebrew worship, government, and national life; heaven; the people of Israel; the church of God.

Zionism, zī'un-izm, *n.* A movement dedicated to the establishment and maintenance of the state of Israel.

zircon, zėr'kon, *n.* A hard lustrous mineral, one of the gems, called also jargon.

zither, zithern, zit'ėr, zit'ėrn, *n.* A flat musical instrument with from twenty-nine to forty-two strings, played with the fingers.

zodiac, zō'di-ak, *n.* An imaginery belt or zone in the heavens, within which the apparent motions of the sun, moon, and principal planets are confined, divided into twelve equal parts or signs. **zodiacal,** zō-dī'a-kal, *a.* Pertaining to the zodiac.

zombi, zom'bi, *n.* A West Indian superstition that a dead being may be brought back to life; such a person.

zone, zōn, *n.* A girdle or belt; one of the five great divisions of the earth, bounded by circles parallel to the equator; any well-defined belt. **zonule,** zōn'ūl, *n.* A little zone.

zoo, zō, *n.* An area designed to house wild animals, birds, &c., for public viewing.

zoology, zō-ol'o-ji, *n.* The science of the natural history of animals. **zoologist,** zō-ol'o-jist, *n.* One who is versed in zoology. **zoological,** zō"o-loj"i-kal, *a.* Pertaining to zoology.

zoon, zō'on, *n.* An animal.

zoophyte, zō'o-fīt, *n.* A name applied to many plant-like animals, as sponges.

Zoroastrianism, zō'rō-as"tri-an-izm, *n.* The ancient Persian religion founded by Zoroaster, one feature of which was a belief in a good and an evil power perpetually at strife; the religion of the Parsees; fire-worship. **Zoroastrian,** zō'rō-as"tri-an, *a.* Pertaining to Zoroaster or Zoroastrianism.—*n.* A believer in this religion.

Zouave, zō-äv', *n.* A French infantry soldier dressed after the Turkish fashion.

Zulu, zō'lö, *n.* A member of a warlike branch of the Kaffir race in South Africa.

zymic, zi'mik, *a.* Pertaining to fermentation.

zymology, zī-mol'o-ji, *n.* The doctrine of ferments and fermentation.

zymotic, zi-mot'ik, *a.* Pertaining to fermentation; applied to epidemic and contagious diseases, supposed to be produced by germs acting like a ferment.